Handbook of Archaeological Sciences

Handbook of Archaeological Sciences

Edited by

D.R. Brothwell
University of York

and

A.M. Pollard
University of Bradford

JOHN WILEY & SONS, LTD
Chichester • New York • Weinheim • Brisbane • Singapore • Toronto

Other Wiley Editorial Offices

John Wiley & Sons, Inc., 605 Third Avenue,
New York, NY 10158-0012, USA

WILEY-VCH Verlag GmbH, Pappelallee 3,
D-69469 Weinheim, Germany

John Wiley and Sons Australia, Ltd, 33 Park Road, Milton,
Queensland 4064, Australia

John Wiley & Sons (Asia) Pte Ltd, 2 Clementi Loop #02-01,
Jin Xing Distripark, Singapore 129809

John Wiley & Sons (Canada) Ltd, 22 Worcester Road,
Rexdale, Ontario M9W 1L1, Canada

Library of Congress Cataloging-in-Publication Data

Handbook of archaeological sciences / edited by D.R. Brothwell and A.M. Pollard.
    p. cm.
Includes bibliographical references and index.
ISBN 0-471-98484-1 (alk. paper)
1. Archaeology—Methodology. I. Brothwell, Don R.   II. Pollard, A.M.

CC75 .H34 2001
930.1'028—dc21   00-043916

British Library Cataloguing in Publication Data

A catalogue record for this book is available from the British Library

ISBN 0-471-98484-1

Typeset in 9/11 pt Times from the author's disks by C.K.M. Typesetting, Salisbury, Wiltshire.
Printed and bound in Great Britain by Bookcraft (Bath) Ltd, Midsomer Norton.
This book is printed on acid-free paper responsibly manufactured from sustainable forestry,
in which at least two trees are planted for each one used for paper production.

Contents

List of Contributors   *ix*

Foreword: Martin Aitken FRS   *xiii*

Acknowledgements   *xv*

Introduction: Archaeological science: a current perspective. D. Brothwell and A.M. Pollard   *xvii*

SECTION 1. DATING   1

Overview – Dating in archaeology; past, present and future   3
      R.E.M. Hedges
1   Quaternary geochronological frameworks   9
      J.J. Lowe
2   Radiocarbon dating   23
      R.E. Taylor
3   Dendrochronology and other applications of tree-ring studies in archaeology   35
      P.I. Kuniholm
4   Trapped charge dating (ESR, TL, OSL)   47
      R. Grün
5   Uranium-series dating   63
      A.G. Latham
6   Magnetic properties and archaeomagnetism   73
      R.S. Sternberg
7   Obsidian hydration dating   81
      W.R. Ambrose
8   *In situ* cosmogenic isotopes: principles and potential for archaeology   93
      F.M. Stuart

SECTION 2. QUATERNARY PALAEOENVIRONMENTS   101

Overview – Environmental reconstruction   103
      K.J. Edwards
9   Modelling Quaternary environments   111
      A. Wise
10   Insects as palaeoenvironmental indicators   121
      M. Robinson
11   Non-marine mollusca and archaeology   135
      R.C. Preece
12   Mammals as climatic indicators   147
      D.W. Yalden

13   Peat stratigraphy and climate change   155
     K. Barber and P. Langdon
14   Archaeology and soil micromorphology   167
     D.A Davidson and I.A. Simpson
15   Taphonomic investigations   179
     R.A. Nicholson
16   Global biogeochemical cycles and isotope systematics – how the world works   191
     A.M. Pollard and L. Wilson

SECTION 3. HUMAN PALAEOBIOLOGY   203

Overview – Human palaeobiology: then and now   205
     J.E. Buikstra
17   Pleistocene and Holocene hominid evolution   213
     D.R. Brothwell
18   Human palaeobiology as human ecology   219
     H. Schutkowski
19   Disease ecology   225
     D.J. Ortner
20   Assessment of age at death and sex in the adult human skeleton   237
     M. Cox
21   The study of preserved human tissue   249
     M.R. Zimmerman
22   Palaeodemography   259
     A.T. Chamberlain
23   Body tissue chemistry and palaeodiet   269
     J. Sealy
24   Cremated bone   281
     J.I. McKinley and J.M. Bond

SECTION 4. BIOMOLECULAR ARCHAEOLOGY   293

Overview – Archaeological science in the biomolecular century   295
     A.M. Pollard
25   Ancient DNA   301
     T.A. Brown
26   Blood residues in archaeology   313
     P.R. Smith and M.T. Wilson
27   Survival and interpretation of archaeological proteins   323
     A.M. Gernaey, E.R. Waite, M.J. Collins, O.E. Craig and R.J. Sokol
28   Lipids in archaeology   331
     R.P. Evershed, S.N. Dudd, M.J. Lockheart and S. Jim
29   Archaeological microbiology   351
     G. Grupe

SECTION 5. BIOLOGICAL RESOURCE EXPLOITATION   359

Overview – At the beginning of the task: the archaeology of biological remains   361
     C. Higham
30   Biological resource exploitation: problems of theory and method   365
     M. Charles and P. Halstead

31   Human impact on vegetation   379
       L. Dumayne-Peaty
32   Archaeobotany and the transition to agriculture   393
       M.K. Jones and S. Colledge
33   Dietary evidence from the coprolites and the intestinal contents of ancient humans   403
       T.G. Holden
34   Vertebrate resources   415
       A.K.G. Jones and T.P. O'Connor
35   The exploitation of invertebrates and invertebrate products   427
       K.D. Thomas and M.A. Mannino

SECTION 6. INORGANIC RESOURCE EXPLOITATION   441

Overview – Materials study in archaeology   443
       M.S. Tite
36   Ceramic petrology, clay geochemistry and ceramic production – from technology to the
       mind of the potter   449
       I.K. Whitbread
37   Lithic exploitation and use   461
       M. Edmonds
38   Glass and glazes   471
       J. Henderson
39   Science, speculation and the origins of extractive metallurgy   483
       D. Killick
40   Pyrotechnology   493
       J.G. McDonnell
41   The provenance hypothesis   507
       L. Wilson and A.M. Pollard

SECTION 7. ARCHAEOLOGICAL PROSPECTION   519

Overview – The role and practice of archaeological prospection   521
       A. David
42   Surface collection techniques in field archaeology: theory and practice   529
       T.J. Wilkinson
43   Geophysical prospection in archaeology   543
       Y. Nishimura
44   Remote sensing   555
       D.N.M. Donoghue
45   Geochemical prospecting   565
       C. Heron
46   Archaeological data integration   575
       M. Van Leusen

SECTION 8. BURIAL, DECAY AND ARCHAEOLOGICAL CONSERVATION   585

Overview – Degradation, investigation and preservation of archaeological evidence   587
       C. Caple
47   Defining the burial environment   595
       R. Raiswell

48   Electrochemical processes in metallic corrosion   605
      M. McNeil and L.S. Selwyn
49   Post-depositional changes in archaeological ceramics and glasses   615
      I.C. Freestone
50   The deterioration of organic materials   627
      J.M. Cronyn
51   The deterioration of bone   637
      A. Millard
52   Maximizing the life span of archaeological objects   649
      D. Watkinson

SECTION 9. STATISTICAL AND COMPUTATIONAL METHODS   661

Overview – Numbers, models, maps: computers and archaeology   663
      R.D. Drennan
53   Spatial information and archaeology   671
      M. Gillings
54   Multivariate analysis in archaeology   685
      M.J. Baxter
55   Applications of the Bayesian statistical paradigm   695
      C.E. Buck
56   Animal bone quantification   703
      T.P. O'Connor
57   Quantification of broken objects   711
      M.J. Shott
58   Numerical modelling in archaeology   723
      M.W. Lake
59   Synthesizing analytical data – spatial results from pottery provenance   733
      H. Neff

General Index   749

Site Index   759

Species names and Taxonomic groups index   761

List of Contributors

Martin Aitken, Le Garret, 63 930 Augerolles, Puy-de-Dome, France

Wal R. Ambrose, Dept. of Archaeology and Natural History, Research School of Pacific and Asian Studies, Canberra, ACT 0200 Australia

Keith Barber, Dept. of Geography, University of Southampton, University Road, Highfield, Southampton, SO17 1BJ

Mike J. Baxter, Dept. of Mathematics, Statistics and Operational Research, Nottingham Trent University, Clifton Lane, Clifton, Nottingham NG11 8NS

Julie M. Bond, Dept. of Archaeological Sciences, University of Bradford, Richmond Road, Bradford, BD7 1DP

Don R. Brothwell, Dept. of Archaeology, University of York, Kings Manor, York, YO1 2EP

Terry A. Brown, Dept. of Biomolecular Sciences, UMIST, PO Box 88, Manchester, M60 1QD

Caitlin E. Buck, School of History and Archaeology, University of Wales, Cardiff, PO Box 494, CF1 3XU

Jane E. Buikstra, Dept. of Anthropology, University of New Mexico, Albuquerque, NM 87131 USA

Chris Caple, Dept. of Archaeology, University of Durham, South Road, Durham, DH1 3LE

Andrew T. Chamberlain, Dept. of Archaeology and Prehistory, University of Sheffield, S1 4ET

Michael Charles, Dept. of Archaeology and Prehistory, University of Sheffield, Northgate House, West Street, Sheffield, S1 4ET

Susan Colledge, Institute of Archaeology, University College London, 31–34 Gordon Square, London, WC1H 0PY

Matthew J. Collins, Fossil Fuels and Environmental Geochemistry, Drummond Building, University of Newcastle, Newcastle, NE1 7RU

Margaret Cox, Dept. of Conservation Sciences, Bournemouth University, Fern Barrow, Poole, BH12 5BB

Oliver E. Craig, Fossil Fuels and Environmental Geochemistry, Drummond Building, University of Newcastle, Newcastle, NE1 7RU

Janey M. Cronyn, Institute of Archaeology, University College London, 31–34 Gordon Square, London WC1H 0PY

Andrew David, English Heritage Centre for Archaeology, Fort Cumberland, Eastney, Portsmouth PO4 9LD

Donald A. Davidson, Dept. of Environmental Sciences, University of Stirling, Stirling, FK9 4LA

Daniel N.M. Donoghue, Dept. of Geography, University of Durham, South Road, Durham, DH1 3LE

Robert D. Drennan, Dept. of Anthropology, University of Pittsburgh, Pittsburgh, PA 15260 USA

Stephanie N. Dudd, School of Chemistry, University of Bristol, Bristol, BS8 1TS

Lisa Dumayne-Peaty, School of Geography, University of Birmingham, Edgbaston, Birmingham B15 2TT

Mark Edmonds, Dept. of Archaeology and Prehistory, University of Sheffield, Northgate House, West Street, Sheffield S1 4ET

Kevin J. Edwards, Dept. of Geography, University of Aberdeen, Aberdeen AB24 3UF

Richard P. Evershed, School of Chemistry, University of Bristol, Bristol, BS8 1TS

Ian C. Freestone, Dept. of Scientific Research, British Museum, Great Russell Street, London

Angela M. Gernaey, Fossil Fuels and Environmental Geochemistry, Drummond Building, University of Newcastle, Newcastle, NE1 7RU

Mark Gillings, School of Archaeological Studies, University of Leicester, University Road, Leicester, LE1 7RH

Rainer Grün, Quaternary Dating Research Centre, Research School of Pacific and Asian Studies, Australia National University, Canberra, ACT 0200, Australia

Gisela Grupe, Institut für Anthropologie und Humangenetick, Ludwig Maximilians Universitat, Richard Wagner Strasse 10/l, 80333 München, Germany

Paul Halstead, Dept. of Archaeology and Prehistory, University of Sheffield, Northgate House, West Street, Sheffield, S1 4ET

Robert E.M. Hedges, Research Laboratory for Archaeology and the History of Art, University of Oxford, 6 Keble Road, Oxford, OX1 3QJ

Julian Henderson, Dept. of Archaeology, University of Nottingham, University Park, Nottingham, NG7 2RD

Carl Heron, Dept. of Archaeological Sciences, University of Bradford, Richmond Road, Bradford, BD7 1DP

Charles Higham, Anthropology Department, University of Otago, PO Box 56, Dunedin, New Zealand

Timothy G. Holden, Howden Farm, Gifford, Haddington, East Lothian, EH41 4JS

Susan Jim, School of Chemistry, University of Bristol, Bristol, BS8 1TS

Andrew K.G. Jones, Dept. of Archaeological Sciences, University of Bradford, Richmond Road, Bradford, BD7 1DP

Martin K. Jones, Dept. of Archaeology, University of Cambridge, Downing Street, Cambridge, CB2 3DZ

Dave Killick, Dept. of Archaeology, University of Arizona, Tuscon AZ 85721 USA

Peter I. Kuniholm, Dept. of the History of Art and Archaeology, Cornell University, B-48 Goldwin Smith Hall, Ithaca, New York 14853-3201 USA

Mark W. Lake, Institute of Archaeology, University College London, 31–34 Gordon Square, London WC1H 0PY

Pete Langdon, Dept. of Geography, University of Southampton, University Road, Highfield, Southampton, SO17 1BJ

Alf G. Latham, School of Archaeology, Classics and Oriental Studies, Hartley Building, University of Liverpool, Liverpool, L63 3BX

Martijn Van Leusen, Groningen Institute of Archaeology, Poststraat 6, 9712 ER Groningen, The Netherlands

Matthew J. Lockheart, School of Chemistry, University of Bristol, Bristol, BS8 1TS

John J. Lowe, Centre for Quaternary Research, Royal Holloway College, University of London, Egham, Surrey TW20 0EX

Marcello A. Mannino, Institute of Archaeology, University College London, 31–34 Gordon Square, London WC1H 0PY

J. Gerry McDonnell, Dept. of Archaeological Sciences, University of Bradford, Richmond Road, Bradford, BD7 1DP

Jacqueline I. McKinley, 12 Victoria Road, Warminster, Wiltshire, BA12 8HE

Michael McNeil, Office of Research, USNRC Mail Stop T10E10, Washington, DC 20555 USA

Andrew Millard, Dept. of Archeology, University of Durham, South Road, Durham, DH1 3LE

Hector Neff, Research Reactor, University of Missouri – Columbia, Columbia, MO 65211 USA

Rebecca A. Nicholson, Dept. of Archaeological Sciences, University of Bradford, Bradford, BD7 1DP

Yashusi Nishimura, Nara Cultural Properties, Research Institute, 9-1, 2 Chrome Nijychô, Nara-shi 630 Japan

Terry P. O'Connor, Dept. of Archaeology, University of York, Kings Manor, York, YO1 2EP

Don J. Ortner, Dept. of Anthropology, National Museum of Natural History, Washington DC 20560 USA

A. Mark Pollard, Dept. of Archaeological Sciences, University of Bradford, Richmond Road, Bradford, BD7 1DP

Richard C. Preece, Dept. of Zoology, University of Cambridge, Downing Street, Cambridge, CB2 3EJ

Rob Raiswell, School of Earth Sciences, The University of Leeds, Leeds, LS2 9JT

Mark Robinson, University Museum, Parks Road, Oxford, OX1 3PW

Holger Schutkowski, Dept. of Archaeological Sciences, University of Bradford, Richmond Road, Bradford, BD7 1DP

Judy Sealy, Dept. of Archaeology, University of Cape Town, Private Bag, Rondesbosch 7700, South Africa

Lyndsie S. Selwyn, Canadian Conservation Institute, 1030 Innes Road, Ottawa, Ontario, 1A OC8 Canada

Michael J. Shott, Dept. of Sociology, Anthropology and Criminology, University of Northern Iowa, Cedar Falls, IA 50614-0513 USA

Ian A. Simpson, Dept. of Environmental Sciences, University of Stirling, Stirling, FK9 4LA

Patricia R. Smith, Dept. of Biological and Chemical Sciences, University of Essex, Wivenhoe Park, Colchester, CO4 3SQ

Robert J. Sokol, Regional Blood Transfusion Centre, Longley Lane, Sheffield, S5 7JN

Robert S. Sternberg, Dept. of Geosciences, Franklin and Marshall College, Lancaster PA 17604-3003 USA

Finlay M. Stuart, Scottish Universities Environmental Research Centre, East Kilbride, Glasgow, G75 0QU

R.E. Taylor, Radiocarbon Laboratory, Dept. of Anthropology, Institute of Geophysics and Planetary Physics, University of California, Riverside, CA 92521 USA

Michael S. Tite, Research Laboratory for Archaeology and the History of Art, Oxford University, 6 Keble Road, Oxford, OX1 3QJ

Ken D. Thomas, Institute of Archaeology, University College London, 31–34 Gordon Square, London WC1H 0PY

Emma R. Waite, Fossil Fuels and Environmental Geochemistry, Drummond Building, University of Newcastle, Newcastle, NE1 7RU

David Watkinson, School of History and Archaeology, University of Wales, Cardiff, PO Box 494, CF1 3XU

Ian K. Whitbread, Fitch Laboratory, British School of Athens, 52 Odos Souedias, GR 106 76 Athens, Greece

Tony J. Wilkinson, University of Chicago, Oriental Institute, 1155 East Fifty-Eighth Street, Chicago, Illinois 60637 USA

Lyn Wilson, Dept. of Archaeological Sciences, University of Bradford, Richmond Road, Bradford, BD7 1DP

Michael T. Wilson, Dept. of Biological and Chemical Sciences, University of Essex, Wivenhoe Park, Colchester, CO4 3SQ

Alicia Wise, DNER Office, JISC, King's College London, Old Library, Strand, London WC2R 2LS

Derek W. Yalden, School of Biological Sciences, 3–239 Stopford Building, University of Manchester, Manchester, M13 9PL

Michael R. Zimmerman, Dept. of Anthropology, University of Pennsylvania, Philadelphia, PA, USA

Foreword

Almost fifty years ago there was publication of what may be considered as the essential forerunner of the present compendium: this was *La Découverte du Passé* under the editorship of Annette Laming (Editions A. et J. Picard 1952). Among the contributors were R.J.C. Atkinson, A. France-Lanord, A. Leroi-Gourhan, H.L. Movius, K.P. Oakley, and J.F.S. Stone. When I joined the field in 1957 this was the 'bible' that the late Professor Christopher Hawkes placed in my hands. In those days the emphasis was on scientific aids to archaeology notably in the use of chemical analysis of artefacts for study of ancient technology and trade routes, dating by radiocarbon and archaeomagnetism, and location of buried remains by resistivity surveying as pioneered by Atkinson. These were the initial foci of interest in the journal *Archaeometry* when it was first published, in 1958, and these aspects were still dominant in the landmark publication *Science and Archaeology* (Brothwell and Higgs 1963, 1969).

In looking at the contents of these publications one may note the gradual evolution, culminating in the present publication, of biological effects from being interfering factors in the aids provided by physics and chemistry to being the studies themselves. This would seem to be appropriate given the biological nature of humans! But irrespective of any such generalizations the editors are to be congratulated on assembling a veritable feast for all having an interest in things past whether as active practitioners or, as now is the case for myself, observers on the sidelines.

Martin Aitken FRS
Le Garret, France

Acknowledgements

The editors would first of all like to thank their respective families for their patience and support during the production of this book. We would also like to thank all the contributors for responding promptly (well, most of them!) and patiently (all of them!) to increasingly desperate demands for various drafts, corrections, queries, etc. Many people have contributed in various ways to the production of this volume, but particularly Shirley Haigh, who tried to keep the correspondence in some sort of order, and Simon Blockley, who consistently rescued one of the editors (MP) from his incompetent efforts to deal with electronic figures. Simon Blockley and Kirsten Ward also re-drew some of the figures. Becky Nicholson stepped in at the last minute to resuscitate the species index. Holger Schutkowski attempted to make up for MP's appalling lack of skill in European languages. Any errors which remain, of course, are the sole responsibility of the editors. Finally, apologies are due to the cleaners, who have had to work round a mountain of paper on MP's office floor for the last three years!

We are particularly grateful to all those who have given permission to reproduce figures and data. The book is, of course, dedicated to all those giants on whose shoulders we have attempted to stand.

Introduction

Archaeological Science: a Current Perspective

D.R. BROTHWELL and A.M. POLLARD

The collection of papers in this volume reflects the range of scientific studies currently being undertaken in archaeology. The chapters are grouped in sections representing a particular theme (chronometric, palaeoenvironmental, and so forth). Having said that, we do not suggest that this volume is fully comprehensive of the enormous range of research which has been carried out over the past thirty years, since the second edition of *Science in Archaeology* (Brothwell and Higgs 1969). These decades have seen considerable growth in archaeology as science, and the appearance and successful establishment of journals such as *Archaeometry* and the *Journal of Archaeological Science* (both of which have recently expanded), and indeed a number of more specialist journals are now being published. So to attempt a fully comprehensive review of science in archaeology would have demanded a multi-volume encyclopaedic-style of publication. We did not have such a gargantuan task in mind. What we hope is presented here is a reasonably balanced representation of the major areas of scientific activity in world archaeology. Each contribution could have been expanded in various directions, had space allowed, and each one presents something of the personal interests of the individual authors. Few of us in science would present our subjects exactly as our colleagues might. But to recognize different positions, different points of view, between those working in a particular area, is to see the nature of science and recognize its potential for advance. The final choice of what to include (and therefore what to omit) was dictated by several factors, not least of which was the personal interests of the editors, combined with what we could actually persuade our friends and colleagues to produce! No doubt each reader (and reviewer) will produce a list of crucial topics wantonly omitted. So be it, but we hope that those areas selected will serve the next generation of archaeological scientists as well as those identified in the 1960s.

Some of the applications of science in archaeology can now be viewed as relatively mature sciences – radiocarbon must be a prime example, with dedicated laboratories, conferences and specialist literature, but there are others, including the long history of the study of biological remains. The application of some newer sciences to the resolution of archaeological problems is clearly still in its infancy. As with all infants, we can look forward to considerable growth and maturation. The rate of growth will depend on nutrition (i.e., resources) and parental (i.e., archaeological) nurturing. At a global level, growth in archaeological science has been variable, although in Britain at least, academic posts are slowly on the increase (but still modest in total number). As the addresses of some of our contributors show, much essential scientific work is still undertaken outside institutions of archaeology or anthropology. This will of course always happen to some extent, because archaeology is such a broadly-based science subject that it will always call on new lines of scientific research in the 'pure' sciences, if there is potential in applying such new techniques and lines of investigation to archaeological problems.

Nevertheless, the 'embeddedness' of a scientific approach to archaeology within mainstream archaeological thinking remains an important indicator of the vitality of archaeological science. On this measure, much has been achieved in the last 30 years.

Part of our strength and future, however, lies in our essential 'impurity'; what some might term our 'mongrelism'. We are continually attracting 'exotic' science, and applying it to the understanding of earlier human populations. And make no mistake, archaeology, if it is to mature in the new millennium, has to view itself as one of the most difficult but also the most challenging and fascinating of all the sciences, because it is ultimately concerned with the nature of our own species. This requires a high standard of scientific research, and has major implications for our philosophical approach to the subject (e.g., Pollard 1995), especially in the context of teaching. We are, of course, aware of differences of opinion about the relationship between archaeology and archaeological science. Is archaeology basically an 'Arts' subject which occasionally allows in bits of scientific expertise? Is it just about the ruins of sites such as Knossos, or the art of Pompeii? While we all get pleasure and inspiration from these sites, and the scientist is no less romantic than the poet(!), archaeology is concerned with populations through time, and their dispassionate assessment by methodologies which can be adopted and repeated by other researchers. We contend that evaluation means very little if it is not placed on a rigorous scientific basis, so that we all understand, without buzz words and jargon, the standards, methodology and precise nature of the evaluation. We would argue that the philosophy of science is equally applicable to the analysis of cultural phenomena through space and time as to that of soils or bones. Whatever we do as humans, how we perish or survive, migrate, make war, trade stone axes, or paint erotica, requires precise and critical evaluation. This is not to deny the personal hopes, hates, jealousies, pain, fear and irrational beliefs of each one of us, and of those in the past. But it is only by careful analysis of what remains of the past, and its consideration in relation to the modern evidence of ethology, psychology and ethnography, that we can hope for more lasting images of the past. There will always be the need for imagination and evaluation of a range of probabilities in interpreting the past (and we must always avoid projecting our own beliefs and value system backwards in time), but fictional reconstruction (i.e., that which is unconstrained by evidence), whilst no doubt a worthy art form, is not good archaeology. Culture, whether as a material or social component of a

society, can only be understood by dissecting its complexity in a precise fashion. The various levels of human conflict may be viewed in soap opera terms, or in a scientific way at a family, group and population level (Brothwell 1999).

The scientific attitude does not deny the complexity of human culture and society, and its role in determining human responses to environmental and technological change. Perhaps the next step in the expansion of archaeological science will be a critical evaluation of what cultural knowledge and culture-related behaviour amounts to in terms of its adaptive value, or as a means of consolidating group cohesion, or in maximizing fertility in a group, or in ensuring the differential survival of an elite. We may well be sorely tested in casting such a scientific eye at the origins of the Victorian bustle or the post-war craze for the hoola hoop. The application of ethological principles to the scientific study of human behaviour, past and present, may be one of the ways in which further progress in archaeology can be made (Hinde 1991).

In writing this introduction we are very well aware that there has occasionally been criticism of science in archaeology within some theoretical archaeologies. It can be very difficult to understand archaeological colleagues when they express blanket anti-science views. For instance, Whitely (1998:21) writes; 'Because science has failed as a social force, and because its knowledge has been a source of oppression, its grand theories and methods need to be questioned, if not rejected outright... . This reflects the conclusion that alternative modes of knowledge, and means for gaining knowledge, should be explored and adapted, to replace those of a normally bankrupt western science.' Although perhaps a fair reflection of the current wave of popular anti-scientism, we do not recognize or accept this description. Such thinking reinforces the image of the caricature scientist, as a white-coated unimaginative boffin or technician. Nothing could be further from the truth, and the truly great scientists are as creative as any composer or poet. Indeed it seems to stem from a complete misconception of the nature of scientific thinking. In fact we would predict, contrary to such remarks, that science over the next few decades will help to transform current archaeological theory. At present, to those of us concerned with the science within archaeology, the literature on archaeological theory is surprisingly lacking in the integration of scientific theory. Admittedly, this is partly our own fault in not contributing more often to general archaeological theorizing. Another reason may be that certain current theories are not attractive to some working in areas of archaeological science. The ethos of science demands constraint in theorizing. 'Creative' jumps are allowed in science, if constrained by observation and with the expectation of eventual verification. Indeed, the history of scientific thought is punctuated by such paradigm shifts, of which evolution and quantum theory are but two obvious examples. But we do not wish to expand further on this question of good theorizing here, except to hope that the assembled range of studies will show that theory is as relevant and central to archaeological science as any other part of archaeology.

Surely one of the most important problems for us in the future will be the continued funding of scientific research in archaeology. On this point, there seems increasing cause for concern, especially as laboratory costs get higher and higher. The problem is complex and much time is wasted in this new form of hominid-hunting behaviour – for grants. In an ideal world, of course, research planning and funding of important primary research should be international, but, beyond aspects of medical and nuclear research, this remains an unlikely prospect. But perhaps, even if research must remain regional, there is a need for more sharing of experiences – if not frustrations – at an international level. Perhaps because funding is limited and highly competitive, there is a tendency to exercise caution in seeking collaboration. The big challenge to archaeology is to demonstrate coherence in research planning, especially in the identification of those topics of the highest importance in particular research areas. Larger disciplines than ours (such as the Earth sciences) can produce agreed and reasoned national statements identifying the five most important areas for research over the coming five years. Although this might be seen as a sterile intellectual exercise, it demonstrates commonality of purpose and, at a more basic level, that evaluative dialogue is taking place. Such arguments win funding battles. A good example of the lack of agreed common purpose is the way in which applications to study the taphonomy and survival of microbial DNA in specific bone pathology have generally not attracted significant funding. Yet it remains potentially one of the most important aspects of bioarchaeology and medical history.

In Britain between 1994 and 1999, there was a considerable upsurge in interest in ancient biomolecules as a result of substantial and welcome funding by the Natural Environment Research Council (NERC). Looking back at this important endeavour from another millennium, are there lessons to be learnt? The project was entitled the 'Ancient Biomolecules Initiative', but although the technologies were new in archaeology, the research tended to follow established lines of enquiry such as the domestication of plants and animals, or the recent spread of human populations. There was sometimes poor incorporation of the existing knowledge of relevant prehistoric archaeology and linguistic evaluations, as well as rather playing down the real complexity of the situation. It is clear now, after the event, that taphonomic aspects should have been investigated as a first stage, far more thoroughly and in more directions. Availability of samples does not always guarantee results. Ultimately, the problem with such funding models is that after this burst of research effort, earmarked funding diminishes and much of the research ceases. High-level science cannot be turned on and off in such a way. What is needed, as a viable second stage, is the establishment of one or two national laboratories to further such research into the future. Fortunately, in the UK, this is exactly what has happened with the recent establishment of the Ancient Biomolecules Centre, Oxford University as a result of the Joint Infrastructure Fund (which has also funded a replacement accelerator in the Oxford Radiocarbon Accelerator Unit, and a new accelerator at the Scottish Universities Environmental Research Centre, East Kilbride, with a capacity for other cosmogenic nuclei). Radiocarbon laboratories are now established facilities within archaeology, but other important lines of work also deserve long-term support.

Perhaps the greatest change in the thirty years since *Science in Archaeology* has been the wider availability of computers. Information technology has been transformed into a vast global network. But this transformation still seems to leave much to be done, and in particular there are still few well-defined and assembled databases. Some of the future of computational analyses depends on this organization of vastly increasing amounts of data. To take one simple example; there is considerable variation in the osteometric data just on ancient European dogs, and the question is what was this pattern of diversity through Europe in time and space? Indeed, was there selection of specific varieties? With a European canid database, it would be easy enough to undertake multivariate analysis to answer such questions, but such a data base has still to be assembled and thus the questions remain unanswered. Clearly we are at a critical level in data analysis, where often the computer technology is in position but the data is scrambled all over the place, and is in no position to be used effectively.

For all the difficulties which may currently be perceived, there is no doubt in our minds that science will continue to contribute massively to the survival of our species and towards increasing our understanding of its development. The physical remains of the past have huge importance to contemporary life, not only because of their inherent aesthetic qualities, but also because of their relevance to future economic development. Their preservation and interpretation increasingly demands the input of scientific knowledge. We also echo (and extrapolate from) the remarks made by Martin Aitken in 1982 – 'archaeological science does not only serve archaeology.' Many of our sister historical sciences benefit from an input of archaeological information, not least in the form of tighter chronologies and evidence of human response to environmental change. We therefore recommend the papers in this volume to you as examples of how science is contributing significantly to just one academic discipline, archaeology.

On a practical level, the contributions are structured in nine major themes, but a cursory glance will show that these are intersecting and mutually interactive. We have deliberately avoided extensive discussion of techniques, or descriptions of instrumentation – these become rapidly outdated, and are extensively covered elsewhere (e.g., Pollard and Heron 1996:20, or Ciliberto and Spoto 2000). Instead we have encouraged extensive referencing, and have in each section highlighted selected texts for further reading. We trust this approach will allow an appreciation of how the science which originates in a wide range of parent disciplines has enriched our study and understanding of ourselves,

as well as sometimes feeding back to inform the parent discipline. Each section is prefaced by an essay intended to overview and introduce it. Each author has approached his or her task differently, but each essay gives a broader context to the papers which follow.

REFERENCES

Aitken, M.J. (1982). Archaeometry does not only serve archaeology. In Olin, J.S. (ed.) *Future Directions in Archaeometry*, 61. Smithsonian Institution Press: Washington DC.

Brothwell, D. (1999). Biosocial and bio-archaeological aspects of conflict and warfare. In Carman, J. and Harding, A. (eds) *Ancient Warfare, Archaeological Perspectives*, 25–38. Sutton: Stroud.

Ciliberto, E. and Spoto, G. (2000). *Modern Analytical Methods in Art and Archaeology*. John Wiley: New York.

Hinde, R.A. (1991). A biologist looks at anthropology. *Man*, **26**:583–608.

Pollard, A.M. (1995). Why teach Heisenberg to archaeologists? *Antiquity*, **69**:242–247.

Pollard, A.M. and Heron, C. (1996). *Archaeological Chemistry*. Royal Society of Chemistry: Cambridge.

Whitley, D.S. (1998). New approaches to old problems: archaeology in search of an ever-elusive past. In Whitley, D. (ed.) *Reader in Archaeological Theory: Post-processual and Cognitive Approaches*, 1–28. Routledge: London.

SECTION 1

Dating

Overview – Dating in Archaeology; Past, Present and Future

R.E.M. HEDGES

Research Laboratory for Archaeology and the History of Art, University of Oxford.

In several ways dating appears to be one of the most straightforward deployments of archaeological science. From the perspective of even the most ardent post-processualist the objectivity of a chronological framework is seen as important; and for most archaeologists, dating gives a foundation which, although numerically fallible, is not altered by the vagaries of philosophical movements. But this detachment from the messiness of understanding past human behaviour comes at a price. Firstly, published dates of the archaeological record, perceived as so independent of interpretation, can all the more easily acquire a sense of permanence which they may not deserve; and it is very difficult to erase or replace the effect of wrong dates. So dating results, which are inherently difficult to confirm by direct methods, must be right – and this places a serious demand on corroborative support. Secondly, archaeology is nothing if not deliciously interpretative, resting as it does on unavoidably flimsy evidence and the insights of anthropology. A link must be established between an event dateable by physics or chemistry, and the interesting events of human behaviour. This may be subtle and indirect – the section on dendrochronology cites one example of potential problems in the construction of a crannog; the apparent 'curation' of bovid skulls in the radiocarbon dating of the 'Neolithic phase' of Stonehenge is another (Ramsey and Allen 1995) – but in any case it is a link in which both the interpreting archaeologist and the dating scientist must participate.

Another source of complication is the vast range of time which archaeology encompasses. On the one hand culture may change in a generation; dating methods with a precision of, say, 10 years are sought – only dendrochronology, so far, can respond to this. On the other, hominid behaviour can be traced back to beyond four million years. No single general method seems remotely possible to register the complete range, and so the framework of dating is necessarily a mixture of overlapping patches, varying in its robustness and ease of use. Without the fabric of supporting methods, any single method would indeed be rather weak, and although dating is presented here as distinct chapters, the strength of the whole exceeds that of the sum of the parts.

A fourth, and inevitable, aspect of archaeological dating based on the physical sciences, is the need to engage with the 'given' material. Such material, at least, must record some memory of the past, must have survived in recognizable form over time, and must be relevant to the archaeological issues. It comes as a bonus that a chosen sample also happens demonstrably to manifest precisely all the fundamental

Handbook of Archaeological Sciences. Edited by D.R. Brothwell and A.M. Pollard.
© 2001 John Wiley & Sons, Ltd.

assumptions on which a dating method is based. More usually, much of its past history is not recoverable in important ways (thermal history for obsidian; uranium uptake history in bone; biochemical degradation for radiocarbon; solar irradiation history of sediments for optical luminescence, etc.). So more often than not judgement and compromise also play a part; it is part of the dating scientist's role to develop methods to minimize the need for these, but none would deny that experience as well as science is a necessary ingredient in the production of dates.

THE DATING METHODS COVERED

Comparison with the dating methods included in the 1963 and 1969 editions of *Science in Archaeology* edited by Brothwell and Higgs (1963, 1969) is reminiscent of returning to a family group after a generation. Some old friends are still there – most are changed and, we hope, older and wiser. Some are missing, while some have grown surprisingly. Perhaps the main shock is to see how Emiliani's prescient account of deep sea cores (Emiliani 1963) has become the most fundamental chronological framework of all, and quite rightly occupies the first place in the current dating section. Even had one imagined the significance and usefulness of Oxygen Isotope Stratigraphy (OIS), who would have imagined that it could be calibrated by the most basic process of all, which also provides the very basis of our calendar? It is nevertheless unfortunate that the method is necessarily stratigraphic (a single measurement at best tells us only if we are dealing with an even or uneven numbered Stage), and that the primary records are remote from archaeological (even, to an extent, from terrestrial) sites. Therefore dating in most cases depends on a chain of correlations, usually with the common theme of a climatic agency. Such correlations may involve quite different types of evidence, however, as in biostratigraphy and geomorphology, as well as sediment lithology, and these help to provide a better 'fix'. The application to dating Boxgrove (Roberts 1994) is a good example of the clarity the OIS framework has provided, while not necessarily answering the question particularly well. But it does point up the essential role of stratigraphic correlations, and it is somewhat disappointing to find these so little represented in the compilation of dating methods within this volume. Such methods, especially of biostratigraphy but including magnetic stratigraphies, tephrostratigraphy and lithostratigraphies, are bound to become

increasingly useful now that they have a common temporal reference. Does OIS now retire on its laurels, having set up the framework – what more can we expect? For one thing, the OIS has helped to demonstrate the potential of annual archives, especially ice cores, but also lake varves and, we may hope, tree rings. Back in 1969 Shackleton showed a beginning, studying signals from short term archives preserved in molluscs. In this volume, Lowe points out the very rapid short term climatic changes now being discovered in marine and ice cores. As things develop, we can expect an accumulating survey and discovery of novel archives recording stratigraphic blips, perhaps eventually providing not just decadal but even seasonal resolution. How to exploit these will be an interesting challenge for the next generation of archaeologists. In any case, the interpretation of terrestrially-derived, climatically-driven stable isotope records has so far progressed but a little way into this rich territory.

Stratigraphic signals need not, of course, be viewed only in relation to climatic fluctuation. Magnetic changes (which are briefly discussed here) and volcanic events also help to establish connection on a quite large regional scale, while biostratigraphy has the potential for great refinement (for example in tracking changes in insect populations). Therefore almost any technique that produces a date at one specific point may find itself playing a crucial role on another part of the planet. The potential application of Greenland ice core stratigraphy in the dating of the eruption of Thera in the Aegean in the sixteenth century BC illustrates well this kind of long distance linkage (Aitken 1990:25). Powerful examples of this approach result from the accumulating infilling of dendrochronological opportunities, in which archaeologically significant events can have a chance of being registered to within a frighteningly close precision. This depends entirely upon preservation conditions, but it is good to see that more than wetlands or deserts can be exploited; that charcoal can sometimes be dated; and that the whole enterprise becomes more powerful as it grows. The precision of dendrochronology brings quite new, and so far scarcely exploited, potential for archaeological inferences, but in any case the linkage between culturally defined stratigraphy and dendrochronological dating, at least in the later prehistoric periods, does engender a particularly close relationship between archaeology and the dating specialist. I for one am quite converted – from an initial position where the main value of dendrochronology seemed to be in providing a calibration for radiocarbon dating.

The methods considered so far have been essentially stratigraphic – a linkage of simultaneity must be made over a region, from which eventually the environmentally generated signal can be identified against a dated master series. Dating the master series must ultimately refer to either a nuclear-electronic 'clock' or an astronomical clock. Neither the regularity of the solar system, nor the disintegration rate of unstable atomic nuclei is easy to perturb. Both types of clocks, and their dependent dating methods, therefore can be called 'absolute' in principle – but the absolute nature of the cosmogenic radioactive methods becomes in practice subject to environmentally-dependent assumptions – hence the need, to cite one example, for 'calibrating' radiocarbon. In general, nuclear-electronic methods are 'analogue' and linear – the date tends to depend directly on the magnitude of a small set of measurements, and an error in the result is in proportion to the extent to which assumptions are misplaced. In contrast, stratigraphic methods are 'digital' and cyclical with a far less straightforward sense of what determines the possible size of error. Therefore the role of assumptions in the two types of method are quite different. Assumptions can be on any scale; from global, to that of the site, to that of the sample; e.g., from the production rates of a cosmogenic nuclide, or the formation processes of a sedimentary formation, to the extent of extraneous and misleading material in a particular sample. It follows that errors have also to be treated at different levels, and it is, not surprisingly, at the level of the individual sample where an estimate of the likely error is most difficult to make. A main way to manage these difficulties is to exercise an increasingly rigorous selection on the sample itself.

SAMPLE SELECTION

One of the striking features of developments in dating is how critical this question of sample selection has become, and we see it at work in several of the most important methods. For example in potassium–argon dating, by using a focused laser to liberate the trapped radiogenic gas it is now possible to measure the nuclide abundance ratio for a single rock grain (e.g., Maluski and Schaeffer 1982). So a volcanic deposit containing reworked older sediment – which would previously have dominated the argon signal and produced far too old an age – can now be dissected and dated particle by particle. The same approach can be taken in the luminescent dating of sediment; indeed it has allowed

the notoriously early dating of the Australian site of Jinmium to be re-dated to a far less exciting and eccentric date; more details for this example are given by Grün in his chapter. Similarly in radiocarbon dating, the 'third revolution' identified by Taylor has been effective largely because the possibility to use much smaller amounts of material makes it feasible for a crude organic sample to be chemically dissected. A good example is provided by a potsherd which can contain several carbon sources all of different age (from the clay before firing, the temper, the firesmoke, food residues and other such usage, or from the soaking up of mobile soil organics during burial). Here separation of chemical sources is not at all easy, but one elegant possibility is the gas-chromatographic separation of lipids extracted from the cooking residues into single molecular compounds such as palmitic and stearic acids. A fourth example is provided by U series measurements. As the radiocarbon sample size has been reduced by a factor of 1000 by employing mass spectrometric in place of radioactive detection methods, so has the sample size for uranium-daughter measurements. A particular challenge is to apply this method to bone and tooth, where it would have the greatest relevance to the site archaeology. The problem here is that uptake of uranium by bone is so obviously a chemically open system that far more information is needed before the geochemical situation can be modelled and the method applied. It is now possible to supply this information from measurements of the daughter product in profiles across a bone, using thermal ionization or inductively coupled plasma mass spectrometry (Millard and Hedges 1996, Pike and Hedges in press). No doubt this process of continuing refinement will carry on – even radiocarbon has about a factor of ten to go in sample size reduction before it reaches a theoretical limit. However, to set against this is the effort involved – only the most important problems can expect to be tackled; although it would be foolish to predict, from current technology, what would count as effort in 30 years time.

In neither edition of *Science in Archaeology* (Brothwell and Higgs 1963, 1969) was there any notion of cosmogenic nuclides other than radiocarbon. So the 'other nuclides' are very much new kids on the block, and, like many teenagers, their application to dating has not been especially fulfilling, at least from the point of view of archaeology. This is largely because only radiocarbon has a global mixing mechanism (i.e., carbon dioxide in the atmosphere and the oceans); as the chapter by Stuart explains, hopes for the technically difficult isotope ^{41}Ca were dashed when its ratio to

^{40}Ca was found to vary in contemporary fauna; and this had seemed to be the nuclide with the greatest promise of archaeological application. Nevertheless, a lot of valuable geomorphological work has been done with exposure ages measured, for example, on moraines (Gosse *et al.* 1995), or on soil erosion, with the most commonly applied nuclide ^{10}Be, often in conjunction with ^{26}Al. Actually, the long term records of ^{10}Be deposition have helped to separate cosmic ray production rate from geomagnetic shielding effects, so helping to understand the causes of variation in the radiocarbon calibration curve – another example of how different methods, often in unexpected ways, interact to strengthen each other.

Luminescent methods were, however, quite definitely a gleam in the eye of their 1960s contributors. It is quite marvellous to see how much things have changed since then. While the clock still ticks (mainly) to nuclear disintegrations, the processes that start and stop it, and the way in which the record of accumulated radiation damage is revealed, have, along with the material and the events being studied, evolved in unpredictable directions. Dating Roman pottery has given way to establishing the antiquity of anatomically modern humans in Australia through a careful analysis of site formation processes. No other member of the family of dating methods has been able to help in this. On the other hand, the very important application of thermoluminescence to burnt flint in the Mount Carmel caves of the Levant (Mercier *et al.* 1993) is able to be corroborated by such related methods as Electron Spin Resonance (ESR) on such different material as tooth enamel. But burnt flint is not common, and a great strength of ESR, by contrast, is its application to abundant and critical material. Helped also by uranium-series dating of calcite deposits (mainly travertines and flowstones in stratigraphic association), these methods have raised great beacons back into the time when our own species was forming itself. If uranium-series dating can also be reliably applied to bone, and there is some hope for this, a very powerful combination of methods will be available to document thoroughly this most critical period in human development.

One could fancy that uranium-series dating of bone was foreshadowed in Oakley's article on dating through bone chemistry (Oakley 1969), in which uranium uptake over time was demonstrated. Alas, like most chemical methods, this had a good run for its money before succumbing eventually to uncooperative reality. The problem, of course, is that few chemical clocks are independent of the chemical environment,

and none are independent of temperature. This last difficulty is not fatal, however, and the case of obsidian hydration demonstrates how both difficulties can be circumvented in favourable circumstances. But one would never choose chemical clocks except in desperation, although where radiocarbon dating is inadequate (the young archaeology of New Zealand makes a good example), or out of reach, then it has been worth the try, provided corroboration is available. One naturally thinks of amino acid racemization; unfortunately it was, at an early stage, applied to the most difficult material of all – bone – and the seductive but ultimately disillusioning results (see Pollard and Heron 1996:271) have deterred others. However, results on apparently less charismatic material such as ostrich shell promise real success (Miller *et al.* 1999). Actually ostrich shell turns out to be a rich source of information in those same African Middle Stone Age sites where the technologies developed by early modern humans are first manifested. If ostrich shells, why not molluscs? The disarmingly named 'aminostratigraphy' of molluscs from raised beaches, etc., (Bowen 1999) which therefore correlate well with isotope stages since the chemistry is slowed down during the cold stages, while not without ambiguities, does also provide additional links in the dating framework. And – who knows? – one day we may understand enough about the degradation of proteins in bone to show that some changes – maybe amino acid racemization, maybe not – are sufficiently clock-like to provide a determination of age.

I have left radiocarbon dating to last. This was firmly established by the 1960s, and already prominent in the first edition of Brothwell and Higgs (1963). Methods are much more prominent now, and having undergone three revolutions, radiocarbon dating seems set to enjoy a dominant but comfortable maturity. Probably 95 per cent of all archaeological dates have been determined by radiocarbon, which attests to the match between the ^{14}C half-life and world growth in population, as well as to the ubiquity of suitable material. But maturity should not include complacency, and radiocarbon dating is still a long way from being a fully satisfactory method. For a start, the construction of a dating chronology inevitably invites new dates, which build on existing ones, to achieve that much higher resolution and penetrate that much further. So improved accuracy and precision is always sought, though now is unfortunately limited by the calibration curve. This can be partially defeated on occasion by 'wiggle matching', or by the statistical combination of additional chronological information (e.g., from stratigraphy) but in general the curve can't be bucked. Although great progress has been made in continuing the curve into the Pleistocene, at this stage results so far serve more as warnings of troubles to come in the interpretation of dates in the 30–40 ka time period. A chronology based on uncalibrated radiocarbon dates will at best be distorted and at worst treacherously ambiguous. Within the Holocene the situation is now fairly clear and calibration limitations are accepted. Other sources of error become relevant, and there is, for example, no general way to demonstrate that a given sample, even after chemical processing, does not contain a level of contamination of different age carbon sufficient to alter the date significantly. Experience has shown that some materials can be treated to give far more reliable dates than others, but it remains a major challenge to be able to date important classes of material. For example, bone from hot continental environments more than a few millennia old usually contains a sufficient amount of carbon to date, but no one has found a way to separate exogenous from endogenous material when so much has degraded so badly. The list could be continued. A related problem which has retreated only slightly is the ability to date beyond about eight half lives (> 46 ka BP). So far, AMS methods have promised more than they have delivered – much of the problem lies in laboratory-derived contamination which gets worse the smaller the sample. But also verifying that dates of $c.$ 50 ka age are correct, are corroborated with proper stratigraphic behaviour, and have adequate precision for real testing, is a major effort. These problems partly arise from the prevalence and versatility of carbon chemistry in our world – the very advantage that gives radiocarbon dating such a wide range of application. As more different kinds of material are studied, another difficulty is encountered in the complexity of biological carbon flows from atmosphere to sample. It is now clear that many food webs may contain carbon from different ages – perhaps derived from organic matter in the soil and transported via aquatic food webs. So in many cases it becomes necessary to understand the ecological setting of an archaeological sample, in addition to its taphonomic and geochemical setting.

HOW WILL OUR DATING FAMILY LOOK IN ANOTHER 30 TO 40 YEARS?

Of course not all the family is here in this volume – some absences have already been noted. One potential member whose relationship might not yet be recognized is the evidence provided by molecular genetic analysis of modern (and perhaps even ancient) populations. It is possible to construct 'coalescence times' for genetic types which are descended without recombination (such as mitochondrial and Y chromosome variants) so that, give or take a few basic assumptions about population demographic history, the temporal origins for the separation populations can be assigned. It would be surprising if much of the chronological evidence for human evolution and population dispersal in the next edition was not based on genetic data.

The gap beyond radiocarbon is not well-filled. This is critical for our understanding of the advent of anatomically modern humans, from 'Out of Africa' to 'into Australia', and indeed much of the Old World. Whether existing techniques will sufficiently fill this gap remains to be seen – most of the difficulties are soluble by present methods, given enough detailed information about the specific situation under study; also, perhaps other as yet unconceived chemical methods can be made to work. It would be surprising if new and precise stratigraphic markers, whether climate related or perhaps signals of glitches in the solar wind, were not to be discovered and used to bind together the whole gamut of dating opportunities.

Many of our major current dating questions, within the radiocarbon period, seem as much a question of archaeology and application as of dating. This includes migration into the Americas, the dynamics of Neolithicization in Europe, and the co-existence of Neanderthal with modern humans. But if dating could be made far more precise, (and this seems unlikely for radiocarbon), then many entirely new archaeological questions – for example, featuring demography – would present themselves. Again, such a possibility is more likely to come from stratigraphic methods, perhaps in combination – if wiggle matching could be made to work on 5 or 10 year intervals, for (an unrealistic!) example – and a reader in 30 years time might be as interested to see how the latest method had evolved out of those we know today as we are looking back on the first *Science in Archaeology*.

I started by emphasizing the objective nature of establishing a date, and how the result has its own independent significance. To finish I would like to balance this, by recalling how methods of dating form a complex community within themselves, and are embedded in a wider context of environmental scientific knowledge. The requirement for an overall frame of reference, and the need for corroboration between methods, work to ensure that the whole is far more powerful than the sum of the parts.

REFERENCES

Aitken, M.J. (1990). *Science-based Dating in Archaeology*. Longman: London.

Bowen, D.Q. (1999). Only four major 100-ka glaciations during the Brunhes Chron? *International Journal of Earth Sciences*, **88**:276–284.

Brothwell, D. and Higgs, E. (eds) (1963). *Science in Archaeology*. Thames and Hudson: London.

Brothwell, D. and Higgs, E. (eds) (1969). *Science in Archaeology*, (2nd edn). Thames and Hudson: London.

Emiliani, C. (1963). The significance of deep-sea cores. In Brothwell, D. and Higgs, E. (eds), *Science in Archaeology*, 99–107. Thames and Hudson: London.

Gosse, J., Klein, J., Evenson, E.B., Lawn, B. and Middleton, R. (1995). Be-10 dating of the duration and retreat of the last Pinedale glacial sequence. *Science*, **268**:1329–1333.

Maluski, H. and Schaeffer, O.A. (1982). Ar-39-Ar-40 laser probe dating of terrestrial rocks. *Earth and Planetary Science Letters*, **59**:21–27.

Mercier, N., Valladas, H., Bar-Yosef, O., Vandermeersch, B., Stringer, C. and Joron, J.L. (1993). Thermoluminescence date for the Mousterian burial site of Es-Skhul, Mt. Carmel. *Journal of Archaeological Science*, **20**:169–174.

Millard, A.R. and Hedges, R.E.M. (1996). A diffusion-adsorption model of uranium uptake by archaeological bone. *Geochimica et Cosmochimica Acta*, **60**:2139–2152.

Miller, G.H., Beaumont, P.B., Deacon, H.J., Brooks, A.S., Hare, P.E. and Jull, A.J.T. (1999). Earliest modern humans in southern Africa dated by isoleucine epimerization in ostrich eggshell. *Quaternary Science Reviews*, **18**:1537–1548.

Oakley, K.P. (1969). Analytical methods of dating bones. In Brothwell, D. and Higgs, E. (eds), *Science in Archaeology*, (2nd edn), 35–45. Thames and Hudson: London.

Pike, A.W.G. and Hedges, R.E.M. (in press). Sample geometry and U-uptake in archaeological teeth: implications for U-series and ESR dating. *Quaternary Geochemistry*.

Pollard, A.M. and Heron, C. (1996). *Archaeological Chemistry*. Royal Society of Chemistry: Cambridge.

Ramsey, C.B. and Allen, M.J. (1995). Analysis of the radiocarbon dates and their archaeological significance. In Cleal, R.M.J., Walker, K.E. and Montague, R. (eds) *Stonehenge in its Landscape*. Archaeological Report 10, 526–535. English Heritage: London.

Roberts, M.B. (1994). How old is Boxgrove Man – reply. *Nature*, **371**:751.

Shackleton, N. (1969). Marine mollusca in archaeology. In Brothwell, D. and Higgs, E. (eds) *Science in Archaeology* (2nd edn), 407–414. Thames and Hudson: London.

1

Quaternary Geochronological Frameworks

J.J. LOWE

Centre for Quaternary Research, Department of Geography, Royal Holloway,
University of London.

There is growing evidence to suggest that the Earth experienced pronounced cooling between approximately 2.8 and 2.4 million years ago (Ma). Because this change is reflected in a diverse range of geological records from both continental and ocean realms, many scientists take this to mark the onset of the Quaternary period (e.g., Lowe and Walker 1997, Williams *et al.* 1998). The earliest major expansions of continental ice sheets in the northern hemisphere date to around 2.75 Ma (Shackleton *et al.* 1984, Willis *et al.* 1999). Layers of ice-rafted debris in sediments on the floor of the North Atlantic Ocean become more conspicuous and widespread around 2.5 Ma (Ruddiman and Raymo 1988, Ruddiman *et al.* 1989). The vast thickness of loess that blankets the Loess Plateau of northern China began to accumulate about 2.5 to 2.3 Ma (Heller and Liu 1982, Kukla *et al.* 1990), whilst the deserts of Africa, Australia and South America appear to have expanded at around the same time (Williams *et al.* 1998). Lake sediment sequences in such widely separated localities as Israel, Japan and Colombia all record significant environmental change at around 2.4 Ma (Kukla 1989). It is interesting, then, that the earliest skeletal remains of primates that were beginning to resemble modern humans (hominids) also date to about, or shortly after, this time (Deacon and Deacon 1999; see Chapter 17). This has led to speculation on the possible connections between the pace of human evolution and climatic impacts on the environment (e.g., Vrba *et al.* 1995, Vrba 1996).

While an environmentally deterministic explanation of human evolution remains debatable, it is nonetheless clear that the record of human history, from the skeletal fragments of hominids of late Pliocene to early Quaternary age, to the rich cultural legacy of classical to modern times, must be viewed against the backcloth of climatic change. This seems axiomatic for at least two reasons. Firstly, climate almost certainly had a significant influence on human endeavours and on the path of human history. It governs the thresholds, rates and magnitudes of so many environmental processes on which human survival and economy depend (e.g., vegetation succession, faunal distributions, oceanic circulation and temperature, rates and types of soil formation, global volume of ice and hence global or eustatic sea levels, etc.). The second reason is related to geochronology: global climate variations during the Quaternary appear to have been orchestrated by regular changes in the geometrical disposition of the Sun and the Earth (so-called 'astronomical variables'), and these temporal rhythms are reflected in the geological record. They provide the basis for one of the most important chronometers employed today for the dating and correlation of Quaternary successions and events: the 'SPECMAP timescale'.

Handbook of Archaeological Sciences. Edited by D.R. Brothwell and A.M. Pollard.
© 2001 John Wiley & Sons, Ltd.

In this chapter, the focus is on the principles that have led to the construction of the SPECMAP timescale and, to a lesser extent, on a second important dating method that has been employed to test some of the SPECMAP assumptions, as well as to date some of the early hominid records – *magnetic reversal stratigraphy* (the 'palaeomagnetic timescale'). These two topics together provide an overarching geochronological framework for the dating and correlation of Quaternary environmental changes, the history of human evolution and the archaeological record. There are, of course, many other methods available for dating Quaternary sequences and events, as well as any archaeological horizons and remains associated with them. Some of these are addressed in other chapters in this section. For a summary of the comprehensive range of dating and correlation methods available, see Aitken (1990), Smart and Frances (1991) and Lowe and Walker (1997).

ASTRONOMICAL THEORY (MILANKOVITCH HYPOTHESIS)

The 'Astronomical Theory' of global climate change was developed by a Scotsman, James Croll, over 100 years ago and subsequently elaborated by a Serbian geophysicist, Milutin Milankovitch, in 1924. The 'Milankovitch Hypothesis', as it has become popularly known, is based on the notion that the Earth's climate varies over the long (millennial) term due to regular and predictable changes in the Earth's orbit and axis (Berger *et al.* 1984). Planetary gravitational forces alter;

(i)   the shape of the Earth's orbit, which varies from almost circular to elliptical and back again over a cycle of approximately 100 ka, a process referred to as the *eccentricity of the orbit,*

(ii)   the tilt of the Earth's axis relative to the ecliptic (the Earth's orbital plane) which inclines between extremes of 21° 39' and 24° 36' over a cycle of c. 41 ka, a phenomenon known as the *obliquity of the ecliptic,* and

(iii)   a rotational movement of the Earth around its axis (the Earth's 'wobble'), which leads to a constant shift in the season of the year in which the Earth is nearest the sun, since this is determined by the prevailing geometry of the Earth's inclination and its orbital path. This third process, known as *precession of the equinoxes* or *precession of the solstices,* varies over cycles with durations of 19 and 23 ka. A fuller account of these

variations can be found in Lowe and Walker (1997), Williams *et al.* (1998), and Wilson *et al.* (1999).

Milankovitch argued that these astronomical cycles, working in combination, drive long-term climatic variations at the surface of the Earth. The total amount of radiation received by the Earth is mainly determined by the eccentricity of the Earth's orbit, whilst the other variables affect the way in which incoming radiation is distributed over the Earth's surface. He used mathematical constants to define each of the three orbital mechanisms, and made assumptions about their radiative effects on the surface of the Earth, and thus computed their integrated (net) radiative effect which, he argued, provided the best explanation of global temperature variations over the recent geological past. The basic principles developed by Milankovitch are still widely held to be valid today, although the harmonics of the orbital motions and the scale of their radiative effects on the Earth have been re-calculated many times, e.g., Berger and Loutre (1994) and Berger *et al.* (1999). The mathematical calculations are likely to be refined even further, but in broad terms the three main Milankovitch rhythms appear to provide a robust, general explanation for long-term, cyclic climate oscillations during the Quaternary (Rial 1999). Cyclic phenomena with similar periodicities have been detected in a diverse range of marine and terrestrial records. The earliest clear evidence to support the theory arose from a series of pioneering studies of oxygen isotope variations in deep marine sedimentary sequences, the results of which were published during the 1960s (Imbrie and Imbrie 1979).

OXYGEN ISOTOPE STRATIGRAPHY OF DEEP MARINE CORES

In parts of the deep ocean floors, marine 'oozes' – fine-grained muds that consist largely of the remains of marine microfossils and fine (clay-grade) clastic particles – have accumulated continuously (albeit slowly) over millions of years. Numerous cores have been recovered from these deposits over the past four decades or so, using specially designed ships and drilling apparatus, and their microfossil content, as well as a range of sedimentological properties, have been analysed in great detail. Most attention, however, has been devoted to the analysis of one parameter in particular: the *oxygen isotope ratio* of selected marine microfossils. This is because the results have consistently revealed cyclic variations with periodicities that match those of the dominant Milankovitch rhythms of eccentricity, obliquity and precession (Shackleton 1987, Berger 1988).

Many marine organisms secrete or construct carbonate or siliceous hard parts during their life cycle, for which oxygen is derived directly from the sea water which they inhabit. The fossil remains of these marine organisms accumulate on the sea floor, and successive fossil accumulations provide a record of temporal changes in oxygen isotope ratios within the oceans. There are three isotopes of oxygen in nature, of which the heaviest is ^{18}O and the lightest is ^{16}O. The third isotope (^{17}O) can be ignored in the present context. The ratio of ^{18}O to ^{16}O (denoted as δ^{18}O: the deviation of ^{18}O content of a sample relative to an agreed international laboratory standard; see Chapter 16) from microfossils in a long marine sediment sequence varies in a quasi-cyclic fashion (see below and Figure 1.1). Furthermore, the quasi-cyclical patterns (isotope 'traces' or profiles) obtained from numerous core sequences recovered from different ocean basins, and which are based on a variety of fossil types, are frequently very similar. This suggests that the cyclical isotope variations preserved in marine microfossil records reflect widespread factors that have affected the oceans *en masse*.

The oxygen isotope ratio of ocean water is altered through a *fractionation* process, which is the preferential removal or enrichment of the lighter isotope. The process is in part a direct result of global climate variations, because ocean δ^{18}O is partly temperature-dependent. Over the long term, however, the dominant influence is the volume of the world's ice sheets (Shackleton and Opdyke 1973, Shackleton 1987), which expanded markedly during cold (*glacial*) episodes and contracted during warm (*interglacial*) episodes. This process alters the balance of water stored within the oceans and on land, which in turn leads to shifts in the ratio of heavy to light isotopes of oxygen in both the oceans and in the ice sheets.

During the water cycle (see Chapter 16), evaporation of water from the sea surface leads to the preferential removal of the lighter H_2^{16}O molecules, because slightly more energy is required to remove the heavier H_2^{18}O molecules. During glacial stages, as the ice sheets expand, water is removed from the oceans and stored in the ice, and since atmospheric water is preferentially enriched in H_2^{16}O, the ice sheets are composed of water that has a much lower δ^{18}O than sea water. With the progressive selective removal of H_2^{16}O from the oceans during glacial stages, sea water becomes enriched in ^{18}O: it becomes *isotopically heavy*. Thus the larger the ice sheets grow, the 'heavier' becomes the oxygen isotope ratio of sea water. Conversely, when the ice sheets melt during interglacial stages, large volumes of water enriched in H_2^{16}O are delivered back to the oceans, thus making sea water isotopically lighter than during glacial stages. Figure 1.1 shows two typical 'saw-toothed' isotopic traces from marine microfossil records which span the last 2.6 million years. The successive oscillations between heavier and lighter ratios reflect directly the alternate waxing and waning of the world's ice sheets. Such palaeoenvironmental interpretations of isotopic profiles generally assume that marine biota secrete or construct carbonate or silicate structures with an oxygen isotope ratio identical to that of the sea water in which they live, though this need not always be the case (see Patience and Kroon 1991).

In order to establish the periodicity of the quasi-cyclic variations reflected in marine microfossil records, two things are necessary; (i) some means of establishing the age of key horizons within the sequence, in order to define an age range spanning several cycles, and (ii) a mathematical basis for calculating the strength and wavelength of any cycles represented. In the pioneering studies of these records, the first requirement was met by the application of palaeomagnetic reversal dating (see below and Chapter 6) whilst the second was effected by *spectral analysis* of the time-series data. In a classic publication Hays *et al.* (1976) used spectral analysis on a marine oxygen isotope record to demonstrate that the dominant cycles had periodicities of 100, 41, 24 and 19 ka. They concluded that astronomical cycles were the primary driving mechanism behind long-term climate changes during the Quaternary (Imbrie and Imbrie 1979), an influence which we now refer to as *orbital forcing*.

THE OXYGEN ISOTOPE STAGE SCHEME

As argued above, the characteristic peaks and troughs in marine isotope traces reflect the relative extent of global palaeoglaciation, which indirectly reflects global temperature variations, with the 'peaks' of lighter ratios reflecting warmer conditions (i.e., high sea-levels and reduced glacial cover). Isotope traces are conventionally divided into *oxygen isotope stages (OIS)*, counting from the top of each core sequence (Figures 1.1 and 1.2). Warm episodes are allocated odd numbers, counting consecutively from the current warm episode, the Holocene interglacial (OIS-1). Even numbers denote

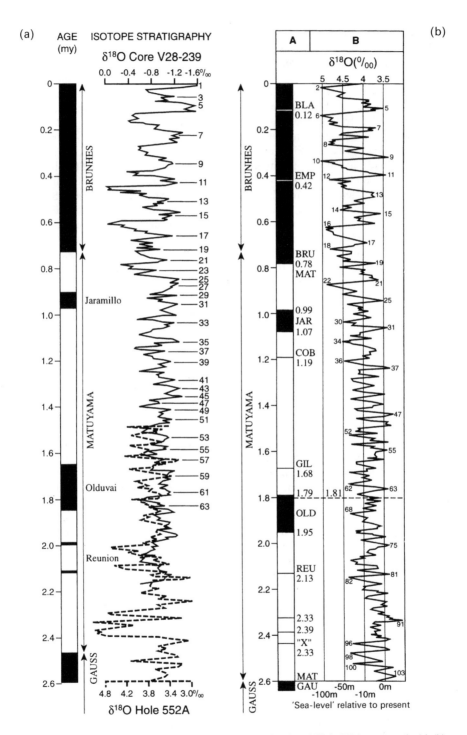

Figure 1.1   (a) Composite oxygen isotope profiles from Pacific cores V28-239 and Hole 552A compared with (b) oxygen isotope profile from ODP (677) (modified after several sources, but mainly Shackleton *et al.* 1990). The numbers on each curve are oxygen isotope stages. The palaeomagnetic reversal scale (shown to the left of each curve) for (a) is constructed using 'raw' (radiometric) ages, while that for (b) has been calibrated to the orbital timescale. See text for explanation of these terms.

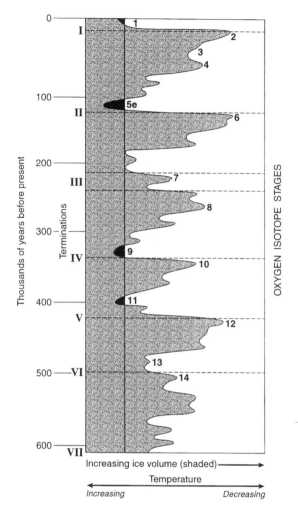

Figure 1.2 Schematic representation of oxygen isotope variations for the past 600 ka, drawn with lighter isotope values to the left and heavier values to the right, so that increase in shading represents increase in global glaciation. Arabic numerals denote oxygen isotope stages; Roman numerals to left indicate positions of *Terminations* (after Lowe and Walker 1997).

cold stages. Because it is a 'count-from-top' method, the application of this scheme for dating and correlation can be problematic where there are hiatuses in the marine records, where sequences have been subject to deformation, or where the isotope variations are subdued (Jansen 1989). An important feature of the OIS notation system is that, whereas the odd and even numbers generally indicate warm and cold episodes of interglacial and glacial status respectively, this is not the case for oxygen isotope stages 2 to 5. During the initial defi-

nition of the OIS scheme, the peak labelled OIS-3 was incorrectly assumed to have interglacial status. Subsequent research, however, has shown that the last interglacial–glacial cycle (OIS-5 to OIS-2; roughly 130 to 18 ka) is represented in much more stratigraphic detail than the preceding stages, due to less compression of the more recent, near-surface sediments. OIS-5 can thus be subdivided into a number of sub-stages (5e to 5a), of which only sub-stage 5e is now considered to reflect true interglacial conditions (the last, Eemian or Ipswichian interglacial, approximately 130–120 ka). The other sub-stages of 5, as well as OIS-4, OIS-3 and OIS-2, represent shorter-lived climatic oscillations superimposed on the overall trend of cooling between the last interglacial thermal maximum (OIS-5e) and the thermal minimum of the last glacial stage (OIS-2).

Since all of the oceans are affected simultaneously by the fractionation effects which result from changes in the volume of global ice sheets, the isotope profiles obtained from different marine cores can be correlated by matching equivalent peaks and troughs, since these should be contemporaneous. The matching process is aided by the characteristic asymmetric ('saw-tooth') shape of the profiles. The start of each interglacial stage is abrupt, with very steep changes to lighter isotopic values, probably reflecting rapid melting of the ice sheets. By comparison, the changes to heavier isotope values in the oceans during glacial stages is more gradual, probably as a result of a slow build-up of continental ice sheets (Lowe and Walker 1997:151). The sharp boundaries between glacial and interglacial stages are termed *Terminations* (Figure 1.2). Note that *Termination II* marks the start of the Last Interglacial (the lower boundary of OIS-5e, dated approximately to 130 ka) and *Termination I* the beginning of the present (Holocene) interglacial (OIS-1: *c.* 11.5 ka BP). The number of terminations represented in the profiles, the fact that some terminations are more pronounced than others (e.g., *Termination IV*) and the overall shape of the profiles (the number and the clarity of oxygen isotope stages recognized) all aid in the matching process. It was, however, the development of magnetic reversal dating that provided the first opportunity to establish whether core-matching in this way provides reliable and consistent results.

MAGNETIC REVERSAL (POLARITY) STRATIGRAPHY

The Earth's magnetic field is in a constant state of flux, varying in both strength and direction due to a number of internal and external geophysical influences (Tarling 1983). The geomagnetic poles migrate relative to the geographic poles (occasionally termed *polar wandering*) and, from time to time, experience complete reversal, with the N and S geomagnetic poles switching positions. Recent changes in field strength and in the positions of the geomagnetic poles can be reconstructed from direct instrumental measurements and historical records (Thompson and Oldfield 1986). Beyond this, the longer-term pattern of geomagnetic changes can be inferred from archaeomagnetic measurements (e.g., fire-baked bricks, tiles, pottery and hearths: Chapter 6) and from geological data (volcanic strata, deep-marine sediments, lake sediments) because crystals or fine-grained suspended sediment particles will often align in the direction of the prevailing magnetic field. Thus, for example, crystals in magma that are rich in ferromagnetic material can become aligned during cooling, while clay particles in marine or lake sediments, which become aligned during suspension, may retain their preferred orientation after settling. The former strength, declination, inclination and polarity of the Earth's magnetic field can be inferred by measuring the *natural remanent magnetism (NRM)* locked in the archaeological and geological archives.

The study of variations in magnetic properties through a sequence of rocks or sediments is termed *magnetostratigraphy*. This encompasses three different approaches to the measurement of lithological magnetic properties for the purposes of correlation and dating. The first is based on the measurement of the *mineral magnetic potential* or *magnetic susceptibility* of samples (the magnetic properties inherent in, or that can be induced in, a unit sample volume), which varies with the concentration, size and chemical composition of 'magnetizable' particles present within different lithological units. The resulting information can provide much useful insight into past environmental history, as well as a basis for correlation of sequences at a local (within-site) scale (Thompson and Oldfield 1986, Walden *et al.* 1999). The second approach is the reconstruction of *secular variations* in declination (polar wandering), inclination and strength of the Earth's magnetic field. This information can provide the basis for correlation of geological successions at the regional scale (e.g., Thompson 1986). Both of these approaches are discussed in more detail in Aitken (1990) and in Chapter 6. The third approach, based on the history of geomagnetic polarity reversals, provides a scheme for dating and correlating Quaternary as well as pre-Quaternary strata at a global scale. The focus here is on this third aspect only.

Deep-sea sediments, long lake sediment sequences and certain volcanic strata retain long-term histories of changes in the Earth's magnetic field. These archives reveal that the Earth's polarity is subject to frequent and very sudden reversals, the reasons for which are still not fully understood, though they appear to relate to progressive changes in field intensity (Valet and Meynadier 1993). The present-day magnetic field is conventionally considered to exhibit *normal polarity*, whilst the opposite configuration is termed *reversed polarity*. Records of polarity reversal, which extend back to the Cretaceous and beyond, show long periods during which the dipole (the N–S field axis) tends to remain locked in one of these alignments. For example, the Earth's magnetic dipole has tended to adopt the normal configuration for the last 800 000 years or so (see below). These long periods of preferred polarity, with durations of around 10^5 to 10^7 years, are designated *polarity epochs*. They were far from stable periods, however, for they were frequently interrupted by much shorter episodes of reversal termed *polarity events*, as well as by *polarity excursions*, which are short-lived migrations of the positions of the poles through 45° or more. Since polarity reversals have global impacts, polarity epochs and events can be used as a basis for world-wide geological correlations.

Where the epoch boundaries can be detected in volcanic strata, the host rock can be dated using the potassium–argon (K-Ar) method (Aitken 1990), thereby enabling a *palaeomagnetic reversal timescale* to be established (Figure 1.3). Dates for the last three epoch boundaries, the Brunhes/Matuyama (*c.* 0.73 Ma), the Matuyama/Gauss (*c.* 2.47 Ma) and the Gauss/Gilbert (*c.* 3.41 Ma), are fairly secure, as they are based on a large number of age determinations (Thompson 1991). By comparison, the ages of the polarity events are less secure, due to the limited number and lower precision of available K-Ar dates. In the majority of these cases, therefore, their ages have been estimated by interpolation (Berggren *et al.* 1980).

The magnetic reversal timescale provides an independent basis for dating and correlating marine oxygen isotope records (Cande and Kent 1995). Due to their fine-grained nature, and because they generally settle under very tranquil conditions, clastic marine sediments often retain a *detrital remanent magnetism*. Analysis of the magnetostratigraphy of deep marine deposits, therefore, will often show the imprint of the series of magnetic polarity reversals which have affected the sediments during their deposition. In places where the marine sediment record extends over a million years or more, epoch boundaries are easily detected.

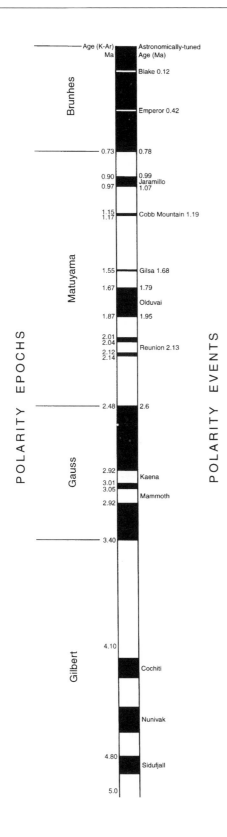

However, the detection of magnetic events, especially those that were very short-lived, is less straightforward. Where sedimentation has been particularly slow, the sequence may be so compressed that polarity events are difficult to resolve. Conversely, where sedimentation rates have been relatively high (*c.* 0.25 to 0.5 m/1000 years or more), it is frequently difficult to obtain cores of sediment that extend below the Brunhes/Matuyama transition.

The polarity epoch boundaries provide useful marker horizons for testing correlations based on oxygen isotope stratigraphy. For example, the two isotope traces shown in Figure 1.1, which span the whole of the Quaternary, can be correlated by magnetostratigraphy. In both cases the Brunhes/Matuyama boundary coincides with OIS-19, which supports the notion that oxygen isotope stages are broadly synchronous. Since the boundary has been dated radiometrically, this also provides an age for OIS-19, and thus an age-span for the interval between oxygen isotope stages 1 to 19, which in turn provides a basis for calculating the periodicities of cyclic changes reflected in isotope variations. These useful applications notwithstanding, the palaeomagnetic reversal timescale can only provide age estimates for epoch boundaries and some of the geomagnetic events that have been dated by independent geochronological methods. Ages of horizons that fall between these events are estimated by interpolation. The SPECMAP timescale, on the other hand, provides a continuous timescale for estimating the age of any horizon in the marine oxygen isotope record.

THE SPECMAP TIMESCALE

Since the isotopic stage boundaries (especially the clearly-defined Terminations) are essentially synchronous, and since time series analysis shows them to have periodicities which approximate the astronomical (Milankovitch) frequencies of 23 ka, 41 ka and 100 ka, then the ages of any stage boundary can be computed by extrapolating back from the present day using the

Figure 1.3 The palaeomagnetic timescale for the last 5 Ma. Shaded segments indicate periods of normal polarity while unshaded segments denote reversed polarity. Polarity epochs are named on left, and events on the right. Radiometric ages for polarity epoch boundaries and events are indicated on the left, while ages calibrated by orbital tuning are shown on the right. (Based on several sources – see Lowe and Walker 1997.)

astronomical constants. Imbrie *et al.* (1984) developed a standard, high-resolution chronology for oxygen isotope records, known as the *SPECMAP timescale*, by 'tuning' the isotope records to the astronomical timescale (*orbital tuning*). The procedure involved the following steps. In order to avoid any bias associated with an individual isotope record, a standardized curve was derived by 'stacking' a number of records in which the isotopic stages were well defined. The resulting composite (master) curve was then smoothed and filtered to reduce statistical 'noise', and spectral analysis was then performed. Cyclic phenomena thus revealed were then aligned with the equivalent astronomical cycles (the process of 'tuning') using six key reference points of established age (five based on radiocarbon dating, and the sixth – the Brunhes/Matuyama boundary – dated by K-Ar) as chronological markers. The SPECMAP timescale constructed for the last 300 000 years of the Pleistocene by Martinson *et al.* (1987) is illustrated in Figure 1.4. A number of other detailed compilations have been developed for the Middle and Early Pleistocene periods (Ruddiman *et al.* 1986, 1989, Raymo *et al.* 1989, Shackleton *et al.* 1990), while other recent work has extended the astronomical timescale into pre-Quaternary times (e.g., Shackleton *et al.* 1995, Naish *et al.* 1998).

Tuning to the orbital timescale alters the age estimates of important stratigraphic markers suggested by other methods, such as radiometric dating. Thus, for example, the Brunhes/Matuyama polarity reversal is dated to 0.73 Ma by K-Ar dating, but orbital tuning suggests an age closer to 0.8 Ma for this event. When examining published data, therefore, care should be taken to establish whether 'raw' (e.g., radiometric) or orbitally-tuned ages have been employed, as confusion can arise when comparing between different records if this has not been made clear, or if different approaches have been employed.

SIGNIFICANCE OF THE SPECMAP TIMESCALE

The SPECMAP timescale, and the assumptions upon which it is based, are pivotal to current theories about the nature and timing of environmental changes during the Quaternary period. It provides the only *continuous* chronometer that extends through the whole of the Quaternary, and it underpins many recent attempts to correlate terrestrial and marine records. Furthermore,

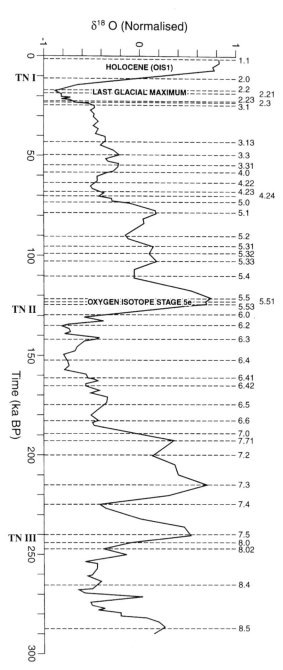

Figure 1.4   The orbitally-tuned timescale for the last 300 000 years based on Martinson *et al.* (1987). The dashed horizontal lines denote distinct features in the oxygen isotope profile for which SPECMAP ages are shown at the right-hand edge of the diagram. Note that Martinson *et al.* have employed a numeric system for sub-stages rather than the more traditional alphanumeric system (e.g., 5.5 for OIS 5e). TN I to TN III show the approximate positions of the last three *Terminations*.

spectral analysis of isotopic variations, upon which the SPECMAP scheme is based, indicates that there were significant changes in the wavelength and amplitude of the dominant climate cycles during the Pliocene and Quaternary. These phase changes suggest the influence of non-Milankovitch factors on the course of climate history. These two issues have an important bearing on ideas concerning the possible relationships between human evolution and behaviour on the one hand, and global climate changes on the other.

Marine-continental correlations

It is now well established that many terrestrial sequences which span the whole or a considerable part of the Quaternary also show clear evidence of cyclic variations and, moreover, spectral analysis of the continental records also reveals the dominant stamp of orbital forcing. Examples include the thick loess-palaeosol successions of China and elsewhere (e.g., Kukla *et al.* 1990, Ding *et al.* 1994, Porter and An 1995, Liu *et al.* 1999), growth increments and chemical variations in speleothem (cave calcite) deposits (e.g., Schwarcz *et al.* 1982, Kashiwaya *et al.* 1991), long sediment sequences in deep lakes (e.g., Hooghiemstra and Sarmiento 1991, Hooghiemstra *et al.* 1993, Tzedakis 1993, 1994), and ice-core records (Petit *et al.* 1999). Close comparisons between the loess and marine records for the past 2.5 Ma, using palaeomagnetic horizons as 'tie-lines' between the profiles, shows very close correspondence, not only in the number of major oscillations recognized during the Quaternary, but also in important phase changes in amplitude and dominant cycle, as indicated by the independent application of spectral analysis to each record (e.g., Liu *et al.* 1999). The close similarity between marine and continental palaeoenvironmental records suggests a very strong coupling between global ice volume changes (since the marine oxygen isotope record predominantly reflects global palaeoglaciation) and the strength of the monsoon system over Asia. Such close similarity between continental and marine records also provides support for the notion that tuning to the SPECMAP timescale provides reliable age estimates and a robust basis for correlation at a global scale. This hypothesis has been very much strengthened by the discovery of a generally close correspondence between Milankovitch insolation rhythms and climate variations reflected in Antarctic ice core records for the period of the last 400 ka (Sowers *et al.* 1993, Petit *et al.* 1999).

Phase changes in the rhythm of climate change during the Quaternary

Spectral analysis of both deep marine and long continental records indicates that the pulse of global climate variations has shifted in pace and strength during the Pliocene and Quaternary (Prell 1982, Ruddiman and Raymo 1988, Raymo and Ruddiman 1992). In the Pliocene, prior to around 2.8 to 2.6 Ma, the 19 to 23 ka cycle predominated. The 41 ka cycle became the dominant influence between *c.* 2.6 and 0.8 Ma (broadly equivalent to the Matuyama geomagnetic epoch). By contrast, the Brunhes epoch (post 800 ka) has been dominated by the 100 ka cycle, while the amplitude of climate oscillations has greatly increased during this period (Ruddiman *et al.* 1986, De Menocal 1995, Liu *et al.* 1999). These phase shifts in the periodicity of major climatic variations cannot be explained by orbital forcing alone, but are assumed to reflect a number of feedback processes in the climate system. A combination of factors, such as, *inter alia*, differential thermal response of land and ocean to insolation changes, changes in albedo, changes in atmospheric gas ratios and dust content, and global tectonism, may lead to modulation of the effects of orbital variations (either accentuating or dampening their effects) as well as to significant time-lags between insolation change and environmental responses (see Williams *et al.* 1998:98, Lowe and Walker 1997:361). The marked increase in the amplitude of climatic oscillations during the last 800 ka, for example, is thought to reflect an intensification of global glaciation, with very much more extensive ice sheets on the continents of the northern Hemisphere than during the preceding Quaternary cold stages.

HUMAN EVOLUTION AND GLOBAL CLIMATE CHANGE

There is much speculation in the scientific literature about the factors that may have influenced the origin and evolution of humans, as well as significant changes in their behaviour, with the sharpest focus directed to such significant 'milestones' as the original divergence of hominids from pongids during the Pliocene (Tattershall 1995, Leakey *et al.* 1995), and the development of stone tools at *c.* 2.5 Ma (Deacon and Deacon 1999). In many recent accounts, global climate change is advanced as one of the probable major causal factors of such developments, either as a direct agent, or acting indirectly by influencing other environmental processes. For example, the transition from the Pliocene to the Quaternary was a time of marked global cooling, with increased seasonality and significant dessication in some tropical areas, such as eastern and southern Africa, the region within which early hominids appear to have emerged. These changes may have brought about the gradual fragmentation of tropical forest and an expansion of more open woodland and savanna grassland (Williams *et al*. 1998). These habitat changes may, in turn, have exerted selective pressures upon hominid populations, forcing them to adapt in order to increase their chances of survival. Speculation on such matters is one thing, but testing the underlying assumptions is an altogether different matter.

There are a number of reasons why such claims remain (for now) rather difficult to affirm. First of all, the number of skeletal remains, especially for certain key periods and sites, is really rather limited. There are major gaps in the hominid-human lineage, while the exact stratigraphic position of the remains is frequently uncertain (Williams *et al*. 1998). Secondly, the precise nature of climatic conditions associated with hominid remains, or with artifactual assemblages, has to be inferred from associated geological information; the various methods employed for this are either difficult to quantify or are subject to wide statistical uncertainty (Lowe and Walker 1997). Thirdly, a new perspective on the rate and pattern of global climate change has emerged within the last decade or so. High-resolution studies of marine and continental sequences, especially of ice cores obtained from the polar ice sheets, has demonstrated that the orbitally-driven climate cycles of the last few hundred thousand years were frequently interrupted by irregular, short-lived climate oscillations of surprisingly large amplitude (e.g., GRIP Project Members 1993, Bond *et al*. 1993, Bond and Lotti 1995). The most detailed evidence currently available is for the last glacial-interglacial cycle (OIS-5 to OIS-1). At least 24 abrupt oscillations, from cold stadial conditions to warm interstadial conditions (almost as warm as those of the present day) and back to cold conditions again, characterize the interval between 110 and 14 ka BP (Dansgaard *et al*. 1993). Some of these irregular oscillations lasted only 1 to 3 ka, while some of the cold-warm transitions occurred within a few decades (Alley *et al*. 1993). These short-lived '*sub-Milankovitch events*', which cannot be explained by orbital forcing mechanisms, may have had important influences on the survival, distribution and migration of human populations.

A fourth difficulty is that of ascertaining the precise age of human remains and of associated artifacts.

Beyond the limits of radiocarbon dating (*c*. 40 to 60 ka; see Chapter 2), certain techniques, such as ESR and U-series dating, can be employed to date human fossils directly (Chapters 4 and 5). Other methods can date the sediments in which the remains are embedded (e.g., OSL and TL methods, and cosmogenic nuclide dating – Chapters 4 and 8). Some hominid remains occur within sediments that are interstratified with volcanic layers, and the latter can be dated using the K-Ar method (e.g., Clark 1992). In such instances, limiting dates can be obtained from the overlying and underlying volcanic strata, between which the age of the fossil human remains should lie. However, the statistical uncertainties associated with radiometric dates tend to be large, while age estimates derived using different dating methods frequently diverge. Approximate ages for some skeletal remains have been inferred by reference to the palaeomagnetic reversal scheme. This approach has proved especially useful for estimating the antiquity of some early stages in hominid development, in sites where there is little scope for adopting alternative methods (e.g. Parés and Pérez-Gonzalez 1995, Partridge *et al*. 1999). Without the application of additional methods, however, this approach cannot provide precise ages, but merely establishes the magnetic epoch within which the fossils accumulated, or their age relative to magnetic epoch boundaries or events.

An increased understanding of the rate and pathway of human evolution, and the possible influences of global climate change upon the process, is therefore dependent upon significant headway being made in all four of the above-mentioned scientific endeavours – i.e., closing the gaps in the archaeological record, refining palaeoclimate methods, achieving a fuller understanding of the nature and impact of sub-Milankovitch climate variability, and increasing the accuracy and precision of the relevant geochronological methods. A wide range of technical and methodological advances are indeed developing within the current research which is addressing each of these concerns, but one development perhaps merits special mention. That is the work currently under way to link archaeological records in Africa and Asia more closely to the SPECMAP timescale (e.g., De Menocal 1995, De Menocal and Bloemendal 1995). The potential dividend from this research will be an improved geochronological framework for assessing the archaeological records, as well as a much sharper resolution of the precise way in which important evolutionary stages match on to the climate record (e.g., Potts 1998). We eagerly await the new ideas and perspectives that will undoubtedly emerge from this exciting line of research.

REFERENCES

*Recommended for further reading

*Aitken, M.J. (1990). *Science-based Dating in Archaeology*. Longman: London.

Alley, R.B., Meese, D.A., Shuman, C.A., Gow, A.J., Taylor, K.C., Grootes, P.M., Whitell, J.W.C., Ram, M., Waddington, E.D., Mayewski, P.A. and Zielinski, G.A. (1993). Abrupt increase in Greenland snow accumulation at the end of the Younger Dryas event. *Nature*, **362**:527–529.

Berger, A. (1988). Milankovitch theory and climate. *Review of Geophysics*, **26**:624–657.

Berger, A. and Loutre, M.F. (1994). Precession, eccentricity, obliquity, insolation and paleoclimates. In Duplessy, J.-C. and Spyridakis, M.-T. (eds), *Long-Term Climatic Variations: Data and Modelling*. NATO ISI Series I, vol. 22, 107–151. Springer-Verlag: Berlin.

Berger, A., Imbrie, J., Hays, G., Kukla, G. and Saltzman, B. (eds) (1984). *Milankovitch and Climate*. Reidel: Dordrecht.

Berger, A., Li, X.S. and Loutre, M.F. (1999). Modelling northern hemisphere ice volume over the last 3 Ma. *Quaternary Science Reviews*, **18**:1–11.

Berggren, W.A., Burckle, L.H., Cita, M.B., Cooke, M.B.S., Funnell, B.M., Gartner, S., Hays, J.D., Kennett, J.P., Opdyke, N.D., Pastouret, L., Shackleton, N.J. and Takayanagi, Y. (1980). Towards a Quaternary timescale. *Quaternary Research*, **13**:277–302.

Bond, G. and Lotti, R. (1995). Iceberg discharge into the North Atlantic on millennial time scales during the Last Glaciation. *Science*, **267**:1005–1010.

Bond, G., Broecker, W., Johnsen, S., McManus, J., Labeyrie, L., Jouzel, J. and Bonani, G. (1993). Correlations between climate records from North Atlantic sediments and Greenland ice. *Nature*, **365**:143–147.

Cande, S. and Kent, D.V. (1995). Revised calibration of the geomagnetic polarity timescale for the Late Cretaceous and Cenozoic. *Journal of Geophysical Research*, **100**:6093–6095.

Clark, J.D. (1992). African and Asian perspectives on the origins of modern humans. *Philosophical Transactions of the Royal Society of London*, **B337**:201–215.

Dansgaard, W., Johnsen, S.J., Clausen, H.B., Dahl-Jensen, D., Gundestrup, N.S., Hammer, C.U., Hvidberg, C.S., Steffensen, J.P., Sveinbjornsdottir, A.E., Jouzel, J. and Bond, G. (1993). Evidence for general instability of past climate from a 250-kyr ice-core record. *Nature*, **364**:218–220.

*Deacon, H.J. and Deacon, J. (1999). *Human Beginnings in South Africa*. David Philip: Cape Town.

De Menocal, P.B. (1995). Plio-Pleistocene African climate. *Science*, **270**:53–59.

De Menocal, P.B. and Bloemendal, J. (1995). Plio-Pleistocene climatic variability in subtropical Africa and the palaeoenvironment of hominid evolution: a combined data-model approach. In Vrba, E.S., Denton, G.H., Partridge, T.C. and Burckle, L.H. (eds), *Paleoclimate and Evolution, with Emphasis on Human Origins*, 262–288. Yale University Press: New Haven.

Ding, Z., Yu, Z., Rutter, N. and Liu, T.S. (1994). Towards an orbital time scale for Chinese loess deposits. *Quaternary Science Reviews*, **13**:39–70.

GRIP Project Members (1993). Climate instability during the last interglacial period recorded in the GRIP ice core. *Nature*, **364**:203–207.

*Hays, J.D., Imbrie, J. and Shackleton, N.J. (1976). Variations in the Earth's orbit: pacemaker of the Ice Ages. *Science*, **194**:1121–1132.

Heller, F. and Liu, T.S. (1982). Magnetostratigraphic dating of loess deposits in China. *Nature*, **300**:431–433.

Hooghiemstra, H. and Sarmiento, G. (1991). Long continental pollen record from a tropical intermontane basin: Late Pliocene and Pleistocene history from a 540-meter core. *Episodes*, **14**:107–115.

Hoogheimstra, H., Melice, J.L., Berger, A. and Shackleton, N.J. (1993). Frequency spectra and palaeoclimatic variability of the high precision 30-1450 ka Funza I pollen record (Eastern Cordillera, Colombia). *Quaternary Science Reviews*, **12**:141–156.

*Imbrie, J. and Imbrie, K.P. (1979). *Ice Ages – Solving the Mystery*. MacMillan: London.

Imbrie, J., Hays, J.D., Martinson, D.G., McIntyre, A., Mix, A.C., Morley, J.J., Pisias, N.G., Prell, W.L. and Shackleton, N.J. (1984). The orbital theory of Pleistocene climate: support from a revised chronology of the marine $\delta^{18}O$ record. In Berger, A., Imbrie, J., Hays, G., Kukla, G. and Saltzman, B. (eds), *Milankovitch and Climate*, 296–306. Reidel: Dordrecht.

Jansen, E. (1989). The use of stable oxygen and carbon isotope stratigraphy as a dating tool. *Quaternary International*, **1**:151–166.

Kashiwaya, K., Atkinson, T.C. and Smart, P.L. (1991). Periodic variations in Late Pleistocene speleothem abundance in Britain. *Quaternary Research*, **35**:190–196.

Kukla, G. (1989). Loess stratigraphy in Central China. *Palaeogeography, Palaeoclimatology, Palaeoecology*, **72**:203–225.

Kukla, G., An, Z.S., Melice, J.L., Gavin, J. and Xiao, J.L. (1990). Magnetic susceptibility record of Chinese loess. *Transactions of the Royal Society of Edinburgh: Earth Sciences*, **81**:263–288.

Leakey, M.D., Feibel, C.S., McDougall, I. and Walker, A. (1995). New four-million-year-old hominid species from Kanapoi and Allia Bay, Kenya. *Nature*, **376**:565–571.

Liu, T., Ding, Z. and Rutter, N. (1999). Comparison of Milankovitch periods between continental loess and deep sea records over the last 2.5 Ma. *Quaternary Science Reviews*, **18**:1205–1212.

*Lowe, J.J. and Walker, M.J.C. (1997). *Reconstructing Quaternary Environments*, (2nd edn). Addison Wesley Longman: Harlow.

Martinson, D.G., Pisias, N.G., Hays, J.D., Imbrie, J., Moore, T.C. and Shackleton, N.J. (1987). Age dating and the orbital theory of the ice ages: development of a high resolution 0-300,000 year chronostratigraphy. *Quaternary Research*, **27**:1–29.

Naish, T.R., Abbott, S.T., Alloway, B., Beu, A.G., Carter, R.M., Edwards, A.R., Journeaux, T.D., Kemp, P.J.J., Pillans, B.J., Saul, G.S. and Woolfe, K.J. (1998). An astronomical calibration of a Southern Hemisphere reference section, Wanganui Basin, New Zealand. *Quaternary Science Reviews*, **17**:695–710.

Partridge, T.C., Shaw, J., Heslop, D. and Clarke, R.J. (1999). The new hominid skeleton from Sterkfontein, South Africa: age and preliminary assessment. *Journal of Quaternary Science*, **14**:293–298.

Patience, A.J. and Kroon, D. (1991). Oxygen isotope chronostratigraphy. In Smart, P.L. and Frances, P.D. (eds), *Quaternary Dating Methods – A User's Guide*. Technical Guide 4, 199–222. Quaternary Research Association: London.

Parés, J.M. and Pérez-Gonzalez, A.P. (1995). Paleomagnetic age for hominid fossils at Atapuerca archaeological site, Spain. *Science*, **269**:830–832.

Petit, J.T., Jouzel, J., Raynaud, D., Barkov, N.I., Barnola, J.M., Basile, I., Benders, M., Chappellaz, J., Davis, M., Delaygue, G., Delmolte, M., Kotlyakov, V.M., Legrand, M., Lipenkov, V.Y., Lorius, C., Pepin, L., Ritz, C., Saltzman, E. and Stievenard, M. (1999). Climate and atmospheric history of the past 420,000 years from the Vostok ice core, Antarctica. *Nature*, **399**:429–436.

Porter, S.C. and An, Z. (1995). Correlation between climate events in the North Atlantic and China during the last glaciation. *Nature*, **375**:305–308.

Potts, R. (1998). Environmental hypotheses of hominin evolution. *Yearbook of Physical Anthropology*, **41**:93–136.

Prell, W.L. (1982). Oxygen and carbon isotopic stratigraphy for the Quaternary of hole 502B: evidence for two modes of isotopic variability. *Initial Reports of Deep Sea Drilling Project*, **68**:455–464.

Raymo, M.E. and Ruddiman, W.F. (1992). Tectonic forcing of the Cenozoic climate. *Nature*, **359**:117–122.

Raymo, M.E., Ruddiman, W.F., Backman, J., Clement, B.M. and Martinson, D.G. (1989). Late Pleistocene evolution of the northern hemisphere ice sheets and North Atlantic deep water circulation. *Paleoceanography*, **4**:413–446.

Rial, J.A. (1999). Pacemaking the Ice Ages by frequency modulation of the Earth's orbital eccentricity. *Science*, **285**:564–568.

Ruddiman, W.F. and Raymo, M.E. (1988). Northern hemisphere climate regimes during the past 3 Ma: possible tectonic connections. *Philosophical Transactions of the Royal Society of London*, **B318**:411–430.

Ruddiman, W.F., Raymo, M.E. and McIntyre, A. (1986). Matuyama 41 000-year cycles: North Atlantic ocean and Northern Hemisphere ice sheets. *Earth and Planetary Science Letters*, **80**:117–129.

Ruddiman, W.F., Raymo, M.E., Martinson, D.G., Clement, B.M., and Backman, J. (1989). Pleistocene evolution: northern hemisphere ice sheets and North Atlantic Ocean. *Paleoceanography*, **4**:353–412.

Schwarcz, H.P., Gascoyne, M. and Harmon, R.S. (1982). Applications of U-series dating to problems of Quaternary climate. In Ivanovich, M. and Harmon, R.S. (eds), *Uranium Series Disequilibrium: Applications to Environmental Problems*, 326–350. Clarendon Press: Oxford.

Shackleton, N.J. (1987). Oxygen isotopes, ice volume and sea level. *Quaternary Science Reviews*, **6**:183–190.

Shackleton, N.J. and Opdyke, N.D. (1973). Oxygen isotope and palaeomagnetic stratigraphy of equatorial Pacific core V28-238: oxygen isotope temperatures and ice volume on a 10^5 and 10^6 year scale. *Quaternary Research*, **3**:39–55.

Shackleton, N.J., Backman, J., Zimmerman, H., Kent, D.V., Hall, M.A., Roberts, D.G., Schnitker, D., Baldauf, J.G., Desprairies, A., Homrighausen, R., Huddlestun, P., Keene, J.B., Kaltenback, A.J., Krumsiek, K.A.O., Morton, A.C., Murray, J.W. and Westbergsmith, J. (1984). Oxygen isotope calibration of the onset of ice-rafting in DSPD site 552A: a history of glaciation in the North Atlantic region. *Nature*, **307**:620–623.

Shackleton, N.J., Berger, A. and Peltier, W.R. (1990). An alternative astronomical calibration of the lower Pleistocene timescale based on ODP Site 677. *Transactions of the Royal Society of Edinburgh: Earth Sciences*, **81**:251–261.

Shackleton, N.J., Crowhurst, S., Hagelberg, T., Pisias, N.G. and Schneider, D.A. (1995). A new late Neogene timescale: application to leg 138 sites. In Pisias, N.G., Mayer, L.A. and Stewart, S.K. (eds), *Proceedings of the Ocean Drilling Program Scientific Results*, **138**:73–104.

*Smart, P.L. and Frances, P.D. (1991). *Quaternary Dating Methods – A User's Guide*. Technical Guide 4, Quaternary Research Association: London.

Sowers, T., Bender, M., Labeyrie, L., Martinson, D., Jouzel, J., Raynaud, D., Pichon, J.J. and Korotkevich, Y. (1993). 135,000 year Vostok-SPECMAP common temporal framework. *Paleoceanography*, **8**:737–766.

Tarling, D.H. (1983). *Palaeomagnetism*. Chapman and Hall: London.

Tattershall, I. (1995). *The Last Neanderthal: the Rise, Success and Mysterious Extinction of our Closest Human Relatives*. Macmillan: London.

Thompson, R. (1986). Palaeomagnetic dating. In Berglund, B.E. (ed.) *Handbook of Holocene Palaeoecology and Palaeohydrology*, 313–327. John Wiley: Chichester.

Thompson, R. (1991). Palaeomagnetic dating. In Smart, P.L. and Frances, P.D. (eds), *Quaternary Dating Methods – A User's Guide*. Technical Guide 4, 177–198, Quaternary Research Association: London.

*Thompson, R. and Oldfield, F. (1986). *Environmental Magnetism*. Allen and Unwin: London.

Tzedakis, P.C. (1993). Long-term tree populations in northwest Greece through multiple Quaternary climatic cycles. *Nature*, **364**:437–440.

Tzedakis, P.C. (1994). Vegetation change through glacial-interglacial cycles: a long pollen sequence perspective.

Philosophical Transactions of the Royal Society of London, **B345**:403–432.

Valet, J.-P. and Meynadier, L. (1993). Geomagnetic field intensity and reversals during the past four million years. *Nature*, **366**:234–238.

Vrba, E.S. (1996). Climate, heterochrony and human evolution. *Journal of Anthropological Research*, **52**:1–28.

*Vrba, E.S., Denton, G.H., Partridge, T.C. and Burckle, L.H. (1995). *Paleoclimate and Evolution, with Emphasis on Human Origins*. Yale University Press: New Haven.

Walden, J., Oldfield, F. and Smith, J. (eds) (1999). *Environmental Magnetism: a Practical Guide*. Technical Guide 6, Quaternary Research Association: London.

*Williams, M., Dunkerley, D., De Deckker, P., Kershaw, P. and Chappell, J. (1998). *Quaternary Environments*, (2nd edn). Arnold: London.

Willis, K.J., Kleczkowski, A., Brigg, K.M. and Gilligan, C.A. (1999). The role of sub-Milankovitch climate forcing in the initiation of the Northern Hemisphere glaciation. *Science*, **285**:568–571.

*Wilson, R.C.L., Drury, S.A. and Chapman, J.J. (1999). *The Great Ice Age*. Routledge: London.

2

Radiocarbon Dating

R.E. TAYLOR

Radiocarbon Laboratory, Department of Anthropology, Institute of Geophysics and Planetary Physics, University of California, Riverside.

Radiocarbon ^{14}C dating, after a half century of use and continuing technical refinement, remains the most widely employed method of inferring chronometric age for late Pleistocene and Holocene organic materials. The influence of ^{14}C dating in archaeology has been profound, especially in prehistoric studies, and more recently, in providing the principal time scale for reconstructing the history of late Quaternary environments. The late Glyn Daniel (1967:266) equated the discovery of the ^{14}C method in the twentieth century with the discovery of the antiquity of the human species in the nineteenth century. Grahame Clark (1970:38) pointed to ^{14}C dating as making a *world* prehistory possible by contributing the first world-wide chronometric time scale that transcended local and regional boundaries. Radiocarbon dating made a significant impact even in areas with previously very well-defined archaeological chronologies such as the ancient Near East (Pritchard 1967:viii).

Recent extended discussions of the application of ^{14}C dating in archaeology can be found in Aitken (1990), Bowman (1990) and Taylor (1996, 1997, 2000). A brief but excellent technical overview can be found in Geyh and Schleicher (1990:162). A comprehensive discussion of low-level counting technology as applied to ^{14}C dating can be found in Theodórsson (1996). Compendia of the primary ^{14}C calibration data include Stuiver and Kra (1986) and Stuiver *et al.* (1993, 1998a). Stuiver *et al.* (1998b) present an overview of the INTCAL98 radiocarbon age calibration data. Currently, the principal computer-based approaches to calibration include CALIB (Stuiver and Reimer 1993), CAL25 (van der Plicht 1993), CalibETH (Nicklaus *et al.* 1992) and OxCal (Bronk Ramsey 1994). A conference in 1990 and the resulting volume (Taylor *et al.* 1992) summarized the major contributions that ^{14}C has made not only as a dating but also as a biological and environmental tracer isotope over its first 40 years of use. An annotated bibliography of radiocarbon dating literature from 1947–1968 can be found in Polach (1988). The journal *Radiocarbon*, originally intended as the means of publishing ^{14}C date lists from various laboratories, now primarily publishes research articles and reviews and, as regular numbers of *Radiocarbon*, proceedings of the approximately triannual International Radiocarbon Conferences.

THE RADIOCARBON DATING MODEL

The natural production of ^{14}C is a secondary effect of cosmic-ray interactions with atmospheric gas molecules which results in the production of neutrons (Figure

---

Handbook of Archaeological Sciences. Edited by D.R. Brothwell and A.M. Pollard.

2.1). Radiocarbon is formed by the reaction of thermalized, lower energy, neutrons with ^{14}N. It is then rapidly oxidized to form $^{14}CO_2$. In this form, ^{14}C is distributed throughout the Earth's atmosphere by stratospheric winds, becoming generally well-mixed by the time ^{14}C-tagged CO_2 molecules reach the Earth's surface. Most ^{14}C is absorbed in the oceans, while 1–2 per cent becomes part of the terrestrial biosphere, primarily by means of photosynthesis. Plant materials and animals which are, directly or indirectly, dependent on plants, are thus 'tagged' with ^{14}C.

Metabolic processes in living organisms maintain the ^{14}C content in approximate equilibrium with atmospheric ^{14}C concentrations, i.e., while ^{14}C decays in living tissue, it is continually replaced through the ingestion of plant or animal tissue. Once metabolic processes cease, as at the death of an animal or plant, the amount of ^{14}C begins to decrease by radioactive decay – in the case of ^{14}C, by beta decay – at a rate measured by the ^{14}C half-life (Taylor 1987, 1997).

The *radiocarbon age* of a sample is based on a measurement of its residual ^{14}C content. For a ^{14}C age to be equivalent to its actual or solar/calendar age

at a reasonable level of precision, a set of assumptions need to be satisfied. These are that;

(i)   the $^{14}C/^{12}C$ ratio in each carbon reservoir has remained essentially constant over the ^{14}C time scale,

(ii) complete and rapid mixing of ^{14}C occurs throughout the various carbon reservoirs on a worldwide basis,

(iii) carbon isotope ratios (e.g., $^{13}C/^{12}C$) in samples have not been altered except by ^{14}C decay since the death of an organism,

(iv) the half-life of ^{14}C is accurately known with reasonable precision, and

(v)   natural levels of ^{14}C can be measured to appropriate levels of accuracy and precision (Taylor 1996).

A significant portion of contemporary ^{14}C studies, especially as they relate to archaeological applications, fall into one of two categories. First, there are investigations designed to examine and compensate for the effects of violations of these primary assumptions as applied to specific sample types or compartments of the carbon reservoirs. Second, there are highly focused efforts to document explicitly the association between the organic sample on which a ^{14}C age estimate is obtained and the archaeological object, feature, or geological context for which an age determination is desired.

Radiocarbon age estimates are generally expressed in terms of a set of characteristic parameters that define a *conventional radiocarbon age*. These parameters, introduced in the mid-1970s and explicitly defined by Stuiver and Polach (1977), include:

(i)   the use of 5568 (±30) years as the ^{14}C half-life (8033 year mean life) used to calculate age, although the actual half-life value is probably closer to 5730 (±40) years;

(ii) the use of one of the United States National Institute of Standards and Technology (formerly US National Bureau of Standards, NBS)-distributed oxalic acid preparations – or a secondary standard (e.g., sucrose) with a known relationship to a primary standard – as a contemporary or modern reference standard to define a 'zero' ^{14}C age;

(iii) the use of AD 1950 as the zero point from which to count ^{14}C time;

(iv) to account for fractionation effects, a normalization of ^{14}C in all samples to a common $^{13}C/^{12}C$ ($\delta^{13}C$) value of $-25\permil$, and finally,

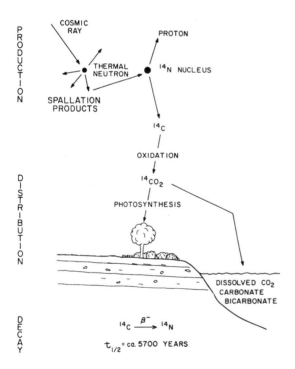

Figure 2.1 Radiocarbon dating model: production, distribution and decay of ^{14}C (based on Taylor 1997:Fig. 3.1).

(v) an assumption that $^{14}C/^{12}C$ ratios in all reservoirs have remained constant over the ^{14}C time scale.

In addition, each ^{14}C determination is expected to be accompanied by an expression which provides an accurate estimate of the overall *experimental* or *analytical uncertainty*. Since counting statistics associated with the measurement of ^{14}C concentrations in samples are usually the dominant component of the analytical uncertainty, this value is informally referred to as the *statistical error*. This '±' term is suffixed to all appropriately documented ^{14}C age estimates and is typically expressed as plus or minus one standard deviation ($\pm 1\,\sigma$). For samples from some carbon reservoirs, conventional contemporary standards may not define a zero ^{14}C age. A *reservoir corrected radiocarbon age* can sometimes be calculated by documenting the apparent age exhibited in appropriate control samples and correcting for this observed deviation. Reservoir effects are most often observed in samples from fresh water lakes and marine environments.

A *calibrated radiocarbon age* takes into consideration the fact that ^{14}C activity in living organisms which, in most cases, directly reflects atmospheric ^{14}C levels, has not remained constant over the ^{14}C time scale because of changes in ^{14}C production rates or reservoir mixing parameters in the carbon cycle. The study of the various factors responsible for the variability in ^{14}C production rates and changes in the worldwide distribution of ^{14}C in various carbon reservoirs over the late Pleistocene and Holocene has occupied the attention of many in the ^{14}C research community for over four decades. The various issues raised by the nature of the variability over time in the ^{14}C time scale – with the documentation of this variability now extended into the late Pleistocene – is discussed in greater detail below.

In the current nomenclature of the journal *Radiocarbon*, '^{14}C years BP' is expressed only as 'BP' with the '^{14}C years' implied (e.g., 2510 ± 50 BP). Calibrated ages, i.e., calendar or solar years, are expressed with only the 'cal' designation attached (e.g., cal AD 1520, 3720 cal BC) with the 'years' implied. The journal *American Antiquity* adopted the nomenclature of *Radiocarbon* except for punctuation (B.P. rather than BP). In the early 1970s, the journal *Antiquity* adopted a terminology whereby 'bp' and 'ad/bc' designate conventional (uncalibrated) ^{14}C values whilst 'BP' and 'AD/BC' designate calibrated ^{14}C values (Daniel 1972).

The ^{14}C time scale now extends from about 300 years ago to between 40 000 and 60 000 years. The limitations on the young end of the ^{14}C time scale are a consequence of the complex interplay of various recent natural 'warps' – de Vries effects – in the ^{14}C time scale and anthropogenic, e.g., 'bomb' ^{14}C, effects. The maximum ^{14}C ages that can be inferred using decay counting technology depend on characteristics of different laboratory instrumentation and experimental configurations – e.g., background and sample blank values, counter size, length of counting – and, to some degree, the amount of sample available for analysis. Currently, for laboratories with counters designed to work with older samples, routine upper limits using moderate sample sizes (3–7 g of carbon) range upward to about 55 000 years. Employing relatively large sample sizes, typically not available from archaeological contexts, a few laboratories have developed the capability to obtain age estimates up to about 70 000 years. With isotopic enrichment – again using relatively large (>15 g of carbon) amounts of sample material – ages up to 75 000 years have been reported on a small number of samples (Grootes *et al.* 1975, Stuiver *et al.* 1978, Erlenkeuser 1979). Efforts have now begun to exploit accelerator mass spectrometry (AMS) technology (see below) to extend the ^{14}C time scale out to as much as 70 000–90 000 years using sample weights of less than a gram of carbon.

DEVELOPMENT OF RADIOCARBON DATING STUDIES

Stages in the history of the development of ^{14}C dating and its application in archaeology can be distinguished partly by the type of detection technology employed and, partly, on understandings concerning the relationship between radiocarbon and 'real' or solar/calendar time. The first generation of archaeological ^{14}C applications, the 'First Radiocarbon Revolution' (Renfrew 1973:48), began with the appearance of the first ^{14}C 'date list' in 1950 (Arnold and Libby 1950, 1951). In the early 1970s, second generation studies began with the recognition of the need to calibrate ^{14}C data – comparing ^{14}C-inferred ages with those that reflected solar or 'real time', i.e., dendrochronology or calendar-based systems. The result was the 'Second Radiocarbon Revolution' (Renfrew 1973). In the late 1970s, the 'Third Radiocarbon Revolution' in ^{14}C studies was ushered in by a new technology, the development of AMS for ^{14}C measurement (Muller 1977, Linick *et al.* 1989).

Several recent technical and methodological advances have provided contexts for a series of significant applications of the ^{14}C method in archaeological studies. In addition to the application of AMS, these include the extension of the calibrated ^{14}C time scale into the late Pleistocene and a more detailed characterization of Holocene 'time warps' – de Vries effects – where relatively rapid changes in atmospheric ^{14}C concentrations complicate the inherent precision with which ^{14}C content can be converted into inferred age. The extension of the calibration of the ^{14}C time scale beyond that provided by tree ring data has been accomplished primarily by the use of paired uranium–thorium (U-series, see Chapter 5) and AMS-based ^{14}C measurements on marine coral samples.

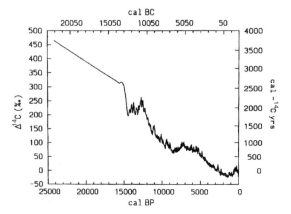

Figure 2.2 Characterization of Late Pleistocene and Holocene deviation of ^{14}C from dendrochronological, uranium-series and varve-counted marine sediment-based age expressed in $\Delta^{14}C‰$ (left margin) and cal-^{14}C years (right margin) from INTCAL98 data base: 0-24 000 cal BP (Stuiver *et al.* 1998b). Figure produced by P. Reimer, University of Washington, Seattle.

Extending the calibration of the ^{14}C time scale

Comparisons of ^{14}C with dendrochronological data based on Irish oak and German oak and pine for the earliest portion and Douglas fir, sequoia and bristlecone pine for later periods now document about 11 800 years of solar time (Stuiver *et al.* 1998a). Most of the ^{14}C measurements comprising these data sets are characterized as 'high-precision', referring to carefully measured counting uncertainties typically at the $\pm 1\sigma$ level of <20 years ($\pm 2.5‰$) for the ^{14}C values used to provide the dendrochronologically-based calibration data. The validity of the stated uncertainties has been extensively examined by detailed interlaboratory comparisons among a number of the laboratories producing the calibration data (Scott *et al.* 1990). For the period before dendrochronological controls are available, paired uranium/thorium ($^{234}U/^{230}Th$) and ^{14}C samples from cores drilled into coral formations (Edwards *et al.* 1993, Bard 1998, Bard *et al.* 1998, Burr *et al.* 1998) provide the principal data on which a late Pleistocene ^{14}C calibration curve has been extended to 24 000 cal BP or, as expressed in ^{14}C time, to 20 300 BP (Stuiver *et al.* 1998b).

With this extension, it has now become apparent that the 'sine-wave'-like characterization of the Holocene ^{14}C calibration curve was an artifact of the limited time frame documented by the initial Holocene tree-ring/^{14}C data. Figure 2.2 shows a plot of the off-set between ^{14}C and assumed 'true' ages for the last 24 000 years based primarily on the most current combined dendrochronological/^{14}C and coral uranium-series/^{14}C data, as presented in the INTCAL98 data set (Stuiver *et al.* 1998b, Stuiver and Reimer pers. comm. 1998). Based on the expanded calibration data, it now appears that the long-term secular variation ^{14}C anomaly over about the last 25 000 years can be char-

acterized as representing a slow-decay function on which has been superimposed middle- and short-term de Vries effects perturbations.

For the period before about 25 000 cal BP, age estimates obtained from ^{14}C and other Quaternary dating methods applied to samples obtained from a variety of contexts are, to some degree, inconsistent with regard to indications of the magnitude of the ^{14}C age offsets. For example, comparisons between ^{14}C values (adjusted by 3 per cent to take into consideration the most likely ^{14}C half-life) and thermoluminescence age estimates on materials from hearths at Lake Mungo, Australia suggest deviations in the range of 3500 to 5000 years between 27 000 and 31 000 cal BP (Bell 1991). Studies of variations in the intensity of the Earth's dipole magnetic field – a major cause of the long-term ^{14}C secular variation trend – as well as comparisons of precisely determined ^{14}C and associated $^{40}Ar/^{39}Ar$ values from volcanic deposits, suggest somewhat less age offsets for this period. However, the geomagnetic data suggest an increasing ^{14}C/solar time offset in the range of 1500 to 2700 years between 25 000 and 40 000 years, but predicts that there will be good agreement between ^{14}C and solar time at about 45 000–50 000 years (Mazaud *et al.* 1992, Southon *et al.* 1995). In addition, there also may have been a major 'spike' in atmospheric ^{14}C concentrations between 30 000 and 35 000 cal BP (Voelker *et al.* 1998:fig. 6). Further detailed studies are necessary to clarify the magnitude of the offsets in ^{14}C activity for this period (Geyh and Schlüchter 1998).

Holocene de Vries effects

A fuller rendering of the entire Holocene ^{14}C time scale permits researchers to review more precisely the timing and characteristics of the de Vries 'wiggles' over the last ten millennia. Figure 2.3 plots the series of defined Holocene 'time warps' reflecting the time ranges of the de Vries effect perturbations in the calibration curve (Taylor *et al.* 1996:fig. 3). Figure 2.3A represents 0 to 5000 BP and Figure 2.3B represents the 5000 to 10 000 BP period in ^{14}C years. The inherent uncertainties and fluctuations in the calibration curve cause discrete cal ages to broaden into ranges, even when, as in Figures 2.3A and 2.3B, the ^{14}C ages are plotted with a hypothetical zero variance. Thus, ^{14}C age determinations deriving from time periods with larger calibration range values will be inherently less precise. For example, on the average, calibrated age values for 8000–10 000 BP are inherently much less precise than those in the 0–2500 BP period because of the large ^{14}C 'time warps' occurring during those periods.

In Figure 2.3, 12 major and five intermediate de Vries effect perturbations can be identified. Major de Vries effects have been defined as warps exceeding 250 cal years; intermediate de Vries effects are those that exhibit ranges in excess of 140 cal years, and minor de Vries effects have ranges of less than 140 cal yr. The 17 major and intermediate de Vries perturbations have

been assigned roman numeral and letter combinations. Roman numerals identify the ^{14}C millennium, i.e., I = 0 to 1000 BP, II = 1000 to 2000 BP, while lower case letters identify the perturbation in chronological order within each ^{14}C millennial period. It should be noted that the INTCAL98 calibration data set shifts slightly the time scale for early Holocene ^{14}C time warps but does not effect their magnitude (Stuiver pers. comm. 1998).

Various strategies to increase the precision of ^{14}C-based age inferences in the light of the variable effects of de Vries-type secular variations include the use of Bayesian statistical approaches to calibration procedures (Buck *et al.* 1991, Buck and Christen 1998) and 'wiggle-matching'. An example of the latter includes the determination of a cutting date for timber from a Japanese tomb to AD 320 with a precision of ±5 years (Kojo *et al.* 1994). When precision at the level of < ±30 years can be statistically justified, concerns about latitude dependent differences in ^{14}C atmospheric concentrations become relevant. For example, for southern hemispheric samples, there is a suggestion that a ^{14}C age reduction of 24 ± 3 ^{14}C years prior to calibration appears to be appropriate (Stuiver *et al.* 1998b).

Accelerator Mass Spectrometry

From the initiation of ^{14}C studies until the late 1970s, the basis of inferring ^{14}C concentrations, and thus the ^{14}C age of samples, employed exclusively *decay counting* technology. In decay counting, isotopic

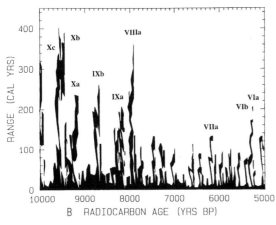

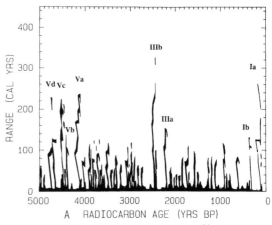

Figure 2.3 Holocene de Vries effects: ranges ('warps') in cal years obtained from the calibration of conventional ^{14}C ages. Figure taken from Taylor *et al.* (1996) based on data from Stuiver and Reimer 1993:figs. 3A-D. Figure 2.3A represents 0–5000 radiocarbon years BP and Figure 2.3B 5000–10 000 radiocarbon years BP. Ranges produced for ideal hypothetical samples with zero ^{14}C sample standard deviation that had been formed during a 20 year or shorter interval and with the youngest cal age obtained for each ^{14}C age set at zero.

concentrations are measured by counting decay events in an ionization or scintillation detector and comparing the count rate observed in an unknown-age sample to that exhibited by appropriate standards under a common set of experimental conditions. For ^{14}C, this involves counting beta particles, i.e., negatively charged electrons emitted from the ^{14}C nucleus. In decay counting, only a relatively small fraction of the ^{14}C atoms present in a carbon sample are actually detected during the course of measurement. Whilst there are approximately 5.9×10^{10} atoms of ^{14}C in 1 g of modern 'pre-bomb' carbon, on the average, over a one minute period, less than 14 of these atoms will decay and be available for detection. In large part, it was this inherent inefficiency in decay counting that gave impetus to efforts to develop *direct* or *ion counting* technology using a form of mass spectrometry.

Within a year of the initial publication of the concept underlying AMS technology (Muller 1977), the first published AMS-based ^{14}C determination on an archaeologically-related sample was obtained using the 88-inch (224-cm) cyclotron at the University of California Lawrence Berkeley Laboratory (Muller *et al.* 1978). Because of technical problems of using cyclotron-based AMS systems for natural level measurements, all routine AMS measurements are now undertaken on another type of particle accelerator, an electrostatic tandem accelerator. Although initially HEMS (High Energy Mass Spectrometry) was used to refer to this technology, typically, TAMS (Tandem Accelerator Mass Spectrometry) is now used. 'Tandem' here refers to the fact that particle acceleration in electrostatic systems is accomplished in a two-step 'pull-push' process. In 1977, two groups of physicists simultaneously published proposals of how a tandem accelerator could be employed to measure ^{14}C and other cosmogenic isotopes at natural concentrations using milligram amounts of carbon (Nelson *et al.* 1977, Bennett *et al.* 1977, 1978). This approach proved to be a practical AMS technology for a wide range of rare, cosmogenic isotopes including ^{14}C and, to date, almost all AMS ^{14}C age determinations have been obtained on a TAMS instrument (see Chapter 8 for other isotopes). By way of an historical footnote, the question of who first conceived the idea that led directly to the development of AMS technology is the subject of continuing discussion (Gove 1996, 1999, Taylor 1999).

Three advantages of AMS technology in the measurement of ^{14}C were anticipated as a result of the greatly enhanced detection efficiency. First, major reductions in sample sizes are possible – from gram amounts of carbon to milligram amounts and, with additional efforts, to the level of less than 100 micrograms. Second, major reductions in counting times are possible. Reductions from several days for conventional systems and even weeks and months with micro- and mini-decay counting systems could be achieved with several minutes of counting for AMS systems to achieve ± 1 per cent counting statistics. Finally, it was anticipated that there might be a significant increase in the applicable dating time frame – from the currently routine 40 000/50 000 years out to as much as 100 000 years (Muller 1977, Gove 1992).

The first two of the three originally-anticipated benefits of AMS technology – major reductions in sample size and counting times – have been fully realized over the last decade (Taylor *et al.* 1984, Hedges and Gowlett 1986, Taylor 1991). For both sample sizes and counting times, order-of-magnitude reductions have been made possible on a routine basis. However, the third advance has not, as yet, occurred due to the current inability to exclude micro-contamination of samples, primarily with modern carbon introduced during sample preparation. A significant portion of this contamination results from the current requirement in most laboratories that samples must be converted to graphitic carbon for use in the ion source of an AMS system. Parts per million of modern carbon contamination translates into background levels which generally limit the maximum ages that can be resolved to between 40 000 and 50 000 years. One laboratory has developed a CO_2 gas source but reports similar background values (Bronk Ramsey and Hedges 1987). To date, the oldest age reported on an actual sample background blank (Pliocene wood) is 60 500 BP (Kirner *et al.* 1997).

The development of AMS technology has provided the technical means by which very low organic carbon content sample types, such as organic extracts from bone and ceramics, along with micro-sample materials such as single seeds and small amounts of hair, can now be routinely dated. It should be emphasized that AMS-based ^{14}C age determinations are not necessarily more or less accurate or precise than decay counting. Currently, the principal advantage of AMS technology for ^{14}C applications is the ability to obtain meaningful dates with samples containing microgram amounts of carbon (e.g., Kirner *et al.* 1995).

CASE STUDIES: ARCHAEOLOGICAL APPLICATIONS

Over the last decade, the expanding use of AMS-based ^{14}C analysis has continued to create new and expanded areas of research, where ^{14}C data have yielded important new understandings which would have not been possible with decay counting. In archaeology, there have been a variety of issues and topics which have been significantly advanced by the capability to obtain ^{14}C measurements on milligram amounts of sample.

Hedges (1995) has noted that the advantages of micro-sample ^{14}C analysis include the ability to increase the reliability of ^{14}C-inferred age estimates in addition to the generation of new chronological information. With regard to the former, the ability to re-measure problematical samples, the feasibility of undertaking highly selective chemical pretreatment strategies, the ability to compare different chemical fractions of the same sample, and select the most relevant sample material have all been made routinely feasible as a result of AMS-based ^{14}C analyses.

Some AMS-based ^{14}C values have been obtained in situations where larger amounts of sample were available. However, those having responsibility for a unique archaeological or historic object would consent to the removal of only a small portion of the larger sample. Such was the case with the AMS ^{14}C dating of the Shroud of Turin. This 4.3 by 1 metre rectangular-shaped linen cloth housed in the Cathedral of St. John the Baptist in Turin, Italy is alleged to have been, since 1353 when its existence is first documented, the 'True Burial Sheet of Christ'. The calibrated ^{14}C age of this sample measured by three AMS laboratories indicates that the flax from which the linen was fabricated was most probably growing sometime during the later part of the thirteenth or during the fourteenth century, exactly the period during which the shroud was first historically documented (Damon et al. 1989). Arguments that ^{14}C activity in portions of the shroud could have been altered by exchange of atmospheric CO_2 with the linen as the result of high temperature effects ('scorching') or other postulated chemical reactions (e.g., Kouznetsov et al. 1996) have been refuted by experiments specifically designed to test the validity of the purported mechanisms (Jull et al. 1996, Long 1998, Hedges et al. 1998a).

A good illustration of the effect of being able to target the most relevant sample is illustrated by a study of maize specimens excavated from two rock shelters in the Tehuacán Valley, Mexico. Samples of Zea mays from these sites had been regarded as the earliest example of cultivated maize in the New World. In the early 1970s, their age had been estimated on the basis of conventional ^{14}C determinations obtained on charcoal assumed to be stratigraphically associated with the maize samples in the Tehuacán

Valley sites. In contrast to the 5350 to 7000 BP values on the associated charcoal, the range in ^{14}C values directly obtained on milligram amounts of maize using AMS-based ^{14}C analysis is 1560 to 4700 BP for the samples from San Marcos Cave and 450 to 4090 BP for the specimens from Coxcatlan Cave (Long et al. 1989). This significantly later occurrence of maize at Tehuacán raises questions concerning assumptions about where the centre(s) of maize domestication in Mesoamerica may have been.

AMS ^{14}C technology has been applied to a wide array of archaeological and historical issues and problems including determination of the recent age of purported Palaeolithic art objects such as the 'Sherborne bone' (Stringer et al. 1995, d'Errico et al. 1998), direct dates identifying eighth millennium ceramics in the New World (Roosevelt et al. 1991) and the documentation of the re-use of timbers in the Al-Aqsa Mosque in Jerusalem (Liphschitz et al. 1997). The Oxford AMS Laboratory, probably the laboratory most focused on archaeological dating, has examined a lengthy series of human bone samples from various European Palaeolithic and later contexts. In some cases, the originally-assigned Pleistocene age has been affirmed, e.g., hominid skeletons from Gough's Cave (Hedges et al. 1991). In other cases, what was once thought to be a Pleistocene age human skeleton turned out to be, in the case, for example, of Hunstanton Woman, of Saxon age (Hedges et al. 1994). Measurements of AMS ^{14}C have also advanced attempts to obtain accurate dates on organics associated with rock paintings in several areas of the world although the problems are complex and the results often controversial (Hedges et al. 1998b).

A further example of usefulness of AMS technology in ^{14}C studies is the use of such data as part of efforts to address one of most acrimonious debates in New World archaeology – the nature and timing of the peopling of the Western Hemisphere. Historically, this debate has centred on two issues: the scientific validity of data offered as evidence for human presence, and the accuracy of the age estimates associated with these data (Dillehay and Meltzer 1991). A number of discussions have focused on questions concerning the validity of purported Paleoindian materials with assigned ages reportedly in excess of the well-documented terminal Pleistocene Clovis period occupation of North America (Haynes 1992) with documented associated ^{14}C ages in the range of 11 570 ($\pm$70) to 10 890 ($\pm$50) BP (Taylor et al. 1996). Of the more than 100 sites in North America that have, over the last 100 years, been reported to contain evidence of 'pre-Clovis' occupation, only a relatively small number currently remain under active consideration. Of these remaining alleged pre-Clovis sites in North America (Payen 1982) or South America (Lynch 1990, Meltzer *et al*. 1994), either the cultural nature of the material or the adequacy of the geochronological data associated with the remains – or both – have been questioned.

In South America, ^{14}C values on materials from Caverna da Pedra Pintada at Monte Alegre, Brazil have been used to argue that the earliest human occupation there overlapped in time with Clovis in North America (Roosevelt *et al*. 1996). However, reservations have been expressed concerning several aspects of the reports on this site including interpretations of the ^{14}C data (Tankersley 1997). The late Pleistocene age of human occupation at Monte Verde, Chile dated by a suite of ^{14}C values to about 12 500 BP – i.e., about 1000 years before Clovis (Dillehay 1989, 1997) – has recently been supported by a number of investigators (Adovasio and Pedler 1997, Meltzer *et al*. 1997, Taylor *et al*. 1999) although there have been renewed concerns about the integrity of the stratigraphic contexts at the site (e.g., Fiedel 1999), with strong rejoinders by site excavators (Dillehay *et al*. 1999, Collins 1999).

It is generally accepted that debates concerning the validity of dating frameworks associated with Paleoindian materials – and particularly purported pre-Clovis materials – were substantively transformed with the introduction of the ^{14}C method. For almost all archaeologists, the ^{14}C method has acquired the status of the final arbiter of the accuracy of chronological inferences for materials associated with actual or purported Paleoindian contexts. However, there is a recognition that the validity of ^{14}C-inferred ages can depend most directly on the type of sample material being dated. One of these problematical sample types is bone and there has developed an extensive literature on problems of obtaining valid ^{14}C-based age estimates on bone (Hedges and Law 1989, Stafford *et al*. 1991, Taylor 1992).

Measurements of AMS ^{14}C on milligram amounts of carbon provided the technical capability to undertake a direct examination of bone from a series of human skeletons from North American sites that, on various grounds, had been declared to date to a period before 11 000–12 000 BP; i.e., allegedly pre-Clovis in age. A detailed analysis was carried out of the validity of ^{14}C age estimates on a range of different fractions from bone including individual amino acids and other highly specific organic constituents. To date, no directly ^{14}C-dated North American human skeleton has yielded published ages in excess of the known age of the

Clovis period (Taylor *et al*. 1985, Taylor 1994). Currently, the oldest published directly ^{14}C-dated North American human skeletal sample is from Anzick in Montana. Radiocarbon values ranging from 10 940 ± 90 (AA-2981) to 10 240 ± 120 (AA-2978) have been obtained on various amino acid fractions (Stafford *et al*. 1991, Stafford 1994). Other directly ^{14}C-dated New World human skeletal materials reported in excess of 10 000 ^{14}C years BP include those from Buhl, Idaho (10 675 ± 95 [BETA-43055/ ETH-7729]; Green *et al*. 1998), Mostin, California (10 470 ± 490 [UCLA-2171]; Kaufman 1980) and Arroyo Frias River, Argentina (10 300 ± 60 [NSRL-1893/CAMS-16598]; A. H. Hicks pers. comm., 1996).

In part because of the technical studies conducted as part of the examination of these skeletons, there now appears to be a general consensus among investigators concerning the reliability of bone ^{14}C values. Where appropriate biochemical purification procedures are employed, accurate ^{14}C age estimates can be obtained on bone samples retaining significant amounts of intact collagen, the principal organic component of bone (Taylor 1992). However, bones seriously depleted in protein (mostly collagen) content (< 5 per cent of the original amount) have the potential to yield anomalous ^{14}C values (Hedges and Law 1989). Various investigations have examined other non-collagen organic components in bone that might resist contamination during bone diagenesis but, to date, the results have not been promising despite extensive research (e.g., Ajie *et al*. 1992, Burky *et al*. 1998).

CONCLUSION

The impact of ^{14}C dating on archaeological research has been, in some aspects, clear and explicit and, in others, subtle. In addition to providing a common chronometric time scale for the entire late Quaternary, an important contribution of the ^{14}C method for archaeology is that the technique provides a chronometric time scale which is completely independent of any assumptions about cultural processes and totally unrelated to any type of manipulation of artifact data. It has also been suggested that the introduction of ^{14}C dating led to a noticeable improvement in archaeological field methods (Johnson 1965:764) and was, at least in part, responsible for the increasing focus on statistical approaches in the evaluation of archaeological data (Thomas 1978:323).

Radiocarbon data continues to provide the foundation on which most of the prehistoric archaeological time scales in most areas of the world for the last 40 000 years are, directly or indirectly, constructed. Although currently not often stressed, the influence of ^{14}C data on the pursuit of archaeological studies continues to be profound and pervasive for those interested in supporting their assertions about the past with empirically-based data.

ACKNOWLEDGEMENTS

The UCR Radiocarbon Laboratory is supported by the National Science Foundation, the Gabrielle O. Vierra Memorial Fund, and the College of Humanities, Arts, and Social Sciences, University of California, Riverside. The author wishes to thank A. H. Hicks for his unpublished radiocarbon determination, Minze Stuiver and Paula Reimer (University of Washington) for providing information on the INTCAL98 calibration data base, and the comments of Joan Schneider on an earlier draft of this manuscript. This is contribution 98/10 of the Institute of Geophysics and Planetary Physics, University of California, Riverside.

REFERENCES

*Recommended for further reading

Adovasio, J.M. and Pedler, D.R. (1997). Monte Verde and the antiquity of humankind in the Americas. *American Antiquity*, 71:573–580.
*Aitken, M.J. (1990). *Science-based Dating in Archaeology*. Longman: London.
Ajie, H.O., Kaplan, I.R., Hauschka, P.V., Kirner, D., Slota, P.J. Jr. and Taylor, R.E. (1992). Radiocarbon dating of bone osteocalcin: isolating and characterizing a non-collagen protein. *Radiocarbon*, 34:296–305.
Arnold, J.R. and Libby, W.F. (1950). *Radiocarbon Dates (September 1, 1950)*. Institute for Nuclear Studies, University of Chicago: Chicago.
Arnold, J.R. and Libby, W.F. (1951). Radiocarbon dates. *Science*, 113:111–120.
Bard, E. (1998). Geochemical and geophysical implications of the radiocarbon calibration. *Geochimica et Cosmochimica Acta*, 62:2025–2038.
Bard, E., Arnold, M., Hamelin, B., Tisnerat-Laborde, N. and Cabioch, G. (1998). Radiocarbon calibration by means of mass spectrometric ^{230}Th/^{234}U and ^{14}C ages of corals. An updated database including samples from Barbados, Mururoa and Tahiti. *Radiocarbon*, 40:1085–1092.
Bell, W.T. (1991). Thermoluminescence dates for the Lake Mungo aboriginal fireplaces and the implication for the radiocarbon time scale. *Archaeometry*, 33:43–50.

Bennett, C.L., Beukens, R.P., Clover, M.R., Gove, H.E., Liebert, R.B., Litherland, A.E., Purser, K.H. and Sondheim, W.E. (1977). Radiocarbon dating using accelerators: negative ions provide the key. *Science*, 198:508–509.
Bennett, C.L., Beukens, R.P., Clover, M.R., Elmore, D., Gove, H.E., Kilius, L., Litherland, A.E. and Purser, K.H. (1978). Radiocarbon dating with electrostatic accelerators: dating of milligram samples. *Science*, 201:345–347.
*Bowman, S.G.E. (1990). *Interpreting the Past: Radiocarbon Dating*. British Museum Publications: London.
Bronk Ramsey, C. (1994). Analysis of chronological information and radiocarbon calibration: the program OxCal. *Archaeological Computing Newsletter*, 41:11–16.
Bronk Ramsey, C. and Hedges, R.E.M. (1987). A gas ion source for radiocarbon dating. *Nuclear Instruments and Methods in Physics Research*, B29:45–49.
Buck, C.E. and Christen, J.A. (1998). A novel approach to selecting samples for radiocarbon dating. *Journal of Archaeological Science*, 24:303–310.
Buck, C.E., Kenworthy, J.B., Litton, C.D. and Smith, A.F.M. (1991). Combining archaeological and radiocarbon information: a Bayesian approach to calibration. *Antiquity*, 65:808–821.
Burky, R.R., Kirner, D.L., Taylor, R.E., Hare, P.E. and Southon, J.R. (1998). Radiocarbon dating of bone using gamma-carboxyglutamic acid and alpha-carboxyglycine (aminomalonate). *Radiocarbon*, 40:11–20.
Burr, G.S., Beek, J.W., Taylor, F.W., Recy, J., Edwards, R.L., Cabioch, G., Correge, T., Donahue, D.J. and O'Malley, J.M. (1998). A high-resolution radiocarbon calibration between 11 700 and 12 400 calendar years BP derived from ^{230}Th ages of corals from Espiritu Santo Island, Vanuatu. *Radiocarbon*, 40:1093–1105.
Clark, G. (1970). *Aspects of Prehistory*. University of California Press: Berkeley.
Collins, M.B. (1999). Reply to Fiedel, Part II. *Discovering Archaeology* [Special Report], 1(6):14–15.
Damon, P.E., Donahue, D.J., Gord, B.H., Hatheway, A.L., Jull, A.J.T, Linick, T.W., Sercelo, P.J., Toolin, L.J., Bronk, C.R., Hall, E.T., Hedges, R.E.M., Housley, R., Law, I.A., Perry, C., Bonani, G., Trumbore, S., Wolli, W., Ambers, J.C., Bowman, S.G.E., Leese, M.N. and Tite, M.S. (1989). Radiocarbon dating the shroud of Turin. *Nature*, 337:611–615.
Daniel, G. (1967). *The Origins and Growth of Archaeology*. Crowell: New York.
Daniel, G. (1972). Editorial. *Antiquity*, 46:265.
Dillehay, T.D. (1989). *Monte Verde: A Late Pleistocene Settlement in Chile 1: Paleoenvironment and Site Context*. Smithsonian Institution Press: Washington DC.
Dillehay, T.D. (1997). *Monte Verde: A Late Pleistocene Settlement in Chile 2: The Archaeological Context*. Smithsonian Institution Press: Washington DC.
Dillehay, T.D. and Meltzer, D.J. (eds) (1991). *The First Americans: Search and Research*. CRC Press: Boca Raton.

Dillehay, T.D., Pino, M., Rossen, J., Ocampo, C., Rivas, P.L., Pollack, D. and Henderson, G. (1999). Reply to Fiedel, Part 1. *Discovering Archaeology* [Special Report], **1(6)**:12–14.

Edwards, R.L., Beck, J.W., Burr, G.S., Donahue, D.J., Chappell, J.M.A., Bloom, A.L., Druffel, E.R.M. and Taylor, F.W. (1993). A large drop in atmospheric $^{14}C/^{12}C$ and reduced melting in the Younger Dryas, documented with ^{230}Th ages of corals. *Science*, **260**:962–968.

Erlenkeuser, H. (1979). A thermal diffusion plan for radiocarbon isotope enrichment from natural samples. In Berger, R. and Suess, H.E. (eds) *Radiocarbon Dating*, 216–237. University of California Press: Berkeley.

d'Errico, F., Williams, C.T. and Stringer, C.B. (1998). AMS dating and microscopic analysis of the Sherborne Bone. *Journal of Archaeological Science*, **25**:777–787.

Fiedel, S.J. (1999). Artifact provenience at Monte Verde: confusion and contradictions. *Discovering Archaeology* [Special Report], **1(6)**:1–12.

*Geyh, M.A. and Schleicher, H. (1990). *Absolute Age Determination: Physical and Chemical Dating Methods and their Application*. Springer-Verlag: Berlin.

Geyh, M.A. and Schlüchter, C. (1998). Calibration of the ^{14}C time scale beyond 22 000 BP. *Radiocarbon*, **40**:475–482.

Gove, H. (1992). The history of AMS, its advantages over decay counting: applications and prospects. In Taylor, R.E., Kra, R. and Long, A. (eds) *Radiocarbon After Four Decades: An Interdisciplinary Perspective*, 214–229. Springer-Verlag: New York.

Gove, H. (1996). *Relic, Icon or Hoax? Carbon Dating the Turin Shroud*. Institute of Physics: Bristol.

Gove, H. (1999). *From Hiroshima to the Iceman: The Development and Applications of Accelerator Mass Spectrometry*. Institute of Physics: Bristol.

Green, T.J., Cochran, B., Fenton, T.W., Woods, J.C., Titmus, G.L., Tieszen, L., Davis, M.A. and Miller, S.J. (1998). The Buhl burial: a Paleoindian woman from southern Idaho. *American Antiquity*, **63**:457–476.

Grootes, P.M., Mook, W.G., Vogel, J.C., de Vries, A.E., Haring, A. and Kismaker, J. (1975). Enrichment of radiocarbon for dating samples up to 75 000 years. *Zeitschrift für Naturforschung*, **30A**:1–14.

Haynes, C.V. Jr. (1992). Contributions of radiocarbon dating to the geochronology of the peopling of the New World. In Taylor, R.E., Kra, R. and Long, A. (eds) *Radiocarbon after Four Decades: An Interdisciplinary Perspective*, 355–374. Springer-Verlag: New York.

Hedges, R.E.M. (1995). Radiocarbon dating by accelerator mass spectrometry. *American Journal of Archaeology*, **99**:105–108.

Hedges, R.E.M. and Gowlett, J.A.J. (1986). Radiocarbon dating by accelerator mass spectrometry. *Scientific American*, **254**:100–107.

Hedges, R.E.M. and Law, I.A. (1989). The radiocarbon dating of bone. *Applied Geochemistry*, **4**:249–253.

Hedges, R.E.M., Housley, R.A., Ramsey, C.B. and van Klinken, G.J. (1991). Radiocarbon dates from the Oxford AMS system: Archaeometry datelist 13. *Archaeometry*, **33**:279–296.

Hedges, R.E.M., Housley, R.A., Bronk Ramsey, C. and van Klinken, G.J. (1994). Radiocarbon dates from the Oxford AMS system: Archaeometry datelist 18. *Archaeometry*, **36**:337–374.

Hedges, R.E.M., Bronk Ramsey, C. and van Klinken, G.J. (1998a). An experiment to refute the likelihood of cellulose carboxylation. *Radiocarbon*, **40**:59–60.

Hedges, R.E.M., Bronk Ramsey, C., van Klinken, G.J., Pettitt, P.B., Nielsen-Marsh, C., Etchegoyen, A., Fernandez Niello, J.O., Boschin, M.T. and Llamazares, A.M. (1998b). Methodological issues in the ^{14}C dating of rock paintings. *Radiocarbon*, **40**:35–44.

Johnson, F. (1965). The impact of radiocarbon dating upon archaeology. In Chatters, R.M. and Olson, E.A. (eds) *Proceedings of the Sixth International Conference Radiocarbon and Tritium Dating*, 762–780. Clearinghouse for Federal Science and Technical Information: Springfield, Virginia.

Jull, A.J.T., Donahue, D.J. and Damon, P.E. (1996). Factors affecting the apparent radiocarbon age of textiles: a comment on 'Effects of fires and biofractionation of carbon isotopes on results of radiocarbon dating of old textiles: the Shroud of Turin'. *Journal of Archaeological Science*, **23**:157–160.

Kaufman, T.S. (1980). *Early Prehistory of the Clear Lake Area, Lake County, California*. Unpublished Ph.D. Dissertation, University of California, Los Angeles.

Kirner, D., Taylor, R.E. and Southon, J.R. (1995). Reduction in backgrounds of microsamples for AMS ^{14}C dating. *Radiocarbon*, **37**:697–704.

Kirner, D., Burky, R. Taylor, R.E. and Southon, J.R. (1997). Radiocarbon dating organic residues at the microgram level. *Nuclear Instruments and Methods in Physics Research*, **B123**:214–217.

Kojo, Y., Kalin, R.M. and Long, A. (1994). High-precision 'wiggle-matching' in radiocarbon dating. *Journal of Archaeological Science*, **21**:475–479.

Kouznetsov, D.A., Ivanov, A.A. and Veletsky, P.R. (1996). Effects of fires and biofractionation of carbon isotopes on results of radiocarbon dating of old textiles: the Shroud of Turin. *Journal of Archaeological Science*, **23**:109–121.

Linick, T.W., Damon, P.E., Donahue, D.J. and Jull, A.J.T. (1989). Accelerator mass spectrometry: the new revolution in radiocarbon dating. *Quaternary International*, **1**:1–6.

Liphschitz, N., Biger, G., Bonani, G. and Wolfli, W. (1997). Comparative dating methods: botanical identification and ^{14}C dating of carved panels and beams from the Al-Aqsa Mosque in Jerusalem. *Journal of Archaeological Science* **24**:1045–1050.

Long, A. (1998). Attempt to affect the apparent ^{14}C age of cotton by scorching in a CO_2 environment. *Radiocarbon*, **40**:57–58.

Long, A., Benz, B.F., Donahue, D.J., Jull, A.J.T. and Toolin, L.J. (1989). First direct AMS dates on early maize from Tehuacán, Mexico. *Radiocarbon*, **31**:1035–1040.

Lynch, T.F. (1990). Glacial-age man in South America: a critical review. *American Antiquity*, **55**:12–36.

Mazaud, A., Laj, C., Bard, E., Arnold, M. and Tric, E. (1992). A geomagnetic calibration of the radiocarbon time-scale. In Bard, E. and Broecker, W.S. (eds) *The Last Deglaciation: Absolute and Radiocarbon Chronologies*, 163–169. Springer-Verlag: Berlin.

Meltzer, D.J., Adovasio, J.M. and Dillehay, T.D. (1994). On a Pleistocene human occupation at Pedra Furada, Brazil. *Antiquity*, **68**:695–714.

Meltzer, D.J., Grayson, D.K., Ardila, G., Barker, A.W., Dincauze, D.F., Haynes, C.V. Jr., Mena, F., Nunez, L. and Stanford, D.J. (1997). On the Pleistocene antiquity of Monte Verde, southern Chile. *American Antiquity*, **62**:659–663.

Muller, R.A. (1977). Radioisotope dating with a cyclotron. *Science*, **196**:489–494.

Muller, R.A., Stephenson, E.J. and Mast, T.S. (1978). Radioisotope dating with an accelerator: a blind measurement. *Science*, **201**:347–348.

Nelson, D.E., Korteling, R.G. and Scott, W.R. (1977). Carbon-14: direct detection at natural concentrations. *Science*, **198**:507–508.

Nicklaus, T.R., Bonani, G., Simonius, M., Suter, M. and Wolfli, W. (1992). CalibETH: An interactive computer program for the calibration of radiocarbon dates. *Radiocarbon*, **34**:483–492.

Payen, L.A. (1982). *The pre-Clovis of North America: temporal and artifactual evidence*. Unpublished Ph.D. Dissertation, University of California, Riverside.

Polach, D. (1988). *Radiocarbon Dating Literature, The First 21 Years, 1947–1968*. Academic Press: London.

Pritchard, J.B. (1967). *Archaeological Discoveries in the Holy Land*. Bonanza Books: New York.

Renfrew, C. (1973). *Before Civilization: the Radiocarbon Revolution and Prehistoric Europe*. Alfred A. Knopf: New York.

Roosevelt, A.C., Housley, R.A., Imazio da Silveira, M., Maranca, S. and Johnson, R. (1991). Eighth millennium pottery from a prehistoric shell midden in the Brazilian Amazon. *Science*, **254**:1621–1624.

Roosevelt, A.C., Lima da Costa, M., Lopes Machado, C., Michab, M., Mercier, N., Valladas, H., Feathers, J., Barnett, W., Imazio da Silveira, M., Henderson, A., Sliva, J., Chernoff, B., Reese, D.S., Holman, J.A., Toth, N. and Schick, K. (1996). Paleoindian cave dwellers in the Amazon: the peopling of the Americas. *Science*, **272**:373–384.

Scott, E.M., Long, A. and Kra, R. (eds) (1990). Proceedings of the International Workshop on Intercomparison of Radiocarbon Laboratories. *Radiocarbon*, **32**:253–397.

Southon, J.R., Deino, A.L., Orsi, G., Terrasi, R., and Campajola, L. (1995). Calibration of the radiocarbon time scale at 37 ka BP. *Abstract of Papers* 10, 209th American Chemical Society National Meeting, Part 2.

Stafford, T.W. (1994). Acclerator C-14 dating of human fossil skeletons: assessing accuracy and results on New World specimens. In Bonnichsen, R. and Steele, D.G. (eds) *Method and Theory for Investigating the Peopling of the Americas*, 45–55. Corvallas, Center for the Study of the First Americans: Oregon State University.

Stafford, T.W., Hare, P.E., Currie, L., Jull, A.J.T. and Donahue, D.J. (1991). Accuracy of North American human skeleton ages. *Journal of Archaeological Science*, **18**:35–72.

Stringer, C.B., d'Errico, F., Williams, C.T., Housley, R. and Hedges R. (1995). The solution to the Sherborne problem. *Nature*, **378**:452.

Stuiver, M. and Kra, R.S. (eds) (1986). Calibration Issue. *Radiocarbon*, **28**:805–1030.

Stuiver, M. and Polach, H.A. (1977). Discussion: reporting of ^{14}C data. *Radiocarbon*, **19**:355–363.

Stuiver, M. and Reimer, P.J. (1993). Extended ^{14}C data base and revised CALIB 3.0 ^{14}C age calibration program. *Radiocarbon*, **35**:215–230.

Stuiver, M., Heusser, C.H. and Yang, I.C. (1978). North American glacial history extended to 75 000 years ago. *Science*, **200**:16–21.

Stuiver, M., Long, A. and Kra, R.S. (eds) (1993). Calibration 1993. *Radiocarbon*, **35**:1–244.

Stuiver, M., van der Plicht, J. and Long, A. (eds) (1998a). INTCAL 98: Calibration Issue. *Radiocarbon*, **40**(3):1041–1159.

Stuiver, M., Reimer, P.J., Bard, E., Beck, J.W., Burr. G.S., Hughen, K.A., Kromer, B., McCormac, G., van der Plicht, J. and Spurk, M. (1998b). INTCAL98 Radiocarbon age calibration 24 000-0 cal BP. *Radiocarbon*, **40**:1041–1083.

Tankersley, K.B. (1997). Keeping track of time: dating Monte Alegre and the peopling of South America. *The Review of Archaeology*, **18**:28–34.

Taylor, R.E. (1987). *Radiocarbon Dating, an Archaeological Perspective*. Academic Press: Orlando.

Taylor, R.E. (1991). Radioisotope dating by accelerator mass spectrometry: archaeological and paleoanthropological perspectives. In Göksu, H.Y., Oberhofer, M. and Regulloi, D. (eds) *Scientific Dating Methods*, 37–54. Kluwer: Dordrecht.

Taylor, R.E. (1992). Radiocarbon dating of bone: to collagen and beyond. In Taylor, R.E., Kra, R. and Long, A. (eds) *Radiocarbon After Four Decades: An Interdisciplinary Perspective*, 375–402. Springer-Verlag: New York.

Taylor, R.E. (1994). Radiocarbon dating of bone using accelerator mass spectrometry: current discussions and future directions. In Bonnichsen, R. and Steele, D.G. (eds) *Method and Theory for Investigating the Peopling of the Americas*, 27–44. Corvallas, Center for the Study of the First Americans: Oregon State University.

*Taylor, R.E. (1996). Radiocarbon dating: the continuing revolution. *Evolutionary Anthropology*, **4**:169–181.

*Taylor, R.E. (1997). Radiocarbon dating. In Taylor, R.E. and Aitken, M.J. (eds) *Chronometric Dating in Archaeology*, 65–96. Plenum Press: New York.

Taylor, R.E. (1999). Review of 'From Hiroshima to the Ice Man: The Development and Applications of Accelerator Mass Spectrometry' by Gove, H.E. *Physics World*, **12**:47–48.

*Taylor, R.E. (2000). The contribution of radiocarbon dating to New World archaeology. *Radiocarbon*, **42**:1–21.

Taylor, R.E., Donahue, D.J., Zabel, T.H., Damon, P.E. and Jull, A.J.T. (1984). Radiocarbon dating by particle accelerators: an archaeological perspective. In Lambert, J.B. (ed.) *Archaeological Chemistry III*, 333–356. American Chemical Society: Washington DC.

Taylor, R.E., Payen, L.A., Prior, C.A., Slota, P. Jr., Gillespie, R., Gowlett, J.A.J., Hedges, R.E.M., Jull, A.J.T., Zabel, T.H., Donahue, D.J. and Berger, R. (1985). Major revisions in the Pleistocene age assignments for North American human skeletons by C-14 accelerator mass spectrometry: none older than 11,000 C-14 years BP. *American Antiquity*, **50**:136–140.

*Taylor, R.E., Kra, R. and Long, A. (eds) (1992). *Radiocarbon After Four Decades: an Interdisciplinary Perspective*. Springer-Verlag: New York.

Taylor, R.E., Stuiver, M. and Reimer, P.J. (1996). Development and extension of the calibration of the radiocarbon time scale: archaeological applications. *Quaternary Science Reviews*, **15**:655–668.

Taylor, R.E., Haynes, C.V. Jr., Kirner, D.L. and Southon, J.R. (1999). Radiocarbon analysis of modern organics at Monte Verde, Chile: no evidence for a local reservoir effect. *American Antiquity*, **64**:455–460.

Thomas, D.H. (1978). The awful truth about statistics in archaeology. *American Antiquity*, **43**:231–244.

*Theodórsson, P. (1996). *Measurement of Weak Radioactivity*. World Scientific: Singapore.

van der Plicht, J. (1993). The Groningen radiocarbon calibration program. *Radiocarbon*, **35**:231–237.

Voelker, A.H.L., Sarnthein, M., Grootes, P.M., Erlenkeuser, H., Laj, C., Mazaud, A., Nadeau, M.-J. and Schleicher, M. (1998). Correlation of marine ^{14}C ages from the Nordic seas with the GISP2 isotope record: implications for ^{14}C calibration beyond 25 ka BP. *Radiocarbon*, **40**:517–534.

3

Dendrochronology and Other Applications of Tree-ring Studies in Archaeology

P.I. KUNIHOLM

Department of the History of Art and Archaeology, Cornell University.

Tree-ring dating, as Bannister said in the 1963 edition of *Science in Archaeology*, is deceptively simple. Some species of trees add their annual growth increments in two parts: spring wood and then summer wood cells ('early wood' and 'late wood'). These pairs of growth increments, when seen on the end-grain, look like 'rings': hence the term. When trees in a given climatic region are similarly affected by yearly changes in the climate, their rings can be matched ('crossdated') with one another so that a given ring can be assigned to a specific calendar year. Sometimes a felling time within a year can be identified. Figure 3.1 shows a piece of structural oak from a tower in north Greece, the construction document of which survives. Work was begun on the monument in May 1597 and finished in December 1597. The timber itself was cut in late April/early May 1597 as only the springwood vessels of 1597 have formed. Clearly the timber was felled within a very narrow window of time and was used (as we know from the document) almost immediately thereafter. Dendrochronology is the only form of archaeometric dating with this kind of annual or sub-annual resolution. The method works only with species having clear, annual growth rings; it works with dry wood, wet wood (bog sites or shipwrecks), and burned wood (charcoal). Figure 3.2 shows two crossdatable pieces of sanded charcoal from a Middle Bronze Age

palace in Turkey (nineteenth century BC). Species in which the annual ring-boundaries are non-existent or indistinct, e.g., tropical trees, and most fruit or orchard trees (whose ring-growth may reflect merely the assiduity or the laziness of the gardener), cannot be crossdated.

Crossdating is the fundamental principle upon which all dendrochronology is based and therefore deserves further explanation. The researcher has to be assured that rings from two or more specimens were formed in the same year. Simple ring-counts are not sufficient. Neither is a single pattern of co-variation in ring-width (a 'signature'). In order to avoid the possibility of an accidental (but spurious) 'match' dendrochronologists try to compare samples which have at least 100 rings and multiple signatures rather than shorter-lived specimens which may not preserve enough signatures to guarantee the fit. These ring-patterns may be generated by a wide variety of causes. Fritts (1976), in one graph alone, lists eighteen possible causes for one narrow ring. The ring-patterns which are most usually crossdatable are the trees' mutual response to some mutual climatic stimulus; in some regions principally rainfall or lack of it; in others principally temperature; in yet others some combination of the two. This stimulus-and-response is therefore specific to a climatic region: i.e., the south-western USA, the extreme

Figure 3.1 Oak chain-beam from the Frourio Vardari in Thessaloniki, North Greece. Earlywood vessels from 1597 had just formed when the tree was felled, indicating a cutting-date of late April/early May 1597.

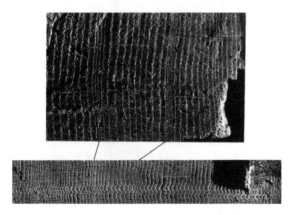

Figure 3.2 Two crossdated pieces of charcoal from a Middle Bronze Age palace in Turkey (nineteenth century BC). Note the two extraordinary signatures. Several dozen other signatures confirm the correctness of the crossdating.

northern timber-line (>∼60°N), northern Europe, the eastern Mediterranean, etc. The climatic boundaries for crossdating have been best determined, in practice, by trial and error. Sometimes they fit the map, sometimes not, and then an explanation for the apparent anomaly must be sought. Wood cut from a forest site in Calabria in southern Italy, for example, crossdates with wood from Greece and Turkey, but it does not crossdate with wood from Spain, or over the Alps, or even Sicily. The first two non-fits are no surprise, but the non-fit with Mount Etna in Sicily, only 80 km away, is, and therefore requires explanation. Sicily appears to belong more to the North African climate system rather than to that of the central/eastern Mediterranean.

Caveats to the dendrochronological method include:

(i)   the possibility of re-used wood: e.g., the Arizona mesas where wood cut in pre-Columbian times is still in use today (for comments on dendrochronological interpretation see Bannister 1962);

(ii)   changing habits of users of wood: e.g., Renaissance painters who in different centuries tended to let their panels dry out for two, to five, to eight, to 10 years before painting on them;

(iii)   heavily trimmed wood: e.g., cut boards or musical instruments;

(iv)   wood imported from some other climatic region, e.g., *Abies* (fir) at Herculaneum imported from the Alps, or *Quercus* (oak) panel paintings in England and the Low Countries which were imported as cut boards from the Baltic;

(v)   wood which is so badly degraded that its ring- and cell-structures are not preserved;

(vi)   'complacent' ring-sequences, i.e., little or no significant change from year to year;

(vii)   wood that has such erratic ring-sequences that they appear to fit in more than one place, and

(viii)   no wood preserved at all, e.g., the Baths of Caracalla or Diocletian in Rome with their hundreds of empty beam-holes.

The standard cautions that govern an archaeologist's activities in the field apply to dendrochronology as well. Beware of singleton samples, wood from mixed fills, a single lump of charcoal selected randomly from a large pile, etc. A small bag of charcoal collected and submitted to the author as a single sample included as many as five different species of trees. Further basic explanations of the dendrochronological method and useful illustrative material are to be found in Stokes and Smiley (1968), Ferguson (1970), Eckstein *et al.* (1984), and Baillie (1982, 1995). A series of international meetings have brought the dendrochronological community together at irregular intervals, and allowed free exchange of information and data. The latest proceedings were published in 1998 by Stravinskiene and Juknys.

BRIEF HISTORY OF THE METHOD

Tree-ring dating was discovered by the astronomer Andrew Ellicott Douglass in the early years of the twentieth century in the course of his search for a pattern of plant responses to solar phenomena. If he had been a biologist, he probably would have considered all the reasons why the method ought not to work and would have abandoned it at the outset. It is a curiosity that 'the Douglass Method', as it was called for decades after he practically singlehandedly dated the American south-west (see Haury 1962, also Webb 1983), is still relevant and in use today. One needs only a razor blade to surface the wood, a pin to mark off the decades, graph paper on which to note down the micro-rings and other significant morphological details (unusually heavy or light latewood, partial rings, missing rings or rings missing on a particular radius, frost damage, outbreaks of insect infestation, etc.), and then the patience to match the pieces of graph paper until crossdating is achieved, confirmed by holding the two pieces of wood against each other.

Douglass's simple but highly-effective method (*skeleton-plotting*), used today principally in the American south-west, does not work everywhere. In many other regions of the world where trees are not so highly-stressed, each ring has to be measured and the resulting graphs compared. A variety of measuring instruments are in use, and software packages for the statistical analysis of tree-ring information are announced regularly, but nothing quite replaces the human eye. Figure 3.3 shows two boards from an Egyptian sarcophagus in the Boston Museum of Fine Arts. Clearly, they were cut from the same tree. No statistical manipulation, no chi-squared tests, no r^2 calculations are necessary. The danger in dendrochronology-by-the-numbers ought to be self-evident, yet there are still inexperienced workers who believe in the computer and a packaged software program rather than in the wood itself. Whether a low-technology or a high-technology method is used, the final result should be the same: a date that is accurate to the year and that can be replicated by other workers. For other cautions see Appendix III in Baillie (1982).

TECHNIQUES

Sampling

Full cross-sections provide the greatest amount of information. When cutting these is either impossible or forbidden (from a living tree or from an important architectural monument), the dendrochronologist is obliged to resort to coring. A Swedish increment corer is used to extract thin radial cores from standing trees, and a variety of commercially-available drillbits are used to extract similar radial cores from intact architectural timbers. Klein and colleagues in the Hamburg laboratory have had good success with some 2000 oil paintings painted on wooden panels by surfacing the end-grain with a razor blade and measuring directly from the panel (Eckstein *et al.* 1983, Klein 1980, 1986, 1993, 1994). On rare occasions a good, high-contrast photograph of the end-grain has allowed a piece of wood to be dated. The disadvantage of

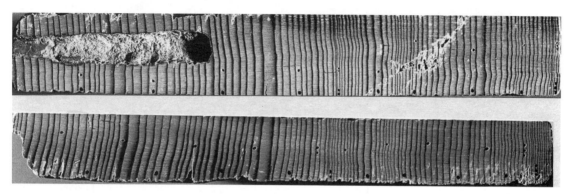

Figure 3.3   Two cedar boards from a Dynasty XII sarcophagus in the Boston Museum of Fine Arts. The signatures and other similarities in the ring-patterns show that the boards were cut from the same tree.

photographs is that microscopically-small rings are almost impossible to discern unless the photographer had the forethought to do some sanding and polishing before taking the photograph. For both sections and cores it is important to include as much of the sapwood as possible where it is extant and to avoid knots, cracks, and other blemishes which distort the patterns of ring-growth. On any sample, if the bark is present (Figure 3.4A), or the 'waney edge' (an Anglicism for the surface immediately beneath the bark), the date when the tree was felled can be determined to the year. For oaks (which have estimable even if region-specific amounts of sapwood), if a significant amount of sapwood is preserved (Figure 3.4B), the felling date can be estimated with varying degrees of precision to within several years. In other species, or in oaks with little or no sapwood and an unknown amount of missing heart-wood (Figure 3.4C), only a *terminus post quem* date is possible.

Analytical

The surface of the sample to be studied is prepared with fine sandpaper or a razor blade so that every ring can be measured and morphological oddities noted, usually under a binocular dissecting microscope. Then,

whether a low-technology ('the Douglass method') or a more high-technology method is used, the latter including complete measurement of the ring-series and various kinds of statistical analyses (see the more recent handbooks identified above), the rings have to be matched to one another. Once wood or charcoal specimens have been crossdated, they are then set in order (Figure 3.5), beginning with an absolutely-dated tree, and a chronology is built in step-wise fashion into the past as far back as the evidence will allow.

BUILDING THE LONG CHRONOLOGIES

The backbone of all tree-ring research is the long chronologies to which all the dates are pinned. For North America the longest archaeological tree-ring chronologies, both *Abies* and *Pinus* (fir and pine) go back to about 300 BC, and the *Pinus longaeva* (bristlecone pine) chronology is now over 8400 years with a tentative extension to near 10 000. The European *Quercus* (oak) chronology is 10 479 years long, extending to 8480 BC (Pilcher *et al.* 1984, Becker 1993; published numbers updated from Spurk *et al.* 1998). A 2012-year chronology of *Pinus silvestris* (Scots pine) when Europe was still too cold for oaks to grow (but

Figure 3.4   Three dating possibilities from a single cross-section of Greek oak. A is the most desirable sample with all the sapwood rings preserved out to the waney edge in 1439. B is the next-best sample with some, but not all, of the sapwood rings present. The felling date therefore has to be estimated within five or 10 years. C is the least desirable sample with all of the sapwood rings and an unknown number of heartwood rings missing. The felling date cannot be estimated.

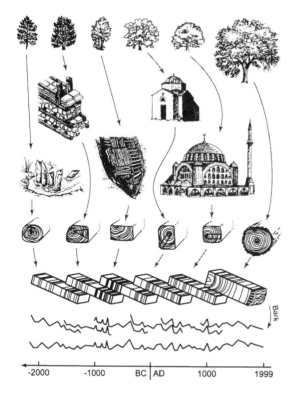

Figure 3.5 Schematic demonstration of chronology-building, from a living tree sampled in 1999, to a Turkish mosque, to a Byzantine church, to a Roman shipwreck, to an Iron Age/Bronze Age wall, to a prehistoric pile-dwelling.

which overlaps with the beginning of the oak chronology for more than 500 years) gives the European workers a complete tree-ring sequence from the present back into the last glaciation (numbers again updated from Kromer and Spurk 1998). The chronologies are expected to be lengthened in the very near future to include both the Lower and Upper Dryas. Aegean chronologies, principally *Quercus*, *Juniperus*, and *Pinus* (oak, juniper, and pine), total over 6500 years with the longest single segment 1636 years (Kuniholm 1996). In the southern hemisphere, the southern Andes has a *Fitzroya cupressoides* (alerce) sequence extending back to 1634 BC, and New Zealand now has a 1200 year chronology for *Lagarostrobus colensoi* (silver pine). In Tasmania a chronology of over 4100 years has been developed for *Lagarostrobus franklinii* (Huon pine), but its archaeological significance is limited by the fact that exploitation of this tree dates back to only the early nineteenth century. Southern Africa's longest chronology is one of 413 years for *Widdringtonia cedarbergensis* or Clanwilliam cedar.

The northern hemisphere tree-ring chronologies currently have greater relevance to archaeology because they co-exist with vast amounts of archaeological activity. Tree-ring dates have been cited at annual archaeological meetings for the better part of a century for North America, for almost half a century for Europe, and for a couple of decades for the Aegean and the Near East. North America's lead in using tree-ring dates has a lot to do with the pioneering efforts of Douglass and his followers and also a lot to do with the lack of king-lists, written records, and other chronological indicators on which Old World archaeologists have so long relied.

Some 573 tree and shrub species have been investigated for tree-ring studies. Of these some 180 can be crossdated within the same species, but also at times between and among species. Some of the important genera for archaeological research are (species known to crossdate/species investigated): *Pinus* or pine (54/63), *Quercus* or oak (27/44), *Abies* or fir (21/34), *Picea* or spruce (19/21), *Juniperus* or juniper (15/21), *Larix* or larch (9/9), *Populus* or poplar (7/10), *Acer* or maple (6/10), *Betula* or birch (5/15), *Tsuga* or hemlock (5/7), and *Cedrus* or cedar (4/4). Grissino-Mayer (1993) gives the complete listing as well as an assessment of each species' importance in dendrochronology.

PROGRESS FROM 1963–1999

At this point the seriously-interested reader should consult two fundamental articles: Bannister (1963) and Dean (1997). Bannister's is the classic exposition, and yet he forecast 'rapid future progress'. Dean's recent summary of that progress shows how prescient Bannister was and how the application of the dendrochronological method has practically exploded in the last generation to include a variety of sophisticated forms of climate and environmental reconstruction. Grissino-Mayer's website (http://web.utk.edu/ ˜grissino) with links to several dozen laboratories around the world shows 6752 bibliographic entries as of September 1999, and references are added regularly. Two journals devoted exclusively to dendrochronological subjects are the *Tree-Ring Bulletin* (1934–present) and *Dendrochronologia* (1983–present). Over 1500 archived tree-ring data sets are in the International Tree Ring Data Bank in Boulder, Colorado (http:// www.ngdc.noaa.gov/paleo/ftp-treering.html), and a polyglot cross-referenced guide to dendrochronological terminology in seven languages is to be found in Kaennel and Schweingruber (1995).

As archaeology has grown from its rather primitive beginnings, so, too, dendrochronology has evolved from a relatively limited focus on the dating of monuments or archaeological strata. In addition to the simple ring-width measurements pioneered by Douglass (1919, 1928, 1936), whether skeleton-plotted or measured, new analytical techniques include X-radiography, X-ray densitometry, and neutron activation analysis, among others, to study morphological and chemical changes within particular rings or cells or to detect the presence of specific trace-elements and isotopes.

Applied dendrochronological topics now include the study of changes in both the immediate and distant environment (Dean 1988), the history and effects of pollution (summarized in Schweingruber 1988), stream erosion and infill (LaMarche 1966), forest fires (Swetnam 1993), earthquakes (LaMarche and Wallace 1972, Jacoby *et al.* 1992), glacial movement (LaMarche and Fritts 1971, Schneebeli and Röthlisberger 1976, Kaiser 1993), volcanoes (LaMarche and Hirschboeck 1984, Kuniholm *et al.* 1996), tsunamis, seasonal river flooding, insect lifecycles, human intervention in the forest, and changes in wood utilization and exploitation (Billamboz 1988, Dean 1978), and so on. Schweingruber (1988) provides an extraordinary illustrated listing, with bibliography, of many of these fields and sub-fields into which dendrochronological research has evolved. See also Schweingruber (1993, 1996) and Schweingruber and Schoch (1992) for the most recent work on dendroecology and the environment.

CASE STUDIES IN DENDROCHRONOLOGY

In contrast to some of the other archaeometric techniques where the laboratory scientists interact very little with the archaeologists, dendrochronology from its very beginning has been typified by close collaboration between laboratory and field workers. In practice the dendrochronologist has visited the site, discussed its problems and interpretation with the excavator, and only then has taken the sample. An ideal sample will be of value to both parties, i.e., datable and from a significant archaeological context. Instances where dendrochronology has been applied with noteworthy results to the interpretation of archaeological sites and archaeological or art-historical artifacts include the following, selected from the three principal regions where tree-ring dating has been done extensively.

North America

At Pueblo Bonito (New Mexico) and other nearby sites Douglass not only provided absolute dates for forty-five monuments for the first time ever (Douglass 1929, 1935), but he also made observations on the possible use of dead timbers, or re-use of timbers, and on the effects of a great drought between AD 1276–1299, as well as over a dozen other droughts which must have had significant effects on the local population. In this ecumenical outlook Douglass, as a field archaeologist, was decades ahead of his time.

At Betatakin, Kiet Siel, and eleven neighbouring sites in north-eastern Arizona, Dean took Douglass's work a step further by providing dates for specific rooms and clusters of rooms (Dean 1969, Dean *et al.* 1978), as well as integrating the tree-ring dates with the interpretation of the ceramic evidence. He also was able to make a number of inferences:

(i)   that the environment of Betatakin has not changed in 700 years while that of Kiet Siel has,
(ii) that one site exhibits the practice of stockpiling timbers before use and the other does not,
(iii) that at both sites the re-use of old wood is common, and
(iv) that patterns of population growth, of immigration, and of population decline can be demonstrated.

Finally, Dean was able to make a number of inferences about the social organization of the villages – all beginning with the tree-rings!

In an early work that is little-known to European archaeologists, Giddings studied sea-side settlements in northern Alaska at Point Hope and along the Bering Strait (Giddings 1942). Here he was able to show that some of these whalebone and wood buildings were made of trees that had drifted about the Arctic Circle for more than a century before they were incorporated into house walls.

Europe

Here the chronologies are longer and the story is more complicated. In the Bodensee (Lake Constance) and other early lake-settlements near the Alps (Billamboz 1988, 1990, 1996, Schlichtherle 1990), not only have the earliest Neolithic levels been dated to the year, but the very shape of each oak post is an indication of its likely date, even before measurement (Billamboz 1987). In the first phase of the Neolithic all timbers are little more than saplings and must have been collected from near the lakeshore. In the second phase of the Neolithic the timbers are always halved or quartered, suggesting both that the supply of small-dimension wood was exhausted and that the technology to split somewhat larger trees had been developed. In the third phase even larger trees are cut into multiple segments. Technology had continued to develop so that the forest on the hillsides away from the lake could be exploited.

In Zürich and the Swiss lake district the work of Huber and Merz at Zug-Sumpf, Thayngen-Weier, and the Burgäschisee, and culminating now in the work of the Ruoff group has been exemplary. The Pfahlbauland exhibit at Zürich in 1990 was a creative setting-forth of the whole prehistoric past of the lakes: architecture, agriculture, animal domestication, ecological and environmental studies, and technological practices of all kinds (multiple references in Schweizerisches Landesmuseum Zürich 1990; Pfahlbauland videos 1990), all dated by dendrochronology.

Riverine Europe has been studied dendrochronologically from the headwaters of the Rhine (Kramer and Schlichtherle 1995, Billamboz and Martinelli 1996), Mosel, and Danube (Billamboz and Schlichtherle 1986) all the way to the Baltic, from the living oaks of the Spessart Forest back to the last ice age (Becker 1982, Becker et al. 1984, with references to the work of Huber, the German analogue to Douglass). New work includes studies of the medieval and prehistoric Netherlands (Jansma 1995), the prehistoric trackways across the lower Rhineland (Schmidt 1987), and the early medieval and Viking settlements at Haithabu (Eckstein 1972, Eckstein et al. 1983). It also includes the analysis of a long series of medieval buildings in the Rhineland (Hollstein 1980), a thorough study of private houses in the Mosel Region (Schmidt et al. 1990), and the identification of the imported Polish oak which served as supports for Netherlandish panel paintings (Baillie et al. 1985, Eckstein et al. 1986) as well as for wainscoting in English country houses.

Insular Europe is being studied by the Belfast group, as well as the Sheffield and Nottingham groups. The islands, as does the Continent, have wooden trackways such as the Sweet Track in Somerset dated by dendrochronology (Morgan 1988, Coles and Coles 1986), bogs, submerged forests, sunken boats, but also horizontal mills (Baillie 1982) and crannogs, small artificial islands formed inside circles of oak posts driven into lakebeds (Baillie 1995). The latter are split sections of enormous trees, often subdivided radially in halves or thirds with the result that 'phantom phasings' result: the interior third ends without sapwood, as does the

middle third some years later. Only the exterior third (with its sapwood present) reveals the true state of affairs. All three 'phases' are one. Indiscriminate radiocarbon analysis of the three sets of sections would have yielded nonsensical results. The Bodensee analyses by Billamboz (1987; especially the timbers from his Neolithic III) are analogous to this.

Archaeological dendrochronology in Russia, notably at Novgorod (Kolchin 1963, 1967), in addition to providing firm dates for the churches and houses, also revealed a remarkable set of split-log roadways which, as they sank into the soft substrate, showed many signs of conflagrations. Novgorod, which we know from the chronicles was never attacked by anybody, suffered a catastrophic burning about once every twenty-four years over several centuries, not altogether surprising for a town built largely of wood (Kolchin 1963). So much for some of the 'destruction levels' about which Near Eastern archaeologists so often read and write! Study of the Scythian kurgans from Pazyryk in the High Altai to western Russia is still in its infancy and remains largely a project for the future, but the potential is considerable.

Aegean and the Near East

Dendrochronological analysis of approximately two hundred medieval buildings in Greece and Turkey has been carried out since 1973 (Kuniholm and Striker 1987, Kuniholm 1994). One striking example of how the method can change old ways of thinking is the Church of the Holy Apostles in Thessaloniki where a puzzling, long-misunderstood monogram which suggested a date of AD 1310–1314 is contradicted by the dendrochronological date of 1329 (Kuniholm and Striker 1990). 'Dendroprovenancing' as mentioned above for exported Polish oak in northern Europe is possible in the Aegean as well with Alpine fir and spruce found in a Renaissance palace in Dubrovnik on the Dalmatian Coast, Black Sea oak found in medieval monuments in Istanbul and Thessaloniki, and Alpine fir and spruce found in the destroyed Roman towns of Pompeii and Herculaneum (Kuniholm forthcoming).

In the pre- and proto-historic Near East a series of dates for the Iron Age and the Bronze Age is available (Kuniholm 1996, Kuniholm et al. 1996). The earliest work is at the Neolithic site of Çatal Höyük where a 576-year chronology, wiggle-matched by radiocarbon (see below) fairly closely to an end date of 6449 BC is in place (Kuniholm and Newton 1997, Newton and Kuniholm 1999).

CASE STUDIES IN ENVIRONMENTAL AND CLIMATIC RECONSTRUCTION

North America

Although climate reconstruction may be considered by some archaeologists as outside the scope of their immediate concerns, the successful study and analysis of palaeoclimate is having an increasing impact on archaeological thinking. For the method in general see Fritts (1976), Hughes *et al.* (1982) and Schweingruber (1996); for the south-west US in general see Douglass (1914, 1919, 1928, 1936) and Schulman (1956); for western North America see Schweingruber *et al.* (1991); for the southern Colorado plateau see Dean and Funkhouser (1995); for the Sierra Nevada see Graumlich (1993); for the Medieval warm period see Hughes and Diaz (1994); for the south-eastern USA see Reams and Van Deusen (1996) and Stahle and Cleaveland (1992); for Jamestown see Stahle *et al.* (1998); for fire history and climate change in the California sequoia groves see Swetnam (1993).

Europe

For Europe in general see Bartholin *et al.* (1992) and Briffa *et al.* (1986); for western Europe see Schweingruber *et al.* (1990, 1991); for Fennoscandia see Briffa *et al.* (1990); for the Medieval warm period see Hughes and Diaz (1994); and for southern Europe see Urbinati and Carrer (1997).

Aegean and the Near East

For an early resumé see Kuniholm (1990), and now Hughes *et al.* (in press).

RADIOCARBON CALIBRATION AND WIGGLE-MATCHING

The story of the tree-ring calibration of the radiocarbon time-scale is or should be well known to most archaeologists (see Chapter 2). What is less well-understood is the application of 'wiggle-matching', where selected decade-long slices cut from a piece of wood at specific intervals are individually radiocarbon-dated, and then the whole array of dates is matched to the radiocarbon curve (Kuniholm 1996). Figure 3.6 shows an example of wiggle-matching from the Early Bronze Age site of Lavagnone di Brescia in northern Italy. The work is still in progress, but even a casual reader of graphs

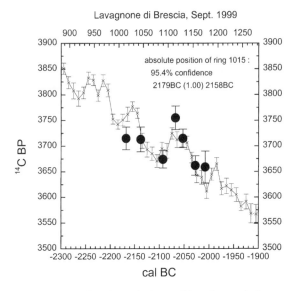

Figure 3.6 Radiocarbon wiggle-matching of an Early Bronze Age site. The seven decadal ring-sequences were sliced from a log at selected intervals. Since the exact number of rings between each set of samples is known, it is possible to consider them as a single group. The radiocarbon counting errors are thereby minimized.

should be able to see that the seven radiocarbon dates, as wiggle-matched to the calibrated radiocarbon curve, limit the possibilities of placement of the chronology to about a decade either way. The fourth (or middle) date, about 3755 years BP, could just as easily be placed about 70–130 years earlier because of the wiggles that the radiocarbon curve takes at those points. However, because we know the relationship of the fourth sample to the other six, there is only one likely range on the curve where all seven samples can sit in comfort. Thus the two sets of 'wiggles', both those of the master radiocarbon curve and those from the Lavagnone sequence, may be said to 'match' each other at that one placement with a very small margin of error.

FUTURE PROSPECTS

Baillie (1995) said: 'In many ways people have been unprepared for the injection, into a predominantly radiocarbon-based chronological framework, of precise calendar dates...'. This is equally true for parts of the archaeological world where chronologies traditionally have been based on king-lists, pottery types, and the written records where such exist. The fact that there are four different chronologies for Egypt, all based on the 'historical record' (Åström 1987, Kitchen 1996), should give one pause for thought.

There is continued reason, however, to be highly optimistic about future prospects in dendrochronology and its evolving applications. As the long tree-ring chronologies are extended and their relationships to one another are more clearly understood, as geographical gaps are filled in to create a web of absolutely-dated and interlinked chronologies world-wide, and as new methods of their interpretation are developed, projections on a hemispheric scale will become possible. Soon we will see in print when the Upper Dryas happened and exactly how many years it lasted in southern Germany. Before the pioneering forty years of work by Huber and Becker and their followers this would have been unimaginable. In 1976 this writer was assured that there were four oak chronologies in Germany that would never match each other. Now there is one. Seventeen years ago Baillie (1983) asked rhetorically 'Is there a single British Isles oak tree-ring signal?' We now know that the answer is yes, and that the British and German chronologies match each other. Indeed, all of western European oak from the Pyrenees to the Baltic can be crossdated. The accomplishments of the last thirty-six years, as the list of case studies above should show, have been just what Bannister predicted in 1963. The effects that tree-ring dating ought to have on archaeology in the next generation and the refinements in archaeological thinking that will thereby be required are indeed going to be revolutionary.

REFERENCES

*Recommended for further reading

Åström, P. (1987). *High, Middle, or Low? Acts of an International Colloquium on Absolute Chronology Held in Gothenburg 20–22 August 1987, Vol. 1.* Paul Åströms Forlag: Gothenburg.
*Baillie, M.G.L. (1982). *Tree-Ring Dating and Archaeology.* University of Chicago Press: Chicago.
Baillie, M.G.L. (1983). Is there a single British Isles tree-ring signal? In Aspinall, A. and Warren, S.E. (eds) *Proceedings of the 22nd Symposium on Archaeometry*, 73–82. University of Bradford Press: Bradford.
*Baillie, M.G.L. (1995). *A Slice Through Time: Dendrochronology and Precision Dating.* Batsford Press: London.
Baillie, M.G.L., Hillam, J., Briffa, K.R. and Brown, D.M. (1985). Re-dating the English art-historical tree-ring chronologies. *Nature*, **315**:317–319.
Bannister, B. (1962). The interpretation of tree-ring dates. *American Antiquity*, **27**:508–514.

Bannister, B. (1963). Dendrochronology. In Brothwell, D. and Higgs, E. (eds) *Science in Archaeology*, 162–176. Basic Books: New York.
Bartholin, T.S., Berglund, B.E., Eckstein, D. and Schweingruber, F.H. (eds) (1992). *Tree Rings and Environment*. Lundqua Report 34, Lund University: Lund.
Becker, B. (1982). Dendrochronologie und Paläoökologie subfossiler Baumstämme aus Flussablagerungen: ein Beitrag zur nacheiszeitlichen Auenentwicklung im südlichen Mitteleuropa. *Mitteilungen der Kommission für Quartärforschung der österreichischen Akademie der Wissenschaften*, Band 5.
Becker, B. (1993). An 11 000-year German oak and pine dendrochronology for radiocarbon calibration. *Radiocarbon*, **35**:201–213.
Becker, B., Billamboz, A., Keefer, E., Liese-Kleiber, H., Rösch, M., Schlichtherle, H., Schmidt, B. and Schmitt, K. (1984). *Berichte zu Ufer- und Moorsiedlungen Südwestdeutschlands 1.* Landesdenkmalamt Baden-Württemberg: Stuttgart.
Billamboz, A. (1987). Le bois raconte l'histoire des hommes et de la forêt. *Archeologia*, **222**:30–38.
Billamboz, A. (1988). Jahresringe im Bauholz. *Archäologie in Württemberg: Ergebnisse und Perspektiven archäologischer Forschung von der Altsteinzeit bis zur Neuzeit*, 515–529. Theiss Verlag: Stuttgart.
Billamboz, A. (1990). Das Holz der Pfahlbausiedlungen Südwestdeutschlands: Jahrringanalyse aus archäodendrologischer Sicht. 5. Kolloquium der Deutschen Forschungsgemeinschaft. *Bericht der Römisch-Germanischen Kommission*, **71**:187–207.
Billamboz, A. (1996). Tree-rings and pile-dwellings in southern Germany: following in the footsteps of Bruno Huber. In Dean, J.S., Meko, D.M. and Swetnam, T.W. (eds) *Tree Rings, Environment and Humanity*, 471–483. University of Arizona: Tucson.
Billamboz, A. and Martinelli, N. (1996). La recherche dendrochronologique en Europe pour l'âge du bronze ancien. In Mordant, C. and Gaiffe, O. (eds) *Cultures et Sociétés du Bronze Ancien en Europe*, 85–96. CTHS: Paris.
Billamboz, A. and Schlichtherle, H. (1986). Le Néolithique des bords de lac et des tourbières du Sud-Ouest de l'Allemagne. *Première Céramique, Premier Métal du Néolithique à l'Âge du Bronze dans le domaine Circum-Alpin*, 23–35. Musée d'Archéologie: Lons-le-Saunier.
Briffa, K.R., Wigley, T.M.L., Jones, P.D., Pilcher, J.R. and Hughes, M.K. (1986). *The Reconstruction of Past Circulation Patterns over Europe Using Tree-Ring Data*. Contract No. CL111 UK Final Report, Commission of the European Communities: Brussels.
Briffa, K.R., Bartholin, T.S., Eckstein, D., Jones, P.D., Karlen, W., Schweingruber, F.H. and Zetterberg, R. (1990). A 1400-year tree-ring record of summer temperatures in Fennoscandia. *Nature*, **346**:434–439.
Coles, B. and Coles, J. (1986). *Sweet Track to Glastonbury: the Somerset Levels in Prehistory*. Thames and Hudson: London.

Dean, J.S. (1969). Chronological analysis of Tsegi Phase sites in Northeastern Arizona. *Papers of the Laboratory of Tree-Ring Research 3*. University of Arizona Press: Tucson.

Dean, J.S. (1978). Tree-ring dating in Archaeology. *University of Utah Anthropological Papers*, **24**:129–163.

Dean, J.S. (1988). Dendrochronology and paleoenvironmental reconstruction on the Colorado Plateaus. In Gumerman, G.J. (ed.) *The Anasazi in a Changing Environment*, 119–167. Cambridge University Press: Cambridge.

*Dean, J.S. (1997). Dendrochronology. In Taylor, R.E. and Aitken, M.J. (eds) *Chronometric Dating in Archaeology*, 31–64. Plenum Press: New York.

Dean, J.S. and Funkhouser, G.S. (1995). Dendroclimatic reconstructions for the southern Colorado Plateau. In Waugh, W.J. (ed.) *Climate Change in the Four Corners and Adjacent Regions: Implications for Environmental Restoration and Land-Use Planning*, 85–104. Grand Junction Projects Office, US Department of Energy.

Dean, J.S., Lindsay, A.J. Jr. and Robinson, W.J. (1978). Prehistoric settlement in Long House Valley, northeastern Arizona. In Euler, R.C. and Gumerman, G.J. (eds) *Investigations of the Southwestern Anthropological Research Group: An Experiment in Archaeological Cooperation*, 25–44. Museum of Northern Arizona: Flagstaff, AZ.

Douglass, A.E. (1914). A method of estimating rainfall by the growth of trees. In Huntington, E. (ed.) *The Climatic Factor as Illustrated in Arid America*, 101–121. Publication 192, Carnegie Institution of Washington: Lancaster, Pennsylvania.

Douglass, A.E. (1919). *Climatic Cycles and Tree Growth: A Study of the Annual Rings of Trees in Relation to Climate and Solar Activity*. Publication 289, Carnegie Institute: Washington, DC.

Douglass, A.E. (1928). *Climatic Cycles and Tree Growth II*. Publication 289:2. Carnegie Institute: Washington, DC.

Douglass, A.E. (1929). The secret of the Southwest solved by talkative tree rings. *National Geographic Magazine*, **56**:736–770.

Douglass, A.E. (1935). *Dating Pueblo Bonito and Other Ruins of the Southwest*. Technical Papers, Pueblo Bonito Series 1, National Geographic Society: Washington, DC.

Douglass, A.E. (1936). *Climatic Cycles and Tree Growth: A Study of Cycles*. Publication 289:3, Carnegie Institute: Washington, DC.

Eckstein, D. (1972). Tree-ring research in Europe. *Tree-Ring Bulletin*, **32**:1–18.

Eckstein, D., Wrobel, S. and Aniol, R.W. (eds) (1983). *Dendrochronology and Archaeology in Europe: Proceedings of a Workshop of the European Science Foundation*. Mitteilungen der Bundesforschungsanstalt für Forst- und Holzwirtschaft, Nr. 141, Kommissionsverlag: Hamburg.

*Eckstein, D., Baillie, M.G.L. and Egger, H. (1984). *Dendrochronological Dating. Handbooks for Archaeologists No. 2*. European Science Foundation: Strasbourg.

Eckstein, D., Wazny, T., Bauch, J. and Klein, P. (1986). New evidence for the dendrochronological dating of Netherlandish paintings. *Nature*, **320**:465–466.

Ferguson, C.W. (1970). Concepts and techniques of dendrochronology. In Berger, R. (ed.) *Scientific Methods in Medieval Archaeology*, 183–200. University of California Press: Berkeley.

*Fritts, H.C. (1976). *Tree Rings and Climate*. Academic Press: London.

Giddings, J.L. Jr. (1942). Dendrochronology in Northern Alaska. *Laboratory of Tree-Ring Research Bulletin* **9:1**. University of Arizona Press: Tucson.

Graumlich, L.J. (1993). A 1000-year record of temperature and precipitation in the Sierra Nevada. *Quaternary Research*, **39**:249–255.

Grissino-Mayer, H.D. (1993). An updated list of species used in tree-ring research. *Tree-Ring Bulletin*, **53**:17–43.

Haury, E.W. (1962). HH-39: recollections of a dramatic moment in Southwestern archaeology. *Tree-Ring Bulletin*, **24(3-4)**:11–14.

Hollstein, E. (1980). *Mitteleuropäische Eichenchronologie: Trierer Grabungen und Forschungen, Band XI*. Philipp von Zabern: Mainz.

Hughes, M.K. and Diaz, H.F. (eds) (1994). *The Medieval Warm Period*. Kluwer Academic Publishers: Dordrecht.

Hughes, M.K., Kelly, P.M., Pilcher, J.R. and LaMarche, V.C. Jr. (1982). *Climate from Tree Rings*. Cambridge University Press: Cambridge.

Hughes, M.K., Kuniholm, P.I., Eischeid, J., Garfin-Woll, G., Griggs, C.B. and Latini C. (in press). Aegean tree-ring signature years explained. *Tree-Ring Bulletin*.

Jacoby, G.C., Williams, P.L. and Buckley, B.M. (1992). Tree ring correlation between prehistoric landslides and abrupt tectonic events in Seattle, Washington. *Science*, **258**:1621–1623.

Jansma, E. (1995). *RemembeRINGs: The Development and Application of Local and Regional Tree-Ring Chronologies of Oak for the Purposes of Archaeological and Historical Research in the Netherlands*. Nederlandse Archeologische Rapporten 19.

Kaennel, M. and Schweingruber, F.H. (1995). *Multilingual Glossary of Dendrochronology: Terms and Definitions in English, German, French, Spanish, Italian, Portuguese and Russian*. Paul Haupt: Berne.

Kaiser, K.F. (1993). Growth rings as indicators of glacier advances, surges and floods. *Dendrochronologia*, **11**:101–122.

Kitchen, K.A. (1996). The historical chronology of Ancient Egypt. A current assessment. In Randsborg, K. (ed.) *Absolute Chronology: Archaeological Europe 2500–500 B.C. Acta Archaeologica 67*, 1–14. Munksgaard: Copenhagen.

Klein, P. (1980). Dendrochronologische Untersuchungen an Eichenholztafeln von Rogier Van der Weyden. *Jahrbuch der Berliner Museen*, **23**:113–123.

Klein, P. (1986). Dendrochronological analysis of early Netherlandish panels in the National Gallery of Art. In

Hand, J.O. and Wolff, M. *Early Netherlandish Painting*, 259–260. Systematic Catalogue of the Collections, National Gallery of Art: Washington, DC.

Klein, P. (1993). Dendrochronological analysis of German panels in the National Gallery of Art. In Hand, J.O. *German Paintings of the Fifteenth through Seventeenth Centuries*, 195–197. National Gallery of Art: Washington, DC.

Klein, P. (1994). Lucas Cranach und seine Werkstatt. Holzarten und dendrochronologische Analyse. In Grimm, C., Erichsen, J. and Brockhoff, E. (eds) *Lucas Cranach. Ein Maler-Unternehmer aus Franken*. Haus der Bayerischen Geschichte: Augsburg.

Kolchin, B.A. (1963). *Novii Metodi v Arkheologii Trudi Novgorodskoi Ekspeditsii, Tom III*. Akademiya Nauk SSSR: Moscow.

Kolchin, B.A. (1967). Dendrochronology. In Artsikhovsky, A.V. and Kolchin, B.A. *Novgorod the Great: Excavations at the Medieval City*, 23–34. Frederick A. Praeger: New York.

Kramer, W. and Schlichtherle, H. (1995). Unterwasser-Archäologie in Deutschland. *Antike Welt*, **26**:3–16.

Kromer, B. and Spurk, M. (1998). Revision and tentative extension of the tree-ring based ^{14}C calibration, 9200–11 855 cal BP. *Radiocarbon*, **40**:1117–1125.

Kuniholm, P.I. (1990). The archaeological record: evidence and non-evidence for climatic change. In Runcorn, S.K. and Pecker, J.-C. (eds) *The Earth's Climate and Variability of the Sun Over Recent Millennia*. Philosophical Transactions of the Royal Society of London A, 645–655.

Kuniholm, P.I. (1994). Long tree-ring chronologies for the eastern Mediterranean. In Demirçi, S., Özer, A.M. and Summers, G.D. (eds) *Archaeometry '94: Proceedings of the 29th International Symposium on Archaeometry*, 401–409. TÜBITAK: Ankara.

Kuniholm, P.I. (1996). The Prehistoric Aegean: dendrochronological progress as of 1995. In Randsborg, K. (ed.) *Absolute Chronology: Archaeological Europe 2500–500 BC*, 327–335. Acta Archaeologica 67, Munksgaard: Copenhagen.

Kuniholm, P.I. (forthcoming). Dendrochronological investigations at Herculaneum and Pompeii. In Jashemski, W.F. (ed.) *The Natural History of Pompeii and Other Vesuvian Sites*. Cambridge University Press: Cambridge.

Kuniholm, P.I. and Newton, M.W. (1997). Interim dendrochronological progress report 1995/6. In Hodder, I. (ed.) *On the Surface: Çatalhöyük 1993–95*, 345–347. British Institute of Archaeology at Ankara/McDonald Institute: Cambridge.

Kuniholm, P.I. and Striker, C.L. (1987). Dendrochronological investigations in the Aegean and neighboring regions, 1983–1986. *Journal of Field Archaeology*, **14**:385–398.

Kuniholm, P.I. and Striker, C.L. (1990). Dendrochronology and the architectural history of the Church of the Holy Apostles in Thessaloniki. *Architectura: Zeitschrift für Geschichte der Baukunst*, **20**:1–26.

Kuniholm, P.I., Kromer, B., Manning, S.W., Newton, M.W., Latini, C.E. and Bruce, M.J. (1996). Anatolian tree rings and the absolute chronology of the eastern Mediterranean, 2220–718 BC. *Nature*, **381**:780–783.

LaMarche, V.C. Jr. (1966). An 800-year history of stream erosion as indicated by botanical evidence. Professional Paper 550-D, US Geological Survey, D83-D86.

LaMarche, V.C. Jr. and Fritts, H.C. (1971). Tree rings, glacial advance, and climate in the Alps. *Zeitschrift für Gletscherkunde und Glazialgeologie*, **7**:125–131.

LaMarche, V.C. Jr. and Hirschboeck, K.K. (1984). Frost rings in trees as records of major volcanic eruptions. *Nature*, **307**:121–126.

LaMarche, V.C. Jr. and Wallace, R.E. (1972). Evaluation of effects of past movements on the San Andreas Fault, Northern California. *Geological Society of America Bulletin*, **83**:2665–2676.

Morgan, R. (1988). *Tree-Ring Studies of Wood used in Neolithic and Bronze Age Trackways from the Somerset Levels*. BAR 184, British Archaeological Reports: Oxford.

Newton, M.W. and Kuniholm, P.I. (1999). Wiggles worth watching – making radiocarbon work: the case of Çatal Höyük. *MELETEMATA: Studies in Aegean Archaeology presented to Malcolm H. Wiener as he enters his 65th year*, 527–536. Université de Liège: Liège.

Pfahlbauland videos (1990). *Pfahlgeschichten: Die Entwicklung des Pfahlbaubildes und die moderne Archäologie*. Zürich: Ateliers für Didaktik.

Pilcher, J.R., Baillie, M.G.L., Schmidt, B. and Becker, B. (1984). A 7272-year tree-ring chronology for western Europe. *Nature*, **312**:150–152.

Reams, G.A. and Van Deusen, P.C. (1996). Detection of a hurricane signal in bald cypress tree-ring chronologies. In Dean, J.S., Meko, D.M. and Swetnam, T.W. (eds) *Tree Rings, Environment and Humanity*, 265–271. University of Arizona: Tucson.

Schlichtherle, H. (1990). Aspekte der siedlungsarchäologischen Erforschungen von Neolithikum und Bronzezeit im südwestdeutschen Alpenvorland. 5. Kolloquium der Deutschen Forschungsgemeinschaft. *Bericht der Römisch-Germanischen Kommission*, **71**:208–244.

Schmidt, B. (1987). *Dendrochronologie und Ur- und Frühgeschichte*. Habilitationschrift: Köln.

Schmidt, B., Köhren-Jansen, H. and Freckmann, K. (1990). *Kleine Hausgeschichte der Mosellandschaft: Band 1 der Schriftenreihe zur Dendrochronologie und Bauforschung*. Rheinland-Verlag: Köln.

Schneebeli, W. and Röthlisberger, F. (1976). *8000 Jahre Walliser Gletschergeschichte: Ein Beitrag zur Erforschung des Klimaverlaufs in der Nacheiszeit*. Die Alpen: Zeitschrift des Schweizer Alpen Club, Luzern.

Schulman, E. (1956). *Dendroclimatic Change in Semiarid America*. University of Arizona Press: Tucson.

*Schweingruber, F.H. (1988). *Tree Rings: Basics and Applications of Dendrochronology*. D. Reidel: Dordrecht.

Schweingruber, F.H. (1993). *Trees and Wood in Dendrochronology*. Springer-Verlag: Berlin.

*Schweingruber, F.H. (1996). *Tree Rings and Environment: Dendroecology*. Paul Haupt: Berne.

Schweingruber, F.H. and Schoch, W.H. (1992). *Holz, Jahrringe und Weltgeschehen*. Lignum: Dietikon (CH).

Schweingruber, F.H., Eckstein, D., Serre-Bachet, F. and Bräker, O.U. (1990). Identification, presentation and interpretation of event years and pointer years in dendrochronology. *Dendrochronologia*, **8**:9–38.

Schweingruber, F.H., Briffa, K.R. and Jones, P.D. (1991). Yearly maps of summer temperatures in western Europe from AD 1750 to 1975 and western North America from 1600 to 1982. *Vegetatio*, **92**:5–71.

Schweizerisches Landesmuseum Zürich (1990). *Die ersten Bauern: Pfahlbaufunde Europas, Band 1 & 2: Einführung, Balkan und angrenzende Regionen der Schweiz*. Schweizerisches Landesmuseum: Zürich.

Spurk, M., Friedrich, M., Hofmann, J., Remmele, S., Frenzel, B., Leuschner, H.H. and Kromer, B. (1998). Revisions and extension of the Hohenheim oak and pine chronologies: new evidence about the timing of the Younger Dryas/ Preboreal transition. *Radiocarbon*, **40**:1107–1116.

Stahle, D.W. and Cleaveland, M.K. (1992). Reconstruction and analysis of spring rainfall over the southeastern U.S. for the past 1000 years. *Bulletin of the American Meteorological Society*, **73**:1947–1961.

Stahle, D.W., Cleaveland, M.W., Blanton, D.B., Therrell, M.D. and Gay, D.A. (1998). The Lost Colony and Jamestown droughts. *Science*, **280**:564–567.

*Stokes, M.A. and Smiley, T.L. (1968). *An Introduction to Tree-Ring Dating*. University of Chicago Press: Chicago.

Stravinskiene, V. and Juknys, R. (eds) (1998). *Proceedings of the International Conference: Dendrochronology and Environmental Trends*. Vytautas Magnus University: Kaunas.

Swetnam, T.W. (1993). Fire history and climate change in giant sequoia groves. *Science*, **262**:885–889.

Urbinati, C. and Carrer, M. (1997). *Dendroecologia: una Scienza per l'Ambiente fra Passato e Presente*. Atti del XXXIV Corso di Cultura in Ecologia, Università degli Studi di Padova: Padova.

Webb, G.E. (1983). *Tree Rings and Telescopes: The Scientific Career of A.E. Douglass*. University of Arizona Press: Tucson.

4

Trapped Charge Dating (ESR, TL, OSL)

R. GRÜN

Research School of Earth Sciences, Australian National University.

Trapped charge dating techniques – electron spin resonance, commonly abbreviated to ESR, thermoluminescence (TL) and optically stimulated luminescence (OSL) – have played a major role in the establishment of chronologies in archaeology, particularly in the pre-radiocarbon time range. In archaeological applications, ESR is mostly used for dating tooth enamel, TL for sediments and burnt flint and the latest method, OSL, for sediments. TL and ESR have been instrumental in documenting the early evolution of modern humans in Israel (Valladas *et al.* 1988, Mercier *et al.* 1995, Grün and Stringer 1991). OSL allows the age estimation of sediments that were only exposed to dim sunlight for short time periods. At present, OSL dating is not yet routinely applied in archaeological studies but one can expect that this technique will lead to a breakthrough of knowledge similar to the revolution achieved by radiocarbon dating in the 1950s and 1960s. Recent reviews on ESR dating in archaeology were published by Rink (1997) and Grün (1997), and on luminescence dating by Aitken (1997, 1998) and Roberts (1997).

BASIC PRINCIPLES

Trapped charge dating (TCD) comprises a family of dating methods which are based on the same principle, namely the time-dependent accumulation of electrons and holes in the crystal lattice of certain common

minerals (Figure 4.1). The minerals are acting as natural radiation dosimeters. When a mineral is formed or reset, all electrons are in the ground state. Naturally occurring radioactive isotopes (U, Th, and K) emit a variety of rays which ionize atoms. Negatively charged electrons are knocked off atoms in the ground state (valence band) and transferred to a higher energy state (conduction band); positively charged holes remain near the valence band. After a short time of diffusion, most electrons recombine with holes, thus returning the mineral back to its original state. However, all natural minerals contain defect sites (e.g., lattice defects, interstitial atoms, etc.) at which electrons and holes can be trapped. The trapped electrons and holes form paramagnetic centres which can be detected with an ESR spectrometer, giving rise to a characteristic ESR signal. For the measurement of a luminescence signal, the trapped electrons have to be either thermally (by heating) or optically (by light exposure) activated. The electrons return to the conduction band and most of them will recombine with the holes. If such holes are luminescence centres, light emission (luminescence) is observed.

Figure 4.2 shows the basic principles of the dating process. A *zeroing event* resets any previously stored trapped electrons – this resetting may be heating, exposure to sunlight or mineral formation. After zeroing, new electrons and holes are trapped as a result of natural radiation (Figure 4.1), thus increasing the

Handbook of Archaeological Sciences. Edited by D.R. Brothwell and A.M. Pollard.

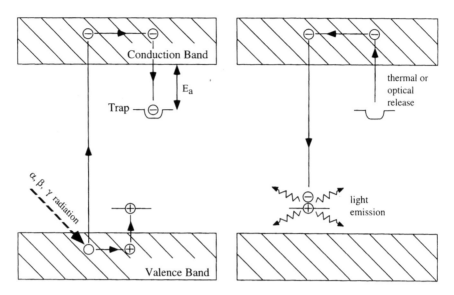

Figure 4.1   The basis for trapped charge dating (from Grün 1997). Left: ionizing radiation knocks off negative electrons from atoms, which are transferred to the conduction band; positively charged holes are left near the valence band. Most electrons recombine with holes, but some are trapped in the crystal lattice. These trapped electrons can be directly measured by ESR. Right: subsequent heating (TL) or light exposure (OSL) releases the electrons and light emission (luminescence) is observed. $E_a =$ activation energy or trap depth.

TCD signal which grows to the *natural intensity*, I_N, as measured in the laboratory. The sample is then irradiated with known doses (the *additive dose method* – see below) generating more trapped electrons and increasing the TCD signal. The measured signal intensity is plotted against the defined laboratory doses (the *dose response curve*) and these data points are used to extrapolate to I_0, the initial signal (which may be zero, depending on the efficiency of the resetting mechanism). The intersection with I_0 yields the *equivalent dose*, D_E, which the sample has received in the past. A TCD age, T, is derived from the simple relationship:

$$D_E = \int_0^T D(t)\, dt \qquad (1)$$

If the dose rate, $D(t)$ or $\dot{D}$, is constant, Equation (1) is reduced to:

$$T = \frac{D_E}{\dot{D}} \qquad (2)$$

The determination of the D_E value is the actual ESR/TL/OSL part of the dating procedure. The dose rate is calculated from an analysis of the radioactive elements in the sample and its surroundings. The concentrations of the radioactive elements are converted into dose

rates by published tables (see below and Table 4.1). The determination of the radioactivity that influences the sample is rather complex and has to be carefully evaluated.

ESR measurement

In an ESR spectrometer, the sample is placed into a microwave cavity which is located in a strong external magnetic field. A paramagnetic centre (i.e., the trapped electron or hole) has a magnetic moment, and this has the same orientation as the magnetic field. In resonance, the magnetic moment is flipped into the opposite direction by absorption of microwave energy which is conducted to the sample from a microwave generator. The amount of absorbed microwave energy is directly proportional to the number of paramagnetic centres, and, in the end, to the age of the sample.

The ESR spectrometer records the microwave absorption with respect to the magnetic field, resulting in characteristic ESR spectra (see Figure 4.5, below). The ESR signal is usually shown as the first derivative. In order to become independent of specific equipment configurations, the position of an ESR line in a spectrum is described by the g-value, which is proportional to the ratio of microwave frequency over magnetic

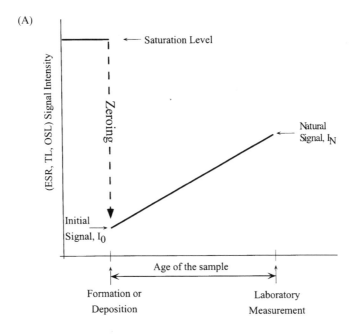

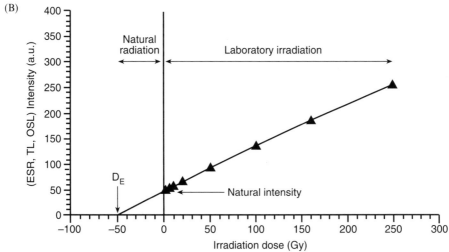

Figure 4.2 Basic principles of the dating process (modified from Aitken 1998:fig. 1.1). A: I_0 is the experimentally determinable *initial intensity*, I_N the *natural signal* or *natural intensity*. After measurement of I_N, the sample is irradiated in the laboratory (B). The *equivalent dose* (D_E) value results from fitting the data points of the dose response with an exponential function and extrapolation to I_0. Reproduced by permission of Oxford University Press.

field strength. The *g*-value is characteristic for a given paramagnetic centre and is usually near the value of 2 (which corresponds approximately to the *g*-value for free electrons). For more details on ESR spectroscopy in dating applications see Grün (1989), Ikeya (1993) and Jonas (1997).

Luminescence measurement

The difference between TL and OSL is the method of re-activating the trapped electrons. For TL the sample is heated, leading to light emission from the sample when electrons recombine with luminescence centres

(Figure 4.1). Figure 4.3 shows the equipment used for TL and OSL measurements. A mineral component of the sample is deposited on a disk which is placed on a heater for TL measurements (Figure 4.3A). At elevated temperatures, electrons are evicted from the traps (see Figure 4.1) and upon recombining with luminescence centres, the sample emits light. The photons are converted into electric pulses with a photomultiplier. The light emission is then plotted versus the heating temperature, resulting in a *glow curve* (see also Figure 4.5C). The configuration for OSL measurements is very similar (Figure 4.3B). Light in a narrow frequency range (green light for measuring quartz, red for feldspars) is shone on to the sample. This activates the electrons in those traps that are light sensitive. When the electrons combine with luminescence centres, the sample emits light. The colour filters in front of the photo-multiplier are used to eliminate quantitatively the light emitted from the light source. The light emission is plotted against the time elapsed after the light source was switched on, resulting in a *shine-down curve* (see also Figure 4.5E). In most cases, the light emission

used for dating lies in the ultra violet range, but other colours have also been investigated (Krbetschek *et al.* 1997). For more details on the basic principles of luminescence see McKeever and Chen (1997), for instrumentation Bøtter-Jensen (1997) and for OSL measurements Aitken (1998).

Determination of the dose value, D_E

In order to provide reliable results the measured TCD signal must have the following properties:

(i)   when the sample is reset it contains an initial signal that can be either experimentally determined or assumed to be zero,

(ii) the signal intensity grows in proportion to the dose received,

(iii) the signals must have a stability time which is at least one order of magnitude higher than the age of the sample,

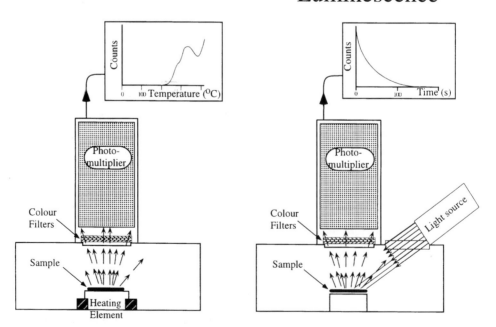

(A) Thermoluminescence (B) Optically Stimulated Luminescence

Figure 4.3   The basic instrumental components for luminescence measurements (after Aitken 1985, 1998). (A) TL measurements, (B) OSL measurements. Reproduced by permission of Oxford University Press.

(iv) the number of traps is constant or changes in a predictable manner,

(v) recrystallization, crystal growth or phase transitions must not have occurred,

(vi) the signals should not show anomalous fading, and

(vii) the signal is not influenced by sample preparation (grinding, exposure to laboratory light, etc.).

The term, equivalent dose, stems from the fact that the laboratory procedures utilize mono-energetic β or γ sources whereas the dose the sample has received in the past is the sum of multi-energetic α, β, γ and cosmic rays (see below). Thus, the experimentally determined dose value is the β or γ equivalent of the naturally received dose which is frequently called *palaeodose*, P.

There are several basic techniques for the determination of the D_E value (Figure 4.4). The *additive dose method* is most widely used (Figure 4.2B and 4.4A), and is described above. In many circumstances, I_0 is demonstrably zero or assumed to be zero. In TL studies of sediments, I_0 is often a significant percentage of I_N and has to be determined experimentally. This is either done with a sunlight simulator (Aitken 1985) or a surface sample is collected and its natural intensity is used as I_0 for the samples collected further down in a sedimentary profile (e.g., Readhead 1988). In ESR studies, the additive dose method is almost exclusively used. For the fitting of the data points, the dose response curve has to be mathematically described. Usually it is assumed that the data points are best fitted by a single saturating function. Grün and Brumby (1994) discuss the magnitude of errors involved in the

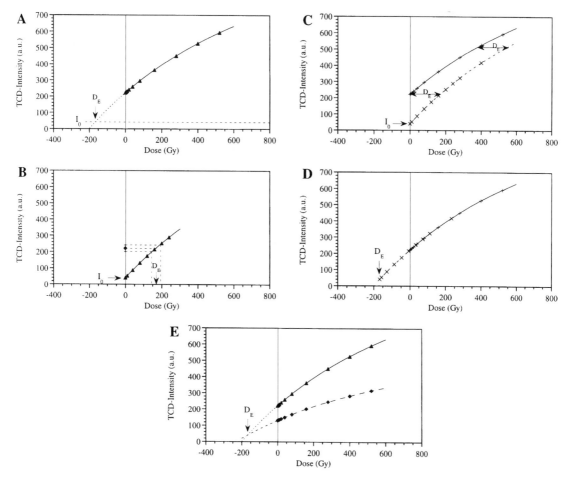

Figure 4.4 Methods for dose determination. (A) Additive dose method (see also Figure 4.2), (B) regeneration method, (C and D) slide method and (E) partial bleach method.

extrapolation procedures. However, many samples show different dose responses, such as a saturating plus linear function (Berger 1990) or inflexion points (Katzenberger and Willems 1988). In these cases, the application of an inappropriate model for curve fitting may lead to erroneous D_E values.

The *regeneration technique* is an alternative for D_E estimation (Figure 4.4B). First I_N is measured and the subsequent aliquots are reset to I_0. These aliquots are then irradiated with defined laboratory doses and the projection of I_N on to the regenerated dose response curve yields D_E. The regeneration method has the advantage of involving smaller errors than the additive dose method and, furthermore, the D_E result is little dependent on the mathematical model used for the fitting of the data points (in contrast to the additive and partial bleach techniques). However, some samples show sensitivity changes after resetting and the regeneration D_E value may differ from the additive D_E value. This problem is addressed in the *slide technique* (Figures 4.4C and 4.4D; Prescott *et al.* 1993): the natural and reset aliquots are irradiated so that the additive dose response curve overlaps significantly with the regenerated dose response curve. The horizontal distance between the two curves yields the D_E value. The overlapping parts of the two dose response curves can be used for the recognition of sensitivity changes, and re-scaling of the regenerated dose response curve can be carried out, if necessary.

The *partial bleach technique* is used in TL studies of sediments where insufficient light bleaching is suspected (i.e., it is not possible to determine I_0). First, a conventional additive dose response curve is established, then irradiated aliquots are exposed to light for a relatively short time and a second dose response curve is produced (Figure 4.4E). The intersection of both curves yields the D_E value.

The *single aliquot regeneration* (SAR) method for OSL dating is an alternative to the multi-aliquot techniques described above (Murray and Roberts 1998, Murray and Wintle 2000). Rather than using several aliquots for the establishment of the regeneration dose response curve, the SAR protocol carries all measurements out on the same sample. First, the natural intensity is measured; after this, the sample is irradiated with defined doses. Sensitivity changes are monitored and corrected for by giving the sample a test dose and measuring its response to it. For dating, the SAR protocol is carried out on a range of sub-samples which allows recognition of sample inhomogeneity as well as partial bleaching (Olley *et al.* 1998). The precision of the SAR protocol (≈ 2 per cent) for OSL is significantly better than any of the multi-aliquot techniques described above.

ESR spectra and TL glow curves contain components which are not thermally stable, i.e., the use of such D_E values would lead to age underestimations. ESR spectra may contain signals that are not radiation sensitive at all and TL glow curves may contain peaks that are not light sensitive. For the recognition of such areas, *plateau tests* were introduced in early TL studies and later adopted in ESR and OSL. Rather than determining a single value, D_E values are continuously determined over the whole ESR/TL/OSL spectrum range (Figure 4.5) and thermally unstable or radiation insensitive components can be recognized. TL glow curves (Figures 4.5C and 4.5D) contain many unstable signals (e.g., around 100°C). The plateau between about 300 and 400°C can be used for dating; at higher temperatures light insensitive signals lead to higher doses and noise to a larger scatter. In ESR studies (4.5A,B) the region between 3455 and 3465 10^{-4} T yields a plateau indicating little interference (the large scatter in the centre is due to the zero-passing of the ESR spectrum, that at higher and lower magnetic fields is due to signal noise). In OSL studies (4.5E and 4.5F), the plateau contains some information about the kinetics involved in the measurement (Bailey 1998).

Determination of the dose rate, $\dot{D}$

The dose rate is calculated from the concentrations of radioactive elements in the sample and its surroundings (only the U and Th decay chains and the ^{40}K decay are of relevance; a minor contribution comes from ^{87}Rb in the sediment), plus a component of cosmic rays. There are three different ionizing rays which are emitted from the radioactive elements: (i) gamma rays have a range of about 30 cm, (ii) beta rays (electrons) have a range of about 2 mm, (iii) alpha rays have only a very short range of about 20 μm because of the large size of the particles. Alpha particles are not as efficient in producing ESR/TL/OSL intensity as beta and gamma rays, therefore the alpha efficiency, which is usually in the range of 0.05 to 0.2, has to be determined (Aitken 1985).

The concentrations of radioactive elements in the sample are usually very different from those of its surroundings. Thus, *internal dose rates* and *external dose rates* have to be assessed independently. Furthermore, it is necessary to estimate the cosmic dose rate, which is about 300 μGy/a at sea-level and decreases with depth

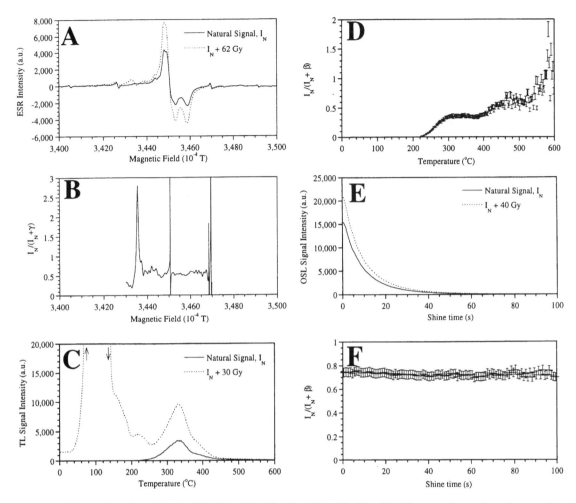

Figure 4.5 Plateau dose determination. ESR (A and B), TL (C and D), OSL (E and F). The upper figures show the natural and irradiated signals recorded, and the lower the ratio of the two. (TL and OSL data were kindly provided by N.A. Spooner, Canberra).

below ground, and is also dependent on altitude as well as geographic latitude (Prescott and Hutton 1988).

The conversion of the elemental analysis into dose rates are shown in Table 4.1. For example, if a large

Table 4.1 Dose rates calculations for the U and Th decay chains and K (Adamiec and Aitken 1998).

Concentration of radioactive elements	$\dot{D}_\alpha$	$\dot{D}_\beta$	$\dot{D}_\gamma$
1 ppm ^{238}U + ^{235}U	2780	146	113 μGy/a
1 ppm ^{232}Th	732	27	48 μGy/a
1% K		782	243 μGy/a

sample, such as a burnt flint, contains 2 ppm U, 5 ppm Th and 1% K, and an α-efficiency (k) of 0.1 is assumed or measured, the total internal dose rate is generated by alpha and beta particles:

$$\dot{D}_{\text{internal}} = k\dot{D}_\alpha + \dot{D}_\beta$$
$$= (2 \times 0.1 \times 2780 + 5 \times 0.1 \times 732)$$
$$+ (2 \times 146 + 5 \times 27 + 1 \times 782) \, \mu\text{Gy/a}$$
$$= 2133 \, \mu\text{Gy/a} \tag{3}$$

If an *external γ-dose rate* of 1500 μGy/a was measured and a *cosmic dose rate* of 150 μGy/a was calculated from the depth of the sample below surface, the total dose rate is:

$$\dot{D}_{\text{total}} = \dot{D}_{\text{internal}} + \dot{D}_{\text{external}}$$

$$= 2133 + 1500 + 150 \; \mu\text{Gy/a}$$

$$= 3783 \; \mu\text{Gy/a} \tag{4}$$

Dose rate calculations become more complicated when disequilibrium in the U-decay chains or attenuation factors have to be considered (Aitken 1985, 1998, Grün 1989; see also Chapter 5). Typical errors in the estimation of the total dose rate are in the range of 4–7 per cent.

External dose rate

The calculation of the external dose rate is dependent on the size of the samples (Figure 4.6). The removal of the outer 50 μm of the sample eliminates all the externally alpha irradiated volume. If the outer 2 mm can be removed, the external beta dose is eliminated. In this case the external dose rate consists of gamma and cosmic rays only. If the samples are smaller, it receives external beta radiation which decreases with depth and therefore attenuation factors have to be considered (Aitken 1985, Grün 1989). Cosmic rays are high energy particles and are attenuated once they penetrate the

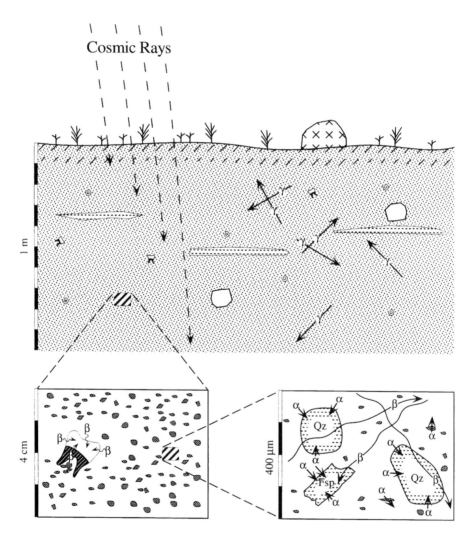

Figure 4.6   The different components of natural radiation relevant for dose rate calculations (based on S. Stokes as shown in Aitken 1998:fig. 2.2). Reproduced by permission of Oxford University Press.

sedimentary layers. For practical purposes, the cosmic dose rate becomes negligible at a depth of about 20 metres.

The external beta dose rate has to be calculated separately from the external gamma dose rate because the beta dose rate is generated from the sediment immediately attached to the sample, whereas the gamma dose rate originates from all sediment that is within a radius of about 30 cm around the sample (see Figure 4.6). The beta dose rate from the sediment is derived from a chemical analysis of U, Th, and K. In homogeneous sediments, the gamma dose rate can be calculated from a chemical analysis of the bulk sediment. However, if the sediment contains boulders or intercalation of layers with different radioactivity, the gamma dose rate should be measured *in situ* with a portable, calibrated gamma spectrometer or TL dosimeters. *In situ* measurements have the advantage that they include the present-day water contents. Water absorbs some β and γ rays and its presence in the surrounding sediment has to be considered in the calculation of the beta and gamma dose rate (Aitken and Xie 1990).

Internal dose rate

This parameter is mainly generated by alpha and beta rays emitted from elements in the sample. In luminescence studies, it is often assumed that quartz is free of radioactive elements. This assumption will cause only small errors if the external dose rate is relatively high. However, in low dose rate environments, e.g., quartz sand dunes (Prescott and Hutton 1995), the internal dose rate originated by small amounts of radioactive elements may constitute a significant part of the total dose rate. Feldspars are usually free of U and Th, but K has to be measured. Similar considerations as for quartz apply. Quaternary calcitic samples, including speleothems, shells and corals, but also tooth enamel and dentine, display disequilibrium in the U-decay chains which is actually the basis for U-series dating (see Chapter 5). U-series disequilibrium affects the average dose rates and has to be taken into account mathematically (Grün 1989).

Alpha efficiencies range from 0.13 (ESR of tooth enamel) to 0.03 (OSL of quartz; Rees-Jones and Tite 1997). Note that alpha efficiencies can not only change from sample to sample but also from technique to technique on the same samples (e.g., Lang and Wagner 1996). Alpha efficiencies can be routinely measured in luminescence studies whereas the size requirements for ESR measurements make its assess-

ment difficult (Grün and Katzenberger-Apel 1994). If the samples are small, the internal alpha and beta dose rates are not 100 per cent absorbed and self-absorption factors have to be calculated (1 minus the external attenuation factors).

The dose rate can be measured with a precision of about 5 per cent. The overall uncertainty of a trapped charge dating result may be as low as 6 to 7 per cent.

APPLICATIONS OF TRAPPED CHARGE DATING TECHNIQUES

When reviewing the literature, one finds many cases where trapped charge dating results have challenged conventional ideas, as have, for example, the TL and ESR results from early modern hominid sites in the Levant (Valladas *et al.* 1988, Mercier *et al.* 1995, Grün and Stringer 1991). One immediate reaction was the dismissal of the results. This partly relates to the fact that there are very few other dating techniques available in archaeology for the pre-radiocarbon time range of older than 40 000 years. Thus, conventional chronological wisdom is sometimes based on preconception. On the other hand, in some cases it has turned out that TCD results have been erroneous because all TCD methods are still in a rapid phase of development and some of the pitfalls have not yet been recognized. However, before disregarding any evidence one has to keep in mind that reliable chronologies are the result of the synthesis of all evidence available, in an ideal case based on detailed archaeological, palaeoanthropological, palaeontological, palynological, sedimentological, geochemical and geochronological analysis.

ESR dating of tooth enamel

This is the main application of ESR dating in archaeological studies. ESR dating of speleothems, spring deposited travertines and shells in archaeological contexts has been recently reviewed (Grün 1997) and there is little to add in this respect.

ESR dating of tooth enamel has been applied to a variety of archaeological and palaeoanthropological sites (see Grün and Stringer 1991, Grün 1997, Rink 1997). The method is applicable between a few thousand years and, in exceptional circumstances, up to a few million years (Schwarcz *et al.* 1994). For details on sample preparation, spectrum evaluation and dose rate determination see Grün (1989, 1997) and Rink (1997).

ESR dating of teeth encompasses a particular problem: U-uptake. Teeth, bones and some shells show post-depositional U-uptake and this effect further complicates the dose rate determination. The process of uranium uptake cannot normally be determined exactly (see Chapter 5). Dentine usually accumulates much more U than enamel (by a factor of 10 to 100; Grün and Taylor 1996). For teeth, two models have been suggested (Ikeya 1982); (i) U-accumulation shortly after burial of the tooth (*early U-uptake*, EU), (ii) continuous U-accumulation (*linear U-uptake*, LU).

As long as the U-concentrations in the components of a tooth are low (< 2 ppm in dentine) the discrepancy between EU and LU ages is less than 10 per cent. With increasing U-concentrations this intrinsic uncertainty increases very rapidly. In the extreme, the LU model age is twice the EU age estimate. New developments in ESR and U-series dating have shown a strategy to overcome this problem (see below). However, if there are no specific indications to justify a particular U-uptake model, age estimates for both models ought to be given. The most probable age of most samples is somewhere between the two estimates (for a compilation of ESR results on teeth see Grün and Stringer 1991). Most teeth older than the last interglaciation, which is widely accompanied by a more pluvial climate, have accumulated considerable amounts of uranium. Therefore most ESR age estimates of such teeth are associated with large uncertainties (> 25 per cent). It is important to note that the EU age estimate is the minimum possible age. An overall precision of better than 7 per cent can be obtained for teeth with low U-concentrations (e.g., Grün et al. 1990).

The application of ESR dating to the site of Hexian (Grün et al. 1998) is a prime example which illustrates the limited value of stand-alone ESR and U-series analysis on faunal materials. However, the combination of both methods can lead to very precise results. Portions of several human crania were found at the site of Hexian, Anhui Province, China (Huang et al. 1982). The human remains were attributed to *Homo erectus* and, based on some progressive features, correlated with the specimen HIII found in Layer 3 of Zhoukoudian (Wu and Dong 1985). The site had previously been dated by Huang et al. (1995a, 1995b) who obtained ESR ages in the range of 160 to 220 ka (EU) and 250 to 350 ka (LU), and Chen and Yuan (1988) who reported U-series results of 130 to 220 ka (combined $^{231}Pa/^{230}Th$). The ESR results of Grün et al. (1998) are shown in Figure 4.7A. These cover a large time span of 344 ± 48 ka (EU) to 465 ± 94 ka (LU). Even though these ages span the time range of about

300 to 550 ka, they were considerably older than the previously obtained results. Grün et al. (1998) also carried out U-series analyses on different constituents of two teeth obtaining U-series ages of between 150 and 550 ka (Figure 4.7B). If these results were reported without further consideration they would clearly demonstrate the very limited value of ESR and U-series analysis of faunal materials (mainly due to the unknown U-uptake history).

Grün et al. (1988) developed a model that can combine ESR and U-series data and solve for U-uptake history (see also McDermott et al. 1993, Grün and McDermott 1994). Both techniques are dependent on uranium uptake, but to a different extent. With the independent measurement of ESR and U-series dating results it becomes possible to establish two equation systems that can solve (i) for age and (ii) for a single parameter U-uptake equation. Two teeth from Hexian were analysed by ESR and U-series and the combination of both methods can explain the very different U-uptake history that both teeth have experienced (Figure 4.7C). The combined U-series/ESR data result in a very tight age estimation of 412 ± 25 ka (Figure 4.7B).

This result was first greeted with scepticism, because it implied that the Hexian calvaria were contemporaneous with the morphologically less advanced *Homo erectus* specimen from Zhoukoudian (LI-LIII) rather than more similar HIII (Wu et al. 1985). However, new precise TIMS U-series results on speleothem layers from layer 2 and 3 at Zhoukoudian (Shen et al. 1996) show that these layers are also considerably older than originally proposed by Wu et al. (1985). As a result, a morphological correlation between Hexian and Zhoukoudian HIII is now supported by chronological evidence, but both specimens are considerably older than previously thought (Grün 2000).

TL dating of burnt flint

The most comprehensive review of luminescence applications in archaeology was recently published by Roberts (1997). Thermoluminescence dating was developed in the late 1960s and early 1970s for the dating of pottery (Aitken 1985). TL readers are very sensitive to light emission and samples with ages of a few tens of years can be reliably dated. One of the main applications of TL pottery analysis lies in provenance authentication (Stoneham 1983). Wintle and Huntley (1982) pioneered TL dating of sediments in the late 1970s. For sediment dating, TL has been replaced by OSL in recent years, mainly because OSL selectively measures

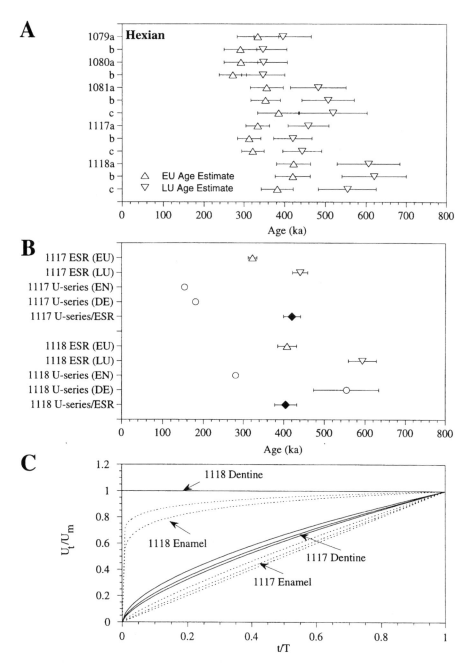

Figure 4.7 (A) ESR age estimates on teeth from Hexian (after Grün *et al.* 1998). (B) Age estimates for samples 1117 and 1118 (EN = Enamel; DE = dentine). Both the ESR and U-series estimates imply that the two teeth have distinctively different ages. The combined U-series/ESR age estimates are virtually indistinguishable and give the best age estimate for the site (412 ± 25 ka). (C) Modelled U-uptake histories. Sample 1118 shows U-uptake which is near to a closed system model whereas the constituents of sample 1117 are closer to a linear uptake model.

the electrons caught in light sensitive traps whereas the TL signal results from a series of traps with different light sensitivities (see below).

Today, dating of burnt flint is the main application of TL in archaeological contexts. The method is applicable between a few hundred years and a few hundred thousand years, covering the time span of the controlled use of fire by humans. For details on TL sample collection and preparation as well as dose rate evaluation see Aitken (1985), for spectrum evaluation and other laboratory procedures see Wintle (1997) and for specific details on TL dating of burnt flint see Mercier *et al.* (1995).

TL dating of burnt flint from the site of Qafzeh, Israel, revolutionized our thinking on modern human evolution (Valladas *et al.* 1988). It has been known for many years that modern humans evolved from or replaced Neanderthals in Europe at sometime in the range of 35 000 to 40 000 years. This Eurocentric picture was then transposed to other areas and it was therefore thought that Neanderthal sites in the Levant, such as Kebara and Tabun, were somewhat older than 45 000 years and that the sites where early modern humans were found, Qafzeh and Skhul, were somewhat younger.

The site of Qafzeh contained remains of at least 20 hominids which are generally regarded as early modern humans. The publication of TL age estimates of 92 ± 5 ka carried out on 20 burnt flint samples from layers XVII to XXIII (Figure 4.8; Valladas *et al.*

1988) caused a serious disturbance in palaeoanthropological circles. Although Bar-Yosef and Vandermeersch (1981) had already suggested that the site may be as old as 100 000 years, others rejected the TL dates because it was felt that the dates could not be verified independently and may be inaccurate, were still experimental, or would not stand the test of time (Grün and Stringer 1991). Subsequent ESR (Schwarcz *et al.* 1988) and U-series (McDermott *et al.* 1993) dating studies on animal teeth as well as non-destructive U-series dating of the human remains (Yokoyama *et al.* 1997) confirmed the antiquity of the site. Today, the early arrival of modern humans in the Levant is widely accepted. For a summary of the dating results of palaeoanthropological sites in the Levant see Grün and Stringer (1991), Mercier *et al.* (1995) and Grün (1997).

OSL dating of sediment

OSL dating was introduced by Huntley *et al.* (1985). In recent years, OSL has replaced TL for the dating of sediments, because;

(i)   OSL uses the same methods as nature to reset the sample (light activation rather than thermal activation),

(ii) OSL measures the light sensitive traps only and the signal is not overlapped by light insensitive signals, thus in OSL I_0 is very close to zero whilst in TL I_0 is usually a high percentage of I_N, and

(iii) the OSL signals are far more light sensitive than TL (e.g., Godfrey-Smith *et al.* 1988).

For details on sample collection and preparation, as well as dose rate evaluation, see Aitken (1998), for spectrum evaluation and other laboratory procedures see Wintle (1997). Luminescence dating of sediment can be applied between a few years and about one million years (Huntley *et al.* 1994).

Luminescence dating of sediments has found wide applications in archaeology (Roberts 1997). Luminescence dating was decisive in demonstrating that the early colonization of Australia took place well before 40 000 years ago, i.e., prior to the invasion of *Homo sapiens* into Europe (see above). Roberts *et al.* (1990) used TL dating of sediments at the Malakunanja II shelter in Arnhem Land, Northern Territory, Australia, demonstrating that the earliest artifacts at that site were deposited around 55 ka. Subsequently, a luminescence study was carried out at Deaf Adder Gorge (Roberts *et al.* 1994), a site about 70 km south

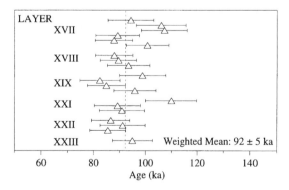

Figure 4.8   TL dating of burnt flint from Qafzeh (after Valladas *et al.* 1988). 20 samples from Layers XVII to XXIII into which more than 20 skeletons of early modern humans were buried. The dates show no trend with depth indicating rapid deposition of the layers. The weighted mean age is 92 ± 5 ka. Reprinted with permission from *Nature*, **331**:614–616, copyright (1988) Macmillan Magazines Limited.

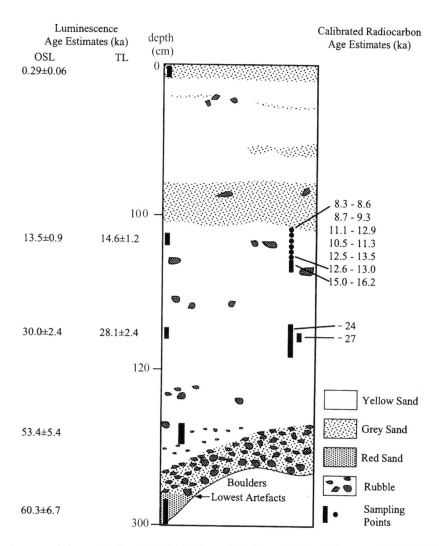

Figure 4.9 Luminescence dating results from Deaf Adder Gorge, NT, Australia (after Roberts *et al.* 1994). The luminescence data show near complete resetting at the top of the sedimentary column. Within the radiocarbon dating range, both luminescence methods yield very good agreement with the calibrated radiocarbon age estimates. The lowest artifacts are bracketed between 53.4 ± 5.4 and 60.3 ± 6.7 ka, supporting the earlier claim of Roberts *et al.* (1990) that the Australian continent was colonized well before 40 000 years ago.

of Malakunanja II. As shown in Figure 4.9, both luminescence methods show very good agreement with calibrated radiocarbon results. In contrast to radiocarbon, the lower layers can be dated with OSL (and TL) and the earliest artifacts are bracketed between 53.4 ± 5.4 and 60.3 ± 6.7 ka. The rubble found in the lower levels at the site could make TL dating questionable, but the short exposure times required for OSL make age overestimations unlikely. The early arrival of anatomically fully modern humans was confirmed in multi-dating

studies (U-series, ESR, OSL) of the Lake Mungo 3 skeleton which involved direct dating of the human material (Thorne *et al.* 1999).

Recently, it was claimed by Fullager *et al.* (1996) that the site of Jinmium, NT, may be as old as 116 ka. The TL results of this study were indeed obstructed by rubble that decayed in the sedimentary layers without being sufficiently exposed to sunlight. Analysis of the TL glow curves (Spooner 1998) predicted that the maximum age of the site was between 10 and 30 ka. Roberts *et al.*

(1998) confirmed with AMS radiocarbon and OSL dating that the site was younger than 10 000 years.

OUTLOOK

Trapped charge dating will play an increasing role for the establishment of archaeological chronologies in the pre-radiocarbon time scale. Considering the nearly universal applicability of OSL dating, the routine application of this method should lead to a revolution in our understanding of archaeological processes similar to the introduction of radiocarbon dating in the 1950s and 1960s.

The main advance in ESR dating of tooth enamel lies in the direct dating of human material using enamel fragments (Grün *et al.* 1996) and, possibly, whole teeth. Uranium of enamel fragments can be measured using laser ablation ICP-MS which allows the precise analysis of very small samples (Eggins *et al.* 1998) and can be used to establish uranium profiles along very thin holes (50 μm diameter) which are nearly invisible. New generation multi-collector ICP sector mass spectrometers (Halliday *et al.* 1998) will significantly reduce laboratory preparation for U-series dating. Thus, combined ESR/U-series dating could develop as a routine method within the next few years. ESR measurements can also provide important restraints when hominid fossils are dated non-destructively by gamma spectrometric U-series dating (Simpson and Grün 1998). The key for the establishment of reliable chronologies for a given site lies in the application of as many dating techniques as possible (e.g., Abeyratne *et al.* 1997, Thorne *et al.* 1999).

ACKNOWLEDGEMENTS

I thank N.A. Spooner, Canberra, for corrections.

REFERENCES

*Recommended for further reading

Abeyratne, M., Spooner, N., Grün, R. and Head, J. (1997). Multidating studies of Batadomba Cave, Sri Lanka. *Quaternary Science Reviews*, 16:243–255.
Adamiec, G. and Aitken, M.J. (1998). Dose-rate conversion factors: update. *Ancient TL*, 16:37–50.
*Aitken, M.J. (1985). *Thermoluminescence Dating*. Academic Press: New York.
*Aitken, M.J. (1997). Luminescence dating. In Taylor, R.E. and Aitken, M.J. (eds) *Chronometric and Allied Dating in Archaeology*, 183–216. Plenum: New York.
*Aitken, M.J. (1998). *Optical Dating*. Oxford University Press: Oxford.
Aitken, M.J. and Xie, J. (1990). Moisture correction for annual gamma dose. *Ancient TL*, 8:6–9.
Bailey, R.M. (1998). *The Form of the Optically Stimulated Luminescence Signal of Quartz: Implications for Dating*. Unpublished PhD Dissertation, Royal Holloway, University of London.
Bar-Yosef, O. and Vandermeersch, B. (1981). Notes concerning the possible age of the Mousterian layers in Qafzeh Cave. In Cauvin, J. and Sanlaville, P. (eds) *Préhistoire du Levant*, 281–286. CNRS: Paris.
Berger, G.W. (1990). Regression and error analysis for a saturating-exponential-plus-linear model. *Ancient TL*, 8:23–25.
Bøtter-Jensen, L. (1997). Luminescence techniques: instrumentation and methods. *Radiation Measurements*, 27:749–748.
Chen, T.M. and Yuan, S. (1988). Uranium-series dating of bones and teeth from Chinese Palaeolithic sites. *Archaeometry*, 30:59–76.
Eggins, S.M., Kinsley, L.P.J. and Shelley, M. (1998). Deposition and elemental fractionation processes during atmospheric pressure laser sampling for analysis by ICP-MS. *Applied Surface Science*, 127–129:278–286.
Fullagar, R.L.K., Price, D.M. and Head, L.M. (1996). Early human occupation of northern Australia: archaeology and thermoluminescence dating of Jinmium rock-shelter, Northern Territory. *Antiquity*, 70:751–773.
Godfrey-Smith, D.I., Huntley, D.J. and Chen, W.H. (1988). Optical dating studies of quartz and feldspar sediment extracts. *Quaternary Science Reviews*, 7:373–380.
*Grün, R. (1989). Electron spin resonance (ESR) dating. *Quaternary International*, 1:65–109.
*Grün, R. (1997). Electron spin resonance dating. In Taylor, R.E. and Aitken, M.J. (eds) *Chronometric and Allied Dating in Archaeology*, 217–261. Plenum: New York.
*Grün, R. (2000). Electron spin resonance dating. In Ciliberto, E. and Spoto, G. (eds) *Modern Analytical Methods in Art and Archaeology*, 641–679. John Wiley: New York.
Grün, R. and Brumby, S. (1994). The assessment of errors in the past radiation doses extrapolated from ESR/TL dose response data. *Radiation Measurements*, 23:307–315.
Grün, R. and Katzenberger-Apel, O. (1994). An alpha irradiator for ESR dating. *Ancient TL*, 12:35–38.
Grün, R. and McDermott, F. (1994). Open system modelling for U-series and ESR dating of teeth. *Quaternary Science Reviews*, 13:121–125.
*Grün, R. and Stringer, C.B. (1991). ESR dating and the evolution of modern humans. *Archaeometry*, 33:153–199.
Grün, R. and Taylor, L. (1996). Uranium and thorium in the constituents of fossil teeth. *Ancient TL*, 14:21–25.
Grün, R., Schwarcz, H.P. and Chadam, J.M. (1988). ESR dating of tooth enamel: coupled correction for U-uptake and U-series disequilibrium. *Nuclear Tracks and Radiation Measurements*, 14:237–241.

Grün, R., Beaumont, P. and Stringer, C.B. (1990). ESR dating evidence for early modern humans at Border Cave in South Africa. *Nature*, **344**:537–539.

Grün, R., Brink, J.S., Spooner, N.A., Taylor, L., Stringer, C.B., Franciscus, R.G. and Murray, A.S. (1996). Direct dating of Florisbad hominid. *Nature*, **382**:500–501.

Grün, R., Huang, P.H., Huang, W., McDermott, F., Stringer, C.B., Thorne, A., and Yan G. (1998). ESR and U-series analyses of teeth from the palaeoanthropological site of Hexian, Anhui Province, China. *Journal of Human Evolution*, **34**:555–564.

Halliday, A.N., Lee, D.-C., Christensen, J.N., Rehkämper, M., Yi, W., Luo, X., Hall, C.M., Ballentine, C.J., Pettke, T. and Stirling, C. (1998). Applications of multiple collector-ICPMS to cosmochemistry, geochemistry, and paleoceanography. *Geochimica et Cosmochimica Acta*, **62**:919–940.

Huang, H.P., Fang, D.S. and Ye, Y.X. (1982). Preliminary study of the fossil hominid skull and fauna of Hexian, Anhui. *Vertebrata Palasiatica*, **20**:248–256.

Huang, P.H., Zheng, L.Z., Quan, Y.C., Liang, R.Y., Xu, Y.H, Fang, Y.S. and Fang, D.S. (1995a). Preliminary study on ESR dating of Hexian Man and its fauna. *Nuclear Techniques*, **18**:491–494 (in Chinese).

Huang, P.H., Zheng, L.Z., Quan, Y.C., Liang, R.Y., Xu, Y.H., Fang, Y.S., and Fang D.S. (1995b). Study on age of Hexian Man of *Homo erectus*. *Acta Anthropologia Sinica*, **14**:262–265 (in Chinese).

Huntley, D.J., Godfrey-Smith, D.I. and Thewalt, M.L.W. (1985). Optical dating of sediments. *Nature*, **313**:105–107.

Huntley, D.J., Hutton, J.T. and Prescott, J.R. (1994). Further thermoluminescence dates from the dune sequence in the south-east of South Australia. *Quaternary Science Reviews*, **13**:201–207.

Ikeya, M. (1982). A model of linear uranium accumulation for ESR age of Heidelberg, Mauer, and Tautavel bones. *Japanese Journal of Applied Physics*, **21**:L690–692.

Ikeya, M. (1993). *New Applications of Electron Spin Resonance – Dating, Dosimetry and Microscopy*. World Scientific: Singapore.

Jonas, M. (1997). Concepts and methods of ESR dating. *Radiation Measurements*, **27**:943–948.

Katzenberger, O. and Willems, N. (1988). Interferences encountered in the determination of AD of mollusc samples. *Quaternary Science Reviews*, **7**:485–489.

Krbetschek, M.R., Götze, J., Dietrich, A. and Trautmann, T. (1997). Spectral information from minerals relevant for luminescence dating. *Radiation Measurements*, **27**:695–748.

Lang, A. and Wagner, G.A. (1996). Infrared stimulated luminescence dating of archaeosediments. *Archaeometry*, **38**:129–141.

McDermott, F., Grün, R., Stringer, C.B. and Hawkesworth, C.J. (1993). Mass-spectrometric U-series dates for Israeli Neanderthal/early modern hominid sites. *Nature*, **363**:252–255.

McKeever, S.W.S. and Chen, R. (1997). Luminescence models. *Radiation Measurements*, **27**:625–661.

Mercier, N., Valladas, H. and Valladas, G. (1995). Flint thermoluminescence dates from the CFR laboratory at Gif: contributions to the study of the chronology of the Middle Palaeolithic. *Quaternary Science Reviews*, **14**:351–364.

Murray, A.S. and Roberts, R.G. (1998). Measurement of the equivalent dose in quartz using a regenerative-dose single-aliquot protocol. *Radiation Measurements*, **29**:503–515.

*Murray, A.S. and Wintle, A.G. (2000). Luminescence dating of quartz using an improved single-aliquot regenerative-dose protocol. *Radiation Measurements*, **32**:57–73.

Olley, J., Caitcheon, G. and Murray, A. (1998). The distribution of apparent dose as determined by optically stimulated luminescence in small aliquots of fluvial quartz: implications for dating young sediments. *Quaternary Science Reviews*, **17**:1033–1040.

Prescott, J.R. and Hutton, J.T. (1988). Cosmic ray and gamma ray dosimetry for TL and ESR. *Nuclear Tracks and Radiation Measurements*, **14**:223–227.

Prescott, J.R. and Hutton, J.T. (1995). Environmental dose rates and radioactive disequilibrium from some Australian luminescence dating sites. *Quaternary Science Reviews*, **14**:439–448.

Prescott, J.R., Huntley, D.J. and Hutton, J.T. (1993). Estimation of equivalent dose in thermoluminescence dating – the *Australian slide* method. *Ancient TL*, **11**:1–5.

Readhead, M.L. (1988). Thermoluminescence dating study of quartz in aeolian sediments from southeastern Australia. *Quaternary Science Reviews*, **7**:257–264.

Rees-Jones, J. and Tite, M. (1997). Optical dating results for British archaeological sediments. *Archaeometry*, **39**:177–187.

*Rink, W.J. (1997). Electron spin resonance (ESR) dating and ESR applications in Quaternary science and archaeometry. *Radiation Measurements*, **27**:975–1025.

*Roberts, R.G. (1997). Luminescence dating in archaeology: from origins to optical. *Radiation Measurements*, **27**:819–892.

Roberts, R.G., Jones, R. and Smith, M.A. (1990). Thermoluminescence dating of a 50 000 year-old human occupation site in northern Australia. *Nature*, **345**:125–129.

Roberts, R.G., Jones, R., Spooner, N.A., Head, M.J., Murray, A.S. and Smith M.A. (1994). The human colonization of Australia: optical dates of 53 000 and 60 000 years bracket human arrival at Deaf Adder Gorge, Northern Territory. *Quaternary Science Reviews*, **13**:575–583.

Roberts, R., Bird, M., Olley, J., Galbraith, R., Lawson, E., Laslett, G., Yoshida, H., Jones, R., Fullagar, R., Jacobson, G. and Hua, Q. (1998). Optical and radiocarbon dating at Jinmium rock shelter in northern Australia. *Nature*, **393**:358–362.

Schwarcz, H.P., Grün, R., Vandermeersch, B., Bar-Yosef, O., Valladas, H. and Tchernov, E. (1988). ESR dates for the hominid burial site of Qafzeh in Israel. *Journal of Human Evolution*, **17**:733–737.

Schwarcz, H.P., Grün, R. and Tobias, P.V. (1994). ESR dating studies of the australopithecine site of Sterkfontein, South Africa. *Journal of Human Evolution*, **26**:175–181.

Shen, G., Ku, T.L., Gahleb, B. and Yuan, Z. (1996). Preliminary results on U-series dating of Peking Man site with high precision TIMS. *Acta Anthropologica Sinica*, **15**:210–217.

Simpson, J.J. and Grün, R. (1998). Non-destructive gamma spectrometric U-series dating. *Quaternary Science Reviews*, **18**:1009–1022.

Spooner, N.A. (1998). Human occupation at Jinmium, northern Australia: 116 000 years ago or much less? *Antiquity*, **72**:173–178.

Stoneham, D. (1983). Porcelain dating. *PACT*, **9**:227–239.

Thorne, A., Grün, R., Mortimer, G., Spooner, N.A., Simpson, J.J., McCulloch, M.T., Taylor, L. and Curnoe, D. (1999). Australia's oldest human remains: age of the Lake Mungo 3 skeleton. *Journal of Human Evolution*, **36**:591–612.

Valladas, H., Reys, J.L., Joron, J.L., Valladas, G., Bar-Yosef, O. and Vandermeersch, B. (1988). Thermoluminescence dating of Mousterian 'Proto-Cro-Magnon' remains from Israel and the origin of modern man. *Nature*, **331**:614–616.

Wintle, A.G. (1997). Luminescence dating: laboratory procedures and protocols. *Radiation Measurements*, **27**:769–817.

Wintle, A.G. and Huntley, D.J. (1982). Thermoluminescence dating of sediments. *Quaternary Science Reviews*, **1**:31–53.

Wu, R.K. and Dong, X.R. (1985). *Homo erectus* in China. In Wu, R.K. and Olson, J.W. (eds) *Palaeoanthropology and Palaeolithic Archaeology in the People's Republic of China*, 79–89. Academic Press: Orlando.

Wu, R.K., Ren, M.E., Zhu, X.M., Yang, Z.G., Hu, C.K., Kong, Z.C., Xie, Y.Y. and Zhao, S.S. (1985). *Multidisciplinary Study of the Peking Man Site at Zhoukoudian*. Science Press: Beijing (in Chinese).

Yokoyama, Y., Falgueres, C. and de Lumley, M.A. (1997). Datation directe d'un crâne Proto-Cro-Magnon de Qafzeh par la spectrométrie gamma non déstructive. *Comptes Rendus de l'Académie des Sciences Serie IIa*, **324**:773–779.

5

Uranium-series Dating

A.G. LATHAM

School of Archaeology, Classics and Oriental Studies, University of Liverpool.

In archaeology, the U-series methods have found use in dating secondary chemical deposits such as cave speleothems and hot spring deposits and, less reliably, bones, teeth and molluscs. U-Series, ESR and TL constitute a powerful array of methods for providing chronological data on cave sites (see Chapter 4). Many caves represent hominid sites, and the stalagmites and flowstones within them are often associated with cultural layers and, at the very least, these layers serve to provide maximum or minimum dates for a given cultural layer. U-series methods have provided dates for deposits from the Lower-Middle Pleistocene/late-Lower Palaeolithic (c. 500 000 yr) to the present and, hence, the methods are germane to an understanding of hominid evolution itself, to major changes in lithic use and toward the provision of a chronological framework for palaeoenvironmental change (Chapter 1). Together with ESR and TL, the U-Th method has played a significant role in helping to establish the temporal overlap between Archaic *Homo sapiens* (Neanderthals) and anatomically modern humans, particularly in the Near East (Aitken *et al.* 1993). The standard reference work for U-series dating and for other applications of U-series disequilibria is Ivanovich and Harmon (1992), especially the contribution of Schwarcz and Blackwell (1992) which discusses archaeological applications. The reader is also referred to the review by Schwarcz (1989).

BASIS FOR U-SERIES DATING

The U-series methods derive from the radiogenesis of long-lived radioactive daughters of the two uranium isotopes, ^{238}U and ^{235}U, these being the thorium isotope, ^{230}Th and the protactinium isotope, ^{231}Pa. The half-life of ^{230}Th is 75 200 years and of ^{231}Pa, 34 300 years (Figure 5.1). Because of the greater abundance of ^{238}U, the most frequently used method is based on the isotopes ^{238}U, the intermediate ^{234}U, and the daughter, ^{230}Th. The dating limits of this method are from a few hundred years to 350 000 years by alpha-particle spectrometry, and up to about 500 000 years by mass-spectrometry (see below). The ^{231}Pa-^{235}U method (Gascoyne 1985, Whitehead *et al.* 1999) is occasionally used to check for concordance, mostly of bone U-Th ages where the U content is sufficiently high (e.g., Chen and Yuan 1988). It has a dating limit of about 200 000 years.

All the U-series methods are based on the natural chemical separation of daughters from parent U isotopes. This separation begins with the solutional weathering of U isotopes from the source material, transport by groundwater, and redeposition in secondary minerals such as speleothem calcite. The daughter isotopes, ^{230}Th and ^{231}Pa, are precipitated as insoluble hydroxides and so are not transported in groundwater. For buried bones or teeth there is often direct

Handbook of Archaeological Sciences. Edited by D.R. Brothwell and A.M. Pollard.

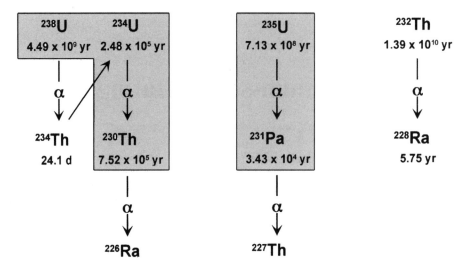

Figure 5.1   The principal isotopes in the two long-lived uranium series and thorium series alpha-decay relationships, with half-lives. Some short-lived intermediate isotopes are not shown. The three series end in stable ^{206}Pb, ^{207}Pb and ^{208}Pb respectively. The boxes show the principal isotopes in U-series dating.

absorption of uranium from percolating groundwater without absorption of the daughters. It is the predictable re-establishment of radioactive equilibrium with time between parents and daughters that provides the clock. The lapse of time since the formation of the deposit is measured by how close the isotopic ratios are to their equilibrium value of 1 (Figures 5.2 and 5.3). In the U-Th method, the measured isotope ratios are ^{234}U/^{238}U and ^{230}Th/^{234}U. Due to the peculiar nature of the weathering of U isotopes from source

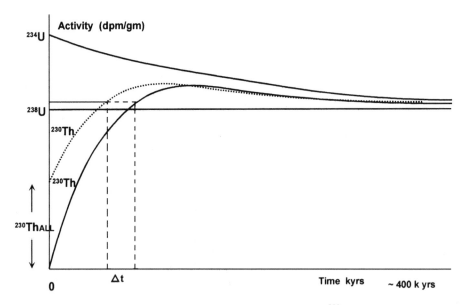

Figure 5.2   A sketch of the growth in activity (disintegrations per minute per gram) of ^{230}Th, from an initial value of zero, towards equilibrium, first with parent ^{234}U and then with ^{238}U, as a function of time. The dotted curve sketches the growth of ^{230}Th if the sample is already contaminated by some allogenic thorium. In such a case, the isotope ratios give an apparently increased age, Δt.

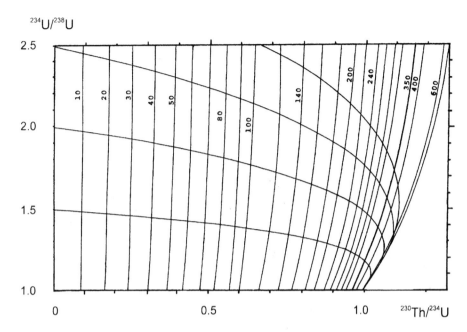

Figure 5.3 The isochron equivalent of Figure 5.2 with $^{234}U/^{238}U$ activity ratio plotted against $^{230}Th/^{234}U$ activity ratio. The isochrons are labelled in ka.

there is frequently a slight excess of ^{234}U over ^{238}U above their equilibrium value of 1. This is because of the fact that ^{234}U, occupying an alpha-recoil damaged site, is more susceptible to mobilization than is ^{238}U.

The equation yielding the age from the isotope ratios, and which is equivalent to a point on an isochron in Figure 5.3, is given by:

$$\frac{^{230}Th}{^{234}U} = \frac{1 - e^{-\lambda_{230}t}}{^{234}U/^{238}U} + \frac{\lambda_{230}}{\lambda_{230} - \lambda_{234}}$$

$$\times \left(1 - \frac{1}{^{234}U/^{238}U}\right)(1 - e^{-(\lambda_{230}-\lambda_{234})t}) \qquad (1)$$

and t has to be worked out by an iterative method using a computer program. λ_{230} and λ_{234} are the decay constants of ^{230}Th and ^{234}U.

ASSUMPTIONS OF THE METHOD AND PROBLEM SAMPLES

From the discussion above, a new layer of calcite on a speleothem should contain only uranium and no daughter ^{230}Th; thus the radiometric clock is reset to zero at time zero. This assumption of initial conditions has been borne out reasonably well by several studies (e.g., Latham et al. 1986). Whitehead et al. (1999) have

shown that it is possible for ^{230}Th and ^{231}Pa isotopes to be deposited with the newly precipitated calcite from the feedwater; the isotopes were presumably carried by soil-derived colloids. The study samples, however, had very low amounts of U (<0.1 ppm) and the effect in very young, and zero-age, samples was to increase the apparent age by a few thousand years.

A more serious exception to the Th-free assumption arises from contamination of the secondary precipitates by dust, clays and mud brought in by wind and cave floods. This material is referred to as *detritus* and the accompanying 'common' or *allogenic* isotopes are often impossible to separate out physically from the radiogenic isotopes in the calcite itself. As ^{232}Th is present in detritus but not in pure calcite, the degree of ^{230}Th, ^{234}U and ^{238}U contamination is estimated by the amount of ^{232}Th as revealed during the analysis (Figure 5.2; for illustrative purposes, only contamination by ^{230}Th, the dotted curve, is considered). The apparent increases in age can be up to 10 ka in some cases. Multiple-sample leaching techniques, and techniques based on the dissolution of several coeval samples, have been developed to obviate the problem (Schwarcz and Latham 1989, Luo and Ku 1991, Bischoff and Fitzpatrick 1991). In these methods, the isotopic ratios of the carbonate fraction and detrital isotope ratios are distinguished from each other using so-called isochron plots. The isotope ratios from the carbonate fraction are input into the dating equation, as before, in order to yield the age.

The second assumption of the method is that the system has remained closed from time zero to the time when the isotopes are measured. This assumption has also been found to be sound for the vast majority of secondary precipitates. There are known to be exceptions but they become obvious from the isotopic analysis. Unfortunately, such open-system behaviour is much less easy to allow for, and some calcite samples have yielded unreliable dates (usually too old), or no dates at all. The problem seems to arise when another crystalline form of calcium carbonate, aragonite, converts to calcite in the presence of water and some of the uranium is lost. The problem was first highlighted by attempts to date interglacial corals that are formed originally of aragonite (Kaufman 1986).

In the case of bone and teeth, we are never sure exactly when a given sample acquired its U. This is a special case of the open-system problem. For such material, extra model assumptions are introduced and different modelled ages are compared to see how sensitive the ages are to the new assumptions. Usually each sample has to be examined on its merits. Even tooth enamel, as hard as it is, may not be immune to open-system behaviour throughout the time of burial (Bischoff *et al.* 1988). It is frequently the case that the higher the concentration of U in bone the less reliable the date. A great amount of effort has been expended in finding out the conditions under which bone and teeth (enamel and dentine) are likely to give reliable results, not only for U-Th (Millard and Hedges 1995) but also for the ESR method (Chapter 4) and for ^{14}C dating of collagen (Chapter 2). ESR dating of teeth and bone relies heavily on model assumptions for the uptake of U (Latham 1997, Millard and Pike 1999). Similar problems also beset the dating of molluscs (e.g., Kaufman and Broecker 1965).

LABORATORY TECHNIQUES

The abundances of the relevant isotopes can be estimated either from monitoring the α particles emitted as the radioactive nuclei decay (α spectrometry), or by direct measurements of the abundances using mass spectrometry (usually TIMS – thermal ionization mass spectrometry). These techniques are discussed below, but the following considerations apply to both.

Because of their generally low abundance and because thorium and uranium isotopes overlap in the measured spectra, the isotopes of interest are concentrated and separated from each other and from the matrix prior to measurement. This necessitates wet chemistry using acid dissolution, ion-exchange resins and the addition of a yield monitor (spike) of the two elements. (In geology and in environmental radioactivity studies, the use of artificial isotopes to monitor the differing yields of sets of isotopes is also known as *isotope dilution*). The isotope peaks are then counted from the alpha- or mass-spectra recorded in the instrument memory. The peak area counts are input into the dating equation, together with a number of other factors such as the efficiency of the counters and calibration factors that estimate the concentration of isotopes in the original material. A computer program is used to work out the isotope ratios, the chemical yield of U and Th, the concentration of U, the age and the standard deviation on the age (Ivanovich and Harmon 1992). Interlaboratory calibrations using a specially prepared ^{232}U-^{228}Th spike were run to confirm standardization between alpha-labs (Ivanovich *et al.* 1984). Rosholt (1984) introduced the ^{236}U and ^{229}Th spikes to speed up the analysis of contaminated samples; these spikes are also used in mass-spectrometric U-series dating.

Age estimate errors

As in radiocarbon dating, the errors quoted in U-series work are based on counting statistics and are propagated first through the isotope ratios and then as age equivalents. They are quoted as either 1 sigma (1 standard deviation) or 2 sigma on the age and, because of the shape of the ^{230}Th growth curve (Figure 5.2), the upper age bound is larger than the lower one. When leaching techniques and isochron plots have to be used for contaminated samples, the isotope ratio errors are, in fact, correlated to each other. Ludwig and Titterington (1994) have presented an error estimation method for these correlated errors.

Alpha-spectrometry

Alpha particles emitted by the radioisotopes are quickly attenuated in air so the discs containing the samples are placed next to the semiconductor detector in a vacuum chamber. Peak counting is done automatically by a multi-channel analyser connected to a computer. One U-Th sample measurement usually takes a few days to count from initial dissolution to final counting, and analysis is often carried out in batches. The alpha-counting equipment is generally trouble-free, though the semiconductor detectors eventually have to be replaced as they acquire a build-up of alpha-emitting contaminants.

Mass spectrometry

Using a thermal ionization mass spectrometer (TIMS), the actual counting may take hours rather than days but this does not take into account demands on the machine for other purposes and greater down-time. The samples are chemically loaded on to filaments, together with standards, in batches, around the inside of an ionization turret at the front of the mass-spectrometer, and a large electromagnet separates the isotopes according to their mass. Commercial thermal ionization mass-spectrometers ionize each filament in turn and the Th and U beams are measured on an array of sensitive ion detectors.

In the comparison of alpha-counting with mass spectrometry there is a trade-off in cost against precision on the quoted age. Mass-spectrometric U-Th dates are about ten times more precise than those produced by routine alpha-spectrometry (Edwards *et al.* 1987), but a mass spectrometer is ten times more expensive, and a skilled technician is required to maintain the machine at optimum performance. Mass spectrometry has the added advantage that it requires only milli-grams rather than grams of sample, which is important where tooth enamel is being analysed or where samples are precious as, for example, when a hominid bone is the only available datable material. Consequently, many analyses are still carried out on alpha-counters, but strategically important samples can be identified and sent on to be re-analysed by mass spectrometry.

RECENT DEVELOPMENTS AND APPLICATIONS

In the dating of bone, the ^{235}U–^{231}Pa pair is used occasionally as a concordance check on ^{238}U–^{230}Th dates, and has been applied to a number of archaeological sites in China (Chen and Yuan 1988). An uptake model is required to describe how and when the U was absorbed into the bone. Generally two uptake models are considered and results compared with each other. In the *early uptake* (EU) case the bone (or tooth) is considered to have acquired its measured amount of U soon after burial. The U-Th age, as given by the normal age equation, is thus the *EU age*.

It is often observed however that buried bone can contain great amounts of U, up to tens of parts per million (ppm), and the bone probably acquired this U over a period of time commensurate with the age of the sediment itself. The outcome is that the normally derived age is too young for the associated sediments. This scenario is then modelled as a *linear uptake* (LU) of U.

For ancient tooth enamel, measurement of ^{238}U–^{230}Th gives the isotope ratio of the system now, whereas ESR, which measures accumulated radiation dose from burial to now, gives a kind of dose-average over the whole burial period. If the two are used together they can give an estimate for the age which is, to some extent, independent of the modelled U uptake assumptions (see Chapter 4). To this end, John Chadam (McMaster University) has developed a series of uptake models controlled by a single parameter, *p*. The family of models is given by:

$$U_t = U_0[t/T]^{p+1} \tag{2}$$

where T is the age of the sample and *t* is any time between 0 and T; U_t and U_0 are the amounts of U at time *t* and the final measured value, and *p* is an adjustable parameter (Schwarcz *et al.* 1988a). Thus, the EU scenario is characterized by $p = -1$, whereas for LU, $p = 0$. By comparing the ESR and U–Th ages it is possible to adjust *p* until both sets of analyses give the same age. Thus the comparison gives both the U uptake history and the model age. Clearly, this approach assumes smooth monotonic (regularly increasing) uptake histories, and U-loss cannot be modelled. The possibility that U-uptake, of any kind, was delayed after burial of the bone, cannot be tested.

The U uptake problem also besets attempts to date precious bone samples by non-destructive *gamma-ray counting*. In this variation, the sample is held in front of a sensitive gamma-detector for counting of the isotope peaks. γ particles are emitted as a by-product of α emission. Unlike alpha particles, gamma rays are not attenuated to any great extent by air; thus, important bone and tooth samples do not have to be destroyed to be dated. The arrangement is calibrated using an identically-shaped cast having known quantities of the U series isotopes (Yokoyama and Nguyen 1981, Simpson and Grün 1998). In addition to uncertainty about U uptake, some isotope peaks (e.g., ^{230}Th and ^{234}U) have very low intensities above background and so, where feasible, some isotope ratios are taken from mass-spectrometric data of allied samples (Schwarcz *et al.* 1998b). A recent attempt to date the Swanscombe skull calvaria fragments was not successful using this method (Barton and Stringer 1997), largely because of uncertainty about U uptake. One calvaria fragment had a different U content than the other two showing that it had a different U uptake history (Latham 1997; see below). Stringer and Hublin (1999), arguing from geomorphological evidence, consider the skull fragments to be about 400 ka in age. Because of the very long half-life (4.5 Gyr) of ^{238}U, U–Pb techniques can only be applied to date old rocks but Getty and DePaolo (1995) showed that under favourable circumstances (high U content, and radiogenic lead that is sufficiently in excess of concentrations of 'common' lead), it would be possible to date young rocks (recalling that ^{206}Pb is the end product of the ^{238}U decay chain but that most rocks already contain some common, that is, non-radiogenic, ^{206}Pb). Richards et al. (1998) have shown that calcite samples having high U and deposited at or before the Middle Pleistocene (>200 ka) could be dated by U–Pb and that the dates were concordant with U–Th dates. This opens up the possibility of U–Pb dating some secondary calcites, into the Middle Pleistocene (that is, down to 200 ka), where the U–Th method takes over. The U–Th and U–Pb methods together could then potentially cover the whole of the Quaternary and beyond (see below).

The U–Th method was used on corals to calibrate the ^{14}C method beyond the range of dendrochronological calibration (Bard et al. 1990; see Chapter 2). The result is that the age of the last glacial maximum, previously dated by ^{14}C to be 18 000 years, is recalibrated to 20 000 years. Similarly, it is suspected that the radiocarbon ages at around 36 000 years are likely to be nearer 40 000 years (Bischoff et al. 1994). Among other consequences, this will lead to a modified timescale for Upper Palaeolithic transitions.

The study of palaeoenvironment is highly relevant to the archaeology of hominid sites. U-series ages have been used in many studies for palaeoenvironmental purposes; a few examples follow.

Delineating interglacial and interstadial periods

A great many age estimates were made on speleothems of caves in northern temperate zones in order to delineate periods when annual average groundwater temperatures were above freezing (Gascoyne et al. 1983, Gascoyne and Harmon 1992). These ages were sometimes accompanied by stable isotope analyses (δ^{18}O) of calcite and fluid inclusions in attempts to derive palaeotemperatures directly from oxygen isotopic fractionation (see Chapter 16), though with mixed success

(Schwarcz and Yonge 1983, Gascoyne 1992). Complementary studies on speleothems which formed during glacial low sea-stands, and which are now submerged in caves in the Bahamas, yielded complementary age estimates for glaciations (Li et al. 1989). Periods of increased rainfall in desert environments have been estimated from U–Th dates of speleothems (Brook et al. 1990); this work also clearly showed that pollen spectra from speleothems can be used to infer prevailing ecological conditions.

Dating pollen entrapped in speleothems

The exterior exine of pollen grains degrades as groundwaters become more alkaline. It is therefore surprising that sufficient numbers of recognizable pollen grains survive trapped in the calcite of some speleothems. Bastin (1978) measured pollen in six speleothems of Holocene and Weichselian ages from Belgian caves with some success. Contrasting conditions between subatlantic and glacial stages were clearly distinguishable. In a study of a very old, possibly Cromerian-age, speleothem from the Mendip Hills, Baker et al. (1997) counted interglacial pollen and inferred that it had been carried on to the precipitating calcite in the dripwater. The age of the sample was bracketed by TIMS ages greater than 400 ka and a palaeomagnetic analysis (Chapter 6) which showed the sample to be younger than 780 ka.

CASE STUDIES

There are a great many important archaeological sites that have now been dated by U-series methods. The great majority of these have been concerned with hominid evolution from the Middle Palaeolithic (500 ka) to the Mesolithic (10–12 ka), and the importance of these sites has been a major factor in pushing the development of U-series, ESR and TL techniques on new materials and testing novel approaches; the following three studies are selected to illustrate the variation in technique and comparison with other methods.

Vertesszöllos, Hungary

This site is a quarry on the side of the Tata river, a tributary to the Danube. A hominid part-skull (occiput; where the skull joins the spinal column) was found in loess-contaminated, spring-deposited, travertine, together with fragments of teeth belonging to a child. In one of the earliest applications of U-series dating methods, Cherdyntsev *et al.* (1963) found that samples of the travertine contained ^{232}Th, a sure indicator that the samples were heavily contaminated. The age estimates ranged from about 160 to over 300 ka. Schwarcz and Latham (1984) used leaching techniques on several approximately coeval samples and produced a combined age estimate of 203 ± 24 ka. The Biharian fauna of the site is not easily reconciled with the younger U–Th dates (e.g., Wolpoff 1999).

Israeli cave sites

Originally, microfaunal data (e.g., Bar-Yosef 1989) indicated that there was probably an overlap in time in the occupation of the region by Neanderthals and anatomically modern humans (AMHs); the sites are, chiefly, Kebara and Tabun for Neanderthals, and Qafzeh and Es Skhul for AMHs. Although there are doubts concerning the stratigraphic assignation of the Tabun 1 skeleton (see Bar-Yosef and Callendar 1999), the temporal overlap has been confirmed by TL, ESR and U/Th dates on a variety of materials from these sites. For example, McDermott *et al.* (1993) have shown that U/Th and ESR dates of tooth enamel and dentine yield a series of U-uptake ages which indicate that the Qafzeh AMHs pre-date the Kebara Neanderthals. For Qafzeh, the ages are estimated to be from 110–85 ka, whereas burnt flint TL dates for Kebara range from 45 to 65 ka (Valladas *et al.* 1987). It should be noted, however, that the dating of the various layers at Tabun is still problematic in that the modelled U-uptake ages of U–Th and ESR of teeth are significantly younger than the TL dates from burnt flint (e.g., Bar-Yosef 1989), and also that the distinction between Levantine Neanderthals and AMHs is still under debate. Some workers suggest that they may be variations within a single species (e.g., Bar Yosef and Callendar 1999).

Atapuerca, Spain

Sima de los Huesos is an important Middle Pleistocene (200 to 525 ka) cave site in the Sierra de Atapuerca, Burgos, Spain, containing hominid bones below a stratum of the remains of the cave bear *Ursus deningeri*. The upper layer also contains thin calcite coatings, and the lower layers contain more massive pieces of stalagmitic material, generally all of reliably datable quality. However, the massive speleothem has provided

only maximum ages of mostly greater than 350 ka, whereas the capping calcite ranges in age from about 46 to 200 ka. The preferred age of the hominid remains is based upon a comparison of modelled uptake ages from both ESR and U–Th analyses of slivers of bear bone, hominid bone (limited) and of other fauna. Using the approach of Schwarcz *et al.* (1988a), Bischoff *et al.* (1997) used the combined ESR and U–Th analyses to find the most likely uptake history and model ages. For one group of analyses of bear bones, they found the uptake history to be nearer to LU than to EU with $p = -0.18$, and the true age of the oldest set of bear bones to be near to 320 ka. The limited analysis of hominid bones gave a minimum age of 200 ka, and so they inferred that the hominid and earliest bear bones were in place from between 350 to 320 ka. This site and the nearby, and even older, Gran Dolina, continue to receive a great deal of attention as they are among the oldest hominid sites in Europe.

SUMMARY AND PROSPECTS

The U-series methods continue to occupy a prominent position in providing age estimates for climatic events in the later Quaternary. Target projects have included the dating of corals, for high sea-stands, drowned speleothems, for low sea stands, and speleothems in temperate caves, such as those in the limestone areas of the British Isles, for interglacial ages. Early on, pioneers like Cherdyntsev realized the potential of the method for dating hominid sites where there were secondary deposits of calcite associated with bone or with artifacts. From about the 1980s onward, this application of the technique has expanded greatly to cover cave sites in several regions of the world. Further developments have included occasional cross-calibration with ESR, TL and ^{14}C techniques, application to dating bone and teeth, and the dating of more precious bone samples using gamma-ray methods. For such materials, there is often uncertainty about the exact U-uptake history; the uptake history, consequently, has to be modelled in some way. With mass-spectrometry and smaller samples, it might be possible in future to use only those samples that show an unequivocal diffusion profile, that is, a sample that shows no evidence of subsequent U-leaching. Even so, apart from testing the robustness of the estimated age to variations in uptake, there is seldom an opportunity to test the model rigorously by other means or by other information. Therefore, with sites like Tabun and Kebara, in Israel, the aim of the archaeologists and archaeological scientists has been to obtain dates by a number of techniques, and this kind of multi-technique approach is becoming almost universal. In this regard, it is unfortunate that some archaeologists still send samples for analysis to scientists who have no knowledge of the site. It is usually preferable for the archaeologist and the scientist to collect the samples together.

Where sufficiently high U concentrations allow, perhaps one of the most exciting recent developments has been the application of the long-established sister technique of U–Pb dating to young secondary minerals and, perhaps, also to bone and teeth. A recent attempt to use the U–Pb technique on a layer of calcite just above a newly discovered Australopithecine find at Sterkfontein, South Africa, yielded an isochron age of about 3.1 Ma (Cliff and Latham, unpublished data). This is in agreement with an age of 3.3–3.5 Ma assigned to the hominid using magnetostratigraphy (Partridge et al. 1999).

In the early 1990s, magnetic sector inductively-coupled plasma mass-spectrometers were applied to U/Th analysis (e.g., Halliday et al. 1998), with the advantage of an increased precision on the estimated age. This has meant a higher age limit for the method of 500 000 years, and it has also meant that small samples, such as those from fossil tooth dentine, can now be analysed.

ACKNOWLEDGEMENTS

I thank Dan Barnes for his assistance in compiling some of the material in this section.

REFERENCES

*Recommended for further reading

*Aitken, M.J., Stringer, C.B. and Mellars, P.A. (eds) (1993). The Origin of Modern Humans and the Impact of Chronometric Dating. Princeton University Press: Princeton.

Baker, A., Caseldine, C., Hawkesworth, C., Latham, A.G. and Hatton, J. (1997). A Cromerian Complex stalagmite from the Mendip Hills. Journal of Quaternary Science, 12:533–537.

Bar-Yosef, O. (1989). Geochronology of the Levantine Middle-Palaeolithic. In Mellars, P. and Stringer, C.B. (eds) The Human Revolution: Behavioural and Biological Perspectives on the Origin of Modern Humans, 589–610. Edinburgh University Press: Edinburgh.

Bar-Yosef, O. and Callendar, J. (1999). The woman from Tabun: Garrod's doubts in historical perspective. Journal of Human Evolution, 37:879–885.

Bard, E., Hamelin, B., Fairbanks, R.G. and Zinder, A. (1990). Calibration of the ^{14}C timescale over the past 30 000 years using mass-spectrometric U–Th ages from Barbados corals. Nature, 345:405–410.

Barton, J.C. and Stringer, C.B. (1997). An attempt at dating the Swanscombe skull bones using non-destructive gamma-ray counting. Archaeometry, 39:205–216.

Bastin, B. (1978). L'analyse pollinique des stalagmites: une nouvelle possibilité d'approche des fluctuations climatiques du quaternaire. Annales de la Societé Géologique de Belgique 101:13–19.

Bischoff, J.L. and Fitzpatrick, J.A. (1991). U-series dating of impure carbonates: an evaluation of the isochron technique using total-sample dissolution. Geochimica et Cosmochimica Acta, 55:543–554.

Bischoff, J.L., Rosenbauer, R.J., Tavoso, A. and de Lumley, H. (1988). A test of uranium-series dating of fossil tooth enamel: results from Tournal Cave, France. Applied Geochemistry, 3:145–151.

Bischoff, J.L., Ludwig, K., Garcia, J.F, Carbonell, E., Vaquero, M., Stafford, T.W. and Jull, A.J.T. (1994). Dating of basal Aurignacian sandwich at Abric Romani (Catalunya, Spain) by radiocarbon and uranium-series. Journal of Archaeological Science 21:541–551.

Bischoff, J.L., Fitzpatrick, J.A., Leon, L., Arsuaga, J.L., Falgueres, C., Bahain, J.J. and Bullen, T. (1997). Geology and preliminary dating of the hominid-bearing sedimentary fill of the Sima de los Huesos chamber, Cueva Mayor of the Sierra de Atapuerca, Burgos, Spain. Journal of Human Evolution, 33:129–154.

Brook, G.A., Burney, D.A. and Cowart, J.B. (1990). Desert palaeoenvironmental data from cave speleothems with examples from the Chihuahan, Somali-Chalbi, and Kalahari deserts. Palaeogeography, Palaeoclimatology and Palaeoecology, 76:311–329.

Chen, T.-M. and Yuan, S.-X. (1988). Uranium-series dating of bones and teeth from Chinese palaeolithic sites. Archaeometry, 30:59–76.

Cherdyntsev, V.V., Kazachevskii, I.V. and Kuzmina, E.A. (1963). Dating of Pleistocene carbonate formations by the thorium and uranium isotopes. Geochemistry International, 2:794–801.

Edwards, R.L., Chen, J.H. and Wasserburg, G.J. (1987). ^{238}U ^{234}U-^{230}Th-^{232}Th systematics and the precise measurement of time over the past 500 000 years. Earth and Planetary Science Letters, 81:175–192.

Gascoyne, M. (1985). Application of the ^{227}Th/^{230}Th method to dating Pleistocene carbonates and comparison with other methods. Geochimica et Cosmochimica Acta, 49:1165–1171.

Gascoyne, M. (1992). Palaeoclimate determination from cave calcite deposits. Quaternary Science Reviews, 11:609–632.

Gascoyne, M. and Harmon, R.S. (1992). Palaeoclimatology and palaeosea levels. In Ivanovich, M. and Harmon, R.S.

(eds) *Uranium-Series Disequilibrium: Applications to Earth, Marine and Environmental Sciences*, 553–582. Oxford University Press: Oxford.

Gascoyne, M., Schwarcz, H.P. and Ford, D.C. (1983). Uranium-series ages of speleothem from northwest England: correlation with Quaternary climate. *Philosophical Transactions of the Royal Society*, **B301**:143–164.

Getty, S.R. and DePaolo, D. (1995). Quaternary geochronology using the U-Th-Pb method. *Geochimica et Cosmochimica Acta*, **59**:3267–3272.

Halliday, A.N., Lee, D.-C., Christensen, J.N., Rehkämper, M., Yi, W., Luo, X.Z., Hall, C.M., Ballentine, C.J., Pettke, T. and Stirling, C. (1998). Applications of multiple collector-ICPMS to cosmochemistry, geochemistry, and paleoceanography. *Geochimica et Cosmochimica Acta*, **62**:919–940.

*Ivanovich, M. and Harmon, R.S. (1992). *Uranium-Series Disequilibrium: Applications to Earth, Marine and Environmental Sciences*, (2nd edn). Oxford University Press: Oxford.

Ivanovich, M., Ku, T.-L., Harmon, R.S. and Smart, P. (1984). Uranium series intercomparison project (USIP). *Nuclear Instrumentation and Methods in Physics Research*, **223**:446–471.

Kaufman, A. (1986). The distribution of ^{230}Th/^{234}U ages in corals and the number of last interglacial high-sea stands. *Quaternary Research*, **25**:55–62.

Kaufman, A. and Broecker, W. (1965). Comparison of Th^{230} and C^{14} ages for carbonate materials from lakes Lahontan and Bonneville. *Journal of Geophysical Research*, **70**:4039–4054.

Latham, A.G. (1997). Uranium-series dating of bone by gamma-ray spectrometry: comment. *Archaeometry*, **39**:217–219.

Latham, A.G., Schwarcz, H.P. and Ford, D.C. (1986). The paleomagnetism and U-Th dating of Mexican stalagmite, DAS2. *Earth and Planetary Science Letters*, **79**:195–207.

Li, W.-X., Lundberg, J., Dickin, A.P., Ford, D.C., Schwarcz, H.P., McNutt, R. and Williams, D. (1989). High precision mass-spectrometric uranium-series dating of cave deposits and implications for palaeoclimate studies. *Nature*, **339**:534–536.

Ludwig, K.R. and Titterington, D.M. (1994). Calculation of ^{230}Th/U isochrons, ages and errors. *Geochimica et Cosmochimica Acta*, **58**:5031–5042.

Luo, S. and Ku, T.-L. (1991). U-series isochron dating: a generalized method employing total sample dissolution. *Geochimica et Cosmochimica Acta*, **55**:555–564.

McDermott, F., Grün, R., Stringer, C.B. and Hawkesworth, C.J. (1993). Mass-spectrometric U-series dates for Israeli Neanderthal/early modern hominid sites. *Nature*, **363**:252–254.

Millard, A.R. and Hedges, R.E.M. (1995). The role of the environment in the uranium uptake by buried bone. *Journal of Archaeological Science*, **22**:239–250.

Millard, A.R. and Pike, A.W.G. (1999). Uranium-series dating of the Tabun Neanderthal: a cautionary note. *Journal of Human Evolution*, **36**:581–585.

Partridge, T.C., Shaw, J., Heslop, D. and Clarke, R.J. (1999). The new hominid skeleton from Sterkfontein: age and preliminary assessment. *Journal of Quaternary Science*, **14**:293–298.

Richards, D.A., Bottrell, S.H., Cliff, R.A., Stroehle, K. and Rowe, P.J. (1998). U-Pb dating of a speleothem of Quaternary age. *Geochimica et Cosmochimica Acta*, **62**:3683–3688.

Rosholt, J.N. (1984). Radioisotope dilution analyses of geological samples using ^{236}U and ^{229}Th. *Nuclear Instrumentation and Methods in Physics Research*, **223**:572–576.

*Schwarcz, H.P. (1989). Uranium series dating of Quaternary deposits. *Quaternary International*, **1**:7–17.

*Schwarcz, H.P. and Blackwell, B. (1992). Archaeological applications. In Ivanovich, M. and Harmon, R.S. (eds) *Uranium-Series Disequilibrium: Applications to Earth, Marine and Environmental Sciences*, 513–552. Oxford University Press: Oxford.

Schwarcz, H.P. and Latham, A.G. (1984). Uranium-series age determination of travertines from the site of Vertesszöllos, Hungary. *Journal of Archaeological Science*, **11**:327–336.

Schwarcz, H.P. and Latham, A.G. (1989). Dirty calcites 1: uranium series dating of contaminated calcite using leachates alone. *Chemical Geology*, **80**:327–336.

Schwarcz, H.P. and Yonge, C. (1983). Isotopic composition of palaeowaters as inferred from speleothem and its fluid inclusions. In *Palaeoclimates and Palaeowaters; a Collection of Environmental Isotope Studies*, 115–133. Publication 621, International Atomic Energy Agency: Vienna.

Schwarcz, H.P., Grün, R. and Chadam, J. (1988a). ESR dating of tooth enamel: coupled correction for U-uptake and U-series disequilibrium. *Nuclear Tracks and Radiation Measurements*, **14**:237–241.

Schwarcz, H.P., Simpson, J.J. and Stringer, C.B. (1998b). Neanderthal skeleton from Tabun: U-series data by gamma-ray spectrometry. *Journal of Human Evolution*, **35**:635–645.

Simpson, J.J. and Grün, R. (1998). Non-destructive gamma spectrometric U-series dating. *Quaternary Science Reviews*, **17**:1009–1022.

Stringer, C.B. and Hublin, J.-J. (1999). New age estimates for the Swanscombe hominid, and their significance for human evolution. *Journal of Human Evolution*, **37**:873–877.

Valladas, H., Joron, J.L., Valladas, G., Arensburg, B., Bar-Yosef, O., Belfer-Cohen, A., Goldberg, P., Laville, H., Meignen, L., Rak, Y., Tchernov, E., Tillier, A.M. and Vandermeersch, B. (1987). Thermoluminescence dates for the Neanderthal burial site at Kebara in Israel. *Nature*, **330**:159–160.

Whitehead, N.E., Ditchburn, R.G., Williams, P.W. and McCabe, W.J. (1999). ^{231}Pa and ^{230}Th contamination at zero age: a possible limitation on U/Th dating of speleothem material. *Chemical Geology*, **156**:359–366.

Wolpoff, M.H. (1999). *Paleoanthropology*. McGraw Hill: Boston.

Yokoyama, Y. and Nguyen, H.V. (1981). Direct dating of Tautavel Man by nondestructive gamma-ray spectrometry of fossil human skull Arago XXI. *Comptes Rendus de l'Academie des Sciences Serie III*, **292**:741–744.

6

Magnetic Properties and Archaeomagnetism

R.S. STERNBERG

Department of Geosciences, Franklin and Marshall College.

Magnetic applications in archaeology and palaeoanthropology traditionally fall into three areas. Magnetic dating has been used to date sites from the past few millennia using the phenomenon of geomagnetic secular variation. Magnetic dating has also been used to date older hominid sites using the geomagnetic reversals recorded by the sediments forming or related to the site matrix (see Chapter 1). The magnetic anomalies generated by features and artifacts at archaeological sites are the basis of magnetic prospection (see Chapter 43). This paper will give an overview of the use of magnetic properties of archaeological materials for examining site formation processes and artifact characterization, and the application of magnetization to problems of archaeomagnetic secular variation dating and magnetic reversal dating. A detailed treatment of palaeomagnetism can be found in Tarling (1983), and a review of archaeomagnetic dating in Eighmy and Sternberg (1990).

MAGNETIC PROPERTIES

All materials have an intrinsic magnetic susceptibility. The application of a magnetizing field will induce a magnetization in the material that is proportional to the strength of the magnetizing field. The constant of proportionality is the *magnetic susceptibility*. Induced magnetization is reduced to zero if the magnetizing material is removed. For example, a paper clip will acquire an induced magnetization in the presence of the magnetic field of a permanent magnet, and will be attracted to the magnet.

Magnetite (Fe_3O_4) has the highest susceptibility among common minerals, with a value of 500×10^{-6} $m^3 \, kg^{-1}$ (SI unit of mass specific susceptibility). Haematite (Fe_2O_3), another common iron oxide, has a susceptibility of $0.6 \times 10^{-6} \, m^3 \, kg^{-1}$. These minerals, like most, are *paramagnetic*, which means they have positive susceptibilities. Some minerals, for example quartz (SiO_2), calcite ($CaCO_3$), as well as other materials like plastic, are *diamagnetic*, which means they have small negative susceptibilities, with absolute values less than $0.01 \times 10^{-6} \, m^3 \, kg^{-1}$.

Some paramagnetic materials are also *ferromagnetic*, which means they can acquire a *permanent*, or *remanent*, magnetization. Magnetite and hematite are the two most common minerals that can acquire a remanence. Remanence is the basis of palaeomagnetism, the study of the history of the Earth's magnetic field through examination of the remanence in rocks of different ages (Tarling 1983). Heating is the most common mechanism for imparting a remanence to archaeological samples (and igneous rocks), which is then called a *thermoremanent magnetization* (TRM). Sediments can also acquire a *depositional remanent*

Handbook of Archaeological Sciences. Edited by D.R. Brothwell and A.M. Pollard.
© 2001 John Wiley & Sons, Ltd.

magnetization (DRM) when settling magnetic grains are torqued into alignment with the geomagnetic field. A stable archaeomagnetic remanence records the direction of the Earth's magnetic field at the time the remanence was acquired, even though the geomagnetic direction has changed since that time. Thus, *in situ* oriented samples can reveal past directions of the Earth's magnetic field. Properties of the remanence such as its strength are a complex function of mineralogy, grain sizes and shapes, as well as of the geomagnetic field. However, the strength of a TRM is linearly proportional to the strength of the ambient field; the constant of proportionality is a function of the magnetic minerals. Thorough discussions of the magnetic properties of minerals and rocks can be found in Thompson and Oldfield (1986) and Dunlop and Özdemir (1997).

ARCHAEOMAGNETISM

The spatial and temporal variation of the Earth's magnetic field (Merrill *et al.* 1996) allow for the possibility of archaeomagnetic dating. About 85 per cent of the spatial variation of the geomagnetic field at the Earth's surface can be attributed to the pattern expected for a dipolar field. For example, the magnetic field strength is twice as strong at the magnetic poles as at the equator; a compass needle swinging in the horizontal plane will point towards magnetic north; a compass needle swinging in the vertical plane will be horizontal at the magnetic equator and vertical at the poles. The non-dipole field consists of all the higher order spatial variations of the field, yielding anomalies in the magnetic field with wavelengths up to several thousand kilometres.

Temporal changes in the field occur at different scales. Two phenomena are important for archaeomagnetism. Magnetic reversals occur several times every million years, are globally synchronous, and change the direction of the magnetic field at any location by 180°. The polarity of the present field is called normal; when the field is inverted from the present polarity it is reversed. Within a particular polarity interval, the field direction typically changes at a rate of 1° every few decades, and field strength changes several per cent per century. These changes, termed *secular variation*, are due to both dipole and non-dipole field behaviour, variable over time, and variable over space.

Archaeomagnetic dating is based on the recording of magnetic field changes in the remanence carried by rocks or archaeological materials. These changes may be secular variation of direction recorded by baked *in situ* archaeological features, secular variation of field strength recorded by baked archaeological features or artifacts, or reversals in polarity of the field recorded by the sedimentary matrix of palaeoanthropological sites. The pattern of magnetic field changes is not predictable, so archaeomagnetic dating becomes an exercise in building up the pattern of temporal changes using other dated material, then pattern matching of this master chronology with the materials to be dated (Sternberg 1990). These patterns are globally synchronous for magnetic reversals, but regionally specific for secular variation.

Dating applications

Archaeomagnetism is inherently a co-operative endeavour between geophysicists interested in the history of the geomagnetic field, and archaeologists wishing to apply that information to archaeological problems. These goals are not identical, but complementary. It benefits each discipline to help the other. Archaeologists working at a firmly dated site may not need archaeomagnetic dates, but can help geophysicists by providing well-dated features recording magnetic field information. Once the secular variation pattern has been well-established, geophysicists can assist archaeologists with archaeomagnetic dates.

Hongre *et al.* (1998) and Ohno and Hamano (1993) indicate the value to geophysics of comprehensive secular variation data sets. Hongre *et al.* (1998) used archaeomagnetic, sedimentary and volcanic secular variation data covering the past two millennia to infer that the dipole moment of the geomagnetic field has been decreasing for the past 2000 years, the non-dipole part of the field varies with characteristic periods of several centuries, and the axial quadrupole component of the field may be persistently different from zero. Ohno and Hamano (1993) complement longer Holocene sedimentary records with archaeomagnetic data to indicate three periods of high dipole moment strength, and a predominantly westward elliptical, albeit irregular, motion of the geomagnetic pole position.

One region where archaeomagnetic dating has been commonly used is in the American southwest, particularly for the Hohokam culture (Dean 1991). Archaeological sites and their associated features on the Colorado Plateau in northeastern Arizona have been accurately and precisely dated using dendrochronology. However, in the Sonoran Desert adjacent to the Plateau, tree-ring and carbon-14 dating of wood is problematic because of the potential for long-term preservation before use (Schiffer 1986). The secular variation pattern for the southwestern geomagnetic field can be largely compiled on the Colorado Plateau where there is good independent age control, but can then be applied to archaeomagnetic dating in the desert where magnetic field behaviour will be the same.

Archaeomagnetists have used different methods for the construction of secular variation curves from discrete data having uncertainties in both age and magnetic direction, and for the interpretation of dates by comparison of such results to a secular variation curve that is itself uncertain. Thus, different methods of interpretation result in different archaeomagnetic dates and uncertainties, even if the raw data are the same (Sternberg and McGuire 1990a, Wolfman 1990, Batt 1997).

Figure 6.1 shows the archaeomagnetic secular variation of the virtual geomagnetic pole for the American southwest from Sternberg (1989; see also Sternberg and McGuire 1990b). The view is looking down upon the north geographic pole. The uncertainty of the curve is not shown. The ovals represent archaeomagnetic results on five lava flows from the Sunset Crater area, outside Flagstaff, Arizona (Champion 1980). Comparison with the curve yields archaeomagnetic dates of AD 1000–1175 for Vent 512 and Gyp Crater; AD 1100–1175 for Bonito, and AD 1100–1325 for Sunset Crater (Sternberg 1989). No date was interpreted for Kana-a because its direction was too far from the curve. (Archaeomagnetic dates can also yield multiple date possibilities because the secular variation curve can bend back upon itself.) These results are reasonable in that the flows track around the curve in the same sequence as their stratigraphic order, and narrow tree rings in the region suggest the possibility of growth disturbed by volcanic eruptions between AD 1065–1067 (Breternitz 1967). This date is within the archaeomagnetic age range for both Vent 512 and Gyp Crater.

Relative archaeomagnetic dates may be interpreted even when there is not a detailed enough master curve for absolute dating. If archaeomagnetic directions are different from one another, this suggests that the features must have different ages. Tarling and Downey (1990) compared archaeomagnetic directions from Minoan sites in eastern and central Crete with results from Akrotiri on Thera (Santorini). Each set indicated a different magnetic direction cluster. This was interpreted to mean that the sites were last used (before the sites were abandoned) at different times, and could thus not be due to a single cataclysmic volcanic eruption of Santorini during the seventeenth century BC, or an earthquake or tsunami related to an eruption.

Archaeomagnetic *palaeointensities* give the strength or intensity of the magnetic field at the time the remanence was acquired. Absolute archaeointensities can be derived from samples bearing a TRM using Thellier or Shaw-type palaeointensity experiments (Thomas 1983). The strength of the magnetization does not depend upon sample orientation, so artifacts no longer *in situ*, such as ceramics, can be used for archaeointensity measurements (Shaw *et al.* 1995). Kovacheva (1991) routinely uses palaeointensities along with magnetic directions on baked hearth samples to narrow down the possibilities for archaeomagnetic dating. This is at the expense of the considerable time and care needed for the palaeointensity experiment.

The depositional remanence acquired by archaeological sediments can occasionally be used for archaeomagnetic dating, although DRM is generally less reliable than TRM. Eighmy and Howard (1991) used archaeomagnetic directions from canal sediments along with stratigraphic, ceramic, and radiocarbon information to examine the history of the construction and use of Hohokam irrigation canals over a period of about 500 years. They found the declinations to be more reliable than the inclinations, which can shallow as grain alignments with the geomagnetic field are flattened by the pull of gravity.

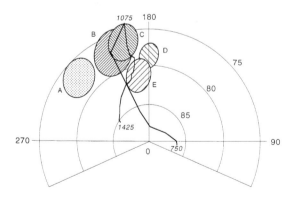

Figure 6.1 Secular variation of the virtual geomagnetic north pole for the American Southwest from AD 750–1425 (after Sternberg 1989). Several dates in years AD along the curve are labelled. Ovals are poles with two standard errors of the mean for lava flows from Sunset Crater, Arizona (Champion 1980): area A = Kana-a; B = Vent 512; C = Gyp Crater; D = Bonito; E = Sunset Crater. Copyright for this figure is held by the Academic Press, San Diego, CA.

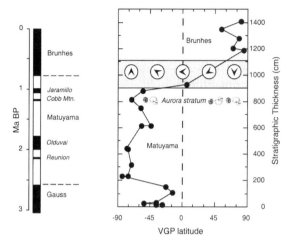

Figure 6.2 The magnetic reversal time scale, with normal chrons and subchrons in black, and reversed chrons and subchrons in white (left). Palaeomagnetic site directions at Gran Dolina, Atapuerca, Spain (right; Parés and Pérez-Gonzalez 1995). The zone where the magnetic field is reversing is indicated in grey. The age of the Aurora stratum, where hominid fossils and artifacts were found, is older than the Brunhes-Matuyama transition at 780 ka. After Sternberg (1997). Copyright for this figure is held by the American Geophysical Union.

Palaeomagnetic reversals have been used to date sedimentary sequences bearing hominid bones and artifacts. One of the outstanding questions of hominid dispersal is when and by what route they arrived in Europe. Did they arrive after 500 ka, or considerably earlier? Evidence favouring a longer chronology comes from the Gran Dolina site in Atapuerca, northern Spain (Parés and Pérez-Gonzalez 1995). Abundant human fossil remains, perhaps a form of *Homo heidelbergensis* or a new species, were found in association with rich faunal and lithic assemblages. The fossil-bearing Aurora stratum is found just below a polarity transition zone (Figure 6.2). Small mammal fossils and comparison with younger strata dated to 350 ka by ^{230}Th-^{234}U indicate the reversal is the Brunhes-Matuyama transition at 780 ka. These data support a longer hominid occupation of Europe.

MAGNETIC PROSPECTION

Magnetic prospection is covered elsewhere in this volume (Chapter 43). However, the relationship between magnetic prospection and archaeomagnetism

should be emphasized. Magnetic anomalies of baked features can be caused by either enhanced susceptibility due to mineralogical change, or to acquisition of thermoremanent magnetization (Tite and Mullins 1971, Morinaga *et al.* 1999). Dipolar anomalies aligned parallel to magnetic north–south are consistent with either induced magnetization or an *in situ* object carrying a recent remanent magnetization; a dipolar anomaly not aligned north–south must be due to a much older remanence when the field direction was different, or material no longer *in situ* (von Frese 1984). Consideration of the magnetic properties of archaeological features can help model magnetic anomalies (Jakobsen and Abrahamsen 1985, Sternberg 1987). Bevan (1994) has shown how vector addition of remanent and induced magnetization can lead to the irregular magnetic anomalies over historic brick walls.

OTHER ARCHAEOLOGICAL APPLICATIONS OF MAGNETIC MEASUREMENTS

Magnetic properties can be related to archaeological site formation processes (Sternberg 1998, 1999). Magnetic minerals may serve as palaeoclimatic indicators. Climate can affect magnetic susceptibility of sediments through pedogenesis and/or dilution by an influx of non-magnetic minerals. Ellwood *et al.* (1997, 1998) interpret susceptibility changes in Quaternary sediments in Albanian and Portuguese caves in terms of climatic change. Pedogenesis and mineralogical change outside the cave during times of warm climate enhance magnetic susceptibility. These minerals are eroded and washed into the cave where they are preserved. Magnetic susceptibility can be measured quickly in the field, or under more controlled conditions in the laboratory. If susceptibility proves to be a reliable proxy for palaeoclimate, this method should see wider use. Magnetic susceptibility, along with laboratory-induced remanence which is dependent on composition and grain-size, is also useful in considering the geoarchaeological sedimentary context of archaeological sites (Dalan and Banerjee 1998, Jing and Rapp 1998).

Archaeomagnetic remanence has also been used to examine site formation processes. Sternberg *et al.* (1999) discussed how archaeomagnetic results from hearths and walls that are unreliable for determining ancient geomagnetic directions may alternatively be useful for inferring other processes, such as magnetization by lightning strikes, or mechanical movement since the primary magnetization was acquired. Bellomo (1993), Morinaga *et al.* (1999) and Peters and

Thompson (1999) used field and laboratory evidence to indicate how specific firing mechanisms can affect the magnetic properties of soils. Shaffer (1993) examined the magnetization in burned daub from the walls of a Neolithic building in Italy. Coherence in archaeomagnetic directions from fallen daub walls suggests the walls were intentionally burned while standing to increase the durability of the daub, which was later used as a construction material for other buildings.

Magnetism has also been used as an indicator of provenance for obsidians (McDougall et al. 1983, Church and Caraveo 1996), stone (Williams-Thorpe and Thorpe 1993, Williams-Thorpe et al. 1996), and ceramic paste (Burakov and Nachasova 1986, Moskowitz et al. 1987). These studies include the use of susceptibility, as well as natural and laboratory-induced remanences. Figure 6.3 illustrates how remanence properties can differentiate obsidian sources (McDougall et al. 1983). The magnetic properties discriminated fairly well between three groups of geological source rocks and archaeological artifacts (Sardinia A, B, and C) that were also identifiable from their chemical signatures derived by neutron activation analysis. A fourth group, Sardinia D, previously unknown from chemical analyses, was also identified by the magnetic data, later corroborated by neutron activation. Magnetic measurements are quicker and less destructive than chemical methods of provenance determination.

Technological processes, especially those involving heat treatment, can also be inferred from magnetic measurements. Heat treatment of cherts makes it easier to work these lithic resources by flaking. Borradaile et al. (1993) experimentally determined that susceptibility and remanence properties of cherts are altered by heating in the laboratory. These changes are large enough such that heat treatment could be inferred if artifacts were compared with known source material.

FUTURE DIRECTIONS

Geophysically-oriented archaeomagnetists will continue to fill in the gaps in the secular variation record. The applications of archaeomagnetism to non-traditional problems such as relative dating and site formation processes should increase. Better studies of the remanence properties of archaeological features and artifacts will enable more successful archaeointensity experiments, which would be helpful for full-vector archaeomagnetic dating, and for complementing increasingly abundant palaeointensity records from sedimentary sequences. Field and laboratory studies of susceptibility will be further considered as proxies for climatic and anthropogenic influences. Dating of hominid sites in different parts of the world will be improved by the use of palaeomagnetic reversal stratigraphy and other chronological methods to improve the understanding of the spatial-temporal patterns of human origins.

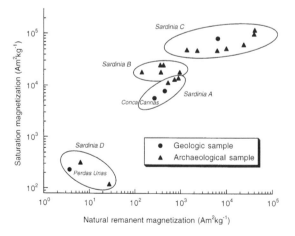

Figure 6.3 Remanence properties of obsidians from Sardinia (after McDougall et al. 1983). Circle symbols represent geologic samples; triangles are archaeological samples. Groups A–D have been differentiated by chemical composition. Two geological provenances are labelled. Permission to reproduce this figure is by R.E. Taylor and M.J. Aitken (eds), Plenum Press, 1997.

REFERENCES

*Recommended for further reading

Batt, C.M. (1997). The British archaeomagnetic calibration curve: an objective treatment. *Archaeometry*, **39**:153–168.

Bellomo, R.V. (1993). A methodological approach for identifying archaeological evidence of fire resulting from human activities. *Journal of Archaeological Science*, **20**:525–553.

Bevan, B.W. (1994). The magnetic anomaly of a brick kiln. *Archaeological Prospection*, **1**:93–104.

Borradaile, G.J., Kissin, S.A., Stewart, J.D., Ross, W.A. and Werner, T. (1993). Magnetic and optical methods for detecting the heat treatment of chert. *Journal of Archaeological Science*, **20**:57–66.

Breternitz, D.A. (1967). The eruption(s) of Sunset Crater: dating and effects. *Plateau*, **40**:72–76.

Burakov, K.S. and Nachasova, I.E. (1986). The possibility of determining the place of origin of ancient ceramics by rock magnetism. *Izvestiya, Earth Physics*, **22**:779–782.

Champion, D.E. (1980). *Holocene Geomagnetic Secular Variation in the Western United States*. Open-File Report 80–824, US Geological Survey: Washington DC.

Church, T. and Caraveo, C. (1996). The magnetic susceptibility of Southwestern obsidian: an exploratory study. *North American Archaeologist*, **17**:271–285.

Dalan, R.A. and Banerjee, S.K. (1998). Solving archaeological problems using techniques of soil magnetism. *Geoarchaeology*, **13**:3–36.

Dean, J.S. (1991). Thoughts on Hohokam chronology. In Gumerman, G.J. (ed.) *Exploring the Hohokam: Prehistoric Desert People of the American Southwest*, 61–149. University of New Mexico Press: Albuquerque.

Dunlop, D.J. and Özdemir, Ö. (1997). *Rock Magnetism*. Cambridge University Press: Cambridge.

Eighmy, J.L. and Howard, J.B. (1991). Direct dating of pre-historical canal sediments using archaeomagnetism. *American Antiquity*, **56**:88–102.

*Eighmy, J.L. and Sternberg, R.S. (eds) (1990). *Archaeomagnetic Dating*. University of Arizona Press: Tucson.

Ellwood, B.B., Petruso, K.M. and Harrold, F.B. (1997). High-resolution paleoclimatic trends for the Holocene identified using magnetic susceptibility data from archaeological excavations in caves. *Journal of Archaeological Science*, **24**:569–573.

Ellwood, B.B., Zilhão, J., Harrold, F.B., Balsam, W., Burkart, B., Long, G.J., Debénath, A. and Bouzouggar, A. (1998). Identification of the last glacial maximum in the Upper Paleolithic of Portugal using magnetic susceptibility measurements of Caldeirão Cave sediments. *Geoarchaeology*, **13**:55–71.

Hongre, L., Hulot, G. and Khokhlov, A. (1998). An analysis of the geomagnetic field over the past 2000 years. *Physics of the Earth and Planetary Interiors*, **106**:311–335.

Jakobsen, P.-E. and Abrahamsen, N. (1985). Magnetic mapping of kiln remnants at Bistrup, Denmark. In Edgren, T. and Jungner, H. (eds) *Proceedings of Third Nordic Conference on the Application of Scientific Methods in Archaeology*, 321–328. Finnish Antiquarian Society: Helsinki.

Jing, Z. and Rapp, J.G. (1998). Environmental magnetic indicators of the sedimentary context of archaeological sites in the Shangqiu area of China. *Geoarchaeology*, **13**:37–54.

Kovacheva, M. (1991). Prehistoric sites from Bulgaria studied archaeomagnetically. In Pernicka, E. and Wagner, G.A. (eds) *Archaeometry '90*, 559–567. Birkhäuser Verlag: Basel.

McDougall, J.M., Tarling, D.H. and Warren, S.E. (1983). The magnetic sourcing of obsidian samples from Mediterranean and Near Eastern sources. *Journal of Archaeological Science*, **10**:441–452.

Merrill, R.T., McElhinny, M.W. and McFadden, P.L. (1996). *The Magnetic Field of the Earth*. Academic Press: San Diego.

Morinaga, H., Inokuchi, H., Yamashita, H., Ono, A. and Inada, T. (1999). Magnetic detection of heated soils at Paleolithic sites in Japan. *Geoarchaeology*, **14**:377–399.

Moskowitz, B.M., Lindsay, J., Hemphill, P. and Judson, S. (1987). A magnetic study of Etruscan Bucchero pottery: an application of rock magnetism to archaeometry. *Geoarchaeology*, **2**:285–300.

Ohno, M. and Hamano, Y. (1993). Global analysis of the geomagnetic field: time variation of the dipole moment and the geomagnetic pole in the Holocene. *Journal of Geomagnetism and Geoelectricity*, **45**:1455–1466.

Parés, J.M. and Pérez-Gonzalez, A. (1995). Paleomagnetic age for hominid fossils at Atapuerca archaeological site, Spain. *Science*, **269**:830–832.

Peters, C. and Thompson, R. (1999). Superparamagnetic enhancement, superparamagnetism, and archaeological soils. *Geoarchaeology*, **14**:401–413.

Schiffer, M.B. (1986). Radiocarbon dating and the 'old wood' problem: the case of the Hohokam chronology. *Journal of Archaeological Science*, **13**:13–30.

Shaffer, G.D. (1993). An archaeomagnetic study of a wattle and daub building collapse. *Journal of Field Archaeology*, **20**:59–75.

Shaw, J., Yang, S. and Wei, Q.Y. (1995). Archaeointensity variations for the past 7500 years evaluated from ancient Chinese ceramics. *Journal of Geomagnetism and Geoelectricity*, **47**:59–70.

Sternberg, R.S. (1987). Archaeomagnetism and magnetic anomalies in the American Southwest. *Geophysics*, **52**:368–371.

Sternberg, R.S. (1989). Secular variation of archaeomagnetic direction in the American Southwest, AD 750–1425. *Journal of Geophysical Research*, **94**:527–546.

Sternberg, R.S. (1990). The geophysical basis of archaeomagnetic dating. In Eighmy, J.L. and Sternberg, R.S. (eds) *Archaeomagnetic Dating*, 5–28. University of Arizona Press: Tucson.

*Sternberg, R.S. (1997). Archaeomagnetic dating. In Taylor, R.E. and Aitken, M.J. (eds) *Chronometric Dating in Archaeology*, 323–356. Plenum Press: New York.

Sternberg, R. (1998). Introduction: magnetism and site formation processes. *Geoarchaeology*, **13**:1.

Sternberg, R. (1999). Introduction: magnetism and site formation processes in archaeology-2. *Geoarchaeology*, **14**:375.

Sternberg, R.S. and McGuire, R.H. (1990a). Techniques for constructing secular variation curves and for interpreting archaeomagnetic dates. In Eighmy, J.L. and Sternberg, R.S. (eds) *Archaeomagnetic Dating*, 109–134. University of Arizona Press: Tucson.

Sternberg, R.S. and McGuire, R.H. (1990b). Archaeomagnetic secular variation in the American Southwest, AD 700–1450. In Eighmy, J.L. and Sternberg, R.S. (eds) *Archaeomagnetic Dating*, 199–225. University of Arizona Press: Tucson.

Sternberg, R., Lass, E., Marion, E., Katari, K. and Holbrook, M. (1999). Anomalous archaeomagnetic directions and site formation processes at archaeological sites in Israel. *Geoarchaeology*, **14**:415–439.

*Tarling, D.H. (1983). *Palaeomagnetism: Principles and Applications in Geology, Geophysics, and Archaeology*. Chapman and Hall: London.

Tarling, D.H. and Downey, W.S. (1990). Archaeomagnetic results from Late Minoan destruction levels on Crete and the 'Minoan' tephra on Thera. In Hardy, D.A. (ed.) *Thera and the Aegean World III*, 146–159. Thera Foundation: London.

Thomas, R. (1983). Review of archaeointensity methods. *Geophysical Surveys*, **5**:381–393.

Thompson, R. and Oldfield, F. (1986). *Environmental Magnetism*. Allen and Unwin: London.

Tite, M.S. and Mullins, C. (1971). Enhancement of the magnetic susceptibility of soils on archaeological sites. *Archaeometry*, **13**:209–219.

von Frese, R.R.B. (1984). Archaeomagnetic anomalies of midcontinental North American archaeological sites. *Historical Archaeology*, **18**:4–19.

Williams-Thorpe, O. and Thorpe, R.S. (1993). Magnetic susceptibility used in non-destructive provenancing of Roman granite columns. *Archaeometry*, **35**:185–195.

Williams-Thorpe, O., Jones, M.C. and Thorpe, R.S. (1996). Magnetic susceptibility variations at Mons Claudianus and in Roman columns: a method of provenancing to within a single quarry. *Archaeometry*, **38**:15–42.

Wolfman, D. (1990). Retrospect and prospect. In Eighmy, J.L. and Sternberg, R.S. (eds) *Archaeomagnetic Dating*, 313–364. University of Arizona Press: Tucson.

7

Obsidian Hydration Dating

W.R. AMBROSE

Department of Archaeology and Natural History, Research School of Pacific and Asian Studies,
Australian National University.

The introduction of a new chronometric method in the late 1950s, based on the time dependent increase in thickness of an obsidian's hydrating surface layer, led to the rapid 'dating' of thousands of obsidian artifacts. Later research into the factors controlling the hydration reaction tempered this initial enthusiasm. The role of chemistry in both the composition and reactive surroundings of obsidian is better understood after related research into the permanence of nuclear waste glasses. Despite this, a fully predictive chemical model for hydration growth rates is still elusive. Temperature is a crucial factor, with various methods proposed for determining the rate constants. The related more difficult measurement of the thermal status of an archaeological site, and its extrapolation over a long time frame, is progressing through detailed site monitoring and modelling with time-dependent heat-transfer equations. The measurement of micrometre-scale hydration depths has improved greatly with the application of techniques such as ion beam reactions, Fourier transform interference analysis, and digital microscopy. Such systems can measure the hydration of artifacts, and establish basic rate constants from experimentally exposed obsidians for finite temperature and time. Hydration is one aspect of a complex natural weathering process and, when combined with the related contribution of erosion, can provide a measure of the surface dissolution rate. Some of the problems in calibrating obsidian hydration dates with other chronometric systems may arise from neglecting the surface loss that can occur while hydration is developing. The improvements of the last forty years will continue as more attention is given to the chemistry, surface weathering reactions, site temperature response, and measurement accuracy.

ORIGINS OF OBSIDIAN HYDRATION DATING

Obsidian is a relatively rare volcanic glass produced in flows of silica-rich rhyolite lava. The concentration gradient of water in magmatic solution has a major affect on the form of the eruption, its products and their weathering characteristics. Obsidian may be present as microscopic shards in volcanic ash, zonally as vesicular pumice, compressed as glassy pumice, or occasionally as massive deposits from deeper levels or later stages in the eruption. Eventually, over hundreds of millennia, hydration can convert glassy pumice and obsidian to *perlite* (Nasedkin 1987), where the water content can reach 9 per cent (Epel'baum and Salova 1987). The development of hydration dating followed the observation of Ross and Smith (1955) of a sharp

Handbook of Archaeological Sciences. Edited by D.R. Brothwell and A.M. Pollard.
© 2001 John Wiley & Sons, Ltd.

boundary between water-rich perlite and glassy obsidian. Friedman and Smith (1960) first demonstrated that this provided a means for dating obsidian artifacts. Volcanic glass fragments in both ash and pumice have been the subject of obsidian hydration dating of volcanic events (Davis 1984, Friedman and Peterson 1971), but compact glassy obsidians of interest to archaeologists have been the predominant focus for hydration dating research.

PROCESS AND COMPOSITION

Typical obsidian includes about 80 to 90 per cent major glass network forming oxides, with a range between about 65 to 78 per cent SiO_2 and 10 to 15 per cent Al_2O_3. The remaining major elements are the glass intermediate and network modifiers at usually less than a few per cent each. The appropriate magma composition may not yield obsidian if thermodynamic conditions during an eruption are unfavourable, such as the temperature gradient and cooling rate (Manley 1992), or vapour pressure and melt viscosity. Water, an important volatile in glassy obsidian, is usually within 0.1 to 2.0 per cent by weight of total oxides.

The amount of water at equilibrium vapour pressure in the glass-forming magma at high temperature can only be retained if high pressure is maintained until temperatures below the glass transition range are reached (Newman *et al.* 1988). With cooling, the obsidian becomes under-saturated, with an affinity for additional water (Friedman and Long 1984). The basis of hydration dating is the capacity of the obsidian to restore an equilibrium water content by slow diffusion at normal ground temperature. A gradient of retained water in the flow (Newman *et al.* 1988) can affect the refractive index and density (Ross and Smith 1955, Long and Friedman 1968), and, more importantly, the hydration rates of obsidian from different parts of a single flow (Mazer *et al.* 1992, Stevenson *et al.* 1993a).

THE DATING BASICS

A newly fractured hydrophilic obsidian surface is a boundary between the dry and the wet. Water absorption into the glass produces an hydration zone (Figure 7.1), with a higher refractive index and density than the interior, with its depth giving a measure of time since the surface was exposed. The system first described by Friedman and Smith (1960) was applied to 600 artifacts from Dynastic Egypt, Pleistocene East Africa, Japan,

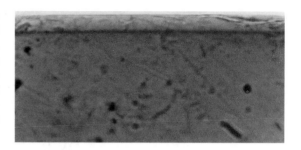

Figure 7.1 Microscope image of a typical hydrated obsidian surface at $\times 400$ magnification. The mean hydrated layer thickness in this specimen is $5.47 \pm 0.17\,\mu m$.

North and Central America and Alaska. Petrological thin sections were used to display profiles from the surface to the interior (Friedman *et al.* 1997), with microscopic measurement of the hydration depth (X) being related to the square root of time (*t*), by a rate constant (*k*) as:

$$X = kt^{0.5} \qquad (1)$$

The radiocarbon age of associated material usually provided the time base and the calculated value for the constant *k* then allowed other obsidians from related sites or climate zones to be dated.

Temperature dependence

Friedman and Smith (1960) accounted for the exponential relationship of the hydration rate to temperature with seven climatic zones, each with appropriate rate constants from the Arctic to the tropics. The measurement of site temperature was not a priority since the value for *k*, for any location, was usually found by dividing the hydration thickness by the age of associated radiocarbon-dated material. In experimental studies of accelerated hydration at temperatures from 95°C to 245°C, Friedman and Long (1976) demonstrated that the Arrhenius equation gave an appropriate empirical solution to the relationship of temperature to the hydration rate *k* using:

$$k = A\exp^{-E/RT} \qquad (2)$$

where *T* is Kelvin temperature, *R* the universal gas constant, *E* the activation energy, and the pre-exponential *A* is related to the particular physical and chemical characteristics of an obsidian. The activation energy is sufficiently high at 70 to 90 kJ (Stevenson *et al.* 1993a) to make the hydration reaction so temperature sensitive that a $\pm 1°C$ change produces around ± 10 per cent difference in the rate.

Chemical composition effects

Other studies show that obsidians with different chemical compositions also hydrate at different rates. The basis for these differences has been addressed by several authors (Ericson 1981, 1988, Friedman and Long 1976, Stevenson and Scheetz 1989, Suzuki 1973), all endeavouring to isolate the key chemical and physical determinants in the hydration reaction. None of the alternative rate-controlling formulations was applied in an operational dating program. There was also some doubt about the basic diffusion process: variants on the square root of time function were proposed, with a simple arithmetic rate $X = kt^{1.0}$ being one contender (Meighan 1988). Controlled laboratory experiments have consistently shown a $kt^{0.5}$ function.

Effective hydration temperature (EHT)

The measurement of ground temperature to determine the site-specific rate constant k is an essential part of the dating equation (Lynch and Stevenson 1992). The simple division of the world into seven temperature zones, or *effective hydration temperatures* (EHTs), was replaced by efforts to measure site-specific ground temperatures. This employed standard thermometry (Suzuki 1973) as well as models based on air temperature records (Friedman 1976). Water vapour diffusion across a polycarbonate barrier was proposed as a thermal cell for hydration dating purposes (Ambrose 1976, Trembour *et al.* 1988). A problem with these analogue devices in a variable temperature regime, both diurnal and seasonal, is that the integrated hydration response of obsidian will be higher than that of the cells because of their lower activation energy. Analogue cells can therefore create an error in the calculated effective hydration temperature depending on the amplitude of the temperature range. For palaeotemperature calculations extending to the Pleistocene in the temperate latitudes of Japan, Suzuki (1973) proposed using climatic indicators from pollen cores, sea-sediment isotopic values, and obsidian fission-track dates.

Mathematical modelling of effective hydration temperature has been advanced as a solution to the problem of site-specific monitoring (Stevenson *et al.* 1989, Ridings 1996). A comprehensive review of the difficulties of reducing the dynamic temperature variable to a single site EHT was carried out in a year-long survey in the temperate New Zealand climate between 34 and 38°S (Jones *et al.* 1997). This showed that even at a micro-regional scale the temperature variable could account for dating errors of 38 per cent so that temperature estimates should be targeted to single locations or sites.

Humidity and hydration rate relationship

The relative water vapour pressure at the obsidian surface can have a significant effect on the hydration reaction under high temperature experimental conditions (Abrajano *et al.* 1989). There is a rapid reduction in obsidian hydration velocity below 90 per cent RH between 150°C and 175°C (Mazer *et al.* 1991). This is supported by laboratory exposure of obsidian powders at temperatures of 40°C and 70°C with RH of 28 per cent to 100 per cent (Friedman *et al.* 1994). However, a problem with sterile laboratory studies is a lack of direct application to specific conditions within an archaeological site. The diurnal temperature changes in soil at shallow depth can create dew point conditions daily, while obsidian may be a substrate for microbiological activity that can alter the immediate surface vapour pressure. Saturation vapour pressure occurs even in superficially dry soils below a depth of 0.25 m (Friedman *et al.* 1994). Field monitoring at Easter Island shows 100 per cent RH at 0.1 m soil depth (Stevenson *et al.* 1993b, 1998). The relationship between humidity and hydration rates needs further examination under a range of soil conditions at archaeological sites. Evidence for the formation of water on silicates is present in nanometre scale imaging of surfaces by Scanning-Probe Microscopy (Salmeron *et al.* 1997). Glass can be analysed by SPM at normal air pressure and controlled humidity, to yield information on the hydration process and other induced surface changes.

EARLY APPLICATIONS

Despite serious doubts about the basics of hydration dating, due to the unpredictable nature of soil and environmental weathering effects (Zeuner 1960), the system was widely adopted in the United States Great Basin, California, and Central America. Early problems of conflicting standards were endemic, with multiple rate constants proposed to reconcile the obsidian results with radiocarbon dating (Findlow *et al.* 1975). A proliferation of hydration rates showed that one Californian source had at least 13 different values, with another having at least 10 (Ericson 1988). While some of the rate differences could result from different EHT values, others were attributed to inherent obsidian differences. The ease of sample preparation has produced thousands of hydration readings that were variously transformed to a chronology (e.g., Michels 1971).

Work in Japan, while confirming the generally accepted $t^{0.5}$ hydration growth rate function, included a systematic review of hydration dating and fore-shadowed improvements in the assessment of site temperature and rate constants across the Holocene–Pleistocene boundary (Katsui and Kondo 1976, Suzuki 1973). Smaller projects were undertaken in East Africa (Michels *et al.* 1983a), and Sardinia (Dyson *et al.* 1990), but the extensive research in obsidian trade and technology in Europe (Williams-Thorpe 1995) has no equivalent in hydration dating. According to one author, the method is too imprecise compared with radiocarbon dating (Pollmann 1993:10). Despair, based on inconsistent site temperature data for Pot Creek Pueblo, is shown by Ridings (1996) who was at a loss to explain differences between obsidian dates and those from tree-rings and radiocarbon. Others dismiss all previous hydration dates as worthless (Anovitz *et al.* 1999). Braswell (1992) suggested that hydration dating should not be relied upon as a chronometric technique, due to problems of EHT estimates and unrecognized effects of soil chemistry. But citing the same data other authors defend their interpretation of settlement history at Copán, Honduras, based on hydration dating of more than 2000 obsidian artifacts (Webster *et al.* 1993). Conflicting interpretations of obsidian hydration dates are widespread in the literature.

A 1988 catalogue presented over 13 000 hydration readings from the University of California obsidian dating laboratory (Meighan and Scalise 1988). In the same year a general review of hydration dating showed it produced a wider error margin and generally younger results than other methods, and that some of the discrepancies could be explained by solution chemistry of the obsidian surface (McGrail *et al.* 1988).

often used with simple ocular measuring graticules, or image splitting devices (Michels *et al.* 1983b). The best control of light microscopy still leaves optical resolution at about $\pm 0.2\,\mu m$ (Stevenson *et al.* 1987). Added to this is an operator observation error, and variation between operators, with inter-laboratory comparison showing significant differences (Stevenson *et al.* 1998).

Better measurement is possible by combining microscopy with digital imaging software that applies pixel statistics across the hydration zone (Ambrose 1994, 1998, Stevenson *et al.* 1996, Jones *et al.* 1998). Improvement is achieved by arbitrarily defining the hydration front as the point of inflection in the pixel grey-scale profile. The optical resolution zone of $0.2\,\mu m$ can be subdivided by the imaging system to define a boundary within a pixel dimension of $0.1\,\mu m$ or less at $\times 1000$ magnification. Image scans can be stored as computer files for statistical treatment. A typical scan is shown in Figure 7.2.

Direct surface measurement for small hydration depths, with a precision better than $\pm 0.02\,\mu m$, is achievable with Fourier-transform spectrophotometry (Kondo and Matsui 1992), and Secondary Ion Mass Spectrometry (SIMS) (Anovitz *et al.* 1999). Acoustic microscopy is another technique capable of measuring micrometre dimensions (Briggs and Kolosov 1996) and may be applicable to hydration dating (C.M. Stevenson pers. com.). These non-destructive techniques are attractive alternatives to microscopy by avoiding artifact damage from cutting thin obsidian sections.

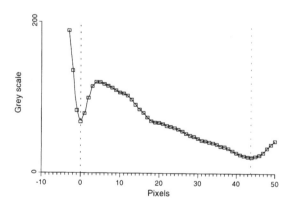

Figure 7.2 Average pixel density compiled from seven digitized scans across an obsidian section. The surface is taken as zero while the transition to the non-hydrated body of the obsidian is a distance of 43.8 ± 1.3 pixels. This converts to a thickness of $4.83 \pm 0.14\,\mu m$.

RATE DETERMINATION

Hydration measurement

Accurate hydration measurement is essential for both rate and age determinations. Optical microscopy is

Ambient temperature rates

The most direct method for rate determination exposes obsidians in controlled normal air temperature and humidity, but even after a year obsidian would develop an hydration thickness below the optical microscopy range; decades would be necessary to induce clearly measurable hydration depths. Ion beam techniques offer alternatives to optical microscopy (Lee *et al.* 1974, Clark *et al.* 1994, Anovitz *et al.* 1999). Although these systems are not readily available where large collections are to be dated, their major potential lies in measuring very small hydration depths from short-term experiments at ambient temperatures.

Powder based rates

It is generally accepted that molecular water is the diffusing species in low temperature glass hydration (Lee *et al.* 1974, Newman *et al.* 1988, Silver *et al.* 1990) and silica (Doremus 1995). Therefore the weight gain of a large surface area obsidian powder, exposed to normal air temperature and humidity, can indicate hydration velocity on the assumption that the gain is attributable to diffusion of molecular water.

High temperature induced rates

As optical microscopy is unsuited for short-term hydration at normal temperatures, an alternative high-temperature strategy for determining hydration rate constants has become widely adopted. Friedman and Long (1976) exposed freshly flaked obsidians to water vapour between 95°C and 245°C where observable hydration thicknesses of several μm can be generated in days. The exponential temperature dependence of the growth rate (Equation 2) can be used to extrapolate to normal archaeological site temperatures using Equation 3 (Michels *et al.* 1983b):

$$k' = k \exp[E/R(1/T - 1/T')] \qquad (3)$$

where k' is the extrapolated hydration rate at the archaeological site temperature T' (in Kelvin), k is the experimental rate constant at elevated temperature T, E is the activation energy from a series of laboratory high temperature exposures, and R is the gas constant. This system was applied to dating obsidians from East Africa (Michels *et al.* 1983a).

A basic assumption in extrapolating from high temperature to site temperatures is that no change in the process occurs between high temperature and pressure and low temperature at atmospheric pressure, but a change in silica reactions to water at 100°C is reported (Marshall 1980). While this question remains open, the use of the high temperature system has led to important research on the influence of chemical and physical differences in controlling the hydration rate.

Water-content based rates

As well as being a major factor in the formation of obsidian, compositional or *connate* water influences the diffusion rate of molecular water into obsidian. Haller (1963) proposed that the diffusion of water in glass is positively correlated with the original water content. Around 200 induced hydrations on different obsidians and tektites at temperatures between 75°C and 230°C, for up to 400 days, showed a correlation of $r = 0.95$ between the activation energy of hydration and the water content of each source set (Mazer *et al.* 1992). From this, the activation energy of archaeological obsidians could be predicted from their water content. Extrapolation from Equation 3 to the EHT of archaeological sites provides the appropriate rate constants for calculating the final hydration rates.

The water content and high temperature activation energy system for rate calculation has been applied to archaeological sites in North America (Stevenson *et al.* 1998), Easter Island (Stevenson *et al.* 1993b) and New Zealand (Stevenson *et al.* 1996). These projects derived the water content mainly from Fourier transform infrared spectroscopy, FTIR, using the protocol of Newman *et al.* (1986), but is only suited to relatively transparent obsidians. As obsidian density and refractive index are affected by water content (Ross and Smith 1955) they offer an alternative assay.

A plot of water content and density in a range of obsidians from America and the south-west Pacific (Figure 7.3) shows a two-phase curve indicating a rapid change around 2.35 g/cm^3, and a water content of about 0.2 per cent (Ambrose and Stevenson unpublished data), but this interdependence has significant uncertainty. A similar inflection occurs between the presence of hydroxyl groups and molecular water in obsidians as shown by FTIR at around 0.4 per cent H_2O (Newman *et al.* 1986), and 0.3 per cent H_2O by IR analysis (Ross and Smith 1955). The higher density lower water content obsidians of the south-west Pacific should have more uniform slower hydration rates, compared with the water-rich faster hydrating obsidians of North America. But it would be surprising if water content was the sole determinant of hydration velocity between obsidian flows with different major chemical

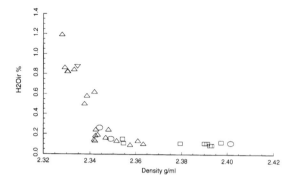

Figure 7.3 The two-phase curve demonstrates a break in the relationship of connate water to density. The source of each specimen is shown by the symbols as; △ America, □ Papua New Guinea, ○ New Zealand, ▽ Turkey. The lower density obsidians have a large range of water values, while conversely the Southwest Pacific obsidians have a wide density range and a narrow range of lower water content. Reproduced by permission from Christopher Stevenson, Virginia Dept. of Historic Resources, Petersburg, VA23803, USA.

compositions. Further research is needed on the importance of connate water and other chemical variables in the hydration process.

OBSIDIAN WEATHERING

The problem of a dating system based on the weathering of obsidian has not been seriously considered by many proponents. Glass is inherently unstable and will convert to a devitrified product at a rate dependent on its composition, temperature, water vapour pressure, and chemical affinity of the surrounding medium (Bourcier 1994). Obsidian may be reduced through dissolution to products other than hydrous perlite. The extensive experimental research into the permanence of nuclear waste glasses (Roy 1997) gives useful insights into their short-term surface reactions in a range of environments. The analysis of manufactured historical glasses has aided understanding of the weathering process (Bates and Buck 1994). However, research on obsidian hydration, as an analogue to long term weathering of nuclear waste glasses (Mazer 1994), has not fully utilized archaeological information spanning tens of thousands of years. For example, in the appendix listing the first 600 obsidians measured by Friedman and Smith (1960) are many regarded as of little value because of surface loss, although the artifact ages are known from other information. Practically

every published work on obsidian dating contains inconsistencies often cited as evidence of artifact re-use, disturbance in site stratigraphy, differences in obsidian chemistry (Adams *et al.* 1992), or failure from unrecognized causes (Ridings 1996), but surface loss is rarely considered.

The exposure of obsidian to humid soil conditions in an archaeological site will lead to dissolution of its surface, even in silica-saturated sedimentary deposits where chemical conditions for preservation seem favourable. Alteration proceeds by hydrolysis of oxygen bonds in the glass network-modifier ions, mainly Na^+ and K^+. With moist surface conditions and ion exchange these elements among others can be reconstituted into different mineral phases, while the hydrated layer may remain intact through the relatively stable aluminosilicate glass network formers (Clark *et al.* 1994:109). Al and Si can also be lost with their alteration products forming in the surrounding medium, or being retained as a clay at the glass surface (White 1988:231). Clay itself can accelerate surface dissolution by ion exchange (Aertsens 1997). Under these conditions the hydrated surface can be reduced or entirely lost with fundamental consequences for the dating system.

Short-term laboratory-based tests on the dissolution rates of glasses do not match the diverse, changing and long-term effects of archaeological burial for thousands of years. Soil micro-organisms are excluded from laboratory trials, but endolithic bacteria have been identified as agents in the dissolution of natural basalt glasses (Thorseth *et al.* 1992). Soil humic acids are also active in glass dissolution (Wei and Van Isegem 1997). In some circumstances the weathered obsidian surface may become deeply etched (Figure 7.4), in other cases the alteration may give little hint that weathering has

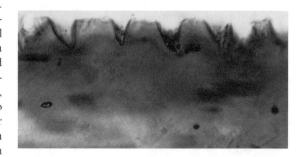

Figure 7.4 Severely weathered obsidian surface from the Pamwak site, Papua New Guinea. The largest etch pit is about 11 μm deep with some residual hydration of variable thickness.

Table 7.1 Obsidian from the Sasi site, in the Manus Islands of Papua New Guinea, showing larger hydration thickness readings from the interior fracture surfaces compared with the exposed outer surfaces (Ambrose 1988).

Index No.	Fissure (µm)	Surface (µm)	Difference (µm)	Loss rate (µm/ka)	Total loss (µm)
5056	5.40	4.54	−0.86	0.7	1.5
5057	5.57	4.52	−1.05	0.8	1.7
5058	5.41	5.17	−0.23	0.2	0.4
Means	5.46 ± 0.10	4.74 ± 0.37	−0.72	0.6	1.2

occurred. High temperature experimental conditions can produce fast dissolution rates for modelling the effect of some environmental variables (Jones *et al.* 1998), but heterogeneous archaeological deposits can contain additional aggressive biochemical factors.

Loss rate measurement

The difficulty of calculating surface loss to determine an unaffected hydration thickness arises from the conflicting rates of hydration and dissolution. The hydration rate is exponentially related to temperature. The dissolution rate is also temperature dependent but, due to the complexity of natural weathering processes, without a simply predicted rate at any particular site. The hydration front proceeds into the obsidian at a rate that reduces as a function of the depth of the existing hydration. Therefore any hydration reduction will accelerate the hydration growth rate. In time, under a steady rate of surface dissolution the hydration thickness can reach an asymptote regardless of its age. It is therefore not possible to measure an erosion-reduced hydration layer and correct its dimension with the simple addition of an amount equal to the apparent loss. An exception is when internal fractures from the time of artifact manufacture, that are protected from erosion, can be compared with outer exposed flake surfaces (Ambrose 1994).

The comparative thicknesses of obsidian hydration on weathered flake surfaces and unweathered fissures can illustrate the problem of surface dissolution. The Sasi site, from Lou Island in the Manus Islands of Papua New Guinea, is an obsidian workshop deposit buried beneath five metres of volcanic ash and pumice until it was exposed by beach erosion in 1985. The eruption is dated by radiocarbon on charcoal to 2095 ± 55 BP (Ambrose 1988). The deep deposits of siliceous ash and pumice embedding the mass of obsidian flakes should be favourable for obsidian preservation. Against this, the site has an annual mean air temperature of about 27° ± 2°C and rainfall up to

3800 mm/yr where humic acid mobilization and microbiological activity would be supported.

The results (Table 7.1) show larger hydration thickness readings from the interior fracture surfaces compared with the exposed outer surfaces. A main implication is that any hydration rate based on the outer surface measurements and the radiocarbon age would be in error for readings outside the age of the site, or at any other site of the same age with different dissolution rates. The apparent mean loss at 0.6 µm/ka represents a real mean loss of 1.2 µm from the external surfaces, according to an iterative computer algorithm that calculates the changing balance between the hydration and loss rates (J. Chappell pers. com.). The loss over 2140 years (from 1995) shows a significant 520 year discrepancy between the dates calculated for the internal and external surfaces (Figure 7.5). In comparison the difference at 500 years is within the possible reading error of optical microscopy.

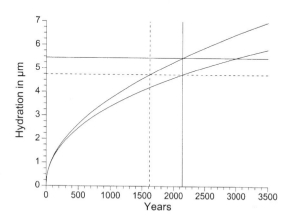

Figure 7.5 Calculated mean hydration thickness over time for (upper) unimpeded growth and (lower) erosion affected growth for obsidian from the 2100 BP Sasi site. The mean arithmetic loss of 0.6 µm/kyr converts to a computed difference of 0.7 µm between the internal and external surface measurements, and this would translate into an approximate 520 year discrepancy in the age calculation.

Table 7.2 The hypothetical growth of hydration at 100, 1000 and 10 000 years at 20°C for an obsidian with the hydration rate $k = 0.011$. With a reading error of ± 0.1 μm, the translated error at the three time slices increases with older specimens but produces a less significant error in percentage terms.

'True' age in years	100	1000	10 000
Hydration (μm)	1.05	3.32	10.49
Growth for nth year (μm)	0.005	0.0017	0.0005
Age error at ± 0.1 μm (yr)	± 19	± 60	± 380

Surface loss can produce significant errors in an age calculation. The other two major contributors to dating errors are temperature and hydration measurement.

ERROR ESTIMATES

The fall-off in hydration growth rate with time means that the error from thickness measurement and temperature uncertainty becomes more apparent with older age samples (Table 7.2). This can be simply demonstrated by considering the hypothetical growth of hydration at 100 years compared with growth at 1000 and 10 000 years at 20°C for an obsidian with the hydration rate $k = 0.011$. With the reading error of ± 0.1 μm, the translated error at the three time slices increases with older specimens but produces a less significant error in percentage terms. For dates calculated for higher or lower EHTs, the same measurement uncertainty produces relatively larger age-error estimates. The most pervasive error is that associated with uncertainty in temperature estimates with a ± 1.0°C temperature difference resulting in an obsidian hydration age difference of about ± 10 per cent.

RECENT APPLICATIONS

Geological

In a geological application of hydration dating, Adams *et al.* (1992) measured 459 sand grains from glacio-fluvial river terrace sediments extending to 160 000 years ago in West Yellowstone, Montana. The sites had an estimated effective hydration temperature of 1.4°C, and a very slow hydration rate. A detailed statistical analysis of the frequency distribution of hydration thicknesses between 5 to 15 μm concluded that they recorded three major glacial events. A potential problem with the surface attrition of the obsidian sand was avoided by reading only clean conchoidal

flake surfaces. Apart from overlapping hydration readings for the major events, a recalculation of the rate constant for a temperature of 0°C would increase the calculated age of one terrace from 26 000 to 29 100 years, again emphasizing the critical need for accurate effective hydration temperature calculation. The spread of hydration readings was wider than the authors could explain by events such as sediment reworking, from which they conclude that the chemistry of each specimen differs sufficiently from the parent flow to alter its hydration rate. They propose that each specimen be chemically analysed to determine more specific hydration rates.

Archaeological

In a review of hydration dates on 15 000 obsidian specimens from Mesoamerica, Freter (1993) makes a distinction between three approaches to achieving age estimates. Firstly, the experimental method, as at the West Yellowstone terraces, attempts to be independent of other dating systems by using laboratory-based experimental rate determination coupled with site temperature assessment. The second, empirical, method makes use of associated dated materials such as radiocarbon to provide the time base for determining the hydration rate constants. The third, relative method, relies on serially ordering a site's obsidian artifacts into a relative chronology for correlation of periods and events. All three approaches have been employed on research projects in Mesoamerica. For the Copán Project in the Maya Lowlands, which aims to more clearly define the history of settlement, population growth and decline in the region, Freter (1992) adopted the experimental approach in calculating more than 2500 hydration dates. Comparisons between chronologies based on radiocarbon, archaeomagnetism and ceramics series indicated that hydration dates gave better matches with the ceramic and archaeomagnetic dates than with radiocarbon for the earlier phase of the settlement. The study concluded that given the difficulty of finding samples in the same context, the obsidian dates are generally in good agreement with other methods.

The hydration dating chronology of the Copán settlement complex has been critically reviewed because of its use as an absolute dating technique. The validity of the system was questioned on the familiar grounds of experimental rate determination, site temperature and relative humidity assessment, soil chemistry, obsidian composition, and microscope measuring imprecision

(Braswell 1992). This elicited a spirited defence of the initial research results (Webster *et al.* 1993). To an interested observer the debate encapsulates the wide range of problems inherent in hydration dating. There have nevertheless been significant advances by accepting the need for further research into the complex issues governing the system.

Research in New Zealand has addressed some of the recurring issues in hydration dating, with an emphasis on site temperature assessment and microscopy reading accuracy. New Zealand's 900 year settlement history spans an archaeologically important period that radiocarbon dating can have some difficulty in calibrating, particularly for the last 500 years or so. The short time span of human settlement, and plentiful obsidian sources, provides an ideal test for the hydration dating system. The temperate, high-rainfall climate, and a major obsidian source that is inherently slow to hydrate, places a premium on accurate hydration measurements. The New Zealand study (Stevenson *et al.* 1996) employed a computer-based image digitizing system giving a ratio of 0.075 μm per pixel. This precision is important when hydration depths are generally less than 1.5 μm. Hydration rates were determined from experimentally induced hydration between 150°C to 180°C. The site rate constants were determined by detailed and regional site temperature survey, using thermal cells (Jones *et al.* 1997). By isolating the micro and macro-environmental variables, and coupling these to soil surface-energy-balance equations, effective hydration temperature values can be extended to longer time-temperature series. Calculated EHT values should account for site variables such as rainfall, albedo, exposure, burial depth, vegetation, and soil type. Data from ten thermal cells exposed to a depth of 40 cm at a meteorological station, and the surface energy-balance model applied to the station data, gave good predictive agreement between the meteorological record and the calculated cell temperatures (Jones *et al.* 1998). The use of a blind sampling procedure, digitized hydration readings, experimental rate constants, and a surface-energy balance model applied to 31 obsidians from an eighteenth to nineteenth century site produced results within the expected historical age range.

FURTHER PROSPECTS

The derivation of rate constants from high temperature induced hydration, extrapolated to ambient temperatures, is widely used. It would be useful to verify that the extrapolation suffers no low temperature divergence by using the same technology for measuring hydration over the entire temperature range. A likely candidate for measuring a wide range of hydration depths is SIMS (Anovitz *et al.* 1999) from short-term induced hydration at ambient site temperatures, to deeper hydration induced at high temperature.

The importance of water in moderating the hydration rate is indicated in several studies. However, water content alone is unlikely to account for the differences in the hydration rates between obsidian sources that do not share the same chemical composition. The relative contributions of all physical and chemical variables need to be quantified in order to construct rate-predicting indices.

The basic problem of assessing site temperature needs to be overcome before hydration dating can be an independent chronometric system. The annual mean temperature from meteorological observations, or as an exponential value from some analogue system, will not equate to the exponential mean temperature of the hydration process. On the other hand a complete annual meteorological record can be used to calculate an exponential mean. A site temperature record can be similarly integrated over time as an exponential value at the activation energy of hydration for the obsidian being dated. The calculation of an effective mean temperature is a problem common to all chemical-rate dating systems, including amino-acid racemization, but rather than establishing primary temperature-based reaction rate constants it relies mainly on empirical calibration constants from radiometric dating of associated materials (Hare *et al.* 1997). Unless an accurate integrated temperature can be calculated for obsidian at an archaeological site, an independent radiometric system will also be needed to provide an empirical time base for establishing longer range rate constants. The re-working of the hydration equation to find a site temperature is fraught with difficulty, because its derivation from the exponential response also requires details of temperature history. There is the possibility that an obsidian's temperature history is recorded in the water concentration of its hydrated layer (Lee *et al.* 1974). It is also likely that the concentration reflects an equilibrium reached at the most recent hydration temperature.

The reading error, temperature assessment, and reducing growth rate with thickness, indicate that obsidian hydration dating will have maximum potential under certain conditions. These include; a younger age specimen when hydration growth is most rapid; warmer climates where the hydration rate is faster;

sites with the least temperature variation; sites with a high moisture level; and exposure in the least aggressive soils. These constraints can suggest optimal conditions but they do not rule out hydration dating in less favourable conditions.

There have been tens of thousands of obsidians measured for their hydration, and dates have been attributed to these. This has only been possible when assumptions were made about a collection's common chemistry, rate constants, temperature and diagenetic history. The obsidian hydration process, and the variability of site micro-climate and weathering, requires greater attention to the analysis of each obsidian submitted for dating, rather than the common bulk sampling strategy where large numbers of obsidians have been used in an effort to overwhelm the complexity of the system.

ACKNOWLEDGEMENTS

I am grateful to John Chappell, Research School of Earth Sciences, Australian National University for the computer algorithm used to calculate obsidian erosion rates in Figure 7.5, and Christopher Stevenson, Virginia Dept. of Historic Resources, Petersburg, VA 23803, USA for permission to reproduce Figure 7.3.

REFERENCES

*Recommended for further reading

Abrajano, T., Bates, J. and Mazer, J. (1989). Aqueous corrosion of natural and nuclear waste glasses: II. Mechanisms of vapour hydration of nuclear waste glasses. *Journal of Non-Crystalline Solids*, **8**:269–288.

Adams, K.D., Locke, W.W. and Rossi, R. (1992). Obsidian-hydration dating of fluvially reworked sediments in the West Yellowstone Region, Montana. *Quaternary Research*, **38**:180–195.

Aertsens, M. (1997). Modelling glass dissolution in clay with analytic and stochastic methods. In Gray, W.J. and Triay, I.A. (eds) *Scientific Basis for Nuclear Waste Management XX*, 197–204. MRS Symposium Proceedings 465, Materials Research Society: Pittsburgh.

Ambrose, W.R. (1976). Intrinsic hydration rate dating of obsidian. In Taylor, R.E. (ed.) *Advances in Obsidian Glass Studies: Archaeological and Geochemical Perspectives*, 81–105. Noyes Press: New Jersey.

Ambrose, W.R. (1988). An early bronze artefact from Papua New Guinea. *Antiquity*, **62**:483–491.

Ambrose, W.R. (1994). Obsidian hydration dating of a Pleistocene age site from the Manus Islands, Papua New Guinea. *Quaternary Science Reviews*, **13**:137–142.

Ambrose, W.R. (1998). Obsidian hydration dating at a recent-age obsidian mining site in Papua New Guinea. In Shackley, M.S. (ed.) *Archaeological Obsidian Studies: Method and Theory*, 205-222. New York: Plenum.

Anovitz, L.M., Elam, J.M., Riciputi, L.R. and Cole, D.R. (1999). The failure of obsidian hydration dating: sources, implications, and new directions. *Journal of Archaeological Science*, **26**:735–752.

Bates, J.K. and Buck, E.C. (1994). Waste glass weathering. In Barkatt, A. and Van Konynenburg, R.A. (eds) *Scientific Basis for Nuclear Waste Management XVII*, 41–53. MRS Symposium Proceedings 333, Materials Research Society: Pittsburgh.

Bourcier, W.L. (1994). Waste glass corrosion modelling: comparison with experimental results. In Barkatt, A. and Van Konynenburg, R.A. (eds) *Scientific Basis for Nuclear Waste Management XVII*, 69–82. MRS Symposium Proceedings 333, Materials Research Society: Pittsburgh.

Braswell, G.E. (1992). Obsidian hydration dating, the Coner Phase, and revisionist chronology at Copán, Honduras. *Latin American Antiquity*, **3**:130–147.

Briggs, A. and Kolosov, O. (1996). Acoustic microscopy for imaging and characterization. *Materials Research Society Bulletin*, **21**:30–35.

Clark, D.E., Schulz, R.L., Wicks, G.G. and Lodding, A.R. (1994). Waste glass alteration processes, surface layer evolution and rate limiting steps. In Barkatt, A. and Van Konynenburg, R.A. (eds) *Scientific Basis for Nuclear Waste Management XVII*, 107–122. MRS Symposium Proceedings 333, Materials Research Society: Pittsburgh.

Davis, J.O. (1984). Tephra hydration rinds as indicators of age and effective hydration temperature. In Hughes, R. (ed.) *Obsidian Studies in The Great Basin*, 91–101. Contributions of the University of California Archaeological Research Facility 45, University of California: Berkeley.

*Doremus, R.H. (1995). Diffusion of water in silica glass. *Journal of Materials Research*, **10**:2379–2389.

Dyson, S.L., Gallin, L., Klimkiewicz, M., Rowland, R.J. Jr. and Stevenson, C.M. (1990). Notes on some obsidian hydration dates in Sardinia. *Quaderni*, **7**:25–42.

Epel'baum, M.B. and Salova, T.P. (1987). Experimental study of volcanic glasses: water specification, application to perlite genesis and vesiculation. In Konta, J. (ed.) *2nd International Conference on Natural Glasses*, 73–80. Charles University: Prague.

Ericson, J.E. (1981). *Exchange and Production Systems in Californian Prehistory. The Results of Hydration Dating and Chemical Characterization of Obsidian Sources*. BAR International Series 110, British Archaeological Reports: Oxford.

Ericson, J.E. (1988). Obsidian hydration rate development. In Sayre, E.V., Vandiver, P., Druzik, J. and Stevenson, C. (eds) *Materials Issues in Art and Archaeology*, 215–224. MRS Symposium Proceedings 123, Materials Research Society: Pittsburgh.

Findlow, F.J., Bennett, V.C., Ericson, J.E. and DeAtley, S.P. (1975). A new hydration rate for certain obsidians in the American Southwest. *American Antiquity*, **40**:344–348.

Freter, A. (1992). Chronological research at Copán, methods and implications. *Ancient Mesoamerica*, **3**:117–133.

Freter, A. (1993). Obsidian-hydration dating: its past, present, and future application in Mesoamerica. *Ancient Mesoamerica*, **4**:285–303.

Friedman, I. (1976). Calculations of obsidian hydration rates from temperature measurements. In Taylor, R.E. (ed.) *Advances in Obsidian Glass Studies: Archaeological and Geochemical Perspectives*, 173–180. Noyes Press: New Jersey.

Friedman, I. and Long, W.D. (1976). Hydration rate of obsidian. *Science*, **191**:347–352.

Friedman, I. and Long, W. (1984). Volcanic glasses, their origins and alteration processes. *Journal of Non-Crystalline Solids*, **67**:127–133.

Friedman, I. and Peterson, N. (1971). Obsidian hydration dating applied to dating of basaltic volcanic activity. *Science*, **171**:1028.

Friedman, I. and Smith, R.L. (1960). A new dating method using obsidian: Part 1, the development of the method. *American Antiquity*, **25**:476–522.

Friedman, I., Trembour, F.W., Smith F.L. and Smith G.I. (1994). Is obsidian hydration dating affected by relative humidity? *Quaternary Research*, **41**:185–190.

*Friedman, I., Trembour, F.W. and Hughes, R.E. (1997). Obsidian hydration dating. In Taylor, R.E. and Aitken, M.J. (eds) *Chronometric Dating in Archaeology*, 297–321. Plenum: New York.

Haller, W. (1963). Concentration-dependent diffusion coefficient of water in glass. *Physics and Chemistry of Glasses*, **4**:217–220.

Hare, P.E., von Endt, D.W. and Kokis, J.E. (1997). Protein and amino acid diagenesis dating. In Taylor, R.E. and Aitken, M.J. (eds) *Chronometric Dating in Archaeology*, 261–296. Plenum: New York.

Jones, M., Sheppard, P.J. and Sutton, D.G. (1997). Soil temperature and obsidian hydration dating: a clarification of variables affecting accuracy. *Journal of Archaeological Science*, **24**:505–516.

Jones, M.D., Sheppard, P.J. and Sutton, D.G. (1998). Recent developments in obsidian hydration dating. *Records of the Australian Museum*, **50**:235–240.

Katsui, Y. and Kondo, Y. (1976). Variation in obsidian hydration rates for Hokkaido, northern Japan. In Taylor, R.E. (ed.) *Advances in Obsidian Glass Studies: Archaeological and Geochemical Perspectives*, 120–140. Noyes Press: New Jersey.

Kondo, Y. and Matsui, S. (1992). Application of obsidian hydration dating with the Hitachi Model U-6000 microscopic Fourier-Transform Spectrometer – dating of stone implements by using a new nondestructive analysis. *Hitachi Scientific News*, **35**:3577–3580.

Lee, R.R., Leich, D.A., Tombrello, T.A., Ericson, J.E. and Friedman, I. (1974). Obsidian hydration profile measurements using a nuclear reaction technique. *Nature*, **250**:44–47.

Long, W. and Friedman, I. (1968). The refractive index of experimentally hydrated rhyolite glass. *American Mineralogist*, **53**:1754–1756.

Lynch, T.F. and Stevenson, C.M. (1992). Obsidian hydration dating and temperature controls in the Punta Negra Region of northern Chile. *Quaternary Research*, **37**:117–124.

Manley, C.R. (1992). Extended cooling and viscous flow of large, hot rhyolite lavas: implications of numerical modeling results. *Journal of Volcanology and Geothermal Research*, **53**:27–46.

Marshall, W.L. (1980). Amorphous silica solubilities-1. Behaviour in aqueous sodium solutions; 25–300°C, 0–6 molal. *Geochimica et Cosmochimica Acta*, **44**:907–913.

Mazer, J.J. (1994). The role of natural glasses as analogues in projecting the long term alteration of high-level nuclear waste glasses: Part 1. In Barkatt, A. and Van Konynenburg, R.A. (eds) *Scientific Basis for Nuclear Waste Management XVII*, 159–165. MRS Symposium Proceedings 465, Materials Research Society: Pittsburgh.

Mazer, J.J., Stevenson, C.M., Ebert, W.L. and Bates, J.K. (1991). The experimental hydration of obsidian as a function of relative humidity and temperature. *American Antiquity*, **56**:504–513.

Mazer, J.J., Bates, J.K., Stevenson, C.M. and Bradley, C.R. (1992). Obsidians and tektites: natural analogues for water diffusion in nuclear waste glasses. In Sombret, C.G. (ed.) *Scientific Basis for Nuclear Waste Management*, 513–520. MRS Symposium Proceedings 257, Materials Research Society: Pittsburgh.

McGrail, B.P., Pederson, L.R., Strachan, D.M., Ewing, R.C and Cordell L.S. (1988). Obsidian hydration dating field, laboratory and modeling results. In Sayre, E.V., Vandiver, P., Druzik, J. and Stevenson, C. (eds) *Materials Issues in Art and Archaeology*, 263–269. MRS Symposium Proceedings 123, Materials Research Society: Pittsburgh.

Meighan, C.W. (1988). Progress in obsidian dating studies. In Meighan, C.W. and Scalise, J.S. (eds) *Obsidian Dates IV*, 3–9. Monograph 29, Institute of Archaeology, University of California: Los Angeles.

*Meighan, C.W. and Scalise, J.L. (1988). *Obsidian Dates IV: a Compendium of Obsidian Hydration Determinations made at the UCLA Obsidian Hydration Dating Laboratory*. Monograph 29, Institute of Archaeology, University of California: Los Angeles.

Michels, J.W. (1971). The colonial obsidian industry of the Valley of Mexico. In Brill, R.H. (ed.) *Science and Archaeology*, 251–271. MIT Press: Cambridge, Mass.

Michels, J.W., Tsong, I.S.T. and Nelson, C.M. (1983a). Obsidian dating and East African archaeology. *Science*, **219**:361–366.

Michels, J.W., Tsong, I.S.T. and Smith, G.A. (1983b). Experimentally derived hydration rates in obsidian dating. *Archaeometry*, **25**:107–117.

Nasedkin, V.V. (1987). Hydration types, minerals and geology of volcanic glasses. In Konta, J. (ed.) *2nd International Conference on Natural Glasses*, 65–71. Charles University: Prague.

Newman, S., Stolper, E.M. and Epstein, S. (1986). Measurement of water in rhyolite glasses: calibration of an infrared spectroscopic technique. *American Mineralogist*, **71**:1527–1541.

Newman, S., Epstein, S. and Stolper, E. (1988). Water, carbon dioxide, and hydrogen isotopes in glasses from the ca. 1340 A.D. eruption of the Mono Craters, California: constraints on the degassing phenomena and initial volatile content. *Journal of Volcanology and Geothermal Research*, **35**:75–96.

Pollmann, H.-O. (1993). *Obsidian im nordwestmediterranen Raum: Seine Verbreitung und Nutzung im Neolithikum und Aeneolithicum*. BAR International Series 585, British Archaeological Reports: Oxford.

Ridings, R. (1996). Where in the world does obsidian hydration dating work? *American Antiquity*, **61**:136–148.

Ross, C.S. and Smith, R.L. (1955). Water and other volatiles in volcanic glasses. *American Mineralogist*, **40**:1071–1089.

Roy, R. (1997). Science underlying radioactive waste management: status and needs – twenty years later. In Gray, W.J. and Triay, I.A. (eds) *Scientific Basis for Nuclear Waste Management XX*, 3–14. MRS Symposium Proceedings 465, Materials Research Society: Pittsburgh.

Salmeron, M., Xu, L., Hu, J. and Dai, Q. (1997). High-resolution imaging of liquid structures: wetting and capillary phenomena at the nanometer scale. *Materials Research Society Bulletin*, **22**:36–41.

Silver, L.A., Ihinger, P.D. and Stolper, E. (1990). The influence of bulk composition on the speciation of water in silicate glasses. *Contributions to Mineralogy and Petrology*, **104**:142–162.

Stevenson, C.M. and Scheetz, B.E. (1989). Induced hydration rate development of obsidians from the Coso Volcanic Field: a comparison of experimental procedures. In Hughes, R.E. (ed.) *Current Directions in California Obsidian Studies*. Contributions of the University of California Archaeological Research Facility, University of California at Berkeley: California, **48**:24–30.

Stevenson, C., Freeborn, W. and Scheetz, B. (1987). Obsidian hydration dating: an improved optical technique for measuring the width of the hydration rim. *Archaeometry*, **29**:120–123.

Stevenson, C.M., Carpenter, J. and Scheetz, B.E. (1989). Obsidian dating: recent advances in the experimental determination and application of hydration rates. *Archaeometry*, **31**:193–206.

Stevenson, C.M., Knaus, E., Mazer, J.J., and Bates, J.K. (1993a). Homogeneity of water content in obsidian from the Coso Volcanic Field: implications for obsidian hydration dating. *Geoarchaeology*, **8**:371–384.

Stevenson, C.M., Friedman, I. and Miles, J. (1993b). The importance of soil temperature and relative humidity in obsidian dating, with case examples from Easter Island. In Fischer, S.R. (ed.) *Easter Island Studies, Contributions to the History of Rapanui in Memory of William T. Malloy*, 96–102. Monograph 32, Oxbow Books: Oxford.

*Stevenson, C.M., Sheppard, P.J. and Sutton, D.G. (1996). Advances in the hydration dating of New Zealand obsidian. *Journal of Archaeological Science*, **23**:233–242.

Stevenson, C.M., Mazer, J.J. and Scheetz, B.E. (1998). Laboratory obsidian hydration rates. In Shackley, M.S. (ed.) *Archaeological Obsidian Studies: Method and Theory*, 181–204. Plenum: New York.

Suzuki, M. (1973). Chronology of prehistoric human activity in Kanto, Japan. Part 1 – framework for reconstructing prehistoric human activity in obsidian. *Journal of the Faculty of Science, University of Tokyo*, **IV(3)**:241–318.

Thorseth, I.H., Furness, H. and Heldal, M. (1992). The importance of microbiological activity in the alteration of natural basaltic glass. *Geochimica et Cosmochimica Acta*, **56**:845–850.

Trembour, F., Smith, F.L. and Friedman, I. (1988). Diffusion cells for integrating temperature and humidity over long periods of time. In Sayre, E.V., Vandiver, P., Druzik, J. and Stevenson, C. (eds) *Materials Issues in Art and Archaeology*, 245–251. MRS Symposium Proceedings 123, Materials Research Society: Pittsburgh.

Webster, D., Freter, A. and Rue, D. (1993). The obsidian dating project at Copán: a regional approach and why it works. *Latin American Antiquity*, **4**:303–324.

Wei, J. and Van Iseghem, P. (1997). The effect of humic acids on the element release from high level waste glass. In Gray, W.J. and Triay, I.A. (eds) *Scientific Basis for Nuclear Waste Management XX*, 189–196. MRS Symposium Proceedings 465, Materials Research Society: Pittsburgh.

White, W.B. (1988). Glass hydration mechanisms with application to obsidian hydration dating. In Sayre, E.V., Vandiver, P., Druzik, J. and Stevenson, C. (eds) *Materials Issues in Art and Archaeology*, 225–236. MRS Symposium Proceedings 123, Materials Research Society: Pittsburgh.

Williams-Thorpe, O. (1995). Obsidian in the Mediterranean and the Near East: a provenancing success story. *Archaeometry*, **37**:217–248.

Zeuner, F.E. (1960). Advances in chronological research. In Heizer, R.F. and Cook, S.F. (eds) *The Application of Quantitative Methods in Archaeology*, 325–343. Quadrangle: Chicago.

8

In situ Cosmogenic Isotopes: Principles and Potential for Archaeology

F.M. STUART

Isotope Geosciences Unit, Scottish Universities Environmental Research Centre.

The 'cosmic rays' that are responsible for the production of ^{14}C in the atmosphere (see Chapter 2) survive with enough energy to impact into the uppermost layers of the Earth's surface. The interaction of these high energy neutrons with atoms in soil and rock generate new (*in situ*) isotopes in the uppermost metre or so. When the production rate of these 'cosmogenic' isotopes outstrips their natural abundance, and where the production rate is known, the abundance of these isotopes can be exploited to provide quantitative constraints on the exposure age of the surface. While studies of *in situ* cosmogenic isotopes are providing absolute chronologies for many branches of Earth sciences that have previously lacked them – such as geomorphology, neotectonics and glaciology – they have not been routinely applied to archaeology. This is largely a consequence of the low production rates of the cosmogenic isotopes that are most commonly used. However, continued technical developments are leading to the ability to measure progressively smaller numbers of atoms, opening the field of archaeology to the application of exposure chronologies by *in situ* cosmogenic isotopes.

This chapter outlines the controls on the production of *in situ* cosmogenic isotopes in exposed surfaces and reviews the factors of relevance to exposure dating archaeological material. Cerling and Craig's (1994) review article is an excellent treatment of the theory and application of *in situ* cosmogenic isotopes to geomorphology-based study as well as providing an informative history of cosmogenic isotope research. Bierman (1994) presents a thorough review of the use of the radioactive *in situ* cosmogenic isotopes for geomorphological research, with a useful discussion on the problems of exposure dating. The mathematical basis for the application of *in situ* cosmogenic isotopes to exposure dating and the measurement of erosion rates is presented by Lal (1988, 1991). Dickin's review of the use of cosmogenic isotopes in Earth sciences is a useful starting point for general information (Dickin 1995:360–393). The state of the art in accelerator mass spectrometric measurement of low abundance isotopes in nature, including the radioactive cosmogenic isotopes, is reviewed by Fifield (1999).

MECHANISMS OF *IN SITU* COSMOGENIC ISOTOPE PRODUCTION

In situ cosmogenic isotopes are generated by nuclear reactions induced by high energy neutrons interacting with atomic nuclei in material at the Earth's surface (Lal and Peters 1967). The high energy neutrons result from the collision of cosmic ray nucleons, primarily

Handbook of Archaeological Sciences. Edited by D.R. Brothwell and A.M. Pollard.

protons and alpha particles, with atmospheric nuclei. Cosmic ray nucleons are galactic and solar in origin. Galactic cosmic rays are dominantly protons which originate outside our solar system and have energies of up to 100 GeV (1 GeV = 10^9 eV; 1 eV = 1.602 × 10^{-19} J; Reedy 1987). The origin of galactic cosmic rays is unclear, but the very high energies suggest an origin in supernovae. The flux to Earth is dominantly modulated by the activity of the Sun's magnetic field. Solar cosmic rays are emitted irregularly by flare events on the Sun. They are also primarily protons which have lower energies, in the range 1–50 MeV (1 MeV = 10^6 eV). The solar cosmic ray flux (100 protons/cm^2/s) is significantly higher than from galactic cosmic rays (3 protons/cm^2/s).

On entering the atmosphere, high energy cosmic rays collide with a target nucleus fragmenting it, producing one or more daughter isotopes (with smaller total mass than the target nucleus) and one or more fundamental particles (such as protons and neutrons). These are termed *spallation reactions*. While the charged secondary particles are slowed by ionization, the secondary neutrons lose energy principally during collisions. The secondary particles still retain enough energy to cause further spallation reactions in the atmosphere, triggering a cascade of high energy neutrons which bathe the Earth's surface. For the commonly exploited *in situ* cosmogenic isotopes, production is dominated by neutrons derived from galactic protons, as the energy of secondary neutrons derived from solar cosmic rays

tend to be lower than the binding energy of most atomic nuclei (7.4–8.8 MeV).

The *in situ* cosmogenic isotopes which are most commonly exploited in timescale studies are ^{3}He, ^{10}Be, ^{14}C, ^{21}Ne, ^{26}Al and ^{36}Cl (Cerling and Craig 1994). Spallation reactions are the dominant production mechanism for all the commonly used *in situ* cosmogenic isotopes. In general the higher the mass of the cosmogenic isotope, the greater the dependence of the production rate on the target element mass. For instance, the production of ^{3}He is virtually isochemical while the production of ^{36}Cl is largely restricted to spallation reactions on Ca and K atoms. The chemical control on cosmogenic isotope production results in a mineralogical control on the application of each isotope. Table 8.1 summarizes the main target elements for each of the commonly used *in situ* cosmogenic isotopes, as well as recording the minerals most commonly used for study. The other important control on the suitability of mineral phases is the absence of elements which may interfere with the analysis of the cosmogenic isotope (Table 8.1).

Spallation reactions are restricted to fast neutrons (energy >0.5 eV). However, a number of the isotopes commonly used for establishing exposure chronologies are produced from the capture of lower energy thermal neutrons (<0.5 eV). Thermal neutrons are generated both from the slowing of the fast neutrons produced from the cosmic ray flux, and from the interaction between the nuclei of light elements and alpha particles

Table 8.1 The half-life, target isotopes and minerals used for the commonly used *in situ* cosmogenic isotopes.

Isotope	Half-life (yr)	Production rate (atoms/g/yr)*	Target element	Minerals	Comments
^{3}He	Stable	115–121	All rock forming elements	Olivine, pyroxene, garnet	Highly diffusive in common minerals. Requires correction for thermal neutron capture ^{3}He.
^{10}Be	1.5×10^6	5–7	O (Mg, Al, Si)	Quartz, olivine	Absorbed 'meteoric' ^{10}Be must be chemically removed.
^{14}C	5730	~21	O	Quartz	Absorbed 'meteoric' ^{14}C must be chemically removed.
^{21}Ne	Stable	15–45	Na, Si, Mg, Al	Quartz, olivine, pyroxene	Requires correction for nucleogenic ^{21}Ne in old surfaces and atmospheric Ne.
^{26}Al	7.1×10^6	15–40	Al, Si	Quartz, olivine	Isobaric interference from ^{26}Mg restricts application to low Mg minerals.
^{36}Cl	3.0×10^5	7–30	K, Ca, Cl	Calcite, olivine, whole rock basalts	Isobaric interference from ^{36}S.

* Surface production scaled to sea level at >70°N or S, expressed per gramme of parent rock/mineral. With the exception of ^{3}He, isotope production rates are strongly dependent on the chemical composition of the target mineral.

(α) which result from radioactive decay of ^{238}U, ^{235}U, ^{232}Th and ^{147}Sm, and the spontaneous fission of ^{238}U. Nucleogenic isotope production rates are highest when the target isotope has a high cross-section for thermal neutron capture. These reactions are particularly important in the production of ^{3}He, ^{21}Ne and ^{36}Cl, via ^{6}Li(n,α)^{3}He (Kurz 1986), ^{24}Mg(n,α)^{21}Ne (Wetherill 1954) and ^{35}Cl(n,γ)^{36}Cl reactions (Zreda *et al.* 1991) respectively. In the case of the stable cosmogenic isotopes, nucleogenic production becomes important in old rocks which have a long time to accumulate the non-cosmogenic isotopes.

CONTROLS ON THE PRODUCTION RATE OF *IN SITU* COSMOGENIC ISOTOPES

For the conventional radiometric decay schemes used in Earth and environmental sciences, such as the ^{40}K decay to ^{40}Ar, the production rate of the daughter isotope is controlled by the half-life of the radioactive parent isotope. The radioactive half-life is a physical constant which is unaffected by temperature or pressure and leaves the absolute production rate of the daughter isotope dependent on the abundance of the parent isotope. However, cosmogenic isotopes are formed from high energy particles which ultimately originate beyond the Earth. Cosmogenic isotope production rates are dependent on factors which moderate the flux and energy of the cosmic ray-derived neutrons, as well as, in the case of some isotopes, the chemistry of the surface material.

The intensity of the cosmic ray flux decreases as it penetrates deeper into the atmosphere. The decrease is exponential with depth in the Earth's atmosphere, by approximately a factor of three every 1.5 km. Consequently, the *in situ* cosmogenic isotope production rate is strongly dependent on elevation (normalized to sea level). As an example, *in situ* cosmogenic isotope production rates in surfaces at 3 km above sea level at 60°N or S are approximately 11 times higher than production rates at sea level at the same latitude.

The primary cosmic rays which produce the high energy neutrons responsible for cosmogenic isotope production are charged particles which are deflected by the magnetic field of the Earth prior to penetrating the atmosphere. In general charged particles require greater energy to penetrate the stronger equatorial magnetic field than the polar field, thus the primary cosmic ray flux is lowest at the equator and highest at the geomagnetic poles. This results in higher *in situ* cosmogenic isotope production rates at higher latitudes. The effect is significant, with, for example, production rates at the equator being approximately 50 per cent of those at 60°N or S. Lal and Peters (1967) used cosmic ray induced nuclear disintegration data collected at various latitudes and altitudes in the atmosphere to generate scaling factors for cosmogenic isotopes production at the Earth's surface which are commonly used to calculate isotope production rates across the globe.

Despite being massively more energetic than solar cosmic rays, the flux of galactic cosmic rays is strongly affected by the solar cycle. Geomagnetic storms, which occur when clouds of solar plasma interact with the geomagnetic field during times of high solar activity, tend to decrease the cosmic ray flux to Earth. This process is most effective in attenuating the lowest energy galactic cosmic rays (<1 GeV) and decreases cosmogenic isotope production at high altitude and latitude to the greatest extent. Sunspot intensity cycles fluctuate on periods of 11 years resulting in variation in the sea level neutron flux by 20 per cent between solar maxima and minima (Lal and Peters 1967). Further, two hundred year period changes in solar activity are thought to be responsible for 1–2 per cent changes in the ^{14}C production rate, the so-called 'Suess wiggles' (Suess 1986; see also Chapter 2).

The above effects have a significant effect on the pursuit of absolute exposure ages from accumulated *in situ* cosmogenic isotopes. That is, temporal changes in the geomagnetic field strength, solar activity and the galactic cosmic ray flux result in changes in the production rate of cosmogenic isotopes at the Earth's surface. The long exposure duration of surfaces sampled in, for instance, geomorphological studies (>10^5 years) result in the averaging out of the short time scale variations in *in situ* cosmogenic isotope production which result from solar activity. However, the future application of *in situ* cosmogenic isotopes to short exposure durations, such as are applicable to archaeological time scales, will require calibration of isotope production rates in the same manner as for ^{14}C.

Long time scale variation in the Earth's dipole field is known to have significant effect on cosmogenic isotope production rates. For example, atmospheric ^{14}C concentrations over the last 9000 years show a sinusoidal variation that suggests that 6000–7000 years ago the main geomagnetic field was significantly weaker than the present day. Past geomagnetic field strengths are known from direct measurements of archaeological material and marine cores back to 160 ka (McElhinny and Senanayake 1982, Meynadier *et al.* 1992). Beyond 160 ka it is likely that enhanced cosmogenic isotope production may result from geomagnetic field reversals and excursions and it is difficult to correct cosmic ray fluxes and exposure ages. While the current production rate of most cosmogenic isotopes are fairly well established there remains a dearth of data on integrated production rates beyond the last 15 ka due to the lack of exposed surfaces with well-established ages and the calibration of production rates remains one of the key focuses of much terrestrial cosmogenic isotope research (e.g., Kurz *et al.* 1990, Licciardi *et al.* 1999). Consequently a significant uncertainty (±10–15 per cent) is assumed on exposure ages beyond this time.

In the same way that atmospheric depth results in a decrease in the overall energy of the secondary neutrons, so does the penetration into rock surfaces. The greater density of rock compared to atmosphere results in a rapid attenuation of the secondary neutron flux. Attenuation is principally dependent on the density of the rock, and in most rocks cosmogenic isotope production by spallation ceases to be significant beyond approximately 1.5 metres. The exponential decrease of cosmogenic isotope production means that exposure ages are sensitive to the depth sampled and it is crucial that accurate depth information is taken during sampling. Partial burial of a surface during its exposure results in a decrease – a slowing of the isotope 'clock'. Residence of a rock mass or artifact within the upper 1.5 metres prior to exposure at the Earth's surface may result in the 'inheritance' of a significant quantity of cosmogenic isotopes which, if not corrected for, may result in a significant overestimation of the exposure age.

SURFACE EXPOSURE DATING USING *IN SITU* COSMOGENIC ISOTOPES

Of the cosmogenic isotopes most commonly used for surface exposure dating, two are stable (^{3}He and ^{21}Ne) while the other four (^{10}Be, ^{14}C, ^{26}Al and ^{36}Cl) are radioactive and decay to daughter isotopes with time (Table 8.1). A number of other cosmogenic isotopes have been considered for dating purposes but are not currently exploited routinely (e.g., ^{41}Ca; Taylor *et al.* 1988).

The concentration of stable cosmogenic isotopes increases in an exposed material with time if no losses occur via diffusion or chemical breakdown of the host mineral. Thus, the concentration of the stable isotope is directly proportional to the exposure duration (Figure 8.1). This is not necessarily the true exposure age as exposed surfaces and objects at the Earth's surface

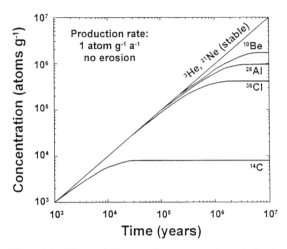

Figure 8.1 The evolution of the concentration of the six commonly used cosmogenic isotopes in a surface with time, modified slightly from Cerling and Craig (1994). With permission, from the *Annual Review of Earth and Planetary Sciences*, Volume 22, © 1994, by Annual Reviews (www.AnnualReviews.org).

are liable to be covered for periods which result in a slowing of the cosmogenic isotope production, or, in the case of burial below 1.5 metres, its complete cessation (Figure 8.2). In contrast, the accumulation of the radioactive cosmogenic isotopes in exposed surfaces is ultimately balanced by their decay. While an exposed surface usually starts with lower initial concentrations of the radioactive cosmogenic isotopes than the stable ones, the abundance of the radioactive isotopes approach a steady-state concentration after approximately five half-lives. This puts upper limits on the use of radioactive isotopes for exposure dating purposes to approximately three half-lives of the isotope decay (Figure 8.1) and has a practical limitation on studies. However, this is unlikely to be a concern in the application of *in situ* cosmogenic isotopes for archaeological purposes as the timescales are unlikely to extend beyond the range of use of the shortest lived isotope, ^{14}C. A more significant problem for future archaeological studies is that the time scales of interest to archaeology are not long enough to accumulate measurable quantities of most isotopes. Current technology means that the short time scales during which archaeologically relevant material has been exposed to cosmic radiation probably restricts exposure dating studies to ^{3}He (Kurz 1986, Licciardi *et al.* 1999), ^{14}C (Jull *et al.* 1992) and ^{36}Cl (Zreda *et al.* 1991).

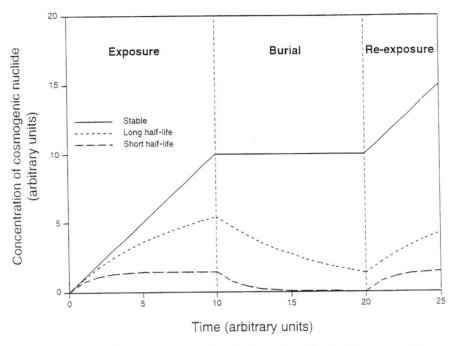

Figure 8.2 Schematic evolution of the concentration of stable, long half-life and short half-life cosmogenic isotopes through an exposure-burial-re-exposure cycle.

Following Cerling and Craig (1994), the general equation for the accumulation of stable *in situ* cosmogenic isotopes in an exposed surface is given as:

$$C_0(t) = J_0 T^*[1 - \exp(-t/T^*)] \qquad (1)$$

where $C_0(t)$ is the concentration of a stable cosmogenic isotope C at the altitude of the exposed surface ($z = 0$) at present time (t), and J_0 is the appropriate cosmogenic isotope production rate. T^* is a time constant which is defined as:

$$T^* = 1/(U/h + E/z) \qquad (2)$$

where U is the change in elevation of the surface between the time of exposure and present day, and E is the erosion rate of the surface. The h and z terms are factors which take account of the attenuation of the cosmic radiation in the atmosphere and exposed material. Although surfaces of interest to archaeologists are unlikely to have been subjected to significant erosion or uplift since their exposure, *in situ* cosmogenic isotopes provide a powerful tool to measure regional surface denudation rates, both in exposed rock surfaces (Summerfield *et al.* 1999) and in sedimentary detritus (Granger *et al.* 1996), and constrain uplift rates of mountain belts (Brook *et al.* 1995).

Equation (1) assumes that all the measured isotopes are cosmogenic in origin and that no non-cosmogenic isotopes are present in the samples. The production of cosmogenic [10]Be, ^{14}C and [36]Cl in the atmosphere is high enough that the adsorption of these isotopes on to mineral surfaces can be significant in comparison to the abundance of *in situ* cosmogenic isotopes. While this can be exploited as a chronometer of soil formation (Monaghan *et al.* 1992) it poses a problem for *in situ* cosmogenic isotope dating studies. Atmospherically-derived [10]Be and [36]Cl can be removed by successive acid leaches of mineral samples (Zreda *et al.* 1991, Kohl and Nishizumi 1992) while organic matter contaminated by atmospheric ^{14}C can be removed from minerals by oxidation.

We can summarize whether the accumulated *in situ* cosmogenic isotopes can be used to date the exposure of surfaces by highlighting certain criteria that must be met;

(i)   the surface being dated has not inherited cosmogenic isotopes prior to exposure,
(ii) the surface has not been shielded from cosmic rays during the exposure history,
(iii) the surface has not suffered more than a few centimetres of erosion since exposure,

(iv) the duration of the exposure event – i.e., the time the material spent between 1.5 metres and the surface – was negligible in comparison to the duration of surface exposure,

(v) suitable minerals (or bulk chemical composition) are present,

(vi) the surface has been exposed for long enough for a measurable quantity of the cosmogenic isotope to have accumulated, and for short enough for the abundance of the radioactive isotopes not to have reached equilibrium, and

(vii) non-cosmogenic isotopes, such as those produced by thermal neutron capture (^{3}He, ^{21}Ne and ^{36}Cl), adsorbed from the atmosphere (^{10}Be, ^{14}C and ^{36}Cl), and as trapped primordial species (^{3}He) are removed or corrected for.

Sample preparation and isotopic analysis

Cosmogenic ^{10}Be, ^{14}C, ^{26}Al and ^{36}Cl abundances are measured by accelerator mass spectrometry (AMS; see Chapter 2). Extensive chemical preparations of samples are necessary prior to analysis. ^{10}Be and ^{26}Al are measured in pure quartz aliquots of up to 50 g which are obtained by a combination of heavy liquid, magnetic separation and acid dissolution. Sample preparation for mass spectrometry involves the dissolution of the mineral separate in HF (e.g., Kohl and Nishizumi 1992). Cosmogenic ^{14}C and ^{36}Cl analyses do not generally require mineral separation; chemical separation procedures rely mainly on acid dissolution of whole rock samples (Zreda et al. 1991, Jull et al. 1992). Based on counting statistics, the 1σ precision of cosmogenic ^{10}Be, ^{14}C, ^{26}Al and ^{36}Cl determinations by AMS is usually <7 per cent. Of the 45 AMS facilities presently in operation worldwide, approximately 10 routinely measure in situ-produced cosmogenic isotopes.

Cosmogenic ^{3}He and ^{21}Ne abundances are measured in pure separates of one mineral type. Minerals with low He diffusivities, such as olivine, pyroxene and garnet, are necessary for the retention of cosmogenic ^{3}He (which is not retained by quartz or feldspar). Cosmogenic ^{21}Ne is commonly measured in 0.1–1 g aliquots of quartz (e.g., Niederman et al. 1993, 1994). Isotope abundance measurements are made using conventional noble gas isotope mass spectrometry (Niederman et al. 1993). This typically involves in vacuo crushing of each mineral separate to extract magmatic, atmospheric and nucleogenic He and Ne components from fluid inclusions prior to the extrac-

tion of the lattice-hosted cosmogenic isotopes, by incremental heating or fusion of the powdered sample. Analytical precision is controlled by the reproducibility of precisely known volumes of the isotope and are typically better than ±3 per cent (Kurz et al. 1990, Niederman et al. 1993), although uncertainties in the absolute abundances of cosmogenic ^{3}He and ^{21}Ne are usually greater than this because of the corrections for the non-cosmogenic isotopes (Niederman et al. 1994).

POSSIBLE ARCHAEOLOGICAL APPLICATIONS AND POTENTIAL PITFALLS

The burial of small artifacts, such as pottery sherds and implements, will result in exposure ages that are lower than the fabrication age. Consequently in situ cosmogenic isotope abundances in artifacts are unlikely to yield absolute chronological information. However, it is conceivable that the acquisition of cosmogenic isotopes in shallowly-buried material may provide the basis for authenticity tests.

In the upper metre of the Earth's surface ^{41}Ca ($T_{1/2} \sim 100$ ka) is produced by the capture of cosmogenic thermal neutrons by ^{40}Ca. Calcium in animal bones is acquired by the ingestion of plants which have acquired the Ca from soil waters which originates from the breakdown of minerals. Calcium is incorporated into bone while the animal is alive with a ^{41}Ca/^{40}Ca ratio similar to that of the local rocks. After the death of the animal the reduction of the ^{41}Ca/^{40}Ca by ^{41}Ca decay can, in principle, be used to date bones – in a manner analogous to the ^{14}C technique. However, unlike the ^{14}C method, soil waters at the Earth's surface do not form an isotopically uniform reservoir and the resulting ^{41}Ca/^{40}Ca of bone samples is highly variable (Middleton et al. 1989, Kutschera et al. 1989). Consequently, the ^{41}Ca technique has not been routinely developed for dating bones.

Cosmogenic exposure dating is likely, in the first instance, to be restricted to large structures that have been continually exposed since construction, such as buildings, monuments and standing stones. Where the stone used for construction was available at the time, such as erratic boulders, there is the likelihood of encountering surfaces which have significant pre-use exposure and therefore contain inherited in situ cosmogenic isotopes. Ancient structures made from quarried rock provide a better chance of minimizing the contribution of inherited cosmogenic isotopes, although it must be borne in mind that cosmogenic isotopes are produced down to 1.5 metres in rocks and that even quarried rock may be susceptible to inheritance.

Natural events which expose rock surfaces are unlikely to be temporally associated with human activity, but may provide a constraint on its timing. For example, exposure dating of rock surfaces will provide a maximum possible age of petroglyphs engraved on the rock surface. In a study of the ^{36}Cl content of petroglyph panels from the Côa valley, Portugal, Phillips *et al.* (1997) showed that the surfaces have been exposed long enough to have been engraved during Palaeolithic times. This countered previous radiocarbon evidence that the engravings are Holocene (e.g., Watchman 1996). The study also demonstrated that erosion rates of the nearby hill slopes are low enough to support the preservation of Palaeolithic rock art (Phillips *et al.* 1997). In a critical response, Watchman (1998) argued that the original work did not take account of the possibility that atmospheric ^{36}Cl may have been deposited on the rock surfaces from groundwater.

In their review, Cerling and Craig (1994) finish with a discussion of the potential of *in situ* cosmogenic isotopes to archaeology, in particular to dating the Sphinx. They concluded that technical developments remained to be made before such a study can be performed with any degree of accuracy but their parting words are appropriate and bear repeating here: 'Egyptologists, relax: you have nothing to fear for the moment. But let your scientific progeny beware! The time will come for this study.' Cosmogenic isotope exposure dating holds great potential for archaeology and the time is fast approaching when both communities must come together and design the simple experiments that will test the important hypotheses.

REFERENCES

*Recommended for further reading

*Bierman, P.R. (1994). Using *in situ* cosmogenic isotopes to estimate rates of landscape evolution: a review from the geomorphic perspective. *Journal of Geophysical Research*, **99**:13885–13896.

Brook, E.J., Brown, E.T., Kurz, M.D., Ackert, R.P., Raisbeck, G.M. and Yiou, F. (1995). Constraints on age, erosion and uplift of Neogene glacial deposits in the Transantarctic Mountains determined from *in situ* cosmogenic ^{10}Be and ^{26}Al. *Geology*, **23**:1063–1066.

*Cerling, T.E. and Craig, H. (1994). Geomorphology and *in situ* cosmogenic isotopes. *Annual Reviews of Earth and Planetary Sciences*, **22**:273–317.

*Dickin, A.P. (1995). *Radiogenic Isotope Geology*. Cambridge University Press: Cambridge.

*Fifield, L.K. (1999). Accelerator mass spectrometry and its applications. *Reports of Progress in Physics*, **62**:1223–1274.

Granger, D.E., Kirchner, J.W. and Finkel, R. (1996). Spatially averaged long-term erosion rates measured from *in situ*-produced cosmogenic nuclides in alluvial sediment. *Journal of Geology*, **104**:249–257.

Jull, A.J.T., Wilson, A.E., Burr, G.S., Toolin, L.J. and Donahue, D.J. (1992). Measurements of cosmogenic ^{14}C produced by spallation in high-altitude rocks. *Radiocarbon*, **34**:737–744.

Kohl, C.P. and Nishizumi, K. (1992). Chemical isolation of quartz for measurement of *in situ*-produced cosmogenic nuclides. *Geochimica et Cosmochimica Acta*, **56**:3583–3587.

Kurz, M.D. (1986). Cosmogenic helium in a terrestrial igneous rock. *Nature*, **320**:435–439.

Kurz, M.D., Colodner, D., Trull, T.W., Moore, R. and O'Brien, K. (1990). Cosmic ray exposure dating with *in situ* produced cosmogenic ^{3}He: results from young Hawaiian lava flows. *Earth and Planetary Science Letters*, **97**:177–189.

Kutschera, W., Ahmad, I., Billquist, P.J., Glagola, B.G., Furer, K., Pardo, R.C., Paul, M., Rehm, K.E., Slota, P.J. Jr., Taylor, R.E. and Yntema, J.L. (1989). Studies towards a method for radiocalcium dating of bones. *Radiocarbon*, **31**:311–322.

*Lal, D. (1988). *In situ* produced cosmogenic isotopes in terrestrial rocks. *Annual Reviews of Earth and Planetary Sciences*, **16**:355–388.

*Lal, D. (1991). Cosmic ray labeling of erosion surfaces: *in situ* nuclide production rates and erosion models. *Earth and Planetary Science Letters*, **104**:424–439.

Lal, D. and Peters, B. (1967). Cosmic-ray produced radioactivity in the Earth. *Handbook of Physics*, **46**:551–612.

Licciardi, J.M., Kurz, M.D., Clark, P.U. and Brook E.J. (1999). Calibration of cosmogenic ^{3}He production rates from the Holocene lava flows in Oregon, USA, and the effects of the Earth's magnetic field. *Earth and Planetary Science Letters*, **172**:261–271.

McElhinny, M.W. and Senanayake, W.E. (1982). Variations in the geomagnetic dipole 1: the past 50 000 years. *Journal of Geomagnetism and Geoelectricity*, **34**:39–51.

Meynadier, L., Valet, J.-P., Weeks, R., Shackleton, N. and Hagee, V.L. (1992). Relative geomagnetic intensity of the field in the last 140 ka. *Earth and Planetary Science Letters*, **114**:39–57.

Middleton, R., Fink, D., Klein, J. and Sharma, P. (1989). ^{41}Ca concentrations in modern bone and their implications for dating. *Radiocarbon*, **31**:305–310.

Monaghan, M.C., McKean, J., Dietrich W. and Klein, J. (1992). ^{10}Be chronometry of bedrock-soil conversion rates. *Earth and Planetary Science Letters*, **111**:483–492.

Niederman, S., Graf, T. and Marti, K. (1993). Mass spectrometric identification of cosmic ray-produced neon in terrestrial rocks with multiple neon components. *Earth and Planetary Science Letters*, **118**:65–73.

Niederman, S., Graf, T., Kim, J.S., Kohl, C.P., Marti, K. and Nishizumi, K. (1994). Cosmic ray produced ^{21}Ne in terrestrial quartz: the neon inventory of Sierra Nevada quartz separates. *Earth and Planetary Science Letters*, **125**:341–355.

Phillips, F.M., Flinsch, M., Elmore, D. and Sharma, P. (1997). Maximum ages of the Côa valley (Portugal) engravings measured with Chlorine-36. *Antiquity*, **71**:100–104.

Reedy, R.C. (1987). Predicting the production rates of cosmogenic nuclides in extraterrestrial matter. *Nuclear Instruments and Methods in Physics Research*, **B29**:251–261.

Summerfield, M.A., Stuart, F.M., Cockburn, H.A.P., Dunai, T., Sugden, D.E., Marchant, D.R. and Denton, G. (1999). Long-term rates of denudation in the Dry Valleys region of the Transantarctic Mountains, southern Victoria Land, Antarctica: preliminary results based on *in situ*-produced cosmogenic ^{21}Ne. *Geomorphology*, **27**:113–129.

Suess, H.E. (1986). Secular variations of cosmogenic ^{14}C on Earth: their discovery and interpretation. *Radiocarbon*, **28**:259–265.

Taylor, R.E., Slota, P.J. Jr., Henning, W., Kutschera, W. and Paul, M. (1988). Radiocalcium (^{41}Ca) dating; recent developments and current issues. In Farquhar, R.M., Hancock, R.G.V. and Pavlish, L.A. (eds) *Proceedings of the 26th International Archaeometry Symposium*, 58–61. University of Toronto: Toronto.

Watchman, A. (1996). A review of the theory and assumptions in the AMS dating of the Foz Côa petroglyphs, Portugal. *Rock Art Research*, **13**:883–901.

Watchman, A. (1998). Some observations on the radiocarbon and cosmogenic isotope dating of petroglyphs, Foz Côa, Portugal. *Antiquity*, **72**:197–200.

Wetherill, G.W. (1954). Variations in the isotopic abundances of neon and argon from radioactive mineral. *Physics Reviews*, **96**:679–683.

Zreda, M., Phillips, F.M., Elmore, D., Kubik, P.W. and Sharma, P. (1991). Cosmogenic chlorine-36 production rates in terrestrial rocks. *Earth and Planetary Science Letters*, **105**:94–109.

SECTION 2

Quaternary Palaeoenvironments

Overview – Environmental Reconstruction

K.J. EDWARDS

Department of Geography, University of Aberdeen.

The Quaternary geological period covers more than two million years of Earth history, and the study of Quaternary environments embraces an impressive suite of disciplines between which there is interaction if not full-blown integration. Climatology, glaciology, oceanography, sedimentology, palaeoecology, primatology and archaeology are just a few of the sciences which benefit Quaternary science and which profit from its existence. While a (diminishing) number of archaeologists might find it difficult to see the Quaternary as a framework, embracing the 'environment' in the broadest terms to include the natural and the social worlds, neither is it simply a context for human activity. As recent publications have stressed, changing environments were integral to life in the past, and they were not the 'noise' in the creation of societies (Bell and Walker 1992, Chambers 1993, Edwards and Ralston 1997, Edwards and Sadler 1999).

The papers in this section provide a taste of what Quaternary science can contribute to the overall picture of archaeological science. Other sections may be claimed to serve the same purpose – for instance, dating, aspects of human palaeobiology, and certainly resource exploitation, are all frequent components of mainstream Quaternary study. Single volumes have been devoted to Quaternary palaeoenvironments (e.g.,

Simmons and Tooley 1981, Williams *et al.* 1993, Lowe and Walker 1997, Roberts 1998), and, indeed, to many core approaches (e.g., Birks and Birks 1980, Berglund 1986, Delcourt and Delcourt 1991, Jones and Keen 1993, Elias 1994, Ashworth *et al.* 1997, Yalden 1999). It is not possible to cover the whole field in one section, but a number of key elements are taken up by the contributors.

THE CONTRIBUTIONS – A SELECT DISCUSSION

In her contribution, Alicia Wise takes a broad perspective which suggests that climate models could provide a unifying backdrop for studying Quaternary environments. The astronomical theory of the orbital forcing of solar insolation proposed by Scottish autodidact James Croll in the nineteenth century and given quantitative elaboration by Serbian mathematician Milutin Milankovitch in the last century, has promulgated a scientific industry (e.g., Imbrie and Imbrie 1979, Kutzbach and Guetter 1986, Huntley 1999, Willis *et al.* 1999) which has largely by-passed archaeology (but see Gamble 1993). In that the majority of archaeologists are not concerned with pre-Holocene events,

---

Handbook of Archaeological Sciences. Edited by D.R. Brothwell and A.M. Pollard.

this is perhaps understandable. Wise is able to plead the potential utility of climate models at superficially more manageable scales (e.g., General Circulation Models (GCMs) and Regional Circulation Models (RCMs)), even if their archaeological application is sparse (Wise and Thorme 1995). Her extended example of the North African Sahara enables a series of questions to be posed which embraces faunal and floral domestication, settlement location and the role of climate. As she acknowledges, however, the GCMs provide 'insights' (e.g., into seasonality and magnitude of climatic events), but they are crude and cannot give site-specific information. Furthermore, 'GCMs are not going to replace detailed pollen core, palaeo-lake level reconstruction, and other proxies for specific archaeological locales for a long time to come'. In stating that 'environment does not determine human behaviour now, nor did it in the past', Wise is espousing a view that is not discordant with her final comment that 'archaeologists interested in modelling the environment also need to embrace more post-processual ideas and theories'. Quite apart from the difficulties and pitfalls of meshing environment and phenomenology (e.g., O'Connor 1991, Edwards 1998), the former statement is rather too sweeping. It is more than likely that human behaviour would have been influenced by a transition from the final stages of glaciation to the Holocene interglacial which may have lasted little more than a decade (e.g., Taylor et al. 1993), while the eruption of Santorini (Buckland et al. 1997a), desertification in present-day Africa or flooding in Bangladesh would serve to concentrate the mind powerfully!

Insects can be fine proxy indicators of climate (Coope 1959, Atkinson et al. 1987, Coope and Lemdahl 1995, Wagner 1997) and the climatic response of short-lived, fast migrating faunas represents a remarkable bonus. The use of insects to archaeology goes beyond this to include habitat type and human-environment interactions (Ashworth et al. 1997). In his contribution, Mark Robinson reports that about one million species of insects have been described with perhaps as many again awaiting attention. The Coleoptera (beetles) are the largest order of insects and the animal group with the greatest palaeoecological value, occurring in almost every conceivable terrestrial and aquatic habitat (Buckland et al. 1997b, Dinnin and Sadler 1999). Many beetles are free-ranging carnivores, but dung, carrion, decaying vegetable material and dead wood all support large associations and many plant-feeders are host-specific (Elias 1994). Insect remains will also survive in anoxic environments, especially waterlogged contexts or where conditions are very

cold or dry. This can include archaeological contexts (e.g., Hall et al. 1980, Buckland et al. 1983) as well as natural ones (Coope et al. 1971, Buckland et al. 1998, Whittington et al. 1998).

Robinson also summarizes the ubiquity and utility of insects other than beetles (e.g., dragonflies, earwigs, lice, true bugs, fleas, caddis flies, midges, wasps and ants). It is unfortunate that the study of insects within Quaternary science is not as widespread as that of pollen – who knows what we might be missing? Indications are provided in the edited volume by Ashworth et al. (1997). Brooks (1997) uses the head capsules of the aquatic larvae of the Chironomidae (non-biting midges; order Diptera) to show that chironomids may equal Coleoptera as indicators of Late-glacial climatic oscillations (e.g., Walker 1995). Elsewhere, Brooks et al. (1997) had shown that chironomids at Whitrig Bog in the Scottish Borders reflected a 10°C crash in summer temperatures over a few decades at the start of the Loch Lomond Stadial. Sadler and Jones (1997), also using chironomids, demonstrate how community changes in the Holocene relate to water acidification and eutrophication. For the Falkland Islands and South Georgia, Buckland and Hammond (1997) argue that circumantarctic distributions of Coleoptera owe more to ice- and drift-wood-rafting and to later anthropochorous dispersal than to long-term survival in refugia (e.g., Buckland and Dugmore 1991, Skidmore 1997; but see Crawford 1999). A study of beetle faunas on the Lower Trent floodplain (Dinnin 1997) and the Humberhead Levels (Whitehouse 1997) respectively, emphasizes the mosaic and transient nature of distributions, with changes wrought by woodland clearance, drainage, fire and the Little Ice Age, and relative stability in floodplain hydroseres. In a thoughtful paper, Kenward (1997) argues that occupation sites, with their synanthropic faunas, act as 'islands' of 'invasion', producing data of relevance to both archaeology and island biogeography.

In Derek Yalden's examination of mammals as climate indicators, it is quite clear that extrapolations from current distributions provide less than precise proxies. This does not, of course, affect their usefulness as indicators of faunal presence or palaeodiet. An assumption that the present ranges of mammals offer a reasonable indication of climatic tolerances may be compromised by human impacts on distributions and habitats, quite apart from changes with evolutionary time. It is unlikely that many distributions are determined directly by climatic considerations and the ranges of numerous mammals are latitudinally broad.

There are, however, some (partial) exceptions including the wild boar which depends on mast crops (beech and oak) for its overwinter diet and it is averse to excessive winter snow depth. Lemming remains can also be useful as climatic indicators – collared lemmings occur in drier, colder conditions, while brown lemmings prefer wetter places. It is necessary, however, to be aware that current mammal distributions may not provide good climatic analogues and may be disjunct because of human impacts. Late-glacial climates, particularly during the interstadials, were probably unlike any climate now existing. They may have been very cold and dry in winter, but they would also have been much warmer and possibly moister in summer than present-day Arctic climates, with longer growing seasons and a much greater production of biomass. This could partly explain how large megafaunal populations (including woolly mammoth, woolly rhinoceros, bison and reindeer), themselves sufficient to sustain populations of human hunters, survived in such apparently inhospitable times. The Bering land-bridge, for example, was host to such communities, and important for allowing humans to enter North America. During cold intervals, such as the Late Glacial Stadial (cf. the Younger Dryas), the assumed absence of people in places like Scotland was more probably a reflection of the low carrying capacity of mid-latitude tundra for large vertebrate prey than the cold, to which human populations had long been adapted. It might be noted, for instance, that conditions more extreme than in Late-glacial Scotland were met by the palaeoeskimo Independence I people who occupied the Greenland–Ellesmere Island High Arctic area *c.* 4300–3800 BP (Schledermann 1996), where minimum and maximum temperatures reach around $-33°C$ and $11°C$ respectively (Edwards forthcoming).

The use of ombrotrophic (rain-fed) peat bogs (mainly raised and blanket mires) for reconstructing climates has a long history (e.g., Lewis 1905, Sernander 1908, Walker and Walker 1961, Aaby 1976, Godwin 1981) and, after many decades of doubts, is enjoying a resurgence (Barber 1981, Wijmstra *et al.* 1984, Blackford 1993, 1998). Keith Barber and Pete Langdon describe how the accumulation of peat above the groundwater limit means that there is a fairly direct relationship between the mean water-table of the bog and precipitation. There is also a link between the mean water-table and the abundance of different species (especially *Sphagna*) on the bog surface, as well as the humification (decomposition) of the peat. Analyses of the peat allow the reconstruction of past surface wetness of the bog. Sample resolution can be of

the order of around 10 years cm^{-1} and bogs also yield multi-proxy records such as plant macrofossils, testate amoebae, pollen, non-pollen microfossils and isotope geochemistry. Of particular value from a climatic stance is the prominent indications of wetter and/or colder conditions during the time periods 4700–4500 cal BC, 3700–3500 cal BC, 3000–2600 cal BC, 2200–1500 cal BC, 800–500 cal BC, cal AD 500–700, cal AD 1350–1500, and the later part of the Little Ice Age, between cal AD 1650 and 1800. Some of these intervals are corroborated at other sites (Anderson *et al.* 1998) and by other indicators (e.g., Gear and Huntley 1991), but not all (Anderson 1998, Tipping 1999), and research is progressing on inter- and intra-site variability. These data relate to Britain, but comparisons with the Netherlands (Dupont 1986, Kilian *et al.* 1995) and Ireland (van Geel and Middeldorp 1988, Blackford and Chambers 1995), for instance, are possible. A challenge for archaeology is to assess its evidence in relation to such climate reconstructions – not in a deterministic sense, but in terms of the degree of relationship, if any, between respective data sets.

The contribution of Donald Davidson and Ian Simpson is devoted to soil micromorphology (Kubiena 1953, Brewer and Sleeman 1988) – a topic which has been embraced by archaeology (e.g., Courty *et al.* 1989, Canti 1998), though not without controversy (Carter and Davidson 1998, Macphail 1998). Microscopic-scale soil examination enables the investigator to study soil fabric in a way impossible to the field observer and in a more intimate fashion than routine physical or chemical analyses. On- and off-site studies typically permit inferences regarding land use practices such as slash-and-burn, up-rooting, ploughing, manuring, irrigation, horticultural practices and pasturing-herding. The validation of such inferences is clearly of importance to the process and traditional approaches based on comparison and analytical experience (e.g., manuring as indicated by charcoal fragments in old cultivated topsoils), with perhaps experimental control where undisturbed or 'natural' soils are available locally, are being supplemented by studies which have interpretational validation as their prime objective. These seek to apply rigour by making quantitative comparisons with a wide range of samples and reference materials. Key conclusions from the investigation of soils buried for 32 years beneath the Overton Down experimental earthworks (Crowther *et al.* 1996), are the rapidity and magnitude of soil change following burial and the importance of obtaining as many samples as possible from buried soils in order to include all local microenvironments. Studies of abandoned field systems may allow longer time periods to be investigated (Davidson and Carter 1998), but results are not always informative, other than to provide confirmation that tillage had occurred in soils known to have been cultivated! Exciting potential is shown by lipid biomarkers which have been used to identify grassy turf and human manure inputs to fossil early cultivated soils in Orkney (Simpson *et al.* 1998) as well as to distinguish between omnivorous and herbivorous manure sources, and between pig and human sources in anthropogenic soils, thereby validating and developing earlier interpretations of formation processes based *inter alia* on micromorphology (Simpson *et al.* 1999; covered more extensively in Chapter 28). Of considerable interest is the application of soil micromorphology to elucidate fundamental questions relating to soil pollen analysis. Davidson and Simpson report that biological activity is the most important factor in the incorporation and redistribution of pollen in a wide range of common upland British soil profiles and supporting some previous palynological findings (e.g., Havinga 1974, Andersen 1979, Aaby 1983). The depth of incorporation is especially determined by the depth of activity of earthworms, with the transporting of grains via their excrement. There is no evidence for significant downwashing of palynomorphs (*pace* Dimbleby 1985), even though the soils studied exhibited great contrasts in hydrological regime and degree of water-table fluctuation. In podzols, which are largely lacking in earthworms, pollen incorporation is limited to surface organic horizons by shallow bioturbation, which creates a mixed-age assemblage of indeterminate duration at the soil surface. Palynologists will await the full publication of this research with great interest. Of particular concern will be judgements regarding its general applicability and its significance for both shallow profiles (or samples from immediately beneath archaeological features) and deeper ones which appear to preserve a stratified palynological record.

Rebecca Nicholson reviews the complex issue of taphonomy – the investigation of the processes which act upon living entities after death and before fossilization. This is a massive topic involving the burial of (sub)fossils, perhaps after aeolian, aquatic or faunal/human transport, and the influence of physical and chemical processes at any stage between the formation of life and death assemblages. The importance of taphonomy has long been known to those working in Quaternary and archaeological science (e.g., Kenward 1978, Lowe 1982, Osborne 1983, Havinga 1984, Patterson *et al.* 1987, Brothwell 1990, Carter 1990, Bell *et al.* 1996, Gaudzinski 1998) and the topic is dis-

cussed implicitly at least by other papers in this section (i.e., those by Robinson, Yalden, Barber and Langdon, and Davidson and Simpson). Recovery procedures, sampling strategies and subsequent analysis all influence data availability, but ultimately there is still the need to interpret those data. Progress is likely to continue within constituent disciplines because it is from them that much of the demand for solutions and rigour will probably arise. A major strength of Quaternary science, however, is its multi- and frequent interdisciplinarity, and it would be surprising if well-conceived multidisciplinary projects were unable to produce major advances in our understanding of taphonomic processes at all levels from the molecular to the landscape scale.

If taphonomy is a 'massive topic', that of global biogeochemical cycles and isotope systematics is truly vast. Mark Pollard and Lyn Wilson set out to show 'how the world works', and in this endeavour they enlist the familiar overlapping subsystems of the global ecosystem, *viz.* the atmosphere, hydrosphere, lithosphere, and biosphere, together with an examination of the principal elements which control life on earth (mainly carbon, nitrogen, oxygen and hydrogen). Their account is not only a masterfully succinct revision course, but also manages to point out the applicability of such fundamental topics to the world of archaeological science. Sinks and sources, stable isotopes, palaeodiet, palaeotemperature, radiocarbon, photosynthesis and metabolic pathways rub shoulders with SMOWs, SLAPs and MRTs. Although global scale considerations of biogeochemical cycling may appear only distantly relevant to archaeological considerations, Pollard and Wilson maintain rightly that its principles can inform our understanding of the accumulation and deterioration of the archaeological record.

ADDITIONAL COMMENTS

Many fields pervade the conglomerate discipline of Quaternary science (e.g., Lowe and Walker 1997), of which dating and pollen analysis are perhaps the best examples. In this volume dating is a section in its own right, while pollen analysis in the service of anthropogenic history forms the subject of the paper by Dumayne-Peaty, and palynology is frequently mentioned in other contributions. In terms of the Earth sciences, there may justifiably have been major contributions on geomorphology, land-sea interactions, limnology, tephrochronology, ice-core and cave studies, while the life sciences could offer the study of molluscs, ostracods, foraminifera, diatoms, and broader scale considerations of biodiversity and bio-geographical conservation. However, space is limited, the muse is often weak, and a number of useful recent accounts are already in existence (e.g., Brown 1997, Bayley 1998, Andrews and Banham 1999, Shennan and Andrews 2000). It is asking far too much to expect those engaged in specific parts of Quaternary and archaeological science to be fully cognizant with all the approaches which constitute Quaternary environmental study. For the uninitiated, however, a general familiarity is unlikely to breed contempt and would probably reap valuable insights.

REFERENCES

Aaby, B. (1976). Cyclic climatic variation in climate over the last 5500 yr reflected in raised bogs. *Nature*, **263**:281–284.

Aaby, B. (1983). Forest development, soil genesis and human activity illustrated by pollen and hypha analysis of two neighbouring podzols in Draved forest, Denmark. *Danmarks geologiske Undersøgelse II*, **114**:1–114.

Andersen, S.Th. (1979). Brown earth and podzol: soil genesis illuminated by microfossil analysis. *Boreas*, **8**:59–73.

Anderson, D.E. (1998). A reconstruction of Holocene climatic changes from peat bogs in north-west Scotland. *Boreas*, **27**:208–224.

Anderson, D.E., Binney, H.A. and Smith, M.A. (1998). Evidence for abrupt climatic change in northern Scotland between 3900 and 3500 calendar years BP. *The Holocene*, **8**:97–103.

Andrews, P. and Banham, P. (eds) (1999). *Late Cenozoic Environments and Hominid Evolution: a Tribute to the Late Bill Bishop*. Geological Society: London.

Ashworth, A.C., Buckland, P.C. and Sadler, J.P. (eds) (1997). *Studies in Quaternary Entomology: an Inordinate Fondness for Insects*. Quaternary Proceedings No. 5, John Wiley: Chichester.

Atkinson, T.C., Briffa, K.R. and Coope, G.R. (1987). Seasonal temperatures in Britain during the past 22 000 years, reconstructed using beetle remains. *Nature*, **325**:587–592.

Barber, K.E. (1981). *Peat Stratigraphy and Climatic Change*. Balkema: Amsterdam.

Bayley, J. (ed.) (1998). *Science in Archaeology: an Agenda for the Future*. English Heritage: London.

Bell, M. and Walker, M.J.C. (1992). *Late Quaternary Environmental Change: Physical and Human Perspectives*. Longman: London.

Bell, M., Fowler, P.J. and Hillson, S.W. (1996). *The Experimental Earthwork Project 1960–1992*. Research Report 100, Council for British Archaeology: York.

Berglund, B.E. (ed.) (1986). *Handbook of Holocene Palaeoecology and Palaeohydrology*. John Wiley: Chichester.

Birks, H.J.B. and Birks, H.H. (1980). *Quaternary Palaeoecology*. Edward Arnold: London.

Blackford, J. (1993). Peat bogs as sources of proxy climatic data: past approaches and future research. In Chambers, F.M. (ed.) *Climate Change and Human Impact on the Landscape*, 47–56. Chapman and Hall: London.

Blackford, J.J. (1998). Holocene climatic variability in the North Atlantic Region as shown by peat bog records. *Fróðskaparrit*, **46**:155–162.

Blackford, J.J. and Chambers, F.M. (1995). Proxy climate record for the last 1000 years from Irish blanket peat and a possible link to solar variability. *Earth and Planetary Science Letters*, **133**:145–150.

Brewer, R. and Sleeman, J.R. (1988). *Soil Structure and Fabric*. CSIRO Publications: Melbourne.

Brooks, S.J. (1997). The response of Chironomidae (Insecta: Diptera) assemblages to Late-glacial climatic change in Kråkenes Lake, Western Norway. In Ashworth, A.C., Buckland, P.C. and Sadler, J.P. (eds) *Studies in Quaternary Entomology: an Inordinate Fondness for Insects*, 49–58. Quaternary Proceedings No. 5, John Wiley: Chichester.

Brooks, S.J., Mayle, F.E. and Lowe, J.J. (1997). Chironomid-based Lateglacial reconstruction for southeast Scotland. *Journal of Quaternary Science*, **12**:161–167.

Brothwell, D. (1990). Environmental and experimental studies in history. In Robinson, D.E. (ed.), *Experimentation and Reconstruction in Environmental Archaeology*, 1–24. Oxbow Books: Oxford.

Brown, A.G. (1997). *Alluvial Archaeology: Floodplain Archaeology and Environmental Change*. Cambridge University Press: Cambridge.

Buckland, P.C. and Dugmore, A.J. (1991). 'If this is a refugium, why are my feet so bloody cold?' The origins of the Icelandic biota in the light of recent research. In Maizels, J.K. and Caseldine, C.J. (eds) *Environmental Change in Iceland: Past and Present*, 107–125. Kluwer: Dordrecht.

Buckland, P.C. and Hammond P.M. (1997). The origins of the biota of the Falkland Islands and South Georgia. In Ashworth, A.C., Buckland, P.C. and Sadler, J.P. (eds) *Studies in Quaternary Entomology: an Inordinate Fondness for Insects*, 59–69. Quaternary Proceedings No. 5, John Wiley: Chichester.

Buckland, P.C., Sveinbjarnardóttir, G., Savory, D., McGovern, T.H., Skidmore, P. and Andreasen, C. (1983). Norsemen at Nipáitsoq, Greenland: a palaeoecological investigation. *Norwegian Archaeological Review*, **16**:86–98.

Buckland, P.C., Dugmore, A.J. and Edwards, K.J. (1997a). Bronze Age myths? Volcanic activity and human response in the Mediterranean and North Atlantic regions. *Antiquity*, **71**:581–593.

Buckland, P.C., Coope, G.R. and Sadler, J.P. (1997b). A bibliography of Quaternary entomology. In Ashworth, A.C., Buckland, P.C. and Sadler, J.P. (eds) *Studies in Quaternary Entomology: an Inordinate Fondness for Insects*, Diskette. Quaternary Proceedings No. 5, John Wiley: Chichester.

Buckland, P.C., Edwards, K.J. and Sadler, J.P. (1998). Early Holocene investigations at Saksunardalur and the origins of the Faroese biota. *Fróðskaparrit*, **46**:259–266.

Canti, M.G. (1998). The micromorphological identification of faecal spherulites from archaeological and modern materials. *Journal of Archaeological Science*, 25:435–444.

Carter, S.P. (1990). The stratification and taphonomy of shells in calcareous soils: implications for land snail analysis in archaeology. *Journal of Archaeological Science*, **17**:495–507.

Carter, S.P. and Davidson, D.A. (1998). An evaluation of the contribution of soil micromorphology to the study of ancient arable agriculture. *Geoarchaeology*, 13:535–547.

Chambers, F.M. (ed.) (1993). *Climate Change and Human Impact on the Landscape*. Chapman and Hall: London.

Coope, G.R. (1959). A Late Pleistocene insect fauna from Chelford, Cheshire. *Proceedings of the Royal Society of London*, **B151**:70–86.

Coope, G.R. and Lemdahl, G. (1995). Regional differences in the Lateglacial climate of northern Europe based on coleopteran analysis. *Journal of Quaternary Science*, **10**:391–395.

Coope, G.R., Morgan, A. and Osborne, P.J. (1971). Fossil Coleoptera as indicators of climatic fluctuations during the last glaciation in Britain. *Palaeogeography, Palaeoclimatology, Palaeoecology*, **10**:87–101.

Courty, M.A., Goldberg, P. and Macphail, R. (1989). *Soils and Micromorphology in Archaeology*. Cambridge University Press: Cambridge.

Crawford, R.M.M. (1999). The Arctic as a peripheral area. In Nordal, I. and Razzhivin, V.Y. (eds) *The Species Concept in the High North – a Panarctic Flora Initiative*, 131–153. Det Norske Videnskaps – Akademi I. Matematisk Naturvitenskapelig Klasse, Skrifter, Ny serie 38.

Crowther, J., Macphail, R.I. and Cruise, G.M. (1996). Short-term, post-burial change in a humic rendzina soil, Overton Down experimental earthwork, Wiltshire, England. *Geoarchaeology*, **11**:95–117.

Davidson, D.A. and Carter, S.P. (1998). Micromorphological evidence of past agricultural practices in cultivated soils: the impact of a traditional agricultural system on soils in Papa Stour, Shetland. *Journal of Archaeological Science*, 25:827–838.

Delcourt, H.R. and Delcourt, P.A. (1991). *Quaternary Ecology, a Paleoecological Perspective*. Chapman and Hall: London.

Dimbleby, G.W. (1985). *The Palynology of Archaeological Sites*. Academic Press: London.

Dinnin, M. (1997). Holocene beetle assemblages from the Lower Trent floodplain at Bole Ings, Nottinghamshire, UK. *Quaternary Proceedings*, 5:83–104.

Dinnin, M.H. and Sadler, J.P. (1999). 10 000 years of change: the Holocene entomofauna of the British Isles. In Edwards, K.J. and Sadler, J.P. (eds) *Holocene Environments of Prehistoric Britain*, 545–562. Quaternary Proceedings 7 (*Journal of Quaternary Science*, **14**(6)), John Wiley: Chichester.

Dupont, L.M. (1986). Temperature and rainfall variation in the late Holocene based on comparative palaeoecology and isotope geology of a hummock and a hollow (Bourtangerveen, The Netherlands). *Review of Palaeobotany and Palynology*, **48**:71–159.

Edwards, K.J. (1998). Detection of human impact on the natural environment: palynological views. In Bayley, J. (ed.) *Science in Archaeology: an Agenda for the Future*, 69–88. English Heritage: London.

Edwards, K.J. (forthcoming). Palaeoenvironments of Late Upper Palaeolithic and Mesolithic Scotland and the North Sea area: new work, new thoughts. In Saville, A. (ed.) *Mesolithic Scotland: the Early Holocene Prehistory of Scotland and its European Context*. Society of Antiquaries of Scotland: Edinburgh.

Edwards, K.J. and Ralston, I.B.M. (eds) (1997). *Scotland: Environment and Archaeology, 8000 BC–AD 1000*. John Wiley: Chichester.

Edwards, K.J. and Sadler, J.P. (eds) (1999). *Holocene Environments of Prehistoric Britain*. Quaternary Proceedings 7 (*Journal of Quaternary Science*, **14**(6)), John Wiley: Chichester.

Elias, S.A. (1994). *Quaternary Insects and their Environments*. Smithsonian Institution Press: Washington DC.

Gamble, C. (1993). *Timewalkers: the Prehistory of Global Colonization*. Alan Sutton: Stroud.

Gaudzinski, S. (1998). Large mammal hunting strategies in the Palaeolithic of Europe: a taphonomic approach. In Bayley, J. (ed.) *Science in Archaeology: an Agenda for the Future*, 47–62. English Heritage: London.

Gear, A.J. and Huntley, B. (1991). Rapid changes in the range limits of Scots pine 4000 years ago. *Science*, **251**:544–547.

Godwin, H. (1981). *The Archives of the Peat Bogs*. Cambridge University Press: Cambridge.

Hall, A.R., Kenward, H.K. and Williams, D. (1980). *Environmental Evidence from Roman Deposits in Skeldergate*. The Archaeology of York Fascicule 14/3, Council for British Archaeology: London.

Havinga, A.J. (1974). Problems in the interpretation of pollen diagrams from mineral soils. *Geologie en Mijnbouw*, **53**:449–453.

Havinga, A.J. (1984). A 20-year experimental investigation into the corrosion susceptibility of pollen and spores in various soil types. *Pollen et Spores*, **26**:541–558.

Huntley, B. (1999). Climatic change and reconstruction. In Edwards, K.J. and Sadler, J.P. (eds) *Holocene Environments of Prehistoric Britain*, 513–520. Quaternary Proceedings 7 (*Journal of Quaternary Science*, **14**(6)), John Wiley: Chichester.

Imbrie, J. and Imbrie, K.P. (1979). *Ice Ages: Solving the Mystery*. Macmillan: London.

Jones, R.L. and Keen, D.H. (1993). *Pleistocene Environments in the British Isles*. Chapman and Hall: London.

Kenward, H.K. (1978). *The Analysis of Archaeological Insect Assemblages: a New Approach*. Archaeology of York Fascicule 19/1, Council for British Archaeology: London.

Kenward, H.K. (1997). Synanthropic decomposer insects and the size, remoteness and longevity of archaeological occupation sites: applying concepts from biogeography to past 'islands' of human occupation. In Ashworth, A.C., Buckland, P.C. and Sadler, J.P. (eds) *Studies in Quaternary Entomology: an Inordinate Fondness for Insects*. Quaternary Proceedings No. 5, 135–151. John Wiley: Chichester.

Kilian, M.R., van der Plicht, J. and van Geel, B. (1995). Dating raised bogs: new aspects of AMS ^{14}C wiggle matching, a reservoir effect and climate change. *Quaternary Science Reviews*, **14**:959–966.

Kubiena, W.L. (1953). *The Soils of Europe*. Murphy: London:

Kutzbach, J.E. and Guetter, P.J. (1986). The influence of changing orbital parameters and surface boundary conditions on climatic simulations for the past 18 000 years. *Journal of the Atmospheric Sciences*, **43**:1726–1759.

Lewis, F.J. (1905). The plant remains in Scottish peat mosses. Part I. The Scottish Southern Uplands. *Transactions of the Royal Society of Edinburgh*, **41**:699–723.

Lowe, J.J. (1982). Three Flandrian pollen profiles from the Teith Valley, Perthshire, Scotland. II. Analysis of deteriorated pollen. *New Phytologist*, **90**:371–385.

Lowe, J.J. and Walker, M.J.C. (1997). *Reconstructing Quaternary Environments* (2nd edn). Addison Wesley Longman: London.

Macphail, R.I. (1998). A reply to Carter and Davidson's 'an evaluation of the contribution of soil micromorphology to the study of ancient agriculture'. *Geoarchaeology*, **13**:549–564.

O'Connor, T.P. (1991). Science, evidential archaeology and the new scholasticism. *Scottish Archaeological Review*, **8**:1–7.

Osborne, P.J. (1983). An insect fauna from a modern cesspit and its comparison with probable cesspit assemblages from archaeological sites. *Journal of Archaeological Science*, **10**:453–463.

Patterson, W.A. III, Edwards, K.J. and Maguire, D.J. (1987). Microscopic charcoal as a fossil indicator of fire. *Quaternary Science Reviews*, **6**:3–23.

Roberts, N. (1998). *The Holocene: an Environmental History*, (2nd edn). Blackwell: Oxford.

Sadler, J.P. and Jones, J.C. (1997). Chironomids as indicators of Holocene environmental change in the British Isles. In Ashworth, A.C., Buckland, P.C. and Sadler, J.P. (eds) *Studies in Quaternary Entomology: an Inordinate Fondness for Insects*, 219–232. Quaternary Proceedings No. 5, John Wiley: Chichester.

Schledermann, P. (1996). *Voices in Stone: a Personal Journey into the Arctic Past*. Komatik Series 5, Arctic Institute of North America, University of Calgary: Calgary.

Sernander, R. (1908). On the evidence of Post-glacial changes of climate furnished by the peat-mosses of Northern Europe. *Geologiska Föreningens i Stockholm Förhandlingar*, **30**:467–478.

Shennan, I. and Andrews, J. (eds) (2000). *Holocene Land-Ocean Interaction and Environmental Change Around the North Sea*. Special Publications 166, Geological Society: London.

Simmons, I.G. and Tooley, M.J. (eds) (1981). *The Environment in British Prehistory*. Duckworth: London.

Simpson, I.A., Dockrill, S.J., Bull, I.D. and Evershed, R.P. (1998). Early anthropogenic soil formation at Toft Ness, Sanday, Orkney. *Journal of Archaeological Science*, **25**:729–746.

Simpson, I.A., van Bergen, P.F., Perret, V., Elhmmali, M., Roberts, D.J. and Evershed, R.P. (1999). Lipid biomarkers of manuring practice in relict anthropogenic soils. *The Holocene*, **9**:223–229.

Skidmore, P. (1997). Zoogeographical notes on the muscid fauna of Greenland and the North Atlantic. In Ashworth, A.C., Buckland, P.C. and Sadler, J.P. (eds) *Studies in Quaternary Entomology: an Inordinate Fondness for Insects*, 245–253. Quaternary Proceedings No. 5, John Wiley: Chichester.

Taylor, K.C., Alley, R.B., Doyle, G.A., Grootes, P.M., Mayewski, P.A., Lamorey, G.W., White, J.W.C. and Barlow, L.K. (1993). The flickering switch of the Late Wisconsin climate change. *Nature*, **361**:432–436.

Tipping, R.M. (ed.) (1999). *The Quaternary of Dumfries and Galloway. Field guide*. Quaternary Research Association: London.

van Geel, B. and Middeldorp, A.A. (1988). Vegetational history of Carbury Bog (Co. Kildare, Ireland) during the last 850 years and a test of the temperature indicator value of ^{2}H/^{1}H measurements of peat samples in relation to historical sources and meteorological data. *New Phytologist*, **109**:377–392.

Wagner, P.E. (1997). Human impact or cooling climate? The 'Little Ice Age' and the beetle fauna of the British Isles. In Ashworth, A.C., Buckland, P.C. and Sadler, J.P. (eds) *Studies in Quaternary Entomology: an Inordinate Fondness for Insects*, 269–276. Quaternary Proceedings No. 5, John Wiley: Chichester.

Walker, D. and Walker, P.M. (1961). Stratigraphic evidence of regeneration in some Irish bogs. *Journal of Ecology*, **49**:169–185.

Walker, I.R. (1995). Chironomids as indicators of past environmental change. In Armitage, P.D., Cranston, P.S. and Pinder, L.C.V. (eds) *The Chironomidae: Biology and Ecology of Non-Biting Midges*, 405–422. Chapman and Hall: London.

Whitehouse, N.J. (1997). Insect faunas associated with *Pinus sylvestris* L. from the mid-Holocene of the Humberhead Levels, Yorkshire, U.K. In Ashworth, A.C., Buckland, P.C. and Sadler, J.P. (eds) *Studies in Quaternary Entomology: an Inordinate Fondness for Insects*, 293–303. Quaternary Proceedings No. 5, John Wiley: Chichester.

Whittington, G., Connell, R.E., Coope, G.R., Edwards, K.J., Hall, A.M., Hulme, P.D. and Jarvis, J. (1998). Devensian organic interstadial deposits and ice sheet extent in Buchan, Scotland. *Journal of Quaternary Science*, **13**:309–324.

Wijmstra, T.A., Hoekstra, S., De Vries, B.J. and van der Hammen, T. (1984). A preliminary study of periodicities in percentage curves dated by pollen density. *Acta Botanica Neerlandica*, **33**:547–555.

Williams, M.A.J., Dunkerley, D.L., de Dekker, P., Kershaw, A.P. and Stokes, T. (1993). *Quaternary Environments*. Edward Arnold: London.

Willis, K.J., Kleczkowski, A., Briggs, K.M. and Gilligan, C.A. (1999). The role of sub-Milankovitch climatic forcing in the initiation of the Northern Hemisphere glaciation. *Science*, **285**:568–571.

Wise, A.L. and Thorme, T. (1995). Global palaeoclimate modelling approaches: some considerations for archaeologists. In Huggett, J. and Ryan, N. (eds) *Computer Applications and Quantitative Methods in Archaeology*, 127–132. BAR International Series 600, British Archaeological Reports: Oxford.

Yalden, D. (1999). *The History of British Mammals*. Poyser: London.

9

Modelling Quaternary Environments

A. WISE

JISC, King's College London.

The Quaternary – the last two million years of Earth's history – is of special interest to archaeologists because it is during this time that the expansion of *Homo* took place. The challenges humans faced on their journeys were many, and adapting to a wide variety of environments was by no means the least of these. For this reason the Quaternary environment has been the focus of much research from a number of theoretical perspectives and with a wide array of methods.

It is not only archaeologists and other scientists who are interested in the Quaternary environment. International interest has been focused on past environments generally because of the story they tell about Earth's ecosystem responses to change (Adams and Woodward 1992). The prospect of dramatic environmental change in our own time, spurred on by anthropogenic greenhouse gases (see Chapter 16), means that information from the past is needed in order to plan for the future. A change in environment, depending on its magnitude and rapidity, could have significant effects. Human reactions to such changes in the past, known through archaeology and related disciplines, can inform predictions of human response to future global change. There are a variety of sources of evidence about the Quaternary environment (Chapter 1; see also Lowe and Walker 1997). Fluctuating lake levels, depositional sequences in glaciers and sediment, and tree ring growth are some of the ways the Earth records information about its environmental history.

WHEN EVIDENCE ISN'T ENOUGH

Palaeoenvironmental evidence is often difficult to collect, involving a spectrum of disciplines. It is also a confusing body of evidence to interpret and synthesize. The ultimate cause of the changes recorded in bodies of environmental evidence is rarely obvious, though the proximal causes sometimes are. Tree ring growth, for example, is affected by the temperature and precipitation in any given year. The cause of these temperature and precipitation fluctuations, however, is not recorded in the tree ring evidence, and it is this ultimate cause of change that is most useful in understanding past environments and environmental change. Confusingly, the proximal causes of change suggested by various sources of evidence may point to varying ultimate causes. For example, how are we to interpret a region in which tree rings suggest high precipitation for 10 years but evidence from lakes suggests that water levels were falling and that it therefore may have been drier?

In general, it is difficult to relate palaeoenvironmental change to its ultimate causes because of the following factors:

(i) feedback between parts of the environmental system,
(ii) lag times in response obscure cause and effect relations,

(iii) spatial and temporal discontinuity of the palaeoenvironmental record,

(iv) difficulty in obtaining absolute dates, and

(v) variability in the ultimate causes of environmental change.

Environmental scientists often need an independent way of testing different explanatory hypotheses to understand the complex system behind environmental evidence. This is where modelling comes in.

MODELS; THEIR USES AND LIMITATIONS

In science a model is usually a simplified representation that allows better understanding of something complex in the natural world. Some of the earliest scientific models were physical. For example, little models of the solar system were built by early astronomers trying to understand the way planets move in relationship to each other. These kinds of physical models are still used, but more abstract kinds of models are now also available.

Analogy is the process of arguing from similarity in some traits to similarity in other traits. Archaeologists use analogy, sometimes indiscriminately or unwisely (Ascher 1961) to construct explanatory models. The use of ethnographic analogy, or making arguments about the way people lived in the past based on ethnographic observation of people from different cultures in the present, is particularly widespread in American archaeology as it is closely allied with anthropology. A relatively new kind of analogy has appeared recently in the archaeological literature and is based on the adaptation of ideas drawn from phenomenology. Here experiences obtained by interacting with ancient monuments in the present are used to argue by analogy for the way people may have interacted with these monuments in the past (Tilley 1994).

Some models shape the questions we ask in archaeology and how we attempt to answer them. For example, French historians of the *Annales* school suggested that rural social history is structured in the short, medium, and long term. Relatively long-term structures, for example the ecology of a region, are thought to affect medium and short-term human relations and therefore multi-temporal and multi-scalar regional analyses are advocated as the best ways of understanding social history. This has been successfully tested and adopted by some archaeologists (Crumley and Marquardt 1987, Bintliff 1991).

Another main class of model, used in both archaeology and environmental sciences, is numerical modelling (see Chapter 58). There is a range of types of numerical models including deterministic models for which inputs and outputs are rigidly controlled, stochastic models in which probability is factored, dynamic models that accommodate change through time, and a variety of multivariate models. Stochastic and multivariate models are probably the most familiar to archaeologists as many of our most cherished statistical techniques (e.g., linear regression, variance analysis, multiple regression) are included in these categories.

Economic models are also frequently used in archaeology, and the precise kinds of economies being modelled range widely. Ways of modelling human economic behaviour in our late twentieth century global capitalist economy (e.g., supply and demand) are not appropriate for many populations studied through the archaeological record and for this reason other models have been developed. For example, economic models such as optimal foraging are frequently used to assist archaeologists studying those who live by hunting, gathering, and fishing (Winterhalder and Smith 1981). Population modelling has been with us since the late eighteenth century (Chapman 1988) and underpins much discussion of past economies as do models of kinship and socio-political organization drawn from anthropology (Clarke 1972).

What all models have in common is the ability to simplify some aspect or aspects of the complex world allowing study of dynamic systems or other things that cannot be effectively reproduced in a lab, experimented upon, or studied in the field. Models are often used to decrease the time scale required to observe complex interactions in nature, and thus make such systems more appreciable by, and accessible to, human study. Models are also used to facilitate the integration and testing of a variety of data and may be useful at any stage of research; and intuition, experimentation and theory all have their roles. Models change from *a priori* to *a posteriori* types as the modelling process moves from enabling depiction of complex data to ordering them and then to explaining them (Hardisty *et al.* 1993). Creating models can thus be useful in moving projects through the process of researching minutiae and detail, and then on to the creation of broader explanatory frameworks.

CLIMATE MODELS – A UNIFYING BACKDROP FOR STUDYING THE QUATERNARY ENVIRONMENT?

Climate models can help us answer questions about the ultimate causes of environmental change as well as its seasonality, pace, and scale. This is because climate itself results from interactions in the atmosphere, biosphere, cryosphere, and oceans; and solar radiation is the primary source of energy input for this system. For this reason climate models provide a unifying backdrop for studying the Quaternary environment (Wise and Thorme 1995).

We know some of the reasons that climate changes (see Chapter 1). There are regular changes in the Earth's orbit called Milankovitch cycles which affect the seasonal and spatial distribution of solar radiation. The Earth's orbit is slightly eccentric rather than purely elliptical and changes approximately every 105 000 years; the tilt of Earth's axis changes approximately every 41 000 years, and the time of the equinoxes changes approximately every 21 000 years (Wright 1993). Solar radiation is the main external source of energy input to Earth's environmental system. It interacts with a variety of internal mechanisms and feedback loops on Earth to produce our climate. Examples of some of these internal mechanisms and feedback loops include the melting of glaciers and polar ice caps, the introduction of aerosols into the atmosphere as the result of dust storms or volcanic eruptions, the introduction of sulfate and carbon to the atmosphere from slash and burn agriculture. Although the relative importance of volcanic controls and astronomical controls on incoming solar radiation is debated in climatology, researchers agree that both play important roles and act at different time scales (see Crowley and North 1991:102).

Variations in the Earth's orbit and properties of land, atmosphere, oceans, ice sheets, and biota affect how and where incoming solar energy is absorbed or reflected. Gases and particles in the atmosphere may reflect solar energy back to space or prevent heat escaping from Earth's surface to space. The reflectivity of the ground surface, or albedo, changes with land cover. For example, snow reflects much more energy to space than green forest canopies. The different thermal properties of oceans and continents result in different parts of the climate system reacting to changes in forcing variables at different time scales.

There are two types of climate models in widespread use. The first are General Circulation Models (GCMs) and the second are Energy Budget Models (EBMs).

GENERAL CIRCULATION MODELS

These complex, global-scale, three-dimensional dynamic numerical models are based on physical principles like the law of thermodynamics. GCMs represent change in Earth's atmosphere and oceans in order to model large-scale climate systems including precipitation, temperature, wind circulation, and pressure on a scale of minutes or hours over time periods ranging from a few years to hundreds of years (Kutzbach 1985).

The various components of the climate system can be either initially specified or calculated during the model run. The effect and importance of the various forcing variables are monitored for each model. For example, using variable soil moisture values (where the calculations from Time 1 in the model produce the values for Time 2) rather than prescribed soil moisture allows more accurate modelling of past climates by enabling calculation of evaporation rates which influence Earth's hydrology, temperature and circulation (Gallimore and Kutzbach 1989:177).

Calculating many variables makes the GCM more realistic, but also makes it more complicated to construct and expensive to run. A great deal of effort has been expended to link coupled atmospheric and oceanic GCMs with global models of surface variables such as biome distribution or soils (Foley 1994). Coupled GCMs were already so computer intensive, however, that these newer versions push the limits of available computing technology.

GCMs are especially useful in conjunction with palaeoenvironmental studies of times in the recent past with relatively accurate time control, especially the Pleistocene and Holocene. Discrepancies between simulations and field data can point to areas of weakness in the models, so systematic comparison of model output with field observations is extremely useful for fine-tuning models. GCM simulations of past global climates can be tested against the archaeological, geological, palaeobotanical, palaeozoological, and other records (COHMAP 1988, Huntley 1999, Huntley et al. 1995, Kalkstein 1991, Wright et al. 1993).

What this testing tells us is that the accuracy of model output varies by region and variable. For example, there is good correlation between palaeolake-level evidence and GCM runs for the last 18 000 years in Africa (Street-Perrott and Perrott 1993) though precipitation is the least accurately modelled component of climate in GCMs. The models seem to work best in the northern hemisphere, especially in the area of the North Atlantic. This is partly due to the greater concentration of land mass in the northern hemisphere, the greater amount of research which has been done on northern high latitude areas, and the better quality and quantity of input records (e.g., sea ice).

GCMs are not commercially available, and instead are produced through national research and development programmes. Access to GCM output is often free to academic researchers. A good source of information about available data is the Intergovernmental Panel on Climate Change (IPCC) GCM Archive Gateway available online at http://ipcc-ddc.cru.uea.ac.uk. Also helpful are the Natural Environment Research Council's data centres, especially the British Atmospheric Data Centre and the British Oceanic Data Centre. See http://www.nerc.ac.uk/environmental-data/data/directory.htm for more information.

A clearer sense of GCMs can be obtained by considering one in detail, for example the HadCM3 (see http://www.meto.govt.uk/sec5/sec5pg1.html for more information). This is a coupled atmosphere-ocean GCM developed at the Hadley Centre in Britain and funded by the Meteorological Office (Gordon *et al.* 2000). The atmospheric component of the model has 19 levels with a horizontal resolution of 2.5° latitude by 3.75° longitude. The oceanic component of the model has 20 levels with a horizontal resolution of 1.25×1.25 degrees. The model is initialized from ocean observations (Levitus and Boyer 1994) with appropriate atmospheric and sea ice states. The atmosphere and ocean exchange information once per model-day. The effects of minor greenhouse gases, CO_2, water vapour, ozone, and background aerosols are represented. Modelled

processes include the freezing and melting of soil moisture, surface runoff and soil drainage, evaporation, snow depth, and vegetation type.

Outputs from GCMs are large numeric files, but the data in these files are generally displayed through a variety of graphics packages. There is therefore no standard look or feel to GCM outputs. For example, GCM data might be displayed as maps showing different sized arrows to represent direction and strength of atmospheric and oceanic flows, or might be displayed as animated videos.

Finer spatial resolution is offered by Regional Circulation Models (Giorgi *et al.* 1993), which combine the physics of climate modelling with the detailed dynamics of weather forecasting. One application simulates the late glacial climate of the south-western United States and demonstrates the contribution of both large-scale and local-scale climate features (Hostetler *et al.* 1994). The horizontal resolution in this model is 60 km which is extremely promising.

ENERGY BUDGET MODELS

EBMs are easy to use, inexpensive numerical models based on the laws of mass and energy conservation. They require some knowledge of climatology, mathematics, and physics to construct. These models

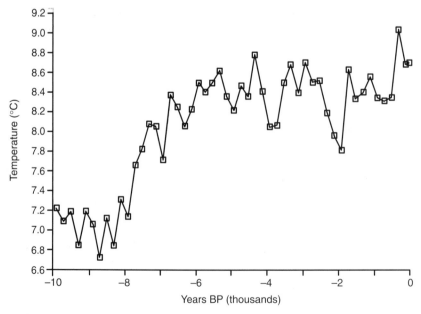

Figure 9.1 Sample EBM output as graphical display, showing average annual temperature over the last 10 000 years at the site of Trimontium (Roman Newstead, southern Scotland, UK; Wise 2000).

calculate the temperature characteristics of the Earth's atmosphere from information about the amount of incoming solar radiation reaching the Earth (Crowley and North 1991:7).

Zero-dimensional EBMs are the most simple models because they do not resolve differences at varying latitudes and longitudes and are based only on the assumption that on Earth there is a balance between incoming absorbed solar radiation and outgoing terrestrial radiation. One-dimensional EBMs are based on the additional piece of knowledge that the Earth receives more solar radiation at low latitudes than it does near the poles. As a result excess heat flows from equatorial regions to higher latitudes via the atmosphere and the ocean. Two-dimensional EBMs take geography and seasonal radiation changes into account for a more accurate depiction of global circulation patterns. Experiments run with two dimensional EBMs yielded temperature results which measure up to those given by GCMs (Hyde *et al.* 1989).

One archaeological example of the application of an EBM is in the macrophysical model developed by Reid Bryson (Bryson 1984). The structure of this model is a combination of the physics underlying global atmospheric circulation patterns and modern site-specific weather information such as rainfall, surface temperature, and wind direction/speed. The amount of solar radiation reaching the Earth provides the foundation of this model, as is the case with all GCMs and EBMs, but the macrophysical model also takes account of volcanic aerosol modulation of incoming radiation for the last 30 000 years. Output of the model can be displayed mathematically or graphically (see Figure 9.1 for an example of EBM graphical output).

CASE STUDY

Both descriptions and explanations of the early Holocene archaeology of North Africa are closely entwined with climate change. This is not unexpected given the restrictive climate and relatively harsh environment that people living there face today. Much work has been done on the palaeoenvironments, palaeoclimatology, and archaeology of North Africa making it a useful region in which to explore the archaeological/environmental modelling interface.

North Africa today is dominated by the Sahara desert where virtually no rain falls, but 9000 years ago it was very different with conditions wetter than present. Large lakes spread across the North African landscape (Hastenrath and Kutzbach 1983, Street-Perrott and Perrott 1993). Rivers carried water through the southern Sahara into the Nile River (Pachur and Kropelin 1987). Changes in flow carved the Nile valley into a deep, uninhabitable channel (Close and Wendorf 1992, Stanley and Warne 1993). Most strikingly, the Sahara seems to have been much more widely covered by grasslands at the time (Neumann and Schulz 1987, Petit-Maire *et al.* 1991, Ritchie and Haynes 1987) and palaeozoological and botanical evidence indicate the now-barren landscape once sustained diverse life (Gautier 1987, Hassan 1986).

At the end of the Last Glacial Maximum, the area now covered by the Sahara desert supported no human life (Close and Wendorf 1992) and the Nile valley in northern Egypt was not hospitable for living creatures as its channel was deep and floodplain limited. Archaeological evidence shows settlement concentrations in the Nile valley of southern Egypt and areas further south. Subsistence activities focused on fishing, hunting, and gathering (Close and Wendorf 1992, Gautier 1987). By 9500 BP archaeological evidence suggests renewed occupation of the Saharan region (Close and Wendorf 1992). People in what is now the central Sahara hunted hare, porcupine, hedgehog, birds, wild sheep, gazelle, and possibly wild cattle. They caught fish in the lakes which then dotted the southern Saharan landscape, gathered wild plants and processed them on grinding stones, utilized blade technologies, and decorated their pottery with a dotted wavy line pattern (Barich 1987). Gaps in occupation occurred at many sites (variably dated, but generally falling between 8500 and 6000 BP) and then people re-occupied the Sahara. In the intervening period their subsistence behaviours seem to have changed from fishing/hunting/gathering to cattle pastoralism. The earliest actual evidence for domesticated cattle comes from the site of Bir Kiseiba in southeast Egypt (Close and Wendorf 1992). This is deduced not from skeletal evidence, as domesticated status is morphologically unclear, but the ecological context of faunal remains. In archaeological assemblages large quantities of small animals and small quantities of cattle have been found. No middle-sized or other large animals have been found, suggesting that the environment could not support cattle-sized creatures without human intervention. There is some evidence for cultivation and perhaps a trend toward domestication of sorghum and millet by around 8500 BP from the Egyptian site of Nabta Playa (Close and Wendorf 1992, Wendorf *et al.* 1992). No archaeological evidence for a full agricultural economy has been found prior to the introduction of Near Eastern domesticates (wheat and barley) around 6000 BP.

The current consensus on the early North African adoption of cattle domestication is that it had something to do with climate change. Some suggest that pastoralism was an adaptation of hunter/gatherers across North Africa to climatic deterioration in the mid-Holocene (Barich 1987). Others agree that pastoralism developed across North Africa at approximately the same time, but argue this occurred during the wet early Holocene. During the following arid phase, places like Dahkla Oasis are thought to have become cultural centres from which pastoralism was transmitted to people living in the Nile Valley. A third suggestion is that cattle were domesticated during the early Holocene re-settlement of the Sahara in the face of precarious environments. The cattle provided a reliable source of protein in the form of their milk and blood (Close and

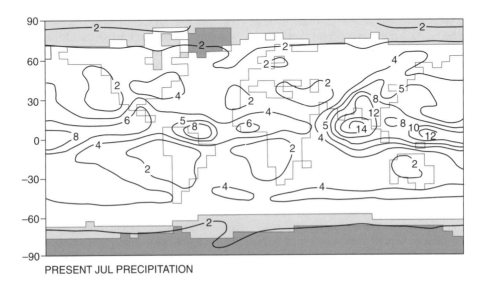

PRESENT JUL PRECIPITATION

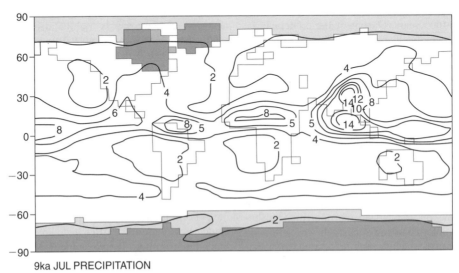

9ka JUL PRECIPITATION

Figure 9.2 GCM output showing modern precipitation and model runs for 9000 years BP. Note the change in precipitation in North Africa with almost no precipitation recorded currently, and a monthly average of 8 mm per day 9000 years ago (after Kutzbach *et al.* 1993:fig. 4.11).

Wendorf 1992). Another proposed scenario is one of mutualism in which wet conditions during the early Holocene led to a northward spread of Sahel-type grasslands after which the climate began to decline and water became scarce forcing human, animal, and plant populations to cluster around remaining bodies of water. Here close proximity instigated the long process of cultivation and selection which subsequently ended in domestication. Climate plays an important role in all of these domestication theories, but they often conflict with one another about the direction of climate change and its importance for human populations.

Reconstructing the palaeoclimate and palaeoenvironment of North Africa is difficult because of a scarcity of absolute dates, the challenges of doing fieldwork in the Sahara, and the necessity of collating evidence collected at a variety of spatial and temporal scales. Differential preservation of organic remains means that much more information is available for places like the Nile Valley than for the central Sahara. Climate models can be useful in untangling such a situation.

GCMs cannot give us detailed, site-specific information. We are unable to use them to reconstruct the early to mid-Holocene climates of Bir Kiseiba, Nabta Playa, or Dahkla Oasis. They can, however, provide insight into the regional climatic patterns that were prominent in the past and can offer helpful insights into the seasonality, magnitude, and tempo of past climate changes. GCMs show that the main difference between modern and early Holocene solar radiation rests with the date the Earth is closest to the sun, although obliquity of Earth's axis and the eccentricity of its orbit were also different (Kutzbach 1981). Currently the Earth is closest to the sun in the northern hemisphere winter. Nine thousand years ago the Earth was closest to the sun in northern hemisphere summer resulting in 7 per cent more solar radiation reaching the Earth in boreal summer and 7 per cent less solar radiation reaching the Earth in boreal winter, although the yearly average was about the same as it is today.

In North Africa the major climatic control, today and 9000 years ago, is differential heating of the continental land mass and the Atlantic and Indian oceans. The oceans have a greater thermal capacity than land, and sea surface temperatures respond more conservatively to changes in incoming radiation than do land surface temperatures. In winter the land quickly loses heat while oceans remain relatively warm. In summer, the land heats relatively quickly while the oceans remain relatively cool. These differences in response

underlie the timing and distribution of monsoonal rains. GCM runs suggest that in Africa 9000 years ago there was greater precipitation in summer as the monsoonal rain belt moved northwards, and cooler conditions due to increased cloudiness (Kutzbach et al. 1996). GCMs tell us that a large portion of North Africa probably experienced improved climates at the same time (roughly 12 000 – 6000 BP) and for the same global reasons (orbital geometry changes). EBMs confirm GCM simulations. For example, an energy budget experiment by Hastenrath and Kutzbach (1983) supports the idea that lake level changes in Africa were the result of precipitation differences in the past, and not primarily temperature-related evaporation differences.

The advance of people into the eastern Sahara took place c. 9500 BP (Close and Wendorf 1992). GCMs suggest this was a warm wet period (see Figure 9.2) which contradicts the idea that cattle pastoralism was a response by humans to increasing aridification or other climatic deterioration. It is possible that pastoralism spread northwards in Africa with the monsoonal rain belt, however current evidence suggests that pastoral sites farther south post-date those to the north (Close and Wendorf 1992). Overall, GCMs support the idea that cattle domestication occurred either during the warm wet early Holocene (perhaps as a result of cultural interaction between North Africa and the Near East) or during the subsequent arid phase as water became scarce and human, animal, and plant populations clustered around bodies of water.

IMPORTANT CONSIDERATIONS AND FUTURE DIRECTIONS

Given the complex changes to incoming solar radiation experienced by Earth, it is not surprising that aspects of the environmental system react in different ways and at different speeds and that interpreting palaeoenvironmental evidence can be difficult. Models are very useful for helping us to understand this complexity. For archaeologists interested in human behaviour, the detail of daily or seasonal weather regimes in the past might be more informative than long term climatic trends. Current models provide information only about these longer trends. The good news is that these trends can help archaeologists understand the long-term environmental variation people contended with in the past.

Though the causes of climate change proceed both gradually (e.g., the Milankovitch cycles) and suddenly (e.g., volcanic eruptions emitting gas and particles into the atmosphere), the climate itself often changes very quickly. For example, the change between glacial and interglacial periods appears to take place in only a few thousand years and may represent the resolution of gradually building stresses in the climate system. A quick short-lived climate change, for example two or three years of flood or drought, could have had serious consequences for individuals. It is these rapid changes that are most difficult to learn about with General Circulation or Energy Budget Models as it is too expensive to run model experiments at fine enough time resolution. Some sense of the range of variance and the frequency and magnitude of extremes can however be obtained.

Scale is important in determining how useful GCMs can be to archaeologists. GCMs are not useful for determining what the climate was like at a particular spot on the ground in a particular century in the past because their output is difficult to relate precisely to points on the ground. GCMs will not replace detailed pollen core, palaeolake level reconstruction, and other proxies for specific archaeological locales. Rather, GCMs can provide information about past climates in areas lacking proxy data and can clarify some of the major reasons why climates changed in the past. GCMs also provide information on the seasonality and magnitude of past climate states, changes from winter to summer precipitation regimes for example. GCMs and other palaeoenvironmental models can provide a 'reality check' for the consistency of assertions made about affects of climate change upon human populations.

Archaeologists need to articulate their requirements for finer time and scalar resolution in paleoenvironmental models. Finer scalar resolution may require a new breed of modelling. Options include meso-scale models, coupling of GCMs and EBMs, or the discovery of new statistical relationships between climate patterns and the weather. In future, interpretation of these complicated models will be aided by increased application of visualization and virtual reality.

It is also important that archaeologists do not accept palaeoclimatic reconstructions at face value, and it may be desirable for more archaeologists to undertake modelling themselves. Archaeologists interested in using models of the environment will, however, need to embrace more post-processual ideas and theories (Lock 1995, McGlade 1995). Human groups have a wide range of behavioural strategies, and socio-cultural relationships such as kinship and political organization on which to rely, so our responses to climate change are probably more complex than conceived in other scientific disciplines. Environment does not determine human behaviour now, nor did it in the past, and this message is one that archaeologists are well-placed to contribute to international palaeoclimate modelling.

ACKNOWLEDGEMENTS

Research that contributed to this paper was undertaken while the author was a fellow in the Climate, People and Environment Program at the University of Wisconsin's Climatic Research Center. Discussions with Reid Bryson, Jon Foley, John Kutzbach, and Trisha Thorme were particularly interesting and formative. Thanks are also due to Ian Barnes, Don Brothwell, Carole Crumley, Joel Gunn, Mark Pollard, and Bruce Winterhalder for reading and commenting on drafts of this paper.

REFERENCES

*Recommended for further reading

Adams, J.M. and Woodward, F.I. (1992). The past as a key to the future: the use of palaeoenvironmental understanding to predict the effects of man on the biosphere. *Advances in Ecological Research*, **22**:257–314.

Ascher, R. (1961). Analogy in archaeological interpretation. *Southwestern Journal of Anthropology*, **17**:317–325.

Barich, B.E. (1987). *Archaeology and Environment in the Libyan Sahara: the Excavations in the Tadrart Acacus, 1978–1983*. BAR International Series 368, British Archaeological Reports: Oxford.

Bintliff, J. (ed.) (1991). *The Annales School and Archaeology*. Leicester University Press: Leicester.

Bryson, R.A. (1984). Late Quaternary volcanic modulation of Milankovitch climate forcing. *Theoretical and Applied Climatology*, **39**:115–125.

Chapman, J. (1988). Putting pressures on populations: social alternatives to Malthus and Boserup. In Bintliff, J., Davidson, D.A. and Grant, E.G. (eds) *Conceptual Issues in Environmental Archaeology*, 291–310. Edinburgh University Press: Edinburgh.

Clarke, D.L. (ed.) (1972). *Models in Archaeology*. Methuen: London.

*Close, A.E. and Wendorf, F. (1992). The beginnings of food production in the Eastern Sahara. In Gebauer, A.B. and Price, T.D. (eds) *Transitions to Agriculture in Prehistory*, 63–72. Prehistory Press: Madison, Wisconsin.

COHMAP (1988). Climatic changes of the last 18 000 years: observations and model simulations. *Science*, **241**:1043–1052.

Crowley, T.J. and North, G.R. (1991). *Paleoclimatology*. Oxford University Press: New York.

Crumley, C. and Marquardt, W.A. (eds) (1987). *Regional Dynamics: Burgundian Landscapes in Historical Perspective*. Academic Press: San Diego.

Foley, J.A. (1994). The sensitivity of the terrestrial biosphere to climate change: a simulation of the mid-Holocene. *Global Biogeochemical Cycles*, **8**:405–425.

Gallimore, R.G. and Kutzbach, J.E. (1989). Effects of soil moisture on the sensitivity of a climate model to Earth orbital forcing at 9000 yr BP. *Climatic Change*, **14**:175–205.

Gautier, A. (1987). Fishing, fowling and hunting in Late Paleolithic times in the Nile Valley in Upper Egypt. *Palaeoecology of Africa*, **18**:429–440.

Giorgi, F., Bates, G.T. and Nieman, S.J. (1993). The multiyear surface climatology of a regional atmospheric model over the western United States. *Journal of Climate*, **10**:75–95.

Gordon, C., Cooper, C., Senior, C.A., Banks, H., Gregory, J.M., Johns, T.C., Mitchell, J.F.B. and Wood, R.A. (2000). The simulation of SST, sea ice extents and ocean heat transports in a version of the Hadley Centre coupled model without flux adjustments. *Climate Dynamics*, **16**:147–168.

Hardisty, J., Taylor, D.M. and Metcalfe, S.E. (1993). *Computerised Environmental Modelling: A Practical Introduction*. John Wiley: Chichester.

Hassan, F.A. (1986). Desert environment and origins of agriculture in Egypt. *Norwegian Archaeological Review*, **19**:63–76.

Hastenrath, S. and Kutzbach, J.E. (1983). Paleoclimatic estimates from water and energy budgets of East African lakes. *Quaternary Research*, **19**:141–153.

Hostetler, S.W., Giorgi, F., Bates, G.T. and Bartlein, P.J. (1994). Lake-atmospheric feedbacks associated with paleolakes Bonneville and Lahontan. *Science*, **263**:665–668.

Huntley, B. (1999). Climatic change and reconstruction. *Journal of Quaternary Science*, **14**:513-520.

Huntley, B., Berry, P.M., Cramer, W. and McDonald, A.P. (1995). Modelling present and potential future ranges of some European higher plants using climate response surfaces. *Journal of Biogeography*, **22**:967–1001.

Hyde, W.T., Crowley, T.J., Kim, K. and North, G.R. (1989). Comparison of GCM and Energy Balance Model simulations of seasonal temperature changes over the past 18 000 years. *Journal of Climate*, **2**:864–887.

Kalkstein, L.S. (ed.) (1991). *Global Comparisons of Selected GCM Control Runs and Observed Climate Data*. Report prepared for the United States Environmental Protection Agency, Washington DC.

Kutzbach, J.E. (1981). Monsoon climate of the early Holocene – climate experiment with the Earth's orbital parameters for 9000 years ago. *Science*, **214**:59–61.

Kutzbach, J.E. (1985). Modeling of paleoclimates. *Advances in Geophysics*, **28A**:159–196.

Kutzbach, J.E., Guetter, P.J., Behling, P.J. and Selin, R. (1993). Simulated climatic changes: results of the COHMAP climate-model experiments. In Wright, H.E., Kutzbach, J.E., Webb, T., Ruddiman, W.F., Street-Perrott, F.A. and Bartlein, P.J. (eds) *Global Climates Since the Last Glacial Maximum*, 24–93. University of Minnesota Press: Minneapolis.

Kutzbach, J.E., Bonan, G., Foley, J. and Harrison, S.P. (1996). Vegetation and soil feedbacks on the response of the African monsoon to orbital forcing in the early to middle Holocene. *Nature*, **384**:623–626.

Levitus, S. and Boyer, T.P. (1994). *World Ocean Atlas 1994, Volume 4: Temperature*. NOAA/NESDIS E/OC21, US Department of Commerce: Washington DC.

Lock, G. (1995). Archaeological computing, archaeological theory and moves toward contextualism. In Huggett, J. and Ryan, N. (eds) *Computer Applications and Quantitative Methods in Archaeology*, 13–18. BAR International Series 600, British Archaeological Reports: Oxford.

Lowe, J.J. and Walker, M.J.C. (1997). *Reconstructing Quaternary Environments*, (2nd edn). John Wiley: New York.

McGlade, J. (1995). Archaeology and the ecodynamics of human-modified landscapes. *Antiquity*, **69**:113–132.

Neumann, K. and Schulz, E. (1987). Middle Holocene savanna vegetation in the Central Sahara – a preliminary report. *Palaeoecology of Africa*, **18**:163–166.

Pachur, H.J. and Kropelin, S. (1987). Wadi Howar: paleoclimatic evidence from an extinct river system in the southeastern Sahara. *Science*, **237**:298–300.

Petit-Maire, N., Fontugne, M. and Rouland, C. (1991). Atmospheric methane ratio and environmental changes in the Sahara and Sahel during the last 130 kyrs. *Palaeogeography, Palaeoclimatology, Palaeoecology*, **86**:197–204.

Ritchie, J.C. and Haynes, C.V. (1987). Holocene vegetation zonation in the eastern Sahara. *Nature*, **330**:645–647.

Stanley, D.J. and Warne, A.G. (1993). Sea level and initiation of Predynastic culture in the Nile Delta. *Nature*, **363**:435–438.

*Street-Perrott, F.A. and Perrott, R.A. (1993). Holocene vegetation, lake levels, and climate of Africa. In Wright, H.E., Kutzbach, J.E., Webb, T., Ruddiman, W.F., Street-Perrott, F.A. and Bartlein, P.J. (eds) *Climatic Changes During the Past 18 000 Years: Regional Syntheses, Mechanisms and Causes*, 318–356. University of Minnesota Press: Minneapolis.

Tilley, C. (1994). *A Phenomenology of Landscape: Places, Paths and Monuments*. Berg Press: Oxford.

Wendorf, F., Close, A.E., Schild, R., Wasylikowa, K. Housley, R.A., Harlan, J.R. and Krolik, H. (1992). Saharan exploitation of plants 8000 years BP. *Nature*, **359**:721–724.

Winterhalder, B. and Smith, E.A. (1981). *Hunter-Gatherer Foraging Strategies: Ethnographic and Archeological Analyses*. University of Chicago Press: Chicago.

Wise, A.L. (2000). *Late Prehistoric Settlement and Society in Southeastern Scotland*. Unpublished Doctoral Dissertation, University of North Carolina – Chapel Hill.

Wise, A.L. and Thorme, T. (1995). Global palaeoclimate modelling approaches: some considerations for archaeologists. In Huggett, J. and Ryan, N. (eds) *Computer Applications and Quantitative Methods in Archaeology*, 127–132. BAR International Series 600, British Archaeological Reports: Oxford.

Wright, H.E. (1993). Environmental determinism in Near Eastern prehistory. *Current Anthropology*, **34**:458–469.

*Wright, H.E., Kutzbach, J.E., Webb, T., Ruddiman, W.F., Street-Perrott, F.A. and Bartlein, P.J. (1993). *Global Climates Since the Last Glacial Maximum*. University of Minnesota Press: Minneapolis.

10

Insects as Palaeoenvironmental Indicators

M. ROBINSON

Oxford University Museum of Natural History.

Insects occur in a very wide range of terrestrial and freshwater aquatic habitats. Although there are few fully marine species, there are many from brackish and strand-line habitats. Insect species feed on a wide range of living, dead and decomposing biological material. Associations with bacteria, which live in the gut of some species, enable them to digest cellulose and lignin. Most plants are attacked by insects, while there are both carnivores and parasites which feed on other animals. There are more species of insect than any other arthropod; about one million species have already been described and it is estimated that over a million are yet to be described. An important characteristic of insects is that they have an exoskeleton of chitin, an amino-polysaccharide.

INSECTS IN ARCHAEOLOGICAL CONTEXTS

Nine orders of the class Insecta are regularly found in archaeological deposits although there have been occasional finds from other orders. The orders Odonata (dragonflies), Dermaptera (earwigs), Phthiraptera (lice) and Hemiptera (true bugs) are conveniently grouped into the non-taxonomic unit Exopterygota. They undergo incomplete metamorphosis. The orders Coleoptera (beetles), Siphonaptera (fleas), Diptera (flies), Trichoptera (caddis flies) and Hymenoptera (bees, ants and wasps) all belong to

the taxonomic sub-division Endopterygota, whose members show complete metamorphosis, i.e., a larva very different in morphology from the adults hatches from the egg. The insect undergoes substantial internal re-organization within the pupa before the winged adult emerges. The adult often has a different food source from the larva.

Order Odonata (dragonflies)

The Odonata have aquatic predatory nymphs and adults which hunt their prey in the air. Remains of both nymphs and adults are sometimes found in aquatic deposits (e.g., Robinson 1991).

Order Dermaptera (earwigs)

The Dermaptera are terrestrial insects which mostly feed on dead and decaying plant and animal material. Their remains, including their characteristic cerci (pincers), are quite often abundant in waterlogged deposits (e.g., Robinson 1986) but their palaeoecological value is limited because there are so few species.

Order Phthiraptera (biting and sucking lice)

The Phthiraptera are wingless, obligate ectoparasites at all stages of their life. Most biting lice are associated with birds but the sucking lice (suborder Anoplura) just feed on the blood of mammals, often being host-specific. Anoplura remains are sometimes found in waterlogged organic material where there has been close contact with humans or domestic animals.

Order Hemiptera (true bugs)

The Hemiptera have mouthparts adapted for piercing and sucking. The great majority of them feed on the sap of plants but a few suck blood. Most are terrestrial although there are some aquatic, including marine skimming, species. Hemipteran remains are never as abundant in waterlogged sediments as coleopteran remains but many fragments are readily identifiable. Useful supplementary palaeoecological information can be obtained from them and some are host-specific in their food.

Order Coleoptera (beetles)

The Coleoptera are the largest order of insects, indeed of any animals. With the exception of some lake deposits, Coleoptera are by far the most abundant, closely identifiable insects from organic sediments, in part because the adults are so heavily sclerotized (protein molecules in the exoskeleton are cross-linked). They occur in almost every conceivable terrestrial and aquatic habitat and a few brackish habitats. Many are free-ranging carnivores but dung, carrion, decaying vegetable material and dead wood all support large associations of decomposer Coleoptera. Several families of Coleoptera feed on plants, some species being host-specific. The aquatic Coleoptera range from species of stagnant water through to those which are extremely fastidious in their requirement for clean, well-oxygenated flowing water. The very diverse assemblages of Coleoptera from some Pleistocene sites and some rural archaeological sites contrast strongly with the restricted range, mostly of synanthropic species including pests, which can be found in some urban deposits. Coleoptera have proved to be the order with the greatest palaeoecological value.

Order Siphonaptera (fleas)

Siphonaptera are hard-bodied, laterally-compressed, wingless, jumping insects which feed on the blood of birds and mammals. They tend to have preferred host species and are found in the same type of deposits as Phthiraptera (e.g., Girling 1984).

Order Diptera (flies)

The Diptera are a large order of insects. Their distinguishing feature is the possession of only a single pair of wings. The larvae of flies can be either terrestrial or aquatic, a high proportion feeding on decaying organic material although some are parasitic. Adults have sucking mouthparts, the food of different species ranging from nectar, through liquid exuded by decaying organic material, to blood. Remains of larvae, puparia and adults are preserved in waterlogged organic sediments but they often present great problems of identification, the remains of adults tending to be fragmentary while the immature stages are often taxonomically undescribed. However, identifiable larval head capsules of Chironomidae (midges) can be very common in lake sediments (Walker 1987). This family is very sensitive to water quality and temperature. Puparia, especially of Muscidae (house flies, etc.) and Sphaeroceridae (sewage and seaweed flies) have proved useful in characterizing waterlogged deposits of organic refuse, including middens and cesspits (Belshaw 1988). Fly larvae and puparia are also susceptible to calcium phosphate mineralization in cesspits.

Order Trichoptera (caddis flies)

The Trichoptera are moth-like insects with aquatic larvae. The larvae have diverse feeding habits but many feed on organic detritus. Both cases and larval sclerites survive in aquatic sediments. Some larval cases can be identified (e.g., Kelly and Osborne 1963–4) but the larvae themselves have more potential (Wilkinson 1987). The main palaeoecological value of Trichoptera is that some species are fastidious in their water quality requirements.

Order Hymenoptera (bugs, wasps and ants)

The Hymenoptera are characterized by two pairs of wings which are linked in flight. Some are social and live in colonies. The larvae of many feed on plants, or are fed on protein-rich foods or are parasitic on other insects. Many of the adults feed on nectar. The remains of the adults, especially the heads, which tend to be more heavily sclerotized than the remainder of the body, are commonly preserved in waterlogged organic sediments. They have, however, proved exceedingly difficult to identify. An exception to this is *Apis mellifera* (honey bee) which is a species of particular interest in its own right (Allen and Robinson 1993). One of the social groups of Hymenoptera, the

Formicidae (ants) is, however, sufficiently distinctive and small that the members can readily be identified (e.g., Robinson 1986). Some Hymenoptera, including the Cynipidae (gall wasps) induce the formation of galls, clusters of enlarged or additional cells in plants, to provide food and protection for their larvae. These galls, which are morphologically distinct and host-specific, are preserved in waterlogged sediments along with other plant remains (Robinson 1980a).

THE PRESERVATION OF INSECT REMAINS IN ARCHAEOLOGICAL AND OTHER QUATERNARY DEPOSITS

Chitin is quite resistant to decay although it is attacked by fungi. In aerobic environments dead insects soon decay unless conditions are very dry or cold. However, the permanent waterlogging of a fine sediment reduces the diffusion of oxygen sufficiently to limit the decay of any organic material in it, and rapidly results in the deposit becoming anaerobic (anoxic). These conditions are hostile to the organisms which decay chitin. Preservation is probably best in circum-neutral to slightly acidic organic silts, whereas in very acidic peat, specimens are sometimes rendered flimsy and pale. Inevitably, the most heavily sclerotized remains are the best preserved. Under good conditions of preservation, fine detail survives including surface microsculpturing, scales and setae (hairs).

Structural colours which result from thin films of epicuticle creating interference patterns with light, or surface irregularities scattering light, are usually retained. These are the metallic or iridescent colours shown particularly by Odonata, Coleoptera and Hymenoptera. Not all pigments survive so well; reds for example, tending to be fugitive but the blacks and browns due to heavy sclerotization do not deteriorate. One curious effect of this is that because sclerotization enhances preservation only the black spots survive from the elytra of some coccinellid beetles (ladybirds) when conditions for preservation are poor. Although freshly extracted, well-preserved beetle sclerites (skeletal units) can appear almost identical to modern examples when wet, there has in fact been a loss of protein from them and they will often shrivel or crack on drying.

As a general guide, if conditions are suitable for the preservation of macroscopic plant remains by waterlogging, insect remains will also survive. These conditions are likely to occur in natural situations such as lake beds, palaeochannel sediments and peat bogs.

They will also be present in archaeological features which extend below the water table such as pits, well bottoms and ditches. A rising water table can result in the preservation of insects in deposits which are not usually waterlogged, for example floor layers and true soils. In north-west Europe there have been episodes in the lives of some towns, for example Dublin and York, where the rate of deposition of organic refuse, against the background of a cool wet climate, has exceeded the rate of decay. The organic material has then held water in the manner of an ombrogenous peat bog. Insect remains will also be preserved in organic sediments where conditions are so cold that the rate of decay is very much reduced, for example Norse settlement sites in Greenland (McGovern et al. 1983).

Insect remains can also be preserved by mineralization. Girling (1979) reported the discovery of calcium carbonate-replaced arthropod remains from archaeological deposits but a brief re-examination of this material showed the insect remains had in fact experienced calcium phosphate mineralization; see Green (1979) for a discussion of this process as it affects seeds. Subsequently, many finds have been made of calcium phosphate-replaced insects, usually from cesspits and particularly of Diptera puparia. Calcium phosphate mineralization appears to occur rapidly after insects have been incorporated into sediments with a liquid rich in phosphate ions, such as sewage, against a background of calcium carbonate, for example a limestone lining to a cesspit. Mineralization most usually occurs by the infiltration of voids within specimens, producing an internal cast, rather than the replacement of hard parts. This can create considerable problems for identification. True calcium carbonate-replaced insect remains have occasionally been noticed in tufa deposits, for example cases of Trichoptera.

Metal corrosion products sometimes result in the preservation of insect remains. In the case of iron it is predominantly by replacement or the formation of an external cast, whereas with bronze it seems largely to be due to its biocidal action. Both types of preservation are perhaps most frequently encountered on grave goods accompanying inhumations, where the remains preserved are usually Diptera puparia.

Insect remains can be preserved by desiccation in very arid regions, for example parts of Egypt. This type of preservation is rarely perfect and the remains have often been damaged by the nibbling of invertebrates. A special category of desiccated insect remains can be found in middens of the packrat (Neotoma spp.) in the deserts of western North America (Elias 1994:24). The middens accumulate in rock shelters used by the packrats and the contents are cemented together with urine. Desiccated insect remains are occasionally encountered in wetter regions from inside buildings. Such remains have been found in late Medieval, soot-blackened thatch and from cob-walling in Britain. Insects can be preserved as a result of charring, but they are by no means as ubiquitous as carbonized crop remains on settlements. They have been found beneath volcanic ash on the Greek island of Santorini (Panagiotakopulu *et al.* 1995) while a deposit of Roman burnt grain from England contained charred grain beetles (Osborne 1977).

SAMPLING, EXTRACTION AND IDENTIFICATION OF INSECT REMAINS

The sampling and extraction of insect remains from waterlogged sediments has been covered in detail elsewhere (Coope 1986, Buckland and Coope 1991, Elias 1994:25). For most insect groups, including Coleoptera, sequential samples divided at 50 mm to 200 mm intervals and usually of 1 kg to 10 kg weight are taken from freshly cut sections. The sampling interval is in part related to the rate of sedimentation but the difficulty of establishing contemporaneity over the large surface area necessary for samples of this size and problems with mixing during sedimentation mean that sample intervals closer than 50 mm are rarely practicable. Great care must be taken not to sample across stratigraphic boundaries because it can result in spurious intermediate assemblages. The highest concentrations of remains are often found in organic muds that accumulated on river channel margins and in steep sided archaeological features, such as wells. In contrast, samples well in excess of 10 kg have proved necessary for some Pleistocene studies. Chironomidae (midge) larvae are analysed from very much smaller samples; 5-10 g is generally adequate from lake sediments (Hofmann 1986). This means that sampling can be undertaken by coring and it is recommended that cores are taken from the deepest part of the lake.

The standard technique for the recovery of most insect remains from organic sediments is paraffin flotation, first described by Coope and Osborne (1967). Samples are disaggregated in water, drained on a 0.2 or 0.3 mm sieve, mixed with paraffin and water added. Insect remains either float to the surface or are stuck there by surface tension whereas most plant debris will sink. Once the plant debris has settled, the insect remains can be poured off on to the sieve. The procedure is repeated until no more insect remains are

recovered. The technique is extremely effective for the recovery of insect remains from organic muds such as palaeochannel sediments and well bottoms. However, much plant debris will also float from some peats, Cyperaceae (sedges) and *Sphagnum* spp. (bog moss) being particularly problematic. The flot is washed with hot water and detergent, sorted in water under a binocular microscope and the insect fragments either stored in 70 per cent ethanol or glued on to card to await identification. Identifications are made by direct comparison of the sclerites with reference specimens. This is done using a binocular microscope at magnifications of up to ×100. Useful characters for identification range from gross morphology to fine details of microsculpture. The most usually identified sclerites of Coleoptera are head capsules, pronota (thorax carapaces) and elytra (wing cases) but other sclerites can be very diagnostic. Genitalia are particularly characteristic although it is often necessary for them to be associated with other sclerites to hint at the taxonomic group they are from. Occasionally, scanning electron microscopy is used to examine critical details at higher magnifications. Species descriptions and the final couplets of identification keys can be useful aids to identification but they are no substitute for good reference material. It is usually possible to identify almost all Coleoptera from an assemblage to genus and at least half to species. The results are tabulated to give for each sample the minimum number of individuals of each taxon represented by the sclerites identified from it.

Samples for chironomid analysis are deflocculated in hot 10 per cent potassium hydroxide solution and sieved down to 0.1 mm (Hofmann 1986). They are then sorted under a binocular microscope for chironomid larval head capsules, which are mounted on microscope slides. In contrast to the analysis of most insect groups, there are numerous descriptions and identification keys which can be used to identify them.

Insect remains preserved by mineralization, desiccation and charring are generally recovered from samples along with macroscopic plant remains. Samples of the order of 1 kg are wet-sieved down to 0.5 mm, dried and sorted for mineralized remains. Samples of perhaps 4 litres for desiccated remains and 10 to 50 litres for carbonized remains are floated in water on to a 0.3 to 0.5 mm mesh. The flots are dried and sorted under a binocular microscope for remains including insects.

ASPECTS OF INTERPRETATION

Pleistocene studies of sub-fossil insect remains have tended to emphasize biogeography and palaeoclimatology. Holocene studies have tended to concentrate on general palaeoenvironmental reconstructions, settlement conditions and evidence for human activities. Underlying both categories of study is the morphological and apparent ecological constancy of insect species throughout the Quaternary. To quote Coope (1970) 'One of the most outstanding facts to emerge from the study of Quaternary insect fossils is that those skeletal elements which possess distinctive features match precisely those of species which are still living at the present. No fossil has yet shown intermediate features between known species.' This observation still holds true. It is likely that some Quaternary insect remains that so far defy identification do belong to species now extinct but, on experience to date, many more of them will eventually be matched to species which are still extant somewhere in the world. It is rather harder to demonstrate ecological constancy but species generally kept the same company earlier in the Quaternary as they do today (Buckland and Coope 1991:10). It must also be remembered that some habitats, and therefore the insect communities associated

with them, which existed in the past no longer occur today. The example of the fly *Thoracochaeta zosterae* in latrines is given below.

Taphonomic considerations for Pleistocene biogeographic and palaeoclimatic studies tend to be rather limited other than establishing that all the remains from a sample are contemporaneous with the deposit and that re-worked material is absent. For more general palaeoenvironmental reconstructions, however, detailed considerations are needed of how the insects came together in the death assemblage and the preservational factors which acted on it. For example, a deposit which accumulated under water may contain insects which lived in the water itself, terrestrial species from the surrounding environs which fell in and species in refuse which had been dumped in the water by humans. A particular problem can arise with some rather barren urban environments which supported little insect life, with the result that the majority of insect remains that are preserved in such situations comprise a 'background fauna' of insects which had flown in from the surrounding countryside (Kenward 1975a). Any simple environmental reconstruction based on them could be very misleading.

EXAMPLES OF THE STUDY OF QUATERNARY INSECT REMAINS

Biogeography and species constancy

The studies of Coope showed that the response of insects to the environmental instability of the Quaternary was migration rather than evolution (Coope 1970, Buckland and Coope 1991). One of the most numerous scarabaeid dung beetles from Devensian (last glacial) deposits at Dorchester on Thames, England was *Aphodius holdereri* which is now restricted to the High Tibetan Plateau (Coope 1973). Not all migrations were over such long distances; many of the Coleoptera which occurred in Britain during cold episodes of the Devensian are now to be found in the European Arctic tundra. The beetle *Helophorus glacialis*, which occurs in snow meltwater pools, is particularly characteristic of Late Devensian Zone III (*c.* 10 500 BP) insect assemblages in England (Briggs *et al.* 1985:63, Osborne 1976). With the climatic amelioration of the Holocene, it retreated northwards and up mountains. It is now to be found in northern Scandinavia, on mountains in southern Scandinavia and on mountains in southern Europe above 2000 m such as the Pyrenees (Figure 10.1).

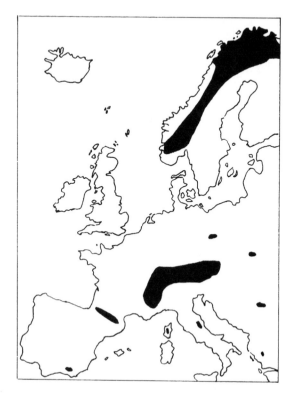

Figure 10.1 Present-day distribution of *Helophorus glacialis*, a small water beetle which commonly occurs on Late-glacial (Late Devensian Zone III) sites in England.

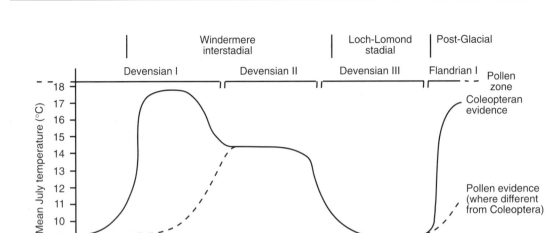

Figure 10.2   Changes in the average July temperatures in the English Midlands during the Late Glacial and Early Post-Glacial as suggested by insect (Coope 1986) and palynological data.

Palaeoclimate

The response by insects to climatic change of migration, combined with the large number of insect species, many of which have limited climatic tolerances, gives a powerful means of palaeoclimatic reconstruction. All biological groups can respond to sudden severe climatic deterioration with death, but the good dispersive power of many insects and their short generation time enables new insect faunas to colonize more rapidly than most other biological groups following environmental change. Thus insects have given some of the best evidence for the abrupt climatic changes which characterize the Quaternary. For example, Coleoptera showed the slight degree of warming of the Chelford Interstadial in Britain (a brief warm episode around 62 000 BP during the Devensian; Coope 1977). A thermophilous fauna of Coleoptera dated to 43 000 BP from Isleworth in the Lower Thames Valley, England, showed that at the height of the Upton Warren Interstadial, summer temperatures were warmer than at present but the vegetation had not had sufficient time to respond to the climatic amelioration and there was no evidence from the insects for temperate woodland (Coope and Angus 1975).

Probably the best sequence of rapid climatic change which has been demonstrated from coleopteran evidence is for the Late Devensian (Late Glacial) and early Holocene of Britain (Coope 1977, 1986, Osborne

1976). Figure 10.2 shows average July temperatures as suggested by insect evidence for the period compared with botanical evidence as suggested by pollen analysis. Of particular interest is the replacement around 13 000 BP of an arctic fauna by a temperate insect fauna which included many Carabidae (ground beetles) and water beetles typical of lowland England. However, tree-dependent insects are absent and the pollen still suggests an arctic flora. Only around 12 000 BP, when climatic deterioration has already set in and the insect fauna has been replaced by one characteristic of northern Britain, does the pollen give evidence for climatic amelioration and the development of woodland. Both insects and pollen show the return of arctic conditions around 11 000 BP at the end of the Windermere Interstadial. The arctic insect fauna of the Loch Lomond Stadial was very rapidly displaced by the temperate insect fauna of the Holocene around 10 000 BP. A closely dated sequence from West Bromwich, Staffordshire suggested a very abrupt transition to mean summer temperatures similar to those of the present day over a period of perhaps less than 50 years (less than the error on a radiocarbon date; Osborne 1980). There were no certain intermediate faunas from the sequence. In contrast, the pollen evidence shows woodland colonization and succession by more thermophilous trees occurring over 2000 years.

Results from North America also show a plant migration lag in comparison with insect evidence for climatic amelioration at the end of the Wisconsin (Late Glacial) (Schwert and Ashworth 1988, Elias 1994:84). For example, changed insect faunas showed climatic amelioration to conditions suitable for tree colonization in the Midwest of the United States from 15 300 BP onwards but the vegetation remained tundra.

The reconstruction of past climate from beetle remains has been refined with the Mutual Climatic Range method (Atkinson *et al.* 1986, 1987). Principal component analysis shows over 96 per cent of the variance in thermal climate of the Palaeoarctic (Europe and Asia) is described by the warmth of the summer (TMAX) combined with the temperature range between the warmest and coldest months (TRANGE). They express the warmth of the climate and its degree of continentality. These parameters were plotted for species of Carabidae (ground beetles), water beetles and scarabaeoid dung beetles which occur as Pleistocene fossils, using data from meteorological stations throughout their modern geographic range. (Phytophagous beetles, whose distributions might reflect that of their host plants, were not used.) This gave a climatic range envelope for each species of TMAX against TRANGE. To estimate past climate by this method, the modern climatic range envelopes for all the relevant species in a Quaternary assemblage are compared and the area of greatest overlap is found. This gives a plot of TMAX against TRANGE most likely to correspond with the climatic conditions at the time the deposit was laid down.

Packrat middens and environmental change in the northern Chihuahuan Desert

Insects have also given evidence of environmental change in arid regions at the end of the Pleistocene. As part of a wider study of fossil insects from the interior continental desert which spans the border between Mexico and the United States, the contents of packrat middens were investigated from the northern Chihuahuan Desert in Texas and New Mexico (Elias 1994:212). The insects from them were mostly species which normally dwell in the open which had ventured into the middens and had then been preserved in desiccated packrat urine. Cool, moist conditions were suggested from the faunas which dated from 22 000–18 000 BP, the full Wisconsin glaciation, but there was a gradual increase in grassland taxa until 12 500 BP. There was then a transition from the temperate Wisconsin fauna to the more xeric (tolerant of dry conditions) postglacial fauna. Many temperate species

persisted until 7500 BP after which date the desert environment was firmly established and the last temperate species were lost by 2500 BP, after which desert scrub prevailed.

British old woodland fauna

The woodland succession of the Holocene was reflected not just in the arrival of host-specific tree-feeding insects as their host trees colonized but in the occurrence of specialized insects of over-mature trees and esoteric dead-wood habitats as woodland aged. Many of the latter have poor dispersive powers and were dependent on almost continuous tree cover from continental Europe to England prior to the severance of land connections by 8500 BP. The weevil *Dryophthorus corticalis*, for example, was identified from a palaeochannel of the Thames at Runnymede of Mesolithic date (Robinson unpublished) and has been recorded from several other sites with old woodland faunas (Buckland 1979:109). This beetle is now only known from Britain in Windsor Forest, where it occurs in damp wood inside old oak trees, often in the company of the ant *Lasius brunneus*. Some of these assemblages include species which are now extinct in Britain, for example Mesolithic deposits at Hampstead Heath, London contained the beetles *Pycnomerus terebrans* and *Isorhipis melasoides* (Girling 1989). Both now have a disjunct distribution in Central Europe (Figure 10.3) and are regarded as relict species of old woodland. Girling (1982) listed fourteen 'old woodland' beetles identified from Mesolithic to Bronze Age deposits that are now extinct in Britain, but many more have now been discovered. This 'old woodland' fauna survived Neolithic clearance but by the end of the Bronze Age, areas of suitable habitat were so broken up as to prevent colonization between them. One of the last examples of such a fauna was discovered at Thorne Moors, Humberside and dated to 2980 ± 110 BP (Buckland and Kenward 1973, Buckland 1979).

Insects as indicators of human activity

Clearance at Hampstead Heath, England

A sequence of organic deposits at Hampstead Heath, England was shown by pollen analysis to span the Elm Decline, which gave a marker horizon of 5200 BP, enabling a division to be made between the Mesolithic sediments below this level and the

Figure 10.3   Present distribution in Western Europe (shaded) and Mesolithic, Neolithic and Bronze Age records from England (+) of the wood-boring beetle *Isorhipis melasoides* (Buckland 1979:80 with additions).

Neolithic to Bronze Age sediments above (Girling 1989).

One problem with the interpretation of coleopteran results from rural deposits is the very high species diversity, so that even if large assemblages are identified in terms of minimum number of individuals, most species are only represented by a few individuals. A series of habitat-related species groups have been devised to overcome this problem (Robinson 1981:279, 1991:278). Some species of Coleoptera are eurytopic (occur in many different habitats) so not all beetles can be classified in these groups. The results are expressed as a percentage of the minimum number of individuals of terrestrial Coleoptera in each assemblage, excluding the aquatic species. This is because many assemblages accumulated under water and it enables some of the differences due to the environment of the deposit itself to be removed. (Pollen analysts often express their results as a percentage of the dry land pollen for similar reasons). Only around 40 per cent of the terrestrial Coleoptera from a site will fall

into a species group, so their sum does not add up to 100 per cent.

The results from Hampstead Heath have been expressed in Figure 10.4 by species group. Members of Species Group 4, Coleoptera which feed on wood in various stages of decay, leaves, fruits and bark of trees and shrubs, plus fungal feeders and predators which are strictly associated with wood, were very abundant in the pre-Elm Decline deposits (WHS1). In contrast, Species Group 2, scarabaeoid dung beetles such as *Aphodius* spp., which mostly occur in the dung of large herbivores in the field rather than in manure heaps and therefore provide a good indication for pasture grazed by domestic animals, was absent. Species Group 4 showed a decline above the level of the Elm Decline (WHS2, WHS3) whereas there was a significant presence of Species Group 2. This suggested that woodland was being cleared for grazing. Insects which tend to be favoured by human habitation, Species Groups 8 to 10, were entirely absent.

The clearance at Hampstead Heath was only partial. A very open pastoral landscape was suggested by insect assemblages from an Iron Age settlement on the floodplain of the River Thames at Farmoor, Oxfordshire, where the wood and tree-dependent beetles of Species Group 4 comprised less than 0.1 per cent of the terrestrial Coleoptera whereas the scarabaeoid dung beetles of Species Group 2 comprised about 28 per cent of the terrestrial Coleoptera (Robinson 1981:280).

The impact of settlement: the rural to urban transition at Oxford

There are many insects that are favoured by settlements, particularly those associated with organic refuse and structural timbers. Figure 10.5 shows a coleopteran sequence from the Hamel, Oxford, which spans the transition from rural to urban conditions when a suburb of the town spread on to the site in the late twelfth century AD (Robinson 1980b). The bottom sample in the sequence (645) pre-dated urbanization and the scarabaeoid dung beetles of Species Group 2 suggested pasture on the site. Sample 769 and above gave strong evidence of human settlement nearby. Beetles which readily infest structural timbers, particularly *Anobium punctatum* (woodworm beetle) (Species Group 10) rose to over 7 per cent of the terrestrial Coleoptera. There was a major presence of synanthropic beetles (beetles which thrive in close company with humans; Species Group 9a) such as *Ptinus fur*. These beetles naturally live in such habitats as birds' nests and

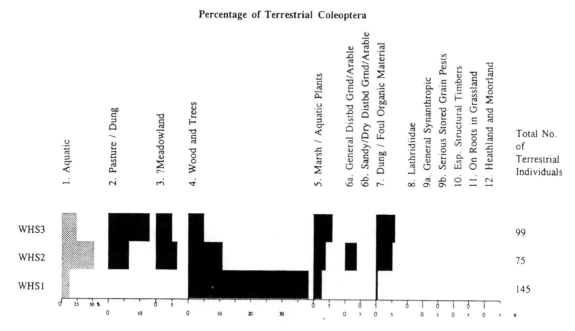

Percentage of Terrestrial Coleoptera

Species groups expressed as a percentage of the total terrestrial Coleoptera (i.e. aquatics excluded). Not all the terrestrial Coleoptera have been classified into groups.

Figure 10.4   Species groups of Coleoptera from West Heath Spa, Hampstead Heath.

have been able to find suitable conditions inside buildings. Members of the Lathridiidae (Species Group 8), which feed on moulds on such material as old thatch and damp hay were also plentiful.

The impact of settlement on water quality; Chironomidae in Lake Ontario

Chironomid larvae were analysed from sediment cores extending back 2800 years from the Bay of Quinte, Lake Ontario, Canada (Warwick 1980). The fauna suggested an episode of eutrophication related to the Hopewell Indian settlement around 2000 BP. Much greater eutrophication followed British colonization at the end of the eighteenth century, which resulted in organic waste reaching the water. However the trend towards eutrophication was then reversed as clearance and agriculture caused erosion, resulting in sediment being washed into the lake.

Introduction of insects

Trade and colonization by humans resulted in the spread of some insect species in antiquity, particularly pests of stored products and ectoparasites of humans and their domestic animals. The Romans were apparently responsible for the dispersal of grain beetles over much of Western Europe (Buckland 1981). A late first century AD Roman military granary at York, England experienced a severe infestation of exotic grain beetles including *Oryzaephilus surinamensis* (saw-tooth grain beetle) and *Sitophilus granarius* (grain weevil; Kenward and Williams 1979). The Romans introduced *Blatta orientalis* (oriental cockroach) to late Roman Lincoln (Kenward pers. comm.). As the Norse colonized Iceland and Greenland, they inadvertently brought *Pediculus humanus humanus* (human body louse) and *Melophagus ovinus* (sheep ked) with them (Sveinbjarnardóttir and Buckland 1983, Sadler 1990, Amorosi *et al.* 1994). International trade in the post-Medieval period brought insects from the tropics to Western Europe, for example the wreck of the Dutch East Indiaman *Amsterdam* contained a jar of tamarind

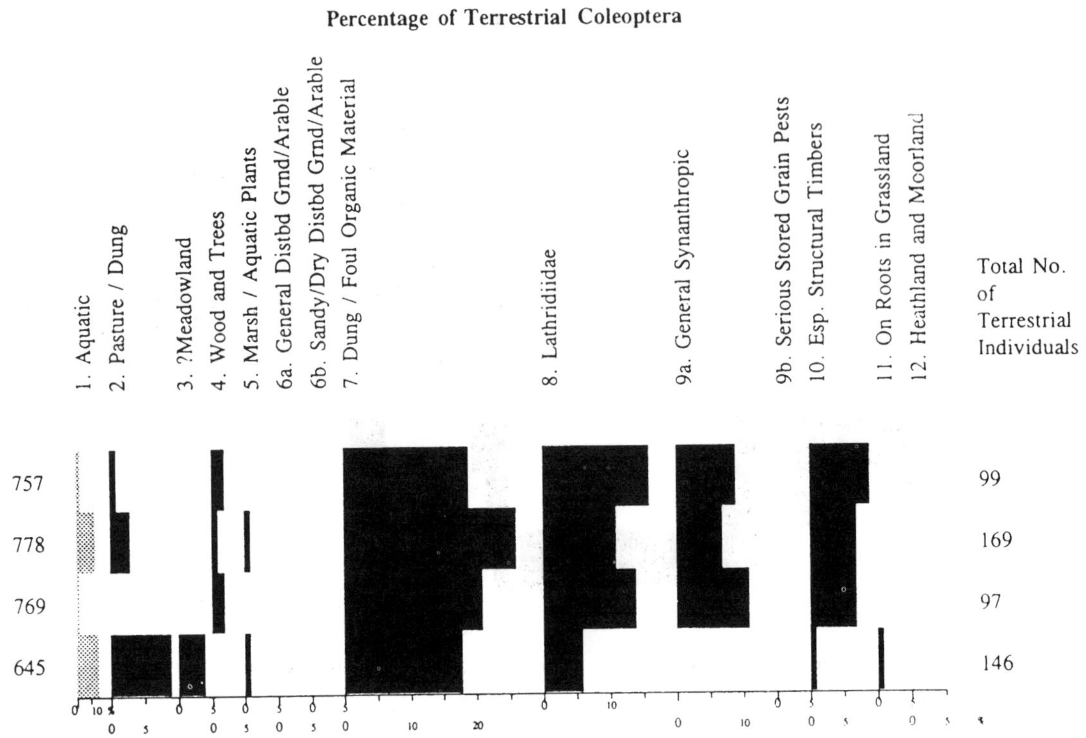

Percentage of Terrestrial Coleoptera

Species groups expressed as a percentage of the total terrestrial Coleoptera (i.e. aquatics excluded). Not all the terrestrial Coleoptera have been classified into groups.

Figure 10.5   Species groups of Coleoptera from The Hamel, Oxford.

pods infested with large numbers of the beetle *Sitophilus linearis*, originally from India (Hakbijl 1986).

Aspects of urban living conditions

Palaeoentomology has given much information on urban living conditions particularly from towns with extensive waterlogged deposits such as York, England. Whereas Roman York was kept relatively clean, much organic refuse accumulated in the Anglo-Scandinavian town. Trampled organic material in floor layers provided an ideal habitat for the small flightless beetle *Aglenus brunneus*, which flourished in vast numbers (Kenward 1975b). The study of species associations of decomposer communities can be used to characterize different categories of organic refuse (Kenward 1982) while the species diversity of death assemblages can assist in the separation of indoor assemblages from mixed and outdoor assemblages (Kenward 1978, 1985). The same synanthropic and

wood-boring beetles that infested the early Medieval buildings of Oxford (Robinson 1980b) occurred in abundance at Anglo-Scandinavian Coppergate, York (Kenward and Hall 1995:62).

Mixed assemblages of ectoparasitic insects resulted from humans living in close proximity to their domestic animals or processing skins from them. One assemblage from Coppergate contained *Damalina ovis* (sheep louse), *Pediculus humanus* (human head or body louse), *Felicola subrostratus* (cat louse) and *Haematopinus apri* (pig louse) (Kenward and Hall 1995:596). In addition to *P. humanus*, *Pthirus pubis* (crab louse), *Pulex irritans* (human flea) and *Cimex columbarius* or *lectularius* (pigeon or bed bug) were found partly preserved by calcium phosphate replacement and partly by waterlogging in an early eighteenth century cesspit in the City of London (Girling 1984). They imply a low level of hygiene of the occupants of the site; the human flea lives in dirty houses and the crab louse is spread by sexual contact.

Flies thrived on urban refuse. Numerous puparia of *Stomoxys calcitrans* (stable fly) and *Musca domestica* (house fly) were found in a dump of processed dye-plants at Anglo-Scandinavian Coppergate (Kenward and Hall 1995:552). Both humans and their domestic animals are bitten by *S. calcitrans*. Puparia of the same flies were identified from the Hamel, Oxford, where they were probably breeding in their more usual habitat of straw enriched with animal urine and faeces (Robinson 1980b). Even the upper class inhabitants of early post-Medieval towns were troubled by flies. Numerous puparia of Sphaeroceridae were found in a contemporaneous latrine inside the lodging of Robert Saye, Provost of Oriel College, Oxford in the late seventeenth century (Robinson and Wilson 1987:71). Every time he lifted the lid, small flies would have flown up to the light.

Latrines and Thoracochaeta zosterae

Probably the most commonly encountered and numerous Diptera puparia from Medieval and early post-Medieval cesspits in England belong to *Thoracochaeta zosterae* (seaweed fly) (e.g., Belshaw 1988). They are preserved either by waterlogging or calcium phosphate mineralization. It is a small fly which can now be found breeding around the coast of Britain and rarely occurs inland. The nitrogen isotope ratio of some of these puparia from two thirteenth to fourteenth century waterlogged cesspits at Oxford was investigated, which established that the flies had derived their nitrogen from a terrestrial food chain rather than from feeding on material of marine origin (Webb *et al.* 1998). It is possible that the *T. zosterae* larvae were particularly well-adapted to conditions in cesspits because the high concentration of salt in the urine created an osmotic tension similar to that from seawater and the decaying faeces had similar characteristics to decaying seaweed. Once cesspits ceased to be used, so the fly retreated to its maritime habitat.

Insects as food and providers of food

Insects are still eaten in many cultures and they have been a food source in the past (see Chapter 35). Desiccated human coprolites from caves in North America have given evidence for the use of insects in the diet. Coprolites dated to 9500 BP from Dirty Shame Rockshelter, Oregon contained remains of termites (Elias 1994:127), while grasshopper fragments were reported from coprolites from the Ocampo Caves, Tamaulipas, Mexico (Callen 1969).

There are now many archaeological finds of *Apis mellifera* (honey bee) from Britain. Such large numbers of honey bee remains were found at Anglo-Scandinavian Coppergate as to suggest bee-keeping (Kenward and Hall 1995:765). Individual finds of honey bees from Iron Age and late Bronze Age deposits (e.g., Allen and Robinson 1993) show that honey and beeswax were available resources in late prehistoric Britain although it is possible they were from wild colonies.

CONCLUSIONS AND FUTURE POTENTIAL

This review has demonstrated the versatility of insect studies in Quaternary and archaeological research. The information that can be gained from them ranges from the details of climatic oscillations during an interstadial to the fleas that infested the houses of a settlement. Although the procedures are time-consuming and most research requires access to extensive reference collections which are only held by a few institutions, the results can well justify the effort.

There is much potential for the combination of insect studies with other palaeoenvironmental techniques. For example, pollen analysis can show the composition of woodland, insects of old woodland can indicate the character of the woodland. Pollen might show the extent of grassland while insects can differentiate whether it was used for pasture or hay meadow.

There is the potential to analyse other taxonomic groups of insect, for example Hymenoptera (bees, wasps, etc.) other than Formicidae (ants), even though at present the prospect seems daunting. Studies could also be taken to other regions of the world, for example the tropics, although species diversity and incomplete knowledge of the modern fauna would present major problems.

The success of statistical techniques of analysis has already been demonstrated by the Mutual Climatic Range (MCR) method and some of the techniques of Kenward. There is certainly potential for the use of correspondence analysis to detect species associations. The analysis of the stable isotope ratio for nitrogen has been used to confirm the food source of insects (Webb *et al.* 1998), and other isotope studies are possible. The use of AMS radiocarbon dating on chitin of individual sclerites of climatically sensitive insects could provide a means of investigating the time scale of stadial-interstadial transitions during the Pleistocene. DNA studies might show the degree to which morphological stability of insect species with time is linked to genetic stability at the molecular level.

Quaternary and archaeological entomology has developed rapidly since its modern inception 40 years ago. It is likely that advances will continue to be made with the subject.

ACKNOWLEDGEMENT

Part of this chapter has been taken from an unpublished review of palaeoentomology in southern England which was funded by the Ancient Monuments Laboratory of English Heritage.

REFERENCES

*Recommended for further reading

Allen, T.G. and Robinson, M.A. (1993). *The Prehistoric Landscape and Iron Age Enclosed Settlement at Mingies Ditch, Hardwick-with-Yelford, Oxon.* Oxford University Committee for Archaeology: Oxford.

Amorosi, T., Buckland, P.C., Magnússon, K., McGovern, T.H. and Sadler, J.P. (1994). An archaeozoological investigation of the midden at Nesstofa, Reykjavik, Iceland. In Luff, R. and Rowley-Conwy, P. (eds) *Whither Environmental Archaeology?*, 69–80. Monograph 38, Oxbow: Oxford.

*Atkinson, T.C., Briffa, K.R., Coope, G.R., Joachim, J.M. and Perry, D.W. (1996). Climatic calibration of coleopteran data. In Berglund, B.E. (ed.) *Handbook of Holocene Palaeoecology and Palaeohydrology*, 851–858. John Wiley: Chichester.

Atkinson, T.C., Briffa, K.R. and Coope, G.R. (1987). Seasonal temperatures in Britain during the past 22 000 years, reconstructed using beetle remains. *Nature*, **325**:587–592.

Belshaw, R.D. (1988). A note on the recovery of *Thoracochaeta zosterae* (Haliday) (Diptera: Sphaeroceridae) from archaeological deposits. *Circaea*, **6**:39–41.

Briggs, D.J., Coope, G.R. and Gilbertson, D.D. (1985). *The Chronology and Environmental Framework of Early Man in the Upper Thames Valley.* BAR 137, British Archaeological Reports: Oxford.

Buckland, P.C. (1979). *Thorne Moors: a Palaeoecological Study of a Bronze Age Site.* Occasional Publication 8, Department of Geography: Birmingham.

Buckland, P.C. (1981). The early dispersal of insect pests of stored products as indicated by archaeological records. *Journal of Stored Product Research*, **17**:1–12.

*Buckland, P.C. and Coope, G.R. (1991). *A Bibliography and Literature Review of Quaternary Entomology.* Collis Publications: Sheffield.

Buckland, P.C. and Kenward, H.K. (1973). Thorne Moor: a palaeoecological study of a Bronze Age site. *Nature*, **241**:405–406.

Callen, E.O. (1969). Diet as revealed by coprolites,. In Brothwell, D. and Higgs, E.S. '(eds) *Science in Archaeology*, 235–243 (2nd edn). Thames and Hudson: New York.

*Coope, G.R. (1970). Interpretation of Quaternary insect fossils. *Annual Review of Entomology*, **15**:97–120.

Coope, G.R. (1973). Tibetan species of dung beetle from Late Pleistocene deposits in England. *Nature*, **245**:335–336.

Coope, G.R. (1977). Fossil coleopteran assemblages as sensitive indicators of climatic changes during the Devensian (Last) cold stage. *Philosophical Transactions of the Royal Society of London*, **B280**:313–337.

*Coope, G.R. (1986). Coleoptera analysis. In Berglund, B.E. (ed.) *Handbook of Holocene Palaeoecology and Palaeohydrology*, 703–713. John Wiley: Chichester.

Coope, G.R. and Angus, R.B. (1975). An ecological study of a temperate interlude in the middle of the last glaciation, based on fossil Coleoptera from Isleworth, Middlesex. *Journal of Animal Ecology*, **44**:365–391.

Coope, G.R. and Osborne, P.J. (1967). Report on the coleopterous fauna of the Roman well at Barnsley Park, Gloucestershire. *Transactions of the Bristol and Gloucestershire Archaeological Society*, **86**:84–87.

*Elias, S.A. (1994). *Quaternary Insects and their Environments.* Smithsonian Institution Press: Washington DC.

Girling, M.A. (1979). Calcium carbonate-replaced arthropods from archaeological deposits. *Journal of Archaeological Science*, **6**:309–320.

Girling, M.A. (1982). Fossil insect faunas from forest sites. In Bell, M. and Limbrey, S. (eds) *Archaeological Aspects of Woodland Ecology*, 129–146. BAR International Series 146, British Archaeological Reports: Oxford.

Girling, M.A. (1984). Eighteenth century records of human lice (Pthiraptera, Anoplura) and fleas (Siphonaptera, Pulicidae) in the City of London. *Entomologist's Monthly Magazine*, **120**:207–210.

Girling, M.A. (1989). Mesolithic and later landscapes interpreted from the insect assemblages of West Heath Spa Hampstead. In Collins, D. and Lorimer, D. (eds) *Excavations at the Mesolithic Site on West Heath, Hampstead 1976–1981*, 72–89. BAR 217, British Archaeological Reports: Oxford.

Green, F.J. (1979). Phosphate mineralization of seeds from archaeological sites. *Journal of Archaeological Science*, **6**:279–284.

Hakbijl, T. (1986). Remains of insects. In Gawronski, J.H.G. (ed.) *Amsterdam Project*, 72–73. Annual Report 1995, VOC Ship Amsterdam Foundation: Amsterdam.

Hofmann, W. (1986). Chironomid analysis. In Berglund, B.E. (ed.) *Handbook of Holocene Palaeoecology and Palaeohydrology*, 715–728. John Wiley: Chichester.

Kelly, M. and Osborne, P.J. (1963–4). Two faunas and floras from the alluvium at Shustoke, Warwickshire. *Proceedings of the Linnaean Society of London*, **176**:37–65.

Kenward, H.K. (1975a). Pitfalls in the environmental interpretation of insect death assemblages. *Journal of Archaeological Science*, **2**:85–94.

Kenward, H.K. (1975b). The biological and archaeological implications of the beetle *Aglenus brunneus* (Gyllenhall) in ancient faunas. *Journal of Archaeological Science*, **2**:63–69.

Kenward, H.K. (1978). *The Analysis of Archaeological Insect Assemblages: A New Approach*. Archaeology of York Fascicule 19/1, York Archaeological Trust: York.

Kenward, H.K. (1982). Insect communities and death assemblages, past and present. In Hall, A.R. and Kenward, H.K. (eds) *Environmental Archaeology in the Urban Context*, 71–78. Research Report 43, Council for British Archaeology: London.

Kenward, H.K. (1985). Outdoors – indoors? The outdoor component of archaeological insect assemblages. In Fieller, N.R.J., Gilbertson, D.D. and Ralph, N.G.A. (eds) *Palaeobiological Investigations: Research Design, Methods and Data Analysis*, 97–104. BAR S266, British Archaeological Reports: Oxford.

*Kenward, H.K. and Hall, A.R. (1995). *Biological Evidence from 16–22 Coppergate*. Archaeology of York Fascicule 14/7, York Archaeological Trust: York.

Kenward, H.K. and Williams, D. (1979). *Biological Evidence from the Roman Warehouses in Coney Street*. Archaeology of York Fascicule 14/2, Council for British Archaeology: London.

McGovern, T.H., Buckland, P.C., Savory, D., Sveinbjarnardóttir, G., Andreasen, C. and Skidmore, P. (1983). A study of the faunal and floral remains from two Norse farms in the Western Settlement, Greenland. *Arctic Anthropology*, **20**:93–120.

Osborne, P.J. (1976). Evidence from the insects of climatic variations during the Flandrian period: a preliminary note. *World Archaeology*, **8**:150–158.

Osborne, P.J. (1977). Stored product beetles from a Roman site at Droitwich, England. *Journal of Stored Products Research*, **13**:203–204.

Osborne, P.J. (1980). The Late Devensian–Flandrian transition depicted by serial insect faunas from West Bromwich, Staffordshire, England. *Boreas*, **9**:139–147.

Panagiotakopulu, E. Buckland, P.C., Day, P.M., Sarpaki, A. and Doumas, C. (1995). Natural insecticides and insect repellents in antiquity: a review of the evidence. *Journal of Archaeological Science*, **22**:705–710.

Robinson, M.A. (1980a). Archaeological finds of wasp galls. *Journal of Archaeological Science* **7**:93–95.

Robinson, M.A. (1980b). Waterlogged plant and invertebrate evidence. In Palmer, N.J., Beaker burial and medieval tenements in the Hamel, Oxford. *Oxoniensia*, **45**:199–206.

Robinson, M.A. (1981). The Iron Age to early Saxon environment of the Upper Thames Terraces. In Jones, M. and Dimbleby, G. (eds) *The Environment of Man: the Iron Age to the Anglo-Saxon Period*, 251–286. BAR 87, British Archaeological Reports: Oxford.

Robinson, M.A. (1986). Waterlogged plant and invertebrate evidence. In Miles, D. (ed.) *Archaeology at Barton Court Farm, Oxon*. Research Report 50, Council for British Archaeology: London, microfiche chapters VIII, IX and XI.

Robinson, M.A. (1991). The Neolithic and Late Bronze Age insect assemblages. In Needham, S.P. (ed.) *Excavation and Salvage at Runnymede Bridge, 1978: the Late Bronze Age Waterfront Site*, 277–326. British Museum Press: London.

Robinson, M.A. and Wilson, R. (1987). A survey of environmental archaeology in the South Midlands. In Keeley, H.C.M. (ed.) *Environmental Archaeology: a Regional Review*, 16–100. Occasional Paper 1, Historic Buildings and Monuments Commission: London.

Sadler, J.P. (1990). Records of ectoparasites on humans and sheep from Viking Age deposits in the former western settlement of Greenland. *Journal of Medical Entomology*, **27**:628–631.

Schwert, D.P. and Ashworth, A.C. (1988). Late Quaternary history of the northern beetle fauna of North America: a synthesis of fossil and distributional evidence. *Memoirs of the Entomological Society of Canada*, **144**:93–107.

Sveinbjarnardóttir, G. and Buckland, P.C. (1983). An uninvited guest. *Antiquity*, **58**:127–130.

Walker, I.R. (1987). Chironomidae (Diptera) in palaeoecology. *Quaternary Science Reviews*, **6**:29–40.

Warwick, W.F. (1980). Paleolimnology of the Bay of Quinte, Lake Ontario: 2800 years of cultural influence. *Canadian Bulletin of Fisheries and Aquatic Sciences*, **206**:1–117.

Webb, S.C., Hedges, R.E.M. and Robinson, M. (1998). The seaweed fly *Thoracochaeta zosterae* (Hal.) (Diptera: Sphaerocidae) in inland archaeological contexts: δ^{13}C and δ^{15}N solves the puzzle. *Journal of Archaeological Science*. **25**:1253–1259.

Wilkinson, B.J. (1987). Caddis fly (Trichoptera) remains. In Balaam, N.D., Levitan, B. and Straker, V. (eds) *Studies in Palaeoeconomy and Environment in South-West England*, 247–248. BAR British Series 181, British Archaeological Reports: Oxford.

11

Non-marine Mollusca and Archaeology

R.C. PREECE

Department of Zoology, University of Cambridge.

The shells of land and freshwater snails are abundant in a range of Quaternary sediments and are especially common in archaeological deposits in limestone regions. They have attracted scientific attention for nearly 300 years but it is only since the late 1950s that they have been subject to more rigorous quantitative analysis. The study of the past distributions, occurrences and associations of non-marine Mollusca in the Quaternary has two main aims. First, to find out as much as possible about such Mollusca for their own sake. Second, to use them to determine the age of the sediments containing them and to shed light on the environmental and climatic conditions under which such sediments accumulated. Detailed knowledge of faunal history not only allows us to reconstruct the ecological successions that have given rise to modern communities but it also provides the factual basis for understanding the origins of modern distributions (historical biogeography).

Mollusca are useful because of their wide distribution and their occurrence in a variety of sediments, including many (e.g., loess, hillwash, tufa) that may be strongly oxidized and lacking in organic fossils, such as plant or insect remains. This brief account reviews the ways in which the shells of land and freshwater molluscs have been used in palaeoenvironmental reconstruction and have provided data central to other issues, such as the tempo and mode of evolution.

TAPHONOMY AND DIAGENESIS

Fossil assemblages rarely represent living communities. In many instances there is likely to have been differential loss of certain elements that consequently fail to enter the fossil record. For obvious reasons, slugs are poorly represented as fossils but even these produce internal plates (limacid or milacid taxa) or small granules (arionid slugs) made of calcite that commonly occur in Quaternary deposits. Neither type of remain is reliably identifiable below generic level, so that individual species of slug cannot usually be distinguished. Other organisms, such as earthworms, also produce calcitic granules and it is likely that many of the reports of arionid remains in the literature actually relate to structures produced by lumbricid worms (Canti 1998).

Preservation varies enormously not only between deposits but also horizontally and vertically within a single sequence. Leaching is a serious problem that can cause shells to become severely corroded, rendering their identification difficult or impossible. For example, at Holywell Coombe, Folkestone, ground-water had reacted with iron sulfides (pyrite and marcasite) to form acids that attacked shells, causing severe damage, occasionally leaving only internal moulds (Preece 1998). In extreme cases, there might be almost complete loss of aragonitic shells, only calcitic elements, such as slug plates, surviving. Such a situation occurred at the

---

Handbook of Archaeological Sciences. Edited by D.R. Brothwell and A.M. Pollard.
© 2001 John Wiley & Sons, Ltd.

early Middle Pleistocene hominid site at Boxgrove, Sussex, where molluscan assemblages from certain de-calcified horizons were composed almost entirely of slug plates (Preece and Bates 1999). The same horizon only a few metres away, however, furnished more diverse land snail assemblages with a good representa-tion of delicate thin-shelled species, such as *Vitrinobrachium breve*, showing that the decalcification was extremely patchy. At other sites, the calcium carbonate of the shells has vanished leaving only the periostraca, the organic outer shell coverings, as evidence of their occurrence. Percolating water does not always lead to decalcification but may actually precipitate calcium carbonate, which may not be suffi-cient to cement the shells into the deposit, but may nevertheless encrust and obscure diagnostic features of the shell.

Mechanical damage can also occur during transport and after burial, although some species seem more prone to this than others. Crushing can severely affect large shells during compaction. For example, the shells of freshwater mussels (*Unio* and *Anodonta* spp.) fre-quently disintegrate into a mass of nacreous flakes. Identification is possible if the umbones, on which the diagnostic features occur, remain more or less intact (Kennard *et al.* 1925). Very occasionally the parasitic glochidial larvae of freshwater mussels are also pre-served and since they show species-specific characters, they can be used to establish the species of mussel pre-sent (Aldridge and Horne 1998). Small tightly coiled shells, on the other hand, may remain relatively unda-maged. Breakage does not necessarily preclude specific identification, because the shells of many species possess diagnostic microsculpture (see Preece 1981), so that most apical shell fragments are identifiable provided that the preservation is reasonably good.

There has been relatively little work on the processes that lead to the incorporation of shells into soils. One notable exception is the work undertaken by Carter (1990), who attempted to quantify the taphonomic effects controlling the incorporation, mixing and sub-sequent destruction of shells in buried soils. He con-ducted field experiments that suggested that the mean residence time for various species of land snail ranged from about 5.7 years for *Cochlicopa lubricella* to 335 years in the case of robust shells such those of *Helicella itala*. Where the surface casting rate is high (5–10 mm yr^{-1}), assemblages from the A horizon will span only 20–30 years giving excellent temporal resolution (1–4 years in a 1 cm spit). In most cases far lower casting rates were observed and the temporal and ecological resolutions of land snail assemblages were poor in comparison.

RESPONSES OF NON-MARINE MOLLUSCS TO ENVIRONMENTAL CHANGE

Faced with changed environmental circumstances, such as occur throughout the Quaternary, organisms have three basic options. First, they can adapt to the new circumstances. Second, they can move out of trouble, maintaining their positions with respect to environmen-tal gradients by 'tracking the environment'. Third, they can admit defeat and become extinct. Amongst the invertebrates, molluscs are unusual in having a relatively good fossil record so that it is possible to establish which of these options occurs most commonly.

Evolution

The quality of evidence needed to show that evolution has taken place in response to climatic or environmen-tal changes is demanding. Ideally, we need to know precisely when and where such changes occurred and also that they are indeed evolutionary, and not a consequence of movement of a stable geographical cline nor the increase of population or expansion following a speciation event elsewhere (Bennett 1997). Knowledge about the situation throughout the entire geographical range of a species is necessary, rather than information from only one or two fossil sequences. The only places where such stringent requirements can potentially be realized are small islands.

Oceanic islands in many parts of the world are inhabited by endemic species of land snail. The faunas existing today are generally impoverished compared to those that existed before the arrival of humans. This is especially true of many islands in the Pacific, where the losses have been catastrophic. In the Hawaiian islands, for example, it is estimated that only 25 per cent of the 763 native species survive today (Solem 1990). These particular losses have been attributed to habitat destruction, over-collecting and the deliberate intro-duction of carnivorous snails in well intentioned but ill-conceived attempts to control the introduced Giant African land snail *Achatina fulica* (Hadfield 1986).

The scale of these extinctions obscures the natural diversity that once existed on such islands but it is still possible to learn much about evolutionary history from the fossil records from oceanic islands. Aeolianite (dune) deposits containing fossil snails occur on several islands, such as Bermuda (Gould 1969) or those in the Madeiran group (Cook *et al.* 1993). Here it has been possible to detect the existence of new species with the confidence that they evolved at or near the site of deposition and cannot have moved in after an origin at some distant point.

The study of molluscan successions has contributed important information relating to issues such as the tempo and mode of evolution. The Cenozoic molluscan succession of the eastern Turkana basin, for example, has been critical in the debate centred on whether evolution proceeds rapidly at certain brief intervals followed by long periods of stasis ('punctuated equilibrium') or whether the primary mode is by phyletic gradualism. Williamson (1981, 1985) argued strongly for the former mode, although others remained sceptical about his claims, preferring to interpret his simultaneous 'speciation events' in no fewer than 10 different lineages as ecophenotypic consequences of environmental stress (e.g., Fryer *et al.* 1985).

All organisms are continually subject to natural selection but microevolutionary processes seldom lead to speciation during the Quaternary, at least in mid latitude continental regions, such as north-west Europe. Several species of land snail are polymorphic with respect to shell colour and the occurrence and nature of banding. The two common species of *Cepaea* (*nemoralis* and *hortensis*) are perhaps the best known examples amongst the European fauna. There is now an enormous literature on the factors controlling this polymorphism, both from genetic and ecological standpoints. Colour is seldom preserved in the shells of fossil land snails but banding is more durable and often does survive. This has allowed people to study temporal changes in banding patterns over thousands of years and to relate these to climatic or other environmental causes (e.g., Currey and Cain 1968, Cain 1971).

Other species of land snail exhibit morphological changes through time. Late-glacial specimens of *Pupilla muscorum*, for example, are frequently larger, both taller and broader, than specimens from Holocene levels from the same sites (Kerney *et al.* 1964, Preece 1998). Rousseau and Laurin (1984) and Rousseau (1989, 1997) reported similar findings in older Quaternary sequences in France, where detailed morphometric analyses were undertaken, suggesting a link between shell morphology (chiefly height and outline of the aperture) and climate. Rousseau (1997) regarded this morphological plasticity as the result of ecophenotypic adaptation but the coexistence of different shell morphs within sympatric populations suggests that the situation may be more complex (Preece 1998). A clearer relationship between shell size and climate (i.e., mean annual rainfall) has been reported in the case of *Pleurodonte lucerna* on Jamaica (Goodfriend 1992).

Distributional changes

The most common biotic response to changes of environment is not evolution but shifts in geographical distribution. Such shifts may be either spatial, involving changes in latitude or longitude, or altitudinal or both. Some of the range shifts seen during the Quaternary are very spectacular. For example, a regular member of Devensian (Last) glacial beetle assemblages is *Aphodius holdereri*, a species that is today restricted to Tibet (Coope 1973). There are several other examples of Asiatic and arctic-alpine beetles occurring in northwest Europe during cold stages of the Quaternary (see Chapter 10). Conversely, species with southern ranges today were widespread during temperate periods. Comparable, although less spectacular, changes in geographical range can be observed amongst Quaternary non-marine molluscs. No strictly Asiatic species are known, but taxa with arctic-alpine modern ranges, such as *Vertigo genesii* and *Columella columella*, were common during certain glacial stages. The occurrence of such taxa have often been taken to indicate cold climates but such an interpretation may not always be valid. *Columella columella* is extinct in Britain but is known to have survived into the early Holocene both in southern England (Preece 1998) and in Ireland (Preece *et al.* 1986), whereas *Vertigo genesii* still lives at sites in northern England and Scotland (Coles and Colville 1980, Colville 1998). The occurrence of these snails therefore appears to be not related directly to the thermal environment but rather to its effect on maintaining the openness of the habitat (Preece 1997).

During temperate stages of the Quaternary various species, which today inhabit southern regions, spread northwards in north-west Europe. Perhaps the most famous of these is the bivalve *Corbicula fluminalis*, which has a modern range extending from north-east Africa through Syria and Asia Minor to Kashmir. *Belgrandia marginata*, a small prosobranch gastropod, was also frequent in north-west Europe during interglacial periods, although today it is confined to a few localities in southern France and Spain (Boeters 1987).

Large distributional shifts are also seen among the land snails, which include several species that occur far beyond their modern range.

MOLLUSCA AS INDICATORS OF THE AGE OF A DEPOSIT

Some people believe that because there has been relatively little faunal turnover amongst invertebrates during the Quaternary, they are therefore worthless in indicating the age of particular deposits. It is true that Quaternary snails, for instance, are not ideal zone fossils, since they neither possess planktonic larvae capable of cosmopolitan dispersal nor undergo rapid speciation, at least in mid to high latitudes of continental regions. It is therefore not possible to erect a series of range zones applicable globally, such as the ammonite zones defined from the Jurassic and Cretaceous.

Such a handicap does not, however, render the group useless for biostratigraphy. Certain species, for instance, do appear to be limited to one horizon. In Britain, *Viviparus diluvianus* and *Theodoxus danubialis* are currently known only from the Hoxnian Interglacial, whereas *Tanousia runtoniana* has been recorded only from the 'Cromerian'. Caution needs to be exercised here because in Britain these species are known from only a few localities, so that knowledge of their complete stratigraphical ranges must await the discovery of other sites. Such deposits will need to be dated independently for obvious reasons. On the continent, these taxa are all known from other horizons, *V. diluvianus* and *T. danubialis* occurring in the Late Tiglian and *T. runtoniana* occurs in the stratotype of the Bavel Interglacial (Meijer 1990).

A species that occurred during several different stages may also be useful, provided that it did not occur in all stages. For example, the extinct bivalve *Pisidium clessini* (=*astartoides* auctt.) is known in Britain from the Norwich Crag and then every interglacial from the Cromerian up to the penultimate interglacial but is unknown from either the Last Interglacial or the Holocene. Similarly, *Corbicula fluminalis*, another bivalve, also occurs as drifted shells in the Norwich Crag but then is absent from the Cromerian Complex, returning in all interglacial stages up to but not including the Last (Ipswichian) Interglacial. Like *P. clessini*, it too seems to have been absent in north-west Europe during the Last Interglacial and the Holocene (Meijer and Preece 2000). Obviously when using negative evidence in this way it is important to ensure that the absences are 'real' and not the result of facies

differences or collection failure. Usually other taxa are present that suggest correlation with a particular period. Therefore it is frequently the presence of some taxa, combined with the absence of others, that imparts a distinctive character to a particular assemblage.

For many interglacials, at least those studied in north-west Europe, it is not usually possible to use non-marine molluscs to place their occurrence within any particular part of the interglacial cycle. This stems from the fact that most shell-bearing interglacial sites studied in NW Europe are fluvial, which therefore provide more fragmentary records with poorer stratigraphical resolution than other depositional settings. An exception is the fluvial molluscan assemblages from the Hoxnian Stage at famous Palaeolithic sites such as Swanscombe and Clacton-on-Sea. A striking feature of the Swanscombe sequence is the change in character of the freshwater fauna that occurs between the Lower and the Middle Gravels (Kerney 1971). Assemblages from the upper part of the Swanscombe aggradation contain a number of species that no longer live in Britain including *Theodoxus danubialis* (=*serratiliniformis*), *Viviparus diluvianus*, *Valvata naticina*, *Belgrandia marginata*, *Corbicula fluminalis* and *Pisidium clessini*. These are the so-called 'Rhenish fauna', which Kennard (1942) believed demonstrated linkage between the Thames and Rhine river systems only after the deposition of the Lower Gravel.

A similar pattern occurs at Clacton-on-Sea, the type site of the Clactonian Palaeolithic industry, where the molluscan succession can be related, in part, to different sub-stages of the Hoxnian by means of pollen analysis (Turner and Kerney 1971). Apart from *Pisidium clessini*, members of the 'Rhenish fauna' are absent from the lowermost freshwater beds (Ho IIb), *B. marginata* occurs in their upper levels (Ho IIIa) and *Corbicula* and *V. diluvianus* are unknown before the estuarine stage late in the interglacial (Ho IIIb) (Kerney 1971). Several members of the 'Rhenish fauna' have recently been discovered at East Hyde near Tillingham (Essex), 20 km south-west of Clacton. As at Clacton these also occur in the late temperate sub-stage of the Hoxnian (Ho IIIb), together with occasional brackish species (Roe and Preece 1995, Roe 1999).

The faunas from glacial stages pose a particular problem because, unlike those from interglacials, they are generally composed of the same small group of hardy species that recur during successive cold periods. This is exemplified by the restricted land snail faunas from loess, which are dominated by *Pupilla muscorum* with subordinate *Columella columella* and *Vertigo genesii*.

These are commonly associated with marsh species, such as *Succinea oblonga*, or with a limited aquatic fauna consisting of *Anisus leucostoma*, *Pisidium obtusale lapponicum* and occasionally *P. stewarti* (=*vincentianum*). Not all these species may exist at a single site but this fauna is known from several periods during the Last Glacial stage (Devensian/Weichselian), as well as from much earlier glacial stages. Slightly richer faunas are known from loess sequences in central and eastern Europe, which typically include additional species of *Pupilla* (e.g., *sterri*, *loessica*), as well as *Vallonia tenuilabris* (Lozek 1964). Another recurrent fauna is the pioneer *Gyraulus laevis–Armiger crista* facies, typical of 'ecologically young' lacustrine environments that existed during late-glacial phases of both the Devensian and Anglian and at other times. It is possible to distinguish assemblages that lived during the coldest periods (stadials) from those that existed during the more temperate interstadials. A relatively small number of species (commonly 10 or less) are known from the former, whereas two dozen or more are known from the latter (Kerney 1977a, Holyoak 1982). Interstadial deposits pre-dating the Devensian Late-glacial are known chiefly from fluvial contexts, where it can be difficult to decide whether a particular shell has been reworked (Holyoak 1982).

During the Late-glacial and Holocene land snail assemblages can provide good evidence for the age of particular deposits, although without independent corroboration there are dangers of circular reasoning. For these critical periods, radiocarbon dating has provided the necessary independent support. Calcareous slope-deposits formed by incremental accumulation often provide valuable records not only for the Late-glacial but also for the periods following forest clearance from the Neolithic onwards. The later sediments can also provide stratified sequences of artefacts (e.g., Bell 1983, Bennett *et al.* 1998). Tufas, which formed in low-energy environments around springs, provide excellent successions of land snail assemblages during the early to mid Holocene. These are also of direct archaeological interest since tufas commonly yield Mesolithic artefacts, such as at Blashenwell, Dorset (Clark 1938, Preece 1980), Prestatyn, North Wales (Clark 1938), Cherhill, Wiltshire (Evans and Smith 1983) and Newlands Cross, County Dublin (Preece *et al.* 1986).

There are now a number of good molluscan successions spanning the Late-glacial–Holocene transition and extending virtually up to the present day. Most of these sequences are in southern England and result from work undertaken through the infill of chalkland

valleys (e.g., Kerney 1963, Kerney *et al.* 1964, Evans 1966) or from tufa sequences (e.g., Evans *et al.* 1978, Kerney *et al.* 1980, Preece 1980, Preece and Day 1994). Despite some minor regional variation, land snails appeared to recolonize Britain in an ordered succession, in much the same way as did plants. This observation prompted the definition of a series of molluscan assemblage zones that could be applied to comparable sequences in southern Britain (Kerney 1977b, Kerney *et al.* 1980). In most cases these zones are characterized by their faunal composition, rather than by the presence of a single species. Two Late-glacial zones (y and z) and six Holocene zones (a–f) were defined (Table 11.1), from a type succession at Holywell

Table 11.1 Molluscan zonation scheme defined at Holywell Coombe, Folkestone, Kent (modified from Kerney 1977b, Kerney *et al.* 1980, Preece 1998). Note that zone z extends into the very early Holocene and that zone d is no longer subdivided into subzone d^1 and d^2. The ages for the zone boundaries are based on radiocarbon dates obtained during the Eurotunnel project (Preece 1998).

Zone f: From sometime before 2870 ± 70 BP (shell date based on first appearance of *H. aspersa*). Archaeological evidence indicates a Romano–British age for much of this zone. Open ground fauna; as zone e but with appearance of *Helix aspersa*.

Zone e: Lower boundary appears to be diachronous and has produced dates ranging from 5620 ± 90 to 3980 ± 70 BP. Open ground fauna; decline of shade-demanding species; re-expansion of *Vallonia*.

Zone d: 7650 ± 80 BP until sometime before 5620 ± 90 BP. Woodland fauna; expansion of *Oxychilus cellarius*, *Spermodea*, *Leiostyla*, *Acicula*.

Zone c: 8630 ± 120 BP until just before 7650 ± 80 BP. Woodland fauna: replacement of *Discus ruderatus* by *Discus rotundatus*.

Zone b: Slightly before 9460 ± 140 until 8630 ± 120 BP. Woodland fauna: expansion of *Carychium tridentatum* and *Aegopinella*; *Discus ruderatus* characteristic.

Zone a: 9760 ± 100 BP until sometime before 9530 ± 75 BP. As zone z, but with decline of bare soil species (notably *Pupilla*) and corresponding expansion of catholic species; appearance of *Carychium tridentatum*, *Vitrea*, *Aegopinella*.

Zone z: Slightly before $11\,530 \pm 160$ until 9820 ± 90 BP. Open ground fauna; restricted periglacial assemblage with *Pupilla*, *Abida*, *Vallonia*, *Trichia*, *Columella columella*, *Nesovitrea hammonis*.

Zone y: $13\,160 \pm 400$ BP until shortly before $11\,530 \pm 160$ BP. Impoverished fauna dominated by *Pupilla*, *Vallonia* and *Vitrina*.

Coombe, Folkestone (Kent). In fact, in the original study (Kerney *et al.* 1980) zone y had not been found at Holywell Coombe, but new work conducted in advance of the construction of the Channel Tunnel demonstrated its occurrence there in its expected stratigraphical position (Preece 1998, Preece and Bridgland 1999). This new work is important for three reasons. First, it provided better resolved molluscan data from several different profiles, that could be linked to the results from other fossil groups. Second, it enabled the molluscan succession to be related, in part, to the vegetational history by means of pollen analysis. Third, it yielded more radiocarbon dates, which provide a better chronological framework for the molluscan zonation scheme. It is important to stress that the zonation scheme is unlikely to be applicable over large areas (see Preece *et al.* 1984) and the zone boundaries, even if they can be recognized, will almost certainly prove to be diachronous.

Many archaeologists are interested in more recent periods of time and will wonder whether molluscs can be used to help them date their deposits. The two largest British land snails, *Helix pomatia* and *Helix aspersa*, are unknown with certainty before the Roman period (Kerney 1966). Indeed, the appearance of *H. aspersa* at Holywell Coombe, which defines the base of zone f (Kerney *et al.* 1980), coincides with a unit that has yielded Roman and later artefacts (Preece 1998). Likewise the two most common species of helicelline snail, *Cernuella virgata* and *Candidula intersecta*, are also late immigrants. In Britain *C. virgata* is known from interglacial deposits but during the Holocene is unknown with certainty before the Roman period. *Candidula intersecta* has been reported from a few Bronze Age sites but most of the records are later, as are those for *Candidula gigaxii* and *Monacha cantiana* (Kerney 1966, Evans 1972). Many of these species, which in Britain are largely or entirely confined to the Holocene, are xerophilous and have been found mainly in colluvial deposits at the foot of Chalk slopes or, more often, directly associated with archaeological sites.

Great caution needs to be exercised when using non-marine molluscan assemblages to provide an estimate of the age of particular deposits. Although they do not show an evolutionary sequence of species, such as the succession of ammonites species seen in the Mesozoic, they can nevertheless be used to give an approximate idea about age. It is generally not possible to do so from the assemblages recovered from cold stage deposits, but they can often provide a clue as to the age of a particular interglacial, whereas in the Late-glacial and Holocene they can be used to constrain the age to within much narrower limits.

MOLLUSCA AS INDICATORS OF CLIMATE

Traditionally inferences about the contemporary climate during which a deposit accumulated have been based on the modern geographical ranges of organisms contained in the deposit. Geographical data for land and freshwater molluscs is fortunately rather good, at least for most of northern Europe (Kerney *et al.* 1983). For many countries, the British Isles included, distributions have been mapped using the National 10 kilometre grid (e.g., Kerney 1999) and for some regions the level of detail is even better, information being available on a 2 km grid basis (e.g., Killeen 1992). Such information provides a firm basis from which to consider the possible effects of climate as a cause of distributional changes.

Many species have wide geographical distributions, occurring throughout much of the Palaearctic. *Vallonia pulchella*, for example, has a range from the Ahaggar region of the central Sahara to within the Arctic Circle in Scandinavia and also in North America (Sparks 1963). Such species are of little use when attempting to reconstruct palaeoclimates. Fortunately, a few species have more restricted ranges and if such distributions are controlled by climate, then these species offer much better prospects. The problem can be approached in two ways, either by considering the presence or absence of certain species or by considering the overall composition of the fauna.

In Britain there are no species of land or freshwater mollusc that are known uniquely from cold stages, but several species occur overwhelmingly in such contexts. *Columella columella* and *Vertigo genesii* are typical examples of land snail, but each occurs in the early Holocene in both southern Britain (Preece 1998) and Ireland (Preece *et al.* 1986). Their arctic-alpine modern ranges seem to be governed as much by the openness of the habitat, as by the cold climate. As with the land snails, no aquatic species are confined to cold stages, although the bivalve *Pisidium stewarti* is known principally from such contexts but also occurs in the early Holocene (Stelfox *et al.* 1972).

Conversely there are many species that are known only from interglacial stages. Most famous amongst these are the bivalve *Corbicula fluminalis* and the minute gastropod *Belgrandia marginata* mentioned earlier. Amongst the non-British land snails commonly encountered in interglacial deposits, several now occur in southern (e.g., *Vallonia enniensis*) or in central Europe (e.g., *Clausilia pumila*). Species that are today at the northern limit of the range in Britain were common, occurring at interglacial sites beyond their present ranges. Such species include *Helicodonta obvoluta*, *Ena montana* and *Truncatellina cylindrica*. Some rarer species are known in Britain principally from the Hoxnian tufas at Hitchin, Hertfordshire (Kerney 1959) and Beeches Pit, West Stow (Kerney 1976, Preece *et al.* 1991). These include taxa such as *Platyla similis* (=*Acicula diluviana*), now living in south-east Europe, *Laminifera pauli* (Pyrenean), *Ruthenica filograna* (east European) and *Retinella* (*Lyrodiscus*), a subgenus known living only on the Canaries. The extreme disjunction of their modern ranges means that it is impossible to find a modern analogue for these Middle Pleistocene assemblages.

The presence of such species indicates climatic conditions at least as warm or possibly slightly warmer than those now prevailing in Britain today. When reaching such a conclusion it is important to remember that there is likely to have been a lag between the amelioration of climate and the arrival of thermophilous species in northern Europe. Sparks (1963) contrasted the delayed appearance of thermophiles during the early part of the 'Last Interglacial', when the climate already appears to have been suitable for them, with their persistence towards its end, when the climate had clearly deteriorated. Many of these occurrences are based on records from fluvial contexts, so that it is difficult to exclude the possibility of reworking. Derivation does not, however, provide the only explanation and some species genuinely did persist. There are various reasons why such species may have lingered on. Some may have survived in some particularly favourable habitat, perhaps on a south-facing slope, where the microclimate may have been substantially different from the prevailing regional climate.

Certain species of land snail, with somewhat southern modern ranges, were absent during the early part of the Late-glacial, only appearing in southern England about 11 500 BP (Kerney 1963). *Abida secale*, a xerophilous species with a range that does not reach Scandinavia today, was one of these. Interestingly in Kent this species survived right through the Younger Dryas and into the early Holocene (Kerney 1963, Preece 1998). It is now extinct on the North Downs, where it succumbed only as the result of the increasing shade cast by the spreading Holocene forests. *Abida secale* does not appear to be controlled by severe cold (it also lives at relatively high elevations in the Alps) but rather by lack of heavy shade. Such evidence serves as a warning against the uncritical use of modern distributions to infer climatic limitation.

Other species of land snail have modern ranges that are more convincingly suggestive of climatic limitation. The distribution of *Lauria cylindracea*, for example, closely matches those for frost-sensitive plants, such as holly *Ilex aquilinum* and ivy *Hedera helix*. Since the thermal tolerances of these plants have been determined precisely (Iversen 1944), it is likely that *Lauria* is also susceptible to periods of prolonged winter cold (Kerney 1968). Likewise, the modern range of *Ena montana* is very similar to that of the mistletoe *Viscum album*, a plant limited by the lack of summer warmth. The occurrence of *E. montana* and *L. cylindracea* in a sample therefore suggests accumulation during a period when the summers were warm and the winters mild (Kerney 1968).

The precise climatic tolerances of most species of land snail have never been determined experimentally and this is a handicap when using them to reconstruct palaeoclimate. Experimental studies have, however, been undertaken on some of the larger helicid species. In one recent study the local extinction of *Arianta arbustorum* from sites around Basle in Switzerland, could be linked directly to increased thermal radiation caused by urbanization since 1908 (Baur and Baur 1993).

It may not be possible to trace in any detail the history of such critical 'indicator species' through a sequence because they may occur only at low frequencies. An alternative way to derive useful climatic information is therefore to consider the assemblages as a whole. Such an approach was adopted by Sparks, who divided the assemblages into four distributional groups based on modern ranges. These were:

(i)   species reaching to, or almost to, the Arctic Circle,
(ii) species reaching approximately 63°N,
(iii) species reaching 60–61°N (i.e., approximately the limit of oak), and
(iv) species reaching the very south of Scandinavia or being confined to the continental mainland.

By plotting the frequencies of species in each group, he was able to discern climatic trends of increasing warmth at the beginning of interglacials or cooling towards their end. These simple interpretations are clearly complicated by the effects of delayed immigration, persistence and derivation discussed earlier. Despite these complications, an experienced malacologist should be able to gain a shrewd idea of the climatic history from changes in faunal composition.

Attempts have recently been made to obtain quantitative climatic data from non-marine molluscs. Two approaches have been adopted. The first uses a climatic transfer method based on quantitative analyses of modern land snail assemblages from sites with associated climatic records along a north–south transect (Rousseau 1991). This provides a training set against which fossil assemblages can be matched using multivariate techniques. Various climatic reconstructions using this method have now been published (e.g., Rousseau *et al.* 1993, 1994) but the underlying assumption is that the modern communities are governed principally by climate, and this may not always be so.

The second approach involves geochemical analyses of individual shells. Stable isotope analyses are increasingly being employed. Thus variations in the $^{18}O/^{16}O$ ratios measured in certain species of land snail from a Late-glacial sequence in Switzerland were found to compare closely with the main temperature oscillations inferred for the sequence from other biostratigraphical data (Kaiser and Eicher 1987). Detailed isotope studies have also been used on shells from middens to establish the season of collection of particular species of marine shell. In this way it may be possible to confirm whether the human occupation at the midden site was continuous or episodic. Such an approach could be used on shells of large land snails that may also have served as food.

Most recent studies have undertaken analysis of ^{18}O values of shell carbonate to reconstruct trends in the oxygen isotope composition of rainfall. Such data obtained from the shells of relatively long-lived species (e.g., *Limicolaria*) have provided high resolution records of past seasonal climate variability (e.g., Leng *et al.* 1998). Analyses of ^{13}C values of the organic matter in fossil shells are harder to interpret but they have been used to reconstruct former C_4 plant distributions from which past rainfall amounts can be inferred (Goodfriend 1990). A good review of the use of land shells in palaeoenvironmental reconstruction is provided by Goodfriend (1992).

MOLLUSCA AS INDICATORS OF LOCAL CONDITIONS

Just as many non-marine molluscs have fairly wide geographical ranges, so do many have equally broad ecological tolerances. Such species are uninformative regarding the reconstruction of climate or environment,

at least from straightforward faunal analyses. Most assemblages contain species that are more exacting in their requirements and it is these that provide the main evidence for palaeoenvironmental reconstruction.

One of the great virtues of molluscs is the fact that they can provide information about very local environments. Clearly, fluvial assemblages are likely to contain mixtures of species from a variety of both freshwater and terrestrial habitats. These have been indiscriminately brought together by the action of the river and may have been transported some distance from their sources. Such fluvial assemblages provide a regional view of faunas living in the catchment, although in such situations one must always be alert to the possibility of reworking of shells from older deposits. This information may nevertheless be helpful, especially when attempting to establish the age and character of particular interglacial deposits.

Sparks (1961, 1963) found it useful to allocate each species of freshwater mollusc to one of four ecological groups:

(i)   Slum species, i.e., those which will stand exceedingly poor water conditions, such as poor aeration, periodic drying, large temperature changes consequent upon the small size of the body of water. Only certain species can stand such conditions, although such species may be found elsewhere.

(ii) Catholic species, i.e., those which are found in practically every type of freshwater environments, except the worst 'slums'.

(iii) Ditch species: a term designed to cover those species which prefer plant-rich slow-flowing streams.

(iv) Moving water species, i.e., those more commonly found in larger bodies of water, streams or ponds, where movement is assumed either by currents or by winds.

He plotted the varying frequencies of these ecological groups through a number of sequences and was reassured by the consistency of the results and their compatibility with the conclusions drawn from other evidence.

Lacustrine sequences often provide more continuous sedimentary records but their aquatic molluscan faunas can be extremely monotonous, especially from sites close to the centre of the lake basin (e.g., Sparks, 1962). More informative sequences, that have a bearing on lake-level changes, can be obtained from marginal areas, even though these records are generally less continuous. It is often sensible to take multiple cores from different parts of the lake basin in order to undertake a comprehensive palaeoenvironmental reconstruction.

Many terrestrial sequences yield records that provide extremely local indications of the immediate environment. Such information can obviously be of enormous value to archaeologists who are more interested in the local rather than the regional picture. The main problem concerns the temporal resolution attainable in such deposits. Buried soils, as discussed earlier, may contain assemblages that are severely time-averaged (Carter 1990). In other situations, such as actively accreting tufa surfaces, far better temporal resolution may be possible. The sampling strategy should naturally be designed to address the problems of specific research projects.

Land snail assemblages can also be divided into various ecological groups, depending on the nature of the environment. In wetland habitats it might be helpful to plot the frequency of aquatic, marsh and dry-ground taxa. In this way it would be possible to recognize flooding horizons and their immediate consequences. Alternatively, in drier contexts, the openness of the environment might be important, so the land snails could be grouped into those that are intolerant of shade, those indifferent to it and those that are shade-demanding. Such a classification may be useful in demonstrating human impact on the landscape, such as the recognition of forest clearance episodes (e.g., Evans 1972).

CONCLUSIONS

The shells of land and freshwater molluscs are common in a range of Quaternary deposits and they can be extremely helpful in assessing former climates and environments. They are especially useful in calcareous deposits and in such cases may represent the only source of palaeoenvironmental evidence. They can provide useful information about local environments and with caution may be able to provide clues to the age of particular deposits. Future work is likely to see an increase in their use in high resolution palaeoclimate studies involving stable isotope analyses.

REFERENCES

*Recommended for further reading

Aldridge, D.C. and Horne, D.C. (1998). Fossil glochidia (Bivalvia, Unionidae): identification and value in palaeoenvironmental reconstructions. *Journal of Micropalaeontology*, **17**:179–182.

Baur, B. and Baur, A. (1993). Climatic warming due to thermal radiation from an urban area as possible cause for the local extinction of a land snail. *Journal of Applied Ecology*, **30**:333–340.

Bell, M. (1983). Valley sediments as evidence of prehistoric land-use on the South Downs. *Proceedings of the Prehistoric Society*, **49**:119–150.

Bennett, K.D. (1997). *Evolution and Ecology: the Pace of Life*. Cambridge University Press: Cambridge.

Bennett, P., Ouditt, S. and Rady, J. (1998). The prehistory of Holywell Coombe. In Preece, R.C. and Bridgland, D.R. (eds) *Late Quaternary Environmental Change in Northwest Europe: Excavations at Holywell Coombe, South-east England*, 261–314. Chapman and Hall: London.

Boeters, H.D. (1987). Westeuropäische Moitessieriidae und westeuropäische Hydrobiidae. I Spanien und Portugal. *Archiv für Molluskenkunde*, **118**:181–261.

Cain, A.J. (1971). Colour and banding morphs in subfossil samples of the snail *Cepaea*. In Creed, R. (ed.) *Ecological Genetics and Evolution*, 65–92. Blackwell: Oxford.

Canti, M. (1998). Origin of calcium carbonate granules found in buried soils and Quaternary deposits. *Boreas*, **27**:275–288.

Carter, S.P. (1990). The stratification and taphonomy of shells in calcareous soils: implications for land snail analysis in archaeology. *Journal of Archaeological Science*, **17**:495–507.

Clark, J.G.D. (1938). Microlithic industries from tufa deposits at Prestatyn, Flintshire and Blashenwell, Dorset. *Proceedings of the Prehistoric Society*, **4**:330–334.

Coles, B. and Colville, B. (1980). A glacial relict mollusc. *Nature*, **286**:761.

Colville, B. (1998). The status and conservation of *Vertigo geyeri* Lindholm, 1925 and *V. genesii* (Gredler, 1856) in the British Isles. *Journal of Conchology Special Publication* No 2, 303–306.

Cook, L.M., Goodfriend, G.A. and Cameron, R.A.D. (1993). Changes in the land snail fauna of eastern Madeira during the Quaternary. *Philosophical Transactions of the Royal Society of London*, **B339**:83–103.

Coope, G.R. (1973). Tibetan species of dung beetle from Late Pleistocene deposits in England. *Nature*, **245**:335–336.

Currey, J.D. and Cain, A.J. (1968). Studies on *Cepaea*. IV. Climate and selection of banding morphs in *Cepaea* from the climatic optimum to the present day. *Philosophical Transactions of the Royal Society of London*, **B253**:483–498.

Evans, J.G. (1966). Late-glacial and Post-glacial subaerial deposits at Pitstone, Buckinghamshire. *Proceedings of the Geologists' Association*, **77**:347–364.

*Evans, J.G. (1972). *Land Snails in Archaeology*. Seminar Press: London.

Evans, J.G. and Smith, I.F. (1983). Excavations at Cherhill, North Wiltshire 1967. *Proceedings of the Prehistoric Society*, **49**:43–117.

Evans, J.G., French, C. and Leighton, D. (1978). Habitat change in two Late-glacial and Post-glacial sites in southern Britain: the molluscan evidence. In Limbrey, S. and Evans, J.G. (eds) *The Effect of Man on the Landscape: the Lowland Zone*, 63–75. Research Report No. 21, Council for British Archaeology: London.

Fryer, G., Greenwood, P.H. and Peake, J.F. (1985). The demonstration of speciation in fossil molluscs and living fishes. *Biological Journal of the Linnean Society*, **26**:325–336.

Goodfriend, G.A. (1990). Rainfall in the Negev Desert during the mid-Holocene, based on ^{13}C of organic matter in land snail shells. *Quaternary Research*, **34**:186–197.

*Goodfriend, G.A. (1992). The use of land snail shells in paleoenvironmental reconstruction. *Quaternary Science Reviews*, **11**:665–685.

Gould, S.J. (1969). An evolutionary microcosm: Pleistocene and Recent history of the land snail *P. (Poecilozonites)* in Bermuda. *Bulletin of the Museum of Comparative Zoology*, **138**:407–532.

Hadfield, M.G. (1986). Extinction in Hawaiian achatinelline snails. *Malacologia*, **27**:67–81.

Holyoak, D.T. (1982). Non-marine Mollusca of the last glacial period (Devensian) in Britain. *Malacologia*, **22**:727–730.

Iversen, J. (1944). *Viscum, Hedesa* and *Ilex* as climate indicators. *Geologiska Føreningens i Stockholm Førhhandlingar*, **66**:463–483.

Kaiser, K.F. and Eicher, U. (1987). Fossil pollen, molluscs and stable isotopes in the Dättnau Valley, Switzerland. *Boreas*, **16**:293–304.

Kennard, A.S. (1942). Faunas of the High Terrace at Swanscombe. *Proceedings of the Geologists' Association*, **53**:105.

Kennard, A.S., Salisbury, A.E. and Woodward, B.B. (1925). Notes on the British Post-Pliocene Unionidae, with more especial regard to the means of identification of fossil fragments. *Proceedings of the Malacological Society*, **16**:267–285.

Kerney, M.P. (1959). An interglacial tufa near Hitchin, Hertfordshire. *Proceedings of the Geologists' Association*, **70**:322–337.

Kerney, M.P. (1963). Late-glacial deposits on the Chalk of south-east England. *Philosophical Transactions of the Royal Society of London*, **B246**:203–254.

Kerney, M.P. (1966). Snails and man in Britain. *Journal of Conchology*, **26**:3–14.

Kerney, M.P. (1968). Britain's fauna of land Mollusca and its relation to the Post-glacial thermal optimum. *Symposia of the Zoological Society of London* No 22, 273–291.

Kerney, M.P. (1971). Interglacial deposits at Barnfield pit, Swanscombe, and their molluscan fauna. *Journal of the Geological Society*, **127**:69–93.

Kerney, M.P. (1976). Mollusca from an interglacial tufa in East Anglia, with the description of a new species of *Lyrodiscus* Pilsbry (Gastropoda: Zonitidae). *Journal of Conchology*, **29**:47–50.

Kerney, M.P. (1977a). British Quaternary non-marine Mollusca: a brief review. In Shotton, F.W. (ed.) *British Quaternary Studies: Recent Advances*, 31–42. Clarendon Press: Oxford.

Kerney, M.P. (1977b). A proposed zonation scheme for Late-glacial and Post-glacial deposits using land Mollusca. *Journal of Archaeological Science*, **4**:387–390.

Kerney, M.P. (1999). *Atlas of the Land and Freshwater Molluscs of the British Isles*. Harley Books: Colchester.

Kerney, M.P., Brown, E.H. and Chandler, T.J. (1964). The Late-glacial and Post-glacial history of the Chalk escarpment near Brook, Kent. *Philosophical Transactions of the Royal Society of London*, **B248**:135–204.

Kerney, M.P., Preece, R.C. and Turner, C. (1980). Molluscan and plant biostratigraphy of some Late Devensian and Flandrian deposits in Kent. *Philosophical Transactions of the Royal Society of London*, **B291**:1–43.

Kerney, M.P., Cameron, R.A.D. and Jungbluth, J.H. (1983). *Die Landschnecken Nord- und Mitteleuropas*. Paul Parey: Hamburg.

Killeen, I.J. (1992). *The Land and Freshwater Molluscs of Suffolk. An Atlas and History*. Suffolk Naturalists' Society: Ipswich.

Leng, M.J., Heaton, T.H.E, Lamb, H.F. and Naggs, F. (1998). Carbon and oxygen isotope variations within the shell of the African land snail *Limicolaria kambeul chudeaui* (Germain): a high-resolution record of climate seasonality? *The Holocene*, **8**:407–412.

Lozek, V. (1964). Quartärmollusken der Tschechoslowakei. *Rozpravy Ustredního Ustavu Geologichého*, **31**:1–374.

Meijer, T. (1990). Notes on Quaternary freshwater Mollusca of the Netherlands, with descriptions of some new species. *Mededelingen van de Werkgroep voor Tertiaire en Kwartaire Geologie*, **26**:145–181.

Meijer, T. and Preece, R.C. (2000). A review of the occurrence of *Corbicula* in the Pleistocene of North-west Europe. *Geologie en Mijnbouw*, **79**:241–255.

Preece, R.C. (1980). The biostratigraphy and dating of the tufa deposit at the Mesolithic site at Blashenwell, Dorset, England. *Journal of Archaeological Science*, **7**:345–362.

Preece, R.C. (1981). The value of shell microsculpture as a guide to the identification of land Mollusca from Quaternary deposits. *Journal of Conchology*, **30**:331–337.

Preece, R.C. (1997). The spatial response of non-marine Molluscs to past climate changes. In Huntley, B., Cramer, W., Morgan, A.V., Prentice, H.C. and Allen, J.R.M. (eds) *Past and Future Rapid Environmental Responses of the Terrestrial Biota*, 163–177. NATO ASI Series I, Vol. 47, Springer-Verlag: Berlin.

*Preece, R.C. (1998). Mollusca. In Preece, R.C. and Bridgland, D.R. (eds) *Late Quaternary Environmental Change in North-west Europe: Excavations at Holywell Coombe, South-east England*, 158–212. Chapman and Hall: London.

Preece, R.C. and Bates, M.R. (1999). Mollusca. In Roberts, M.B. and Parfitt, S.A. (eds) *Boxgrove: a Middle Pleistocene Hominid Site at Eartham Quarry, Boxgrove, West Sussex*,

170–175. Archaeological Report 17, English Heritage: London.

Preece, R.C. and Bridgland, D.R. (1999). Holywell Coombe, Folkestone: a 13 000 year history of an English chalkland valley. *Quaternary Science Reviews*, **18**:1075–1125.

Preece, R.C. and Day, S.P. (1994). Comparison of the molluscan and vegetational successions from a radiocarbon-dated tufa in Oxfordshire. *Journal of Biogeography*, **21**:463–478.

Preece, R.C., Bennett, K.D. and Robinson, J.E. (1984). The biostratigraphy of an early Flandrian tufa at Inchrory, Glen Avon, Banffshire. *Scottish Journal of Geology*, **20**:143–159.

Preece, R.C., Coxon, P. and Robinson, J.E. (1986). New biostratigraphic evidence of the Post-glacial colonization of Ireland and for Mesolithic forest disturbance. *Journal of Biogeography*, **13**:487–509.

Preece, R.C., Lewis, S.G., Wymer, J.J., Bridgland, D.R. and Parfitt, S. (1991). Beeches Pit, West Stow, Suffolk (TL 798719). In Lewis, S.G., Whiteman, C.A. and Bridgland, D.R. (eds) *Central East Anglia and the Fen Basin*, 94–104. Field Guide, Quaternary Research Association: London.

Roe, H.M. (1999). Late Middle Pleistocene sea-level change in the southern North Sea: the record from eastern Essex, UK. *Quaternary International*, **55**:115–128.

Roe, H.M. and Preece, R.C. (1995). A new discovery of the Middle Pleistocene 'Rhenish fauna' in Essex. *Journal of Conchology*, **35**:272–273.

Rousseau, D.-D. (1989). Réponses des malacofaunes terrestres quaternaires aux contraintes climatiques en Europe septentrionale. *Palaeogeography, Palaeoclimatology, Palaeoecology*, **69**:113–124.

Rousseau, D.-D. (1991). Climatic transfer functions from Quaternary molluscs in European loess deposits. *Quaternary Research*, **36**:195–209.

Rousseau, D.-D. (1997). The weight of internal and external constraints on *Pupilla muscorum* L. (Gastropoda: Stylommatophora) during the Quaternary in Europe. In Huntley, B., Cramer, W., Morgan, A.V., Prentice, H.C. and Allen, J.R.M. (eds) *Past and Future Rapid Environmental Responses of the Terrestrial Biota*, 303–318. NATO ASI Series I, Vol. 47, Springer-Verlag: Berlin.

Rousseau, D.-D. and Laurin, B. (1984). Variations de *Pupilla muscorum* L. (Gastropoda) dans le Quaternaire d'Achenheim (Alsace): une analyse de l'interaction entre espèce et milieu. *Geobios, Mémoire Spécial*, **8**:349–355.

Rousseau, D.-D., Limondin, N. and Puisségur, J.-J. (1993). Holocene environmental signals from mollusk assemblages in Burgundy (France). *Quaternary Research*, **40**:237–253.

Rousseau, D.-D., Limondin, N., Magnin, F. and Puisségur, J.-J. (1994). Temperature oscillations over the last 10 000 years in western Europe estimated from terrestrial mollusc assemblages. *Boreas*, **23**:66–73.

Solem, A. (1990). How many Hawaiian land snails are left and what can we do for them? *Bishop Museum Occasional Papers*, **30**:27–40.

Sparks, B.W. (1961). The ecological interpretation of Quaternary non-marine Mollusca. *Proceedings of the Linnean Society of London*, **172**:71–80.

Sparks, B.W. (1962). Post-glacial Mollusca from Hawes Water, Lancashire, illustrating some difficulties of interpretation. *Journal of Conchology*, **25**:78–82.

Sparks, B.W. (1963). Non-marine Mollusca and archaeology. In Brothwell, D. and Higgs, E. (eds) *Science in Archaeology*, 395–406. Thames and Hudson: London.

Stelfox, A.W., Kuiper, J.G.J., McMillan, N.F. and Mitchell, G.F. (1972). The Late-glacial and Post-glacial Mollusca of the White Bog, Co. Down. *Proceedings of the Royal Irish Academy*, **72B**:185–207.

Turner, C. and Kerney, M.P. (1971). A note on the age of the freshwater beds of the Clacton Channel. *Journal of the Geological Society*, **127**:87–93.

Williamson, P.G. (1981). Palaeontological documentation of speciation in Cenozoic molluscs from Turkana Basin. *Nature*, **293**:437–443.

Williamson, P.G. (1985). Punctuated equilibrium, morphological stasis and the palaeontological documentation of speciation: a reply to Fryer, Greenwood and Peake's critique of the Turkana Basin mollusc sequence. *Biological Journal of the Linnean Society*, **26**:307–324.

12

Mammals as Climatic Indicators

D.W. YALDEN

School of Biological Sciences, University of Manchester.

Archaeological sites that preserve human bones are likely also to contain bones of other mammals, and this is particularly true of cave sites, where other sources of climatic information are sparse. Mammals, especially lemmings and other rodents, have long been used as indicators of habitat and therefore indirectly of climate. Ungulates, often the prey of the human inhabitants, also serve this function. Being *endotherms* ('warm-blooded'), mammals are less sensitive than plants and invertebrates as climatic indicators, but the better knowledge of their detailed ecological requirements compensates for this in practical terms. In particular, mammals indicate very clearly the peculiar climatic conditions of glacial times, which have no modern analogues in either steppe or tundra conditions.

The use of mammals as climatic indicators for archaeological sites goes well back into Victorian times, when the occurrence of Reindeer *Rangifer tarandus* in Britain was taken by Dawkins and Sanford (1866) as confirming the severity of winter weather in Europe mentioned by Julius Caesar; that they had totally confused concepts of the timing and complexity of Pleistocene climatic changes had yet to be appreciated. Large mammals such as Hippopotamus *Hippopotamus amphibius*, Woolly Mammoth *Mammuthus primigenius*, Woolly Rhinoceros *Coelodonta antiquitatis* and Spotted Hyaena *Crocuta crocuta* attracted most attention from early archaeologists, but the smaller mammals, particularly the rodents, offer better resolution, and a more certain climatic indication, than the few large mammals that occur at most sites. Their use demands a proper screening (sieving) sampling regime, to extract a sufficient sample of the small mammal fauna. Fortunately isolated teeth and jaws can often be identified with sufficient accuracy to obtain an adequate assessment of the fauna and therefore its ecological implications.

The most obvious way to use mammal remains as indicators of past climate is to extrapolate from their current distributions. This assumes that present ranges offer a reasonable indication of climatic tolerances (an assumption that may be defeated by the severe impact of human disturbance to distributions and habitats), and that such tolerances have not changed with evolutionary time. These assumptions are less firmly justified the further back in time one goes. A second route, more useful with palaeontological (i.e., older) faunas than archaeological ones, is to make direct inferences from anatomy of the fossils, both from their skeletons and, more particularly, from their teeth. Good reviews of the Quaternary mammalian faunas of North America (Kurtén and Anderson 1980), Europe (Kurtén 1968) and of Britain in particular (Stuart 1982) are available as guides to the distribution and significance of mammals in archaeological contexts. The standard

Handbook of Archaeological Sciences. Edited by D.R. Brothwell and A.M. Pollard.
© 2001 John Wiley & Sons, Ltd.

taxonomic works (Corbet 1978, Hall 1981) include useful distribution maps, as do many popular field guides (e.g., Burt and Grossenheider 1952, Corbet and Ovenden 1980), though none covers the Palaearctic as a whole. The impact of humans in perturbing distributions and habitats of mammals in the British Isles is specifically reviewed by Yalden (1999).

EXTRAPOLATING CLIMATE FROM MAMMALIAN DISTRIBUTIONS

Most large mammals, and many smaller ones, have ranges that are latitudinally broad, and implicitly therefore wide climatic tolerances. For example, the European deer provide a good south–north sequence, of Roe *Capreolus capreolus* and Red Deer *Cervus elaphus* in the south, Elk (Moose) *Alces alces* in middle latitudes, and Reindeer *Rangifer tarandus* in the north. (A similar sequence in North America has Roe replaced by White-tailed and Mule Deer *Odocoileus virginianus* and *O. hemionus*.) However, their ranges are so extensive that one could easily misinterpret the presence of any one of them in an archaeological site (Table 12.1). In fact, they do not overlap in Europe to the extent that all four occur in any one place (they do all overlap in Siberia), and the apparent overlap of latitudinal range is partly due to the northward extension of the southern species in the maritime climate of Norway, matched by the southward extension of the northern species in the continental interior. In other words, the presence of *Rangifer* may be correctly assumed to indicate a cold site and the presence of *Cervus* or *Capreolus* similarly indicates a warm site, but deriving precise indications of temperature is not possible. Table 12.1 indicates very roughly (using the *Times Atlas* to derive isotherms that match the northern and southern limits of ranges as shown in Corbet (1978) and Burt and Grossenheider

(1952)) the wide climatic tolerances shown by these species. It is unlikely that their distributions are determined directly by climatic considerations, though the depth of winter snow may limit their ability to survive in the north, and rainfall, determining summer forage in Mediterranean climates, may limit the southwards extensions of the southern species. Unfortunately for present purposes, little research on the factors limiting the ranges of mammals has been undertaken. One useful exception is the Wild Boar *Sus scrofa*, which has been shown to depend on mast crops (beech and oak) for its overwinter diet, and to be very sensitive to winter snow depth (Okarma *et al.* 1995). Thus it is largely dependent on deciduous woodland in Europe, and furthermore limited in its range north and eastwards. The mild winters of the last decades have allowed it to expand its range into Finland (Saez-Royuela and Telleria 1986). However, snow depth also has an indirect but complicated effect on other ungulates; by altering the ease with which wolves hunt them. Though wolves normally kill weak or vulnerable deer, under conditions of deep snow cover Red Deer are more vulnerable and even healthy deer may be killed (Okarma 1984). Snow depth hinders the deer but allows the lighter wolves to hunt more effectively, so long as there is a crust on the snow that supports the wolves but not the deer. However, very soft snow hinders the shorter legged wolves even more than the deer (Peterson 1977).

In practical terms, there is in both the Palaearctic and Nearctic a small suite of species that are, currently, essentially confined to high Arctic latitudes, north of about 65°N in the Palaearctic and 55°N in the Nearctic. They include Arctic Fox *Alopex lagopus*, Reindeer/Caribou *Rangifer tarandus*, Polar Bear *Ursus maritimus* (formerly *Thalarctos maritimus*), Collared Lemmings *Dicrostonyx torquatus/groenlandicus/hudsonius*, Brown and Norway Lemmings *Lemmus trimucronatus/sibiricus/lemmus* and Musk Ox *Ovibos*

Table 12.1 The latitudinal ranges and implied climatic tolerances of northern deer Cervidae. Latitudinal distributions are estimated from maps in Corbet (1978) and Burt and Grossenheider (1952). These are extrapolated to climatic tolerances (mean monthly July and January temperatures) from the maps in the *Times Atlas*. While there is a gradient of temperature tolerance from south to north, the overlap between species is complete: there is no mean summer which would be unacceptable to all species, and only a narrow band around −10°C that might be too warm for the northern species yet too cold for one of the southern species in winter.

	Europe (°N)	Asia (°N)	N. America (°N)	July (°C)	January (°C)
Rangifer tarandus	60–70	52–78	48–83	2–22	−45 – −12
Alces alces	53–70	46–70	43–68	5–22	−40 – −12
Cervus elaphus	35–63	28–58	46–55	10–27	−18 – +8
Capreolus capreolus	35–65	28–60	—	12–27	−8 – +8
Odocoileus virginianus	—	—	8–49	15–27	−18 – +15

moschatus. Most of these are also very distinctive skeletally (Polar Bear remains may be hard to distinguish from Brown/Grizzly Bear *U. arctos*), and their presence in an archaeological site is a reliable indicator of cold conditions. This is not to argue that their southern limits are necessarily controlled by temperature; the Arctic Fox, for example, is limited by competition from the Red Fox *Vulpes vulpes* which can readily kill its smaller relative, but needs more food, especially in winter. Clearly, all are tolerant of severe cold, however, and a fauna containing them is likely to have experienced average January temperatures of below freezing. The lemmings are particularly useful as climatic indicators, because their ecologies differ; Collared Lemmings feed especially on dwarf shrubs (willows and Mountain Avens) and occur in drier, colder conditions, while Brown Lemmings prefer wetter places and feed on mosses, grasses and sedges (Batzli 1993). Although their geographical ranges overlap extensively, they do not always co-occur in archaeological sites, and in Belgium their relative numbers changed sharply in successive periods during the Late-glacial; *Lemmus* was numerous there during the Allerod Interstadial, but was virtually replaced during the Younger Dryas by *Dicrostonyx* (Cordy 1991).

Associated with them in both modern and archaeological faunas may be a much wider range of species that range widely from south to north; in Europe as in North America. Such species as the Masked Shrew *Sorex caecutiens* and Common Shrew *S. araneus*, Muskrat *Ondatra zibethica* and Water Vole *Arvicola terrestris* extend from Mediterranean to Arctic latitudes. The use of such species for climatic reconstruction is less refined than for beetles, but there is within this group of mammals sufficient variation in range that the methods used by Atkinson *et al.* (1987) could be applied. In western Europe, the three common rodents, *Apodemus sylvaticus*, *Clethrionomys glareolus* and *Microtus agrestis* overlap widely, but the former occurs further south and the latter further north (Figure 12.1), so that collectively they provide a gradient of occurrence and abundance from south to north, like that of the deer mentioned above. The typical moles Talpidae of both Europe and North America depend upon digging a burrow system to trap earthworms and insect larvae; this is impossible in frozen soils, and their ranges are constrained in the north to around 60°N in Europe and 50°N in North America; only the semi-aquatic *Condylura cristata* extends a little further north, in North America, to about 55°N, and *Desmana moschata* similarly ranges north to about 60°N in Europe.

The opposite group to the Arctic specialists should be a group of semi-tropical species that denote much warmer conditions. This group is very obvious in North America, where it comprises species typically regarded as South or Central American in origin, and confined at present to the southern United States. A typical and distinctive member is the Nine-banded Armadillo *Dasypus septemcinctum*, which is confined south of about 35°N. Moreover, although the species has been spreading northwards in recent decades, it is frost-sensitive, indeed suffers from frostbite, and is limited northwards by 24 annual freeze days per year and a mean January temperature of −2°C. It also needs >38 cm of rainfall annually, limiting its range westwards (Taulman and Robbins 1996). Peccaries *Tayassu tajacu*, Coati *Nasua nasua*, Cacomistle *Bassariscus astutus*, various southern felids (Margay *Felis weidii*, Jaguarondi *F. yagouarondi*, Ocelot *F. pardalis*, Jaguar *Panthera onca*) and skunks (*Conepatus leuconotus*, *Mephitis macroura*) are other examples, along with numerous rodents (e.g., *Sigmodon hispidus*, *S. ochrognathus*, *Baiomys taylori*). The equivalent group is less evident in Europe, where the Mediterranean Sea has been a barrier to immigration from the south throughout archaeological time. There are some characteristically southern species, notably the white-toothed shrews *Crocidura suaveolens*, *C. russula*, *C. leucodon* and *Suncus etruscus*. Other species which might be regarded as members of this group (*Atelerix algirus*, *Genetta genetta*, *Herpestes ichneumon*, *Macaca sylvanus*) are surely human introductions (Dobson 1998), in relatively recent times, and therefore of little use as climatic indicators in any archaeological sense. The mammals of the Balkan peninsula do have somewhat more of a southern cast (the Mouse-tailed Dormouse *Myomimus personatus*, Broad-toothed Mouse *Apodemus mystacinus*, Mole Rat *Spalax leucodon*, Golden Jackal *Canis aureus*), but there are more Turkish or Levantine species missing than there are in common, and the Bosphorus has also been a patent barrier to mammal migration.

This attempt to divide mammals into northern and southern components is confused if not frustrated in Europe by a large number of species that have instead east–west limits to their distributions. Obvious examples with archaeological relevance are the Common Hamster *Cricetus cricetus*, the Saiga *Saiga tatarica* and Steppe Pika *Ochotona pusillus*. These species occur in archaeological sites along with such obvious cold-indicators as collared lemming and reindeer. They are found now on the arid steppes and semi-deserts of Central Asia, but their ranges are typically both dry

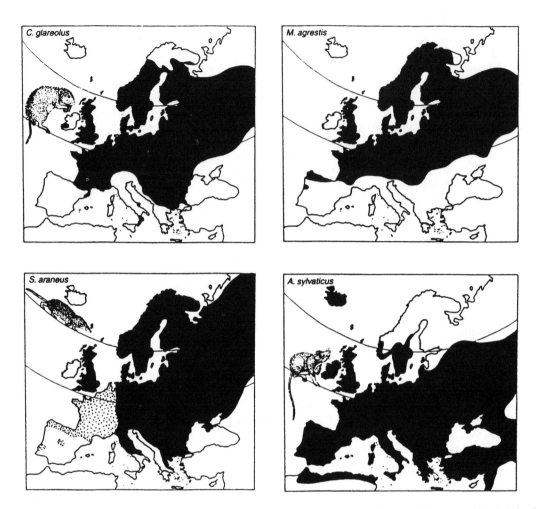

Figure 12.1   The distributions in Europe of the most common small mammals, to indicate the variable extent of their latitudinal ranges (from Yalden 1999). Reproduced by permission of the Academic Press, London.

and cold in winter. It is surely relevant that the Narrow-headed Vole *Microtus gregalis* (*M. anglicus* of British authors), often found in Late-glacial sites with these species, has a split range. It occurs now in an arctic zone, along with Collared Lemmings, and in a steppe zone in central Asia, along with such species as Saiga. This serves as a warning, and a reminder, that Late-glacial climates were unlike any climate now existing. They may indeed have been very cold, in winter, and probably at times very dry; but they would also have been much warmer in summer than present-day Arctic climates, may have been seasonally more moist, and certainly will have had longer growing seasons (earlier springs and later autumns) with much greater production of biomass. This in part explains the mystery of

how large populations of large mammals (Woolly Mammoth, Woolly Rhinoceros, Bison, Saiga, Reindeer), themselves sufficient to sustain populations of human hunters, survived in such apparently inhospitable times. This topic has been extensively discussed in particular in relation to the ecology of the Bering land-bridge, which was clearly host to these communities, and important for allowing humans to enter North America. It has been pointed out that shrubs such as willows would have been particularly productive in such environments (Bliss and Richards 1982). In turn, it may explain the specifically European puzzle of the abundance of the Spotted Hyaena *Crocuta crocuta* in the earlier part of the Last Glaciation. Now confined to Africa south of the Sahara, it is easy to suppose that it is too intolerant of cold to survive in Europe, now or during a glacial period. The earlier part of the Devensian/Weichselian was a period when large ungulates were certainly abundant, and as a specialist predator of such species, it was perhaps the loss of its food supply, rather than temperature as such, that caused its retreat from Europe.

Back before the Last Glaciation, Britain and other parts of western Europe clearly experienced a warmer climate during the last Interglacial. The most notable species for climatic reconstruction was undoubtedly the Hippopotamus, which occurred as far north as the Nile Delta in Pharaonic times, but is now restricted south of the Sahara. It certainly requires warm water as a refuge from both climate and predators, suffering both from drought and sunburn in hot dry conditions, and from frostbite in cold conditions. Other southern mammals also occur as far north as Britain during interglacials, including the Fallow Deer *Dama dama* (native only in the Middle East, but now introduced to many places outside its original range) and Barbary Macaque *Macaca sylvana*. The Rabbit *Oryctolagus cuniculus*, now like the Fallow Deer a familiar species in so many parts of the world, is native only to Iberia and southern France. It was a member of the Hoxnian Interglacial fauna at Swanscombe, along with *Macaca* and *Dama* (Stuart 1982), and part of the mammalogical argument for a much warmer, perhaps Mediterranean, climate then. Despite their wide distribution in modern Britain, Rabbits are most abundant in areas of drier soils and warmer climates in south-eastern Britain, and their spectacular success in the drier areas of Australia is indicative of their climatic preferences.

ANATOMICAL EXTRAPOLATION

The skeletal and dental adaptations of mammals are well described and sometimes researched in minute detail. A good general overview is provided by Carroll (1988) and a popular summary by Savage and Long (1986). Although only indirectly indicative of climate, limb structure is a good and sensitive indicator of the extent to which woodland or grassland dominates a site, and the similar dental differentiation between browsers and grazers is well documented. The crude dichotomy between low-crowned (brachyodont) molars characteristic of browsers and the high-crowned (hypsodont) molars of grazers is now supported by electron-microscopic examination of the pits (in browsers) or striae (in grazers) on the enamel

surface of the teeth, and the carbon isotope content of the enamel (see Chapter 23).

Hypsodont molars evolved in parallel in several evolutionary lines of mammals. Among the most obvious are the sequences from mastodons to true elephants, from hamster-like to vole or lemming-like rodents, from woodland to grassland pigs like warthogs, from forest antelopes to sheep and cattle, and the horse lineage from *Parahippus* to *Merychippus-Pliohippus-Equus*. At the same time, limbs elongated, and the length of the metapodials (metacarpals and metatarsals) either relative to other limb bones or, in the absence of complete skeletons, relative to their own width, gives a good indication of their function. Forest mammals have shorter, broader limbs, relative to those of open habitats, because of softer soils and slower more deliberate movements. These changes coincide with the evolution of extensive grasslands in the mid-Miocene, about 15 Ma. The consequence is a more diverse modern fauna in which browsing forest animals, intermediate forms and specialist grazers may co-exist. This provides ample scope for detailed analysis.

A good example of the application of this subject is offered by Collinson and Hooker (1987). Although applied to Eocene faunas, much older than any of archaeological interest, it provides a model that could readily be applied to later faunas. The mammals occurring in the deposits were examined against three criteria: diet, size and locomotor type. Diet was judged from tooth morphology and the known diets of modern mammals with analogous teeth. Size was judged from tooth size, or from skeletal size if skeletons were available. Skeletal anatomy, particularly the types of joint surfaces at the critical joints (knee, ankle, elbow, wrist) indicated locomotor type; the anatomy of near relatives was used when species were only known from teeth. The percentages of mammal species in each of these three categories were then compared with those in similar analyses of modern, mostly African, faunas. At the extremes, higher proportions of browsing and grazing herbivores, larger mammals, and large ground mammals typify open habitats, whereas higher proportions of insectivores and frugivores, smaller mammals, and arboreal or scansorial types typify forested communities. Open habitats, modern grasslands and tundra, imply drier and/or colder climates, whereas forested localities must be wetter and warmer. The resolution of these methods is certainly sufficient to discriminate intermediate habitats, as shown by the changes recognized as the British Palaeocene tropical forest changed through the Eocene into the Oligocene to drier, semi-forested habitat (Figure 12.2).

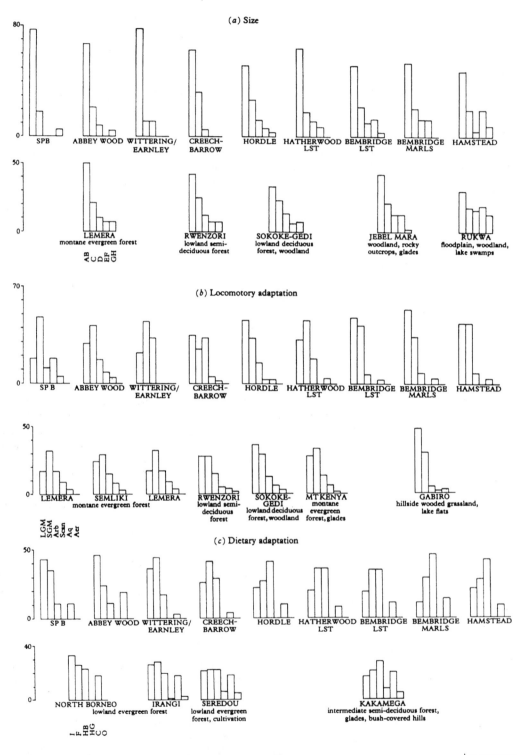

(a) Size

SPB   ABBEY WOOD   WITTERING/EARNLEY   CREECH-BARROW   HORDLE   HATHERWOOD LST   BEMBRIDGE LST   BEMBRIDGE MARLS   HAMSTEAD

LEMERA
montane evergreen forest

RWENZORI
lowland semi-deciduous forest

SOKOKE-GEDI
lowland deciduous forest, woodland

JEBEL MARA
woodland, rocky outcrops, glades

RUKWA
floodplain, woodland, lake swamps

(b) Locomotory adaptation

SP B   ABBEY WOOD   WITTERING/EARNLEY   CREECH-BARROW   HORDLE   HATHERWOOD LST   BEMBRIDGE LST   BEMBRIDGE MARLS   HAMSTEAD

LEMERA   SEMLIKI   LEMERA
montane evergreen forest

RWENZORI
lowland semi-deciduous forest

SOKOKE-GEDI
lowland deciduous forest, woodland

MT KENYA
montane evergreen forest, glades

GABIRO
hillside wooded grassland, lake flats

(c) Dietary adaptation

SP B   ABBEY WOOD   WITTERING/EARNLEY   CREECH-BARROW   HORDLE   HATHERWOOD LST   BEMBRIDGE LST   BEMBRIDGE MARLS   HAMSTEAD

NORTH BORNEO
lowland evergreen forest

IRANGI

SEREDOU
lowland evergreen forest, cultivation

KAKAMEGA
intermediate semi-deciduous forest, glades, bush-covered hills

PALEOCENE   EOCENE   OLIGOCENE

CHRONOLOGICAL VALUE OF MAMMALS

An important additional value of the mammals contained in the archaeological record is their stratigraphic value, since the evolutionary changes of such lineages as voles and elephants have been well studied. The changes are linked to climatic changes, in that the evolutionary changes are for northern species that equipped them better to withstand the extreme conditions of successive glaciations. This is most obvious for the mammoth lineage, evolving from the generalist Pliocene *Archidiskodon meridionalis* through *Mammuthus trogontherii* to *M. primigenius*. The sequences of rodents, especially voles, are more valuable for stratigraphic purposes, because it is easier to obtain adequate samples, and being smaller they have evolved faster. The water vole lineage *Mimomys–Arvicola* is particularly well studied and useful in Eurasia (Chaline 1987). Other voles and lemmings, as well as small insectivores, are also valuable; Stuart (1982) discusses these species, their diagnostic characters and stratigraphic ranges in a useful and accessible manner.

CONCLUSION

The mammalian faunas accompanying archaeological remains of humans and their artifacts are of direct interest to archaeologists as the food and sometimes raw materials for the artifacts and inspiration for the art. They have a considerable additional value as indicators of climate and habitat. This value is only available if adequate sampling is in place to obtain a full and balanced range of taxa, including the smaller species whose abundance and diagnostic value is considerable. Sieving or screening for specimens down to the size of small mammal teeth should be a part of every archaeologist's routine. Sub-sampling of deposits may be adequate, but ignoring this important part of the evidence is not.

REFERENCES

*Recommended for further reading

Atkinson, T.C., Briffa, K.R. and Coope, G.R. (1987). Seasonal temperatures in Britain during the past 22 000 years, reconstructed using beetle remains. *Nature*, **325**:587–592.

Batzli, G.O. (1993). Food selection by lemmings. In Stenseth, N.C. and Ims, R.A. (eds) *The Biology of Lemmings*, 281–301. Linnean Society Symposium 15, Academic Press: London.

Bliss, L.C. and Richards, J.H. (1982). Present-day Arctic vegetation and ecosystems as a predictive tool for the Arctic-steppe mammoth biome. In Hopkins, D.M., Matthews, J.V., Schweger, C.E. and Young, S.B. (eds) *Paleoecology of Beringia*, 241–258. Academic Press: New York.

Burt, W.H. and Grossenheider, R.P. (1952). *A Field Guide to the Mammals*. Houghton Mifflin: Boston.

Carroll, R.L. (1988). *Vertebrate Paleontology and Evolution*. W.H. Freeman: New York.

Chaline, J. (1987). Arvicolid data (*Arvicolidae, Rodentia*) and evolutionary concepts. *Evolutionary Biology*, **21**:227–310.

Collinson, M.E. and Hooker, J.J. (1987). Vegetational and mammalian faunal changes in the Early Tertiary of southern England. In Friis, E.M., Chaloner, W.G. and Crane, P.R. (eds) *The Origins of Angiosperms and their Biological Consequences*, 259–304. Cambridge University Press: Cambridge.

*Corbet, G.B. (1978). *The Mammals of the Palaearctic Region: a Taxonomic Review*. British Museum (Natural History): London.

Corbet, G.B. and Ovenden, D. (1980). *The Mammals of Britain and Europe*. Collins: London.

Cordy, J.-M. (1991). Palaeoecology of the Late Glacial and early Postglacial of Belgium and neighbouring areas. In Barton, N., Roberts, A.J. and Roe, D.A. (eds) *The Late Glacial in North-west Europe*, 40–47. CBA Research Report 77, Council for British Archaeology: London.

Dawkins, W.B. and Sanford, W.A. (1866). *British Pleistocene Mammalia. Introduction*. Palaeontographical Society: London.

Dobson, M. (1998). Mammal distribution in the western Mediterranean: the role of human intervention. *Mammal Review*, **28**:77–88.

*Hall, E.R. (1981). *The Mammals of North America*, (2nd edn). John Wiley: New York.

Figure 12.2 The reconstructed mammal faunas of early Tertiary England (Palaeocene SPB through Eocene to Oliogocene Hamstead) compared with recent faunas from Africa and Asia, to illustrate the change from forest to more open faunas, and the value of this analysis. Faunas are assessed by size, locomotor type and diet of the contained species (from Collinson and Hooker 1987). Reproduced by permission of the Cambridge University Press, Cambridge. Size: AB <1 kg; C 1–10 kg; D 10–45 kg; EF 45–180 kg; GH >180 kg. Locomotor Type: LGM large ground mammal; SGM small ground mammal; Arb arboreal: Scan scansorial; Aq aquatic; Aer aerial (but bats were omitted because they are so rare as fossils). Diet: I insectivore; F frugivore; HB herbivore browser; HG herbivore grazer; C carnivore; O omnivore.

*Kurtén, B. (1968). *Pleistocene Mammals of Europe*. Weidenfeld and Nicolson: London.

*Kurtén, B. and Anderson, E. (1980). *Pleistocene Mammals of North America*. Columbia University Press: New York.

Okarma, H. (1984). The physical condition of Red Deer falling as prey to the Wolf and Lynx and harvested in the Carpathian Mountains. *Acta Theriologica*, **29**:283–290.

Okarma, H., Jedrzejewska, B., Jedrzejewski, W., Krasinski, Z.A. and Milkowski, L. (1995). The roles of predation, snow cover, acorn crop and man-related factors on ungulate mortality in Bialowieza Primeval Forest, Poland. *Acta Theriologica*, **40**:197–217.

Peterson, R.O. (1977). *Wolf Ecology and Relationships on Isle Royale*. Scientific Monograph 11, National Park Service: Washington DC.

Saez-Royuela, C. and Telleria, J.L. (1986). The increased population of the Wild Boar (*Sus scrofa* L.) in Europe. *Mammal Review*, **16**:97–101.

Savage, R.J.G. and Long, M.R. (1986). *Mammal Evolution, an Illustrated Guide*. British Museum (Natural History): London.

*Stuart, A.J. (1982). *Pleistocene Vertebrates in the British Isles*. Longman: London.

Taulman, U.F. and Robbins, I.W. (1996). Recent range expansion and distributional limits of the nine-banded armadillo (*Dasypus novemcinctus*) in the United States. *Journal of Biogeography*, **23**:635–648.

*Yalden, D.W. (1999). *The History of British Mammals*. T. and A.D. Poyser: London.

13

Peat Stratigraphy and Climate Change

K. BARBER and P. LANGDON

Palaeoecology Laboratory, Department of Geography, University of Southampton.

Ombrotrophic (rain-fed) peat bogs are a well-established source of sequential proxy-climate data, but records have been produced by different methods and have been difficult to replicate. Estimating the abundance of the different peat components by eye gives a reasonable first approximation of change and has been used successfully in archaeological contexts. A new quantitative method of plant macrofossil analysis has been developed which provides data suitable for further analysis by multivariate statistics, especially Weighted Averages Ordination (WAO), Detrended Correspondence Analysis (DCA) and Time-Series Analysis (TSA). Application of these methods, together with analyses of humification and testate amoebae, to over thirty sites in Britain and Europe shows that there are a number of periods of climatic change of regional importance. Prominent amongst the changes to wetter and/or colder conditions are the time periods (calibrated radiocarbon years) 4700–4500 BC, 3700–3500 BC, 3000–2600 BC, 2200–1500 BC, 800–500 BC, AD 500–700, AD 1350–1500, and especially the later part of the Little Ice Age, between AD 1650 and 1800, which was the most severe climatic event of the last 2000 years. It is clear that strong (even amplified) proxy-climate signals exist in ombrotrophic bogs, and these signals would have been reflected in changes that would have been particularly important for less-developed agricultural communities, such as changes in water-tables and growing seasons.

BACKGROUND

'As a botanical field investigator for many years past interested in bogs and fens I have often had occasion to notice that these areas appeal very differently to different persons: to some I fear they do not appeal at all, and I fancy that many an archaeologist at heart prefers the dry chalk trench to the soaking black peat face.'
(Godwin 1946)

Peat bogs preserve a unique record of not only their own past vegetation, in the form of the subfossil remains of the plants that make up the peat, but also act as archives of other environmental information (Godwin 1981, Barber 1981, 1993). In particular pollen analyses have long been used to reconstruct past natural vegetation history and human impact upon the environment around such bogs. Raised bogs, those which have accumulated peat above the ground-water table, are also valuable in that they contain a proxy-climate record, and the first division of the Holocene period, into phases of warm and dry or cool and wet climate, was originally based on the peat stratigraphy of Scandinavian bogs. Modern work,

Handbook of Archaeological Sciences. Edited by D.R. Brothwell and A.M. Pollard.
© 2001 John Wiley & Sons, Ltd.

involving detailed macro- and microfossil analyses of the peat, humification analyses, and more and better radiocarbon age estimates, are now allowing us to better separate the climatic 'signal' from the inevitable ecological 'noise' inherent in any biological system (Barber 1994). This contribution sets out the rationale and methodology behind recent research on the peat stratigraphic archive as it relates to climate reconstruction. Some results of recent work are presented and the implications for agriculture in the past are briefly discussed. The archaeology to be found in peatlands is a separate field which has been the subject of much recent research and excavation (Coles 1992, Brown 1997).

RATIONALE AND METHODOLOGY

The main peatlands that form the proxy-climate archive are *ombrotrophic* or 'rain-fed', the accumulation of peat over the millennia having raised the surface like a flattened dome above the mineral groundwater limit. This means that there is a relatively direct relationship between the mean water-table of the bog and precipitation, and there is also a relationship between the mean water-table and the abundance of different species on the bog surface, especially the bog mosses (Sphagna) as well as the humification of the peat. We can, therefore, by analysing the peat for the remains of plants and other sub-fossils, and for humification, reconstruct the past surface wetness of the bog – a proxy-climate record which, in the uppermost peat, can be related to independently-known climatic changes of the last few hundred years. Raised bogs are linked to, and usually derive from, the other main type of peatland, the *minerotrophic* or 'rock-fed' kind, which occur in valleys and basins, or on floodplains, and which are nourished by inflowing streams as well as by precipitation. They are subject to many influences due to natural and cultural changes in their catchments, and analyses of their peats therefore gives a complex picture of environmental changes (Brown 1997), rather than the simple proxy-climate signal of raised bogs. A third type of peatland, *blanket bogs*, are a mixture of ombrotrophic and minerotrophic areas. They also may contain Sphagna but they also may be dominated by sedges, and the generally higher degree of humification means that the plant tissues in the peat may not be recognizable. However their humification record is a valuable proxy-climate record, especially as they dominate the peatland landscape of the Atlantic fringes of northern Europe (Blackford and Chambers 1995).

The proxy-record, in undamaged bogs, is both continuous (and can extend from 9500 years BP; Hughes *et al.* 2000) and of quite high resolution, with average accumulation rates in wet Atlantic bogs of about 10 to 12 yr cm^{-1}. Raised bogs yield multi-proxy records in the form of plant macrofossils, testate amoebae and humification of the peat itself, as well as pollen, non-pollen microfossils, magnetic properties, and isotope geochemistry. Added to these attributes raised bogs are relatively amenable to dating by conventional and AMS radiocarbon assay, though this may not be without its problems (Kilian *et al.* 1995) and where present, distal Icelandic tephras can provide more precise pinning-points in the stratigraphy (Dugmore *et al.* 1995, Pilcher *et al.* 1996).

Early work on deriving proxy-climate signals from peat stratigraphy utilized open peat sections where the stratigraphic relationships could be easily observed (Walker and Walker 1961, Barber 1981). With the mechanization of peat winning from the 1970s onwards such sections are now rare and often overgrown, and there is a need to demonstrate that data can be replicated from core profiles. Replication of results is of course very important, but palaeoecological methods are very time-consuming, and the proxy-climate 'signal' is subject to ecological 'noise'. However, there is now a great deal of corroboration in proxy-climate reconstructions from nearby sites (Barber *et al.* 1994b, Mauquoy and Barber 1999a), and from distant sites (Van Geel *et al.* 1996, Barber *et al.* 2000), and recently the degree of replicability between cores from the same site has been explicitly tested (Barber *et al.* 1998, Woodland *et al.* 1998, Charman *et al.* 1999). These studies concluded that the main features of the record could be adequately replicated, and that cores from the central parts of bogs show a coherent series of changes. Barber *et al.* (1998) also discuss a standard approach to fieldwork involving aerial and ground survey, the coring of at least two intersecting transects, and the careful examination of the peat stratigraphy in the field before more detailed laboratory analyses.

PLANT MACROFOSSILS

In their natural state European raised bogs are dominated by species of the genus *Sphagnum*, the bog-moss, of which there are about 40 species in Europe (Daniels and Eddy 1990) though most individual bogs contain less than ten in varying proportions. These mosses underlie, as a more or less continuous carpet, a top layer of vascular plants such as cotton sedges

(*Eriophorum* species) and various heathers (Ericaceae family) of which the common heather or ling, *Calluna vulgaris*, often dominates. Sphagna grow from the tip or capitulum of the plant, at a rate determined by the species and the regional climate, but generally averaging 1–3 cm yr^{-1}. However these few centimetres of living plant break down to much less by way of peat. Active bogs contain two layers – *acrotelm* and *catotelm* (Ingram 1978). The former is a surface layer of a few centimetres which is relatively well-oxygenated and has some water movement, both vertically and laterally. As growth of the mosses packed together at the bog surface proceeds, the lower parts of each plant are shaded and die, and there is decomposition, loss of structure and compaction of the remains, which then pass into the waterlogged, anoxic catotelm, where the rate of decay slows dramatically and peat accumulation takes place at a rate of about 100 cm in 1000 to 2000 years (Clymo 1991).

Besides the relatively direct relationship between the bog's mean water table and effective precipitation (the balance of precipitation less evapotranspiration), there is also an observable relationship between the mean water table and the zonation of Sphagna and other species such as sedges and heathers on the bog surface (Boatman 1983, Andrus *et al.* 1983). The peat formed by these various species, when washed and sieved, reflects the occurrence and abundance of the past surface vegetation. There are however changes due to differential decay of species, though this can be over-emphasized – in peat of low humification it is often possible to pick out whole *Sphagnum* shoots. What is mainly lost is mass and structural integrity, for in much of the late-Holocene peats of the temperate zone many of the sub-fossils are recognizable to species or sub-genus level. Most of the loss of mass is due to the decay of the living contents of cells and the decay of aerial parts of vascular plants such as cotton sedges (*Eriophorum* spp.) and heather (*Calluna vulgaris*). However, with regard to the bog mosses, as long as the leaf size and shape and the diagnostic cellular details are still discernible then the major part of the original moss community can be reconstructed with some accuracy.

Laboratory procedures

Two methods of peat macrofossil analysis are employed. The *Abundance Estimate* method involves a five-point scale estimate of the washed and sieved remains of a small block of peat. The peat is placed on a fine sieve and washed with a jet of tap water to break it up and free the subfossil remains from the organic matrix. The remains are then transferred to a petri dish or glass trough and examined under a low-power stereo microscope. The remains are scored as 1 = rare, 2 = occasional, 3 = frequent, 4 = common and 5 = abundant (Figure 13.1). This method is rapid and can be employed to give a useful overview of the development of a site and as a reconnaissance tool to help choose a master core for more detailed analyses. It was the method used by Walker and Walker (1961) and by Barber (1981).

The master core is analysed by the more quantitative *Quadrat and Leaf Count* (QLC) method developed at Southampton (Barber *et al.* 1994b). This is much more time-consuming (by a factor of three or so) but allows the data to be subject to multivariate analyses. Peat samples, $4 \times 1 \times 1$ cm, are extracted from wide-diameter cores and washed with a strong jet of water over a 125-micron sieve. The remains are placed in a rectangular glass trough and enough water added to provide a monolayer of remains. In a similar manner to an ecologist throwing quadrats to estimate present vegetation, peat components are then estimated from 15 averaged quadrat counts under low power magnification ($\times 10$) using a 10×10 square grid graticule in the microscope. A high-quality stereozoom microscope is preferable for these repetitive analyses. The advantage of this is that many fragments of plant tissue can be quickly identified by zooming in, though inevitably some have to be removed from the sample trough and identified under high power microscopy. A random selection of *Sphagnum* leaves (>100 per sample interval) are then removed from the trough, stained and mounted in parallel lines under a large coverslip, and identified at high magnification ($\times 400$) to the lowest possible taxonomic level and expressed as percentages. The diagrams produced (Figure 13.3) then give information on peat components and the make-up of the identifiable *Sphagnum* component.

While it is possible then to interpret these data qualitatively in terms of changing wetness conditions on the bog surface – and by implication the conditions experienced on nearby farmed land (Barber 1982) – because of the quantified nature of these data it is also possible to process them using multivariate techniques (see Chapter 54). For example, by giving each of the components of such diagrams an indicator value with respect to the water table, and performing Weighted Averages Ordination (WAO), a single line graph of the climate proxy, bog surface wetness, can be derived (Dupont 1986, Barber *et al.* 1994b). Figure

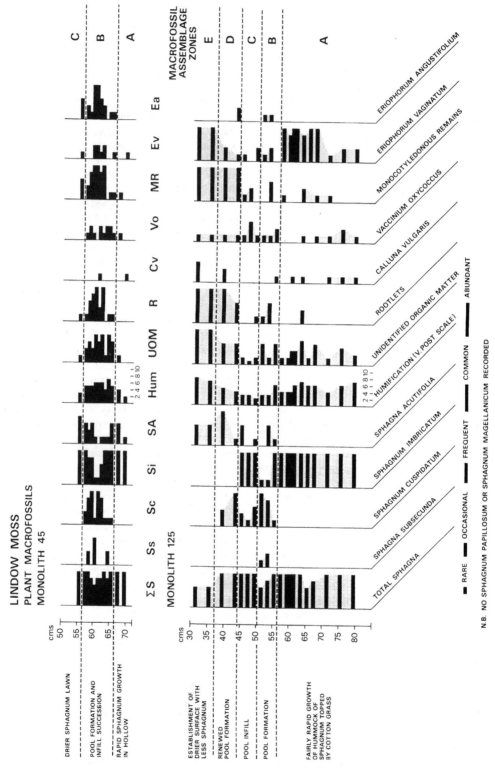

Figure 13.1   Peat macrofossil diagrams from Lindow Moss produced using the Abundance Estimates method.

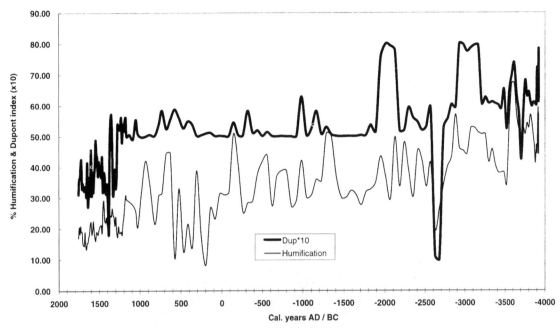

Figure 13.2 Proxy-climate records from Bolton Fell Moss, Cumbria. The upper line is a plot of Weighted Averages Ordination scores (following Dupont 1986) and the lower line is percentage humification, both against calibrated radiocarbon years. (Modified from Barber *et al.* (1994c)).

13.2 shows such a graph, allied to the humification values for the same profile. There is however an element of subjectivity in this procedure, in that the indicator values, usually ranging from 1 to 8 (Dupont 1986), are chosen to reflect the position of a taxon with respect to average water-level, but the field data used to support these indicator values are neither extensive nor unequivocal.

More objective techniques of multivariate analysis include Detrended Correspondence Analysis (DCA), Generalized Linear Modelling (GLIM – used to develop a Climate Response Model by relating species changes in the recent peat to known climate changes), and Time-Series Analysis, all of which have been applied to data from Bolton Fell Moss, Cumbria (Barber *et al.* 1994a). All these techniques confirmed that the data possess coherent and robust structure and that the variations in the data are related to the bog water table and through that to climate.

HUMIFICATION

The decomposition of peat involves many physical and chemical changes. The combined activities of the faunal and microbial populations in mire ecosystems result in the decomposition and humification of the plant remains. The degree of humification has been used to classify peat types since the early work on peat stratigraphy. Von Post devised, in the 1920s, a simple ten point scale based on the visual characteristics of wet peat squeezed by hand (English translation in Davies 1944:Appendix 1). This is still useful in field descriptions, although the more comprehensive system of Troels-Smith (1955) is now more commonly used. However, as quantifiable changes occur within the peat matrix as plant matter decomposes, measurements on a continuous numeric scale are more accurate for the detection of small scale, more subtle changes (Blackford and Chambers 1993).

Colorimetric peat humification analysis appears to represent a semi-quantitative measure of average summer effective rainfall, since the decomposition state is dependent on the time the plant remains take to pass from the biologically active acrotelm into the almost inert catotelm. This is controlled by water table depth; where it is shallow, under regimes of high effective precipitation, there is less scope for decomposition before peat passes into the catotelm. This assumption forms the basis of many palaeoclimatic reconstructions

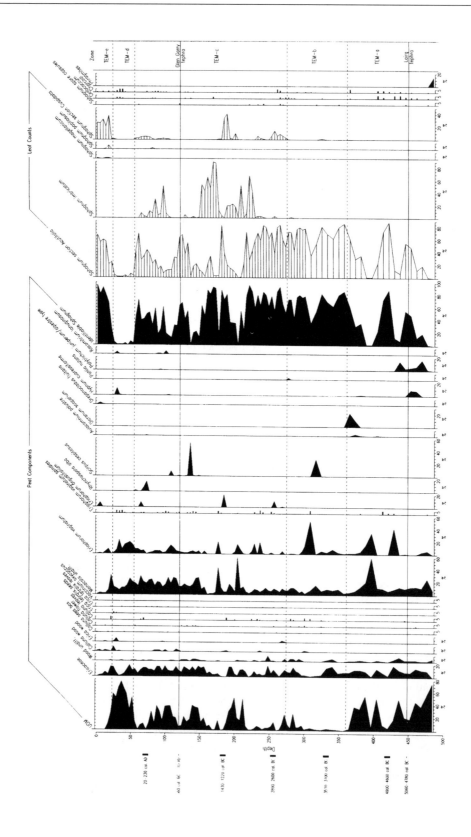

(e.g., Blackford and Chambers 1991, 1995, Chambers *et al.* 1997, Anderson *et al.* 1998). Interpretation of humification data must be undertaken with care, and should be carried out in the presence of plant macrofossil data, as the possibility of a species signal within the data is conceivable.

Colorimetric analysis of peat humification

Measuring the degree of humification involves the alkaline extraction of humic acids from peats, which are produced from the decomposition of organic material, the proportion of which increases as the peat decomposes further. A dark coloured extract would be indicative of well-humified peat, and suggest a drier mire surface, whereas a lighter colour would indicate peat which has been less humified, suggesting a wetter mire surface.

The methods used follow Blackford and Chambers (1993). Subsamples of 4 cm^3 are taken from the peat cores and dried under an infra-red lamp, then ground with a pestle and mortar, and 200 mg of peat weighed out. This sample is then brought to boiling point in 100 ml of freshly mixed 8 per cent caustic soda (NaOH) and simmered gently for one hour. After cooling the samples are transferred into a 200 ml flask, topped up to the mark with distilled water, and shaken well. Samples are filtered through Whatman Qualitative 1 paper into a beaker. 50 ml of the solution is then diluted 1:1 with distilled water into a 100 ml flask and shaken well. Four hours after the initial mixing the samples are measured three times on a Spectrophotometer. The absorbance is recorded at 540 nm, and the average reading calculated.

TESTATE AMOEBAE ANALYSIS

Testate amoebae (Protozoa, Rhizopoda), also known as Testacea or thecamoebae, are unicellular animals with a discrete shell enclosing the cytoplasm and are the most common group of single celled organisms living in surface peat. Moisture is the main ecological variable governing variations in distribution and abundance of Testacea outside aquatic habitats (Tolonen 1986) and therefore peatland testate amoebae are

important indicators of hydrology in fossil studies (Charman and Warner 1997).

There has recently been an increase in the production of quantitative testate data as transfer functions have been employed in an attempt to ascertain the past mean water table depths from ombrotrophic bogs (Charman 1997, Woodland *et al.* 1998). Transfer functions are used as regression techniques in which the dependent variable is the environmental factor of interest, which is used to calibrate fossil species data so as to derive the estimates of the unknown environmental variable (Charman 1997). In developing transfer functions, modern training sets must first be derived, and can then be subjected to Canonical Correspondence Analysis (CCA). These modern testate data have shown that moisture variables, most significantly, depth to the water table, were strongly associated with the main axis of variation, while the secondary axis appeared most strongly correlated with pH (Warner and Charman 1994). Reconstructions of past mire water table depths can be based on these modern training data sets, and are comparable around the world. They include results from England (Charman *et al.* 1999), northern America and Canada (Charman and Warner 1997), and New Zealand (Charman 1997). The results can also be tested against other techniques of proxy-climate reconstruction, specifically plant macrofossil data (DCA analysis) and humification (Chiverrell and Atherden 1999, Mauquoy and Barber 1999a).

Methodology

There has been a long debate – since the early 1900s – on the taxonomy and identification of testate amoebae. Useful keys have been produced, notably by Corbet (1973) and Ellison and Ogden (1987). However, confusion still exists in the literature on the identification of some species. Charman *et al.* (in press) have recently produced a comprehensive taxonomic key including illustrations, which they suggest should form the basis for future research into Testacea from British oligotrophic mires.

The method of preparing the testates follows that of Hendon and Charman (1997). A sample of 2 cm^3 is broken up in a beaker and three *Lycopodium* tablets (Stockmarr 1971) are added to enable concentrations

Figure 13.3   Peat macrofossil diagram from Temple Hill Moss, Scotland, produced using the Quadrat and Leaf Count method. Peat components (black curves) are estimated from microscope quadrat data and leaf counts (bar graphs) are percentages of 100+ moss leaves mounted on microscope slides – see text for details.

of Testacea to be calculated. The peat is boiled for 10 minutes in 100 ml of distilled water and the cooled samples are then sieved and the fraction between 300 μm and 15 μm retained. This material is then washed, centrifuged, and stained with safranin. Another wash is followed by storing the remains in glycerol in a glass vial. A small amount of material is mounted on a slide and two drops of water added, as this improves the definition of the Testacea under the microscope (Charman pers. comm.). The slides are then sealed with nail varnish but it is best to analyse them within a few hours as they may dry out. At least 150 tests are counted per slide where possible (Woodland *et al.* 1998). Levels are rejected when over 1000 *Lycopodium* spores are counted before 100 tests (Charman pers. comm.).

CASE STUDIES

Lindow Man

Lindow Moss, Cheshire is the site of the most celebrated Bog Body yet found in Britain (Stead *et al.* 1986). As part of the multi-proxy investigations into this important find Abundance Estimate macrofossil analyses were conducted on two peat monoliths (Barber 1986). It was assumed at the time, on field stratigraphic evidence, that the body had been dumped into a pool after death. The macrofossil results (Figure 13.1) show a fairly wet bog surface dominated by *Sphagnum imbricatum* with cotton sedges (*Eriophorum vaginatum*), succeeded by the pool at about 300 BC, and the inference was therefore drawn that 'For a short time before Lindow Man's death, and for some decades afterwards, the surface of the bog was distinctly wetter with widespread pools . . . as a result of a change to a wetter and/or cooler climate . . . [which] undoubtedly would have had severe effects on the harvest' (Barber 1986:89). One could speculate on whether or not Lindow Man's peculiar demise and interment was a human sacrifice and therefore linked to this natural decline in crop fertility shown independently by the peat macrofossils.

However, as the radiocarbon dating evidence accumulated it became clear that the body was some 400–500 years younger than the peat it was laid on, and alternative views were aired (Buckland 1995, Barber 1995). The fact that the body had not been colonized by insects – which was not known to Barber in 1986 – led Buckland (1995) to conclude that the body had been pushed down into a deep pool in winter. However, the

stratigraphic and macrofossil evidence points to only a shallow pool existing on Lindow Moss *c.* 300 BC, and Barber (1995) therefore suggested that a simpler explanation would be that Lindow Man's body was inserted into the peat of the infilled pool. One can demonstrate how this could be done on the surfaces of modern bogs. For example, Walton Moss and Bolton Fell Moss in Cumbria (Barber *et al.* 1994b) have a pool peat layer only 20 cm below the modern surface which relates to the later part of the Little Ice Age, *c.* AD 1700–1800, and it is possible to cut down to this and to roll the peat back like a carpet – indeed, the peat breaks naturally at the junction of felted pool peat and the infilling lawn peat above. This neatly solves the lack of an insect fauna on the body, as the peat could have been rolled back over the body immediately with such minimal disturbance as to be undetectable almost 2000 years later. This example underlines the need for careful examination of field stratigraphy, for closely sampled macrofossil analyses, and for multi-proxy evidence such as that of the insect fauna. It also demonstrates the usefulness of environmental evidence in the interpretation of past human actions.

The climate of northern Cumbria since the Neolithic

The North West Wetlands Survey has led to much useful and interesting archaeological data being unearthed from the peatlands of north-west England (e.g., Middleton *et al.* 1995). These peatlands, and those of the adjacent Scottish Borders region, have also been one of the primary foci of modern work on the proxy-climate record and a great deal is now known about past climatic trends in the area (e.g., Mauquoy and Barber 1999b). As an example, Figure 13.2 is a plot of Weighted Averages Ordination (WAO), following the indicator values approach of Dupont (1986), of the macrofossil data from a 5 m deep core at Bolton Fell Moss, Cumbria (NGR NY 490690) as well as the percentage humification values. The records show a good degree of correspondence in the amplitude and phase of the two signals, but there are a number of places where they diverge, for reasons which are still under investigation. The time scale is based upon the rounded mid-points of the 2σ calibrated range of 22 high-precision radiocarbon dates and indicates an almost constant rate of peat accumulation of just over 12 years per cm (Barber *et al.* 1994a).

From about 4000 BC until 2900 BC (all dates are calibrated), the climate was relatively dry, though with a wet period around 3700 BC, and a very dry phase between 3200 and 2900 BC. The massive change to a very wet and probably cold climatic phase following 2900 BC ushered in a long period of dominance of *Sphagnum imbricatum* as the main peat former. Here we see an interesting difference in the two proxy-records. *S. imbricatum* was the major peat-former in most Atlantic raised bogs during the late Holocene but declined dramatically and became extinct at many sites in recent centuries (Mauquoy and Barber 1999b), and this leads to difficulties with assigning an indicator value for the purposes of Weighted Averages Ordination. There is good evidence, from the associated species and humification analyses, that *S. imbricatum* inhabited a wider niche in the past, including low hummock and lawn microforms (Stoneman *et al.* 1993), and by assigning a lower indicator value the upper graph in Figure 13.2 can be made to parallel the humification trace more closely. Using Dupont's (1986) original weighting for this reconstruction has the advantage of separating the two plots to give a clearer picture, and it can be seen that a number of the dry-indicating peaks in humification between 1500 BC and 100 BC are reflected in the ordination values, but the humification results point to a rather wetter/ cooler climate, especially around AD 200 to AD 600. The beginning of the Little Ice Age shows up well at AD 1300.

The peaks and troughs in these graphs must have been reflected in lower and higher groundwater tables in northern Cumbria, and with a cooler climate and shorter growing season, there must have been effects on prehistoric agriculture. The drastic change at 2900 BC (range at 2σ: 3080–2780 cal. BC), and the much more favourable conditions either side of this period, should be discernible in the archaeological record.

The climate of the Pentland Hills since 5000 BC

As part of a wider study of the late Holocene climate of Scotland (Langdon 1999) a number of bogs were analysed using all three proxies described above. Data from one of these, Temple Hill Moss (NGR NT 311661), are presented in Figures 13.3 and 13.4. The bog is located on the northern flank of the Pentland Hills, near the village of Balerno, about 16 km southwest of Edinburgh and about 5 km northeast of a Roman fortlet. It has an area of 43 ha, and is structurally intact, although in the past some burning and peripheral drainage has taken place. The plant macrofossil diagram, constructed by the QLC method outlined above is shown in Figure 13.3, and radiocarbon

dates and tephra isochrones (Dugmore *et al.* 1995) have been used to construct an age/depth model, giving an average accumulation rate of *c.* 16.5 years/cm. The interpolated dates from the age/depth model for each sample are used in constructing the timescale in Figure 13.4.

Temple Hill Moss is unusual in that the stratigraphy is dominated by *Sphagnum* section *Acutifolia*, and not the usually ubiquitous *Sphagnum imbricatum* (Figure 13.3) which is only found in three major phases at Temple Hill, the latter two of which (dated to 1250– 920 cal. BC and cal. AD 60–130) appear to have grown under relatively dry climatic regimes as suggested by testate amoebae and humification analyses (Figure 13.4). However, before the initial dry *S. imbricatum* phase, a significant climatic deterioration is shown in all three proxies (Figure 13.4) which has been radiocarbon dated to 1430–1220 cal. BC. Other major climatic deteriorations can be detected in each of the three major proxies around 4700 BC, 3900 BC, 3300 BC, 2300 BC, 500 BC, AD 600, and AD 1600–1700.

CONCLUSIONS

Peat stratigraphic studies have advanced a long way since Godwin's pioneering work (Godwin 1946), and as the examples above show, we are now producing proxy-climate records using three different methods. Research is continuing on deriving more such records from different areas, in replicating them within and between sites, and in correlating the records between distant sites. However, it is still not clear how much of the proxy-climate record is forced by changes in temperature and how much by changes in precipitation. Analysis of long documentary climate records suggests the hypothesis that the temperature signal is more coherent and is dominant over the spatially and temporally incoherent precipitation signal (Barber *et al.* 2000).

Work is now in progress at two sites in Cumbria to test this hypothesis by comparing a chironomid-based proxy temperature record from a lake (Brooks *et al.* 1997) with an effective precipitation record from a nearby peat bog. It is hoped that this will allow us to achieve a greater understanding of climatic forcing mechanisms, to tune the Climate Response Model established from the same area (Barber *et al.* 1994a), and to take an important step towards providing quantitative data for the climate modelling community. However, as mentioned earlier, the relevance of these data to the archaeological community lies in the

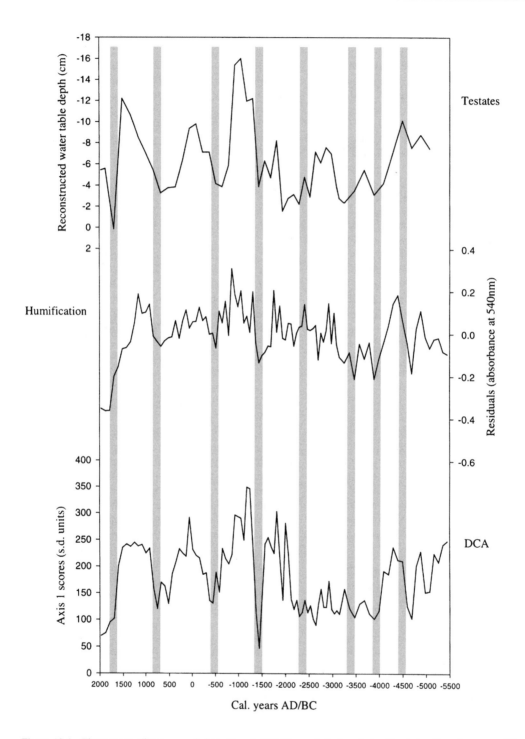

Figure 13.4   Three proxy-climate records from Temple Hill Moss, plotted against calibrated radiocarbon years. The abundances of plant macrofossils in Figure 13.3 have been transformed into a downcore plot of the Detrended Correspondence Analysis (DCA) Axis 1 scores. Testate amoebae counts have been transformed into water table depths using a transfer function and humification values have been detrended – see text for details. The vertical shaded bars highlight periods of cooler/wetter climate.

composite proxy-record from peatlands. The peaks and troughs in Figures 13.3 and 13.4 must have been reflected in fluctuations in the groundwater tables of prehistoric fields. Furthermore, our new methodology gives us a means of comparing changes from one region to another – from west to east across northern England, for example. One must bear in mind that not every core will record all the possible climatic changes that have occurred in an area (Barber *et al.* 1998) but as the amount of new standardized data grows so does our understanding of past environmental change, and it may soon be time to draw together a consolidated picture of the regional climates of the past.

REFERENCES

*Recommended for further reading

Anderson, D.E., Binney, H.A. and Smith, M.A. (1998). Evidence for abrupt climatic change in northern Scotland between 3900 and 3500 calendar years BP. *The Holocene*, **8**:97–103.

Andrus, R.E., Wagner, D.J. and Titus, J.E. (1983). Vertical zonation of *Sphagnum* mosses along hummock-hollow gradients. *Canadian Journal of Botany*, **61**:3128–3139.

*Barber, K.E. (1981). *Peat Stratigraphy and Climatic Change: a Palaeoecological Test of the Theory of Cyclic Peat Bog Regeneration*. Balkema: Rotterdam.

Barber, K.E. (1982). Peat-bog stratigraphy as a proxy climatic record. In Harding, A.F. (ed.) *Climatic Change in Later Prehistory*, 103–113. Edinburgh University Press: Edinburgh.

Barber, K.E. (1986). Peat macrofossil analyses as indicators of the bog palaeoenvironment and climatic change. In Stead, I.M., Bourke J.B. and Brothwell, D.R. (eds) *Lindow Man: The Body in the Bog*, 86–89. British Museum Publications: London.

Barber, K.E. (1993). Peatlands as scientific archives of biodiversity. *Biodiversity and Conservation*, **2**:474–489.

Barber, K.E. (1994). Deriving Holocene palaeoclimates from peat stratigraphy: some misconceptions regarding the sensitivity and continuity of the record. *Quaternary Newsletter*, **72**:1–9.

Barber, K.E. (1995). Two views on peat stratigraphy and the age of the Lindow Bodies. B: Peat stratigraphy and the Lindow Bog Body: a reconsideration of the evidence. In Turner, R.C. and Scaife, R.G. (eds) *Bog Bodies: New Discoveries and New Perspectives*, 50–51. British Museum Press: London.

Barber, K.E., Chambers, F.M., Maddy, D., Stoneman, R. and Brew, J.S. (1994a). A sensitive high resolution record of late Holocene climatic change from a raised bog in northern England. *The Holocene*, **4**:198–205.

Barber, K.E., Chambers, F.M., Dumayne, L., Haslam, C.J., Maddy, D. and Stoneman, R.E. (1994b). Climatic change

and human impact in north Cumbria: peat stratigraphic and pollen evidence from Bolton Fell Moss and Walton Moss. In Boardman, J. and Walden, J. (eds) *The Quaternary of Cumbria: Field Guide*, 20–54. Quaternary Research Association: Oxford.

Barber, K.E., Chambers, F.M. and Maddy, D. (1994c). The climate of Northern Cumbria since the Neolithic. In Middleton, R. and Newman, R. (eds) *North West Wetlands Survey, Annual Report 1994*, 17–20. English Heritage: Lancaster.

Barber, K.E., Dumayne-Peaty, L., Hughes, P.D.M., Mauquoy, D. and Scaife, R.G. (1998). Replicability and variability of the recent macrofossil and proxy-climate record from raised bogs: field stratigraphy and macrofossil data from Bolton Fell Moss and Walton Moss, Cumbria, England. *Journal of Quaternary Science*, **13**:515–528.

Barber, K.E., Maddy, D., Rose, N., Stevenson, A.C., Stoneman, R.E. and Thompson, R. (2000). Replicated proxy-climate signals over the last 2000 years from two distant UK peat bogs: new evidence for regional palaeoclimate teleconnections. *Quaternary Science Reviews*, **19**:481–487.

Blackford, J.J. and Chambers, F.M. (1991). Proxy records of climate from blanket mires: evidence for a Dark Age (1400 BP) climatic deterioration in the British Isles. *The Holocene*, **1**:63–67.

Blackford, J.J. and Chambers, F.M. (1993). Determining the degree of peat decomposition for peat based palaeoclimatic studies. *International Peat Journal*, **5**:7–24.

Blackford, J.J. and Chambers, F.M. (1995). Proxy climate record for the last 1000 years from Irish blanket peat and a possible link to solar variability. *Earth and Planetary Science Letters*, **133**:145–150.

Boatman, D.J. (1983). The Silver Flowe National Nature Reserve, Galloway, Scotland. *Journal of Biogeography*, **10**:163–274.

Brown, A.G. (1997). *Alluvial Geoarchaeology: Floodplain Archaeology and Environmental Change*. Cambridge University Press: Cambridge.

Brooks, S.J., Mayle, F.E. and Lowe, J.J. (1997). Chironomid-based Lateglacial climatic reconstruction for southeast Scotland. *Journal of Quaternary Science*, **12**:161–167.

Buckland, P.C. (1995). Two views on peat stratigraphy and the age of the Lindow Bodies. A: Peat stratigraphy and the age of the Lindow Bodies. In Turner, R.C. and Scaife, R.G. (eds) *Bog Bodies: New Discoveries and New Perspectives*, 47–50. British Museum Press: London.

Chambers, F.M., Barber, K.E., Maddy, D. and Brew, J.S. (1997). A 5500-year proxy-climate and vegetational record from blanket mire at Talla Moss, Borders, Scotland. *The Holocene*, **7**:391–399.

Charman, D.J. (1997). Modelling hydrological relationships of testate amoebae (Protozoa: Rhizopoda) on New Zealand peatlands. *Journal of the Royal Society of New Zealand*, **27**:465–483.

Charman, D.J. and Warner, B.G. (1997). The ecology of testate amoebae (Protozoa: Rhizopoda) in oceanic peatlands in Newfoundland, Canada: Modelling hydrological relationships for palaeoenvironmental reconstruction. *Ecoscience*, **4**:555–562.

Charman, D.J., Hendon, D. and Packman, S. (1999). Multi-proxy surface wetness records from replicate cores on an ombrotrophic mire: implications for Holocene palaeoclimate records. *Journal of Quaternary Science*, **14**:451–463.

*Charman, D.J., Woodland, W.A. and Hendon, D. (in press). *The Identification of Testate Amoebae from Peatlands.* Technical Guide, Quaternary Research Association: Oxford.

Chiverrell, R.C. and Atherden, M.A. (1999). Climate change and human impact – evidence from peat stratigraphy at sites in the eastern North York Moors. In Bridgland, D.R., Horton, B.P. and Innes, J.B. (eds) *The Quaternary of North-East England: Field Guide*, 113–130. Quaternary Research Association: London.

Clymo, R.S. (1991). Peat Growth. In Shane, L.C.K. and Cushing, E.J. (eds) *Quaternary Landscapes*. Belhaven Press: London.

Coles, B.J. (ed.) (1992). *The Wetland Revolution in Prehistory*. The Prehistoric Society and WARP: Exeter.

Corbet, S.A. (1973). An illustrated introduction to the testate rhizopods in *Sphagnum*, with special reference to the area around Malham Tarn, Yorkshire. *Field Studies*, **3**:801–838.

*Daniels, R.E. and Eddy, A. (1990). *A Handbook of European Sphagna*. Natural Environment Research Council: Swindon.

Davies, E.G. (1944). Figyn Blaen Brefi: a Welsh upland bog. *Journal of Ecology*, **32**:147–166.

Dupont, L.M. (1986). Temperature and rainfall variation in the late Holocene based on comparative palaeoecology and isotope geology of a hummock and a hollow (Bourtangerveen, The Netherlands). *Review of Palaeobotany and Palynology*, **48**:71–159.

Dugmore, A.J., Larsen, G. and Newton, A.J. (1995). Seven tephra isochrones in Scotland. *The Holocene*, **5**:257–266.

Ellison, R.L. and Ogden, C.G. (1987). A guide to the study and identification of fossil testate amoebae in Quaternary lake sediments. *International Revue der Gesamten Hydrobiologia*, **72**:639–652.

Godwin, H. (1946). The relationship of bog stratigraphy to climatic change and archaeology. *Proceedings of the Prehistoric Society*, **12**:1–11.

*Godwin, H. (1981). *The Archives of the Peat Bogs*. Cambridge University Press: Cambridge.

Hendon, D. and Charman, D.J. (1997). The preparation of testate amoebae (Protozoa: Rhizopoda) samples from peat. *The Holocene*, **7**:199–205.

Hughes, P.D.M., Mauquoy, D., Barber, K.E. and Langdon, P.G. (2000). Mire development pathways and palaeoclimatic records from a full Holocene peat archive at Walton Moss, Cumbria, England. *The Holocene*, **10**:465–479.

Ingram, H.A.P. (1978). Soil layers in mires: function and terminology. *Journal of Soil Science*, **29**:224–227.

Kilian, M.R., van der Plicht, J. and Van Geel, B. (1995). Dating raised bogs: new aspects of AMS ^{14}C wiggle matching, a reservoir effect and climate change. *Quaternary Science Reviews*, **14**:959–966.

Langdon, P.G. (1999). *Reconstructing Holocene climate change in Scotland utilizing peat stratigraphy and tephrochronology*. Unpublished PhD Thesis, University of Southampton.

Mauquoy, D. and Barber, K.E. (1999a). A replicated 3000 year proxy-record from Coom Rigg Moss and Felecia Moss, The Border Mires, northern England. *Journal of Quaternary Science*, **14**:263–275.

Mauquoy, D. and Barber, K.E. (1999b). Evidence for climatic deteriorations associated with the decline of *Sphagnum imbricatum* Hornsch Ex Russ. in six ombrotrophic mires from Northern England and the Scottish Borders. *The Holocene*, **9**:423–437.

Middleton, R., Wells, C.E. and Huckerby, E. (1995). *The Wetlands of North Lancashire*. Lancaster Imprints 4, North West Wetlands Survey: Lancaster.

Pilcher, J.R., Hall, V.A. and McCormac, F.G. (1996). An outline tephrochronology for the Holocene of the north of Ireland. *Journal of Quaternary Science*, **11**:485–494.

Stead, I.M., Bourke, J. and Brothwell, D.R. (1986). *Lindow Man. The Body in the Bog*. British Museum Publications: London.

Stockmarr, J. (1971). Tablets with spores used in absolute pollen analysis. *Pollen et Spores*, **13**:615–621.

Stoneman, R.E., Barber, K.E. and Maddy, D. (1993). Present and past ecology of *Sphagnum imbricatum* and its significance in raised peat-climate modelling. *Quaternary Newsletter*, **70**:14–22.

Tolonen, K. (1986). Rhizopod analysis. In Berglund, B.E. (ed.) *Handbook of Holocene Palaeoecology and Palaeohydrology*, 645–666. John Wiley: Chichester.

Troels-Smith, J. (1955). Karakterisering af løse jordater (Characterization of unconsolidated sediments). *Danmarks Geologiske Undersøgelse IV Series*, **3(10)**:1–73.

Van Geel, B., Buurman, J. and Waterbolk, H.T. (1996). Archaeological and palaeoecological indications of an abrupt climate change in The Netherlands, and evidence for climatological teleconnections around 2650 BP. *Journal of Quaternary Science*, **11**:451–460.

Walker, D. and Walker, P.M. (1961). Stratigraphic evidence of regeneration in some Irish bogs. *Journal of Ecology*, **49**:169–185.

Warner, B.G. and Charman, D.J. (1994). Holocene changes on a peatland in northwestern Ontario interpreted from testate amoebae (Protozoa) analysis. *Boreas*, **23**:270–279.

Woodland, W.A., Charman, D.J. and Sims, P.C. (1998). Quantitative estimates of water tables and soil moisture in Holocene peatlands from testate amoebae. *The Holocene*, **8**:261–273.

14

Archaeology and Soil Micromorphology

D.A. DAVIDSON and I.A. SIMPSON

Department of Environmental Science, University of Stirling.

A fundamental tenet of pedology is that past and present soil processes are reflected in field morphology. The investigation of soil development and human impacts on soils over time has relied heavily on characterization of soil morphological properties supplemented by data derived from laboratory analysis. Soil micromorphology extends this approach to the microscopic scale through the collection of undisturbed samples. The manufacture of soil thin sections involves the drying of samples (by air and oven drying or acetone replacement or freeze-drying), impregnation of resin under reduced pressure and curing of blocks, and sawing, lapping and mounting on glass slides. The final results are thin sections *c.* 30 μm thick, which can be examined under a petrological microscope. In this chapter we briefly summarize the development of thin section micromorphology, highlight applications in archaeological contexts and emphasize the need for validation of features observed in thin section.

DEVELOPMENT OF SOIL MICROMORPHOLOGY

W.L. Kubiena is widely regarded as the father figure to soil micromorphology and is best known for his book *The Soils of Europe* (Kubiena 1953). He very much established micromorphology's contribution to soil classification and our understanding of soil formation processes. Other benchmark contributions have been by Brewer and Sleeman (1988) in terms of the first attempt to systematize terminology, FitzPatrick (1993) for pedological interpretation and Bullock *et al.* (1985) for devising an international description system. The provision of full descriptions is extremely instructive since the investigator has to systematically examine all thin section attributes. It is inevitably a time-consuming process but with experience, greater attention can be paid to those attributes of thin sections relevant to specific research questions. Basic concepts from the international descriptive system are summarized in Tables 14.1–14.3.

In recent decades the overall contribution of micromorphology to soil science has been subject to substantial change. The trend over the last 20 years or so has been to exploit micromorphology and its associated techniques for providing new insights into soil processes as induced by physical, biological and land use mechanisms (Miedema 1997). For example, it has been used to determine the effects of different cultivation techniques on soils (Drees *et al.* 1994) and the interactions of soil and the soil biota (Kooistra 1991). There is increasing use of image analysis techniques as demonstrated by Terribile and Fitzpatrick (1995) which

Handbook of Archaeological Sciences. Edited by D.R. Brothwell and A.M. Pollard.

Table 14.1 Terminology in thin section micromorphology.

SOIL FABRIC
Total organization of a soil as expressed by the spatial arrangements of the soil constituents (solids and voids)

SOIL STRUCTURE
Size, shape and arrangement of primary particles and voids in both aggregated and nonaggregated material and size, shape and arrangement of any aggregates present

SOIL MICROSTRUCTURES – structures evident at magnifications $> \times 5$

COARSE AND FINE MATERIAL
A division between coarse and fine material – division e.g., at 10 μm or 2 μm

BASIC COMPONENTS
These are the simplest mineral and organic particles seen in thin section. They form the building blocks to the soil organization.

GROUNDMASS
General term to describe the coarse and fine material which forms the base material of soil

MICROMASS
General term for finer material

PEDOFEATURE
A distinct fabric unit; stands out in contrast to adjacent soil material, e.g. clay coating in void, nodules of iron oxides

Table 14.2 Standardized descriptive criteria used in thin section micromorphology.

1. SIZE, SHAPE, NATURE OF BOUNDARIES, SHARPNESS

2. DISTRIBUTION PATTERNS:
   Basic distribution
      Distribution with respect to other individuals of the same type, e.g., random, clustered
   Referred distribution
      Distribution with respect to specific features, e.g., planar voids or root channels
   Related distribution
      Distribution with respect to individuals of a different type, e.g., gefuric coarse units linked by braces of finer material

3. AGGREGATED MATERIAL
   Types of peds, size, grade

4. MICROSTRUCTURE
   Type e.g., bridged grain structure

5. VOIDS
   packing voids
   vugh – large void, spherical to elongate, not interconnected
   vesicle – similar to vugh, but smoother in outline
   channel – elongated, cylindrical
   chamber – nearly spherical, connected by channels

permits, for example, the quantification of soil structure (Ringrose-Voase 1991). These changes in emphasis have also been reflected in the application of micromorphology to archaeology. The early work on micromorphology as applied to archaeology is typified by Cornwall (1958) who very much focused on the palaeoenvironmental interpretation of buried soils as a means of providing environmental contexts for archaeological sites. This remains a key concern, but since the early 1980s increasing attention has been given to site taphonomy and the wider impact of anthropogenic activity on soil landscapes. In an evaluation of soil micromorphology and archaeology, Davidson *et al.* (1992) identified a change to a greater emphasis on investigating sediment type, anthropogenic features, and nature of disturbance during occupation and post-depositional processes. Courty *et al.* (1994) highlight the ways by which micromorphology can assist with understanding the relationships between environment and behaviour. They summarize intra-site analysis (anthropogenically structural transformations, animal effects, anthropogenic deposits and spatial and temporal variability) and off-site analysis (land use

practices and human-induced soil alteration and effects on landscape dynamics). As an example, they list micromorphological features and fabrics associated with such land use practices as slash and burn, uprooting, ploughing, manuring, irrigation, horticultural practices and pasturing-herding. Thus ploughing, for example, results in fragmented slaking crusts, dusty silty clay intercalations and coatings, mixing of horizons, loss of the fine fraction, decrease in biological activity and changes in biological fabrics (see for example Figure 14.1 in colour plates). Courty *et al.* (1994:266) conclude that 'integration of micromorphological data with archaeological, chronological and other environmental data now illustrates the considerable precision that can be achieved in defining spatial patterns of past human activities...'. Such an integrative approach is illustrated in the study by Macphail *et al.* (1998) who studied thin sections derived from an Iron Age funerary shaft at St Albans. The results when combined with data derived from SEM/EDXRA and diatom analysis allowed the identification of five sedimentological units (termed microfabric types). Such micromorphological characterization clearly

Table 14.3 Descriptive framework for thin section micromorphology.

1. STRUCTURE

2. GROUNDMASS – subdivided into coarse material and micromass

3. ORGANIC COMPONENTS

   (a) plant residues (> 5 cells connected in original tissues)
   (b) organic fine material (< 5 cells and includes amorphous components)
   (c) organic pigment staining – whole or part of micromass

   Excrement pedofeatures can also be described under this heading.

4. TEXTURAL CONCENTRATION FEATURES
   Features associated with an increase in concentration of material of a particular size, e.g., coatings, infillings, cappings

5. AMORPHOUS CONCENTRATION FEATURES
   Appear amorphous in plane polarized light (PPL), isotropic in cross polarized light (XPL). Three types identified under oblique incident light are:

   (a) white or dark brown colours – organic components
   (b) black to yellowish brown – oxides and hydroxides of manganese
   (c) yellowish brown to reddish brown – oxides and hydroxides of iron

   These occur as e.g., nodules, segregations (e.g., mottles) which are impregnative

6. CRYSTALLINE CONCENTRATION FEATURES
   e.g., features consisting of Fe oxides, gypsum, gibbsite

added descriptive data to the site record. As another example of combining micromorphological and diatom analyses, Grave and Kealhofer (1999) investigated the extent of bioturbation in ditch infill at a site in northwestern Thailand; they were able to show that the impact of insect activity is highly localized and does not affect the overall sequence of microbotanical changes.

Soil micromorphology has similarly contributed to Quaternary science, primarily through the investigation of buried soils. Kemp (1998) overviews the contribution of micromorphology to palaeopedological research and stresses the importance of relying on a combination of such features as channels, faunal excrements, calcitic root pseudomorphs, and illuvial clay coatings. He highlights fundamental challenges posed by the polygenetic nature of soils and the fact that in contemporary soils, attributes may not be in equilibrium with current environmental conditions. This leads him to discuss the

equifinality problems – the same end result can come from varying combinations of processes. He illustrates this with reference to argillic horizons; in Quaternary studies the traditional view is to regard the accumulation of illuvial clay as occurring under (interglacial) temperate, seasonally dry climates under stable forest cover. Kemp (1998) argues that such illuviation can occur under a range of environmental conditions and thus it would be erroneous to propose a particular palaeoenvironmental condition because of evidence of translocated clay. In conclusion, Kemp (1998) stresses the importance of adequate sampling and the need to validate particular interpretations through the study of present-day processes; similar priorities also urged for soil micromorphological work in relation to archaeology.

Despite the interpretational difficulties, micromorphological analysis is widely perceived to yield results of distinctive value to aid archaeological interpretation. The investigation of soil thin sections as collected from sections on archaeological sites can be viewed as a direct extension of field description and interpretation of site stratigraphy. Furthermore, the slides can be studied in the comfort of a laboratory and retained for examination by other micromorphologists. Further investigation is also possible through the manufacture of new slides from the original impregnated blocks. The subject of micromorphology and archaeology is now moving into a more analytical development phase, based on better sampling strategies and more emphasis on validation of micromorphological interpretation. There are high costs associated with the production and analysis of soil thin sections; as a result there is a continuing need to demonstrate to archaeologists the interpretational payoff from micromorphology.

APPLICATIONS OF MICROMORPHOLOGY TO ARCHAEOLOGY – SELECTED EXAMPLES

Over the last two decades, thin section micromorphology has been used to address a wide range of archaeological questions ranging in scale from the site to the landscape. To illustrate the diversity of archaeological applications, we first highlight site formation processes, emphasizing occupation surfaces, cave sediments and waste midden deposits. All archaeological sequences are subject to modification during formation as well as in subsequent abandonment. The elucidation of such site formation or taphonomy is central to archaeological interpretation and the investigation of soil micromorphology can result in the provision of important evidence that can address key archaeological questions. As a second example we highlight the role of micromorphology in evaluating the incorporation of pollen into soil matrixes, and the implications that this has for palaeo-environmental interpretation.

Site formation processes

Matthews *et al.* (1997) demonstrate that integrated microstratigraphic and micromorphological analyses can be of particular value in the investigation of occupation sites. For a range of sites in the Middle East, they illustrate the distinctive contribution which micromorphology can make to an understanding of pre-depositional histories of components, depositional agencies and processes and post-depositional alterations. They provide a list of micromorphological attributes characteristic of domestic and ritual activities; interpretation was aided by the integration of results from wet-sieving. They conclude that micromorphology provides a means for integrating a range of geoarchaeological, bioarchaeological and artifactual evidence from occupation sites though they also stress the need for adequate sampling strategies and further experimental investigations to assist with interpretation.

Cave sites present particular challenges to archaeological interpretation given the extent to which diagenetic processes can modify deposits. Such processes can have marked influences on stratigraphic integrity, preservation of bones and other organic materials, dating evidence, artifact concentrations and site occupation records. The study of the micromorphology in combination with the mineralogy and sedimentology has proved very useful for the investigation of cave deposits. As one example, Karkanas *et al.* (1999) studied Theopetra cave in central Greece, occupied from the middle Palaeolithic onwards. The particular aim of the study was the investigation of mineral alteration and this was tackled by analyzing bulk samples by spectrometry and X-ray diffraction; undisturbed samples were examined for micromorphology supplemented by microprobe determinations. The particular value of the micromorphological research was the characterization of the different lithostratigraphic units; fine-grained stratification was evident in some deposits indicating water deposition in a low energy environment. As another example, microscopic seams of spherulites were present in particular deposits. Through collating the various strands of analytical evidence for the various deposits, Karkanas *et al.* (1999) were able to

identify a sequence both vertically and laterally of increasing diagenetic alteration. Diagenetic pathways were thus identified which could be used to predict change in other analogous cave deposits.

Investigation of occupation sites using thin section micromorphology integrated with archaeological excavation has also been pursued in coastal areas of the North Atlantic region by Simpson and co-workers, with particular focus on identifying the development of specialized fishing activity sites. Specialized fishing and fish trade in this region is thought to be critical to understanding the transformation from Viking age to Middle Ages and to the incorporation of peripheral polities such as northern Norway, Iceland and the Northern Isles of Scotland into Medieval Christian Europe (Barrett *et al.* 2000). Intensification of seasonal fishing and fish processing activities has been considered through the micromorphological investigation of midden deposits at key sites in Caithness and Orkney, Scotland, and in Vesterålen, northern Norway. Here the goal has been to determine whether midden deposits formed as a result of fish processing on a commercial scale or as a result of fishing activity for local or domestic use. This problem has been approached through two assumptions. If the midden is relatively uniform in composition, found to be the only form of waste disposal on the site and discontinuous in its pattern of deposition, it may be reasonable to view it as a result of a specialized fish processing activity. Alternatively, if the midden is highly variable in composition and continuous in its deposition, it is more probable that it was associated with a farmstead that merely included fishing within a wider economic base. It was therefore necessary to identify variation in composition and potential source of the sediments in the midden, while the identification and analysis of textural pedofeatures within the deposits might establish whether the middens developed through sporadic or continuous deposition. Micromorphological evidence of continuous deposition would suggest the existence of a permanent settlement while sporadic deposition could imply seasonal or temporary use of the site. The latter is perhaps more consistent with a commercial fishery than the former if one envisions a seasonal fishing station such as those known from Medieval Norway.

At Robert's Haven, Caithness, Scotland, contrasting midden deposits were examined from the site using thin section micromorphology (Simpson and Barrett 1996). One of the midden deposits contained a large proportion of fish bone; here thin section micromorphology revealed a wide range of domestic waste material, including burnt and unburnt grassy and peaty turves as well as the calcium spherulite remains of herbivorous dung. The limited occurrence of textural pedofeatures in this midden suggested that it developed predominantly on a short term, possibly seasonal cycle, of deposition and non-deposition. Micromorphological evidence from a second, nearby, midden deposit indicated a similar accumulation of domestic waste materials, but lacked fish bone and textural pedofeatures, suggesting that here deposition was virtually continuous. It is possible to conclude therefore that the fish bone midden represents one activity area associated with specialized fishing activity in an economically diverse permanent settlement, an interpretation validated through zoo-archaeological analysis together with the recovery of pottery and carbonized cereal grain. Similar analyses have also been undertaken at the Quoygrew site in Westray, Orkney (Simpson *et al.* 1998a). Here, micromorphological analyses of the cliff face midden deposits indicate that much of the matrix material is peat ash within which fish bones and shells were embedded. The occurrence of non-laminated dusty clay coatings as well as silty clay crusts associated with phytoliths indicates that there were relatively short periods of time when there was no deposition of midden material. When these observations are considered in conjunction with the large extent and uniformity of the midden, the interpretation is that the area functioned as a specialized fish processing area. These observations are in contrast to the midden deposits elsewhere on the site which are more akin to the persistent deposition of a range of domestic waste materials. This suggests that, like Robert's Haven, Quoygrew was the site of a large household that included specialized fishing for export within a wider economic base, rather than a commercial fishing station.

Micromorphology and associated microprobe analyses has also contributed to the understanding of early fishing site formation at Langenesværet, Vesterålen, northern Norway (Simpson *et al.* in press). Here four sedimentary types could be identified based on fine mineral and organic material characteristics, on coarse organic material and on microstructure characteristics. Type 1 sediments are characterized by weathered subangular and subrounded coarse mineral material, black organo-mineral fine material and intergrain micro-aggregate microstructures. They also have occasional to many phosphatic pedofeatures as distinctive coatings and void infills (see Figure 14.2 in colour plates); Proton Induced X-ray Emission (PIXE) analyses of these features clearly indicate that they are Ca-Fe-phosphates, although the ratios of these three elements vary markedly between different sub-samples.

Jenkins (1994) suggests the origin of such features is release of P and Ca from bone hydroxyapatite into ionic solution with subsequent re-adsorption on to active ferric hydroxides. Such a view is supported by the similar element distribution in the pedofeatures and weathered bone fragments found in the same thin section. Marine fish bone is the most likely local origin of these features, given the high strontium trace element values derived from PIXE analyses. These sediments are found in the lower part of the stratigraphies, corresponding to the earliest phase of site formation, and are considered to be consistent with a periodically utilized shoreline fishing activity area.

Type 2 sediments from Langenesværet are characterized by dominant fine organic material and spongy microstructures, corresponding to the middle phases of sediment accumulation and are consistent with the introduction of peaty turves that were wet heath in origin. Fish bone and birch charcoal are embedded in the peat material and suggest that the peats were once part of wall structures associated with permanent or semi-permanent fishing settlement. Similarly, Type 3 sediments are also characterized by spongy microstructures associated with peat turves used for structures, but which are also associated with lignified coarse organic material predominantly birch in origin which may be interpreted as being introduced to the site for fish curing purposes. Type 4 deposits are characterized by organomineral fine material of different colours and subangular blocky microstructures. Narrow bands and small, isolated micro-stratigraphies together with varying colours of fine organo-mineral material in thin section imply a range of materials making up these sediments. These include charcoal and fuel ash wastes and both wet and dry peaty turves. Fish bone is evident throughout these deposits, emphasizing the pre-eminence of the marine element in resource exploitation. The microstructure is indicative of an open area and, taken together, these observations suggest that the later phases of site formation were dominated by waste material accumulation associated with fishing activity. Although full archaeological excavation still remains to be undertaken to test these interpretations, the micromorphological observations serve to highlight the evolving nature of this site, from open, shoreline activity, through to constructed settlement phases and waste material accumulation. They also serve to demonstrate the contrasting nature of specialized fishing site formation in the southern and arctic areas of the North Atlantic region, providing a basis from which to discuss social, economic and environmental parameters in the development of coastal fishing communities.

Validation of soil pollen analysis from micromorphology

Soil pollen is an important source of evidence in palaeoenvironmental research associated with archaeological projects. However, interpretation of results is beset with difficulties as a result of the impact of bioturbation, translocation, differential destruction and anthropogenic disturbance on pollen in soils (Davidson *et al.* 1999). Despite a wide awareness of the interpretational problems in soil pollen analyses, Keith-Lucas (1994) summarized an enormous increase in the use of soil pollen analysis in conjunction with archaeological excavations. Thus it is particularly surprising that there is a dearth of experimental research that validates interpretation of soil pollen results in terms of age-stratification, vertical translocation, coherence of assemblages and non-biased preservation. Overall, it can be hypothesized that pollen is moved and transformed in soils as a result of a combination of processes which depend upon particular soil and vegetation conditions. A key research need is thus to devise experiments that can generate information on the particular processes of pollen incorporation and redistribution in different soils. Soil micromorphology can play a key role in providing the necessary evaluation. Davidson *et al.* (1999) report a project involving pollen and micromorphological analysis for a range of soils typical of upland cool maritime environments *viz.* humic orthic gley, ground-water orthic gley, ferric podzol, cambic stagnogley, typical orthic brown soil.

The results show biological activity to be the most important factor in the incorporation and redistribution of pollen in a range of common upland British soil profiles, supporting the findings of Aaby (1983), Andersen (1979), Havinga (1974) and Odgaard (1988). The depth of incorporation of pollen grains in the soil is determined by the depth of activity of soil invertebrates capable of transporting whole grains. Pollen, as identified in thin section, is very strongly associated with larger invertebrate excrement. Pollen deposited on the soil surface is consumed, digested and excreted by macrofauna, particularly large surface organic matter feeding invertebrates. It is moved laterally and vertically by organo-mineral feeding earthworms, if present. Pollen grains are too large to be moved in the same way by mesofauna such as enchytraeids although these can constitute a high proportion of the total soil biomass in many northern ecosystems (Dawod and FitzPatrick 1993). Enchytraeids are therefore neutral in terms of pollen redistribution.

Earthworms are the main agents of incorporation at the ground-water orthic gley, the cambic stagnogley and the typical orthic brown sites where they are very dominant in the upper horizons. In the ferric podzol, pollen is incorporated at the soil surface within excrement of surface feeding insects. However, earthworms are absent and therefore pollen is not transported deeper into the profile. Enchytraeids are present in the upper horizons but they are too small to transport pollen. In the humic orthic gley there is no evidence for pollen incorporation processes operating in the profile at present.

Pollen grains within the examined soils do not appear to behave as coherent assemblages. All tetrad pollen grains observed in thin section occurred as isolated individuals with each undergoing individual processes of incorporation. There is no evidence from micromorphological observations for the existence of 'humic complexes' (Dimbleby 1985). Also there is no evidence that downwashing of pollen is significant in these soils despite the soils exhibiting great contrasts in hydrological regime and degree of water-table fluctuation. The results also suggest that pollen is retained in the surface organic horizon of the ferric podzol with no detectable downward transfer to mineral horizons. Given the strong relation between pollen incorporation and biological activity, and the absence of evidence for downwashing, it is unlikely that pollen grains are totally removed by translocation from the profiles.

Pollen is incorporated into soils if suitable soil invertebrates are present to ingest, transport and excrete whole pollen grains. This process does not result in age stratification of pollen assemblages but creates a single mixed-age assemblage down to the maximum depth of relevant invertebrate activity. In soils with active soil-ingesting earthworm populations, this depth may be considerable. In podzols and other profiles lacking earthworms, pollen incorporation and mixing are limited to surface organic horizons by shallow bioturbation. This creates a highly compressed, mixed-age assemblage at the soil surface. The temporal resolution of any mixed-age assemblage will be determined by the duration of the process that has created it; this could range from decades to millennia depending on the history of profile evolution. In all cases sub-sampling for pollen within that mixed-age horizon will not improve the temporal resolution of the data or yield time sequences. Age-stratification is only present in soils with surface accumulating organic horizons – effectively operating as shallow peats. Here, in the absence of invertebrates capable of transporting pollen, age stratified assemblages of pollen can be extracted and interpreted.

The micromorphological results show that the interpretation of pollen data from soils must be based on a clear understanding of the soil processes resulting in the incorporation of pollen. The analysis of pollen in soils can be a useful technique for environmental reconstruction, although its use is limited to specific situations. In the vast majority of cases, soils will contain mixed-age assemblages and the value of any analysis will be dependent on the temporal resolution required by the analysis and the time period represented by the assemblage. This latter point may prove impossible to determine. In accumulating organic horizons (O and potentially H horizons), pollen remains temporally stratified and may be interpreted palaeoecologically. Soil pollen analysis may therefore be of greatest value in the accumulating peaty horizons of peaty soils or in accumulating litter layers of podzols.

VALIDATION OF MICROMORPHOLOGICAL INTERPRETATION

Traditionally thin sections from archaeological contexts are investigated using an holistic approach whereby key micromorphological components are first described and then interpreted on the basis of the analyst's experience. However, it is apparent that such interpretations often lack validation, and is an issue that is now increasingly attracting the attention of micromorphologists. Experimental approaches and approaches which rely on sampling from known historical contexts are currently being developed as a way of validating the interpretations of features observed in thin section from archaeological contexts.

Experimental approaches to cultivation impacts on soil micromorphology

Archaeologists often challenge soil micromorphologists for evidence of cultivation prior to site formation. This involves sampling soils at the base of sites and for subsequent interpretation of micromorphological features. This important topic has been reviewed by Macphail *et al.* (1990), but has been the subject of more recent controversies (Carter and Davidson 1998, Macphail 1998, Carter and Davidson 2000). One research approach is to investigate the micromorphology of soils which have been subject to particular tillage systems. Gebhart (1992) undertook micromor-

phological analysis of soils which had been tilled using a hoe, ard, spade and cultivator. The results illustrate the complexity of the problem, key issues being the duration of the experiments, varying responses from different soils and the persistence of diagnostic structural features following burial or bioturbation. She concluded that there is the critical need for more studies of this type in order that results are representative of wider environmental conditions. Lewis (1998) undertook laboratory and field experiments as well as investigations from archaeological contexts in order to determine the impact of cultivation on soil micromorphology. She discussed such key problems as the effect of cultivation implements on the distribution of dusty clay coatings, the relationship of depth of tillage to structural boundaries or textural pedofeatures, the transient nature of soil structure as induced by tillage, and the occurrence of dusty clay coatings in particular untilled profiles whilst all tilled samples do not possess such pedofeatures. Through the combined investigation of experimental and archaeological contexts, she was able to identify variation in loose and dense zones, mixing of fabrics, occurrence of aligned linear or planar void spaces, and the presence of lenses of fine marking cuts as indicative of tillage. Overall she argued the need for much better interpretational security in terms of proposing evidence for past cultivation from micromorphological evidence. It can thus be concluded that it is difficult to associate particular soil structural or pedofeatures with specific tillage techniques though the combination of various micromorphological attributes may provide stronger evidence for past tillage. As discussed below, the clearest evidence of past cultivation comes from the legacy of manuring inputs.

Experimental earthworks and buried soils

The Overton Down Experimental Earthworks provide a unique opportunity to investigate changes in soils as a result of burial after 32 years (Crowther *et al.* 1996). A critical archaeological question is the extent to which on-site processes have modified environmental evidence; the soil environment is clearly transformed following burial and the result could well be substantial modification to many soil properties. At Overton Down there was the opportunity to investigate a humic rendzina which had been buried under a turf stack and chalk rubble. Central to the approach was comparison with a local control site. Soil thin sections were divided into 5 mm squares and within each, estimates were made of flint, chalk, calcareous soil, decalcified soil, voids and plant residues. The conclusion was that '...the characteristics of a humic rendzina soil can alter quite rapidly over the first few decades following burial' (Crowther *et al.* 1996:114). This is explained primarily as a result of compaction resulting in reduced void space and organic decomposition. Crowther *et al.* (1996) stress the importance of microenvironmental conditions in influencing the nature of buried soils. For example, the buried rendzina under the turf stack continued to be subject to leaching and acidification with a corresponding decline in bioturbation. In contrast the rendzina buried under the chalk rubble became more alkaline, better aerated and retained its earthworm population. The key conclusions from this investigation relate to the magnitude of soil change following burial and stress the importance of obtaining as many samples as possible from buried soils in order to include all local microenvironmental conditions.

Experimental validation of a specific feature – faecal spherulites

Microscopic calcium carbonate spherulites are frequently observed in thin sections from many archaeological contexts and have distinctive optical properties because of the crystallization of calcium carbonate. They occur in archaeological sections where animal dung is abundant and alkaline conditions have been maintained. They vary in diameter from c. 5 to 15 μm and are thought to be formed in the gut of sheep, goats or cows. The inevitable problem is the interpretation of such spherulites from archaeological contexts and the need is to distinguish faecal spherulites from similar materials (e.g., coccoliths) and related biominerals. As a first step Canti (1998) provided details of faecal spherulite morphology as derived from modern animal dung. Using accessory plates on a petrological microscope and different illuminations, he was able to demonstrate that true faecal spherulites can be distinguished. He also reports varying relationships between maximum retardation and diameter according to different animals. As a result the interpretation of spherulites from archaeological contexts is now on a more secure basis, though Canti (1998) stresses the importance of examining loose materials at varying orientations and under different analytical systems.

Sampling from known historical contexts

Although there are clear merits in adopting an experimental approach to soil micromorphology and archaeology, a fundamental problem is the extent to which the inevitably short experimental time scale is sufficient to mimic archaeological circumstances. If the objective is to understand the impact of cultivation on soils, an alternative approach is to investigate soils from recently abandoned and well-documented traditional agricultural systems. Viewing such systems as analogues of past practice has the merit of being more realistic in an archaeological sense; also, the impact of greater time periods can be assessed than in the purely experimental approach. Surprisingly there have been few studies of this type with the one major exception being plaggen soils in central and western Europe (Blume 1998, Carter and Davidson 1998, Conry 1974, Davidson and Simpson 1984, Mucher *et al.* 1990, Simpson 1997). Plaggen soils are distinguished by the presence of a deep topsoil (>50 cm), formed as a result of manuring with peaty or grassy turves over many centuries. Ethnographic and other documentary records must be examined in order to establish relationships between recorded agricultural practices of a 'traditional' system and the nature of soils as expressed in micromorphology. Central to the approach must be the preservation of the impact of the traditional system on soils either through abandonment or burial. Even following agricultural abandonment, soil transformations will inevitably continue. The approach can be illustrated with reference to one case study; full details are given by Davidson and Carter (1998).

There are clear advantages in selecting a study area where there has been considerable continuity of agricultural practice; this is the case with the small island of Papa Stour, located on the west coast of Shetland in the north of Scotland. The other outstanding merit of this island for archaeological and micromorphological investigations is that pioneering ethnographic studies of Fenton (1978) in the 1960s recorded the final years of the traditional mixed farming system based on cattle and sheep with crops of cereals, kale and potatoes. Thirty years later, an historically low human population in the island and sheep-dominated agriculture involving a grass-based forage system have ensured that most of the former arable land has gone out of cultivation, thereby preserving substantial areas of old arable soils unaffected by current agricultural practices. Therefore the island offers the opportunity to study cultivated soils that were the product of a distinctive set of traditional agricultural practices, unaffected by recent changes in farming.

From the Papa Stour investigation, no diagnostic micromorphological evidence was obtained from cultivated horizons relating to tillage. The history of changing tillage methods over the past three centuries from single-stilted plough, through spade to mould-board plough is not detectable in soil thin sections. It is widely recognized that characteristic microstructure and textural pedofeatures, which are the principal source of evidence for tillage, will only develop in certain soils and are then susceptible to destruction by bioturbation (Courty *et al.* 1989). The former cultivated soils in Papa Stour have a high level of biological activity and their structure and fabric has been totally re-worked by invertebrates. In fact, the biological activity has been promoted by the long history of soil manuring and therefore is positively correlated with cultivation. On the basis of the results from Papa Stour, micromorphology appears to have little to offer in the study of tillage compared to other sources of information such as the surviving features of old field systems. The implication is that should arable soils be buried, for example under stone structures within a short timespan of field abandonment (< 40 years), then there may well be an absence of soil structural evidence indicative of former tillage.

In contrast to the lack of results relating to tillage and structure, clear and diagnostic evidence was obtained on the impacts of manuring practice on micromorphological features. In part this was due to the exceptional geological circumstances and distinctive turf-stripping tradition on the island. Because manuring involves the addition of mineral and organic components to the soil, it is more likely than tillage to have a lasting impact on the soil. The impact on the soil in any specific case will be determined by the stability of manure inputs. In addition, the presence of artifact scatters in fields has long been recognized by archaeologists as evidence for manuring and is of particular value in determining the extent and duration of manuring. Validation of manuring practice may also be reinforced by comparison with other analytical methods of determining organic applications to early agricultural soils. Analysis of free soil lipids has, for example, served to identify grassy turf and human manure inputs to fossil early cultivated soils at Tofts Ness, Orkney (Bull *et al.* 1999a, 1999b, Simpson *et al.* 1998b). Further, recent, developments in biomarker analysis have enabled distinctions to be made between omnivorous and herbivorous manure sources, and between pig and human sources in anthropogenic soils, validating and developing earlier interpretations of formation processes based on phosphorus chemistry and thin section micromorphology (Simpson *et al.* 1999). Integration of micromorphology and biomarker analyses appears to hold promise for the comprehensive

analysis and interpretation of early agricultural soils and their place in the cultural landscape.

The central aim of the study on Papa Stour was to take a well-documented system and to test the ways in which known cultivation practices have impacted on the micromorphology of the cultivated soils. The results highlight the partial nature of the evidence that survives for this system in the cultivated soils. No information was obtained about the nature or impact of tillage, other than confirmation that it had occurred in soils known to have been cultivated. The most successful results were obtained on manuring practice which can be clearly linked to the recorded techniques in Papa Stour. Such views very much accord with those of Courty (n.d.) who writes '... the features recognized to be diagnostic of ancient cultivation (e.g., internal slaking, dusty clay coatings, microstructural disturbances) are rarely striking evidences. It is only when ancient farmed soils have been rapidly protected from subsequent alteration by burial that the microscopic evidence for ancient cultivation is unequivocal.' The important conclusion is that micromorphology will only elucidate certain aspects of agricultural practice.

CONCLUSION

As discussed in this chapter, the changes in use of micromorphology in soil science are mirrored in archaeological applications. The development of semi-automated methods for the manufacture of thin sections, combined with image analysis systems linked to mechanical stages with auto sampling facilities and micro-spatial statistical routines, opens new and exciting research possibilities for research in soils and archaeology. However, some cautionary comments are required. The importance of validating interpretations through experimental or conventional microscopic techniques cannot be underestimated. Confidence in ultimate results can also be increased when micromorphological analysis is combined with other techniques drawn from pollen analysis, magnetic susceptibility, and organic geochemistry or microprobe analysis. Convergence of evidence using different techniques applied to the same question remains the most appropriate approach to issues in archaeological science. Despite the plea for larger sample sizes, the use of complementary analytical techniques and the need for interpretational validation, it is likely that micromorphology will continue to play a key role in the investigation of old land surfaces and archaeological deposits. In such circumstances, limited sample numbers are inevitable and as a consequence it is all the more important for the small group of micromorphologists working on archaeological deposits to electronically exchange images of slides and proposed interpretations. Such exchange of expertise combined with continuing research using samples from known contexts will ensure the continuing centrality of micromorphology in archaeological science.

ACKNOWLEDGEMENT

Thanks are expressed to Dr. Paul Adderley for comments on a draft of this chapter.

REFERENCES

*Recommended for further reading

Aaby, B. (1983). Forest development, soil genesis and human activity illustrated by pollen and hypha analysis of two neighbouring podzols in Draved Forest, Denmark. *Danmarks Geologiska Undersøgelse II*, **114**:1–114.

Andersen, S.T. (1979). Brown earth and podzol: soil genesis illuminated by microfossil analysis. *Boreas*, **8**:59–73.

Barrett, J.H., Beukens, R., Simpson, I.A., Ashmore, P., Poaps, S. and Huntley, J. (2000). What was the Viking age and when did it happen? A view from the periphery. *Norwegian Archaeological Review*, **33**:1–39.

Blume, H.-P. (1998). History and landscape impact of plaggen soils in Europe. *16th World Congress of Soil Science*. (CD-ROM) ISSS-AISS-IBG-SICS: Montpellier.

*Brewer, R. and Sleeman, J.R. (1988). *Soil Structure and Fabric*. CSIRO Publications: East Melbourne.

Bull, I.D., Simpson, I.A., Dockrill, S.J. and Evershed, R.P. (1999a). Organic geochemical evidence concerning the origin of ancient anthropogenic soil deposits at Tofts Ness, Sanday, Orkney. *Organic Geochemistry*, **30**:535–556.

Bull, I.D., Simpson, I.A., van Bergen, P.F. and Evershed, R.P. (1999b). Muck 'n' molecules: organic geochemical methods for detecting ancient manuring. *Antiquity*, **73**:86–96

Bullock, P., Fedoroff, N., Jongerius, A., Stoops, G., Tursina, T. and Babel U. (1985). *Handbook for Soil Thin Section Description*. Waine Research Publications: Wolverhampton.

Canti, M.G. (1998). The micromorphological identification of faecal spherulites from archaeological and modern materials. *Journal of Archaeological Science*, **25**:435–444.

Carter, S.P. and Davidson, D.A. (1998). An evaluation of the contribution of soil micromorphology to the study of ancient arable agriculture. *Geoarchaeology*, **13**:535–547.

Carter, S.P. and Davidson, D.A. (2000). A reply to Macphail's comments on 'An evaluation of the contribution of soil micromorphology to the study of ancient arable agriculture.' *Geoarchaeology*, **15**:499–502.

Conry, M.J. (1974). Plaggen soils: a review of man-made raised soils. *Soils and Fertilizers*, **37**:319–326.

Cornwall, I.W. (1958). *Soils for the Archaeologist*. Phoenix House: London.

Courty, M.A. (n.d.) Application of soil micromorphology in archaeology. In Kooistra, M.J. (ed.) *European Training Course on Soil Micromorphology*. Agricultural University: Wageningen.

*Courty, M.A., Goldberg, P. and Macphail, R. (1989). *Soils and Micromorphology in Archaeology*. Cambridge University Press: Cambridge.

Courty, M.A., Goldberg, P. and Macphail, R.I. (1994). Ancient people – lifestyles and cultural patterns. *15th World Congress of Soil Science*, 250–259.

Crowther, J., Macphail, R.I. and Cruise, G.M. (1996). Short-term, post-burial change in a humic rendzina soil, Overton Down experimental earthwork, Wiltshire, England. *Geoarchaeology*, **11**:95–117.

Davidson, D.A. and Carter, S.P. (1998). Micromorphological evidence of past agricultural practices in cultivated soils: the impact of a traditional agricultural system on soils in Papa Stour, Shetland. *Journal of Archaeological Science*, **25**:827–838.

Davidson, D.A. and Simpson, I.A. (1984). The formation of deep topsoils in Orkney. *Earth Surface Processes and Landforms*, **9**:75–81.

Davidson, D.A., Carter, S.P. and Quine, T.A. (1992). An evaluation of micromorphology as an aid to archaeological interpretation. *Geoarchaeology*, **7**:55–65.

Davidson, D.A., Carter, S., Boag, B., Long, D., Tipping, R. and Tyler, A. (1999). Analysis of pollen in soils: processes of incorporation and redistribution of pollen in five soil profile types. *Soil Biology and Biochemistry*, **31**:643–653.

Dawod, V. and FitzPatrick, E.A. (1993). Some population sizes and effects on the Enchytraeidae (Oligochaeta) on soil structure in a selection of Scottish soils. *Geoderma*, **56**:173–178.

Dimbleby, G.W. (1985). *The Palynology of Archaeological Sites*. Academic Press: London.

Drees, L.R., Karathanasis, A.D., Wilding, L.P. and Blevins, R.L. (1994). Micromorphological characteristics of long-term no-till and conventionally tilled soils. *Soil Science Society of America Journal*, **58**:508–517.

Fenton, A. (1978). *The Northern Isles: Orkney and Shetland*. John Donald: Edinburgh.

*FitzPatrick, E.A. (1993). *Soil Microscopy and Micromorphology*. John Wiley: Chichester.

Gebhart, A. (1992). Micromorphological analysis of soil structure modifications caused by different cultivation implements. In Anderson, P.C. (ed.) *Préhistoire de l'Agriculture: Nouvelles Approches Expérimentales et Ethnographiques*, 373–381. Monographie du CRA no 6, CNRS: Paris.

Grave, P. and Kealhofer, L. (1999). Assessing bioturbation in archaeological sediments using soil morphology and phytolith analysis. *Journal of Archaeological Science*, **26**:1239–1248.

Havinga, A.J. (1974). Problems in the interpretation of pollen diagrams of mineral soils. *Geologie en Mijnbouw*, **53**:449–453.

Jenkins, D.A. (1994). Interpretation of interglacial cave sediments from a hominid site in north Wales: translocation of Ca-Fe-phosphates. In Ringrose-Voase, A.J. and Humphreys, G.S. (eds) *Soil Micromorphology: Studies in Management and Genesis*, 293–305. Elsevier: Amsterdam, 293-305.

Karkanas, P., Kyparissi-Apostolika, N., Bar-Yosef, O. and Weiner, S. (1999). Mineral assemblages in Theopetra, Greece: a framework for understanding diagenesis in a prehistoric cave. *Journal of Archaeological Science*, **26**:1171–1180.

Keith-Lucas, D.M. (1994). Pollen analysis of archaeological soils (and mineral sediments). *Seesoil*, **10**:37–60.

Kemp, R.A. (1998). Role of micromorphology in paleopedological research. *Quaternary International*, **51/52**:133–141.

Kooistra, M.J. (1991). A micromorphological approach to the interactions between soil structure and soil biota. *Agriculture, Ecosystems and Environment*, **34**:315–328.

Kubiena, W.L. (1953). *The Soils of Europe*. Murphy: London.

Lewis, H. (1998). *The Characterization and Interpretation of Ancient Tillage Practices through Soil Micromorphology: a Methodological Study*. Unpublished PhD thesis, University of Cambridge.

Macphail, R.I. (1998). A reply to Carter and Davidson's 'An evaluation of the contribution of soil micromorphology to the study of ancient agriculture'. *Geoarchaeology*, **13**:549–564.

Macphail, R.I., Courty, M.A. and Gebhardt, A. (1990). Soil micromorphological evidence of early agriculture in north-west Europe. *World Archaeology*, **22**:53–69.

Macphail, R.I., Cruise, G.M., Mellalieu, S.J. and Niblett, R. (1998). Micromorphological interpretation of a 'turf-filled' funerary shaft at St Albans, United Kingdom. *Geoarchaeology*, **13**:617–644.

Matthews, W., French, C.A.I., Lawrence, T., Cutler, D.F. and Jones, M.K. (1997). Microstratigraphic traces of site formation processes and human activities. *World Archaeology*, **29**:281–308.

Miedema, R. (1997). Applications of micromorphology of relevance to agronomy. *Advances in Agronomy*, **59**:119–169.

Mucher, H.J., Slotboom, R.T. and Ten Veen, W.J. (1990). Palynology and micromorphology of a man-made soil. A reconstruction of the agricultural history since late-Medieval times of the Posteles in the Netherlands. *Catena*, **17**:55–67.

Odgaard, B.V. (1988). Heathland history in western Jutland, Denmark. In Birks, H.H., Birks, H.J.B., Kanland, P.E. and Moe, D. (eds) *The Cultural Landscape – Past, Present and Future*, 311–320. Cambridge University Press: Cambridge.

Ringrose-Voase, A.J. (1991). Micromorphology of soil structure: description, quantification, application. *Australian Journal of Soil Research*, **29**:777–813.

Simpson, I.A. (1997). Relict soil properties of anthropogenic deep top soils as indicators of infield management in Marwick, West Mainland, Orkney. *Journal of Archaeological Science*, **24**:365–380.

Simpson, I.A. and Barrett, J.H. (1996). Interpretation of midden formation processes at Robert's Haven, Caithness, Scotland, using thin section micromorphology. *Journal of Archaeological Science*, **23**:543–556.

Simpson, I.A., Milek, K.B. and Barrett, J.H. (1998a). *Geoarchaeological Investigations at Quoygrew, Westray, Orkney: The formation of Midden Deposits and Cultivated Anthropogenic Soils*. Unpublished Report, Department of Environmental Science, University of Stirling.

Simpson, I.A., Dockrill, S.J., Bull, I.D. and Evershed, R.P. (1998b). Early anthropogenic soil formation at Toft Ness, Sanday, Orkney. *Journal of Archaeological Science*, **25**:729–746.

Simpson, I.A., van Bergen, P.F., Elhmmali, M., Roberts, D.J. and Evershed, R.P. (1999). Lipid biomarkers of manuring practice in relict anthropogenic soils. *The Holocene*, **9**:223–229.

Simpson, I.A., Perdikaris, S., Cook, G., Campbell, J.L. and Teesdale, W.J. (in press). Cultural sediment analyses and transitions in early fishing activity at Langenesværet, Vesterålen, northern Norway. *Geoarchaeology*.

Terribile, F. and Fitzpatrick, E.A. (1995). The application of some image analysis techniques to recognition of soil micromorphological features. *European Journal of Soil Science*, **46**:29–45.

15

Taphonomic Investigations

R.A. NICHOLSON

Department of Archaeological Sciences, University of Bradford.

The remains of animals and plants provide samples of once dynamic living systems. Inevitably, samples provide less than the whole story and this is particularly true in the case of organic remains, which by their very nature are destined to decay. The investigation of the processes which act upon living entities after death and before complete fossilization or decomposition is termed taphonomy. Pioneered in the first half of the twentieth century by German palaeontologists Richter, Hecht and Weigelt, it was not until the later decades of the twentieth century that taphonomy became a major issue in archaeology. Taphonomy as applied to archaeology has been considered in relation to a range of organic materials and even, occasionally, to inorganic artifacts (Hiscock 1990). As originally defined by the Russian palaeontologist I.A. Efremov (1940:85) taphonomy is a very specific discipline: 'the study of the transition of animal remains from the biosphere into the lithosphere', but the principles have clear application to other materials. Since the common archaeological application of taphonomy extends beyond faunal remains, this chapter considers a wider definition of taphonomy, following Gifford (1981:366) who describes it as the area of research which 'defines, describes and systemises the nature and effects of processes that act on organic remains after death'. As modifications cease only either with lithification or total destruction, all organic archaeological materials are, by definition, undergoing taphonomic modification both prior to and subsequent to excavation. Taphonomy can therefore be considered as a set of transformations which an organism may or may not pass through in the transition between life and complete decomposition or eventual fossilization (Figure 15.1). Taphonomic investigations are designed to aid in the interpretation of fossil assemblages by exploring the effects of various cultural and environmental forces which may affect an organism's remains after death.

TERMINOLOGY

Taphonomy is essentially multidisciplinary and encompasses research in biological, chemical and geosciences as well as in palaeontology and archaeology. Hence the literature is potentially enormous and wide-ranging. In a synthetic paper entitled 'Taphonomy's contribution to paleobiology', Behrensmeyer and Kidwell (1985:109) noted that a large proportion of papers incorporating the study of processes between death and final burial did not include 'taphonomy' as a key word. This is in part an inevitable consequence both of the confusion which has arisen around the exact meaning of the term and of the proliferation of synonyms for different aspects of taphonomy. It has been argued that much of what is commonly called taphonomy is in fact

Handbook of Archaeological Sciences. Edited by D.R. Brothwell and A.M. Pollard.

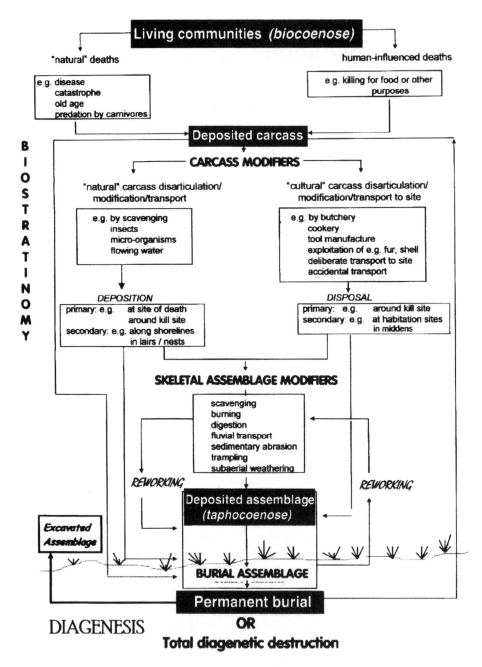

Figure 15.1   Taphonomic pathways causing modifications to skeletal assemblages.

'*actuopalaeontology*', a term coined by Richter and defined in Efremov's paper of 1940.

Actuopalaeontology incorporates the uniformitarian assumption that biases in the palaeontological (and archaeological) record can be understood by studying present-day processes of modification. A range of terms have been developed to describe stages or processes which can be subsumed under the general discipline of taphonomy. Of those more commonly used, *biostratinomy* explores factors which affect organic remains between death and final burial, whilst *diagenesis* relates to transformations occurring after final deposition (Lawrence 1968, 1971). Clarke *et al.* (1967) called these *pertothaxic* and *taphic* factors respectively, while other authors have coined a selection of specialized terms for assemblages formed by individual processes (Denys 1985). As the literature expands such a profusion of nomenclature could prove a hindrance to key word searches, so the overarching term 'taphonomy', incorporating 'biostratinomy' and 'diagenesis', all as defined above, are here proposed as standard.

TAPHONOMIC PROCESSES

An appreciation of taphonomy is an essential prerequisite to any investigation of ancient organic remains, since only if the formation processes are understood is it possible to judge the significance of the organisms represented. While some fossils are buried *in situ*, the majority are selectively transported some distance, by water, wind or animal (including human) action. Distinguishing *primary* from *secondary* or *derived* fossils is crucial to palaeoenvironmental and archaeological reconstructions. Between death and burial a considerable number of processes may have taken place which although distorting the original death assemblage may invest it with additional information. Whilst many of these processes could be considered to bias assemblages, taphonomic investigations aim not only to compensate for missing information, by modelling the pathways taken as assemblages form, but also to identify and investigate the formation processes themselves as these may have archaeological or environmental value in their own right. Lawrence (1968:1316) discussed the need to 'strip away the taphonomic overprint', but it is often the 'taphonomic overprint' itself which can yield vital information about human and non-human actions which have occurred on or off-site and which have transformed the animal and plant remains.

Archaeologically a range of other factors also influence the visibility of materials: sampling strategies, recovery procedures and analytical selection. Incorrect sampling and analysis may bias an assemblage more than any other taphonomic process. The importance of on-site soil sieving for the recovery of representative samples of bones is now well known, but any recovery mechanism which selects against smaller or more fragile items can potentially invalidate subsequent analysis. Rough handling of botanical remains during sampling and flotation can, for example, result in the loss of very fragile weed seeds and chaff fragments, to the detriment of palaeobotanical interpretation. Incorrect storage of samples may accelerate decomposition and in the worst cases lead to total destruction.

Taphonomic processes act on material remains during a period of time which may vary greatly. Both intrinsic and extrinsic factors act to determine whether an item will survive into the archaeological record. Intrinsic factors include size, internal structure and composition, extrinsic factors before burial include variables such as place and manner of death, climate and the action of humans or other animals. Generally, the longer something remains above ground the greater the number of biostratinomic processes which may act upon it and the less likely it is to be preserved. Before burial organic materials may be subjected to physical, chemical and biological attrition. Corpses of animals and plants may be disarticulated either slowly, by micro-organisms, or rapidly by humans or other animals. The remains may be transported by humans, other scavengers, wind, water or the effects of gravity. Organic materials may be modified by one or a number of physical and/or chemical processes such as abrasion, burning, passage through an animal's gut, and fracturing resulting from applied pressure. Exposure to the climatic elements may cause the physical and chemical breakdown of tissues, and micro-organisms may penetrate, creating channels which subsequently allow access to other animal or chemical forces.

After burial, soil temperature, moisture, aeration, pH and levels of activity of micro-organisms all contribute to diagenesis. Animal and plant remains may be fragmented by movement within the sediment, eroded and leached by groundwater, and penetrated by soil micro-organisms and roots. These diagenetic factors can completely destroy all forms of organic material within a timespan varying from days to many years, unless particular circumstances such as waterlogging, permanent freezing or extreme aridity obtain. Organic material survives best in conditions which inhibit the activity of micro-organisms and the movement of groundwater. Waterlogged, anaerobic conditions promote preservation and are responsible for the long-term survival of organic remains ranging from relict forests to the remains of lice and mites.

The immediate *post-mortem* burial environment in most cases predicates against survival. Decomposition by bacterial action is the normal consequence of death, maintaining the recycling of nutrients in the biosphere (see Chapter 16). It is only in exceptional circumstances that organic remains will survive into the archaeological and palaeontological record.

ARCHAEOLOGICAL OVERVIEW

Considerable advances have been made during the last 25 years or so in the fields of biostratinomy and diagenesis in relation to archaeology, although earlier archaeologists were well aware of post-depositional alterations to bone (Brothwell 1990). The publication of two volumes, *Fossils in the Making* (Behrensmeyer and Hill 1980) and *Life History of a Fossil* (Shipman 1981), reflected a growing concern with understanding formation processes, since it was recognized that the palaeontological (and archaeological) record represents a picture of the past influenced as much by environmental degradation processes as by culturally mediated ones.

Many of the most comprehensive and influential taphonomic studies have focused on vertebrate remains, culminating in a synthetic volume devoted to the subject (Lyman 1994). No such archaeological synthesis exists for invertebrate or plant taphonomy (though for a synthetic paper on plant taphonomy see Beck 1989), but both are active areas of palaeontological interest (Allison and Briggs 1991a). The degradation of organic biomolecules (proteins, lipids, carbohydrates, nucleic acids including DNA) has traditionally been a topic for geochemical research, although recent archaeological applications are discussed elsewhere (Section 4).

Although taphonomic investigations cover a wide range of topics, most can be considered in terms of the following aims:

(i) to distinguish between allochthonous and autochthonous assemblages,
(ii) to identify and characterize individual agents of modification and attrition and to identify the effects of these agents on contemporary, and by analogy on ancient, materials,
(iii) to assess and better understand the extent to which organic remains or assemblages have been modified or lost from the archaeological record,
(iv) to separate material of direct cultural significance from material accumulated by agents other than humans, and
(v) by examining modifications to archaeological material, to identify individual formation processes of cultural or of environmental significance.

Both contemporary observation and experiment have played a key role in developing models to explain the processes of post-mortem modifications, decomposition and fossilization. These approaches can be described as *actualistic investigations*, from the term 'actuopalaeontology' (Solomon 1990). Such studies have proved essential to archaeological interpretation, examples including the palaeoecological reconstructions based on an understanding of formation processes in Plio-Pleistocene vertebrate assemblages (Behrensmeyer 1975) and the identification of non-human agents of bone accumulation in cave deposits (Klippel *et al.* 1987). It has also become commonplace to work in the reverse direction, by recording attributes of archaeological material in order to try to reconstruct aspects of the taphonomic pathway. Whilst this may be a natural response to the problem of interpreting large and diverse assemblages, any groups defined within the archaeological material can only be properly understood in taphonomic terms by reference to contemporary observation and experiment. The following sections provide a necessarily brief overview of the extensive literature, but the divisions are essentially fairly arbitrary. As in many areas of science, the most successful research often combines several different approaches.

OBSERVATIONAL INVESTIGATIONS

Vertebrates

Observation-based research can be considered as a branch of ethnography, since the researcher is an observer moving in after an event has taken place to record the material remains. Based on the uniformitarian premise that the present is the key to the past, this area of research is epitomized by the work of Johannes Weigelt, who in the mid-1920s recorded in detail the death and burial of a large range of vertebrates in modern depositional environments in order to understand better the Quaternary fossil record (Weigelt 1989). In common with most actualistic research, observational research should fulfil the requirement to isolate cause and effect. Presuming adequate monitoring of all relevant parameters (which is often extremely difficult) the processes involved in assemblage formation can be easily identified. Application of such observations to archaeological assemblages may be more difficult, since archaeological assemblages are seldom formed by a single process, and several processes may cause similar modifications ('equifinality'). To archaeologists, perhaps the best known observational investigations are those of Lewis Binford, whose investigations into the actions of both human and non-human modifiers of bone extrapolized patterning observed in modern Nunamiut eskimo camps to bone assemblages recovered from archaeological sites in Africa (Binford 1981).

Brain, working in Africa, quantified the composition of, and damage to, assemblages of bones accumulated by porcupines and other mammalian predators (Brain 1981). Scanning electron microscopy has been used to separate different types of marks on bones and so distinguish human-derived cut or tooth marks from those resulting from gnawing by other animals, trampling or natural environmental forces (Shipman 1981, Olsen and Shipman 1988). Research of this kind has helped to distinguish hominid hunting from scavenging activity, and hominid scavenging from that prosecuted by other mammals. While some archaeologically recovered bone assemblages may be of little or no cultural significance, the elucidation of the agent or agencies of deposition may be of considerable relevance to palaeo-ecological and palaeoenvironmental studies. Small mammal bone accumulations from contemporary bird pellets and carnivore scats have been used to identify the predators responsible for bone accumulations in early cave deposits, while other bone groups appeared abraded in a manner consistent with fluvial transport (Andrews 1990, 1995). Trampling as a particular biostratinomic process has a considerable literature, as researchers have examined not only modification to bones but also their dispersal (Andrews and Cook 1985, Gifford 1981).

Degreasing, cracking and flaking all follow subaerial exposure, but the rate at which they occur depends upon the climate, extent of exposure and the substrate as well as upon the morphology of the bone(s) involved. Behrensmeyer (1978) systematically studied and classified into six stages the effects of subaerial weathering on the bones of large vertebrates over time in a relatively arid environment, but it is clear that the rate at which bones will weather depends on bone size and structure as well as local climate (Lyman and Fox 1989, Andrews

1995). Neighbouring bones or even different parts of the same bone will weather at different rates depending upon the micro-climates to which they are exposed.

Invertebrates

Palaeoenvironmental reconstruction depends upon the correct identification of autochthonous (i.e., non-transported, or *in situ*) assemblages. The species and species-diversity represented in an assemblage of Mollusca or Coleoptera can provide important environmental and ecological information (see Chapters 10 and 11). While some species may be indicative of specific habitats, investigations of insect faunas from a range of different contemporary environments has revealed the richness of the 'background fauna' which can complicate palaeoenvironmental and palaeoecological analysis (Kenward 1978).

Assemblages of land snails have been shown to be particularly vulnerable to selective fragmentation and degradation, particularly in the A soil horizon (Carter 1990). Briggs *et al.* (1990) found selective species preservation in floodplain deposits when compared with living assemblages from similar environments. Earthworm activity at the soil surface has been shown to mix together snail assemblages accumulated over 20 to 30 years (Carter 1990) and similar effects may be expected for assemblages of seeds, small bones and insect remains. Similarly, time averaging also affects assemblages subject to bioturbation by wind, water and rodent activity, as well as by some human activities such as ploughing.

Plants

Floral as well as faunal assemblages are affected by differential transport and differential preservation. Pollen spectra have traditionally been interpreted with regard to observations into the relative dispersal rates from different taxa (Moore and Webb 1978). The small size of pollen, spores and seeds renders them particularly susceptible to vertical and lateral mixing and so homogenization. That mixing occurs in the organic horizons even of acidic upland podsols has been demonstrated by Tipping *et al.* (1999), who observed the incorporation into the soil of non-local pollen from plants introduced within the last 150 years. Such homogenization has clear implications for the interpretation of pollen spectra. Seeds, like pollen, are produced in greatly different quantities by different plant taxa, and have shapes and sizes related to their mode of dispersal, but archaeobotanical reports concentrate largely upon cultural influences on seed distribution. Wood and seed preservation on many sites is a consequence of charring, which is largely determined by the frequency and use of fires by the human inhabitants. Observation of traditional systems of crop processing has demonstrated marked differences in weed seed distributions and concentrations depending upon the stage of processing: cleaning, winnowing, parching and storing. These have allowed predictive models to be constructed which define the modes of charring and the types of residue expected after each procedure (Jones 1981, Hillman 1981).

EXPERIMENT-BASED INVESTIGATIONS

Experiment has a crucial role in taphonomic study. Since most formation processes which act on ancient assemblages do so over a considerable timespan, experiments can simulate processes which otherwise would occur at a rate too slow for convenient study. In simulated environments it is possible to investigate single processes in a manner which would be impractical or impossible in the field under everyday conditions. By contrast, field experiments can be designed to enable researchers to document in detail processes which would be otherwise difficult to observe, under conditions more analogous to those of archaeological interest.

Degradation generally involves many processes and it is often far from straightforward to separate out the effects of individual variables. A quick search through the archaeological literature reveals numerous field-based and laboratory-based experiments into a wide range of biostratinomic and diagenetic processes.

Experimental studies can be divided into four groups:

(i) *laboratory experiments*, which are used to investigate in detail the effects of a single, controlled, process,

(ii) *short-term field investigations*, which are usually restricted to the action of a single, or small groups of, controlled variables,

(iii) *long-term field-based experiments*, which may be relatively slow and necessarily involve more than one variable, and

(iv) *computer modelling*, which can simulate the effects of one or many variables over time; this form of experimental taphonomy has received little attention to date.

Experiments have been used to investigate both the effect of the intrinsic structure of organic materials and to examine the effects of individual taphonomic processes (Robinson 1990). Until very recently the majority of publications in the archaeological literature concerned biostratinomic processes; diagenesis has received relatively little coverage outside palaeontology, as illustrated by Lyman (1994) who devotes to it a mere 17 pages out of a total of 465 pages concerned with bone taphonomy. Recent developments discussed below and in Chapter 51 show that this situation is changing.

Biostratinomic experiments

A range of bone modifications have been investigated with the aim of attributing distinctive marks or bone accumulations to specific causes. Fracturing experiments using stone tools have revealed features which may identify bones smashed for marrow from those broken by carnivores or by trampling (Blumenschine and Selvaggio 1988). Experiments into damage and movement of bones resulting from trampling are discussed by, among others, Gifford-Gonzalez *et al.* (1985), Fiorillo (1989) and Jones (1990).

Transport

Abrasion to bones may result from trampling, aeolian action or water transport as well as from bone tool usage. To distinguish each mode of abrasion, bones have been tumbled in various sedimentary matrices (Korth 1979, Shipman and Rose 1983, Nicholson 1992) and rubbed with a range of different physical and chemical media (Bromage 1984). Using flume experiments Behrensmeyer (1975, 1982) demonstrated how bones of varying density are differentially transported, leading to spatially sorted collections which may not, however, exhibit any significant amount of rounding as a consequence.

Exposure

While it is intuitively obvious that organic materials suffer as a result of prolonged exposure to the climatic elements, Brain was the first to experimentally monitor subaerial weathering. By placing the bones of a pig in the open and in the shade for seven years and monitoring their degradation, he was able to demonstrate very real differences in decomposition resulting from the exposure to sunlight (Brain 1981:115). These experiments have been augmented by actualistic research using a range of animals and depositional environments (see above); however it may not always be possible to distinguish subaerial from post-depositional weathering, since in temperate environments microbial action may be primarily responsible for bone degradation both above and below ground.

Heating

The dates and developmental stages at which hominids first harnessed fire and subsequently developed a preference for cooked meat are issues central to the study of human evolution. Yet although much bone utilized by humans must have been cooked, at the present time there is no convincing means of distinguishing cooked but uncharred bone from uncooked bone archaeologically. Where collagen survives, changes to its structure may hold the key to the determination of low-temperature heating (Richter 1986, Nielsen-Marsh 1999). Burned bone is commonly identified archaeologically and may result from accidental burning, roasting, rubbish disposal or intentional cremation. The effect of different kinds of cremation on humans and other animals has been studied experimentally (see Chapter 24). Very occasionally bones may appear unheated externally but blackened internally in a manner consistent with charring (Figure 15.2). The cause of this phenomenon is as yet unclear, but bone stained by manganese or iron oxides may be mistaken for burned bone and the distinction is important for Pleistocene sites where recognition of hominid activity may rely on the correct identification of burned bone. Bones heated to high temperatures in the presence of oxygen show characteristic colour changes with increasing temperature and, when viewed at very high magnifications, surface modifications (Shipman et al. 1984). However some similar surface changes were also found on unheated but weathered bone (Nicholson 1993). A range of other techniques have been utilized to identify heated bone, including X-ray diffraction, carbon-nitrogen ratios, electron spin-resonance, infra-red spectroscopy and thermoluminescence. So far none has proved a useful tool for routinely and unequivocally identifying cooked as opposed to burned bone. Stiner et al. (1995) have convincingly established the difficulty even of identifying burned bone using infra-red and X-ray diffraction, since recrystallization due to burning may be impossible to distinguish from recrystallization due to weathering above and below ground.

Chewing, gnawing and digestion

Contemporary assemblages of vertebrate remains modified by the feeding habits of other animals have been a popular subject for experimental study. Modifications include damage by jaw action (chewing and tearing) and by the actions of acids and enzymes secreted during digestion in the gut. A range of experiments have been used to investigate the effects of digestion on organic materials (usually bones, but exceptionally other materials, e.g., Calder 1977) in order to better understand archaeologically-recovered assemblages and also to aid in the identification of fossilized coprolites. Raptor and carnivore feeding habits and the contents of their pellets and scats have been comprehensively reviewed by Andrews (1990; see above); this work details a number of experimental investigations concerned not only with pellet formation but also with pellet dispersal and degradation. The effects on vertebrate and invertebrate skeletal parts of ingestion and digestion by dogs, pigs, rats and humans have also been the subject of several experiments since Steenstrup (1862) fed bones to dogs to compare the damage incurred with that seen on bones from Mesolithic Danish middens. The very rapid loss of skeletal material as a result of scavenging by dogs was demonstrated experimentally by Payne and Munson (1985). Similarly, Jones (1990) recorded a huge loss of bone, and characteristic distortions to bones recovered in faeces after feeding fish to a dog, pig, rat and a human. Since most organic rubbish would in the past probably have been fed to, or scavenged by, domestic or commensal animals, there is a

Figure 15.2 Horse metatarsal from Old Scatness Broch, Shetland, showing apparently unheated (but butchered, gnawed, pitted and eroded) cortical bone surrounding blackened, apparently charred, cancellous bone.

potential for the selective loss of those bones most likely to be ingested. Given a well-preserved assemblage, the corroding, pitting and polishing action of gut enzymes can sometimes be observed on surviving bone fragments, though detailed inspection is required since bones eroded by water action and corroded by acidic groundwater may exhibit similar damage.

Invertebrates

Once dead, invertebrates may be subjected to many of the same processes which disperse and degrade vertebrates and their skeletons. Much of the palaeontological research into invertebrate taphonomy has been aided by experiments, for example the processes involved in fossilization have been studied by monitoring the decomposition of marine invertebrates in a range of aquatic environments (Allison and Briggs 1991b). Kidwell and Boscence (1991) and Claasen (1998) have discussed shell taphonomy, with reference to experimental studies involving heating, tumbling and trampling.

Plants

Plant remains recovered archaeologically are generally preserved by charring, waterlogging, mineralization or desiccation. Whether part of a plant is preserved is determined not only by extrinsic factors such as the nature of the soil and the climate but also by intrinsic physical properties (size, shape, surface morphology). Cultural factors are clearly critical, since some plant parts are much more likely to be charred than others and once charred some plant parts may be rendered unidentifiable. Some woods, for example, when burned produce better charcoal than others, whilst some burn completely to ash. A number of experiments have demonstrated how different types of grain, seeds and tubers may be selectively carbonized, dependent upon variables such as temperature, humidity and the size and shape of the plant components (Renfrew 1973, Boardman and Jones 1990, Dickson 1990, Gustafsson 2000).

Plant tissues are liable to movement by wind and water, but there has been little archaeologically-motivated experimentation involving the transportation of plants and their parts. The palaeontological literature reveals both observations and experiments into relative dispersal rates and decay of leaves, seeds and wood (Spicer 1991), and experiments in ruminant digestion from early agricultural texts have been used

by Anderson and Ertug-Yaras (1998) in a comprehensive review of plant preservation in dried and burned animal dung. Beck (1989) investigated differences in the breakage patterning of fresh and aged cycad seed as part of an experiment-based project looking at distinguishing human processed, from naturally fragmented, seeds. The differential preservation of plant tissues is an area of considerable research potential and challenge to archaeobotanical analysis.

Diagenetic experiments

Bone diagenesis is dealt with in more detail in Chapter 51. After burial, bone is subject to decay by microbial and chemical processes. Key variables include the internal structure of the bone, its size, macroporosity and microporosity and degree of mineralization. The burial environment affects bone decay in terms of groundwater flow rate, chemical composition of the groundwater, temperature and the microbiological potential of the sediment. In practice these variables are inter-related. Von Endt and Ortner (1984) used different sized pieces of crushed bovine bone to assess the effects of temperature and bone size on rates of decay, concluding that the larger the piece the slower the decay rate. This led them to conclude that small bones are liable to decay in preference to large ones. They also noted that the porosity of the skeletal tissue exerted an important influence on decay rate, a factor which might explain why, if less porous, small bones do not always seem to decay as fast as larger bones from larger species (Nicholson 1996). Bacterial decomposition has been initiated experimentally as a means of better understanding bone decomposition both before and after burial (Child *et al.* 1993, Child 1995).

The *post-mortem* processes of mineralization are poorly understood in archaeology. The term can describe the process whereby after death, if exposed to water, an organic matrix is gradually replaced by new minerals, which preserve the original shape of the organic item, in some cases even down to individual cells. A range of mineralized organic materials, most usually seeds or wood, are recovered archaeologically from a range of soil environments. Electron microprobe analysis of mineralized seeds from Potterne has demonstrated that the tissues had been replaced by a form of calcium phosphate (Carruthers unpublished) and similar results have been found elsewhere. It has traditionally been thought that mineralization occurs in deposits rich in urine and faecal waste (Green 1979), or in deposits where waterlogging preserved the items long enough for calcium phosphate replacement to occur. Given damp conditions, where calcium and phosphorus are available perhaps from bone and/or ash, it has been suggested that mineral-rich solution percolates into the plant tissues, where the calcium phosphate crystallizes out and forms a cast of the object (Green 1979). Some plant tissues and seed types seem more susceptible to this kind of preservation, and assemblages are frequently dominated by a restricted range of species (Carruthers 1993). Occasionally, where seeds have a thick seed coat, the coat is preserved in a non-mineralized state surrounding the mineralized centre. Outside the archaeological literature, palaeontologists have had a long-standing interest in the process of *phosphatization* as the key to fossilization, recently enhanced by experiments into the decay and mineralization of invertebrate soft tissue in aqueous environments (Allison and Briggs 1991a) and the experimental fossilization of phosphatic, non-phosphatic and non-mineralized organic remains (Lucas and Prevot 1991).

Like seeds, pollen survival is clearly influenced by grain size and morphology and Vuorela (1977) designed experiments to test the potential for long-term relative survival of several pollen types. The resistant wall material found in the spores of *pteridophytes* (ferns and liverworts) and in the pollen grains of gymnosperms and angiosperms is termed sporopollenin, and its decay has been investigated experimentally by Havinga who in 1964 deposited mixtures of 19 pollen and spore species in various soils in order to trace their survival or decay over time (Havinga 1967, 1971). His results showed that decay was slow in sphagnum peat, more evident in *Carex* peat and in podsolized sandy soil, and was very rapid in both river clay and leaf mould. Where deterioration was rapid, there was a marked change in the relative frequencies of species.

Long-term field-based experiments

The experimental earthwork programmes at Overton Down and Wareham in southern England are widely known field-based experimental studies. Started in the 1960s, the experiments involved the construction of large earthworks (bank and ditch) in a chalk environment (Overton Down) and an acidic heathland environment (Wareham), with the deliberate burial of a range of organic and inorganic materials at each site. The aim of the projects was to study the processes of decay and decomposition over many years, with periodic excavation of samples for detailed study.

Most recently the Overton earthwork was excavated in 1992 (Bell *et al.* 1996), following which the next excavation will be in 2024. Whilst the timescale of the investigations is unrivalled, inevitably with hindsight some shortcomings are now apparent, in particular the very limited range of animal and plant remains which were buried.

Other long-term field experiments include periodic observations on bone degradation using an entire buried ram (Ovis) (van Wijngaarden-Bakker 2000) and on the degradation of hair utilizing a range of burial environments and a pig (Sus) as a human cadaver analogue (Wilson *et al.* forthcoming). This author conducted a series of experimental burials using a range of vertebrate remains (mammal, bird and fish, cooked and uncooked) in a range of different soils and sediments, but in the first instance utilizing a more limited timescale of seven years between burial and excavation (Nicholson 1996, 1998). These experiments have indicated the complexity of diagenesis. Whilst rates of bone destruction did not seem to be clearly correlated with soil pH or with soil type, the local soil microfauna (itself related to soil type and very local pH) appeared to play a critical role in decomposition, as did the treatment the carcass had undergone prior to burial.

TAPHONOMY INTO THE FUTURE

The second half of the twentieth century has seen great progress in our understanding of individual taphonomic processes, but the results have been slow to influence archaeological method and theory. As we enter the twenty-first century there is a clear need to move towards synthetic and archaeologically-integrated taphonomic studies. Archaeological sites are disappearing at an ever increasing rate, and to protect our heritage it is essential that the processes of degradation are better understood. Beyond the study of single process and effect, integrated studies are now starting to address globally important themes, such as the relationship between geological and climatic conditions and biomolecular preservation (Nielsen-Marsh 1999). Greater understanding of groundwater movement both within archaeological sediments and at the level of the interaction between buried bone and its surrounding water (Hedges and Millard 1995) promise the possibility of developing models by which diagenetic effects may be predicted, allowing greater archaeological awareness of the processes of formation and loss of sites and the artifacts and ecofacts within them.

REFERENCES

*Recommended for further reading

*Allison, P. and Briggs, D.E.G. (eds) (1991a). *Taphonomy. Releasing the Data Locked in the Fossil Record.* Plenum Press: New York.

Allison, P. and Briggs, D.E.G. (1991b). The taphonomy of soft-bodied animals. In Donovan, S.K. (ed.) *Fossilization: the Process of Taphonomy*, 120–140. Belhaven Press: London.

Anderson, S. and Ertug-Yaras, F. (1998). Fuel, fodder and faeces: an ethnographic and botanical study of dung fuel use. *Environmental Archaeology*, 1:99–110.

*Andrews, P. (1990). *Owls, Caves and Fossils*. University of Chicago Press: Chicago.

Andrews, P. (1995). Experiments in taphonomy. *Journal of Archaeological Science*, 22:147–153.

Andrews, P. and Cook, J. (1985). Natural modifications to bone in a temperate setting. *Man*, 20:675–691.

Beck, W. (1989). The taphonomy of plants. In Beck, W., Clarke, A. and Head, L. (eds) *Plants in Australian Archaeology*, 31–53. University of Queensland: St Lucia.

Behrensmeyer, A.K. (1975). The taphonomy and paleoecology of Plio-Pleistocene vertebrate assemblages east of Lake Rudolf, Kenya. *Bulletin of the Museum of Comparative Zoology*, 146:473–578.

Behrensmeyer, A.K. (1978). Taphonomic and ecologic information from bone weathering. *Paleobiology*, 4:150–162.

Behrensmeyer, A.K. (1982). Time resolution in fluvial vertebrate assemblages. *Paleobiology*, 8:211–228.

*Behrensmeyer, A.K. and Hill, A.P. (1980). *Fossils in the Making: Vertebrate Taphonomy and Paleoecology*. University of Chicago Press: Chicago.

Behrensmeyer, A.K. and Kidwell, S.M. (1985). Taphonomy's contribution to paleobiology. *Paleobiology*, 11:105–119.

*Bell, M., Fowler, P.J. and Hillson, S.W. (1996). *The Experimental Earthwork Project 1960–1992*. Research Report 100, Council for British Archaeology: York.

*Binford, L.R. (1981). *Bones: Ancient Men and Modern Myths*. Academic Press: New York.

Blumenschine, R.J. and Selvaggio, M. (1988). Percussion marks on bone surfaces as a new diagnostic of hominid behaviour. *Nature*, 333:763–765.

Boardman, S. and Jones, G. (1990). Experiments on the effects of charring on cereal plant components. *Journal of Archaeological Science*, 17:1–11.

Briggs, D.J., Gilbertson, D.D. and Harris, A.L. (1990). Molluscan taphonomy in a braided river environment and its implications for studies of Quaternary cold stage river deposits. *Journal of Biogeography*, 17:623–637.

Brain, C.K. (1981). *The Hunters or the Hunted? An Introduction to African Cave Taphonomy*. University of Chicago Press: Chicago.

Bromage, T.G. (1984). Interpretation of scanning-electron microscope images of abraded forming bone surfaces. *American Journal of Physical Anthropology*, 64:161–178.

Brothwell, D. (1990). Environmental and experimental studies in history. In Robinson, D.E. (ed.) *Experimentation and Reconstruction in Environmental Archaeology*, 1–24. Oxbow Books: Oxford.

Calder, A.M. (1977). Survival properties of organic residues through the human digestive tract. *Journal of Archaeological Science*, 4:141–152.

Carruthers, W. (1993). Carbonised, mineralised and waterlogged plant remains. In Hawkes, J. and Heaton, M.J. (eds) *A Closed Shaft Garderobe and Associated Medieval Structures at Jennings Yard, Windsor, Berkshire*, 82–90. Report 3, Wessex Archaeology: Salisbury.

Carter, S.P. (1990). The stratification and taphonomy of shells in calcareous soils: implications for land snail analysis in archaeology. *Journal of Archaeological Science*, 17:495–507.

Child, A. (1995). Taphonomy of archaeological bone. *Studies in Conservation*, 40:19–30.

Child, A.M., Gillard, R.D. and Pollard, A.M. (1993). Microbial attack on collagen II: isolation of the micro-organisms and the detection of their enzymes. *Journal of Archaeological Science*, 20:159–164.

Claasen, C. (1998). *Shells*. Cambridge University Press: Cambridge.

Clarke, J., Beerbower, J.R. and Kietzke, K.K. (1967). Oligocene sedimentation, stratigraphy, paleoecology and paleoclimatology in the Big Badlands of South Dakota. *Fieldiana Geology Memoir*, 5:1–158.

Denys, C. (1985). Nouveaux critères de reconnaissance des concentrations de microvertébrés d'après l'étude des pelotes de chouettes du Botswana (Afrique australe). *Bulletin of the National Museum of Natural History, Paris 4th series*, 7:879–933.

Dickson, C. (1990). Experimental processing and cooking of emmer and spelt wheats and the Roman army diet. In Robinson, D.E. (ed.) *Experimentation and Reconstruction in Environmental Archaeology*, 33–40. Oxbow Books: Oxford.

Efremov, I.A. (1940). Taphonomy: a new branch of paleontology. *Pan-American Geologist*, 74:81–93.

Fiorillo, A.R. (1989). An experimental study of trampling: implications for the fossil record. In Bonnichsen, R. and Sorg, M.H. (eds) *Bone Modification*, 61–71. Center for the Study of the First Americans, Orono: Maine.

Gifford, D.P. (1981). Taphonomy and paleoecology: a critical review of archaeology's sister disciplines. In Schiffer, M. (ed.) *Advances in Archaeological Method and Theory Vol. 4*, 365–438. Academic Press: New York.

Gifford-Gonzalez, D.P., Damrosch, D.B., Prior, J. and Thunen, R.L. (1985). The third dimension in site structure: an experiment in trampling and vertical dispersal. *American Antiquity*, 50:803–818.

Green, F. (1979). Phosphate mineralisation of seeds from archaeological sites. *Journal of Archaeological Science*, 6:279–284.

Gustafsson, S. (2000). Carbonized cereal grains and weed seeds in prehistoric houses – an experimental perspective. *Journal of Archaeological Science*, 27:65–70.

Havinga, A.J. (1967). Palynology and pollen preservation. *Review of Palaeobotany and Palynology*, 2:81–98.

Havinga, A.J. (1971). An experimental investigation into the decay of pollen and spores in various soil types. In Brooks, J., Grant, P.R., Muir, M., van Guzel, P. and Shaw, G. (eds) *Sporopollenin*, 446–479. Academic Press: London.

Hedges, R.E.M. and Millard, A.R. (1995). Bones and groundwater: towards the modelling of diagenetic processes. *Journal of Archaeological Science*, 22:155–164.

Hillman, G.C. (1981). Reconstructing crop husbandry practices from charred remains of crops. In Simmons, I.G. and Tooley, M.J. (eds) *Farming Practice in British Prehistory*, 183–191. Duckworth: London.

Hiscock, P. (1990). A study in scarlet: taphonomy and inorganic artefacts. In Solomon, S., Davidson, I. and Watson, D. (eds) *Problem Solving in Taphonomy*, 34–49. University of Queensland: St. Lucia.

Jones, A.K.G. (1990). Experiments with fish bones and otoliths. In Robinson, D.E. (ed.) *Experimentation and Reconstruction in Environmental Archaeology*, 143–146. Oxbow Books: Oxford.

Jones, G.E.M. (1981). Crop processing at Assiros Toumba: a taphonomic study. *Zeitschrift für Archaeologie*, 15:105–111.

Kenward, H.K. (1978). *The Analysis of Archaeological Insect Assemblages: a New Approach*. Archaeology of York Fascicule 19/1, Council of British Archaeology: London.

Kidwell, S.M. and Bosence, D.W. (1991). Taphonomy and time-averaging of marine shelly faunas. In Allison, P. and Briggs, D.E.G. (eds) *Taphonomy. Releasing the Data Locked in the Fossil Record*, 116–188. Plenum Press: New York.

Klippel, W.E., Snyder, L.M. and Parmalee, P.W. (1987). Taphonomy and archaeologically recovered mammal bone from southeast Missouri. *Journal of Ethnobiology*, 7:155–169.

Korth, W.W. (1979). Taphonomy of microvertebrate fossil assemblages. *Annals of the Carnegie Museum*, 48:235–285.

Lawrence, D.R. (1968) Taphonomy and information losses in fossil communities. *Geological Society of America Bulletin*, 79:1315–1330.

Lawrence, D.R. (1971). The nature and structure of paleoecology. *Journal of Paleontology*, 45:593–607.

Lucas, J. and Prevot, L.E. (1991). Phosphates and fossil preservation. In Allison, P. and Briggs, D.E.G. (eds) *Taphonomy. Releasing the Data Locked in the Fossil Record*, 389–411. Plenum Press: New York.

*Lyman, R.L. (1994). *Vertebrate Taphonomy*. Cambridge University Press: Cambridge.

Lyman, R.L. and Fox, G.L. (1989). A critical evaluation of bone weathering as an indicator of bone assemblage formation. *Journal of Archaeological Science*, 16:293–317.

Moore, P.D. and Webb, J.A. (1978). *An Illustrated Guide to Pollen Analysis*. Hodder and Stoughton: London.

Nicholson, R.A. (1992). Bone survival: the effects of sedimentary abrasion and trampling on fresh and cooked bone. *International Journal of Osteoarchaeology*, 2:79–90.

Nicholson, R.A. (1993). A morphological investigation of burnt animal bone and an evaluation of its utility in archaeology. *Journal of Archaeological Science*, 20:411–428.

Nicholson, R.A. (1996). Bone degradation, burial medium and species representation: debunking the myths, an experiment-based approach. *Journal of Archaeological Science*, 23:13–33.

Nicholson, R.A. (1998). Bone degradation in a compost heap. *Journal of Archaeological Science*, 25:393–403.

Nielsen-Marsh, C. (1999). Ancient Biomolecules Group, University of Newcastle. *Osteoarchaeology Research Group Newsletter*, 20:7–11.

Olsen, S.L. and Shipman, P. (1988). Surface modification on bone: trampling versus butchery. *Journal of Archaeological Science*, 15:535–553.

Payne, S. and Munson, P.J. (1985). Ruby and how many squirrels? In Fieller, N.R.G., Gilbertson, D.D. and Ralph, N.R.A. (eds) *Paleobiological Investigations: Research Design, Methods and Data Analysis*, 31–40. BAR International Series 266, British Archaeological Reports: Oxford.

Renfrew, J.M. (1973). *Palaeoethnobotany. The Prehistoric Food Plants of the Near East*. Methuen: London.

Richter, J. (1986). Experimental study of heat-induced morphological changes in fish bone collagen. *Journal of Archaeological Science*, 13:477–481.

*Robinson, D.E. (ed.) (1990). *Experimentation and Reconstruction in Environmental Archaeology*. Oxbow Books: Oxford.

*Shipman, P. (1981). *Life History of a Fossil: an Introduction to Taphonomy and Paleoecology*. Harvard University Press: Cambridge, Mass.

Shipman, P., Foster, G. and Schoeninger, M.J. (1984). Burnt bones and teeth: an experimental study of color, morphology, crystal structure and shrinkage. *Journal of Archaeological Science*, 11:307–325.

Shipman, P. and Rose, J. (1983). Early hominid hunting, butchering and carcass processing behaviour: approaches to the fossil record. *Journal of Anthropological Archaeology*, 2:57–98.

Solomon, S. (1990). What is this thing called taphonomy? In Solomon, S., Davidson, I. and Watson, D. (eds) *Problem Solving in Taphonomy*, 25–33. University of Queensland: St. Lucia.

Spicer, R.A. (1991). Plant taphonomic processes. In Allison, P. and Briggs, D.E.G. *Taphonomy. Releasing the Data Locked in the Fossil Record*, 72–108. Plenum Press: New York.

Steenstrup, J.J. (1862). *Et Blik paa Natur og Oldforskningens Forstudier til Besvarelsen af Spörgsmaalet om Menneskeslægtens tidlgste Optræden I Europa*. Inbydelsesskrift til Kjøbenhavns Universitets Aarfest: Kjøbenhavn.

Stiner, M.C., Kuhn, S.L., Weiner, S. and Bar-Yosef, O. (1995). Differential burning, recrystallization, and fragmentation of archaeological bone. *Journal of Archaeological Science*, **22**:223–237.

Tipping, R., Long, D., Carter, S., Davidson, D., Tyler, A. and Boag, B. (1999). Testing the potential of soil-stratigraphic palynology in podsols. In Pollard, A.M. (ed.) *Geoarchaeology: Exploration, Environments, Resources*, 79–90. Special Publication No. 165, Geological Society: London.

van Wijngaarden-Bakker, L. (2000). Experimental taphonomy. In Huntley, J.P. and Stallibrass, S. (eds) *Taphonomy and Interpretation*, 85–90. Oxbow Books: Oxford.

von Endt, D.W. and Ortner, D.J. (1984). Experimental effects of bone size and temperature on bone diagenesis. *Journal of Archaeological Science*, **11**:247–253.

Vuorela, I. (1977). Preservation of pollen types in long-term storage and physical stress tests. *Memoranda Society of Fauna Flora Fennica*, **53**:25–33.

Weigelt, J. (1989). *Recent Vertebrate Carcasses and their Paleobiological Implications*. University of Chicago Press: Chicago (translation).

Wilson, A.S., Dixon, R.A., Edwards, H.G.M., Farwell, D.W., Janaway, R.C., Pollard, A.M. and Tobin, D.J. (forthcoming). Towards an understanding of the interaction of hair with the depositional environment. *Proceedings of III World Congress of Mummy Studies. Arica, Chile*.

16

Global Biogeochemical Cycles and Isotope Systematics – How the World Works

A.M. POLLARD and L. WILSON

Department of Archaeological Sciences, University of Bradford.

Over recent decades, it has become increasingly clear that the traditional disciplinary studies of physics, chemistry, biology, and so on, are inadequate, when considered in isolation, to explain many natural systems. Processes such as the corrosion of metallic surfaces in contact with groundwater, for example, can be described electrochemically, but the rates of many reactions are not explained by thermodynamics alone. Microbial mediation has often been identified as the cause of such deviations from 'pure chemical' behaviour (see Chapter 48). The term 'biogeochemistry' was coined more than 50 years ago to denote the study of chemical reactions taking place within the atmosphere, oceans and freshwater, the Earth's crust and all living organisms, and the interactions between them. The goal of biogeochemistry, according to Schlesinger (1997:4) is 'to understand the processes controlling the chemical environment in which we live'.

The global ecosystem consists of four overlapping and interrelated subsystems – termed the *atmosphere*, *hydrosphere*, *geosphere*, and *biosphere* – and is powered principally by energy from the sun. These subsystems act as 'sinks' and 'sources' for all the elements which circulate within and between them. The principal elements which control life on earth are carbon, nitrogen, oxygen and hydrogen, and to a lesser extent phosphorus and sulfur. Each element is cycled between subsystems by a wide range of physical, chemical and biological processes. These processes are collectively termed the *biogeochemical* and *hydrological cycles*. It is now widely accepted that human impact on these cycles, particularly the carbon cycle, is increasingly affecting the global ecosystem. A consideration of stable isotope systematics fits very well within the concept of biogeochemical cycling (Fontes and Fritz 1980, O'Neil *et al.* 1991, Hoefs 1997). The use of stable isotope geochemistry to reconstruct modern ecosystems is a rapidly developing field known as 'isotope ecology' (Wada *et al.* 1991, Lajtha and Michener 1994, Griffiths 1998).

These cycles all have significant relevance to a wide range of sciences, including archaeology. For example, the carbon cycle is well-known archaeologically because of its role in ensuring rapid mixing of cosmogenic ^{14}C, which is an essential pre-requisite for radiocarbon dating (Chapter 2). The overall rate of decay of organic matter in the ground is controlled by variations in the rate of carbon cycling, which therefore affects taphonomic processes (Chapter 15). The fractionation of carbon and nitrogen isotopes as they are cycled around the biosphere is used to facilitate dietary reconstruction from bone chemistry (Chapter 23). The fractionation of oxygen (and hydrogen) isotopes during the meteoric cycle of water is used for palaeotemperature reconstructions from ice cores (Chapter 1) and, to a lesser extent, mammalian tooth enamel. The fixation of phosphorus into soils as part of the phosphorus cycle is used as a geochemical location technique to identify human activity (Chapter 45).

This chapter summarizes the water, carbon and nitrogen cycles, and more briefly the phosphorus and sulfur cycles, highlighting points of archaeological importance. Passing comment is also made on other inorganic cycles.

BIOGEOCHEMICAL CYCLES

A clear picture has emerged over the past decade, which shows that the basic materials required to sustain the biosphere (water, carbon, nitrogen, etc.) are not static, but are constantly being cycled between the four main 'reservoirs' (biosphere, atmosphere, lithosphere and hydrosphere). As in any dynamic system, the mass of any substance (e.g., water) in any one of these 'reservoirs' is constant providing the rates of input and output ('fluxes') are constant. Any change to either will cause a shift in the system equilibrium, resulting in a net transfer of that substance between one reservoir and another. Components of a system which lock up material for a long period of time are called 'sinks'. For example, limestone ($CaCO_3$) acts as a sink for oceanic carbonate, in that it effectively removes it from the ocean system. In the much longer term, however, uplift and terrestrial weathering of surface rocks will eventually liberate the carbonate again. Components of a system which liberate a material into that system are called 'sources' – for example, decaying organic matter is a source of carbon and nitrogen into the terrestrial ecosystem. The 'Mean Residence Time' (MRT) of a material in a particular reservoir is a particularly important parameter which can be calculated as follows (Schlesinger 1997:51):

$$MRT = \text{Mass in reservoir/flux} \qquad (1)$$

Biogeochemical cycles are quantified from a knowledge of the mass of a particular substance in each of the relevant reservoirs, and the flux of that material between each of the reservoirs. It is often possible to write down a simplified chemical equation which encapsulates the reaction by which the material is transferred from one reservoir to another. This allows quantification of the effects of such reactions. For example, if one mole of organic matter (taken to be represented by the generic formula CH_2O, with a molecular mass of 30 g) is oxidized (transferring mass from the biosphere to the atmosphere), the reaction can be summarized as follows:

$$CH_2O + O_2 \rightarrow CO_2 + H_2O \quad \Delta G^0 = -475\,\text{kJ/mol} \quad (2)$$

Thus 30 g of organic material oxidized will release 44 g of carbon dioxide (one mole of CO_2) and liberate 475 kJ of energy (i.e., an exothermic reaction). The same reaction (albeit a highly simplified version of the true biochemical reactions) can be considered to represent the conversion of organic carbon back to carbon dioxide and water as a result of the metabolic action (respiration) of microbes and higher animals

THE WATER CYCLE

Water is cycled around the surface of the Earth in huge quantities (Schlesinger 1997; Figure 16.1). Using the units of 10^{18} g (Exagrams), the oceans have a mass of 1 350 000 Eg, and lose 425 Eg/yr in evaporation, of which 385 Eg/yr returns to the ocean as precipitation, and 40 Eg/yr is transported to the land. Evapotranspiration by plants contributes a further 71 Eg/yr to the atmosphere, and therefore 111 Eg/yr falls as terrestrial precipitation. Put in slightly more relevant terms, this corresponds to an average rainfall of 70 cm/yr if it fell evenly across the Earth's land surface. It is not, of course, evenly distributed. The mass of water in the atmosphere is 13 Eg, so the mean residence time of water in the atmosphere is 13/111, or 0.117 years (roughly six weeks). Mean residence time in the ocean is more complicated to calculate. Simplistically, it is 1 350 000/425, or approximately 3200 years, but this does not take into account the complex structure of the world's oceans. Only the surface layer of the ocean is well-mixed with the atmosphere as a result of wave action. This layer varies from 75 to 200 metres in depth, depending on latitude, and has a global average annual temperature of 18°C. The boundary between the warm surface waters and the much colder deep waters is known as the *thermocline*, and is marked by a rapid change in the temperature profile and density of the water column. Below this, the temperature is a relatively constant 3°C. Deep waters constitute about 95 per cent of the ocean volume, and so the effective residence time for water in the surface ocean is nearer to 160 years.

The cycling of water is important archaeologically because there is a good deal of evidence to suggest that, in some parts of the world at least, the supply, control and management of water has been critical in the rise

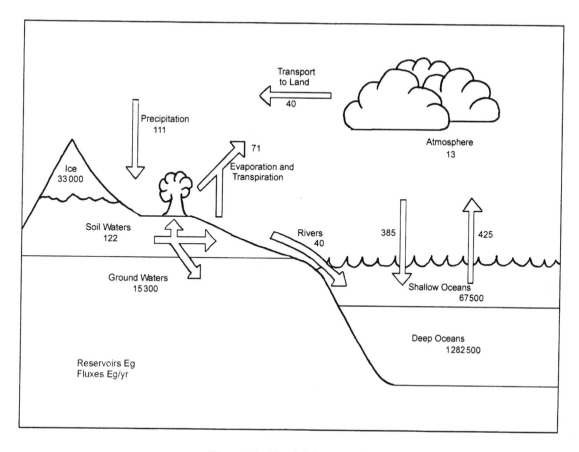

Figure 16.1   The global water cycle.

and fall of civilizations. The relatively rapid demise of the Classic Maya civilization around AD 800, for example, has been attributed to numerous economic and environmental factors (Sabloff 1995). However, a recent study of light stable isotopes from local lacustrine sediment cores (Hodell *et al.* 1995) has provided evidence that palaeoclimatic change, involving the onset of a 200 year period of dryness, ultimately led to decline. It appears the widespread shortage of water, coupled with pre-existing stresses was sufficient to topple this once-great society. A similar phenomenon occurred during the mid-Holocene with the desertification of the Sahara (Roberts 1998:115). Until the third millennium BC, lakes were plentiful in the Saharan region, as attested by finds of aquatic micro and macro fauna. The archaeological record is abundant for this period and is particularly rich in rock art. Again, palaeoclimatic change resulted in the disappearance of vital water resources and the consequent depletion of food supplies, creating the inhospitable

landscape which dominates the region today. A good deal of dendroclimatology, particularly in the southwestern USA, is dedicated to reconstructing changes in past water availability (e.g., Knox 1993, Brockway and Bradley 1995, Cleaveland 2000).

The water cycle is, however, important archaeologically and environmentally for quite another reason – isotopic fractionation of both oxygen and hydrogen can occur each time water goes through a phase change or is transported across a membrane. For physical processes, this fractionation is linearly dependent on the temperature at which this process occurs. Thus the hydrogen or oxygen isotope ratio is a direct measure of the temperatures involved in the process.

Hydrogen and oxygen (like many other light elements) occur naturally in more than one isotopic form. The most common form of hydrogen is the simplest of atomic structures – a single proton (charge +1, mass 1) in the nucleus, orbited by a single electron (charge −1, mass negligible). This isotope of hydrogen is symbolized by ^{1}H. Much less abundant, but naturally occurring and stable, is the heavy isotope known as ^{2}H, or deuterium (D). This has an additional neutron in the nucleus, with zero charge but a mass of $+1$, making this isotope twice as heavy as the lighter isotope. A third isotope (^{3}H, or tritium [T]) is even less abundant, and is radioactively unstable. In nature, on average only 0.0156 per cent of all hydrogen atoms are the heavier isotope ^{2}H (roughly 3 in 20 000 atoms). The most abundant stable isotope of oxygen is ^{16}O, with eight protons and eight neutrons in the nucleus, but two other heavier stable isotopes exist – ^{17}O, with nine neutrons, and ^{18}O, with ten neutrons. The abundance of ^{17}O is low (0.04 per cent) compared with 0.2 per cent for ^{18}O, but it can be seen that the lighter isotope is still the most abundant (99.76 per cent) (see Table 16.1 for a more complete list of relevant stable isotope abundances).

As water is cycled round the natural system, small changes occur in the ratio of both ^{2}H/^{1}H and ^{18}O/^{16}O. This is because the increased mass of the heavier isotope renders it slightly less likely to take part in processes such as evaporation, enriching slightly the remaining liquid in the heavier isotope whilst depleting the resulting vapour of the same isotope. Such processes are termed *fractionation*, and are critically dependent on the mass difference between the two isotopes. Hydrogen should therefore be expected to show the largest fractionation effects, since the heavier isotope is twice the mass of the lighter, whereas in oxygen it

is only heavier by 12.5 per cent. Even for hydrogen, however, the effects are small. As stated above, the average abundance ratio of ^{2}H to ^{1}H is 0.0156:99.98, or 0.000156, and therefore any changes to this ratio are only detected in the last digit of this small number. In order to simplify this problem, isotope geochemists have adopted a relative notation known as the δ notation, defined for hydrogen as follows:

$$\delta^2 H = \left(\frac{(^2H/^1H)_{sample} - (^2H/^1H)_{standard}}{(^2H/^1H)_{standard}} \right) \times 1000$$

(3)

In this notation, the ratio of ^{2}H to ^{1}H in the sample is compared to the same ratio in an internationally agreed sample material. If the ratio in the sample is identical to that in the standard, then the δ value (δ^2H, or δD as it is also called) is zero. If the sample is isotopically heavier than the standard, the ^{2}H/^{1}H ratio in the sample is greater than that in the standard, and the value of δ becomes positive. The units (because of the multiplication by 1000) are known as 'per mil', symbolized as '‰'. If the sample is isotopically lighter, then the top line becomes negative, and δ becomes negative. The beauty of the δ notation is that if δ becomes more positive as it is fractionated, then the sample is getting isotopically heavier, and vice versa. The standard used for hydrogen isotopic measurements in water is VSMOW (Vienna Standard Mean Ocean Water) or SLAP (Standard

Table 16.1 Isotope systems used archaeologically, other than those used primarily for dating (after Pollard 1998:286).

Element	Isotope ratio	Natural isotopic abundance (%)	Substances studied	Application
Hydrogen	^{2}H/^{1}H	^{1}H = 99.985 ^{2}H(D) = 0.015	Water, organic matter (cellulose, collagen, lipids, chitin, peat)	Climate, plant-water metabolism
Carbon	^{13}C/^{12}C	^{12}C = 98.89 ^{13}C = 1.11	Organic matter, carbonates, biomineralized tissue, soil, CO_2	Diet, plant water-use efficiency, climate and habitat, provenance (ivory and marble)
Nitrogen	^{15}N/^{14}N	^{14}N = 99.633 ^{15}N = 0.366	Organic matter, soil, dissolved NO_3^- and NH_4^+, groundwater	Diet, nitrogen fixation pathways, animal water use, climate, groundwater pollution
Oxygen	^{18}O/^{16}O	^{16}O = 99.759 ^{17}O = 0.037 ^{18}O = 0.204	Water, biomineralized carbonates and phosphates, sedimentary phosphates and carbonates, silicates, organic matter	Climate, plant and animal water metabolism, ocean temperature, provenance (marble), chronostratigraphy
Sulfur	^{34}S/^{32}S	^{32}S = 95.00 ^{33}S = 0.76 ^{34}S = 4.22 ^{36}S = 0.014	Organic matter, hydrocarbons, sulfates, sediments	Diet, pollution

Light Antarctic Precipitation) (Coplen 1994, 1995). The equation for $\delta^{18}O$ is identical to that given above, with the ratio $^{18}O/^{16}O$ replacing the ratio for hydrogen. The same standards are used for measurement of oxygen isotope ratios in water, but different standards are used for oxygen isotopes in rocks and biominerals.

The importance of oxygen and hydrogen isotope ratios in the water cycle was first demonstrated by Dansgaard (1964), in a classic paper which showed a simple linear relationship between $\delta^{18}O$ in precipitation and the average annual air temperature. Craig (1961) had already demonstrated, through the isotopic analysis of a large number of meteoric water samples collected at different latitudes, that a simple relationship existed between $\delta^{18}O$ and δD in precipitation:

$$\delta D = 8\,\delta^{18}O + 10 \qquad (4)$$

This is called the 'meteoric water line', and generally explains the relationship for most cases. Exceptions are called 'closed basins', where excessive evaporation perturbs the system. Dansgaard then compared the annual mean $\delta^{18}O$ value of precipitation with the average annual air temperature and obtained a straight line of equation:

$$\delta^{18}O = 0.695\,T - 13.6 \qquad (5)$$

Thus $\delta^{18}O$ in the precipitation becomes increasingly positive (i.e., isotopically heavier) as the average air temperature rises. This relationship (or subsequent variants of it) have been used to convert the $\delta^{18}O$ record obtained from ice cores in Greenland (GRIP and GISP2) and Antarctic ice cores (Vostok) into palaeo-temperature records (e.g., Johnsen *et al.* 1997, Dowdeswell and White 1995, O'Brien *et al.* 1995), thus giving a climatic framework to the past 420 000 years (Chapter 1).

THE CARBON CYCLE

The global carbon cycle (Figure 16.2) is well-known to archaeologists because of its importance in cycling cosmogenic ^{14}C throughout the biosphere, and also because of increased atmospheric CO_2 as a result of human activity. Because of these latter concerns, it is the best-studied global cycle, but it is still the case that many of the reservoir and flux estimates are subject to considerable uncertainty.

The vast majority of the 10^{23} g of carbon present on Earth is sequestered in sedimentary rocks (inorganic carbonates and organic sediments), and is therefore unavailable for global cycling on anything other than a geological timescale. The active carbon pool is estimated as 40 000 petagrams (Pg, or 10^{15} g), of which 38 000 Pg resides in the oceans. The atmospheric pool contains 750 Pg, the land plants 560 Pg, and the soil biomass 1500 Pg. Fluxes into the atmosphere are estimated (for the 1980s) to be 60 Pg/yr each from plant and soil biota respiration, 6 Pg/yr from industrial sources, 0.9 Pg/yr from net vegetation destruction (e.g., burning of rainforest), and 90 Pg/yr from exchange with the surface ocean. The model is currently out of equilibrium, with the atmospheric pool estimated to be increasing by 3.2 Pg/yr.

The mean residence time for oceanic carbon (as CO_2) with respect to the atmosphere can be estimated as 38 000/92, or around 400 years, but considerations of the structure of the ocean (as above) and better estimates of the partition of carbon between surface and deep waters reduce the figure for surface waters to around 11 years (Schlesinger 1997:361). The MRT for atmospheric carbon taking into account fluxes into the ocean and uptake by photosynthesis is 750/(92 + 120), or about 3.5 years, which is commensurate with the mixing time of the atmosphere. In fact, more careful estimates (Houghton *et al.* 1995) put the MRT for atmospheric CO_2 at between 50 and 200 years, which is the best current estimate for the time taken for the atmospheric system to regain equilibrium if human perturbation were to cease immediately. Many of the features of our current understanding of the global carbon cycle are directly mirrored in our understanding of the use of ^{14}C as a dating tool – the rapid atmospheric mixing, the sequestration of ^{14}C into the deep oceans giving a 'marine offset', etc. (Chapter 2).

Isotopic fractionation of carbon as it is cycled has been studied in great detail for many years. Carbon has two stable isotopes ^{12}C, with six protons and six neutrons, and ^{13}C, with seven neutrons. The expression for $\delta^{13}C$ is obtained from that given above by inserting $^{13}C/^{12}C$ for $^2H/^1H$. The internationally agreed standard for carbon is the CO_2 produced from a Cretaceous belemnite rock in South Carolina, called the Vienna Peedee Belemnite Formation (VPDB) (Coplen 1994, 1995).

Measurements of $\delta^{13}C$ have become particularly important in archaeology for two principal reasons. One is that $\delta^{13}C$ measurements can be used to correct radiocarbon dates obtained on organic material for fractionation effects, (on the assumption that ^{14}C fractionates twice as much as ^{13}C because it is two units

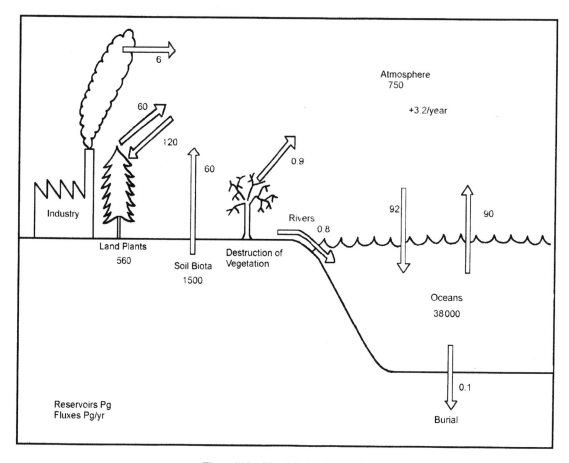

Figure 16.2   The global carbon cycle.

heavier than ^{12}C rather than one). The other is because δ^{13}C measurements (often combined with δ^{15}N) made on bone collagen (and occasionally bone mineral or lipid) can be used to reconstruct an average diet for the animal (Chapters 23 and 28).

Fractionation begins when green plants photosynthesize, and combine CO_2 from the atmosphere with H_2O taken up by the root system to produce sugars and eventually cellulose. Farquhar *et al.* (1982) showed that the isotopic composition of plant material ($\delta^{13}C_p$) as a result of this process can be expressed as:

$$\delta^{13}C_p = \delta^{13}C_{atm} - a - (b - c)c_i/c_a \qquad (6)$$

where a is the discrimination against $^{13}CO_2$ compared to $^{12}CO_2$ during diffusion of CO_2 through air, and b is the discrimination in a particular plant species against ^{13}C during the carboxylation reaction. The isotopic value of atmospheric CO_2 is $\delta^{13}C_{atm}$, and c_i and c_a

are the partial pressures of CO_2 within the intercellular spaces of the leaf and in the atmosphere respectively. The value of $\delta^{13}C_{atm}$ is around $-7\permil$ (although this value changes with latitude and time), a is 4.4$\permil$ and b is typically around 30$\permil$.

For the majority of land plants, which photosynthesize using the C_3 metabolic pathway (Schlesinger 1997:129), this results in a range of $\delta^{13}C_p$ values between about $-19\permil$ and $-29\permil$, with an average value of $-26.5\permil$ (van der Merwe and Medina 1991). The C_3 metabolic pathway is used by all trees and woody shrubs and temperate grasses, in which Rubisco (ribulose biphosphate carboxylase-oxygenase) is the carboxylating agent. A second photosynthetic pathway was discovered as a result of isotopic studies of plants, termed C_4, in which the primary carboxylating enzyme is phosphoenolpyruvate (PEP). This pathway has a different value of b in the Farquhar equation, and results in plants with $\delta^{13}C_p$ values of $-12\permil$ and

−16‰, with an average of −12.5‰. These characteristics are displayed in many species of subtropical grasses (Ehleringer and Monson 1993).

Plants are the base of the terrestrial food chain. The body tissue of animals feeding on these plants, and subsequently of omnivores and carnivores, is dependent on the isotopic composition of the plant material ingested, modified by further metabolically-induced fractionations as the food is processed and incorporated into body tissue. There has been considerable debate over recent years about the exact amount of fractionation induced by the fixation of ingested carbon into body tissue − a debate which has been hampered by a lack of detailed knowledge about the routing of various elements of the diet into body tissue (see Chapter 23). At its simplest, it is assumed that the bone collagen of a herbivore is +5‰ enriched relative to the plant tissue consumed, and the bone collagen of a carnivore is further enriched by +7‰ relative to the meat it consumes.

Such interpretations are no more than relatively long-term averages, and allow discrimination of the sources of dietary input at the level of C_3 terrestrial vs. C_4 terrestrial vs. marine. Models such as these have allowed many researchers to reconstruct the relative diets of individuals within cemeteries, reflecting status or gender difference with respect to food availability (e.g., Ubelaker et al. 1995, White and Schwarcz 1989, Katzenberg and Weber 1999), or to look at variations of diet over time. The original study by van der Merwe and Vogel (1978) is a classic example, which investigated temporal changes in $\delta^{13}C$ values in the bone collagen of a North American prehistoric population (see Chapter 23). Other studies have attempted to find evidence for weaning in female skeletons, or changes in nutritional status as a result of disease (e.g., Herring et al. 1998, Wright and Schwarcz 1999). A further extension of this work is the use of differential information available within a single skeleton. This has been exploited most clearly in historic material from South Africa (Sealy et al. 1995; see Chapter 23).

Carbon isotopes retrieved from lipid fractions of organic residues embedded within ceramic matrices are increasingly playing a role in dietary reconstruction (see Chapter 28). Using the same principles as bone collagen isotopy, specific plant species have been identified (Evershed et al. 1994), distinctions between ruminant and non-ruminant animal fats have been made (Evershed et al. 1997) and direct evidence for milk usage has recently been found (Dudd and Evershed 1998).

Certain systems allow high resolution studies of isotopic change, such as climatic reconstruction from measurements of δD, $\delta^{13}C$ and $\delta^{18}O$ in annual or even sub-annual growth rings in trees (Robertson et al. 1996). Another application has been the determination of the harvesting season of oysters via the analysis of $\delta^{13}C$ and $\delta^{18}O$ in annual growth rings (Andrus and Crowe 2000).

One other important aspect of the carbon cycle in archaeology is the observation that the degradation of buried organic material is an integral part of the cycle. Thus the rates governing the loss of organic evidence in archaeology − part of the taphonomic process (Chapter 15) − should be predictable from an understanding of the inputs and outputs of the cycle. There has been considerable study in the literature of the factors which control the rates of decay of organic matter in environments such as temperate and tropical forests, and these observations should be directly applicable to archaeological evidence in similar environments (e.g., Hopkins 1998).

THE NITROGEN CYCLE

Nitrogen (and phosphorus) control and limit many of the vital reactions of the biosphere, such as photosynthesis and respiration. It is likely that nitrogen and phosphorus availability have controlled the size of the biosphere itself over geological time. The nitrogen cycle is driven by microbial activity, which can for example convert inert N_2 gas from the atmosphere into inorganic forms such as NH_4^+ and NO_3^- in the soil, which can then be assimilated by plants. At the other end of the cycle, denitrifying bacteria convert these forms back to inert N_2 gas (Schlesinger 1997:384).

The atmosphere contains the largest reservoir of nitrogen (estimated at 3.9×10^{21} g), but this vast quantity is unavailable to the majority of organisms because of the relative chemical inactivity of the N_2 molecule. Figures for fluxes in the nitrogen cycle are relatively poorly constrained. Lightening produces up to 3 Tg (teragrams; 10^{12} g) per year of bioavailable nitrogen, but biological fixation by soil bacteria accounts for about 140 Tg/yr. The mean residence time for nitrogen in the terrestrial biosphere appears to be around 700 years. From the net primary terrestrial production of carbon (60×10^{15} g/yr), and assuming a mean C/N ratio of 50 for primary production biomass, the annual nitrogen requirement for land plants is around 1200 Tg/y. Thus the biological fixation of nitrogen only supplies a little over a tenth of the required nitrogen for terrestrial plant growth. The remainder is assumed to come from internal recycling and from the decomposition of dead biomass in the soil. Consideration of the rate of turnover of biomass in the soil suggests that the mean residence time for nitrogen in the soil is around 100 years (Schlesinger 1997:387), which is substantially longer than that of carbon (nine years on average; Schlesinger 1997:142).

Human activity has impacted considerably on the nitrogen cycle, both as a result of fossil fuel emissions into the atmosphere (about 20 Tg/yr), and also from artificial fertilizer directly into the soil (80 Tg/yr). Most of the atmospheric nitrogen is deposited almost immediately as NO_3^- on the land, since it has a very short residence time in the atmosphere. This contributes to the phenomenon know as 'acid rain'. Thus about 40 per cent of the nitrogen (100/240 Tg/yr) which enters the soil each year is a direct result of human activity. Some of this influx is carried away by river flow (36 Tg/yr) and into the groundwaters (11 Tg/yr). Bacterial denitrification also removes a large amount of nitrogen back to the biosphere, estimated as up to 200 Tg/yr. The oceans receive 36 Tg/yr from river inflow, 15 Tg/yr from biological nitrogen fixation in surface waters, and 30 Tg/yr from direct precipitation. Denitrification removes around 110 Tg/yr back to the atmosphere. Surface waters contain little nitrogen, but the deep oceans contain as much as 570 000 Tg.

Cycling of nitrogen, like carbon, can be followed by observing small changes in the isotopic ratio, this time of $^{15}N/^{14}N$ (defined as $\delta^{15}N$, where the international standard is atmospheric nitrogen (AIR); Mariotti 1983). Nitrogen isotope systematics in the biosphere are less well understood than those of carbon, but are frequently used in parallel with carbon to reconstruct diet from the isotopic analysis of skeletal collagen (Ambrose 1991; see Chapter 23). The nitrogen isotope ratios in bone can also reflect the differential utilization of nitrogen-fixing plants (e.g., legumes) and non-nitrogen fixing plants. The principal variation, however, is between terrestrial and marine ecosystems. Terrestrial mammals and birds have a mean bone collagen $\delta^{15}N$ value of $+5.9‰$, whereas marine mammals have an average value of $+15.6‰$ (Scheoninger et al. 1983). Subsequent studies (Wada et al. 1991) have shown clear trophic level discrimination against nitrogen in marine ecosystems. This results in a marked distinction in $\delta^{15}N$ between humans who live predominantly on marine resources (e.g., North American Inuit) and display $\delta^{15}N$ values between $+17$ and $+20‰$, and terrestrial agriculturists who have values in the range $+6$ to $+12‰$ (e.g., DeNiro 1987, Richards and Mellars 1998). When combined with carbon isotope data, this can therefore be a powerful tool.

THE PHOSPHORUS AND SULFUR CYCLES

Phosphorus in the terrestrial ecosystem is nearly all derived from the weathering of phosphatic rocks, and in recent times by human mining activity and the subsequent use of phosphorus fertilizers. There is no equivalent to microbial fixation of nitrogen in the phosphorus cycle, and therefore the level of phosphorus available to the biosphere is small in both terrestrial and ocean environments. The main mechanism of phosphorus transport is by rivers, which deposits about 21 Tg (teragrams; 10^{12} g) into the oceans per year, mostly as insoluble particles which are rapidly deposited on the continental shelf. Most of the available phosphorus in the surface oceans is rapidly recycled in a period of a few days. The rest is eventually deposited on the ocean floor, which forms the largest reservoir of phosphorus.

In terrestrial soils, the cycling of phosphorus is important archaeologically, since it forms the basis of one of the most common chemical survey techniques (Chapter 45). In modern artificial fertilizers, soluble inorganic phosphates are added which are directly available to plants, although much is rapidly lost by 'fixation' (conversion to insoluble minerals) in the soil (Larsen 1967). Most inputs, however, are in the form of organic phosphates (animal and plant debris, dung, etc.), which subsequently undergo 'mineralization' processes, converting them into inorganic phosphates (Dalal 1977). In this context, the term 'mineralization' differs from its normal geochemical usage, and implies a procedure which releases nutrients in inorganic forms (i.e., P becomes PO_4^{3-}). Although the general trend is for organic phosphates to convert to inorganic forms with time (Brady and Weil 1999), under some circumstances models predict increases of organic forms with time, such as the work of Parton et al. (1988), which predicted changes in C, N and P over 10 000 years of soil development in grasslands. This showed a decrease in inorganic phosphorus by about 50 per cent, and a commensurate increase in organic phosphorus.

Most of the Earth's sulfur is distributed between three reservoirs – the oceans (where it exists as dissolved sulfates), and two components of the sedimentary environment, either as the oxidized form (gypsum, $CaSO_4$) or the reduced form (sulfides). It is cycled from oxidized to reduced species by microbial redox reactions, which introduce large isotopic fractionations.

Hence isotopic studies (where the ratio of ^{34}S to ^{32}S is used to define $\delta^{34}S$, using the Canyon Diablo Troilite (CDT) meteorite as the internationally-agreed standard) are widely used to study the cycling of sulfur (Schlesinger 1997:407). Gaseous sulfur compounds have a very short residence time in the atmosphere, and hence most of the mobility of sulfur relates to either emissions into the atmosphere (from anthropogenic sources, periodic events such as volcanic activity and dust storms), and terrestrial run-off via rivers, both of which result in deposition into the ocean. Wave action and gas production in the surface oceans return most of this deposition back into the atmosphere, where it is re-deposited on the land surfaces.

The archaeological importance of the sulfur cycle is that under anaerobic waterlogged environments such as are encountered in lake deposits and in peat bogs, sulfur reducing bacteria of the genera *Desulfovibrio* and *Desulfotomaculum* can use the sulfate ion (SO_4^{2-}) as an electron acceptor during the oxidation of organic matter (generalized as CH_2O; Caple 1998). This produces various sulfur-containing gases, but predominantly hydrogen sulfide (H_2S), which gives these environments a characteristic smell:

$$2H^+ + SO_4^{2-} + 2(CH_2O) \rightarrow 2CO_2 + H_2S + 2H_2O \tag{7}$$

Much of the H_2S produced is not released to the atmosphere, but goes on to react with inorganic soil components, particularly Fe^{2+}, precipitating pyrrhotine (FeS), which gives anaerobic soils their dark colour. Further reactions might follow:

$$H_2S + FeS \rightarrow FeS_2 + 2H^+ + 2e^- \tag{8}$$

This can result in masses of pyrite forming in the deposit (Chapter 47) and these minerals are often observed either as a coating on material recovered from anaerobic sediments, or as inclusions (framboidal pyrites) in buried material such as bone. Pyrites may be particularly damaging in the context of archaeological conservation (Chapter 50) because if conditions become sufficiently oxidizing (e.g., as the deposit dries out, or the object is removed archaeologically), then other bacteria may re-oxidize the sulfide to release sulfate, which in turn increases the pH of the material, potentially causing damage.

Sulfur isotope ratios have yet to be exploited to any extent in archaeological applications, but $\delta^{34}S$ should, in theory, be characteristic of the sulfur source (Schwarcz 1991:267). Differentiation between marine

sulfates (^{34}S-rich) and igneous or sedimentary sulfides (^{34}S-depleted; Hoefs 1997) is of potential use in palaeo-dietary applications.

OTHER INORGANIC CYCLES

Broader studies of biogeochemical cycling, including the influence of inorganic species such as Ca, and Si, suggest that biotic activity controls and regulates the chemical conditions of the Earth's surface. The current oxidizing atmosphere (21 per cent oxygen) was created about 2 billion years ago, as a result of the establishment of photosynthesizing organisms (Schlesinger 1997:36). There even appears to be a link between the total storage capacity of the various compartments of the Earth's system, such that if for example the weathering rate of surface limestones increases, then there must be a concomitant increase in sedimentation rate on the ocean floor, since geochemical evidence suggests that the ocean composition has not changed dramatically over geologically recent time. There may even be a link between the size of the biosphere and the rates of weathering and deposition of various minerals on the surface of the Earth (Schlesinger 1997:189). Thus there may be a regulatory link between the capacity of the Earth to support life and the rates of inorganic cycling.

SUMMARY

Biogeochemical cycling is at the heart of many of the processes regarded as valuable to an interpretation of the archaeological record, such as ^{14}C dating and the isotope ecology of humans. At the human scale, many of the wider considerations may appear to be irrelevant, but there does seem to be considerable scope for applying the principles of biogeochemical cycling, with all the associated control and feedback mechanisms that this implies, to aid our understanding of the accumulation and deterioration of the archaeological record.

REFERENCES

*Recommended for further reading

Ambrose, S.H. (1991). Effects of diet, climate and physiology on nitrogen isotope abundances in terrestrial foodwebs. *Journal of Archaeological Science*, **18**:293–317.
Andrus, C.F.T. and Crowe, D.E. (2000). Geochemical analysis of oysters as a method to determine season of capture. *Journal of Archaeological Science*, **27**:33–42.

Brady, N.C. and Weil, R.R. (1999). *The Nature and Properties of Soils*, (12th edn). Prentice Hall: New Jersey.

Brockway, C.G. and Bradley, A.A. (1995). Errors in stream flow drought statistics reconstructed from tree-ring data. *Water Resources Research*, **31**:2279–2293.

Caple, C. (1998). Parameters for monitoring anoxic environments. In Corfield, M., Hinton, P., Nixon, T. and Pollard, A.M. (eds) *Preserving Archaeological Remains In Situ*, 113–123. Museum of London Archaeological Service: London.

Cleaveland, M.K. (2000). A 963-year reconstruction of summer (JJA) streamflow in the White River, Arkansas, USA, from tree-rings. *The Holocene*, **10**:33–41.

Coplen, T.B. (1994). Reporting of stable hydrogen, carbon and oxygen isotopic abundances. *Pure and Applied Chemistry*, **66**:273–276.

Coplen, T.B. (1995). Discontinuance of SMOW and PDB. *Nature*, **375**:285.

Craig, H. (1961). Isotopic variations in meteoric waters. *Science*, **133**:1702–1703.

Dalal, R.C. (1977). Soil organic phosphorus. *Advances in Agronomy*, **29**:83–117.

Dansgaard, W. (1964). Stable isotopes in precipitation. *Tellus*, **16**:436–468.

DeNiro, M.J. (1987). Stable isotopy and archaeology. *American Scientist*, **75**:182–91.

Dowdeswell, J.A. and White, J.W.C. (1995). Greenland ice cores and rapid climate change. *Philosophical Transactions of the Royal Society of London*, **A352**:359–371.

Dudd, S.N. and Evershed, R.P. (1998). Direct demonstration of milk as an element of archaeological economies. *Science*, **282**:1478–1480.

Ehleringer, J.R. and Monson, R.K. (1993). Evolutionary and ecological aspects of photosynthetic pathway variation. *Annual Review of Ecology and Systematics*, **24**:411–439.

Evershed, R.P., Arnot, K.I., Collister, J., Eglinton, G. and Charters, S. (1994). Application of isotope ratio monitoring gas chromatography-mass spectrometry to the analysis of organic residues of archaeological origin. *Analyst*, **119**:909–914.

Evershed, R.P., Mottram, H.R., Dudd, S.N., Charters, S., Stott, A.W., Lawrence, G.J., Gibson, A.M., Connor, A., Blinkhorn, P.W. and Reeves, V. (1997). New criteria for the identification of animal fats preserved in archaeological pottery. *Naturwissenschaften*, **84**:402–406.

Farquhar, G.D., O'Leary, M.H. and Berry, J.A. (1982). On the relationship between carbon isotope discrimination and the inter-cellular carbon-dioxide concentration in leaves. *Australian Journal of Plant Physiology*, **9**:121–137.

*Fontes, J.C. and Fritz, P. (1980). *Handbook of Environmental Isotope Geochemistry*. Elsevier: Amsterdam.

*Griffiths, H. (ed.) (1998). *Stable Isotopes: Integration of Biological, Ecological and Geochemical Processes*. Bios Scientific Publishers: Oxford.

Herring, D.A., Saunders, S.R. and Katzenberg, M.A. (1998). Investigating the weaning process in past populations. *American Journal of Physical Anthropology*, **105**:425–439.

Hodell, D.A., Curtis, J.H. and Brenner, M. (1995). Possible role of climate in the collapse of Classic Maya civilization. *Nature*, **375**:391–394.

*Hoefs, J. (1997). *Stable Isotope Geochemistry*, (4th edn). Springer: Berlin.

Hopkins, D.W. (1998). The biology of the burial environment. In Corfield, M., Hinton, P., Nixon, T. and Pollard, A.M. (eds) *Preserving Archaeological Remains In Situ*, 73–85. Museum of London Archaeological Service: London.

Houghton, R.A., Meira Filho, L.G., Bruce, J., Lee, H., Callander, B.A., Haites, E., Harris, N. and Maskell, K. (1995). *Climate Change 1994*. Cambridge University Press: Cambridge.

Johnsen, S.J., Clausen, H.B., Dansgaard, W., Gundestrup, N.S., Hammer, C.U., Andersen, U., Andersen, K.K., Hvidberg, C.S., Dahl-Jensen, D., Steffensen, J.P., Shoji, H., Sveinbjörnsdottir, A.E., White, J., Jouzel, J. and Fisher, D. (1997). The delta O-18 record along the Greenland Ice Core Project deep ice core and the problem of possible Eemian climatic instability. *Journal of Geophysical Research-Oceans*, **102**:26397–26410.

Katzenberg, M.A. and Weber, A. (1999). Stable isotope ecology and palaeodiet in the Lake Baikal region of Siberia. *Journal of Archaeological Science*, **26**:651–659.

Knox, J.C. (1993). Large increases in flood magnitudes in response to modest changes in climate. *Nature*, **361**:430–432.

*Lajtha, K. and Michener, R.H. (eds) (1994). *Stable Isotopes in Ecology and Environmental Science*. Blackwell: Oxford.

Larsen, S. (1967). Soil phosphorus. *Advances in Agronomy*, **19**:151–210.

Mariotti, A. (1983). Atmospheric nitrogen is a reliable standard for natural ^{15}N abundance measurements. *Nature*, **303**:685–687.

O'Brien, S.R., Mayewski, P.A., Meeker, L.D., Meese, D.A., Twickler, M.S. and Whitlow, S.I. (1995). Complexity of Holocene climate as reconstructed from a Greenland ice core. *Science*, **270**:1962–1964.

*O'Neil, J., Taylor, R., Kaplan, H.P. and Isaac, R. (1991). *Stable Isotope Geochemistry*. Special Publication No. 3, Geochemical Society: San Antonio.

Parton, W.J., Stewart, J.W.B. and Cole, C.V. (1998). Dynamics of C, N, P and S in grassland soils: a model. *Biogeochemistry*, **5**:109–131.

Pollard, A.M. (1998). Archaeological reconstruction using stable isotopes. In Griffiths, H. (ed.) *Stable Isotopes: Integration of Biological, Ecological and Geochemical Processes*, 285–301. Bios Scientific Publishers: Oxford.

Richards, M.P. and Mellars, P.A. (1998) Stable isotopes and the seasonality of the Oronsay middens. *Antiquity*, **72**:178–184.

Roberts, N. (1998). *The Holocene: An Environmental History*, (2nd edn). Blackwell Publishers: Oxford.

Robertson, I., Pollard, A.M., Heaton, T.H.E. and Pilcher, J.R. (1996). Seasonal changes in the isotopic composition of oak cellulose. In Dean, J.S., Meko, D.M. and Swetnam, T.W. (eds) *Tree Rings, Environment, and Humanity: Proceedings of the International Conference, Tucson, Arizona*, 617–628. University of Tucson: Arizona.

Sabloff, J.A. (1995). Drought and decline. *Nature*, **375**:357.

*Schlesinger, W.H. (1997). *Biogeochemistry: an Analysis of Global Change*, (2nd edn). Academic Press: London.

Schoeninger, M., DeNiro, M. and Tauber, H. (1983). Stable nitrogen isotope ratios of bone collagen reflect marine and terrestrial components of prehistoric human diet. *Science*, **220**:1381–1383.

Schwarcz, H.P. (1991). Some theoretical aspects of isotope paleodiet studies. *Journal of Archaeological Science*, **18**:261–275.

Sealy, J., Armstrong, R. and Schrire, C. (1995). Beyond lifetime averages: tracing life histories through isotopic analysis of different calcified tissues from archaeological human skeletons. *Antiquity*, **69**:290–300.

Ubelaker, D.H., Katzenberg, M.A. and Doyon, L.G. (1995). Status and diet in precontact Highland Ecuador. *American Journal of Physical Anthropology*, **97**:403–411.

van der Merwe, N.J. and Medina, E. (1991). The canopy effect, carbon isotope ratios and foodwebs in Amazonia. *Journal of Archaeological Science*, **18**:249–259.

van der Merwe, N.J. and Vogel, J.C. (1978). Carbon content of human collagen as a measurement of prehistoric diet in Woodland North America. *Nature*, **276**:815–816.

Wada, E., Mizutani, H. and Minagawa, M. (1991). The use of stable isotopes for food web analysis. *Critical Reviews in Food Science and Nutrition*, **30**:361–371.

White, C. and Schwarcz, H.P. (1989). Ancient Maya diet as inferred from isotopic and chemical analyses of human bone. *Journal of Archaeological Science*, **16**:451–474.

Wright, L.E. and Schwarcz, H.P. (1999). Correspondence between stable carbon, oxygen and nitrogen isotopes in human tooth enamel and dentine: infant diets at Kaminaljuyu. *Journal of Archaeological Science*, **26**:1159–1170.

SECTION 3

Human Palaeobiology

Overview – Human Palaeobiology: Then and Now

Department of Anthropology, University of New Mexico.

'The biological study of earlier human remains is ... a multi-faceted discipline which can tell us far more than that population A had shorter heads or longer faces than population B. Indeed it is vital to the complete understanding of man's cultural and social development.'

(Brothwell and Higgs 1969:27)

During the 1960s, as illustrated by this epigram, scientists engaged in the archaeological study of human remains were eagerly embracing a biology of humankind's past that extended well beyond an earlier preoccupation with skulls and craniometry. Chapters from the Brothwell and Higgs (1963, 1969) volumes exemplify this trend. Genovés (1969a, 1969b) firmly identified the bony pelvis as key in the identification of sex, while also describing macroscopic, microscopic, and chemical features that provide evidence of age-at-death. Stature as a characteristic attribute of human groups was considered by Wells (1969), while Gejvall (1969) emphasized positive rewards for efforts taken to study cremated remains. A population perspective on human health or (palaeo)epidemiology was advocated by Goldstein, although most of his discussion of

palaeopathology focused upon specific diseases such as tuberculosis, syphilis, yaws, and leprosy. In closing, however, he called for both increased diagnostic precision and contextualized regional perspectives for future studies of ancient disease. A.T. Sandison (1969) recommended extensive use of histology in the study of mummified remains, while other authors such as Garlick (1969) and Brothwell *et al.* (1969) advocated applications of various chemical and radiographic methods, including scanning electron microscopy. These topical and methodological foci were considered state-of-the-art and even prescient for skeletal biologists of the 1960s. As such, they comprise a useful landmark against which to reflect the current cluster of papers that comprise Section 3: Human Palaeobiology.

There are clear parallels in the organization of the present volume's section on human palaeobiology and the earlier version, entitled 'Man'. The separate chapters by Genovés on sex determination and age estimation are topically combined into a single offering by Cox: Assessment of Age at Death and Sex in the Adult Human Skeleton (Chapter 20). Recognizing the increased significance of population approaches to the past, further discussion of population structure appears in a chapter entitled Palaeodemography by

Handbook of Archaeological Sciences. Edited by D.R. Brothwell and A.M. Pollard.
© 2001 John Wiley & Sons, Ltd.

Chamberlain (Chapter 22). Advances in the investigation of cremated bone are considered by McKinley and Bond (Chapter 24) whose offering includes both humans and other mammals. The chapter by Ortner (Chapter 19) treats palaeopathology as Disease Ecology, which is followed by Zimmerman's Study of Preserved Human Tissue (Chapter 21). Brief reviews of hominid adaptations and Holocene microevolution by Brothwell (Chapter 17) and human ecology by Schutkowski (Chapter 18) draw together themes that were dispersed throughout the earlier Brothwell and Higgs (1963, 1969) volumes. Topics such as stature are no longer afforded chapter status, whilst taphonomy is dealt with separately elsewhere (a general review in Chapter 15, and a specific review of bone taphonomy in Chapter 51). Appropriately, bone chemistry (Sealy Chapter 23) assumes a prominence never envisioned by 1960s scholarship. Bone chemistry and aDNA analyses (Chapter 25) thus replace radiography, histology, and microscopy as the 'hot' new contemporary methods whose future seems bright indeed.

In the introductory chapter to this section, Brothwell presents an overview of Pleistocene and Holocene hominid evolution, primarily from an historical perspective. In so doing, he observes that 'the demographic and pathological aspects of fossil hominids have been particularly neglected, in comparison with the considerable work now undertaken on skeletal series of the last few thousand years'. He also notes that there has been little research on evidence of environmental stresses in fossil hominids, including Neanderthals.

The few demographic and health-related studies that *have* occurred provide tantalizing, if sometimes controversial results. Cook and co-workers (1983) have proposed acrobatic behaviours for gracile australopithecines, based upon end plate remodelling of thoracic vertebrae. In studies of trauma among European and western Asian late archaic *Homo sapiens*, Berger and Trinkaus (1995) found relatively high frequencies of head and neck injuries that parallel those of American rodeo competitors. The authors interpret the Neanderthal examples as a likely result of agonistic encounters with medium-sized ungulates (see also Jurmain 1999). Comprehensive demographic studies have also focused upon Neanderthals (Trinkaus 1995) and the early archaic *Homo sapiens* from Atapuerca, Spain (Bermúdez de Castro and Nicolás 1997). Mortality schedules for these two groups are said to resemble each other, but contrast with patterns common to modern hunter-foragers (Bermúdez de Castro and Nicolás 1997).

As Brothwell emphasizes, dietary reconstructions are crucial for explaining human evolution. Various authors have been applying bone chemistry methods to fossil materials, beginning with Sillen's landmark studies (1981, 1986, 1992 but see Sillen *et al.* 1989). Lee-Thorp *et al.* (1994) have also used bone chemistry to elucidate australopithecine diets, arguing the robust australopithecines consumed quantities of C_4 grasses (see also Chapter 23). As a reflection of general health status, linear enamel hypoplasias (LEH, see following discussion on non-specific stress indicators) have been studied in Neanderthals and early archaic *Homo sapiens* (Bermúdez de Castro and Pérez 1995, Larsen 1997, Ogilvie *et al.* 1989). The permanent dentitions of the Krapina Neanderthals present significantly more evidence of LEH than do those from the Atapuerca early archaic human sample, for example, suggesting differences in young juvenile health for the two groups.

In other studies, histological techniques have identified relatively small osteons in Neanderthal bone (Trinkaus and Thompson 1987) and have been used to establish mortality patterns for Neanderthals who apparently show a youthful death profile (Abbott *et al.* 1996). Ruff *et al.* (1993) have used temporally sequential samples from the genus *Homo* to establish a trend for decreased mechanical loading through time, beginning with Neanderthals (see also Jurmain 1999). Among the most startling of results is the fact that Neanderthal DNA has recently been amplified by two laboratories (Krings *et al.* 1997, Ovchinnikov *et al.* 2000). Such studies well illustrate more ancient applications of methods most commonly applied to recent materials, in the manner called for by Brothwell.

In his contribution entitled Disease Ecology (Chapter 19), Ortner explores a fascinating evolutionary issue: what is the ecological context of human disease and how has it changed throughout human prehistory and history? Recognizing the complex interrelationship of environmental and cultural factors that affect the human condition, Ortner chooses to focus upon five variables that may place human groups at risk for acquiring infectious diseases: animal vectors, quantity and quality of food resources, human population size and density, environmental conditions, and cultural factors.

Focusing primarily, but not exclusively on Old World examples, Ortner underscores the role of animal vectors in the origin of diseases such as tuberculosis, as well as their contemporary significance in the life cycle of pathogens that cause echinococcosis and brucellosis in humans. Dietary diversity is cited as an advantage for hunter-gatherers, with agriculturalists at greater risk for nutritional deficiency due to their narrow resource base. Population aggregation may also place human groups at risk, as can cultural practices that limit access to vital resources, including food. The role of the environment in the evolution of disease is illustrated by two examples: the treponematoses and malaria.

Like Goldstein's earlier consideration of palaeopathology (1969), Ortner champions a population-based approach. His presentation has also benefited from the contextually grounded, regional studies of ancient disease that Goldstein recommended over 30 years before. Not specified here are the various methods commonly used by students of ancient disease to make diagnoses and to develop models of population health. While there still exist many of the 'lacunae' Goldstein (1969:486) recognized in the diagnoses of lesions in dry bone, Ortner himself (Ortner and Putschar 1985) has been a leader in the development of rigorous procedures for the diagnosis of specific conditions. Other recent contributions to this endeavour include publications by Aufderheide and Rodríguez-Martín (1998), Buikstra and Ubelaker (1994), Lovell (2000), and Roberts and Manchester (1995).

Another facet of palaeopathology, the attempt to reconstruct population health through the use of non-specific stress indicators, has become immensely popular since Goldstein's presentation. Especially useful for developing the regional histories Goldstein recommended, attributes such as Harris Lines, linear enamel defects, stature attainment, and cortical thickness have proved important for characterizing population health (Buikstra and Cook 1980, Cohen and Armelagos 1984, Larsen 1997). Although critiques of this method have appeared (Wood et al. 1992), carefully constructed research designs remain convincing, e.g., Storey (1999). The impact of the Wood et al. (1992) critique has been evaluated in the context of more recent studies (Buikstra 1997, Milner et al. 2000).

Studies of mummified human tissues were considered by Sandison (1969). Egyptian and Basket-Maker (Southwest US) examples dominated his text. Today, as emphasized by Zimmerman in Chapter 21, investigations of mummies have become increasingly visible crossroads for medical scientists and anthropologists. Stimuli for such initiatives, which have included collaborative and interdisciplinary mummy 'autopsies', have been many, all grounded in a heightened interest in studies of ancient disease which began during the 1960s (Brothwell and Sandison 1967, Buikstra and Cook 1980, Jarcho 1966, Ubelaker 1982). As Zimmerman notes, tangible evidence of this trend included the development of the Paleopathology

Association, the Paleopathology Club, and the courses in palaeopathology offered at the Smithsonian Institution.

As the study of mummified tissues has become increasingly visible, cross-cultural summary volumes have been published and reissued (Cockburn and Cockburn 1980, Cockburn et al. 1998). These and other works typically describe either isolated cases of specific diseases or changing patterns of body treatment. A complementary trend has been contextual study, heavily integrated with population-based, archaeological investigations. Much of this work is grounded in the Andean region, including comprehensive studies of the earliest prepared mummies in the world, those of the Chinchorro culture (Guillén 1992, Arriaza 1995). As Zimmerman emphasizes, mummies are significant sources of biological data that ranges from aDNA to coprolites (see Chapters 25 and 33). This rich resource is therefore likely to assume even greater significance for future investigations of humankind's history.

Cox's chapter (20) focuses upon the attribution of age and sex in adult remains. Like Genovés (1969a), she emphasizes the pelvis as the key location of accurate information for sex diagnosis. She is also careful to emphasize that she is offering methods for estimating biological sex, a basis for gender-based inferences but not necessarily isomorphic with the social construct. As Cox notes, aDNA methods (Stone et al. 1996) hold promise for sex diagnosis in juvenile remains, previously considered an intractable problem for bioarchaeologists.

In an exhaustive review of methods for estimating chronological age from biological age, Cox discusses both dental and skeletal attributes. She also provides a balanced perspective on the significance of the critique of palaeodemography levelled by Bocquet-Appel and Masset (1982). Maximum likelihood estimation methods, as a means of overcoming biases introduced by reference samples, are cited here and further discussed by Chamberlain (Chapter 22).

Cox also emphasizes, as have many authors, that an inability to estimate age-at-death in older adults severely limits palaeodemographic inferences. There is one newly developed technique that may overcome this limitation. It combines replicable observations of the pubic symphysis, the auricular surface, and cranial vault sutures with the statistical rigor of transition analysis (Boldsen 1997, Boldsen and Milner 1999, Milner et al. 1997, Milner and Boldsen 1999, Milner et al. 2000). While further testing is warranted, it appears that the Milner-Boldsen method will facilitate accurate age estimates extending well into the older adult years.

Cox does not consider methods for age-at-death estimates in juvenile materials. While there are many standard sources for such determinations (Hillson 1986, 1996, Moorrees *et al.* 1963a, 1963b, Smith 1991, Ubelaker 1989), readers are well-advised to appreciate certain recently developed critiques, especially of estimates based on long bone diaphyseal length, e.g., Konigsberg and Holman (1999) and Saunders (2000). Microscopic dental techniques may also increase precision for age estimates in subadult remains. These methods have been most commonly applied in evolutionary contexts (Bromage and Dean 1985), but they are also applicable in more recent materials (Fitzgerald and Rose 2000).

Chamberlain's discussion of palaeodemography (Chapter 22) explicitly addresses the issues of biases introduced by the nature of archaeological data and the imprecision of age estimation in archaeological samples. Appropriate distinctions between archaeological and forensic applications are made. Bayesian statistical methods are considered as a method for removing the effect of reference sample age structure upon estimation techniques. The iterative approach favoured by Konigsberg and Frankenberg (1992; see also Konigsberg *et al.* 1997, Holman *et al.* 1997) is deemed effective but cumbersome, with Chamberlain favouring the use of uninformative priors (prior probabilities) for sex estimation and fixed model priors for age-at-death computations.

Three other palaeodemographic topics are also briefly considered by Chamberlain. He is optimistic about results obtained through the estimation of population size based upon such variables as residence size, quantities of food residues, and volumes of storage pits. He is less sanguine about the archaeologist's ability to detect firm evidence for migration. The use of genetic data to infer demographic history is also noted.

Sealy's discussion of bone chemistry and palaeodiet (Chapter 23) is an elegant summary of current perspectives on a topic that has developed immense popularity since the Brothwell and Higgs (1969) publication. Initial excitement over the use of trace elements has now been tempered by the realities of diagenesis and expanded knowledge of the complex relationships between environment, diet, and bone composition (Sandford 1993, Sandford and Weaver 2000). Today, the only trace elements that appear useful are the alkaline earths, barium and strontium (Burton and Price 1990, 1991).

More reliable as indicators of diet are stable isotopes. When there is appropriate knowledge of the local food web and if diagenetic change can be ruled out, stable isotopes of carbon provide evidence of marine diets and/or the consumption of tropical grasses such as millet, maize, sorghum, and sugarcane. Spacing between the carbon isotope ratios (transformed as $\delta^{13}C$ values) in bone apatite and collagen can measure dietary protein. Similarly, $\delta^{15}N$ values assess relative amounts of dietary protein and have also been used in studies of weaning. Oxygen isotopes are useful measures in hydrology and climatology. Both oxygen and strontium isotopes vary across geological units and thus, by comparing the composition of teeth and bones, residential histories can be estimated. Other less commonly used isotopes for dietary and residential reconstructions include hydrogen, sulfur, and lead.

Sealy is properly conservative in her evaluation of bone chemistry in inferences of diet and residence. Trace elements had been used uncritically as dietary markers for many years by researchers whose enthusiasm was fuelled by the glamour of sophisticated technology and the seeming precision of numerical output carried to several decimal places. On the other hand, when applied in the context of appropriately rigorous research designs, light and heavy isotope analyses has excellent potential for elucidating dietary and locational histories.

As did Gejvall (1969), McKinley and Bond (Chapter 24) consider both contemporary crematoria and ancient pyres in their discussion of cremated bone. Recent experimental studies allow McKinley and Bond increased precision in their characterization of bone shrinkage and the macroscopic appearance of bone burned fleshed, 'green' but defleshed, and dry. Histological methods for estimating age-at-death in cremated materials have been added to the skeletal biologist's toolkit since Gejvall's publication, as have additional models for sexual dimorphism throughout the skeleton. To apply these methods, however, the issue of shrinkage must be addressed. That the use of fire in funerary rituals of the past is incompletely understood and that there is yet unrealized potential in the study of cremated human bone were conclusions drawn by Gejvall. These same points are forcefully raised and effectively illustrated in the present study.

There are two additional subjects not represented in Section 3 that are significant aspects of palaeobiological research: (i) biological distance, and (ii) taphonomy (but see Chapters 15 and 51). Recent developments in both of these arenas will be discussed briefly and appropriate references cited.

While it is clear that aDNA holds promise (see Chapter 25) for advancing palaeobiological knowledge of human population structures and even health, the limitations imposed by degradation are profound. Measurements and other observations of heritable features of teeth and bones are unlikely to be replaced immediately as fundamentally important for models of biological (genetic) relationships. Recent publications have focused upon defining heritability and variation in dental features (Scott and Turner 1997) and non-metric traits (Buikstra and Ubelaker 1994, Hauser and DeStefano 1989). Cranial dimensions continue to serve as sources of information about heritage, e.g., Pietrusewsky (2000).

Although observational techniques may have changed little over previous decades, statistical methods for characterizing population structure and segmentation are markedly different from those employed at the time of the Brothwell and Higgs publications. Influenced by archaeological studies of regions and communities, as well as by investigations of residence patterning and epigenetic (non-metric) traits in historical contexts (Lane and Sublett 1972), bioarchaeologists have placed increased emphasis upon defining local kin relationships. In parallel, population genetic models have been incorporated into studies of ancient groups (Konigsberg and Buikstra 1995, Relethford and Lees 1982). These 'model-bound' approaches contrast with the *post hoc* interpretations common to earlier multivariate algorithms such as Mahalanobis' generalized distances. The latter are termed 'model-free'. Although studies of biological relationships decreased during the mid-twentieth century for a variety of reasons ranging from the stigma associated with craniometry to the 'New Archaeology' with its emphasis upon ecology and human adaptation, they appear to have been increasing in more recent decades (Buikstra *et al.* 1990).

Chapter 43 of the Brothwell and Higgs volume by Garlick (1969) focused upon experimental evidence of diagenetic change in buried bone. Since that time taphonomy has become an increasingly visible subject, especially among forensic anthropologists (Haglund and Sorg 1997). While those who study the recently dead are primarily concerned with issues such as post-mortem interval, diagenetic changes that alter bone chemistry are crucial to bioarchaeological characterizations of ancient diet, for example. Although taphonomy has clearly been more prominent in zooarchaeology than in the study of archaeologically recovered human remains, it has become increasingly important to bioarchaeologists over recent years, a trend that is likely to continue.

In sum, Section 3 includes state-of-the-art treatment

of subjects that have been of long-standing interest to students of palaeobiology: palaeopathology, palaeodemography, and cremation. These topics were considered by the 1963 and 1969 Brothwell and Higgs volumes and also appear in this compilation. Techniques never envisioned at mid-twentieth century are also included, importantly bone chemistry methods that have refined our perspectives on diet and human residence patterns. Biomolecular approaches that have facilitated the recovery and amplification of ancient DNA also promise to markedly change, if not revolutionize our perspective on humankind's past.

REFERENCES

Abbott, S., Trinkaus, E. and Burr, D.B. (1996). Dynamic bone remodeling in later Pleistocene fossil hominids. *American Journal of Physical Anthropology*, **99**:585–601.

Arriaza, B.T. (1995). *Beyond Death: The Chinchorro Mummies of Ancient Chile*. Smithsonian Institution Press: Washington DC.

Aufderheide, A.C. and Rodríguez-Martín, C. (1998). *The Cambridge Encyclopedia of Human Paleopathology*. Cambridge University Press. Cambridge

Berger, T. and Trinkaus, E. (1995). Patterns of trauma among the Neandertals. *Journal of Archaeological Science*, **22**:841–852.

Bermúdez de Castro, J.M. and Pérez, P.J. (1995). Enamel hypoplasia in the middle Pleistocene hominids from Atapuerca (Spain). *American Journal of Physical Anthropology*, **96**:301–314.

Bermúdez de Castro, J.M. and Nicolás, M.E. (1997). Paleodemography of the Atapuerca-SH Middle Pleistocene hominid sample. *Journal of Human Evolution*, **33**:333–355.

Bermúdez de Castro, J.M. and Pérez, P.J. (1997). Paleodemography at Atapuerca-SH Middle Pleistocene hominid sample. *Journal of Human Evolution*, **33**:333–335.

Bocquet-Appel, J.P. and Masset, C. (1982). Farewell to paleodemography. *Journal of Human Evolution*, **12**:353–360.

Boldsen, J.L. (1997). Transition analysis: a method for unbiased age estimation from skeletal traits. *American Journal of Physical Anthropology Supplement*, **24**:76 (abstract).

Boldsen, J.L. and Milner, G.R. (1999). Age estimation through transition analysis: an introduction and software demonstration. Paper presented at mathematical modeling for paleodemography: Coming to consensus. Rostock, Germany.

Bromage, T.G. and Dean, M.C. (1985). Re-evaluation of the age at death of immature fossil hominids. *Nature*, **317**:525–527.

Brothwell, D. and Higgs, E. (1963). *Science in Archaeology*. Thames and Hudson: London.

Brothwell, D. and Higgs, E. (1969). *Science in Archaeology*, (2nd edn). Thames and Hudson: London.

Brothwell, D. and Sandison, A.T. (eds.) (1967). *Disease in Antiquity*. Charles C. Thomas: Springfield.

Brothwell, D., Molleson, T., Harcourt, R. and Gray, P.H.K. (1969). The application of X-rays to the study of archaeological material. In Brothwell, D. and Higgs, E. (eds) *Science in Archaeology* (2nd edn), 513–525. Thames and Hudson: London.

Buikstra, J.E. (1997). Paleodemography: context and promise In Paine, R.R. (ed.) *Integrating Archaeological Demography: Multidisciplinary Approaches to Prehistoric Population*, 367–380. Occasional Paper No. 24, Center for Archaeological Investigations: Carbondale, IL.

Buikstra, J.E. and Cook, D.C. (1980). Paleopathology: an American account. *Annual Review of Anthropology*, 9:433–470.

Buikstra, J.E. and Ubelaker, D.H. (eds) (1994). *Standards for Data Collection from Human Skeletal Remains*. Research Series No. 44, Arkansas Archaeological Survey: Arkansas.

Buikstra, J.E., Frankenberg, S.R. and Konigsberg, L.W. (1990). Skeletal biological distance studies in American physical anthropology: recent trends. *American Journal of Physical Anthropology*, 82:1–8.

Burton, J.H. and Price, T.D. (1990). The ratio of barium to strontium as a paleodietary indicator of consumption of marine resources. *Journal of Archaeological Science*, 17:547–557.

Burton, J.H. and Price, T.D. (1991). Paleodietary applications of barium in bone. In Pernicka, E. and Wagner, G.A. (eds) *Proceedings of the 27th International Symposium on Archaeometry*, 787–795. Birkhäuser Verlag: Basel.

Cockburn, A. and Cockburn, E. (1980). *Mummies, Disease and Ancient Cultures*. Cambridge University Press: Cambridge.

Cockburn, A., Cockburn, E. and Reyman, T.A. (eds) (1998). *Mummies, Disease and Ancient Cultures*, (2nd edn). Cambridge University Press: Cambridge.

Cohen, M.N. and Armelagos, G.G. (1984). *Paleopathology at the Origins of Agriculture*. Academic Press: Orlando.

Cook, D.C., Buikstra, J.E., de Rousseau, C.J. and Johanson, D.C. (1983). Vertebral pathology in the Afar australopithecines. *American Journal of Physical Anthropology*, 60:83–101.

Fitzgerald, C.M. and Rose, J.C. (2000). Reading between the lines: development and subadult age assessment using the microstructural growth markers of the teeth. In Katzenberg, M.A. and Saunders, S.R. (eds) *Biological Anthropology of the Human Skeleton*, 163–186. Wiley-Liss: New York.

Garlick, J.D. (1969). Buried bone. In Brothwell, D. and Higgs, E. (eds) *Science in Archaeology*, (2nd edn), 503–512. Thames and Hudson: London.

Gejvall, N.G. (1969). Cremations. In Brothwell, D. and Higgs, E. (eds) *Science in Archaeology*, (2nd edn), 468–479. Thames and Hudson: London.

Genovés, S. (1969a). Sex determination in early man. In Brothwell, D. and Higgs, E. (eds) *Science in Archaeology*, (2nd edn), 429–439. Thames and Hudson: London.

Genovés, S. (1969b). Estimation of age and mortality. In Brothwell, D. and Higgs, E. (eds) *Science in Archaeology*, (2nd edn), 440–452. Thames and Hudson: London.

Goldstein, M.S. (1969). The paleopathology of human skeletal remains. In Brothwell, D. and Higgs, E. (eds) *Science in Archaeology*, (2nd edn), 480–489. Thames and Hudson: London.

Guillén, S. (1992). *The Chinchorro Culture: Mummies and Crania in the Reconstruction of Preceramic Coastal Adaptation in the South Central Andes*. Unpublished PhD Dissertation, University of Michigan.

Haglund, W.D. and Sorg, M.H. (eds) (1997). *Forensic Taphonomy: the Postmortem Fate of Human Remains*. CRC Press: Boca Raton.

Hauser, G. and De Stefano, G.F. (1989). *Epigenetic Variants of the Human Skull*. Schweizerbart'sche Verlagsbuchhandlung: Stuttgart.

Hillson, S. (1986). *Teeth*. Cambridge University Press: Cambridge.

Hillson, S. (1996). *Dental Anthropology*. Cambridge University Press: Cambridge.

Holman, D.J., O'Connor, K.A., Wood, J.W. and Boldsen, J.L. (1997). Correcting for nonstationarity in paleodemographic mortality models. *American Journal of Physical Anthropology Supplement*, 24:132 (abstract).

Jarcho, S. (ed.) (1966). *Human Palaeopathology*. Yale University Press: New Haven.

Jurmain, R. (1999). *Stories from the Skeleton. Behavioral Reconstruction in Human Osteology*. Gordon and Breach: Langhorne.

Konigsberg, L.W. and Buikstra, J.E. (1995). Regional approaches to the investigation of past human biocultural structure. In Beck, L.A. (ed.) *Regional Approaches to Mortuary Analysis*, 191–219. Plenum: New York.

Konigsberg, L.W. and Frankenberg, S.R. (1992). Estimation of age structure in anthropological demography. *American Journal of Physical Anthropology*, 89:235–256.

Konigsberg, L.W. and Holman, D.J. (1999). Estimation of age-at-death from dental emergence and implications for studies of prehistoric somatic growth. In Hoppa, R.D. and Fitzgerald, C.M. (eds) *Human Growth in the Past: Studies from Bones and Teeth*, 264–289. Cambridge University Press: Cambridge.

Konigsberg, L.W., Frankenberg, S.R. and Walker, R.B. (1997). Regress what on what? Paleodemographic age estimation as a calibration problem. In Paine, R.R. (ed.) *Integrating Archaeological Demography: Multidisciplinary Approaches to Prehistoric Population*, 64–88. Occasional Paper No. 24, Center for Archaeological Investigations: Carbondale, IL.

Krings, M., Stone, A., Schmitz, R.W., Krainitzi, H., Stoneking, M. and Pääbo, S. (1997). Neandertal DNA sequences and the origin of modern humans. *Cell*, 90:19–30.

Larsen, C.S. (1997). *Bioarchaeology. Interpreting Behavior from the Skeleton*. Cambridge University Press: Cambridge.

Lane, R.A. and Sublett, A.J. (1972). The osteology of social organization: residence pattern. *American Antiquity*, **37**:186–201.

Lee-Thorp, J.A., van der Merwe, N.J. and Brain, C.K. (1994). Diet of *Australopithecus robustus* at Swartkrans from stable carbon isotopic analysis. *Journal of Human Evolution*, **27**:361–372.

Lovell, N.C. (2000). Paleopathological description and diagnosis. In Katzenberg, M.A. and Saunders, S.R. (eds) *Biological Anthropology of the Human Skeleton*, 217–248. Wiley-Liss: New York.

Milner, G.R. and Boldsen, J.L. (1999). A validation of transition analysis from known-age skeletons. Paper presented at Mathematical Modeling for Palaeodemography. Coming to Consensus. Rostock, Germany.

Milner, G.R., Boldsen, J.L. and Usher, B.M. (1997). Age-at-death determination using revised scoring procedures for age-progressive skeletal traits. *American Journal of Physical Anthropology Supplement*, **24**:170 (Abstract).

Milner, G.R., Wood, J.W. and Boldsen, J.L. (2000). Paleodemography. In Katzenberg, M.A. and Saunders, S.R. (eds) *Biological Anthropology of Human Skeleton*, 467–497. Wiley-Liss: New York.

Moorrees, C.F.A., Fanning, E.A. and Hunt, E.E. (1963a). Formation and resorption of three deciduous teeth in children. *American Journal of Physical Anthropology*, **21**:205–213.

Moorrees, C.F.A., Fanning, E.A. and Hunt, E.E. (1963b). Age formation by stages for ten permanent teeth. *Journal of Dental Research*, **42**:1490–1502.

Ogilvie, M.D., Curran, B.K. and Trinkaus, E. (1989). Incidence and patterning of dental hypoplasia among the Neandertals. *American Journal of Physical Anthropology*, **79**:25–41.

Ortner, D.J. and Putschar, W.G.J. (1985). *Identification of Pathological Conditions in Human Skeletal Remains*. Smithsonian Institution Press: Washington DC.

Ovchinnikov, I.V., Götherström, A., Romanova, G.P., Kharitonov, V.M., Lidén, K. and Goodwin, W. (2000). Molecular analysis of Neanderthal DNA from the northern Caucasus. *Nature*, **404**:490–493.

Pietrusewsky, M. (2000). Metric analysis of skeletal remains: methods and applications. In Katzenberg, M.A. and Saunders, S.R. (eds) *Biological Anthropology of the Human Skeleton*, 375–416. Wiley-Liss: New York.

Relethford, J.H. and Lees, F.C. (1982). The use of quantitative traits in the study of human population structure. *American Journal of Physical Anthropology*, **25**:113–132.

Roberts, C. and Manchester, K. (1995). *The Archaeology of Disease*, (2nd edn). Cornell University Press: Ithaca, New York.

Ruff, C.B., Trinkaus, E., Walker, A. and Larsen, C.S. (1993). Postcranial robusticity in Homo I. Temporal trends and mechanical interpretation. *American Journal of Physical Anthropology*, **91**:21–53.

Sandison, A.T. (1969). The study of mummified and dried human tissues. In Brothwell, D. and Higgs, E. (eds) *Science in Archaeology*, (2nd edn), 490–502. Thames and Hudson: London.

Sandford, M.K. (1993). *Investigations of Ancient Human Tissue: Chemical Analyses in Anthropology*. Gordon and Breach: Langhorne.

Sandford, M.K. and Weaver, D.S. (2000). Trace element research in anthropology: new perspectives and challenges. In Katzenberg, M.A. and Saunders, S.R. (eds) *Biological Anthropology of the Human Skeleton*, 329–350. Wiley-Liss: New York.

Saunders, S.R. (2000). Subadult skeletons and growth-related studies. In Katzenberg, M.A. and Saunders, S.R. (eds) *Biological Anthropology of the Human Skeleton*, 135–162. Wiley-Liss: New York.

Scott, G.R. and Turner II, C.G. (1997). *The Anthropology of Modern Human Teeth*. Cambridge University Press: Cambridge.

Sillen, A. (1981). Strontium and diet at Hayonim cave. *American Journal of Physical Anthropology*, **56**:131–137.

Sillen, A. (1986). Biogenic and diagenetic Sr/Ca in Plio-Pleistocene fossils of the Omo Shungura formation. *Paleobiology*, **12**:311–323.

Sillen, A. (1992). Strontium-calcium (Sr/Ca) of *Australopithecus robustus* and associated fauna from Swartkrans. *Journal of Human Evolution*, **23**:495–516.

Sillen, A., Sealy, J.C. and van der Merwe, N.J. (1989). Chemistry and paleodietary research: no more easy answers. *American Antiquity*, **54**:504–512.

Smith, B.C. (1991). Changes in perikymata and their significance to a postmortem dental identification. *Journal of Forensic Sciences*, **36**:166–178.

Stone, A.C., Milner, G.R., Pääbo, S. and Stoneking, M. (1996). Sex determination of ancient human skeletons using DNA. *American Journal of Physical Anthropology*, **99**:231–238.

Storey, R. (1999). Late classic nutrition and skeletal indicators at Copán, Honduras. In White, C. (ed.) *Reconstructing Ancient Maya Diet*, 169–179. University of Utah Press: Salt Lake City.

Trinkaus, E. (1995). Neanderthal mortality pattern. *Journal of Archaeological Science*, **22**:121–142.

Trinkaus, E. and Thompson, D. (1987). Femoral diaphyseal histomorphometric age determination for the Shanidar 3, 4, 5 and 6 Neandertals and Neandertal longevity. *American Journal of Physical Anthropology*, **72**:123–129.

Ubelaker, D.H. (1982). The development of American paleopathology. In Spencer, F. (ed.) *A History of American Physical Anthropology: 1930–1980*, 337–356. Academic Press: New York.

Ubelaker, D. (1989). *Human Skeletal Remains: Excavation, Analysis and Interpretation*. Aldine Publishing Co.: Chicago.

Wells, L.H. (1969). Stature in earlier races of mankind. In Brothwell, D. and Higgs, E. (eds) *Science in Archaeology*, (2nd edn), 453–467. Thames and Hudson: London.

Wood, J.W., Milner, G.R., Harpending, H.C. and Weiss, K.M. (1992). The osteological paradox: problems in inferring prehistoric health from skeletal samples. *Current Anthropology*, **33**:343–370.

17

Pleistocene and Holocene Hominid Evolution

D.R. BROTHWELL

Department of Archaeology, University of York.

There is little doubt that human palaeontology is the oldest of the archaeological sciences. Discoveries of human fossils go back to early in the nineteenth century, and although the significance of some finds was not appreciated until later in the century, it was at least indicative of a growing interest in human remains. Moreover, these human skeletal finds were of a range of periods, so that even remains as recent as the last thousand years began to be considered in considerable detail.

Fossil hominids began to appear nearly two hundred years ago (Paviland Cave, 1822; Engis Cave, 1830), with the famous neandertal calotte accidentally found in 1856. Sir Charles Lyell was quick to see the significance of the Engis and neanderthal finds (Lyell 1863), and so was T. H. Huxley (1863), who provided a good description of the find and concluded that this Neandertal individual did not represent a 'missing link', but it did clearly indicate a fossil form unlike modern human populations. Huxley remained intrigued by this neanderthaler, and returned to its morphology and affinities in his detailed study of late prehistoric skeletal material from Caithness (Huxley 1866).

Further discoveries in 1868 at the rock-shelter of Cro-Magnon provided good evidence of an Upper Palaeolithic group, with clear morphological affinities with Holocene European groups (Quatrefages 1883). It was also apparent at the end of that century, that the associated fossil mammal bones and teeth, some of extinct species, suggested a fauna in marked contrast to that in modern Europe. Moreover, there was growing interest in and evidence of climatic changes through time, from river terraces, cave deposits and other sediments (Wright 1893); and finally, the discoveries of stone tools from such deposits provided evidence of material cultures of the distant past. Dating was to remain a serious problem but studies on the growth of stalagmites in fossil producing caves at least suggested a considerable antiquity for the deposits.

Before the close of the century, evidence of another fossil hominid group had been discovered between 1891–94 in Java, and is now accepted as part of the widely dispersed *Homo erectus* group. So as the century ended, prehistorians and anthropologists were already discussing three of the morphologically distinctive fossil hominid groups (Keane 1896). And as regards Holocene populations, tombs and cemeteries in Europe, Egypt, the New World and elsewhere, were beginning to reveal micro-evolutionary diversity. The detailed study of changes in early British populations by Davis and Thurnam (1865) is a particularly good example of this early research on Holocene populations.

The twentieth century has seen an enormous outpouring of studies on fossil and sub-fossil hominids,

---

and a bibliography would run into volumes. In the history of human palaeontology, the most significant discoveries of this century have been concerned with fossils broadly referred to as australopithecines or other, possibly basal, representatives of the genus *Homo*. The distinctiveness of the australopithecines was early emphasized by Dart (1925) and Broom (1936). These and further discoveries resulted initially in the defining of three separate genera for these fossils, *Australopithecus*, *Plesianthropus* and *Paranthropus*.

Debate has continued over the years as to what this variation means in terms of true speciation versus sexual dimorphism or within-group variation. Clearly there is a degree of sexual dimorphism greater than recent hominids, and there is a consensus of opinion that there is a gracile and robust form.

EVOLUTIONARY TREES

Sir Arthur Keith (1915) was the first to provide a reasonably balanced evolutionary tree for the higher primates, and especially the hominids. Today, of course, there are major errors, in that his geological divisions are wrong (*Homo erectus* diverges in the Miocene), and the Pleistocene occupies only 200 000 years. Boule and Vallois (1957) considered alternative evolutionary relationships for *Homo erectus*, remaining surprisingly reluctant to see this species as ancestral to later hominids. A part of the australopithecine range of variation (four or five species?) is now seen to give rise to early *Homo* species (Grine 1988), and it is generally accepted that the 'classic' neandertalers did not contribute significantly, in terms of their genes, to more recent human groups. But there are still problems in determining where the 'archaic' hominids, such as seen in the Kabwe (Broken Hill) and Ngandong (Solo) specimens, should be placed.

DATING FOSSIL HOMINIDS

Very considerable improvements in dating hominids have occurred in the past fifty years. From reliance on stratigraphy and zone fossils, the situation was transformed by radiocarbon dating and subsequent techniques (see Section 1). It is now clear that the australopithecines have a range from *c*. 5 to 1 million years ago, overlapping with the emergence of *Homo*, 2 million years ago. The most debatable issue is surely when our own species emerged, as yet not at all clear from skeletal morphology and tool technology.

ENVIRONMENTAL CONTRASTS AND HOMINID ADAPTATIONS

A vast literature has grown detailing the environmental changes, climatic and biological, which have occurred during the Pleistocene and Holocene periods (for example, Cushing and Wright 1967, Lowe and Walker 1984, Roberts 1989, Bell and Walker 1992). The problem, therefore, is not establishing environmental change over the critical period of the evolution and differentiation of *Homo*, but in understanding how environmental change provided selection pressures which influenced physiological and structural adaptations.

Over a century ago, Wright (1893:292) understood that species in the past 'adjusted to quite different climatic conditions from those which now seem necessary to their existence'. But how such adaptation occurred remained unanswered. Surprisingly, Darwin (1871) seems to be equally uncertain about the mechanisms producing variation in humans. He writes: 'man resembles those forms, called by naturalists ... polymorphic, which have remained extremely variable, owing, as it seems, to such variations being of an indifferent nature, and to their having thus escaped the action of natural selection' (p. 198). Four decades later, Semple (1911) was forcefully pointing out that such geographic factors as temperature, altitude, island isolation, and rainfall influenced the biology of human populations. Ironically, she saw Darwinism, evolution by natural selection, as the critical determining factor behind human variation. Since then, recent human adaptability has been well-studied at a physiological and population level (e.g., Baker and Weiner 1966, Harrison 1977), but the relationship between hominid structural changes and the environmental backgrounds, remains largely enigmatic.

A major problem, of course, has been the paucity of good information on environments associated with fossil hominids, particularly with the earlier groups. Contributions to the reconstruction of these palaeoenvironments have been especially important by Butzer (1971, 1978, 1982,) and Andrews (1992, 1996). As regards the differentiation of the australopithecines, Vrba (1988) suggested that on available evidence, major global cooling was occurring near 2.5 Ma, with the development of more open and arid environments in at least the more eastern African area, but probably extending into South Africa as well. By 0.9 Ma, geological sequences suggest further environmental changes which caused the 'robust' australopithecines to become extinct, and perhaps promoted the considerable geographic expansion of *Homo erectus*. Roberts (1984) argued that these changes resulted in fluctuating environmental stress, which could have adaptively challenged the early hominids more than other mammals.

These early hominid environments in Africa were by no means all the same, and currently it is considered that while the early (3.6–2.6 Ma) Hadar region in Ethiopia had a lake and floodplain setting, at Omo in Ethiopia, by 2 Ma, there was drier savannah, with associated river systems, and some forest. Early Olduvai, Tanzania (1.9–1.5 Ma) had a salt lake with river systems and dry woodland savannah, but this changed radically after a tectonic phase resulted in the drying up of the lake. In contrast again, the australopithecine sites of the South African Transvaal, were mosaic environments which together suggest a trend to drier conditions (Andrews 1992). It is possible that the contrasting forms of early australopithecine may be due to some geographic isolation and strong selection in these early contrasting environments. It is of course easy to suggest, but it remains debatable whether these changing environments really provided critical stress levels for morphological change to have occurred. Indeed Butzer (1978:211) stated that 'no case has yet been made to the effect that environmental changes promoted biological, social or cultural adaptations in late Tertiary or early Pleistocene times'.

Whatever reservations are retained in the evaluation of structural changes in relation to environmental stresses through time, the fact remains that we must consider further the adaptive significance of bipedalism, brain size increase (beyond that correlated with body size changes), tooth variation and size decrease, and so on. By the later Middle- and Upper Pleistocene, physical changes are generally less marked, with at least the exception of the 'classic' neandertalers. Howell's (1952) now-classic hypothesis that the robust and 'stocky' build of this population was related to cold adaptation remains an interesting matter for further investigation. Finally, if the variation in modern populations is derived from micro-evolution of only the last 80–120 ka (Stringer 1993), then we might be tempted to think that no adaptive changes have occurred in that relatively short geological time. But from physiological rather than skeletal evidence, it is clear that micro-adaptations continued in such variables as climatic adaptation, with thermoregulatory needs influencing body size and form, solar radiation load linked to skin pigmentation, and yet other variables being probably associated with cold acclimatization (Barnicot 1959).

BIPEDALISM

The human palaeontologist Franz Weidenreich realized early on that our posture and method of locomotion is perhaps the most significant change in our species – 'the fundamental specialisation by which man differs from any other mammals ... is the perfectly erect position and the complete release of the forelimbs from use in the locomotion of the body' (Weidenreich 1947). He acknowledges that 'bipeds' occur in other species, but only in the hominid line have there been profound structural changes at the cranial base, in vertebral curvature, pelvic remodelling and reorientation, and adaptational changes in the limbs and feet, with repositioning of the centre of gravity.

Bipedalism was certainly well established by australopithecine times, although skeletally still distinctive from modern humans. The most impressive changes are in the pelvis, with an increasing basin form, iliac remodelling and increased hip joint size. The femur changes under the influence of leg positioning needs, with a greater angulation into midline and expansion of the linea aspera (in line with changes in muscle size and emphasis).

Reasons for the evolution of bipedalism are not hard to find; to increase running speed, to free the hands, for ease in looking for predator dangers, even to cut down on direct surface exposure to the sun. Unfortunately, it is another matter to confirm these theories experimentally. 'A great challenge for evolutionary kinesiologists is to detail this novel (locomotory) pattern on the basis of sound biomechanical principles instead of analogies with the condition in extant forms' (Tuttle 1981). That the evolution of a perfectly adapted bipedalism has not been achieved, and now may never be, is well summed up by Straus (1962). He concludes that since the Middle Pleistocene, 'precious little progress toward its (postural) perfection seems to have occurred. For modern men all too plainly and too often are subject to pathologic modifications – in the form of herniated or shrunken intervertebral disks, flat feet, varicose veins, haemorrhoids and inguinal or femoral hernia ... that bear witness to the imperfect transmutation of a pronagrade, quadrupedal primate into an erect, bipedal one' (Straus 1962).

BRAIN AND BEHAVIOUR

'No one, I presume', wrote Darwin (1871), 'doubts that the large proportion which the size of a man's brain bears to his body, compared to the same proportion in the gorilla or orang, is closely connected with his higher mental powers.' Weidenreich (1948), having considered brain size, convolutions and fissure complexity in different mammals, as well as fossil hominids and recent people, nevertheless concluded that 'neither the size nor the form of the brain or the surface of the hemispheres ... furnishes a reliable clue to the amount and degree of general or special mental qualities'. Le Gros Clarke (1958) was similarly guarded and pointed out that modern human brain size in people of 'normal' intelligence could vary from 900 cm^3 to about 2300 cm^3. The problem, he rightly said, was that brain size 'can tell us nothing of the intrinsic neural organisation which may be supposed to be much more closely related to intellectual functions than mere mass of nervous tissue'. In the four decades which have followed this comment, a mass of new hominid material has been discovered which at least confirms the gradual increase in average brain size during hominid evolution.

Research emphasis has changed during this time, and much attention is now being given to human behavioural evolution (as indicated for instance by Foley 1991, Noble and Davidson 1996, Mithen 1996). For it is the brain, large or small, which is ultimately linked to the capacity for language, and for the development of an increasingly complex social life. Changes in behaviour, with extensive migrations at the *Homo erectus* level, in contrast to the restricting ranges of australopithecine social groups, enabled the widespread peopling of the Old World by earlier Middle Pleistocene times (Gamble 1993). But the ultimate problem concerned with brain and behaviour remains; that is, what small scale but critical behavioural factors in hominid groups with modestly larger brains, permitted the secular trend to ever larger human brain size? Was it a dietary change?

SIZE AND SHAPE VARIATION

Even with the limited amount of fossil hominid material available for comparison during the nineteenth century, it was clear to Lyell (1863), Huxley (1863) and others that there were significant morphological differences. And as in the case of those working on excavated skeletons of the past few millennia, such as Davis and Thurnam (1865), the variation was recorded by measurements. This tradition of osteometry has been criticized from time to time, but is robust enough to survive and be of value today. Sir Arthur Keith (1915) was one of the best early proponents of measurement and comparison in fossil hominids, with Sollas

(1933) indicating the value of skull contours in the comparative evaluation of shape.

By 1940, with the increasing discoveries of *Homo erectus* (Sinanthropus, Pithecanthropus) and australopithecine fossils, there were clearly four major divisions of hominids, on crude size and shape – namely australopithecines, *Homo erectus*, later Middle Pleistocene (neandertals and others) and advanced *Homo sapiens* forms.

Variations within these groups suggested changing degrees of sexual dimorphism (Genovés 1963, Pilbeam and Zwell 1972) through time, as well as more than one species of australopithecine. It could be that earlier *Homo erectus* evolved into more than one later species (Rightmire 1993). There is now little doubt, on dating and morphological grounds, that neanderthal evolution was parallel with the emergence of an advanced ancestor of modern peoples. In these changes through time, we see macro-evolutionary transformation, but studies on later Pleistocene and Holocene skeletal series have shown that micro-evolution has also continued (Suzuki 1969, Jantz 1972, Howells 1973, 1989).

DISEASE AND THE EARLIER HOMINIDS

While Holocene populations have now received considerable attention as regards their demography and health, (e.g., Ortner and Putschar 1981, Aufderheide and Rodríguez-Martín 1998) there is no doubt that fossil hominids have been seriously neglected as regards their pathology and morbidity. While this may be partly explained by the fragmentary nature of fossil material, it is also somewhat of a reflection of current interests within the field of human palaeontology.

Very few fossil hominids, with the exception of cases such as the 'old man' of La Chapelle-aux-Saints, are likely to have died of old age. There is thus a need to search minutely for any evidence of abnormality. Yet I know of no search for evidence of orbital cribra for instance, although this area of the skull survives well. Other evidence of environmental stress is neglected, although abnormal cranial thickness is known in *Homo erectus* and one Krapina neandertal fragment displays pitting and vault changes suggestive of nutritional hyperparathyroidism.

Mortality clearly indicates that earlier hominid groups had survival problems. Some 58 per cent of australopithecines died before maturity (Mann 1975), 43 per cent of the Chinese *Homo erectus* group (Mann, 1981), and 49 per cent of neandertals (Hassan 1981).

These percentages will, however, be influenced (and reduced) by taphonomic factors.

Oral pathology was certainly becoming a health problem by later Pleistocene times (Brothwell 1963) and a detailed survey still has to be undertaken. Trauma, evidence of which was noted in the original Neander valley specimen, is particularly well in evidence in the Shanidar neanderthals (Trinkaus 1983), and Weidenreich (1939) considered that trauma was responsible for some of the deaths in individuals from both lower and upper caves at Zhoukoudien (Chou kou-tien), in China. The La Chapelle-aux-Saints skeleton found in 1908, displays severe arthropathy of vertebrae and hip joints and since then further cases of joint disease have appeared, especially at Shanidar. Hyperostosis frontalis interna is present in the original 1848 Gibraltar neanderthal. Surprising, if not enigmatic, finds include a 1.7 million year old *Homo erectus* (KNM-ER 1808) with possible hypervitaminosis A (Walker *et al.* 1982), and a parietal from Lazaret Cave, Nice (*c.* 120 000 BP), which could display a reaction to a meningioma (Duplay *et al.* 1970). Considering the vast amount of Pleistocene skeletal material, albeit incomplete, which is now available for study, it is surprising that more detailed studies on disease evidence have not been forthcoming.

CONCLUSIONS

This has been an attempt to digest a vast literature on human skeletal populations, Pleistocene and Holocene, into a brief review. The primary reason for this is because human palaeontology, within which I would include sub-fossil studies, can certainly be seen as one of the earliest archaeological sciences. The study of such human remains reveals both macro-evolutionary changes through time but also, in the case of Holocene groups, smaller-scale micro-evolutionary differences. The most significant changes have been in brain size increase and the adoption of bipedalism, which have resulted in cranial, spinal, pelvic and leg adaptations in particular. But although we are far better informed of environmental changes associated with earlier hominid groups, how these have really influenced structural changes remains enigmatic. Thus, the most significant scientific advance in the future of this field will surely be to understand the mechanisms by which environmental and genetic factors result in skeletal and dental changes through time. Finally, the demographic and pathological aspects of fossil hominids have been particularly neglected, in comparison with the considerable work now undertaken on skeletal series of the last few thousand years. So in this respect also, there are interesting challenges for the future.

REFERENCES

*Recommended for further reading

Andrews, P. (1992). Reconstructing past environments. In Jones, S., Martin, R. and Pilbeam, D. (eds) *The Cambridge Encyclopaedia of Human Evolution*, 191–195. Cambridge University Press: Cambridge.

*Andrews, P. (1996). Palaeoecology and hominoid palaoenvironments. *Biological Review*, **71**:257–300.

Aufderheide, A. and Rodríguez-Martín, C. (1998). *The Cambridge Encyclopaedia of Human Paleopathology*. Cambridge University Press: Cambridge.

Baker, P.T. and Weiner, J.S. (eds) (1966). *The Biology of Human Adaptability*. Clarendon: Oxford.

Barnicot, N.A. (1959). Climatic factors in the evolution of human populations. *Cold Spring Harbour Symposia on Quantitative Biology*, **24**:115–129.

Bell, M. and Walker, M.J. (1992). *Late Quaternary Environmental Change*. Longman: Harlow.

Boule, M. and Vallois, H.V. (1957). *Fossil Men: a Textbook of Human Palaeontology*. Thames and Hudson: London.

Broom, R. (1936). A new fossil anthropoid skull from South Africa. *Nature*, **138**:486–488.

Brothwell, D.R. (1963). The macroscopic dental pathology of some earlier human populations. In Brothwell, D.R. (ed.) *Dental Anthropology*, 271–288. Pergamon: London.

Butzer, K.W. (1971). *Environment and Archaeology*. Methuen: London.

Butzer, K.W. (1978). Geoecological perspectives on early hominid evolution. In Jolly, C. (ed.) *Early Hominids of Africa*, 191–217. Duckworth: London.

*Butzer, K.W. (1982). *Archaeology as Human Ecology*. Cambridge University Press: Cambridge.

Cushing, E.J. and Wright, H.E. (1967). *Quaternary Paleoecology*. Yale University Press: New Haven.

Dart, R. (1925). *Australopithecus africanus*: the man-ape of South Africa. *Nature*, **115**:195–199.

Darwin, C. (1871). *The Descent of Man, and Selection in Relation to Sex*. Murray: London.

Davis, J.B. and Thurnam, J. (1865). *Crania Britannica*. Taylor and Francis: London.

Duplay, J., De Lumley, M.A. and Julliard, G. (1970). Un pariétal anténéandertalien: probléme diagnostique. *Neuro-Chirurgie*, **16**:5–13.

*Foley, R.A. (ed.) (1991). *The Origins of Human Behaviour*. Unwin Hyman: London.

Gamble, C. (1993). *Time-walkers. The Prehistory of Global Colonisation*. Sutton: Stroud.

Genovés, S. (1963). Sex determination of earlier man. In Brothwell, D. and Higgs, E. (eds) *Science in Archaeology*, 343–352. Thames and Hudson: London.

Grine, F.E. (1988). Australopithecus. In Tattersall, I., Delson, E. and Van Couvering, J. (eds) *Encyclopaedia of Human Evolution and Prehistory*, 67–74. Garland: London.

Harrison, G.A. (ed.) (1977). *Population Structure and Human Variation*. Cambridge University Press: Cambridge.

Hassan, F.A. (1981). *Demographic Archaeology*. Academic Press: London.

Howell, F.C. (1952). Pleistocene glacial ecology and the evolution of 'Classic Neandertal' man. *South-western Journal of Anthropology*, **8**:377–410.

Howells, W.W. (1973). Cranial variation in man: a study by multivariate analysis of patterns of difference among recent human populations. *Papers of the Peabody Museum of Archaeology and Ethnology*, **67**:1–259.

Howells, W.W. (1989). Skull shapes and the map: craniometric analyses in the dispersion of modern homo. *Papers of the Peabody Museum of Archaeology and Ethnology*, **79**:1–189.

Huxley, T.H. (1863). *Man's Place in Nature and Other Essays*. Dent: London (collected 1906).

Huxley, T.H. (1866). Notes upon the human remains from Keiss. In Laing, S. (ed.) *Prehistoric Remains of Caithness*, 83–161. Williams and Norgate: London.

Jantz, R.L. (1972). Cranial variation and microevolution in Arikara skeletal populations. *Plains Anthropologist*, **17**:20–35.

Keane, A.H. (1896). *Ethnology*. Cambridge University Press: Cambridge.

Keith, A. (1915). *The Antiquity of Man*. Williams and Norgate: London.

Le Gros Clark, W. (1958). Bones of contention. *Journal of the Royal Anthropological Institute*, **88**:1–15.

Lowe, J.J. and Walker, M.J.C. (1984). *Reconstructing Quaternary Environments*. Longman: Harlow.

Lyell, C. (1863). *The Antiquity of Man*. Dent: London.

Mann, A.E. (1975). *Paleodemographic Aspects of the South African Australopithecines*. University of Pennsylvania: Philadelphia.

Mann, A. (1981). The significance of the Sinanthropus casts, and some paleodemographic notes. In Sigmon, B.A. and Cybulski, J.S. (eds) *Homo Erectus: Papers in Honor of Davidson Black*, 41–62. University of Toronto Press: Toronto.

Mithen, S. (1996). *The Prehistory of the Mind*. Pheonix: London.

Noble, W. and Davidson, I. (1996). *Human Evolution, Language and Mind*. Cambridge University Press: Cambridge.

Ortner, D. and Putschar, W. (1981). *Identification of Pathological Conditions in Human Skeletal Remains*. Smithsonian Institution Press: Washington DC.

Pilbeam, D.R. and Zwell, M. (1972). The single species hypothesis, sexual dimorphism, and variability in early hominids. *Yearbook of Physical Anthropology*, **16**:69–79.

Quatrefages, A.D. (1883). *The Human Species*. Paul, Trench and Trübner: London.

Rightmire, G.P. (1993). Variation among early Homo crania from Olduvai Gorge and the Koobi Fora region. *American Journal of Physical Anthropology*, **90**:1–33.

Roberts, N. (1984). Pleistocene environments in time and space. In Foley, R. (ed.) *Hominid Evolution and Community Ecology*, 25–53. Academic Press: London.

Roberts, N. (1989). *The Holocene. An Environmental History*. Blackwell: Oxford.

Semple, E.C. (1911). *Influences of Geographic Environment*. Constable: London.

Sollas, W.J. (1933). The sagittal section of the human skull. *Journal of the Royal Anthropological Institute*, **63**:389–431.

Straus, W.L. (1962). Fossil evidence of the evolution of the erect, bipedal posture. *Clinical Orthopaedics*, **25**:9–19.

*Stringer, C.B. (1993). Reconstructing recent human evolution. In Aitken, M., Stringer, C. and Mellars, P. (eds) *The Origin of Modern Humans and the Impact of Chronometric Dating*, 180–195. University Press: Princeton.

Suzuki, H. (1969). Microevolutional changes in the Japanese population from the prehistoric age to the present day. *Journal of the Faculty of Science, Tokyo, Section 5*, **3**:279–309.

Trinkaus, E. (1983). *The Shanidar Neandertals*. Academic Press: London.

Tuttle, R.H. (1981). Evolution of hominid bipedalism and prehensile capabilities. *Philosophical Transactions of the Royal Society*, London, **B292**:89–94.

*Vrba, E.S. (1988). Late pliocene climatic events and hominid evolution. In Grine, F.E. (ed.) *Evolutionary History of the 'Robust' Australopithecines*, 405–425. Aldine: New York.

Walker, A., Zimmerman, M.R. and Leakey, R.E.F. (1982). A possible case of Hypervitaminosis A in *Homo Erectus*. *Nature*, **296**:248–250.

Weidenreich, F. (1939). The duration of life of fossil man in China and the pathological lesions found in his skeleton. *The Chinese Medical Journal*, **55**:34–44.

Weidenreich, F. (1947). The trend of human evolution. *Evolution*, **1**:221–236.

Weidenreich, F. (1948). The human brain in the light of its phylogenetic development. *The Scientific Monthly*, **67**:103–109.

Wright, G.F. (1893). *Man and the Glacial Period*. Paul, Trench and Trübner: London.

18

Human Palaeobiology as Human Ecology

H. SCHUTKOWSKI

Department of Archaeological Sciences, University of Bradford.

Major recent achievements contributing to the progress in different fields of human palaeobiology have been made through the application and increasing refinement of modern analytical methods. A great deal of our present knowledge about dietary patterns and food resource utilization of extinct hominids and modern humans is a result of stable isotope and elemental analyses of human remains. Mobility and migration can be traced, and palaeoclimatic evidence is revealed by directly investigating the chemical composition of human skeletal remains (see Katzenberg and Harrison 1997 for a recent overview). Following up this theme, the impact of seasonality on the availability of foodstuffs and residential shift, and their reflection in bone chemistry will be among future research themes, as it entails the perspective of studying both intra- and inter-individual variation in more detail. Connected with this will be extended and more intensified studies pursuing the routing of dietary carbon and nitrogen to further clarify the translation of food components into diet-indicating isotopic signals in various body tissues (see Chapter 23).

The improved quality of skeletal diagnoses by, for example, histomorphological analyses of bone microstructure and cyclical appositional growth patterns in tooth roots add great benefit to the development of refined palaeodemographic models (see Chapters 20 and 22). The study of ancient DNA (aDNA; see Chapter 25) provides information by any reproducibly positive result, which is unambiguous in a way never achievable through other methods and the full range of applications has yet to be explored (Herrmann and Hummel 1994).

By the same token, palaeopathology has already and will further gain significant contributions from molecular analyses (e.g., Greenblatt 1998), as to the aetiology of infectious diseases such as tuberculosis or treponemal disease through molecular identification of the causative pathogen. Progress in the detection of hereditary disease may significantly add to our understanding of palaeoepidemiology (see Chapter 25).

AN ECOLOGICAL FRAMEWORK

Human palaeobiology, as represented here, reflects the implications of data gathered through an assessment of basic and derived biological information from various kinds of human remains of a wide range of provenance, as well as the technical and analytical means to do so. Translated into an ecological context, the whole of this section of the volume is about identifying biological parameters characteristic of human individuals and populations as they relate to conditions of energy, matter, space and time in their respective habitats (for general aspects see for example Odum (1973)).

Evolutionary change, distribution and prevalence of disease, demographic structures, or dietary patterns, each of those can be, at least in part, regarded as the result of adaptational variation in response to environmental constraints and inter-relations between humans and the various biotic and abiotic components of the ecosystem. However, as humans are involved, the nature of this context is essentially biocultural rather than merely biological.

Generally, wherever humans are part of ecosystems they share the same kind of geochemical cycles and are subject to the same kind of processes and principles as other organisms. The spatial distribution of human populations is related to resource density, they participate in flows of matter and energy within the system and are part of food webs. Like any other organism, they are tied into structural and functional relations with the living and the inanimate environment. Hence, the ecosystem can be regarded as the complex totality within which adaptation occurs (e.g., Moran 1990, Orlove 1980, Schulze and Zwölfer 1987). However, one characteristic of humans is their ability to deliberately influence, change and govern these relations by the implementation of social and cultural systems. Rather than just reacting to given conditions of the habitat occupied, they themselves change these conditions by altering their environment. Part of the human ecological niche, therefore, is to alter landscapes, manipulate biodiversity and alter flows of energy and matter, for example in order to increase the sustainability and efficiency of resource utilization (see Butzer 1982). It is obvious that humans do so, but part of the human niche is also related to how it happens and what effects it causes.

Information in an ecological sense usually refers to genetic structures underlying morphology and behaviour, and the fact that this genetic information is subject to evolutionary change. In order to achieve manipulation of flows within their ecosystems, humans make use of non-genetic information in a clearly unique way by transforming possibilities of shaping the environment into strategies, rules and arrangements, which are in turn part of their cultures and institutions. Culture, in all its complexity, stores information that allows short-term retrieval and change. Because information can be passed on tradi-genetically across generations, humans are able to stretch the time category within ecosystems and bridge it over periods longer than their average lifetimes. In doing so, they also perpetuate culture into a continuously exploitable, yet sustaining resource, making this a hallmark of their ecological niche. In utilising this capacity, no other

organism is able to alter its own environment with such an impact and in such an enormously lasting way. Ecosystems of this kind, shaped by humans, can only come into being because we are in part highly emancipated from our purely biological nature and because, instead, human life is essentially reliant on sets of rules regulating socio-cultural arrangements. Nevertheless, there are immediate consequences to the biology of humans, for example with regard to health or nutritional options or, in general terms, with regard to survival and reproduction (Moran and Gillet-Netting 2000).

Immediate outcomes of culturally determined actions and decisions that have an impact on human biology may not only be recognized in the living, but can be directly traced in ancient populations as well. Age structures, sex ratios, distribution of disease, diet – as discussed elsewhere in this section, all provide ample evidence of exactly such outcomes. Human skeletal finds, therefore, are biocultural archives, whose information can be deciphered by analytical methods and interpreted within an ecological framework. Human palaeobiology thus differs from the palaeobiology of any other living organism in that it is tightly connected with the impact of culture as a decisive ecological category that adds to the traditional notion. This, in turn, implies that human palaeobiology deals with the impact of human-made or at least human-altered landscapes. Biology and culture constitute the inseparable dual nature of humans. Hence, human palaeobiology will be able to make use of a genuine biological approach, the ecosystem concept and, as it incorporates culture as an ecological category, address the biocultural context within an integrative and consistent framework.

The interaction of humans and their environments, i.e., how they act as the hinges between socio-cultural, biotic and abiotic components of their ecosystems, can be very briefly described by addressing three issues: diet, demography, and disease.

Diet

Humans managed to successfully inhabit virtually all of the Earth's biomes. Their omnivorous nutritional behaviour is a necessary, but not a sufficient, assumption to explain how this came about. As a response to general ecological circumstances and specifically to limiting factors in their habitats humans develop strategies of food procurement that usually entail meshing in flows of energy and matter. In order to implement and sustain these strategies, socio-cultural arrangements and mechanisms of resource management become necessary and effective and can be regarded as adaptive solutions within the community to allow adjustment to the habitat for long-term survival.

The scope of existing modes of production, therefore, results from close integration of environmental conditions and the linkage of ecological factors and economic structures (Ellen 1982). They act back on modes of social organization and, by this token, constitute dependence of socio-cultural structures on qualities of the natural environment. However, not as stereotype responses, but in terms of probabilistic cultural mediation of environmental conditions as a typical feature of human communities. The more people depart from subsistence economies, the efficiency of food production is increasingly determined by being integrated into complex processes of energy transfer between various populations and habitats. Energetic efficiency and resource reliability become crucial factors of subsistence and require more and more elaborate resource management (Ulijaszek 1995).

Demography

Variance in the efficiency of resource management in turn has an effect on differential probabilities of survival and fertility. Because populations are tied into ecological relationships with their environment, operational decisions of manipulating flows of energy and matter occur and can be analysed in regard to reproductive effects. Individuals are likely to utilize the availability of energy as a means of increasing fitness. Human reproductive patterns are therefore tightly connected to economic options and strategies, i.e., to modes of production. Choice and exercise of a certain subsistence mode relates to options of a population to expand and thus to possibilities and conditions of reproduction. These, in turn, relate to resource distribution in a given habitat. Reproduction and resource supply are mutually interdependent.

Demographic structures of populations are the direct outcome of accumulated individual reproductive decisions in response to given ecological constraints and resource options. Population in an ecological sense refers to groups of individuals who reproductively interact, settle in the same habitat, and utilize a common resource basis. Population structure and dynamics is affected by common or different environmental settings that human populations are exposed to and

against which strategies evolve that serve to adjust size and composition of the population to the conditions of the respective habitat (Rogers 1992).

Change of characteristic population traits, such as density, size, fertility or mortality can thus be seen as being directly dependent of biotic, abiotic and cultural factors of the environment. Climate, soil quality or geomorphology, as well as the supply of animal and plant resources are connected with the possibilities of use and availability of resources in socio-ecological human ecosystems. This holds in particular for cultural factors, including technological skills to enhance efficiency of exploitation strategies and socio-cultural regulations relating to division of labour. Since these factors eventually aim at long-term survival in the habitat, adaptations to the ecological conditions of resource availability will affect cultural solutions to the basic biological problems of survival and reproduction. Genetic information is not sufficient here, but tradigenetic, cultural responses will eventually be decisive to the selective success of optimal resource utilization (see also Durham 1991).

A given population structure results from local environmental conditions and reactions to certain stressors present in the habitat, and availability of food resources is central to population size (e.g., Malthus 1798). Populations and the natural resources they use grow at different rates. As resources can only be increased in a linear fashion and populations have the intrinsic capacity of exponential growth, both curves will eventually diverge so that the available resources can no longer sustain the growing population. Checks, such as epidemics, war or famine will counteract and decimate population size to a number sustainable again by the available resources. Such external events, shortage of supply but also climatic change and disease vectors can be referred to as extrinsic factors.

Intrinsic factors influencing size and distribution of a population add to it. They result from such different variables as options of resource utilization due to membership of a social group, distribution of food within a family or household, attitudes of differential preference towards offspring of certain sex or contraceptive birth control. This entails taking a view of the limitation of population size in terms of natural selection. Basically, all organisms have the potential of unlimited amplification. However, hardly any species makes complete use of this potential, but instead, natural population sizes can be found. They are a result of selection, which in human populations not only acts on biological but also on socio-cultural traits.

Accordingly, any measure taken by an individual, any behaviour or characteristic put through by preferential selection within a population and thereby depressing population growth, will have a regulatory effect.

None of either extrinsic or intrinsic factors is effective in every population to the same degree or constantly across time. However, in changing combinations they add to maintain the overall stability of an ecosystem. Especially, the effect of intrinsic factors is suggestive of efficient mechanisms allowing for a flexible adjustment of population size or density to the available resources. If this leads to equilibrium on a local scale it can be regarded as a hint to adaptive population regulation (Wood 1998). And to put the case further, the adjustment of populations to certain densities may be seen as the cumulative effect of individual or familial reproductive decisions, which in sum lead to dynamic equilibria.

Disease

In the case of extrinsic factors, diseases especially contribute to the biotic components influencing probabilities of survival and reproduction. Within a general ecological explanatory model, therefore, the origin and diffusion of diseases is seen as an evolutionary interaction between pathogen, human host and the given environmental conditions supporting this interrelation. The notion of environment has to be enlarged by socio-cultural components within a human ecological context, which facilitate alterations of the natural habitats into ecosystems shaped by human activity and which constantly create modified settings for a co-evolution of pathogens and humans. Through selection of adaptive mechanisms, organisms are designed to achieve internal steady states in reaction to specific external conditions, which will allow survival with or despite the pathogen and ensure regular physiological and biochemical processes. In situations where an organism is not able to adequately react to the stressor, i.e., cannot provide an adaptive response (or not quickly enough), this will lead to the outbreak of a disease. Disease, therefore, is the result of insufficient adaptation of organisms to existing environmental conditions under the influence of pathogenic stressors (Goodman *et al.* 1988). Thus, within the co-evolutionary inter-relation of environment, host and pathogen, a balanced selection towards dynamic equilibria between these components may be expected.

Taking this into consideration, the diversity of environments created by humans resulted in regionally and temporally different disease patterns. Dependent on the conditions of natural units, contact with other populations, resource supply and subsistence techniques evolving from it, these environments sustain different population densities. Growth and density of populations are therefore correlated with the appearance of certain diseases and allow conclusions to be drawn about ecological conditions. This may even go as far as to predict marriage patterns and pathogen stress to be correlated in human populations for ultimate reasons of distributing genetic risk, in that areas of the world with high and varied pathogen prevalence tend to show higher rates of polygamy (e.g., Low 1990). Hence, in conditions where the habitat has a high pathogen load that may lead to considerable impairment of reproductive options, socio-culturally governed variance in marriage patterns aims at high genetic variability of offspring. The adaptive advantage is to ensure that even in the case of higher mortality caused by infectious diseases reproductive success can be optimized.

THE RESOURCE BASE

Given the scope of these and other topics discussed elsewhere in this section, human palaeobiology obviously represents mainstream avenues of epistemological and research interests as part of archaeological science. To achieve this, human palaeobiology needs reliable access to and availability of the most valuable resource we have at our disposal, the human remains themselves, be it on an evolutionary, historic or subrecent scale of our past. They are the most immediate and direct sources which can be researched for human strategies of coping with survival in different and changing environments through time. Even for those periods where written sources are available, no other archive allows for the scrutiny of hypotheses and data comparable in quality and potential message. This is why the curation of human remains collections is of paramount importance.

Claims for re-burial are increasingly raised and can lead to a significant impairment and shrinkage of what may be called the skeletal legacy of our past. Admittedly, this is a significant ethical issue – and no less so a political issue – and nobody would seriously ignore or question it. But two things should be kept in mind. Firstly, results arising from the study of human remains are of mutual interest to both the scientific community and the wider public. There is an immense general interest in exactly the same questions that are also at the focus of human palaeobiological research, revolving around human variation and adaptability. People are interested to learn why we are different, yet alike, and archaeological science has the means to serve this curiosity through meticulous and timely conceptual and methodological approaches. And there is no other way of achieving it. Archaeology without humans is like a stage without actors. Therefore, secondly, the responsible curation of human skeletal collections has only one justification – because we need to work with them and utilize them as an invaluable and unique biocultural archive. The outcome of this commitment is by no means confined to academia, but rather serves as a bridge between scientific and public interest. In this respect, the chapters in this section provide excellent examples to assure that human palaeobiology will be further able to attract broad scientific and public interest.

SUMMARY

Concluding from this brief outline, it appears to be evident that major fields of human palaeobiology are highly suitable to be analyzed and their results be interpreted as outcomes of the dynamic interaction of humans and their environments against the background of an ecological framework. Sophisticated analytical tools already allow deciphering parts of the complex nature of past human dietary patterns. This is the foundation to pursue this towards increasingly refined approaches, which will eventually reveal the quantification of ancient foodstuffs and detailed provenance in terms of position within human food webs or in terms of food items. This, of course, is a giant leap towards a more comprehensive understanding of palaeodietary behaviour in past human communities and will be the basis to relate differential resource utilization to environmental and population data.

As a prerequisite, quantitative ageing and molecular sexing techniques will provide the necessary quality of data needed to, more realistically, reconstruct past population structure and dynamics (see Chapters 20 and 25). Studies of aDNA will eventually provide kinship and genealogies (e.g., Gerstenberger et al. 1999) and will allow for the reconstruction of reproductive patterns. Taking these data into the context of dietary reconstruction, modes of production in past human populations and nutritional behaviour of individuals can finally be monitored against reproductive patterns. Differential reproductive success is in the reach of becoming explicable against patterns of past resource utilization. Likewise, this applies to the analysis of differential survival caused by environmentally-triggered disease vectors (Chapter 19).

The potential of an ecosystemic approach to the analysis and interpretation of human palaeobiological data is twofold. As has been shown, it provides an integrative conceptual framework to correlate the complex interaction of humans within their habitats, and it relatively straightforwardly relates to a limited number of well-defined categories being effective in governing ecosystem relationships. The addition of culture as a typically human ecological category and the modification of the time category enhance the application of the concept rather than violate it. Finally, combining different ecological viewpoints, such as system, population, and behaviour enables directly relating, for example, patterns of resource exploitation to the sustainability of populations and reproductive decisions. This, in turn, adds a new quality, in that proximate goals in human populations, related for example to subsistence and survival can be interpreted on a generic level of questions dealing with adaptation, e.g., in terms of ultimate goals relating to reproductive success and fitness differentials. This will eventually allow integrating the impact of modes of production and modes of reproduction in past human societies.

REFERENCES

*Recommended for further reading

*Butzer, K.W. (1982). *Archaeology as Human Ecology.* Cambridge University Press: Cambridge.
*Durham, W.H. (1991). *Coevolution. Genes, Culture and Human Diversity.* Stanford University Press: Stanford.
Ellen, R. (1982). *Environment, Subsistence and System. The Ecology of Small-Scale Social Formations.* Cambridge University Press: Cambridge.
Gerstenberger, J., Hummel, S., Schultes, T., Häck, B. and Herrmann, B. (1999). Reconstruction of a historical genealogy by means of STR analysis and Y-haplotyping of ancient DNA. *European Journal of Human Genetics*, 7:469–477.
Goodman, A.H., Brookes Thomas, R., Swedlund, A.C. and Armelagos, G.H. (1988). Biocultural perspective and stress in prehistoric, historical and contemporary population research. *Yearbook of Physical Anthropology*, **31**:169–202.
Greenblatt, C.L. (ed.) (1998). *Digging for Pathogens.* Center for the Study of Emerging Diseases, Jerusalem, Balabat Publishers: Rehovot.
Herrmann, B. and Hummel, S. (eds) (1994). *Ancient DNA. Recovery and Analysis of Genetic Material from Paleontological, Archeological, Museum, Medical, and Forensic Specimens.* Springer-Verlag: New York.

Katzenberg, M.A. and Harrison, R.G. (1997). What's in a bone? Recent advances in archaeological bone chemistry. *Journal of Archaeological Research*, **5**:265–293.

Low, B.S. (1990). Marriage systems and pathogen stress in human societies. *American Zoologist*, **30**:325–339.

Malthus, T. (1798). *Essay on the Principle of Population*. Pickering: London (reprinted 1986).

Moran, E.F. (1990). Ecosystem ecology in biology and anthropology: a critical assessment. In Moran, E.F. (ed.) *The Ecosystem Approach in Anthropology. From Concept to Practice*, 3–40. University of Michigan Press: Ann Arbor.

*Moran, E.F. and Gillet-Netting, R. (eds) (2000). *Human Adaptability. An Introduction to Ecological Anthropology*. Westview Press: Boulder.

Odum, E.P. (1973). *Fundamentals of Ecology*, (3rd edn). W.B. Saunders and Co.: Philadelphia.

Orlove, B.S. (1980). Ecological anthropology. *Annual Reviews of Anthropology*, **9**:235–273.

Rogers, A.R. (1992). Resources and population dynamics. In Smith, E.A. and Winterhalder, B. (eds) *Evolutionary Ecology and Human Behaviour*, 375–402. Aldine de Gruyter: New York.

Schulze, E.D. and Zwölfer, H. (eds) (1987). *Potentials and Limitations of Ecosystem Analysis*. Springer-Verlag: Berlin.

Ulijaszek, S.J. (1995). *Human Energetics in Biological Anthropology*. Cambridge University Press: Cambridge.

Wood, J.W. (1998). A theory of pre-industrial population dynamics. *Current Anthropology*, **39**:99–135.

19

Disease Ecology

D.J. ORTNER

Department of Anthropology, National Museum of Natural History, Smithsonian Institution
and
Department of Archaeological Sciences, University of Bradford.

Pathogenic agents are a ubiquitous part of the environment in which we live, including the air we breath, the water we drink, the plants and animals we eat, and the ground on which we walk. Pathogens include infectious organisms and non-living toxic materials that can cause disease either by their presence or their presence in excessive amounts. Disease can also be caused by the lack of substances in the environment, such as trace elements, that are necessary for health. Infectious agents include prions, viruses, fungi, bacteria, protozoa, and multicelled parasites.

Humans, far more than any other species, modify the natural environment in ways that affect our own health. Cultural innovation often creates new conditions in the environment that can have a major impact on the prevalence of disease in a given human society. The development of agriculture, for example, meant interacting with the soil in ways that greatly increased the exposure of agriculturists to soil-borne infectious agents such as fungi. Irrigation, whilst providing a more controllable source of water needed for farming, supplied a more favourable environment for many disease organisms. Domestication of animals brought mankind a more predictable source of protein. It also created a much closer relationship with animal *vectors* (carriers) of infectious diseases and increased the ex-

posure of people to these diseases, often with serious consequences. These factors highlight the complexity of disease and the environmental conditions that affect its expression. Although culture is the creation of people, its impact on the environment is so substantial that no attempt to understand the ecological context of human disease can overlook this dimension of human existence (Brown *et al.* 1996).

Environmental factors that contribute to human disease include:

  (i) infectious organisms,
 (ii) climate,
(iii) vegetation,
 (iv) food (both type and abundance) available to a human group,
  (v) potentially toxic substances in the environment,
 (vi) lack of essential elements in the soil and/or water, and
(vii) cultural traits, both within a human society and the cultural elements of other societies that impact in some way on the health of a given human society.

These variables also interact in many different ways and this contributes to the complexity that makes

Handbook of Archaeological Sciences. Edited by D.R. Brothwell and A.M. Pollard.
© 2001 John Wiley & Sons, Ltd.

understanding the role of the environment in human disease a challenging exercise. Our knowledge of disease in human communities is further complicated by the dimension of time and the evolutionary changes that occur through time. The following paragraphs emphasize the importance of infectious agents as a critical factor in the environment of human groups. However, it is important to remember that other environmental variables have an important impact on the prevalence and severity of human disease.

The presence of a specific pathogen in a specific human environment is highly variable and subject to many factors, including temperature, humidity, rainfall, and the daily, as well as seasonal, variation of all three. How the human organism interacts with an infectious agent, toxic substances, and the dietary absence of elements critical to normal body metabolism is modulated by several factors that determine if illness (*morbidity*) and/or death (*mortality*) will occur. The most fundamental of these factors is the immune response of the individual to an infectious organism. The immune response includes all the biological mechanisms the body uses to defend itself against infectious agents and toxic substances. Our genetic heritage plays a significant role in determining the effectiveness of the immune system and the immunity or lack of immunity to one or more organisms that occurs in some human individuals and populations (Janeway and Travers 1994, Ewald 1994).

In a typical, pre-industrial, archaeological cemetery, between 40 and 50 per cent of the individuals died before reaching sexual maturity. Infectious disease, or complications from infection, probably was the most common cause of death. Natural selection operating on genetic variability in the immune response provides a mechanism for infectious disease to be a significant factor in human evolution. Because of major cultural and demographic changes during the past 10 000 years that increased exposure of people to infectious pathogens, infection probably has accounted for a higher percentage of mortality during this period than in earlier stages of human evolution. However, the evidence needed to support this hypothesis is difficult to obtain and interpret. Most of the biological response to infectious pathogens occurs at the cellular and molecular levels of organization in the living individual and rarely affects the human skeletal remains recovered from an archaeological site. Recent research on ancient DNA and other biomolecules recovered from archaeological human skeletons is a promising methodological development for studying disease in past human populations (Kolman and Tuross 2000) but preserva-

tion of bone tissue is often inadequate for this type of analysis (see Chapter 25).

Despite the current paucity of hard evidence for disease in antiquity, the general principles of the relationship between disease, particularly infectious disease, and human groups or populations are both plausible and well known. Our hunter-gatherer ancestors probably had a very different relationship with infectious disease than did the early sedentary agriculturists (Cockburn 1963:46). The advent of cities in human history and the emergence of larger and more dense human occupation of habitation sites greatly changed the role of disease in human society (e.g., Cohen and Armelagos 1984a). Two likely effects were an increase in the number of pathogens that affected human groups and an increased likelihood of exposure to those pathogens that were present.

The fundamental question explored here is what is the ecological context of human disease and how has it changed throughout human prehistory and history? This is not a new question. Hooton, a biological (physical) anthropologist at Harvard University, published a remarkable study of a large archaeological human skeletal sample from the American south-west. In this report he speculated on disease trends through time (Hooton 1930:320) that certainly had an important ecological context. Angel (1946), a student of Hooton and a biological anthropologist, made a plausible case for a relationship between cultural growth and increased human biological diversity using data from human skeletal samples from archaeological sites in the Eastern Mediterranean. Cockburn (1963), a physician with international experience in public health, explored the relevance of evolutionary processes on the history and evolution of human infectious disease. Hudson (1968:9) and Hackett (1963:31) showed a link between the four syndromes of treponematosis and different environmental conditions. McNeill (1976) dealt with many similar issues in his historical study of epidemic infectious diseases that had such a dramatic impact on human populations. Cohen, an archaeologist, and Armelagos, a biological anthropologist, co-edited a major work (1984b) that explored the relationship between changing economy and health of human populations. Evolutionary perspectives on human health and disease have been the focus of two fairly recent publications (Ewald 1994, Nesse and Williams 1994). More recently, Larsen (1997), a biological anthropologist, demonstrated a link between increased social stress and a decline in health based on evidence from the human remains associated with archaeological sites in the American south-east.

The ecological context in which human groups exist is a complex, interrelated mixture of many factors that affect the human response to disease. A comprehensive treatment of this subject would fill a large book. The objectives of this chapter are more modest and limited to a few illustrative highlights of environmental factors that affect human vulnerability to disease. These include:

(i) animal vectors, particularly those related to domesticated animals,
(ii) the quantity, quality, and utilization of food resources,
(iii) demographic factors, particularly population size and density,
(iv) environmental conditions, and
(v) cultural factors including the patterns of interaction between individuals and groups of people as well as cultural innovations such as irrigation.

ANIMAL VECTORS IN HUMAN DISEASE

One of the important cultural innovations linked to agriculture is the domestication of animals that, among other things, provide a more regular source of food directly with meat but also from secondary animal products such as milk and eggs. However, animals are common vectors in the transmission of infectious disease to humans (Brothwell 1991). In more recent history the devastating depopulation brought about by infectious epidemics provides eloquent testimony regarding the impact infectious pathogens can have on human societies. Plague, caused by a bacterial infectious agent (*Yersinia pestis*) that is transmitted to humans by fleas carried by rats, resulted in the death of as much as a third of the population in Medieval England (Howe 1997:90). Today, malaria, a disease caused by protozoa transmitted by mosquitoes, is a major public health problem in many developing countries. Angel's (1966) research supports the hypothesis that malaria was a significant cause of illness and death at least 8000 years ago.

Animals undoubtedly have been a vector for human infection well before the advent of agriculture. However, the intensity of human/animal vector interaction increased dramatically with domestication. The history of animal domestication is still being clarified through archaeological research. Dogs probably were domesticated as long ago as 12 000 BP and goats around 9900 BP (Zeder pers. comm.). Current evidence traces sheep and pig domestication to about 9000 BP

and cattle shortly thereafter, certainly by 8000 BP. All of these animals transmit infectious pathogens to mankind. The remainder of this section reviews briefly three diseases in people that are linked at least initially to domestic animal vectors: (i) tuberculosis, (ii) brucellosis, and (iii) echinococcosis. These diseases can also affect the human skeleton and anatomical evidence of pathological lesions may be apparent in archaeological human skeletons.

Aurochs, the wild ancestor of cattle, were domesticated in the Near East by about 8000 BP (Smith 1995:65). Before the domestication of cattle, tuberculosis was uncommon; the infected animals quickly died from the disease or were killed by predators before they could pass the disease to very many other animals within their species (Cockburn 1963:220). Bringing more animals together in relatively small spaces increased their risk of infectious disease (Hare 1967:117) and protection from predators permitted sick animals to survive longer and transmit their diseases to more animals and people. The evidence of possible tuberculosis in human skeletal remains dating to the Late Neolithic and Early Bronze Age (Ortner 1979) suggests that the disease was probably present in cattle herds early in the process of domestication. Following domestication, tuberculosis most likely became a much more serious problem for both cattle and the human groups who domesticated them (Manchester 1984:163). The closer contact between domesticated animals and their human caretakers increased the exposure of these people to infectious diseases carried by the animals. Bovine tuberculosis is caused by *Mycobacterium bovis* and normally enters the human host via the gastrointestinal portal. However, there is no reason why the infection could not have been transmitted to the human respiratory tract of the herders by droplets from infected cattle as they coughed or sneezed.

Although the close proximity of human cattle herders to infected animals would have made them more vulnerable to tuberculosis, non-herders could have acquired the disease by eating contaminated meat. When milk became a common source of food around 5–7000 years ago (Simoons 1979:62) human exposure to tuberculosis became even greater. However, the greatest threat to humankind from tuberculosis probably occurred when the organism adapted for human to human transmission (Daniel 1981:35). This adaptation by the tubercle bacillus (*Mycobacterium tuberculosis*) when combined with increasing population size and greater concentrations of people in cities provided optimum conditions for the maintenance of the organism in the host population and for the transmission of the disease between people. Determining when this adaptation occurred is a difficult problem since the most typical skeletal lesions of tuberculosis are in the vertebrae (Figures 19.1 and 19.2) and both bovine and human variants are similar. The evolutionary development of tuberculosis in its relationship with the human host illustrates how cultural innovations, in this case domestication of cattle, can change the relationship between mankind and the environment. However, this initial change may be further complicated by adaptation of the organism to other modes of transmission (human to human) that can be even more serious.

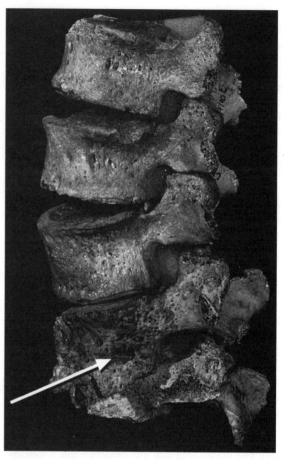

Figure 19.2 Lateral view of the lumbar vertebrae seen in Figure 19.1. Note the reactive bone formation apparent on the fourth vertebral body that contains an opening for draining pus (arrow) from the chronic infection.

The development of PCR methods for copying DNA segments from archaeological human remains offers the potential for clarifying the history and evolution of tuberculosis and other infectious diseases (see Chapter 25). There are reports about the recovery and identification of DNA from infectious pathogens extracted from human skeletal remains (e.g., Salo *et al.* 1994, Spigelman and Donoghue 1999, Zink *et al.* 1999). However, the cautionary comments about the problems of contamination need to be taken seriously (Kolman and Tuross 2000). There is an additional complication in that DNA is often not preserved well enough in archaeological human skeletal remains for this methodology to be used.

Brucellosis is an infectious disease that in humans is caused by any one of three strains of the bacterium

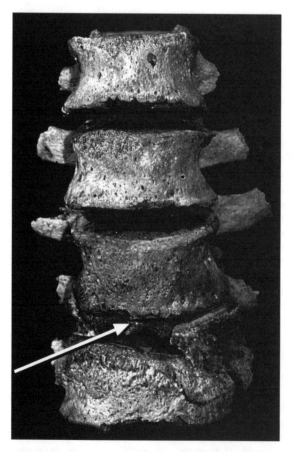

Figure 19.1 Anterior view of a case of probable tuberculosis of the lower spine in an adolescent skeleton excavated from the Early Bronze Age (*c.* 3100 BC) site of Bab edh-Dhra' in Jordan (BD '77, burial A100E-73). The focus of the destructive process is the fourth lumbar vertebral body (arrow) which has collapsed.

Brucella melitensis. There are several potential animal vectors, including pigs, goats and cattle. The disease can be acquired by eating poorly cooked, contaminated meat of any of these vectors. Today the disease most often is caused by ingesting contaminated cows' milk or milk products such as cheese. Unlike tuberculosis, brucellosis regularly involves more than one site within the skeleton and in the spine (Figures 19.3 and 19.4) the destructive processes associated with the disease rarely cause collapse of the vertebral bodies (Ortner and Putschar 1985:138, Bishop 1939).

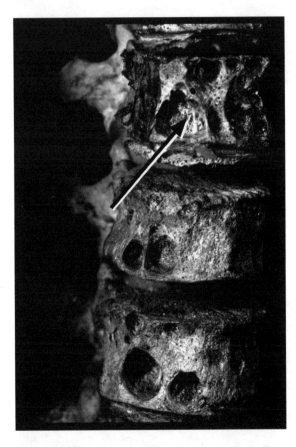

Figure 19.3 Anterior view of three thoracic vertebrae (T10–T12) with multiple destructive sites in the vertebral bodies and evidence of considerable repair within the destructive lesions. The case is from the Schreiner Collection (Catalogue no. 1338), Anatomy Institute University of Oslo. The skeleton is an adult male about 19 years of age at the time of death from the site of Tysfjord, Nordland, Norway. Note that the vertebral bodies have not collapsed. The multiple sites, the repair within the lesion, and the absence of vertebral body collapse support a diagnosis of brucellosis or possibly echinococcosis but not tuberculosis.

Anderson (1968:996, 1028) provides a brief description of a fragmentary skeleton from Nubia (Site 117, Burial 17) that is tentatively dated, by stone tool association (Qadan industry) to between 13 000 and 5000 BC (Wendorf 1968:990). Anderson notes a Swiss cheese-like destructive process of T12–L2 vertebrae that he associates with early spinal tuberculosis. There is no mention of vertebral body collapse, kyphosis, or involvement of the vertebral arches. Circular destructive lesions of the vertebral body without collapse could be an early manifestation of tuberculosis but are more suggestive of brucellosis or echinococcosis. Since one of the potential vectors of brucellosis is the goat, this disease may occur earlier in human history than tuberculosis.

Echinococcosis is a disease caused by the larval stage of a tapeworm *Echinococcus granulosus*. The tapeworm normally occupies the small intestine of dogs including wild varieties. Intermediate hosts include sheep, pigs, cattle, deer, and humans. The eggs containing the larvae of the tapeworm are passed to the environment via dog faeces. After being ingested by an intermediate host, the tissue shell containing the larvae dissolves freeing the larvae which penetrate the intestinal walls of the host and enter the blood or lymphatic system. They most often affect the liver or lungs but can affect any tissue including bone although this is a relatively rare occurrence. In bone the most common site is marrow, particularly the spongy bone of the vertebral column and pelvis (Resnick and Niwayama 1995:2540).

In archaeological human burials echinococcus may be expressed in two ways. The first of these is the mineralized connective tissue shell created by the body of the host to isolate the larvae that have invaded soft tissue or an organ. These mineralized shells tend to be ovoid and range in size from two centimetres to many centimetres in their long axes. Because of the predilection by the larvae for the liver and lungs these shells will most often occur in the region of the abdominal or chest cavity. They can easily be overlooked during excavation of a human burial which may account for relatively few cases in published reports. The mineralized remains of this tissue (Figure 19.5) are virtually diagnostic of echinococcosis and a few archaeological cases of this disease have been published (Wells and Dallas 1976, Ortner and Putschar 1985:229).

If the larvae invade bone marrow they normally do not stimulate the formation of a connective tissue shell. However, the larvae tend to cluster and create a destructive zone in spongy bone around the cluster. Compact bone may form at the margins of the destructive lesion creating the sclerotic margin apparent in

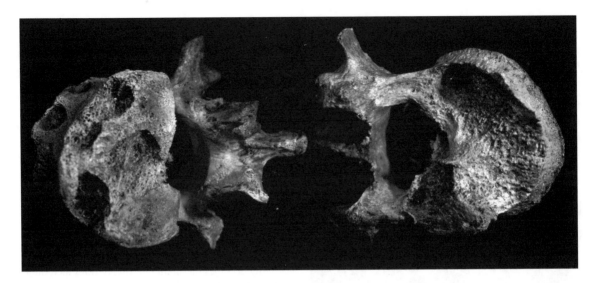

Figure 19.4   Reflected view of L1–L2 vertebrae from the Schreiner Collection (Catalogue no. 1338) showing multiple destructive lesions of the vertebral body. Despite the extensive destruction there is no evidence of vertebral body collapse.

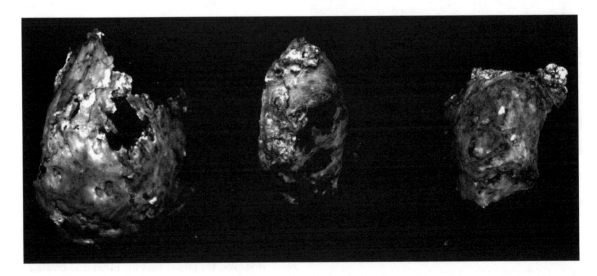

Figure 19.5   Mineralized hydatid cysts from Kodiak Island, Alaska, USA, associated with the skeleton of an adult female. Skeleton formerly in the collections of the National Museum of Natural History (Catalogue no. 374623), now repatriated and reburied.

radiographs. Because destructive lesions in bone often occur in the lower spine, the lesions can easily be confused with tuberculosis or brucellosis. However, similar to brucellosis and unlike tuberculosis, multiple sites of infection are common.

Because the most common vector of echinococcosis is the dog the disease will be linked with the domestication of dogs which, as noted earlier, occurred as early as 12 000 BP. The complex life history of the pathogen also involves the intermediate hosts and exposure to humans would have increased when sheep were domesticated (by 9000 BP) and dogs used in managing the sheep herds.

ECONOMIES AND FOOD RESOURCES: THEIR EFFECT ON HUMAN DISEASE

Throughout most of human prehistory, food was obtained by hunting and gathering. Indeed this type of economy remains a significant way of obtaining food resources in many human societies today. In some of these societies the food resources obtained from hunting and gathering are supplemented with slash-and-burn agriculture (Neel 1983:79). There are important dimensions of a hunting/gathering economy that affect human disease prevalence. Hunter/gatherer societies tend to be fairly small and isolated from other human societies. Many infectious diseases and particularly those caused by some viruses depend on relatively large host population size for survival and reproduction and would not have been extant in hunter/gatherer societies when this was the only economy present (Cockburn 1963). Today, of course, hunter/gatherers do come in contact with people from agricultural and industrial economies where population sizes are sufficient to maintain diseases caused by agents that require large host populations. The effect of these contacts often results in tragic illness and death (Neel 1982).

Another aspect of typical hunter/gatherer societies that affects disease prevalence is a diet that tends to be more varied than agricultural societies. This diversity of diet reduces the risk of dietary deficiencies and starvation (Cohen and Armelagos 1984a). This, in turn, reduces the risk of disease from infectious agents. Agricultural economies are linked to critical cultural and social changes that profoundly affect the relationship between infectious pathogens and human groups. Agriculturists are sedentary and tend to live in larger clusters of people. Because of the sedentary nature of an agricultural economy, disposal of garbage and human waste is a more serious problem than with

hunter/gatherers and this increases exposure to infectious pathogens.

Agricultural economies tend to be much more specialized in their reliance on food sources. Reduced dietary diversity increases the risk of nutritional deficiencies although creating the potential of increased caloric input per person. The other risk was famine and the lack of backup food sources if the crop failed. The diverse food resources of the hunter/gatherer provides greater flexibility when confronted by diminished food supplies.

DEMOGRAPHIC FACTORS IN HUMAN DISEASE

Age distribution, sex distribution, and population size are demographic factors that influence the type and prevalence of diseases found in human groups. Sex distributions have probably remained relatively constant throughout human history although short-term variation due to biological and culturally-defined differences between the sexes would certainly have occurred. Until very recently life expectancy has varied within a relatively narrow range with high infant mortality and very few people living past fifty years of age. Infectious pathogens have the most serious impact on infants, children and the very old. Some of the other diseases such as cancer and arthritis predominantly affect people after age fifty. In societies where few people live past fifty these diseases will be much less common. The much greater life expectancy enjoyed by people living today in developed countries is a very recent development in human history and has greatly increased the prevalence of diseases associated with ageing.

Population size is the major demographic factor that has changed dramatically in the past 10–15 000 years of human history (Hassan 1983). The increase in population size and density increases the risk of person-to-person transmission of infectious diseases but also provides a greater supply of hosts enhancing the ability of a pathogen to survive in a host population. The relationship between the host population size and the survival of a type of disease organism in a human host population depends on several factors. One of these is the mode of transmission which may be water-borne, vector-borne, air-borne, and person-to-person. There are organisms that can survive in fairly small and isolated human groups (Neel 1983:77). However, many viruses that are pathogenic to mankind need a fairly large human host population to provide the pool of hosts needed to survive and propagate (Cockburn 1963:84). Such viruses were unlikely to have been a significant source of infection before the development of urbanism about 8000 years ago.

ENVIRONMENTAL FACTORS IN HUMAN DISEASE

The classic epidemiological studies of treponematosis by Hackett (1963) and Hudson (1968) demonstrated a geographical distribution of the four syndromes that strongly suggests a link to different environmental conditions. The authors used modern data as the basis for speculating on the evolution of these syndromes. The four syndromes are: (i) pinta, (ii) yaws, (iii) bejel (also called endemic syphilis), and (iv) syphilis. Yaws is seen mostly in tropical regions of the world, bejel in the dry, grassland areas, and syphilis in the temperate zones. The fourth syndrome, pinta, is seen only in the tropical areas of South America.

Three of the four syndromes (yaws, bejel, and syphilis) cause skeletal lesions in some patients. Pinta is mostly a skin disease and does not affect the skeleton. Skeletal lesions in yaws, bejel, and syphilis are similar although there has been some effort to distinguish between the bone changes in the three syndromes (e.g., Steinbock 1976:86). However, the morphological overlap between the three syndromes is great and assigning a case of archaeological skeletal treponematosis to a specific syndrome on the basis of anatomical evidence is speculative at best. Recent research (Centurion-Lara et al. 1998) demonstrates variation in DNA between two of the syndromes of treponematosis so it may be possible to distinguish these syndromes in well-preserved archaeological cases of this disease. The question remains regarding whether or not environmental differences associated with these syndromes were the determining factor in the clinical differences that exist or whether the clinical differences are the result of other factors such as the age of onset and chance variation in the history of the syndromes.

Powell (1988:168) reviewed the evidence for pre-Columbian treponematosis in North American skeletal samples from Illinois and Alabama. The most typical pathological feature was a bone-forming lesion of the lower extremity. The presence of these lesions, when combined with other evidence for treponematosis, does argue for the presence of this disease in pre-Columbian skeletal samples. However, other pathological conditions can produce these lesions as well and caution is needed in interpreting the data.

The link between standing water and particularly marshy environments and the vector of malaria (caused by protozoa of the genus Plasmodium), carried by mosquitoes of the genus Anopheles, has been established since Sir Ronald Ross described the life cycle of the parasite in the latter part of the nineteenth century (Krogstad 1999:737). The evolutionary dynamics between the parasite and the human host have been the focus of major research and speculation for almost as long. The abnormal haemoglobins in the human host that interfere with the life cycle of the parasite are one of the adaptive mechanisms that exist within some human host populations. Two abnormal haemoglobins are those that cause the diseases sickle cell anaemia and thalassaemia. These diseases have significant morbidity and mortality and the genes for these diseases would normally be eliminated through natural selection. However, since the protozoa are less able to reproduce in individuals having these abnormal blood proteins, people with the partial (heterozygous) expression of the gene are less affected by malaria. The abnormal haemoglobin in the red blood cells stimulates increased red blood cell turnover and the demand for increased space within the skeleton for blood formation (haematopoietic marrow). The anatomical evidence of this disease is largely limited to the skeletons of children. The occurrence of affected skeletons provides evidence of anaemia in archaeological burial sites. Angel (1966) used this anatomical feature to trace the history of anaemia and malaria back in time in the Eastern Mediterranean.

Very local environmental conditions may have a significant effect on human health. Smoke from open fires may be the cause of the increased prevalence of naso-pharyngeal cancer in societies where this type of fire is used for cooking or heating (Wells 1964:75). Toxic levels of fluorine occur in the water supply in some regions of the world and result in disease affecting people living in these regions (Ortner and Putschar 1985:288). The lack of iodine in the soil and water in high elevations, including some areas of the Alps, can cause hypothyroidism and the dwarfism and mental deficiency associated with this disease.

CULTURAL FACTORS IN HUMAN DISEASE

Cultural factors impact on human disease in multiple ways that range from relatively direct influence to those that are indirect. In many, although certainly not all, traditional human societies, there is a definite social hierarchy in access to food (Ortner 1998). Adult men tend to be at the top of this hierarchy followed by boys, women and, lastly, girls. In times of plenty, the effect of this hierarchy is probably minimal but in situations where protein/calorie resources are inadequate the effect on women and girls may result in malnutrition or starvation as a direct effect of this cultural tradition. However, poor nutrition is also an indirect factor in disease through its linkage with an increased vulnerability to infectious and other diseases.

There are also gender related differences in exposure to infectious disease that are the result of culturally determined roles for men and women. In hunter/gatherer societies men tend to do the hunting and women the gathering. In agricultural societies men usually do the heavy work of ploughing in which exposure to soil-borne diseases, particularly those caused by fungi, is great. This gender difference is true in developed countries and is a major factor in the much greater prevalence of mycotic diseases in men (Utz 1989). It is likely that gender difference in mycotic disease prevalence is characteristic of earlier agricultural communities as well.

Cultural innovation is one of the defining features of human evolution. We have already highlighted some of the problems that resulted from large scale cultural changes such as sedentism, the development of agricultural economies, and urbanism. Smaller scale cultural innovations also affect mankind's vulnerability to disease. Water is critical to agriculture so it is not surprising that enhancing access to and control of this resource was an early innovation. Irrigation extends back in time to at least the Chalcolithic period (Helms 1981) in the Near East (c. 4000–3000 BC). Schistosomiasis is a human disease caused by flat worms in which sheep and goats are common vectors but with a mollusc as an intermediate host. Because of the importance of water in the life cycle of the parasite, irrigation canals and other artificial water reservoirs are an ideal place for these organisms to thrive (Brown et al. 1996:208). Herd animals like sheep and goats drink the water and, through their faecal droppings contaminate other water sources. Human exposure in such an environment is inevitable and schistosomiasis is very prevalent in developing countries where herd animals and irrigation are used. It seems likely that water-borne diseases would have increased significantly in past human populations with the introduction of irrigation.

Perhaps the most dramatic example of cultural influence on disease is the relationship between cannibalism and kuru. This disease was first described amongst the Fore of Papua New Guinea and initially was thought to be caused by a virus. It is transmitted when tribal

members eat the brain of another member who died with the disease. It is now known to be one of a group of similar diseases caused by prions, an infectious protein, that includes Kreutzfeldt-Jakob disease that affects humans and the animal disease scrapie (Prusiner 1998). All affect the nervous system and all are fatal.

CONCLUSIONS

The preceding paragraphs have provided some examples of the interaction between various components of the environment and human disease. These examples highlight the fact that the environment is an important factor. This is particularly the case with infectious diseases where the relationship between infectious agents and human hosts is a continuously evolving competition between two organisms played out in a constantly changing environment. The biological adaptation that takes place involves co-evolution in which the pathogen responds to the adaptive adjustments of the host as the host population develops a more effective immune response to the infectious agent.

This co-evolution involves different strategies by both the pathogen and the host. Ewald (1994:34) notes that death is rarely a good defence mechanism against infection and the death of the host rarely benefits the pathogen. Earlier thinking on the subject hypothesized that host/pathogen co-evolution is characterized by attenuation of virulence in the pathogen and improved immune response by the host (Cockburn 1963:35, McNeill 1976:9) leading to an increasingly benign relationship and chronic disease. More recently other hypotheses have been proposed that address the biological complexity of this relationship (Ewald 1994, Nesse and Williams 1994). Basically pathogen virulence is related to trade-offs associated with different levels of virulence. In other words, there are situations where increased virulence is beneficial to the pathogen species even when the host dies if the pathological process provides an effective method of infecting new hosts. Diarrhoea, for example, is a host response to infectious agents that can, and often does, result in the death of the host primarily because of severe dehydration. Organisms that stimulate this response will normally die with the host but if they infect other hosts before the primary host dies, severe diarrhoea may be beneficial to the pathogen species as is the case in cholera and some other infectious diseases. The important point is that pathogen species survival is the evolutionary objective and there are several strategies for achieving this objective many of which are part of or affected by environmental conditions.

ACKNOWLEDGEMENTS

I greatly appreciate the assistance of Mrs Agnes Stix, Department of Anthropology, National Museum of Natural History (NMNH), Smithsonian Institution in preparing the figures and conducting bibliographic searches. The author also appreciates the contribution of Mrs Marcia Bakry, Department of Anthropology, NMNH who was responsible for preparing the final version of the figures. Dr Melinda A. Zeder, Department of Anthropology, NMNH provided the information on the archaeological dating for the earliest evidence of domestication of various animals.

REFERENCES

*Recommended for further reading

Anderson, J.E. (1968). Late Paleolithic skeletal remains from Nubia. In Wendorf, F. (ed.) *The Prehistory of Nubia*, 996–1040. Southern Methodist University Press: Dallas.

Angel, J.L. (1946). Social biology of Greek culture growth. *American Anthropologist*, **48**:493–533.

Angel, J.L. (1966). Porotic hyperostosis, anemias, malarias, and marshes in the Prehistoric Eastern Mediterranean. *Science*, **153**:760–763.

Bishop, W.A. (1939). Vertebral lesions in undulant fever. *Journal of Bone and Joint Surgery*, **21**:665–673.

Brothwell, D.R. (1991). On zoonoses and their relevance to paleopathology. In Ortner, D.J. and Aufderheide, A.C. (eds) *Human Paleopathology*, 18–22. Smithsonian Institution Press: Washington DC.

Brown, P.J., Inhorn, M.C. and Smith, D.J. (1996). Disease, ecology, and human behavior. In Sargent, C.F. and Johnson, T.M. (eds) *Handbook of Medical Anthropology*, 183–218. Greenwood Press: Westport, Connecticut.

Centurion-Lara, A., Castro, C., Castillo, R., Shaffer, J.M., Van Voorhis, W.C. and Lukehart, S.A. (1998). The flanking region of sequences of the 15-kDa lipoprotein gene differentiate pathogenic treponemes. *Journal of Infectious Diseases*, **177**:1036–1040.

*Cockburn, T.A. (1963). *The Evolution and Eradication of Infectious Diseases*. Johns Hopkins Press: Baltimore.

Cohen, M.N. and Armelagos, G.J. (1984a). Paleopathology at the origins of agriculture: editors' summation. In Cohen, M.N. and Armelagos, G.J. (eds) *Paleopathology at the Origins of Agriculture*, 585–601. Academic Press: Orlando.

Cohen, M.N. and Armelagos, G.J. (eds) (1984b). *Paleopathology at the Origins of Agriculture*. Academic Press: Orlando.

Daniel, T.M. (1981). An immunologist's view of the epidemiology of tuberculosis. In Buikstra, J.E. (ed.) *Prehistoric Tuberculosis in the Americas*, 35–38. Northwestern University Archeological Program: Evanston, Illinois.

*Ewald, P.W. (1994). *Evolution of Infectious Disease*. Oxford University Press: Oxford.

Hackett, C.J. (1963). On the origin of the human treponematoses. *Bulletin of the World Health Organization*, **29**:7–41.

Hare, R. (1967). The antiquity of diseases caused by bacteria and viruses, a review of the problem from a bacteriologist's point of view. In Brothwell, D. and Sandison, A.T. (eds) *Diseases in Antiquity*, 115–131. Charles C. Thomas: Springfield, Illinois.

Hassan, F.A. (1983). Earth resources and population: an archeological perspective. In Ortner, D.J. (ed.) *How Humans Adapt: A Biocultural Odyssey*, 191–226. Smithsonian Institution Press: Washington DC.

Helms, S.W. (1981). *Jawa: Lost City of the Black Desert*. Cornell University Press: Ithaca, New York.

Hooton, E.A. (1930). *The Indians of Pecos Pueblo*. Yale University Press: New Haven.

Howe, G.M. (1997). *People, Environment, Disease and Death*. University of Wales Press: Cardiff.

Hudson, E.H. (1968). Christopher Columbus and the history of syphilis. *Acta Tropica*, **25**:1–16.

Janeway, C.A. and Travers, P. (1994). *Immunobiology*. Garland Publishing: New York.

Kolman, C.J. and Tuross, N. (2000). Ancient DNA analysis of human populations. *American Journal of Physical Anthropology*, **111**:5–23.

Krogstad, D.J. (1999). Malaria. In Guerrant, R.L., Walker, D.H. and Weller, P.F. (eds) *Tropical Infectious Diseases*, 736–766. Churchill Livingstone: Philadelphia.

*Larsen, C.S. (1997). *Bioarchaeology: Interpreting Behavior from the Human Skeleton*. Cambridge University Press: Cambridge.

Manchester, K. (1984). Tuberculosis and leprosy in antiquity: an interpretation. *Medical History*, **28**:162–173.

McNeill, W.H. (1976). *Plagues and Peoples*. Anchor Press: Garden City, New York.

Neel, J.V. (1982). Infectious disease among amerindians. *Medical Anthropology*, **6**:47–55.

Neel, J.V. (1983). Some base lines for human evolution and the genetic implications of recent cultural developments. In Ortner, D.J. (ed.) *How Humans Adapt: A Biocultural Odyssey*, 67–93. Smithsonian Institution Press: Washington DC.

Nesse, R.M. and Williams, G.C. (1994). *Why We Get Sick*. Times Books: New York.

Ortner, D.J. (1979). Disease and mortality in the Early Bronze Age people of Bab edh-Dhra', Jordan. *American Journal of Physical Anthropology*, **51**:589–598.

Ortner, D.J. (1998). Male/female immune reactivity and its implications for interpreting evidence in human skeletal paleopathology. In Grauer, A. and Stuart-Macadam, P.

(eds) *Sex and Gender in Paleopathological Perspective*, 79–92. Cambridge University Press: Cambridge.

*Ortner, D.J. and Putschar, W.G.J. (1985). *Identification of Pathological Conditions in Human Skeletal Remains*. Smithsonian Institution Press: Washington DC.

*Powell, M.L. (1988). *Status and Health in Prehistory*. Smithsonian Institution Press: Washington DC.

Prusiner, S.B. (1998). Prions. *Proceedings of the National Academy of Science of the USA*, **95**:13363–13383.

Resnick, D. and Niwayama, G. (1995). Osteomyelitis, septic arthritis, and soft tissue infection: organisms. In Resnick, D. (ed.) *Diagnosis of Bone and Joint Disorders*, (3rd edn), 2448–2558. WB Saunders: Philadelphia.

Salo, W.L., Aufderheide, A.C., Buikstra, J. and Holcomb, T.A. (1994). Identification of *mycobacterium-tuberculosis* DNA in a pre-Columbian Peruvian mummy. *Proceedings of the National Academy of Sciences of the USA*, **91**:2091–2094.

Simoons, F.J. (1979). Dairying, milk use, and lactose malabsorption in Eurasia: a problem in culture history. *Anthropos*, **74**:61–80.

Smith, B.D. (1995). *The Emergence of Agriculture*. Scientific American Library: New York.

Spigelman, M. and Donoghue, H.D. (1999). Mycobacterium tuberculosis DNA in archaeological specimens. In Pálfi, G., Dutour, O., Deák, J. and Hutás, I. (eds) *Tuberculosis Past and Present*, 353–360. Golden Book Publisher Ltd.: Szeged, Hungary.

Steinbock, R.T. (1976). *Paleopathological Diagnosis and Interpretation*. Charles C. Thomas: Springfield, Illinois.

Utz, J.P. (1989). Blastomycosis. In Hoeprich, P.D. and Jordan, M.C. (eds) *Infectious Diseases*, (4th edn), 510–516. JB Lippincott: Philadelphia.

Wells, C. (1964). *Bones, Bodies, and Disease*. Frederick A. Praeger: New York.

Wells, C. and Dallas, C. (1976). Romano-British pathology. *Antiquity*, **59**:425–427.

Wendorf, F. (1968). Site 117: A Nubian final Paleolithic graveyard near Jebel Sahaba, Sudan. In Wendorf, F. (ed.) *The Prehistory of Nubia*, 954–995. Southern Methodist University Press: Dallas.

Zink, A., Haas, C.J., Hagedorn, H.G., Szeimies, U. and Nerlich, A.G. (1999). Morphological and molecular evidence for pulmonary and osseous tuberculosis in a male Egyptian mummy. In Pálfi, G., Dutour, O., Deák, J. and Hutás, I. (eds) *Tuberculosis Past and Present*, 379–382. Golden Book Publisher Ltd.: Szeged, Hungary.

20

Assessment of Age at Death and Sex in the Adult Human Skeleton

M. COX

School of Conservation Sciences, Bournemouth University.

Determination of the sex of an individual and their age at death are crucial components of scientific archaeology, biological and forensic anthropology and palaeodemography. Both are also vital in understanding the biocultural and epidemiological significance of trauma and disease. This paper briefly reviews current methods for the estimation of age and sex in adult skeletal material, highlighting areas of strength and concern. For a more detailed review of ageing and sexing, see Cox (2000) and Mays and Cox (2000) respectively.

DETERMINATION OF SEX

The use of the term *gender* instead of *biological sex* is now creeping into the scientific literature (e.g., Sutton *et al.* 1996). Gender is a value-laden term describing culturally constructed attributes related to perceptions of 'maleness' and 'femaleness' and should not be confused with biological sex. Biological sex is, however, the essential base point from which to infer gendered attributes. Although all foetuses begin as female, the difference between males and females is established at conception; the female having two X chromosomes and the male one X and one Y. At about six weeks the Y chromosome triggers the development of the testes and the process of masculinization begins. Sexual differen-

tiation is determined by hormonal differences between males and females.

When determining sex from the skeleton, it is desirable to examine the whole skeleton, and the reliability is contingent upon the completeness of the remains (Meindl *et al.* 1985), particularly when levels of dimorphism are low. Most researchers report higher accuracy in blind tests when using the whole skeleton rather than single elements: e.g., 96 per cent (Meindl *et al.* 1985); 97 per cent (Molleson and Cox 1993). However, some elements, particularly the pelvis and skull, are more important than others. Even so, sex determination is not straightforward since characteristics indicating sex can be influenced by genetics, disease and environmental factors. Further to this, although rarely so, some individuals are affected by disorders of sexual differentiation (Mays and Cox 2000) which might affect skeletal form.

The pelvis

Differences in the pelvis are the most significant sexing indicators as they represent functional modification and evolutionary adaptation. The pelvis has evolved to ensure biomechanically successful upright gait and bipedality, but in females modification has taken place to ensure that obstetric success is also possible (Cox 1989). The male pelvis is generally a high and narrow

Handbook of Archaeological Sciences. Edited by D.R. Brothwell and A.M. Pollard.

structure of android shape. Ideally, but subject to nutritional and pathological modification, the female pelvis is gynacoid in shape with a transversely oval and relatively wide inlet, and wider greatest pelvic diameter and outlet than that of the male. The criteria employed by anthropologists to determine sex are all reflections of this functional adaptation with its resultant metrical and morphological differences (Budinoff and Tagg 1990).

Criteria for females include: the developed ventral arch (Phenice 1969), the wide and shallow greater sciatic notch (Hager 1996), sub-pubic concavity and the ridged medial border of the inferior pubic ramus. Sacral criteria also play a part and the ratio between the width of the sacral body and alas, and the extent of the sacro-iliac joint are also diagnostic (Bass 1987, Hoyme and Işcan 1989). The presence or absence of preauricular sulci and pubic pitting are now known to reflect pelvic size and shape (Cox 1989, MacLaughlin and Cox 1989), and can be found on both sexes.

Reliability of the pelvis in determining sex in adults is generally good for the experienced osteologist. Phenice's criteria (1969) were tested by Sutherland and Suchey (1991) with 96 per cent accuracy ($n = 1284$), though less successfully (Lovell 1989) on a smaller sample ($n = 50$). However, some samples are less dimorphic than others and challenge even the most experienced osteologist. Further, methods that work on one sample may not work on another (MacLaughlin and Bruce 1986). In the United Kingdom, some urban Medieval samples are far less dimorphic than both earlier and later material.

Metrical analysis, specifically using discriminant functions, has also been evaluated ($n = 100$) for sexing the pelvis (Schulter-Ellis et al. 1985) achieving 95 per cent accuracy using an acetabulum/pubis index and 97 per cent accuracy when this was combined with femoral head diameter. It is important to remember that the use of discriminant functions for sexing or ageing should be reserved for cases where ancestry and socio-economical status are the same as that of the sample on which the method was developed.

The skull

It is probably the face and jaw, rather than the cranium, which possess the most sexually dimorphic traits. In late adolescence, craniofacial changes start to occur in males. This hormonally mediated phenomenon leads to an elongation of the face, an enlargement of the brow ridges and an accentuation of the chin. Changes in the

angle of the ramus and the mandibular body also occur. The upper orbital margins become thicker and blunter and the orbital shape becomes squarer. The supra-orbital notch becomes deeper and changes in brow ridge size also change the nasal bridge profile, rather than its actual shape. Females, however, retain the more or less gracile juvenile form. Their foreheads are generally vertical in profile with well-defined frontal eminences, whilst the glabellar region is smooth in comparison to the prominence of the males. Muscle markings on the nuchal crest, temporal bone, around the zygomatic roots, and temporal crest are larger and heavier in males. Various authors have advocated the use of such features (e.g., Brothwell 1981, Bass 1987, Mays 1998). Such features are correlated with robusticity and size – the male considered more robust, rugged and muscle-marked than the female. Nevertheless, absolute differences seldom exist and many intermediate forms are found. Furthermore, cultural practice (e.g., Tomenchuk and Mayhall 1979) can affect morphology.

Many authors feel secure in claiming 80 per cent accuracy for sex identification from the adult cranium alone (Hoyme and Işcan 1989) increasing to 90 per cent if the mandible is included (Meindl et al. 1985). Maat et al. (1997) have indicated that mandibular criteria should be used with caution. This is supported by the different results achieved by such authors as Donnelly et al. (1998).

Metrical analysis of the skull and dentition

Discriminant functions have been used to determine sex from metrical analysis of the skull and dentition. Hanihara (1959) reported an accuracy of 90 per cent using three dimensions from the skull. Using the mandible, Hanihara reported 85 per cent accuracy from four dimensions, while Giles (1964) achieved 84 per cent from eight measurements. Hunter and Garn (1972) found that, metrically, sexual dimorphism is pronounced and localized in the mandibular ramus. This is linked to continuing postpubertal mandibular growth in males (Walker and Kowalski 1972).

Many researchers regard dentition as being sexually dimorphic (e.g. Mayhall and Kanazawa 1989). This has been attributed to protracted amelogenesis in the developing male tooth crowns, resulting in thicker enamel. The X chromosome promotes growth of both enamel and dentine while the Y chromosome only influences enamel (Alvesalo 1997) but this can be influenced by individual variation. Such dimorphism also has application in sexing juveniles.

A multivariate approach has been explored by Garn *et al.* (1979) with a success rate of 87 per cent. Rösing (1983) tested dental discrimination in archaeological material, sexed independently using the pelvis, and obtained 90 per cent concurrence. It is important to remember that the actual size differences between the sexes in individual teeth are very small (*c.* 0.4-0.5 mm; Hillson 1996) and intra- and inter-observer error can be significant. Furthermore, population differences in tooth size are independent of sample differences in tooth size dimorphism. Dimorphism in the permanent dentition is variable and, in most living samples, lower canines show the greatest dimorphism (up to 7.3 per cent) followed by the upper canine (Perzigian 1976). Assessment of the size of the dental arcade as an indicator of sex (e.g., Porter 1998) has shown that males have larger arcades and that there are inter-population differences.

There have been several inconclusive studies conducted on the dimorphism of non-metric dental traits (e.g., Perzigian 1976). Some differences have been shown for the metaconule (Harris and Bailit 1980) and for third molar and second upper incisor agenesis (Davies 1967).

Metrical variation of post cranial elements

In order to enable fragmentary remains to be sexed, discriminant function analysis of metrical variation of a wide range of bones has been attempted (e.g., Seidemann *et al.* 1998, Cologlu *et al.* 1998), with varying degrees of accuracy.

Deoxyribonucleic acid (DNA)

With the development of polymerase chain reaction (PCR; see Chapter 25), molecular archaeology has provided a wide range of information about ancient human material, including biological sex. DNA can survive in archaeological human bone and analysis of chromosome X- and Y- specific sequences can then determine the sex of remains (e.g., Brown 2000). Faerman *et al.* (1998) have obtained useful results using the amelogenin gene. DNA analysis has enormous potential to provide sex data for gender studies, infants and juveniles, incomplete skeletons, material with low levels of dimorphism, and as a test of the reliability of other methods on samples from varied temporal and spatial contexts. However, DNA does not always survive and

is presently only considered about 80 per cent reliable. Furthermore, it is relatively expensive and, as such, is unlikely to become commonly employed.

ESTIMATION OF AGE AT DEATH

Without knowledge of the age (and sex) of individuals and samples recovered from archaeological contexts, the significance of cultural practice and trends becomes inherently encumbered with our own cultural values to the detriment of the 'real' significance of the archaeology (Cox 2000). There is increasing agreement amongst practitioners that estimating age of adults is fraught with problems, not least because we are seeking to determine a constant linear progression (i.e., chronological age) from a range of fluctuating biological criteria. Add to this that age and sex determination share a mutable dependency on one another and on ancestry, and that characteristics determining both can be affected by genetic, environmental and socio-economic variables, as well as disease processes, and the complexity of this subject area is apparent.

A further consideration is the derivation of the sample upon which a method has been developed. Many methods were based on archaeological material of unknown age, (e.g., dental attrition; Miles 1962, Brothwell 1981), large samples of individuals of low socio-economic status, some of whom lack documented age and sex (e.g., the Hamann-Todd and Terry collections), or that from small numbers of modern willed body or dissection room samples. Some methods have been tested and 'validated' against ages derived from the application of other ageing criteria, rather than known age and sex, which results in the propagation of systematic errors rather than establishing methods based on reliable criteria. Concordance of results using different methods should be recognized as such and not attributed with any greater significance (Scheuer and Black 2000). Of particular significance to forensic cases is the fact that most of the ageing methods discussed here were primarily developed for use on samples, not individuals. Systematic errors within each method are less significant amongst the sample than when dealing with individuals and this is clearly of considerable importance forensically. A less well-understood bias was first brought to the attention of anthropologists in the 1980s (Bocquet-Appel and Masset 1982, 1985, 1996). They argued that developing an ageing method on any sample would result in the replication of the original sample's mortality profile in samples to which the method is applied.

Recent research trends

Despite historical and epigraphic evidence from the last two millennia to the contrary, prior to the 1980s, palaeodemographic analysis consistently and unquestioningly reported low life expectancy with few individuals apparently living beyond their fifth decade (Weiss 1973). This trend largely reflected the low upper age limits of easily applied and inexpensive ageing methods in use until recently. Examples are Brothwell's dental attrition phasing (1981), and methods using the pubic symphysis (McKern and Stewart 1957, Gilbert and McKern 1973). The application of these, by the scope and distribution of their phases and ranges, determined the mean age and age range of any sample to which they were applied.

The designation and acceptance by practitioners of such low upper age limits reflected contemporary misconceptions about longevity in past populations. Perspectives began to change in the 1980s when experienced practitioners frequently saw evidence of pathological conditions (e.g., Paget's Disease) known clinically to affect only the elderly, in skeletons with assessed ages that were considerably younger.

Bocquet-Appel and Masset's work (1982, 1985) provoked a considerable if unconvincing rebuttal in the literature (e.g., Buikstra and Konigsberg 1985). Nevertheless, several researchers continue to argue that, whatever the precise mechanisms involved, methodological bias is serious, leading particularly to an under-representation of the over-40s in our interpretation of the archaeological record (e.g., Paine and Harpending 1998, Aykroyd et al. 1999). Such researchers are currently developing statistical devices such as 'maximum likelihood estimation techniques' to remove this bias.

Ageing methods

Fundamental to ageing characteristics and methods is the fact that living bone is a dynamic tissue subject to resorption and remodelling in response to a host of stressors and stimulants. Bone can adapt its form, to a limited extent, to cope with physical demands made upon it and can remodel in response to stress, trauma and disease. Bone health and status in adults is maintained by a balanced relationship between osteoblasts and osteoclasts, a relationship that changes with such factors as levels of exercise as well as increasing age. Physical ageing processes centre on progressive denaturation of protein in collagen fibrils (Angel et al. 1989) and the death of non-replaceable neurons and other cells. Age related changes include both hypertrophy and atrophy.

During the early years of life, estimating age is relatively straightforward, because the development of the dentition and the appearance and the fusion of growth centres of bone offer relatively dependable indicators of age occurring within a comparatively short age range (e.g., Mays 1998). Fortunately, some of these continue into adulthood and are discussed here. Once skeletal maturation is complete, estimation is dependent on degenerative changes that occur at differing rates between and within different bones in individuals, different samples and populations. Variables that increase the complexity of this difficult area of research and application include random individual variation in maturation and degeneration, and the systematic effects of environmental, nutritional, endocrine and genetic factors on growth and senescence.

Currently-employed methods of ageing adult skeletons are based on four biological criteria: final stages of skeletal maturation, changes to dentition, morphological change at joints where movement is either limited or non-existent, and changes to bone structure including osteon frequency. Another approach is that of multi-factorial application. Less commonly applied criteria such as the ossification of hyaline cartilage and arachnoid granulation are discussed elsewhere (Cox 2000).

Final stages of skeletal maturation

Several areas of the skeleton complete maturation during or about the third decade of life and consequently have value in identifying those dying in early adulthood. These include the ventral rings of the vertebrae, petroexoccipital articulation and fusion of the medial clavicle.

(i) Ventral rings of the vertebrae
The superior and inferior ventral rings of the vertebrae were first considered to be of value in ageing by McKern and Stewart in 1957. Albert and Maples (1995) suggested that complete fusion occurs around 24 to 25 years and seems to occur earlier in females than in males.

(ii) Petroexoccipital articulation

Fusion of the jugular growth plate (petroexoccipital articulation) was examined by Maat and Mastwijk

(1995) who noted that fusion was not observed in individuals of below 22 years with bilateral fusion occurring in females by 34 and males by 36. Evaluation of a much larger sample by Hershkovitz *et al.* (1997a) demonstrated that closure can occur up to the age of 50, and that in up to 9 per cent of cases did not occur at all. This clearly demonstrates the inherent problems that arise when devising methods on small sample sizes (i.e., where ranges of human variation are reduced).

(iii) Medial clavicle

The clavicle is the last bone to complete epiphyseal fusion. Black and Scheuer (1996) demonstrated that fusion was always complete by 29 years. Webb and Suchey (1985) noted that in Caucasoids this was 28 years with 34 years for Negroids.

Dentition

Teeth undergo continuous change from approximately twenty weeks gestation to death or complete loss of dentition (Costa 1986). However, they are not subject to extensive remodelling processes rendering them relatively impervious to many of the variables that increase the complexity of using bone for ageing. Furthermore, dental remains are amongst the most resistant parts of the human body and will survive most diagenetic processes and burial environments (cremation and extremes of pH excepted). For a detailed review of this subject see Whittaker (2000).

(i) Dental attrition

Attrition of the occlusal surfaces through use is assessed in permanent dentition (Miles 1962, Brothwell 1981). Dental attrition was far greater in some periods of the past than it is today, relating to the abrasive nature of food and food processing methods. As changes have occurred in diet through time with transition from coarser to more refined foodstuffs (currently being reversed in some western cultures), the occurrence of dentine exposure decreases, and vice versa. However, factors such as individual idiosyncrasies, the use of teeth as tools, malocclusion and pathology can also affect the rate and pattern of wear.

Probably the most widely used scoring scheme for archaeological samples is that developed by Brothwell (1981), developed upon UK archaeological samples of unknown age. Also using archaeological material,

Miles (1962) produced a system for age assessment based on the idea that rates of wear can be calibrated against dental eruption.

Opinions vary as to the reliability and importance of dental wear in age determination (e.g., Johansson *et al.* 1993). Molleson and Cohen (1990) demonstrated that attrition stages do not represent a series through which all dentition passes in ordered and steady sequence and consequently their application under-ages older individuals.

(ii) Histological and biochemical analysis

Gustafon (1950) pioneered this approach to age determination using six features: attrition of the occlusal surface, secondary dentine deposition, periodontosis, cementum apposition, root resorption and root dentine sclerosis. However, his method was not statistically supported and was eventually discredited. Many researchers have, however, attempted to refine this method (e.g., Johanson 1971). Later studies have shown that root dentine transparency is probably the most reliable of these methods, which are time-consuming, expensive, destructive and require special expertise. For these reasons, although regularly employed on forensic material, they are only rarely used in archaeology. Three areas merit further discussion but all require further work on large samples of known age to determine their reliability.

(a) Root dentine sclerosis

Dentine transparency develops as dentine tubules fill with calcium phosphates of the apatite family. This results in a change in the refractive index so that in transmitted light sclerotic areas appear transparent and normal areas opaque. Commencing in the late teens near the apex of the root at the cement–dentine junction, this process gradually spreads to create a complex three-dimensional form. It is this arrangement that is responsible for generating the main obstacle encountered in recording the extent of the area of the sclerosis. A further problem lies with attempts to standardize the sclerosis for overall root size (Drusini *et al.* 1991). Various authors report varying levels of inaccuracy with this method (e.g., Johanson 1971, Lucy *et al.* 1995).

(b) Cementum annulation

Cementum is the calcified tissue immediately surrounding the dentine of the root and neck of the tooth. It is continuously deposited during life and so a 'growth ring' effect is established. Work conducted on small samples (e.g., Miller *et al.* 1988) has produced promising results. Areas of concern are intra- and inter-tooth variability within individuals and that the biological basis for annulation in humans is unclear. Damage to dentition is a problem and is difficult to evaluate without a surviving peridontal ligament (Charles *et al.* 1986).

(c) Amino acid racemization

An alternative chemical approach to age at death estimation concerns amino acid racemization. Racemization proceeds fast enough at body temperature for detectable amounts of D-enantiomers to accumulate during life. It is possible that D:L ratios in dentine might be useful to determine age at death (e.g., Gillard *et al.* 1990).

Various researchers claim limited success with studies on very small samples which are usually of unknown age, e.g., Child *et al.* (1993) reported the unreliability of this method when applied to older, and therefore potentially degraded, material. One problem is that the rate of racemization is temperature dependent and consequently it should only be used where it is safe to assume that burial conditions have remained constant.

Morphological change at joints with limited or no movement

(i) Cranial suture closure

The correlation of cranial suture closure with increasing age has received the attention of many throughout this century (e.g., Hershkovitz *et al.* 1997b), collectively producing equivocal but generally discouraging results. While it is known that cranial sutures can (but do not always) progressively close (though not necessarily at a reliable or constant rate) and become obliterated, the underlying biological processes determining if and when closure occurs are not understood (Key *et al.* 1994). Consequently, we have no understanding of if, or which, extrinsic factors can affect closure rates (Mays 1998) and cannot therefore meaningfully apply this method to archaeological material. This principle applies to most biological processes utilized in age determination.

(ii) Pubic symphysis morphology

Todd (1920) first explored systemic changes to the symphysial face of the pubis and his method was reappraised by McKern and Stewart (1957). The young age span of this sample was a problem, as was the lack of female standards. Gilbert and McKern (1973) produced a schema for females based on a small sample of reliably documented individuals but which was found to be wanting in 1979 by Suchey. Work has continued (e.g., Brooks and Suchey 1990) and increasingly demonstrated unacceptably wide and overlapping age ranges for each stage. On a practical level, pubic symphyses rarely survive in large numbers in archaeological samples (*c.* 30 per cent; Waldron 1987), its anterior position rendering it prone to weathering and mechanical damage – a serious limitation.

(iii) Rib end morphology

Ribs are united to the sternum by lengths of cartilage. Işcan and colleagues (Işcan and Loth 1984, Işcan *et al.* 1985) consider these to become increasingly irregular in morphology as age increases. When tested on material from Belleville, Ontario, this method under-aged individuals with amounts increasing with real age. This method also showed the greatest degree of interobserver disparity of all methods applied to this sample (Saunders *et al.* 1992). Loth (1995) evaluated her method on the Christ Church, Spitalfields' material (*n* = 75) which is also of known age (Molleson and Cox 1993). The results suggest that those below 18 and in the 40s were aged to the correct decade, but all others were under-aged. Utilization of this method on archaeological material is seriously hampered by the need to be able to identify the fourth rib. Ribs are often incomplete and fragmentary in archaeological material, and consequently extremely difficult to identify.

(iv) Auricular surface of the ilium

Age related changes to the auricular surface were first schematically associated with age ranges by Lovejoy *et al.* (1985a). This method is reviewed in detail by Jackes (1992). Bedford *et al.* (1993) considered it to be superior to the pubic symphysis. An assessment of the method by Murray and Murray (1991) found it wanting as a single indicator of age and the age ranges too large for forensic applications. Evaluation on material from Belleville, Ontario (*n* = 49), indicated that its reliability decreases with age (by under-ageing), particularly from the mid-30s (Saunders *et al.* 1992) and that it is subject to inter-observer error. The biological process of change to this articulation is also little understood. There is little doubt that this joint, like cranial sutures, survives better than the pubic symphysis or the ribs in archaeological material. As such, it merits further evaluation on a large documented sample.

Bone microstructure and involution

Several authors have reviewed the literature concerned with examining age at death from bone histomorphometry (e.g., Stout 1992). Results from assessments of methods vary enormously, in part reflecting the size and site of the sample and the relationship of the assessment vehicle with that upon which the method was devised. Recent work has focused on the clavicle in association with either the femur or ribs (e.g., Stout *et al.* 1996). Stout and Paine (1992) found the rib and clavicle in combination to be accurate to 5.5 years.

Semi-automatic image analysis of cross sections of 101 femoral diaphyseal bone sections (forensic material aged between 18 and 87) reported a standard deviation of 12.58 years (Wallin *et al.* 1994). These authors concluded that such analysis is less precise than suggested by the literature, as did Macchiarelli and Bondioli (1994). A recent study of cortical porosity of the entire mid-shaft femur (Feik *et al.* 1997) showed age-related sex differences in the pattern of bone loss but concluded that the method had little value as a predictor of age in forensic applications.

A limiting factor with such methods is that there appears to be a strong relationship between bone remodelling rates and a range of genetic and environmental factors (Stout 1992). Further, the application of histological methods to archaeological material can be affected by diagenesis (see Chapter 51). This and other approaches to ageing are potentially compromised by the work of Belkin *et al.* (1998). Their study demonstrated the magnitude of environmental effects, particularly temperature and humidity on thermo-regulation and consequently basal metabolism rate, circulatory and endocrine functions ($n = c.\ 7500$). The implications of such work for assessment of age in archaeological samples are very important considering spatial and temporal climatic change in the past.

Multifactorial methods

First proposed in 1970 (Acsádi and Neméskeri), the perceived advantages of using multifactorial approaches to assigning age at death to archaeological material rest upon the minimization of errors in individual methods. Jackes (1992) considers the multifactorial approach to ageing in considerable critical detail. It is difficult to be convinced by the arguments put forward for the use of multifactorial approaches when there are so many inherent problems within individual methods employed. It is also possible that such an approach will compound rather than minimize systematic errors. Combine this with the fact that most methods have been developed on a small number of samples, particularly samples selected using different criteria from the Hamann-Todd collection, upon which many of the methods have been tested for reliability (e.g., Lovejoy *et al.* 1985b).

Evaluation of the reliability of such methods on archaeological material of known age is limited. The Complex Method was found wanting with less than 30 per cent of adults aged to within five years and a systematic error whereby most older adults were underaged and vice versa (Molleson and Cox 1993). Saunders *et al.* (1992) found Lovejoy *et al.*'s method to perform badly. Interestingly, and contrary to these results, Bedford *et al.* (1993) found Lovejoy *et al.*'s method to work well on the modern Grant collection producing a smaller error than with individual methods.

CONCLUSIONS

Where adult skeletons survive in good and relatively intact condition and levels of dimorphism are high, it is unusual for there to be difficulty in attributing biological sex using secondary sex characteristics (i.e., pelvic and cranial criteria). Where remains are not intact or where levels of dimorphism are low, a range of metrical and statistical criteria can be applied, but should be determined on a sample that can be sexed using secondary sex characteristics. Resources permitting, DNA analysis has the potential to be the most reliable method to apply to incomplete cases, juveniles or where levels of dimorphism are low.

In terms of ageing, it seems reasonable to conclude that we can identify young adults ($< c.\ 30$ years) within archaeological and forensic assemblages. For older adults, ascribed ages can fall within extremely large age brackets with a considerable and unacceptable degree of overlap. Assessment of methods on the small number of archaeological samples of known age available to us suggests that current methods tend to overage the 30 to 40 year age-group and under-age the older groups by unacceptably large margins.

The reasons for our difficulties in ageing lie in that we are attempting to predictively correlate non-linear biological changes (largely processes we do not fully understand, and influenced by genetics and environment), with a linear and constant phenomenon – passing time. Given the vast range of variation within and between families, samples and populations, this may not be possible within meaningful confidence limits that provide useful data capable of addressing our current research agendas. Work examining climatic variables on bone loss suggests that this is a significant consideration affecting rates of change, and one that clearly needs to be considered in future work.

Methodologically, in both developing and testing methodologies there has been an over-reliance on a small number of samples, some of which are not entirely or even largely comprised of reliably documented sex and age. In the last decade or so, more reliable material has become available, largely from autopsy rooms. However, generally such sample sizes are small, particularly when broken down into sub-sets of ancestry, sex and parity status. Further, the arguments for sample bias influencing application outcomes are convincing. Microscopic dental methods are presently considered most reliable by the forensic fraternity, but they have yet to be tested on large samples, so it behoves us to be cautious in their application.

For this area to develop, it is imperative that large samples of reliably documented skeletal material become available for both developing and testing methods. Such a scenario is unlikely, which makes a case for the creation of large samples by the amalgamation of a number of small ones. Ideally, samples of different ancestry, socio-economic and climatic groups should include equal numbers of all ages, and both sexes. Concurrent to that, further research needs to be undertaken examining the biological processes underlying age-related change and the influence thereon of genetic and environmental variables. Without this, the issue of applying methods developed upon modern material to archaeological (and forensic) material, which can be of unknown or at best uncertain genetic and environmental context, is questionable. A tall order it may be, but the potential gain is immeasurable, enriching and enabling archaeology, anthropology and the judicial process.

ACKNOWLEDGEMENTS

The cranial suture and dental ageing and sexing components of this paper are based upon and extended from an unpublished paper 'Ageing and sexing the skull: the anthropologists' contribution', presented at the Cranio-Facial Reconstruction Conference, held at Windsor in July 1997. Linda O'Connell is thanked for her input to that paper.

REFERENCES

*Recommended for further reading

Acsádi, G. and Nemeskéri, J. (1970). *History of Human Life Span and Mortality*. Akademiai Kiado: Budapest.

Albert, A.M. and Maples, W.R. (1995). Stages of epiphyseal union for thoracic and lumbar vertebral centra as a method of age determination for teenage and young adult skeletons. *Journal of Forensic Sciences*, **40**:623–633.

Alvesalo, L. (1997). Sex chromosomes and human growth, a dental approach. *Human Genetics*, **101**:1–5.

Angel, J.L., Suchey, J.M., Isçan, M.Y. and Zimmerman, M.R. (1989). Age at death estimation from the skeleton and viscera. In Zimmerman, M.R. and Angel, J.L. (eds) *Dating and Age Determination of Biological Materials*, 179–220. Croom Helm: London.

Aykroyd, R.G., Lucy, D., Pollard, A.M. and Roberts, C.A. (1999). Nasty, brutish, but not necessarily short. *American Antiquity*, **64**:55–70.

Bass, W.M. (1987). *Human Osteology. A Field Guide and Manual*, (3rd edn). Archaeological Society: Missouri.

Bedford, M.E., Russell, K.F., Lovejoy, C.O., Meindl, R.S., Simpson, S.W. and Stuart-Macadam, P.L. (1993). Test of the multifactorial ageing method using skeletons with known ages-at-death from the Grant collection. *American Journal of Physical Anthropology*, **91**:287–297.

Belkin, V., Livshits, G., Otremski, I. and Kobyliansky, E. (1998). Aging bone score and climatic factors. *American Journal of Physical Anthropology*, **106**:349–359.

Black, S. and Scheuer, L. (1996). Age changes in the clavicle: from the early neonatal period to skeletal maturity. *International Journal of Osteoarchaeology*, **6**:425–434.

Bocquet-Appel, J.P. and Masset, C. (1982). Farewell to paleodemography. *Journal of Human Evolution*, **11**:321–333.

Bocquet-Appel, J.P. and Masset, C. (1985). Paleodemography: resurrection or ghost? *Journal of Human Evolution*, **14**:107–111.

Bocquet-Appel, J.P. and Masset, C. (1996). Paleodemography: expectancy and false hope. *American Journal of Physical Anthropology*, **99**:571–583.

Brooks, S.T. and Suchey, J.M. (1990). Skeletal age determination based on the os pubis: a comparison of the Acsádi-Nemeskéri and Suchey-Brooks methods. *Human Evolution*, **5**:227–238.

Brothwell, D.R. (1981). *Digging up Bones*. British Museum (Natural History): London.

Brown, K. (2000). Ancient DNA – applications in human osteoarchaeology: achievements, problems and potential. In Cox, M. and Mays, S. (eds) *Human Osteology in*

Archaeology and Forensic Science, 455–474. Greenwich Medical Media: London.

Budinoff, L.C. and Tague, R.G. (1990). Anatomical and developmental bases for the ventral arc of the human pelvis. *American Journal of Physical Anthropology*, **82**:73–79.

Buikstra, J.E. and Konigsberg, L.W. (1985). Palaeodemography: critiques and controversies. *American Anthropologist*, **87**:316–333.

Charles, K., Charles, D., Cheverud, J. and Buikstra, J. (1986). Estimating age at death from growth layers in cementum. In Zimmerman, M. and Angel, J.L. (eds) *Age Determination of Biological Materials*, 277–301. Charles C. Thomas: Springfield.

Child, A.M., Gillard, R.D., Hardman, S.M., Pollard, A.M., Sutton, P. and Whittaker, D. (1993). Preliminary microbiological investigations of some problems relating to age at death determinations in archaeological teeth. In Fankhauser, B.L. and Bird, J.R. (eds) *Archaeometry: Current Australasian Research*, 85–90. Australian National University: Canberra.

Cologlu, A.S., Isçan, M.Y., Yavuz, M.F. and Sari, H. (1998). (1998). Sex determination from the ribs of contemporary Turks. *Journal of Forensic Sciences*, **43**:273–276.

Costa, R.L. (1986). Determination of age at death: dental analysis. In Zimmerman, M.R. and Angel, J.L. (eds) *Dating and Age Determination of Biological Materials*, 248–269. Croom Helm: London.

Cox, M.J. (1989). *Evaluation of the Significance of Scars of Parturition in the Christchurch, Spitalfields Sample*. Unpublished PhD thesis, University College London.

*Cox, M.J. (2000). Ageing adults from the skeleton. In Cox, M. and Mays, S. (eds) *Human Osteology in Archaeology and Forensic Science*, 61–82. Greenwich Medical Media: London.

Davies, P.L. (1967). Agenesis of teeth: a sex limited trait. *Journal of Dental Research*, **46**:1309.

Donnelly, S.M., Hens, S.M., Rogers, N.L. and Schneider, K.L. (1998). A blind test of mandibular ramus flexure as a morphological indicator of sexual dimorphism in the human skeleton. *American Journal of Physical Anthropology*, **107**:363–366.

Drusini, A., Calliari, I. and Volpe, A. (1991). Root dentine transparency: age determination of human teeth using computerized densitometric analysis. *American Journal of Physical Anthropology*, **85**:25–30.

Faerman, M., Bar-Gal, G.K., Filon, D., Greenblatt, C.L., Stager, L., Oppenheim, A. and Smith, P. (1998). Determination of sex of infanticide victims from the Late Roman era through ancient DNA analysis. *Journal of Archaeological Science*, **25**:861–865.

Feik, S.A., Thomas, C.D.L. and Clement, J.G. (1997). Age-related changes in cortical porosity of the mid-shaft of the human femur. *Journal of Anatomy*, **191**:407–416.

Garn, S.M., Cole, P.E. and van Astine, W.L. (1979). Sex discriminatory effectiveness using combinations of root lengths and crown diameters. *American Journal of Physical Anthropology*, **50**:115–118.

Gilbert, B.M. and McKern, T.W. (1973). A method for ageing the female os pubis. *American Journal of Physical Anthropology*, **38**:31–38.

Giles, E. (1964). Sex determination by discriminant function analysis of the mandible. *American Journal of Physical Anthropology*, **22**:129–135.

Gillard, R.D., Pollard, A.M., Sutton, P.A. and Whittaker, D.K. (1990). An improved method for age determination from the measurement of D-aspartic acid in dental collagen. *Archaeometry*, **32**:61–70.

Gustafon, G. (1950). Age determinations of teeth. *Journal of the American Dental Association*, **41**:45–54.

Hager, L. (1996). Sex differences in the sciatic notch of great apes and modern humans. *American Journal of Physical Anthropology*, **99**:287–300.

Hanihara, K. (1959). Sexual diagnosis of Japanese long bones by means of discriminant functions. *Journal of the Anthropological Society of Nippon*, **67**:21–27.

Harris, E.F. and Bailit, H.L. (1980). The metaconule: a morphologic and familial analysis of a molar cusp in humans. *American Journal of Physical Anthropology*, **53**:349–358.

Hershkovitz, I., Latimer, B., Dutour, O., Jellema, L.M., Wish-Baratz, S., Rothchild, C. and Rothchild, B.M. (1997a). The elusive Petroexoccipital articulation. *American Journal of Physical Anthropology*, **103**:365–373.

Hershkovitz, I., Latimer, B., Dutour, O., Jellema, L.M., Wish-Baratz, S., Rothchild, C. and Rothchild, B.M. (1997b). Why do we fail in ageing the skull from the sagittal suture? *American Journal of Physical Anthropology*, **103**:393–399.

Hillson, S. (1996). *Dental Anthropology*. Cambridge University Press: Cambridge.

Hoyme, L.E. St and Isçan, M.Y. (1989). Determination of sex and race: accuracy and assumptions. In Isçan, M.Y. and Kennedy, K.A.R. (eds) *Reconstruction of Life from the Skeleton*, 53–93. Alan Liss: New York.

Hunter, W.S. and Garn, S.M. (1972). Disproportionate sexual dimorphism in the human face. *American Journal of Physical Anthropology*, **36**:133–138.

Isçan, M.Y. and Loth, S.R. (1984). Determination of age from sternal rib in white males. A test of the phase method. *Journal of Forensic Sciences*, **31**:122–132.

Isçan, M.Y., Loth, S.R. and Scheuerman, E.H. (1985). Determination of age from the sternal rib in white females. A test of the phase method. *Journal of Forensic Sciences*, **31**:990-999.

Jackes, M. (1992). Palaeodemography: problems and techniques. In Saunders, S.R. and Katzenberg, M.A. (eds) *Skeletal Biology of Past Peoples*, 189–224. John Wiley: New York.

Johanson, G. (1971). Age determinations from human teeth. *Odontologisk Revy*, **22**:1–126.

Johansson, A., Haraldson, T., Omar, R., Kiliaridis, S. and Carlsson, G.E. (1993). A system for assessing the severity and progression of occlusal tooth wear. *Journal of Oral Rehabilitation*, **20**:125–131.

Key, C.A., Aiello, L.C. and Molleson, T.I. (1994). Cranial suture closure and its implications for age estimation. *International Journal of Osteoarchaeology*, 4:193–207.

Loth, S.R. (1995). Age assessment of the Spitalfields cemetery population by rib phase analysis. *American Journal of Human Biology*, 7:465–474.

Lovejoy, C.O., Meindl, R.S., Pryzbeck, T.R. and Mensforth, R.P. (1985a). Chronological metamorphosis of the auricular surface of the ilium: a new method for the determination of adult skeletal age at death. *American Journal of Physical Anthropology*, 68:15–28.

Lovejoy, C.O., Meindl, R.S., Mensforth, R.P. and Barton, T.J. (1985b). Multifactorial determination of skeletal age at death: a method and blind tests of its accuracy. *American Journal of Physical Anthropology*, 68:1–14.

Lovell, N.C. (1989). Test of Phenice's technique for determining sex from the os pubis. *American Journal of Physical Anthropology*, 79:117–120.

Lucy, D., Pollard, A.M. and Roberts, C.A. (1995). A comparison of three dental techniques for estimation of age at death in humans. *Journal of Archaeological Science*, 22:417–428.

Maat, G.J.R. and Mastwijk, R.W. (1995). Fusion status of the jugular growth plate: an aid for age at death determination. *International Journal of Osteoarchaeology*, 5:163–167.

Maat, G.J.R., Mastwijk, R.W. and Van der Velde, E.A. (1997). On the reliability of non-metrical morphological sex determination of the skull compared with that of the pelvis in the low countries. *International Journal of Osteoarchaeology*, 7:575–580.

MacChiarelli, R. and Bondioli, L. (1994). Linear densitometry and digital image processing of the proximal femur radiographs: implications for archaeological and forensic anthropology. *American Journal of Physical Anthropology*, 93:109–122.

MacLaughlin, S.M. and Bruce, M.F. (1986). The sciatic notch/acetabulum index as a discriminator of sex in European skeletal remains. *Journal of Forensic Sciences*, 31:1380–1390.

MacLaughlin, S.M. and Cox, M.J. (1989). The relationship between body size and parturition scars. *Journal of Anatomy*, 164:258.

Mayhall, J.T. and Kanazawa, E. (1989). Three-dimensional analysis of the maxillary first molar crowns of Canadian Inuit. *American Journal of Physical Anthropology*, 78:73–78.

*Mays, S. (1998). *The Archaeology of Human Bones*. Routledge: London.

*Mays, S. and Cox, M. (2000). Sex determination in skeletal remains. In Cox, M. and Mays, S. (eds) *Human Osteology in Archaeology and Forensic Science*, 117–130. Greenwich Medical Media: London.

McKern, T.W. and Stewart, T.W. (1957). *Skeletal Age Changes in Young American Males Analysed from the Standpoint of Age Identification*. Technical Report No. EP-45, Environmental Protection Research Division: Natick, MA.

Meindl, R.S., Lovejoy, C.O., Mensforth, R.P. and Carlos, L.D. (1985). Accuracy and determination of error in the sexing of the skeleton. *American Journal of Physical Anthropology*, 68:79–85.

Miles, A.E.W. (1962). Assessment of the ages of a population of Anglo-Saxons from their dentitions. *Proceedings of the Royal Society of Medicine*, 55:881–886.

Miller, C., Dove, S. and Cottone, J. (1988). Failure of use of cemental annulations in teeth to determine the age of humans. *Journal of Forensic Sciences*, 33:137–143.

Molleson, T.I. and Cohen, P. (1990). The progression of dental attrition stages used for age assessment. *Journal of Archaeological Science*, 17:363–371.

Molleson, T. and Cox, M. (1993). *The Spitalfields Project Volume 2. The Anthropology. The Middling Sort.* Research Report 86, Council for British Archaeology: York.

Murray, K.A. and Murray, T. (1991). A test of the auricular surface ageing techniques. *Journal of Forensic Sciences*, 36:1162–1169.

Paine, R.R. and Harpending, H.C. (1998). Effect of sample bias on palaeodemographic fertility estimates. *American Journal of Physical Anthropology*, 105:231–240.

Perzigian, A.J. (1976). The dentition of the Indian Knoll skeletal population: odontometrics and cusp number. *American Journal of Physical Anthropology*, 44:113–122.

Phenice, T.W. (1969). A newly developed method of sexing the os pubis. *American Journal of Physical Anthropology*, 30:297–302.

Porter, A.M.W. (1998). The dental arcade and human morphology. *International Journal of Osteoarchaeology*, 8:66–74.

Rösing, F.W. (1983). Sexing immature human skeletons. *Journal of Human Evolution*, 12:149–155.

Saunders, S.P., Fitzgerald, C., Rogers, T., Dudar, C. and McKillop, H. (1992). A test of several methods of skeletal age estimation using a documented archaeological sample. *Canadian Society of Forensic Science Journal*, 25:97–117.

Scheuer, L. and Black, S. (2000). Development and ageing of the juvenile skeleton. In Cox, M. and Mays, S. (eds) *Human Osteology in Archaeology and Forensic Science*, 9–22. Greenwich Medical Media: London.

Schulter-Ellis, F.P., Hayek, L.C. and Schmidt, D.J. (1985). Determination of sex with a discriminant analysis of new pelvic bone measurements: part II. *Journal of Forensic Sciences*, 30:178–185.

Seidemann, R.M., Stojanowski, C.M. and Doran, G.H. (1998). The use of the supero-inferior femoral neck diameter as a sex assessor. *American Journal of Physical Anthropology*, 107:305–313.

Stout, S.D. (1992). Methods of determining age at death using bone microstructure. In Saunders, S.R. and Katzenberg, M.A. (eds) *Skeletal Biology of Past Peoples*, 21–35. John Wiley: New York.

Stout, S.D. and Paine, R.R. (1992). Histological age estimation using rib and clavicle. *American Journal of Physical Anthropology*, **87**:111–115.

Stout, S.D., Parro, M.A. and Perotti, B. (1996). A test and correction of the clavicle method of Stout and Paine for histological age estimation of skeletal remains. *American Journal of Physical Anthropology*, **100**:139–142.

Suchey, J.M. (1979). Problems in the ageing of females using the os pubis. *American Journal of Physical Anthropology*, **51**:467–471.

Sutherland, L.D. and Suchey, J.M. (1991). Use of the ventral arc in pubic sex determination. *Journal of Forensic Sciences*, **36**:501–511.

Sutton, M.Q., Malik, M. and Ogram, A. (1996). Experiments on the determination of gender from coprolites by DNA analysis. *Journal of Archaeological Science*, **23**:263–267.

Todd, T.W. (1920). Age changes in the pubic bone. Part I. The male white pubis. *American Journal of Physical Anthropology*, **3**:285–339.

Tomenchuk, J. and Mayhall, J.T. (1979). A correlation of tooth wear and age among modern Igloolik Eskimos. *American Journal of Physical Anthropology*, **51**:67–78.

Waldron, T. (1987). The relative survival of the human skeleton: implications for palaeodemography. In Boddington, A., Garland, A.N. and Janaway, R.C. (eds) *Death, Decay and Reconstruction*, 55–64. Manchester University Press: Manchester.

Walker, G.F. and Kowalski, C.J. (1972). On the growth of the mandible. *American Journal of Physical Anthropology*, **36**:111–118.

Wallin, J.A., Tkocz, I. and Kristensen, G. (1994). Microscopic age determination of human skeletons including an unknown but calculable variable. *International Journal of Osteoarchaeology*, **4**:353–362.

Webb, P.A.O. and Suchey, J.M. (1985). Epiphyseal union of the anterior iliac crest and medial clavicle in a modern multi-racial sample of American males and females. *American Journal of Physical Anthropology*, **68**:457–466.

Weiss, K.M. (1973). *Demographic Models for Anthropology*. Memoir No. 27, Society for American Archaeology, Washington DC.

*Whittaker, D. (2000). Ageing from the dentition. In Cox, M. and Mays, S. (eds) *Human Osteology in Archaeology and Forensic Science*, 83–100. Greenwich Medical Media: London.

21

The Study of Preserved Human Tissue

M.R. ZIMMERMAN

Department of Anthropology, University of Pennsylvania, Philadelphia.

Disease and death are integral parts of the history not only of individuals but also of whole populations. Palaeopathological studies are aimed at improving our understanding of the evolution of diseases and their role in human biological and social history. The father of modern palaeopathology is considered to be Sir Marc Armand Ruffer and his definition, 'the science of the diseases which can be demonstrated in human and animal remains of ancient times' (1921) is the one generally accepted today.

Pathogenic organisms and patterns of disease can evolve, as do larger organisms, but there is evidence, on the other hand, for considerable stability in host-parasite relationships. Even 'new' diseases are often found to antedate initial clinical descriptions. Information on ancient disease patterns is obtained from ancient pathological material and several other sources, including historic records such as Egyptian medical papyri, studies of the great plagues of Medieval Europe, and works of art, such as paintings, pottery effigies, figurines, religious statuary, and figures and faces on coins.

The most reliable palaeopathological information derives from the examination of skeletal material and mummies. Mummies are defined as bodies preserved either naturally, as by drying or freezing, or artificially. Naturally preserved bodies have been found in bogs and in arctic and arid areas. Artificially preserved mummies are classically Egyptian, but are also found in the Aleutian Islands, South America, ancient Scythia, the islands of the Torres Strait, Italy, the Canary Islands, Japan and China (Cockburn *et al.* 1998). From studies of these mummies, a number of diseases have been diagnosed. Many of the diagnoses offered have been presumptive, a necessary limitation considering the degree of preservation usually encountered, although experimental studies do indicate that mummification is effective in preserving pathological change (Brier and Wade 1997, Zimmerman *et al.* 1998).

HISTORICAL ASPECTS OF THE EXAMINATION OF MUMMIES

The first of the truly modern palaeopathologists was Sir Marc Armand Ruffer (1859–1917). Ruffer was an English experimental pathologist and bacteriologist of some note when an illness forced him to Egypt for recuperation. He developed the rehydration technique that is still in use for preparing microscopic sections of mummies, and made a number of important diagnostic contributions. Unfortunately, he was lost at sea in World War I.

Handbook of Archaeological Sciences. Edited by D.R. Brothwell and A.M. Pollard.
© 2001 John Wiley & Sons, Ltd.

The mid-twentieth century was characterized in the United States by only sporadic contributions from individual physicians and in Great Britain by the work of Don Brothwell and A.T. Sandison, who published *Diseases in Antiquity* (Brothwell and Sandison 1967). The field was revitalized in the 1970s by the activities of three groups. The Paleopathology Association was founded in Detroit by Eve and the late Aidan Cockburn and 12 charter members. The association publishes the quarterly *Paleopathology Newsletter*, presents symposia and meets on occasion to examine a mummy. These studies, performed at a number of museums and medical centres in the United States and Canada, have gone far towards improving the difficulties that were experienced in interpreting lesions in the past, and a wide variety of new techniques have come into play, including sophisticated radiographic studies such as computed tomographic scanning, electron and scanning electron microscopy, fluorescent antibody and other serological techniques, neutron activation analysis and other chemical and microbiological techniques.

A second group, headed by Marvin Allison and Enrique Gerszten of the Pathology Department, Medical College of Virginia, Richmond, has conducted an extensive survey of Peruvian and Chilean mummies. They have published many articles and monographs (e.g, Gerszten *et al.* 1998) and the Paleopathology Club of the International Academy of Pathology has developed from this group.

A full length course in palaeopathology, held at the Smithsonian Institution from 1971–1974, under the direction of the late J. Lawrence Angel and Don Ortner and with the co-operation of Lent Johnson, Walter Putschar and T.D. Stewart, provided a third major impetus in palaeopathology. The seminar provided training for a number of people and was at least indirectly responsible for the publication of Steinbock's *Paleopathological Diagnosis and Interpretation* (1976), which focuses primarily on skeletal material, as does the text prepared by Ortner and Putschar (1985). Most recently, the Armed Forces Institute of Pathology, also in Washington, has sponsored several seminars in palaeopathology. As interest in the field increases, the number of journals accepting palaeopathology articles also increases. *Science*, the *American Journal of Physical Anthropology*, and the *Paleopathology Newsletter* publish many relevant articles. There are also a number of new books in the field (e.g., Aufderheide and Rodríguez-Martín 1998, Roberts and Manchester 1995).

TECHNICAL CONSIDERATIONS

Examination of a mummy is best performed by a team approach, beginning with radiological examination (Harris and Wente 1980, Cockburn *et al.* 1998). Egyptian mummies require Egyptologists for unwrapping and interpretation of the objects and hieroglyphics (Smith and Dawson 1991, Taylor 1995). A physical anthropologist should be part of the team and the actual autopsy must be performed by a pathologist. Careful labelling of specimens is needed, as it may be difficult or impossible to identify tissue types after rehydration. Extensive photography is essential and should include infrared photography to identify tattoos, which have been found in Scythians, Inuit and European mummies (Zimmerman and Smith 1975, Spindler 1994, Hart Hansen 1998). The soot used for ancient tattoos results in a dark blue or black tattoo, easily seen in the living but difficult to discern in the dark brown skin of a mummy. As blue objects are darkened when photographed with infrared film, the use of infrared photography has proved invaluable in the detection and evaluation of tattoos in mummies. Similarity of motifs between tattoos and artifacts can provide some reassurance that both are from the same general time period. The utility of this approach is limited by the accuracy of the dating of the artifacts and by the innate conservatism of aboriginal art and motifs for hundreds or thousands of years.

Rehydration of mummy tissues dates to the nineteenth century, when a few investigators soaked mummified tissue in caustic potash, checking the process at the desired state with formalin. Formalin coagulates the proteins in tissues, thus deactivating the enzymes that are responsible for tissue breakdown. In the early twentieth century, Ruffer developed his rehydrating solution, which is still in use. Ruffer's solution, 50 parts water, 30 parts absolute alcohol, and 20 parts 5 per cent sodium carbonate solution, is most easily prepared by dissolving 0.6 g of sodium carbonate in 42 ml of water and adding 18 ml of absolute (100 per cent) alcohol. In Ruffer's technique, one-third of the solution was removed and replaced with absolute alcohol for three successive days. The rehydrated tissue was then immersed in absolute alcohol for three more days. Allison simplified the process by immersing the tissues in Ruffer's solution till they were fully rehydrated to visual inspection (usually 24–48 hours). The solution always develops a dark brown turbidity. The tissue is then fixed in alcohol and processed in the same fashion as are normal tissues. Elimination of the changes of solution greatly decreases the trauma to which these delicate tissues are subjected.

A variety of special stains can be used to demonstrate specific features of the tissues. In general, connective tissue and any foreign elements, such as pigments, bacteria, or parasites, are best preserved, whilst epithelial tissues fare less well. Connective tissue stains are those used most, including the Masson trichrome, which stains muscle red and fibrous tissue blue or green, and phosphotungstic acid hematoxylin, for the cross striations of muscles. Standard hematoxylin and eosin, which stains nuclei blue and cytoplasm pink, is useful only in a very general sense. Some other techniques that have been applied to rehydrated tissue include plastic embedding of bone specimens, which would otherwise have to be decalcified, and scanning and transmission electron microscopy.

It is also possible to estimate the dating and age at death of a mummy (Zimmerman and Angel 1986). In adults, a rough estimate of early, middle or late can be made, usually based on the degree of atherosclerosis, but more precise techniques are available through a study of teeth and bone (see Chapter 20). The expected accuracy of age-related variation in mummified soft tissue is far less than that obtained from the skeletal system and teeth, and radiological examination is most useful for age estimation in children.

MUMMY TYPES AND FINDINGS

Mummies have been found in many parts of the world. Artificial mummies have been prepared in classic Egyptian society and by indigenous island populations, including the Canary Islands, Aleutian Islands and Melanesia. Frozen mummies (human and animal) are found in Alaska, Greenland and Russia. Desiccated bodies are found in North and South America, Australia, China and Japan, and bog bodies have been found in northern Europe and Britain (Fischer 1998). The palaeopathological findings in these bodies (Tyson 1997) fall into a number of broad general categories.

Skeletal deformities, such as spina bifida, are generally diagnosed by gross or radiological examination. A rare condition, alkaptonuric arthritis (or ochronosis), was diagnosed radiologically in several mummies in the 1960s, but it has become apparent that increased radiodensity of intervertebral cartilage is seen in many Egyptian mummies as an artifact of mummification. Calculus, or stone formation has been described in the gall bladder and urinary tract. Microscopic confirmation for these diagnoses is unnecessary.

Traumatic injuries have included frostbite in a pre-Columbian Chilean mummy and fractures in Peruvian, Alaskan and Egyptian mummies. Some of the fractures are either post-mortem or 'embalmer's fractures'. Aspiration of foreign material has been seen in two mummies. A Peruvian mummy of AD 950 was found to have aspirated a molar tooth, which, firmly impacted in a left bronchus, resulted in fatal pneumonia (Allison et al. 1974a). A mummy from St Lawrence Island, Alaska, died 1600 years ago of asphyxiation due to aspiration of moss. It appeared that this woman had been trapped in her house during an earthquake or landslide and buried under the moss roof (Zimmerman and Smith 1975).

There have been many reports of inflammatory processes. Osteomyelitis has been seen in Peruvian and Egyptian mummies. Zimmerman and Clark (1976) diagnosed a skin disorder, subcorneal pustular dermatosis, in a 3200 year old Egyptian mummy. This condition was not described in modern patients until 1956.

Periodontal disease and caries have been noted in Pharaohs and fellahs as well as mummies from other areas of the world. X-ray and mineralogical analysis of ancient Egyptian bread reveals sufficient abrasive particles to account for the dental attrition seen in these ancient teeth (Leek 1972). We have virtually no evidence of dental surgery by the ancient Egyptians, indicating that what therapy was available was directed at the soft tissues, to little avail. Dental disease such as periodontal disease or caries, can lead to infection of the middle ear and mastoid sinuses, and bilateral perforation of the ear drums has been found in an Egyptian mummy.

Infectious disease is categorized by the etiologic agents, i.e., viruses, bacteria, fungi, protozoan and metazoan parasites, and insects. Viruses have not been seen in the few electron microscopic studies performed on mummies. However, two viral diseases that have been noted in ancient Egyptian material, poliomyelitis and smallpox, do show diagnostic lesions grossly and on light microscopy. As early as 1900, Mitchell noted a shortened leg in an elderly male of 3700 BC as indicative of poliomyelitis (Mitchell 1900). Ruffer (1921) reported a characteristic deformity of the foot of the Pharaoh Siptah of the XIXth Dynasty, with X-ray examination showing overall shortening of the entire right leg and atrophy of the soft tissues, indicating the presence of a neuromuscular disease in childhood, almost certainly poliomyelitis. Whilst infection by the polio virus is almost universal in developing countries, the clinical disease is rare.

Infection usually occurs early in life, when maternal antibodies prevent the development of the disease, allowing the virus to set up a commensal relationship in the intestinal tract of the host. With improved sanitation, the result of infection by the virus is more likely to be disease than a commensal state. The finding of this disease in a Pharaoh can be attributed to the isolation of the Royal Family and provides historical verification for this concept of the pathogenesis of poliomyelitis.

A smallpox-like eruption has been noted on the mummy of Rameses V (Hopkins 1980) and the characteristic microscopic features of the vesicles of smallpox have been identified in a XXth Dynasty mummy, attesting to the antiquity of this disease (Ruffer 1921).

Pneumonia, one of the most common of the bacterial infectious processes, and a major cause of death in the pre-antibiotic era, has been identified in Alaskan, Peruvian and Egyptian mummies. Pneumonia can be complicated by the entry of micro-organisms into the blood stream and the development of metastatic abscesses in other organs. Such abscesses were noted in an Aleut mummy in the heart, lungs, and kidneys (Zimmerman et al. 1971). The heart valves can become involved, and healed endocarditis has been reported in an Egyptian mummy (Long 1931) and an Inuit mummy (Zimmerman and Aufderheide 1984).

The question of the origin of syphilis has always aroused much controversy (see Chapter 19). Although characteristic skeletal lesions have been described in ancient material from both sides of the Atlantic, not a single case of syphilis has ever been diagnosed in a mummy (Zimmerman and Kelley 1982).

The Medical College of Virginia group was the first to stain and identify *Mycobacterium tuberculosis* in a mummy, in their description of a case of advanced disease in a Peruvian child of AD 700 (Allison et al. 1973). The characteristic lesions of tuberculosis present in this child, caseous necrosis, spinal deformity and psoas abscess, had been amply demonstrated in other mummies, but not the organisms. A review by Morse et al. (1964) established the presence of tuberculosis in ancient Egypt, and Zimmerman (1977a) was able to stain tubercle bacilli in the mummy of an Egyptian child who died of pulmonary haemorrhage. Of interest is the failure of Elliot Smith to find any examples of tuberculosis in 6000 predynastic Nubian skeletons and mummies, suggesting the Dynastic period for the evolution of human tuberculosis in the Nile Valley.

No specific fungal infections have been identified in mummies. The St Lawrence Island Inuit mummy

(Zimmerman and Smith 1975) did have a chronic granulomatous process affecting the lymphatic system, suggesting histoplasmosis.

Our evidence for protozoan parasites is mostly indirect. Coprolites from the American south-west contain Charcot–Leyden crystals, which are seen in diarrhoeal states, particularly in cases of amebiasis (Heizer 1969). Splenic changes have been diagnosed as malarial in Egyptian mummies (Ruffer 1921, Reyman et al. 1977). Angel (1966) noted a geographical overlap between malaria and porotic hyperostosis of the skull, which fits in well with current thinking on the protective effects of hereditary anaemias against malaria.

We are on much firmer ground in diagnosing metazoan infections and infestations, as parasitic worms and their ova remain well preserved for millennia. The ova of *Ascaris lumbricoides, Schistosoma hematobium,* and *Taenia solium* have been reported in Egyptian mummies (Ruffer 1921, Reyman et al. 1977, Cockburn et al. 1998), and the ova of ascaris, trichuris and fish tapeworm have been seen in 2000 year old European bog bodies (Fischer 1998).

Parasitic infestations have also been seen in the New World. Trichuriasis appears to have been a world-wide infestation (Pizzi and Schenone 1955). Adult hookworms, *Ancylostoma duodenale,* have been seen in Peruvian mummies (Allison et al. 1974b). Western American coprolites dating from 10 000 years ago have yielded pinworm ova (Fry and Moore 1969), and thorny headed worm ova (Moore et al. 1969). The latter probably represents an accidental infestation of the individual by this rodent parasite, as does the finding of a fish trematode in the St Lawrence Island Inuit woman's mummy (Zimmerman and Smith 1975).

A number of degenerative processes have been identified in mummies, primarily involving the skeletal, vascular and pulmonary systems. Osteoarthritis, easily identified by damage to the vertebrae and other joints, has been diagnosed in Egyptian, Coptic and Nubian mummies. Its presence in the hot dry climate of Egypt and Nubia belies the folk attribution of the disease to damp climates. Rameses II suffered from severe osteoarthritis of the hips and the disease has been found in Peruvian mummies, completing the documentation of its geographical and social ubiquity.

A more life threatening disorder, atherosclerosis, has been very well documented in mummies, again showing a ubiquitous distribution. A sudden death depicted on an Egyptian tomb relief has been interpreted as evidence of coronary artery disease and myocardial infarction (Breutsch 1959). This historic evidence is well-substantiated by the finding of atherosclerosis in many Egyptian mummies, including the Pharaohs Merneptah, Amenhotep II and Rameses II. Atherosclerosis has also been seen in New World mummies from the Aleutian Islands and St Lawrence Island. The condition has been found in only a few of the many Peruvian mummies studied, suggesting a possible lower incidence in ancient Peru or shorter life spans. The diagnosis of the various disturbances of circulation resulting from atherosclerosis (thrombosis, embolization, myocardial or pulmonary infarction, etc.) has not been made in any mummy. This is surprising in view of the historical and anatomical evidence of atherosclerosis, but may be the result of a problem in preservation. Acutely infarcted tissue is autolysed *in situ*, and as such would not be distinguishable from postmortem autolysis (Zimmerman 1978).

Another common degenerative process is the accumulation of foreign material, particularly in the lungs. The deposition of carbon pigment (anthracosis) has been seen in mummies from all areas, including Alaska, the Canary Islands and Egypt. The combination of carbon and silica particles (anthracosilicosis) is seen in Egyptian mummies. The ubiquity of anthracosis is attributed to life-long exposure to open fires, for heating and cooking, whilst the silicosis is probably due to inhalation of sand during the storms common to Egypt. Several mummies have shown lung damage as a result of these exposures.

Trace elements can also accumulate in the tissues. An autopsy was performed on Charles Francis Hall, an Arctic explorer who died and was buried in Greenland in 1871. Hair and nail samples removed from the frozen body a century later showed high levels of arsenic and the presumption is that he was poisoned by his crew (Paddock *et al.* 1970).

There have only been a few tissue diagnoses of neoplasms in mummified remains. Possible reasons for the few diagnoses of cancer in mummies include poor preservation, early age at death and a relative rarity of cancer in antiquity (Zimmerman 1977b).

THE INTEGRATION OF PALAEOPATHOLOGY AND ARCHAEOLOGY

The second major focus of palaeopathology is the integration of palaeopathological findings with archaeological information, resulting in an improved picture of the health status of ancient populations. Examples are found in studies of Egyptian and Alaskan mummies.

Egyptian mummification developed from the natural preservation of unembalmed bodies buried in the hot, dry sands of the desert in Predynastic times. The history of ancient Egypt is conventionally divided into the Predynastic (prehistoric) and Dynastic periods. The Dynastic Period begins at 3100 BC with the invention of writing and terminates with the conquest of Egypt by Alexander the Great in 332 BC, followed by the Roman Period, after 30 BC. All deceased Egyptians were mummified until the Christian era, about AD 200 to 400. Egyptian mummies have been studied in Egypt itself and in museums in North America and Europe. A typical example is the investigation of mummies found in the Theban tomb of a New Kingdom priest, Nebwenenef, the first of Rameses' High Priests, who died about 1290 BC (Zimmerman 1977a). Fifty secondary burials were recovered from the tomb, broken by tomb robbers into over 12 000 fragments. The remains found in this tomb do not constitute a population in the usual anthropological sense, but rather a collection deposited in the tomb over a number of centuries.

The specimen of most pathological interest was the mummy of an approximately five-year-old child, who was found to have suffered from tuberculosis of the bone and lungs, with recurrent and finally fatal pulmonary haemorrhage (Zimmerman 1979a), firmly establishing the presence of tuberculosis in dynastic Egypt. The inferences on social conditions and habitation patterns derived from this diagnosis are of special value in view of the almost exclusively monumental emphasis in Egyptian archaeology. The presence of tuberculosis in ancient Egypt verifies the impression that most ancient Egyptians lived in crowded living conditions, the disease being much more readily transmitted in crowded communities. Childhood tuberculosis is acquired by exposure to an individual whose sputum contains many infective organisms. Persons with recently acquired disease, i.e., children and young adults, of the parental age group, are relatively non-infectious, in contrast to elderly persons (such as grandparents) with reactivated disease. Childhood tuberculosis is thus indirect evidence suggestive of multi-generational rather than bi-generational households in ancient Egypt; this pattern persists today.

Anthracosis in this young child confirms the presence of an open fire in the dwelling place. In the hot climate of Thebes, this was probably an oven fire for baking bread rather than a heating fire. The documentation of this condition in many mummies has made it apparent that air pollution, once thought to be limited to modern, industrialized societies, has been a feature of human settlements for millennia.

Atherosclerosis was noted in a number of arterial samples, but evidence of neoplastic disease was minimal, with only two benign tumours identified and no lytic lesions suggestive of metastatic cancer. In another field study of 14 mummies, the Dakhleh Oasis Project in the western desert of Egypt, two malignant tumours were identified, involving the rectum and bladder. The relatively good preservation of the tumours found in these mummies is consistent with the preservation of tumours noted in experimental mummification studies (Zimmerman 1979b). The rarity of such diagnoses in the palaeopathological literature implies that factors existing in the modern world only are involved in the causation of cancer. In contrast, atherosclerosis is clearly of great antiquity.

A picture emerges from such studies of a society whose members, of all classes, lived in close proximity, in multi-generational households and shared exposure to the same pathogens. Although there is little evidence of the malignant tumours that plague the twentieth century, the living conditions of ancient Egypt ensured transmission of infectious diseases. The chronic anaemia of parasitic diseases such as schistosomiasis, compounded by the debilitating effects of under-nutrition, tuberculosis and other acute and chronic infections must have resulted in a population with a marginal health status, although still capable of extraordinary architectural and military exploits. This background of disease and under-nutrition may have been a factor in the association of episodic political and administrative difficulties and agricultural failures with foreign military setbacks known to have occurred in ancient Egypt. It is a tribute to the abilities of the Egyptian administrators that she was able to play the role she did on the stage of the ancient world.

In contrast to the many studies of Egyptian mummies, only a few mummies have been found in the Arctic (Hart Hansen 1998). The frigid climate results in frozen mummies with remarkable histological detail, but bodies are preserved only under extraordinary circumstances. The frozen ground makes winter burials impossible, and the permafrost layer, only a few centimetres below the surface, discourages deep burials even in summer. Cycles of freezing and thawing tend to bring summer burials to the surface, exposing bodies to the ravages of animals and the weather.

Human bodies have been found on St Lawrence Island in the Bering Sea and in Barrow, the northernmost point of North America. The St Lawrence Island mummy, found in 1972, was that of a middle aged Inuit woman who died a traumatic death 1600 years ago (Zimmerman and Smith 1975). As noted above, her air passages were packed with moss and associated

microscopic foci of haemorrhage indicated death by asphyxiation. Antemortem fracture of the right temporal bone confirmed the role of trauma in her death. It was concluded that she had been trapped in her semi-subterranean house by a landslide or earthquake, struck by the stone used to hold the roof flap down, buried alive and asphyxiated. Other findings included atherosclerosis, anthracosis, healed pneumonia and emphysema.

Ten years later, the remains of five people were found in a crushed winter house in the ancient village of Utqiagvik on a bluff overlooking the Arctic Ocean in the modern town of Barrow, the northernmost point of Alaska (Zimmerman and Aufderheide 1984). Their deaths, dated to 500 years ago, were attributed to the well-documented phenomenon of *ivu*, an enormously powerful inland incursion of large amounts of wind- and tide-driven broken sea ice, which crushed their winter house.

The three youngest individuals had been skeletonized. The others, both adult females, were very well preserved and showed fatal crushing chest injuries. Both had rib fractures, collapsed lungs and bloody chest fluid. The younger woman, in her mid-twenties, also had a skull fracture. The older woman, in her forties, was found near the exit from the house, with a roof beam across her chest. The lungs of both showed massive anthracosis, related to the intensely smokey atmosphere of houses heated by seal oil lamps, and severe osteoporosis (demineralization) of the bones, due to an almost totally meat-based diet.

The older woman had coronary and aortic atherosclerosis but had still been reproductively active. Her breasts, prominent on gross examination, showed the histological appearance of lactation and other evidence indicated that she had delivered some two to six months before death. No infant's body was found, however. Her body also showed evidence of previous bouts of pneumonia, complicated by pleuritis, infection involving the heart and kidney failure, followed, rather surprisingly, by recovery. Cystic structures in the diaphragm indicated trichinosis, which infects Arctic populations through the meat of the polar bear.

Most recently, in 1994, the frozen body of a six year old Inuit girl was found adjacent to the site of the frozen family described above. The archaeological context and radiocarbon dates suggest that the little girl was a member of the semi-nomadic Thule culture (*c.* AD 800–1200). She had been buried in a meat cellar dug partly through an abandoned house floor, and appeared to have died of starvation. Her intestine was filled with gravel, sand, pebbles and animal hair, indicating that normal food sources were unavailable. The terminal event was pulmonary edema, probably secondary to hypoproteinemia, with the accumulation of bloody fluid in the chest cavities and collapse of the left lung.

A severe degree of emphysema was a contributing cause to her death. Emphysema, common in long time cigarette smokers, is rare in children. This child's emphysema was a complication of a rare genetic disorder, alpha-l-antitrypsin (AlAT) deficiency, evidenced by the accumulation in her liver of an abnormal form of the AlAT. The pathogenetic sequence in this disorder is initiated by lung infection. Inflammatory cells enter the lungs from the blood and release destructive enzymes such as trypsin aimed at the invading bacteria. To prevent destruction of the lung itself alpha-l-antitrypsin is released by the liver into the blood stream. Individuals with an inherited deficiency of AlAT are unable to inactivate trypsin and other enzymes in their lungs, leading to destruction of elastic tissue and the development of emphysema.

She had suffered multiple bouts of illness during her brief life, as evidenced by numerous growth arrest lines ('Harris lines') observed by X-ray in her long bones. A sled buried with the child was probably used when she was too weak or ill to walk. Her deliberate burial is a rare find in ancient Inuit populations and is evidence that this chronically ill child was kept alive and treated with care in life and in death.

Another group of frozen Inuit bodies, radiocarbon dated to the fifteenth century, was found in Greenland in 1972, near the abandoned settlement of Qilakitsoq (Hart Hansen and Gullov 1989). These eight mummies, preserved by low temperature and humidity in two adjacent sheltered grave sites, were living at the same time as the last descendants of Erik the Red in Greenland, and are representative of the Skrellings described in Icelandic and Norwegian sagas.

Pathological diagnoses included anthracosis, Down's syndrome in a severely disabled child, and a case of nasopharyngeal carcinoma, a relatively common disease amongst the Inuit of Greenland. A wide range of studies was performed on the mummies, including studies of teeth, eyes, skin, intestinal contents, skeletons, trace metals, fungi, bone mineral, etc., demonstrating the value of the interdisciplinary approach to such rare finds.

In the Aleutian Islands, the cool damp climate would seem to be poorly suited to mummification but cultural practices have supervened to produce artificial mummies. The Aleuts of the eighteenth century, from the immediate pre-Russian era, mummified their dead by drying the cadaver in the air or over a fire. The mummy was then dressed, bound with the hips, elbows and knees flexed, wrapped in sea lion skins and placed in a burial cave on Kagamil Island. A number of mummies were removed from the island in the late nineteenth and early twentieth centuries. The mummy of a middle aged male now in the Smithsonian Institution and a middle aged female from the Peabody Museum of Archaeology and Ethnology of Harvard University have been examined.

The male mummy was found to have died of lobar pneumonia caused by a gram-negative bacillus, complicated by septicaemia and diffuse metastatic abscesses (Zimmerman et al. 1971). Other findings included pulmonary anthracosis and mild atherosclerosis. There was evidence of severe dental stress and periodontal disease. The female mummy, which had been quite literally in dead storage in the museum for over a century, showed marked pulmonary anthracosis (Zimmerman et al. 1981). Her death appeared to be due to pneumonia and pleuritis. She also suffered from chronic otitis media and mastoiditis. Remarkable also was preservation of lice, providing clear evidence of the antiquity and ubiquity of *pediculosis capitis*. No lead was found in this cadaver, in marked contrast to findings in modern persons.

Rare finds such as those described above give us a glimpse into the prehistoric Arctic and show health hazards shared by past and present inhabitants of a once remote area. Diseases such as pneumonia, anthracosis, osteoporosis and trichinosis have well-known natural histories and are relatively easily explained in the context of the Arctic and Aleutian ecosystems.

CONCLUSION

Examination of preserved human remains in the field and in museum collections has demonstrated the value of the use of current techniques. Although gross and light microscopic pathological techniques remain essential, the application of radiology, electron microscopy, neutron activation analysis, and biochemical and other special studies represents a major advance in palaeopathology, allowing a whole new range of diagnostic possibilities. The availability of these techniques and the co-operation of archaeologists and museum directors in allowing study of their valuable specimens has coincided with the interests of a sizeable group of scientists of many disciplines in providing integration of archaeological and historical information and a much-needed historical perspective on the evolution of many of the diseases that afflict modern humans.

REFERENCES

*Recommended for further reading

Allison, M.J., Mendoza, D. and Pezzia, A. (1973). Documentation of a case of tuberculosis in pre-Columbian America. *American Review of Respiratory Diseases*, **107**:985–991.

Allison, M.J., Pezzia, A., Gerszten, E., Giffler, R.F. and Mendoza, D. (1974a). Aspiration pneumonia due to teeth – 950 AD and 1973 AD. *Southern Medical Journal*, **67**:479–483.

Allison, M.J., Pezzia, P., Hasegawa, I. and Gerszten, E. (1974b). A case of hookworm infestation in a pre-Columbian American. *American Journal of Physical Anthropology*, **41**:103–106.

Angel, J.L. (1966). Porotic hyperostosis, anemias, malarias, and marshes in the prehistoric eastern Mediterranean. *Science*, **153**:760–763.

*Aufderheide, A.C. and Rodríguez-Martín, C. (1998). *The Cambridge Encyclopaedia of Human Palaeopathology*. Cambridge University Press: Cambridge.

Breutsch, W.L. (1959). The earliest record of sudden death possibly due to atherosclerotic coronary occlusion. *Circulation*, **20**:438–441.

Brier, B. and Wade, R.S. (1997). The use of natron in human mummification: a modern experiment. *Zeitschrift für Ägyptische Sprache und Altertumskunde*, **124**:89–100.

*Brothwell, D.R. and Sandison, A.T. (eds) (1967). *Diseases in Antiquity: A Survey of the Diseases, Injuries and Surgery of Early Populations*. Charles C. Thomas: Springfield, Illinois.

*Cockburn, A., Cockburn, E. and Reyman, T.A. (eds) (1998). *Mummies, Disease, and Ancient Cultures*, (2nd edn). Cambridge University Press: Cambridge.

Fischer, C. (1998). Bog bodies of Denmark and northwestern Europe. In Cockburn, A., Cockburn, E. and Reyman, T.A. (eds) *Mummies, Disease and Ancient Cultures*, (2nd edn), 237–262. Cambridge University Press: Cambridge.

Fry, G.F. and Moore, J.G. (1969). *Enterobius vermicularis*: 10 000-year-old human infection. *Science*, **166**:1620.

Gerszten, P.C., Gerszten, E. and Allison, M.J. (1998). Diseases of the skull in pre-Columbian South American mummies. *Neurosurgery*, **42**:1145–1151.

Harris, J.E. and Wente, E.F. (eds) (1980). *An X-ray Atlas of the Royal Mummies*. University of Chicago Press: Chicago.

Hart Hansen, J.P. (1998). Bodies from cold regions. In Cockburn, A., Cockburn, E. and Reyman, T.A. (eds) *Mummies, Disease and Ancient Cultures*, (2nd edn), 336–350. Cambridge University Press: Cambridge.

Hart Hansen, J.P. and Gullov, H.C. (eds) (1989). *The Mummies from Qilakitsoq – Eskimos in the 15th Century.*

Man and Society 12, Meddelelser om Grønland: Copenhagen.

Heizer, R.F. (1969). Anthropology of Great Basin coprolites. In Brothwell, D.R. and Higgs, E. (eds) *Science in Archaeology*, (2nd edn), 244–250. Thames and Hudson: London.

Hopkins, D.R. (1980). News from the field: Egypt. *Paleopathology Newsletter*, **31**:6.

Leek, F.F. (1972). Bread and teeth in ancient Egypt. *Journal of Egyptian Archaeology*, **58**:126–132.

Long, A.R. (1931). Cardiovascular renal disease: report of a case of 3000 years ago. *Archives of Pathology (Chicago)*, **12**:92–94.

Mitchell, J.K. (1900). Study of a mummy affected with anterior poliomyelitis. *Transactions of the Association of American Physicians*, **15**:134–136.

Moore, J.G., Fry, G.F. and Englert, E. Jr. (1969). Thorny-headed worm infection in North American prehistoric man. *Science*, **163**:1324–1325.

Morse, D., Brothwell, D.R. and Ucko, P.J. (1964). Tuberculosis in ancient Egypt. *American Review of Respiratory Diseases*, **90**:524–541.

*Ortner, D.J. and Putschar, W.G.J. (1985). *Identification of Pathologic Conditions in Human Skeletal Remains*. Smithsonian Institution Press: Washington DC.

Paddock, F.K., Loomis, C.C. and Perkons, A.K. (1970). An inquest on the death of Charles Francis Hall. *New England Journal of Medicine*, **282**:784–786.

Pizzi, T. and Schenone, H. (1955). Trichuris in an Inca. *Tropical Medicine and Hygiene News*, **4**:6–7.

Reyman, T.A., Zimmerman, M.R. and Lewin, P.K. (1977). Autopsy of an Egyptian mummy. 5. histopathologic examination. *Canadian Medical Association Journal*, **117**:470–471.

*Roberts, C. and Manchester, K. (1995). *The Archaeology of Disease*, (2nd edn). Cornell University Press: Ithaca, New York.

*Ruffer, M.A. (1921). *Studies in the Palaeopathology of Egypt*. University of Chicago Press: Chicago.

Smith, G.E. and Dawson, W.R. (1991). *Egyptian Mummies*. Kegan Paul International: London.

Spindler, K. (1994). *The Man in the Ice*. Weidenfeld and Nicolson: London.

Steinbock, B.T. (1976). *Paleopathological Diagnosis and Interpretation: Bone Diseases in Ancient Human Populations*. Charles C. Thomas: Springfield, Illinois.

Taylor, J.H. (1995). *Unwrapping a Mummy: The Life, Death and Embalming of Horemkenesi*. British Museum Press: London.

Tyson, R. (ed.) (1997). *Human Paleopathology and Related Subjects: An International Bibliography*. San Diego Museum of Man: San Diego.

Zimmerman, M.R. (1977a). The mummies of the tomb of Nebwenenef: paleopathology and archaeology. *Journal of the American Research Center in Egypt*, **14**:33–36.

Zimmerman, M.R. (1977b). An experimental study of mummification pertinent to the antiquity of cancer. *Cancer*, **40**:1358–1362.

Zimmerman, M.R. (1978). The mummified heart: a problem in medicolegal diagnosis. *Journal of Forensic Sciences*, **23**:750–753.

Zimmerman, M.R. (1979a). Pulmonary and osseous tuberculosis in an Egyptian mummy. *Bulletin of the New York Academy of Medicine*, **55**:604–608.

Zimmerman, M.R. (1979b). Paleopathologic diagnosis based on experimental mummification. *American Journal of Physical Anthropology*, **51**:235–254.

Zimmerman, M.R. and Angel, J.L. (eds) (1986). *Dating and Age Determination of Biologic Materials*. Croom Helm: London.

Zimmerman, M.R. and Aufderheide, A.C. (1984). The frozen family of Utqiagvik: the autopsy findings. *Arctic Anthropology*, **21**:53–64.

Zimmerman, M.R. and Clark, W.H. Jr. (1976). A possible case of subcorneal pustular dermatosis in an Egyptian mummy. *Archives of Dermatology*, **112**:204–205.

Zimmerman, M.R. and Kelley, M.A. (1982). *Atlas of Human Paleopathology*. Praeger: New York.

Zimmerman, M.R. and Smith, G.S. (1975). A probable case of accidental inhumation of 1600 years ago. *Bulletin of the New York Academy of Medicine*, **51**:828–837.

Zimmerman, M.R., Yeatman, G.W., Sprinz, H. and Titterington, W.P. (1971). Examination of an Aleutian mummy. *Bulletin of the New York Academy of Medicine*, **47**:80–103.

Zimmerman, M.R., Trinkaus, E., LeMay, M., Aufderheide, A.C., Reyman, T.A., Marrocco, G.R., Ortel, R.W., Benitez, J.T., Laughlin, W.S., Horne, P.D., Schultes, R.E. and Coughlin, E.A. (1981). The paleopathology of an Aleutian mummy. *Archives of Pathology and Laboratory Medicine*, **105**:638–641.

Zimmerman, M.R., Brier, B. and Wade, R.S. (1998). 20th century replication of an Egyptian mummy – implications for paleopathology. *American Journal of Physical Anthropology*, **107**:417–420.

22

Palaeodemography

A.T. CHAMBERLAIN

Department of Archaeology and Prehistory, University of Sheffield.

Demography is the study of the size, structure and dynamics of populations, and palaeodemography is distinguished from 'regular' demography only in that its subject matter encompasses the populations of the past rather than those of the present day. The term 'population' refers to a group of living individuals, but the meaning of this concept depends on whether it is used in a biological or a socio-cultural context. A biological population is a group of interbreeding organisms, or (in a formal sense) a cluster of individuals which have a high probability of mating with each other compared to their probability of mating with members of some other population. In the human sciences the population is also viewed as a social unit with membership determined by shared linguistic, cultural or historical experience. This kind of population, sometimes labelled a 'community', a 'culture' or a 'people', refers to a group united by their mutual social recognition of ancestry and kinship, by other cultural affinities and usually by co-residence or geographical proximity. According to this viewpoint socio-economic and socio-cultural factors are paramount in the formation and maintenance of human populations. In considering archaeological populations both the biological and the social perspectives are important. Economic factors are often deeply implicated in the determination of patterns of migration and in reproductive decisions exercised by individuals and families, while at the same time the constraints of biology are evident in regular patterns of fertility and mortality that are common to all human and animal populations.

Demography considers the population as a singular object for quantitative analysis, and seeks to explain variations in population size, density, structure and dynamics. Population size and density refer respectively to the absolute number of individuals and the number of individuals per unit area of territory. Population structure describes the distribution of the individuals across designated categories, principally those of age and sex. Population dynamics refers to the growth or decline in the size of the population, and/or changes in its structure over time. Dynamic change is potentially complex because of its dependence on the separate factors of fertility, mortality and migration: in all populations these factors vary substantially across age and sex categories, and they also change over time. As a result, quantitative demographic models of real populations are often complex, and population parameters sometimes change in a counter-intuitive fashion.

There is no quick and easy route by which population size and structure can be inferred from archaeological data. A multitude of confounding factors, including the differential deposition, preservation and recovery of archaeological remains (see Chapters 15 and 51), conspire to render samples incomplete and unrepresentative, whilst indirect evidence for population numbers (such as settlement size: see below) are open to a variety of conflicting interpretations. In addition to these problems of data quality (which are encountered in most archaeological data) palaeodemography has had to grapple with its own special methodological problems, in particular the difficulties surrounding methods of age estimation (see Chapter 20) and the sometimes questionable practice of applying stable and stationary demographic models to past populations.

DEMOGRAPHIC METHODS

In both contemporary and historical demography much use is made of census data, which provides direct information about the size and structure of living populations – and of vital statistics, that is records of events such as births and deaths from which measures of fertility and mortality can be calculated. These sources of data are usually unavailable to the palaeodemographer. The primary data for palaeodemography consists either of indirect proxy measures of population size (such as settlement size, or resource availability), or of estimates of the population's age structure derived from an analysis of a sample of deaths using stable or stationary population models. It is important to note that the age structure of a mortality sample will generally differ from that of the living population within which the deaths occur because in most populations the risk of death varies significantly with age. Only in the special case of catastrophic mortality, in which every member of a population has an equal chance of dying, will the mortality profile resemble the age profile of the living community.

The age structure of a living population can be reconstructed from a mortality sample using a stable population model and standard life table calculations. In a population that is closed to inward and outward migration the age and sex distribution is determined by the population's current and recent history of mortality and fertility. If age-specific birth and death rates are constant over a period of time the population will eventually converge on a stable age structure with population size increasing or decreasing at a constant rate. In a stable population the numbers of individuals in each age category increase or decrease at the same rate as the whole population. It takes a few generations, perhaps 50–100 years, for the age distribution of a human population to achieve stable structure (Coale 1957, Weiss 1975), and in practice any given closed population will show in its age structure the cumulative

effects of up to a century of intrinsic demographic events. For example, present day US and western European populations show the effects of increased fertility post-World War II (the 'baby-boom'), and its demographic consequences for fertility in the 1980s (the 'baby boom echo'). Stable populations are idealized constructs because no real population maintains unchanging fertility and mortality schedules for long periods of time (and few real-life populations are truly closed to migration). However, pre-industrial human populations may approximate stable populations, as the wide-scale and rapid changes in fertility and mortality rates associated with demographic transitions appear to be a recent historical phenomenon.

The life table, sometimes known as survival analysis, is a mathematical device for representing the mortality experience of a population and for exploring the effects on survivorship of age-specific probabilities of death. The central concepts in life table analysis are age-specific mortality and the probability of survivorship to specific ages. A cohort of individuals of a given age will experience a predictable number of deaths during a finite interval of time, with the proportion dying depending on the length of the time interval and on the population's age-specific probability of death. The number of survivors at the end of the time interval will equal the original cohort minus the individuals who have died. Thus survivorship decreases at each successive age interval, from a maximum value at birth to zero at the age at which the last survivor dies (Table 22.1, Figure 22.1).

In a cross-sectional analysis of a sample of deaths, palaeodemographic data in the form of the age-specific number of deaths in each age category are entered directly into the D_x column of a life table under the simplifying assumption that the population is stationary (birth rate equal to death rate). However, it is often more realistic to assume that the population is stable rather than stationary, as in many populations overall birth rates slightly exceed death rates and such populations therefore will show small or moderate rates of intrinsic growth. Population growth has a marked effect on life table parameters, for example it inflates the number of juvenile deaths (and hence it appears to reduce average life expectancy at birth) simply because the birth cohorts of individuals born in more recent decades will be larger than cohorts of individuals who were born in earlier decades when the population was smaller in size (Boddington 1987). These effects of population growth on mortality can be compensated for by adjusting the number of age-specific deaths in proportion to the predicted change in size of the

Table 22.1 Life Table for the Carlston Annis (Bt-5) Late Archaic Skeletal Population (data taken from Mensforth 1990).

Age class (x)	Number of deaths (D_x)	Percentage of deaths (d_x)	Percentage of survivors (l_x)	Probability of death (q_x)	Person-yrs in age class (L_x)	Person-yrs remaining (T_x)	Expectancy of Life (e_x)
0–	105	29.66	100.00	0.30	425.85	2281.07	22.81
5–	17	4.80	70.34	0.07	339.69	1855.23	26.38
10–	14	3.95	65.54	0.06	317.80	1515.54	23.13
15–	27	7.63	61.58	0.12	288.84	1197.74	19.45
20–	35	9.89	53.95	0.18	245.06	908.90	16.85
25–	34	9.60	44.07	0.22	196.33	663.84	15.06
30–	31	8.76	34.46	0.25	150.42	467.51	13.57
35–	22	6.21	25.71	0.24	112.99	317.09	12.34
40–	20	5.65	19.49	0.29	83.33	204.10	10.47
45–	18	5.08	13.84	0.37	56.50	120.76	8.72
50–	13	3.67	8.76	0.42	34.60	64.27	7.34
55–	9	2.54	5.08	0.50	19.07	29.66	5.83
60–	6	1.69	2.54	0.67	8.47	10.59	4.17
65+	3	0.85	0.85	1.00	2.12	2.12	2.50

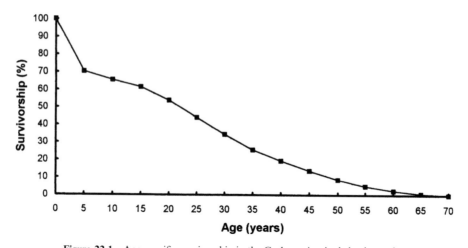

Figure 22.1 Age-specific survivorship in the Carlston Annis skeletal sample.

population through time. This is accomplished by estimating the average intrinsic rate of natural increase, r, (alternatively r can be calculated by using settlement data as a proxy for population numbers – see below) and then each value of D_x is corrected for population growth by multiplying by $(1 + r)^x$, where x is age in years and r is the rate of population growth per annum. This effectively inflates the number of deaths in the older age categories to compensate for the fact that the birth cohorts of these age categories were originally smaller in size than the cohorts that contributed the younger deaths in the mortality sample.

For the purposes of modelling of non-stable populations and for the projection of the age structure of

closed populations it is desirable to take account of fertility as well as mortality. As with mortality, human fertility is strongly age-structured particularly in females. Human female age-specific fertility shows a characteristic pattern of change with age, peaking in the decade 20–29 years and declining rapidly after 40 years of age. In population projection calculations (see below) the number of daughters born to mothers, rather than the number of children, provide a more accurate basis for predicting population trends (the term 'reproductivity' designates the rate of production of female offspring).

The demographic behaviour of a closed, age-structured population can be modelled in a simple manner by using matrix arithmetic (Leslie 1945, 1948, Weiss 1975). For simplicity the analysis of population projection is confined to females distributed across equal-length age categories and assumes fixed age-specific rates of reproduction and mortality. The age distribution of the female population at time t is represented by a column vector $P(t)$ containing the numbers of individuals P_x in each age category x. The age specific female reproductivity data (f_x) and survival probabilities (s_x) are contained in a square projection matrix M (sometimes known as a Leslie matrix) in which each row and column corresponds to a single age category. The first row of the projection matrix contains the age-specific reproductivities, or rates of production of female offspring f_x (these rates are set at zero for the age categories outside the reproductive period of 15 to 49 years of age). The sub-leading diagonal of the projection matrix contains the age-specific probabilities of survival $s_x = 1 - q_x$, calculated from the life table values of q_x, for each age category up to the penultimate category (individuals in the last age category do not contribute to the future population). All other cells in the matrix are set to zero. Then the population at future time $t' = t + \delta x$ (where δx is the duration of a single age category) is given by the matrix multiplication $P(t') = M \times P(t)$ (Table 22.2). The operation can be repeated to give the projected population at time $t + 2\delta x$, $t + 3\delta x$, and so on. The projection matrix is easily implemented on a computer spreadsheet and provides a useful but simple tool for modelling non-stable populations, for example when a pioneering community colonizes a new territory, or for a population undergoing a demographic transition.

Table 22.2 Simplified population projection matrix for a high fertility/high mortality population. The first row of the matrix contains female age-specific reproductivity, while the sub-leading diagonal contains the female age-specific probabilities of survival. Female population structure can be predicted at 15 year intervals by successively multiplying the matrix by a column vector containing the current female age structure. Population growth rate for this projection matrix is approximately 1.5 per cent per annum.

Age Class	0–14	15–29	30–44	45–59	60–74	75+
0–14	0	1.8	1.2	0	0	0
15–29	0.55	0	0	0	0	0
30–44	0	0.8	0	0	0	0
45–59	0	0	0.75	0	0	0
60–74	0	0	0	0.5	0	0
75+	0	0	0	0	0.25	0

THE PROBLEM OF SAMPLE BIAS

The straightforward application of standard demographic modelling to archaeological data is confounded by sample bias and by the inaccuracy of methods of estimating life history variables. Age at death distributions obtained from mortuary data will clearly be influenced by any selectivity that may occur in burial practices and by any sampling biases that are introduced by the process of discovery and excavation of archaeological remains. Biases in demographic data from archaeological samples can be detected by the method of 'pattern matching', an approach described by Milner et al. (1989) and Paine (1989) in which the archaeological data are compared to model life table mortality schedules in order to reveal discrepancies between the demographic structures of the archaeological and the reference populations. This technique requires a uniformitarian assumption that the age structure of the archaeological population must have originally resembled that of a model stable population. The assumption may be justified: the age structure and mortality levels observed in carefully-censused foraging communities (e.g., Hill and Hurtado 1995) match the low-to-medium life expectancy survivorship curves of model stable populations (Figure 22.2), thus giving confidence to the belief that the modern population models might also be applicable to communities known only through the archaeological record.

A major source of bias in palaeodemographic data is the under-representation of the youngest age classes, which is a very common property of assemblages of human skeletal remains from archaeological contexts (Acsádi and Nemeskéri 1970). The shortfall in numbers of children, particularly infants and young children, is manifest even when large samples of skeletons are recovered from the cemeteries of communities in which deceased individuals of all ages are expected to receive normative funerary rites. The skeletal remains of infants and children have a lower preservation potential (children's skeletons are smaller, their bones are less robust to physical damage and bioturbation, and their graves are more easily disturbed or truncated) and a lower likelihood of recovery (children's remains are less easily recognized, they may have less elaborate graves, they may be overlooked when commingled with the remains of adults). The pattern of under-representation of infants in archaeological assemblages is not confined to human examples: archaeozoological samples of the skeletal remains of wild and domestic mammals may also show deficiencies in the youngest age classes.

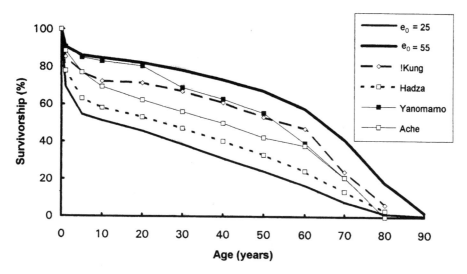

Figure 22.2 Age-specific survivorship in four hunter-gatherer populations. Survivorship in these populations matches the Coale and Demeny 'West' model life table populations with average life expectancy at birth (e_0) of between 25 and 55 years.

THE PROBLEM OF AGE ESTIMATION

The methodology of age estimation from skeletal indicators (Chapter 20) also contributes bias to palaeodemographic data. Age at death in skeletal samples is estimated by observing the state of morphological indicators which are known to co-vary with age. The quantitative relationship between age and morphological indicator is usually determined using a reference series comprised of a large number of individuals each of whose age and indicator state is known. By means of a uniformitarian assumption (that the age/indicator relationship is constant across samples and populations) the age of any unknown or target individual can then be estimated from observations of the morphological indicator.

Much of the research on the estimation of age at death from the skeleton has been undertaken for the purposes of forensic anthropology, and archaeologists have tended to apply these methods without adapting them to the special circumstances of palaeodemography. First, in reconstructing the age distribution of an archaeological sample the palaeodemographer is not primarily interested in accurate age estimates for target individuals, but intends instead to recover the *distribution* of ages that is responsible for the spread of indicator data observed in the study sample (Jackes 1985, 1992, Konigsberg and Frankenberg 1992). This differs from the objective of a forensic investigation, in which

regression or calibration techniques can be used to obtain an optimal point estimate of the age of a target individual. A second problem with traditional methods of age estimation in palaeodemography is that the resultant age estimates are frequently influenced by the age structure of the reference sample (Bocquet-Appel and Masset 1982, Konigsberg and Frankenberg 1992). In some applications of skeletal age determination this is not problematic because the target individual can be assumed to be from a population resembling the reference population (for example, where reference series have been obtained by aggregating data from previous forensic investigations). However the distribution of ages at death in some reference series is highly aberrant when compared to natural mortality profiles. Some forensic anthropological reference series are dominated by deaths among young adults, whereas in natural stable populations the adult deaths tend to be concentrated in the older age categories.

The influence of the age structure of the reference series on the estimation of age from skeletal samples can be eliminated by using Bayesian statistical methods (Konigsberg and Frankenberg 1992, Lucy *et al.* 1996; see Chapter 55). Applying Bayes' theorem, and given a parameter (in this case age) and some data (in this case the state of the morphological indicator) that are held to influence the probability of the parameter, then the posterior probability of the parameter is equal to its prior probability multiplied by the standardized likelihood of the data:

$$p(A|I) = \frac{p(I|A)}{p(I)} \times p(A_{\text{prior}}) \qquad (1)$$

where $p(\alpha|\beta)$ is the conditional probability of α, given β.

In plain words, the probability of being in a particular age category A, given a particular state of the indicator I, is equal to the conditional probability of possessing that indicator state, given the age category, divided by the overall probability of possessing the indicator state, multiplied by the prior probability of being in the age category. Crucial to this approach is the selection of appropriate prior probabilities of age [$p(A_{\text{prior}})$], and here there are several options. The use of the reference series as a source of priors can be ruled out for the reasons given above (reference series rarely exhibit natural age distributions). Similarly, the approach advocated by Konigsberg and Frankenberg (1992) in which the priors are obtained iteratively from the distribution of indicator states in the target population by an expectation-maximization algorithm cannot be recommended. Whilst Konigsberg and Frankenberg's method is an effective way of removing the effects of reference series age structure, it is computationally difficult, and it relies on the target population being an unbiased sample of its parent population. Age estimates obtained by their method cannot, therefore, be used to detect and quantify bias in the target population sample. The remaining options are to assume a uniform prior probability of age (an 'uninformative prior'; Konigsberg and Frankenberg 1992) or to select fixed model priors based on an age distribution taken from a family of stable populations or from ethnographic or historical demographic sources. Uninformative priors are appropriate in sex estimation

(where the default presumption is that deaths are derived from approximately balanced sex populations) but are usually inappropriate in age estimation because of the large variance in age-specific probability of death.

The application of fixed model priors in age estimation is demonstrated in Tables 22.3 and 22.4. Since broad age categories and discrete indicator states are typically utilized in archaeology, the complete distributions of age categories and indicator states in the reference series can normally be presented in a concise manner in a contingency table. Table 22.3 gives the distribution of morphological stages of the pubic symphysis, a commonly used age indicator, in a reference series of 273 females whose age was documented from birth and death certificates (Suchey et al. 1986, Brooks and Suchey 1990: the reference series was obtained from routine autopsies and its age structure is biased towards young adults).

For each cell in the contingency table we can calculate a Bayesian posterior probability of age, given indicator, using the formula:

$$p(A|I) = \frac{p(I|A)}{\sum [p(I|A) \times p(A_f)]} \times p(A_f) \qquad (2)$$

where $p(I|A)$ is the cell contents divided by the row total, $p(A_f)$ is the fixed model prior probability of age and the denominator summates the product $p(I|A) \times p(A_f)$ across all age categories for the particular indicator. The values of these posterior probabilities, calculated using prior probabilities taken from high and medium-mortality model life tables, are shown in Table 22.4. These posterior probabilities of age, when applied to distributions of pubic symphysis stages recorded in archaeological samples, generate realistic distributions of age at death that are not influ-

Table 22.3 Age (10 year categories) and pubic symphyseal stage in a reference series of 273 females. Data taken from Brooks and Suchey (1990).

Age\Stage	Stage I	Stage II	Stage III	Stage IV	Stage V	Stage VI	Row Sum
15–24 yrs	47	26	10	0	0	0	83
25–34 yrs	1	18	26	17	7	0	69
35–44 yrs	0	3	5	14	13	4	39
45–54 yrs	0	0	2	4	11	13	30
55–64 yrs	0	0	1	2	8	19	30
65–74 yrs	0	0	0	2	1	10	13
75–84 yrs	0	0	0	0	3	2	5
85–94 yrs	0	0	0	0	1	3	4
Col Sum	48	47	44	39	44	51	Tot = 273

Table 22.4 (a) Probability of age given symphysis stage using fixed priors from model life table with average life expectancy $e_0 = 20$. (b) Probability of age given symphysis stage using fixed priors from model life table with average life expectancy $e_0 = 50$.

(a)

Age\Stage	I	II	III	IV	V	VI
15–24	0.98	0.46	0.16	0	0	0
25–34	0.02	0.42	0.54	0.28	0.08	0
35–44	0	0.12	0.17	0.38	0.25	0.05
45–54	0	0	0.08	0.13	0.26	0.21
55–64	0	0	0.05	0.07	0.21	0.33
65–74	0	0	0	0.14	0.05	0.33
75–84	0	0	0	0	0.14	0.06
85–94	0	0	0	0	0.01	0.01

(b)

Age\Stage	I	II	III	IV	V	VI
15–24	0.97	0.41	0.11	0	0	0
25–34	0.03	0.44	0.47	0.15	0.02	0
35–44	0	0.15	0.19	0.26	0.09	0.02
45–54	0	0	0.13	0.13	0.13	0.09
55–64	0	0	0.10	0.10	0.15	0.21
65–74	0	0	0	0.35	0.06	0.38
75–84	0	0	0	0	0.49	0.19
85–94	0	0	0	0	0.07	0.12

enced by the strongly skewed age distribution of the Brooks and Suchey reference series.

SETTLEMENT AND RESOURCE UTILIZATION EVIDENCE

Methods for estimating population size from the floor areas of dwellings and the areal extent of settlements have been reviewed by Hassan (1981). The most frequently used measures of settlement size are the cumulated floor space of roofed habitation areas and the total area of the settlement. Much currency has been given to the results of a comparative ethnographic study of 18 globally distributed societies by Naroll (1962), who proposed a constant ratio of roofed dwelling floor space to population, giving an average floor space of 10 m^2 per person. Roughly similar figures have been confirmed in a number of separate ethnographic studies, although these studies have been concentrated in low latitude regions and it is likely that higher average densities of room occupation may be typical in regions where lower temperatures are prevalent. In applying such formulae to the archaeological evidence it is also important to distinguish habitation space from storage and livestock housing space, and to take into account the proportion of buildings or rooms that are occupied at any given time.

In many archaeological investigations it is difficult or impossible to assess the area of dwelling space but the overall spatial extent of the settlement can be estimated. The estimation of population size from settlement area is complicated by the likely allometric relationship between the two variables, with the allometric exponent itself differing for different classes of settlement (Wiessner 1974). Thus Wiessner proposed

the following model for the relationship between settlement area and population size:

$$Area = constant \times (Population)^b \tag{3}$$

where the exponent $b = 2$ for open camps, 1 for enclosed or defended villages and $\frac{2}{3}$ for urban areas.

The exponent of two for open settlements, indicating that settlement area increases as the square of population size, may result from an increase in the frequency of inter-individual interactions with increasing population size, necessitating either an increase in the proportion of space allocated to social activities or a reduction in the overall average density of people within the settlement. The hypothesis that in hunter-gatherer camps the settlement area is proportional to (Population)^2 has been reaffirmed by theoretical modelling (Read 1978), and is corroborated by an extensive comparative study which showed that the maximum residential density in hunter-gatherer communities decreases markedly as community size increases (Fletcher 1990).

Quantitative measures of the production and consumption of resources, including amounts of food residues, artifact quantities and volumes of storage pits, can also be used as proxies for population size (see reviews by Hassan 1981 and Schact 1981). As with estimates of population size from settlement evidence, the analysis of resource utilization can be useful for determining long-term rates of population growth, a necessary prerequisite for the accurate application of stable population models in the investigation of past population structure.

MIGRATION

Migration refers to the process whereby individuals enter or leave a population other than through birth and death. As with fertility and mortality, migration is influenced by age and sex but in a more complex and less consistent fashion. The analysis of migration requires that the population has recognizable boundaries, usually defined for human populations in terms of the individual's place of permanent residence. Migration also implies the existence of two populations (donor and recipient) and as migrants' mortality and fertility characteristics may differ from those of both donor and recipient populations it is likely that migration will have appreciable effects on population structure. Migration is usually regarded as a voluntary process, but there are many historical examples of enforced migration and the term in its broadest sense could include the transport and enslavement of members of a conquered population.

Human migration is difficult to model and predict because it depends on individual decision making as well as the fluctuating demographic, economic and political circumstances in both donor and recipient populations. Migration tends to be age structured, with adults around mean-age-at-first-marriage (usually in the early twenties) together with their dependent infant offspring exhibiting the highest mobility and hence the highest probabilities of migration (Rogers and Castro 1984). A population receiving migrants may experience higher than average fertility because peak fertility occurs at about the same age as peak migration potential (Paine 1997).

The rate of migration is also usually an inverse function of the distance migrated, and some demographers have developed gravity models in which migration is proportional to the size of the donor and recipient populations and inversely proportional to a function of intervening distance between donor and recipient populations (Plane and Rogerson 1994). A special instance of large-scale migration is the colonization of effectively vacant habitats, which can be simulated using the 'wave of advance model'. This model has been employed to explain the transition to agriculture in Europe (Ammerman and Cavalli-Sforza 1984), the expansion of modern humans 'Out of Africa' (Young and Bettinger 1995) and the postglacial human occupation of North America (Steele et al. 1998). The wave of advance model postulates locally high birth rates among pioneer colonizers in a frontier zone, which continually moves forward into areas of lower population density through a process of successive short-distance migration. Migration rates under this model are a function of the rate of population growth which is predicted to be higher than in non-migrating populations. As mentioned above, elevated fertility is a general property of migrating populations, and would be expected in pioneering communities quite apart from any population increase contingent on the higher carrying capacity permitted by the colonization of unexploited territories.

The role of migration in the explanation of culture change is highly contentious (Anthony 1990) and the question is difficult to resolve using traditional demographic approaches to mortuary data. The presence of migrants in a skeletal population can be detected by isotopic analysis of skeletal remains (Price et al. 1994, Ezzo et al. 1997, White et al. 1998; see Chapter 23) and through the analysis of ancient DNA and other genetic markers (e.g., Colson et al. 1997). Postmarital residence practices in which the separate sexes have different migration rates are predicted to cause sex differences in genetic diversity, and in theory this might be detected through the analysis of skeletal non-metric traits (Lane and Sublett 1972, Konigsberg 1988).

BIOMOLECULAR ANTHROPOLOGY AND GENETIC ARCHAEOLOGY

Information about the demographic history of a population can also be obtained from genetic data (see Chapter 25), as genetic diversity is influenced by population size and migration as well as the intrinsic mutation rates of the genes themselves. Spatial variations in the frequency of classical genetic markers (mainly variants in the structural genes encoded by nuclear DNA) have been used to reconstruct large-scale prehistoric population movements (Cavalli-Sforza et al. 1994, Sokal et al. 1991). Also useful in this regard are haploid genetic loci, including the maternally-inherited mitochondrial DNA and the male-specific non-recombining parts of the Y chromosome (Donnelly and Tavaré 1995, Harpending et al. 1998). These parts of the genome can be used to define distinct genetic lineages with the divergence between the lineages being proportional to the time since the lineages shared a most recent common genetic ancestor. This allows the investigator to reconstruct the phylogenetic history of a group of related populations, and the divergence between populations may correspond to major demographic events such as large-scale migrations and colonizations.

Periods of rapid population expansion also leave a distinctive genetic signature, for example in the distribution of pairwise differences between the DNA sequences of individuals in a population (Harpending et al. 1993, Rogers 1995) and in the geometric patterns of lineage relationships (Richards et al. 1996). If a population has expanded rapidly from a much smaller group of founding individuals at an early point in its history, then most of the genetic mutations in the population will have occurred post-expansion in separate genetic lineages and each mutation will be present in just one or two copies in the population. Comparisons between the DNA of pairs of individuals will show a narrow distribution of differences and a phylogeny of the genetic lineages in the population will be 'starlike' with the lineages radiating from one or a few ancestral sequences. In contrast, in a population that has not undergone a rapid expansion there will be a greater proportion of shared ancestral mutations and the distribution of pairwise sequence differences between individuals will be broader.

REFERENCES

*Recommended for further reading

*Acsádi, G. and Nemeskéri, J. (1970). *History of Human Life Span and Mortality.* Akadémiai Kiadó: Budapest.

Ammerman, A.J. and Cavalli-Sforza, L.L. (1984). *Neolithic Transition and the Genetics of Populations in Europe.* Princeton University Press: Princeton.

Anthony, D.W. (1990). Migration in archaeology: the baby and the bathwater. *Current Anthropology,* **92**:895–914.

Bocquet-Appel, J.-P. and Masset, C. (1982). Farewell to paleodemography. *Journal of Human Evolution,* **11**:321–333.

Boddington, A. (1987). From bones to population: the problem of numbers. In Boddington, A., Garland, A.N. and Janaway, R.C. (eds) *Death, Decay and Reconstruction,* 180–197. Manchester University Press: Manchester.

Brooks, S. and Suchey, J.M. (1990). Skeletal age determination based on the os pubis: a comparison of the Acsádi-Nemeskéri and Suchey-Brooks methods. *Human Evolution,* **5**:227–238.

*Cavalli-Sforza, L.L., Menozzi, P. and Piazza, A. (1994). *The History and Geography of Human Genes.* Princeton University Press: Princeton.

Coale, A.J. (1957). How the age distribution of a human population is determined. *Cold Spring Harbor Symposia on Quantitative Biology,* **22**:83–88.

Colson, I.B., Richards, M.B., Bailey, J.F., Sykes, B.C. and Hedges, R.E.M. (1997). DNA analysis of seven human skeletons excavated from the terp of Wijnaldum. *Journal of Archaeological Science,* **24**:911–917.

Donnelly, P. and Tavaré, S. (1995). Coalescents and genealogical structure under neutrality. *Annual Review of Genetics,* **29**:401–421.

Ezzo, J.A., Johnson, C.M. and Price, T.D. (1997). Analytical perspectives on prehistoric migration: a case study from east-central Arizona. *Journal of Archaeological Science,* **24**:447–466.

Fletcher, R. (1990). Residential densities, group sizes and social stress in Australian aboriginal settlements. In Meehan, B. and White, N. (eds) *Hunter-Gatherer Demography,* 81–95. Oceania Monographs 39, University of Sydney: Sydney.

Harpending, H.C., Sherry, S.T., Rogers, A.R. and Stoneking, M. (1993). The genetic structure of ancient human populations. *Current Anthropology,* **34**:483–496.

Harpending, H.C., Batzer, M.A., Gurven, M., Jorde, L.B., Rogers, A.R. and Sherry, S.T. (1998). Genetic traces of ancient demography. *Proceedings of the National Academy of Sciences of the USA,* **95**:1961–1967.

*Hassan, F.A. (1981). *Demographic Archaeology.* Academic Press: New York.

*Hill, K. and Hurtado, A.M. (1995). *Ache Life History, the Ecology and Demography of a Foraging People.* Aldine de Gruyter: Chicago.

Jackes, M.K. (1985). Pubic symphysis age distributions. *American Journal of Physical Anthropology,* **68**:281–299.

Jackes, M. (1992). Paleodemography: problems and techniques. In Saunders, S.R. and Katzenberg, M.A. (eds) *Skeletal Biology of Past Peoples,* 189–224. John Wiley: New York.

Konigsberg, L.W. (1988). Migration models of prehistoric post-marital residence. *American Journal of Physical Anthropology,* **77**:471–482.

Konigsberg, L.W. and Frankenberg, S.R. (1992). Estimation of age structure in anthropological demography. *American Journal of Physical Anthropology,* **89**:235–256.

Lane, R.A. and Sublett, A. (1972). The osteology of social organization. *American Antiquity,* **37**:186–201.

Leslie, P.H. (1945). On the use of matrices in certain population mathematics. *Biometrika,* **33**:183–212.

Leslie, P.H. (1948). Some further notes on the use of matrices in population mathematics. *Biometrika,* **35**:213–245.

Lucy, D., Aykroyd, R.G., Pollard, A.M. and Solheim, T. (1996). A Bayesian approach to adult human age estimation from dental observations by Johanson's age changes. *Journal of Forensic Sciences,* **41**:189–194.

Mensforth, R.P. (1990). Paleodemography of the Carlston Annis (Bt-5) late archaic skeletal population. *American Journal of Physical Anthropology,* **82**:81–99.

Milner, G.R., Humpf, D.A. and Harpending, H.C. (1989). Pattern matching of age-at-death distributions in paleodemographic analysis. *American Journal of Physical Anthropology,* **80**:49–58.

Naroll, R. (1962). Floor area and settlement population. *American Antiquity,* **27**:587–589.

Paine, R.R. (1989). Model life table fitting by maximum likelihood estimation: a procedure to reconstruct paleodemographic characteristics from skeletal age distributions. *American Journal of Physical Anthropology,* **79**:51–61.

Paine, R.R. (1997). Uniformitarian models in osteological paleodemography. In Paine, R.R. (ed.) *Integrating Archaeological Demography: Multidisciplinary Approaches to*

Prehistoric Population, 191–204. Southern Illinois University: Carbondale.

Plane, D.A. and Rogerson, P.A. (1994). *The Geographical Analysis of Population, with Applications to Planning and Business*. John Wiley: New York.

Price, T.D., Johnson, C.M., Ezzo, J.A., Ericson, J. and Burton, J.H. (1994). Residential mobility in the prehistoric southwest United States: a preliminary study using strontium isotope analysis. *Journal of Archaeological Science*, **21**:315–330.

Read, D.W. (1978). Towards a formal theory of population size and area of habitation. *Current Anthropology*, **19**:312–337.

Richards, M., Côrte-Real, H., Forster, P., Macauley, V., Wilkinson-Herbots, H., Demaine, A., Papiha, S., Hedges, R., Bandelt, H.J. and Sykes, B. (1996). Paleolithic and Neolithic lineages in the European mitochondrial gene pool. *American Journal of Human Genetics*, **59**:185–203.

Rogers, A.R. (1995). Genetic evidence for a Pleistocene population explosion. *Evolution*, **49**:608–615.

Rogers, A. and Castro, L.J. (1984). Model migration schedules. In Rogers, A. (ed.) *Migration, Urbanism and Spatial Population Dynamics*, 41–91. Westview Press: Boulder.

Schact, R.M. (1981). Estimating past population trends. *Annual Review of Anthropology*, **10**:119–140.

Sokal, R.R., Oden, N.L. and Wilson, C. (1991). Genetic evidence for the spread of agriculture in Europe by demic diffusion. *Nature*, **351**:143–145.

Steele, J., Adams, J. and Sluckin, T. (1998). Modelling Paleoindian dispersals. *World Archaeology*, **30**:286–305.

Suchey, J.M., Wisely, D.V. and Katz, D. (1986). Evaluation of the Todd and McKern-Stewart methods of ageing the male os pubis. In Reichs, K. (ed.) *Forensic Osteology: Advances in the Identification of Human Remains*, 33–67. Charles C. Thomas: Springfield.

Weiss, K. (1975). Demographic disturbance and the use of life tables in anthropology. *American Antiquity*, **40**:46–56.

White, K., Spence, M.W., Stuart-Williams, H.L.Q. and Schwarcz, H.P. (1998). Oxygen isotopes and the identification of geographical origins: the Valley of Oaxaca versus the Valley of Mexico. *Journal of Archaeological Science*, **25**:643–655.

Wiessner, P. (1974). A functional estimator of population from floor area. *American Antiquity*, **39**:343–349.

Young, D.A. and Bettinger, R.L. (1995). Simulating global human expansion in the late Pleistocene. *Journal of Archaeological Science*, **22**:89–92.

23

Body Tissue Chemistry and Palaeodiet

J. SEALY

Department of Archaeology, University of Cape Town.

The distributions of certain stable isotopes and trace elements in foodwebs make it possible to use them as natural tracers of foodstuffs. Their measurement in archaeological human skeletons provides a direct record of diet, supplementing conventional approaches which rely on reconstruction of diet from identification of excavated food residues. Analysis of animal bones offers a powerful means of palaeoenvironmental reconstruction. Early work in this field was on trace elements, but in the last two decades the focus has shifted to stable isotope measurements. Stable carbon isotopes ($^{13}C/^{12}C$) are the best understood and most widely applied palaeodietary tracer, followed by nitrogen isotopes ($^{15}N/^{14}N$) and determinations of the abundance of elemental strontium or strontium/calcium ratios. There is growing interest in applications of $^{87}Sr/^{86}Sr$ and $^{18}O/^{16}O$. Other trace elements and isotopes of elements such as hydrogen, sulfur and lead have been explored to a much lesser extent.

For the stable light isotopes of carbon, nitrogen, oxygen, hydrogen and sulfur, the mass difference between the two isotopes is sufficiently large that physical and chemical reactions cause isotopic fractionation; i.e., there is a change in the proportions of the isotopes in the products of the reaction, compared with the starting materials, as long as the process is non-quantitative (see Chapter 16). These fractionations are complex, incorporating physical effects (e.g.,

evaporation, diffusion), equilibrium effects (e.g., phase changes) and kinetic effects (fractionation during unidirectional processes such as photosynthesis). Overall, the chemical reactions continuously in process in the world around (and within) us act as isotopic separators. If we understand these processes and the resultant isotopic patterning, we can use the isotopic composition of archaeological body tissues to track the foods consumed by ancient people or animals, answering questions about possible dietary changes in the past. Further, it is sometimes possible to deduce, from these observations, aspects of landscape use. Reconstruction of certain characteristics of palaeoenvironments and palaeoclimates can be achieved in this way.

There are two basic requirements for the exploitation of isotopes or trace elements as natural tracers: we need to know:

(i) the distribution, in the foodweb, of the isotopes or elements under investigation, and
(ii) in the analysis of archaeological samples, that we can measure biogenic isotopic or trace element compositions; i.e., that the signals are not compromised by *post-mortem* alteration ('diagenesis') or contamination.

For most chemical and isotopic techniques of dietary tracing, early applications to archaeological

Handbook of Archaeological Sciences. Edited by D.R. Brothwell and A.M. Pollard.

problems relied upon an understanding of the natural distribution of the relevant isotopes or trace elements culled from life or Earth sciences. As the archaeological questions become more complex, archaeologists need to carry out more precise mapping of these distributions, ideally, focusing on items known to have been important in the diets of the humans or animals who form the ultimate subject of study. The nature of human diets, which usually incorporate a wide range of foods, means that this groundwork can be challenging.

Recognizing diagenetic signals in archaeological and fossil specimens, and finding ways to separate diagenetic and biogenic material, has become a field of study in its own right (see Chapter 51). Most palaeodietary studies are of bones or teeth, although soft tissues are sometimes available (e.g., White 1993, Aufderheide *et al.* 1994; see Chapter 21). The organic fraction of bone (bone 'collagen': strictly speaking, acid-insoluble bone protein) generally preserves well in material of Holocene age, and may last much longer in cool climates. Palaeodietary studies have used modified versions of the collagen isolation procedures developed by radiocarbon laboratories, with good results. Attempts to isolate biogenic material from the inorganic fraction of archaeological bone have been much more problematic. Most interest has centred on carbonate in bone apatite (for analysis of $\delta^{13}C$) and on strontium (for determination of Sr/Ca and $^{87}Sr/^{86}Sr$). The inorganic fraction of bone is subject to contamination and to the incorporation of extraneous material during recrystallization processes which occur after burial. There is, however, general agreement that it is possible to remove at least some of this diagenetic mineral by washing in weakly acidic solutions (Lee-Thorp and van der Merwe 1987, 1991, Lee-Thorp *et al.* 1997, Sillen 1986). The extent to which these protocols are effective depends upon the burial environment. It is up to the researcher to decide whether, in the case in question, it is possible to isolate sufficiently pure biogenic material to yield reliable analyses. This is usually assessed by applying the technique to a range of faunal species whose diets are well-understood. If these yield the expected results, then the protocols can be extended to species whose diets are in question. Investigation of the structure of the sample material, e.g., through infra-red spectroscopy, can also be helpful. Increasingly, researchers prefer to measure the inorganic fraction of tooth enamel, rather than bone, since its greater density and crystallinity make it more resistant to diagenesis (Quade *et al.* 1992, Wang and Cerling 1994, Koch *et al.* 1997, Lee-Thorp *et al.* 1997, Budd *et al.* 2000).

Stable isotope measurements are usually reported using the delta notation, where (using nitrogen as an example):

$$\delta^{15}N = \left(\frac{(^{15}N/^{14}N)_{sample}}{(^{15}N/^{14}N)_{standard}} - 1 \right) \times 1000‰ \qquad (1)$$

The standard for $\delta^{15}N$ measurements is generally atmospheric N_2, which by definition has $\delta^{15}N = 0‰$ (parts per mil, or parts per thousand). Values of $\delta^{13}C$ are reported relative to Peedee Belemnite (PDB), a marine limestone. Most organic compounds contain less ^{13}C than marine limestones, so their $\delta^{13}C$ values are negative. Values of $\delta^{18}O$ may be expressed relative to PDB, or sometimes relative to Standard Mean Ocean Water (SMOW).

CARBON ISOTOPES

Isotopic patterning in living organisms

The carbon isotope patterning of the biosphere is determined primarily by isotopic fractionation associated with photosynthesis. Atmospheric CO_2 has $\delta^{13}C$ of about $-8‰$. As CO_2 diffuses into the pores on plant leaves, the lighter isotope diffuses slightly faster, leading to enrichment in ^{12}C compared with ^{13}C within plant tissues. Enzymes involved in photosynthesis select for ^{12}C, introducing additional fractionation. Thus plants contain less ^{13}C – they have lower $^{13}C/^{12}C$ ratios – than air. Most plants photosynthesize by the *Calvin–Benson*, or C_3 pathway, in which the first product of photosynthesis is a 3-carbon compound. These plants discriminate very strongly against ^{13}C, so that their mean $\delta^{13}C$ value is $-27‰$, range -22 to $-34‰$ (O'Leary 1995). A smaller group of plants, mostly tropical grasses, utilize a different pathway: the *Hatch–Slack* or C_4 pathway, in which carbon is fixed initially into a 4-carbon compound. C_4 photosynthesis also discriminates against ^{13}C, but to a lesser extent than C_3 photosynthesis. The mean $\delta^{13}C$ for C_4 plants is $-13‰$, range -8 to $-16‰$.

C_3 plants include almost all species native to temperate environments, such as north-western Europe and eastern North America. Trees and most shrubs are C_3. The important crop plants of the Near East, such as wheat, barley, oats and rye, are all C_3, as are fruits and vegetables. Rice, too, is C_3. C_4 plants include maize, sugarcane, sorghum and millet – the domesticated tropical grasses.

A few plants have the ability to switch between the C_3 and C_4 pathways. This mode of photosynthesis is termed *Crassulacean Acid Metabolism* (CAM) and is found mainly in succulents. It may yield $\delta^{13}C$ values in between the C_3 and C_4 ranges, or if one pathway dominates, the values may mimic those of C_3 or C_4 plants. Since few succulents are important sources of food for humans, CAM photosynthesis is of limited relevance here.

Carbon isotope ratios of animals depend upon the food they eat. Large herbivores eating a C_3 diet have bone collagen $\delta^{13}C$ of about $-22‰$, i.e., about 5‰ more positive than their diet. In savannah grasslands where the trees are C_3 and the grasses are C_4, browsing animals have bone collagen $\delta^{13}C$ of about $-22‰$, grazing animals of around $-8‰$ (Vogel 1978, Lee-Thorp and van der Merwe 1987). The diet-to-collagen shift is probably rather less for small animals such as rats and mice, and may depend upon the isotopic composition of different dietary components (DeNiro and Epstein 1978, Ambrose and Norr 1993, Tieszen and Fagre 1993). Diet-to-muscle tissue spacing is about $+3‰$, so that the meat of large C_3-consuming herbivores is $c. -24‰$. Adipose tissue is more negative than diet, by about $-3‰$. Fractionation is a stepwise process, so that carnivores have isotope ratios still more enriched than those of their prey, although the diet-to-tissue isotope spacings for carnivores are probably rather smaller than those for herbivores. The shift between diet and inorganic carbonate in bone apatite is much larger, $c.$ 12 to 14‰ for large animals (Lee-Thorp *et al.* 1989, Cerling *et al.* 1997). Once again, values are probably lower for small animals: 9–11‰ for the experimental rat and mouse studies (Ambrose and Norr 1993, Tieszen and Fagre 1993). All diet-to-tissue isotopic shifts result from the metabolic processes involved in the conversion of food to body tissue, discussed further below.

Carbon isotope patterning in the oceans is complex. There is constant exchange between dissolved carbon dioxide, bicarbonate and carbonate ions, with associated isotopic fractionation. The enzymes associated with both C_3 and C_4 photosynthesis have been identified in marine algae, and factors such as depth influence algal isotope ratios. Fortunately, these variations tend to average out as one moves up the food chain. Most marine organisms important in human diets are animals, rather than plants. A reasonable estimate of mean $\delta^{13}C$ for marine animals from temperate oceans is around $-16‰$.

Archaeological case studies

There are by now many case studies; for reviews, see Schwarcz and Schoeninger (1991), Katzenberg (1992), Katzenberg and Harrison (1997) and Schoeninger and Moore (1992). A few especially successful applications are worth mentioning here. The first use of stable carbon isotope measurements to solve an archaeological problem was the study of the introduction of maize agriculture to eastern North America (Vogel and van der Merwe 1977, van der Merwe and Vogel 1978). Eastern North America is a C_3 environment, and human skeletons from this region which pre-date the adoption of maize agriculture have C_3-derived isotopic signals in their bone collagen, around $-21.5‰$. Maize, as a C_4 crop, has an isotopic composition quite distinct from indigenous foods. After maize agriculture was introduced, $\delta^{13}C$ of human bone collagen rose steeply, reaching values more positive than $-10‰$. This change occurred only $c.$ AD 1000, much later than many archaeologists had thought. Subsequent studies have documented regional variations in the process (reviewed in Buikstra and Milner 1991). This approach has also been applied to tracking the spread of maize into South America, and the adoption of C_4 African grain crops in parts of Europe (Murray and Schoeninger 1988).

In areas with terrestrial C_3 vegetation, there is a significant difference between terrestrial and marine $\delta^{13}C$ values. Carbon isotopes have been used successfully to investigate the importance of marine foods in the diets of coastal-dwellers in many parts of the world (see reviews cited above, also Pate and Schoeninger 1993, Aufderheide *et al.* 1994, McGovern-Wilson and Quinn 1996, Ambrose *et al.* 1997). Note that these are *comparative, qualitative* studies, comparing marine food consumption in skeletons from different areas, or of different ages. For reasons outlined below, it is currently not possible to determine what percentage of food was marine.

There are latitudinal variations in $\delta^{13}C$ values, both in the sea and on land. Van Klinken *et al.* (1994) have documented a shift of almost 3‰ in tree wood charcoal from northern Scotland to the Mediterranean, due to temperature effects on fractionation during CO_2 uptake. This phenomenon has been used to identify probable recent immigrants from warmer climates to the Roman camp at Poundbury in Dorset, England (Richards *et al.* 1998).

These studies have relied primarily upon isotopic measurements of bone collagen. Collagen has been isolated successfully from European Pleistocene materials, including Neanderthal skeletal remains and associated fauna (Bocherens *et al.* 1991, 1995, 1999, Fizet *et al.* 1995, Ambrose 1998). It tends to be poorly preserved in very ancient material, and in samples from warmer environments. Carbon isotope measurements on Plio-Pleistocene, or even older, bones are made on carbonate in bone or tooth apatite.

Measurements of $\delta^{13}C$ in carbonate from tooth enamel have been used to investigate the diet of *Australopithecus robustus* from Swartkrans. The strongly-developed jaws and molar teeth, indicating crushing and grinding of food, have long been considered to point to a specialized vegetarian dietary niche. Since the likely plant foods (fruits, pods and nuts) are C_3, *A. robustus* tooth enamel was expected to yield a C_3-derived isotope value. In fact, the results showed a significant proportion of C_4-derived food. Dental morphology and microwear studies are inconsistent with the direct consumption of grass, so the likely sources of C_4-based carbon are animals which fed on the abundant C_4 grasses of this environment (Lee-Thorp *et al.* 1994). *Australopithecus robustus* was probably more omnivorous than most recent studies have allowed. The same seems to be true of *A. africanus* (Sponheimer and Lee-Thorp 1999a). Similar analyses of other fossil hominids promise new insights into the ways in which dietary specializations (or lack thereof) helped shape evolutionary trajectories.

Carbon isotopes in tooth enamel have been measured in even older material, helping to answer questions about the diets of fossil animals, and contributing to studies of long-term climate change (e.g., Thackeray *et al.* 1990). For a review of applications of isotope techniques in palaeontology and palaeo-environmental reconstruction, see Koch (1998). Apatite $\delta^{13}C$ is also of interest in more recent material, in that it may reflect different components of the diet than those incorporated into bone collagen (see below).

NITROGEN ISOTOPES

Isotopic patterning in living organisms

Atmospheric nitrogen is incorporated into biological systems through nitrogen fixation by bacteria and soil microorganisms. Soil nitrogen values are generally slightly greater than 0‰, as a result of the cumulative effect of the fractionations associated with fixation and denitrification (Shearer and Kohl 1986). Plants have $\delta^{15}N$ values between about -5 and $+20$‰ (data compiled by Ambrose 1991), but very positive values are rare, restricted to desert and saline environments. Animal $\delta^{15}N$ may range from $+1$ or $+2$‰ to around $+20$‰. The spread of values within an ecosystem is, however, much narrower. In temperate, well-watered situations, terrestrial animals generally have $\delta^{15}N$ below 10‰. As for carbon, there is stepwise enrichment of the heavy isotope at higher trophic levels, usually considered to be of the order of 3–4‰ (Schoeninger 1985, Ambrose and DeNiro 1986, Ambrose 1991). Enrichment with increasing trophic level is greater for nitrogen than for carbon.

In arid areas, much more positive $\delta^{15}N$ values have been documented (Schwarcz *et al.* 1999 and references therein). Soil $\delta^{15}N$ is higher, and Heaton (1987) has shown that plant $\delta^{15}N$ correlates with climate, with more positive values in dry or saline surroundings. The increase in animal $\delta^{15}N$ with aridity, at least for some species, is even more marked, so that physiological processes within animals must be involved. There have been several suggestions as to what these might be; the most powerful model centres around the function of urea in animals under drought stress. For most mammals, the majority of excreted nitrogen is in the form of urea in urine. Urea is depleted in ^{15}N. Animals under heat stress, especially drought-tolerant species, tend to increase their urea (and thus their ^{14}N) output, and retain more of the heavy ^{15}N isotope in their bodies (Ambrose 1991).

In the oceans $\delta^{15}N$ values depend mostly on the balance of nitrification and denitrification. Nitrification (nitrogen fixation) occurs both on land and in the sea, with ^{14}N fixed preferentially, by a small margin. Denitrification occurs mostly in the oceans. It is associated with a much stronger selection for ^{14}N, leaving the oceans enriched in ^{15}N compared with terrestrial systems. Smaller contributions to enriched marine $\delta^{15}N$ values are made by: (i) terrestrial runoff into the sea, which contributes isotopically enriched organic nitrogen, and (ii) marine food-chains tend to be longer than those on land, incorporating several carnivorous trophic levels with associated stepwise isotopic fractionation. Thus marine $\delta^{15}N$ values are more positive than terrestrial ones, except where the terrestrial system is arid.

Archaeological case studies

Nitrogen is found in bone collagen and other protein-aceous tissues such as muscle and hair. It is not present in significant quantities in the inorganic fraction of bone, so that nitrogen isotope analyses of archaeological bones are at present limited to specimens with good collagen preservation. Values of $\delta^{15}N$ are valuable in studying marine/terrestrial diets among coastal populations, alone or in combination with $\delta^{13}C$ (see references above). Nitrogen isotopes are particularly useful in areas where the terrestrial vegetation includes C_4 plants, so that carbon isotopes do not clearly discriminate between marine and terrestrial foods.

The increase in $\delta^{15}N$ with trophic level means that nitrogen isotope ratios can also give information on whether diets were primarily plant- or animal food-based. This is possible only in isotopically homogeneous environments; attempts to extract this information from bones from a number of African populations were complicated by the influence of aridity in some areas (Ambrose 1986, Ambrose and DeNiro 1986). Iacumin et al. (1998), analysing skeletons from the Kerma necropolis of ancient Nubia, concluded that meat from cattle was probably more important in the Ancient Kerma period (c. 4450–4000 BP) than in the Middle or Classic periods (4000–3450 BP). Measurements of $\delta^{15}N$ in the bones of children have been used successfully to investigate age of weaning, because suckling infants are effectively a trophic level higher than their mothers. Thus breast-fed babies have high $\delta^{15}N$ values, which decrease as they are weaned, usually to diets richer in plant foods. A number of studies are reviewed in Katzenberg et al. (1996), see also Schurr (1997, 1998). Since duration of nursing is related to rate of population growth, this approach should provide useful insights into palaeodemography.

OXYGEN ISOTOPES

The ratio of $^{18}O/^{16}O$ in precipitation varies with temperature (and hence latitude), with altitude, amount of precipitation and distance from the ocean also exerting some influence (see Chapter 16). Water $\delta^{18}O$ is therefore a useful measurement in hydrology and climatology. Animal $\delta^{18}O$ depends upon the composition of drinking water, food and atmospheric oxygen. The latter is relatively constant, so oxygen isotope ratios in body tissues are determined by climate, ecology and the animal's physiology (Kolodny et al. 1983, Luz et al. 1984, Luz and Kolodny 1985). Measurements of $\delta^{18}O$ in archaeological or palaeontological animals of selected species offer a means of investigating past hydrological and climatological regimes. It may be possible to use $\delta^{18}O$ to deduce something of the behaviour of fossil species, especially in

relation to water use. For relatively recent periods in which conditions are likely to be similar to those of the present, $\delta^{18}O$ can be helpful as a sourcing tool, as in the studies mentioned below.

Oxygen occurs in all body tissues, but analytical work has focused on $\delta^{18}O$ in bone phosphate, with some investigation of bone and enamel carbonate. Phosphate has been preferred because the stability of the phosphate bond promises good prospects for extracting biogenic oxygen. Carbonate oxygen is more subject to post-depositional exchange, thus obscuring the biogenic signal. As procedures for pre-treatment of samples to remove diagenetic carbonates come into wider use, analysis of $\delta^{18}O$ in carbonate is likely to become more popular (as for carbon isotopes in carbonate) (Sponheimer and Lee-Thorp 1999b). The oxygen isotopic compositions of phosphate and carbonate in mammal bone are closely correlated, since both derive from the same pool of body water (Bryant et al. 1996, Iacumin et al. 1996). Modern deer bones collected from across North America show a range of about 12‰ in phosphate $\delta^{18}O$, with higher values from areas of lower relative humidity (Luz et al. 1990). The $\delta^{18}O$ spacing between drinking water and bone depends upon the relative rates of drinking and respiration, especially because of the loss of ^{18}O-depleted water vapour during respiration. Samples for palaeoclimatic studies should therefore be taken from species that drink water copiously and have low metabolic rates (Luz et al. 1984).

Oxygen isotope measurements of human skeletons have been used to investigate the origins of archaeological populations. Skeletons from Teotihuacán, from barrios thought to have been occupied by ethnic communities from different parts of Mesoamerica, yielded clustered phosphate $\delta^{18}O$ values consistent with the occupation of different areas of the city by people with diverse places of origin (Stuart-Williams et al. 1996, White et al. 1998). Attempts to match $\delta^{18}O$ of putative Oaxacan immigrants with samples from Oaxaca were, however, unsuccessful. Schwarcz et al. (1991) used oxygen isotopes to explore the origins of soldiers killed in the War of 1812, and buried at the Snake Hill cemetery at Fort Erie, Ontario. The $\delta^{18}O$ values of all the individuals in the group were very similar, so they probably came from the same geographical region, perhaps the north-eastern USA. Fricke et al. (1995) showed that oxygen isotopes in the teeth of Norse and Inuit people from Greenland preserved a record of rapid environmental cooling from about AD 1400 to 1700 – the time of the Little Ice Age.

TRACE ELEMENTS

The first attempts to use bone chemistry for palaeo-dietary reconstruction relied upon trace element concentrations, especially strontium (Brown 1974, Gilbert 1975), and drew on previous palaeontological studies (Toots and Voorhies 1965, Parker and Toots 1970). This approach had the advantage of being able to use the large data-base of elemental strontium measurements in natural systems, accumulated after World War II as a result of concern about adverse effects of radioactive ^{90}Sr fallout from atomic bomb testing. The chemical similarity between strontium and calcium means that strontium is incorporated into bone, in small quantities, in place of calcium. There is biopurification of calcium – that is, discrimination against strontium – in the mammalian digestive tract. In addition, mammalian kidneys excrete Sr more rapidly than Ca, leading to stepwise reduction in Sr/Ca at higher trophic levels. Many plants have relatively high Sr/Ca. Herbivores eating those plants have lower Sr/Ca, and carnivores preying on the herbivores have further reduced Sr/Ca (Elias et al. 1982).

Brown (1974) reported higher bone strontium in female skeletons, and suggested that females had less access to meat foods than males. (It may be, however, that females have higher values because of reduced discrimination against strontium during pregnancy and lactation; Sillen and Kavanagh 1982). Schoeninger (1979) showed that skeletons from Chalcatzingo, Mexico, buried with large quantities of grave goods, had lower strontium levels than skeletons with few or no grave goods. She inferred that higher-status individuals ate more meat.

Subsequent work highlighted several issues of concern. Since strontium resides mainly in the inorganic fraction of bone, diagenesis is a possible complicating factor. After a good deal of argument in the literature as to whether bone strontium levels are or are not susceptible to post-depositional contamination, Sillen (1981) resolved the issue. He demonstrated that, at Hayonim Cave in Israel, carnivores in the Natufian levels had lower Sr/Ca than herbivores. In the lower, Aurignacian, levels Sr/Ca for carnivores and herbivores converged as a result of greater diagenetic change in older material. He then developed a washing procedure (the 'solubility profile') to attempt to isolate biogenic material which would give reliable Sr/Ca measurements (Sillen 1986; see also Nelson et al. 1986, Tuross et al. 1989, Sillen 1990, Sealy et al. 1991, Koch et al. 1992, Sillen and Sealy 1995, Koch et al. 1997, Elliott et al. 1998).

The Sr/Ca ratio is reduced in a predator compared with its prey. As archaeologists moved beyond this basic premise, and measured Sr/Ca in the wide range of food items which potentially form part of human diets, it became apparent that there is considerable variability in Sr/Ca at any one trophic level. Sr/Ca in a carnivore picked at random is not necessarily lower than in a herbivore (Sealy and Sillen 1988), so that the method does not provide a simple measure of meat/plant food. There is, however, as yet no detailed survey of Sr/Ca in an archaeological human food web. Burton and Wright (1995) have pointed out that, because Sr is incorporated into bone as a trace constituent in the wake of Ca, bone Sr/Ca is strongly influenced by the presence of high calcium foods in the diet, even if these are present in small quantities.

Thus interpretation of Sr/Ca in archaeological bones is much more complicated than initially realized. Successful applications with rigorously defined parameters include Sillen and Smith's (1984) measurements of Sr/Ca in juvenile skeletons to study weaning age, since human milk is very low in Sr/Ca, whereas weaning foods (usually gruel) are higher. Broader studies require careful assays of likely food sources. Sillen's (1992) analysis of Australopithecus robustus and associated fauna from Swartkrans concurs with the results of the carbon isotope analyses mentioned above, in concluding that robust australopithecines are unlikely to have been purely herbivorous. Increasingly, however, studies of Sr/Ca are carried out in conjunction with strontium isotope analyses (e.g., Sillen et al. 1995).

Buikstra et al. (1989) and Sandford (1992), amongst others, have reviewed studies of other trace elements. In general, these have been hampered by:

(i)   lack of data on the distribution of many elements in various possible foodstuffs,
(ii) poor understanding of the mechanisms by which trace elements are incorporated into bone, and
(iii) diagenesis.

Lambert and Weydert-Homeyer (1993) addressed some of these shortcomings by carrying out controlled feeding experiments, using rats. Diets with different trace element compositions were fed to different groups of rats, and the rats' bones analysed. In addition to the elemental composition of the diet, factors such as the amount of dietary fibre influenced bone chemistry. Ezzo (1994) surveyed a range of trace elements as potential palaeodietary indicators, and concluded that, apart from strontium and barium (which follows strontium), the difficulties listed above, especially (ii), preclude the use of trace element measurements for reliable palaeodietary reconstructions.

STRONTIUM ISOTOPES

Strontium isotope analysis ($^{87}Sr/^{86}Sr$) differs from the approaches described above, in that there is no biological fractionation of strontium isotopes. There are, however, substantial differences in $^{87}Sr/^{86}Sr$ in different geological formations. The ^{87}Sr is formed by radioactive decay of ^{87}Rb, with a half-life of 4.9×10^{10} years, whilst ^{86}Sr is not radiogenic. Both isotopes are stable, so that $^{87}Sr/^{86}Sr$ increases through geological time. Old rocks, especially those rich in rubidium, have $^{87}Sr/^{86}Sr$ as high as 0.720, whilst young volcanic rocks have values around 0.703. Marine $^{87}Sr/^{86}Sr$ is 0.709. Although strontium isotope values change through geological time, they are effectively constant for the relatively short windows of time of interest to most archaeologists. Strontium isotope measurements are generally expressed as the ratio $^{87}Sr/^{86}Sr$, although some authors use an ε notation analogous to the δ values used for stable isotope ratios (Ezzo et al. 1997, Price et al. 1994a).

Bone $^{87}Sr/^{86}Sr$ is identical to that of dietary strontium. Thus bone strontium isotope composition can be used to source humans or animals to the geological substrates on which they lived and obtained their food. In regions with more than one geological formation with different $^{87}Sr/^{86}Sr$, bone strontium tells us whether people or animals lived on one formation or the other, or whether they moved between them. Note, however, that bones register $^{87}Sr/^{86}Sr$ of biologically available strontium, which may differ from the whole-rock or mineral values usually measured by geologists (Sillen et al. 1998). For archaeological samples, care must be taken to measure biogenic, rather than diagenetic strontium, as for Sr/Ca. Most studies use a leaching procedure, such as the solubility profiles mentioned above, to remove diagenetic mineral (see references cited above, also Price et al. 1994a).

Ericson (1985) first proposed that strontium isotope ratios in tooth enamel, compared with bone tissue could yield information on the area in which people lived in their childhood, compared with their adult years. He suggested that archaeologists could detect patrilocal vs. matrilocal residence patterns in this way. Price et al. (1994a) and Ezzo et al. (1997) used this approach to study residential mobility in the prehistoric US southwest. Price et al. (1994b) and Grupe et al. (1997) investigated the question of whether

Central European Beaker people were immigrants to the areas where they were buried. Sillen et al. (1998) mapped the strontium isotope ratios of the surroundings of Swartkrans Cave, South Africa, and compared the results of $^{87}Sr/^{86}Sr$ determinations on seven robust australopithecine and two early Homo specimens from the site. Most had strontium isotope compositions very similar to the local veld, but one individual, a large male robust australopithecine (SK 876), had significantly different $^{87}Sr/^{86}Sr$. The authors suggested that he might have moved into the area from elsewhere.

RESEARCH IN PROGRESS

The techniques outlined above can be combined, and analysis of multiple samples from different parts of the skeleton of a single individual can yield information on diet at different stages during life. In rapidly growing tissues, seasonal signals can sometimes be identified in cyclic variations in isotope ratios (e.g., White 1993, Fricke and O'Neil 1996). This approach is in its infancy, but has a number of archaeological applications. Comparison of isotopic ratios in tooth, cortical and cancellous bone, each containing tissue formed during a different period of an individual's life, has been used to identify the skeletons of slaves imported to the Cape Colony during the eighteenth and nineteenth centuries (Sealy et al. 1995, Cox and Sealy 1997). It would be valuable to know more about rates of bone synthesis and resorption, at different stages of life and under different dietary regimes, in order to fine-tune this approach. Improved ways of separating bone laid down some time before death from that formed very late in life also promise advances in this area (Bell et al. 1999).

A fundamental problem in reconstructing palaeodiet from body tissue chemistry is our lack of understanding of biochemical mechanisms involved in the conversion of food to body tissues, and how these produce isotopic fractionation. The biochemical pathways have been studied only at the molecular scale, whereas the questions archaeologists would like to answer are at a much more general level. The problem is best illustrated in relation to the fate of dietary carbon.

Carbon is ubiquitous in foods; it occurs in proteins, fats and carbohydrates. Early studies of carbon isotopes and palaeodiets assumed that all dietary carbon contributed equally to bone collagen: the 'scrambled egg' model. We now know that this is not the case. Some dietary components are preferred in collagen synthesis, so that their carbon is preferentially included in collagen, and their isotopic composition has a disproportionately large effect on collagen $\delta^{13}C$. We now have preliminary results from experiments designed to investigate this issue, through controlled feeding of laboratory animals. Both Ambrose and Norr (1993) and Tieszen and Fagre (1993), working with rats and mice respectively, found that dietary protein was the major contributor to bone collagen. Bone apatite was a better indicator of average dietary $\delta^{13}C$. The details of these processes, and the extent to which patterns seen in small animals can be generalized to larger organisms such as humans, remain to be worked out.

Relatively few studies have thus far attempted to trace variations in isotope ratios at the molecular level. Stott *et al.* (1999) used $\delta^{13}C$ of cholesterol extracted from bones to monitor dietary $\delta^{13}C$ shortly before death (see Chapter 28). Studies of proteins show that there is considerable variation in both $\delta^{13}C$ and $\delta^{15}N$ between different amino acids (Macko *et al.* 1983, Hare and Estep 1983, Hare *et al.* 1991, Turban-Just and Schramm 1998). Only once we understand isotopic fractionation at the metabolic level will we be able to achieve *quantitative* reconstructions of diet – a long-standing goal of bone chemistry studies.

REFERENCES

*Recommended for further reading

Ambrose, S.H. (1986). Stable carbon and nitrogen isotope analysis of human and animal diet in Africa. *Journal of Human Evolution*, **15**:707–731.

Ambrose, S.H. (1991). Effects of diet, climate and physiology on nitrogen isotope abundances in terrestrial foodwebs. *Journal of Archaeological Science*, **18**:293–317.

Ambrose, S.H. (1998). Prospects for stable isotopic analysis of later Pleistocene hominid diets in west Asia and Europe. In Akazawa, T., Aoki, K. and Bar-Yosef, O. (eds) *Neandertals and Modern Humans in Western Asia*, 277–289. Plenum Press: New York.

Ambrose, S.H. and DeNiro, M.J. (1986). Reconstruction of African human diet using bone collagen carbon and nitrogen isotope ratios. *Nature*, **319**:321–324.

Ambrose, S.H. and Norr, L. (1993). Experimental evidence for the relationship of the carbon isotope ratios of whole diet and dietary protein to those of bone collagen and carbonate. In Lambert, J.B. and Grupe, G. (eds) *Prehistoric Human Bone: Archaeology at the Molecular Level*, 1–37. Springer-Verlag: Berlin.

Ambrose, S.H., Butler, B.M., Hanson, D.B., Hunter-Anderson, R.L. and Krueger, H.W. (1997). Stable isotopic analysis of human diet in the Marianas Archipelago, Western Pacific. *American Journal of Physical Anthropology*, **104**:343–361.

Aufderheide, A.C., Kelley, M.A., Riviera, M., Gray, L., Tieszen, L.L., Iversen, E., Krouse, H.R. and Carevic, A. (1994). Contributions of chemical dietary reconstruction to the assessment of adaptation by ancient highland immigrants (Alto Ramirez) to coastal conditions at Pisagua, North Chile. *Journal of Archaeological Science*, **21**:515–524.

Bell, L., Sealy, J. and Cox, G. (1999). Isotopic studies of dietary change: a new approach using bone density fractionation. Paper presented at the 4th World Archaeology Conference, Cape Town, 10–14 January.

Bocherens, H., Fizet, M., Mariotti, A., Lange-Badre, B., Vandermeersch, B., Borel, J.P. and Bellon G. (1991). Isotopic biogeochemistry (^{13}C, ^{15}N) of fossil vertebrate collagen: application to the study of a past food web including Neandertal man. *Journal of Human Evolution*, **20**:481–492.

Bocherens, H., Fogel, M.L., Tuross, N. and Zeder, M. (1995). Trophic structure and climate information from isotopic signatures in Pleistocene cave fauna from southern England. *Journal of Archaeological Science*, **22**:327–340.

Bocherens, H., Billiou, D., Mariotti, A., Patou-Mathis, M., Otte, M., Bonjean, D. and Toussaint, M. (1999). Palaeoenvironmental and palaeodietary implications of isotopic biogeochemistry of last interglacial Neanderthal and mammal bones in Scladina Cave (Belgium). *Journal of Archaeological Science*, **26**:599–607.

Brown, A.B. (1974). Bone strontium as a dietary indicator in human skeletal populations. *Contributions to Geology*, **13**:47–48.

Bryant, J.D., Koch, P.L., Froelich, P.N., Showers, W.J. and Genna, B.J. (1996). Oxygen isotope partitioning between phosphate and carbonate in mammalian apatite. *Geochimica et Cosmochimica Acta*, **60**:5145–5148.

Budd, P., Montgomery, J., Barreiro, B. and Thomas, R.G. (2000). Differential diagenesis of strontium in archaeological human dental tissues. *Applied Geochemistry*, **15**:687–694.

Buikstra, J.E. and Milner, G.R. (1991). Isotopic and archaeological interpretations of diet in the Central Mississippi Valley. *Journal of Archaeological Science*, **18**:319–329.

*Buikstra, J.E., Frankenburg, S., Lambert, J.B. and Xue, L. (1989). Multiple elements: multiple expectations. In Price, T.D. (ed.) *The Chemistry of Prehistoric Human Bone*, 155–210. Cambridge University Press: Cambridge.

Burton, J.H. and Wright, L. (1995). Nonlinearity in the relationship between bone Sr/Ca and diet: palaeodietary implications. *American Journal of Physical Anthropology*, **96**:273–282.

Cerling, T.E., Harris, J.M., MacFadden, B.J., Leakey, M.G., Quade, J., Eisenmann, V. and Ehleringer, J.R. (1997). Global vegetation change through the Miocene/Pliocene boundary. *Nature*, **389**:153–158.

Cox, G. and Sealy, J. (1997). Investigating identity and life histories: isotopic analysis and historical documentation of slave skeletons found on the Cape Town foreshore,

South Africa. *International Journal of Historical Archaeology*, **1**:207–224.

DeNiro, M.J. and Epstein, S. (1978). Influence of diet on the distribution of carbon isotopes in animals. *Geochimica et Cosmochimica Acta*, **42**:495–506.

Elias, R.W., Hirao, Y. and Patterson, C.C. (1982). The circumvention of the natural biopurification of calcium along nutrient pathways by atmospheric inputs of industrial lead. *Geochimica et Cosmochimica Acta*, **46**:2561–2580.

Elliott, T.A., Forey, P.L., Williams, C.T. and Werdelin, L. (1998). Application of the solubility profiling technique to recent and fossil fish teeth. *Bulletin de la Société Géologique de France*, **169**:443–451.

Ericson, J.E. (1985). Strontium isotope characterization in the study of prehistoric human ecology. *Journal of Human Evolution*, **14**:503–514.

Ezzo, J.A. (1994). Putting the 'chemistry' back into archaeological bone chemistry analysis: modeling potential paleodietary indicators. *Journal of Anthropological Archaeology*, **13**:1–34.

Ezzo, J.A., Johnson, C.M. and Price, T.D. (1997). Analytical perspectives on prehistoric migration: a case study from east-central Arizona. *Journal of Archaeological Science*, **24**:447–466.

Fizet, M., Mariotti, A., Bocherens, H., Lang-Badre, B., Vandermeersch, B., Borel, J.P. and Bellon, G. (1995). Effect of diet, physiology and climate on carbon and nitrogen stable isotopes of collagen in a Late Pleistocene anthropic paleoecosystem: Marillac, Charente, France. *Journal of Archaeological Science*, **22**:67–79.

Fricke, H.C., O'Neil, J.R. and Lynnerup, N. (1995). Oxygen isotope composition of human tooth enamel from medieval Greenland: linking climate and society. *Geology*, **23**:869–872.

Fricke, H.C. and O'Neil, J.R. (1996). Inter- and intra-tooth variation in the oxygen isotope composition of mammalian tooth enamel phosphate: implications for palaeoclimatological and palaeobiological research. *Palaeogeography, Palaeoclimatology, Palaeoecology*, **126**:91–99.

Gilbert, R.I. (1975). *Trace Element Analyses of Three Skeletal Amerindian Populations at Dickson Mounds*. Unpublished PhD dissertation, University of Massachusetts, Amherst.

Grupe, G., Price, T.D., Schröter, P., Söllner, F., Johnson, C.M. and Beard, B.L. (1997). Mobility of Bell Beaker people revealed by strontium isotope ratios of tooth and bone: a study of southern Bavarian skeletal remains. *Applied Geochemistry*, **12**:517–525.

Hare, P.E., Fogel, M.L., Stafford, T.W. Jr., Mitchell, A.D. and Hoering, T.C. (1991). The isotopic composition of carbon and nitrogen in individual amino acids isolated from modern and fossil proteins. *Journal of Archaeological Science*, **18**:277–292.

Hare, P.E. and Estep, M.L.F. (1983). Carbon and nitrogen isotopic composition of amino acids in modern and fossil collagens. *Carnegie Institution of Washington Yearbook*, **82**:410–414.

Heaton, T.H.E. (1987). The $^{15}N/^{14}N$ ratios of plants in South Africa and Namibia: relationship to climate and coastal/saline environments. *Oecologia*, **74**:236–246.

Iacumin, P., Bocherens, H., Mariotti, A. and Longinelli, A. (1996). An isotopic palaeoenvironmental study of human skeletal remains from the Nile valley. *Palaeogeography, Palaeoclimatology, Palaeoecology*, **126**:15–30.

Iacumin, P., Bocherens, H., Chaix, L. and Marioth, A. (1998). Stable carbon and nitrogen isotopes as dietary indicators of Ancient Nubian populations (Northern Sudan). *Journal of Archaeological Science*, **25**:293–301.

*Katzenberg, M.A. (1992). Advances in stable isotope analysis of prehistoric bones. In Saunders, S.R. and Katzenberg, M.A. (eds) *Skeletal Biology of Past Peoples: Research Methods*, 105–119. Wiley-Liss: New York.

*Katzenberg, M.A. and Harrison, R.G. (1997). What's in a bone? Recent advances in archaeological bone chemistry. *Journal of Archaeological Research*, **5**:265–293.

Katzenberg, M.A., Herring, D.A. and Saunders, S.R. (1996). Weaning and infant mortality: evaluating the skeletal evidence. *Yearbook of Physical Anthropology*, **39**:177–199.

*Koch, P.L. (1998). Isotopic reconstruction of past continental environments. *Annual Reviews of Earth and Planetary Science*, **26**:573–613.

Koch, P.L., Halliday, A.N., Walter, L.M., Stearley, R.F., Huston T.J. and Smith G.R. (1992). Sr composition of hydroxyapatite from recent and fossil salmon: the record of lifetime migration and diagenesis. *Earth and Planetary Science Letters*, **108**:277–287.

Koch, P.L., Tuross, N. and Fogel, M.L. (1997). The effects of sample treatment and diagenesis on the isotopic integrity of carbonate in biogenic hydroxylapatite. *Journal of Archaeological Science*, **24**:417–429.

Kolodny, Y., Luz, B. and Navon, O. (1983). Oxygen isotope variations in phosphate of biogenic apatites, I. Fish bone apatite – rechecking the rules of the game. *Earth and Planetary Science Letters*, **64**:398–404.

Lambert, J.B. and Weydert-Homeyer, J.M. (1993). Dietary inferences from element analyses of bone. In Lambert, J.B. and Grupe, G. (eds) *Prehistoric Human Bone: Archaeology at the Molecular Level*, 217–228. Springer-Verlag: Berlin.

Lee-Thorp, J.A. and van der Merwe, N.J. (1987). Carbon isotope analysis of fossil bone apatite. *South African Journal of Science*, **83**:71–74.

Lee-Thorp, J.A. and van der Merwe, N.J. (1991). Aspects of the chemistry of modern and fossil biological apatites. *Journal of Archaeological Science*, **18**:343–354.

Lee-Thorp, J.A., Sealy, J.C. and van der Merwe, N.J. (1989). Stable carbon isotope ratio differences between bone collagen and bone apatite, and their relationship to diet. *Journal of Archaeological Science*, **16**:585–599.

Lee-Thorp, J.A., van der Merwe, N. and Brain, C.K. (1994). Diet of *Australopithecus robustus* at Swartkrans from stable carbon isotopic analysis. *Journal of Human Evolution*, **27**:361–372.

Lee-Thorp, J.A., Manning, L. and Sponheimer, M. (1997). Problems and prospects for carbon isotope analysis of very small samples of fossil tooth enamel. *Bulletin de la Société Géologique de France*, **168**:767–773.

Luz, B. and Kolodny, Y. (1985). Oxygen isotope variations in phosphate of biogenic apatites, IV. Mammal teeth and bones. *Earth and Planetary Science Letters*, **75**:29–36.

Luz, B., Kolodny, Y. and Horowitz, M. (1984). Fractionation of oxygen isotopes between mammalian bone phosphate and environmental drinking water. *Geochimica et Cosmochimica Acta*, **48**:1689–1693.

Luz, B., Cormie, A.B. and Schwarcz, H.P. (1990). Oxygen isotope variations in phosphate of deer bones. *Geochimica et Cosmochimica Acta*, **54**:1723–1728.

Macko, S.A., Estep, M.L.F., Hare, P.E. and Hoering, T.C. (1983). Stable nitrogen and carbon isotopic composition of individual amino acids isolated from cultured microorganisms. *Carnegie Institution of Washington Yearbook*, **82**:404–410.

McGovern-Wilson, R. and Quinn, C. (1996). Stable isotope analysis of ten individuals from Afetna, Saipan, Northern Marianas Islands. *Journal of Archaeological Science*, **23**:59–65.

Murray, M.L. and Schoeninger, M.J. (1988). Diet, status and complex social structure in Iron Age central Europe: some contributions of bone chemistry. In Gibson, D.B. and Geselowitz, M.N. (eds) *Tribe and Polity in Late Prehistoric Europe: Demography, Production and Exchange in the Evolution of Complex Social Systems*, 155–176. Plenum Press: New York.

Nelson, B.K., DeNiro, M.J., Schoeninger, M.J. and DePaolo, D.J. (1986). Effects of diagenesis on strontium, carbon, nitrogen and oxygen concentration and isotopic composition of bone. *Geochimica et Cosmochimica Acta*, **50**:1941–1949.

O'Leary, M.H. (1995). Environmental effects on carbon isotope fractionation in plants. In Wada, E., Yoneyama, T., Minigawa, M., Andao, T. and Fry, B.D. (eds) *Stable Isotopes in the Biosphere*, 78–91. Kyoto University Press: Kyoto.

Parker, R.B. and Toots, H. (1970). Minor elements in fossil bones. *Geological Society of America Bulletin*, **81**:925–932.

Pate, F.D. and Schoeninger, M.J. (1993). Stable carbon isotope ratios in bone collagen as indicators of marine and terrestrial dietary composition in southeastern South Australia: a preliminary report. In Fankhauser, B.L. and Bird, J.R. (eds) *Archaeometry: Current Australasian Research*, 38–44. Australian National University: Canberra.

Price, T.D., Johnson, C.M., Ezzo, J.A., Ericson, J. and Burton, J.H. (1994a). Residential mobility in the prehistoric southwest United States: a preliminary study using strontium isotope analysis. *Journal of Archaeological Science*, **21**:315–330.

Price, T.D., Grupe, G. and Schröter, P. (1994b). Reconstruction of migration patterns in the Bell Beaker

period by stable strontium isotope analysis. *Applied Geochemistry*, **9**:413–417.

Quade, J., Cerling, T.E., Barry, J.C., Morgan, M.E., Pilbeam, D.R., Chivas, A.R., Lee-Thorp, J.A. and van der Merwe, N.J. (1992). A 16-Ma record of palaeodiet using carbon and oxygen isotopes in fossil teeth from Pakistan. *Chemical Geology*, **94**:183–192.

Richards, M.P., Hedges, R.E.M., Molleson, T. and Vogel, J.C. (1998). Stable isotope analysis reveals variations in human diet at the Poundbury Camp cemetery site. *Journal of Archaeological Science*, **25**:1247–1252.

*Sandford, M.K. (1992). A reconsideration of trace element analysis in prehistoric bone. In Saunders, S.R. and Katzenberg, M.A. (eds) *Skeletal Biology of Past Peoples: Research Methods*, 79–104. John Wiley: New York.

Schoeninger, M.J. (1979). Diet and status at Chalcatzingo: some empirical and technical aspects of strontium analysis. *American Journal of Physical Anthropology*, **51**:295–310.

Schoeninger, M.J. (1985). Trophic level effects on $^{15}N/^{14}N$ and $^{13}C/^{12}C$ ratios in bone collagen and strontium levels in bone mineral. *Journal of Human Evolution*, **14**:515–525.

*Schoeninger, M.J. and Moore, K. (1992). Bone stable isotope studies in archaeology. *Journal of World Prehistory*, **6**:247–296.

Schurr, M. (1997). Stable nitrogen isotopes as evidence for the age of weaning at the Angel site: a comparison of isotopic and demographic measures of weaning age. *Journal of Archaeological Science*, **24**:919–927.

Schurr, M. (1998). Using stable nitrogen isotopes to study weaning behaviour in past populations. *World Archaeology*, **30**:327–342.

*Schwarcz, H.P. and Schoeninger, M.J. (1991). Stable isotope analyses in human nutritional ecology. *Yearbook of Physical Anthropology*, **34**:283–321.

Schwarcz, H.P., Gibbs, L. and Knyf, M. (1991). Oxygen isotopic analysis as an indicator of place of origin. In Pfeiffer, S. and Williamson, R.F. (eds) *Snake Hill: an Investigation of a Military Cemetery from the War of 1812*, 263–268. Dundurn Press: Toronto.

Schwarcz, H.P., Dupras, T.L. and Fairgrieve, S.I. (1999). ^{15}N enrichment in the Sahara: in search of a global relationship. *Journal of Archaeological Science*, **26**:629–636.

Sealy, J.C. and Sillen, A. (1988). Sr and Sr/Ca in marine and terrestrial foodwebs in the southwestern Cape, South Africa. *Journal of Archaeological Science*, **15**:425–438.

Sealy, J.C., van der Merwe, N.J., Sillen, A., Kruger, F.J. and Krueger, H.W. (1991). $^{87}Sr/^{86}Sr$ as a dietary indicator in modern and archaeological bone. *Journal of Archaeological Science*, **18**:399–416.

Sealy, J., Armstrong, R. and Schrire, C. (1995). Beyond lifetime averages: tracing life histories through isotopic analysis of different calcified tissues from archaeological human skeletons. *Antiquity*, **69**:290–300.

Shearer, G. and Kohl, D.H. (1986). N_2 fixation in field settings: estimations based on natural ^{15}N abundance. *Australian Journal of Plant Physiology*, **13**:699–756.

Sillen, A. (1981). Strontium and diet at Hayonim Cave. *American Journal of Physical Anthropology*, **56**:131–137.

Sillen, A. (1986). Biogenic and diagenetic Sr/Ca in Plio-Pleistocene fossils of the Omo Shungura formation. *Paleobiology*, **12**:311–323.

Sillen, A. (1990). Response to N. Tuross, A.K. Behrensmeyer, and E.D. Eanes. *Journal of Archaeological Science*, **17**:595–596.

Sillen, A. (1992). Strontium-calcium ratios (Sr/Ca) of *Australopithecus robustus* and associated fauna from Swartkrans. *Journal of Human Evolution*, **23**:495–516.

*Sillen, A. and Kavanagh, M. (1982). Strontium and palaeo-dietary research: a review. *Yearbook of Physical Anthropology*, **25**:67–90.

Sillen, A. and Sealy, J.C. (1995). Diagenesis of strontium in fossil bone: a reconsideration of Nelson *et al.* (1986). *Journal of Archaeological Science*, **22**:313–320.

Sillen, A. and Smith, P. (1984). Weaning patterns are reflected in strontium-calcium ratios of juvenile skeletons. *Journal of Archaeological Science*, **11**:237–245.

Sillen, A., Hall, G. and Armstrong, R. (1995). Strontium calcium ratios (Sr/Ca) and strontium isotopic ratios (^{87}Sr/^{86}Sr) of *Australopithecus robustus* and *Homo* sp. from Swartkrans. *Journal of Human Evolution*, **28**:277–285.

Sillen, A., Hall, G., Richardson, S. and Armstrong, R. (1998). ^{87}Sr/^{86}Sr ratios in modern and fossil food-webs of the Sterkfontein Valley: implications for early hominid habitat preference. *Geochimica et Cosmochimica Acta*, **62**:2463–2473.

Sponheimer, M. and Lee-Thorp, J.A. (1999a). Isotopic evidence for the diet of an early hominid, *Australopithecus africanus*. *Science*, **283**:368–370.

Sponheimer, M. and Lee-Thorp, J.A. (1999b). Oxygen isotopes in enamel carbonate and their ecological significance. *Journal of Archaeological Science*, **26**:723–728.

Stott, A.W., Evershed, R.P., Jim, S., Jones, V., Rogers, J.M., Tuross, N. and Ambrose, S. (1999). Cholesterol as a new source of palaeodietary information: experimental approaches and archaeological applications. *Journal of Archaeological Science*, **26**:705–716.

Stuart-Williams, H. le Q., Schwarcz, H.P., White, C.D. and Spence, M.W. (1996). The isotopic composition and diagenesis of human bone from Teotihuacan and Oaxaca, Mexico. *Palaeogeography, Palaeoclimatology, Palaeoecology*, **126**:1–14.

Thackeray, J.F., van der Merwe, N.J., Lee-Thorp, J.A., Sillen, A., Lanham, J.L., Smith, R., Keyser, A. and Monteiro, P.M.S. (1990). Changes in carbon isotope ratios in the late Permian recorded in therapsid tooth apatite. *Nature*, **347**:751–753.

Tieszen, L.L. and Fagre, T. (1993). Effect of diet quality and composition on the isotopic composition of respiratory CO_2, bone collagen, bioapatite and soft tissues. In Lambert, J.B. and Grupe, G. (eds) *Prehistoric Human Bone: Archaeology at the Molecular Level*, 121–155. Springer-Verlag: Berlin.

Toots, H. and Voorhies, M.R. (1965). Strontium in fossil bones and the reconstruction of food chains. *Science*, **149**:854–855.

Turban-Just, S. and Schramm, S. (1998). Stable carbon and nitrogen isotope ratios of individual amino acids give new insight into bone collagen degradation. *Bulletin de la Société Géologique de France*, **169**:109–114.

Tuross, N., Behrensmeyer, A.K. and Eanes, E.D. (1989). Strontium increases and crystallinity changes in tapho-nomic and archaeological bone. *Journal of Archaeological Science*, **16**:661–672.

van der Merwe, N.J. and Vogel, J.C. (1978). ^{13}C content of human collagen as a measure of prehistoric diet in woodland North America. *Nature*, **276**:815–816.

van Klinken, G.J., van der Plicht, H. and Hedges, R.E.M. (1994). Bone ^{13}C/^{12}C ratios reflect (palaeo-)climatic variations. *Geophysical Research Letters*, **21**:445–448.

Vogel, J.C. (1978). Isotopic assessment of the dietary habits of ungulates. *South African Journal of Science*, **74**:298–301.

Vogel, J.C. and van der Merwe, N.J. (1977). Isotopic evidence for early maize cultivation in New York state. *American Antiquity*, **42**:238–242.

Wang, Y. and Cerling, T.E. (1994). A model of fossil tooth and bone diagenesis: implications for paleodiet reconstruction from stable isotopes. *Palaeogeography, Palaeoclimatology, Palaeoecology*, **107**:281–289.

White, C.D. (1993). Isotopic determination of seasonality in diet and death from Nubian mummy hair. *Journal of Archaeological Science*, **20**:657–666.

White, C.D., Spence, M.W., Stuart-Williams, H. le Q. and Schwarcz, H.P. (1998). Oxygen isotopes and the identification of geographical origins: the Valley of Oaxaca versus the Valley of Mexico. *Journal of Archaeological Science*, **25**:643–655.

24

Cremated Bone

J.I. McKINLEY

Warminster, Wilts.

and J.M. BOND

Department of Archaeological Sciences, University of Bradford.

The use of the term 'cremated' indicates that the bone is the product of a series of ritual acts comprising disposal of the dead by the mortuary rite of cremation. Consequently, in addition to the standard osteological objectives of ascertaining demographic and pathological data, analysis also aims to deduce evidence pertaining to pyre technology, and indications of the rites and rituals attendant on the funerary practice.

This chapter analyses the characteristic form and nature of cremated bone and outlines the process of cremation – an understanding of which is essential to the analysis of cremated bone – comparing modern crematoria and pyre cremation, including results from experimental work. Analytical methods for the recovery of demographic, anthropological and pathological data specific to cremated remains is discussed, with consideration of how this data may be used to assess aspects of the technology, rituals and, thereby, the rites of cremation.

THE FORM AND NATURE OF CREMATED BONE

Cremated bone is often described as 'burnt', 'calcined' or 'oxidized'; whilst each may be an accurate description, incomplete calcination/oxidation is not uncommon, and not all burnt bone (human or animal) has been cremated. The cremation process comprises dehydration and oxidation of the organic components of the body, including the $c.$ 30 per cent organic component of the skeleton (Glorieux 1982). The macroscopic appearance of the bone and its microstructure are variably altered, dependent on a number of factors; reviews of which have been presented by Wahl (1982:6), Lange et al. (1987:17) and McKinley (1994a:76).

The macroscopic appearance of bone is altered as dehydration leads to shrinkage, fissuring and sometimes twisting, generally following patterns dictated by bone morphology and the stresses imposed by soft tissue attachments (e.g., 'U' shaped fissures along the length of long bone shafts (Figure 24.1), or concentric fissuring in humeral/femoral heads). Small bones, such as carpals and phalanges, often survive whole (Figure 24.1). Laboratory experiments and observations (Baby 1954, Binford 1963, Thurman and Wilmore 1981) have demonstrated that dehydration effects differ between dry and 'green' (fresh) bone, but that in 'green' bone there is no conclusively discernible difference in appearance between fleshed and de-fleshed cadavers (McKinley 1994a:78).

Experimental investigations of bone shrinkage have mostly been undertaken in laboratories using parts of cadavers. Various shrinkage factors have been suggested – an 'overall' factor of 12 per cent (Rösing 1977); 'a maximum mean' of c. 15 per cent (Shipman et al. 1984); a cross-sectional shrinkage of 25–30 per cent for femur shafts, 5 per cent longitudinal long bone shrinkage and 12 per cent for a femoral head (Lange et al. 1987:19), and Holck (1986:76) showing factors of 0–25 per cent. Preliminary observations taken from dissection room cadavers in crematoria (McKinley unpublished) indicate, for example, 1.9–2.5 per cent cross-sectional shrinkage in the radius shaft and 3.8–5.0 per cent in the radial head. This indicates that there is no reliable 'overall' shrinkage factor, there being substantial variation within and between individual skeletons, which is almost certainly a product of vari-able temperature. Shrinkage is related to changes in crystal structure which is directly affected by temperature (see below) and, in the cremation of an entire cadaver, different bones may be subject to different temperatures, particularly in pyre cremation. The biological age of the individual will also have an effect – 'the cross-linking of collagen with age,... providing resistance to movement' (Holden et al. 1995a).

Bone colour ranges between the brown or black of slightly charred bone, through hues of blue and grey, to the buff/white associated with oxidized bone, often varying within the individual, even from a modern crematorium. Within a given time span, bone with substantial soft tissue coverage will not cremate as fully as that with less, and some bone has a higher organic component than others (e.g., compact versus spongy) and consequently takes longer to oxidize. Shipman et al. (1984) and Holden et al. (1995b) found a correlation between the colour of the bone and the temperatures attained during experimental cremation. Observations by the latter clearly demonstrated that the maximum temperature indicated by the condition of a single bone fragment may not necessarily reflect the temperature affecting the entire corpse, recording a 'gradual decrease in temperature ... as a function of the radial distance from the outer cortical bone surface'.

Microscopic changes affecting the crystal structure of the calcium phosphate, hydroxyapatite

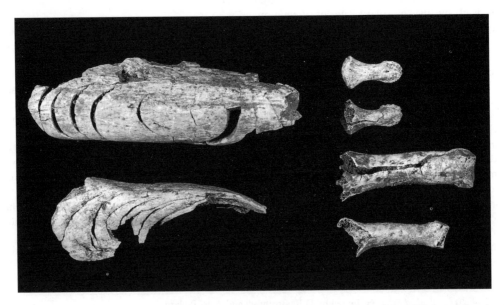

Figure 24.1 Characteristic fissuring: right – complete or almost complete finger phalanges; left – 'U'-shaped fissuring in the femur and humerus shafts.

$(Ca_{10}(PO_4)_6(OH)_2)$, forming 70 per cent of the bone mass (Glorieux 1982; see also Chapter 51), have been observed by a number of authors and linked to specific temperatures (e.g., Shipman *et al.* 1984). Whilst there is general agreement on the basic process, experimentally-derived temperature thresholds and the detail of observed changes do vary. As the hydroxyapatite crystals dehydrate in heating, the crystals remineralize in a different size and form. Holden *et al.* (1995a) observed recrystallization of the mineral commencing at 600°C, with crystal growth between 600–1000°C, a sintering process ('localized melting') occurring at *c.* 1000°C and up to 1400°C, leading to fusion of the crystals. It was also noted that the changes which occurred were not just linked to temperature, but also to the duration of heating and biological age – the latter falling into three broad bands of young (<22 yr), adult (22–60 yr) and old (>60 yr). Pyrophosphate is produced at temperatures above 600°C, leading to the formation of tricalcium phosphate in a variety of crystal forms during sintering (Lange *et al.* 1987, Holden *et al.* 1995a).

MODERN CREMATION

Modern crematoria, with highly efficient technology designed to meet public health criteria, provide monitored data against which archaeological material can be assessed. The technology of British crematoria has been described by, amongst others, Evans (1963). The visible process, and variations due to different cadavers or cremators and working practices etc., have been documented for British (McKinley 1993, 1994a:72, 1994b) and continental European crematoria (Wahl 1982:20, Holck 1986:37).

Cremation in modern crematoria takes approximately 60–90 minutes, although shorter (*c.* 30 minutes) and longer (more than 3 hours) variations have been noted. It aims to effect full oxidation of all the organic components of the body (not necessarily considered a prerequisite to 'cremation' in other contemporary, or in past European, cultures) by monitored control of the temperature and air flows. The thermally efficient ovens (cremators) render the application of an external heat source (gas jets) unnecessary once the minimum working temperature has been achieved (*c.* 700–1000°C), since heat produced by the soft tissue burning increases the temperature within the cremator. The intensity and duration of cremation is not uniform across the corpse, and cremation of the bone itself is affected by the density of soft tissue coverage (which does not conduct heat efficiently and reduces the oxygen supply to the bone), the varying nature of the bone itself (see above) and position relative to the fuel supply (gas jets). After *c.* 45 minutes, although some of the denser soft tissues remain and continue to burn for some time, the intensity of burning, and consequently the temperature, decreases dramatically.

At the end of cremation, a recognizable skeleton remains, including those of neonatal and young infants (Figure 24.2), though the latter are obviously very fragile (McKinley 1994a:75, Holck 1997). The weight of bone recovered from an adult cremation varies

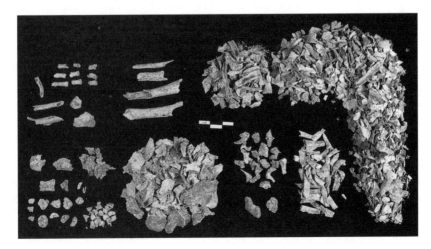

Figure 24.2 Cremated infant; unerupted tooth crowns lower left. (Reproduced by permission from Jacqueline Nowakowski of the Cornwall Archaeological Unit.)

between *c.* 1 kg and 3.6 kg (McKinley 1993). It has been observed that few articular surfaces and generally less spongy bone survive amongst the raked-out remains of some elderly individuals (>80 yr), particularly gracile females, which is believed to reflect the crumbling of osteoporotic bone. The fine-fraction ashes familiar as the remains from crematoria are the product of deliberate pulverization (cremulation) of the cremated bone.

Thermodynamic studies of modern crematoria, including calculations of combustion rates, air and fuel requirements, and the calorific values of various species of wood (Holck 1986), lead to the conclusions that the energy used 'corresponds to approximately 146 kg of pinewood', but that in practice 'a considerably greater amount of fuel is necessary' for pyre cremation. Open pyres do not, for instance, retain or circulate hot gases as in the cremator. Holck also states that: 'The grade of burning is proportional with the applied time, temperature and amount of oxygen.' These three factors, and the relationship between them, represent the necessary criteria for cremation. For example, a corpse burnt at the required temperature but for too short a time will not fully cremate, and insufficient oxygen supply may result in reducing conditions, merely charring the body.

PYRE CREMATION

Evidence for funerary procedures and beliefs associated with cremation may be gleaned from documentary sources and pictorial representations of ancient cremations (Toynbee 1996, Holck 1986:5, McKinley, 1994a:79) and from anthropological data (Dubois and Beauchamp 1943, Wahl and Wahl 1983, Pautreau 1994, Downes 1999). The basic structure of the pyre appears to have been universal: a box-frame of horizontal timbers arranged in layers at right-angles and in-filled with brushwood, providing a fuel source and a stable support for the corpse and pyre goods (i.e., items placed on the pyre not just in the grave) allowing circulation of air (see Chapter 40). Construction may be on a flat surface, such as in the cremation *ghats* of India, or over a shallow scoop or pit such as described in late-eighteenth century Australia (Hiatt 1969), to provide an under-pyre draught.

Observation of experimental pyre cremations have demonstrated the temperatures attainable (>1000°), duration, how the pyre collapses and the thermodynamic efficiency (Pionteck 1976, Lambot *et al.* 1994:249, McKinley 1997a, 1997b). The basic process is the same as in modern crematoria, but pyre crema-

tion is inherently more variable – heat is not retained and recirculated, peripheral areas of the pyre will experience much lower temperatures, wind strength may affect how the pyre burns and how quickly, heavy rain may curtail the whole proceedings. The duration and, thereby, the potential efficiency of cremation is affected by the quantity of wood used to build the pyre, and that this may vary (often in accordance with wealth) is demonstrated by both archaeological (e.g., Homer's *Iliad*) and contemporary accounts (McKinley 1994a:79).

Pyre cremation has variously been observed to take three hours (modern India), 7–8 hours (Pointeck 1976), or 7–10 hours for the pyre to cool sufficient to allow hand collection of the bone (Wahl 1982). There are common references to remains being recovered the day after cremation (Dubois and Beauchamp 1943, Hiatt 1969, Wahl 1982). 'Completion' of cremation depends on how fully oxidized the remains are required to be. After three hours a pyre may be largely burnt down but still too hot to allow manual recovery, and both bone and the soft tissues of the abdomen and thorax will continue to burn slowly on the remnants of the pyre in favourable weather conditions. The pyre collapses slowly upon itself with little outward spread, and, if unmanipulated, the skeletal remains lay in their anatomical order in the final stages, and clearly visible (Méniel 1994, McKinley 1997a).

AIMS AND METHODS OF ANALYSIS: HUMAN BONE

The funerary rite characteristically involved incomplete recovery of skeletal remains from the pyre, with burial often incorporating 50 per cent or less of the bone remaining at the end of cremation, of which only 30–50 per cent may be identifiable to a specific skeletal element. This, together with the degree of bone fragmentation, has a major effect on the quantity and quality of retrievable data. As bone fragment size decreases, precise identification becomes increasingly difficult, although the distinctive form of certain cranial elements renders them recognizable even as very small fragments. The ageing and sexing of cremated human remains is not intrinsically more difficult than with unburnt skeletal remains, the same criteria potentially being applied (Chapter 20), but, inevitably, some of the skeletal elements of greatest assistance may not be available for examination. The following discussion concerns variations in techniques or applicability specific to cremated bone.

Number of individuals

The number of individuals represented within a deposit is illustrated either by age-related differences in bone size and development or by the duplication of identifiable bone fragments (Figure 24.3). The integrity and condition of the deposit must always be considered, e.g., disturbance may have led to mixing of bone from adjacent burials. It has been suggested that bone weights in excess of 2141–2500 g are indicative of multiple burials (Holck 1986, Lange *et al.* 1987). However, higher weights have been recorded from modern crematoria (see above), and undisturbed archaeological burials of single adults have produced weights of 57 g to 3000 g (Wahl 1982:25, McKinley unpublished). Dual adult burials of <2000 g are not infrequent, and those comprising an adult with an immature individual can yield far less.

The use of different colours, unless observed in duplicated bones (see above), is unreliable, as are apparent contradictions in sexually dimorphic traits between different skeletal elements – certainly within British populations (see Chapter 20). Histological analysis of diaphyseal bone structures (Cuijpers 1997) may have some potential, but given the current levels of reliability of the method for ageing cremated remains (Hummel and Schutkowski 1993) it should be viewed with caution.

Ageing

The age of immature individuals may be assessed from unerupted tooth crowns, which often survive cremation intact (Figure 24.2). However, the enamel of erupted teeth shatters as it expands in cremation and generally does not support wear pattern analysis. Bone development and fusion of growth centres are often visible, but, since entire long bones are very rarely, if ever, recovered, recorded patterns of growth (e.g., Bass 1987) cannot be applied, though diaphyseal diameters have been used in some instances (Rösing 1977, Holck 1986:93).

Other morphological methods for ageing adults may rarely, if ever, be applied; the recovery of pubic symphyses is uncommon (a maximum of 4 per cent burials from a *c.* 4000 sample; McKinley unpublished). The sternal ends of ribs have never been noted (Holck 1986:94) and, whilst small parts of the ilium auricular surface are occasionally observed, they are rarely of sufficient size to allow assessment. In the absence of other criteria there is sometimes a reliance on cranial suture fusion – the skull vault being frequently recovered with at least one fragment having evident sutures (Holck 1986:96). Broad age bands are applied (*c.* 30 yr) but the general trend of progressive suture fusion with age always has exceptions and the application of the method in the absence of supporting evidence has been questioned (Chapter 20).

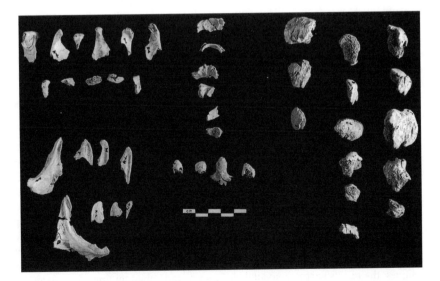

Figure 24.3 Trelowthas Barrow cist grave; multiples of mandibular condyles (upper left), mandibular coronoid processes (lower left), atlas anterior arch (upper centre), axis odontoid process (lower left) and patellae (right).

Histological ageing methods offer the potential to overcome the problems of bone fragmentation and the lack of visible morphologically diagnostic features (Herrmann 1973; see also Chapter 20). Initial consideration of the applicability of histological analysis to cremated bone (Herrmann 1977) concluded that at temperatures <700–800°C bone shrinkage would be minimal and the internal structures maintained; however, methods were developed for specific skeletal elements which may be missing or unidentifiable within cremation burials. The deleterious effect of shrinkage (commencing at 600°C) on any quantitative analyses is generally acknowledged (Herrmann 1977, Holck 1986:98, Holden *et al.* 1995a). Experiments conducted on cremated remains of known age (Hummel and Schutkowski 1993), whilst concluding that the best results were obtained from qualitative analysis, demonstrated that the results were not as good as with unburnt material; the average difference between chronological and assessed age was 8.4 ± 6.5 yr, but there was a tendency to over-age young individuals (by up to 20 years) and under-age older ones (by up to 19 years). This systematic discrepancy has been observed in a number of skeletal and dental age estimation techniques, and may be a consequence of the regression procedures used (Aykroyd *et al.* 1997).

Tooth roots are frequently recovered and, although potentially subject to variable shrinkage the basic structure remains intact after cremation. Early attempts to analyse incremental lines in the dental cementum of cremated teeth failed to produce any useable sections (Holck 1986). More recently Grosskopf (1997) has quoted an accuracy of ± 3.2 yr in ageing, decreasing to ± 6.2 yr where the sex of the individual or the precise tooth being analysed is unknown. The technique is very time consuming (20 cross-sections per tooth) and Grosskopf concluded that the method should not be used in isolation. Problems include indications that the reliability of the technique decreases with age and doubling of lines in 10 per cent of cases (see Chapter 20).

Structural changes to the bone mineral occurring during heating are affected by the age of the individual (Holden *et al.* 1995a), resulting in three broad age groups being detectable. However the lack of reliable results for older adults (> 60 yr) using other histological methods illustrates the potential usefulness of this technique. Whilst offering the potential to provide closer ageing for more adult burials than is possible with macroscopic techniques, the results currently available from histological analysis are of variable reliability (see Chapter 20). In most instances, it is preferable to quote broad adult age groups rather than stating a specific age in years, even where this leads to a restriction in demographic discussion, to avoid basing analysis on potentially unreliable data.

Sexing

Where the full skeletal remains of individuals of known sex have been examined in modern crematoria, a high rate of accuracy (90 per cent, others 'unsexed'; McKinley unpublished) has been achieved in sexing using standard visual methods (see Chapter 20). In archaeological deposits, however, pelvic fragments are uncommon and are often too small to enable confident sexing. Dental metric analysis is not possible other than with unerupted crowns from immature individuals (see above). General observation of the size and robusticity of the bone may give an indication of sex, but many of the standard measurements are not feasible with cremated remains due to fragmentation and incomplete recovery. Skull parts are frequently found and even small fragments of, for example, supra-orbit, mastoid process, mandible, etc., may assist in attribution of sex.

Several schemes of measurements have been devised specifically for use with cremated remains, largely developed using modern cremated remains (i.e., of known age and sex). Gejvall's (1969, 1981) method includes up to seven measurements taken from the skull vault, humerus, radius and femur. It has been argued (Holck 1986:75) that the variability in skull vault and diaphyseal thickness is not sufficiently significant; other potential problems may be linked to the age of the individual, variable bone shrinkage during cremation and correct identification of the precise bone fragment required (McKinley 1993). Despite this, Schutkowski and Hummel (1987), for example, were able to assign sex to 25 per cent previously unsexed adults in one assemblage using the technique. A major problem with the application of both Gejvall's (1969, 1981) and van Vark's (1974, 1975) methods (the latter encompassing a potential 57 suggested measurements) is the incomplete or non-recovery of the required skeletal elements; the humeral head, for example, being recovered intact in only *c.* 4 per cent of burials (sample >4000; McKinley unpublished).

Wahl (1982) devised a series of five measurable variables for the petrous temporal, a frequently recovered skeletal element, easily identified even when fragmentary, and maintaining its form in cremation. Classification values of 91.4 per cent were claimed for unburnt bone, and 80 per cent for cremated bone, though large areas of overlap are apparent within some variables (Wahl 1982:figures 11–16). The technique was devised on a non-homogeneous, unburnt sample group of 125, with standardized shrinkage factors being used to adjust for the effects of cremation. Lower classification values of 67–73.4 per cent were obtained when the technique was tested on the cremated remains of individuals of known sex (Schutkowski and Herrmann 1987).

Metric methods require a statistically viable minimum data base; van Vark (pers. comm.) advocated a minimum assemblage of 10, using between one and five comparable measurements per burial. Consequently, the practical application of some of these methods is, unfortunately, often limited. The potential problem of variable shrinkage must also always be considered. The most secure results are likely to be obtained through a combination of morphological variables and measurements – the use of a single trait, morphological or metric, being unreliable, certainly in British assemblages (see Chapter 20).

The applicability of DNA analysis to cremated remains has, to date, received little attention. The technique requires the retention of sufficient organic components in a suitable condition for analysis (Brown 1998) and the successful extraction of a protein (albumin) from archaeological cremated bone (Cattaneo et al. 1994) suggests that this may occur in some cases. Complete oxidation of all bone was not always attained in ancient cremations and those skeletal elements with the greatest soft tissue coverage may prove suitable for analysis, whilst charred soft tissue residues (Buikstra and Swegle 1988, McKinley 1994a:75, 1997b) may offer further potential.

Skeletal indices

Standard skeletal indices cannot, generally, be calculated for cremated material, although there are very exceptional circumstances where cranial indices have been presented (Wiercinska 1970).

Stature estimations, using standard regression equations, have been made from the estimated lengths of long bones calculated from the diameters of articular heads. Databases of variable size, e.g., 533 unburnt radii (Müller 1958) or 162 Medieval inhumations (Gralla 1964), were used to calculate correlations between head diameter and long bone length (Malinowski 1969), with various shrinkage factors being advocated (0 per cent – Gralla (1964); 1.4 per cent – Müller (1958) and 12 per cent – Rösing (1977)).

Müller (1958) claimed accuracy of ±7.5 cm for individuals of known sex and ±10 cm where the sex was unknown. Conversion tables devised by Rösing (1977) to estimate stature directly from primary data, give a stated error of ± 6.9–8.6 cm.

Potential inaccuracies with the technique, arising chiefly from variations in shrinkage (Wahl 1982:36, Holck 1986:112) and high statistical error, combine with the limited applicability due to the incomplete and fragmentary nature of archaeological material. For example, in more than 4000 British cremation burials complete femoral heads were present in <0.5 per cent of cases (mostly unsuitable for measurement), with the radial head presenting a measurable diameter in c. 5 per cent (McKinley unpublished).

Pathology

The same range of pathological lesions may be observed in cremated remains as in unburnt bone, but, since reliable diagnoses of pathological conditions require full (or near complete) skeletal recovery, the limitations are self-evident. The observation of lesions is at least as dependent on the condition of the bone as on the prevalence of disease.

Some conditions, e.g., osteoporosis, predispose bone to crumble during cremation (McKinley 1993). Identifiable dental diseases tend to be those affecting the supportive structure, but carious lesions may be recognized where the roots were involved (e.g., McKinley 1994a). Cuts have been recognized (Holck 1986:178), but fractures and other injuries are rarely observed (Holck 1986:198). Some less common conditions have been reported, e.g., trepanation (Grimm 1974), weapon injuries (Musgrave 1985), calcified lymph nodes (Garland 1994, McKinley 1994a:114), gall stones (Schutkowski et al. 1986, McKinley 1994a:114), and diffuse idiopathic skeletal hyperostosis (Smits et al. 1997).

AIMS AND METHODS OF ANALYSIS: ANIMAL BONE

Most of the above discussion is as true for studies of animal bone as for human bone; the problems of ageing, sexing and identifying pathologies are very similar, with the added problem of possible multiple species. There are also very real differences between human and animal bone, both in the archaeological occurrence of non-human bone and in its appearance and preservation. 'Calcined' animal bone can be found on domestic sites as well as funerary ones; even a small campfire can reach 800°C (Nicholson 1995) and where the soils are inimical to the preservation of bone, calcined fragments may be the only evidence of the domestic economy of a settlement site. Animal carcasses may be placed on separate pyres or on the fringes of the human's pyre, leading to differential or incomplete burning, which will itself affect preservation (Nicholson 1995), and different degrees of mixing with the human remains (e.g., McKinley 1994a:92, Bond 1994). Animals may also be present only as body parts (i.e., joints of meat) or as amulets (e.g., perforated raptor claws from Spong Hill; Bond 1994:134) or possibly, in the case of bear terminal phalanges (claws) as furs or rugs (Bond 1996).

Inter-species variations in the structure, size and density of bones and the composition of the surrounding flesh means that preservation also varies; whilst cremation of human bone has been well-researched, in non-human bone it is less well-documented. Buikstra and Swegle (1988) experimented with the burning of large mammal bone and Bond (1996) recorded observations on the preservation of large mammal bone from archaeological contexts, but only Nicholson (1993, 1995) has published experiments on the effects of burning on small mammal, bird and fish bone.

These studies suggest that there is considerable variation in the colour and surface appearance of different bones heated to the same temperatures for the same length of time. The combustion of organics seems to take longer in fish bone than in mammal and bird bone, and the fish bones were consistently darker than other bones when heated to the same temperature (Nicholson 1993). A surprising number of fish bones seem to have survived experimental burning, especially the vertebrae and jaw (Nicholson 1995).

Both Buikstra and Swegle's (1988) experimental work and Bond's (1994, 1996) studies of animal bone from Anglo-Saxon cremation cemeteries in England suggest that there are marked differences in preservation between the bones of larger and smaller mammals; those of larger mammals broke into more and smaller pieces on cremation (and subsequent retrieval). This is extremely important from a methodological point of view, because it means that large mammals are probably under-identified in cremation deposits relative to humans and smaller mammals.

The significance of animals in cremation deposits is in the information they carry about human attitudes to the animal world; information not readily available from the normal domestic residue of settlement sites. Crabtree (1995) and Bond (1996) reviewed this evidence for the Anglo-Saxon world, whilst Sigvallius (1997) looked at the evidence for Iron Age Sweden and Gräslund (1980) for Viking age Birka in Sweden. Kühl (1984) reviewed animal remains in Bronze Age to Viking period Schleswig-Holstein, Germany. Cremated animal bone has not been as widely studied as cremated human bone, and its potential significance to funerary studies has yet to be fully explored.

PYRE TECHNOLOGY AND RITUAL

Not all deposits containing cremated bone represent the remains of a cremation burial; pyre sites, with or without pyre debris, have been found (Sjösvärd et al. 1983, Downes 1995, Fitzpatrick 1997) and re-deposited pyre debris is often encountered (Polfer 1993, McKinley 1997a). Each of these deposits represents a ritual act, a component of the wider mortuary rite, and their material and stratigraphic characteristics need to be analysed in that context to understand funerary practices and beliefs. Many facets of the rite, which is obviously expensive in terms of time and effort and which leaves no direct archaeological trace (Wahl 1982:40), may be deduced indirectly from archaeological, historical, osteological, anthropological and comparative data, including corpse position, cremation efficiency, mode of bone collection and deposition. Burial conditions affecting bone survival will have consequences for data interpretation (see Chapter 51) and osteological study cannot be divorced from the archaeological context (Wahl 1982), e.g., was the burial urned or unurned? The positions in which corpses may have been placed on the pyre are illustrated by anthropological data (Wahl 1982:40), the distribution of cremated remains within combined, *in situ* pyre sites/graves (Lambot et al. 1994, Sjösvärd et al. 1983) and the adherence of pyre goods to specific skeletal elements (McKinley 1994a:83). The formation processes, attendant on subsequent stages of the mortuary rites, may also be illustrated (McKinley 1997a:137).

Cremation efficiency and potential technical difficulties may be deduced from data acquired from modern crematoria, experimental work and anthropological sources, whilst temperature variations within the pyre may be gauged using the visual and microscopic methods discussed above, and the appearance of pyre goods and pyre debris (McKinley 1994a:84). Geographic and temporal variations in efficiency have been observed (Holck 1987:131, McKinley 1997b).

References to cremations being deliberately curtailed (Wahl 1982:40) are not wholly corroborated by experimental work (McKinley 1997b), and where there was no urgency of access to a pyre site it would not have been necessary. References to 'quenching' or ritual 'washing' are likely to reflect a more common practice, experiments having demonstrated the naturally 'clean' appearance of bone at the end of cremation (Méniel 1994:figures 2–6, McKinley 1997b).

For reasons which remain unclear, the weight of bone collected for burial varied widely both temporally and geographically (see above; Holck 1986:112, McKinley 1997a). One trend alone appears to have remained universal – the entire cremated remains were not collected for burial. Evidence to suggest male burials on average incorporated larger quantities of bone than those of females (Wahl 1982:24) are not necessarily statistically significant with large overlaps in the weight ranges. Nor does archaeological data support theories that only the largest fragments or about half the cremated remains were collected for burial (Wahl 1982:24). One observation which may be of significance is the *consistently* high weights of bone recovered from the 'primary' burials within British Bronze Age cemeteries (averaging 1525.7 g; McKinley 1997a), the time expended in collecting the bone for burial possibly being a reflection of the deceased's 'status'.

An apparently random selection of skeletal elements appear to be represented in most deposits (Wahl 1982:31). Apparent predominance of skull fragments is, in most cases, representative of the preferential survival and ease of identification of such fragments, whereas rare cases in which skull bones are absent are likely to demonstrate deliberate exclusion. The observation from one British Bronze Age site that certain skeletal elements were more common in burials of one or other sex (Robertson pers. comm.) is currently uncorroborated elsewhere.

Bone fragment size is affected by a number of factors. In Wahl's (1982:30) review, 80 per cent of fragments fell between 10 and 50 mm in length and it was suggested that bones were ritually broken to fit the burial container. Other studies indicate an absence of conclusive evidence for such a practice, demonstrating that much fragmentation occurs after burial along dehydration fissures formed during cremation (McKinley 1994b). It is not unlikely however, that there were geographic and temporal variations in practice affecting fragment size.

The manner in which bone was collected from the pyre for burial has received relatively little attention; it is generally assumed to have involved manual recovery of individual fragments once the pyre had cooled (Wahl 1982:40), a relatively simple task since the buff/white cremated bone is highly visible and accessible. Other possible modes of recovery may have involved raking bone off the pyre and/or winnowing, before or after cooling (McKinley 1994a:86, 1997a). Temporal and geographic variation of practice is again highly likely.

Re-deposition of pyre debris, cleared after collection of the bone for formal burial, may take a variety of forms (McKinley 1997a); analysis of material from these deposits and comparison with that from contemporaneous burials and pyre sites is increasing our understanding of the mortuary rites (Cosack 1982, Polfer 1993). Ordered deposition of skeletal elements in burials has been observed on rare occasions, but the overwhelming majority indicate arbitrary deposition (Wahl 1982:40). Not only skeletal elements, but multiples of individuals and animal bones (pyre goods) have also been found mixed throughout individual burials (e.g., McKinley 1994a).

A terminological distinction must be made between *multiple cremations* (several corpses cremated on the same pyre), *multiple burials* (one vessel/grave used for simultaneous burial of remains from separate cremations) and *multiple graves* (individual burials made into one grave). The first two may be difficult to distinguish from each other. Similar frequencies of dual cremations/burials have been noted in various studies, e.g., 4.4 per cent (Holck 1987:164) and 3 per cent (Sigvallius 1994:121) from Scandinavian assemblages, and 5 per cent from British assemblages (McKinley 1997a). A difference in composition was noted between the two areas, the majority of dual burials from the former comprising two adults (most frequently a female and a male), the latter most commonly an immature individual with an adult of either sex (mostly female).

Theories regarding dual cremations/burials include possible cases where an urn may not have been buried until the remains from a second pyre were included (Wahl 1982:22), such as with a Bronze Age burial from Hampshire (McKinley 1997a, 1999). In most other cases, the evident thorough mixing of the remains suggest dual cremation rather than just dual burial (McKinley 1994a:100). Whatever the reasons, physical closeness in death is likely to mirror close relations in life, though some theories favour sacrifice where females and males occur together (Wahl 1982:22).

CONCLUSION

The development of reliable and accessible methods of ageing and sexing will have a major impact on cremation studies. The archaeologist's need for demographic data to interpret status and gender as reflected through pyre goods and grave goods makes the need for improvements in this field imperative. Advances have undoubtedly been made, but frequently only in the wake of application of methods to unburnt material. More detailed research focusing directly on cremated remains and using more modern reference material of known age and sex may assist in giving the specific problems of cremated remains a higher profile.

Many unanswered questions remain with respect to specific facets of the rites attendant on the mortuary practice of cremation. However, the growing corpus of data from different periods and geographic areas will facilitate meaningful comparison of specific aspects of the cremation rite, less reliant on the materialistic obsessions of artifact analysis.

ACKNOWLEDGEMENTS

The writers are grateful to Elaine Wakefield of Wessex Archaeology for producing Figures 24.1–3 and to Jacqueline Nowakowski of the Cornwall Archaeological Unit for permission to print Figure 24.2.

REFERENCES

*References for further reading

Aykroyd, R.G., Lucy, D., Pollard, A.M. and Solheim, T. (1997). Regression analysis in adult age estimation. *American Journal of Physical Anthropology*, **104**:259–265.

Baby, R.S. (1954). *Hopewell Cremation Practices*. Papers in Archaeology 1–7. Ohio Historical Society: Columbus, Ohio.

Bass, W. (1987). *Human Osteology, a Laboratory and Field Manual*. Missouri Archaeological Society: Columbia.

Binford, L.R. (1963). An analysis of cremations from three Michigan sites. *Wisconsin Archaeologist*, **44**:98–110.

Bond, J.M. (1994). The cremated animal bone. In McKinley, J.I. (ed.) *The Anglo-Saxon Cemetery at Spong Hill, North Elmham Part VIII: The Cremations*, 121–135. East Anglian Archaeology No. 69, Norfolk Museums Service: Dereham.

Bond, J.M. (1996). Burnt offerings: animal bone in Anglo-Saxon cremations. *World Archaeology*, **28**:76–88.

Brown, K.A. (1998) Gender and sex – what can ancient DNA tell us? *Ancient Biomolecules*, **2**:3–15.

Buikstra, J.E. and Swegle, M. (1988). Bone modification due to burning: experimental evidence In Bonnichsen, R. and Sorg, M.H. (eds) *Bone Modification*, 247–258. University of Maine: Orono.

Cattaneo, C., Gelsthorpe, K., Sokol, R.J. and Phillips, P. (1994). Immunological detection of albumin in ancient human cremations using ELISA and monoclonal antibodies. *Journal of Archaeological Science*, **21**:565–571.

Cosack, E. (1982). *Das sächsische Gräberfeld bei Liebenau, Kr. Nienburg (Weser) Teil 1*. Mann: Berlin.

Crabtree, P.J. (1995). The symbolic role of animals in Anglo-Saxon England: evidence from burials and cremations. In Ryan, K. and Crabtree, P.J. (eds) *The Symbolic Role of Animals in Archaeology*, 39–49. MASCA Research Papers in Science and Archaeology 12, University of Pennsylvania: Philadelphia.

Cuijpers, S.A.G.F.M. (1997). Possibilities of histological research on diaphyseal fragments in cremated remains. In Smits, E., Iregren, E. and Drusini, A.G. (eds) *Cremation Studies in Archaeology*, 73–86. Logos Edizioni: Saonara.

Downes, J. (1995). Linga Fold. *Current Archaeology*, **142**:396–399.

Downes, J. (1999). Cremation: a spectacle and a journey. In Downes, J. and Pollard, T. (eds) *The Loved Body's Corruption*, 19–29. Scottish Archaeological Forum: Glasgow.

Dubois, J.A. and Beauchamp, H.R. (1943). *Hindu Manners, Customs and Ceremonies*. Clarendon Press: Oxford.

Evans, W.E.D. (1963). *The Chemistry of Death*. Charles C. Thomas: Springfield, Illinois.

Fitzpatrick, A.P. (1997). *Westhampnett, West Sussex, Volume 2: The Iron Age, Romano-British and Anglo-Saxon Cemeteries excavated in 1992*. Report No. 12, Wessex Archaeology: Salisbury.

Garland, N. (1994). Histological analysis of the calcined masses. In McKinley, J.I. (ed.) *The Anglo-Saxon cemetery at Spong Hill, North Elmham Part VIII: The Cremations*, 135. East Anglian Archaeology No. 69, Norfolk Museums Service: Dereham.

Gejvall, N.G. (1969). Cremations. In Brothwell, D. and Higgs, E. (eds) *Science in Archaeology*, (2nd edn, 468–479). Thames and Hudson: London.

Gejvall, N.G. (1981). Determination of burned bones from Prehistoric graves: observations on the cremated bones from the graves at Horn. *Ossa Letters*, **2**.

Glorieux, F.H. (1982). Mineral. In Cruess, R.L. (ed.) *The Musculoskeletal System*, 97–106. Churchill Livingstone: Edinburgh.

Gralla, G. (1964). Próba Rekonstruckcji Wzrostu ze szczatków ciaopalnych. *Material Prace Antropologiczne*, **70**:95–98.

Gräslund, A.-S. (1980). *Birka 4: The Burial Customs. A study of the Graves on Bjorko*. Almqvist and Wiksell: Stockholm.

Grimm, H. (1974). Anthropologische Ergebnisse der Untersuchung von Leichenbrandresten der Schönfelder,

Einzelgrab- und Kugelamphorenkultur. *Jahresschrift für mitteldeutsche Vorgeschichte*, **58**:265–274.

Grosskopf, B. (1997). Counting incremental lines in teeth – a valid method for age determination in cremations. In Smits, E., Iregren, E. and Drusini, A.G. (eds) *Cremation Studies in Archaeology*, 87–94. Logos Edizioni: Saonara.

Herrmann, B. (1973). Möglichkeiten histologischer Untersuchungen an Leichenbränden. *Mitteilungen der Berliner Gesellschaft für Anthropologie, Ethnologie und Urgeschichte*, **2**:164–167.

Herrmann, B. (1977). On histological investigations of cremated human remains. *Journal of Human Evolution*, **6**:101–103.

Hiatt, B. (1969). Cremation in Aboriginal Australia. *Mankind*, **7**:104–115.

*Holck, P. (1986). *Cremated Bones: A Medical-Anthropological Study of an Archaeological Material on Cremation Burials*. Anthropologiske skrifter Nr. 1, Anatomical Institute, University of Oslo: Oslo.

Holck, P. (1997). Why are small children so seldom found in cremations? In Smits, E., Iregren, E. and Drusini, A.G. (eds) *Cremation Studies in Archaeology*, 33–38. Logos Edizioni: Saonara.

Holden, J.L., Phakey, P.P. and Clement, J.G. (1995a). Scanning electron microscope observations of heat-treated human bone. *Forensic Science International*, **74**:29–45.

Holden, J.L., Phakey, P.P. and Clement, J.G. (1995b). Scanning electron microscope observations of incinerated human femoral bone: a case study. *Forensic Science International*, **74**:17–28.

Hummel, S. and Schutkowski, H. (1993). Approaches to the histological age determination of cremated human remains. In Grupe, G. and Garland, A.N. (eds) *Histology of Ancient Human Bone: Methods and Diagnosis*, 111–123. Springer-Verlag: Berlin.

Kühl, I. (1984). Animal remains in cremations from the Bronze age to the Viking period in Schleswig-Holstein, North Germany. In Grigson, C. and Clutton-Brock, J. (eds) *Animals and Archaeology 4: Husbandry in Europe*, 209–219. BAR International Series 227, British Archaeological Reports: Oxford.

Lambot, B., Friboulet, M. and Méniel, P. (1994). *Le Site Protohistorique d'Acy-Romance (Ardennes) 2: Les nécropoles dans leur contexte régional*. Memoire No. 8, Société Archéologique Champenoise: Reims.

*Lange, M., Schutkowski, H., Hummel, S. and Herrmann, B. (1987). *A Bibliography on Cremations*. PACT: Strasbourg.

Malinowski, A. (1969). Synthéses des recherches Polonaises effectuées jus'que présent sur les os des Tombes à incineration. *Przeglad Antropologiczny*, **35**:141.

McKinley, J.I. (1993). Bone fragment size and weights of bone from modern British cremations and its implications for the interpretation of archaeological cremations. *International Journal of Osteoarchaeology*, **3**:283–287.

*McKinley, J.I. (1994a). *The Anglo-Saxon cemetery at Spong Hill, North Elmham Part VIII: The Cremations*. East Anglian Archaeology No. 69, Norfolk Museums Service: Dereham.

McKinley, J.I. (1994b). Bone fragment size in British cremation burials and its implications for pyre technology and ritual. *Journal of Archaeological Science*, **21**:339–342.

McKinley, J.I. (1997a). Bronze Age 'barrows' and funerary rites and rituals of cremation. *Proceedings of the Prehistoric Society*, **63**:29–145.

McKinley, J.I. (1997b). The cremated human bone from burials and cremation-related contexts. In Fitzpatrick, A.P. (ed.) *Westhampnett, West Sussex, Volume 2: The Iron Age, Romano-British and Anglo-Saxon Cemeteries excavated in 1992*, 55–72. Report No. 12, Wessex Archaeology: Salisbury.

McKinley, J.I. (1999). Human bone and funerary deposits. In Walker, K.E. and Farwell, D.E. (eds) *Twyford Down, Hampshire. Archaeological Investigations on the M3 Motorway Bar End to Compton 1990–1993*, 85–117. Monograph 9, Hampshire Field Club: Salisbury.

Méniel, P. (1994). Les restes animaux du bûcher. In Lambot, B., Friboulet, M. and Méniel, P. (eds) *Le Site Protohistorique d'Acy-Romance (Ardennes) 2: Les nécropoles dans leur contexte régional*, 283–286. Memoire No. 8, Société Archéologique Champenoise: Reims.

Müller, C. (1958). Schätzung der Köperhöhe bei Funden von Leichenbränden. *Ausgrabungen und Funde*, **2**:52–58.

Musgrave, J.H. (1985). The skull of Philip II of Macedon. In Lisney, S.J.W. and Matthews, B. (eds) *Current Topics in Oral Biology*, 1–16. University of Bristol Press: Bristol.

Nicholson, R.A. (1993). A morphological investigation of burnt animal bone and an evaluation of its utility in archaeology. *Journal of Archaeological Science*, **20**:411–428.

Nicholson, R.A. (1995). Out of the frying pan into the fire: what value are burnt fish bones to archaeology? *Archaeofauna*, **4**:47–64.

Pautreau, J.P. (1994). Quelques aspects des cremations contemporaries en Asie de Sud-Est. In Lambot, B., Friboulet, M. and Méniel, P. (eds) *Le Site Protohistorique d'Acy-Romance (Ardennes) 2: Les nécropoles dans leur contexte régional*, 306–315. Memoire No. 8, Société Archéologique Champenoise: Reims.

Pionteck, J. (1976). The process of cremation and its influence on the morphology of bones in the light of results of experimental research. *Archeologia Polski*, **21**:247–280.

Polfer, M. (1993). La nécropole gallo-romaine de Septfontaines-Deckt (Grand-Duché de Luxembourge) et son *ustrinum* central: analyse comparative de matériel archéologique. In Fredière, A. (ed.) *Monde des Mortes, Monde des Vivants en Gaule Rurale*, 173–176. FERACF/La Simarre: Tours.

Rösing, F.W. (1977). Methoden und Aussagemöglichkeiten der anthropologischen Leichenbrandbearbeitung. *Archäologie und Naturwissenschaften*, **1**:53–80.

Schutkowski, H. and Hummel, S. (1987). Variabilitätsvergleich von Wandstärken für die

Geschlechts-zuweisung an Leichenbränden. *Anthropologischer Anzeiger*, **45**:43–47.

Schutkowski, H., Hummel, S. and Gegner, S. (1986). Case report 8 (cremated urinary calculi). *Palaeopathology Newsletter*, **55**:11–12.

Shipman, P., Foster, G. and Schoeninger, M. (1984). Burnt bones and teeth, an experimental study of colour, morphology, crystal structure and shrinkage. *Journal of Archaeological Science*, **11**:307–325.

Sigvallius, B. (1994). *Funeral Pyres. Iron Age Cremations in North Spånga*. Theses and Papers in Osteology 1, Stockholm University: Stockholm.

Sigvallius, B. (1997). Animals in Iron Age cremations in Central Sweden. In Smits, E., Iregren, E. and Drusini, A.G. (eds) *Cremation Studies in Archaeology*, 37–49. Logos Edizioni: Saonara.

Sjösvärd, L., Vretemark, M. and Gustavson, H. (1983). Vendel warrior from Vallentuna. In Lamm, J.P. and Norstrom, H.A. (eds) *Vendel Period Studies: Transactions of the Boat-grave Symposium*, 133–150. Studies 2, Statens Historiska Museum: Stockholm.

Smits, E., Verhart, L.M.B., Cuijpers, S.A.G.F.M. and Grosskopf, B. (1997). The chieftain's grave of Oss. In Smits, E., Iregren, E. and Drusini, A.G. (eds) *Cremation Studies in Archaeology*, 95–102. Logos Edizioni: Saonara.

Thurman, M.D. and Wilmore, L.J. (1981). A replicative cremation experiment. *North American Archaeologist*, **2**:275–283.

Toynbee, J.M.C. (1996). *Death and Burial in the Roman World*. John Hopkins: London.

van Vark, G.N. (1974). The investigation of human cremated skeletal material by multivariate statistical methods. I methodology. *Ossa*, **1**:63–95.

van Vark, G.N. (1975). The investigation of human cremated skeletal material by multivariate statistical methods. II measures. *Ossa*, **2**:47–68.

*Wahl, J. (1982). Leichenbranduntersuchungen. Ein Überblick über die Bearbeitungs- und Aussagemöglichkeiten von Brandgräbern. *Prähistorische Zeitschrift*, **57**:2–125.

Wahl, J. and Wahl, S. (1983). Zur Technik der Leichenverbrennung: I. Verbrennungsplätze aus ethnologischen Quellen. *Archäologisches Korrespondenzblatt*, **13**:513–520.

Wiercinska, A. (1970). The methods of anthropological investigations of cremated bones in Poland. In Filip, J. (ed.) *Actes du VIIe Congrès International des Sciences Préhistoriques et Protohistoriques*, 1296–1299. Institut d'Archéologie de l'Academie Tchecoslavaque des Sciences a Prague: Prague.

SECTION 4

Biomolecular Archaeology

Overview – Archaeological Science in the Biomolecular Century

A.M. POLLARD

Department of Archaeological Sciences, University of Bradford.

In terms of scientific research, it is widely predicted that the twenty-first century will be the century of biology, in contrast to the twentieth century, which was dominated by physics. The great discoveries of that century include quantum theory, relativity and particle physics, all of which changed the trajectory of humankind for ever (for good and ill). In the next, we can look forward to the rapid completion of the Human Genome Project and further developments in genetic manipulation, with all that these promise for our abilities to control our own health, welfare, ageing processes, and, ultimately, the future of the human species (again, probably, for good and ill). Arguably, for the first time, this means that humans are no longer subject to the evolutionary pressures of natural selection, and have the ability to manipulate their own environment in a much more direct and immediate way. Archaeologists, would, of course, argue strongly that neither of these prospects are particularly new, but the scale and immediacy of such technologies will undoubtedly be of a magnitude previously not experienced.

Scientific archaeology has been a microcosm of these revolutions. Although there is a long history of the quantification and description of biological remains in archaeology for chronological, environmental and economic reconstruction, there has been up until relatively recently very little systematic biochemical analysis of these remains. During the second half of the twentieth century the majority of analytical effort was devoted to the study of the inorganic residues of past societies, using the techniques of physics and chemistry (the 'golden age of archaeological chemistry': Pollard and Heron 1996). In fact, it was implicitly taken for granted that biological material (other than mineralized tissue, and certain geological materials, such as jet and amber) did not survive in the archaeological record, other than under exceptional circumstances of extreme aridity or cold. And, of course, what was not looked for was not found.

EARLY AWAKENINGS IN OILY RESIDUES

Even those studies which did analyse organic materials tended to use the techniques of inorganic chemistry rather than the more powerful techniques for organic materials such as chromatography and mass spectrometry. Thus, archaeological objects of jet and shale were characterized by neutron activation analysis and then X-ray fluorescence (e.g., Pollard et al. 1981, but see Watts et al. 1999). Slightly against this trend, amber was successfully characterized by infra-red (Beck

Handbook of Archaeological Sciences. Edited by D.R. Brothwell and A.M. Pollard.

1986), but bone was often analysed as a purely inorganic material, with the intention of using trace elements as indicators of diet. Early pioneers of organic archaeological chemistry were Rolf Rottländer and John Evans (Rottländer and Hartke 1983, Evans and Hill 1983), who used relatively unsophisticated techniques to extract and identify organic residues (lipids) in archaeological ceramics during the late 1970s. These studies, although rather piece-meal in approach, did serve to alert the archaeological community that such material could and did survive in archaeological contexts. In the UK at least, the field of archaeological lipid analysis has been revolutionized by Richard Evershed and his group, originally in Liverpool and now at Bristol (see Chapter 28). The importance of this work cannot be overstated, and it is instructive to look at the roots of this success. In essence it is very simple – it is the bringing together of a fundamental knowledge and experience of natural products biochemistry with a range of well thought out archaeological problems. This, combined with energy and enthusiasm, has resulted in an outstanding series of publications. These have demonstrated the ubiquity and value of organic biomarkers in a wide range of archaeological contexts, ranging from the initial work on lipids preserved in bog bodies, through lipids in ceramics, to the residues of manuring in soils, and more recently the discovery that cholesterol can be recovered from skeletal material and used to give an additional dimension to dietary reconstruction. The value of this work is, of course, not just that such material survives, but that, with a knowledge of modern biochemistry, such survival can be turned into valuable archaeological information.

BONE POINTS THE WAY

Another strand of development was the growing interest in the organic component of bone – largely the proteins of the collagen family. Growing sophistication in the pretreatment of bone for radiocarbon dating had, by the 1970s, demonstrated that 'whole bone' dates, in which the entire bone (mineral, protein and contamination) was combusted to release CO_2 was generally unsatisfactory (Hassan *et al.* 1977), and that much more reliable results were obtained by purifying the organic phase. This development was, of course, facilitated by improving instrumentation for radiocarbon dating, culminating in the use of accelerator technology for measuring milligram quantities of carbon (see Chapter 2). This focus on the bone collagen allowed

van der Merwe and colleagues in South Africa to make the momentous discovery that collagen isotope chemistry in bone was linked to diet, particularly in an environment where plants utilizing both the C_3 and C_4 photosynthetic pathways were present (Vogel and van der Merwe 1977; see Chapter 23). This led in the 1980s to widespread interest in the isotopic chemistry (initially carbon, but subsequently nitrogen) of human and animal bone for the purposes of dietary reconstruction, but, more recently, for consideration of health, nutrition, status and mobility in past populations (see Chapter 23). These studies have blossomed in the last 10 years, and will no doubt continue to grow.

BLOOD OUT OF STONES?

It was, however, the putative survival of another protein, haemoglobin, which created a great deal of excitement when it was first published in the early 1980s. The claim that blood residues could be detected on ancient stone tools and even identified to species (Loy 1983) was greeted with a wide range of reactions. To archaeologists who wished to know more about the use of stone tools, and the range of species being hunted in the distant past, this development seemed to offer a significant, if not revolutionary, advance. To others, including those with an awareness of the contemporary forensic literature (e.g., Fletcher *et al.* 1984), it seemed essentially ludicrous that such material could survive for so long. In forensic analysis, it was deemed worthwhile to publish that blood and saliva could be immunologically identified to species on stains 'up to 16 months old'. The difference between these two interpretations could hardly be more stark, and strongly suggests that mutual co-operation is long, long overdue. A critical factor in the archaeological case, discussed in detail in Chapter 26, is that many of the early observations, using test indicator strips, have subsequently proved to be susceptible to demonstrating false positives in the presence of common contaminating material from the burial environment. Further, some of the other tests applied such as re-precipitation of haemoglobin crystals, have proved either inconsistent or irreproducible. As is shown in Chapter 26, the combination of stringent recovery and analysis protocols, combined with the phenomenal sensitivity of modern immunoassay techniques, now renders the prospect of such work more plausible. The originator of this research, Tom Loy, has been criticized many times for the perceived shortcomings of his methodologies. Whatever the truth of that, I personally take a more constructive view, which is to say that biomolecular research in archaeology would not be nearly so well-advanced (or interesting!) if he had not had the foresight to embark on such a venture. He certainly deserves credit for that.

MICROBIAL REALITIES

One of the other great revelations of the last decade or so has been the realization that microbial processes are relevant to archaeology. Chapter 29 reviews the recent research in this area, focusing principally on the microbiology of human bone. As discussed in Chapter 50, the term 'biodeterioration' has come into common usage to denote the unwanted destruction of objects by microbial and other agencies. One only has to consider those very few situations where the organic part of the archaeological record survives in its entirety (e.g., frozen tombs, the tomb of Tutankhamun, the 'ice man') to realize what a pathetically small portion of the material world of past societies usually survives into the archaeological record. We reconstruct trade routes, for example, largely by tracing the distribution of the containers (i.e., ceramic vessels). The vast bulk of traded items (i.e., food products) are virtually invisible. These difficulties, in great measure, arise as a result of rapid microbiological cycling of organic materials. Apart from sporadic observations of the effects of microbial activity on bone (e.g., Hackett 1983), it is only in the last decade that systematic studies have been undertaken to discover the nature of the organisms responsible for degrading material such as bone, and to investigate the rate and the conditions under which such processes take place. Apart from the need to link these studies into the wider domain of biogeochemical cycling (Chapter 16), a strong impetus for such work has been the fear that microbial activity might alter the isotopic composition of (largely) the carbon in the sample, with major implications for radiocarbon dating, isotopic studies including palaeodiet and palaeoclimate, and other chronological indicators such as amino acid racemization. Although not sufficently well-studied to be completely certain, it appears that such concerns are not without foundation (see Chapter 29).

THE STRANDS OF LIFE

And so to DNA. It is hard to overstate the significance of the scientific revolution caused by our growing understanding of this particular biomolecule (see Chapter 25). It is hard to remember that a mere 20 years ago phylogenetic relationships were measured by the strength of the immunological reaction between antibodies and the proteins of different species (e.g., Lowenstein et al. 1981)! In archaeology and palaeontology, it is still less than 20 years since the first demonstration of DNA survival in a museum sample (Pääbo 1985). Now DNA is being used to explore the genetic relationship between Neanderthal and modern humans (Krings et al. 1997, Ovchinnikov et al. 2000), which has to be one of the big questions in understanding our own evolution. Although Neanderthal DNA has now been replicated (thereby demonstrating that it is not contamination), in the absence of any DNA sequence from contemporary Cro-Magnon humans, it seems to me that the relationship with modern humans is yet to be fully determined. (Perversely, against all the evidence, and based on complete ignorance of the fossil and archaeological record, my own view is that interbreeding must have taken place, but perhaps the next few years will convincingly disprove this!).

The areas in archaeology where DNA analysis has and could contribute have been well-rehearsed elsewhere, as have the caveats resulting from poor DNA survival and contamination (see Chapter 25). In the UK context, there is no doubt that the development of 'Ancient DNA' was given considerable impetus by the adoption of the Natural Environment Research Council of the Ancient Biomolecules Initiative. Its achievements have been documented elsewhere (Eglinton et al. 1998), but I want to dwell on one aspect of this – the interdisciplinarity of the approach. This initiative brought together archaeologists, palaeontologists, organic geochemists and biomolecular geneticists with a common purpose – to document the degree of survival of ancient DNA, and to use these sequences to address many questions which have been around for some time, but not satisfactorily resolved by 'conventional techniques'. Some of the outcomes were disappointing (but not so scientifically), such as the discovery that amber does not preserve DNA over geological time periods (no easy access to Jurassic Park!). As in most things, it is likely that those discoveries of most lasting value will be those which do not immediately grab the headlines, such as the ability to determine sex from DNA, which seems to have huge applicability. The main lesson, however, to learn from the ABI is that there are huge areas of mutual interest between the collaborating scientists, and that significant advances can be made by simply sharing existing knowledge. The fields, for example, of archaeology and palaeobiology/palaeontology have much in common, and yet they have (with a few notable exceptions) tended to develop in isolation from one another. Each has its own terminology and research frameworks, which act as a barrier to the free exchange of ideas – a good example of this is taphonomy, which is central to both disciplines, and yet there is very little leakage of the respective insights across the disciplinary borders. Perhaps the biggest legacy of ABI will be improved communication between related scientific disciplines.

Sadly, and partly through the welcome if sometimes over-enthusiastic interest of the media in such subjects, it seems that expectations often run far ahead of deliverability where DNA studies in archaeology are concerned. To name but one example, it seems to me somewhat misleading (but perhaps good television) to demonstrate that the DNA of a fossil human bone from south-west England can be matched to that of 'Old Fred' living in a nearby cottage, thereby proving substantial continuity of occupation. This might be so, but it leaves a number of substantial questions unanswered – would this DNA sequence match equally well common sequences from continental Europe, or even the Indian sub-continent? One suspects that it might. It is undoubtedly unfair to criticize work intended as entertainment on the grounds that it does not meet the highest standards of scientific rigour, but it does serve as a warning that a scientific tool is only as good as the quality of the question to which it is applied.

BIOMOLECULAR ARCHAEOLOGY IN THE TWENTY-FIRST CENTURY

It is easy to predict that, of all the sections in this volume, the one which is most likely to develop and transform out of all recognition over the next 30 years is this one – biomolecular archaeology. This is assured simply because of the levels of investment going into genomics in the wider world, if for no other reason. Archaeological DNA research will certainly continue to benefit from the rapid insights generated by the Human Genome Project, and the consequential huge investment into technological and methodological developments. We must not, however, lose sight of the importance of non-DNA research, as exemplified by the papers here. There are undoubtedly further applications of lipid analysis yet to be explored, partly by exploiting new compound-specific mass spectrometers, but also by looking at a wider range of samples, and more importantly by defining new research areas

such as exemplified by the recent work on the origin of dairying.

There is still much to do in understanding the mechanisms of biological degradation. Important work has been done on modelling the hydrolysis of unmineralized collagen (Collins *et al.* 1995), but this needs to be extended to mineralized tissue, and hopefully to include considerations of amino acid racemization – thus, perhaps, reviving interest in this much-maligned technique. The exemplary work of the Newcastle group lead by Matthew Collins shows how this can be done. Research on other proteins has yet to go much beyond demonstrating survival under favourable circumstances, but their potential as additional sources of dietary information (if not as alternative dating targets for radiocarbon dating) remains high.

My personal view of the area with highest developmental potential within archaeology is that of archaeological microbiology. Traditionally, microbiologists are either medically-orientated, or interested in soil microbiology as it relates to topsoil processes. Neither of these are directly applicable to archaeological situations, although both of course have substantial contributions to make. Understanding the microbiology of the sedimentary archaeological environment seems to offer considerable challenges to both microbiologists and archaeologists, and yet microbiological activity is undoubtedly fundamental to many taphonomic processes. Significant advances here would undoubtedly open up many new and exciting avenues of enquiry.

REFERENCES

Beck, C.W. (1986). Spectroscopic studies of amber. *Applied Spectroscopy Reviews*, **22**:57–110.

Collins, M.J., Riley, M.S., Child, A.M. and Turner-Walker, G. (1995). A basic mathematical simulation of the chemical degradation of ancient collagen. *Journal of Archaeological Science*, **22**:175–184.

Eglinton, G., Jones, M. and Brown, T. (eds) (1998). Special ABI issue. *Ancient Biomolecules*, **2**:97–280.

Evans, J. and Hill, H.E. (1983). Dietetic information by chemical analysis of Danish Neolithic pot sherds: a progress report. In Aspinall, A. and Warren, S.E. (eds) *Proceedings of 22nd Symposium on Archaeometry*, 224–228. University of Bradford: Bradford.

Fletcher, S.M., Dolton, P. and Harris-Smith, P.W. (1984). Species identification of blood and saliva stains by Enzyme-Linked Immunoassay (ELISA) using monoclonal antibodies. *Journal of Forensic Sciences*, **29**:67–74.

Hackett, C.J. (1983). Microscopic focal destruction (tunnels) in exhumed human bones. *Medicine, Science and the Law*, **21**:243–265.

Hassan, A.A., Termine, J.D. and Haynes, C.V. Jr. (1977). Mineralogical studies on bone apatite and their implications for radiocarbon dating. *Radiocarbon*, **19**:364–374.

Krings, M., Stone, A., Schmitz, R.W., Krainitzi, H., Stoneking, M. and Pääbo, S. (1997). Neandertal DNA sequences and the origin of modern humans. *Cell*, **90**:19–30.

Lowenstein, J.M., Sarich, V.M. and Richardson, B.J. (1981). Albumin systematics of the extinct mammoth and Tasmanian wolf. *Nature*, **291**:409–411.

Loy, T.H. (1983). Prehistoric blood residues: detection on stone tool surfaces and identification of species of interest. *Science*, **220**:1269–1231.

Ovchinnikov, I.V., Götherström, A., Romanova, G.P., Kharitonov, V.M., Lidén, K. and Goodwin, W. (2000). Molecular analysis of Neanderthal DNA from the northern Caucasus. *Nature*, **404**:490–493.

Pääbo, S. (1985). Molecular cloning of Ancient Egyptian mummy DNA. *Nature*, **314**:644–645.

Pollard, A.M. and Heron, C. (1996). *Archaeological Chemistry*. Royal Society of Chemistry: Cambridge.

Pollard, A.M., Bussell, G.D. and Baird, D.C. (1981). The analytical investigation of Early Bronze Age jet and jet-like material from the Devizes Museum. *Archaeometry*, **23**:139–167.

Rottländer, R.C.A. and Hartke, I. (1983). New results of food identification by fat analysis. In Aspinall, A. and Warren, S.E. (eds) *Proceedings of 22nd Symposium on Archaeometry*, 218–223. University of Bradford: Bradford.

Vogel, J.C. and van der Merwe, N.J. (1977). Isotopic evidence for early maize cultivation in New York State. *American Antiquity*, **42**:238–242.

Watts, S., Pollard, A.M. and Wolff, G.A. (1999). The organic geochemistry of jet: pyrolosis-gas chromatography/mass spectrometry (Py-GCMS) applied to identifying jet and similar black lithic materials – preliminary results. *Journal of Archaeological Science*, **26**:923–933.

25

Ancient DNA

T.A. BROWN

Department of Biomolecular Sciences, UMIST.

Ancient DNA was first reported in archaeological material in the mid-1980s (e.g., Pääbo 1985) and has been extensively studied since the discovery, in 1989, that molecules are sometimes present in bones as well as preserved soft tissues (Brown and Brown 1994). Ancient DNA has not, however, had the immediate impact on archaeology that was originally envisaged. This is largely because the extent of the precautions that must be taken to prevent contamination of human specimens with modern DNA was not fully appreciated until 1995 (Handt et al. 1994, Stoneking 1995). Many of the reports of archaeological and palaeontological DNA published before that date are now questioned (e.g., Austin et al. 1998) and, regrettably, the same is also true of a substantial number of papers published since 1995 – the authors of these papers (and the editors of the journals in which they appear) apparently being unaware of the procedures that must be followed to prevent contamination and to authenticate the results of an ancient DNA study. The appropriate procedures are now well-established and when followed enable ancient DNA analyses of archaeological remains to be carried out in such a way that an acceptable degree of confidence can be placed in the validity of the results (Renfrew 1998). The challenge is now to simplify the procedures so that they can be taken out of the molecular biology laboratory and into the hands of mainstream archaeological scientists. The first part of this chapter describes in general terms the information that can be obtained by DNA analysis. The second part presents an overview of the contributions that ancient DNA is currently making, and will make in the future, within archaeology.

DNA ANCIENT AND MODERN

Ancient DNA is relevant to archaeology for two reasons:

(i)   DNA specifies the biological characteristics of living organisms, which means that some of the biological characteristics of an archaeological specimen can be determined by studying its ancient DNA. The range of characteristics that can be addressed is limited, because molecular biologists still have only a poor understanding of the link between DNA structure and biological attributes, and 'archaeologists cannot hope to obtain from ancient DNA information that molecular biologists have not extracted from modern DNA' (Brown and Brown 1992). For human and animal remains, the feature that is most frequently determined is biological sex (Brown 1998), though an increasing amount of research is being devoted to genetic diseases such as thalassaemia (e.g., Filon *et al.* 1995). With plants, biological characteristics such as the breadmaking quality of wheat have been inferred (Brown 1999a).

(ii)   The DNA of a living organism is inherited from its parents and combines features of both the maternal and paternal DNA. DNA is therefore a record of ancestry and ancient DNA can be used to determine kinship relationships within a small group of specimens (Hummel and Herrmann 1996) and the broader population affinities of a larger set of remains (e.g., Merriwether 1999).

To understand how the information contained in ancient DNA is accessed we must look at the structure of DNA and the ways in which this structure is studied.

DNA structure – the importance of the 'nucleotide sequence'

In chemical terms, *deoxyribonucleic acid* or DNA is a relatively simple molecule. It is a polymer in which the individual units are called *deoxyribonucleotides* (Figure 25.1a). There are four different nucleotides in DNA, each with a slightly different chemical structure. These nucleotides are referred to as A, C, G and T, the abbreviations of their full chemical names:

A = 2′-deoxyadenosine 5′-triphosphate,

C = 2′-deoxycytidine 5′-triphosphate,

G = 2′-deoxyguanosine 5′-triphosphate,

T = 2′-deoxythymidine 5′-triphosphate.

a) Chemical structure of DNA

In a DNA molecule, the nucleotides are linked together to form *polynucleotide* chains of immense length, 250 million nucleotides for the longest human DNA molecule. In living cells, pairs of DNA molecules are entwined around one another to form the *double helix* structure, this structure being held together by weak chemical bonds that form between the nucleotides present in the two strands (Figure 25.1a). The bonds form in a very specific manner, so an A in one strand can bond only with a T in the other, and G can bond only with a C. This means that the nucleotide sequences of the two strands are 'complementary', and if the sequence of one is known then that of the other can be predicted. The part of each nucleotide that participates in the intra-strand bonding is called the 'base', and so the lengths of double-stranded DNA molecules are expressed as 'so many base pairs (bp)'. Using this convention, the longest human DNA molecule is 250 million bp, which is the same as 250 thousand kb (kilobase pairs) and 250 Mb (megabase pairs).

The entire human genome – the full set of DNA molecules in a single human cell – consists of 24 double helices, each double helix contained in a single chromosome, making up a total of 3000 Mb of DNA, whose nucleotide sequence will be completely known in the very near future (Collins *et al.* 1998). These 24 chromosomes comprise 22 *autosomes* and 2 *sex chromosomes*. The nucleus of each human cell (with a few exceptions) contains two copies of each of the autosomes and a pair of sex chromosomes – XX for a female and XY for a male. Strictly speaking, these chromosomes make up the *nuclear genome*, because human cells also contain about 8000 identical copies of a second type of DNA, the *mitochondrial genome* (Figure 25.1b). The mitochondrial genome is a short, circular molecule, just 16 569 bp in length, but has been immensely important

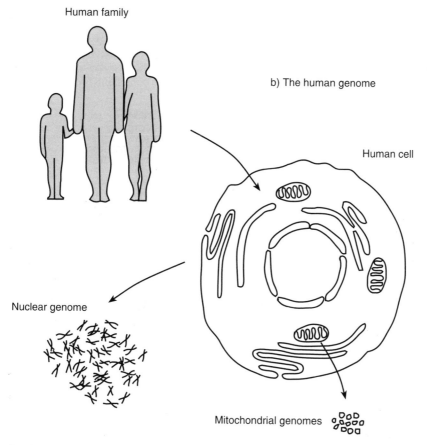

Figure 25.1   DNA and the human genome. (a) The chemical structure of DNA. (b) The nuclear and mitochondrial components of the human genome. Reproduced from T.A. Brown (1999) *Genomes* with permission of BIOS Scientific Publishers Ltd, Oxford.

in studies of human evolution, largely because it evolves relatively rapidly which means that different versions are present in different human populations and comparisons between these *haplotypes* can be used to infer relationships between human groupings.

The key feature of a DNA molecule is its nucleotide sequence. Parts of the nucleotide sequence, the genes, contain the biological information that specifies the characteristics of the living organism. In human DNA there are thought to be about 80 000 genes, each with its unique nucleotide sequence and each specifying a single biological characteristic, usually in conjunction with one or more other genes. At present the biological characteristics specified by only a few thousand of these genes are known, though the figure is increasing rapidly as an outcome of the Human Genome Project, and similar progress is being made in understanding the functions of genes in domesticated animals such as cows and pigs and cultivated plants such as wheat and rice. Unfortunately, for most genes the biological characteristics that they specify are initially understood in terms of the biochemical reactions occurring within cells, additional research being needed to link these reactions to physiological and morphological traits. With humans and animals, this limitation will prevent ancient DNA contributing greatly in areas other than sex identification and genetic disease, at least in the immediate future, but studies of cultivated plants have greater scope, the biochemical and genetic basis to features such as nutritional quality, disease resistance and plant morphology already being understood.

Although the genes are the important part of the DNA, they make up only a small portion of the genomes of most organisms. All the human genes, for example, if placed end to end would give a DNA molecule only 900 Mb in length, about 3 per cent of the total length of the DNA molecules within which they are found. In fact, the 80 000 human genes are separated from one another by vast tracts of nucleotide sequence whose function, if any, has so far eluded molecular biologists. In some of these intergenic regions the DNA sequence changes relatively rapidly through the accumulation of mutations that result in one nucleotide replacing another or short pieces of DNA being inserted or deleted. An example is provided by the DNA sequences called *simple tandem repeats* (STRs) or '*microsatellites*'. There are about 10 000 of these STRs in the human genome, each consisting of a short sequence repeated several times, for example GTGTGTGTGT. Single tandem repeats are prone to mutation by the addition or, less frequently, removal of repeat units, so the 5-unit repeat shown above could

change (due to aberrant DNA replication) to a six- or seven-nucleotide repeat (i.e., GTGTGTGTGTGT or GTGTGTGTGTGTGT). The frequency of STR mutation is small when considered on the timescale of a single human lifetime, but high enough for a number of different versions ('*alleles*') of each STR to be present in the human population as a whole. Each individual has a particular combination of STR alleles and hence a personal '*genetic fingerprint*' that is virtually unique: if just 12 STRs are considered there is only a 1:1 000 000 000 000 000 chance that two individuals other than identical twins will possess the same genetic fingerprint. In forensic science, this specificity enables individuals to be identified from DNA-containing material such as hairs left at crime scenes. In archaeology the importance lies not with the individuality of a genetic fingerprint but the fact that the genetic fingerprint is inherited partly from the mother and partly from the father (Figure 25.2). Two STRs are shown in the top part of this Figure. STR I is a GT-repeat microsatellite with four alleles, consisting of 5, 6, 7 and 8 units respectively; and STR II is a CA-repeat microsatellite with alleles of 9, 10, 11 and 12 units. Each person has two pairs of every chromosome, one inherited from their mother and one from their father, and so has two copies of STR I and two copies of STR

STR number I (GT repeat)

Alleles:	...GTGTGTGTGT...	(5 units)
	...GTGTGTGTGTGT...	(6 units)
	...GTGTGTGTGTGTGT...	(7 units)
	...GTGTGTGTGTGTGTGT...	(8 units)

STR number II (CA repeat)

Alleles:	...CACACACACACACACACA...	(9 units)
	...CACACACACACACACACACA...	(10 units)
	...CACACACACACACACACACACA...	(11 units)
	...CACACACACACACACACACACACA...	(12 units)

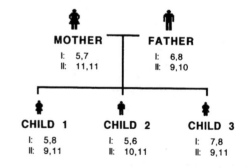

Figure 25.2 Genetic fingerprinting of STRs.

II. In the example shown in the lower part of the figure, the male parent has alleles 6 and 8 for STR I and alleles 9 and 10 for STR II, and the female parent has alleles 5 and 7 for STR I and two copies of alleles 11 for STR II. The male and female parents therefore have distinct genetic fingerprints because they are unrelated (except possibly by marriage). The genetic fingerprint of each child is made up of alleles inherited from the parents. Child 1, for example, has inherited allele 5 of STR I and allele 11 of STR II from her mother, and allele 8 of STR I and allele 9 of STR II from her father. All three children have similar genetic fingerprints, most clearly seen with STR II, where each child has allele 11 and two children have allele 9. If the family relationships between these two adults and three children were unknown, then comparisons of their genetic fingerprints, for these and other STRs, would confirm that the three children could be siblings and that the two adults could be the parents. STR analysis of ancient DNA from a group of human remains therefore enables possible parent-offspring relationships to be inferred, and also enables possible siblings to be identified because their genetic fingerprints, though different, have similarities due to their common ancestry. An interbreeding population is, in genetic terms, simply an extended family so equivalent studies, possibly with STRs but more commonly with less rapidly evolving nucleotide sequences such as those contained in the mitochondrial DNA, enable population affinities to be assessed. The genomes of domestic animals and cultivated plants also contain STRs and other variable sequences, so equivalent studies can be carried out with these species (see below).

The differences between ancient and modern DNA

DNA is not a particularly stable molecule and life as we know it would be impossible if cells did not possess systems for repairing the damage suffered by DNA molecules as a result of attack by chemical and physical agents. One of the most damaging physical agents is heat, which induces water molecules that are tightly bound to the DNA to cleave the covalent bond that links the distinctive base component of the nucleotide to the rest of the structure. The 'baseless' site that is created is unstable and decomposes, resulting in the DNA strand being broken at the point of attack. Each day, some 10 000 baseless sites are created in the DNA of every human cell, but in living cells at least 9999 of these are repaired before a strand break occurs. After death, the repair processes stop working and

water-induced strand breakage occurs unchecked. Strand breakage occurs more rapidly in wet rather than dry specimens (Waite et al. 1997), but extensive DNA fragmentation occurs even in desiccated specimens, as has been shown for plant remains from the desert site of Qasr Ibrim in Upper Egypt (O'Donoghue et al. 1996, Deakin et al. 1998). Rates of fragmentation have been predicted from experiments carried out with DNA in aqueous solution (e.g., Pääbo and Wilson 1991) but the effects of the preservation conditions, which of course might change over time, have never been examined. It is not even known if fragmentation occurs at a uniform rate or, as suggested by some early observations (Pääbo 1989), is more rapid in the period immediately after death. The one certainty is that ancient DNA molecules are much shorter than their modern counterparts. Allaby et al. (1997) concluded that the average size of the ancient DNA molecules in 3000 year old wheat grains, preserved by charring, is only 50–70 bp, and although equivalent experiments have never been carried out with human bones it is clear that these rarely contain molecules longer than 300 bp.

The short length of ancient DNA molecules is not a serious problem in its own right because enough information to identify biological characteristics such as sex, and to infer kinship and population affinities, can usually be obtained from molecules of 100–150 bp. Even if molecules of this length are present only in very small numbers, they can still be studied by the technique called the *polymerase chain reaction* (PCR), which results in multiple copies being made of a specified region of the genome, for example a part of a gene or the sequence spanning an STR. Figure 25.3a illustrates the procedure. In this example a mixture of many DNA fragments has been subjected to a PCR directed at a part of the human amelogenin gene which, as described below, is used in sex identification of human remains. The DNA fragment labelled 'X' is a small part of the X chromosome and contains the target region of the X-specific amelogenin gene: the PCR results in multiple copies of the region being made, each copy being 106 bp in length. The DNA fragment labelled 'Y' contains the target region of the Y-specific amelogenin gene, which is amplified by PCR into 112-bp copies.

At the end of the PCR the selected region has been amplified into many identical copies, giving enough material for examination by gel electrophoresis (see below) or by DNA sequencing. However, there is a problem because a single flake of modern skin or smear of perspiration could contain many more DNA molecules than are present in the ancient DNA

A

Many DNA fragments

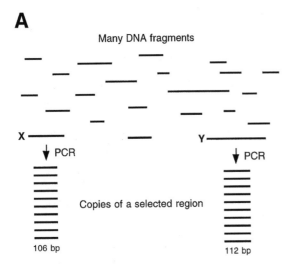

106 bp

Copies of a selected region

112 bp

B

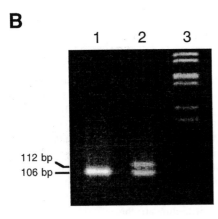

Figure 25.3 The polymerase chain reaction. For a detailed description of PCR and agarose gel electrophoresis, refer to a textbook on molecular biology (e.g., Brown 1999b).

preparation, so if the procedure becomes contaminated in this way the copies made by the PCR will derive mainly or exclusively from the modern DNA contaminants rather than the ancient DNA. This is the underlying cause of the contamination issue that has plagued ancient DNA research down through the years. The solution to the problem is to rigorously exclude modern DNA from specimens destined for DNA analysis. This means that when handling specimens for DNA analysis excavators must wear protective overalls, including gloves and a facemask (Brown 2000), and once in the laboratory the specimens must be accorded the same respect as highly pathogenic viruses, though in the case of ancient DNA the precautions are designed to pre-

vent things getting into the samples rather than out of them. Control procedures must be equally rigorous, with blank extractions performed in parallel with the specimen being tested, to ensure that all reagents and equipment used in the analysis are uncontaminated, and the DNAs of excavators and all others involved in the study must be tested so that the authenticity of the genetic fingerprint obtained from the ancient DNA sample can be checked by comparison with the DNA fingerprints of all individuals who are likely sources of contamination. The problems are less acute with non-human specimens, at least at the excavation stage, though precautions must still be taken to prevent contamination of specimens with airborne DNA contaminants resulting from previous PCRs carried out in the research laboratory.

The technical regime needed to study ancient DNA is difficult but by no means impossible to carry out and good quality research is emerging from an increasing number of laboratories around the world. The range of archaeological specimens now known to contain ancient DNA is shown in Table 25.1.

Table 25.1 Range of material shown to contain ancient DNA.

Type of material	Oldest reliable report (years)*
Human remains	
Bones and teeth	approx 60 000
Mummies	5000
Bog bodies	7500
Hair	2
Fingernails	fresh
Sectioned material on microscope slides	80
Animal remains	
Bone	25 000
Frozen mammoths	40 000
Naturally preserved skins	13 000
Museum skins	140
Specimens kept in formaldehyde	40
Feathers	130
Hair	2
Faeces and coprolites	20 000
Plant material	
Herbaria specimens	118
Charred remains	5000
Desiccated remains	1800

* The Table omits those very old specimens for which there have been controversial and unrepeated claims for DNA preservation: amber specimens (oldest 135 Myr), dinosaur bones (80 Myr) and preserved plant leaves (16 Myr).

THE CONTRIBUTION OF ANCIENT DNA TO ARCHAEOLOGY

This section presents an overview of the areas of archaeology within which ancient DNA is making a contribution, and points out some of the potential though as yet unfulfilled applications of this type of biomolecular archaeology.

Sex identification

The single most important benefit of ancient DNA for archaeologists has been the development of novel methodology for identifying the biological sex of human burials. The traditional method for sexing human skeletal remains makes use of dimorphic bone morphology allied with morphometric data obtained from reference collections of modern or recent human populations (Chapter 20). For adults, approximately 95 per cent accuracy can be achieved if an intact pelvis is available, reduced to 85–90 per cent confidence if the pelvis is crushed but the skull is intact, or 80–90 per cent confidence if sex identification has to be based on post-cranial features such as the robustness of the bones, the size of the feet, or marks of muscle attachments on the bones. With infants and juveniles, sex identification is less accurate because the pre-pubertal skeleton displays relatively little sexual dimorphism. With juveniles, confidence is only 70 per cent if the pelvis is intact, and perhaps as low as 50 per cent (i.e., no better than guesswork) without the pelvis. In fact, much archaeological material is so poorly preserved that morphological identification of sex is simply not attempted. This is particularly true for cremated remains, which usually represent only partial skeletons with the bones cracked and distorted due to heat transformation (McKinley 1994; Chapter 24).

Initial attempts to develop DNA-based methods for sex identification of human remains were based on detection of DNA sequences present only on the Y chromosome, which is possessed by males but not females (Hummel and Herrmann 1991). If a PCR directed at a Y-specific sequence yields a product, as determined by examining the result of the PCR by agarose gel electrophoresis, then the specimen is male. If no PCR product is seen then the specimen might be female, but this result would also be obtained if the specimen contained no ancient DNA or if inhibiting chemicals that prevented the PCR from working were co-extracted with the ancient DNA. This uncertainty has meant that this system has not been widely adopted with ancient DNA, and is generally used only to provide confirmation of sex identifications made by a second method. This second method targets the *amelogenin* gene, which specifies the synthesis of a protein found in tooth enamel, and which is present on both sex chromosomes, X and Y, but with slightly different nucleotide sequences. Several different PCR methods have been developed (reviewed by Brown 1998), most directed at regions of the amelogenin gene where the X sequence contains a few more or less nucleotides than the Y version. For example, in the most widespread system, used in forensic science as well as biomolecular archaeology, the PCR products derived from the copy of the amelogenin gene on the X chromosome are 106 bp in length whereas those from the Y chromosome are 112 bp. After PCR, the DNA mixture is studied by agarose gel electrophoresis, a technique that separates DNA molecules of different lengths. In Figure 25.3b, Lanes 1 and 2 show the results of a PCR with human DNA. In Lane 2, two bands are seen, one of 106 bp and one of 112 bp. This shows that the DNA sample contains both X and Y versions of the amelogenin gene and therefore comes from a male. Lane 1 shows the result of PCR with female DNA, which only has the X version of the amelogenin gene and so gives just the 106 bp PCR product. Lane 3 is a set of DNA size markers.

With modern DNA, PCRs of the amelogenin gene are able to identify sex with virtually 100 per cent accuracy. With ancient DNA the results have been more mixed. For example, Stone et al. (1996) were able to assign a sex to all twenty inhumations at a 700 year old site in the USA, and Lassen et al. (1996) reported only two failures among 30 inhumations up to 1500 years old from three sites in Germany and Switzerland. However, Lassen and colleagues had three failures out of four for much older (6000–7500 year) bones from another German site, and other workers have published success rates for DNA-based sex typing ranging from 44–66 per cent (Brown 2000). As with all ancient DNA work, the underlying message is that results cannot be interpreted in isolation; evidence from other types of analysis is also needed, and that methodological improvements should be sought. As well as these improvements to the human sex identification method, future work will undoubtedly include the development of equivalent sex identification tests for domesticated animals, based on analysis of their amelogenin genes.

Kinship studies

Unlike sex identification, there is currently no reliable way in which kinship can be inferred by morphological examination of human remains. The ease with which this work can be accomplished by STR analysis therefore suggests that this is one area in which ancient DNA can have a major and unique impact on archaeology. The techniques are not difficult: PCR is carried out so that a defined segment of DNA containing an STR is copied. The number of repeats in the STR, and hence the allele type, is then determined from the length of the PCR product, as measured by gel electrophoresis.

The most successful kinship study so far carried out with human DNA is the one that resulted in identification of the remains of the Romanovs, the former Russian ruling family (Gill *et al.* 1994). Although dating only from 1918, and therefore young in archaeological terms, the problems inherent in this project were equivalent to those encountered with much older archaeological material. The group of burials included four male adults and two female adults along with three children, and the question being asked could be precisely phrased as 'could the children be siblings and could any of the adults be parents of the children?' Five STRs were studied but the data from only two of these were needed to show that the three children could be siblings and that only one of the male and one of the female adults could be the parents. As with all kinship studies, the results were not absolutely conclusive because there is always a possibility that the allele combinations detected in the burials occur by chance rather than because the individuals are related to one another. With modern DNA, the frequency of each allele in the population as a whole can be used to calculate a statistical probability for the postulated relationship. This is not possible with archaeological remains because the allele frequencies in the ancient population are unknown and cannot be extrapolated from the frequencies in a modern population descended from it, because over time allele frequencies change in a random manner.

Ancient DNA has also been used to test the hypothesis that close relatives were buried together in tombs from the Kofun era (fifth century AD) in Japan. Genetic fingerprints built up from nine STRs showed that two males from one tomb could have been closely related, but contradicted the hypothesis, based on the ornamentation of the skeletons, that two female skeletons from a second site were mother and daughter (Kurosaki *et al.* 1993). The latter result can be considered definite, presuming the criteria for good quality

ancient DNA work have been satisfied, because STR data that indicate non-relatedness are unambiguous.

Palaeodisease

Palaeodisease is of considerable interest to archaeologists (Chapter 19) and also has potential importance as a means of studying the evolution and epidemiology of modern diseases. Ancient DNA offers possibilities for the study of both genetic and infectious diseases. Genetic diseases are caused by mutations in the genome and as such can be detected by PCRs directed at the mutation-containing regions. Because genetic diseases are of such great importance in clinical research the underlying mutations for many human ones have been identified and more will be characterized as a result of the Human Genome Project. The potential for DNA-based studies of human palaeodisease is therefore vast, but progress depends on appropriate questions being asked. For example, the prevalence of cystic fibrosis in past populations might be of archaeological interest and could be addressed by determining if ancient DNA samples from the relevant specimens contain the mutations that have been shown to cause cystic fibrosis in modern populations. The problem is that meaningful results would depend on ancient DNA tests being carried out on a substantial number of remains, which would be extremely time-consuming, especially if the objective was to chart changes in disease frequency over time, requiring examination of many remains from different periods. At present, such a large-scale ancient DNA project is probably impractical and more feasible palaeodisease studies should be given higher priority.

An example of a more feasible project involving genetic palaeodisease concerns thalassaemia, the inherited form of anaemia or iron deficiency. Anaemias in general – both the inherited and dietary forms – result in the distinctive skeletal features described as porotic hyperostosis, typified by pitting of the skull bones around the eye sockets ('cribra orbitalia') and thickening of other bones. These skeletal features are common in some groups of human remains, but whether they result from dietary or genetic anaemia is not known. Ancient DNA studies could answer this question by determining if mutations in the globin genes, responsible for thalassaemia, are present in these individuals. The practicality of this approach has been demonstrated by Filon *et al.* (1995), who showed that an 8-year-old child from an Ottoman grave (sixteenth–nineteenth century AD) from Israel, whose skull displayed porotic hyperostosis, possessed a mutation for β-thalassaemia and so suffered from genetic anaemia. In fact, this particular genetic defect was so severe that the child should not have survived long after birth, but further examination of the ancient DNA revealed that the child also had a second globin gene mutation, this one compensating for the former by allowing the foetal version of the globin protein to be synthesized for an unusually long time after birth.

The case of the Ottoman child illustrates how ancient DNA analysis can be used to build up a genetic profile of an individual but does not contribute greatly to our general understanding of anaemia in prehistory. More studies are needed to determine if skeletal indications of iron deficiency are generally due to genetic rather than dietary anaemia. Such studies would be of particular interest in the regions and time periods where malaria was thought to have been common, because some thalassaemias, such as sickle cell disease, offer protection against malaria and therefore have a high prevalence in populations in which malaria is endemic. This leads to the second application of ancient DNA in palaeodisease, where the objective is not to identify a defect in human DNA but to determine if ancient DNA from an infectious organism is present. Taylor et al. (1997) have described a method for detection of DNA from the four species of the *Plasmodium* parasite that cause malaria, and have used this method to identify *Plasmodium falciparum* DNA in rib extracts from an individual who died some 60 years ago. These researchers were unable to detect *Plasmodium* DNA in a 1700 year old mummy that had given indications of malaria by other tests, but the feasibility of the analysis with archaeological material has been demonstrated by Sallares et al. (unpublished) who identified malaria DNA in 1500 year old bones from Italy.

Although malaria has considerable potential as an object of ancient DNA study the disease that has received the greatest amount of attention so far is tuberculosis. This is for two reasons. First, tuberculosis was one of the most important diseases in prehistoric and historic times, and indeed was a major cause of human mortality right up until the early decades of the twentieth century. Second, a few tuberculosis victims develop characteristic abnormalities in various parts of their skeletons, abnormalities that are present in archaeological remains, allowing suitable skeletons to be selected as tuberculosis-positive material for the development of the ancient DNA methodology. The causative agent of tuberculosis is *Mycobacterium tuberculosis*, a member of a broad group of micro-organisms

which include non-pathogenic species that inhabit the soil. A PCR test for *M. tuberculosis* DNA must therefore be very specific and avoid cross-reaction with the soil mycobacteria which might be present as contaminants on at least some human skeletal material. This requirement was probably not satisfied in some of the early research carried out on ancient tuberculosis DNA, but there is now a growing body of reliable reports that describe the presence of *M. tuberculosis* DNA in various human remains (e.g., Baron et al. 1996, Faerman et al. 1997). Interestingly, these reports include two for pre-Columbian specimens from the Americas (Salo et al. 1994, Braun et al. 1998), which raises questions about the widely-held hypothesis that human tuberculosis originated from the bovine version of the disease when humans and cattle were brought into close contact after the beginning of farming in the Old World (Manchester 1984).

Population studies

The approach used when ancient DNA is applied to studies of past human populations is rather different to that described above for sex identification, kinship analysis and palaeodisease studies. Extensive information on past populations, not only their genetic characteristics but also their evolutionary and geographical histories, can be inferred from studies of modern human DNA, using the techniques of evolutionary and population biology. In the early 1990s it was thought that ancient DNA would make a significant and widespread contribution to these evolutionary and population studies, but this was before the problems involved in ancient DNA work were fully appreciated. Ancient DNA has indeed been an important factor in the development of ideas regarding the colonization of the New World (Merriwether 1999) and Pacific (Hagelberg et al. 1999) but has had rather less influence on Old World studies. In general, researchers have adopted the strategy whereby a model of some aspect of human prehistory is established through studies of modern DNA and then tested by ancient DNA analysis of a limited number of carefully selected specimens. A case in point concerns the 'Out of Africa' or rapid replacement hypothesis for the origin of modern humans, which postulates that modern humans are descended not from the *Homo erectus* populations that left Africa 1.0–1.5 million years ago, but from a second population that migrated from Africa less than 100 000 years ago. This hypothesis was initially proposed solely as a result of modern DNA studies (Cann *et al.* 1987) and has been modified by subsequent studies also based entirely on modern DNA (Ruvolo 1996). However, it was recognized that an important test would be a comparison between the DNA sequences of Neanderthals, which are accepted as being descendants of the *Homo erectus* migrants, and modern Europeans, who might or might not be descendants of Neanderthals, depending on whether the Out of Africa hypothesis is incorrect or correct. In other words, a carefully defined ancient DNA experiment could be used to test a model devised from the results of a much more extensive series of modern DNA studies. The ancient DNA experiment has been carried out by Krings *et al.* (1997) with a Neanderthal specimen of indeterminate age (but almost certainly the oldest human skeleton to yield ancient DNA), and by Ovchinnikov *et al.* (2000) with a 29 000-year-old specimen from the Caucasus. The conclusion is that there is relatively little genetic similarity between Neanderthals and modern Europeans, and that the latter are therefore almost certainly not descended from the former.

The research strategies used to study past human populations can also be used with other animals and with plants, in particular in order to determine the origins of domesticated species (Brown 1999a). Considerable progress has been made in understanding the relationships between different breeds of cattle and the identity and geographical locations of the original domesticates (MacHugh *et al.* 1999). Similar work has been carried out with dogs (Vila *et al.* 1997) and horses (Lister *et al.* 1998), leading to the interesting conclusion that the latter two animals were domesticated much earlier than previously thought. But these researches have been based mainly on modern DNA studies. It is with cultivated plants that ancient DNA is likely to have the most significant impact. Ancient DNA has been reported in plant remains preserved by desiccation (e.g., Rollo *et al.* 1987) and charring (e.g., Goloubinoff *et al.* 1993), positive results being obtained with a range of cultivated species including various types of wheat as well as rice, maize and sorghum. With each of these species, hypotheses regarding the number of times that the crop was domesticated and the locations of these domestications have been developed from studies of modern plants, and with each crop important questions, such as the timing of a domestication event or the trajectory followed by the crop as its cultivation spread away from its centre of origin, are being addressed by ancient DNA experiments.

CONCLUSIONS

Ancient DNA is having a growing influence on archaeology. In some applications, such as sex identification, kinship analyses and studies of palaeodisease, the potential of ancient DNA is being realized and genetic studies will become increasingly mainstream as methods are refined and simplified and more extensive collaborations between molecular biologists and archaeologists are established. In other areas, such as studies of past human populations and research into the origins and spread of agriculture, ancient DNA work is less widespread but equally important due to the ability of ancient DNA to answer specific questions that cannot be addressed by research based solely on population and evolutionary biology.

REFERENCES

*Recommended for further reading

Allaby, R.G., O'Donoghue, K., Sallares, R., Jones, M.K. and Brown, T.A. (1997). Evidence for the survival of ancient DNA in charred wheat seeds from European archaeological sites. *Ancient Biomolecules*, **1**:119–129.

Austin, J.J. (1998). Ancient DNA from amber inclusions: a review of the evidence. *Ancient Biomolecules*, **2**:167–176.

Baron, H., Hummel, S. and Herrmann, B. (1996). *Mycobacterium tuberculosis* complex DNA in ancient human bones. *Journal of Archaeological Science*, **23**:667–671.

Braun, M., Cook, D.C. and Pfeiffer, S. (1998). DNA from *Mycobacterium tuberculosis* complex identified in North American, pre-Columbian human skeletal remains. *Journal of Archaeological Science*, **25**:271–277.

*Brown, K.A. (1998). Gender and sex – what can ancient DNA tell us? *Ancient Biomolecules*, **2**:3–15.

*Brown, K.A. (2000). Ancient DNA applications in human osteoarchaeology: achievements, problems and potential. In Cox, M. and Mays, S. (eds) *Human Osteology in Archaeology and Forensic Science*, 455–473. Greenwich Medical Media: London.

Brown, T.A. (1999a). How ancient DNA may help in understanding the origin and spread of agriculture. *Philosophical Transactions of the Royal Society of London*, **B354**:89–98.

*Brown, T.A. (1999b). *Genomes*. BIOS Scientific Publishers: Oxford.

Brown, T.A. and Brown, K.A. (1992). Ancient DNA and the archaeologist. *Antiquity*, **66**:10–23.

Brown, T.A. and Brown, K.A. (1994). Ancient DNA: using molecular biology to explore the past. *Bioessays*, **16**:719–726.

Cann, R.L., Stoneking, M. and Wilson, A.C. (1987). Mitochondrial DNA and human evolution. *Nature*, **325**:31–36.

Collins, F.S., Patrinos, A., Jordan, E., Chakravarti, A., Gesteland, R. and Walters, L. (1998). New goals for the

U.S. Human Genome Project: 1998–2003. *Science*, **282**:682–689.

Deakin, W.J., Rowley-Conwy, P. and Shaw, C.H. (1998). Amplification and sequencing of DNA from preserved sorghum of up to 2800 years antiquity found at Qasr Ibrim. *Ancient Biomolecules*, **2**:27–41.

Faerman, M., Jankauskas, R., Gorski, A., Bercovier, H. and Greenblatt, C.L. (1997). Prevalence of human tuberculosis in a medieval population of Lithuania studied by ancient DNA analysis. *Ancient Biomolecules*, **1**:205–214.

Filon, D., Faerman, M., Smith, P. and Oppenheim, A. (1995). Sequence analysis reveals a β-thalassaemia mutation in the DNA of skeletal remains from the archaeological site of Akhziv, Israel. *Nature Genetics*, **9**:365–368.

Gill, P., Ivanov, P.L., Kimpton, C., Piercy, R., Benson, N., Tully, G., Evett, I., Hagelberg, E. and Sullivan, K. (1994). Identification of the remains of the Romanov family by DNA analysis. *Nature Genetics*, **6**:130–135.

Goloubinoff, P., Pääbo, S. and Wilson, A.C. (1993). Evolution of maize inferred from sequence diversity of an *adh2* gene segment from archaeological specimens. *Proceedings of the National Academy of Sciences, USA*, **90**:1997–2001.

Hagelberg, E., Kayser, M., Nagy, M., Roewer, L., Zimdahl, H., Krawczak, M., Lió, P. and Schiefenhövel, W. (1999). Molecular genetic evidence for the human settlement of the Pacific: analysis of mitochondrial DNA, Y chromosome and HLA markers. *Philosophical Transactions of the Royal Society of London*, **B354**:141–152.

Handt, O., Hoss, M., Krings, M. and Pääbo, S. (1994). Ancient DNA: methodological challenges. *Experientia*, **50**:524–529.

Hummel, S. and Herrmann, B. (1991). Y-chromosome-specific DNA amplified in ancient human bone. *Naturwissenschaften*, **78**:266–267.

Hummel, S. and Herrmann, B. (1996). aDNA typing for reconstruction of kinship. *Homo*, **47**:215–222.

Kurosaki, K., Matsushita, T. and Ueda, S. (1993). Individual DNA identifications from ancient human remains. *American Journal of Human Genetics*, **53**:638–643.

Krings, M., Stone, A., Schmitz, R.W., Krainitzi, H., Stoneking, M. and Pääbo, S. (1997). Neandertal DNA sequences and the origin of modern humans. *Cell*, **90**:19–30.

Lassen, C., Hummel, S. and Herrmann, B. (1996). PCR based sex identification of ancient human bones by amplification of X- and Y-chromosomal sequences: a comparison. *Ancient Biomolecules*, **1**:25–33.

Lister, A.M., Kadwell, M., Kaagen, L.M., Jordan, W.C., Richards, M.B. and Stanley, H.F. (1998). Ancient and modern DNA in a study of horse domestication. *Ancient Biomolecules*, **2**:267–280.

MacHugh, D.E., Troy, C.S., McCormick, F., Olsaker, I., Eythórsdóttir, E. and Bradley, D.G. (1999). Early Medieval cattle remains from a Scandinavian settlement in Dublin: genetic analysis and comparison with extant breeds. *Philosophical Transactions of the Royal Society of London, series,* **B354**:99–109.

Manchester, K. (1984). Tuberculosis and leprosy in antiquity: an interpretation. *Medical History*, **28**:162–173.

McKinley, J.I. (1994). Bone fragment size in British cremation burials and its implications for pyre technology and ritual. *Journal of Archaeological Science*, **21**:339–342.

Merriwether, D.A. (1999). Freezer anthropology: new uses for old blood. *Philosophical Transactions of the Royal Society of London*, **B354**:121–129.

O'Donoghue, K., Clapham, A., Evershed, R.P. and Brown, T.A. (1996). Remarkable preservation of biomolecules in ancient radish seeds. *Proceedings of the Royal Society of London*, **B263**:541–547.

Ovchinnikov, I.V., Götherström, A., Romanova, G.P., Kharitonov, V.M., Lidén, K. and Goodwin, W. (2000). Molecular analysis of Neanderthal DNA from the northern Caucasus. *Nature*, **404**:490–493.

Pääbo, S. (1985). Molecular cloning of Ancient Egyptian mummy DNA. *Nature*, **314**:644–645.

Pääbo, S. (1989). Ancient DNA: extraction, characterization, molecular cloning and enzymatic amplification. *Proceedings of the National Academy of Sciences, USA*, **86**:1939–1943.

Pääbo, S. and Wilson, A.C. (1991). Miocene DNA sequences: a dream come true? *Current Biology*, **1**:45–46.

*Renfrew, C. (1998). Applications of DNA in archaeology: a review of the DNA studies of the Ancient Biomolecules Initiative. *Ancient Biomolecules*, **2**:107–116.

Rollo, F., LaMarca, A. and Amici, A. (1987). Nucleic acids in mummified plant seeds: screening of twelve specimens by gel electrophoresis, molecular hybridization and DNA cloning. *Theoretical and Applied Genetics*, **73**:501–505.

Ruvolo, M. (1996). A new approach to studying modern human origins: hypothesis testing with coalescence time distributions. *Molecular Phylogenetics and Evolution*, **5**:202–219.

Salo, W.L., Aufderheide, A.C., Buikstra, J. and Holcomb, T.A. (1994). Identification of *Mycobacterium tuberculosis* DNA in a pre-Columbian Peruvian mummy. *Proceedings of the National Academy of Sciences, USA*, **91**:2091–2094.

Stone, A., Milner, G.R., Pääbo, S. and Stoneking, M. (1996). Sex determination of ancient human skeletons using DNA. *American Journal of Physical Anthropology*, **99**:231–238.

Stoneking, M. (1995). Ancient DNA: how do you know when you have it and what you can do with it? *American Journal of Human Genetics*, **57**:1259–1262.

Taylor, G.M., Rutland, P. and Molleson, T. (1997). A sensitive polymerase chain reaction method for the detection of *Plasmodium* species DNA in ancient human remains. *Ancient Biomolecules*, **1**:193–203.

Vila, C., Savolainen, P., Maldonado, J.E., Amorim, I.R., Rice, J.E., Honeycutt, R.L., Crandall, K.A., Lundeberg, J. and Wayne, R.K. (1997). Multiple and ancient origins of the domestic dog. *Science*, **276**:1687–1689.

Waite, E., Child, A.M., Craig, O.E., Collins, M.J., Brown, T.A. and Gelsthorp, K. (1997). A preliminary investigation of DNA stability in bone during artificial diagenesis. *Bulletin de la Société Géologique de France*, **168**:547–554.

26

Blood Residues in Archaeology

P.R. SMITH AND M.T. WILSON

Department of Biological Sciences, University of Essex.

The study of blood residues, usually on stone tools, began brightly in the early 1980s, but has proved to be a highly controversial field ever since. The mere presence of blood residues on an artifact is, in itself, an important finding as it may assist in the identification of that artifact. If, in addition, it were possible to determine the species of animal butchered many questions could be answered, regarding ancient hunting and animal migratory patterns, and also important dietary information could be obtained. If human blood was detected, genetic studies could be performed. Researchers in this field have utilized many of the techniques now available to biochemists, immunologists and molecular biologists including crystallography, immunoelectrophoresis, radioimmunoassay (RIA), enzyme linked immunosorbent assay (ELISA), radiocarbon dating and, most recently, DNA analysis. These techniques were developed by scientists aware of the pitfalls inherent in their use, particularly with regard to cross-reactivity and contamination, and sensitive to the need to establish a proper set of positive and negative controls. Unfortunately, many of the archaeologists who eagerly adopted these techniques were not so aware of these caveats, and have produced data that, with hindsight, appear open to question. This review aims to provide a critical assessment of the work performed to date on blood residues, to determine which methods are more likely to achieve authentic, reproducible results in the future and to define the limitations of those techniques.

THE STRUCTURE OF HUMAN BLOOD

The average sized adult human male has a total blood volume of approximately 5 litres, constituting about 8 per cent of the total body weight (Fox 1996). Blood is a viscous fluid composed of cells and plasma. The cells, which constitute approximately 40 per cent of the blood volume, comprise the red blood cells or *erythrocytes*, which are the oxygen-carrying cells of the blood, and the white blood cells or *leukocytes*. More than 99 per cent of the cells are the erythrocytes, which are flattened biconcave discs, approximately 7 μm in diameter and 2.2 μm thick, and they do not contain a nucleus. Each erythrocyte contains 200–300 million molecules of haemoglobin, which is made up of the protein globin, and an iron-containing pigment called haem. It is the iron present in the haem that binds oxygen in the lungs and releases it in the tissues.

The other component of the blood, the plasma, is a straw-coloured liquid consisting of water (90 per cent) and a large number of inorganic substances, hormones, enzymes, antibodies and other proteins. The proteins within the plasma fall into three main groups; the *albumins*, which are by far the most abundant, and

Handbook of Archaeological Sciences. Edited by D.R. Brothwell and A.M. Pollard.

Table 26.1 Cellular and protein components of blood.

Constituent	Concentration	Function
Cells		
Erythrocytes	4–6 million/mm^3	Oxygen transport
Leukocytes	4–11 000/mm^3	Fighting disease
Proteins		
Haemoglobin	12–18 g/100 ml	Oxygen transport
Serum Albumin	3–4.5 g/100 ml	Osmotic regulation, transport of fatty acids, bilirubin etc.
α, β and γ Globulins	2.8–3.8 g/100 ml	Antibodies, lipid transport, Cu transport, blood clotting etc.
Fibrinogen	0.3 g/100 ml	Blood clotting.

the *globulins* and *fibrinogen*. The major cellular and protein components of blood, together with their known physiological functions, are given in Table 26.1.

THE USE OF CHEMSTRIPS AND HEMASTIX

In 1983 the detection of prehistoric blood residues on stone tools using the Boehringer Mannheim Chemstrip was reported (Loy 1983). Chemstrips are used medically to test for the presence of haemoglobin in urine, and rely on the reaction of the haem group of haemoglobin with chemicals impregnated on the teststrip. These strips are very sensitive for haemoglobin but, as pointed out by the manufacturers themselves, they are not totally specific, and are affected by oxidizing contaminants such as hypochlorite, and by microbial peroxidases. In 1988, it was reported that Chemstrips gave false positive results when testing archaeological samples (Custer *et al.* 1988). This research demonstrated that soil samples at archaeological sites, and manganese oxide deposits in particular, consistently produced positive chemstrip reactions. Workers then proceeded to use Hemastix, a product closely related to Chemstrips, to determine the presence or absence of blood residues (Loy and Wood 1989). These are again sensitive to contamination from biological and chemical substances other than haemoglobin, and they have since been shown to be highly unreliable when used in an archaeological context (Manning 1994, Downs and Lowenstein 1995).

The major proponent of this technique suggested various ways to circumvent the problems stemming from contamination (Loy 1993). None of these seem

very satisfactory or indeed necessary, given the availability of far superior techniques. In our opinion, the use of Chemstrips and similar colorimetric tests is best confined to the analysis of urine and other clinical samples.

CRYSTALLIZATION OF HAEMOGLOBIN

In 1983 it was also reported (Loy 1983) that haemoglobin could be crystallized from prehistoric blood residues on stone tools and that the species of origin could be determined from the crystal morphology. Crystallization is achieved by a process known as 'salting-out', in which high salt concentrations are added to a solution of protein causing the protein to precipitate out in the form of crystals. The validity of Loy's claim has, however, been questioned in the literature by materials scientists (Gurfinkel and Franklin 1988), biochemists (Smith and Wilson 1992), immunologists (Downs and Lowenstein 1995), physicists (Remington 1994) and archaeologists alike (Fiedel 1996, 1997, Tuross *et al.* 1996). The following objections to the method as a way to identify species may be listed, as follows:

(i) The morphology of a crystal is affected by its chemical environment, and it has been shown that even when pure human haemoglobin solutions and analytical grade reagents are used, a wide variety of crystal shapes may be obtained (Smith and Wilson 1992; see also Figure 26.1). When the crystals obtained from the blood meals of mosquitoes were studied, it was found that salt concentration affected crystal morphology, and that different animal haemoglobins had different solubilities and required different buffer concentrations for crystallization (Washino 1977).

(ii) To identify unambiguously the species of origin of a haemoglobin crystal, the minimum requirement is a complete and accurate analysis of the interaxial angles, and the axial length ratios of the unit cell obtained by X ray diffraction studies. It is not acceptable to make a species identification by a subjective examination of a poorly-formed crystal.

(iii) X ray diffraction analysis requires a protein crystal with approximate dimensions $100 \times 100 \times 100\,\mu m$, containing approximately 0.5 μg of intact correctly-folded protein. It has been shown, however, in control experiments that pro-

Figure 26.1 Crystals of human haemoglobin prepared by 'salting out' (Smith and Wilson 1992) observed at ×6.3 magnification.

(CO-bound) forms of the protein. These spectra should be published.

(vi) If there were sufficient haemoglobin present to form a crystal there would be sufficient to obtain at least a partial amino acid sequence. As there exists a large database of animal haemoglobin sequences, species identification should prove relatively easy.

Notwithstanding these objections Loy has continued to report the identification of a large number of different species by visual inspection of haemoglobin crystals obtained from blood residues. Unfortunately, the crystals are rarely photographed but are, instead, reproduced as line drawings – to quote Fiedel, 'one must assume that this is because the crystals proved to be visible only to Loy' (Fiedel 1997). To the best of our knowledge no independent laboratory has confirmed these reports. In our opinion, this technique has not been authenticated and the results obtained with it to date should be regarded with healthy scepticism.

IMMUNOLOGICAL TECHNIQUES

A variety of immunological techniques have been used to study the survival of blood residues on tool surfaces. These include Ouchterlony, crossover-immuno-electrophoresis (CIEP), radio-immunoassay (RIA) and enzyme linked immunosorbent assay (ELISA). These techniques all rely on the ability of antibodies to react with the protein antigens to form an antibody-antigen complex, but they differ enormously in sensitivity, technical difficulty and reliability.

Ouchterlony

In this technique, antibody and antigen are placed in separate wells in an agarose gel (Hudson and Hay 1989). The proteins diffuse towards each other in the gel, and, where they meet, a white precipitate is formed. This is not generally visible to the naked eye, but can be visualized by staining with the protein stain Coomassie blue (Figure 26.2). This is primarily a qualitative technique giving either a 'yes or no' answer, and one would generally use undiluted anti-serum and antigen at a concentration of approximately 1 mg ml^{-1}.

tein does not survive in those sorts of quantities on buried artifacts (Gurfinkel and Franklin 1988, Cattaneo *et al.* 1995).

(iv) If, surprisingly, *native* haemoglobin did survive in sufficient quantities to be crystallized and analysed by X-ray diffraction, hundreds of reference analyses would need to be performed with animal haemoglobins in order to make a species identification.

(v) If the crystals are indeed of haemoglobin, under suitable experimental conditions they should exhibit the UV/Visible spectra of haemoglobin in the oxygenated, deoxygenated and carboxy

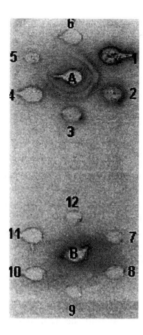

Figure 26.2 Ouchterlony double immunodiffusion of serial dilutions of rabbit antisera raised to human haemoglobin (neat serum in well 1 down to a 1 in 4096 dilution in well 12) reacting with human haemoglobin (A and B, 1 mg ml^{-1}). The Coomassie stained precipitates are clearly visible, and the presence of two lines of precipitation is indicative of an additional protein within the haemoglobin preparation with which the antisera also reacts.

Crossover-Immuno-Electrophoresis (CIEP)

The sensitivity of the Ouchterlony technique has been improved by combining electrophoresis with the immunodiffusion, and CIEP is just one of several immunoelectrophoretic procedures which differ slightly from each other (Culliford 1964). In this technique, the antibody and antigen are again placed in separate wells in an agarose gel but with the antigen in the well nearest the cathode and anti-immunoglobulin antisera placed in the well nearest the anode. Once an electric field is applied, the antigen and antibody migrate towards opposite poles and so towards each other. A precipitate forms where they meet and this can be stained with Coomassie blue. Again, this is primarily a qualitative technique giving either a 'yes or no' answer and, although it is far more sensitive than the Ouchterlony technique, it is relatively unsophisticated compared with RIA or ELISA. Many of the papers detailing the use of CIEP for residue analysis report the original claim made by Culliford (1964) that CIEP can detect

10^{-8} g of protein. This was the limit of sensitivity determined by Culliford for the particular antibodies he used and need not apply to any other antibody preparation. The detection limit of a system has to be determined for each individual antibody used, and will vary very significantly from one antibody preparation to another and from one antigen to another.

Enzyme Linked Immunosorbent Assay (ELISA)

ELISA does not measure the formation of the antibody-antigen complex directly, but uses enzymatic activity to report the presence of the complex and to amplify the signal so enabling much smaller quantities of antigen to be detected. ELISA can take many forms depending on whether one wishes to detect the presence of antibody or antigen in a particular sample. For a comprehensive review of ELISA techniques the reader is referred to Voller *et al.* (1979). A typical assay, however, for the detection of antigen in residues on a tool surface would take the form of the indirect competitive assay illustrated in Figure 26.3. The protein of interest in the residue competes with a sample of the pure known protein for binding sites on the antibody that is bound to the microtitre plate. The pure protein is labelled with an enzyme which reacts with added substrate to yield a coloured product (Figure 26.4 in colour plates). If, therefore, the solution becomes coloured this means that the pure protein has bound to the antibody indicating that there is no protein in the residue competing with it. Alternatively, if the solution remains colourless, there is protein in the residue. The intensity of the colour is directly related to the amount of protein in the residue and so one may determine the exact amount of a particular protein in any given residue by comparison with samples of the pure protein at known concentrations. It should be noted at this point, however, that if the ancient protein is badly degraded it will not compete well with the pure modern protein and so the protein concentration will be underestimated. This semi-quantitative analysis is a distinct advantage over the 'yes or no' answer obtained with Ouchterlony and CIEP. In addition, very small quantities of antibody, typically a 1 in 1000 dilution of neat antiserum, and antigen, ~1 μg ml^{-1}, are required. The chemicals utilized in ELISA are relatively inexpensive, and microplate readers for measuring the colour intensity of the reaction are common pieces of equipment in Biological Sciences departments. ELISA is also quite safe to perform if normal laboratory precautions are taken.

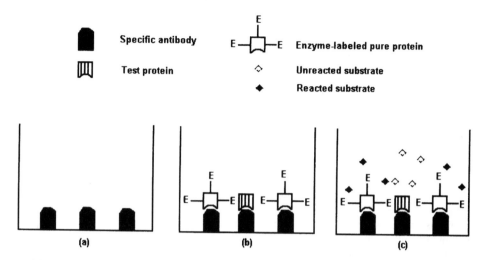

Figure 26.3 The reaction scheme of an indirect competitive ELISA for the detection of antigen.

Radioimmunoassay (RIA)

RIA also measures the formation of the antibody-antigen complex indirectly but, instead of using an enzyme label, RIA uses a radiochemical label to amplify the presence of the complex. Again, the RIA can take many practical forms but a typical assay would involve the solid phase assay as illustrated for ELISA. For a full review of RIA, see Bailey (1994). RIA is as sensitive if not more sensitive than ELISA. It does require quite expensive labelling regents, however, which have a limited shelf life, but most Biological Sciences departments would possess a scintillation counter for measuring the radioactivity. Working with radioactivity is potentially dangerous, but providing all the necessary precautions are taken, RIA is as safe as many other laboratory techniques.

Studies of blood residue analysis using Ouchterlony, CIEP, ELISA and RIA

The initial results obtained with CIEP were most encouraging. Newman and Julig (1989) reported positive reactions with 32 out of 36 artifacts, most of which reacted with more than one antisera. Upon dilution of the antisera only nine artifacts gave positive results, each to a single species. In total six different species were detected. Subsequent studies revealed varying success rates from 18–56 per cent (Petraglia *et al.* 1996, Kooyman *et al.* 1992, Gerlach *et al.* 1996), identifying many different species and often more than

one species on each artifact. The identity of some of the species has, however, been questioned on archaeological (Fiedel 1996, 1997) and technical grounds. This disquiet led to a series of control experiments. A comparative study of Ouchterlony, CIEP and RIA employing a blind test study on 30 ancient unknown residue samples and modern control samples was performed. This found that, although there was almost perfect agreement amongst the three techniques in identifying the modern control samples correctly, of the 20 per cent of the ancient samples that gave a positive reaction there was almost total disagreement and lack of consistency between the three techniques (Downs and Lowenstein 1995). Not one of the positive identifications made by CIEP and RIA agreed with each other. To make matters worse, the most sensitive and discriminatory technique, RIA, produced half as many positive results as the less sensitive technique CIEP. A study using ELISA found that only one tool out of seven gave a positive result for haemoglobin that was convincingly above both the chemical and geological background of the assay (Tuross and Dillehay 1995). This study, in particular, highlighted the importance of considering soil matrix controls in residue analysis. A blind test study of stone artifacts coated with known blood residues and submitted for CIEP analysis found incorrect identification with 73 per cent of the samples (Leach and Mauldin 1995). In another study of blood-stained stone tools which had been buried for up to two years, only one tested positive for albumin by ELISA (Cattaneo *et al.* 1993). As a side issue, none of the CIEP studies claiming success with artifact analysis show photographs of the results and so it is difficult for the reader to form an objective opinion of the results.

All of these studies clearly showed that blood residues do survive on ancient tool surfaces and can be detected by immunological methods. It is much more doubtful, however, whether the assays currently employed will allow species identification. A major concern of the authors of the RIA and ELISA studies is the ability of the polyclonal antibodies used in CIEP to discriminate between species. When a protein is injected into a rabbit, antibodies are produced to very many different regions, or *epitopes*, within that protein. A given protein may have large regions which do not vary in amino acid sequence or structure between species. This means that a polyclonal antibody produced to human albumin will react not only with human albumin but with albumin from dog, cow, horse, etc. The CIEP studies made use of affinity purified polyclonal antibodies produced commercially to supply forensic scientists needing to discriminate between human and animal blood residues. The results of the comparative study by Lowenstein clearly show that these antibodies are not specific when used against ancient residues, giving different answers depending upon the technique used. The study by Tuross *et al.* (1996) showed that in order to attain reasonable species specificity using polyclonal antibodies against blood residues it is necessary to use low protein concentrations and high dilutions of antibody. Antibody/antigen complex formation under such conditions can only be detected by RIA or ELISA. It is now quite clear that, even when using ELISA or RIA, a positive reaction obtained through use of a polyclonal antibody to a particular protein in a blood residue is indicative only of the presence of the protein not of the species from which it originated.

The obvious alternative to polyclonal antibodies is the use of monoclonal antibodies which only react with a single defined epitope of a protein and can be designed to be species specific. However, as has been noted already by others (Tuross *et al.* 1996), there are very few such antibodies, raised to proteins of archaeological interest, available. The preparation of a range of monoclonal antibodies for archaeological use would be extremely expensive and time consuming, but perhaps a better use of these resources than the fruitless analysis of blood residues with polyclonal antibodies using CIEP. A cheaper alternative would be to purify, by affinity chromatography, the polyclonal antibodies to peptides that are species specific. The amino acid sequence of albumin is known for many species and using this information it would be possible to produce

peptides with amino acid sequences corresponding to those regions of the protein that vary most between species. Such peptides, chemically linked to suitable resins, may produce affinity chromatography columns. By passing the polyclonal antibodies down such a column one may isolate an antibody which reacts with one species only.

Dot-blotting using protein A

Dot-blotting is a very sensitive technique in which a sample, thought to contain blood proteins, is applied to a small area (1–2 mm diameter) of nitrocellulose membrane, a type of protein-binding blotting paper. The membrane is then incubated with horseradish peroxidase labelled-Protein A, a *Staphylococcus aureus* derived protein, which binds to immunoglobulin G (IgG) from most mammalian species. If the sample contains IgG a purple/black colour is obtained on addition of substrate (e.g., 1,4-chloronaphthol). This technique has been used to determine the presence of mammalian IgG and therefore blood residues, on tool surfaces (Loy and Wood 1989, Loy *et al.* 1990, Loy and Hardy 1992, Loy 1993, Loy and Dixon 1998). Protein A does not, however, bind just to IgG but also to IgM, which is also restricted to the blood stream, but more importantly to IgA (Patrick *et al.* 1977) which is the predominant immunoglobulin in saliva, milk, and tracheobronchial and genitourinary secretions (Mestecky and McGhee 1987). A control study has shown that if any of these fluids are applied to tool surfaces, a positive result is obtained with protein A (Manning 1994). Positive results were also obtained with tools that had come into contact with dog faeces and saliva, and crushed insects. It is, therefore, clear that casual contact with a tool surface by either an archaeologist, prehistoric or contemporary animals or insects may be sufficient to give a positive reaction with Protein A.

From the above, it is clear that:

(i) CIEP is neither sufficiently sensitive nor discriminatory to be used for blood residue analysis of ancient samples, and we are sceptical of the results obtained with this technique to date. In our opinion the only reliable immunological techniques for this type of analysis are RIA and ELISA. Although ELISA can be performed in the field, the use of radioisotopes means that RIA most definitely cannot. They are both, however, best performed in a laboratory environment in collaboration with scientists who have been trained to recognize inherent technical problems and who have experience of the proper control experiments required to correct for these.

(ii) Polyclonal antibodies should only be used to determine the presence of a particular protein in a blood residue. Species determination should be performed using monoclonal antibodies or peptide-screened polyclonal antibodies.

(iii) Dot-blotting using Protein A cannot be used with complete confidence to indicate the presence of blood residues on tool surfaces.

ISOELECTRIC FOCUSING (IEF)

It has been suggested that isoelectric focusing (IEF) can be used to determine the type and species of origin of proteins within ancient tool residues (Nelson et al. 1986, Loy and Dixon 1998). IEF is a technique that separates proteins according to their net charge (Andrews 1986). Each protein migrates through a gel containing a pH gradient until it reaches the point in the gradient which corresponds to its isoelectric point (pI), i.e., to the pH at which it bears no net charge. At this point migration ceases and the position of the protein can be determined by staining. IEF is an extremely powerful analytical technique, which can separate proteins differing in pI by as little as 0.001 pH unit. However, a change in a single surface amino acid residue in a protein is sufficient to bring about a change in pI of that protein. For example, human haemoglobin A has a pI of 6.87 whereas sickle cell haemoglobin S (with one amino acid difference, βglu6val) has a pI of 7.09. Therefore, in order to monitor the presence of a particular protein, not to mention identify its species of origin, by pI measurements, it would be necessary for that protein to have remained in its original state over the passage of thousands of years. Furthermore, it would need to be present and in sufficient quantities to be visible on an IEF gel. This has been shown not to be the case by immunological and biochemical methods (Ascenzi et al. 1985, Smith and Wilson 1990, Gurfinkel and Franklin 1988, Tuross and Dillehay 1995). We conclude that the technique of IEF is not suitable for blood residue analysis of ancient tool surfaces and the results presented to date using IEF in this context should be interpreted with extreme caution.

RADIOCARBON DATING

There are only a few reports of radiocarbon dating of blood residues, all originating from the same group (Nelson et al. 1986, Loy et al. 1990). One author has since withdrawn his support from one of these papers (Nelson 1993) and the same paper has been heavily criticized in a subsequent report (Gillespie 1997). The main argument centres around whether the carbon date obtained relates to blood residues or contaminating calcium oxalate present at the site, and casts serious doubt on the validity of the dates obtained. There is to date insufficient evidence to determine whether or not radiocarbon dates can be obtained from blood residues.

DNA ANALYSIS

DNA analysis is probably the most powerful technique available for the analysis of blood residues but at the same time the one most susceptible to contamination and misleading results. Archaeological DNA is reviewed elsewhere in this volume (Chapter 25) and so we refer the reader to that section for detailed references and methodology. Briefly, DNA analysis is performed using the Polymerase Chain Reaction (PCR), a technique which takes one piece of DNA and produces up to a million identical copies of that same piece. Consequently, this technique is ideal for the study of blood residues where only a small amount of surviving DNA will be present. If DNA has survived in blood residues in sufficient quantities to be amplified by PCR, it can be sequenced directly and the species of origin determined. However, the blood residue will contain overwhelming quantities of contaminating bacterial and fungal DNA that will also be amplified by the PCR reaction and will overshadow any DNA surviving in the original residue. There are several other technical problems, but none of these are insurmountable, and the study of ancient DNA in general has made enormous advances in recent years. The complications associated with the study of ancient DNA together with the technicalities normally associated with PCR, make it essential that specialist personnel perform the work in a laboratory with dedicated equipment.

PCR and blood residue analysis

Most workers using PCR to study ancient DNA attempt to amplify mitochondrial DNA rather than nuclear DNA, as there are 500–1000 times more copies of mitochondrial DNA in cells and it can be directly sequenced. In fact, over the last 10 years, only a small number of successful studies on nuclear DNA have been reported. These have usually involved bone or mummified material in which the DNA has enjoyed a degree of protection from bacterial and/or chemical damage, and usually required several grams of material. Loy claims to have extracted nuclear DNA from blood residues found on exposed tool surfaces, by simply eluting the DNA into 100 µl water. He then identified the species of origin of the residue by performing species-specific PCR (Loy 1993). A more convincing report has detailed the detection of mitochondrial DNA in blood residues on stone tools 35–65 000 years old (Hardy *et al.* 1997). Here the DNA was cloned prior to sequencing and proper controls were introduced. Given the normal problems reported with detection of ancient tissue and skeletal DNA, the success of this project is quite remarkable. Clearly PCR is potentially a very powerful technique for the study of tool residues but as yet insufficient data has been produced for us to decide whether it has a long-term future in residue analysis.

CONCLUSIONS

An argument often given to justify the use of a particular technique, in particular, CIEP and Hemastix, is that they are routinely used to identify bloodstains or bodily fluids in forensic work and the results are used as evidence in a court of law or in clinical laboratories. This is true, but in these cases the samples have rarely been in the soil for 9000 years, subjected to chemical and microbial attack, but rather have recently been deposited on relatively clean clothing, or other organic or inorganic objects. The archaeological context requires quite a different approach. We have made criticisms of experimental procedure and theory in this review which is, of course, easy to do with hindsight. Nevertheless, when claims are made which run counter to current scientific intuition we feel that the burden of proof weighs heavily on the claimant.

We believe that tool residue analysis is still a worthwhile exercise likely to yield useful archaeological data. The techniques that show the most promise are ELISA, RIA and PCR, but these all require the involvement of specialist personnel and need to be performed under carefully controlled conditions. We feel, therefore, that it is important for archaeologists to establish collaborations with experts in these fields who are interested in archaeological science, willing to undertake the assays and submit these for peer review. There is, however, no reason why the archaeologist trained in sterile technique should not perform the extraction of protein or DNA from residues, and this will also facilitate blind

testing. We suggest the following as guidelines for this procedure:

(i) Only personnel wearing sterile gloves and face-masks should handle the tools, placing these in individual sterile containers. Parallel containers should be prepared containing soil immediately surrounding each particular tool. Samples of soil from within the area, but not likely to be contaminated with blood residues, should also be placed in sterile containers.

(ii) A small blood sample from personnel handling the tools should be retained if DNA analysis is envisaged.

(iii) The elution of proteins or DNA from the tools should be performed in a dedicated laboratory or laboratory area, free from modern contaminating protein or DNA.

(iv) All glassware and plasticware must be kept sterile and dedicated pipettes used with sterile tips, and dedicated devices for concentrating samples (centricons, etc.) employed.

(v) While in its sterile container the tool should be covered with sterile extraction buffer (approximately 50 ml, 5M guanidine HCL, 0.5M Tris, pH 7.4) and incubated on a whirly wheel overnight at room temperature. This buffer will serve to extract both protein and DNA.

(vi) The extract should be centrifuged (10 000 g, 15 mins) to remove any particulates and then split into two fractions, one for protein analysis and one for DNA analysis.

(vii) The aliquot for protein analysis can then be dialysed into phosphate buffered saline and concentrated down to approximately 200 µl using centricon-3 devices (Amicon), which have a molecular weight cut-off of 3000 Daltons. These devices are disposable and a new one should be used for each sample. The DNA aliquot should not be concentrated or dialysed.

(viii) Both the aliquots for DNA and protein analysis should be stored at −80°C until despatch to the collaborating laboratories.

(ix) Exactly the same procedure should be performed with the soil samples.

The above protocol includes an adaptation of the sterile procedures suggested and described by Pääbo (1993) and the buffer systems and reagents are those used by ourselves and others in the field. We believe, therefore, that there is good evidence that these procedures will be effective.

Even allowing for the reservations we have about much of the work performed in this field to date, we are still confident that, if performed properly, artifact analysis as described above is worthwhile. The effort required from the site archaeologists is minimal, in terms of soil collection and maintenance of sterility. The 'extraction' of biological residues from the artifacts and soil is neither expensive nor technically difficult, and well within the capabilities of trained archaeologists. The extracts can then be stored, frozen at −80°C, almost indefinitely and decisions about analysis can be taken at leisure as and when funding becomes available. But remember, one cannot undo what has once been done and any artifact that is scrubbed and cleaned is beyond analysis because contamination cannot then be excluded.

REFERENCES

*Recommended for further reading

*Andrews, A.T. (1986). *Electrophoresis: Theory, Techniques and Biochemical and Clinical Applications*, (2nd edn). Clarendon Press: Oxford.

Ascenzi, A., Brunori, M., Citro, G. and Zito, R. (1985). Immunological detection of haemoglobin in bones of ancient Roman times and of Iron and Eneolithic ages. *Proceedings of the National Academy of Sciences, USA*, **82**:7170–7172.

*Bailey, G.S. (1994). Radioimmunoassay of peptides and proteins. *Methods in Molecular Biology*, **32**:449–460.

Cattaneo, C., Gelsthorpe, K., Phillips, P. and Sokol, R.J. (1993). Blood residues on stone tools – indoor and outdoor experiments. *World Archaeology*, **25**:29–43.

Cattaneo, C., Gelsthorpe, K., Phillips, P. and Sokol, R.J. (1995). Differential survival of albumin in ancient bone. *Journal of Archaeological Science*, **22**:271–276.

Culliford, B.J. (1964). Precipitin reactions in forensic problems. *Nature*, **201**:1092–1094.

Custer, J.F., Ilgenfritz, J. and Doms, K.R. (1988). A cautionary note on the use of Chemstrips for detection of blood residues on prehistoric stone tools. *Journal of Archaeological Science*, **15**:343–345.

*Downs, E.F. and Lowenstein, J.M. (1995). Identification of archaeological blood proteins: a cautionary note. *Journal of Archaeological Science*, **22**:11–16.

Fiedel, S.J. (1996). Blood from stones? Some methodological and interpretative problems in blood residue analysis. *Journal of Archaeological Science*, **23**:139–147.

Fiedel, S.J. (1997). Reply to Newman *et al. Journal of Archaeological Science*, **24**:1029–1030.

Fox, S.I. (1996). *Human Physiology*, (5th edn). Wm C Brown: London.

Gerlach, S.C., Newman, M., Knell, E.J. and Hall, E.S. Jr. (1996). Blood protein residues on lithic artifacts from two archaeological sites in the De Long mountains, northwestern Alaska. *Arctic*, **49**:1–10.

Gillespie, R. (1997). On human blood, rock art and calcium oxalate: further studies on organic carbon content and radiocarbon age of materials relating to Australian rock art. *Antiquity*, **71**:430–437.

Gurfinkel, D.M. and Franklin, U.M. (1988). A study of the feasibility of detecting blood residue on artefacts. *Journal of Archaeological Science*, **15**:83–97.

Hardy, B.L., Raff, R.A. and Raman, V. (1997). Recovery of mammalian DNA from Middle Paleolithic stone tools. *Journal of Archaeological Sciences*, **24**:601–611.

*Hudson, L. and Hay, F.C. (1989). *Practical Immunology*, (3rd edn), Blackwell: Oxford.

Kooyman, B., Newman, M.E. and Ceri, H. (1992). Verifying the reliability of blood residue analysis on archaeological tools. *Journal of Archaeological Science*, **19**:265–269.

Leach, J.D. and Mauldin, R.P. (1995). Additional comments on blood residue analysis in archaeology. *Antiquity*, **60**:1020–1022.

Loy, T.H. (1983). Prehistoric blood residues: detection on tool surfaces and identification of species of origin. *Science*, **220**:1269–1271.

Loy, T.H. (1993). The artefact as site – an example of the biomolecular analysis of organic residues on prehistoric tools. *World Archaeology*, **25**:44–63.

Loy, T.H. and Dixon, E.J. (1998). Blood residues on fluted points from Eastern Beringia. *American Antiquity*, **63**:21–46.

Loy, T.H. and Hardy, B.G. (1992). Blood residue analysis of 90 000 year old stone tools from Tabun Cave, Israel. *Antiquity*, **66**:24–35.

Loy, T.H. and Wood, A.R. (1989). Blood residue analysis at Cayönü Tepesi, Turkey. *Journal of Field Archaeology*, **16**:451–460.

Loy, T.H., Rhys Jones, D.E., Meehan, B., Vogel, J., Southon, J. and Cosgrove, R. (1990). Accelerator radiocarbon dating of human blood proteins in pigments from late Pleistocene art sites in Australia. *Antiquity*, **64**:110–116.

Manning, A.P. (1994). A cautionary note on the use of Hemastix and Dot-blot assays for the detection and confirmation of archaeological blood residues. *Journal of Archaeological Science*, **21**:159–162.

Mestecky, J. and McGhee, J.R. (1987). Immunoglobulin A (IgA): molecular and cellular interactions involved in IgA biosynthesis and immune response. *Advances in Immunology*, **40**:153–245.

Nelson, D.E. (1993). Second thoughts on a rock art date. *Antiquity*, **67**:893–895.

Nelson, D.E., Loy, T.H., Vogel, J.S. and Southon, J.R. (1986). Radiocarbon dating blood residues on prehistoric stone tools. *Radiocarbon*, **28**:170–174.

Newman, M.E. and Julig, P. (1989). The identification of protein residues on lithic artefacts from a stratified boreal forest site. *Canadian Journal of Archaeology*, **13**:119–132.

*Pääbo, S. (1993). Ancient DNA. *Scientific American*, **269**:86–92.

Patrick, C.C., Virella, G. and Koistinen, J. (1977). Differential binding of IgA proteins of different subclasses and allotypes to staphylococcal protein A. *Zeitschrift für Immunitatsforschung*, **153**:466–469.

Petraglia, M., Knepper, D., Glumac, P., Newman, M. and Sussman, C. (1990). Immunological and microwear analysis of chipped-stone artifacts from Piedmont contexts. *American Antiquity*, **61**:127–135.

Remington, S.J. (1994). Identifying species of origin from prehistoric blood residues. *Science*, **266**:298–299.

Smith, P.R. and Wilson, M.T. (1990). Detection of haemoglobin in human skeletal remains by ELISA. *Journal of Archaeological Science*, **17**:255–268.

Smith, P.R. and Wilson, M.T. (1992). Blood residues on ancient tool surfaces: a cautionary note. *Journal of Archaeological Science*, **19**:237–241.

Tuross, N. and Dillehay, T.D. (1995). The mechanism of organic preservation at Monte Verde, Chile, and one use of biomolecules in archaeological interpretation. *Journal of Field Archaeology*, **22**:97–109.

Tuross, N., Barnes, I. and Potts, R. (1996). Protein identification of blood residues on experimental stone tools. *Journal of Archaeological Science*, **23**:289–296.

*Voller, A., Bidwell, D.E. and Bartlett, A. (1979). *The Enzyme Linked Immunosorbent Assay (ELISA)*. Dynatech Europe: Guernsey.

Washino, R.K. (1977). *Identification of Host Blood Meals in Arthropods*. U.S. Army Medical Research and Development Correspondence: Washington DC.

27

Survival and Interpretation of Archaeological Proteins

A.M. GERNAEY, E.R. WAITE, M.J. COLLINS, O.E. CRAIG

University of Newcastle

and R.J. SOKOL

Regional Blood Transfusion Centre, Sheffield.

There have been spectacular, but rare, examples of archaeological protein survival that are well documented. They usually become *cause celèbres* and, directly because of their rarity, are of little general archaeological value. Examples include the frozen Ice Man, the desiccated Peruvian Mummies and the 'pickled' Tollund Man in Denmark. In all these cases, the unusual features of the burial environment have led to a marked suppression of microbial degradation (Child 1995a), and hence the exceptional preservation seen.

Much more typical, and therefore of more widespread value and application to archaeology, are those proteins protected by their natural associations, of which by far the most prevalent are the hard tissue proteins (tooth, bone, antler, shell), because their organization means that they are afforded protection from microbially-mediated enzymolysis until the mineral has been altered diagenetically to allow access of these enzymes (Mayer 1994). Similarly, it is not difficult to envisage that if the protein is associated with a different biopolymer (such as cellulose), the resulting composite will probably be resistant to attack by a single enzyme, so that the degradation of one may not proceed without the decomposition of the other. In the case of mineralized collagen (i.e., bone, tooth and antler), its almost ubiquitous survival has led to its widespread use for ^{14}C dating and whilst the method is routinely successful in samples from the colder latitudes, it is of limited value in samples recovered from warmer climes, due to the rapid loss of collagen (Ambrose 1990).

THE ROLE OF TEMPERATURE

Clearly, then, temperature has a major role to play in the survival of collagen, since temperature will affect rates of chemical reactions (Ortner *et al.* 1972) and microbial growth patterns (Child *et al.* 1993, Child 1995a, b). In temperate climates and under ideal burial conditions, bone collagen could be expected to survive beyond the limits of radiocarbon dating, for example, bones from Joint Mitnor Cave (UK), dated to 120 000

Handbook of Archaeological Sciences. Edited by D.R. Brothwell and A.M. Pollard.
© 2001 John Wiley & Sons, Ltd.

years BP, show good preservation (Hodgins and Hedges in press).

Extrapolating from these data, microbial modifications being limited, Neolithic bones from temperate climates could be expected to contain almost all of their original collagen (indicated by nitrogen content). This hypothesis is supported by bones from the Neolithic site of Bercy, Paris (Bocherens *et al.* 1997); whilst some of the bones from the site were highly degraded, and contained less than 1 per cent of their original nitrogen, others showed 73 per cent of original nitrogen had survived, these latter also having good histology (Pike *et al.* in press). Histology tests for the degree of microbial modification; correlations between protein content and histology have also been noted by previous authors (Hedges *et al.* 1995). In the relatively hotter climate of Utah, good collagen preservation was seen in a Columbian mammoth from Emery County. Dated to 11 200 radiocarbon years BP, microscopy showed well preserved compact and trabecular bone; CNBr peptide mapping of extracted collagen indicated that the major peptides of Type 1 collagen were present, with the same electrophoretic mobility as modern elephant collagen (Schaedler *et al.* 1992). The sites at Bercy and at Emery County illustrate a common observation, that high nitrogen contents and/or good collagen preservation go hand in hand with good histology.

PORE SIZE DISTRIBUTION

This preservation is perhaps to be expected, and can best be explained using the pore protection hypothesis of Mayer (1994). This hypothesis suggests that organic materials in sediments survive for prolonged periods inside small pores, which physically exclude enzymes, however this protection hypothesis discounts any chemical action. Does this hold true for bones? The micro-pores in modern bone have a diameter of <8 nm (Pike *et al.* in press). Enzyme access via micro-pores would be physically restricted (Mayer 1994), since collagenases are large, being between 60–130 kDa (Bond and van Wart 1984). Enzymes of this size would require that the bone mineral first be removed, and laboratory studies support this hypothesis (Krane 1970). Diagenetic alteration enlarges pore size and alters their distribution, so that mesopores (0.5–8 μm) become the major component; with increased diagenetic change, the mean micro-pore size increases also (Pike *et al.* in press), so that enzyme access eventually would not be physically inhibited.

MINERAL INTERACTIONS AND PRESERVATION

Close interaction with the mineral may preserve proteins; some proteins are bound to hydroxyapatite (HAP), others are more closely associated with the collagen (Prigodich and Vesely 1997). Binding studies with osteocalcin (OC) and HAP show that this association is rapid. OC is a small, highly negatively charged protein. In the presence of Ca^{2+}, two helical regions form, so that the acidic residues align (Hauschka and Carr 1982, Collins *et al.* 1999a), preferentially on the (100) face of HAP (Fujisawa and Kuboki 1991).

Recent diagenetic studies have shown that OC could be expected to survive for prolonged (geological) time-spans, but only if its interaction with the bone mineral is uncompromised. The extracted molecule, either alone or bound to HAP, very quickly loses its conformational integrity and, presumably, its preservational ability (Fujisawa and Kuboki 1991). In the same studies, bound albumin was lost much more rapidly than bound OC.

ARCHAEOLOGICAL CERAMICS AND STONE TOOLS

For the reasons mentioned above, proteins would also be expected to be preserved on mineral surfaces from other archaeological contexts. Ceramics, for example, being porous, have large surface areas and may be in contact with protein-rich foodstuffs for prolonged periods of time. Even on ceramics with good preservation of other biomolecules (e.g., lipids; see Chapter 28), reported protein yields are surprisingly low (Evershed and Tuross 1996, Craig *et al.* in press). Although there may be analytical difficulties in extracting proteins from such a context, similar research performed on stone tools have found proteins in abundance (μg amounts) over long time scales (90 000 years; Loy and Hardy 1992, but see Chapter 26). This is surprising considering the lack of protection afforded by a sheer lithic surface, and such claims have given rise to some healthy debate (e.g., Smith and Wilson 1992, Tuross *et al.* 1996, Newman *et al.* 1997; Chapter 26). Many of the early, more spectacular, reports have been criticized for the use of inappropriate methodologies, for lack of controls and poor archaeological interpretation. These are common criticisms, relating to all immunochemical detection methods, and the issues are discussed below.

ANOXIC AND OXIC ENVIRONMENTS

The relationship between preservation and environment of the more 'mundane' samples is much more difficult to define and predict than the extreme examples mentioned above. In general, better preservation of organic remains is found in waterlogged sites and, traditionally, this is attributed to anoxic conditions and the presence of anaerobic micro-organisms, with supposedly highly-reduced efficiency for the degradation of organic materials (see Chapter 50). The degradation of lignin is usually suppressed under anaerobic conditions, since the white rot fungi require oxygen as the terminal electron acceptor. There is no *a priori* reason why anoxic conditions should enhance protein survival. Studies which examined the aerobic and anaerobic bacterial populations present in three different sediment types showed that anaerobic carbon degradation dominated, though cell yield was lowest in the anaerobic zone. Anaerobic productivity still accounted for the majority of cell production, however, as anaerobic degradation processes were so dominant (Wellsbury *et al.* 1996). Indeed, the rate of microbial degradation of mineralized protein may be enhanced under anoxic conditions (Child 1995a).

The site hydrology

Most of the waterlogged ditches and pits that display good bone preservation are stagnant. We suspect that, unlike wood, bone survival is enhanced under waterlogged conditions, not because of the absence of oxygen, but because of the absence of flowing water. The impact of site hydrology on the diagenesis of bone cannot be overstated (for a review see Nielsen-Marsh *et al.* 2000, and Chapter 51). Three models for water movement have been suggested (Hedges and Millard 1995), and subsequently refined (Pike *et al.* in press). Hedges *et al.* (1995), and more recently Nielsen-Marsh and Hedges (1999), have noted that multiple diagenetic parameters (including histology, apatite crystallinity, nitrogen, the ratio of carbonate to phosphate, and the porosity) tend to correlate. Thus good preservation of archaeological protein in the UK (and other regions with similar climatic regimes) can be expected in bones which appear 'well preserved'.

Cave sites probably produce better protein preservation than open sites of equivalent age, particularly where water flow is restricted. Looking at cave sites in Israel, Weiner *et al.* (1997) have observed that the different mineral types present in archaeological bones can indicate the conditions under which the bone may have dissolved.

RATES OF DIAGENETIC REACTIONS

How do proteins fall apart? Processes such as changes in pH and soil ionic strength play an important role, but peptide bond hydrolysis must be key. Can exceptional preservation be explained by an understanding of peptide bond hydrolysis? Hydrolysis constants for single peptide bonds in native proteins can vary over at least 20 orders of magnitude (Krokosynska and Otlewski 1996). Proteins in α-helices are relatively unstable, but the products of protein cleavage leading to the formation of new secondary structural elements are very stable.

Studies with very stable proteins, usually enzymes, show that the major degradation mechanisms are deamidation of asparagine and glutamine, and succinamide formation at aspartate and glutamate leading to racemization (see below) and peptide bond hydrolysis. These reactions are strongly dependent upon conformational freedom of the susceptible amino acid residues (Daniel *et al.* 1996), and van Duin and Collins (1998) report an estimated 10 000 fold reduction in the rate of racemization of aspartic acid in collagen due to conformational constraints. The thermostability of enzymes can be raised by surface attachment (Fernandez-LaFuente *et al.* 1995). It is not possible to state, on the basis of current knowledge, that exceptional preservation of proteins is not possible, only that rigorous procedures are required for their unequivocal demonstration (see below).

RACEMIZATION – PERHAPS A SPECIAL CASE?

Racemization is the interconversion of the D- and L-forms of amino acids. In life, the amino acids making up the proteins of higher eukaryotes consist solely of the L-form. After death, D-forms can accumulate at a rate which is controlled by time and temperature, forming the basis of a dating technique (for a recent review see Johnson and Miller 1997). The advantages of the method are that it is inexpensive and extends beyond the range of radiocarbon (40 to 150 ka BP), but because it is a chemical reaction it can also be affected by fluctuations in the burial environment, e.g., temperature, pH, other ions in solution and, finally, the degree of degradation of the protein.

INTERPRETATION OF DATA

The biochemical content of proteins is used more and more as a source of information for archaeological conclusions. Examples include the palaeoenvironmental and palaeodietary implications of stable isotope ratios in collagen (e.g., Ambrose 1993, Bocherens *et al.* 1995), chiral amino acid ratios for dating (e.g., Collins *et al.* 1999b), and also perhaps as an indicator for DNA survival (Poinar *et al.* 1996), radiocarbon dating (e.g., van Klinken and Hedges 1998) and the immunochemical demonstration of the survival capability of proteins (e.g., biochemically active enzymes; Weser *et al.* 1996). All of these applications require that the diagenetic mechanisms by which the biological signature is altered be properly understood, or at least, that the degree of alteration be identified and the acquired data judged accordingly. Here we concentrate particularly on the problems inherent in the measurements of D:L ratios of amino acids for amino acid racemization dating (AAR) and on the immunochemical demonstration of proteins.

Stable isotope studies

The stable isotopes of nitrogen ($\delta^{15}N$) and carbon ($\delta^{13}C$) present in collagen (and other components) from archaeological bones and teeth have been used for a variety of palaeodietary studies. What degree of fractionation exists in collagen formation and how is this altered by diagenetic factors? For a discussion of these, see Chapter 23.

Amino acid racemization dating and interpretation

The amino acid most commonly used for the dating of bone over the Holocene has been aspartic acid (Asp) because it is the fastest racemizing amino acid in a peptide, giving the required resolution over this timescale, but other amino acids such as alanine, valine and isoleucine have been used for older materials (e.g., Dungworth *et al.* 1973, 1976). Unfortunately, aspartic acid racemization (AAR) dating of archaeological bone has acquired a controversial reputation, mainly due to some spectacular errors made in the mid-1970s. The most famous of these was the erroneous dating of some Californian paleoindian remains to a Pleistocene age (50–60 ka), suggesting an early colonization of North America (Bada *et al.* 1974; see Pollard and Heron 1996:271 for a review). With the advent of AMS carbon-14 dating, the error was corrected and the

skeletons were re-dated to 5–6 ka (Bada 1985). The image of the technique was subsequently damaged, even regarded by some archaeologists as 'some kind of joke' (Marshall 1990). The error was partly due to poor bone preservation, but also to inaccurately dated calibration bone (which is necessary to allow a racemization value to be converted from a relative to an absolute date); the accuracy of this depends upon the calibration material having a similar diagenetic history with respect to temperature and, crucially, protein degradation.

There have been studies where isolation of a discrete protein fraction (collagen) from well-preserved bone has given adequate dates (e.g., Elster *et al.* 1991, Kimber and Hare 1992), but, because bone is an open system, the original amino acids can be lost and contaminating amino acids added, therefore the technique offers little promise for reliable dating. We have shown that leaching of the more soluble proteins and retention and degradation of the insoluble proteins in bone can potentially give any value for a racemization date (Collins *et al.* 1999b). In addition, there is a lack of understanding of the mechanism of AAR – for Asp the rate in proteins depends heavily on conformation. Indeed we can demonstrate that racemization in collagen is driven by degradation of the triple helix, whose intact structure prevents racemization (Julg *et al.* 1987, van Duin and Collins 1998). The recent use of AAR in bone to screen for the survival of DNA (Bada *et al.* 1994, Poinar *et al.* 1996) is misguided, as it does not take into account this mechanism. The analysis of AAR in other biominerals, e.g., mollusc shells (Goodfriend 1991) and ostrich eggshell (Brooks *et al.* 1990) appears to be more reliable, presumably because they approximate to a more closed system with respect to protein leaching and contamination.

IMMUNOCHEMICAL DETECTION AND INTERPRETATION

For immunochemical detection, the target molecule must be able to induce an antibody response when injected into a host animal. Proteins make excellent targets since, generally, they induce antibody responses well; other biomolecules may not be so competent – lipids, for example, are usually poor immunogens. Not all proteins make good immunogens, however, and the more conserved the protein is across species, the less effective it will be as an immunogen.

A wide variety of immunological methods have been applied in archaeological studies, ranging from relatively insensitive immunodiffusion techniques to very sensitive radioimmunoassay and ELISA methods (see Chapter 26). To be successful, studies need close co-operation between immunologists and archaeologists, with a full understanding of the strengths and limitations of each discipline. It must be appreciated, for example, that immunological methods are carefully standardized for a particular use and cannot simply be applied to archaeological material without being validated and standardized for that purpose (Child and Pollard 1992). It is sad to see that some (archaeological) authors still regard this as being solely a problem for the laboratory conducting the analysis and assume that appropriate control procedures are in place (Leach and Mauldin 1995). Poor papers adversely affect the standing of immunological techniques as tools for archaeological research.

Control samples must be included *each time* immunological testing is carried out, and should include fresh and ancient material, and specimens giving positive and negative results. Environmental controls (e.g., soil) are also important. The control results confirm that the test is working properly, that cross-reactivity of the reagents is not a problem and that conditions likely to have been experienced by the test specimens are not interfering with the assay (e.g., Cattaneo *et al.* 1994). The results of the control samples should be given in any article published. The importance of controls cannot be overemphasized; if they are not included, or are inadequate, or give the wrong reaction, then any test result is suspect.

Even with adequate controls, if the test result is questionable, confirmation by non-immunochemical tests must be considered. Cross-reactions, high affinity but non-specificity of antibodies (*heterocliticity*) and loss of epitope integrity (protein conformational change) can all lead to uncertain results. Biochemical (e.g., protein sequencing) or chemical (e.g., chromatographic) confirmation of the demonstrated target molecule may still be required (Child and Pollard 1992).

What value is an understanding of protein degradation to its immunological detection in archaeological materials? A short discussion of a controversial topic may serve to answer this question. Reports over the last ten years of the detection of speciated 'blood' residues (the target is a protein, the Fc fragment of the IgG molecule) on stone tools have excited the archaeological world, tantalizing us all with possibilities. A study on the diagenesis of this molecule (Tuross *et al.* 1996) appears to contradict these reports – using highly sensitive detection methods, IgG does not survive on lithic surfaces if exposed to UV light. There would

appear to be a dichotomy. The central question is the likelihood that IgG will survive.

The hypothesis for survival is sorption to the negatively charged surface of flint (Newman *et al.* 1997). Preservation by association with a mineral surface is a possibility for the Fc fragment of IgG, however, the net charge on that fragment is negative (23/224 positively charged residues and 25/224 negatively charged ones; Edelman *et al.* 1969). Would sorption to a mineral surface (flint) of these residues preserve the species-specific epitope regions of the molecule? A search of the literature did not show that such binding studies have been undertaken, but should be done since flint is cryptocrystalline with a very low surface area compared with clay. This explanation, therefore, can only be hypothetical, and needs testing. If the protein binds to that surface, will this protect it from diagenesis? Experiments suggest it would not (Tuross *et al.* 1996). The Fc region contains some labile bonds (i.e., bonds that are prone to hydrolysis): aspartic acid is next to glycine at residues 280, 385 and 401, and next to serine at residue 399; glutamic acid is next to serine at residue 382. The molecule is not rich in these labile bonds, but those containing aspartic acid are much more labile than those containing glutamic acid (Collins *et al.* 1999a) and the presence of these bonds will promote the chemical degradation of the molecule. For certain immunological detection, amino acid sequencing of the identified targets would be required. This does not seem to have been attempted, to date, but for this, a Western blot would be necessary (see Collins *et al.* 1999a for an explanation).

In summary, an understanding of protein survival has suggested that an immunological target may not survive and immunological detection may need an independent confirmation for definitive proof.

CONCLUSIONS

Archaeological proteins survive variously; spectacular preservations have been recorded, but these are rare. More usually, it is the proteins associated with mineral or other biopolymers that survive. Factors which promote the degradation of proteins are warm climates (although this effect is reduced when deposits are in caves), the flow of water through the site and microbial activity. Studies to characterize archaeological bones show that good protein preservation is highly associated with reduced microbial tunnelling and associated mineral integrity.

Amino acid racemization dating appears fraught with problems principally, the misunderstanding of the mechanisms of aspartic acid racemization and protein diagenesis. Immunological data derived from archaeological proteins must be supported with sufficient controls, adequate test characterization and protein sequencing, where appropriate.

REFERENCES

*Recommended for further reading

Ambrose, S.H. (1990). Preparation and characterisation of bone and tooth collagen for isotopic analysis. *Journal of Archaeological Science*, **17**:431–451.

Ambrose, S.H. (1993). Isotopic analysis of palaeodiets: methodological and interpretive consideration. In Sandford, M.K. (ed.) *Investigations of Ancient Human Tissue. Chemical Analyses in Anthropology*, 59–130. Gordon and Breach: Langhorn, PA.

Bada, J.L. (1985). Aspartic acid racemization ages of California Paleoindian skeletons. *American Antiquity*, **50**:645–647.

Bada, J.L., Schroeder, R.A. and Carter, G.F. (1974). New evidence for the antiquity of man in North America deduced from aspartic acid racemization. *Science*, **184**:791–793.

Bada, J.L., Wang, X.S., Poinar, H.N., Pääbo, S. and Poinar, G.O. (1994). Amino acid racemization in amber-entombed insects – implications for DNA preservation. *Geochimica et Cosmochimica Acta*, **58**:3131–3135.

Bocherens, H., Fogel, M.L., Tuross, N. and Zeder, M. (1995). Trophic structure and climatic information from isotopic signatures in a Pleistocene cave fauna of southern England. *Journal of Archaeological Science*, **22**:327–340.

Bocherens, H., Tressety, A., Wiedemann, F., Giligny, F., Lafage, F., Lanchon, Y. and Marriotti, A. (1997). Diagenetic evolution of mammal bones in two French Neolithic sites. *Bulletin de la Société Géologique de France*, **168**:555–564.

Bond, M.D. and van Wart, H.E. (1984). Characterisation of the individual collagenases from *Clostridium histolyticum*. *Biochemistry*, **23**:3085–3091.

Brooks, A.S., Hare, P.E., Kokis, J.E., Miller, G.H., Ernst, R.D. and Wendorf, F. (1990). Dating Pleistocene archaeological sites by protein diagenesis in ostrich eggshell. *Science*, **248**:60–64.

Cattaneo, C., Gelsthorpe, K., Phillips, P. and Sokol, R.J. (1994). Immunological detection of albumins in ancient human cremations using ELISA and monoclonal antibodies. *Journal of Archaeological Science*, **21**:565–571.

Child, A.M. (1995a). Microbial taphonomy of archaeological bone. *Studies in Conservation*, **40**:19–30.

Child, A.M. (1995b). Towards an understanding of the microbial decomposition of archaeological bone. *Journal of Archaeological Science*, **22**:165–174.

*Child, A.M. and Pollard, A.M. (1992). A review of the applications of immunochemistry to archaeological bone. *Journal of Archaeological Science*, **19**:39–47.

Child, A.M., Gillard, R.D. and Pollard, A.M. (1993). Microbially-induced promotion of amino acid racemization in bone: isolation of the organisms and detection of their enzymes. *Journal of Archaeological Science*, **20**:159–168.

Collins, M.J., Child, A.M., van Duin, A.C.T. and Vermeer, C. (1999a). Is osteocalcin stabilized in ancient bones by adsorption to bioapatite? *Ancient Biomolecules*, **2**:223–238.

*Collins, M.J., Waite, E.R. and van Duin, A.C.T. (1999b). Predicting protein decomposition: the case of aspartic acid racemization kinetics. *Proceedings of the Royal Society of London*, **B354**:51–64.

Craig, O.E., Collins, M.J. and Stacey, R.J. (in press). The ancient potsherd: a unique environment for protein survival? In Millard, A.R. (ed.) *Proceedings of Archaeological Sciences '97*, 47–52. Archaeopress: Oxford.

Daniel, R.M., Dines, M. and Petach, H.H. (1996). The denaturation and degradation of stable enzymes at high temperatures. *Biochemical Journal*, **317**:1–11.

Dungworth, G., Vinken, N.J. and Schwartz, A.W. (1973). Racemization of aliphatic amino acids in fossil collagen of Pleistocene, Pliocene and Miocene ages. In Tissot, B. and Bienner, F. (eds) *Advances in Organic Geochemistry*, 689–700. Technip: Paris.

Dungworth, G., Schwartz, A.W. and van de Leemput, L. (1976). Composition and racemization of amino acids in mammoth collagen determined by gas and liquid chromatography. *Comparative Biochemistry and Physiology*, **53B**:472–480.

Edelman, G.M., Cunningham, B.A., Gall, W.E., Gottlieb, P.D., Rutishauser, U. and Waxdal, M.J. (1969). The covalent structure of an entire γ-G immunoglobulin molecule. *Biochemistry*, **63**:78–85.

Elster, H., Gil-Av, E. and Weiner, S. (1991). Amino acid racemization of fossil bone. *Journal of Archaeological Science*, **18**:605–617.

Evershed, R.P. and Tuross, N. (1996). Proteinaceous material from potsherds and associated soils. *Journal of Archaeological Science*, **23**:429–436.

Fernandez-LaFuente, R., Cowan, D.A. and Wood, A.N.P. (1995). Hyperstabilization of a thermophilic esterase by multipoint attachment. *Enzyme and Microbial Technology*, **17**:366–372.

Fujisawa, R. and Kuboki, Y. (1991). Preferential adsorption of dentine and bone acidic proteins on the (100) face of hydroxyapatite crystals. *Biochimica et Biophysica Acta*, **1075**:56–60.

Goodfriend, G.A. (1991). Patterns of racemization and epimerization of amino-acids in land snail shells over the course of the Holocene. *Geochimica et Cosmochimica Acta*, **55**:293–302.

Hauschka, P.V. and Carr, S.A. (1982). Calcium-dependent α-helical structure in osteocalcin. *Biochemistry*, **21**:2538–2547.

Hedges, R.E.M. and Millard, A.R. (1995). Bones and groundwater: towards the modeling of diagenetic processes. *Journal of Archaeological Sciences*, **22**:155–164.

Hedges, R.E.M., Millard, A.R. and Pike, A.W.G. (1995). Measurements and relationships of diagenetic alteration of bone from three archaeological sites. *Journal of Archaeological Science*, **22**:201–209.

Hodgins, G.W.L. and Hedges, R.E.M. (in press). On the immunological characterisation of ancient collagen. In Millard, A.R. (ed.) *Proceedings of Archaeological Sciences '97*, 61–67. Archaeopress: Oxford.

*Johnson, B.J. and Miller, G.H. (1997). Archaeological applications of amino acid racemization. *Archaeometry*, **39**:265–287.

Julg, A., Lafont, R. and Perinett, G. (1987). Mechanisms of collagen racemization in fossil bones: application to absolute dating. *Quaternary Science Reviews*, **6**:25–28.

Kimber, R.W.L. and Hare, P.E. (1992). Wide range of racemization of amino-acids in peptides from human fossil bone and its implications for amino acid racemization dating. *Geochimica et Cosmochimica Acta*, **56**:739–743.

Krane, S. (1970). Degradation of collagen in connective tissue disease. Rheumatoid arthritis. In Burleigh, P.M.C. and Poole, A.R. (eds) *Dynamics of Connective Tissue Macromolecules*, 309–326. North Holland Publishing Company: Amsterdam.

Krokosynska, I. and Otlewski, J. (1996). Thermodynamic stability effects of single peptide bond hydrolysis of protein inhibitors of serine proteinases. *Journal of Molecular Biology*, **256**:793–802.

Leach, I.D. and Mauldin, R.P. (1995). Additional comments on blood residue analysis in archaeology. *Antiquity*, **69**:1020–1022.

Loy, T.H. and Hardy, B.G. (1992). Blood residue analysis of 90 000 year old stone tools from Tabun Cave, Israel. *Antiquity*, **66**:24–35.

Marshall, E. (1990). Racemization dating: great expectations. *Science*, **247**:799.

Mayer, L.M. (1994). Surface area control of organic carbon accumulation in continental shelf sediments. *Geochimica et Cosmochimica Acta*, **58**:1271–1284.

Newman, M.E., Yohe, R.M. II, Kooyman, B. and Ceri, H. (1997). 'Blood' from stones? Probably: a response to Fiedel. *Journal of Archaeological Science*, **24**:1023–1027.

Nielsen-Marsh, C. and Hedges, R.E.M. (1999). Porosity and the use of mercury intrusion porosimetry in bone diagenesis studies. *Archaeometry*, **41**:165–174.

Nielsen-Marsh, C.M., Gernaey, A.M., Turner-Walker, G., Hedges, R.E.M., Pike, A.G. and Collins, M.J. (2000).

Chemical diagenesis of the protein and mineral fractions of bone. In Cox, M. and Mays, S. (eds) *Human Osteology in Archaeology and Forensic Science*, 439–454. Greenwich Medical Media: London.

Ortner, D.J., von Endt, D.W. and Robinson, M.S. (1972). The effect of temperature on protein decay in bone: its significance in nitrogen dating of archaeological specimens. *American Antiquity*, **37**:514–520.

Pike, A.W.G., Nielsen-Marsh, C. and Hedges, R.E.M. (in press). Modeling bone dissolution and hydrology. In Millard, A.R. (ed.) *Proceedings of Archaeological Sciences '97*, 127–132. Archaeopress: Oxford.

Poinar, H.N., Höss, M., Bada, J. and Pääbo, S. (1996). Amino acid racemization and the preservation of ancient DNA. *Science*, **272**:864–866.

Pollard, A.M. and Heron, C. (1996). *Archaeological Chemistry*. Royal Society of Chemistry: Cambridge.

Prigodich, R.V. and Vesely, M.R. (1997). Characterisation of the complex between bovine osteocalcin and Type I collagen. *Archives of Biochemistry and Biophysics*, **345**:339–341.

Schaedler, J.M. (1992). Studies of collagen in bone and dentin matrix of a Columbian mammoth (late Pleistocene) of central Utah. *Matrix*, **12**:297–307.

Smith, P.R. and Wilson, M.T. (1992). Blood residues on ancient tool surfaces: a cautionary note. *Journal of Archaeological Science*, **19**:237–241.

Tuross, N., Barnes, I. and Potts, R. (1996). Protein identification of blood residues on experimental stone tools. *Journal of Archaeological Science*, **23**:289–296.

van Duin, A.C.T. and Collins, M.J. (1998). The effects of conformational constraints on aspartic acid racemization. *Organic Geochemistry*, **29**: 1227–1232.

van Klinken, G.J. and Hedges, R.E.M. (1998). Chemistry strategies for organic C-14 samples. *Radiocarbon*, **40**:51–56.

Weiner, S., Goldberg, P., and Bar-Yosef, O. (1997). Mineral assemblages in Kebara and Hayonim caves, Israel; a framework for understanding bone and ash preservation. *Abstracts of Papers of the American Chemical Society*, **213**(1), 13-Geoc.

Wellsbury, P., Herbert, R.A. and Parkes, R.J .(1996). Bacterial activity and production in near-surface estuarine and freshwater sediments. *FEMS Microbiological Ecology*, **19**:203–214.

Weser, U., Kaup, Y., Etspuler, H., Kenward, N. and Hedges, R.E.M. (1996). Biochemically and immunologically active alkaline phosphatase in archaeologically important bone samples. *Journal of Archaeological Science*, **23**:723–730.

28

Lipids in Archaeology

R.P. EVERSHED, S.N. DUDD, M.J. LOCKHEART and S. JIM

School of Chemistry, University of Bristol.

Lipids are the animal fats, plant oils, waxes, resins, etc., of the natural world, occurring ubiquitously in plants and animals, now recognized as being preserved under favourable conditions in association with a range of different classes of finds at archaeological sites (Evershed 1993a). The use of lipids as a source of archaeological information rests on molecular analyses aimed at determining their structures and distributions. These properties are then compared systematically with those of specific fauna or flora to determine the identities of natural commodities exploited in the past. This has given rise to the concept of *archaeological biomarker compounds* (Evershed 1993a). The possibility also exists for relating archaeological lipids to specific sources or processes through compound-specific isotope information based on the known biochemistries of extant organisms (Evershed *et al.* 1999). As in any investigations based on ancient biomolecules reliable interpretations require an understanding of the mechanisms underlying possible changes in their structures and distributions arising through either human activity or burial. The relatively high resistance of many lipids to chemical and/or microbiological degradation means that they are more likely to survive in a relatively unchanged state than other classes of biomolecules, e.g. DNA, proteins, carbohydrates, etc. (Eglinton and Logan 1991).

Lipids have been investigated archaeologically as components of:

(i) organic residues in archaeological pottery,
(ii) organic matter in soils and sediments,
(iii) bones and teeth from humans and domesticated animals,
(iv) plant remains, and
(v) amorphous deposits such as resins, tars, pitches, bitumens, etc.

ANALYTICAL TECHNIQUES AND APPROACHES

A typical protocol is summarized in Figure 28.1. Samples are cleaned and crushed, then dissolved in, or extracted with, organic solvent; a mixture of chloroform and methanol is commonly used. The resulting extract, which may be separated further into different lipid classes, is then derivatized, either to improve gas chromatographic properties, or to provide access to specific structure information by means of mass spectrometry. Gas chromatography (GC) is the primary technique used to study lipids from all types of environmental and biological materials. GC provides a very powerful means of separating the complex mixtures

Handbook of Archaeological Sciences. Edited by D.R. Brothwell and A.M. Pollard.

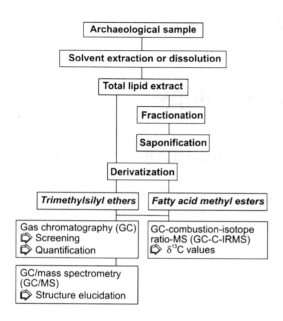

```
┌─────────────────────────────────┐
│      Archaeological sample      │
└─────────────────────────────────┘
┌─────────────────────────────────┐
│  Solvent extraction or dissolution  │
└─────────────────────────────────┘
┌─────────────────────────────────┐
│       Total lipid extract       │
└─────────────────────────────────┘
        ┌──────────────────┐
        │   Fractionation  │
        └──────────────────┘
        ┌──────────────────┐
        │   Saponification │
        └──────────────────┘
    ┌──────────────────┐
    │   Derivatization │
    └──────────────────┘
┌──────────────────────┐  ┌──────────────────────┐
│ Trimethylsilyl ethers│  │ Fatty acid methyl esters│
└──────────────────────┘  └──────────────────────┘
┌──────────────────────┐  ┌──────────────────────┐
│ Gas chromatography(GC)│  │ GC-combustion-isotope │
│ ⇨ Screening          │  │ ratio-MS (GC-C-IRMS)  │
│ ⇨ Quantification     │  │ ⇨ δ¹³C values         │
└──────────────────────┘  └──────────────────────┘
┌──────────────────────┐
│ GC/mass spectrometry │
│ (GC/MS)              │
│ ⇨ Structure elucidation│
└──────────────────────┘
```

Figure 28.1 Typical analytical protocol used in the investigation of lipids in archaeological finds.

of lipids commonly encountered in archaeological materials (Evershed *et al.* 1990). GC separates individual compounds largely according to their different boiling points. Quantitative estimates are obtained from GC analyses by comparing the areas of the GC peaks with those of appropriate internal standard(s) added at the extraction stage of the protocol (Charters *et al.* 1993a, 1997). GC in combination with mass spectrometry (GC/MS) provides structure information that is unobtainable by GC alone, and can also be used as a very sensitive detection technique in trace analysis work (Evershed 2000); GC/MS is vital to biomarker investigations of archaeological materials.

The technique of GC-combustion-isotope ratio-MS (GC-C-IRMS) allows the stable carbon isotope compositions (the ratio of $^{13}C/^{12}C$), expressed as $\delta^{13}C$ values, of biomarkers to be determined at high precision on only 50 to 100 ng of individual compounds (Evershed *et al.* 1994). The GC-C-IRMS instrument comprises a conventional GC linked to an IRMS through a combustion interface, comprising CuO heated to 850°C. As compounds are separated by GC they flow into the combustion interface where they are oxidized to CO_2. The CO_2 is fed into the IRMS and its isotopic composition is measured. The more negative the values obtained the smaller the proportion of ^{14}C in the original compound. Different plant and animal groups, and different classes of biomolecule, exhibit

different $\delta^{13}C$ values, thereby providing the basis for classifying the origins of lipid residues from archaeological finds (Evershed *et al.* 1999).

A recent development has been the use of automated preparative GC with wide-bore capillary columns to isolate individual lipids in high purity and in sufficient amounts (*c.* 500 μg) for radiocarbon analysis by accelerator mass spectrometry (AMS; Stott *et al.* in prep.). This approach has been rigorously tested for lipids derived from archaeological pottery of widely varying age (Medieval to early Neolithic) and shown to yield valid radiocarbon dates with close to the normal precision of AMS. The advantage of using the compound-specific dating approach is that the ^{14}C dates can be directly linked to the plant or animal products from which they derive.

LIPIDS IN ARCHAEOLOGICAL POTTERY

Recent work has shown that unglazed ceramic vessels absorb substantial quantities of lipids from the commodities processed or stored in them during their use (Evershed *et al.* 1992, Heron and Evershed 1993). The fired clay appears to function as a 'molecular sieve' or 'trap' preserving lipids during burial over many millennia. Charred organic deposits, occasionally visible on the surfaces of vessels, may also preserve lipids, but such residues occur with much lower frequency than absorbed residues. Recent work has shown that the chemical analysis of both surface and absorbed residues can provide valuable information concerning the original uses of ancient pottery vessels. The earliest studies of organic residues associated with archaeological ceramics involved the solvent extraction of lipid components, followed by GC analysis to identify the fatty acid components present (e.g., Condamin *et al.* 1976, Patrick *et al.* 1985, Rottländer 1990). Attempts to define the origin of the lipids were based on comparisons between the relative proportions of the fatty acids present in the extracts and those of modern reference fats. Indications are now that this simple approach must be used with caution since fatty acid ratios almost always vary during burial, particularly over prolonged periods (Dudd *et al.* 1998, Dudd and Evershed 1998). Significant advances have been made in the analysis and interpretation of lipid residues, largely by the adoption of high temperature-gas chromatography (HT-GC) and HT-GC/mass spectrometry (HT-GC/MS) which allow a very broad range of lipid classes to be separated within a single analytical run thereby revealing a greater range of lipid residues

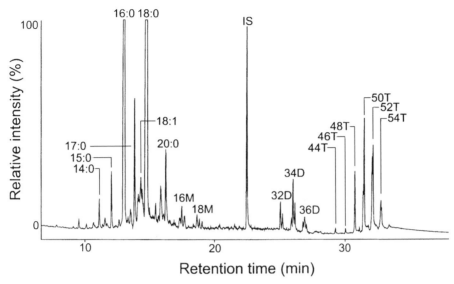

Figure 28.2   HT-GC profile of the trimethysilylated total lipid extract from a Late Neolithic Grooved Ware vessel recovered from excavations in the Welsh Borderlands. The extract contains intact triacylglycerols in the C_{44} to C_{54} acyl carbon number range, C_{32} to C_{36} diacylglycerols, C_{16} and C_{18} monacylglycerols and C_{14} to C_{20} free fatty acids. $C_{18:1}$ is present at low abundance.

than is possible based on fatty acid analyses alone (Figure 28.2). Compound-specific stable isotope analyses ($\delta^{13}C$ values) are proving increasingly valuable in elucidating the origins of lipid residues in archaeological pottery (see below).

Plant epicuticular waxes

One of the early successes of HT-GC and HT-GC/MS was the identification of epicuticular leaf waxes of higher plants. These are composed of various long-chain alkyl compounds in mixtures that have chemotaxonomic value. Moreover, such compounds are especially resistant to degradation compared with other compound classes. One of the most conclusive identifications of a lipid residue in archaeological vessels was made during the investigation of a large number of domestic cooking vessels recovered from the site of the Late Saxon/Medieval settlement of West Cotton (Evershed *et al.* 1991). The extracts yielded a distribution of lipids that comprised three major components including *n*-nonacosane, nonacosan-15-one and nonacosan-15-ol in proportions exactly analogous to those of the epicuticular leaf wax of *Brassica oleracea* (cabbage). Laboratory experiments using replica cooking jars enabled the distribution to be reproduced almost exactly, confirming that the mixture had arisen through the use of the vessels in processing leafy vege-

tables (Charters *et al.* 1997). Supporting data has been obtained from compound-specific stable carbon isotope measurements performed using GC-C-IRMS (Evershed *et al.* 1994) and comparisons made between modern wild type *Brassica* and the archaeological pottery extracts. The $\delta^{13}C$ values for the C_{29} *n*-alkane from two different vessels (−34.8 and −33.1‰) are typical for those of higher plant leaf waxes obtained for the contemporary wild type *Brassica* (−35.8 ± 0.1‰). Whilst these values are in keeping with those for contemporary C_3 plants (Evershed *et al.* 1999), the results served to confirm that the lipid extracts of ancient potsherds contained sufficient lipid to allow high precision $\delta^{13}C$ values to be obtained on individual lipids. This identification provided one of the first examples of the way in which lipids preserved in archaeological ceramics can provide archaeological information that is difficult if not impossible to obtain by other means; namely direct evidence for the consumption of leafy vegetables. Interestingly, we have yet to identify plant leaf waxes of this type in any of the pre-Iron Age pottery we have so far examined, despite many hundreds of vessels having been analysed.

Beeswax

Beeswax is a natural wax of special significance in archaeology (see Chapter 35). The presence of beeswax is readily established by HT-GC and HT-GC/MS analysis which enable the separation of a range of wax esters, long-chain alcohols and *n*-alkanes. Although compounds of this type occur widely as components of plant epicuticular waxes and insect waxes, beeswax can usually be readily identified on the basis of the distribution of *n*-alkanes (C_{23} to C_{33}) and long-chain palmitic acid wax esters (C_{40} to C_{52}). Although beeswax can be recovered from archaeological pottery, and other locations at archaeological sites, in a remarkably well-preserved state, it has recently become apparent that in some instances the composition can be altered such that it is less easily recognized. For example, an investigation of lipid extracts of ceramic vessels used as lamps during the Neopalatial period at the settlement of Mochlos on the north coast of east Crete revealed the presence of beeswax residues in such a highly degraded state (a loss of the shorter chain components) that precluded confident identification via simple distributional analysis (Evershed *et al.* 1997a). The distributions were sufficiently different to suggest another source, possibly a plant wax. As a result the identifications necessitated the use of GC-C-IRMS to determine the $\delta^{13}C$ values of individual components of the lipid extracts. This combination of molecular and isotopic analysis enabled the unambiguous identification of beeswax as the fuel originally burnt in the lamps, a significant finding in view of the perceived wisdom that olive oil was the fuel used in lamps in the Aegean.

Animal adipose fats

Animal fats are the most common class of lipids seen in archaeological pottery. Figure 28.2 shows a typical degraded animal fat distribution that we have observed more commonly than any other organic residue. Laboratory degradation experiments confirmed that this distribution arises through the stepwise hydrolytic degradation shown in Figure 28.3. The presence of animal fats with such a high frequency in pottery assemblages relates to a combination of the large amount of fat derived from the processing of animal products compared with yields of lipids from other commodities, and the high saturated fatty acid content, which increases the likelihood for their survival during burial.

Whilst the recognition of animal fats through the detection of high abundances of $C_{16:0}$ and $C_{18:0}$ fatty acids is straightforward, determination of their specific origin has been the subject of substantial recent research. The molecular characteristics that can be used to differentiate degraded animal fats include:

(i) distributions of fatty acids, including branched-chain and odd carbon-number components,
(ii) compositions of monounsaturated fatty acids,
(iii) stable carbon isotope ratios ($\delta^{13}C$ values) of the saturated $C_{16:0}$ and $C_{18:0}$, and
(iv) triacylglycerol distributions.

Consideration of these properties revealed differences in the origins of fats derived from Medieval lamps and 'dripping' dishes (Evershed *et al.* 1997b, Mottram *et al.* 1999). The distributional data showed the two vessel types to be clearly separable on the basis of *n*-alkanoic acid distributions, with the lamps containing more abundant $C_{18:0}$ than $C_{16:0}$, while the 'dripping dishes' showed a higher abundance of the $C_{16:0}$. Consistent with a ruminant source, the lamp extracts contained a significant abundance of branched-chain and odd carbon numbered, straight-chain components, specifically $C_{15:0}$, $C_{17:0}$ and $C_{19:0}$. In addition, GC-MS analysis of the dimethyl disulfide derivatives of the monounsaturated acids in the extracts of the lamp lipid residues revealed a complex mixture of positional isomers of octadecenoic acid. Such mixtures of isomers appear in the fats of ruminant animals, such as sheep and cattle, as a result of biohydrogenation of unsaturated dietary fats in the rumen (Enser 1991). In marked contrast, only a single isomer, Z-9-octadecenoic acid, was detected in the extracts from the 'dripping' dishes, which is characteristic of the fats of monogastric animals, such as pigs. The high content of saturated *n*-alkanoic acids, the presence of a mixture of positional isomers of monounsaturated alkenoic acids, and branched-chain components, clearly excludes vegetable oils as the potential source(s) of lipid in the ancient lamps and suggests an origin in ruminant animals.

The pronounced differences in the $\delta^{13}C$ values of the individual fatty acids obtained by GC-C-IRMS are entirely consistent with the differences detected in the structures and distributions of the alkanoic and alkenoic acids in the archaeological vessels and modern reference fats. In the lamps the $C_{16:0}$ was enriched in ^{13}C relative to $C_{18:0}$, whereas in the 'dripping dishes' the situation was reversed (Evershed *et al.* 1997b, 1999, Mottram *et al.* 1999). Significantly, the $\delta^{13}C$ values correlated with those of the fats of contemporary animals considered to be the major domesticates in the Medieval period in the UK. These preliminary findings suggested that the lipids preserved in the 'dripping

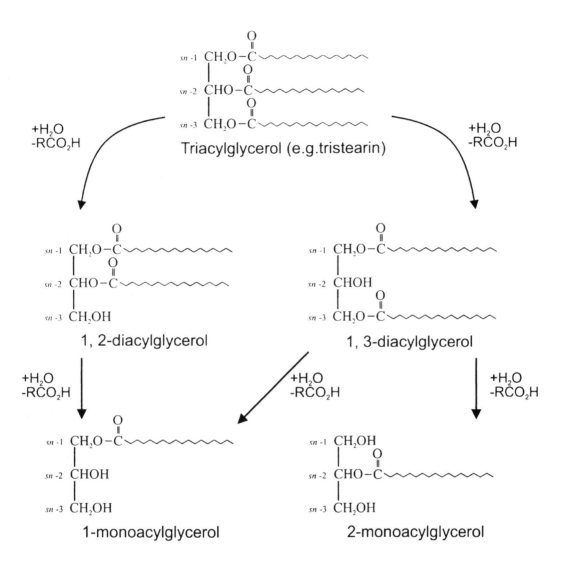

Hydrolysis products

Figure 28.3 Scheme showing the hydrolytic degradation pathway for triacylglycerols through to free fatty acids, that can occur either through microbial or chemical action during both vessel use and burial.

dishes' derived from monogastric animals, such as pigs, while those from the lamps derived from ruminant animals such as sheep and cattle (Evershed *et al.* 1997b, Mottram *et al.* 1999). In the case of the lamps this represents the residue of fuel burned, while its presence in 'dripping dishes' is consistent with their putative use as receptacles for fat collection from carcasses during spit-roasting. The robustness of the $\delta^{13}C$ values of the individual fatty acids has been confirmed through laboratory degradation experiments (Evershed *et al.* 1999). There was essentially no detectable change in animal fats even when >90 per cent had been degraded by micro-organisms.

This approach has recently been applied to the classification of fats in larger assemblages of domestic pottery from archaeological sites. Figure 28.4 is a plot of the stable isotope values of the major saturated fatty acids ($C_{16:0}$ and $C_{18:0}$) in 30 vessels from the Late Saxon/early Medieval site of West Cotton, Northamptonshire, UK, together with the values for the corresponding reference fats from present day farm animals reared on known diets, i.e., similar pastures from the same farm for all the ruminant animals and cereals for the pigs. The data show that both ruminant and non-ruminant fats are present in the archaeological vessels with the mixing of fats being indicated by the points following the mixing line drawn between the mean values for the ruminant and pig reference fats. Distinctions made on the basis of stable carbon isotope data are supported by differences in the distributions of intact triacylglycerols in the extracts (Figures 28.2 and 28.4). The application of these techniques to analyses of pottery from prehistoric periods is beginning to reveal important biases, possibly culturally determined, in the exploitation of different animals (Evershed *et al.* 1997b, Dudd and Evershed 1998, Mottram *et al.* 1999).

Dairy fats

Milk is a valuable resource due to its high protein, nutrient and fat content, and we assume that early humans realized its potential as a renewable resource. It was therefore surprising that milk fat residues had not been recognized with higher frequency in association with ceramic vessels since, just as with the adipose fats, the processing of milk, e.g., pasteurizing, or cooking involving milk or butter, would result in the absorption of appreciable quantities of fat into the walls of unglazed pottery vessels. Significantly, milk fats differ from adipose fats in their fatty acid composition

through the presence of short chain saturated fatty acids in the C_4 to C_{14} carbon number range (McDonald *et al.* 1988:210). Consideration of the chemistry of dairy fats and laboratory degradation studies has shown that dairy fats present in vessels at the time of discard and burial become altered, through decay, in such a way as to make them indistinguishable from adipose fats. The short-chain fatty acyl moieties are more susceptible to hydrolysis than their long-chain counterparts (Laakso 1996). Furthermore, once released from triacylglycerols by hydrolysis the short-chain fatty acids are appreciably more water soluble and volatile than their long-chain counterparts. These two factors explain why milk fat residues cannot be identified by simple comparisons with the fatty acid composition of fresh milk fat.

Stable carbon isotope analyses of the abundant $C_{16:0}$ and $C_{18:0}$ fatty acids provide a convenient means of distinguishing milk fats from adipose fats preserved in pottery vessels. Figure 28.4 shows that a significant number of the vessels studied from the West Cotton assemblages contain fatty acids in which the $C_{18:0}$ fatty acid is significantly depleted in ^{13}C compared with the reference adipose fats. Consideration of the biochemistry and physiology of milk production in ruminant animals and the subsequent analysis of reference milk fats obtained from C_3 pasture-reared sheep and cattle strongly indicates that the origin of these ^{13}C depleted $C_{18:0}$ fatty acids was milk (Dudd and Evershed 1998). The ability to distinguish between milk and adipose fats using the $\delta^{13}C$ values of their $C_{16:0}$ and $C_{18:0}$ fatty acids represents an application of GC-C-IRMS to resolve a long-standing question in archaeology which currently appears intractable by other means, thereby providing a reliable means of recognizing dairying as a component of prehistoric economies.

Plant oils and lipid oxidation products

In many parts of the world plant oils played an important role in human nutrition and culture. In spite of this, surprisingly few reports of the identification of archaeological plant oils exist. The early work of Condamin *et al.* (1976) is illustrative of the problem that exists in making unambiguous identifications. The most abundant fatty acids in the vast majority of plant oils are mono-, di- and triunsaturated and therefore highly susceptible to rapid oxidative degradation. After prolonged burial many vegetable oil residues are dominated by palmitic acid and smaller amounts of stearic acid making the distribution rather undiagnos-

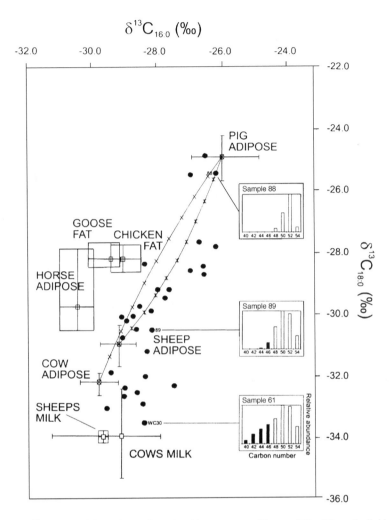

Figure 28.4 Plot of the $\delta^{13}C$ values of the major *n*-alkanoic acid components ($C_{16:0}$ and $C_{18:0}$) from the lipid extracts of potsherds from the Late Saxon/early Medieval site of West Cotton, Northamptonshire, UK. The ringed fields encompass the ranges for present-day reference animal fats with the range bars crossing at the arithmetic mean. A significant number of the archaeological fats cluster near to the reference ruminant adipose and milk fats (bovine and ovine) with fewer plotting in the region of the porcine and chicken adipose fats. The mixing curves have been calculated (Woodbury *et al.* 1995) to illustrate the $\delta^{13}C$ values which would result from the mixing of a theoretical average ruminant adipose fat (based on the mean fatty acid composition of ovine and bovine adipose fats) with average porcine fat. The $\delta^{13}C$ values for our modern reference materials are corrected for the fossil fuel effect, i.e., in accordance with Friedli *et al.* (1986), modern values are increased by 1.2‰ to account for the lighter carbon introduced through fossil fuel burning depleting the $\delta^{13}C$ value of the CO_2 of the present day atmosphere.

tic. Recent work on lipid extracts of pottery from the Near East have shown, however, that some vegetable oils do contain residues that can be unambiguously identified. For example, radish oil is characterized by an abundance of longer chain fatty acids containing up to 24 carbon atoms (both saturated and monoun-saturated components), while caster oil is dominated by ricinoleic acid (Δ^9 12-hydroxy octadecenoic acid; Bland, Horton and Evershed unpublished data). Palm kernel oil characterized by a high abundance of C_{12} and C_{14} saturated fatty acids has also been detected in pottery (Copley and Evershed unpublished data).

Both the unsaturated fatty acid components of both plant oils and animal fats are susceptible to oxidation during vessel use and burial. Interestingly, however, oxidation products, such as hydroxy acids and diacids are rarely if ever seen in lipid extracts of archaeological pottery. This is presumed to be the result of their loss through groundwater leaching. We have performed base (0.5 M sodium hydroxide) treatments of pottery following the conventional solvent extraction step. GC and GC/MS analyses have revealed short-chain dicarboxylic acids, β-hydroxy acids and longer-chain hydroxy and dihydroxy acids (Regert *et al.* 1998). Since these components were only observed following base treatment they are presumed to be covalently bound via ester linkages into the insoluble residues. Such compounds are seen in the free lipid fraction of lipid extracts of potsherds from an exceptionally arid site which concurs with the assertion that they are indeed lost in waterlogged deposits.

Long-chain ketones were discussed above in relation to their occurrence as components of plant epicuticular waxes (Evershed *et al.* 1991, Charters *et al.* 1997). However, some caution is required in using these compounds as biomarkers of such waxes since it has recently been recognized that such long-chain ketones can arise in archaeological pottery as a result of the heating of fatty acids or other fatty acyl lipids to temperatures >300°C (Raven *et al.* 1997) via a free radical-induced dehydration and decarboxylation reaction.

LIPIDS IN ARCHAEOLOGICAL SOILS AND SEDIMENTS

The organic fraction of soil represents the net sum of a complex series of biological, chemical and physical processes which may or may not have been influenced by anthropogenic activities. Whilst the biomolecular composition of morphologically extant archaeological artifacts (e.g., bones, potsherds, etc.) will, by virtue of the objects physical survival, be somewhat constrained, that of a typical soil is diverse. Many lipids found in soils may be ascribed multiple sources making the choice of compounds used to answer clearly defined archaeological questions paramount. Compounds which exhibit a high source specificity potentially may be used as biomarkers for particular organic inputs to the soil environment and, in undisturbed archaeological soils, provide insights into various anthropogenic activities. Changes in soil vegetation cover on a short time scale are often the result of changing agricultural practices. Such changes can affect the soil lipid profile as the composition of source lipids is altered with differing floral growth, an effect which can be detected via

lipid analysis (van Bergen *et al.* 1997a). However, the biomolecular detection of ancient faecal inputs to the soil environment has recently generated most interest (e.g., Bull *et al.* 1999a). The lipid biomarker information obtained from such studies may answer questions ranging from the location of cess-pits, stables and field systems to the faecal origin of manures used to fertilize fields in antiquity. Two chemically distinct, but related, classes of biomarker have been used to detect faecal inputs to archaeological soils with increasing success: 5β-stanols and bile acids.

5β-stanols

This is a class of compounds whose primary origin lies in the microbial reduction of cholesterol and Δ^5-unsaturated phytosterols such as campesterol, stigmasterol and sitosterol, in the guts of higher animals (Figure 28.5). Since, in the natural environment, cholesterol and its congeners if reduced are more likely to form 5α-stanols the occurrence of significant amounts of 5β-stanols, relative to levels in control soils, may be taken as an indicator of faecal deposition. Knights *et al.* (1983) used the presence of coprostanol as an indicator of faecal material in a Roman cess-pit ditch. More recent work has established a set of criteria, based on the specific molecular signature, to assess the presence of faecal matter in soil, independent of the simple occurrence of coprostanol (Bethell *et al.* 1994, Evershed *et al.* 1997c). Analysis of the proportions of 5β-stanols, relative to each other, enables a differentiation to be made between human/porcine and ruminant faecal sources. The greater proportion of vegetable matter in the diet of ruminant animals gives rise to a higher relative abundance of 5β-stanols derived from the phytosterols. This particular technique has been used with success in studies of archaeological midden heaps located on the Isle of Sanday, Orkney where the faecal source was ascribed a human origin (Simpson *et al.* 1998, Bull *et al.* 1999b). Similarly, the faecal origin of manure in a Minoan agricultural terrace on the isle of Pseira, Crete has also been identified as human. At c. 4500 BP this also represents the oldest positive biomolecular detection of faecal material in soil to date (Bull *et al.* 1999c).

Bile acids

These are also products of mammalian gut flora and consequently they represent an additional source of biomolecular information which often complements

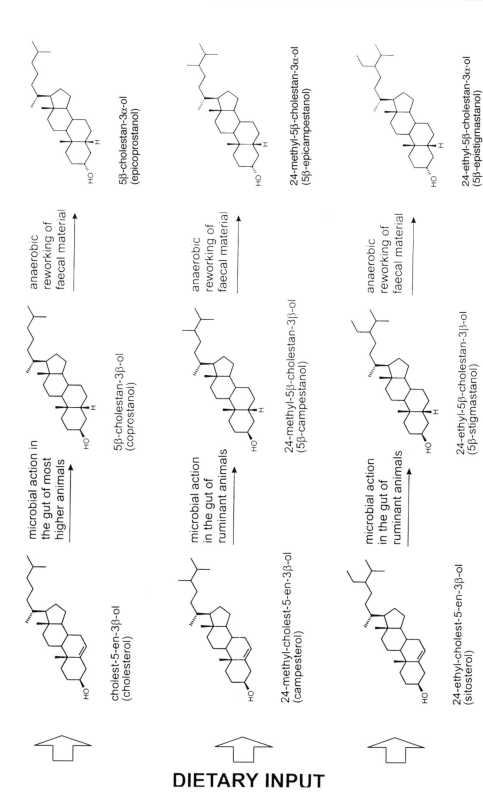

Figure 28.5   Structures, origins and pathways of formation of 5β-stanols.

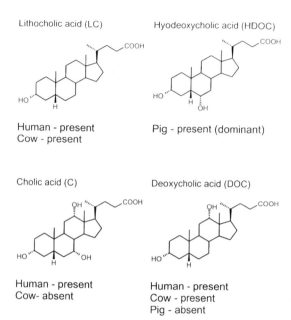

Lithocholic acid (LC)

Human - present
Cow - present

Hyodeoxycholic acid (HDOC)

Pig - present (dominant)

Cholic acid (C)

Human - present
Cow- absent

Deoxycholic acid (DOC)

Human - present
Cow - present
Pig - absent

Figure 28.6 Structures and origins of bile acids.

the sterol/stanol composition of a soil. These compounds (Figure 28.6) provide a more specific means of distinguishing between different faecal inputs as several of the bile acids are only produced in quantity by a particular mammalian species. For instance, hyodeoxycholic acid (HDOC) is a product of the porcine gut. Deoxycholic (DOC), lithocholic (LC) and cholic acids (C) are present in human faecal material, however, while bovine manure has also been shown to contain abundant DOC and LC acids, cholic acid is absent (Simpson et al. 1999).

The concentrations of bile acids may in certain undisturbed archaeological settings provide an indication of the range and intensity of manuring. Analysis of Medieval agricultural soils from Marwick in Orkney have demonstrated an inverse relationship between bile acid concentration and distance from a farmstead where it is presumed that manure was stored prior to application (Simpson et al. 1999). An unexpected finding was the detection of hyodeoxycholic acid, reflecting pig manure deposition, which indicated that historical documentation forms only a partial record of manuring practices.

Aliphatic (straight chain) compounds

n-Alkyl lipids also show some utility in determining whether agricultural activity and/or settlement has

taken place on a particular soil. Simpson and co-workers have ascribed fluctuations in the concentration of even chain length n-alkanols (C_{22} to C_{34}) down a Bronze Age Orcadian mound at Tofts Ness, Sanday, to the incorporation of peaty turves by farmers in order to improve the soil condition. Furthermore, distributions of n-alkanes (C_{27} to C_{33}) and wax esters (C_{36} to C_{60}) in the same soil profile resembled those of the grassy roofing turves which would have been added to the land. A decrease in concentration of n-alkyl lipids with increasing distance from the farmstead was noted in soils surrounding a Medieval farmstead at West Howe, Marwick, Orkney, most likely due to a reduced input of plant-derived manure (Simpson et al. 1999).

LIPIDS IN HUMAN REMAINS

Studies have shown that lipids are preserved in inhumations (Kuksis et al. 1978, Gülaçar et al. 1990, Evershed 1992, Evershed et al. 1995). Work carried out on bog bodies (Evershed and Connolly 1994) and on ancient bones of humans and animals (Evershed et al. 1995) demonstrated that lipids including cholesterol are preserved in appreciable quantities (2–50 µg g^{-1} dry weight of bone). Figure 28.7a shows typical partial HT-GC profiles of the total lipid extracts recovered from archaeological bone of varying age and geographical location. Cholesterol was found to be the most abundant constituent of these bone extracts with cholesteryl fatty acyl esters preserved in smaller amounts. The cholesterol preserved in archaeological bone can be derived from any of the following:

(i)   the remnants of the original blood-borne lipid (in the case of vascular bones),
(ii) the fat component of bone marrow that would be present at the time of death, and
(iii) the cellular lipids present in bone cells (Stott et al. 1997, 1999).

Analyses have been performed to assess whether the $\delta^{13}C$ value of cholesterol determined by GC-C-IRMS could be used in conjunction with existing collagen and apatite stable isotope analyses as a new source of palaeodietary information. These comprised:

(i) the testing of the homogeneity of the $\delta^{13}C$ value preserved within skeletal members and around the skeleton of an ancient individual,
(ii) the analyses of animals raised on isotopically controlled diets in order to gain an understanding

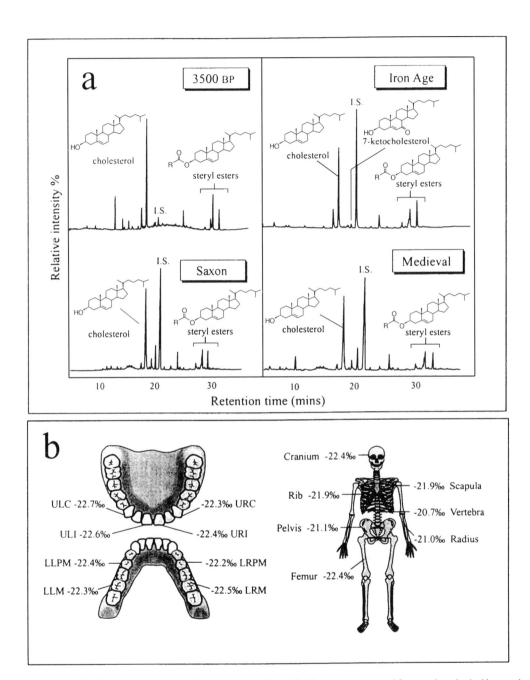

Figure 28.7   (a) Partial high-temperature gas chromatograms of total lipid extracts recovered from archaeological human bones from a wide range of ages and geographical contexts: North America (Archaic); Yarnton Refectory Farm, Oxfordshire (Iron Age); St. Peters Church, Barton-on-Humber, Lincolnshire (Saxon-Medieval); Abingdon Vineyard, Oxfordshire (Medieval) and (b) cholesterol $\delta^{13}C$ values measured around the skeleton and from eight teeth around the jaw of an individual excavated from St Peters Church, Barton-on-Humber, Lincolnshire, UK. Key: ULC = upper left canine, ULI = upper left incisor, LLPM = lower left pre-molar, LLM = lower left molar, URC = upper right canine, URI = upper right incisor, LRPM = lower right pre-molar, LRM = lower right molar.

of the isotopic relationship between diet and bone cholesterol $\delta^{13}C$ values, and

(iii)   the measurement of cholesterol $\delta^{13}C$ values from archaeological populations where the diet had also been assessed through collagen and/or apatite analyses.

Homogeneity of cholesterol $\delta^{13}C$ values

Figure 28.7b shows the bone and teeth cholesterol $\delta^{13}C$ values measured from an individual excavated from St Peter's Church, Barton-on-Humber, Lincolnshire, UK (Saxon-Medieval). Multiple sampling along a femur ($n = 5$; results not shown) and among the teeth ($n = 8$) in the jaw showed that the carbon isotopic composition varied only by 0.7‰, from −22.0‰ to −22.7‰ in both cases. A larger variation of 1.3‰ was observed between different skeletal members ($n = 8$) of the same individual, with $\delta^{13}C$ values ranging from −21.1‰ (pelvis) to −22.4‰ (femur). This demonstrated that the $\delta^{13}C$ of bone cholesterol is essentially homogeneous within one skeletal type and highly consistent between different skeletal members (Stott and Evershed 1996). In practice when studying an archaeological population the same skeletal member is sampled to minimize intra-skeletal variations.

Isotopic relationship between diet and bone cholesterol

Accurate palaeodietary reconstruction requires knowledge of the foodstuffs that were available for consumption, which can be gleaned from floral or faunal remains or from archaeological records, and an understanding of the isotopic relationship between components in the diet and in bone. Isotopically controlled animal feeding experiments have been carried out in recent years to gain more insight into the relationship between the isotopic composition of specific dietary components and bone biochemical components (Hare et al. 1991, Ambrose and Norr 1993, Tieszen and Fagre 1993). The relationship is understandably complex, and thought to be dependent on several factors, including the nutritional status of the animal, the turnover rate of the tissue and its biosynthetic pathway (Koch et al. 1994). Results from these studies have shown the ^{13}C content of apatite reflects that of the whole diet, i.e., its component proteins, carbohydrates and lipids, and that the ^{13}C content of collagen is biased towards the protein intake (see Chapter 23).

Cholesterol isotope analysis performed on the rats from the Ambrose and Norr (1993) study demonstrated that cholesterol also faithfully inherits the isotopic signal of the diet, correlating well with the whole diet $\delta^{13}C$ values. This study also showed that bone collagen, apatite and cholesterol have different turnover rates in the body (Jim et al. in press). Both bone collagen and apatite are slowly re-modelled throughout life and therefore their isotopic compositions are anticipated to be a long term average (10–25 years) of the protein and whole diet intake, respectively (Stenhouse and Baxter 1979). In contrast, cholesterol isolated from rats subjected to diet switch experiments was found to have a turnover rate of c. 300 days. This much shorter rate of turnover for cholesterol allows more subtle changes in diet to be detected, such as seasonal variation in food consumption patterns or migratory behaviour that may be masked in collagen or apatite isotope values. A further advantage that accrues from the isotopic analysis of cholesterol is that it is compound-specific. Cholesterol is a single compound and easy to characterize by gas chromatography-mass spectrometry (GC-MS). The preservation of its carbon skeleton ensures the integrity of its isotopic signal. Therefore, the effects of diagenesis and contamination by other compounds does not alter its biogenic signal. Such effects are more difficult to quantify in the analysis of collagen and apatite as they are both complex biochemical components which are difficult to characterize.

Combined use of collagen and cholesterol isotope analysis

Bone collagen and cholesterol $\delta^{13}C$ values have been measured from ancient populations and compared with rat reference data for two archaeological studies: Illinois River Valley samples spanning from Archaic to Mississippian times, and Barton-on-Humber, Lincolnshire (coastal) and Abingdon Vineyard, Oxfordshire (inland) samples. These archaeological populations were studied to test whether cholesterol $\delta^{13}C$ values can detect isotopically large (introduction of C_4 maize into a C_3 diet) and more subtle (inland versus coastal) differences in diet.

Collagen ($\delta^{13}C$ and $\delta^{15}N$) and apatite isotope analysis have been performed on the Illinois River Valley samples (Ambrose pers. comm.) providing evidence for the introduction of C_4 maize into the diet. Compound-specific $\delta^{13}C$ measurements showed that this change in diet can also be readily detected using cholesterol. Cholesterol was then used to test whether more subtle isotopic differences in diet can be detected in its $\delta^{13}C$ value. An English inland ($n = 9$, Medieval, Abingdon Vineyard, Oxfordshire) and coastal ($n = 9$, Saxon-Medieval, Barton-on-Humber, north Lincolnshire) population were studied. Collagen ($\delta^{13}C$) analysis was also performed. The two populations were indistinguishable from each other using collagen $\delta^{13}C$ values alone. However, mean cholesterol $\delta^{13}C$ values of $-22.0‰$ and $-24.3‰$ were recorded for the coastal and inland site, respectively. This relative enrichment of 2.3‰ suggests an increase in the consumption of marine foodstuffs, which is entirely consistent with the respective geographical locations of the two sites (Stott et al. 1999).

NATURAL BITUMINS, PLANT RESINS AND RELATED PRODUCTS

The identification of the nature and origins of natural bitumens, plant resins and derivatives thereof is highly dependent upon the application of lipid biomarker approaches. Several major contributions have already appeared on this subject (Mills and White 1994, Pollard and Heron 1996) such that only a selection of the most recent examples are covered here to illustrate the overall approach. Most applications in this area involve the characterization of di- and triterpenoid compounds in order to determine the nature, origin and possible means of production of resin or resin derivatives, such as wood tars and pitches. Such materials occur at archaeological sites in association with a variety of artifacts including pottery, lithics and timber where they function as glues, sealants and coating materials (Evershed et al. 1985, Robinson et al. 1987, Beck and Borromeo 1990, Beck et al. 1989, Aveling and Heron 1999, Regert et al. 1998) and more precious medicinal and ritual/funerary substances (van Bergen et al. 1997b, Evershed et al. 1997d).

Since such materials are almost without exception amorphous and homogenous, so that biomarker techniques, such as GC/MS, offer the only reliable means of identifying their origins. Although attempts have been made with the identification of such materials via infrared or nuclear magnetic resonance spectroscopies, such techniques are inherently unsuited to this type of analysis. The multiplicity of compounds typically present means that the spectra are too complex to make meaningful identifications; only GC/MS provides the molecular resolution necessary to achieve rigorous identifications.

Coniferous resin products

Such resins are characteristic of pines and spruces and characterized by the presence of diterpenoid compounds. Whilst the most abundant components of the native tree resins are the abietic and pimaric acids, they may be absent from archaeological samples since the primary products that survive appear to be heated products which comprise a range of altered structures. Although all can be readily related back to their diterpenoid precursors little or none of the native compounds may survive. Figure 28.8 shows the range of compounds detected in tars and pitches from the Mary Rose identified as 'Stockholm' tar, which would have been produced by the destructive distillation of pine wood. Although finds of pine tar are widespread few tar production sites survive from prehistory, but southern and central Europe is rich in production sites dating from the Middle Ages (Beck et al. 1999). These latter sites offer opportunities to learn about the earliest pyrotechnologies such that through careful assessment and experimental studies, production temperatures have been established for the tars based on the degree of decarboxylation and relative amounts of neutral components (Beck et al. 1997).

Coniferous resin products have been recovered as hafting materials (Larsson 1978), linings for transport amphorae (Beck et al. 1989, Beck and Borromeo 1990) and as structural members and rope from shipwrecks (Evershed et al. 1985, Robinson et al. 1987). On some occasions the finds have been very considerable indeed. For example, some 570 kg was recovered from the wreck of a Gallo-Roman trading vessel from the sea bed off the coast of Guernsey. GC/MS analyses showed the tars to be dominated by dehydroabietic acid, with smaller amounts of abietic acid and related diterpenoid acids. The low abundance of defunctionalized neutral components indicates that the 'pitch' must have been produced at relatively low temperatures, thus in composition it more closely resembled a rosin (colophany) than a tar (Stockholm tar) produced by destructive distillation (Evershed 1993b).

Triterpenoid resins and their products

Probably the most widely reported triterpenoid-based products from archaeological sites in Europe are those which derive from the bark of Betula sp. The detection of betulin and lupeol in the tars, together with various pyrolysis products, provides unambiguous evidence for the origin in birch bark. In Europe recent finds of birch bark tar date from the Mesolithic (UK; Aveling

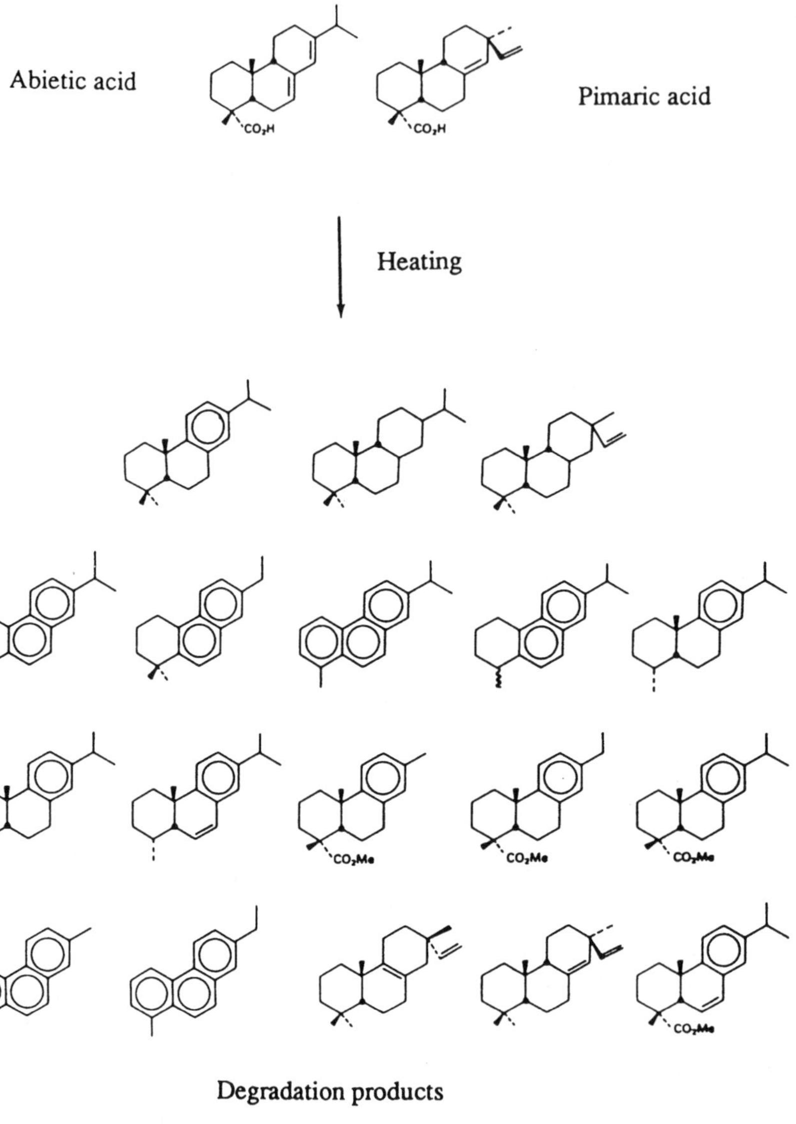

Abietic acid

Pimaric acid

Heating

Degradation products

Figure 28.8 Structure of the major diterpenoid acids comprising coniferous resins and degradation products derived through the heating of pine wood. Variations in the proportions of the carboxylated and decarboxylated forms can provide a measure of the temperatures involved in the preparation of ancient tars and pitches.

and Heron 1999) and Neolithic (France; Regert *et al.* 1999). The utility of birch bark tar was clearly still recognized in the UK in the Romano-British period where an example exists of its use as an adhesive to repair a broken vessel in antiquity (Charters *et al.* 1993b). In this instance, and in another case of a sub-

stantial deposit in an enamelled vessel, possibly a glue pot, GC/MS analyses provided clear evidence for the intentional mixing of the birch bark tar with an animal fat, presumably to provide a substance with more desirable properties (Dudd and Evershed 1999).

It is particularly convenient for the purposes of archaeological interpretations that diterpenoids and triterpenoids are never found together in the same plant. Indeed there are no reports of di- and triterpenoids being found intimately mixed together. The first report of di- and triterpenoid resins at the same site came to light during analyses of samples of amorphous material recovered during sieving of the fill from the cellar of a house at Qasr Ibrim dating to around AD 400–500. The resin fragments were characterized by GC/MS using solvent solubilization, derivatization and pyrolysis techniques (van Bergen *et al.* 1997b, Evershed *et al.* 1997d). Most significantly, the analyses provided the first identification of archaeological frankincense. The trimethylsilylated solvent soluble fraction showed the presence of triterpenoid components present in modern frankincense resin (Figure 28.9). The close similarity between the compositions of the ancient and modern frankincenses is shown through mass chromatograms which reveal virtually identical 'fingerprint' distributions. These data confirmed unambiguously that the archaeological resins were frankincense since the major components detected are the major constituents of the fresh aromatic gum resins from *Boswellia* trees.

Natural bitumens

Natural asphalts (or bitumen) deposits, oil seepage and liquid oil shows are widespread in the Middle East. The work of Connan (1999) has shown that these materials were exploited for a number of purposes by ancient civilizations of the region. Such materials as readily characterized by biomarker techniques routinely applied in petroleum exploration. As with the above

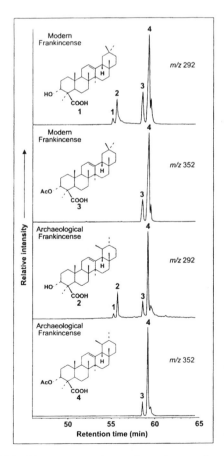
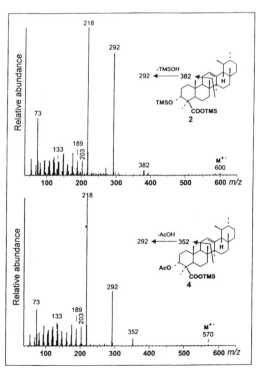

Figure 28.9 Mass spectra and mass chromatograms for modern and archaeological frankincense recovered from Qasr Ibrim, Egypt.

investigation GC, GC/MS and isotopic analyses are vital in this work. Analyses focus on specific bio-markers (particularly steranes and terpanes) in hydro-carbon fractions using mass chromatography to provide characteristic 'fingerprints' for archaeological samples which can be calibrated against well-known natural sources for bitumen in the region. Through this work it has been possible to establish the origins of bitumen from numerous archaeological sites and to document the bitumen trade routes in the Middle-East and the Arabo-Persian Gulf. Analyses of more than 700 samples during the past 10 years have shown natural bitumens to have such varied uses as: building materials, adhesive, decorations, sculpture medium, coatings on roadways, containers (e.g., baskets, earth-enware jars, storage pits), sarcophagi, boats, etc. Evidence for the early use of bitumens by Neanderthal peoples as hafting materials to fix handles on flint tools has come from coatings on implements dated to 40 000 BP (Mousterian period; Boëda *et al.* 1996).

SUMMARY

It is clear from the body of literature accumulated over the past two decades that lipids do survive at archae-ological sites in an association with a range of the most significant classes of find, namely, pottery, animal (especially human) and plant remains, soils and sediments, and as components of various amorphous bituminous or resinous deposits. The major advances in this area have come about by the application of gas chromatography coupled with mass spectrometry. Only these two techniques have the capacity for mole-cular scale resolution and compound identification vital in this field. As a result there is an increasing number of lipid 'signatures' that we can now recognize in the archaeological record and this will inevitably increase as systematic analyses are performed on artifacts from cultures and periods not previously investigated in this way. The ability to obtain compound-specific stable isotope values, up to now only $\delta^{13}C$, has greatly extended the utility of lipids as carriers of archaeologi-cal information. Lipids have been shown to have the potential to answer real archaeological questions, being particularly important in their ability to reveal the exploitation of materials and practices that are fre-quently undetectable by other more traditional archae-ological approaches.

The future of the use of lipids in archaeology is very bright, especially with the prospect of being able to extend the compound specific stable isotope approaches to additional elements, e.g., δD and $\delta^{18}O$ determinations of individual compounds are now feasible. In addition, the first compound-specific radio-carbon analyses have just been performed, by isolating individual compounds by preparative-GC, and submit-ting the trapped compounds to accelerator mass spec-trometry; this refinement of radiocarbon dating will have important applications in resolving outstanding chronological dating questions and addressing issues of indigeneity.

Further outstanding questions concerning the use of lipids are now being resolved by the use of degradation experiments, conducted either in the laboratory or in the field, to reveal the major controls on the preserva-tion/degradation of lipids in association with the most important classes of find, such as pottery. Such experi-ments are leading to a better understanding of why certain commodities, e.g., polyunsaturated plant and fish oils, are difficult to detect in the archaeological record. Experiments of this nature are complemented by analyses of ethnographic artifacts with known his-tories of use. The latter help to bridge the diagenetic time-gap between laboratory and field experiments conducted in real-time, and studies of archaeological artifacts (see Chapter 15). The exploitation of 'bound' lipids as an, as yet, relatively untapped sink of informa-tion has only just begun to be considered, with experi-mental approaches again assisting in the interpretation of results from archaeological artifacts.

REFERENCES

*Recommended for further reading

Ambrose, S.H. and Norr, L. (1993). Experimental evidence for the relationship of the carbon isotope ratios of whole diet and dietary protein to those of bone collagen and carbo-nate. In Lambert, J.B. and Grupe, G. (eds) *Prehistoric Human Bone. Archaeology at the Molecular Level*, 1–37. Springer Verlag: Berlin.

Aveling, E.M. and Heron, C. (1999). Identification of birch bark tar at the Mesolithic site of Starr Carr. *Ancient Biomolecules*, **2**:69–80.

Beck, C.W. and Borromeo, C. (1990). Ancient pine pitch: technological perspectives from a Hellenistic shipwreck. In Biers, A.R. and McGovern, P.E. (eds) *Organic Contents of Ancient Vessels: Materials Analysis and Archaeological Investigation*, 51–58. Research Papers in Science and Archaeology 7, University of Pennsylvania Museum: Philadelphia.

Beck, C.W., Smart, C.J. and Ossenkop, D.J. (1989). Residues and linings in ancient Mediterranean transport amphoras.

In Allen, R.O. (ed.) *Archaeological Chemistry IV*, 369–380, Advances in Chemistry 220, American Chemical Society: Washington DC.

Beck, C.W., Stout, E.C. and Janne, P.A. (1997). The pyrotechnology of pine tar and pitch inferred from quantitative analyses by gas chromatography/mass spectrometry and carbon-13 nuclear magnetic resonance spectroscopy. In Brzezinski, W. and Piotrowsi, W. (eds) *Proceedings of the First International Symposium on Wood Tar and Pitch*, 181–190. State Archaeological Museum: Warsaw.

Beck, C.W., Stout, E.C., Bingham, J., Lucas, J. and Purohit, V. (1999). Central European pine tar technologies. *Ancient Biomolecules*, **2**:281–293.

Bethell, P.H., Ottaway, J., Campbell, G., Goad, L.J. and Evershed, R.P. (1994). The study of molecular markers of human activity: the use of coprostanol in the soil as an indicator of human faecal material. *Journal of Archaeological Science*, **21**:619–632.

Boëda, E., Connan, J., Dessort, D., Muhesen, S., Mercier, N., Valladas, H. and Tisnerart, N. (1996). Bitumen as a hafting material on middle Palaeolithic artifacts. *Nature*, **380**:336–338.

Bull, I.D., Simpson, I.A., van Bergen, P.F. and Evershed, R.P. (1999a). Muck 'n' molecules: organic geochemical methods for detecting ancient manuring. *Antiquity*, **73**:86–96.

Bull, I.D., Simpson, I.A., Dockrill, S.J. and Evershed, R.P. (1999b). Organic geochemical evidence for the origin of ancient anthropogenic soil deposits at Tofts Ness, Sanday, Orkney. *Organic Geochemistry*, **30**:535–556.

Bull, I.D., Betancourt, P.P. and Evershed, R.P. (1999c). Chemical evidence supporting the existence of a structured agricultural manuring regime on Pseira Island, Crete during the Minoan Age. In Betancourt, P.P., Karageorghis, V., Laffineur, R. and Niemeier, W.-D. (eds) *Aegaeum 20, Annales d'Archéologie Aegéene de l'Université de Liège et UT-PASP. Meletemata: Studies in Aegean Archaeology*, 69–73. Université de Liège: Liège.

Charters, S., Evershed, R.P., Goad, L.J., Blinkhorn, P.W. and Denham, V. (1993a). Quantification and distribution of lipid in archaeological ceramics: implications for sampling potsherds for organic residue analysis. *Archaeometry*, **35**:211–223.

Charters, S., Evershed, R.P., Goad, L.J., Heron, C. and Blinkhorn, P.W. (1993b). Identification of an adhesive used to repair a Roman jar. *Archaeometry*, **35**:91–101.

Charters, S., Evershed, R.P., Quye, A., Blinkhorn, P.W. and Denham, V. (1997). Simulation experiments for determining the use of ancient pottery vessels: the behavior of epicuticular leaf wax during boiling of a leafy vegetable. *Journal of Archaeological Science*, **24**:1–7.

Condamin, J., Formenti, F., Metais, M.O., Michel, M. and Blond, P. (1976). The application of gas chromatography to the tracing of oil in ancient amphorae. *Archaeometry*, **18**:195–201.

*Connan, J. (1999). Use and trade of bitumen in antiquity and prehistory: molecular archaeology reveals secrets of past civilizations. *Philosophical Transactions of the Royal Society of London*, **B354**:33–50.

Dudd, S.N. and Evershed, R.P. (1998). Direct demonstration of milk as an element of archaeological economies. *Science*, **282**:1478–1481.

Dudd, S.N. and Evershed, R.P. (1999). Unusual triterpenoid fatty acyl ester components of archaeological birch bark tars. *Tetrahedron Letters*, **40**:359–362.

Dudd, S.N., Regert, M. and Evershed, R.P. (1998). Assessing microbial lipid contributions during laboratory degradations of fats and oils and pure triacylglycerols absorbed in ceramic potsherds. *Organic Geochemistry*, **29**:1345–1354.

Eglinton, G. and Logan, G.A. (1991). Molecular preservation. *Philosophical Transactions of the Royal Society of London*, **B333**:315–328.

Enser, M. (1991). Animal carcass fats and fish oils. In Rossel, J.B. and Pritchard, J.L.R. (eds) *Analysis of Oilseeds, Fats and Fatty Foods*, 329–394. Elsevier: London.

Evershed, R.P. (1992). Chemical composition of bog body adipocere. *Archaeometry*, **34**:253–265.

Evershed, R.P. (1993a). Biomolecular archaeology and lipids. *World Archaeology*, **25**:74–93.

Evershed, R.P. (1993b). Chemical analysis of the pitch. In Rule, M. and Monoghan, J. (eds) *A Gallo-Roman Trading Vessel from Guernsey: Excavation and Recovery of a Third Century Shipwreck*, 115–118. Monograph No. 5, Guernsey Museum: Guernsey.

*Evershed, R.P. (2000). Biomolecular analysis by organic mass spectrometry. In Ciliberto, E. and Spoto, G. (eds) *Modern Analytical Methods in Art and Archaeology*, 177–239. John Wiley: New York.

Evershed, R.P. and Connolly, R.C. (1994). Post-mortem transformations of sterols in bog body tissues. *Journal of Archaeological Science*, **21**:577–583.

Evershed, R.P., Jerman, K. and Eglinton, G. (1985). Pine wood origin for pitch from the *Mary Rose*. *Nature*, **314**:528–535.

Evershed, R.P., Heron, C. and Goad, L.J. (1990). Analysis of organic residues of archaeological origin by high temperature gas chromatography/mass spectrometry. *Analyst*, **115**:1339–1342.

Evershed, R.P., Heron, C. and Goad, L.J. (1991). Epicuticular wax components preserved in potsherds as chemical indicators of leafy vegetables in ancient diets. *Antiquity*, **65**:540–544.

*Evershed, R.P., Heron, C., Charters, S. and Goad, L.J. (1992). The survival of food residues: new methods of analysis, interpretation and application. In Pollard, A.M. (ed.) *New Developments in Archaeological Science*, 187–208. Proceedings of the British Academy 77, Oxford University Press: Oxford.

Evershed, R.P., Arnot, K.I., Collister, J., Eglinton, G. and Charters, S. (1994). Application of isotope ratio monitoring gas chromatography/mass spectrometry to the analysis of organic residues of archaeological interest. *Analyst*, **119**:909–914.

Evershed, R.P., Turner-Walker, G., Hedges, R.E.M., Tuross, N. and Leyden, A. (1995). Preliminary results for the analysis of lipids in ancient bone. *Journal of Archaeological Science*, **22**:277–290.

Evershed, R.P., Vaughan, S.J., Dudd, S.N. and Soles, J.S. (1997a). Fuel for thought? Beeswax in lamps and conical cups from Late Minoan Crete. *Antiquity*, **71**:979–985.

Evershed, R.P., Mottram, H.R., Dudd, S.N., Charters, S., Stott, A.W., Lawrence, G.J., Gibson, A.M., Conner, A., Blinkhorn, P.W. and Reeves, V. (1997b). New criteria for the identification of animal fats in archaeological pottery. *Naturwissenschaften*, **84**:402–406.

Evershed, R.P., Bethell, P.H., Reynolds, P.J. and Walsh, N.J. (1997c). 5β-Stigmastanol and related 5β-stanols as biomarkers of manuring: analysis of experimental materials and assessment of the archaeological potential. *Journal of Archaeological Science*, **24**:485–495.

Evershed, R.P., van Bergen, P.F., Peakman, T.M., Leigh-Firbank, E.C., Horton, M.C., Edwards, D., Biddle, M., Kjolby-Biddle, B. and Rowley-Conwy, P.A. (1997d). Archaeological frankincense. *Nature*, **390**:667–668.

*Evershed, R.P., Dudd, S.N., Charters, S., Mottram, H., Stott, A.W., Raven, A., van Bergen, P.F. and Bland, H.A. (1999). Lipids as carriers of anthropogenic signals from Prehistory. *Philosophical Transactions of the Royal Society*, **B354**:19–31.

Friedli, H., Lotscher, H., Oeschger Siegenthaler, U. and Stauffer, B. (1986). Ice core record of the $^{13}C/^{12}C$ ratio of atmospheric CO_2 in the past two centuries. *Nature*, **324**:237–238.

Gülaçar, F.O., Susini, A. and Klohn, M. (1990). Preservation and post-mortem transformations of lipids in samples from a 4000-year-old Nubian mummy. *Journal of Archaeological Science*, **17**:691–705.

Hare, P.E., Fogel, M.L., Stafford, T.W. Jr., Mitchell, A.D. and Hoering, T.C. (1991). The isotopic composition of carbon and nitrogen in individual amino acids isolated from modern and fossil proteins. *Journal of Archaeological Science*, **18**:277–292.

*Heron, C. and Evershed, R.P. (1993). The analysis of organic residues and the study of pottery use. In Schiffer, M. (ed.) *Archaeological Method and Theory 5*, 247–284. University of Arizona Press: Arizona.

Jim, S., Stott, A.W., Evershed, R.P., Rogers, J.M. and Ambrose, S.H. (in press). Animal feeding experiments in the development of cholesterol as a palaeodietary indicator. In Millard, A. (ed.) *Proceedings of Archaeological Sciences '97*. Archaeopress: Oxford.

Knights, B.A., Dickson, C.A., Dickson, J.H. and Breeze, D.J. (1983). Evidence concerning the Roman Military Diet at Bearsden, Scotland, in the 2nd century AD. *Journal of Archaeological Science*, **10**:139–152.

Koch, P.L., Fogel, M.L. and Tuross, N. (1994). Tracing the diets of fossil animals using stable isotopes. In Lajtha, K. and Michner, R. (eds) *Methods in Ecology: Stable Isotopes in Ecology and Environmental Science*, 63–92. Blackwell Scientific Publications: London.

Kuksis, A., Child, P., Myher, J.J., Marai, L., Yousef, I.M. and Lewin, P.K. (1978). Bile acids of a 3200-year-old Egyptian mummy. *Canadian Journal of Biochemistry*, **56**:1141–1148.

Laakso, P. (1996). Analysis of triacylglycerols approaching the molecular composition of natural mixtures. *Food Review International*, **12**:199–250.

Larsson, L. (1978). *Agerod I:B – Agerod I:D: a Study of Early Atlantic Settlement in Scania*, 117–118. R. Habelt: Lund.

McDonald, P., Edwards, R.A. and Greenhalgh, J.F.D. (1988). *Animal Nutrition*, (4th edn). Longman: Harlow.

*Mills, J.S. and White, R. (1994). *The Organic Chemistry of Museum Objects*, (2nd edn). Butterworths: London.

Mottram, H.R., Dudd, S.N., Lawrence, G.J., Stott, A.W. and Evershed, R.P. (1999). New chromatographic, mass spectrometric and stable isotope approaches to the classification of degraded animal fats preserved in archaeological pottery. *Journal of Chromatography*, **833**:209–221.

Patrick, M., Koning, A.J. and Smith, A.B. (1985). Gas-liquid chromatographic analysis of fatty acids in food residues from ceramics found in the Southwestern Cape. *Archaeometry*, **27**:231–236.

Pollard, A.M. and Heron, C. (1996). *Archaeological Chemistry*. Royal Society of Chemistry: Cambridge.

Raven, A.M., van Bergen, P.F., Stott, A.W., Dudd, S.N. and Evershed, R.P. (1997). Formation of long-chain ketones in archaeological pottery vessels by pyrolysis of acyl lipids. *Journal of Analytical and Applied Pyrolysis*, **40/41**:267–285.

Regert, M., Bland, H.A., Dudd, S.N., van Bergen, P.F. and Evershed, R.P. (1998). Free and bound fatty acid oxidation products in archaeological ceramic vessels. *Proceedings of the Royal Society of London*, **B265**:2027–2032.

Regert, M., Delacotte, J.-M., Menu, M., Petrequin, P. and Rolando, C. (1999). Identification of Neolithic hafting adhesives from two lake dwellings at Chalain (Jura, France). *Ancient Biomolecules*, **2**:81–96.

Robinson, N., Evershed, R.P., Higgs, W.J., Jerman, K. and Eglington, G. (1987). Proof of a pine wood origin for pitch from Tudor (*Mary Rose*) and Etruscan shipwrecks: application of analytical organic chemistry in archaeology. *Analyst*, **112**:637–644.

Rottländer, R.C.A. (1990). Die Resultate der modernen Fettanalytik und ihre Anwendung auf die prähistorische Forschung. *Archaeo-Physika*, **12**:1–354.

Simpson, I.A., Dockrill, S.J., Bull, I.D. and Evershed, R.P. (1998). Early anthropogenic soil formation at Toft Ness, Sanday, Orkney. *Journal of Archaeological Science*, **25**:729–746.

Simpson, I.A., van Bergen, P.F., Perret, V., Elhmmali, M.M., Roberts, D.J. and Evershed, R.P. (1999). Lipid biomarkers of manuring practice in relict anthropogenic soils. *The Holocene*, **9**:223–229.

Stenhouse, M.J. and Baxter, M.S. (1979). The uptake of bomb ^{14}C in humans. In Berger, R. and Suess, H.E. (eds) *Radiocarbon Dating*, 324–341. University of Berkeley Press: Berkeley.

Stott, A.W. and Evershed, R.P. (1996). $\delta^{13}C$ analysis of cholesterol preserved in archaeological bones and teeth. *Analytical Chemistry*, **24**:4402–4408.

Stott, A.W., Davies, E., Evershed, R.P. and Tuross, N. (1997). Monitoring the routing of dietary and biosynthesized lipids through compound-specific stable isotope ($\delta^{13}C$) measurements at natural abundance. *Naturwissenschaften*, **84**:82–86.

Stott, A.W., Evershed, R.P., Jim, S., Jones, V., Rogers, J.M., Tuross, N. and Ambrose, S. (1999). Cholesterol as a new source of palaeodietary information: experimental approaches and archaeological applications. *Journal of Archaeological Science*, **26**:705–716.

Stott, A.W., Berston, R., Evershed, R.P., Bronk Ramsey, C., Humm, M. and Hedges, R.E.M. (in prep.). Compound specific ^{14}C dating of lipids preserved in archaeological pottery. Submitted to *Analytical Chemistry*.

Tieszen, L.L. and Fagre, T. (1993). Effect of diet quality and composition on the isotopic composition of respiratory CO_2, bone collagen, bioapatite and soft tissues. In Lambert, J.B. and Grupe, G. (eds) *Prehistoric Human Bone. Archaeology at the Molecular Level*, 121–155. Springer Verlag: Berlin.

van Bergen, P.F., Bull, I.D., Poulton, P.R. and Evershed, R.P. (1997a). Organic geochemical studies of soils from the Rothamsted classical experiments 1. Total lipid extracts, solvent insoluble residues and humic acids from Broadbalk wilderness. *Organic Geochemistry*, **26**:117–135.

van Bergen, P.F., Peakman, T.M., Leigh-Firbank, E.C. and Evershed, R.P. (1997b). Chemical evidence for archaeological frankincense: Boswellic acids and their derivatives in solvent soluble and insoluble fractions of resin-like materials. *Tetrahedron Letters*, **38**:8409–8412.

Woodbury, S.E., Evershed, R.P., Rossell, J.B., Griffiths, R.E. and Farnell, P. (1995). Detection of vegetable oil adulteration using gas chromatography combustion/isotope ratio mass spectrometry. *Analytical Chemistry*, **67**:2685–2690.

29

Archaeological Microbiology

G. GRUPE

Institut für Anthropologie und Humangenetik, München.

The role of micro-organisms in archaeology is an over-all destructive one. They are responsible for the decomposition of both inorganic and dead organic matter by enzymatic cleavage of organic compounds, hydrolytic and corrosive effects through their production of strong acids, and physical destruction of any material by mechanical forces resulting from microbial growth (Urzi and Krumbein 1994). Microbial activity is therefore likely to dramatically change the native properties of dead plant and animal tissue, artifacts manufactured from these tissues such as parchment, leather and textiles, and is a constant threat for museum specimens, art objects and other objects of cultural heritage. While the micro-organisms themselves may die some time after invasion of a tissue or object, their spores are capable of surviving extremely long times and are potentially hazardous for the excavator. The 'curse of the pharaoh', caused by moulds of the genus *Aspergillus*, is probably the most famous example. Microbial growth and activity depends on several environmental features like humidity, temperature, pH, energy source, etc.

According to Urzi and Krumbein (1994), the interactions between micro-organisms and their substrates in an environment suitable for microbial growth may be differentiated into 'biodegradation' (i.e., the biological process of matter recycling) and 'biodeterioration' (i.e., the harmful attack of micro-organisms towards subjects which are useful or valuable for humans).

With regard to biodeterioration, its prevention plays a key role in conservation and is a major driving force in the development of suitable equipment for storage rooms and display cases (e.g., Maekawa and Valentin 1996). A bibliography on the biodeterioration of cultural property was published a few years ago (Koestler and Vedral 1991), and this aspect is discussed in Chapter 52. This chapter on archaeological microbiology is therefore dedicated to biodegradation and focuses on the most common dead animal tissue being excavated, the archaeological skeleton. As a result of its abundance, and a variety of recently developed archaeometric approaches toward this substrate with high scientific potential, research on microbial decomposition of bone is rather straightforward.

Decomposition of dead organic matter is more a function of the burial environment than of the time elapsed since burial. Normally, the fate of a corpse will be complete disintegration as time goes by, whereby the decomposition process is both a function of physico/chemical parameters such as temperature, water drainage, soil pH, soil pressure and the like, and micro-organisms which actively drive the recycling process. Microbial action on a dead corpse starts very shortly after death and is further governed by the burial environment. Quality and degree of these early stages of decomposition are likely to have a high impact on destruction versus preservation of bodily remains. For

---

Handbook of Archaeological Sciences. Edited by D.R. Brothwell and A.M. Pollard.

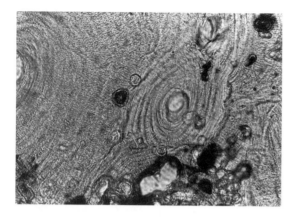

Figure 29.1 Microbial contamination in a thin section of an excavated human bone specimen, after cell stain with methylene blue. Dissolution of the bone mineral resulted in tunnels which still contain the remainders of invading micro-organisms.

example, whilst skeletons from historic and prehistoric times frequently exhibit signs of microbial invasion and destruction (Figure 29.1), such features are rare in fossils which – due to the nature of the fossilization process – must have been buried in preserving environments. Archaeological microbiology is especially crucial for biomolecular archaeology, because microbial decomposition is largely directed towards the organic constituents of a corpse/skeleton, and several expectations raised by the application of biomolecular methods towards archaeological finds, e.g., protein or DNA analysis, are rarely met due to microbial destruction and contamination (Chapters 25 and 28).

MICROBIAL DECOMPOSITION OF CORPSES

According to Child (1995a), microbial decomposition is defined as any deleterious changes to a substrate due to the action of micro-organisms, their by-products and their enzymes. Decomposition of a dead corpse is not a random process, since tissues like intestines or heart, the cells of which are characterized by high rates of biosynthesis, disintegrate first, while connective tissues like bone last longer due to their collagenous matrix (Gill-King 1997). Collagen is a very resistant molecule which is extremely difficult to hydrolyse because of its strong intra- and intermolecular bonds. Also, molecules bigger than water can barely penetrate into the mineral/protein matrix, so bone mineral will protect the collagen (which is an important target protein

for decomposing micro-organisms due to its abundance in bone) against many enzymes (Collins *et al.* 1995). Microbial destruction of a bone manifests itself in tunnels detectable in thin sections (Figure 29.2a), although the origin of these lesions is not yet fully understood and only very few responsible microbial species have been identified (e.g., Bell 1990). However, it is certain that micro-organisms get access to bone protein by the bone's natural internal porosity, therefore the tunnels are not randomly distributed but rather reflect the lamellar microstructure of the bone (Bell 1990). In addition, it cannot be excluded that the acquisition of certain diseases during a lifetime may enhance microbial decomposition after death, since some pathogenic bacteria such as *Mycobacterium tuberculosis* are also capable of solubilizing

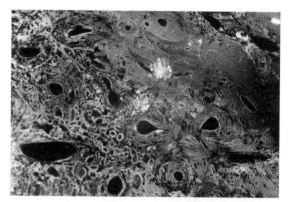

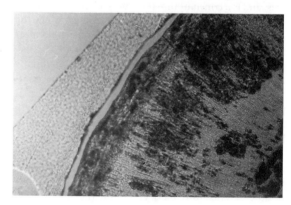

Figure 29.2 (a) (Top) Tunnelling in a thin section (cross section, microradiograph) of an excavated human compact bone as a symptom of microbial invasion and destruction. Tunnels reflect the lamellar structure of Haversian bone. (b) (Bottom) Tunnelling in a thin section (cross section) of excavated human dentine. Microbial invasion took place via the pulp cavity.

collagen. After initial destruction of protein/mineral bondings, decomposition will continue more and more rapidly.

MICROBIAL DECOMPOSITION OF MINERALIZED TISSUE

Once a body is reduced to its mineralized tissues which later may be excavated by archaeologists, microbial decomposition is largely dependent on both mineralization (i.e., production of inorganic ions through the oxidation of organic compounds) and immobilization (i.e., incorporation of inorganic molecules into the microbial protoplasma) (Child 1995b). The problem whether soil fungi or soil bacteria are mainly responsible for bone decomposition has not yet been fully solved. The majority of decomposition processes (liberation of hydrogen and organic acids by the degradation of biomolecules, contribution by humic acids, etc.) leads to an acidic micro-environment which enhances the growth of ubiquituous fungi (Gill-King 1997). While Piepenbrink (1986) succeeded in isolating various species of fungi from excavated skeletons, Child (1995b) was able to demonstrate that such fungi were most likely contaminants due to the environmental changes in the course of the excavation (Figure 29.3). Usually, dead organic matter faces a succession of decomposing micro-organisms, so it is very unlikely that micro-organisms isolated from an excavated bone will belong to the pioneering decomposers.

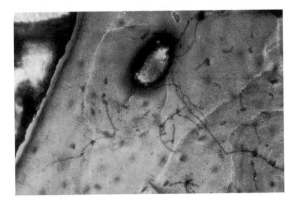

Figure 29.3 A fungus' hyphae detectable in a thin section of an excavated human bone from a desert dry burial environment. Since the microstructure of the specimen is very well preserved without any symptoms of tunnelling, the fungus's growth is most likely a post-excavation phenomenon.

There are some aspects, however, which indicate that soil bacteria should be largely responsible for biogenic decomposition rather than soil fungi: negatively charged cell walls of gram-positive bacteria act in analogy to a loosely packed ion exchange column, so bacteria will change the local ionic milieu. Moreover, many bacteria produce strong acids which can solubilize hydroxyapatite and permit easy access to the bone proteins (Grupe *et al.* 1993). Although trace element analysis of bone mineral is not discussed in this chapter, it is easy to imagine that bacteria (and, in this case, also soil fungi) are capable of significantly altering the original trace element profiles. Most important is the fact that also many non-pathogenic soil bacteria exhibit collagenase activity and are therefore capable of cleaving their target protein. For example, the genus *Streptomyces* produces a collagenase (Endo *et al.* 1987) which is very similar to the respective enzyme produced by *Clostridium histolyticum*, a bacterium which plays the most important role in the collagen breakdown shortly after death (Child 1995a). Interestingly, *Streptomyces* also frequently occurs in biodeteriorated stone (Urzi and Krumbein 1994) – a striking example for the enormous flexibility of certain micro-organisms as a result of their capability of excreting a wide variety of enzymes. Also *Achromobacter iophagus* is capable of cleaving bone matrix collagen in a highly specific way (Berry and Shuttleworth 1988, Vrany *et al.* 1988). It is noteworthy that bacterial collagenases tend to be much more aggressive than mammalian tissue collagenases since bacteria are devoid of collagen. Lastly, so-called pleomorphous bacteria can quickly adapt to changing environments – all features which render bacteria as prime candidates for dead bone decomposition.

The various bacterial species have specific requirements with regard to their environment in terms of oxygen availability, moisture, pH and temperature. As a rule of thumb, the decomposition rate of a buried corpse is approximately eight times slower than above ground, because the soil environment is a barrier to solar radiation, causing low temperatures and also low temperature fluctuations the deeper the corpse is buried (Rodriguez 1997). The average temperature of graves in our temperate climates is around 10°C. While bacterial activity is reduced at low temperatures, it need not necessarily cease at all, and *in vitro* decomposition of bone by soil micro-organisms was successful even at 4°C (Grupe *et al.* 1993). Anyway, within a buried corpse microbial activity will be low, but plenty of time is available for the decomposition process. Whilst bones excavated from dry desert environments scarcely reveal symptoms of microbial decomposition since bacteria require water for their growth and activity, at least some microbial activity must be expected under most circumstances: cold-adapted micro-organisms are responsible for biodegradation even in unfavourable environments (Margesin and Schinner 1997); e.g., living micro-organisms have been recovered from permafrost soils (Gilichinsky *et al.* 1995). Normally, rapid burial and lack of oxygen are judged as prerequisites for exceptionally good tissue preservation, but biogenic decomposition under anoxia is also possible by alternative oxidation of manganese, iron, or sulfate. Even when all oxidants have been completely used, bacteria may switch to fermentation processes (Allison 1988). Lastly, post-excavation microbial contamination should not be neglected.

BIOMOLECULES OTHER THAN COLLAGEN

Since the normal fate of dead matter is complete disintegration and recycling, only in exceptional cases will archaeological organic remains not have suffered from microbial invasion and destruction. Since bacteria possess enzymes for the cleavage of all biomolecular fractions, all archaeometric approaches must be aware of biases due to microbial activity. This does not only necessitate a thorough characterization and identification of an ancient molecule under study, it may also require some efforts to even detect the target molecules which might be simply bound to the bone mineral and therefore retained within the skeleton, but might equally well be hidden and encapsulated in humic acid complexes or might be highly cross-linked to other compounds and therefore not easily set free from the bone matrix.

In the course of the dynamic developments in the field of archaeometry, many classes of biomolecules have been identified which may potentially be preserved in excavated skeletons besides DNA and collagen, including lipids (Evershed *et al.* 1995; see Chapter 28), non-collagenous proteins (Grupe and Turban-Just 1996, Wiechmann *et al.* 1999), and even enzymes with a residual activity (Weser *et al.* 1996). While all such molecules can be destroyed by physico/chemical processes like hydrolysis, all of them are also susceptible to microbial degradation. With the exception of nucleic acids, all of these molecules may accumulate in dead organic matter, but only limited efforts have been undertaken to understand their decomposition histories. For several molecular classes, their unambiguous detection (activity determination in the case of

enzymes, sequencing in the case of DNA) is sufficient to suggest the survival of the target molecules. Investigations therefore mainly focus on the differentiation between native molecules and contamination, or on methodological problems (Handt *et al.* 1996), or on the possibility of an assessment of the presence of target molecules to avoid costly analyses with negative or very limited results (Colson *et al.* 1997). For other molecules, biodegradation may significantly limit the meaning of archaeometric data, even after a successful extraction of the substrate. Whilst lipids are generally degraded by saturation of fatty acids and subsequent cleavage of units consisting of two carbon atoms each, short-chained molecules will prevail in the extract from ancient bone, which may be, however, indistinguishable from naturally-occurring fatty acids. Bacterial enzymes, e.g. of the bacterium *Clostridium welchii* are suggested to be of prime importance in the *post-mortem* hydrolysis and hydrogenation of body fats (Mant 1987). For proteins, immunological methods should be a reliable method to prove the survival of certain target molecules, but very little is known about unspecific cross reactions with contaminating micro-organisms, and the appropriate dilution of antibodies will have to be calculated carefully in every single case.

COLLAGEN

The majority of investigations on microbial decomposition of bone have been performed on bone collagen, because this molecular fraction is very important for several archaeometric approaches such as radiocarbon dating, palaeodietary and palaeoclimatic reconstructions. Because of the abundance of collagen in a bone, most laboratory protocols will lead to some extractable protein from a bone by gentle demineralization or gelatinization. Therefore, archaeometric data like stable carbon or nitrogen isotopic ratios can readily be established from the extracts, but the question remains whether such data will give valid and reliable information. As a consequence, several studies have been made to distinguish between 'good' and 'bad' collagen (e.g., Ambrose 1993), and to understand the decomposition history of extractable protein with the aim of possibly estimating the original biological signal from a degraded substrate.

Cleavage of collagen (like any other protein) leads to peptides and, finally, to free amino acids, which differ considerably in their number of carbon atoms (varying between two for glycine and nine for tyrosine and phenylalanine in proteinogenic amino acids), and to a lesser degree in their number of nitrogen atoms (mostly one in proteinogenic amino acids, but two atoms in lysine and hydroxylysine, three in histidine, and four in arginine). The most important biodegradation pathways by bacteria are simple oxidation of organic matter and denitrification, since both reactions lead to a high yield of free energy per mole of generalized organic components (oxidation: $\Delta G^0 = -475 \, \mathrm{kJ/mol}$, denitrification: $\Delta G^0 = -448 \, \mathrm{kJ/mol}$; Berner 1980). Heterotrophic bacteria gain their energy via the citrate cycle (Michal 1999), thus amino acids with a high number of carbon atoms should be preferentially consumed in the course of biogenic decomposition. Such theoretical expectations were confirmed by inoculating fresh mammalian bone with soil bacteria (Balzer *et al.* 1997), and comparison of the results of such model experiments with degraded collagen from archaeological human bone (Grupe and Turban-Just 1998).

Inoculation of fresh mammalian bone with soil bacteria of the genus *Pseudomonas fluorescens, Alkaligenes piechaudii* and *Bacillus subtilis* under controlled conditions resulted in a biodegradation of collagen in as much as the extractable, insoluble protein fraction was generally depleted in such amino acids which have high numbers of carbon atoms (between five and nine), the relative loss of carbon leading to a depleted C/N ratio in the extract. According to microbial demands, especially the amino acids glutamic acid (an important carbon source, a constituent of the bacterial peptidoglycan mureine, and a precursor molecule for several other amino acids) and proline (precursor for glutamic acid synthesis) were selectively reduced in their abundance, while the small and relatively 'useless' amino acid glycine was retained causing a relative glycine accumulation in the protein (Balzer *et al.* 1997). Such selective removal of specific amino acids from decomposed collagen was also confirmed by amino acid analyses of collagen extracts from archaeological human bones, highly indicative of this decomposition being largely dominated by microbial action, since no such selectivity of breakdown products is to be expected by physico/chemical processes alone. This assumption was further supported by the fact that amino acid profiles of extractable collagen or collagen remnants from a variety of archaeological human bones from different geographical locations and time levels could be grouped into several distinct categories in terms of amino acid profile alteration, indicating that decomposition was no random process (Grupe and Turban-Just 1998).

INFLUENCE ON ARCHAEOMETRIC DATA

How can microbial decomposition bias archaeometric data? Selective breakdown of a protein firstly involves the cleavage of peptide bonds and therefore concerns the nitrogen atom as well as the carboxy (–COOH) carbon atom. Several mechanisms are well-known for significantly changing stable isotopic ratios, like thermodynamic effects (molecules with light isotopes are for instance more volatile), kinetic isotope effects which are caused biochemically and are linked to metabolic processes, and also position effects of elements in a larger molecule do occur. Kinetic isotope effects with regard to nitrogen happen in the course of the cleavage of peptide bonds in as much as the heavy nitrogen isotope, ^{15}N, is preferentially retained within the substrate. Thus, degraded collagen will become heavier in terms of $\delta^{15}N$ compared to the intact molecule. Experimental collagen decomposition by soil bacteria (Balzer *et al.* 1997) in fact resulted in an enrichment of $\delta^{15}N$ up to +5.8‰, which is within the upper range of a trophic level effect (see Chapter 23). Thus, degraded collagen can give a false dietary signal by suggesting a protein-rich, more carnivorous diet by the diagenetically enriched isotopic ratios.

In contrast to stable nitrogen isotopes, experimental collagen degradation showed an overall depletion with the heavy isotope, ^{13}C, resulting in more negative $\delta^{13}C$ value up to −2.9‰. A closer examination of the carboxy carbon atom after decarboxylation revealed that kinetic isotope effects should not be responsible for this alteration of stable carbon isotopes, since the carboxy carbon atom tended to be enriched with the heavy isotope, while the complete molecule was depleted. It is highly probable that the selective collagen degradation by micro-organisms via their preferential removal of certain amino acids is responsible for this phenomenon. It is noteworthy that every single amino acid has its own specific isotopic signature, and the δ-value of the global collagen molecule, which is indicative of ancient dietary habits, is made up from its correct amino acid composition. Whilst only proline is in isotopic equilibrium with the global collagen molecule, all other amino acids are either isotopically heavier or lighter than the collagen, these differences depending on the biosynthesis of the amino acid. In general, such amino acids with a long biosynthetic pathway are isotopically lighter, whilst amino acids with a short biosynthesis are isotopically more positive (e.g., Demmelmair and Schmidt 1993). It could be shown that the altered amino acid compositions after collagen degradation were responsible for the shifts in carbon isotopic ratios: preferential loss of isotopically light amino acids resulted in a more positive δ-value, and vice versa. Again, very misleading data in terms of palaeodiet are likely to result from biodegraded collagen (Grupe and Turban-Just 1998). However, the isotopic shifts detected in less well- to badly-preserved collagen will not cause a significant error with regard to radiocarbon dating, because a shift of 4‰ from the original carbon isotopic ratio will cause an error of about 1 per cent in terms of radioactivity, thus a dating error of 80 years only.

SUMMARY

In summary, microbial decomposition is such a complex phenomenon that it will be very hard if not impossible to tell the exact taphonomic history of a skeletal find. This may be the most important reason why research on this topic is not very straightforward, possibly with the exception of collagen breakdown. However, some general statements can be made with regard to the preservation conditions of biomolecules within an archaeological skeleton, and with regard to laboratory protocols.

Firstly, archaeological tissues which exhibit signs of initial or advanced microbial invasion are less likely to yield intact biomolecules. Moreover, it is questionable whether a skeleton which exhibits considerable tunnelling (Figure 29.2a) would ever have a chance of turning into a fossil. A histological inspection of the bone or tooth specimen prior to archaeometric analysis is very helpful for the assessment of the general state of preservation, and for the assessment of whether exogenous organic material will have contaminated the specimen to a greater or lesser extent. Bone is a very porous tissue and thus constitutes an open system. Choice of bone sample may be crucial, and mostly, the denser compact bone is preferred over trabecular samples, although for example ribs are often of less diagnostic value and are more easily sacrificed for any invasive method of analysis. Many research groups switched from bone to dentine analyses, especially for protein and DNA investigations, because the roots of the teeth are protected by the jaw bones. However, teeth may also be severely affected by microbial decomposition, since the pulp cavity is one of the main entrances for invading micro-organisms (Figure 29.2b). As a cell-free tissue, dental enamel is least susceptible to microbial destruction, but often does not contain the target molecules.

Secondly, micro-organisms do not only destroy a tissue while buried in the soil, but will do so immediately after excavation and especially in the laboratory at room temperature. There is no need to stress that any further contamination of a specimen has to be avoided carefully. Sterilization of the specimen will prevent the further growth of micro-organisms already present, but will not remove the contamination, and heat and/or radiation will destroy the biomolecules. Therefore, all labware, all solutions, etc., have to be as clean as possible, and it is highly recommended to add protease inhibitors, microbial enzyme inhibitors or other appropriate substances dependent on which types of biomolecule are to be analysed. For example, without the use of enzyme inhibitors, freshly extracted collagen from modern bone will exhibit signs of advanced degradation after a few days only (Grupe et al. 2000).

Thirdly, invasion of a bone by soil micro-organisms happens in a largely opportunistic way. Whilst general soil conditions may give some hints as to whether microbial destruction will be progressive or not, state of preservation of the mineralized tissues do vary significantly within one and the same skeleton. Grave goods for instance, which leave a copper impregnation on the bone, will inhibit microbial growth as does any other heavy metal contamination. Therefore, different bone specimens which have been sampled at only a few centimetres distance from each other may or may not contain the preserved target molecule. As a consequence, all analyses should be made at least in duplicate from different specimens of the same skeleton, if only to support a positive signal. Failures in the detection of a target molecule may also be by chance.

Lastly, the state of preservation or degradation of a target molecule is always unpredictable, which is also due to the opportunistic behaviour of soil microorganisms, and especially because of their succession on the substrate. Whilst several reliable laboratory protocols exist for the extraction and identification of preserved proteins, DNA and fatty acids, investigations of ancient biomolecules will hardly ever be routine – protocols will have to be adapted sometimes from one skeletal series to another, and sometimes even from one specimen to another. It is therefore necessary to make every effort possible to confirm the origin of the extracted molecules. Negative signals are disappointing, but not a real problem since what is not preserved cannot be detected. False positive signals and diagenetically-altered signals are much more worrying, and often are due to microbial contamination or destruction.

REFERENCES

*Recommended for further reading

Allison, P.A. (1988). The role of anoxia in the decay and mineralization of proteinaceous macro-fossils. *Paleobiology*, **14**:139–154.

Ambrose, S.H. (1993). Isotopic analysis of paleodiets: methodological and interpretive considerations. In Sandford, M.A. (ed.) *Investigations of Ancient Human Tissue. Chemical Analyses in Anthropology*, 59–130. Gordon and Breach: Langhorne.

*Balzer, A., Gleixner, G., Grupe, G., Schmidt, H.-J., Schramm, S. and Turban-Just, S. (1997). *In vitro* decomposition of bone collagen by soil bacteria: the implications for stable isotope analysis in archaeometry. *Archaeometry*, **39**:415–429.

Bell, L.S. (1990). Palaeopathology and diagenesis: an SEM evaluation of structural changes using backscattered electron imaging. *Journal of Archaeological Science*, **17**:85–102.

Berner, R.A. (1980). *Early Diagenesis. A Theoretical Approach*. Princeton University Press: Princeton.

Berry, L. and Shuttleworth, A. (1988). Bacterial collagenase and collagen identification. *Connective Tissue Research*, **17**:153–158.

Child, A.M. (1995a). Microbial taphonomy of archaeological bone. *Studies in Conservation*, **40**:19–30.

Child, A.M. (1995b). Towards an understanding of the microbial decomposition of archaeological bone in the burial environment. *Journal of Archaeological Science*, **22**:165–174.

Collins, M.J., Ripley, M.S., Child, A.M. and Turner-Walker, G. (1995). A basic mathematical simulation of the chemical degradation of ancient collagen. *Journal of Archaeological Science*, **22**:175–183.

Colson, I.B., Bailey, J.F., Vercauteren, M., Sykes, B.C. and Hedges, R.E.M. (1997). The preservation of ancient DNA and bone diagenesis. *Ancient Biomolecules*, **1**:109–117.

Demmelmair, H. and Schmidt, H.-L. (1993). Precise δ^{13}C-determination in the range of natural abundance on amino acids from protein hydrolysates by gas-chromatography-isotope ratio mass spectrometry. *Isotopenpraxis*, **29**:237–250.

Endo, A., Murakawa, S., Shimizu, H. and Shiraishi, Y. (1987). Purification and properties of a collagenase from a *Streptomyces* species. *Journal of Biochemistry*, **102**:163–170.

Evershed, R.P., Turner-Walker, G., Hedges, R.E.M., Tuross, N. and Leyden, A. (1995). Preliminary results for the analysis of lipids in ancient bone. *Journal of Archaeological Science*, **22**:277–290.

Gilichinsky, D.A., Wagener, S. and Vishnevetskaya, T.A. (1995). Permafrost microbiology. *Permafrost and Periglacial Processes*, **6**:281–291.

*Gill-King, J. (1997). Chemical and ultrastructural aspects of decomposition. In Haglund, W.D. and Sorg, M.H. (eds) *Forensic Taphonomy. The Postmortem Fate of Human Remains*, 93–108. CRC Press: Boca Raton.

Grupe, G. and Turban-Just, S. (1996). Serum proteins in archaeological human bone. *International Journal of Osteoarchaeology*, **6**:300–308.

*Grupe, G. and Turban-Just, S. (1998). Amino acid composition of degraded matrix collagen from archaeological human bone. *Anthropologischer Anzeiger*, **56**:213–226.

Grupe, G., Dreses-Werringloer, U. and Parsche, F. (1993). Initial stages of bone decomposition: causes and consequences. In Lambert, J.B. and Grupe, G. (eds) *Prehistoric Human Bone. Archaeology at the Molecular Level*, 257–274. Springer Verlag: Berlin.

Grupe, G., Balzer, A. and Turban-Just, S. (2000). Modelling protein diagenesis in ancient bone. In Ambrose, S.H. and Katzenberg, M.A. (eds) *Close to the Bone: Biogeochemical Approaches to Paleodietary Analysis in Archaeology*, 173–187. Plenum Press: New York.

Handt, O., Höss, M., Krings, M. and Pääbo, S. (1996). The retrieval of ancient human DNA sequences. *American Journal of Human Genetics*, **59**:368–376.

*Koestler, R.J. and Vedral, J. (1991). Biodeterioration of cultural property: a bibliography. *International Biodeterioration*, **28**:229–340.

Maekawa, S. and Valentin, N. (1996). Development of a prototype storage and display case for the Royal Mummies of the Egyptian Museum in Cairo. In Spindler, K., Wilfing, H., Rastbichler-Zissernig, E., zur Nedden, D. and Nothdurfter, H. (eds) *Human Mummies. The Man in the Ice, Vol. 3*, 47–56. Springer Verlag: Wien.

Mant, A.K. (1987). Knowledge acquired from post-War exhumations. In Boddington, A., Garland, A.N. and Janaway, R.C. (eds) *Death, Decay and Reconstruction. Approaches to Archaeology and Forensic Science*, 65–78. Manchester University Press: Manchester.

Margesin, R. and Schinner, F. (1997). Efficiency of indigenous and inoculated cold-adapted soil microorganisms for biodegradation of diesel oil in alpine soils. *Applied and Environmental Microbiology*, **63**:2660-2664.

Michal, G. (eds) (1999). *Biochemical Pathways*. Spektrum Akademischer Verlag: Heidelberg.

Piepenbrink, H. (1986). Two examples of biogenous dead bone decomposition and their consequences for taphonomic interpretation. *Journal of Archaeological Science*, **13**:417–430.

Rodriguez, W.C. (1997). Decomposition of buried and submerged bodies. In Haglund, W.D. and Sorg, M.H. (eds) *Forensic Taphonomy. The Postmortem Fate of Human Remains*, 459–467. CRC Press: Boca Raton.

*Urzi, C. and Krumbein, W.E. (1994). Microbiological impacts on the cultural heritage. In Krumbein, W.E., Brimblecombe, P., Cosgrove, D.E. and Staniforth, S. (eds) *Durability and Change. The Science, Responsibility, and Cost of Sustaining Cultural Heritage*, 107–135. John Wiley: Chichester.

Vrany, B., Hnátková, Z. and Lettl, A. (1988). Occurrence of collagen-degrading microorganisms in association of mesophilic heterotrophic bacteria from various soils. *Folia Microbiologia*, **33**:458–461.

Weser, U., Knaup, Y., Etspüler, H.M., Kenward, N. and Hedges, R.E.M. (1996). Biochemically and immunologically active alkaline phosphatase in archaeologically important samples. *Journal of Archaeological Science*, **23**:723–730.

Wiechmann, I., Brandt, E. and Grupe, G. (1999). State of preservation of polymorphic plasma proteins recovered from ancient human bones. *International Journal of Osteoarchaeology*, **9**:383–394.

SECTION 5

Biological Resource Exploitation

Overview – At the Beginning of the Task: the Archaeology of Biological Remains

C. HIGHAM

Department of Anthropology, University of Otago.

When asked to write this introduction, I reached for my well-thumbed copy of Grahame Clark's *Prehistoric Europe, the Economic Basis* (1952), to remind myself what was current when I committed myself, 43 years ago, to life as a prehistorian. I had forgotten that he had inscribed my copy 'to Charles Higham, economic prehistorian', a sobriquet which owed much to life in his department. As a volunteer schoolboy on several major excavations in England during the late 1950s, I had experienced a mixed attitude towards the biological remains we were finding. None employed sieves, so only large animal bones, for example, were retained. Their retention at one site lasted only as long as it took to wheelbarrow them to the dump. Hence Clark's survey of economic life in prehistoric Europe came as a welcome antidote, and much of what has happened in the second half of the twentieth century finds antecedents therein. A random opening at page 125, for example, finds him considering the issue of over-wintering cattle in the Swiss lake villages. In 1866, Keller had described the remains of animal ordure in a structure at Robenhausen (Keller 1887), a finding which Clark with typical restraint refused to extend to European sites in general.

The latest issue of the *Journal of Archaeological Science* reveals the extent to which the analysis of such remains has intensified (Nielsen *et al.* 2000). The Neolithic settlement of Weier incorporates a structure with three successive wooden floors, interleaved with layers of animal dung, leaves and twigs. Domestic animals were probably over-wintered in such buildings, and the relative warmth and plentiful food supply attracted beetles, flies and mites. In all, no fewer than 41 taxa of arthropods were identified in one layer alone. They allowed the authors to conclude that the byre was in all probability roofed, and was cleared of accumulated manure from time to time, thus accounting for the low number of beetles which feed on rotting organic material. Such mucking out would in all likelihood have fertilized the cornfields round the settlement.

In 1961, Eric Higgs asked me to proof-read the first edition galleys of *Science in Archaeology* (Brothwell and Higgs 1963). The section on the environment was prefaced with an introduction by John Coles, who was at pains to stress how prehistory at that juncture was becoming less concerned with the typology of artifacts and more with the environment of prehistoric societies. This was part of what might be called the emancipation from typology made possible through radiocarbon dating. Much prehistory at the time was concerned with the minutiae of typology. Whether or not a bronze Hallstatt dagger had a *zwischenstuck* was a matter of grave concern, for its presence and form would determine whether it was Hallstatt B1 or B2, and thereby provide a relative date. Childe and Hawkes traced trade goods from Egypt into

Handbook of Archaeological Sciences. Edited by D.R. Brothwell and A.M. Pollard.

Myceneaen Greece and thence over the Alps into *terra incognita* to obtain a prehistoric chronology. The radiocarbon revolution which followed not only provided for an independent chronological framework, but also freed prehistorians to think differently about their source material.

Eric Higgs and Don Brothwell taught at Cambridge during the late 1950s and early 1960s, and their collegial relationship resulted in that first edition. In it, we find a mix of contributions, many concerned with macro-faunal remains, such as Clutton-Brock on the origins of the domestic dog, Kurtén on the hyaena, Dawson on fish and Sparks on molluscan remains. Hardly surprisingly, the emphasis was very much on European material, although Ryder's consideration of fish incorporated a section on work beyond Europe, travelling as far as Fiji and China for his examples. At least within the cloistered environment of the Cambridge Department, this book had a pervasive effect, for it stimulated the establishment of the British Academy's major research project on the origins of agriculture which was overseen by Clark with Higgs as director. Already Higgs was snaring promising graduate students to his bone room, where he would preside over a growing swarm of enthusiastic followers. He had a string of favourite quotations: 'I can tell you more about a prehistoric society from one bone, than from a box of handaxes' was one such. When an aspiring follower noted that he or she knew nothing about the morphology of bones or plants, he would declaim 'If the experts won't do their homework, then we must do it for them'. Thus Jane Renfrew was metamorphosed into a palaeoethnobotanist, and Paul Wilkinson into the domesticator of the musk ox.

The expansion of this research can be seen in at least two ways. Only six years after the first edition of *Science in Archaeology* appeared, its second and much expanded text was published (Brothwell and Higgs 1969). The contributions in the section on the environment now included a more international repertoire of papers, such as Yarnell on palaeobotany in America. My own contribution, written jointly with Michael Message, reflected the impotence of the palaeozoologist without a modern comparative collection. Having taken books of bone measurements, I had to resolve what they might mean. The solution was to collect the bones of cattle of known age, breed and sex, a procedure which placed strains on my recent marriage as I boiled up in a small kitchen the foot bones of 80 Aberdeen Angus cattle, obtained frozen from northern Australia.

The second major impact of this interest in biological remains, was the development of the flotation machine. I first saw this as a prototype, nicknamed the dustbin, under the control of Tony Legge. I understand that Dr Jim Charles contributed significantly to the original notion. Essentially, water is passed through excavated material in order to attract micro-organic material, which is then trapped in a series of fine-mesh sieves. In my view, every grant-giving agency should require their employment as a condition of funding, but it is a source of amazement that so few archaeologists routinely use this vital technique. I recently visited major excavations in Europe, where not only was flotation avoided, but simple screening was as well.

In the same year as the second edition of *Science in Archaeology* appeared, I undertook my first fieldwork in Thailand. At that juncture, prehistoric research in this part of South-east Asia was in its infancy, and it was often said that due to the nature of the tropical regime, sites had no visible stratigraphy. Even the most casual observer, however, would soon appreciate the importance today, and surely in prehistory too, of a diet of fish and rice. The place of proper data recovery in the analysis of palaeodiets in South-east Asia can be illustrated through a series of sites excavated with different recovery techniques in place. At Non Nok Tha in 1968, no screening took place, and only a handful of fish bones from large and robust species were found. Seven years later at Ban Chiang, ordinary screening was employed, and the number of fish species increased. In 1981 at Ban Na Di, a site of the same date as the previous two, we employed wet sieving with a very fine mesh and fish dominated the faunal spectrum. Jill Thompson was in charge of the flotation machine in 1985 at Khok Phanom Di, and the recovery of micro-organic material was extraordinary (Thompson 1996). Not only rice remains and seeds were captured, but also the remains of insects, fish scales and minute bones and crustacea. Samples of cultural material also yielded forams and ostracodes, vital in reconstructing the changing water regime. The land snails and very small gastropod remains resulted in the identification of over 150 species, each with its preferred habitat. The human faeces incorporated hair from mice, and the remains of a beetle adaptive to life in rice stores: the inhabitants were presumably drawing their rice from stores infested with rodents. Food remains in the digestive tract of a woman included fish scales, bones, and rice husk. Subsequent flotation of the entire contents of pits at the late Neolithic site of Ban Lum Khao have provided samples of fish running to hundreds of individuals from a wide variety of species. There is no excuse for not employing this vital technique.

If it is the task of the field archaeologist to obtain all the available data, it is that of the specialist to analyse and interpret. Each issue of such publications as *Journal of Archaeological Science* brings to our attention new avenues of analysis, new horizons to consider. Many such approaches take us inside our source material. Where we once identified and measured bones, the next generation is now extracting DNA and enormously refining our understanding of prehistory. Barnes *et al.* (2000), for example, have employed DNA to distinguish between domestic and wild species of geese. Matisoo-Smith and co-workers have traced the pattern of human settlement in the Pacific through the DNA of the rat (Matisoo-Smith *et al.* 1998). The DNA of prehistoric dogs in Southeast Asia points to an origin in the Chinese wolf (Tsuda *et al.* 1997). The application of DNA analysis to plant material represents a major advance when it is considered that the first edition of *Science in Archaeology* was a contemporary of Crick and Watson's research on the double helix.

The availability of such tools as the scanning electron microscope has also permitted more intensive research than could have been imagined 50 years ago. The study of scratch patterns on shell knives, for example, or the recovery of tuberous plant remains or blood from stone implements, are now becoming routine.

In his preface to the second edition of *Science in Archaeology*, Grahame Clark stressed that: 'The archaeologist, despite all his triumphs, remains almost at the beginning of his task: immense fields of knowledge remain to be opened up, not merely in remote parts of the world, but in lands where archaeology has passed through its initial stages of development' (Clark 1969:71). Science, he went on, is advancing at an accelerating pace. And so it continues. The following chapters capture the intensity and exhilaration of this advance towards a more complete and illuminating history of the human past.

REFERENCES

Barnes, I., Young, J.P.W. and Dobney, K.M. (2000). DNA-based identification of goose species from two archaeological sites in Lincolnshire. *Journal of Archaeological Science*, **27**:91–100.

Brothwell, D. and Higgs, E.S. (1963). *Science in Archaeology*. Thames and Hudson: London.

Brothwell, D. and Higgs, E.S. (1969). *Science in Archaeology*, (2nd edn). Thames and Hudson: London.

Clark, J.G.D. (1952). *Prehistoric Europe, the Economic Basis*. Methuen: London.

Clark, J.G.D. (1969). Foreword. In Brothwell, D. and Higgs, E.S. (eds) *Science in Archaeology*, (2nd edn). Thames and Hudson: London.

Keller, F. (1887). *The Lake Dwellings of Switzerland and Other Parts of Europe*, (2nd edn). Longmans, Green, and Co.: London.

Matisoo-Smith, E., Roberts, R.M., Irwin, G.J., Allen, J.S., Penny, D. and Lambert, D.M. (1998). Patterns of prehistoric human mobility in Polynesia indicated by mtDNA from the Pacific rat. *Proceedings of the National Academy of Sciences of the USA*, **95**:15145–15150.

Nielsen, B.O., Mahler, V. and Rasmussen, P. (2000). An arthropod assemblage and the ecological conditions in a byre at the Neolithic settlement of Weier, Switzerland. *Journal of Archaeological Science*, **27**:209–218.

Thompson, G.B. (1996). *The Excavation of Khok Phanom Di: a Prehistoric Site in Central Thailand. Vol.4: Subsistence and Environment: the Botanical Evidence*. Research Committee Reports No.53, Society of Antiquaries of London: London.

Tsuda, K., Kikkawa, Y., Yonekawa, H. and Tanabe, Y. (1997). Extensive interbreeding occurred among multiple matriarchal ancestors during the domestication of dogs: evidence from inter- and intraspecies polymorphisms in the D-loop region of mitochondrial DNA between dogs and wolves. *Genes and Genetic Systems*, **72**:229–238.

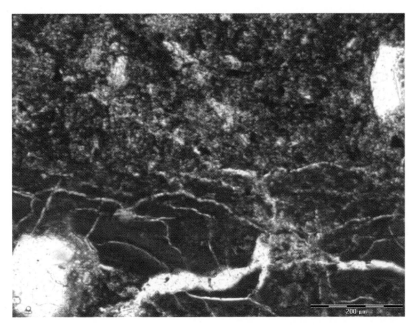

Figure 14.1 Textural pedofeatures from a pre-Columbian Andean caméllon, Ecuador. Viewed in plane polarized light.

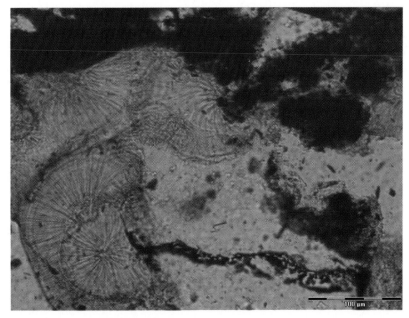

Figure 14.2 Calcium-iron-phosphate crypto-crystalline infills from an early midden site in Verterålen, northern Norway. Viewed in plane polarized light.

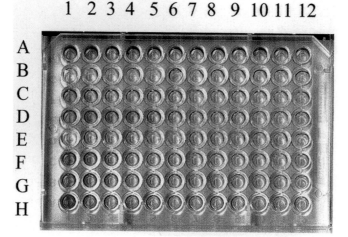

Figure 26.4 An ELISA plate containing different test samples (A-H) which have been serially diluted across the plate (1-12) in an indirect competitive ELISA for the detection of antigen. The intensity of the colour in A-H is a measure of the amount of antigen present in the test samples. In this assay the most coloured well contains the least amount of antigen, see Figure 26.3.

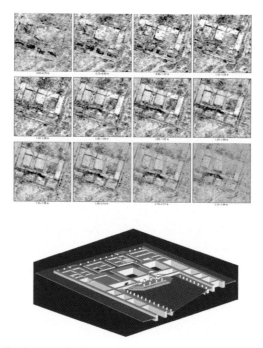

Figure S7.3 GPR time slice images of a Roman building at Carnuntum, Austria, and a 3D model of the archaeological interpretation (from Kandler *et al.* 1999). © Archaeo Prospections.

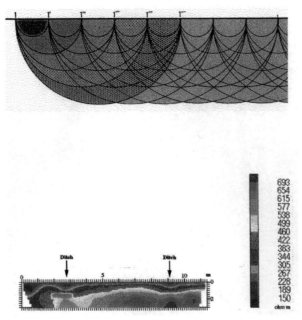

Figure 43.2 An electrical resistivity pseudo-section.

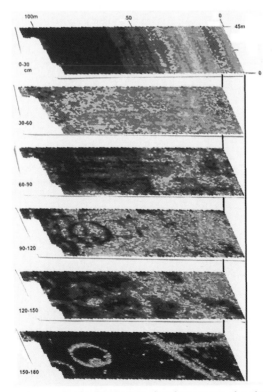

Figure 43.5 A GPR survey in search of subterranean chamber graves, also showing differences in the direction of cultivation and in the boundaries of cultivation.

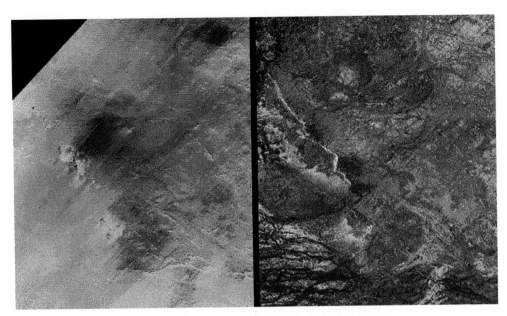

Figure 44.4 Optical and Shuttle Imaging Radar image of the same area of Safsaf Oasis, Egypt showing relict channel features detected by the penetration of the radar beam through very dry smooth desert sand. These images show two views of a region of south-central Egypt, each taken by a different type of spaceborne sensor. On the left is an optical image from the Landsat Thermatic Mapper, and on the right is a radar image from the Spaceborne Imaging Radar-C/X-band Synthetic Aperture Radar (SIR-C/X-SAR). This comparison shows that the visible and infrared wavelengths of Landsat are only sensitive to the materials on the surface, while the radar wavelengths of SIR-C/X-SAR can penetrate the thin sand cover in this arid region to reveal details hidden below the surface (Copyright NASA/JPL).

30

Biological Resource Exploitation: Problems of Theory and Method

M. CHARLES and P. HALSTEAD

Department of Archaeology and Prehistory, University of Sheffield.

In recent years, 'economic archaeology' has been the focus of lively, and often heated, debate concerning its significance, legitimacy, scope and methodological rigour. This debate has been shaped, in part, by ideas permeating archaeology from cognate disciplines such as evolutionary ecology, economic anthropology and sociology, but economy has also been a recurrent 'bone of contention' in paradigmatic disputes within archaeology. During the late 1960s to early 1980s, within the broad climate of the 'New Archaeology', the theoretical and methodological writings on subsistence of Higgs and Binford represented some of the most radical and explicit attempts to theorize the discipline. As a result, economic and ecological archaeology drew much of the fire of the subsequent 'post-processual' critique. Some of the principal (and often interrelated) issues in this theoretical debate are briefly reviewed here, before focusing on their practical implications for the archaeological investigation of resource use.

ECONOMIC ARCHAEOLOGY IN THEORY

For Higgs and the Cambridge 'Palaeoeconomy' school, economy (in particular, the acquisition of food) was the 'primary human adaptation to the environment' (Higgs and Jarman 1975:4) and exercised a determining influence over other aspects of culture, while critics such as Shanks and Tilley (1987:35, 55) have regarded such biological perspectives almost as a denial of humanity. These two sides of this argument, although sometimes presented as mutually exclusive truths, are alternative perspectives on the human past (e.g., Jarman *et al.* 1982:1) which will be found more or less satisfying, depending on the particular question under investigation and on the prejudices of the reader.

More critical is the related argument of the palaeo-economists that economy, as the aspect of human culture most subject to natural selection, should tend in the long term towards optimality (Jarman *et al.* 1982:5). This tendency is implicit in Darwin's concept of the survival of the fittest and similar assumptions have been made with regard to human social behaviour, but there are a number of reasons, practical and theoretical, why optimal adaptations cannot be *achieved* by any organism. First, because the evolutionary goal-posts are constantly moving (e.g., through changes in climate or in the behaviour of other species), a beneficial adaptation at one point in time might subsequently become a threat to survival; the degree of optimality of an adaptation thus depends, in part, on the time scale over which it is evaluated. Secondly, viable adaptations are constrained both by the range of variability (biological or cultural) upon which selection operates and by the need for integration between

Handbook of Archaeological Sciences. Edited by D.R. Brothwell and A.M. Pollard.
© 2001 John Wiley & Sons, Ltd.

different aspects of an adaptive strategy (e.g., dentition, feeding patterns and social behaviour must be mutually compatible). Thirdly, adaptations must be assessed in terms of a specific goal (classically, but not exclusively, reproductive fitness) and specific currency (e.g., energy, protein). As a result, evolutionary ecologists use optimality models heuristically, as a way of measuring actual behaviour in terms of a specified goal, currency and time scale (Foley 1985). Ironically, social scientists who stress our unique status as 'knowledgeable actors' might be thought to offer a theoretical justification for treating humans alone as capable of optimizing behaviour, and it is certainly arguable that human responses to evolutionary problems are unusually goal-directed. In practice, however, the complexity of the real world makes it impossible to predict the future with accuracy, and humans are not yet masters of their own destiny. Archaeologists, therefore, must also restrict themselves to heuristic uses of optimality models.

Economic history and anthropology have been the source of further controversy, which in some respects overlaps with the debate spilling over into archaeology from evolutionary ecology. Polanyi (1957) argued that 'economy' has two meanings. The 'formal' meaning is epitomized by the modern discipline of economics in its concern with how people allocate resources between alternative ends. Underpinning 'formalist' economics is the assumption that resources are scarce and that ends (i.e., wants) are abundant or even infinite. The validity of this assumption for pre-market economies has been widely questioned. For example, Sahlins (1974:1) argues that primitive economies are in fact characterized by abundant resources and limited wants, describing hunter-gatherers as the 'original affluent society'. Formalist economics also assumes that all goods and services are available for purchase in the market and so have a price, whereas Polanyi emphasized the 'substantivist' meaning of economy as the process by which humans procure material resources. This process includes such different mechanisms as reciprocity, redistribution and market exchange, represented in modern capitalist society by housekeeping, taxation/government services and commerce, respectively.

The basic substantivist position, that economic activity is deeply embedded in social relations and moral constraints, is now widely accepted. More contentious is the further argument that the ideal of 'economic man', *Homo economicus*, making rational decisions which maximize benefits and minimize costs, is relevant only to modern market economies. Even in our own capitalist world, economy is deeply embedded in a wider social, political and ideological fabric. For example, few people choose where to shop and what to buy on the basis of cost, quality and convenience only, taking no account of brand names, boycotts, or social relationships with local shopkeepers. Moreover, cultural prescriptions and proscriptions on what can be eaten are very widespread (e.g., Sahlins 1976) and serve, *inter alia*, as markers of ethnic, religious or class affiliation. Nonetheless, 'formalist' cost/benefit analyses can still account for some of our economic activity and, where they fail to do so, can expose 'irrational' (i.e., unpredicted) considerations, such as attraction to designer labels or reluctance to eat horses and dogs. As with the optimality models borrowed from evolutionary ecology, therefore, the formalist ideal, of 'economic man' as the rational decision maker, has heuristic potential in the exploration of both modern and primitive economies. Provided their use is strictly heuristic, formalist analyses do not conflict with the 'substantivist' principle that economy is embedded in social relations and cultural rules.

Archaeologists use the term 'economy' in a variety of ways. For Higgs and Jarman (1975:4), economy referred narrowly to the relationship between human population and resources (primarily staple foods), while Clark (1952:7) regarded economy more broadly, in terms of the interplay between environmental limitations and human aspirations. A critical distinction (Barker and Gamble 1985:5), followed here, is that between subsistence (what people live on) and economy (the management and mobilization of resources). The present chapter is concerned with the exploitation of biological resources, but not only with the nutritional role of such resources. For example, in the early civilizations of both the Old and New World and likewise in Medieval Europe, a primary function of animal husbandry was to produce raw materials for the manufacture of fine textiles, which played a key role in the definition of status and thus, in turn, may have helped to determine access to material resources. Any attempt to understand animal husbandry or land use, which ignored the scale and context of textile production, would plainly be flawed. On the other hand, human nutritional requirements, though complex, are in large part biologically determined (Dennell 1979) and so can be extrapolated to the distant past to an extent not possible for the consumption of fine textiles, the importance of which is inherent to particular historical and cultural contexts. Thus the predictability of human nutritional needs offers a window of inference into the past which archaeologists would be foolish to ignore. Other biological or mechanical parameters with potential for productive extrapolation to the past include the minimum size of population needed for demographic viability and the capacity of human labour to perform particular tasks with a given technology (e.g., Wright 1994).

Hawkes (1954) assigned to 'subsistence-economics' one of the lowest and most accessible rungs on his archaeological 'ladder of inference', because of the material nature of economic existence and the insights offered by natural scientists into the potential of the physical environment. A similar view was pithily expressed in Higgs and Jarman's (1975:1) observation that 'the soul leaves no skeleton', but the most substantial justification was presented by Binford in his discussion of what constitutes good 'middle-range theory' (Binford 1981:25). It is through middle-range theory that the dynamics of human behaviour can be inferred from the static bones, seeds and so on of the archaeological record. Good middle-range theory requires that the relationship between dynamics and statics, observed in the present, should be:

(i)   unambiguous – e.g., only carnivores should be capable of inflicting on bones the patterns of damage attributed to carnivore attrition,

(ii) one of cause and effect rather than mere correlation – e.g., carnivore attrition is shaped by their dental anatomy and function, and

(iii) applicable to the past – e.g., carnivore dental anatomy and function have not changed significantly over the relevant time span.

The last of these requirements entails making a *uniformitarian* assumption about a relationship which can only be observed in the present, leading Binford to stress a fourth characteristic of good middle-range theory – its intellectual independence of the archaeologist's 'general theory' (Binford 1981:29). In effect, this means that, to avoid circular arguments, middle-range theory should be independent of our ideas about human behaviour and so is most securely grounded (as in the example above) in other fields such as biology, non-human ecology, mechanics, etc. (Binford 1981:35). Conversely, for example, the inference of status from grave goods often revolves around potentially circular assumptions concerning human notions of value. Applied strictly, Binford's guidelines would leave most of the human past beyond the scope of archaeological inference, but economic archaeologists should plainly capitalize, where possible, on the opportunities afforded by the biological and ecological sciences for

building robust middle-range theory (Barker and Gamble 1985:6).

The robustness of economic archaeological inference has also been questioned from another perspective. It is argued that all human behaviour is symbolically mediated, such that even the deposition of food waste is informed by culture-specific notions of what is dirty, polluting or otherwise culturally unacceptable. If this viewpoint is accepted, and it is richly exemplified in studies of modern societies, it follows that the ostensibly mundane remains studied by economic archaeologists may in this respect be closer to the value-laden data of the funerary archaeologist than to the unproblematic pollen 'rain' of the palynologist.

Clearly, there has been profound disagreement, between proponents and critics (and indeed among practitioners) of economic archaeology, on a number of general issues of theory and method. The remainder of this chapter, therefore, largely avoids particular questions of process (e.g., domestication, intensification, surplus production, the antiquity of pastoralism) and focuses instead on these more general issues, exploring their practical implications for the archaeological investigation of biological resource use. Attention is drawn to areas where practitioners should proceed with confidence or caution and also to ways in which potential pitfalls may be circumvented.

ECONOMIC ARCHAEOLOGY IN PRACTICE

Inferring resource use: problems of uniformitarianism, equifinality and optimality

It is helpful to start by considering how middle-range theory can be used to infer past dynamics from the static evidence of individual assemblages of, for example, animal bones or charred seeds. Taphonomic analysis, such as discrimination between gnawed and butchered bones (Binford 1981), recognition of digested bone (Payne and Munson 1985), or allowance for differential preservation of cereal parts by charring (Boardman and Jones 1990), depends on our understanding of relatively simple mechanical, physical or chemical processes. Although basic research is still needed into many of these processes, their effects are relatively unambiguous and their uniformitarian extrapolation to the past is unproblematic. Archaeobotanical recognition of the effects of processing (winnowing, sieving) on samples of Old World cereal and pulse crops enjoys similar methodological advantages (Hillman 1984, Jones 1987).

Animals and plants are inherently variable, so that identification of taxon (and, in the case of animals, of age, sex, stature and nutritional state) is subject to greater degrees of imprecision or ambiguity (e.g., Moran and O'Connor 1994, Jones 1998). Uniformitarian assumptions must be made with caution, particularly in the case of taxa (notably domesticates) subject to rapid evolution, but may still be justifiable. For example, morphological comparison of ancient and modern cereal remains can reveal early crop types, which are no longer in widespread cultivation (Jones *et al.* 2000) and the taxonomic status of which may be clarified by analysis of ancient DNA. Likewise, comparison of archaeological and modern mandibles shows that domestication has not altered the order of eruption of teeth in pigs and cattle, thus encouraging faith in dental ageing techniques (e.g., Bull and Payne 1982). Moreover, these identification methods are underpinned by biological principles and, as such, are largely independent of our ideas concerning human behaviour and so pose few risks of circular argument.

Greater problems of *equifinality* (the same pattern being attributable to more than one causal agent) may be posed by the recognition of crop husbandry practices such as irrigation or rotation from the floristic composition of associated weed floras (e.g., Jones *et al.* 1995). Plants respond to a variety of ecological factors (disturbance, fertility, shade, etc.), but it may be possible to discriminate between alternative interpretations of weed floras by considering the 'functional attributes' of plants (Charles *et al.* 1997). The ecological interpretation of weeds also faces significant uniformitarian problems (Behre and Jacomet 1991:82). First, arable weeds are notoriously adaptable and opportunist, but analysis of *suites* of associated taxa may highlight major shifts in the adaptation of individual species, as with the apparent occurrence of present-day marsh and grassland plants as arable weeds at the Roman-period settlement of de Horden in Holland (Lange 1990:94). Secondly, the ecological niche of weeds is affected by the introduction of new competitors, but again diachronic changes to the weed flora of a given region are amenable to archaeobotanical investigation (e.g., Knörzer 1979).

Likewise, the discrimination of different hunting strategies on the basis of the age and sex composition of the prey is complicated by flexibility in the behaviour of animal species. Variability in herd size and social behaviour is systematically related to other variables, however, such as the density of forest, and so may be broadly predictable from independent evidence of vegetation cover (e.g., Legge and Rowley-Conwy 1988). Most critically of all, such models are founded on bodies of ecological theory which are again intellectually independent of archaeological debate concerning the human past and so avoid the risk of circular argument.

The interpretation of animal bone assemblages in terms of 'economic anatomy' (Binford 1978) poses slightly more complex problems. The nutritional value of different body parts is determined by the anatomy of the prey species, and zoology provides both robust and independent grounds for uniformitarian extrapolation of this relationship to the distant past. Carnivore attrition selectively destroys soft body parts, which also tend to be those of high nutritional value (Lyman 1992), but such problems of equifinality may be resolvable by analysis of traces of butchery and gnawing (e.g., Binford 1981). Body part representation offers a useful measure, therefore, of the efficiency with which carcasses were processed and allows a distinction to be drawn between 'bulk' strategies, which intensively extract available nutrients, and 'gourmet' strategies, which select the nutritionally most valuable cuts (Binford 1978:81). These alternative optimality models offer definable yardsticks against which to measure archaeological evidence (Binford 1978:19). Used heuristically, as a measuring device, they do not assume that humans actually behaved optimally or rationally.

The strategy of carcass utilization in a given context may be influenced by practical considerations, such as the number of animals killed, their size, and their condition in the season of death (Binford 1978). These factors can all be determined from evidence other than anatomical representation (e.g., Speth 1983, Legge and Rowley-Conwy 1988). Where they are known, they may be used to explore the degree and nature of rationality in carcass utilization. For example, at the Garnsey site in New Mexico, stratigraphic and faunal evidence suggests the killing of small groups of bison in spring. Anatomical analysis indicates more intensive use of male than female carcasses. The latter would have been in poor condition, and hence of low nutritional value, at this time of year as a result of pregnancy and lactation (Speth 1983) and, in this respect, carcass utilization at Garnsey may be regarded as rational. Thus far, optimality models of carcass utilization have again been used only heuristically. Problems would arise, however, if an attempt was made to identify, solely on the basis of anatomical representation data, the factors which shaped butchery strategy. For example, single and mass kills could be inferred from bulk and gourmet patterns of butchery, respectively, only if rational or optimal behaviour were assumed *a priori*. Such an assumption would violate the principle of intellectual independence and so should be avoided.

Similar caution is needed in the use of mortality profiles to distinguish between management of livestock for meat, milk, wool or traction (Payne 1973). These models rest on the observation that, for well-established biological reasons, animals of different age and sex have differential potential for resource production. In this case, uniformitarian extrapolation to the distant past must take account of the effects of several millennia of selective breeding by humans (Noddle 1990); crop plants pose similar problems (Davies and Hillman 1988). For example, a milk mortality profile is characterized by the slaughter of males during infancy but doubt has been cast on the ability of primitive breeds of cattle, sheep and goats to let down milk in the absence of their offspring (McCormick 1992). Nonetheless, uniformitarian assumptions may be valid, because comparative studies of mammalian lactation suggest that the wild ancestors of these livestock species were pre-adapted to milking and artistic evidence indicates that cultural measures to stimulate let down have long been known (Sherratt 1981). Again problems of equifinality also arise: for example, high mortality among infant calves, lambs or kids might alternatively result from natural deaths or pre-emptive slaughter in the face of a shortage of fodder. Most contentiously of all, however, a slaughter pattern maximizing the *potential* for milk production can only be treated as evidence that dairying *actually* took place if it is assumed that humans made maximum use of this potential (Halstead 1998). Such optimizing models can only be used securely, therefore, as heuristic measures of resource potential, and independent evidence should be sought that this potential was actually exploited. For example, analysis of lipids in ceramics might confirm that a particular species was milked (see Chapter 28), while analysis of animal bone chemistry might confirm whether age of weaning was consistent with management for dairy production.

Modelling resource use: production, exchange and consumption

With due attention to problems of equifinality and to assumptions of uniformitarianism or optimality, archaeologists can explore a number of aspects of past resource use. The synthesis of these individual inferences into broader models of production, exchange

or consumption is a greater challenge, requiring the integration of many complementary strands of evidence.

A pioneering attempt at integration in terms of production was made by Vita-Finzi and Higgs (1970). Noting that the study of animal bones and plant remains could shed no light on the relative importance of these two sources of subsistence, they turned to the analysis of 'site catchments' (the area within a one- or two-hour walk) in such terms as the balance between arable and grazing land or between summer and winter pasture. With allowance for changes in landscape and human technology, this technique provided a simple measure of potential land use around individual sites, coupled with predictions concerning the articulation of complementary seasonal sites on a regional scale. Vita-Finzi and Higgs stressed the need for such predictions to be tested against other classes of evidence, but the low cost of the technique compared to excavation led to a plethora of untested studies which, in effect, treated *resource potential* as a reliable guide to *actual resource use*. In this case, the tacit assumption of economic maximization was underpinned by the contentious argument of Higgs and Jarman (above) that, in the long term, economy should tend towards optimal adaptations. The subsequent use of catchment studies to support the Higgs and Jarman hypothesis (e.g., Jarman *et al.* 1982) illustrates perfectly the danger of circular argument if methods of archaeological inference are founded on assumptions about human behaviour. Nonetheless, some exemplary heuristic applications of locational analysis on this scale are noted below.

The temptation to conflate potential and actual land use has receded as archaeologists have developed a wider array of approaches to the investigation of past cultural landscapes. Many intensive surface surveys record off-site scatters of cultural material, which reveal something of the scale and intensity of human activity in different parts of the landscape. Such scatters were doubtless created by a variety of activities and the pre-eminence of 'middening' (and, hence, of arable farming) as a causal agent has been questioned (Alcock *et al.* 1994), but such ambiguity may be resolved by intensive geoarchaeological study. More fine-grained applications of palynology can expose mosaics of land use, while on-site charcoal offers complementary evidence of such details of the local cultural landscape as the existence of hedges around early farming sites in central Europe (e.g., Kreuz 1988). Intensive and extensive systems of crop husbandry can also be distinguished on the basis of weed floras (e.g., Jones 1992, van der Veen 1992), although attempts to develop similar criteria for intensive and extensive management of livestock (Zeder 1991, Halstead 1996) partly rest on assumptions of economic rationality. There have also been important advances in the use of on-site evidence to locate particular aspects of land use in space. For example, the ecological preferences of marsh plants or arable weeds may shed light on where hay was harvested (e.g., Behre and Jacomet 1991:88) or crops grown (e.g., van der Veen 1992) and, for similar reasons, plant inclusions in dung may indicate which habitats were grazed or browsed by livestock (e.g., Charles 1998). Isotopic analysis of bone may be able to detect longer-distance movements of hunted or herded animals between different drainage systems while, at coastal sites, the balance between littoral and deep-sea fishing may be inferred from the size and species of fish caught (Barrett *et al.* 1999).

The articulation of regional settlement systems, through human mobility or exchange, may be explored in several ways. Perhaps most obviously, plants or animals may be found outside their natural ranges: for example, marine mammals on inland sites in Norse Greenland (McGovern 1992). This biogeographical approach is inevitably biased towards detecting long-distance movements, such as imports of south European grain crops (and weed floras) into Roman northwest Europe (van Zeist 1991) or of exotic plant and animal foods into Roman to early modern London. On a regional scale, however, metric and non-metric variability within an animal species may indicate whether more than one population was represented at a site and so shed light, for example, on the size of hinterland from which early towns were supplied with livestock (e.g., Armitage 1982).

On a similar geographical scale, complementary patterns of anatomical representation in assemblages of animal bones (e.g., Binford 1978) and plant macrofossils (e.g., Jones 1985) can reveal flows of resources in the same way that analysis of lithic reduction sequences can identify the movement of stone. In isolation, such patterns can only be used to identify kill sites and base camps, or producer sites and consumer sites, if human rationality is assumed, but once again the burden of inference can be shared with other categories of evidence. For example, among Mesolithic sites in Denmark, a distinction may be drawn between small, specialized seasonal sites and larger, perennial base camps on the basis of the greater diversity and broader seasonal distribution of hunting activities at the latter (Rowley-Conwy 1999). Distinctive patterns of anatomical representation, such as the under-representation of the rear half of boar at Ringkloster (Rowley-Conwy

1994–95), can then be taken as evidence that seasonal procurement sites supplied meat to base camps without the need to assume human economic rationality. A similar logic underpins the use of complementary or skewed demographic patterns to infer the movement of domestic animals between producer sites, characterized by evidence for infant mortality, and consumer sites, with a lack of breeding stock, for example in early Medieval England (e.g., Crabtree 1994).

Exchange may also be suggested indirectly by the scale of processing or storage facilities. For example, comparison of classical Greek and imperial Roman presses indicates a radical increase in the capacity for production of olive oil on individual estates (Foxhall 1993). Although the realization of this capacity must be demonstrated rather than assumed, the implication of agricultural specialization increasingly geared to exchange is of direct relevance to critical debate concerning the nature of the ancient economy. In a similar vein, Wilkinson (1994) has argued that evidence of local population size (derived from settlement area), the extent of cultivation (inferred from 'manuring scatters') and the frequency of large storage vessels might together identify surplus-producing and surplus-consuming sites in Early Bronze Age Upper Mesopotamia.

While the movement of biological resources, particularly on a regional and inter-regional scale, is beginning to be recognized archaeologically, distinction between different mechanisms of reciprocity, redistribution and (market) exchange remains highly problematic. At Bronze Age Tell el-Amarna in Egypt, the contrast between careful knife-butchery of pigs and goats and careless chopping up of cattle suggests two different methods of meat distribution, and these may plausibly be equated with the domestic economy and central redistribution, respectively, but essentially on contextual grounds (Luff 1994). In Late Bronze Age Greece, textual records of Mycenaean palatial redistributive transactions refer to only two or three cereal crops, implying that most of the cereals and pulses attested archaeobotanically in elite contexts were acquired through undocumented exchange transactions. In this latter case, archaeological evidence has proved invaluable in correcting the strong redistributive bias of the textual evidence but, in isolation, might have shed no light on the institutional mechanisms by which resources were mobilized.

Synthesis in the form of models of consumption is now greatly facilitated by the analysis of human bone chemistry, which has the potential to identify the relative contributions to diet of broad categories of nutritional resources: plants versus animals, marine versus terrestrial foods, C_3 versus C_4 plants (see Chapters 23 and 28). These crude quantitative characterizations neatly complement the finer detail afforded by studies of bone and seed assemblages, which may indicate, for example, the relative abundance of sheep and goat meat or of wheat and barley grain but, for taphonomic reasons, shed little or no light on the relative contributions to diet of such broad categories as domestic mammals and fish. Similarly, while charred plant remains may give a relatively full picture of starchy plant staples, particularly grains but also to some extent tubers, faecal material and especially waterlogged faecal material often demonstrates the range of fruits, stems and leaves which provided essential vitamins and minerals, as well as introducing some variety to the diet (e.g., Tomlinson 1991).

A relatively neglected area has been the interrelationship between animal and plant resources, particularly within farming economies. For example, livestock may provide traction and manure for crop production, while arable crops and crop-processing by-products are widely used as animal fodder. Grassland communities are less well represented than grain crops in the archaeobotanical record, but ecological analysis of available evidence from northwest and central Europe suggests that the development of hay meadows, a distinctive and widespread feature of the recent landscape, can be traced back to the Iron Age (Behre and Jacomet 1991), while provision for earlier livestock included various forms of leaf- and twig-fodder (e.g., Rasmussen 1993). Microwear on animal teeth and plant inclusions in animal faeces provide complementary insights into animal diet. Dental microwear offers a relatively coarse picture of diet, distinguishing between such broad categories as grazing and stall-feeding, but links these insights to individual animals of known species and age and so offers hope of investigating the strategic use of different qualities of pasture by, for example, breeding adult females and non-productive juvenile males (Mainland 1998). Archaeobotanical examination of dung may provide more precise information on dietary components, but perhaps without differentiating species, let alone age and sex, of animal.

There is growing evidence from such studies that grain was widely fed to prehistoric livestock both in the ancient Near East (Charles 1998), where there is also abundant textual evidence of the fattening of animals for sacrifice or feasting, and in Europe. Moreover, in the Near East, comparison of grain finds from dung with those from storage contexts

suggests that a distinction can be drawn between grains such as emmer wheat, used primarily for human consumption, and grains such as barley, used extensively as fodder (Charles 1998). In Europe, where dung was less commonly burnt as fuel, similar inferences may be drawn more cautiously. One negative implication is that the existing archaeobotanical record, which is dominated by food grains in Europe but by dung-derived fodder grains on many Near Eastern sites (Charles 1998), may in each case radically misrepresent the relative abundance of different grain crops. A very positive implication is that archaeobotanists are beginning to identify a cultural hierarchy of 'high-status' (food) and 'low-status' (fodder) grains (Halstead and Jones 1989).

This last observation raises the symbolic dimension of resource use. The widespread role of fine textiles in expressing identity has already been noted and is reflected in archaeobotanical finds of plant macrofossils used in dyeing and mordanting (e.g., Hall 1996). The similar use of furs, feathers, talons, tusks and the like in foraging and farming societies, ancient and modern, has been widely explored. In many societies, the use of horses for riding or to pull chariots has been a privilege of the elite, while exotic pets, park animals and circus animals have served as sources of prestige or political capital. Arguably more universal, however, is the symbolic use of food resources as markers of ethnic identity, religion, rank or class, age and gender, or social context (e.g., Crabtree 1990). For example, in early modern Amsterdam, it may be possible to recognize cess pits belonging to Jewish households on the basis of animal bones compatible, in terms of species and body part composition, with *kosher* rules on meat consumption (Ijzereef 1989).

In traditional African societies, Goody (1982) has argued that high-status consumption is distinguished by the large volume of food and drink provided, whereas Eurasian societies, past and present, have been characterized also by the development of distinctive *cuisines*, differentiated by ingredients or methods of food preparation. For example, in written records from the Late Bronze Age 'palaces' of Mycenaean southern Greece, rations to dependent workers consisted of cereal and figs, whereas provision for elite feasts and ritual offerings included fattened animals, grain, honey, wine and perfumed oil. Likewise, in Medieval England, the abundance of deer bones at castles and their rarity in lower-status urban and rural contexts is consistent with historically documented legal restrictions on hunting (Grant 1988). Culinary practices have attracted less attention than ingredients, but baking and brewing in ancient Egypt have recently been elucidated by micro-scopic analysis (Samuel 1996), while wholemeal and white bread may be distinguishable in bran fragments from human faecal deposits in early modern London (Giorgi 1997:201). In Bronze Age Greece, cooking ves-sel shapes suggest a contrast between a diversified Minoan cuisine, in which baking played a major role, and a more utilitarian Mycenaean tradition dominated by boiling (Borgna 1997). Fine vessels for the ceremo-nial serving and consumption of wine and oil played a major role in many aspects of social life in Bronze Age and early historic Greece.

The rich and diverse symbolic dimension of resource use has been emphasized in recent literature, as an understandable corrective to the materialist bias of much bioarchaeological work during the 1970s and 1980s. Contrary to what is sometimes asserted, how-ever, there is no necessary contradiction between 'cultural' and 'practical' readings of resource use (Sahlins 1976). Meals have both symbolic and nutri-tional value and the inherent superiority of either cultural or practical reasoning cannot be demonstrated *a priori* without agreement on a common currency against which each should be evaluated. Practical reasoning does, however, enjoy the methodological advantage of being more readily verified and this should be exploited. For example, taking account of postglacial changes in shoreline, Shackleton (1988) reconstructed the changing availability of marine molluscs in the vicinity of Franchthi cave in Greece. Shellfish exploitation was not determined by availabil-ity, leading Shackleton to invoke cultural choice. This inferred cultural choice remained stable across the Mesolithic-Neolithic transition, in spite of changes in shoreline, suggesting a degree of cultural continuity which contrasted sharply with the shift from foraging to farming. Because the precise nature of cultural choice is relatively unpredictable, a cultural interpreta-tion of the Franchthi marine molluscs would have been very hard to refute and was plausibly advanced here because a practical interpretation was less open-ended and so could be rejected empirically.

Scales of interpretation

One crucial issue, largely avoided in the preceding discussion, is the spatial *scale* at which resource use is investigated. In *Prehistoric Europe: the Economic Basis*, Graham Clark made frequent heuristic use of a regional or continental scale, for example in noting the association of early farming sites with deciduous

forest in Scandinavia or with fertile loess soils in central Europe (Clark 1952:18, 96). This approach has been used productively to explore such diverse subjects as the ecological context of Bronze Age civilization in the Aegean, or Lower Palaeolithic hunting and scaven-ging strategies and the Neolithic management of live-stock for 'secondary products' of traction, milk and wool in Europe. The suggested linkage between a sec-ondary products revolution, marginal colonization and unstable settlement (Sherratt 1981) has in turn served as a starting point for consideration of patterns of descent, regional alliance and claims to land in later Neolithic Europe. Similarly, the contrast between 'woodland' and 'champion' (open-field) landscapes in lowland England has provoked stimulating discussion of changes in land tenure during the Saxon period (Williamson and Bellamy 1987).

Reacting to the coarseness of resolution at such scales, Vita-Finzi and Higgs (1970) justifiably argued that the immediate catchment of a habitation site was a more appropriate scale at which to explore the relationship between human population and the poten-tial of the environment to yield staple foods. Other resources, however, such as mates, scarce raw materials, prestige goods and arcane knowledge may be drawn from much greater distances and a regional scope is necessary to encompass the range of land-scapes, resources and competing or complementary sites with which individuals might come into contact during the course of a year or a lifetime. Thus, different spatial scales are appropriate to different types of ques-tion (M. Jones 1991).

The substantivist emphasis on the social embedded-ness of economy highlights the need for investigation at a nested series of social scales, from the individual up to the world system (e.g., Flannery 1976). For example, studies of individual skeletons in many parts of the world have revealed the differentiation of production (reflected in skeletal responses to work load and activity patterns) and consumption (inferred from bone chemistry and overall health status) along lines of age, gender or rank (e.g., Larsen 1997). Studies of early farming households in Mesoamerica, the Near East and Europe have underlined the importance of the shift from communal sharing to domestic hoarding, as a co-requisite or correlate of food production and as a possible precondition of the emergence of salient social ranking (e.g., Flannery 1972). Comparative analysis of households or settlements may clarify the extent to which social integration at higher levels was founded on economic specialization or inequality. A fruitful attempt to explore economic inequality on a regional scale is McGovern's demonstration that high-status settlements in Norse Greenland tend to have relatively generous provision for cattle stalling and fodder storage, which is in turn linked to access to abundant local potential for hay meadows (McGovern 1992).

Equally critical and more neglected is the temporal scale of investigation. Temporal and spatial scales are intimately linked, not least because seasonal, inter-annual and longer-term fluctuation or uncertainty in resource availability is widely countered by exploiting spatial variation in resource availability through such basic risk-buffering mechanisms as mobility, exchange and diversification (Halstead and O'Shea 1989). Important changes take place over the *longue durée*, both in the natural and cultural environment and in patterns of human resource use. Partly because of the coarse nature of most archaeological dating, a common temporal unit of investigation is the relative chronological 'phase' or 'period', often spanning centuries or even millennia. At this scale, diachronic trends in resource use may be identified and interpreted in relation, for example, to long-term changes in late Pleistocene climate and vegetation in the Near East or cultural processes such as Roman imperialism in northwest Europe (Kreuz 1999). Chronological precision is often sacrificed to increase sample size, for example by combining animal bones from successive sub-phases to produce a meaningful mortality structure, but finer divisions may be retained for less demanding analytical purposes such as assessment of species composition. For example, changes in the representation of large mammals and edible plants were charted through successive layers at Mesolithic–Neolithic Franchthi cave in Greece in order to explore, rather than assume, the degree of synchrony between the adoption of domestic animals, crops and ceramics (Payne 1975). On lake-side settlements in Switzerland, tree-ring dating affords both a finer (±20 year) chronology and a proxy climate record, which reveals that, over a period of two centuries during the fourth millennium BC, farmers in this agriculturally marginal region responded to climatic deterioration by increased reliance on hunting and gathering (Schibler *et al.* 1997). Individuals take decisions about resource use (or 'economize') against the backdrop of changing responsibilities over the timespan of a human generation (e.g., the transition from childhood to adulthood) and of often dramatic inter-annual fluctuations in the availability of resources (e.g., Sahlins 1974). Studies on an inter-annual timescale are usually, but not always, beyond the resolution of archaeological investigation.

At the fourth millennium BC rural settlement of Sharafabad in Iran, sedimentary and ecofactual evidence from successive layers in a large pit was consistent with a series of seasonal filling episodes over a two-year cycle. Over this cycle, a sharp decline in the rate of discard of animal bone may indicate that the second year was a bad one, perhaps because of drought, while contrasting patterns of artefactual deposition suggest that centrally administered stores were preferentially mobilized in the second year, perhaps to avert food shortage (Wright *et al.* 1989).

Units of analysis: contextual economic archaeology

Preservation and retrieval of archaeobotanical material, at least in regions where charred remains dominate the record, is likely to be the exception rather than the rule, with the result that surviving plant remains tend to be retrieved as discrete samples. Moreover, surviving remains often represent material deliberately discarded during plant processing rather than that destined for consumption and charred accidentally (e.g., Dennell 1976). Each sample must be analysed individually, therefore, in terms of context and composition in order to clarify its processing and depositional history. Processing products need to be distinguished from by-products, and likewise refuse from a single behavioural episode must be distinguished from mixed rubbish, for two primary reasons. First, the recognition of processing is arguably the most effective means of distinguishing which of the plant taxa represented on archaeological sites were intended for consumption, and in what form (Dennell 1976, Hillman 1984). Secondly, because plant processing and taphonomy selectively influence the representation of both plant parts and plant taxa, their effects must be factored out before sample composition is used as evidence for patterns of plant production/gathering or consumption (Jones 1987). For example, the winnowing and sieving of grain crops selectively remove the seeds of weed taxa characteristic of intensive horticulture, leaving behind the 'seed corn' weeds more typical of extensive field cultivation (Jones 1992). A distinction should be drawn, therefore, between the 'unit of interpretation' of varying spatial, temporal and social scale, within which archaeobotanists seek to understand the use of plant resources, and a basic 'unit of analysis' which should correspond, as far as possible, to individual depositional episodes and the more or less discrete behavioural events or processes which lie behind them (G. Jones 1991).

The often severe nature of bone loss is less obvious than in the case of plant remains preserved by charring. Partly for this reason, and partly because bone samples from individual contexts (e.g., a small pit or hearth) are often too small for their composition to be interpreted reliably, there is a widespread tendency to treat the deposition and survival of animal bones on archaeological sites as relatively continuous, such that records from different contexts can be summed to produce 'average' patterns of animal exploitation for an entire period assemblage. Taphonomic studies, however, have shown how gnawing by scavengers and weathering may destroy bone which is not rapidly buried (see Chapter 15). Moreover, single-context bone groups of distinctive and interpretable composition do occur, particularly on urban sites where specialized carcass processing favours the deposition of homogeneous groups of material (e.g., Maltby 1985:49). For example, Roman and later levels at York have yielded individual context groups suggestive of the specialized smoking of shoulders of beef and processing of cattle 'marrow bones' (O'Connor 1988) and perhaps the working of sheep skins. These deposits may represent recurrent deposition over a period of time, but a lens within a pit at the fifteenth century AD village of Raversijde in Belgium comprised head and tail elements from c. 130 plaice and probably represents a single processing and discard event (van Neer and Pieters 1997).

The exceptional and discontinuous nature of bone deposition and survival has been inferred by a different route in studies of Iron Age sites in southern England, where a significant proportion of bone assemblages is often made up by 'special deposits' of articulating skeletons or part-skeletons placed in negative features such as pits (Grant 1991). The number of surviving 'special deposits', divided by the estimated duration of occupation at such sites, suggests that such structured deposition may have taken place very infrequently and thus that the surviving record is substantially shaped by unusual and potentially unrepresentative acts of consumption and deposition. Similarities between 'special deposits' of human and animal bones suggest that some, at least, of the latter should be regarded as ritual depositions, while the difficulty of drawing a clear line between special and ordinary deposits has been seen as evidence that ritual penetrated the most mundane aspects of Iron Age society. In the sense that human behaviour is widely structured by cultural rules, this inference is plausible enough, but claimed empirical support should be regarded with some scepticism. Compared with the *relatively* predictable effects of carcass processing or

taphonomic alteration, structured deposition is highly flexible and so poses severe problems of archaeological recognition and interpretation. For example, the search for structured associations between particular species or particular parts of animals and different types of contexts (e.g., ditch; upper pit fill; basal pit fill – Hill 1995) considers such a large number of variables, and tolerates inversions so freely, that the patterns claimed are quite likely to be fortuitous. Moreover, for many 'special deposits', a taphonomic or practical interpretation is plausible (Wilson 1992). Plainly, it is unwise to identify human activity, practical or cultural, on the basis of an assemblage composition which can be explained adequately in terms of canid gnawing, weathering or soil chemistry, while interpretations in terms of ritual treatment and economic anatomy may not be mutually incompatible. In this context, spatial patterning in left- and right-sided body parts is of particular interest, because the two sides of the body are identical in terms of practical utility and susceptibility to taphonomic processes, so that statistically meaningful associations can confidently be attributed to the symbolic dimension of human behaviour.

On the other hand, some structured deposition is unambiguous and, in addition to its intrinsic interest, may shed positive light on past resource use. For example, at Iron Age Baleshare and Hornish Point in north-west Scotland, bone fragments scattered through occupation deposits, middens and cultivation layers indicated a heavy concentration of cattle mortality among infants and elderly adults. Conversely, a single human burial was associated with two juvenile or sub-adult cattle skeletons, gathered up for deposition after skinning, dismembering, filleting, marrow extraction and carnivore gnawing. Although the consumption and discard of infant and elderly cattle was probably informed by cultural rules, the overtly structured deposition of animal bones in association with this unique human burial suggests the sacrifice during exceptional funerary rituals of animals (perhaps future milk-cows) normally considered too valuable for consumption (Halstead 1998).

Thus investigations of carcass or plant processing, of structured deposition, and of the taphonomic transformations which might mask both of these, have a common need for fine-grained contextual analysis, based on a 'unit of analysis' which, as far as possible, corresponds to individual depositional episodes (G. Jones 1991, Maltby 1985:57). This fundamental point also has practical implications for sampling strategies. While some combination of probabilistic and judgemental sampling is the most reliable way of achieving a representative picture of a particular 'unit of interpretation' (e.g., a site/phase or region/period assemblage; M. Jones 1991), this in no way removes the need to understand the internal variability between constituent 'units of analysis'. For this reason, attempts to achieve representative samples by randomly mixing different 'units of analysis' are misguided.

CONCLUSION

Economic archaeology has been surrounded by theoretical controversy, which has far-reaching and fundamental implications for the archaeological investigation of resource use. The exposure of economic archaeology through the 1980s and 1990s to the heat of theoretical scrutiny has underlined the need for careful use of both concepts and methods. In particular, assumptions of optimality or economic rationality underpin many models and practitioners must take great care to deploy such models heuristically rather than deterministically. Recognition that human use of biological resources is heavily structured by cultural rules, and that the bioarchaeological record is partly shaped by culturally structured deposition, also poses a great challenge.

On the other hand, many of the models used to identify patterns of resource use are founded in biological or ecological theory and are effectively independent of our ideas concerning human behaviour. More generally, in investigating the use of plant and animal resources, archaeologists can exploit many known properties of the biological world as a window on to the human past. The taphonomy of biological resources has been extensively researched and is relatively well understood, while many potential problems of equifinality can be resolved by integrating different types of evidence and complementary techniques of analysis. The arguments over practical versus cultural reasoning will rumble on, but much of the methodology of economic archaeology is of equal value to both schools of thought. There is no necessary conflict between practical and cultural interpretations of past resource use, nor any logical grounds for ascribing primacy to either approach. Practical reasoning enjoys some methodological advantages and is arguably subject to fewer and more soluble problems of equifinality. In the long term, however, economic archaeologists should perhaps move beyond the search for practical versus cultural rationales for resource use and seek to understand the interplay between them. For example, cultural rules play a major role in shaping human identities and these in turn may prescribe obligations of resource procurement and rights to resource use.

ACKNOWLEDGEMENTS

We are grateful to Amy Bogaard and Glynis Jones, for critical comments on an earlier draft of this chapter, and to Andrew Chamberlain, for bibliographical advice.

REFERENCES

*Recommended for further reading

Alcock, S.E., Cherry, J.F. and Davis, J.L. (1994). Intensive survey, agricultural practice and the classical landscape of Greece. In Morris, I. (ed.) *Classical Greece*, 137–170. Cambridge University Press: Cambridge.

Armitage, P.L. (1982). Studies on the remains of domestic livestock from Roman, medieval, and early modern London: objectives and methods. In Hall, A.R. and Kenward, H.K. (eds) *Environmental Archaeology in the Urban Context*, 94–106. Council for British Archaeology: London.

Barker, G. and Gamble, C. (eds) (1985). *Beyond Domestication in Prehistoric Europe*. Academic Press: London.

Barrett, J.H., Nicholson, R.A. and Cerón-Carrasco, R. (1999). Archaeo-ichthyological evidence for long-term socio-economic trends in northern Scotland: 3500 BC to AD 1500. *Journal of Archaeological Science*, 26:353–388.

Behre, K.-E. and Jacomet, S. (1991). The ecological interpretation of archaeobotanical data. In van Zeist, W., Wasylikowa, K. and Behre, K.-E. (eds) *Progress in Old World Palaeoethnobotany*, 81–108. Balkema: Rotterdam.

Binford, L.R. (1978). *Nunamiut Ethnoarchaeology*. Academic Press: New York.

Binford, L.R. (1981). *Bones: Ancient Men and Modern Myths*. Academic Press: New York.

Boardman, S. and Jones, G. (1990). Experiments on the effects of charring on cereal plant components. *Journal of Archaeological Science*, 17:1–11.

Borgna, E. (1997). Kitchen-ware from LM IIIC Phaistos: cooking traditions and ritual activities in LBA Cretan societies. *Studi Micenei ed Egeo-Anatolici*, 39:189–217.

Bull, G. and Payne, S. (1982). Tooth eruption and epiphysial fusion in pigs and wild boar. In Wilson, B., Grigson, C. and Payne, S. (eds) *Ageing and Sexing Animal Bones from Archaeological Sites*, 55–71. BAR 109, British Archaeological Reports: Oxford.

Charles, M. (1998). Fodder from dung: the recognition and interpretation of dung-derived plant material from archaeological sites. *Environmental Archaeology*, 1:111–122.

*Charles, M., Jones, G. and Hodgson, J.G. (1997). FIBS in archaeobotany: functional interpretation of weed floras in relation to husbandry practices. *Journal of Archaeological Science*, **24**:1151–1161.

Clark, J.G.D. (1952). *Prehistoric Europe: the Economic Basis*. Methuen: London.

Crabtree, P. (1990). Zooarchaeology and complex societies: some uses of faunal analysis for the study of trade, social status and ethnicity. In Schiffer, M. (ed.) *Archaeological Method and Theory 2*, 171–181. University of Arizona Press: Tucson.

Crabtree, P. (1994). Animal exploitation in East Anglian villages. In Rackham, J. (ed.) *Environment and Economy in Anglo-Saxon England*, 40–54. Council for British Archaeology: York.

Davies, M.S. and Hillman, G.C. (1988). Effects of soil flooding on growth and grain yield of populations of tetraploid and hexaploid species of wheat. *Annals of Botany*, **62**:597–604.

Dennell, R.W. (1976). The economic importance of plant resources represented on archaeological sites. *Journal of Archaeological Science*, 3:229–247.

Dennell, R.W. (1979). Prehistoric diet and nutrition: some food for thought. *World Archaeology*, 11:121–135.

Flannery, K.V. (1972). The origins of the village as a settlement type in Mesoamerica and the Near East: a comparative study. In Ucko, P.J., Tringham, R. and Dimbleby, G.W. (eds) *Man, Settlement and Urbanism*, 23–53. Duckworth: London.

Flannery, K.V. (ed.) (1976). *The Early Mesoamerican Village*. Academic Press: New York.

*Foley, R. (1985). Optimality theory in anthropology. *Man*, **20**:222–242.

Foxhall, L. (1993). Oil extraction and processing equipment in classical Greece. *Bulletin de Corréspondance Hellénique supplement*, 26:183–200.

Giorgi, J. (1997). Diet in late medieval and early modern London: the archaeobotanical evidence. In Gaimster, D. and Stamper, P. (eds) *The Age of Transition: the Archaeology of English Culture 1400–1600*, 197–213. Oxbow: Oxford.

Goody, J. (1982). *Cooking, Cuisine and Class*. Cambridge University Press: Cambridge.

Grant, A. (1988). The animal resources. In Astill, G. and Grant, A. (eds) *The Countryside of Medieval England*, 149–187. Blackwell: Oxford.

Grant, A. (1991). Economic or symbolic? Animals and ritual behaviour. In Garwood, P., Jennings, D., Skeates, R. and Toms, J. (eds) *Sacred and Profane*, 109–114. Oxford University Committee for Archaeology: Oxford.

Hall, A.R. (1996). A survey of palaeobotanical evidence for dyeing and mordanting from British archaeological excavations. *Quaternary Science Reviews*, 15:635–640.

Halstead, P. (1996). Pastoralism or household herding? Problems of scale and specialization in early Greek animal husbandry. *World Archaeology*, **28**:20–42.

*Halstead, P. (1998). Mortality models and milking: problems of uniformitarianism, optimality and equifinality reconsidered. *Anthropozoologica*, **27**:3–20.

Halstead, P. and Jones, G. (1989). Agrarian ecology in the Greek islands: time stress, scale and risk. *Journal of Hellenic Studies*, **109**:41–55.

Halstead, P. and O'Shea, J. (1989). Cultural responses to risk and uncertainty. In Halstead, P. and O'Shea, J. (eds) *Bad Year Economics*, 1–7. Cambridge University Press: Cambridge.

Hawkes, C. (1954). Archaeological theory and method: some suggestions from the Old World. *American Anthropologist*, **56**:155–168.

Higgs, E.S. and Jarman, M.R. (1975). Palaeoeconomy. In Higgs, E.S. (ed.) *Palaeoeconomy*, 1–8. Cambridge University Press: London.

Hill, J.D. (1995). *Ritual and Rubbish in the Iron Age of Wessex: a Study of a Specific Archaeological Record*. British Archaeological Reports 242, Tempus Reparatum: Oxford.

Hillman, G. (1984). Interpretation of archaeological plant remains: ethnographic models from Turkey. In van Zeist, W. and Casparie, W.A. (eds) *Plants and Ancient Man*, 1–41, Balkema: Rotterdam.

Ijzereef, F.G. (1989). Social differentiation from animal bone studies. In Serjeantson, D. and Waldron, T. (eds) *Diet and Crafts in Towns: the Evidence of Animal Remains from the Roman to the Post-Roman Periods*. BAR 199, 41–53, British Archaeological Reports: Oxford.

Jarman, M.R., Bailey, G.N. and Jarman, H.N. (eds) (1982). *Early European Agriculture*. Cambridge University Press: Cambridge.

Jones, G. (1987). A statistical approach to the archaeological identification of crop processing. *Journal of Archaeological Science*, **14**:311–323.

Jones, G. (1991). Numerical analysis in archaeobotany. In van Zeist, W., Wasylikowa, K. and Behre, K.-E. (eds) *Progress in Old World Palaeoethnobotany*, 63–80. Balkema: Rotterdam.

Jones, G. (1992). Weed phytosociology and crop husbandry: identifying a contrast between ancient and modern practice. *Review of Palaeobotany and Palynology*, **73**:133–143.

Jones, G. (1998). Wheat grain identification – why bother? *Environmental Archaeology*, 2:29–34.

Jones, G., Charles, M., Colledge, S. and Halstead, P. (1995). Towards the archaeobotanical recognition of winter-cereal irrigation: an investigation of modern weed ecology in northern Spain. In Kroll, H. and Pasternak, R. (eds) *Res Archaeobotanicae*, 49–68. Oetker-Voges: Kiel.

Jones, G., Valamoti, S. and Charles, M. (2000). Early crop diversity: a 'new' glume wheat from northern Greece. *Vegetation History and Archaeobotany*, **9**:133–146.

Jones, M. (1985). Archaeobotany beyond subsistence reconstruction. In Barker, G. and Gamble, C. (eds) *Beyond Domestication in Prehistoric Europe: Investigations in Subsistence Archaeology and Social Complexity*, 107–128. Academic Press: New York.

Jones, M. (1991). Sampling in palaeoethnobotany. In van Zeist, W., Wasylikowa, K. and Behre, K.-E. (eds) *Progress in Old World Palaeoethnobotany*, 53–62. Balkema: Rotterdam.

Knörzer, K.-H. (1979). Über den Wandel der angebauten Körnerfrüchte und ihrer Unkrautvegetation auf einer niederrheinischen Lössfläche seit dem Frühneolithikum. *Archaeo-Physika*, **8**:147–163.

Kreuz, A. (1988). Holzkohle-Funde der ältestbandkeramischen Siedlung Friedberg-Bruchenbrücken: Anzeiger für Brennholz-Auswahl und lebende Hecken? In Küster, H.-J. (ed.) *Der prähistorische Mensch und seine Umwelt*, 139–153. Konrad Theiss: Stuttgart.

Kreuz, A. (1999). Becoming a Roman farmer: preliminary report on the environmental evidence from the Romanisation project. *Journal of Roman Archaeology supplementary series*, **32**:71–98.

Lange, A.G. (1990). *Archaeobotanical Research at de Horden: a Numerical Approach*. Rijksdienst voor het Oudheidkundig Bodemonderzoek: Amersfoort.

Larsen, C.S. (1997). *Bioarchaeology: Interpreting Behavior from the Human Skeleton*. Cambridge University Press: Cambridge.

Legge, A.J. and Rowley-Conwy, P.A. (1988). *Starr Carr Revisited: a Re-analysis of the Large Mammals*. London University Department of Extramural Studies: London.

Luff, R. (1994). Butchery at the Workmen's Village (WV), Amarna, Egypt. In Luff, R. and Rowley-Conwy, P. (eds) *Whither Environmental Archaeology?* 158–170. Oxbow Books: Oxford.

Lyman, R.L. (1992). Anatomical considerations of utility curves in zooarchaeology. *Journal of Archaeological Science*, **19**:7–22.

McCormick, F. (1992). Early faunal evidence for dairying. *Oxford Journal of Archaeology*, **11**:201–209.

McGovern, T.H. (1992). Bones, buildings, and boundaries: palaeoeconomic approaches to Norse Greenland. In Morris, C.D. and Rackham, D.J. (eds) *Norse and Later Settlement and Subsistence in the Norse Atlantic*, 193–230. University of Glasgow: Glasgow.

Mainland, I.L. (1998). Dental microwear and diet in domestic sheep (*Ovis aries*) and goats (*Capra hircus*): distinguishing grazing and fodder-fed ovicaprids using a quantitative analytical approach. *Journal of Archaeological Science*, **25**:1259–1271.

Maltby, M. (1985). Patterns in faunal assemblage variability. In Barker, G. and Gamble, C. (eds) *Beyond Domestication in Prehistoric Europe*, 33–74. Academic Press: London.

Moran, N.C. and O'Connor, T.P. (1994). Age attribution in domestic sheep by skeletal and dental maturation: a pilot study of available sources. *International Journal of Osteoarchaeology*, **4**:267–285.

Noddle, B. (1990). Flesh on the bones. *Circaea*, **7**:31–51.

O'Connor, T. (1988). *Bones from the General Accident Site, Tanner Row*. Council for British Archaeology: London.

Payne, S. (1973). Kill-off patterns in sheep and goats: the mandibles from Asvan Kalé. *Anatolian Studies*, **23**:281–303.

Payne, S. (1975). Faunal change at Franchthi Cave from 20,000 BC to 3,000 BC. In Clason, A.T. (ed.) *Archaeozoological Studies*, 120–131. Elsevier: Amsterdam.

Payne, S. and Munson, P.J. (1985). Ruby and how many squirrels? The destruction of bones by dogs. In Fieller, N.R.J., Gilbertson, D.D. and Ralph, N.G.A. (eds) *Palaeobiological Investigations: Research Design, Methods and Data Analysis*, 31–40. BAR International Series 266, British Archaeological Reports: Oxford.

Polanyi, K. (1957). The economy as instituted process. In Polanyi, K., Arensberg, C.M. and Pearson, H.W. (eds) *Trade and Market in the Early Empires: Economies in History and Theory*, 243–270. Free Press: New York.

Rasmussen, P. (1993). Analysis of goat/sheep faeces from Egolzwil 3, Switzerland: evidence for branch and twig foddering of livestock in the Neolithic. *Journal of Archaeological Science*, **20**:479–502.

Rowley-Conwy, P. (1994–95). Meat, furs and skins: Mesolithic animal bones from Ringkloster, a seasonal hunting camp in Jutland. *Journal of Danish Archaeology*, **12**:87–98.

Rowley-Conwy, P. (1999). Economic prehistory in southern Scandinavia. In Coles, J., Bewley, R. and Mellars, P. (eds) *World Prehistory: Studies in Memory of Grahame Clark*, 125–159. Proceedings of the British Academy 99, Oxford University Press: Oxford.

Sahlins, M. (1974). *Stone Age Economics*. Tavistock: London.

Sahlins, M. (1976). *Culture and Practical Reason*. Chicago University Press: Chicago.

Samuel, D. (1996). Investigation of ancient Egyptian baking and brewing methods by correlative microscopy. *Science*, **273**:488–490.

Schibler, J., Jacomet, S., Hüster-Plogmann, H. and Brombacher, C. (1997). Economic crash in the 37th and 36th centuries cal. BC in Neolithic lake shore sites in Switzerland. *Anthropozoologica*, **25–26**:553–570.

Shackleton, J.C. (1988). *Marine Molluscan Remains from Franchthi Cave*. Excavations at Franchthi Cave, Greece, Fascicule 4, Indiana University Press: Bloomington.

Shanks, M. and Tilley, C. (1987). *Reconstructing Archaeology: Theory and Practice*. Cambridge University Press: Cambridge.

Sherratt, A.G. (1981). Plough and pastoralism: aspects of the secondary products revolution. In Hodder, I., Isaac, G. and Hammond, N. (eds) *Pattern of the Past: Studies in Honour of David Clarke*, 261–305. Cambridge University Press: Cambridge.

Speth, J. (1983). *Bison Kills and Bone Counts*. University of Chicago Press: Chicago.

Tomlinson, P.R. (1991). Vegetative plant remains from waterlogged deposits identified at York. In Renfrew, J. (ed.) *New Light on Early Farming*, 109–119. Edinburgh University Press: Edinburgh.

van der Veen, M. (1992). *Crop Husbandry Regimes: an Archaeobotanical Study of Farming in Northern England, 1000 BC–AD 500*. JR Collis: Sheffield.

van Neer, W. and Pieters, M. (1997). Evidence for processing of flatfish at Raversijde, a late Medieval coastal site in Belgium. *Anthropozoologica*, **25–26**:579–586.

van Zeist, W. (1991). Economic aspects. In van Zeist, W., Wasylikowa, K. and Behre, K.-E. (eds) *Progress in Old World Palaeoethnobotany*, 109–130. Balkema: Rotterdam.

Vita-Finzi, C. and Higgs, E. (1970). Prehistoric economy in the Mount Carmel area of Palestine: site catchment analysis. *Proceedings of the Prehistoric Society*, **36**:1–37.

Wilkinson, T.J. (1994). The structure and dynamics of dry-farming states in Upper Mesopotamia. *Current Anthropology*, **35**:483–505.

Williamson, T. and Bellamy, L. (1987). *Property and Landscape*. George Philip: London.

Wilson, B. (1992). Considerations for the identification of ritual deposits of animal bones in Iron Age pits. *International Journal of Osteoarchaeology*, **2**:341–349.

Wright, H., Redding, R. and Pollock, S. (1989). Monitoring interannual variability: an example from the period of early state development in southwestern Iran. In Halstead, P. and O'Shea, J. (eds) *Bad Year Economics*, 106–113. Cambridge University Press: Cambridge.

Wright, K.I. (1994). Ground-stone tools and hunter-gatherer subsistence in southwest Asia: implications for the transition to farming. *American Antiquity*, **59**:238–263.

Zeder, M.A. (1991). *Feeding Cities: Specialized Animal Economy in the Ancient Near East*. Smithsonian Institute Press: Washington DC.

31

Human Impact on Vegetation

L. DUMAYNE-PEATY

School of Geography and Environmental Sciences, University of Birmingham.

The effect of people's activities on vegetation has long been an important theme in environmental archaeology and is an area in which there have been many recent theoretical and methodological advances. This chapter considers the theoretical basis for reconstructing human impact on vegetation by examining a number of methodological issues pertinent to the precision with which these activities can be reconstructed from pollen data. These include the nature of woodland clearance, detection of agriculture in pollen profiles, spatial and temporal resolution, and quantification of human impact using pollen records. These themes are illustrated using examples of Mesolithic human impact on the vegetation of the North York Moors, the Neolithic elm decline, and late prehistoric vegetation change in northern England and central Scotland. The need is stressed for archaeologists and palynologists to work in closer association to assess more fully human impact on the environment.

The value of pollen analysis as a tool for reconstructing and detecting the impact of past human groups on vegetation has been recognized since the pioneering work of Firbas (1934) and Iversen (1941). Subsequently, palynology has become one of the principal methods used in environmental archaeology, to provide information on the ecological setting of human groups and the effect of people and their activities on vegetation (Bell and Walker 1992, Roberts 1998).

Excellent summaries of the principles, theory and applications of pollen analysis can be found in texts such as Berglund (1986), Faegri *et al.* (1989) and Moore *et al.* (1991), and developments specific to cultural palynology are reviewed by Edwards (1979), Birks *et al.* (1988), Harris and Thomas (1991) and Chambers (1993). However, a dichotomy still exists between palaeoecological and archaeological approaches to studying the impact of human activity using palynological data. For example, O'Connor (1998) observed that changes seen in pollen diagrams are interpreted by palynologists in terms of the processes operating in plant communities, whilst the archaeologist might focus upon the meaning of the inferred vegetation change in the context of human groups. The chapter therefore focuses on the recent advances in palynology that have enhanced our understanding of how human groups interacted with their environment and those which make palynological data more relevant to archaeological problems.

PALYNOLOGICAL DATA AND HUMAN IMPACT ON VEGETATION

Human activity may be depicted in pollen diagrams in several ways. The most common palynological evidence for human impact on vegetation is woodland clearance and/or agricultural activity, although it is not always

---

Handbook of Archaeological Sciences. Edited by D.R. Brothwell and A.M. Pollard.
© 2001 John Wiley & Sons, Ltd.

easy to make inferences about vegetation dynamics and archaeological processes from the palynological data.

Woodland clearance

Human activity is most frequently displayed in pollen diagrams by a decrease in tree (arboreal) taxa (e.g., *Quercus, Tilia, Ulmus*), a corresponding increase in open ground indicators (e.g., Poaceae, *Calluna vulgaris*), cultivars (e.g. *Triticum, Hordeum*), weeds of cultivation or pastoralism (e.g., *Plantago lanceolata, Rumex acetosa, Urtica, Succisa*, Chenopodiaceae), and a subsequent increase in pioneering tree species (e.g., *Betula, Corylus*) or those which are light-demanding (e.g., *Fraxinus*). Other woodland taxa (e.g., *Quercus*) regenerate when the cleared area is abandoned. This sequence was identified by Iversen (1973) and became the basis of the 'landnam' or small temporary clearance model (Figure 31.1) which is still used by palynologists. However, Edwards (1979) suggested that human-induced clearance in pollen diagrams may be depicted in other ways (Figure 31.2) and has discussed the shortcomings of traditional clearance models (Edwards 1993).

Agriculture

Archaeologists are often interested in agricultural activity associated with human groups and their settlements. Whilst plant macrofossils and bone assemblages can provide evidence of crop processing, animal husbandry and diet, palynological data can be used to discern the agricultural activity that took place in the wider landscape. Much palynological work has focused upon interpreting herb (non-arboreal) pollen assemblages in the context of agricultural practices which they represent (Behre 1981; Figure 31.3). However, there are problems with this approach.

Non-arboreal pollen types can be represented poorly in pollen diagrams because many herbaceous plants produce and disperse small amounts of pollen or are insect pollinated. As a result, pollen evidence for agriculture may not reach the sampling site, particularly if the landscape surrounding the agricultural area is wooded (Edwards 1982). Pollen production and dispersal differ according to species type which means that the pollen of herbs characteristic of pastoral agriculture is often produced in greater proportions and travels longer distances than pollen of cereals or weeds associated with arable practices, thus leading to bias in the pollen record. Cereals, for example, are often

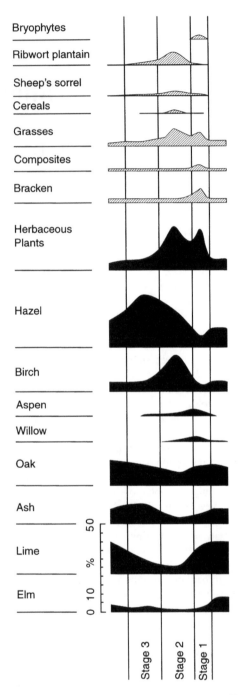

Figure 31.1 Landnam clearance model after Iversen (1973). Stage one is the clearance stage, stage two is a short period of farming and stage three is a period of forest regeneration. The sequence was interpreted as being a result of shifting agriculture undertaken by Neolithic farmers and as lasting between 50 and 100 years.

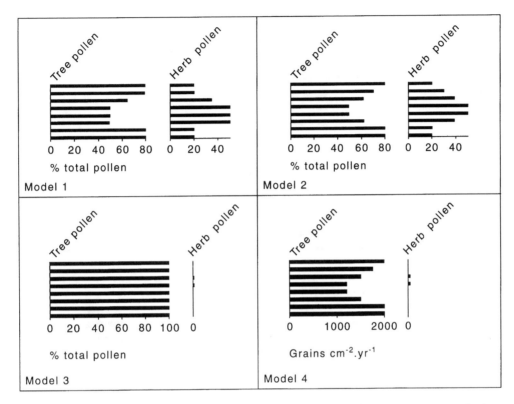

Figure 31.2 Theoretical models of clearance activity after Edwards (1979). Model 1 demonstrates a sudden decline in percentage arboreal pollen as an area of woodland is cleared for the first time by a single group of people. The arboreal pollen percentages in model 2 portray a more gradual clearance as a result of one or several groups of people slowly extending their agricultural area. Models 3 and 4 demonstrate woodland clearance in close proximity to the coring site without disturbance of trees adjacent to the site. Model 3 shows how such activity might be reflected in a percentage pollen diagram where non-arboreal pollen is prevented from reaching the sampling site because of the adjacent woodland. This results in the composition of the pollen rain remaining the same and there is consequently an absence of clearance in the pollen diagram. Model 4 applies where pollen influx is calculated. Here the absolute numbers of woodland taxa decline and non-arboreal pollen increases.

under-represented in pollen profiles because they are poor pollen producers and dispersers. *Triticum, Avena* and *Hordeum* pollen remains in the hulls and is poorly dispersed unless released by human manipulation (Behre 1981). The significance of pollen of such autogamous species is not the same as allogamous species (e.g., *Secale cereale*) (Vuorela 1973, Hall 1988) and it is difficult to determine the share of each type in tillage. Vuorela (1973) noted the sharp decline in cereal pollen with distance from cultivated fields and consequently, a core taken from the edge of a pollen sampling site is more likely to contain pollen evidence for early agriculture than one from the centre (Edwards and MacIntosh 1988). Thus, absence of cereals from a pollen diagram is not conclusive evidence that cultivation did not take place and judicious selection of sampling sites for

reconstructing agricultural activity using palynological data is important. Also, some non-arboreal pollen types are difficult to identify to species level and, in most cases, it is only possible to distinguish a pollen grain to genus or family level. Consequently, an element of subjectivity exists in the interpretation of the curve for that particular pollen type. For example, cereal pollen can be morphologically similar to that of wild grass (e.g., *Aegilops* spp.) and is not always distinguishable.

Furthermore, exclusive indicators of agriculture are rare because many taxa occur in several types of community (Figure 31.3). For example, *Plantago lanceolata* may be found growing in undisturbed grassland, pasture, abandoned arable land or on settlement sites themselves. *Rumex acetosa* is often interpreted as a

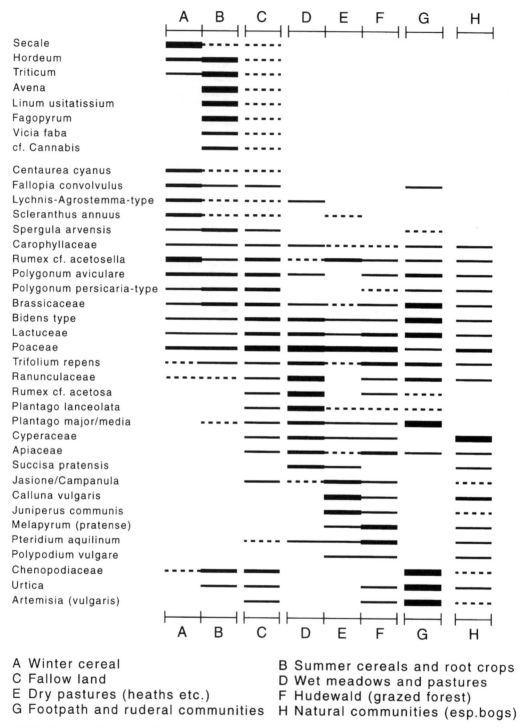

Figure 31.3 The main pollen types, which are indicative of human impact and the communities they might represent (after Behre 1981). Note how indicators with a narrow ecological niche are uncommon and that many pollen types span several types of agriculture and land use.

weed of cultivation, but it may also represent mineral-rich meadows, pastures, footpaths and ruderal communities (Behre 1981). Thus, the narrower the ecological niche of a taxon, the more valuable it is as an indicator of human activity. However, more recently, the allocation of non-arboreal pollen taxa to land use types and agricultural practices has been achieved through multivariate statistical analysis of modern day pollen rain data in relation to current anthropogenic situations. This can then be used as an analogue for past human impact (e.g., Hicks and Birks 1996).

As a result of this, Edwards (1988) concluded that only broad categories of agriculture can be derived from pollen data. These include: (i) mixed farming with the presence of cereals, grass and other herbs, (ii) possible cereal cultivation as part of a mixed agricultural system where weed taxa are common, but cereals are not present, and (iii) non-specific disturbances where weed taxa indicate pasture, husbandry, removal of trees by wind throw or senescence, or settlement. Despite the above shortcomings, pollen analysis is a reliable method for reconstructing broad agricultural activity associated with human groups.

SPATIAL RESOLUTION

Spatial scale is a concept central to interpretation of palynological evidence for human impact. There are two contexts from which human impact on vegetation can be reconstructed, namely on-site and off-site. On-site pollen analysis is where deposits located on the archaeological site itself are studied for their pollen content, whilst off-site pollen analysis is where a lake or a mire not directly associated with, but situated near, archaeological remains is analysed.

On-site pollen analysis

On-site investigations of pollen from organic deposits found on archaeological sites themselves (e.g., wells, ditch-fills, latrines, soils) have been the traditional realm of environmental archaeologists. The technique is used to interpret the ecology of the archaeological site and the activities that took place there, and the resulting data can provide information on diet, way of life, food supply and the economic activities of the occupants. Whilst the study of on-site vegetation change is important for providing information on the environmental context of settlements, there are several limitations discussed by Edwards (1991) and Dumayne-Peaty

and Barber (1997). For example, the dry-land nature of most archaeological sites does not provide the water-logged organic conditions necessary for pollen preservation and, consequently, pollen tends to be poorly preserved, present in low concentrations and biased towards those pollen types which are more resistant to deterioration (e.g., Chenopodiaceae, Lactuceae). Over-representation of pollen derived from the local area precludes vegetation reconstruction beyond the archaeological site itself and there are often considerable constraints on the stratigraphic and temporal resolution of the data because of the short time-span and slow accumulation rates of many deposits. The occupants or subsequent human activity (e.g., back filling of ditches) could also have mixed sediment containing pollen of different ages. Absolute dating of deposits can be difficult, and most are dated by their relative archaeological contexts rather than by radiometric techniques. Consequently, on-site pollen analysis provides a 'snap-shot' of vegetation associated with a particular site at a specific time. There have been several recent regional reviews of on-site pollen analysis (e.g., Caseldine 1989, Huntley and Stallibrass 1995), but much on-site data is annexed to excavation reports and unfortunately not given prominence in the archaeological literature. The visibility and accessibility of such data needs to be increased.

Off-site pollen analysis

The value of off-site pollen analysis is often neglected or disputed by archaeologists (e.g., McCarthy 1995, Hanson 1997, Dumayne-Peaty 1998a) and consequently, the approach has not obtained the place it perhaps merits in routine archaeological work. Pollen analysis of sediment from deposits situated in off-site contexts (e.g., lakes, mires) provides information on the wider environmental and ecological setting of human groups and gives information to supplement on-site palaeoenvironmental and archaeological data where available. The approach aims to reconstruct vegetation at the 'landscape' scale and provides a wider spatial context for the activities of prehistoric people. Pollen preservation and concentration are generally superior to that in on-site contexts, and the more continuous and rapid peat accumulation and sediment deposition rates of mires and lakes respectively enhance the temporal resolution with which vegetation change can be reconstructed (Dumayne-Peaty 1998b). The sediments are usually amenable to radiometric dating. Moreover, off-site contexts may provide information on human presence where archaeological evidence has not yet been discovered or is absent and can, therefore, be used to direct archaeological research and excavation (Whittington and Edwards 1994, Dumayne-Peaty and Barber 1997).

Spatial scale and pollen source area

Recent work has focused on the concept of the pollen source area (i.e., the area around a site from which the pollen deposited at the site is obtained) and its importance when interpreting spatial representation of human activity. The model presented by Jacobson and Bradshaw (1981) developed work by earlier authors (e.g., Tauber 1965, 1977, Oldfield 1970, Andersen 1978) and suggests that the pollen deposited at a sampling site will have been derived from the surrounding landscape and transported to the site by a variety of mechanisms and over a variety of distances that will differ for each pollen type. Three components of pollen rain can be identified:

(i)   local pollen is derived from plants growing within 20 metres of the sampling site,
(ii) extra-local pollen is that from between 20 metres and several hundred metres, and
(iii) regional pollen is transported to the site from greater distances.

The most relevant aspect of the model in terms of spatial representation is that the area from which the pollen deposited at a sampling site is derived is related to the size of that site. Figure 31.4 shows how a site of a particular size (horizontal axis) will contain a certain proportion of pollen rain derived from each component of the pollen rain (vertical axis). For example, pollen deposited at a site over 300 metres in diameter will be derived principally from regional pollen rain, whilst a site smaller than 100 metres in diameter will receive predominantly local pollen. The former site is more likely to record human impact which occurred on a regional or landscape-scale (e.g., substantial clearance of woodland), whilst the latter site would be more appropriate for detecting small-scale, temporary perturbations of woodland close to the sampling site. Models pertaining to spatial representativity of pollen profiles have been refined further by Bradshaw (1988), Prentice (1988), Calcote (1998), Sugita (1994) and Frelich et al. (1998). Modelling and quantification of modern pollen and land use data using multivariate data analysis has been undertaken recently to calibrate fossil pollen assemblages with the aim of evaluating the

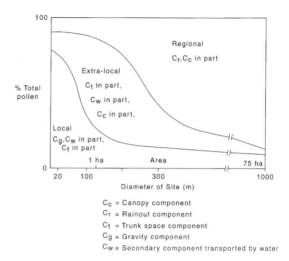

Figure 31.4   The relationship between the size of a site, which has no inflowing stream, and the relative proportions of pollen originating from different areas around the site (after Jacobson and Bradshaw 1981). See text for definitions.

extent of forest clearance in the past (Sugita et al. 1998). Once the relationship between present day plant abundance and area of clearance has been determined, this relationship can be used to infer or reconstruct the past landscape. Gaillard and Berglund (1998) suggest that such an approach is crucial to understanding the effect of human induced woodland clearance on past evapotranspiration, albedo and local, regional and global climatic change and, as a consequence, improve our ability to predict the effect of deforestation on future climate.

Spatial scale and multiple profile studies

Many palynologists depend upon the analysis of one pollen profile from a sampling site to reconstruct human impact on vegetation. However, if pollen diagrams are constructed from a number of locations on an individual mire or lake, or from adjacent deposits, more detailed information on spatial variation in human-induced vegetation change can be obtained, and the location and scale of woodland clearance may be elucidated. This approach was termed 'three dimensional pollen analysis' by Turner (1965) who demonstrated that differences displayed in pollen diagrams from three locations on Tregaron Bog in South Wales were a result of spatial variations in local land use adjacent to the mire. As such, the pollen profile from the centre of a deposit provides a regional 'summary' of those changes detected in profiles from elsewhere on the site.

Recent investigations show that small-scale variability in human impact can be displayed in pollen profiles located as little as 1–10 metres apart (e.g., Turner *et al.* 1989) and, more commonly, at 250 to 400 metres apart (e.g., Edwards 1983, Barber and Twigger 1987, Boyd 1988, Whittington *et al.* 1991). These differences are probably the result of local and extra-local variations in pollen rain which are, in turn, the result of changes in land use and human impact over short distances. For example, the nature of the Late Iron Age landscape has been reconstructed using three pollen diagrams from two adjacent mires in northern Cumbria, namely Walton Moss (WLM) and Bolton Fell Moss [BFM(HI9) and BFM(marginal)] (Dumayne-Peaty and Barber (1998); Figure 31.5). At Walton Moss, the decline in arboreal pollen is more substantial than that in the Bolton Fell Moss (marginal) pollen diagram, where the arboreal pollen curve declines slightly and there is only a small decline in arboreal pollen in the Bolton Fell Moss (HI9) pollen diagram. Variations in pollen representativity suggest that woodland clearance occurred close to Walton Moss, perhaps near the southern margins of the site where there are better quality soils. The Bolton Fell Moss (marginal) diagram records a more localized hazel woodland growing close to the south west margin of the mire, whilst the HI9 profile reflects a regional picture of relatively stable woodland. The differences between the pollen diagrams are probably due to variability in extra-local pollen rain caused by small-scale differences in human activity and demonstrate the value of multiple profile studies – had pollen diagram BFM(HI9) been considered alone, palynologists would have concluded that the Iron Age landscape was well-wooded.

Solving the on-site/off-site dichotomy

Pollen analyses from both on-site and off-site contexts have disadvantages and neither approach is superior, but those studies that combine palynological and archaeological data from on-site and off-site sources are particularly successful at reconstructing vegetation change associated with human groups. The most informative picture of early environments can be obtained where this approach is possible.

A synthesis of disparate studies shows how the results of on-site and off-site pollen analysis could be used together to reconstruct vegetation change associated with human activity more comprehensively.

Dumayne-Peaty (1998b) has synthesized on-site pollen data from Iron Age and Romano-British contexts in the area close to the Antonine Wall, southern Scotland and compared this data with regional off-site pollen diagrams from three mires (Figure 31.6). The regional pollen diagrams from Letham Moss, Blairbech Bog and Fannyside Muir suggest that extensive and substantial woodland clearance occurred during the Late Iron Age. At Letham Moss clearance was rapid and probably associated with an increase in settlement and arable agriculture, at Blairbech Bog clearance was gradual and pastoral agriculture was practised, whilst at Fannyside Muir deforestation was less substantial, more gradual and there is little palynological evidence for agriculture. The regional pollen diagrams suggest clearly that woodland clearance was underway, but provide little information about exact land use practices. However, on-site pollen analyses of ditch infills and turves from Bar Hill fort reveal that woodland was gradually cleared as a result of grazing pressure, rather than deliberate clearance (Boyd 1984). At Mollins, clearance was associated initially with grazing pressure, but intensity of clearance increased as local people felled trees for timber. Grazing pressure then intensified leading to a completely open landscape. Knights *et al.* (1983) and Newell (1983) suggested that the areas around Bearsden fort and Wilderness West respectively were open heathland maintained by grazing and burning with a mosaic of trees. The on-site and off-site profiles indicate that clearance may have been widespread, but the cause and nature of clearance differed at each site.

However, during Romano-British times, distinct contrasts between the regional pollen diagrams emerge. Clearance was sustained around Letham Moss and Fannyside Muir, but woodland regeneration occurred at Blairbech Bog. Heathland expanded at Bar Hill as grazing intensity declined, but at Mollins, Croy Hill, Bearsden and Wilderness Plantation open grazed grassland was maintained. At Croy Hill some birch then invaded the heathland in the wetter areas or as a result of reduced grazing pressure (Newell 1983, Knights *et al.* 1983, Boyd 1984, 1985) whilst at Wilderness Plantation, woodland regeneration occurred (Newell 1983). These results suggest that the landscape was a complex mosaic of vegetation types and the synthesis demonstrates the power of combining on-site and off-site data to elucidate more fully the nature of vegetation change associated with human groups.

It is crucial, therefore, that palynologists and archaeologists co-operate and work in a multidisciplinary manner to overcome the on/off-site dichotomy found in much of the archaeo-palynological literature. There have been several projects that have adopted this approach successfully (e.g., North West Wetlands Survey; Middleton 1994), Severn Estuary (Whittle 1989, Bell 1995, Rippon 1997), Romney Marsh (Eddison 1995) and further studies of this nature should be actively encouraged.

TEMPORAL RESOLUTION

If palynological studies are undertaken at high temporal resolution, the activities of prehistoric people can be examined in more detail and the rate, timing and longevity of vegetation change determined. Many pollen diagrams concerned with human impact have been constructed at coarse sediment sub-sampling intervals (e.g., 4 cm) but, whilst this can give a broad indication of the nature of vegetation change, 4 cm of peat may represent a period of *c.* 40 years or more (Barber *et al.* 1994). This is problematic as many vegetation events (e.g., felling of trees, a phase of shifting agriculture, abandonment of clearances) can occur on shorter time-scales and may be undetected by pollen

analysis undertaken at this resolution. A notable recent methodological advance is fine (or high) resolution pollen analysis, where pollen is analysed from contiguous 1 mm samples of peat or individual lake lamina (e.g., Green and Dolman 1988). Two particularly important studies have been undertaken – the detection of Mesolithic vegetation change in the North Yorkshire Moors (Simmons and Innes 1996a, 1996b) and elucidation of the causes of the Neolithic elm decline in Norfolk (Peglar 1993, Peglar and Birks 1993).

Mesolithic human impact

Fine resolution pollen analysis (FRPA) and multiple profile studies have been used to detect small-scale human impact on the vegetation of the North York Moors during the Mesolithic. The activity of early human groups on vegetation has been notoriously difficult to reconstruct using palynological data because the landscape was predominantly wooded, clearances were small-scale, many Mesolithic groups had transhumance life-styles, and archaeological recovery is often poor.

(a)

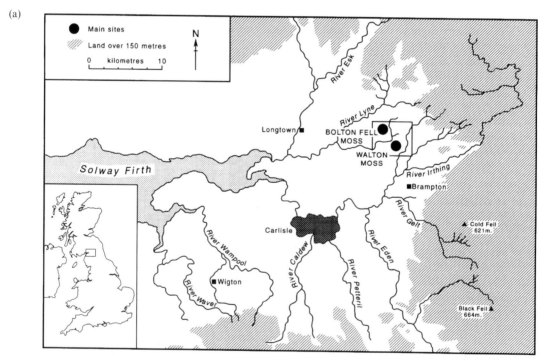

Figure 31.5 (a) Maps showing the location of Bolton Fell Moss and Walton Moss, Cumbria, and (b, opposite) the position of the cores used for pollen analysis. The curves show the summary pollen data and how Iron Age clearance (I) differed at each site.

(b)

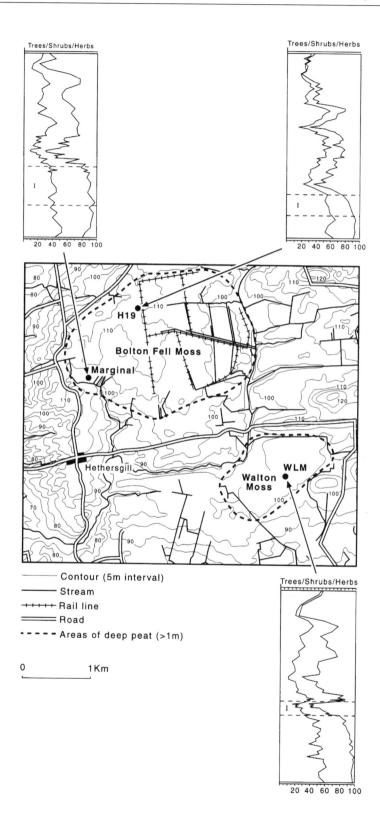

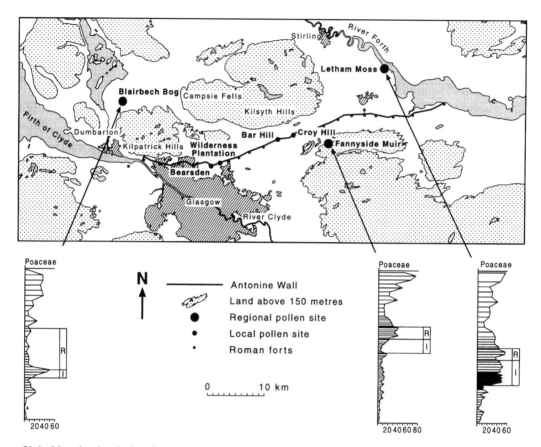

Figure 31.6 Map showing the location of regional and local pollen sites in southern central Scotland. The grass pollen curves showing Iron Age (I) and Romano-British (R) vegetation change at Letham Moss, Blairbech Bog and Fannyside Muir are displayed.

A study of North Gill in the North York Moors (Turner *et al.* 1993, Simmons and Innes 1996a, 1996b) employed FRPA to evaluate the temporal characteristics of Mesolithic disturbance phases and their spatial manifestation. Eleven peat profiles from a 400 metre long transect were analysed for charcoal and pollen and several of these were studied at 1 mm intervals (Figure 31.7). The palynological data suggests that the area was dominated initially by stable forest, but then woodland disturbance that lasted approximately 130 years occurred in some areas. The disturbances are characterized by a decline in tree pollen and a rise in heathland taxa, open ground indicators, cereals and charcoal. Simmons and Innes (1996a, 1996b) suggest that the increase in charcoal implicates the use of fire to create the openings and the high resolution nature of the data allows individual fire events to be discerned. Consequently, woodland clearance is thought to have

been a result of Mesolithic hunter-gatherer populations who used fire to purposely manipulate a pre-existing open area or one which had been cleared by another means (e.g., felling). This would have increased the amount of browsing available to large herbivores (e.g., red deer), increased the amount of hazel (nuts were an important component of Mesolithic diet) and prevented tree regeneration (Simmons and Innes 1996a, 1996b). Clearance was followed by a 50 year period of cultivation in the cleared area, during which the use of fire decreased. Re-examination of some of the pollen diagrams (Simmons and Cundill 1974, Simmons and Innes 1988) using FRPA also demonstrated that what had been previously perceived as an individual clearance was in fact several consecutive clearance episodes separated by short-lived periods of woodland regeneration. The multiple profiles suggest that clearance did not occur in every profile and that the pollen source

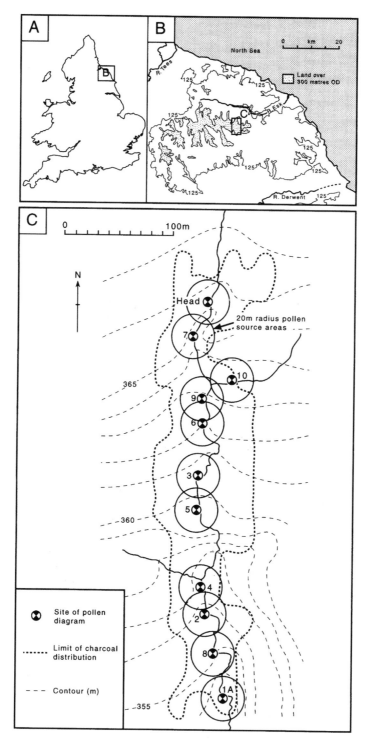

Figure 31.7 Maps showing the location of North Gill, North York Moors, sampling sites and overlapping nature of the pollen source areas during the Mesolithic (after Turner *et al.* 1993, Simmons and Innes 1996a, 1996b).

areas of each site overlapped slightly with adjacent sites. This led Simmons and Innes (1996a, 1996b) to conclude that each clearance was probably tens, rather than hundreds of metres in extent, and that some clearances lasted decades whilst others lasted several hundreds of years. The high resolution results indicate that distinct patches of forest were utilized in different places, at different intensities, at different times and for various uses and durations (Turner *et al.* 1989, 1993).

The Neolithic elm decline

A decline in the percentages of elm pollen is visible in many pollen diagrams from north-west Europe *c.* 5000 BP. Causes of the decline have been debated in the palynological literature since the 1940s and hypotheses which have been proposed to explain it include that of climatic change (e.g., Iversen 1941), soil deterioration (e.g., Sturlodottir and Turner 1985), human impact (e.g., Troels-Smith 1960), pathogenic attack (e.g., Groenman-van-Waateringe 1983) or a combination of these (e.g., Rackham 1990). FRPA and charcoal analysis of laminated lake sediments from Diss Mere, Norfolk have provided a unique opportunity to obtain annual records of land use change which shed further light on the possible causes of the demise in elm pollen (Peglar 1993). The pollen and charcoal data suggest that prior to the elm decline, there was small-scale woodland clearance during which a phase of arable agriculture lasting 50 years occurred. Elm pollen then declined dramatically and the laminated sediments and the high resolution pollen data allowed Peglar (1993) to calculate that elm pollen decreased by 73 per cent in just six years. Such short-lived human activity and rapid decrease in elm would not have been detected using more conventional sampling intervals. According to Peglar (1993), the evidence for human impact prior to the decline and rapid decrease in elm pollen suggests that the elm decline at Diss Mere was a result of pathogen attack in a woodland which had already been disturbed by human activity. Such conclusions were only possible because of the high temporal resolution of the pollen data.

CONCLUSION

The advances in palynology demonstrate its continued importance in environmental archaeology, even though detection and interpretation of human impact on vegetation from palynological data is not straightforward.

If palynologists and archaeologists work in close co-operation from the research design stages of a project, more useful and informative vegetation reconstruction would ensue. For example, defining the archaeological questions which will be asked of the palynological data prior to sampling sediment for pollen analysis would aid selection of sites and methodologies which would best answer archaeological 'needs'. Future challenges include elucidating cause and effect of events displayed in pollen diagrams, determining the precise location and extent of clearance, and quantifying prehistoric human impact on vegetation.

REFERENCES

*Recommended for further reading

Andersen, S.T. (1978). Local and regional vegetational development in eastern Denmark in the Holocene. *Danmarks Geologiske Undersøgelse*, **8**:5–27.

Barber, K.E. and Twigger, S.N. (1987). Late Quaternary palaeoecology of the Severn Basin. In Gregory, K.J., Lewin, J. and Thornes, J.B. (eds) *Palaeohydrology in Practice*, 217–251. John Wiley: Chichester.

Barber, K.E., Chambers, F.M., Maddy, D., Stoneman, R.E. and Brew, J.S. (1994). A sensitive high-resolution record of Late Holocene climatic change from a raised bog in Northern England. *The Holocene*, **4**:198–205.

Behre, K.-E. (1981). The interpretation of anthropogenic indicators in pollen diagrams. *Pollen et Spores*, **23**:225–245.

Bell, M. (ed.) (1995). *Archaeology in the Severn Estuary 1995*. Annual Report of the Severn Estuary Levels Research Committee, University of Wales: Lampeter.

*Bell, M. and Walker, M.J.C. (1992). *Late Quaternary Environmental Change: Physical and Human Perspectives*. Longman: London.

*Berglund, B.E. (ed.) (1986). *Handbook of Holocene Palaeoecology and Palaeohydrology*. John Wiley: Chichester.

*Birks, H.H., Birks, H.J.B., Kaland, P.E. and Moe, D. (eds) (1988). *The Cultural Landscape: Past, Present and Future*. Cambridge University Press: Cambridge.

Boyd, W.E. (1984). Prehistoric hedges: Roman-Iron Age hedges from Bar Hill. *Scottish Archaeological Review*, **3**:32–34.

Boyd, W.E. (1985). Palaeobotanical evidence from Mollins. *Britannia*, **19**:37–48.

Boyd, W.E. (1988). Early Flandrian vegetational development on the coastal plain of north Ayrshire, Scotland: evidence from multiple pollen profiles. *Journal of Biogeography*, **15**:325–337.

Bradshaw, R.H.W. (1988). Spatially precise studies of forest dynamics. In Huntley, B. and Webb, T. (eds) *Vegetation History. Handbook of Vegetation Science* **7**, 725–751. Kluwer: Dordrecht.

Calcote, R. (1998). Identifying forest stand types using pollen from forest hollows. *The Holocene*, **8**:423–432.

Caseldine, A. (1989). *Environmental Archaeology of Wales*. CADW: Lampeter.

*Chambers, F.M. (ed.) (1993). *Climatic Change and Human Impact on the Landscape*. Chapman and Hall: London.

Dumayne-Peaty, L. (1998a). Forest clearance in northern Britain during Romano-British times: re-addressing the palynological evidence. *Britannia*, **26**:315–322.

Dumayne-Peaty, L. (1998b). Human impact on the environment during the Iron Age and Romano-British times: palynological evidence from three sites near the Antonine Wall, Great Britain. *Journal of Archaeological Science*, **25**:203–214.

Dumayne-Peaty, L. and Barber, K.E. (1997). Archaeological and environmental evidence for Roman impact on vegetation near Carlisle, Cumbria: a comment on McCarthy. *The Holocene*, 7:243–245.

Dumayne-Peaty, L. and Barber, K.E. (1998). Late Holocene vegetation change, pollen source areas and pollen variability: a study from Walton Moss and Bolton Fell Moss, Cumbria. *Journal of Quaternary Science*, 13:147–164.

Eddison, J. (ed.) (1995). *Romney Marsh: the Debatable Ground*. Oxford University Committee for Archaeology Monograph 41, Oxbow Books: Oxford.

Edwards, K.J. (1979). Palynological and temporal inference in the context of prehistory, with special reference to the evidence from lake and peat deposits. *Journal of Archaeological Science*, 6:255–270.

Edwards, K.J. (1982). Man space and the woodland edge: speculations on the detection and interpretation of human impact in pollen profiles. In Bell, M. and Limbrey, S. (eds) *Archaeological Aspects of Woodland Ecology*, 5–22. BAR International Series 146 British Archaeological Reports: Oxford.

Edwards, K.J. (1983). Quaternary palynology: multiple profile studies and pollen variability. *Progress in Physical Geography*, 7:587–609.

Edwards, K.J. (1988). The hunter-gatherer/agricultural transition and the pollen record in the British Isles. In Birks, H.H., Birks, H.J.B., Kaland, P.E. and Moe, D. (eds) *The Cultural Landscape – Past, Present and Future*, 253–266. Cambridge University Press: Cambridge.

Edwards, K.J. (1991). Using space in cultural palynology: the value of the off-site pollen record. In Harris, D.R. and Thomas, K.D. (eds) *Modelling Ecological Change: Perspectives from Neoecology, Palaeoecology and Archaeology*, 61–74. Institute of Archaeology: London.

Edwards, K.J. (1993). Models of mid-Holocene forest farming for north-west Europe. In Chambers, F.M. (ed.) *Climate Change and Human Impact on the Landscape*, 133–146. Chapman and Hall: London.

Edwards, K.J. and MacIntosh, C.J. (1988). Improving the detection rate of cereal-type pollen grains in *Ulmus* decline and earlier deposits from Scotland. *Pollen et Spores*, **30**:179–188.

Faegri, K., Kaland, P.E. and Krzywinski, K. (1989). *Textbook of Pollen Analysis*. John Wiley: Chichester.

Firbas, F. (1934). Über die Bestimmung der Walddichte und der Vegetation der Waldbäume. *Natur und Heimat*, **6**:65–73.

Frelich, F., Sugita, S., Reich, P.B., Davis, M.B. and Friedman, S.K. (1934). Neighbourhood effects in forests: implications for within stand patch structure. *Journal of Ecology*, **86**:149–161.

Gaillard, M.-J. and Berglund, B.E. (eds) (1998). *Quantification of Land Surfaces Cleared of Forests During the Holocene*. Palaeoclimate Research Volume 27, European Science Foundation: Strasbourg.

Green, D.G. and Dolman, G.S. (1988). Fine resolution pollen analysis. *Journal of Biogeography*, **15**:685–701.

Groenman-Van-Waateringe, W. (1983). The early agricultural utilization of the Irish landscape: the last word on the elm decline? In Reeves-Smyth, T. and Hammond, F. (eds) *Landscape Archaeology in Ireland*, 217–232, BAR British Series 116, British Archaeological Reports: Oxford.

Hall, V.A. (1988). The role of harvesting techniques in the dispersal of pollen grains of Cerealia. *Pollen et Spores*, **30**:265–270.

Hanson, W.S. (1997). The Roman presence: brief interludes. In Edwards, K.J. and Ralston, B.M. (eds) *Scotland: Environment and Archaeology 8000BC – AD1000*, 195–216. John Wiley: Chichester.

Harris, D.R. and Thomas, K.D. (eds) (1991). *Modelling Ecological Change: Perspectives from Neoecology, Palaeoecology and Environmental Archaeology*. Institute of Archaeology: London.

Hicks, S.P. and Birks, H.J.B. (1996). Numerical analysis of modern and fossil pollen spectra as a tool for elucidating the nature of fine-scale human activities in boreal areas. *Vegetation History and Archaeobotany*, **5**:257–272.

Huntley, J.P. and Stallibrass, S. (1995). *Plant and Vertebrate Remains from Archaeological Sites in Northern England: Data Reviews and Future Directions*. Research Report 4, Architectural and Archaeological Society of Durham and Northumberland: Durham.

Iversen, J. (1941). Land occupation in Denmark's Stone Age. *Danmarks Geologiske Undersøgelse*, **2**:1–68.

Iversen, J. (1973). The development of Denmark's nature since the last glacial. *Danmarks Geologiske Undersøgelse*, **7-C**:1–26.

Jacobson, G.L. and Bradshaw, R.H.W. (1981). The selection of sites for palaeoecological studies. *Quaternary Research*, **16**:80–96.

Knights, B.A., Dickson, C., Dickson, J.H. and Breeze, D.J. (1983). Evidence concerning the Roman military diet at Bearsden, Scotland, in the 2nd century A.D. *Journal of Archaeological Science*, **10**:139–152.

McCarthy, M.R. (1995). Archaeological and environmental evidence for the Roman impact on vegetation near Carlisle, Cumbria. *The Holocene*, **5**:491–495.

Middleton, R. (ed.) (1994). *North West Wetland Survey Annual Report, 1994*. English Heritage: Lancaster.

Moore, P.D., Webb, J.A. and Collinson, M.E. (1991). *Pollen Analysis*. Blackwell: Oxford.

Newell, P.J. (1983). Pollen analysis report. In Hanson, W.S. and Maxwell, G.S. (eds) Minor enclosures on the Antonine Wall at Wilderness Plantation. *Britannia*, **14**:227–243.

O'Connor, T. (1998). Environmental archaeology: a matter of definition. *Environmental Archaeology*, **2**:1–6.

Oldfield, F. (1970). Some aspects of scale and complexity in pollen-analytically based palaeoecology. *Pollen et Spores*, **12**:163–171.

Peglar, S. (1993). The mid-Holocene *Ulmus* decline at Diss Mere, Norfolk, UK: a year-by-year pollen stratigraphy from annual laminations. *The Holocene*, **3**:1–14.

Peglar, S. and Birks, H.J.B. (1993). The mid-Holocene *Ulmus* fall at Diss Mere, South-East England – disease and human impact? *Vegetation History and Archaeobotany*, **2**:61–68.

Prentice, I.C. (1988). Records of vegetation in time and space: the principles of pollen analysis. In Huntley, B. and Webb, T. III (eds) *Vegetation History*, 17–42. Kluwer: Dordrecht.

Rackham, O. (1990). *Trees and Woodland in the British Landscape: the Complete History of Britain's Trees, Woods and Hedgerows*. Weidenfeld and Nicolson: London.

Rippon, S. (ed.) (1997) *Archaeology in the Severn Estuary, 1997*. Annual Report of the Severn Estuary Levels Research Committee, Department of History and Archaeology: Exeter.

*Roberts, N. (1998). *The Holocene: an Environmental History*. Blackwell: Oxford.

Simmons, I.G. and Cundill, P.R. (1974). Late Quaternary vegetational history of the North York Moors. *Journal of Biogeography*, **1**:159–169.

Simmons, I.G. and Innes, J.B. (1988). The later Mesolithic period (6000–5000 bp) on Glaisdale Moor, North Yorkshire. *Archaeological Journal*, **145**:1–12.

Simmons, I.G. and Innes, J.B. (1996a). The ecology of an episode of a period of cereal cultivation on the North York Moors, England. *Journal of Archaeological Science*, **23**:613–618.

Simmons, I.G. and Innes, J.B. (1996b). Disturbance phases in the mid-Holocene vegetation at North Gill, North York Moors. Form and process. *Journal of Archaeological Science*, **23**:183–196.

Sturlodottir, S.A. and Turner, J. (1985). The elm decline at Pawlaw Mire: an anthropogenic interpretation. *New Phytologist*, **99**:323–329.

Sugita, S. (1994). Pollen representation of vegetation in Quaternary sediments: theory and methods in patchy vegetation. *Journal of Ecology*, **82**:879–898.

Sugita, S., Anderson, S.T., Gaillard, M.-J., Odgard, B.V., Prentice, I.C. and Vorren, K.-D. (1998). Modelling and data analysis for the quantification of forest clearance signals in pollen records. In Gaillard, M.-J. and Berglund, B.E. (eds) *Quantification of Land Surfaces Cleared of Forests during the Holocene – Modern Pollen/Vegetation/Landscape Relationships as an Aid to the Interpretation of Fossil Pollen Data*, 125–131. Palaeoclimate Research Volume 27, European Science Foundation: Strasbourg.

Tauber, H. (1965). Differential pollen dispersal and the interpretation of pollen diagrams. *Danmarks Geologiske Undersøgelse*, **89**:1–69.

Tauber, H. (1977). Investigations of aerial pollen transport in a forested area. *Dansk Botanisk Arkiv*, **32**:5–121.

Troels-Smith, J. (1960). Ivy, mistletoe and elm climatic indicators – fodder plants. *Danmarks Geologiske Undersøgelse*, **4**:1–32.

Turner, J. (1965). A contribution to the history of forest clearance. *Proceedings of the Royal Society of London*, **161B**:343–354.

Turner, J., Innes, J.B. and Simmons, I.G. (1989). Two pollen diagrams from the same site. *New Phytologist*, **113**:409–416.

Turner, J., Innes, J.B. and Simmons, I.G. (1993). Spatial diversity in the mid-Flandrian vegetation history of North Gill, North Yorkshire. *New Phytologist*, **123**:599–647.

Vuorela, I. (1973). Relative pollen rain around cultivated fields. *Acta Botanica Fennica*, **102**:1–27.

Whittington, G. and Edwards, K.J. (1994). Palynology as a predictive tool in archaeology. *Proceedings of the Society of Antiquities of Scotland*, **124**:55–65.

Whittington, G., Edwards, K.J. and Cundill, P.R. (1991). Late- and post-glacial vegetational change at Black Loch, Fife, eastern Scotland – a multiple core approach. *New Phytologist*, **118**:147–166.

Whittle, A.W.R. (1989). Two later Bronze Age occupations and an Iron Age channel on the Gwent foreshore. *Bulletin of the Board of Celtic Studies*, **36**:200–223.

32

Archaeobotany and the Transition to Agriculture

M.K. JONES

Department of Archaeology, University of Cambridge

and S. COLLEDGE

Institute of Archaeology, University College London.

Over the last ten thousand years, the food procurement strategies of earlier hominids and humans have been displaced by strategies of food production in which human predators exercised unprecedented control over the lives of their prey species. Understanding this profound ecological transformation in the human past has been a central research goal of archaeobotany. The issue, and the associated domestication of species was brought to the fore by Charles Darwin (1868), and explored in relation to botanical evidence by Alphonse de Candolle (1882). In the following century, Vere Gordon Childe (1936) placed this revolution in food acquisition at the foundation of his model for the subsequent growth of complex societies. Around the same time, Nikolai Vavilov laid the foundations for using plant geography as a guide to supposed 'centres of origin' where this transformation first took place (Vavilov 1992). Carl Ortwin Sauer (1952) further situated this transition within a global context of human geography.

By the 1960s, a series of fieldwork programmes were underway within the 'classic' centres of origin, in particular south-west Asia and Central America (e.g., Braidwood *et al.* 1983, Byers 1967). These programmes incorporated two key methodological advances that would transform our understanding of the issue. One of these was the widespread use of radiocarbon dating (see Chapter 2). The other was the intensive application of archaeobotanical techniques, the focus of this chapter.

A quarter of a century after these fieldwork programmes, a considerable corpus of world-wide research could be drawn upon, brought together in a variety of ways in volumes by Harris (1996), Harris and Hillman (1989), van Zeist *et al.* (1991), Zohary and Hopf (1994) and Smith (1995). These volumes indicate how the focus of interest has broadened considerably from specific transitions in classic centres of origin, to how people were managing and exploiting plant foods in a wide variety of contexts in space and time. The last two volumes are particularly concerned with the plant genetic evidence, and most recently, some strands of plant and human genetics have shifted the focus back more firmly to those classic centres of origin. Within

---

Handbook of Archaeological Sciences. Edited by D.R. Brothwell and A.M. Pollard.

some New World archaeobotany, the focus of study has moved to the social dimension of plant usage (e.g., Hastorf and Popper 1988).

THE KEY ISSUES

In this chapter, we look first at the key issues of debate about the transition, then move to methods for examining them, and briefly describe selected case studies that illustrate their implementation.

Transition from what?

Traditional models of pre-agricultural communities have tended to emphasize the hunting of medium to large sized mammals, as these are the prey species that leave the most conspicuous archaeological trace (see Chapter 34). A small number of Palaeolithic projects have demonstrated that plant foods also formed an important component of pre-agricultural diets, though the data are fragmentary and scattered. Such data however are sufficient to show that we cannot assume that the intensive use of plant food that characterizes agriculture from the outset is entirely new. In many places it followed a long history of wild plant exploitation of which our knowledge is currently limited.

Some of the reason for this scarcity of data may be 'taphonomic', in other words they may arise from the way in which the archaeological record is formed (see Chapter 15). Many plants persist because they are charred (see below), and charred remains accumulate on fixed sites in which hearths and fires are commonplace, and cooking is a major feature of culinary practice. Some of the more diverse pre-agricultural records of food plant arise from other forms of preservation, for example the desiccated cave deposits at Guila Naquitz in Mexico (Flannery 1986), and the waterlogged Jomon middens of coastal Japan (Imamura 1996).

Of those pre-agricultural sites that have yielded archaeobotanical data, a few themes about plant use emerge. First, the taxonomic range of utilized plants can be considerable, with the fruits and seeds from the Upper Palaeolithic site of Abu Hureyra in Syria running to around 150 taxa (Hillman *et al.* 1989). Second, the physiological range of tissues consumed may also have been broad, ranging from seeds, fruits, roots, tubers, flower buds and stems. Not all of these are equally amenable to archaeobotanical detection. In broad terms, seeds and fruits are the most amenable, while our ability to recognize roots and tubers is gradually increasing (Hather 1992, 1994, Hather and Kirch 1991). Third, the appearance of domesticated crops over the last 10 000 years does not signal the first instance either of vegetation management, or of complex culinary practice. There is growing evidence that pre-agricultural stands of wild plants were tended, by such processes as weeding and soil modification. There is also direct and indirect evidence that wild harvests were transformed by such processes as grinding, leaching, cooking, dough or paste preparation, and fermentation. In summary, however great the impact of agriculture using domesticated crops, plant utilization strategies that preceded it were also complex.

What kind of transition?

A central issue of contention has been the geography and pace of the transition. Blumler (1992) has contrasted two models of how it took place as the 'stimulus-diffusion' and 'independent invention' models. The former presupposes a revolutionary transformation, arising from a particular cultural-historical context, not unlike a series of later economic revolutions of the historic period. From that context, the ideas of domestication and agriculture were transferred through time to progressively more distant parts of the world. The latter presupposes a dispersed and gradual evolutionary process, not unlike a series of evolutionary adaptations that proceeded it, in which global environmental pressures steered many cultures in the same direction. Most researchers today envisage something in between, with a widespread and scattered number of origins, some followed by a significant element of expansion and diffusion. There remain, however, differences of view, with implications for how we perceive the relationship between humans and nature, and the relative place of historic agency and environmental pressure in transforming that relationship. Arguments based on traditional bio-archaeological evidence have often lead towards the independent invention model (e.g., Higgs 1972, Barker 1985), while genetic arguments have often leant towards the stimulus-diffusion model (cf. Cavalli-Sforza *et al.* 1994, Smith 1995).

How did agriculture spread?

The two methods of effectively modelling the spread of agriculture are through the direct carbon dating of crop macrofossils from secure archaeological contexts, and through phylogenetic analysis (tree-building) of the genetic variations within living crop species. Ideally the two approaches can be combined through the analysis of ancient DNA from archaeological crop remains (see Chapter 25). Both approaches have superseded the much less secure use of proxy archaeological data, in particular the presence or absence of pottery, on which ideas about agricultural spread still rely in many regions of the world. Interests in the patterns of spread have grown with the proposition that there is a strong association between the spread and diversity of agriculture, genes, and language (Cavalli-Sforza *et al.* 1994, Renfrew 1987).

How did agriculture change?

As emphasized above, there is no single turning point before which people–plant relations were 'simple' and after which they were 'complex'. In evolutionary terms, the point at which a plant becomes dependent upon humans for propagation is clearly significant, and often discernible in the archaeobotanical evidence. This is often taken as the conventional point of 'domestication'. However, transformations in people–plant relationships happened before, and continued after, domestication, and are themselves the focus of much archaeobotanical study. This study has often involved an ecological analysis of weed species (those species that, for one reason or another, accompany crop plants in managed agrarian plots). Weed floras have been used to study a range of aspects of agricultural change, including: cultivation methods, irrigation practice, seasonality of sowing, and maintenance of soil fertility. There have been three broad approaches to using weed evidence in this way, *synecology* (the analysis of communities of taxa), *autecology* (the analysis of individual species), and *FIBS* (Functional Interpretation of Botanical Surveys).

Synecology

Much of the early research in weed floras as a source of information on agricultural methods drew upon the Braun Blanquet school of plant community analysis (cf. Wasylikowa 1981, M. Jones 1988b, G. Jones 1992), which studied plant species as members of ecological communities, rather than individually. Several of these analyses distinguish two basic communities of weeds, one associated with fertile, spring sown hoe plots, the other community associated with extensively cultivated autumn sown fields. In various parts

of Europe, the hoe plot communities have a greater antiquity than the field communities, which did not emerge until late prehistory, suggesting that early agriculture was more horticultural in practice.

Autecology

The British and North American traditions of ecology have been sceptical about natural groupings larger than the species, and taken note of how ephemeral some of those 'communities' are. In the autecological tradition, the analysis of weed floras has drawn on the ecological characteristics of individual species, which independently serve as markers of changing conditions within the agricultural ecosystem (M. Jones 1988a).

FIBS

Functional Interpretation of Botanical Surveys takes a community approach, but not one vulnerable to the ephemerality of synecological communities. Instead it examines functional attributes of the physiological characteristics of different species that share similar environmental contexts, and establishes how those shared attributes connect to changing conditions. FIBS analysis has been profitably applied to a number of problems of agrarian change (cf. Bogaard *et al.* 1999, Charles *et al.* 1997, G. Jones *et al.* 1995).

TYPES OF ARCHAEOBOTANICAL EVIDENCE

Archaeobotanical remains are often categorized in terms of size, which tends to subdivide it according to the forms of methodology employed, and the problems faced in terms of contamination. Remains that are discernible with the naked eye are termed *macrofossils*, are collected by various combinations of sieving, flotation and hand collection (Kenward *et al.* 1980, Pearsall 1989, M. Jones 1991), and contamination can broadly be avoided through simple 'common sense' methods. Remains that are only discernible under an optical microscope are termed *microfossils*, and are collected through various methods of sample cleaning and sample concentration. The avoidance of contamination in this case requires detailed knowledge of how the microfossils can be transported through the air, water, and the sedimentary matrix. At the smallest end of the size scale lies *molecular* and *genetic* evidence, whose extraction and detection methods are discussed in Chapter 25. In these cases, and particularly in the case of ancient DNA, contamination can be a considerable issue, often entailing strict lab protocols, extensive use of control runs, and inter-laboratory cross-checks.

Macrofossils

The most widespread form of macrofossils are variously described as *charred* or *carbonized* remains. These are commonly of wood, seeds, fruits, and a form of soft cell tissue known as *parenchyma*. Charred seeds and fruits have formed the bulk of archaeobotanical crop data from around the world. This has led to a marked bias towards grain crops, particularly cereals and legumes, that has only recently been redressed by the use of parenchyma to detect the root and tuber crops, which are particularly important in tropical and sub-tropical agriculture (Hather 1992, 1994, Hather and Kirch 1991).

The widespread persistence of charred remains in the archaeological record has been attributed to their reduction to elemental carbon, which is not vulnerable to decay. The growth of biomolecular archaeology has shown that not all charred remains are equally transformed. Some may be entirely carbonized, but others much less so. The latter have proven an important source of ancient DNA and other biomolecules (see Chapters 25 and 28).

A second important category of plant macrofossil preservation is through *desiccation*. Here the fossil survives because there is insufficient water to sustain biological decay organisms. Although desiccated remains are geographically more restricted than charred remains, some key centres of origin yield some very dry sites. In Central America, many of the earliest domesticated plants are recovered in desiccated form (e.g., Flannery 1986). The same is true of the less well-studied crops from sub-Saharan and Nilotic Africa (e.g., van der Veen 1996). The sorghum remains from Kasr Ibrim are among the best-preserved crop remains ever recovered from an archaeological site (Deakin *et al.* 1999).

Sometimes, desiccated remains are also partly *mineralized*. The intense evaporation associated with dry sites leads to accumulations of salts within the plant tissue. Such salts as calcium carbonate and calcium phosphate can replace tissue and create a mineral fossil. Where calcium levels are high, for example within building mortar or in a Medieval latrine, such mineralized fossils can also form within predominantly waterlogged contexts (Green 1979, Carruthers 1991).

The final major category of macrofossils persists in *anoxic* conditions, that is, the absence of free oxygen, also required by many of the organisms of decay. The most common occurrence of anoxic conditions is in waterlogged deposits (see Chapter 47). Anoxic macrofossils from such deposits have played a major role in understanding vegetation change (see Chapters 13 and 31), and in elucidating plant exploitation in later prehistory and the historic period (e.g., Lambrick and Robinson 1979, Hall *et al.* 1983, Hall and Kenward 1990, Bouby *et al.* 1999, Maier 1999). However their impact on earlier plant exploitation has been more fragmentary, the most notable examples being in East Asia. The coastal plains of China have yielded some very early waterlogged deposits containing anoxically preserved rice grains (Zhao *et al.* 1986). Such deposits are also an important source of information on plant utilization in the Jomon culture of Japan (Imamura 1996).

Microfossils

Like macrofossils, conditions of preservation and transformation have a strong influence on what microfossils persist in an interpretable form. The persistence of microfossils is also related to their inherent chemical stability. Pollen persists because of its sporopollenin coat. Phytoliths persist because of the inertness of the silica of which they are composed.

The use of pollen analysis in the detection agriculture is discussed in depth in Chapter 31. The point is made in that chapter that a number of key world crops release very little pollen to the air, and such pollen as is released is often identifiable with confidence only to family or genus. For this reason, pollen analysis has played a lesser role than macrofossils in the study of the earliest domesticated crops. It is at some distance from the centres of origin, where the taxa are more exotic, and the indigenous vegetation more profoundly affected, that pollen analysis can sometimes provide the earliest evidence of agriculture. Such is true of northwest Europe, for example. It has also occasionally been argued for specific crops, for example rye in Britain (Chambers and Jones 1984) and maize in North America (Fearn and Liu 1995, but see also Eubanks 1997). However, the more substantial contribution of pollen analysis to studying transitions to agriculture has been to provide information on the ecological context of the transition, rather than specifics of the economic systems themselves.

There is always at least some silica travelling through the vascular (sap) system of any plant. None leaves it through transpiration, so silica invariably accumulates in certain of the plant cells, sometimes forming diagnostic silica bodies, or *phytoliths*, which are among the most durable plant remains in the archaeological record. Both maize and rice have characteristic phytoliths, which have played a role in tracking the spread of maize cultivation into South America, and rice cultivation in East Asia and the Pacific (Piperno 1988).

Prior to the refinement of the analysis of charred soft tissue, the principal archaeobotanical route to tuber agriculture was through the granules of starch that occasionally persisted for considerable periods of time, especially on the surface of artifacts. It is not always clear why they survive as well as they do, but they have been found adhering to the surface of stone tools (Piperno 1988). In broad terms they can be tentatively assigned to species. The morphology of starch grains has provided early evidence for potato in South America (Ugent *et al.* 1982), and taro in the Pacific (Loy *et al.* 1992).

Molecular and genetic evidence

The fast-growing field of molecular evidence is dealt with in depth in Chapters 25 and 28. The most immediate impact on the study of agriculture and its origins has been in lipids and DNA. The lipid outer coating of many plant parts is often highly durable, and sometimes more diagnostic than the tissue it surrounds. Lipids are proving to be valuable in reaching the plant foods that elude both macrofossil and microfossil records (Evershed 1993, Evershed *et al.* 1992, 1999). One key example is the leafy vegetables, such as *Brassica* (Evershed *et al.* 1991).

Ancient and modern DNA are providing direct insight into the problems of agricultural origins and spread. Their use is reviewed in depth in Jones and Brown (2000). At present they support a transition to agriculture intermediate between the stimulus-diffusion and independent-invention models.

SOME APPLICATIONS FROM THE OLD WORLD

Archaeobotanical contrasts within the Fertile Crescent

The area known as the 'Fertile Crescent' within southwest Asia has long been thought of as the context of the first transition to agriculture, and remains the region with the earliest dates for crop domestication.

Collection of plant macrofossils from archaeological sites has continued since the 1960s, and the region now yields a substantial body of archaeobotanical data for early agriculture. These data reveal the transition to agriculture in some detail, and demonstrates that it was not compressed in space and time within a uniform or sudden change. This may be illustrated by reference to a selection of a few of the more recent excavations yielding plant evidence.

Tell Mureybit is situated on the northern bank of the Euphrates river in an area which is today composed of heavily denuded steppe and desert vegetation (van Zeist and Bakker-Heeres 1984). At the time of its occupation, during the Epipalaeolithic and pre-pottery Neolithic periods, the Euphrates valley would have been covered with poplar forest. The site yielded einkorn wheat in a morphologically wild form. Despite its wild form, the accompanying weed seeds tend, as the Pre-Pottery Neolithic progresses, towards the kind of weedy assemblage associated with an arable field. The authors suggest that some form of intervention or management is causing this trend. In other words, the stands of wild cereals are being tended in some way, by watering or weeding perhaps.

Further to the south, in the Damascus Basin lie three more settlement mounds that have been studied and sampled, Tell Aswad, Tell Ghoraifé and Tell Ramad in Syria (van Zeist and Bakker-Heeres 1982). At these three sites, there is evidence both for domesticated crops and for the by-products of crop processing. Aswad contains what is possibly the earliest find of domesticated emmer. The authors infer that wheat, barley, field pea, lentil and linseed were all cultivated. They argue that at Aswad and Ghoraifé dry farming conditions were marginal, while further to the west, Ramad was well within the range of tolerance for rain-fed agriculture. They suggest that the wetter/marshy areas around the sites may have been exploited.

In the Wadi Jilat in the eastern steppic region of Jordan, beyond the limits of dry farming, Garrard *et al.* (1994) excavated two Neolithic settlements associated with seasonal occupation. Wild and domesticated grains of both wheat and barley were recovered. On the basis of the presence of parts of the plant other than the grain, basal culm fragments, culm nodes and barley rachis internodes, Colledge (1994) inferred that these cereals had been locally cultivated. In addition, a number of wild species recovered, for example *Malva* spp., *Capparis* spp., *Centaurea* spp., *Erodium* spp., and *Atriplex* spp. were known to have edible parts that contributed to the food supply. It was also possible to identify the range of types of vegetative storage organs which were present at the sites. These included swollen stems, rhizomes, tubers and roots from monocotyledonous and dicotyledonous plants. Cyperaceae tubers were tentatively identified, *Rheum palaestinum* and roots of *Scorzonera judaica* were recovered. All these taxa could have been exploited as sources of food, and eaten either raw or cooked. It was concluded that the charred remains from these seasonal sites reflected the use, not only of domestic crops, but also a great range of wild plant taxa, many of which were potential sources of food.

These three contrasting data-sets, while displaying a common dependence on wild or domestic cereals clearly display the diversity of plant exploitation practice found across small bands of space and time around the period of the earliest transition to agriculture.

The wider south-west Asian context

Epipalaeolithic sites in south-west Asia were seasonal, transitory settlements. Movements of people were largely dictated by the availability of wild game and wild 'crops'. The few sites pre-dating 10 000 BP that have yielded plant material reflect that reliance on wild plant foods. Although wild, a number of researchers have suggested that certain forms of vegetation management, such as watering and weeding, were practised. Hillman and Davies (1992) refer to 'pre-domestication' cultivation at the end of the Epipalaeolithic.

The earliest and most convincing finds of genetically transformed (domesticated) cereal grains date from the Pre-Pottery Neolithic A period (van Zeist and Bakker-Heeres 1982, Colledge 1994). Sites of this period are found in the Mediterranean zone of the Levant, and in areas where the vegetation was diverse, supporting a rich array of wild cereals and legumes (Bar-Yosef and Belfer-Cohen 1989:484). The centres of origin of several of the 'founder crops' are thought to be in this region of the Levant (Zohary 1996). It is also evident from archaeobotanical remains that the reliance on wild plant food resources continued at this time.

Gopher (1989:81) proposes that the early Pre-Pottery Neolithic of the Levant can be viewed as a single cultural system. He argues that exchange and movement of ideas and artifacts extended over significant geographic distances. Bar-Yosef (1989:58) suggests that the interaction between the early 'farming' communities and contemporary hunter-gatherer groups in the marginal areas would have continued for several millennia. It has been argued that the groups most likely to adopt agriculture as a means of subsistence would have been those in logistically organized settlements within areas suitable for cultivation (Byrd 1992:50). Hillman and Davies (1992:141) suggest that the spread of agriculture to new locations may not always have been successful. They surmise that there would have been instances, where the seed stocks of domesticates were given either to farmers practising 'non-domestication' cultivation or to hunter-gatherers without the requisite knowledge of cultivation techniques or technology, which would have resulted in failure to maintain the domestic strains.

Evidence of exchange throughout the area increases during Pre-Pottery Neolithic B. During this period evidence for exploitation of the steppe/desert regions also increases. In the middle of the Pre-Pottery Neolithic B period (cf. Rollefson 1989:169) numerous sites were founded in the central Levant, and in the southern Levant permanent, so-called, 'agricultural villages' were established for the first time. Domestic cereals and legumes have been identified on many of these settlements in the Mediterranean woodland region of the Levant, as well as on the smaller sites in the arid zone. By the Late Neolithic/Pottery Neolithic there is evidence for the complete adoption of crop- and livestock-based agriculture throughout the Near East.

SOME ARCHAEOBOTANICAL APPROACHES IN THE NEW WORLD

In many ways, the archaeobotany of agricultural transitions has proceeded in similar ways in south-west Asia, and Meso-America, but there are also some notable contrasts. One of these relates to the physical geography of the New World, which inevitably imposes a strong north–south axis on the movement of agriculture and its domesticates from Mexico. As a result, such crops as maize did not have far to travel before entering quite different latitudinal zones from their centre of origin. This opened up a wider variety of methods to track its progress. Another difference relates to the archaeological approach. While archaeobotany in both regions was initially heavily biased towards key cereals, wheat and barley in one, maize in the other, that strong focus upon cereal agriculture was, in the Old World, more intimately tied up with ideas about the progress of civilization. Archaeobotany in the New World has often achieved a broader perspective on plant food usage, as is illustrated by changes in interpretation of the spread of maize.

The pioneering excavations in the Tehuacan valley in Mexico generated a large number of desiccated, and sometimes charred, maize cobs (cf. Byers 1967). Thanks to some erroneous carbon dates, it appeared that the early maize cobs reflected a domestication process on a timescale broadly compatible with what was going on in south-west Asia, although it is now realized that the timetable was more compressed in the New World (cf. Smith 1995). In both parts of the world, the outward spread of these key cereals was seen as a pre-condition for the growth of civilization and complex society. A series of distinct bioarchaeological approaches contributed to tempering this basic stimulus–diffusion model.

South of the Mexican centre of origin, in Panama and further south, a very early presence of maize has been inferred from phytoliths attributed to maize. Piperno and Holst (1998) extracted a range of starch granules and phytoliths from fine cracks in the surface of Panamanian grinding stones of various dates. The earliest, around 7000 years old, thus produced traces of maize, together with those of bottle gourd, squash and leren. Later grindstones add to this list traces of arrowroot, manioc, and some kind of legume. It is not until the first millennium AD that maize comes to dominate the microscopic traces on the grindstone surfaces, in this country on the direct path of maize expansion.

This evidence, from phytoliths and starch granules, resonates with quite independent evidence from the isotopic composition of human bones (see Chapter 23). The study of carbon isotope ratios, which can effectively track maize expansion, has indicated there is a considerable time lag between the first appearances of maize outside its centre of origin, and its eventual move to a prominent position in the human food chain (e.g., Buikstra and Milner 1991). Archaeobotany has shifted its focus from this most obvious of crops to the range of diverse plant foods, some wild, some domesticated, managed in a variety of ways, to constitute the prehistoric diets. Examples of this broader perspective on plant use are seen, for example, in studies by Flannery (1986) and Watson (1989). They each describe rich and diverse ecosystems exploited in a variety of ways, and in which the use of the more familiar crop species is only one element, something comparable with the results from Wadi Jilat (see above). They reflect a general broadening in archaeobotanical approaches to the transition to agriculture, from the core domesticates that dominated earlier research to the wider human ecosystem and the diversity and complexity of its exploitation in the past.

REFERENCES

*Recommended for further reading

Barker, G. (1985). *Prehistoric Farming in Europe*. Cambridge University Press: Cambridge.

Bar-Yosef, O. (1989). The PPNA in the Levant – an overview. *Paléorient*, **15**:57–63.

Bar-Yosef, O. and Belfer-Cohen, A. (1989). The origins of sedentism and farming communities in the Levant. *Journal of World Prehistory*, **3**:447–498.

Blumler, M.A. (1992). Independent inventionism and recent genetic evidence on plant domestication. *Economic Botany*, **46**:98–111.

Bogaard, A., Palmer, C., Jones, G., Charles, M. and Hodgson, J.G. (1999). A FIBS approach to the use of weed ecology for the archaeobotanical recognition of crop rotation regimes. *Journal of Archaeological Science*, **26**:1211–1224.

Bouby, L., Leroy, F. and Carozza, L. (1999). Food plants from late Bronze Age lagoon sites in Languedoc, southern France: reconstruction of farming economy and environment. *Vegetation History and Archaeobotany*, **8**:53–69.

Braidwood, L., Braidwood, R., Howe, B., Reed, C. and Watson, P.J. (eds) (1983). *Prehistoric Archaeology along the Zagros Flanks*. Oriental Institute Publication 105, University of Chicago: Chicago.

Buikstra, J.E. and Milner, G.R. (1991). Isotopic and archaeological interpretations of diet in the Central Mississippi Valley. *Journal of Archaeological Science*, **18**:319–329.

Byers, D.S. (1967). *The Prehistory of the Tehuacan Valley. Volume 1: Environment and Subsistence*. University of Texas Press: Austin.

Byrd, B. (1992). The dispersal of food production across the Levant. In Gebauer, A.B. and Price, T.D. (eds) *Transitions to Agriculture in Prehistory*, 49–61. Monographs in World Archaeology 4, Prehistory Press: Madison, Wisconsin.

Carruthers, W. (1991). Mineralised plant remains: some examples from sites in southern England. In Hajnalova, E. (ed.) *Palaeoethnobotany and Archaeology: Proceedings of 8th Symposium of International Work-Group for Palaeoethnobotany, Nitra-Nove Vozokany 1989*, 75–80. Acta Interdisciplinaria Archaeologica VII, Archaeological Institute of the Slovak Academy of Sciences: Nitra.

Cavalli-Sforza, L.L., Menozzi, P. and Piazza, A. (1994). *The History and Geography of Human Genes*. Princeton University Press: Princeton.

Chambers, F.N. and Jones, M.K. (1984). The antiquity of rye in Britain. *Antiquity*, **58**:219–224.

Charles, M., Jones, G. and Hodgson, J.G. (1997). FIBS in archaeobotany: functional interpretation of weed floras in relation to husbandry practices. *Journal of Archaeological Science*, **24**:1151–1161.

Childe, V.G. (1936). *Man Makes Himself*. Watts: London.

Colledge, S.M. (1994). *Plant Exploitation on Epipalaeolithic and Early Neolithic Sites in the Levant*. Unpublished PhD Thesis, University of Sheffield.

Darwin, C. (1868). *The Variation of Animals and Plants under Domestication. Volume 1*. John Murray: London.

de Candolle, A. (1882). *Origine des Plants Cultivées*. Germer Baillière: Paris.

Deakin, W.J., Rowley-Conwy, P. and Shaw, C. (1999). The sorghum of Qasr Ibrim: reconstructing DNA templates from ancient seeds. *Ancient Biomolecules*, **2**:117–124.

Eubanks, M. (1997). Re-evaluation of the identification of ancient maize pollen from Alabama. *American Antiquity*, **62**:139–145.

Evershed, R.P. (1993). Biomolecular archaeology and lipids. *World Archaeology*, **25**:74–93.

Evershed, R.P., Heron, C. and Goad, L.J. (1991). Epicuticular wax components preserved in potsherds as chemical indicators of leafy vegetables in ancient diets, *Antiquity*, **65**:540–544.

Evershed, R.P., Heron, C., Charters, S. and Goad, L.J. (1992). The survival of food residues: new methods of analysis, interpretation and application In Pollard, A.M. (ed.) *New Developments in Archaeological Science*, 187–208. Proceedings of the British Academy 77, Oxford University Press: Oxford.

Evershed, R.P., Dudd, S.N., Charters, S., Mottram, H., Stott, A.W., Raven, A., van Bergen, P.F. and Bland, H.A. (1999). Lipids as carriers of anthropogenic signals from Prehistory. *Philosophical Transactions of the Royal Society*, **B354**:19–31.

Fearn, M.L. and Liu, K.B. (1995). Maize pollen of 3500 BP from southern Alabama. *American Antiquity*, **60**:109–117.

Flannery, K.V. (1986). *Guila Naquitz*. Academic Press: New York.

Gerrard, A., Baird, D., Colledge, S., Martin, L. and Wright, K. (1994). Prehistoric environment and settlement in the Azraq Basin: an interim report on the 1987 and 1988 excavation seasons. *Levant*, **26**:73–109.

Gopher, A. (1989). Diffusion process in the Pre-Pottery Neolithic Levant: the case of the Helwan Point. In Hershkovitz, I. (ed.) *People and Culture in Change*, 91–105. BAR International Series 508(i), British Archaeological Reports: Oxford.

Green, F.J. (1979). Phosphatic mineralisation of seeds from archaeological sites. *Journal of Archaeological Science*, **6**:279–284.

Hall, A.R. and Kenward, H.K. (1990). *Environmental Evidence from the Colonia*. The Archaeology of York Fascicle 14/6, Council for British Archaeology: London.

Hall, A.R., Kenward, H.K., Williams, D. and Greig, J.R.A. (1983). *Environment and Living Conditions at Two Anglo-Scandinavian Sites*. The Archaeology of York Fascicle 14/4, Council for British Archaeology: London.

*Harris, D.R. (ed.) (1996). *The Origins and Spread of Agriculture and Pastoralism in Eurasia*. UCL Press: London.

*Harris, D.R. and Hillman, G.C. (1989). *Foraging and Farming*. Unwin Hyman: London.

Hastorf, C.A. and Popper, V.S. (1988). *Current Paleoethnobotany: Analytical Methods and Cultural Interpretations of Archaeological Plant Remains*. Chicago University Press: Chicago.

Hather, J.G. (1992). The archaeobotany of subsistence in the Pacific. *World Archaeology*, **24**:70–81.

*Hather, J.G. (ed.) (1994). *Tropical Archaeobotany: Applications and New Developments*. Routledge: London.

Hather, J. and Kirch, P.V. (1991). Prehistoric sweet potato (*Ipomoea batatas*) from Mangaia Island, Central Polynesia. *Antiquity*, **65**:887–893.

Higgs, E.S. (ed.) (1972). *Papers in Economic Prehistory*. Cambridge University Press: Cambridge.

Hillman, G.C. and Davies, M.S. (1992). Domestication rate in wild wheats and barley under primitive cultivation: preliminary results and archaeological implications of field measurements of selection coefficient. In Anderson-Gerfaud, P. (ed.) *Préhistoire de l'Agriculture: Nouvelles Approches Expérimentales et Éthnographiques*, 113–158. Monographie du CRA 6, CNRS: Paris.

Hillman, G.C., Colledge, S. and Harris, D.R. (1989). Plant food economy during the epipalaeolithic period at Tell Abu Hureyra, Syria. In Harris, D.R. and Hillman, G.C. (eds) *Foraging and Farming*, 240–268. Unwin Hyman: London.

Imamura, K. (1996). Jomon and Yayoi: the transition to agriculture in Japanese prehistory. In Harris, D.R. (ed.) *The Origins and Spread of Agriculture and Pastoralism in Eurasia*, 442–464. UCL Press: London.

Jones, G. (1992). Weed phytosociology and crop husbandry: identifying a contrast between ancient and modern practice. *Review of Palaeobotany and Palynology*, **73**:133–143.

Jones, G., Charles, M., Colledge, S. and Halstead, P. (1995). Towards the archaeobotanical recognition of winter cereal irrigation: an investigation of modern weed ecology in northern Spain. In Kroll, H. and Pasternak, R. (eds) *Res Archaeobotanicae. Proceedings of 9th Symposium of International Workgroup for Palaeoethnobotany, Kiel*, 49–68. Oetker-Voges Verlag: Kiel.

Jones, M.K. (1988a). The phytosociology of early arable weed communities, with special reference to southern Britain. In Kuster, H. (ed.) *Der prähistorische Mensch und seine Umwelt. Festschrift fur Udelgard Körber-Grohne zum 65*, 43–51. Konrad Theiss Verlag: Stuttgart.

Jones, M.K. (1988b). The arable field: a botanical battleground. In Jones, M.K. (ed.) *Archaeology and the Flora of the British Isles: Human Influence on the Evolution of Plant Communities*, 86–92. Monograph 14, Oxford University Committee for Archaeology: Oxford.

Jones, M.K. (1991). Sampling in palaeoethnobotany. In van Zeist, W., Wasylikowa, K. and Behre, K.-E. (eds) *Progress in Old World Palaeoethnobotany*, 53–62. AA Balkema: Rotterdam.

Jones, M.K. and Brown, T.A. (2000). Agricultural origins: the evidence of modern and ancient DNA. *The Holocene*, **10**:769–776.

Kenward, H.K., Hall, A.R. and Jones, A.K.G. (1980). A tested set of techniques for the extraction of plant and animal macrofossils from waterlogged archaeological deposits. *Science and Archaeology*, **22**:3–15.

Lambrick, G. and Robinson, M. (1979). *Iron Age and Roman Riverside Settlements at Farmoor, Oxfordshire*. Research Report No. 32, Council for British Archaeology: London.

Loy, T., Spriggs, M. and Wickler, S. (1992). Direct evidence for human use of plants 28 000 years ago: starch residues on stone artifacts from the northern Solomons. *Antiquity*, **66**:898–912.

Maier, U. (1999). Agricultural activities and land use in a Neolithic village around 3900 BC: Hornstaad Hornle IA, Lake Constance, Germany. *Vegetation History and Archaeobotany*, **8**:87–94.

Pearsall, D.M. (1989). *Palaeoethnobotany. A Handbook of Procedures*. Academic Press: London.

Piperno, D.R. (1988). *Phytolith Analysis: an Archaeological and Geological Perspective*. Academic Press: London.

Piperno, D. and Holst, I. (1998). The presence of starch grains on prehistoric stone tools from the humid neotropics: indications of early tuber use and agriculture in Panama. *Journal of Archaeological Science*, **25**:765–777.

Renfrew, A.C. (1987). *Archaeology and Language: the Puzzle of Indo-European Origins*. Jonathan Cape: London.

Rollefson, G.O. (1989). The Late Aceramic Neolithic of the Levant: a synthesis. *Paléorient*, **15**:168–173.

Sauer, C.O. (1952). *Agricultural Origins and Dispersals*. American Geographical Society: New York.

*Smith, B.D. (1995). *The Emergence of Agriculture*. Scientific American Library: New York

Ugent, D., Pozorski, S. and Pozorski, T. (1982). Archaeological potato tuber remains from the Casma Valley of Peru. *Economic Botany*, **38**:417–432.

van der Veen, M. (1996). The plant remains from Mons Claudianus, a Roman quarry settlement in the Eastern Desert of Egypt – an interim report. *Vegetation History and Archaeobotany*, **5**:137–141.

van Zeist, W. and Bakker-Heeres, J.A.H. (1982). Archaeobotanical studies in the Levant 1. Neolithic sites in the Damascus Basin: Aswad, Ghoraifé and Ramad. *Palaeohistoria*, **24**:165–256.

van Zeist, W. and Bakker-Heeres, J.A.H. (1984). Archaeobotanical studies in the Levant 3. Late-Palaeolithic Mureybit. *Palaeohistoria*, **26**:171–199.

*van Zeist, W., Wasylikowa, K. and Behre, K.-E. (eds) (1991). *Progress in Old World Palaeoethnobotany*. AA Balkema: Rotterdam.

Vavilov, N. (1992). *The Origin and Geography of Cultivated Plants*. Cambridge University Press: Cambridge.

Wasylikowa, K. (1981). The role of fossil weeds for the study of former agriculture. *Zeitschrift für Archaologie*, **15**:11–23.

Watson, P.J. (1989). Early plant cultivation in the Eastern Woodlands of North America. In Harris, D.R. and Hillman, G.C. (eds) *Foraging and Farming: the Evolution of Plant Exploitation*, 555–571. Unwin Hyman: London.

Zhao, S. and Wy, W.T. (1986). Early Neolithic Hemodu culture along the Hangzhou estuary and the origin of domestic paddy rice in China. *Asian Perspectives*, **27**:29–34.

Zohary, D. (1996). The mode of domestication of the founder crops of Southwest Asian agriculture. In Harris, D.R. (ed.) *The Origins and Spread of Agriculture and Pastoralism in Eurasia*, 142–158. UCL Press: London.

*Zohary, D. and Hopf, M. (1994). *Domestication of Plants in the Old World*. Clarendon Press: Oxford.

33

Dietary Evidence from the Coprolites and Intestinal Contents of Ancient Humans

T.G. HOLDEN

Headland Archaeology Ltd., Edinburgh.

A knowledge of food and food procurement is central to much archaeological discussion. Unfortunately, however, most foods do not survive well under archaeological conditions and much of our understanding relies on inedible food parts such as shell and bone discarded as midden deposits or as plant remains inadvertently preserved by mechanisms such as charring, desiccation or waterlogging. Under exceptional conditions, however, more direct evidence for diet survives in the form of preserved human faeces.

Within the broad definition of 'palaeofaeces' three distinct classes can be recognized. The first of these is commonly referred to as 'cess' and is recovered as the primary fill of cesspits, latrines and sewers. Such deposits often occur in urban situations and frequently provide large assemblages of human waste yielding good quality evidence on subsistence provided that appropriate recovery and analytical techniques are employed (e.g., Greig 1981, Paap 1983). While the volume of material offers distinct benefits for analysis such contexts also include other domestic waste including animal faeces so prohibiting detailed analysis relating to daily or even seasonal diet.

The second class of faecal remains consists of individual well preserved human stools, commonly referred to as coprolites. These are occasionally preserved by charring or mineralization (Hillman *et al.* 1989:164, Hillman 1989:228, Jones 1983) but most commonly

survive as a result of having rapidly dried out after deposition and the persistence of extreme aridity. As a consequence there are numerous published analyses of samples from the arid areas of south-western North America, Mexico, Peru and Chile (e.g., Callen 1963, Bryant 1974, Bryant and Williams-Dean 1975, Heizer and Napton 1970, Fry 1985, Holden 1991, Reinhard and Bryant 1992) or dry cave environments in other more humid zones (e.g., Stewart 1974, Yarnell 1974). Detailed analyses of such samples have provided statistically valid dietary data enabling the recognition of patterns of seasonal availability of different foods and changes in diet through time (Sutton and Reinhard 1995).

The third class of faecal remains are those recovered directly from the guts of ancient well-preserved humans (see Chapter 21). It is only under exceptional conditions that human body tissue other than bone is recovered archaeologically. When they are, however, they offer some valuable lines of investigation into many aspects of human existence that are difficult to illuminate by any other means. One important aspect is what people have eaten, primarily by the identification and interpretation of food remains remaining in their alimentary canals. However, even though some bodies provide good evidence for diet, in many cases what they have eaten may have very little to do with everyday food. In other cases the significance of the last meals is hard to evaluate, primarily because of the small number of events represented.

Human bodies can be preserved in a variety of different ways but, as with coprolites, the most common method of preservation is by desiccation. Consequently, in areas such as the Pacific coast of Chile and Peru and in North Africa whole cemeteries of buried individuals are often recovered. Numerous examples have been analysed for their intestinal contents notably from Huaca Prieta, Peru (Callen 1963:189, Callen and Cameron 1960:39); northern Chile (Holden 1991, 1994, Holden and Núñez 1993); and from cave sites in North America (Wakefield and Dellinger 1936, Yarnell 1974 and Robbins 1971).

Less frequently bodies are preserved by freezing or by waterlogging and analyses of such samples have been undertaken on the bog bodies of northern Europe (Brandt 1950, Brothwell *et al.* 1990, Helbæk 1950, 1958, Hillman 1986, Holden 1986, 1995, 1999, van der Sanden 1990) and from frozen bodies from Greenland (Lorentzen and Rordam 1989) and the Alps (Spindler 1995). The following discussion relates primarily to the study of the last two categories of material, coprolites and human gut contents.

PALAEOFAECAL ANALYSIS

The composition of faeces

Human faeces are complex assemblages containing a variety of organic and inorganic inclusions from different sources. Cammidge (1914), for example, lists eight different classes of material present in faeces:

(i)   remnants of food which has escaped digestion and absorption,

(ii) remnants of foods which are totally or partially resistant to digestion,

(iii) breakdown products of foods,

(iv) secretions of the mucous membrane and digestive glands,

(v)   cellular elements and amounts of blood, mucus, leucocytes some of which become particularly noticeable during pathological conditions,

(vi) excretory products of the intestinal mucous membrane, (mineral salts, etc.),

(vii) bacterial flora of the large intestine – this makes up the bulk of most faeces, and

(viii) adventitious additions to the stools such as intestinal parasites, or their eggs, enteroliths, gall stones, etc.

To this list can be added accidental contaminants of food such as insects and other invertebrates, pollen, grit, charcoal and a chemical component produced as by-products of the metabolic activity of gut flora. These add to both the complexity of the assemblage and to its potential for answering archaeological questions provided that appropriate analytical techniques are applied. The following represent some of the most commonly addressed areas for study.

Diet

Palaeofaecal analysis represents one of the best ways of obtaining direct dietary data. In most cases we can be certain that what is recovered has at least been consumed even though contaminants such as grit and storage pests are also present. This has obvious advantages over other forms of analysis where interpretation of bone or other biological remains such as mollusc shell or insect parts, is often dependent on differing perceptions of what is edible or not.

Food storage

Storage of foods can be identified where foods that are available during different seasons are present in the same samples. The presence of certain pests that are specific to storage contexts can also be used to suggest methods of storage.

Food processing

The size of the identified food fragments can be used to suggest something of the processing techniques used. Fine fragment size is indicative of pounding and grinding, larger fragment size of less processed foods. In some cases the presence of grit may derive from processing tools such as stone querns or mortars. The presence of charred food remains reveals the use of fire for cooking and in some cases sophisticated techniques such as ESR (Electron Spin Resonance) can provide evidence for temperatures reached and the duration of cooking. Using this technique it has, for example, been possible to distinguish boiled from roasted or baked foods (Hillman *et al.* 1984). The presence of pests of storage such as acarid mites have also, for example, been used to infer the consumption of dried meat products (Baker 1990).

Status

Access to favoured resources may be indicative of high status individuals. On the other hand, the presence of low-status food with, for example, quantities of poorly processed and fibrous food elements, could identify low status individuals but might also represent famine food or food prepared for captives or criminals.

Ritual

Where well-preserved human bodies have been the result of ritual killings the presence of drugs or special foods have been used to throw light on the nature of the rituals.

Medicines

The analysis of coprolites represents one of the few ways in which the use of medicines can be demonstrated with certainty. From gut samples it may even be possible to correlate data from palaeofaecal analysis with pathological conditions that can be observed on the corpse.

Season of deposition

The presence of pollen or seasonally available foods in samples can be used to determine when foods were consumed. In the case of coprolites this will identify when a sample was deposited and, in the case of ancient bodies, the season of death.

Trade and transport

The presence of foods which are unlikely to have been grown locally provide good evidence for trade, transport or movement of people. This can be used to identify long distance trade of preserved foods or, in other cases, the movement of people between local resource zones during, for example, seasonal transhumance.

Health

Intestinal parasites are frequently recovered from faecal samples and can provide data on aspects of health.

Sample preparation

The basic methodologies used in palaeofaecal analysis were developed in the 1950s and 1960s. The use of aqueous solutions of trisodium phosphate as a rehydration medium for desiccated samples was first used by Callen and Cameron (1960) and is now a commonly used technique (Holden 1990). This solution converts otherwise brittle desiccated remains into more manipulable assemblages that can, if required, be dissected and mounted on microscope slides.

Identification of food remains

The identification of the majority of faecal debris requires a detailed knowledge of microscopy, and plant and animal anatomy (Figures 33.1–33.8). Through the use of these well-established disciplines such delicate remains as flower petals, muscle fibres (Figure 33.3), small fragments of pulverized seed testa (Figures 33.4 and 33.5) and cereal bran (Figure 33.6) can all be identified. Optical equipment has clearly improved somewhat since the early days of coprolite research but the same basic microscope skills are required and most of the best reference books are still those produced earlier last century (Winton and Winton 1932, 1935, Gassner 1973, Vaughan 1970, 1979) when plant anatomy was a more fashionable area of botanical study. These sources do, however, tend to concentrate on commercially exploited foods and little comparable work has been undertaken on collected foods (e.g., wild plants, invertebrates).

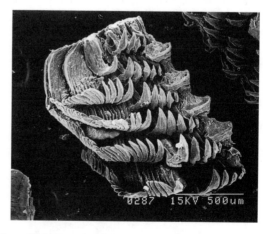

Figure 33.1 Scanning electron micrograph of a fragment of the radula from a species of *Chlorostoma*, a marine mollusc, from El Morro, North Chile. (Photo: T.G. Holden).

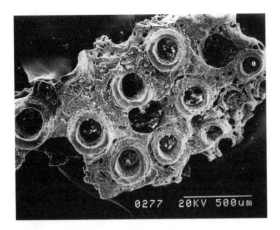

Figure 33.2 A fragment of what is thought to be pharageal teeth sockets of a species of marine fish from Camarones, North Chile. (Photo: T.G. Holden).

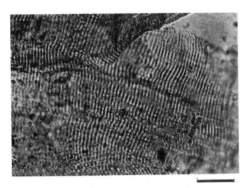

30 μm

Figure 33.3 Muscle fibres from a coprolite from the midden at Tulán 54, North Chile. (Photo: T.G. Holden).

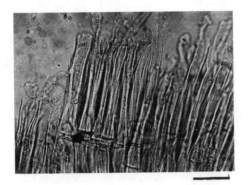

30 μm

Figure 33.4 Small pieces of palisade tissue from a species of legume, from Azapa, North Chile. (Photo: T.G. Holden).

200 μm

Figure 33.5 Fragments of testa of hazel nut (*Corylus avellana*) from the gut of the Lindow III bog body. (Photo: T.G. Holden).

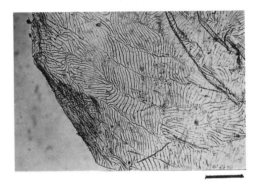

200 μm

Figure 33.6 Fragments of the testa of oat (*Avena* sp.) from the gut of the Zweeloo bog body. (Photo: T.G. Holden).

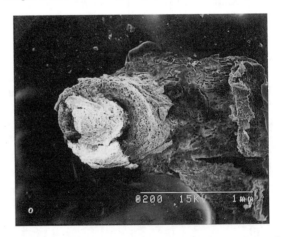

Figure 33.7 Scanning electron micrograph of a fragment of the rhizome of a species of rush, (*Schoenoplectus/Scirpus* sp.) from Tarapacá, North Chile. (Photo: T.G. Holden).

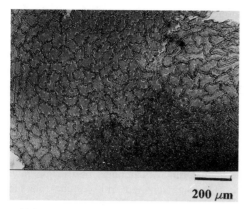

Figure 33.8   A fragment of the testa of an *Opuntia* cactus seed from Tulán 54, North Chile. (Photo: T.G. Holden).

The use of polarized light microscopy is of value in some circumstances, particularly if starch grains are thought to survive. A characteristic Maltese cross is produced by grains from different sources and this can be used in their identification. The Scanning Electron Microscope now also provides an invaluable tool that has only become readily available in recent years. As with the other techniques used it is, however, totally reliant on the existence of a broad range of modern reference material and it is frequently this, as much as anything else, that restricts the level to which identifications can be taken.

The fine palaeofaecal detritus (i.e., the less than 250 μm fraction) has received more attention in recent analyses. This fraction consists largely of bacterial detritus but items of possible diagnostic value such as plant crystals (e.g., druse crystals, raphides), phytoliths, plant hairs and individual or small groups of cells might be expected to contribute to other lines of evidence. The fine detritus also contains chemical traces and techniques are now also being applied that can identify foods that leave little visible trace. These techniques have the potential for producing good results and, although in their infancy, the identification of waxes from coprolites has already been undertaken (Wales *et al.* 1991). Analyses of species-specific animal proteins have also been undertaken with success (Newman *et al.* 1993, Sutton and Reinhard 1995) and offer significant potential for the future. The use of DNA analysis is also of possible value particularly where part-digested muscle fibres and the like have been identified microscopically. No successful analyses on such material have yet been undertaken to the knowledge of the author.

Quantification

The quantification of identifiable food debris from palaeofaecal analyses has always proved problematic. In many cases a subjective system has provided the most practical way of recording the different elements but in other cases measurements of weight and volume, following time consuming separation of the different components, has been undertaken. Rarely, however, do the results provide an accurate value of the proportions of different foods eaten. Foods with distinctive indigestible components are continually over-represented while many of the low fibre foods which often provide a significant calorific input to the diet hardly register. Some attempts have been made to rectify this by manipulating the basic data such that it more closely represents the equivalent dry weights of food consumed. Ideally, one should aim to equate weight or volume of faecal debris to grams (dry weight) of undigested food. Attempts have been made to achieve this by using published values for dietary fibre in different foods as rough analogues for digested foods. In this way the rye bran (*Secale cereale*) to corn spurrey seed testa (*Spergula arvensis*) recovered from the gut of the Huldremose Woman was used to suggest that the original food had contained a ratio of three parts rye to one part corn spurrey (Holden 1994, 1999). In most cases, however, the diversity of plant remains present and the lack of suitable published data on dietary fibre prohibit this sort of interpretation and for many samples a subjective estimate of abundance is as much as can be expected.

Interpretation

At the level of interpretation, the use of statistical techniques with large assemblages of coprolites has proved of benefit. Cluster analysis has, for example, been applied to samples from Antelope House, Arizona and revealed different patterns of food combinations which were thought to represent seasonal availability of different foods (Sutton and Reinhard 1995).

Of extreme relevance to the interpretation of palaeofaecal samples is a knowledge of food taphonomy during the digestive process and in post-depositional environment. Different processing techniques can dramatically alter the likelihood of foods surviving digestion and many factors can affect the efficiency of digestion. There is an existing literature on the changes that food undergoes during processing. Stahl (1989:181), for example, itemizes some of the chemical and physical changes that occur and the nutritional benefits that accrue as a result of pounding/grinding/grating, soaking/leaching, fermentation and heat treatment of plant foods. Some of the effects of heat treatment of food are also discussed with respect to archaeological studies by Holden (1994).

Surprisingly little work has been undertaken into the effects of digestion on foods but it is clear that many different factors can affect its efficiency. A limited amount of experimental work has been undertaken and useful descriptions of the anatomy of digested foods have been made by Calder (1977), Schel *et al.* (1980) and Bock *et al.* (1988). The results of such experiments go some way to enabling us to predict those food components that would always be expected to survive digestion in an identifiable form, those tissues that may survive depending on conditions and those tissues that are very unlikely to survive digestion (Holden 1995). Table 33.1 summarizes some of the commonly consumed plant and animal tissues and how they are likely to survive during digestion.

KEY-HOLE SAMPLING OF HUMAN BODIES

The sampling of faecal traces from well-preserved humans is one area that has seen some changes in the last 10 years. The use of CT scanning (Computed Tomography) and endoscopy has enabled the sampling of faecal material with minimal destruction to body tissues. This was achieved with considerable success on the Danish Bog Body from Huldremose (Brothwell *et al.* 1990) and should enable the sampling of more bodies from museum collections. These bodies are of particular importance because they enable the integration of data from the gut contents with data

Table 33.1 Summary of food elements likely to survive human digestion.

Tissues usually surviving digestion

	Tissue description	*Examples*
Plant	Tissues with lignified, suberized or strongly cutinized cell walls	Protective and structural tissues including thickened seed coats, fibrous tissues (e.g., vascular fibre, xylem tracheary elements); sclereids (e.g., stone cells); cutinized epidermal tissues (e.g., fruit epicarp); suberized tissues (e.g., secondarily thickened stem tissues such as cork layers)
Fungi	Tissues constructed largely of chitin	Most fungal tissues
Animal	Soft tissues containing high concentrations of elastin	Large tendons and cartilage
	Hard tissues containing deposited minerals and those based upon large resistant molecules like keratin and chitin	Bone, insect and other arthropod skeletal elements, hair, mollusc radulae, feathers

Tissues that may or may not survive digestion depending on conditions

Plant	Tissues with thickened cellulose walls but with only slight lignification or a loose association with a cuticle	Tissues such as leaf or stem epidermal tissue will normally be destroyed by digestion, in some cases leaving behind only the remains of a distinctive, detached cuticle
	Dense storage parenchyma rich in oil and protein	Dense parenchyma can prevent digestive enzymes passing to the inner parts of the tissue such as the embryos of some seeds, nut kernels, etc.

Tissues that will not survive digestion under normal circumstances

Plant	Ground tissue of most plant organs	Most metabolically active cells including mesophyll, root, stem and storage parenchyma
Animal	Soft animal tissues and animal products	No evidence would be expected for muscle, non-fibrous organs such as liver, eggs or milk products

Evidence for these last categories, notably starch grains or muscle fibres, has been encountered under exceptional conditions such as where large pieces of meat or whole seeds have been swallowed so protecting the inner muscle fibres and starchy parenchyma respectively or where the transit time through the body has been exceptionally fast.

from palaeopathological studies and chemical analysis of the body tissues.

Problems and potential

One of the primary aims in undertaking this type of research is to try and obtain evidence for diet that might be considered typical of a particular population. This is frequently asking too much of the data but in order to illustrate some of the potential and some of the problems associated with palaeofaecal analyses several recent examples from well-preserved human corpses are presented below.

The circumstances surrounding the death and interment of individuals often sets them aside from ordinary people. The majority of people do not die unexpected deaths, their intestinal contents are therefore part of the story relating to their deaths and may be anything but ordinary. They may not therefore be able to answer questions directly relating to a full range of typical foods but still represent important opportunities to study other aspects of prehistoric life and death. In order to be able to assess the significance of these finds and to determine how representative they are it is essential to know more about the circumstances surrounding their death.

Ritual Meals? – the European bog bodies

The European bog bodies represent a unique category of archaeological find. Much of the evidence suggests that their deaths were linked to ritual killings and deliberate disposal of the body in bogs (see Chapters 13 and 21). What therefore can we glean from an analysis of their intestinal contents? Some of their last meals such as those from the Lindow bog bodies (Holden 1986, 1995) would appear to be very ordinary in composition. Cereals were represented by the bran and only minor levels of contamination by weed seeds were observed. From the Lindow II body the composition, fragment size and the use of ESR to record the thermal history of the cereals lead us to believe that the meal had been eaten in the form of an unleavened bread. There were however, a small number of pollen grains of mistletoe (*Viscum album*) also present giving a tantalizing hint at the possible ritual aspects of his demise (Scaife 1986). The Lindow III body also contained cereal bran but this time with quantities of hazel (Figure 33.5). Similar apparently ordinary meals were also recovered from the Dutch Zweeloo body. In this case millet (*Panicum miliaceum*), blackberry pips (*Rubus* sp.) and

cereal bran (Figure 33.6) were identified (van der Sanden 1990). Few other components were present. In contrast to these all of the Danish examples contained a high proportion of wild species as well as cereal remains.

The Huldremose Woman from Djursland, Denmark has been studied in some detail (Holden 1999). Examination of the body revealed a number of interesting observations. Dated to 1920 ± 100 BP, she had severe lacerations to her legs, amputation of one of her arms and injuries to her hand at, or close to, the time of death. Her head appeared to have been shaved. The overall condition of the body was, however, remarkable considering that she was recovered in the last century and had been allowed to dry semi-naturally in the basement of the National Museum, Copenhagen. Approximately two grams of material were removed from the intestines for analysis (Brothwell *et al.* 1990).

As with the other bog bodies from Denmark the Huldremose body contained cereals, bran, this time rye (*Secale cereale*) and a substantial weed seed element. This was, however, dominated by the seeds of only one species, corn spurrey (*Spergula arvensis*) and was calculated to have made up about one-third of the total meal. These seeds must represent more than mere accidental inclusions in the meals of the Grauballe, Tollund, Borremose and Huldremose people. At the very least, they must have been a tolerated component of recognized nutritive value but were, more probably, included deliberately. The literature indicates that there are three ways in which these weed seeds could possibly have been procured for consumption: (i) deliberate collection from fields, fallow land or waste land (Helbæk 1958:114), (ii) recovered from the waste fraction of crop processing (Hillman 1986:102), (iii) deliberate cultivation (Steensberg pers. comm.). Most probably, all three of the methods of procurement were important during the Iron Age. The presence of certain chaff elements such as those recovered from the Grauballe sample (i.e., even whole spikelets of wheat) would, however, tend to support Hillman's suggestions in that case. With the Huldremose Woman the case is less clear. The rye/corn spurrey mixture could represent a rye crop that had been heavily infested with corn spurrey which was then consumed before being thoroughly cleaned. The total absence of rye chaff in contrast to the presence of vegetative parts of corn spurrey, however, imply that the two elements were collected or possibly just processed separately only to be combined during food preparation.

There is little from the macroscopic plant remains regarding the composition of these last meals to indicate that they had any special significance, ritual or other. It would, however, be very difficult for us to identify this even if it was the case. Perhaps the Danish examples from Borremose, Tollund, Grauballe and Huldremose reflect a more fragile agricultural system commonly beset by crop failure and the weed seeds represent attempts to stretch failing supplies of cereal grain. There is plenty of ethno-historical evidence to suggest that this practice was commonplace in many parts of Europe. If this is the case, it would be tempting to link the ritual killings from Denmark with periods of particular famine. The very ordinariness of examples from other parts of Europe, however, suggests that this is probably too simplistic to explain all of the available information. In any event, it does appear as though certain trends are beginning to manifest themselves and it can only be hoped that as the present database is enlarged upon the relevance of these may become more apparent.

Illness

Most people die as a result of disease rather than physical trauma. Perhaps as many as 10 per cent of all the bodies investigated appear to contain little or no identifiable food remains in the gut. There may be several reasons for this but in many cases it is probably because they had not been eating for some days prior to death or because they had been eating easily-digested low fibre foods suitable for the infirm. Other observations of the food remains can also be explained as being the result of illness but the beauty of these well-preserved cadavers is that they enable detailed palaeopathological examination and a more complete story relating to the individual is available. By way of examples, two very different cases are given.

The first is one of a number of bodies recovered from the valley of Azapa, Chile. It was that of an infant some two years old (Ref. AZ141 T-12) who was believed, on the basis of the palaeopathological evidence, to have died of Acute Bacterial Colitis (Aufderheide pers. comm.). During autopsy samples thought to be either blood clots or food debris were presented for analysis. At higher magnification it transpired that these were, in fact, highly degraded food remains containing quantities of the fragmented palisade layer from the seed of a species of legume (Figure 33.4). There are a number of South American *Phaseolus* species or other large legumes which would contain structures like these. Clearly the food had been

highly processed and is likely to have been specially prepared in an attempt to sustain a sick or dying infant.

By contrast some diseases can result in abnormally large quantities of foods in the intestines. One such condition is chagas disease which today and apparently also in the past was endemic in parts of South America (Rothhammer *et al.* 1984). In cadavers this can often be recognized by the presence of mega-cardia (an enlarged heart) and mega-colon (distended lower intestines) which is caused by the partial paralysis of the lower bowel. Sample TR-40A T-6, a middle aged female from Tarapacá, Chile and dated to roughly AD 300 exhibited all the major symptoms of chagas disease. The massively distended colon provided over half a kilo of coarse botanical fibre (Holden and Núñez 1993). The dominant food component in this case was roughly processed algarrobo (*Prosopis* sp.). These are still eaten today but usually after grinding and removal of the inner hard segments to produce a flour. In this case the whole pods must have been chewed and swallowed and it is a distinct possibility that both the quantity and the composition of the foods recovered were related to chagas disease.

Typical food

In many respects, samples from victims that were unexpectedly killed offer the most likely chances of providing the best evidence of this. One of the clearest examples of this is the case of the Chinchorro fisherman (Sample T18, dated to 2000–500 BC) from the site of El Morro 1–6 on the northern coast of Chile. He was killed by numerous penetrating wounds to the body and blows to the head (Aufderheide pers. comm.). He was buried with his harpoon and fishing net and his gut was packed with the remains of shell fish (*Chlorostoma* sp.; Figure 33.1), fish bone and the underground organs of a species of rush (probably *Scirpus americanus*).

It has to be recognized that one of the main flaws in many of these analyses is that they represent single or small groups of individuals and although they provide a wealth of useful information do not normally provide a good picture of ordinary diet. At the site of Tulán 54, northern Chile (dated to approximately 3200 BP) however, it was possible to provide something approaching this. Here, in the Atacama desert, preservation of organic remains is exceptional. Everything discarded in the hyper-arid environment is preserved. At Tulán this included, not only the inhabitants and their gut contents, but also middens of up to two metres in depth consisting of every fragment of refuse ever discarded on the site. The samples of gut contents from the contemporary cemetery were found to contain considerable quantities of the starch-rich cactus seed (*Opuntia* cf. *atcamensis*; Figure 33.8) and rush rhizomes (*Scirpus americanus*; Figure 33.7); proof that the inhabitants had been consuming them. Their composition matched well with the composition of the hundreds of coprolites from the nearby midden thereby indicating that they too must be human in origin and that the samples taken from the bodies were representative. The coprolites also added additional items to the list of identifications already made such as rodent hair, meat, amphibian and probable camelid bones. In addition to this, rodent skins and bones were present in the midden and even the tops of the tubers which had been cut off could be identified providing additional information regarding the full extent of the foods consumed and how they had been processed. All the plant parts that were not in the gut had been left on the midden. Tools used for food processing lay scattered around the site. The archaeological data, food remains and the present weather patterns suggest that this was only a seasonally occupied camp; preservation at other potential camps are, unfortunately, characterized by charred remains only. Nevertheless, there now exists an excellent, but probably still incomplete, picture of the wild resources that the inhabitants consumed during their stay, how they processed their foods, and something of their personal hygiene and waste disposal patterns.

CONCLUSION

Those samples which are most likely to provide the best evidence of population diet have been recovered from situations that enable the integration of data from several sources of evidence. This is all too often not possible, leaving us uncertain about how typical identified food components are. Improved methods of identification of the less obvious food elements by microscopic or chemical analysis are essential but on their own these may not dramatically improve our ability to interpret the remains. In cases where the samples were taken from well-preserved corpses the body itself can provide a good deal of information and enable us to put the food remains into some sort of context. The information produced by these analyses is, however, almost too detailed for understanding prehistoric diet *per se*. The chemistry of body tissues potentially has a lot to offer (see Chapter 23). Most importantly this would help us to place the detailed evidence relating to the composition of the last meals

into a broader dietary pattern and would have a significant impact on our understanding and significantly increase the value of the data produced to date.

ACKNOWLEDGEMENTS

Thanks are due to John Taylor, National History Museum, Prof. Arthur Aufderheide, Prof. David Harris, Don Brothwell and Gordon Hillman for their support over a number of years. Grateful thanks are also given to the Science and Engineering Research Council (SERC) for their financing much of the work presented here and to Dawn Holmes and Paul Currie for their help in the production of this paper.

REFERENCES

*Recommended for further reading

Baker, A.S. (1990). Two new species of *Lardoglyphus* Oudemans (Acari: Lardoglyphidae) found in the gut contents of human mummies. *Journal of Stored Product Research*, **26**:139–147.

Bock, J.H., Lane, M.A. and Norris, D.O. (1988). *Identification of Plant Food Cells in Gastric Contents for Use in Forensic Investigations: A Laboratory Manual*. U.S. Dept. of Justice: Washington DC.

Brandt, J. (1950). Planterester fra et moselig fra ældre jernalder: Borremose. *Årbøger for Nordisk Oldkyndighed og Historie*, **1950**, 348–350.

Brothwell, D.R., Holden, T.G., Liversage, D., Gottlieb, B., Bennike, P. and Bosen, J. (1990). Establishing a minimum damage procedure for the gut sampling of intact human bodies: the case of the Huldremose Woman. *Antiquity*, **65**:830–835.

Bryant, V.M. (1974). Diet in southwest Texas: the coprolite evidence. *American Antiquity*, **39**:407–420.

Bryant, V.M. and Williams-Dean, G. (1975). The coprolites of man. *Scientific American*, **232**:100–109.

Calder, A.M. (1977). Survival properties of organic residues through the human digestive tract. *Journal of Archaeological Science*, **4**:141–151.

Callen, E.O. (1963). Diet as revealed by coprolites. In Brothwell, D.R. and Higgs, E. (eds) *Science in Archaeology*, 186–194. Thames and Hudson: London.

Callen, E.O. and Cameron, T.W.M. (1960). A prehistoric diet revealed in coprolites. *New Scientist*, **9(190)**:35–40.

Cammidge, P.J. (1914). *The Faeces of Children and Adults*. William Wood and Co.: New York.

*Fry, G.F. (1985). Analysis of fecal material. In Gilbert, R. and Mielke, J.I. (eds) *The Analysis of Prehistoric Diets*, 127–148. Academic Press: New York.

Gassner, G. (1973). *Mikroskopische Unterschung pflanzlicher Lebensmittel*. Gustav Fischer Verlag: Stuttgart.

Greig, J. (1981). The investigation of a Medieval barrel-latrine from Worcester. *Journal of Archaeological Science*, **8**:265–282.

Heizer, R.F. and Napton, L.K. (1970). Archaeology and the prehistoric Great Basin lacustrine subsistence regime as seen from Lovelock Cave, Nevada. *Contributions of the University of California Archaeological Research Facility*, **10**.

Helbæk, H. (1950). Tollundmandens sidste måltid. *Årbøger for Nordisk Oldkyndighed og Historie*, **1950**:328–341.

Helbæk, H. (1958). Grauballemandens sidste måltid. *KUML*, **1958**:83–116.

*Hillman, G.C. (1986). Plant foods in ancient diet: the archaeological role of palaeofaeces in general and Lindow Man in particular. In Stead, I.M., Bourke, J.B. and Brothwell, D.R. (eds) *Lindow Man: The Body in the Bog*, 99–115. British Museum Publications: London.

Hillman, G.C. (1989). Late palaeolithic plant foods from Wadi Kubbaniya in upper Egypt: dietary diversity, infant weaning and seasonality in a riverine environment. In Harris, D.R. and Hillman, G.C. (eds) *Foraging and Farming: The Evolution of Plant Exploitation*, 207–239. Unwin Hyman: London.

Hillman, G.C., Robins, G.V., Oduwole, D., Sales, K.D. and McNeil, D.A.C. (1985). The use of electron-spin resonance spectroscopy to determine the thermal histories of cereal-grains. *Journal of Archaeological Science*, **12**:49–58.

Hillman, G.C., Madeyska, S.M. and Hather, J. (1989). Wild plant foods and diet at late palaeolithic Wadi Kubbaniya: the evidence from charred remains. In Wendorf, F., Schlid, R. and Close, A. (eds) *The Prehistory of Wadi Kubbaniya Vol. 2. Stratigraphy, Palaeoeconomy and Environment*, 162–242. Southern Methodist University Press: Dallas.

Holden, T.G. (1986). Preliminary report on the detailed analysis of the macroscopic remains from the gut of Lindow Man. In Stead, I.M., Bourke, J.B. and Brothwell, D.R. (eds) *Lindow Man: The Body in the Bog*, 116–125. British Museum Publications: London.

Holden, T.G. (1990). The rehydration of coprolites using trisodium phosphate: colour reaction and smell. *Paleopathology Newsletter*, **71**:9–12.

Holden, T.G. (1991). Evidence of prehistoric diet from northern Chile: coprolites, gut contents and flotation samples from the Tulán quebrada. *World Archaeology*, **22**:320–331.

*Holden, T.G. (1994). Dietary evidence from the intestinal contents of ancient humans with particular reference to desiccated remains from northern Chile. In Hather, J.G. (ed.) *Tropical Archaeobotany: Applications and New Developments*, 66–85. Routledge: London.

Holden, T.G. (1995). The last meals of the Lindow Men. In Turner, R. and Scaife, R. (eds) *Bog Bodies: New Discoveries and New Perspectives*, 76–82. British Museum Publications: London.

Holden, T.G. (1999). Food remains from the gut of the Huldremose bog body. *Journal of Danish Archaeology*, **13**:49–56.

Holden, T.G. and Núñez, L. (1993). An analysis of the gut contents of well-preserved human bodies from the Tarapacá region of Northern Chile. *Journal of Archaeological Science*, **20**:595–611.

Jones, A.K.G. (1983). A coprolite from 6-8 Pavement. In Hall, A.R., Kenward, H.K., Williams, D. and Greig, J.R.A. (eds) *Environment and Living Conditions at Two Anglo-Scandinavian Sites*, 225–229. The Archaeology of York Fascicule 14/4, Council for British Archaeology: London.

Lorentzen, B. and Rordam, A.M. (1989). Investigation of faeces from a mummified Eskimo woman. *Meddelelser om Grønland*, **12**:139–143.

Newman, M.E., Yohe, R.M. II, Ceri, H., and Sutton, M.Q. (1993). Immunological protein analysis of non-lithic archaeological materials. *Journal of Archaeological Science*, **20**:93–100.

Paap, N.A. (1983). Palaeobotanical investigations in Amsterdam. In van Zeist, W. and Casparie, W.A. (eds) *Plants and Ancient Man: Studies in Palaeoethnobotany*, 339–344. Balkema: Rotterdam.

*Reinhard, K.J. and Bryant, V.M. Jr. (1992). Coprolite analysis; a biological perspective on archaeology. In Schiffer, M.B. (ed.) *Archaeological Method and Theory 4*, 245–288. University of Arizona Press: Tucson.

Robbins, L.M. (1971). A woodland mummy from Salts Cave Kentucky. *American Antiquity*, **36**:200–206.

Rothhammer, F., Standen, V., Nûñez, L., Allison, M.J. and Arriaza, B. (1984). Origen y desarrollo de la tripanosomiasis en el area centro-sur Andina. *Chungará*, **12**:155–160.

Scaife, R. (1986). Pollen in human palaeofaeces; and a preliminary investigation of the stomach and gut contents of Lindow man. In Stead, I.M., Bourke, J.B. and Brothwell, D.R. (eds) *Lindow Man: The Body in the Bog*, 126–135. British Museum Publications: London.

Schel, J.H.N., Stasse-Wolhuis, M., Katan, M.B. and Willemse, M.T.M. (1980). Structural changes of wheat bran after human digestion. *Mededelingen Landbouwhogeschool Wageningen*, **80(14)**:1–9.

*Spindler, K. (1995). *The Man in the Ice*. Phoenix: London.

Stahl, A.B. (1989). Plant food processing: implications for dietary quality. In Harris, D.R. and Hillman, G.C. (eds) *Foraging and Farming: The Evolution of Plant Exploitation*, 171–196. Unwin Hyman: London.

Stewart, R.B. (1974). Identification and quantification of components in Salts Cave paleofeces, 1970–1972. In Watson, P.J. (ed.) *Archaeology of the Mammoth Cave Area*, 41–47. Academic Press: New York.

Sutton, M.Q. and Reinhard, K.J. (1995). Cluster analysis of the coprolites from Antelope House: implications for Anasazi diet and cuisine. *Journal of Archaeological Science*, **22**:741–750.

van der Sanden, W.A.B. (1990). De laaste maaltijd (1): de macro-resten. In van der Sanden, W.A.B. (ed.) *Mens en Moeras: Veenlijken in Nederland van de bronstijd tot en met de Romeinse Tijd*, 151–157, 232. Drents Museum: Assen.

Vaughan, J.G. (1970). *The Structure and Utilisation of Oil Seeds*. Chapman and Hall: London.

Vaughan, J.G. (1979). *Food Microscopy*. Academic Press: London.

Wakefield, E.G. and Dellinger, S.C. (1936). Diet of dwellers of the Ozark Mountains and its skeletal effects. *Annals of Internal Medicine*, **9**:1412–1418.

Wales, S., Evans, J. and Leeds, A.R. (1991). The survival of waxes in coprolites: the archaeological potential. In Budd, P., Chapman, B., Jackson, C., Janaway, R. and Ottaway, B. (eds) *Archaeological Sciences '89*, 340–344. Monograph 9, Oxbow: Oxford.

Winton, A.L. and Winton, K.B. (1932, 1935). *The Structure and Composition of Foods, Volumes 1 and 2*. John Wiley: New York.

Yarnell, R.A. (1974). Intestinal contents of the Salts Cave mummy and analysis of the initial Salts Cave flotation series. In Watson, P.J. (ed.) *Archaeology of the Mammoth Cave Area*, 109–112. Academic Press: New York.

34

Vertebrate Resources

A.K.G. JONES

Department of Archaeological Sciences, University of Bradford

and T.P. O'CONNOR

Department of Archaeology, University of York.

The dry bones that dominate many archaeological collections are not the prime focus of this chapter. Instead, the biology of living animals – their anatomy, physiology, ethology and ecology – is the starting point for considering human interactions with other animal populations, and the archaeological study of those interactions. The techniques and results of comparative anatomy, much of it undertaken in the nineteenth century, are well known and invaluable sources for archaeologists in establishing which animals were present at a particular time and place. More recent developments in the biological sciences have done much to inform those responsible for conserving animal populations, whether for food or sport, or to maintain the biodiversity of the planet, and there is much here that is relevant to studies of past predation, colonization, and extinction. Current biochemical and biomolecular research promises to add much to our understanding of the origins of species, demes, and domestic forms of vertebrates. Here, archaeology gives an important temporal context to studies of modern populations. The archaeological study of past vertebrate populations as resources utilized by people thus draws upon the biological sciences in a number of ways, but also contributes a long perspective that is beyond the reach of field biology.

Bones are amongst the most common and bulky finds encountered on archaeological excavations and these remains provide the raw data for understanding human diet, animal husbandry and the exploitation of wild populations. Much research has concentrated on the processes by which the bones of living animals become specimens on the analyst's bench – taphonomy (Lyman 1994; see Chapter 15) – and no less effort has been directed to counting and analysing the numbers of these bones to extract meaning from them (Chapter 56). Our concern here, though, is with the study of bones as a means to an end, not as an end in itself.

ANATOMICAL ATTRIBUTES

Animals with backbones – vertebrates of the phylum Chordata – can be divided into five classes; fishes, amphibians, reptiles, birds and mammals. In all but a few aquatic forms, the backbone and other skeletal elements are mineralized in adult individuals. Vertebrates range in size when fully grown from

---

creatures such as the dwarf pygmy goby *Pandaka pygmaea* just 8 mm long and weighing only 4 mg, to the blue whale *Balaenoptera musculus* at 30 metres in length and 160 tonnes. Obviously, large animals have large bones while small species possess small skeletal elements, and so the remains of vertebrates do not stand an equal chance of being recovered from archaeological sites. Two main factors influence retrieval. First, the methods of excavation and recovery influence the number and size of specimens retrieved (Shaffer and Sanchez 1994, Stahl 1996, James 1997, Shaffer and Baker 1999). Second, the nature of the animal's skeleton, in particular the number of identifiable skeletal elements per individual will influence a species' archaeological visibility. Bones, teeth, scales, distinctive spines and other vertebrate hard tissues are now recovered in greater quantities than was formerly the case, as a result of improved recovery methods such as the systematic sieving and sorting of large samples of earth. None the less, vertebrates that produce large robust remains, such as large ungulates, are far more likely to be archaeologically recoverable and recovered than small taxa such as most passerine birds and many fishes.

While the physical remains of animals will inevitably be the primary focus for archaeologists, animals were, and continue to be, utilized as a diverse resource, for products such as meat, milk, hide, wool, eggs, and traction. Animals are also a cultural resource in less tangible ways. The control or possession of certain vertebrates might consign and confirm status, or reflect the moral and aesthetic values of the society (Manning and Serpell 1994). Animals, in particular domesticated species, are socially embedded to much the same degree as artifacts such as pottery or jewellery, while other species frequently assume symbolic or mythic status.

Even if archaeologists sieved and sorted all sediment to less than 1 mm, some animals would continue to be under-represented in the archaeological record. Although most vertebrate skeletons are composed of bone, some, notably the Agnatha – jawless fishes such as lampreys and hag fishes – do not possess mineralized skeletal tissue. The only parts of these animals likely to be preserved in archaeological sites are their chitinous teeth and finds are very rare. The Elasmobranchii – cartilaginous fishes – produce weakly mineralized skeletal tissue which is strong enough to survive as museum specimens when carefully prepared and curated, but when the protein binding the mineral particles degenerates, the tissue crumbles to dust. None the less, most elasmobranchs produce mineralized vertebral centra, and the recovery and identification of archaeological specimens is becoming more routine

(e.g., Reese 1984, Kozuck and Fitzgerald 1989). A few sharks and rays also produce distinctive robust spines (Rosenlund 1986), and most are covered in dermal denticles, some of which may be large enough to be recovered by hand during excavation, although most will only be recovered in samples processed on fine (<1 mm) mesh (Wheeler and Jones 1989). Compared with the Teleostii – bony fishes – elasmobranchs are poorly represented in the fossil record.

The degree of mineralization of the bones of teleosts varies considerably. Some species produce very well mineralized bone which is as dense and robust as the bone of mammals. Others, such as the lumpfish *Cyclopterus lumpus*, lays down bones which are paper-thin even in the most mature individuals. Furthermore, bone can be demineralized during life. Atlantic salmon *Salmo salar* dissolve much of their bone as they swim upstream to their spawning grounds, and so their visibility in archaeological material may depend upon the time of year at which the fish were exploited. Similarly, fish scales vary greatly in size, robustness and thus archaeological visibility. Eel (Apodes) typically produce minute scales that are deeply embedded in the skin and scarcely visible to the naked eye. Most teleosts are covered with conspicuous, transparent or translucent scales that protect the animal and record its life history in incremental growth rings. The sturgeons (Acipenseridae) are covered in large bony scutes, while gars (Lepisosteidae) are protected by distinctive, usually diamond-shaped, ganoid scales. Otoliths ('ear stones') are composed of calcium carbonate and, like scales, record the growth of fish in incremental rings. When found in large numbers, they can provide detailed insights into fish exploitation.

Amphibian and reptile bone ranges from rather fibrous, poorly-mineralized tissue in newly-metamorphosed amphibians, to large, dense structures in heavy reptiles such as monitor lizards and turtles (Sobolik and Steele 1996). Tortoises and turtles may more commonly be represented in archaeological samples by the heavily keratinized carapace, which has been used in many cultures as a raw material for containers, musical instruments, and decorative inlay. Our own experience indicates that a major reason for non-recovery of amphibian and reptile bone is the failure to recognize it as bone when sieved residues are being sorted. Certainly there are no empirical or experimental grounds to expect amphibian and reptile bones to be less well-preserved than the bones of other classes of vertebrates in the same deposits, and much the same must be said of bird bones. Immature bird bone is soft and poorly mineralized: the bird skeleton grows remarkably rapidly in order to attain something close to adult body size by the time that the bird leaves the nest. Immature bird bone is vulnerable to damage during deposition, burial, and excavation. However, the immature stage constitutes a small proportion of the lifetime of most birds, and immature bones are generally uncommon other than at nesting sites, or human occupation sites where unfledged birds have been predated, such as coastal Inuit sites (e.g., Gotfredson 1997:273). In general, then, the structure and composition of bird bones does not militate against their preservation and recovery.

Within mammals, bones are particularly poorly mineralized in neonatal individuals, and are generally much less robust in immature individuals than in those that have attained skeletal maturity. As this maturation is a much slower process in most mammals than in birds, immature mammals are more commonly encountered as the prey of humans, and so the effect of low mineralization in compromising their preservation and recovery is more significant. The bones of adult mammals may also undergo a degree of demineralization at times of physiological stress, as in lactating females, and in old age.

Teeth have to be sharp and hard to cut food stuffs and grind other biological materials, and so are amongst the most robust parts of the skeleton of most vertebrates and therefore survive better than most other parts in archaeological samples (Hillson 1986). The number of teeth per individual varies across vertebrate classes. Fish typically carry simple, undifferentiated teeth on the dentary, premaxilla, and maxilla, with additional teeth on the palatine bone and as pharyngeal teeth in the 'throat' in some families. Some orders of reptiles and amphibians have teeth on the upper and lower jaw bones, and some, such as the extinct tetrapod *Dimetrodon*, have pharyngeal teeth. Reptilian teeth are generally simple structures, though highly adapted in some snakes. Birds, of course, lack teeth. Mammals have relatively small numbers of highly differentiated teeth (heterodonty), typically divisible into incisors, canines, premolars, and molars on both upper and lower jaw, and often carried as successive deciduous and permanent sets. The variation in tooth form and numbers in the main families of mammals is summarized by Hillson (1986), and Wheeler and Jones (1989) review the variation of teeth in fishes. An important point to make about teeth is that the often highly-adapted nature of mammalian dentition means that teeth are often the most diagnostic part of the skeleton. In some difficult groups, notably the Rodentia, identification to species, or even

to genus, may only be reliable on the basis of dental morphology.

Variation in the size, morphology, number, and durability of skeletal and dental elements in vertebrates means that different taxa do not have an equal chance of surviving the processes of death, burial, excavation, and analysis. Archaeologists have long accepted that the larger mammals, especially adults, are over-represented in archaeological samples. However, with the increased use of sieving, and greater attention being paid to the remains of other classes of vertebrates, it is essential to model the biases that are inherent in the diversity of vertebrate structure, and to be alert to all of the skeletal, dental and dermal structures which might survive into the archaeological sample.

The study of vertebrate skeletal anatomy was largely undertaken in the nineteenth century by pioneer zoologists such as Cuvier, Owen, and Agassiz. Older text books of zoology often provide excellent illustrations of the bones and teeth of species 'typical' of most vertebrate orders (e.g., Romer 1962, Goodrich 1930, Barone 1966, Kent 1987). For fishes in particular, classic vertebrate anatomy works include Harder (1975). While these works present a clear picture of the main characteristics of the vertebrate skeletal template, they are rarely of much value in identifying ancient specimens, because they illustrate articulated skeletons of only a small number of species. Archaeological remains are nearly always disarticulated and fragmentary.

To allow the identification of vertebrate remains, zooarchaeologists build a modern comparative collection by acquiring the corpses of accurately identified, recently deceased animals and reducing them to skeletons by a range of processes, some slow, some smelly, and most laborious (Reitz and Wing 1999:362). By spending long hours preparing comparative material, osteologists become familiar with the three dimensional character of vertebrate skeletons and the relationship of form and function, and also come to appreciate the variability found between individuals of one species. This is essential to understanding the distinctive features on which specific identifications are based. Collections of skeletons in major museums of natural history are an important resource for zooarchaeology, and museums employ experienced researchers who may help train new scholars as well as curating collections of identified archaeological material. These are particularly important when examining assemblages that may include extinct forms, or specimens of ambiguous or disputed taxonomy.

While comparative collections are a fundamental resource, a number of publications have been written specifically to assist with the identification of ancient vertebrate remains. These generally deal with one particular class or order of vertebrates, or may be restricted in their geographical scope. Table 34.1 lists some of the more widely-used of these sources, and summarizes their remit. The obvious danger of any such publication is that hard-pressed zooarchaeologists will base identifications solely on the published description if reference specimens are not readily available. This can lead to an over-representation in the literature of species that happen to have been described and illustrated, at the expense of closely-related species which have not. Some identifications require bones to be measured, to obtain size ranges or diagnostic ratios. Sources such as von den Driesch (1976) and Morales and Rosenlund (1979) describe and illustrate standard measurements to give consistency between different workers.

One source of intra-species variation is sexual dimorphism. In some species, primary or secondary sexual characteristics are manifest in the skeleton. Some species of ray, such as the thornback ray *Raja clavata*, produce teeth of different shape and size in males and females, although it is not normally possible to ascribe sex to fish remains. Only rather rarely are dimorphic characters unambiguous: the clear difference in the size and morphology of the canine teeth in male and female pigs is one of the few exceptions. Features such as the presence of 'spurs' on the tarsometatarsal bones of galliform birds are more typical: useful dimorphic characters if we are prepared to accept that a few per cent of specimens will be misidentified (West 1982). More often, we see sexual dimorphism reflected in gross size or some index of skeletal robusticity. Using these criteria, we might infer with some confidence the ratio of males to females, but would have much less confidence in the attribution of an individual specimen. After all, tall, robust females and gracile males are not unusual in our own species. An important point about sexual dimorphism is that it is adaptive, and therefore subject to selection pressures. In some populations of a particular species, dimorphism in size may be particularly marked, or depressed to the point where it is negligible. In studies of archaeological material, we have to take care not to transfer what are, in fact, population-specific dimorphic characters across populations that are widely separated in time and space. Grigson (1984) gives a good example of the complications that sexual dimorphism introduces

Table 34.1 A summary of major published sources of illustrations and keys to aid in the identification of archaeological specimens. The list excludes unpublished theses (but see Stewart and Carrasquilla 1997) and those works limited to the discrimination of two or three taxa.

Source	Geographical remit	Zoological remit
Schmid 1972	Europe	Limited range of mammals
Walker 1985	East Africa	Mammals (post-cranial only)
Scarlett 1972	New Zealand	Mostly marine mammals and birds
Sobolik and Steele 1996	North America	Chelonians
Gaffrey 1939	Europe	Mammal skulls
Böhme 1977	Europe	Anuran pelves
Cohen and Serjeantson 1996	Great Britain	Limited range of mostly larger birds
Cannon 1987	North America	Five representative taxa of fish
Gilbert 1973	North America	Limited range of mostly larger mammals
Glass 1973	North America	Limited range of mammals; skulls only
Olsen 1964	North America	Limited range of mostly larger mammals
Olsen 1968	North America	Limited range of fish, amphibians, reptiles
Olsen 1972	North America	Major bird families; skulls only
Wolsan 1982	Europe	Ungulates; ribs only
Carter 1977	Europe	Ungulates; vertebrae only
Prummel 1987	Europe	Foetal cattle, horse, sheep, pig
Helmer and Rocheteau 1994	Near East and Mediterranean	Smaller ungulates; postcranial only
Pieper 1982	Europe	Ducks of genus Aythya; postcranial only
Vigne 1995	Europe	Four genera of rodent; postcranial only
Yalden and Morris 1989	Great Britain	Mostly rodents and insectivores; limited range of elements
Stewart and Carrasquilla 1997	Europe	A guide to published and thesis sources for birds
Woolfenden 1961	SE North America	Ducks and other waterfowl; postcranial only
Moreno 1985, 1986, 1987	SW Europe	Passeriform birds

to comparisons of early domestic cattle and wild aurochs *Bos primigenius*. The difficulty that we have in confidently attributing sex to disarticulated archaeological material, limits our interpretation of sex-selection of prey animals by hunters, information that might be crucial to understanding a hunting strategy.

The mortality profile of prey or livestock will reflect in part the population ecology of the animals concerned, and in part the decisions taken by hunters or pastoralists. Age at death is reflected in the skeleton of different vertebrates in a number of different ways, and this is not the place to review these procedures in detail (see Reitz and Wing 1999:178, O'Connor 2000:80 for surveys of principles and applications). In general, the attribution of age at death to an individual specimen may be based upon recognizing stages of incremental growth in structures such as the scales or otoliths of fishes (Desse and Desse-Berset 1992) or mammalian dental cementum (Lieberman and Meadow 1992), or upon the state of specific developmental indicators, such as the eruption of the permanent teeth in mammals. In the first instance, the validity of the technique depends upon the consistency of the incremental growth, and the probability that external factors such as food supply or water temperature, or individual factors of disease or injury, might have interrupted the 'normal' growth periodicity. Interpretation of incremental growth data in archaeological material therefore requires us to understand in detail the extent and direction of the growth effects that external or physiological factors might have. That said, the quality of information that can be obtained is quite remarkable. van Neer *et al.* (1993) use inferred growth rate variation in tilapia *Oreochromis niloticus* from the late Palaeolithic site of Makhadma in Egypt to establish the season of fishing, and hence the scheduling of fishing activity within the flood sequence of the Nile. In the second instance, comparative data show only minor inter-population variability in attributes such as the timing of dental eruption (e.g., see Moran and O'Connor 1994), though management practices such as castration may have a marked effect on skeletal development and therefore on attributes such as epiphysial fusion (Reitz and Wing 1999:189). Again, it is essential not only that modern comparative data are collected, but that the effects of external and physiological factors are understood in detail, in order to model the possible direction and extent of inter-population variation.

In order to infer information about the uses that people have made of vertebrate resources, we have to understand the physiology of the 'typical' individual animal and the extent of variation of that physiology (Noddle 1990). Given that understanding, we can begin to infer the decisions that hunters and pastoralists have made, though a detailed interpretation will also rest on an understanding of the behavioural ecology of the species concerned.

BEHAVIOURAL AND ECOLOGICAL ATTRIBUTES

Animals respond in different ways to changes in their environment. A loud noise may cause a deer to flee, a cat to freeze, and an ostrich to run on the spot in a tight circle whilst bobbing its head up and down. Different behaviours are adaptive: they enable individuals to survive longer and produce more young, or to enable other members of their species to do so. Humans, with their great ability to learn, have exploited various aspects of animal behaviour to their advantage.

Some birds and mammals aggregate in large numbers, utilizing the herd or flock as a means to maximize feeding efficiency and to minimize individual risk from predators. Whereas predators such as wolves or cheetahs have had to develop tactics by which to isolate individual members of a herd, in order to be able to 'target' and kill that individual, humans have used prey aggregation to great advantage. An individual hunter encountering a high concentration of prey animals has a problem. He or she will only be able to kill one or two individuals before the rest flee, and if the prey are aggregated, it is likely that the next aggregation will be some distance away. Communal hunting by humans overcomes this problem, and turns the defensive adaptation of aggregation to the hunters' advantage (Driver 1995). A large group of people can kill far more of the individuals in a prey aggregation, so taking advantage of the concentration of animals. Where the prey are herd mammals such as horses, sheep, or bison, they can be driven into a confined space or trap which further facilitates the capture and killing of prey. This form of strategy is well-known from sites such as the Upper Palaeolithic levels at Abri Pataud, France (Spiess 1979), and from numerous bison kill-sites across the American Plains (Reeves 1990, O'Connor 2000:133). Not all large mammals lend themselves to this sort of predation. For example, guanaco, though associating in small herds, do not aggregate in the sort of numbers which makes communal hunting by people efficient, and guanaco kill-sites from South America typically consist of the remains of only a few individuals in any one stratum (Borrero 1990). Obviously, communal hunting has a number of social benefits for the people involved, but in the end it is an economic activity, and the ethology of the prey species largely dictates whether a hunting strategy will be viable or not.

Other aggregations have been exploited, not least those associated with seasonal movements of fish populations. In the Pacific Northwest, seasonal runs of salmon into the major rivers have been exploited with considerable ingenuity. The probability that seasonal salmon runs would fail occasionally was high enough in some areas to require the development of highly sophisticated risk-management strategies to ensure supplies of oil-rich food (Cannon 2000). Seasonal aggregation is also a feature of some bird populations, particularly marine species in the higher latitudes. Inuit sites in Greenland commonly include abundant bird bones, together with those of seal and caribou (Gotfredson 1997). Occasionally, there is clear evidence of the exploitation of a seasonally-aggregated species, as at Nipisat I (c. 3–4000 BP). Here, numerous bones of Brünnich's guillemot *Uria lomvia* were recovered, including a high proportion of juveniles. This clearly indicated that the species was taken during the nesting period. At the opposite end of the New World, shell matrix sites in southern Patagonia often include quantities of immature cormorant (*Phalacrocorax* spp.) and steamer duck *Tachyeres pteneres* bones, showing targeted exploitation of coastal birds roughly from the end of November to mid-March (Lefevre 1997).

Central American and south-east Asian sites often show evidence of what has been called 'garden hunting' (Linares 1976, Reitz and Wing 1999:287). This strategy is most often associated with the intensive cultivation of crops in small fields or garden plots close to settlements. The crops serve to attract animals from the surrounding uncultivated land, whether herbivores attracted by the crop itself, or omnivores and small-bodied predators attracted by the invertebrate community sustained by the cultivated land. The fields and gardens might also constitute clearings within otherwise closed vegetation, within which potential prey would be more visible. In short, the crops serve to attract, aggregate, and render accessible a range of prey animals which can be hunted without the necessity of making journeys far away from the settlement. In optimal foraging terms, search time is minimized, thus giving a positive calorific return even on quite small vertebrates that would otherwise have been disregarded as prey. It may have been garden hunting that first brought people and guinea pigs *Cavia aperea* into close association in the Central Andes.

Some behavioural attributes may have predisposed certain species towards becoming domestic animals, whether one sees that process as driven primarily by human need and intent, or more as a convergence of mutual benefit (O'Connor 1997). In the Old World, the tendency of cattle, sheep and goats to associate in herds must have facilitated their husbandry, though other herd ungulates, notably gazelles, did not become domestic animals, probably because of their greater tendency to migration, and the territorial nature of males during the rut (Garrard 1984, Martin 2000). There is a fascinating switch in the Levant from often highly specialized hunting of gazelles during the Upper Palaeolithic and Mesolithic, to the domestic husbandry of sheep and goats in the Neolithic: a particularly suitable prey being replaced by two well-adapted domesticates.

Two particular aspects of the ecology of other vertebrates affect their interaction with human populations: the trophic level, and the reproductive strategy. Trophic level is particularly important in so far as it influences abundance, and, to some extent, size and aggressiveness. The attenuation of energy through food chains is one of the fundamentals of our trophodynamic model of terrestrial ecology, and leads inevitably to the familiar pyramid of numbers, by which primary consumers are generally much more numerous than the carnivores that prey on them. The preceding discussion emphasizes humans as predators, the top consumers in terrestrial food webs. Such a trophic position is clearly untenable for such an abundant species, and the remarkable thing about people is their involvement in food webs at different trophic levels. When exploiting vertebrate resources, there are obvious advantages to predating the primary consumers, rather than prey at a higher trophic level which are likely to be much less abundant (and also more likely to bite back!). Throughout prehistory, people have tended to concentrate on herbivorous mammals and scavenger or detritivorous fish and molluscs as prey. Exceptions have tended to be local in extent, and represent places where biotic productivity was particularly high. In later Mesolithic Scandinavia, for example, pike *Esox lucius* were taken in appreciable numbers (Enghoff 1994), despite being a species that occupies a high trophic level.

Reproductive strategy is clearly of some importance when predation is at such a level as to have an impact on prey populations. Some vertebrates breed infrequently, having few young at a time, and often show a relatively long period of dependence of the young on the parents. Termed *equilibrium strategists* or *K-strate-*

gists, such species are adapted to giving the young a high probability of attaining breeding age, and maintaining their population numbers close to the carrying capacity of the habitat. K-strategists are often large, putting much of their physiological effort into growing and maintaining the adult body. Conversely, some species show a short period of growth, and breed prolifically, often frequently. They tolerate a high rate of immature mortality and are often small in size. These *opportunist* or *R-strategist* species are generally short-lived: the emphasis is on ensuring that enough young are produced to constitute the next generation, and to give the population the opportunity to undergo rapid expansion if conditions are favourable (Evans and O'Connor 1999:20).

These conflicting strategies should be seen as the extremes of a range along which vertebrates can be arrayed. The challenge for human populations throughout the world has been to find prey that give a satisfactory calorific return for the energy expended in their location and capture, whilst avoiding a reliance on K-strategist prey that would be vulnerable to rapid extinction. People exploiting coastal birds thus tend to utilize, but not to rely on, such notoriously K-strategist species such as albatross (*Diomedea* spp.) despite their large body size and thus favourable calorific return. Hunters in temperate continental interiors have faced the paradox that terrestrial vertebrate faunas have been dominated by large herbivores such as bison and camelids in the Americas, deer and horses in Eurasia, kangaroos and ratites in Australia, and an assortment of bovids in southern Africa. Behaviourally and trophically these are excellent prey: at a low enough trophic level to be relatively numerous, placid herbivores and so more likely to run from humans than to attack them, and mostly aggregating for at least parts of the year, so facilitating their capture through co-operative or communal hunting. Conversely, these large-bodied mammals are relatively K-selected, often having only single young each year, and often not breeding until several years old. The potential for local extinction through over-predation is obvious.

What the archaeological record from these regions seems to show is that the hunting of large herbivores provided an ecologically stable and sustainable strategy so long as the human population density remained low. Kill-sites are often extensive and archaeologically conspicuous: the piles of horse bones at Dereivka (Levine 1990), red deer at Stellmoor (Grönnow 1987), and the numerous bison kill-sites in the American Plains (Reeves 1990). The number and extent of bison kill-sites could give the impression of wholesale slaughter on a grand scale. However, it is evident that bison hunting was sustainable in at least parts of the Plains through some 10 000 years, and it is simply not credible, on *a priori* ecological grounds, that predation of such a large-bodied K-strategist could have been sustained for so long without widespread extinction unless the predation was at a low level. In other words, the sparse survival of settlement evidence is probably at least as much a genuine reflection of low human population density as it is of archaeological site survival. At times, and in some places, there is evidence of this predator-prey relationship coming under strain. The development of meat storage in the form of pemmican, some 5000 years ago, can be seen as a means of maximizing the utility of each carcass, and Late Prehistoric sites such as Vore, Wyoming (AD 1500–1800), show clear evidence of the systematic recovery of fat and marrow (Reher and Frison 1980). This is a good example of people using a technological 'fix' in order to continue with a pattern of subsistence behaviour that may have been becoming marginal, perhaps because of rising human populations in the northern Plains as native Americans were driven northwards and westwards by European settlement.

Another indication of stress in the predator-prey system is the rapid extinction of the prey, and it is the case that in some parts of the world at various times, hunting activity appears to be associated with the rapid extinction of, in particular, large bodied mammals. This is not the place to rehearse the debate in detail: sources such as Martin and Klein (1989) and Martin and Stuart (1995) give both an introduction and the detailed arguments. In the Americas, the megafaunal extinction appears to coincide with the Pleistocene–Holocene transition, a period of rapid climatic and environmental change. It could be argued that this change alone could have precipitated a wave of extinctions in the geographically isolated and densely niche-packed Rancholabrean fauna of North America. Some, notably Geist (1989), have argued that it is simply inconceivable that a relatively small number of human predators arriving from Beringia could have wrought such damage to an ecosystem which accommodated predators far more abundant and highly adapted than a technology-wielding primate. On the other hand, humans have undeniably brought about the extinction of endemic faunas in New Zealand, Madagascar, Hawaii, and the islands of the Mediterranean (Culliney 1988, Patton 2000). However, these are all island systems, and the vulnerability of island biotas to local extinction is well understood, both in theory and from direct observation

(Quammen 1996). In the end, the North American case hinges on absolute dating. Refined calibration of Paleoindian sites indicates that the period of megafaunal extinctions was less sudden than had previously been thought (Grayson 1989, Steele *et al.* 2000), and we can only date the latest *known* specimen of an extinct species, and assume that extinction of that species followed soon after. Resolution of the megafaunal extinction debate will depend upon more refined palaeoclimate modelling, to show exactly the adaptive challenge faced by the Rancholabrean biota, more (and more reliable) absolute dates from Paleoindian sites, and detailed, evidence-based modelling of that ecosystem to develop an interpretation that is both consistent with as much of the empirical evidence as possible, and ecologically credible. One of the irresistible aspects of the extinction debate is the challenge that it offers to archaeological science as an integrated whole.

DISCUSSION: GENERALIZING ABOUT VERTEBRATE RESOURCES

Our point here about using animal bones to study vertebrate resources is that we can use what we know of the biology of the animals concerned first to identify their remains, then to explain their potential and apparent role as resources in the cultural setting concerned. It is sometimes said of archaeological science that it is explanatory rather than interpretive: that we seek 'rational' explanations for patterns in the archaeological record in preference to attempting a hermeneutic interpretation of the place of, in this case, animals in the cultural mind-set. However, where animals comprise a major part of the food resource of a human population, recurrent non-rational utilization of that resource is likely to be self-limiting. It would be quite wrong to go to the opposite extreme to argue that human interaction with other vertebrates is always rational and optimized. Our own culture is replete with examples to the contrary, and so, no doubt, were virtually all human cultures of the last hundred millennia.

The adoption of livestock husbandry in many parts of the world during the early to mid-Holocene can be argued to have been a rational optimization of resource utilization. By bringing prey animals into aggregations close to human settlements, and then controlling and ensuring their reproduction, the search time component of an optimal foraging model is minimized. Further optimization is achieved by maximizing the resource that can be extracted from the prey. Wild animals can

be eaten just as readily as domestic animals, but domestic animals can also be used for milk, wool, dung, blood, traction, and currency. Seen in this way, animal domestication becomes a rational way of optimizing the utilization of vertebrate animals.

However, that functionalist interpretation does not stand up to close examination. A number of writers have argued that domestication is unlikely to have happened on the grounds of human expediency alone, and have proposed more of a mutualistic co-evolution (e.g., see Reed 1980, O'Connor 1997, Zohary *et al.* 1998). We have noted above that specialized hunting of gazelles in the Levant did not develop into the optimization of that utilization by domestication, nor was the specialized hunting of moa in New Zealand optimized into moa husbandry (Anderson 1983). Furthermore, the adoption of animal husbandry was not a one-way adaptation that permanently replaced hunting. At sites in northern Iraq, Zeder (1994) argues that hunting persisted as an optional means of resource extraction long after the domestication of caprines, cattle, and pigs, and hunting persisted in southern Africa alongside the introduction of pastoralism (O'Connor 2000:144). The obvious advantages of animal husbandry were evidently not always so obvious.

One specialized form of hunting that certainly required a thorough knowledge of the behavioural ecology of the prey species is fishing. Fishing is unlike most other forms of hunting in that the prey live in an environment in which humans cannot live without technological support. If fishing is not to be limited to shallow water and tidal rock-pools, artifacts are required with which fish can be hooked, snared, or netted and drawn out of the water (Brandt 1984). The origins of low-technology fishing are obscure: it seems very likely that early hominids would have scooped fish out of shallow water. The size distribution of fish from sites on the lower Darling River, Australia, led Balme to propose the use of traps and nets at least as early as 25 000 BP (Balme 1983). Upper Palaeolithic assemblages from Europe include objects that could have functioned as hooks, gorges, and fish spears and leisters, though it is always possible to contrive an alternative function for a barbed antler point or fusiform bone rod (e.g., see Radcliffe 1927). In many ways, the development of fishing can be seen in the same terms as the hunting of any other vertebrate prey. There were advantages to targeting species that associated in shoals; seasonal movements of the prey had to be understood, scheduled, and acted upon; and there were benefits to using collective effort to optimize the use of densely-aggregated prey. In terms of human ecology and the use of vertebrate resources, the exploitation of *Tilapia* inferred by van Neer *et al.* (1993) is analogous to the seasonal 'cropping' of coastal seabirds, or seasonal hunting of migrating caribou.

CONCLUSION

We are accustomed to using an analysis of the size and body composition of different taxa as a means of explaining some of the patterning that we see in their abundance in archaeological material. We can extend that process to using an analysis of the ecology and ethology of the taxa concerned to explain why and how they might have been more or less attractive as prey or domesticates, or why and how they might have found us attractive as commensal associates. Animal bone assemblages are snapshots of a dynamic and ongoing co-evolution between humans and other vertebrates. That co-evolution produced our species in the first place, as it is inconceivable that hominid evolution proceeded regardless of the selection pressures imposed by changes in the composition, abundance, and behaviour of the rest of the African fauna. In some parts of the world, humans found a successful and stable niche as predators, whether hunting medium to large mammals or foraging smaller resources. In others, nucleation of human populations in mosaic habitats favoured a more interventionist strategy. Where there was a fitness gain for other vertebrates, animal husbandry resulted. From this point of view, it is an interesting question whether developing animal husbandry might have been beneficial to humans in areas other than the known centres of domestication, but failed to happen for want of a potential domesticate with some benefit to gain. Brothwell's (1983) observation that the nine-banded armadillo *Dasypus novemcinctus* is ideally suited to domestication yet has remained undomesticated still requires a satisfactory explanation.

In discussing vertebrate resources we have focused largely on vertebrates as food, but we also stress the importance of other forms of utility. Amongst these is the symbolic use of animals. When people incorporate a species into the symbolic cultural realm, it is often for some particular attribute (the strength of lions or bears; the transcendent flight of birds) that reflects an attribute of the biology of that species. In other words, the utilization by people of animals as a symbolic resource may be as closely related to the ecology and behaviour of that species as its utilization as food or fur, and just as much an aspect of the co-evolution of ourselves and the species involved.

The study of ancient animal bones is functionalist and explanatory, and is based in a secure understanding of the anatomy, physiology, and ecology of the species concerned. It is 'science' in that we proceed by reasoned, tested deduction, and 'archaeology' in that we are primarily concerned with past human populations. However, the study of how those people used other vertebrates as resources goes far beyond the reconstruction of diet to seek to understand all aspects of the place of those animals in the human world, and of our place in theirs.

REFERENCES

*Recommended for further reading

Anderson, A. (1983). The prehistoric hunting of moa (Aves: Dinornithidae) in the high country of southern New Zealand. In Grigson, C. and Clutton-Brock, J. (eds) *Animals and Archaeology 2: Shell Middens, Fishes and Birds*, 33–51. BAR International Series 183, British Archaeological Reports: Oxford.

Balme, J. (1983). Prehistoric fishing in the lower Darling, western New South Wales. In Grigson, C. and Clutton-Brock, J. (eds) *Animals and Archaeology 2: Shell Middens, Fishes and Birds*, 19–33. BAR International Series 183, British Archaeological Reports: Oxford.

Barone, R. (1966). *Anatomie Comparée des Mammifères Domestiques. Tome 1 Osteologie.* Laboratoire d'Anatomie, École Nationale Vétérinaire: Lyon.

Böhme, G. (1977). Zur Bestimmung quartärer Anuren Europas an Hand von Skelettelementen. *Wissenschaftliche Zeitschrift der Humboldt-Universität zu Berlin, Math-Nat. R.* **26**:283–300.

Borrero, A. (1990). Fuego-Patagonian bone assemblages and the problem of guanaco hunting. In Davis, L.B. and Reeves, B.O.K. (eds) *Hunters of the Recent Past*, 373–399. Unwin Hyman: London.

Brandt, A. (1984). *Fish Catching Methods of the World*, (3rd edn). Fishing News Books: Farnham.

Brothwell, D.R. (1983). Why on Earth the guinea-pig? In Proudfoot, B. (ed.) *Site, Environment and Economy*, 115–119. BAR International Series 173, British Archaeological Reports: Oxford.

Cannon, A. (2000). Faunal remains as economic indicators on the Pacific Northwest coast. In Rowley-Conwy, P. (ed.) *Animal Bones, Human Societies*, 49–57. Oxbow Books: Oxford.

Cannon, D.Y. (1987). *Marine Fish Osteology. A Manual for Archaeologists.* Publication No. 18, Department of Archaeology, Simon Fraser University: Burnaby BC.

Carter, H.H. (1977). Vertebrae of the larger mammals of Western Europe. *Ossa*, **3**/4:109–127.

Cohen, A. and Serjeantson, D. (1996). *A Manual for the Identification of Bird Bones from Archaeological Sites*, (2nd edn). Department of Extra-Mural Studies, University of London: London.

Culliney, J. (1988). *Islands in a Far Sea: Nature and Man in Hawaii*. Sierra Club Books: San Francisco.

Desse, J. and Desse-Berset, N. (1992). Age et saison de mort des poissons: application a l'archéologie. In Baglinière, J.-L., Castanet, J., Conand, F. and Meunier, F.J. (eds) *Tissus Durs et Age Individuel des Vertébrés*, 341–353. ORSTOM: Paris.

Driver, J. (1995). Social hunting and multiple predation. *MASCA Research Papers in Science and Archaeology*, 12:23–38.

Enghoff, I.B. (1994). Fishing in Denmark in the Ertebølle Period. *International Journal of Osteoarchaeology*, 4:23–38.

*Evans, J.G. and O'Connor, T.P. (1999). *Environmental Archaeology, Principles and Methods*. Sutton Publishing: Stroud.

Gaffrey, G. (1939). Die Schädel der mitteleuropäischen Säugetiere. *Abhandlungen und Berichte aus den Staatlichen Museen für Tierkunde und Völkerkunde in Dresden, Reihe A: Zoologie*, 20:5–123.

Garrard, A. (1984). The selection of south-west Asian animal domesticates. In Clutton-Brock, J. and Grigson, C. (eds) *Animals and Archaeology 3. Early Herders and their Flocks*, 117–132. BAR International Series 202, British Archaeological Reports: Oxford.

Geist, V. (1989). Did large predators keep humans out of North America? In Clutton-Brock, J. (ed.) *The Walking Larder*, 282–294. Unwin Hyman; London.

Gilbert, B.M. (1973). *Mammalian Osteo-archaeology: North America*. Missouri Archaeological Society: Columbia.

Glass, B.P. (1973). *A Key to the Skulls of North American Mammals*. Missouri Archaeological Society: Columbia.

Goodrich, E.S. (1930). *Studies on the Structure and Development of Vertebrates*. Dover Books: London.

Gotfredson, A.B. (1997). Sea bird exploitation on coastal Inuit sites, west and southeast Greenland. *International Journal of Osteoarchaeology*, 7:271–286.

Grayson, D. (1989). Explaining Pleistocene extinctions: thoughts on the structure of a debate. In Martin, P.S. and Klein, R.G. (eds) *Quaternary Extinctions: a Prehistoric Revolution*, 807–823. University of Arizona Press: Tucson.

Grigson, C. (1984). The domestic mammals of the earlier Neolithic in Britain. In Schwabedissen, H. (ed.) *Die Anfänge des Neolithikums vom Orient bis Nordeuropa. Teil IX Der Beginn der Haustierhaltung in der 'Alten Welt'*, 205–220. Böhlau Verlag: Cologne.

Grönnow, B. (1987). Meiendorf and Stellmoor revisited: an analysis of late Palaeolithic reindeer exploitation. *Acta Archaeologica*, 56:131–166.

Harder, W. (1975). *Anatomy of Fishes*. Schweizerbartsche Verlagsbuchhandlung: Stuttgart.

Helmer, D. and Rocheteau, M. (1994). *Atlas du Squelette Appendiculaire des Principaux Genres Holocènes de Petits Ruminants du Nord de la Méditerranee et du Proche-Orient*. Fiches D'Ostéologie pour l'Archaeologie Serie B, No. 4, CNRS: Juan-les-Pins.

*Hillson, S. (1986). *Teeth*. Cambridge University Press: Cambridge.

James, S.R. (1997). Methodological issues concerning screen size recovery rates and their effects on archaeological interpretations. *Journal of Archaeological Science*, 24:385–397.

Kent, G.C. (1987). *Comparative Anatomy of the Vertebrates*, (6th edn). Mosby College Publishing: Toronto.

Kozuch, L. and Fitzgerald, C. (1989). A guide to identifying shark centra from southeastern archaeological sites. *Southeastern Archaeology*, 8:146–157.

Lefevre, C. (1997). Seabird fowling in southern Patagonia: a contribution to understanding the annual round of the Canoeros Indians. *International Journal of Osteoarchaeology*, 7:260–270.

Levine, M. (1990). Dereivka and the problem of horse domestication. *Antiquity*, 64:727–740.

Lieberman, D.E. and Meadow, R.G. (1992). The biology of cementum increments (with an archaeological application). *Mammal Review*, 22:57–77.

Linares, O.F. (1976). 'Garden hunting' in the American tropics. *Human Ecology*, 4:331–349.

Lyman, R.L. (1994). *Vertebrate Taphonomy*. Cambridge University Press: Cambridge.

Manning, A. and Serpell, J. (eds) (1994). *Animals and Human Society*. Routledge: London.

Martin, L. (2000). Gazelle (*Gazella* spp.) behavioural ecology: predicting animal behaviour for prehistoric environments in south-west Asia. *Journal of Zoology*, 250:13–30.

*Martin, P.S. and Klein, R.G. (eds) (1989). *Quaternary Extinctions: a Prehistoric Revolution*. University of Arizona Press: Tucson.

Martin, P.S. and Stuart, A.J. (1995). Mammoth extinction: two continents and Wrangel Island. *Radiocarbon*, 37:7–10.

Morales, A. and Rosenlund, K. (1979). *Fish Bone Measurements: an Attempt to Standardize the Measuring of Fish Bones from Archaeological Sites*. Steenstrupia: Copenhagen.

Moran, N. and O'Connor, T.P. (1994). Age attribution in domestic sheep by skeletal and dental maturation: a pilot study of available sources. *International Journal of Osteoarchaeology*, 4:267–285.

Moreno, E. (1985). Clave osteologica para la identificacion de los passeriformes ibericos. *Ardeola*, 32:295–378.

Moreno, E. (1986). Clave osteologica para la identificacion de los passeriformes ibericos. *Ardeola*, 33:69–130.

Moreno, E. (1987). Clave osteologica para la identificacion de los passeriformes ibericos. *Ardeola*, 34:243–374.

Noddle, B.A. (1990). Flesh on the bones. *Circaea*, 7:31–51.

O'Connor, T.P. (1997). On working at relationships: another look at animal domestication. *Antiquity*, 71:149–156.

*O'Connor, T.P. (2000). *The Archaeology of Animal Bones*. Sutton Publishing: Stroud.

Olsen, S.J. (1964). *Mammal Remains from Archaeological Sites: Part 1 – Southeastern and Southwestern United States*. Papers of the Peabody Museum of Archaeology and Ethnology Vol 56 No. 1, Harvard University: Cambridge, Mass.

Olsen, S.J. (1968). *Fish, Amphibian and Reptile Remains from Archaeological Sites: Part 1 – Southeastern and Southwestern United States.* Papers of the Peabody Museum of Archaeology and Ethnology Vol 56 No. 2, Harvard University: Cambridge, Mass.

Olsen, S.J. (1972). *Osteology for the Archaeologist No. 4. North American Birds.* Papers of the Peabody Museum of Archaeology and Ethnology, Harvard University, Vol 56 No 4: Cambridge, Mass.

Patton, M. (2000). Blitzkrieg or Sitzkrieg? The extinction of endemic faunas in Mediterranean island prehistory. In Nicholson, R.A. and O'Connor, T.P. (eds) *People as an Agent of Environmental Change,* 117–124. Oxbow Books: Oxford.

Pieper, H. (1982). Probleme der Artbestimmung an Knochen des Extremitatenskelettes sowie Bemerkungen zur systematischen Gliederung der Gattung *Aythya* (Aves: Anatidae). *Schriften aus der Archäologisch-Zoologischen Arbeitsgruppe Schleswig-Kiel,* 6:63–95.

Prummel, W. (1987). Atlas for identification of foetal skeletal elements of cattle, horse, sheep and pig, parts 1 and 2. *Archaeozoologia,* 1(1):23–30; 1(2):11–42.

Quammen, D. (1996). *The Song of the Dodo.* Hutchinson: London.

Radcliffe, W. (1927). *Fishing from Earliest Times.* John Murray: London.

Reed, C.A. (1980). The beginnings of animal domestication. In Coles, H.H. and Garrett, W.N. (eds) *Animal Agriculture,* 3–20 (2nd edn). WH Freeman: San Francisco.

Reese, D.S. (1984). Shark and ray remains in Aegean and Cypriote archaeology. *Opuscula Atheniensis,* 15:188–192.

Reeves, B.O.K. (1990). Communal bison hunters of the Northern Plains. In Davis, L.B. and Reeves, B.O.K. (eds) *Hunters of the Recent Past,* 168–194. Unwin Hyman: London.

Reher, C. and Frison, G.C. (1980). The Vore Site, 48CK302, a stratified buffalo jump in the Wyoming Black Hills. *Plains Anthropologist Memoir,* 16:1–190.

*Reitz, E.J. and Wing, E.S. (1999). *Zooarchaeology.* Cambridge University Press: Cambridge.

Romer, A.S. (1962). *The Vertebrate Body.* WB Saunders: Philadelphia.

Rosenlund, K. (1986). The sting ray *Dasyatis pastinaca* (L.) in Denmark. In Brinkhuizen, D.C. and Clason, A.T. (eds) *Fish and Archaeology. Studies in Osteometry, Taphonomy, Seasonality and Fishing Methods,* 123–128. BAR International Series 294, British Archaeological Reports: Oxford.

Scarlett, R.J. (1972). *Bones for the New Zealand Archaeologist.* Bulletin No. 4, Canterbury Museum: Christchurch.

Schmid, E. (1972). *Atlas of Animal Bones.* Elsevier: Amsterdam.

Shaffer, B.S. and Baker, B.W. (1999). Comments on James' methodological issues concerning analysis of archaeofaunal recovery and screen size correction factors. *Journal of Archaeological Science,* 26:1181–1182.

Shaffer, B.S. and Sanchez, J.L.J. (1994). Comparison of $\frac{1}{8}''$ and $\frac{1}{4}''$ mesh recovery of controlled samples of small-to-medium mammals. *American Antiquity,* 59:525–530.

Sobolik, K.D. and Steele, D.G. (1996). *A Turtle Atlas to Facilitate Archaeological Identifications.* University of Maine: Orono.

Spiess, A.E. (1979). *Reindeer and Caribou Hunters. An Archaeological Study.* Academic Press: London.

Stahl, P. (1996). The recovery and interpretation of microvertebrate bone assemblages from archaeological contexts. *Journal of Archaeological Theory and Method,* 3:31–75.

Steele, J., Gamble, C. and Sluckin, T. (2000). Estimating the rate of Palaeoindian expansion into South America. In Nicholson, R.A. and O'Connor, T.P. (eds) *People as an Agent of Environmental Change,* 125–133. Oxbow Books: Oxford.

Stewart, J.R. and Carrasquilla, F.H. (1997). The identification of extant European bird remains: a review of the literature. *International Journal of Osteoarchaeology,* 7:364–371.

van Neer, W., Augustynen, S. and Linkowski, T. (1993). Daily growth increments on fish otoliths as seasonality indicators on archaeological sites: the Tilapia from late Palaeolithic Makhmada in Egypt. *International Journal of Osteoarchaeology,* 3:241–248.

Vigne, J.D. (1995). *Détermination Ostéologique des Principaux Éléments du Squelette Appendiculaire d'Arvicola, d'Eliomys, de Glis et de Rattus.* Fiches D'Ostéologie pour l'Archaeologie Serie B, No. 6, CNRS: Juan-les-Pins.

von den Driesch, A. (1976). *A Guide to the Measurement of Animal Bones from Archaeological Sites.* Peabody Museum Bulletin 1, Harvard University: Cambridge, Mass.

Walker, R. (1985). *A Guide to the Post-Cranial Bones of East African Mammals.* Hylochoerus Press: Norwich.

West, B. (1982). Spur development: recognizing caponized fowl in archaeological material. In Wilson, B., Grigson, C. and Payne, S. (eds) *Ageing and Sexing Animal Bones from Archaeological Sites,* 255–260. British Series 109, British Archaeological Reports: Oxford.

*Wheeler, A. and Jones, A.K.G. (1989). *Fishes.* Cambridge University Press: Cambridge.

Wolsan, M. (1982). A comparative analysis of the ribs of ungulates for archaeozoological purposes. *Acta Zoologica Cracoviensis,* 26:167–228.

Woolfenden, G.E. (1961). Postcranial osteology of the waterfowl. *Florida State Museum Bulletin, Biological Science,* 6:1–129.

Yalden, D.W. and Morris, P.A. (1989). *The Analysis of Owl Pellets.* Occasional Publication No. 13, Mammal Society: London.

Zeder, M.A. (1994). After the revolution: post-Neolithic subsistence in northern Mesopotamia. *American Anthropologist,* 96:97–126.

Zohary, D., Tchernov, E. and Horwitz, L.K. (1998). The role of unconscious selection in the domestication of sheep and goats. *Journal of Zoology,* 245:129–135.

35

The Exploitation of Invertebrates and Invertebrate Products

K.D. THOMAS and M.A. MANNINO

Institute of Archaeology, University College London.

The non-vertebrate part of the Animal Kingdom includes an extraordinary diversity of life forms and a vast array of species. The major groups of invertebrates which have been significant as resources to people both in the past and the ethnographic recent are listed in Table 35.1. Some important groups of animals significant in various other ways to past people (and also to be found in the archaeological record) are, however, excluded from Table 35.1. These include parasitic taxa (mainly of the phyla Protozoa, Platyhelminthes and Nematoda), various of which parasitize people, domestic animals or crop plants. Some of the groups included in the table are also important for additional reasons: they include species (e.g., various insects and mites) which are pests of stored foods and other materials, they are useful as palaeoenvironmental indicators (e.g., insects, land snails and other molluscs), or they include bioturbators of the archaeological record (e.g., earthworms, land crabs, termites, etc.). In short, invertebrate zooarchaeology is a broad discipline which includes a number of research themes which we do not consider here.

Here we consider the main categories of use and exploitation of invertebrate animals and their products. Our focus is mainly on material products (including food) and their exploitation, with special emphasis on how various scientific approaches or analytical techniques can inform us about this. We have consciously excluded important social, religious, magical and artistic aspects of the ways in which people in the past perceived invertebrate animals because these are largely outside the realm of scientific analysis. In addition, we have deliberately chosen to emphasize certain areas for discussion in preference to others, paying less attention to those areas well covered in the literature by recent books or review articles.

INVERTEBRATES AS FOOD

Perhaps the main use of invertebrates in the past has been for food and there is a considerable literature on this; for this reason, we devote less space to this aspect. Representatives of many of the taxa listed in Table 35.1 have been used for food in the past or the ethnographic recent, including Oligochaeta, Crustacea, Insecta, Mollusca, Echinodermata and Ascidiacea, although most work has focused on the molluscs and insects. Claassen (1998), Meehan (1982) and Waselkov (1987), among many others, have discussed the role of molluscs in human diets both in the past and in ethnographic studies. Claassen (1991), in particular, has been critical of the 'normative' view of shell middens as representing human food debris, pointing out

Handbook of Archaeological Sciences. Edited by D.R. Brothwell and A.M. Pollard.
© 2001 John Wiley & Sons, Ltd.

Table 35.1   The main groups of non-vertebrate animals which have been used by people in the past (classification based on Webb *et al.* 1978). Sources of evidence are: A = archaeological (including direct remains, representations on pottery, in wall paintings, or mosaics, or as skeuomorphs in pottery or stone); H = historical (textual references); E = ethnographic (including ethnohistorical sources).

PHYLUM	Class	Sub-class or Order	Common name of group	Source of evidence: Archaeological, Historical, Ethnographic
PORIFERA				
	Hexactinellida		Siliceous sponges	A,H,E
	Demospongiae		'Spongey' sponges	A?,H,E
CNIDARIA (= COELENTERATA)				
	Anthozoa	Stolonifera	Organ-pipe corals	A,E
		Gorgonacea	Horny corals	A?,H,E
		Antipatharia	Black corals	A?,H,E
		Madreporaria	True or Stony corals	A,H,E
ANNELIDA				
	Polychaeta	Errantia	Ragworms etc.	A,E
		Sedentaria	Lugworms, etc.	A?,E
	Oligochaeta		Earthworms	E
	Hirudinea		Leeches	E
ARTHROPODA–CRUSTACEA				
	Cirripedia	Thoracica	Barnacles	A,H,E
	Malacostraca	Decapoda	Lobsters & crabs	A,H,E
ARTHROPODA–CHELICERATA				
	Arachnida	Scorpiones	Scorpions	A,H,E
		Araneae	Spiders	A,H,E
ARTHROPODA–INSECTA				
	Pterygota	Dictyoptera	Cockroaches	A,E
		Isoptera	Termites	A,E
		Orthoptera	Grasshoppers	A,E
		Homoptera	True bugs	A,H,E
		Coleoptera	Beetles	A,H,E
		Lepidoptera	Moths and butterflies	A,H,E
		Diptera	True flies	A,H,E
		Hymenoptera	Bees, ants, etc.	A,H,E
MOLLUSCA				
	Amphineura	Polyplacophora	Chitons	A,E
	Scaphopoda		Elephant's tusk shells	A,E
	Gastropoda	Prosobranchia	Mostly 'sea snails'	A,H,E
		Opisthobranchia	Mostly 'sea slugs'	E
		Pulmonata	Mostly 'land snails'	A,H,E
	Bivalvia		Marine and freshwater 'clams'	A,H,E
	Cephalopoda	Nautiloidea	Nautilus	A,H,E
		Coleoidea	Cuttlefish, squid, octopus	A,H,E
ECHINODERMATA				
	Asteroidea		Starfishes	E
	Echinoidea		Sea urchins	A,H,E
	Holothuroidea		Sea cucumbers	E
CHORDATA				
	Ascidiacea		Sea squirts	E

that the huge numbers of shellfish could also have been used as fishing bait, and for other utilitarian or even social or ritual purposes. Sutton (1995) and Posey (1986) have considered the role of insects as food from archaeological and ethnographic perspectives, respectively, and Dufour (1987) has examined the value of insect foods to recent human groups in the Amazon.

Most of the literature on invertebrates as food has focused on their role in foraging and gathering societies (see above), so this aspect is not discussed further. Rather less attention has been given to aspects of the intensification of exploitation of invertebrate animals by techniques ranging from 'cultivation' in the wild to some forms of 'farming' or 'domestication' in captivity.

'Cultivation' of invertebrates

The main feature of the 'cultivation' of invertebrates as food by humans is the creation of local conditions which favour the animals, permitting fast growth ('fattening') and enabling them to reach high local population densities. Dufour (1987) provides an instructive ethnographic example of insect exploitation in the Amazon Basin which involves the cutting down of palm trees for their fruit and then leaving the trunks to rot. The trunks are colonized by wood-eating beetles, whose larvae feed and grow in the wood. Eventually the rotting logs are split open and the fat larvae exploited as food.

An example involving marine molluscs comes from the Roman world of the first century AD: oysters (*Ostrea edulis*) were deliberately collected from the coast near the modern town of Brindisi, Italy, and transported for 'fattening' to 'ostriaria' in the waters of Lago Lucrino, to the north of Naples, which are rich in organic nutrients and phytoplankton (Pliny, cited by Yonge 1984:429). It appears that oysters were suspended on ropes in these 'ostriaria'.

Mussels (*Mytilus edulis*) have also been 'cultivated' in the past. Yonge (1984:431) relates how in the Medieval period this species was cultivated in the shallow muddy waters near La Rochelle, on the French Biscay coast, by growing them on nets suspended in the water. From this the modern *bouchot* system of growing mussels on wattle fences was developed. Analogous systems for growing mussels exist in the Netherlands, in various parts of the Mediterranean and in the Philippines.

Such large scale local production systems could lead to the formation of very large shell midden deposits, but if the shelled molluscs were distributed to other places for consumption the archaeological visibility of these intensive production systems would actually be low. Even where 'megamiddens' are found they need not necessarily indicate localized large-scale production by 'cultivation'. Henshilwood *et al.* (1994) describe 'megamiddens' associated with past hunter-gatherer social groups in the south-western Cape, South Africa, which are dominated by shells of the black mussel *Choromytilus meridionalis*. These authors propose that such huge middens developed at specialized 'drying locations' where the shells of the mussel were accumulated after the flesh had been dried for storage or for transport inland.

Honey bees are another group of animals which have also been cultivated in the wild, as in northern Europe in the Medieval period where a system of 'forest beekeeping' was developed (Crane 1983). The bees nested in hollow trees and each bee tree would be 'owned'. Felling of bee trees was forbidden, regardless of whether they had a bee colony in them or were just empty, in the latter case because they could still be of value if later occupied by a swarm. A small door cut in the side of each tree allowed the honey and beeswax to be collected.

Farming and 'domestication'

There is no evidence that 'cultivation' of invertebrate animals in the wild, or even more intensive exploitation methods akin to 'farming', ever led to the development of morphologically distinct forms which could be described as 'domesticates', in the way that some mammal species have been modified. Lack of control over breeding must have been a major factor which inhibited the formation of 'domesticated' forms in otherwise intensively exploited invertebrate species.

Collecting and cultivating species from the wild could have involved allowing them to breed in captivity before being harvested, thereby creating a local population under human protection and control. Good examples of this are found in Roman-period farming of land snails (practices which persist to the present day), in which snails were collected and concentrated into controlled areas for breeding and 'fattening up'. They were harvested only after the completion of the breeding cycle, ensuring a new captive generation of snails (Emslie 1984). In some instances, farming of land snails involved transportation of snails to areas outside their 'natural' geographical distribution. This applies, for example, to the two edible species of larger land snail found in Britain: the so-called Roman snail *Helix pomatia* and the garden snail *H. aspersa* which were both introduced into Britain, probably in the Roman period. Both are now 'feral' members of the British land snail fauna but both could be considered as having been 'domesticated' in terms of at least one of the criteria which have been applied to mammalian domesticates, namely that their geographical range has been extended by deliberate human transport.

Beekeeping using artificial hives to promote colonization, breeding, comb production and honey storage is another form of farming which verges on domestication. Crane (1983, 1984) believes that the system of forest beekeeping, discussed above, led to the development of beekeeping in which logs containing bee colonies were cut from a tree and transported to a place where they could be guarded and exploited more conveniently. The archaeological visibility of beekeeping has been discussed by Crane (1983) and Crane and Graham (1985); it depends on the nature of the hives used (straw, wood, ceramic (e.g., Rosado and Parreño 1997), etc.), on conditions of preservation, and on the availability of documentary or pictorial evidence. Only very rarely are the physical remains of bees preserved in archaeological deposits and even then they would not be distinguishable from truly wild forms. Kenward and Hall (1995) found high concentrations of sclerites of bees, along with fragments of beeswax, at the Anglo-Scandinavian site of Coppergate, York (northern England), which might suggest local beekeeping.

SHELL TOOLS

Intact and unmodified mollusc shells may be used as tools, e.g. baler shells used in Australia as containers to transport water, or they may be modified in various ways. Where shells are used but not modified (unless modified by wear during their use) the reason for their occurrence in an archaeological deposit might be difficult to interpret. Ethnographic parallels might be useful in offering possibilities for their use (e.g., Safer and Gill 1982) and contextual data might also help. An example of the latter case comes from the Neolithic of the Mediterranean, where scraped patterns on the outer surfaces of 'cardial ware' pottery clearly result from using the ribbed edges of cockle shells (species of the genus *Cerastoderma*, which were until recently classified in the genus *Cardium*; hence 'cardial ware'). Recovery of shells of *Cerastoderma* from a site yielding 'cardial ware' might, therefore, be explicable in terms of

their use as tools, although their initial use as food must also be a strong possibility.

The shells of gastropod and bivalved molluscs, especially of larger species, can be modified in various ways to make a range of tools, from heavy-duty axes, adzes and pounders, to small and well-made items such as knives, fish hooks and spinners (see, for example, Claassen 1998, Safer and Gill 1982). The technology used to make these tools is fairly similar, involving various combinations of operations such as hammering, flaking and grinding. In some cases specific modifications appear to have been made to improve the performance of the material. Ethnographic studies show that some societies artificially 'fossilized' fresh shells by soaking them for some time in sea water (Moir 1990). Shell can also be heated to transform some of the aragonitic components to calcite, as revealed by differences in the X-ray diffraction (XRD) patterns of 'normal' and heat-treated shell (Moir 1990), thereby making it stronger.

OTHER UTILITARIAN USES OF INVERTEBRATE MATERIALS

Filler in pottery

Crushed shell, or crushed fossilized shell, can be added to clay as a 'filler' to prevent shrinkage and cracking during drying and firing (see Chapter 36). Such shell-tempered pottery is known from various parts of the world and the shelly inclusions might have some value in helping to source raw materials (see below).

The siliceous spicules of certain sponges have also been found in ancient pottery. In some cases this reflects the sponge fossils present in a particular clay source, but in others it appears that 'fresh' sponges might have been deliberately added to potting clay as a filler or temper. Adamson *et al.* (1987) discuss sponge tempered pottery from the White Nile, Sudan, dating from around 3500 to 1500 BP. Sponge remains observed in sections of pottery include siliceous skeletal spicules as well as asexual reproductive structures (gemmules). These were examined under the scanning electron microscope and identified as probably coming from the swamp-dwelling sponge *Eunapius nitens*. Sediments from the White Nile were analysed and found to contain siliceous sponge spicules but at far lower densities than found in the pottery. The high density of clusters of fresh-looking spicules and, more significantly, of gemmules in the pottery strongly suggest deliberate addition of sponge material to the clay before pots were made. Equally significant is that some pots were found to have no sponge spicules in them, indicating that the clay source was itself spicule-free. Adamson *et al.* (1987) concluded that whole live sponges were probably collected and burned, after which they were ground to create a gritty filler which was added to the clay paste for the production of certain types of pottery, perhaps those to be subjected to external heat. More recently, McIntosh and MacDonald (1989) have reported fresh water sponge spicules in Iron Age pottery from sites along the Niger River in Mali, West Africa, again raising the possibility of the deliberate use of siliceous sponges as pottery temper.

Lime, construction materials and other uses

Crushed shell may have been spread on soils to improve their base status or structure. It can also be used in mortar or in brick making. Shells may be collected specifically for such purposes, either fresh or from storm-beach deposits, or, as Ceci (1984) has shown, they may be quarried from existing shell midden deposits. Burned shell yields quick lime, used for plaster, mortar, whitewash, and other purposes. Burned shell lime is caustic and has uses in tanning animal skins and for decomposing animal bodies or waste. Such 'caustic lime' is also chewed with various stimulants, such as betel nut in India or coca leaves in the Andes (Ceci 1984). Nations (1979) records how the Maya used lime from the burned shells of freshwater snails to soften maize kernels for consumption.

DECORATIVE OBJECTS

Various categories of invertebrate exoskeletons, especially coral skeletons, the shells of molluscs and the chitinous exoskeletons of insects, are often very attractive and fascinating and have been used for ornamental purposes either directly or in a modified form. Perhaps the best known decorative materials of invertebrate origin are pearls, but these have a low archaeological visibility. It has been suggested that the particular aragonitic mineral structure of pearls does not preserve well, but the 'mother-of-pearl' aragonitic layer inside many shells does preserve in archaeological deposits so it is hard to understand why pearls should not also survive (During-Caspers 1983:23). Perhaps they were rarely discarded? Accumulations of shells of particular species of pearl-yielding bivalves at a site might be interpreted as exploitation for pearls, but they could equally represent food debris. Coral is another material that is and has been highly valued for decorative purposes; a particular archaeological case study is discussed below.

The main scientific areas of interest in invertebrate decorative materials are (i) the identification of the taxa used, especially for inferring likely provenance and hence exchange, distribution or trade networks, and (ii) the processes and technology involved in their production. These aspects are not mutually exclusive because highly modified objects might be difficult to identify to a precise biological taxon, raising problems of provenancing (see below).

The degrees of modification of invertebrate materials and the levels of technology required are highly variable, depending on individual or group skills, on the equipment available, on the particular physical properties (e.g., type of material, size, shape, thickness, etc.) of the materials being exploited, and on the types of artifacts required. In some cases virtually no modification might be necessary. Examples include colourful insect wing cases attached to clothing or basketry, or shells such as those of scaphopod molluscs (*Dentalium* and other genera) which naturally have holes at each end of the slightly curved tapering tubular shell, making them 'natural' beads. Such scaphopod beads might be modified by the simple technique of cutting them into segments, for use as small beads or as bead spacers. Other examples of 'no technology' decorative artifacts are shells collected dead from shores which are either holed by abrasion, or holed by predatory gastropods. These are ready for stringing as pendants or beads. An example is shown in Figure 35.1. Here, naturally eroded umbones of the dog cockle *Glycymeris glycymeris* are shown in Figure 35.1a, which are specimens collected by one of the authors from a modern beach deposit. Figure 35.1b shows specimens of *G. violascens* from a grave in Early Bronze Age Jericho, with identical holes to the beach-abraded specimens, suggesting that they too were collected as 'ready-made' beads or pendants. Taborin (1993) has produced a useful synopsis of shell bead and pendant use in the Palaeolithic of France, including numerous 'no-technology' examples.

Predation holes on shells thought to have been used as beads or pendants might be misinterpreted as showing sophisticated drilling techniques by people in the past. It is, however, quite easy to distinguish predator holes from drill holes, in that the former are usually rather small in diameter and are parallel-sided and smooth because they have been drilled by a

(a)

(b)

Figure 35.1 (a) Modern beach-rolled shells of the bivalve mollusc *Glycymeris glycymeris* from south-west England, showing characteristic holes worn in the umbones. (b) Beads or pendants of shells of *Glycymeris violascens* from an Early Bronze Age grave at Jericho, showing identical damage to the umbones as the shells in (a), suggesting that these too had been collected as beach-rolled, perforated, specimens rather than having been deliberately pierced. Scale: the images are all to scale, the shell on the right of (b) has a length of 33.0 mm. (Photo: S. Laidlaw).

combination of mechanical abrasion and chemical etching. Artificial drill holes are usually of wider diameter and tapering section, reflecting the shape of the drill bits (of stone or metal) used. Sometimes artificial drill holes are bi-conical in section, indicating that drilling was undertaken from both sides until a hole was produced; predator holes are, of course, only drilled from the outside of the shell. Lastly, artificial holes usually have rough edges (when viewed under a reflected-light microscope) which is either due to imperfections in the drill bit used, or due to abrasive powders, such as corundum, which were used in the drilling process.

Some workers have suggested that 'natural' shell beads can be recognized by the generally abraded or eroded nature of the surfaces of beach-rolled specimens. This might often be true, but the authors have experience of working on modern shore populations of molluscs where living individuals have highly worn shells because of high-energy wave action moving around abrasive sand particles. We have also collected naturally holed shell specimens (both predator-holed and abrasion-holed) which otherwise look very fresh. Clearly one has to examine a range of characteristics to determine if a shell has been modified by wholly natural processes or if some level of human technology has been applied.

The two simplest ways of making a hole in a shell are (i) to use a percussion tool to smash a hole (possibly a pointed object to perforate the surface of a shell, or a hammer to knock off the spire of a coiled shell), or (ii) to grind the curved surface of a shell on some hard and abrasive material. More sophisticated operations to work shells include sawing, snapping, drilling and chemical etching. Some of the most sophisticated techniques of working shells to produce decorative effects are in cameo-production, where the outer layer or layers of a shell are cut and ground away, revealing different-coloured inner layers which can be worked into various designs. These various techniques produce a range of artifacts with high archaeological visibility, ranging from caches of as-yet unworked shells, through unfinished objects and assorted debitage, to the finished product. These categories of objects, and their specific contextual associations, can be used to infer likely processing sequences (e.g., Kenoyer 1984). Additional insights into production sequences and the application of technologies and specific tools can be gained from ethnoarchaeological studies of traditional shell working. Finally, experimental approaches might add insights to these processes (e.g., Miller 1996).

All such studies are not, of course, wholly directed to merely finding out how shell artifacts were made in the past; they also inform us about levels of technology, complexities of production processes, and the social contexts of production systems, including craft specialization (e.g., Arnold and Munns 1994) and exchange networks. Species selection and human preferences might also be inferred, as shown in a recent study by Stiner (1999) who examined the food and decorative uses of molluscs and their shells at a Palaeolithic site in Italy. Stiner showed that although food choices changed over time, apparently associated with changes in local ecology, the choice of shells for decorative purposes was more conservative and might reflect aesthetic or social factors.

FIBRES

Compared with plants and mammals, invertebrate animals are relatively minor providers of fibres for human use, although one particular fibre (silk) is and has been one of the most valued and sought-after of all natural fibres.

Silk

Although a range of species of insects and spiders produce silk threads, those produced by certain genera of moths (Lepidoptera) have been most exploited for the production of threads and fabrics. Various species of moths occurring in East Asia, South Asia and western Asia/eastern Europe produce silk, and all these have been exploited by people in the past, in the historic recent and up to the present day (Tazima 1984). Most attention has been given by archaeologists and historians to the high-quality silk of Chinese origin, which was traded, along with other commodities, into Europe via the famous Silk Road (the sites along which constitute a significant archaeological resource).

The most important archaeological questions relating to silk have recently been reviewed by Good (1995). Paramount among these are: when was high quality Chinese silk introduced or traded to the West, and to what extent was the silk attested by Classical western authors far-eastern silk or locally-produced silk from indigenous species of moths? These questions are difficult to address because the proteinaceous silk fibres and fabrics have relatively low archaeological visibility, except in cases of exceptional preservation. A good example of this comes from the well-preserved waterlogged Anglo-Scandinavian site of Coppergate, York, where an off-cut of silk fabric was found which matched the fabric in a silk head-dress from the same site, suggesting that silk material was being cut and stitched locally (Walton Rogers 1997:1779). It is not known if the silk fabric in this case came from Byzantium, the Islamic World, or even further east.

A recent study of a postulated silk worm cocoon preserved in archaeological deposits has opened up a new source of evidence for silk production in the past. The calcified cocoon, from the Minoan site of Akrotiri on the island of Thera in the Aegean, was interpreted by

Panagiotakopulu *et al.* (1997) as probably coming from a local species of moth, *Pachypasa otus* (Linn.). This species is the likely source of 'wild silk' in the Classical world. The identification was based partly on cocoon morphology and size, which made a 'silk worm' species likely, and also on evidence from preserved frescoes from the site showing artistic representations of large moths. Further evidence came from representations of moths on gemstones of the Minoan period as well as textual references interpreted from both Linear B scripts and (much later) Classical sources. This example clearly shows that 'high level' archaeological questions about early long-distance trade of silk from China to Europe cannot be realistically addressed until the taxonomic identity of the silk-producing moths has been established, either through the recovery of palaeoentomological specimens like the Akrotiri cocoon or through some new analytical procedure which will allow minute traces of silk to be detected and sourced. Given the generally poor conditions of preservation of insects on most archaeological sites in western Asia and south-eastern Europe (Akrotiri is, rather like Pompeii, a special case of a site preserved by a massive volcanic explosion), we are not optimistic for any significant archaeological breakthrough in the foreseeable future as far as studies of ancient silk are concerned.

Byssus threads

Some species of bivalved molluscs attach themselves to rocks by proteinaceous byssal threads. These threads are often quite short, and of little use to humans, but in fan-shells (various species of the genus *Pinna*) the threads are long and have been exploited as fibres. *Pinna* lives in deposits near low tide or, more abundantly, in deeper waters. The shell is partly buried in muddy gravels, with long byssus threads attached to stones well below the surface. Yonge (1966:253) reports that *Pinna nobilis* is especially common in the Mediterranean, where its long golden-yellow tough byssal threads ('mussel silk') were woven into cloth in the Roman period.

NATURAL PRODUCTS

Mollusc dyes

Perhaps the best known dye of invertebrate origin is Tyrian Purple, one of a range of purple or red dyes which can be obtained from various species of the gastropod mollusc family Muricidae. Tyrian Purple is of Mediterranean origin, being derived from at least three different species of *Murex*, but other muricid-based dyes are known from many regions of the world, including North and West Africa, China and Japan, north-western Europe and Middle and South America. The precursor of these dyes is a straw-coloured fluid in the hypobranchial gland of the living animal. On exposure to air and sunlight, the fluid gradually acquires the purple or red colour due to the formation of indigoid compounds by oxidative and photochemical changes (Baker 1974).

Archaeological evidence for the extraction and use of muricid dyes comes from three sources:

(i) Large accumulations of shells of muricid species, perhaps on the edges of large settlements or associated with particular types of activity areas. Usually the shells have holes smashed into the body whorl to enable extraction of the anterior part of the animal, giving access to the hypobranchial gland. The problem with such large shell accumulations is that they might represent food debris, although relatively homogeneous muricid accumulations would be unusual if only representing debris from food use.

(ii) An unusual and rather controversial piece of evidence for the concentration of living muricids, and even their possible 'cultivation', prior to dye extraction and production comes from observations of the frequency of predation (possibly cannibalism) in archaeological assemblages of muricid shells. Large numbers of hypobranchial glands must be extracted to yield a usable batch of dye, and this would be most productive if many shells could be processed at the same time. This raises the possibility that living molluscs could have been gathered and kept alive in sea-water tanks (cut into rocks in the littoral zone) until sufficient numbers were available to be processed. This idea has been put forward by Spanier (1986), who observed that rock-cut 'tanks' were not uncommon in various areas of the central and eastern Mediterranean (areas in which Tyrian Purple production was important in the past). Spanier also observed that a significant number of *Murex* shells from sites in Acre and Caesarea (Israel) showed signs of having been predated. It is unlikely that such shells would have been collected 'dead' by dye producers. *Murex* species are predators which bore holes in the shells of other molluscs in order to feed on them and cannibalism is not unlikely, although it would probably be rare in nature. Spanier showed that in experimental tanks with no alternative food, *Murex* do, indeed, predate their own species. He therefore suggested that live *Murex* could have been concentrated in large numbers in tanks, with restricted space and food leading to increased intra-specific predation, before being harvested *en masse* for dye production.

(iii) Recent applications of a complex of chemical analytical techniques to pottery with deposits on the inner surface have demonstrated traces of Tyrian purple, more specifically the compound 6,6'-dibromoindigotin (McGovern and Michel 1990). Working with pottery from the thirteenth-century BC site of Sarepta (midway between Tyre and Sidon on the Levant coast), these authors applied both non-destructive and destructive chemical analyses to the purplish deposits on the insides of the pots. Proton-induced X-ray emission (PIXE) spectrometry showed that bromine was abundant in these deposits but that other elements such as manganese, which might also cause coloration in such traces, were present in insignificant amounts. Electron spectroscopic chemical analysis (ESCA) showed that the bromine was specifically bonded to carbon in organic complexes. The Fourier transform infra-red (FT-IR) spectra of the deposits showed close similarities at a number of critical wavelengths when compared with those of a synthetic dibromoindigotin. Finally a destructive test was applied, based on the fact that indigoid dyes are soluble in sodium hydrosulfite solution, yielding a pale solution which becomes deep purple again on exposure to oxygen. When applied to the deposit on a piece of potsherd, this test confirmed the nature of the purple pigment.

Insect dyes

Dyes, especially red pigments, of insect origin are known from many parts of the world. These are usually extracted from various taxa of true bugs (Homoptera). Female scale insects of various species yield the dye (see Donkin 1977 for a discussion of species). In India and south-east Asia lac dye (as well as the sealant shellac) was extracted from females of the lac insect *Kerria lacca*. Kermes *Kermococcus vermilio*, another dye-yielding scale insect, is found around the Mediterranean and adjacent areas of western Asia. In America, the cochineal insect *Dactylopius coccus* also yielded the red dye cochineal which was traded to various parts

of the world from the middle of the sixteenth century AD. In all these cases, harvesting the tiny female scale insects must have been labour-intensive. The insects were ground into a paste for immediate use, or the paste was dried and made into 'cakes' for trade.

The archaeological visibility of insect dye production and use is relatively low. Ethnographic and ethnohistorical data show that exploitation of these resources was generally 'from the wild', but in cases such as the cochineal (Fleming 1983), insects were 'farmed' on their host plants. Chemical analysis of modern insect extracts and of modern (experimentally) dyed fabrics, using a combination of high performance liquid chromatography (HPLC) and UV-visible spectroscopy, has shown that it is possible to distinguish between different types of insect (and plant) dyes (Wouters 1985). Subsequent work (Wouters and Verhecken 1989) showed that it was possible to detect and identify different insect dyes in a range of ancient fabrics, some as old as the seventh century AD.

Beeswax, mastics and sealants

Beeswax is an additional product (to honey) from exploiting either 'wild' or 'domesticated' bee colonies. It is an important material used as a sealant, polish and fuel. An archaeological example, albeit an exceptional one, of preservation of lumps of beeswax in an archaeological context comes from the Anglo-Scandinavian site of Coppergate, York, where small lumps of wax were identified as beeswax by their characteristic smell when burned with a hot needle. Large concentrations of the remains of bees were also recorded from this site. A nearly-spherical ball of beeswax recovered from one of the Coppergate contexts had grooves in its surface, suggesting that it might have been used to wax string or twine (Kenward and Hall 1995:766).

Other archaeological evidence comes from chemical analysis of lipid residues (e.g., Figure 35.2; see Chapter 28) either on or in artifacts (commonly pottery) by gas chromatography/mass spectrometry (GC/MS). Beeswax has been found in ancient pottery (e.g., Evershed 1993), possibly indicating that it was either stored in pots or that it was rubbed into the inner surface of pots to seal them for storage of liquids. Analysis of organic residues on Late Minoan lamps has revealed traces of beeswax (Evershed *et al.* 1997), indicating its possible use as a light-yielding fuel.

Ethnographic evidence shows that a range of other insects were used to produce mastics and sealants in various parts of the world. The creosote lac scale insect

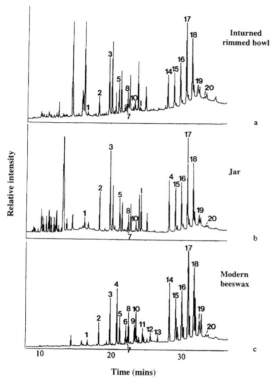

Figure 35.2 Gas chromatograms of lipid extracts from the basal sherds of (a) an inturned rimmed bowl and (b) a jar, both from the Late Saxon/early Medieval occupation site of West Cotton in central England, compared with (c) modern beeswax. From Evershed (1993:fig. 2), who gives details of the chemical identities of the various numbered peaks. Reproduced from World Archaeology by permission of Taylor and Francis, PO Box 25, Abingdon, Oxfordshire, OX14 3UE.

Tachardiella larreae was exploited for its resin in the south-western Great Basin of North America (Sutton 1995). Archaeologically, lac resin has been shown to have been used as a mastic for making composite ornaments, turquoise mosaics, etc., as well as a sealant for storage jars and for basketry water bottles. In some cases these identifications have been confirmed by analytical techniques, notably gas chromatography (Sutton 1995:272). Other species of scale insects were exploited in western North America for waxes and gums which were used on basketry, bows, and tool handles (Sutton 1995:259).

Medicines and poisons

A range of invertebrate species have been used for medicinal purposes. Ethnographic evidence suggests that this use was sometimes based on empirical evidence of real beneficial effects of their use, or in other cases because of some mystical or magical properties they have been deemed to possess. Pliny recorded that sponges were either ground up or burnt and taken as medicines. Certain gorgonacean corals have had medicinal uses (During-Caspers 1986). Leeches (Annelida; Hirudinea) have been used in medicine for the supposedly-beneficial effects of 'bleeding', and more recently extracts of leech anticoagulants ('hirudins') have been used in surgery to prevent blood clotting. A range of insects have been used for medicinal purposes (Cloudsley-Thompson 1976, de Conconi and Moreno 1988, Posey 1986, Sutton 1995) or as hallucinogens (e.g., Groark 1996). In recent western medical practice the larvae of blowflies (Insecta; Diptera) have been used to clean necrotic tissues from wounds. In 'traditional' medical practice, stinging ants and wasps have been used to treat severe arthritis, and the large mandibles of ants have been used as sutures on wounds (the ants are encouraged to bite the two edges of a wound, then their heads are cut off, leaving them in place with the mandibles holding the wound together). Spiders' webs (spiders are arachnids, of course, not insects) have been used to staunch bleeding. Few of these uses are exemplified in the archaeological record, however. Finds of insect remains in human coprolites (e.g., Sutton 1995:280; see Chapter 33) might attest to their being ingested as medicines, but this must be speculative. Most of the evidence inevitably comes from ethnographic and historical sources.

Although a number of invertebrate species are highly poisonous, there is little evidence from ethnography (and none from archaeology) that these poisonous compounds were extracted and utilized. One exception is the use of cone-shell venom applied to spear tips for use in fishing and, possibly, warfare. Cone shells are marine gastropods which are active predators, delivering a neurotoxic venom into their prey via radular teeth modified to form hollow 'needles'. The venom of some *Conus* species can cause serious illness in humans, and the south-west Pacific species *C. geographus* and *C. textile* have been recorded as causing human fatalities. For a general review of the toxins of *Conus* and other invertebrate animals, including their modern therapeutic applications, see Harvey (1999).

EXCHANGE, TRADE AND THE SOURCING OF INVERTEBRATE MATERIALS

The significance of invertebrates, especially mollusc shells, in past exchange and trading systems, and of their potential for enabling archaeologists to link specific geographical areas involved in such systems, has been well known since the pioneering work of Jackson (1917). Durable invertebrate materials which survive and give evidence of past exchange systems include various groups of molluscs (scaphopods, bivalves and gastropods) and the calcareous corals. These appear to have been exchanged between social groups in the past either because they were 'attractive', had symbolic, religious or magical significance, or because they had other values ascribed to them (some shells were used as units of currency up to recent times). A range of case studies is discussed here to show how science-based approaches can contribute to this area of archaeological research, and to highlight problems and future potential.

The exchange and distribution of shell artifacts (bracelets, rings, etc.) made from the marine bivalve species *Spondylus gaederopus* in Neolithic Europe is well known. Recent discussion about this (Halstead 1993) has focused on the social role of such shells both within *Spondylus*-working communities and between these communities and those occupying territories much further from the Aegean coast. Earlier studies were concerned to discover the origins of *S. gaederopus* shell from sites in areas where it is 'alien', and to confirm if the *Spondylus* artifacts found at inland sites were, in fact, made from that species or from local fossil shells of the same genus. Shackleton and Renfrew (1970) used oxygen isotopes to determine if traded *Spondylus* shells could have originated from the (colder) Black Sea or the (warmer) Aegean (see Chapter 16). They confirmed that the shells came from the Aegean, thereby helping to 'align' probable exchange routes. Shackleton and Elderfield (1990) addressed the problem of the identity of the *Spondylus* found at some sites in central Europe. The shell artifacts found had been heavily worked and were not in good condition, making it difficult to determine if they were made from recent *S. gaederopus* of Mediterranean origin, or from fossil *S. crassicosta* derived from local Middle Miocene (*c.* 20 Ma) deposits. By measuring the strontium isotopic compositions ($^{87}Sr/^{86}Sr$) of some archaeological specimens and of fossil shells, Shackleton and Elderfield (1990) were able to show that the archaeological materials were much younger than the fossils and hence must have been obtained through Neolithic exchange systems linking to the Mediterranean.

These examples show the value of specific analytical techniques for sourcing materials of invertebrate origin, but most considerations of past exchange and sources are based on biogeography. Clearly, a material can only be sourced if it has characteristics which relate to a specific, relatively restricted, area of origin and if its archaeological find spot is outside that area. Many invertebrate species have known geographical distributions today which, provided they were not significantly different in the relatively recent ('archaeological') past, can allow us to align exchange routes, or at least to locate likely sources. Such approaches are only reliable if we are able to identify with accuracy the particular biological species involved and if we have reliable knowledge of the recent pattern of distribution of that taxon. Sometimes fairly generalized data are still highly informative, such as the occurrence of artifacts made of corals in later Neolithic sites of the European Alpine region, which could only have been derived from the Mediterranean – although a precise locality could not be determined (Skeates 1993). Other such examples of generalized long-distance contacts come from the frequent occurrence of shells of Indo-Pacific region mollusc species at archaeological sites of various periods in the Mediterranean and central and northern Europe (Reese 1991).

Care must be taken to ensure that specimens are identified with accuracy because imprecise identifications can be very misleading. For example, scaphopod ('elephant's tusk') shells are common finds on sites in the eastern Mediterranean and in the Levant and Mesopotamia. Archaeologists commonly refer to these as 'dentalium' (or, even worse to the purist taxonomist, as 'dentalia' if there is more than one!), with the implication that they are in fact of the genus *Dentalium*. This genus is distributed through the Mediterranean and along the Atlantic coasts of western Europe, and if shells of it are found at an inland site in, say, Syria, they will probably indicate some connection with the Mediterranean littoral. There are, however, other genera of scaphopods which are Indo-Pacific in distribution, and which might indicate connections with the Red Sea, the Gulf, or further afield. Therefore generalized, unconfirmed identifications of scaphopod shells as 'dentalium' should be treated with caution, especially if they are then used to make assumptions about the external contacts of a site.

Taxonomic precision is vital for some purposes, but not for all. The identification of marine shell as a temper in pottery found at an inland site might be valuable for establishing possibly unsuspected connections with coastal communities, as shown in a study by Cleal *et al.* (1994). In this particular case, Grooved Ware pottery of the mid-late third millennium cal. BC from near Stonehenge (central southern England) was found to contain non-fossil marine shell fragments as temper. This suggested either exchange of raw materials (including shell) with coastal areas, or exchange and movement of pottery manufactured at some coastal location. In this case, the latter possibility was discounted because the pottery also contained significant quantities of the mineral glauconite which would probably have come from mineral resources close to the site.

Mention was made above of the problems of localizing certain resources, such as Mediterranean corals, on the basis of biological identity and geographical distribution alone. In this specific case, various coral reefs around the Mediterranean might have been the source of such material. Chemical or isotopic analyses might show that materials derived from the same biological species, but from different locations, have characteristic signatures for those locations. For example, Claassen (1998:213) discusses a study by Katherine Miller who attempted to use chemical element composition, by neutron activation analysis and atomic absorption spectroscopy, to characterize shells of the marine bivalve *Mercenaria mercenaria* collected at various locations in north-eastern USA. Ten elements were identified as being potentially useful for discriminating between localities. A major problem lies in the validity of using present-day elemental data on shells from known localities to compare with archaeological specimens because recent river waters would be carrying different 'loads' of elements due to greater soil erosion and to 'industrial' effluent. Another problem is that variation in elemental composition between different parts of individual shells is often quite wide; using shell fragments for such work would not, therefore, be valid. Despite the apparent potential of such approaches, more basic research in this area is needed.

Insect pests have been of value in giving information about likely origins of traded or transported materials. An insect assemblage from the second century AD Roman site of Alcester, Warwickshire (central England) included a specimen of the Mediterranean wood-boring beetle *Hesperophanes fasciculatus*, probably indicating the importation of high-quality items of wooden furniture (Osborne 1971). Sutton (1995:283) describes how insect pests preserved with a cargo of tobacco in a mid-sixteenth century AD shipwreck were of West Indian rather than North American genera, proving the origin of the cargo.

CONCLUDING COMMENTS

The potential of various scientific analytical techniques for investigating the exploitation and use of inverte-

brates in the past has, we hope, been demonstrated. Although there is a need to develop and apply such powerful techniques further, we believe that this should not be at the expense of traditional approaches, such as accurate identification and taxonomy backed up by biological and ecological knowledge. There is also a need to develop and apply appropriate on-site techniques for the recovery of a range of invertebrate remains as well as proper contextual recording to allow more sophisticated interpretations. Despite possible improvements in these areas of practice, there will always be cases where materials will never survive archaeologically even though their use might be attested ethnographically. Such 'missing resources', including soft-bodied food resources (e.g., squids and other cephalopods, holothurians, ascidians, etc.; see Table 35.1), delicate organic raw materials, and so on, can to some extent be recognized as being of potential significance to people in the past by being incorporated into appropriate ethnobiological and ecological models of resource use and exploitation.

REFERENCES

*Recommended for further reading

Adamson, D.A., Clark, J.D. and Williams, M.A.J. (1987). Pottery tempered with sponge from the White Nile, Sudan. *African Archaeological Review*, **5**:115–127.

Arnold, J.E. and Munns, A. (1994). Independent or attached specialization: the organization of shell bead production in California. *Journal of Field Archaeology*, **21**:473–489.

Baker, J.T. (1974). Tyrian purple: an ancient dye, a modern problem. *Endeavour*, **118**:11–17.

Ceci, L. (1984). Shell midden deposits as coastal resources. *World Archaeology*, **16**:62–74.

Claassen, C. (1991). Normative thinking and shell-bearing sites. *Archaeological Method and Theory*, **3**:249–298.

*Claassen, C. (1998). *Shells*. Cambridge University Press: Cambridge.

Cleal, R.M.J., Cooper, J. and Williams, D. (1994). Shells and sherds: identification of inclusions in Grooved Ware, with associated radiocarbon dates, from Amesbury, Wiltshire. *Proceedings of the Prehistoric Society*, **60**:445–448.

Cloudsley-Thompson, J.L. (1976). *Insects and History*. Weidenfeld and Nicholson: London.

Crane, E. (1983). *The Archaeology of Beekeeping*. Duckworth: London.

Crane, E. (1984). Honeybees. In Mason, I.L. (ed.) *Evolution of Domesticated Animals*, 403–415. Longman: London.

Crane, E. and Graham, A.J. (1985). *Bee Hives of the Ancient World*. International Bee Research Association: Gerrard's Cross.

de Conconi, J.R.E. and Moreno, J.M.P. (1988). The utilization of insects in the empirical medicine of ancient Mexicans. *Journal of Ethnobiology*, **8**:195–202.

Donkin, R.A. (1977). The insect dyes of western and west-central Asia. *Anthropos*, **72**:847–880.

Dufour, D.L. (1987). Insects as food: a case study from the northwest Amazon. *American Anthropologist*, **89**:383–397.

During-Caspers, E.C.L. (1983). Corals, pearls and prehistoric Gulf trade. *Proceedings of the Seminar for Arabian Studies*, **13**:21–29.

During-Caspers, E.C.L. (1986). Of corals and ailments in the ancient Near East. *Proceedings of the Seminar for Arabian Studies*, **16**:25–31.

Emslie, L.J. (1984). Edible snails. In Mason, I.L. (ed.) *Evolution of Domesticated Animals*, 432–433. Longman: London.

Evershed, R.P. (1993). Biomolecular archaeology and lipids. *World Archaeology*, **25**:74–93.

Evershed, R.P., Vaughan, S.J., Dudd, S.N. and Soles, J.S. (1997). Fuel for thought? Beeswax in lamps and conical cups from Late Minoan Crete. *Antiquity*, **71**:979–985.

Fleming, S. (1983). The tale of the cochineal: insect farming in the New World. *Archaeology*, **36**:68–69, 79.

Good, I. (1995). On the question of silk in pre-Han Eurasia. *Antiquity*, **69**:959–968.

Groark, K.P. (1996). Ritual and therapeutic use of harvester ants (*Pogonomyrmex*) in native south-central California. *Journal of Ethnobiology*, **16**:1–29.

Halstead, P. (1993). *Spondylus* shell ornaments from late Neolithic Dimini, Greece: specialised manufacture or marginal accumulation? *Antiquity*, **67**:603–609.

Harvey, A.L. (1999). Deadly remedies. *Biologist*, **46**:102–104.

Henshilwood, C., Nilssen, P. and Parkington, J. (1994). Mussel drying and food storage in the Late Holocene, S.W. Cape, South Africa. *Journal of Field Archaeology*, **21**:103–109.

Jackson, J.W. (1917). *Shells as Evidence of the Migrations of Early Cultures*. Longman: London.

Kenoyer, J.M. (1984). Shell industries at Mohenjo-Daro, Pakistan. In Jansen, M. and Urban, G. (eds) *Interim Reports vol. 1. Reports on Fieldwork Carried out at Mohenjo-Daro, Pakistan 1982-83*, 99–115. German Research Project Mohenjo-Daro/Istituto Italiano per il Medio ed Estremo Oriente: Aachen.

Kenward, H.K. and Hall, A.R. (1995). *Biological Evidence from 16-22 Coppergate*. Archaeology of York Fascicule 14, Council for British Archaeology: York.

McGovern, P.E. and Michel, R.H. (1990). Royal purple dye: its identification by complementary physicochemical techniques. *MASCA Research Papers in Science and Archaeology*, **7**:69–76.

McIntosh, S.K. and MacDonald, K.C. (1989). Sponge spicules in pottery: new data from Mali. *Journal of Field Archaeology*, **16**:489–494.

*Meehan, B. (1982). *Shell Bed to Shell Midden*. Australian Institute of Aboriginal Studies: Canberra.

Miller, M.A. (1996). The manufacture of cockle shell beads at Early Neolithic Franchthi Cave, Greece: a case of craft specialization? *Journal of Mediterranean Archaeology*, **9**:7–37.

Moir, B.G. (1990). Comparative studies of 'fresh' and 'aged' *Tridacna gigas* shell: preliminary investigations of a reported technique for pretreatment of tool material. *Journal of Archaeological Science*, **17**:329–345.

Nations, J.D. (1979). Snail shells and maize preparation: a Locandon Maya analogy. *American Antiquity*, **44**:568–571.

Osborne, P.J. (1971). An insect fauna from the Roman site at Alcester, Warwickshire. *Britannia*, **2**:156–165.

Panagiotakopulu, E., Buckland, P.C., Day, P.M., Doumas, C., Sarpaki, A. and Skidmore, P. (1997). A lepidopterous cocoon from Thera and evidence for silk in the Aegean Bronze Age. *Antiquity*, **71**:420–429.

Posey, D.A. (1986). Topics and issues in ethnoentomology with some suggestions for the development of hypothesis-generation and testing in ethnobiology. *Journal of Ethnobiology*, **6**:99–120.

Reese, D.S. (1991). The trade of Indo-Pacific shells into the Mediterranean basin and Europe. *Oxford Journal of Archaeology*, **10**:159–196.

Rosado, H.B. and Parreño, C.M. (1997). The archaeology of beekeeping in pre-Roman Iberia. *Journal of Mediterranean Archaeology*, **10**:33–47.

Safer, J.F. and Gill, F. (1982). *Spirals from the Sea: an Anthropological Look at Shells*. CN Potter: New York.

Skeates, R. (1993). Mediterranean coral: its use and exchange in and around the Alpine region during the later Neolithic and Copper Age. *Oxford Journal of Archaeology*, **12**:281–292.

Shackleton, N. and Elderfield, H. (1990). Strontium isotope dating of the source of Neolithic European *Spondylus* shell artefacts. *Antiquity*, **64**:312–315.

Shackleton, N. and Renfrew, C. (1970). Neolithic trade routes re-aligned by oxygen isotope analyses. *Nature*, **228**:1062–1065.

Spanier, E. (1986). Cannibalism in muricid snails as a possible explanation for archaeological findings. *Journal of Archaeological Science*, **13**:463–468.

Stiner, M.C. (1999). Palaeolithic mollusc exploitation at Riparo Mochi (Balzi Rossi, Italy): food and ornaments from the Aurignacian through Epigravettian. *Antiquity*, **73**:735–754.

*Sutton, M.Q. (1995). Archaeological aspects of insect use. *Journal of Archaeological Method and Theory*, **2**:253–298.

Taborin, Y. (1993). *La Parure en Coquillage au Paleolithique*. CNRS: Paris.

Tazima, Y. (1984). Silkworm moths. In Mason, I.L. (ed.) *Evolution of Domesticated Animals*, 416–424. Longman: London.

Walton Rogers, P. (1997). *Textile Production at 16–22 Coppergate*. Archaeology of York Fascicule 17/11, Council for British Archaeology: York.

*Waselkov, G.A. (1987). Shellfish and shell midden archaeology. *Advances in Archaeological Method and Theory*, **10**:93–210.

Webb, J.E., Wallwork, J.A. and Elgood, J.H. (1978). *Guide to Invertebrate Animals*, (2nd edn). MacMillan: London.

Wouters, J. (1985). High performance liquid chromatography of anthraquinones: analysis of plant and insect extracts and dyed textiles. *Studies in Conservation*, **30**:119–128.

Wouters, J. and Verhecken, A. (1989). The coccid insect dyes: HPLC and computerised diode-array analysis of dyed yarns. *Studies in Conservation*, **34**:189–200.

Yonge, C.M. (1966). *The Sea Shore*. Collins: London.

Yonge, C.M. (1984). Bivalve molluscs. In Mason, I.L. (ed.) *Evolution of Domesticated Animals*, 429–431. Longman: London.

SECTION 6

Inorganic Resource Exploitation

Overview – Materials Study in Archaeology

M.S. TITE

Research Laboratory for Archaeology and the History of Art, University of Oxford.

The primary aim of materials studies in archaeology is to contribute to the investigation of the overall life cycle or *chaîne opératoire* of surviving artifacts (e.g., stone, ceramics, metals, glass and, when they survive, organic materials). This life cycle starts with production that includes the procurement and processing of the raw materials through to the fabrication and decoration of the artifacts. It then continues through distribution of the artifacts to their use, re-use and ultimate discard (Figure 36.0).

The first stage in such materials studies consists of the *reconstruction* of production, distribution and use. The subsequent second stage is then concerned with the *interpretation* of this reconstructed life cycle in order to provide a better understanding of the behaviour of the people who produced, distributed and used them. This involves attempting to answer questions relating to:

(i)   the mode of production (e.g., household, workshop or factory) or mode of distribution (e.g., down-the-line exchange or central place redistribution),

(ii) the discovery of a new technology (e.g., first production of pottery, copper, iron or glass) and the reasons for its adoption at a particular time and place, and

(iii) the choice of a particular production technology, mode of production and pattern of trade and exchange, and the reasons why these changed.

By combining interpretation with reconstruction, the final goal of materials studies, which is 'not to describe microscale prehistoric *activities*, but to understand microscale social *processes*' (Dobres and Hoffman 1994:213), can be achieved.

RECONSTRUCTION

A starting point for the reconstruction of production, distribution and use is the materials science paradigm (Kingery 1996; Figure S6.1). This states that materials selection and processing associated with production result in an artifact that, in addition to its style, has a particular structure (macro and micro) and composition (mineral, chemical and isotopic). These latter, in turn, give rise to physical properties on which depend the performance characteristics of the artifact in distribution and, more importantly, in use. Thus, in modern materials science, the raw materials and processes are varied in order to achieve a structure and composition that result in the required properties of the finished product. In a prehistoric context, it is rarely, if ever, appropriate to visualize a series of similarly systematic experiments being employed in the development of a production technology. Instead, the materials science paradigm is valuable in providing a basis for making inferences about the raw materials and processes employed in the production of the artifacts from the investigation of their structures and compositions.

Handbook of Archaeological Sciences. Edited by D.R. Brothwell and A.M. Pollard.

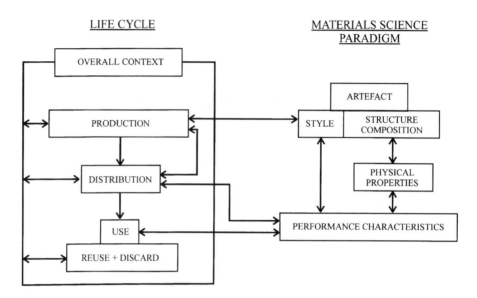

Figure S6.1 The interrelationships between the overall context (environmental, technological, economic, social, political and ideological), the life cycle for artifacts (production, distribution, use, reuse and discard), and the materials science paradigm.

Similarly, inferences regarding the use to which the artifacts were put can sometimes be made from the measurement and assessment of their physical properties, and thus performance characteristics in use.

Thus, the scientific examination of the artifacts used to reconstruct production, distribution and use (Bowman 1991, Pollard and Heron 1996) starts with studying the macrostructure using, for example, low-power binocular microscopy and X-ray radiography. Optical microscopy, in both transmitted and reflected light, scanning electron microscopy and, to a very limited extent, transmission electron microscopy are then used to investigate the microstructure and identify the mineral and other phases present. X-ray diffraction, Fourier transform infrared spectroscopy (FTIR) and Raman spectroscopy can be used to extend the phase identification, with a range of chromatography techniques being extensively used in the identification of organic compounds. A very wide range of analytical techniques are currently available for the determination of chemical composition and of these, inductively coupled plasma mass spectrometry (ICP-MS), neutron activation analysis and X-ray fluorescence spectrometry are of particular importance for the analysis of archaeological artifacts. Finally, mass spectrometry is used to determine the stable isotope compositions for a range of elements with the emphasis at present on lead, carbon, oxygen and strontium. (For a recent review of

analytical techniques applicable to archaeology, see Ciliberto and Spoto 2000.)

In addition to scientific examination, archaeological fieldwork and excavation to locate and investigate the raw materials sources and the sites at which production occurred, and to define the contexts in which the artifacts were used and ultimately discarded are an essential component of any fully convincing reconstruction. Further help in reconstruction can come from contemporary ancient writings and illustrations, and from ethnoarchaeological studies. In addition, the application of the methods of scientific examination to artifacts from an ethnographic context, for which information on production, distribution and use is already available, provides some check on the validity of the results obtained when these same methods are applied in an archaeological context (Skibo 1992). Finally, both full-scale field experiments and laboratory-based experiments to replicate proposed methods of production or use are necessary in order to test the validity of such proposals.

Production

The reconstruction of the production technology involves identifying the raw materials used, together with the tools, energy sources and techniques employed in procuring and processing these raw materials and in fabricating and decorating the artifacts. The complexity of the reconstruction clearly depends on whether one is considering artifacts produced merely through mechanical modification of the raw materials (e.g., wood, bone, stone, pigments) or pyrotechnologies in which the raw materials undergo chemical and microstructural change through the action of heat (e.g., plaster, pottery, metals, glass).

Whenever feasible, the reconstruction should start with archaeological fieldwork and excavation to locate and investigate both the raw material sources, such as the quarries and mines from which stone and metals ores were obtained, and the industrial sites associated with the production of, for example, pottery, metals and glass. Next, the artifacts together with appropriate production debris (e.g., furnace fragments, crucibles, ores, slags, frits) are subjected to scientific examination using the analytical and microscopy techniques outlined above. The data on chemical composition and microstructure thus obtained then provide the basis for elucidating the sequence of processes involved in the production of the artifact. In interpreting these data, the possible effect of cultural and environmental formation processes subsequent to production must be considered. At this stage, it can also be useful to determine, in the laboratory, the physical properties of the raw materials (e.g., clay plasticity, metal alloy melting point, glass viscosity) and, hence, to assess their performance characteristics during the manufacture of the artifacts.

Finally the validity of the reconstruction proposed needs to be tested by experimental replication of the industrial processes (e.g., pottery firing, copper and iron smelting, glass production) or artifact fabrication (e.g., pottery forming, copper and iron working, glass working) in the field or laboratory as appropriate.

Distribution

In the reconstruction of the distribution of artifacts from their production centres (i.e., provenance studies), fieldwork in an attempt to locate all possible sources of the relevant raw material in the predicted production region is again a crucial first step. The second step is to group together those artifacts made from raw material (e.g., flint, marble, clay, copper, iron) from the same source on the basis of the 'fingerprints' provided by their petrography, minor and trace element compositions, or stable isotope compositions. Next, one tries to identify the actual raw material source used by compar-

ison of the compositional 'fingerprints' for the artifact groups with those for the sources located by fieldwork. Finally, one must try to establish the distribution patterns for the artifacts away from the various raw material sources and production centres.

The success of the direct comparison between the artifact groups and the raw material sources depends, of course, on the *between-source* variation exceeding the *within-source* variation, as specified in the so-called 'provenance postulate' (Weigand *et al.* 1977). In addition, one needs to take into account possible changes in the compositional 'fingerprint' of the raw materials during both production of the finished artifact, and its subsequent use and burial.

Use

In establishing the use, as well as the re-use, to which artifacts were put in the past, the first step is a careful assessment of the archaeological context in which they were found. Secondly, one studies any surface wear resulting from use of the artifact, and analyses any residues, principally organic but also inorganic, surviving on or within the body of the artifact. Thirdly, one tries to infer use from the performance characteristics that are determined both by the physical properties and the style of the artifact. In the present context, style is taken to include, in addition to morphology (i.e., dimensions and shape) and decoration, the 'technological style' that is associated with a production process and reflects the sum of the technological choices made (Lechtman 1977, Lemonnier 1986). Finally, as with production technology, the validity of the hypothesized use should be tested by experimental replication of the artifact and its subsequent use in the manner proposed.

INTERPRETATION

The effective interpretation of the life cycle of surviving material culture requires a holistic approach. This must take into account the fact that production, distribution and use are firmly embedded within the overall situational context that includes environmental and technological constraints, the economic and subsistence base, the social and political organization, and the religious and belief systems of the people under consideration (Figure 36.0; Chilton 1999, Sillar and Tite 2000). Thus, one needs to consider, first, how the environmental, technological, economic, social, political and ideological contexts *directly* impinge on (i.e., both constrain and drive) production, distribution and use and, conversely, how these latter impact back on the contexts. Second, because of the strong interdependency between these different stages in the overall life cycle, one needs to consider how the contexts *indirectly* impinge on any one stage (e.g., production) via the other stages (i.e., distribution and use).

In addition, it is important to incorporate within any interpretation an emic approach. In this one tries to understand (or, at the very least, consider) what the artisans thought that they were achieving through their choice of a particular production sequence and what the people using the artifacts thought were the properties of that artifact. For example, to demonstrate that an artifact has certain performance characteristics does not in itself demonstrate that the artisan was consciously operating to achieve these characteristics. Therefore, in seeking an interpretation of production technology, distribution and use of artifacts, ethno-archaeological studies have a definite contribution to make (Longacre 1991). They are particularly valuable in exposing us to other ways of thinking about the material world and reminding us that artifacts are used in creating and expressing social relationships and that rites, myths and taboos can be associated with production, distribution and use (Barley 1994).

Production

First in the interpretation of production, there are questions concerning the mode or organization of production and the extent of craft specialization. Thus, using the parameters of context, concentration, scale and intensity, as defined by Costin (1991), one asks whether the producers were independent or attached to elite groups; whether the production facilities within a region were dispersed or nucleated; whether the production units were small or large scale (i.e., household or factory-based); and whether the artisans worked part-time or full-time (i.e., extent of craft specialization)? Further questions relate to the status of the artisans and the mechanism for transfer of technological practices from one generation to the next. Data relevant to answering these questions are provided by the reconstruction of production and distribution, and include the degree of standardization, the labour requirements and the level of technology, and the pattern of distribution.

Second, there are questions relating to technological discovery, adoption, choice and change. In order to explain how a new technology was discovered, one needs to consider, first, how the necessary raw materials became available. Second, one looks for possible contacts with other technologies that could perhaps have provided the techniques necessary for production and, third, for the existence of a production context in which either chance or deliberate experimentation could have occurred. In turn, to explain how these requirements for the discovery of a new technology might have been met, one needs to consider whether there was a change in the trade and exchange pattern that could have resulted in the acquisition of the new raw materials and/or the new techniques necessary for production. In addition, one looks for a change in the mode of production and the status of the artisans that could have provided contact with other technologies as well as the possibility for chance or deliberate experimentation. Similarly, the adoption of a new technology is dependent on the demand for new materials or new types of artifact for distribution and use. Therefore, in explaining how these demands arose, one looks for the emergence of a new subsistence pattern, a new social elite, a new pattern of trade and exchange, or a new religion.

Again, in explaining technological choice and change (Schiffer and Skibo 1997), the factors that one needs to consider are, first, the availability and performance characteristics of the raw materials, tools, energy sources, and procurement, processing, fabrication and decorative techniques used in production. Second, there are the more social and cultural influences such as the artisan's perception of the raw materials and techniques chosen (i.e., the technological style) and the ability of these to express, for example, some aspect of social identity. Third, the pattern of trade and exchange can *indirectly* influence technological choice, for example, through providing or restricting access to raw materials or by determining the scale and mode of production. Fourth, the intended uses of the artifacts can influence technological choice, again *indirectly*, by determining the performance characteristics and physical properties that are required of the artifacts. In this context, it is important to avoid an over-emphasis on the role of artifacts as purely utilitarian commodities, such as containers, tools and weapons. Instead, one must also consider the social and ideological roles of artifacts in establishing bonds between social groups at all levels from families to states, or as exchange items and gifts used to accrue future benefits. Thus, the value of an artifact was not necessarily associated with its utilitarian performance characteristics. For example, at least in the early stages of metal production, the colour, reflectivity, ductility or power of transformation via melting and recasting of metals could have been more important than their hardness and toughness. Alternatively, the value of an artifact could have been associated with its rarity, its past history or even the ideological significance of the source from which the raw material was obtained.

Distribution

In order to interpret distribution patterns in terms of trade and exchange, it is important to quantify the trends in distribution away from the raw material sources and centres of production. Thus, as discussed by Plog (1977), one needs to establish the scale or intensity, the directionality and symmetry, and the duration of the associated trade or exchange. Further, it should be emphasized that it is rarely satisfactory to consider the distribution of a single artifact type in isolation but that it is desirable, as far as is possible, to consider the full range of artifacts and subsistence products that are included in the trade and exchange system.

The fall-off in the quantity of a particular artifact type with increasing distance from source can, in principle, assist in distinguishing between the different modes of trade or exchange (Renfrew 1975). For example, the fall off with distance from source will tend to be more rapid in the case of down-the-line exchange as compared to 'middleman' trading. Similarly, re-distribution from a central place is likely to produce localized regions of higher concentration along the fall-off curve. However, in attempting to infer the mode of exchange from the fall-off data, it is necessary also to consider the means of transport (i.e., land, river or sea) available since this can significantly affect the distance travelled by the artifact away from source. Further, pottery used for social, political or ideological purposes will tend to have travelled greater distances than that used for utilitarian purposes. Therefore, it is rarely possible to identify unambiguously the mode of exchange or trade from the fall-off data.

Finally, consideration should be given to the reasons for trade and exchange and, in particular, their role in establishing contacts between people and thus contributing towards changes in technology, subsistence, social organization and ideology (Sherratt 1995).

PAST ACHIEVEMENTS AND LIMITATIONS

As is immediately apparent from the results presented in the subsequent chapters, a wide spectrum of methods for scientific examination are now available for the reconstruction of the production technology, distribution and use relating to the full range of surviving archaeological artifacts. Thus, during the past 20–30 years, there have been major developments in scanning electron microscopy, FTIR and Raman spectroscopy, gas chromatography, mass spectrometry and ICP-MS.

There is now a considerable body of data, for a wide range of periods and regions, on the production technology of plaster, pottery, pigments, metals and glass. Progressively increasing emphasis is being given to the interpretation of the production technologies of these materials in terms of their embeddedness in the wider environmental, technological, economic, social, political and ideological contexts and their interdependency on distribution and use. Thus, our overall understanding of technological discovery, adoption, choice and change in antiquity is beginning to be built up.

Second, very extensive distribution (i.e., provenance) studies have been undertaken for a wide range of periods and regions across the world. Again, increasing emphasis is being put on understanding the reasons for trade and exchange, and their role in helping to bring about technological, economic, social, political and ideological change. However, to achieve such an understanding, it is essential that the samples analysed are fully representative of the overall trade and exchange system (i.e., full range of artifacts and subsistence products) of the region under investigation.

Third, in the context of use alteration, the analysis of organic residues, particularly on pottery (Heron and Evershed 1993) but also, to a lesser extent, on stone artifacts, is currently a major area of research. To date, the main efforts have been devoted to developing and establishing the validity of the analytical methods being used. However, the data thus obtained are already adding to our knowledge of both the uses to which the associated artifacts were being put and past human diet. In addition, the data are beginning to make a contribution to our understanding of, for example, the reasons for the adoption of pottery, and the trade and exchange of the otherwise elusive subsistence products for which pottery provided a container.

THE FUTURE

First, in terms of the introduction of new methods for scientific examination, the main requirement for the future is for techniques that both minimize artifact damage and can achieve a high throughput of analyses. Thus, laser ablation ICP-MS for both elemental and isotopic analysis has the potential to make a major contribution in that artifact damage is minimal and, by not requiring any chemical dissolution, throughput is increased. In addition, entirely non-destructive techniques, such as X-ray diffraction tomography, that are possible using the high energy, high flux X-rays generated by synchrotron radiation could be valuable for specific applications.

Second, in terms of reconstruction, it is important that, whenever possible, scientific examination is combined with archaeological fieldwork and excavation, ethnoarchaeology and experimental replication. However, the primary aim for the future must be to put increasing emphasis on the interpretation of production technology, distribution and use in terms of their embeddedness in the wider overall context and their interdependency one to another, with both functional and cultural factors being taken fully into account.

Thus, the ultimate goal is to obtain an overview, first, of the history of technology for different regions of the world and, thus, of human exploitation of the environment in terms of the raw materials used; and, second, of the pattern of trade and exchange and hence of the social, political and cultural contacts between peoples across the world.

REFERENCES

Barley, N. (1994). *Smashing Pots; Feats of Clay from Africa*. British Museum Press: London.

Bowman, S.G.E. (ed.) (1991). *Science and the Past*. British Museum Publications: London.

Chilton, E.S. (ed.) (1999). *Material Meanings*. University of Utah Press: Salt Lake City.

Ciliberto, E. and Spoto, G. (eds) (2000). *Modern Analytical Methods in Art and Archaeology*. John Wiley: New York.

Costin, C.L. (1991). Craft specialization: issues in defining, documenting, and explaining the organization of production. In Schiffer, M.B. (ed.) *Archaeological Method and Theory Vol. 3*, 1–56. Academic Press: New York.

Dobres, M.-A. and Hoffman, C.R. (1994). Social agency and the dynamics of prehistoric technology, *Journal of Archaeological Method and Theory*, 1:211–258.

Heron, C. and Evershed, R.P. (1993). The analysis of organic residues and the study of pottery use. In Schiffer, M.B. (ed.) *Archaeological Method and Theory Vol. 5*, 247–284. Academic Press: New York.

Kingery, W.D. (ed.) (1996). *Learning from Things*. Smithsonian Institution Press: Washington DC.

Lechtman, H. (1977). Style in technology – some early thoughts. In Lechtman, H. and Merrill, R.S. (eds) *Material Culture: Styles, Organization and Dynamics of Technology*, 3–20. West Publishing Company: St. Paul, MN.

Lemonnier, P. (1986). The study of material culture today: towards an anthropology of technical systems. *Journal of Anthropological Archaeology*, 5:147–186.

Longacre, W.A. (1991). *Ceramic Ethnoarchaeology*. University of Arizona Press: Tucson.

Plog, F. (1977). Modeling economic exchange. In Earle, T.K. and Ericson, J.E. (eds) *Exchange Systems in Prehistory*, 127–140. Academic Press: New York.

Pollard, A.M. and Heron, C. (1996). *Archaeological Chemistry*. Royal Society of Chemistry: Cambridge.

Renfrew, A.C. (1975). Trade and interaction. In Sabloff, J.A. and Lamberg-Karlovsky, C.C. (eds) *Ancient Civilizations and Trade*, 3–59. University of New Mexico Press: Albuquerque.

Schiffer, M.B. and Skibo, J.M. (1997). The explanation of artifact variability. *American Antiquity*, **62**:27–50.

Sherratt, A. (1995). Reviving the grand narrative: archaeology and long-term change. *Journal of European Archaeology*, **3**:1–32.

Sillar, B. and Tite, M.S. (2000). The challenge of 'technological choices' for materials science approaches in archaeology. *Archaeometry*, **42**:2–20.

Skibo, J.M. (1992). *Pottery Function: a Use-Alteration Perspective*. Plenum Press: New York.

Weigand, P.C., Harbottle, G. and Sayre, E.V. (1977). Turquoise sources and source analysis: Mesoamerica and the southwestern USA. In Earle, T.K. and Ericson, J.E. (eds) *Exchange Systems in Prehistory*, 15–34. Academic Press: New York.

36

Ceramic Petrology, Clay Geochemistry and Ceramic Production – from Technology to the Mind of the Potter

I.K. WHITBREAD

Fitch Laboratory, British School at Athens, Athens.

Ceramics are synthetic materials and, as such, are sensitive indicators of human decision-making and materials interaction. Potters govern each stage of production, from raw materials selection and preparation, to forming, finishing, decorating and firing, repeatedly affecting the final material with choices and actions that express their cultural symbolism, traditions and individual preferences. Thus, by combining anthropological and physico-chemical research, archaeology can advance studies of past societies through the nature of their ceramic technologies (Sillar and Tite 2000).

Studies of ancient ceramic technologies are numerous, reflecting the diversity of the material (Freestone and Gaimster 1997) and its prominence in the archaeological record. Owing to their wide geographical and temporal occurrence, emphasis here is placed on terracotta and earthenware ceramics (Rice 1987:5), specifically in terms of ancient potters' cognizance of materials properties. This is not what ancient potters thought *of* their materials, which is impossible to discern, but *how* they thought about them (van der Leeuw 1994), determined from comparisons of materials selection in manufacturing processes and properties of the completed artifacts.

CERAMIC ECOLOGY

Technological investigations of archaeological ceramics trace their heritage back to the fundamental works of Shepard and Matson (Bishop and Lange 1991, Kolb 1989). Shepard's *Ceramics for the Archaeologist* (1956) meticulously addresses the analysis of ancient pottery though technological processes. It was Matson, however, who introduced the theoretical framework necessary to export these studies across diverse archaeological domains. He defined ceramic ecology as 'one facet of cultural ecology, that which attempts to relate the raw materials and technologies that the local potter has available to the functions in his culture of the products he fashions' (Matson 1965). Thus, technological studies explicitly look beyond the material itself to the range of human and environmental interactions that affected ceramic production.

Technological choices made by traditional potters are based on an empirical understanding of materials properties. Experience and experimentation are fundamental in this approach, which can be summarized as 'if it works, it's right' (Cuff 1996:83). This encapsulates the observational dependencies of empiricism as structured

---

Handbook of Archaeological Sciences. Edited by D.R. Brothwell and A.M. Pollard.

on the society's system of values (Barley 1994:47, Gosselain 1998) and the potter's perception of desired performance. Moreover, it communicates an inherent conservatism, in that technology may become 'traditional' because it works, thereby joining a network of culturally patterned choices (Vandiver 1988). Arnold's (1971) ethnographic study of potters' clay exploitation at Ticul, Yucatan, differentiated scientific from empirical perspectives in terms of *etic* and *emic* information. Etic information is cross-cultural, external and directly measurable, as in data derived from the scientific analysis of clays. Emic information is culturally embedded, and its context-specific nature must therefore be discovered, such as the ways in which Ticul potters conceptualize clay characteristics and differences.

Although the socially embedded nature of ancient technologies is complex, it is a principal reason for undertaking materials analyses. Archaeology is founded upon artifact remains, and their embedded traces of production technologies are prime routes of access to past societies, notwithstanding the limitations in extractable information (Lemonnier 1986). Within these confines, patterns in ceramic composition and structure can be defined and tested against postulated materials and processes (Kingery 1982). These may be based on modern materials knowledge, studies of traditional potters or technological tendencies, where the same actions and materials re-occur in addressing the same technical problems (Lemonnier 1986). The isochrestic definition of style (Sackett 1990) embraces such studies, where style is viewed as the outcome whenever potters have a choice between equally viable options. These choices may be incorporated into traditions of ceramic manufacture, but whether individual or cultural/traditional, they exist throughout the production process and thus form the basis of technological style (Lechtman 1977). A specific technological style may be defined by an operational sequence, the *chaîne opératoire*, consisting of choices and actions (Sillar and Tite 2000). The sequence itself is as important as the individual stages, so that essential steps can be established and the variations resulting from choices isolated as different styles (Lemonnier 1986). A key advantage of the *chaîne opératoire* is that models for each stage of the production sequence stand as postulates against which future data can be tested. Any adjustment made to the model in one part of the chain can be verified by assessing its effects elsewhere in the sequence (Andrews 1997).

Studies of ancient ceramic technologies call for close integration of the humanities and sciences. Neverthe-

less, the materials component is at the centre of interaction in the production process, and often is all that remains for study. Ancient potters selected and manipulated materials in response to their own patterns of choice, but researchers studying past choices require accurate knowledge of the *specific* types of raw materials and processes employed, so as to avoid basing elaborate conclusions on false premises. Thus, application of analytical methods cannot merely be adopted from the physical sciences, but must be developed to address the key issues in archaeological investigations.

MATERIALS ANALYSIS

To proceed, it is necessary to explore analytical routes to the study of ancient clay bodies, that is, the blend of clays and other materials used to achieve a specific ceramic purpose (Rhodes 1973:24). Such blends are based on the plasticity of clays, brought about through the interaction of clay minerals with water and exchangeable cations, the texture of the material, and the presence of non-plastic inclusions, predominantly silicates, carbonates and organic matter (Grim 1968:3, Rice 1987:54).

Clay minerals belong to the hydrous aluminium phyllosilicates (layer silicates) of which there are several groups, subgroups and species, classified by layer type and charge per formula unit (Moore and Reynolds 1997:130). The subgroups most commonly encountered in the archaeological science literature are kaolins, with a 1:1 layer structure (Figure 36.1) comprising one tetrahedral sheet and one octahedral sheet, and smectites, illites and chlorites, that have a 2:1 structure with an octahedral sheet sandwiched between two tetrahedral sheets. Most naturally occurring clays are mixtures of different clay mineral subgroups, so that clay mineralogy can produce only a general representation of physical performance. A clay body may nevertheless reflect characteristics of the dominant subgroup. For example, kaolinite-rich clay bodies have low drying shrinkage and withstand high temperature firing, but have relatively poor plasticity owing to the tight regular stacking of the kaolin layers. In contrast, smectites have relatively weak bonds between layers, allowing water and loosely attached cations, such as calcium and sodium, into the interlayer area (Pollard and Heron 1996:121). Breakdown of these weakly bonded layers increases water contact, producing 'sticky' or 'fat' clays prone to excessive shrinkage on drying (Cuff 1996:59, Vandiver 1988). Traditional potters

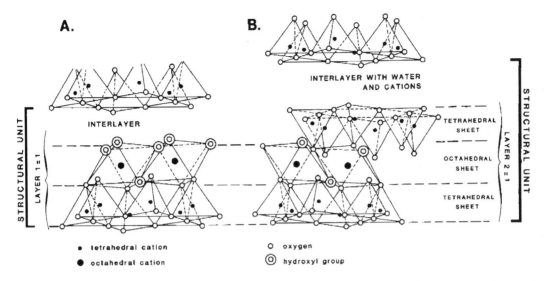

A.

B.

INTERLAYER WITH WATER AND CATIONS

INTERLAYER

STRUCTURAL UNIT

LAYER 1:1

TETRAHEDRAL SHEET

OCTAHEDRAL SHEET

TETRAHEDRAL SHEET

STRUCTURAL UNIT

LAYER 2:1

- • tetrahedral cation
- ● octahedral cation
- ○ oxygen
- ◎ hydroxyl group

Figure 36.1 Clay mineral structures (A) kaolinite, (B) smectite (Chamley 1989). Reproduced by permission of Springer-Verlag, New York.

assess these physical properties without understanding the underlying causes.

X-ray diffraction (XRD) is used to identify clay minerals in natural deposits and unfired bodies (e.g., Arnold 1971), but these minerals cannot normally be identified in ceramics because their lattices are disordered or destroyed during firing. This loss of direct evidence on the specific materials properties with which ancient potters worked has led archaeologists to use alternative analytical methods, principally ceramic petrography and geochemistry (Pollard and Heron 1996:20, Rice 1987:371), to investigate ancient ceramics and potential raw materials.

Ceramic petrology encompasses the study of ceramic materials, technology and provenance, based on *ceramic petrography*, which is the description of ceramic materials in hand specimen and thin section (Whitbread 1995:365). Thin sections are slices ground to 30 microns in thickness so that the translucent rocks and minerals can be identified using a polarizing microscope at low (×25–400) magnification. Scanning electron microscopy generates further detail on microstructure (up to ×50 000; Rice 1987:402) and is used to study the development of vitrification from firing.

Ceramic petrography is a powerful method for technological studies, especially for coarse-grained fabrics. Hand specimen examination enables broad technological traits to be characterized over large assemblages (Peacock 1977), but thin sections enhance inclusion identification and allow direct comparisons with regio-

nal geology. Difficulties arise if the same minerals and rocks occur repeatedly throughout a study area, undermining regional characterization and identification of raw material sources. In these cases, petrographers can exploit micromorphological differences (Whitbread 1995:379) which reflect the potter's working of the clay body. Most micromorphological information is qualitative and, although discrimination by eye can be highly sensitive, results are heavily dependent upon the analyst's experience. Quantification in petrography mainly relies on modal analysis (Stoltman 1989) to classify fabrics by the proportions of different components, and grain-size analysis (Whitbread 1995:388) to reflect potters' choices through the 'feel' of the clay body. Though valuable, these methods are time consuming and fail to capture many significant micromorphological properties.

Geochemical analysis gives quantified data on elemental concentrations, and is especially valuable in studies of fine-grained materials. Clays are composed of the major structural elements Si, Al and O. Minor elements (c. 0.1–10 per cent), such as Ca, Fe, K, Na, Ti and Mg, can be both technological and provenance discriminators. Trace elements (up to 1000 ppm) are generally considered to be accidental, and thus provenance-related (Jones 1986:5). Most common methods of elemental analysis are bulk techniques (e.g., OES, AAS, XRF, NAA, ICP), in which samples are homogenized before analysis. Data from these techniques present a complex combination of provenance and technological information, since the contributions of fired-clay matrix and inclusions cannot be separated (Arnold *et al.* 1991). Alternatively, electron microprobe and other spatially-resolved techniques give elemental data on the structurally-intact ceramic material allowing elemental traits in specific inclusions to be used for provenance and technological research (Shriner and Dorais 1999).

Petrography and geochemistry generate a wide range of structural and compositional data, but they can only reflect technological processes that leave marks in these terms, and rarely is such evidence unequivocal. This handicap strains efforts to interpret scientific results within archaeologically meaningful frameworks. Various approaches have been adopted to mitigate this by broadening the range and contexts of information collected. Thus, laboratory analysis has been augmented by technological examination of ceramic assemblages (e.g., Franken and Steiner 1990), investigations of production sites (e.g., Molera *et al.* 1996), experimental reconstructions (Schiffer and Skibo 1987) and ethnographic studies (Krause 1985, Aronson *et al.* 1994).

RAW MATERIALS PROSPECTION

Clay body characteristics and ceramic performance are based on raw materials, the selection of which is a key stage in the production sequence. Asked what traits were considered most important in clay selection, Kalinga potters of Northern Luzon, Philippines, replied: sticky (plastic), clean (no stones), fine, smooth, no cracks on firing, stands easily, strong/flimsy (too little sand), proximity, resulting pots ring when tapped, and presence of soft stones (Aronson *et al.* 1994). Apart from the last example, the references address physical performance, texture and accessibility rather than composition. Compositional analysis is an indirect route to identifying the selection criteria of ancient potters, but one that is essential in the absence of alternative information.

Raw materials prospection is a common component of ceramic technology studies. Compositional characteristics of 'local' sherds are first determined to indicate the most likely areas for prospection. Samples of potential raw materials are then collected based on traditional methods, such as simple texture and plasticity testing (Cuff 1996:68), and studied in terms of composition, physical attributes and selection patterns. Usually, investigators undertake such fieldwork themselves, as suitable clay sources can rarely be identified from

geological maps alone (Howard 1982; see Chapter 59). Most ancient potters would have derived regional knowledge through several generations (Franken and Steiner 1990:69), but time and funding restrict modern prospection. Given these limitations, a range of workable materials is normally sampled and used to assess the degree of natural variation and the potential choice available to potters in the past.

Clays exploited by traditional potters are a good starting point for identifying ancient raw materials. To take one example, fieldwork at Matacapan, in the Tuxtla Mountains of Veracruz, Mexico, located numerous production sites for Middle Classic (*c.* AD 300–450) Maya Fine Orange pottery (Pool and Santley 1992). The closest likely source in the region was deduced to be Tertiary marine clays of the Concepción Formation, less than 1 km from the site and used by modern potters, rather than the highly plastic smectite clays which dominate the region. XRF analysis of the sherds and clays followed the well-established principles of provenance determination (see Chapter 41) and showed that 97 per cent of the Matacapan ceramics grouped with samples of the Concepción Formation. The present is not always the key to the past, however, and modern potters may not use the same clays as their ancient counterparts. Traditional potters in Messenia, Greece, now choose clays considered to be inferior, requiring additional processing, because the preferred deposits have been worked out (Blitzer 1990).

A major issue in ancient procurement patterns, and a factor in modern prospection, is the proximity of raw materials to production sites. In 111 ethnographic cases noted by Arnold (1985:38), 33 per cent of potters obtained clays within a 1 km radius of their workshops, and 84 per cent within 7 km; similar results were found for temper sources, but potters were prepared to go much further for materials to prepare slips and paints. Distance is a simplistic measure in pre-industrialized production (Peacock 1982:8), where access may, for instance, be socially embedded in visits to distant kin (DeBoer 1984) or based on kinship/political affiliation (Krause 1985:110). Indeed, range is likely to be calculated in travel time rather than distance, and payments for extraction rights (Sillar 1997) may rule out nearby sources.

RAW MATERIALS PROCESSING

Potters often process raw materials to improve their performance. The most common procedures are mixing clays, removing coarse materials through water settling (*levigation*) or sieving, and adding non-plastic materials (*tempering*). Identifying these is critical when relating ceramics to raw materials and in defining the effects of potters' choices on the character of different clay bodies.

Processing may be aimed at attaining a viable clay body from materials that are considered unsuitable in their natural state. This was the case for potters at Kentri, Crete. The bluish white clay they collected, being 'like soap', was considered to be poor for throwing on its own, while deep red earth taken from *terra rossa* soils broke immediately under high heat if used alone, but when the potters mixed these clays they achieved a desired clay body (Blitzer 1984). Mixing at this scale is extremely difficult to detect from the finished products alone. Careful excavation of production sites may allow raw materials to be identified directly (e.g., Molera *et al.* 1996), along with structures from any associated processing facilities, as illustrated in Blitzer's (1984) plan of the Kentri workshop at Tsikalario (Figure 36.2).

Processing also maintains clay-body performance when accommodating changes in the supply of raw materials. Potters at Cuzco, Peru, change raw material resources when the need arises, re-establishing a suitable clay body by adjusting clay mixtures and temper addition (Sillar 1997). An optimal clay body is not defined by raw materials alone, but is subject to potters' preferences. At Archangelos, Rhodes, some potters use one clay, whilst others mix between two and five clays (Jones 1984). In Kenya, some Luo potters use the same combination of clay and temper for the whole range of pottery, whilst others employ different mixtures for different functions (Dietler and Herbich 1989).

Clay mixing may be detected in thin section if clays with distinctive inclusions have been poorly combined (*wedged*) (Franken and Steiner 1990:79). Removal of material, through sieving or levigation, is more difficult to establish without accurate information on the raw materials. Bulk elemental analyses have shown a tendency for trace element concentrations to be increased by refining clays. This is attributed to the relative paucity of trace elements in coarse inclusions compared with the fine fraction of ceramics. Thus, removal of the coarser materials enhances the contribution of the finer fraction in the analytical results (Kilikoglou *et al.* 1988).

Many petrographic studies have addressed the working properties of clay bodies by using coarse inclusions as a technological index, since these can be more readily characterized than the fired clay matrix. The focus of this work is *temper*, which is coarse material (usually non-plastic) added to a clay body by the potter as an opening agent (Shepard 1956:25, Rice 1987:406). It improves workability, reduces drying shrinkage and diminishes heat-induced stresses (Rye 1981:31). It is often difficult to distinguish temper from naturally-occurring inclusions, although the systematic presence of unnatural inclusions such as *grog* (crushed ceramics), slag and bone offers the most secure evidence of deliberate addition.

Relating the physical performance of vessels to inclusion composition is attractive for developing models in ceramic petrology. Calcium carbonate ($CaCO_3$) temper, in the form of limestone and burnt shell, has received considerable archaeological attention following Rye's (1976) landmark study of materials used by Papuan potters to make cooking wares. Many traditional potters remove calcium carbonate inclusions to avoid lime blowing (Rhodes 1973:65). When fired above *c.* 650°C, $CaCO_3$ converts to CaO, releasing CO_2. After firing, CaO re-hydrates to $Ca(OH)_2$, with a significant volume increase, resulting in surface cracks and potentially producing catastrophic failure (Rye 1976, 1981:114). Despite these problems, Rye considered this temper to be optimal for cooking wares that undergo repeated thermal stress over open fires, because the coefficient of thermal expansion of $CaCO_3$ is similar to that of most clays. Using firing experiments on clay samples, Rye (1976) showed that the Papuan potters avoided the problem of lime blowing by adding seawater to the clay body, which interacts with $CaCO_3$ preventing its decomposition.

In contrast, one of the most abundant inclusions in ceramics, quartz (SiO_2), has a thermal expansion coefficient markedly higher than clays, and a structural expansion at 573°C, leading to thermal stress during the firing process and subsequent cooking (Rye 1976). Steponaitis (1984) postulated that in the Moundville region, Alabama, materials use changed to counter such effects and improve mechanical performance: fine sand replaced coarse sand at *c.* 100 BC to diminish thermal stress caused by quartz, crushed pottery temper (grog) was adopted *c.* AD 550 to eliminate differential thermal expansion, and burnt shell temper was introduced, shortly after AD 1000, to exploit its platy character in imparting greater fracture toughness (the ability to remain intact once fracture is initiated) through resistance to crack propagation. There is more to ceramic performance, however, than temper composition. Woods (1986) noted that quartz would not have been so widely tolerated in British prehistoric,

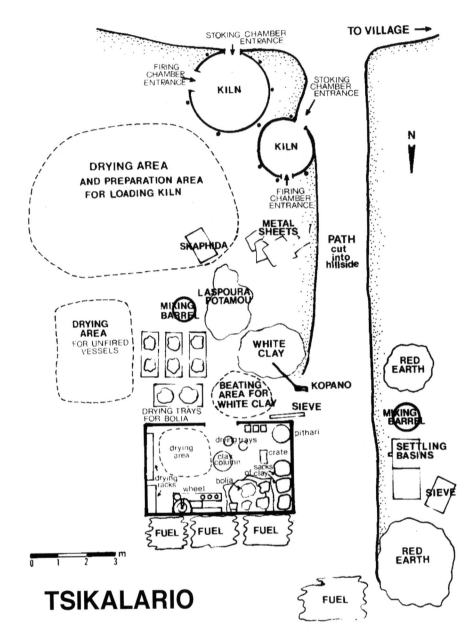

Figure 36.2 Plan of a traditional potter's workshop at Kentri, Crete (Blitzer 1984). Reproduced by permission of University of Pennsylvania Museum, Philadelphia, PA.

Romano-British and Medieval cooking wares if the ceramic limitations posited for it were significant to ancient potters. She concluded that the role of inclusions in opening the fabric was more critical than composition and physical properties. Likewise, Cardew (1969:77) observed that, despite regional differences in the materials used, traditional West African cooking pots were consistent in the coarseness of the body, the very strong 'sticky' plastic clay used and the very low temperatures of firing. Thus, thermal shock was not addressed by controlling inclusion composition, but by using a coarse, open fabric with minimum development of a glassy phase to inhibit crack propagation.

To advance this research, the physical performance of tempering materials within earthenware bodies must be explored, together with traditional potters' assessments of materials properties. Experiments using calcareous clays with quartz inclusions (Kilikoglou *et al.* 1998) have revealed that contraction of the clay matrix on drying, and on cooling after firing, creates zones of microcracks around inclusions, which dissipate fracture energy. These zones effectively act as voids, which suggests that the influence of inclusion composition is limited. Below about 10 per cent inclusion volume catastrophic fracture was found to occur between the damage zones, but at about 20 per cent inclusion volume the damage zones overlap, inhibiting crack propagation but reducing overall strength by about 50 per cent. Thus, the problematic thermal expansion coefficient of quartz does not appear to be significant in practice, as damage zones absorb the induced stresses.

Ethnoarchaeological studies incorporating materials analysis bring numerous insights to questions of materials selection and preparation. In Pabillonis, Sardinia, cooking pots were produced from the 1920s to 1970s and respected for their thermal shock resistance, which was attributed to the particular combination of clay and temper. Annis and Jacobs (1989–90) investigated this using a workshop abandoned in 1968 with equipment, broken pots and prepared clay *in situ*. The potters distinguished two types of raw material, 'earth for soaking' and 'earth for crushing' i.e., temper. Analysis showed the preferred body to have a large amount of inclusions in the fine sand to coarse silt fraction, most of which were derived from temper of sandy clay rich in muscovite mica, quartz and feldspar. Mechanical tests demonstrated that the clay requires 20 per cent fine temper for optimal thermal shock resistance, which is close to the potters' estimates for temper addition. Experiments using substituted quartz temper produced equally good thermal shock properties, suggesting that the combination of clay and temper was not as critical as traditionally claimed.

Arguments promoting one tempering material over another cannot rely on composition alone. They must consider an array of influences, including clay body composition as a whole, vessel form, fabrication techniques and firing methods. Just as critical are differences in pottery use, such as the particular methods of cooking (Skibo 1992:37) and the impact of organic materials, in the form of coatings or vessel contents, on the performance of the ceramic materials (Schiffer *et al.* 1994, Gosselain 1998). Notwithstanding materials performance, the rationale behind temper choice may be purely symbolic. Based on modern materials science, Steponaitis (1984) explained the adoption of grog-temper in the Moundville region in terms of eliminating materials stress. In contrast, Gurensi women, in Ghana, tempered their pottery with grog as a physical act to represent renewal and the life cycle (Gosselain 1998; see also Sillar 1997). This shows that materials analysis generates essential insights into physical performance, but cannot in itself explain the specific rationales of ancient potters, even where these exploit physical advantages.

FORMING, FINISHING AND DECORATING

Application of the *chaîne opératoire* approach to ceramics has focused on forming techniques and construction sequences (van der Leeuw 1993). Basic techniques comprise pinching, press-moulding, slab-building, hammer-and-anvil, coil-building and wheel-throwing (Rye 1981:62). A vessel can be formed using a single technique, a sequence of different techniques, or sections made by different techniques and later joined. These techniques may be identified from various organizational properties of the ceramic material, such as structural discontinuities and preferred orientations in the fabric components.

Macroscopic observation and radiography play a substantial role in determining forming techniques (Vandiver *et al.* 1991), but exploration can be taken further with optical and scanning electron microscopy. Combinations of oriented thin sections have been employed (Whitbread 1996) to discriminate between forming techniques using preferred orientations that survive in low-fired ceramics. Courty and Roux (1995) employed similar methods, with the addition of SEM, in their attempts to differentiate wheel-thrown vessels from coil-made rough-outs subsequently shaped on a wheel. As they note, however, caution is necessary when using structural analysis for this purpose, owing to the procedural difficulties arising from diversity in composition, degrees of firing, and physical interactions of potters in preparing and working bodies.

Like forming, the style of finishing and decorating ceramics is often a function of composition and structure. Middleton's (1987) investigation of Late Bronze and Early Iron Age 'haematite-coated' pottery in south-east England, by optical microscopy, XRD and SEM/EDX, revealed that three different techniques were employed to create the distinctive finish: coatings containing crushed iron oxide, slip coatings and simple burnishing, each representing a specific technological style. Andrews (1997) combined similar analytical techniques with a *chaîne opératoire* approach to explore manufacturing methods and modes of production for Iron Age slip decorated ceramics of the Auvergne, central France.

Forming methods and clay body compositions are interdependent variables and data on either property can be used to elucidate physical characteristics of the other prior to firing (Vandiver 1988). Moreover, by using materials analysis to explore forming, finishing and decorating techniques, archaeologists are able to substantially enhance the definition of technological styles in ceramic production.

FIRING

Firing transforms the clay body into a ceramic, fixing the work of earlier production stages through sintering (Heimann 1989). Earthenware and terracotta were usually produced in open firings (bonfires) and updraft kilns, which have maximum temperatures between 900–1100°C (see Chapter 40). Firing durations of kilns are longer than open firings, but they allow greater control over the rate of heating and the kiln atmosphere (Rye 1981:98).

The relatively low temperatures and short durations of earthenware and terracotta firings mean that thermodynamic equilibrium is rarely attained, and reaction rates (kinetics) largely determine the results (Heimann 1989) as a function of composition, temperature, atmosphere and time. Several elemental and mineralogical techniques have been applied to identify these conditions from the finished ceramics. For example, XRD can chart phase changes under different firing conditions (Maggetti 1982), SEM can record the development of vitrified microstructures in ceramics (Maniatis and Tite 1981), and Mössbauer spectroscopy can reveal firing conditions through the physical and chemical states of iron within the ceramic material (Maniatis *et al.* 1984). Uneven heating and stacking arrangements generate micro-environments during firing, creating varied results even within a single load (Gosselain 1992). As a consequence, identifying firing regimes from ceramics is a complex issue (Kingery 1982, Krause 1985:166) that requires careful sampling of representative materials.

Judgement of firing success depends largely on the potter's purpose and expectations, but can be expressed in terms of colour, strength, density and permeability (Rhodes 1973:18). As with the West African cooking pots discussed above, potters may use firing conditions to control mechanical properties for specific functions. Physical tests can be applied to measure these properties, but colour assessment is more complex as it is subject to individual/cultural preferences. Control of fired colour through materials preparation and firing procedures is well illustrated by Attic black and red figure wares (610–550 BC) from Greece. Potters were able to control the atmosphere in the kiln during firing, changing it from oxidizing to reducing and then back to oxidizing. Provided an adequate temperature was reached, the extremely fine paint used for decoration sintered rapidly during the reduction phase, so that it became sealed from further reaction with the atmosphere, and remained black when the coarser body returned to red on re-oxidation (Maniatis *et al.* 1993). Clearly, the potters recognized the relationship between grain-size of the paint and its performance with respect to temperature and atmosphere, and prepared their raw materials accordingly. Black and red figure vessels displaying problems in this process, such as re-oxidized painted decoration, are widely distributed, showing that a range of success was achieved and to some degree tolerated. Research on the specific details of firing conditions is essential to understanding the techniques employed, but the archaeological significance of these results lies in the broader context of product uniformity achieved by the potters and product variability accepted by consumers.

FUTURE DIRECTIONS FOR SCIENTIFIC ANALYSIS IN CERAMIC TECHNOLOGY STUDIES

Unlike provenance determination, where ceramics are treated as tokens of trade and exchange, technology studies deal directly with the choices of ancient potters embedded within their broader socio-cultural and natural environments. As ethnography illustrates, methods which enable identification of these choices and their contexts are fundamental to developing interpretations of ancient technology based on scientific data (Sillar and Tite 2000).

Much methodological research remains to be done in honing even well-known analytical techniques to address technological questions. Certainly, one way forward lies in examining a wide range of production techniques, individually and as components of a *chaîne opératoire*, with the specific aim of developing analytical methods to identify traces of their use in archaeological remains (Whitbread 1995:392). In addition, production sites need to be excavated with the explicit aim of identifying the technological processes that they represent. Remains of raw materials, processing debris, clay bodies and installations (Figure 36.2) can lead to a far better assessment of techniques and modes of production than can be achieved solely from finished products.

Ceramic production was one of the principal crafts of past societies, reflecting their varied, yet integral, technological components. Embedding materials analyses within archaeological research advances our understanding of the processes, diversity and change in these technologies, and is thus a key to finding the people behind the pots.

ACKNOWLEDGEMENTS

The author thanks N. Brodie and E. Kiriatzi for suggestions in preparing this text. He also thanks the publishers for permission to reproduce Figures 36.1 and 36.2.

REFERENCES

*Recommended for further reading

Andrews, K. (1997). From ceramic finishes to modes of production: Iron Age finewares from Central France. In Cumberpatch, C.G. and Blinkhorn, P.W. (eds) *Not So Much a Pot, More a Way of Life: Current Approaches to Artefact Analysis in Archaeology*, 57–75. Oxbow Monograph 84, Oxbow: Oxford.

Annis, M.B. and Jacobs, L. (1989–90). Cooking ware from Pabillonis (Sardinia): relationships between raw materials, manufacturing techniques and the function of the vessels. *Newsletter, Department of Pottery Technology, University of Leiden*, **7/8**:75–130.

Arnold, D.E. (1971). Ethnomineralogy of Ticul, Yucatan potters: etics and emics. *American Antiquity*, **36**:20–40.

*Arnold, D.E. (1985). *Ceramic Theory and Cultural Process*. Cambridge University Press: Cambridge.

Arnold, D.E., Neff, H. and Bishop, R.L. (1991). Compositional analysis and 'sources' of pottery: an ethnoarchaeological approach. *American Anthropologist*, **93**:70–90.

Aronson, M., Skibo, J.M. and Stark, M.T. (1994). Production and use technologies in Kalinga pottery. In Longacre, W.A. and Skibo, J.M. (eds) *Kalinga Ethnoarchaeology: Expanding Archaeological Method and Theory*, 83–111. Smithsonian Institution Press: Washington DC.

Barley, N. (1994). *Smashing Pots: Feats of Clay from Africa*. British Museum Press: London.

Bishop, R.L. and Lange, F.W. (1991). *The Ceramic Legacy of Anna O. Shepard*. University of Colorado Press: Niwot, Colorado.

Blitzer, H. (1984). Traditional pottery production in Kentri, Crete: workshops, materials, techniques and trade. In Betancourt, P.P. (ed.) *East Cretan Light-On-Dark Ware: Studies on a Handmade Pottery of the Early to Middle Minoan Periods*, 143–157. University Museum Monograph 51, University of Pennsylvania: Philadelphia.

Blitzer, H. (1990). KOPΩNEIKA: storage-jar production and trade in the traditional Aegean. *Hesperia*, **59**:675–711.

Cardew, M. (1969). *Pioneer Pottery*. Longman: London.

Chamley, H. (1989). *Clay Sedimentology*. Springer-Verlag: Berlin.

Courty, M.A. and Roux, V. (1995). Identification of wheel throwing on the basis of ceramic surface features and microfabrics. *Journal of Archaeological Science*, **22**:17–50.

Cuff, Y.H. (1996). *Ceramic Technology for Potters and Sculptors*. A & C Black: London.

DeBoer, W.R. (1984). The last pottery show: system and sense in ceramic studies. In van der Leeuw, S.E. and Pritchard, A.C. (eds) *The Many Dimensions of Pottery: Ceramics in Archaeology and Anthropology*, 527–571. Cingula VII, University of Amsterdam: Amsterdam.

Dietler, M. and Herbich, I. (1989). Tich Matek: the technology of Luo pottery production and the definition of ceramic style. *World Archaeology*, **21**:148–164.

Franken, H.J. and Steiner, M.L. (1990). *Excavations in Jerusalem 1961–1967, vol. II, The Iron Age Extramural Quarter on the South-East Hill*. Oxford University Press: Oxford.

*Freestone, I.C. and Gaimster, D. (1997). *Pottery in the Making: World Ceramic Traditions*. British Museum Press: London.

Gosselain, O.P. (1992). Bonfire of the enquiries. Pottery firing temperatures in archaeology: what for? *Journal of Archaeological Science*, **19**:243–259.

Gosselain, O.P. (1998). Social and technical identity in a clay crystal ball. In Stark, M.T. (ed.) *The Archaeology of Social Boundaries*, 78–106. Smithsonian Institution Press: Washington DC.

Grim, R.E. (1968). *Clay Mineralogy*, (2nd edn). McGraw-Hill: New York.

Heimann, R.B. (1989). Assessing the technology of ancient pottery: the use of ceramic phase diagrams. *Archeomaterials*, **3**:123–148.

Howard, H. (1982). Clay and the archaeologist. In Freestone, I.C., Johns, C. and Potter, T. (eds) *Current Research in Ceramics: Thin-Section Studies*, 145–158. Occasional Paper 32, British Museum Press: London.

Jones, R.E. (1984). Greek potters' clays: questions of selection, availability and adaptation. In Brijder, H.A.G. (ed.) *Ancient Greek and Related Pottery*, 21–30. Allard Pierson: Amsterdam.

Jones, R.E. (1986). *Greek and Cypriot Pottery: a Review of Scientific Studies*. Fitch Laboratory Occasional Paper 1, British School at Athens: Athens.

Kilikoglou, V., Maniatis, Y. and Grimanis, A.P. (1988). The effect of purification and firing of clays on trace element provenance studies. *Archaeometry*, **30**:37–46.

Kilikoglou, V., Vekinis, G., Maniatis, Y. and Day, P.M. (1998), Mechanical performance of quartz-tempered ceramics: part I, strength and toughness. *Archaeometry*, **40**:261–279.

Kingery, W.D. (1982). Plausible inferences from ceramic artifacts. In Olin, J.S. and Franklin, A.D. (eds) *Archaeological Ceramics*, 37–45. Smithsonian Institution Press: Washington DC.

Kolb, C.C. (1989). Ceramic ecology in retrospect: a critical review of methodology and results. In Kolb, C.C. (ed.) *Ceramic Ecology, 1988: Current Research on Ceramic Materials*, 261–375. BAR International Series 426(ii), British Archaeological Reports: Oxford.

Krause, R.A. (1985). *The Clay Sleeps: An Ethnoarchaeological Study of Three African Potters*. University of Alabama Press: University, Alabama.

Lechtman, H. (1977). Style in technology: some early thoughts. In Lechtman, H. and Merill, R.S. (eds) *Material Culture: Style, Organization, and Dynamics of Technology*, 3–20. West Publishing Co: St Paul.

*Lemonnier, P. (1986). The study of material culture today: toward an anthropology of technical systems. *Journal of Anthropological Archaeology*, **5**:147–186.

Maggetti, M. (1982). Phase analysis and its significance for technology and origin. In Olin, J.S. and Franklin, A.D. (eds) *Archaeological Ceramics*, 121–133. Smithsonian Institution Press: Washington DC.

Maniatis, Y. and Tite, M.S. (1981). Technological examination of Neolithic-Bronze Age pottery from central and southeast Europe and from the Near East. *Journal of Archaeological Science*, **8**:59–76.

Maniatis, Y., Aloupi, E. and Stalios, A.D. (1993). New evidence for the nature of Attic black gloss. *Archaeometry*, **35**:23–34.

Maniatis, Y., Jones, R.E., Whitbread, I.K., Kostikas, A., Simopoulos, A., Karakalos, Ch. and Williams, C.K. II (1984). Punic Amphoras found at Corinth, Greece: an investigation of their origin and technology. *Journal of Field Archaeology*, **11**:205–222.

Matson, F.R. (1965). Ceramic ecology: an approach to the study of early cultures of the Near East. In Matson, F.R. (ed.) *Ceramics and Man*, 202–217. Viking Fund Publications in Anthropology 41, Methuen: London.

Middleton, A.P. (1987). Technological investigation of the coatings on some 'haematite-coated' pottery from southern England. *Archaeometry*, **29**:250–261.

Molera, J., García-Vallés, M., Pradell, T. and Vendrell-Saz, M. (1996). Hispano-Moresque pottery production of the Fourteenth-Century workshop of Tester Del Molí (Paterna, Spain). *Archaeometry*, **38**:67–80.

Moore, D.M. and Reynolds, R.C. (1997). *X-ray Diffraction and the Identification and Analysis of Clay Minerals*, (2nd edn). Oxford University Press: Oxford.

Peacock, D.P.S. (1977). Ceramics in Roman and Medieval archaeology. In Peacock, D.P.S. (ed.) *Pottery and Early Commerce: Characterisation and Trade in Roman and Later Ceramics*, 21–33. Academic Press: London.

Peacock, D.P.S. (1982). *Pottery in the Roman World: An Ethnoarchaeological Approach*. Longman: London.

Pollard, A.M. and Heron, C. (1996). *Archaeological Chemistry*. Royal Society of Chemistry: Cambridge.

Pool, C.A. and Santley, R.S. (1992). Middle Classic Pottery economics in the Tuxtla Mountains, Southern Veracruz, Mexico. In Bey, G.J. III and Pool, C.A. (eds) *Ceramic Production and Distribution: An Integrated Approach*, 205–234. Westview Press: Boulder.

Rhodes, D. (1973). *Clay and Glazes for the Potter*. Chilton Book Company: Radnor, Pennsylvania.

*Rice, P.M. (1987). *Pottery Analysis: A Sourcebook*. University of Chicago Press: Chicago.

Rye, O.S. (1976). Keeping your temper under control: materials and the manufacture of Papuan pottery. *Archaeology and Physical Anthropology of Oceania*, **11**:106–137.

*Rye, O. (1981). *Pottery Technology: Principles and Reconstruction*. Taraxacum: Washington DC.

Sackett, J.R. (1990). Style and ethnicity in archaeology: the case for isochrestism. In Conkey, M. and Hastorf, C. (eds) *The Uses of Style in Archaeology*, 32–43. Cambridge University Press: Cambridge.

Schiffer, M.B. and Skibo, J.M. (1987). Theory and experiment in the study of technological change. *Current Anthropology*, **28**:595–622.

Schiffer, M.B., Skibo, J.M., Boelke, T.C., Neupert, M.A. and Aronson, M. (1994). New perspectives in experimental archaeology: surface treatment and thermal response of the clay cooking pot. *American Antiquity*, **59**:197–217.

*Shepard, A.O. (1956). *Ceramics for the Archaeologist*. Publication 609, Carnegie Institution of Washington: Washington DC.

Shriner, C. and Dorais, M.J. (1999). A comparative electron microprobe study of Lerna III and IV ceramics and local clay-rich sediments. *Archaeometry*, **41**:25–49.

Sillar, B. (1997). Reputable pots and disreputable potters: individual and community choice in present-day pottery production and exchange in the Andes. In Cumberpatch, C.G. and Blinkhorn, P.W. (eds) *Not So Much a Pot, More a Way of Life: Current Approaches to Artefact Analysis in Archaeology*, 1–20. Monograph 84, Oxbow: Oxford.

Sillar, B. and Tite, M.S. (2000). The challenge of 'technological choices' for materials science approaches in archaeology. *Archaeometry*, **42**:2–20.

Skibo, J.M. (1992). *Pottery Function: a Use-Alteration Perspective*. Plenum Press: New York.

Steponaitis, V.P. (1984). Technological studies of prehistoric pottery from Alabama: physical properties and vessel function. In van der Leeuw, S.E. and Pritchard, A.C. (eds) *The Many Dimensions of Pottery: Ceramics in Archaeology and Anthropology*, 79–127. Cingula VII, University of Amsterdam: Amsterdam.

Stoltman, J.B. (1989). A Quantitative approach to the petrographic analysis of ceramic thin sections. *American Antiquity*, **54**:147–160.

van der Leeuw, S.E. (1993). Giving the potter a choice: conceptual aspects of pottery techniques,. In Lemonnier, P. (ed.) *Technological Choices: Transformation in Material Cultures Since the Neolithic*, 238–288. Routledge Kegan Paul: London.

van der Leeuw, S.E. (1994). Cognitive aspects of 'technique'. In Renfrew, C. and Zubrow, E.B.W. (eds) *The Ancient Mind: Elements of Cognitive Archaeology*, 135–142. Cambridge University Press: Cambridge.

Vandiver, P. (1988). The implications of variation in ceramic technology: the forming of Neolithic storage vessels in China and the Near East. *Archaeomaterials*, **2**:139–174.

Vandiver, P., Ellingson, W.A., Robinson, T.K., Lobick, J.J. and Séguin, F.H. (1991). New applications of X-radiographic imaging technologies for archaeological ceramics. *Archaeomaterials*, **5**:185–207.

Whitbread, I.K. (1995). *Greek Transport Amphorae: A Petrological and Archaeological Study*. Fitch Laboratory Occasional Paper 4, British School at Athens: Oxford.

Whitbread, I.K. (1996). Detection and interpretation of preferred orientation in ceramic thin sections. In Higgins, T., Main, P. and Lang, J. (eds) *Imaging the Past: Electronic Imaging and Computer Graphics in Museums and Archaeology*, 173–181. Occasional Paper 114, British Museum Press: London.

Woods, A.J. (1986). Form, fabric, and function: some observations on the cooking pot in antiquity. In Kingery, W.D. (ed.) *Technology and Style*, 157–172. Ceramics and Civilization 2, American Ceramic Society: Columbus, Ohio.

37

Lithic Exploitation and Use

M. EDMONDS

Department of Archaeology and Prehistory, University of Sheffield.

The study of lithics has a long history. Once classified as 'elf shot', 'eoliths' and 'thunderbolts', stone tools and waste have been many things, from curiosities to the first collectors to type fossils in early chronologies and markers of distinct cultural traditions. One of the few truly durable traces of prehistory, lithics were instrumental in establishing the antiquity of humanity and they remain crucial for research today. Though much has changed in the ways that we study stone, some issues have been remarkably persistent. Questions of function have always been prominent; informed by analogy and by experiments conducted with varying degrees of control. Equally well-established have been debates regarding the character and significance of artifact distributions, driven in no small part by early successes in identifying patterns of dispersal from known sources.

In the last few decades, these lines of enquiry have been complemented by other concerns. In particular, attention has focused upon the specifics of different technologies or ways of working stone. To some extent, these concerns have been stimulated by the growth of a more sophisticated conception of technology itself, less as hardware determined by an instrumental logic, and more as a social phenomenon. Interest has turned towards exploring how particular traditions of making and using stone tools were caught up in social reproduction (Dobres and Hoffman 1994, 1998, Lemmonier 1993, Schlanger and Sinclair 1990, Tilley 1999). These changes have been encouraged by the development of a sophisticated array of analytical approaches, and a greater concern with combining techniques in an integrated or contextual manner. This chapter follows a common trajectory for stone exploitation. Beginning with characterization and the identification of sources, it looks in turn at approaches to production, distribution and use. In each case, an emphasis is placed upon the analytical techniques at our disposal and the questions they may be used to address.

CHARACTERIZATION

From an early stage, the characterization of raw materials has been a central concern. A wide range of techniques are currently applied to determine the particular character of different stones (Kempe and Harvey 1983, Seiveking and Hart 1986). Some can be identified through direct macroscopic observation and this is often valuable in the initial sorting of assemblages. Things are not always as they seem, however, and it is common to place characterizations on a more detailed and reliable footing. Characterization studies work in different ways to determine the 'fingerprint' of a material by either determining its mineralogy and structure or its elemental composition.

Handbook of Archaeological Sciences. Edited by D.R. Brothwell and A.M. Pollard.

Characterization opens up a range of questions of archaeological interest. At the most basic level, it can help us to understand the mechanical properties of different materials, and their potential for working. The physical structure of different sedimentary, metamorphic and igneous materials conditions the particular ways in which they can be worked (Andrefsky 1998, Luedtke 1992). Some, such as gabbro, have a heterogeneous and coarse-grained structure. Others, such as slate, can be highly laminar. This makes them difficult to work except by grinding, pecking or sawing. Other materials display different properties. Homogenous and isotropic stones such as obsidian or flint have a microcrystalline or cryptocrystalline structure which allows them to be worked in a regular and controlled manner by percussion and pressure flaking (Crabtree 1972). Fundamental to this potential is the property of conchoidal fracture, involving the formation of a Hertzian cone at the point where force is applied to the surface of a suitable piece of material (Cotterell and Kaminga 1987).

Fracturing potentials vary from one material to another. Features such as bedding planes, fissures, voids, fossiliferous or other inclusions can all influence flaking properties. In determining composition and structure, characterization allows us to assess some of the choices made by people in the process of working, and the interplay between technical know-how and raw material potential (Pelegrin 1990). It also helps us to explore patterns of selection adopted by prehistoric communities able to choose from a range of different raw materials. Mechanical properties are by no means the only criteria in this process. Choices made at a variety of levels, from raw material selection to specific flaking techniques, are often conditioned by a wide range of factors. These include the location of sources in broader patterns of landscape occupation, and the historically specific values and associations ascribed to sources, techniques and their products (McBryde 1984, Petrequin and Petrequin 1993).

Petrography

One of the more established approaches, petrography is the characterization of stone in terms of its mineralogy and structure (Kempe and Harvey 1983). The technique involves removing a small piece either by sawing a section or drilling a core. Though the former has a long history, the latter is increasingly common as it has less impact on artifacts that we are reluctant to damage for

aesthetic or other reasons. The ends of a core can be used to plug the hole left by sampling.

Samples are mounted on glass slides and ground down to a thin section of c. 0.5 mm. At this scale, most materials are translucent and can be studied via microscopy. Where cores are used, it is common to cut the core longitudinally, using one half for a thin section and keeping the second for future analysis and/or reference. Using a combination of ordinary, plane polarized and cross polarized light, it is often possible to identify the specific minerals present in particular samples on the basis of size, shape and colour. Since mineralogy often varies according to geological formation, petrography can link products or groups of products with specific sources.

Petrography can characterize a range of raw materials, and has proved valuable in determining the distribution of tools, sculpture and building materials away from their geological sources (Olsen and Alsaker 1984). One of the most successful applications has been the implement petrology programme in Britain and Ireland (Clough and Cummins 1979, 1988, Cooney and Mandal 1998). Concentrating on prehistoric non-flint implements, the programme has characterized several thousand artifacts, among them Neolithic and Bronze Age axes, maceheads, battle axes and axe hammers. This has given a picture of the geographic scale of implement dispersal and the identification of particular locations or sources from which the stone for many of these items was obtained. This, in turn, has stimulated a keen interest in the interpretation of dispersal patterns and the more detailed scrutiny of stone sources themselves (see below). Whilst this technique has been successful on these materials, it is of limited value with others, such as flint.

Geochemical approaches

Often less destructive than petrography, geochemical characterization techniques determine the presence and relative proportions of different elements in particular artifacts or stone samples. As with petrography, where the composition of samples can be matched to specific geological formations, it is often possible to identify both sources and distributions. Stone is generally made up of elements that fall into three frequency ranges (Andrefsky 1998): major elements (2 per cent or more of the material); minor elements (between 2 per cent and 0.1 per cent), and trace elements (less than 0.1 per cent). Often the most useful elements occur only in a few parts per million. Geochemical studies focus on these trace elements as the basis for establishing provenance (see Chapter 41).

Optical Emission Spectroscopy (OES) is a long established technique, particularly in obsidian sourcing studies, but is not the most precise method (c. 20–30 per cent compared to better than 5 per cent in more modern techniques). It was largely displaced by Atomic Absorption Spectrometry (AAS) in the 1970s, which has itself been replaced by Inductively Coupled Plasma Emission Spectroscopy (ICP-OES). X-Ray Fluorescence (XRF) can be a non-destructive technique, although crushing and pelletizing overcomes any problems of surface alteration. XRF can be conducted using a portable machine (Thorpe *et al.* 1991), which gives greater flexibility when working in the field, although the elemental detection limits are significantly poorer. Electron Microprobe Analysis (EMPA) uses a fine beam of electrons to stimulate the emission of characteristic X-rays. The beam can be directed to different points on a sample, allowing the characterization of different phases and inclusions (Kempe and Templeman 1983). Neutron Activation Analysis (NAA) is a much-used technique in geological and archaeological trace element studies: although highly accurate, it is becoming less common because of problems in gaining access to a reactor, and the increased use of plasma techniques, especially indictively-coupled plasma mass spectrometry (ICP-MS) (see Pollard and Heron 1996:chapter 2).

Micropalaeontology

A rather different focus is taken in micropalaeontological approaches. Here the interest shifts from constituent elements to fossils, most notably foraminifera in materials like flint and chert. It is argued that consistent relationships can be identified between the presence and relative frequency of fossil species, and the source of flint and chert. Sampling is destructive, involving either cutting a thin section or dissolving the sample in acid. In the former, the focus is a range of silica, calcite and organic based microfossils. In the latter, surviving organic based microfossils are the primary concern. Though archaeological interest has lagged behind that of geologists, work over the last 20 years suggests considerable potential for the technique, particularly when combined with others (Masson 1984, Mauger 1984, Brooks 1989).

Sources of confusion

The techniques outlined above are crucial for the continued development of many areas of archaeological and geological research. However, our determinations are seldom as distinct and reliable as we sometimes suppose. For example, processes such as glaciation have moved many materials into secondary contexts which were themselves used as sources in prehistory. Examples include flint found in the gravels of many river valleys and in boulder clay deposits, or volcanic rock from specific sources that can be found more widely as erratics in glacial till. Archaeological evidence at many primary geological formations demonstrates that these were exploited as sources in prehistory. In certain cases, however, it is likely that the use of 'derived' material from secondary contexts has also contributed dots to some of our distribution maps. The impact of this variability needs to be considered when interpreting the frequency and distance of artifacts from specific sources, whether these be stone maceheads or the bluestones of Stonehenge (Cunliffe and Renfrew 1997).

There can also be quite basic problems with the naming of certain materials (Andrefsky 1998:57). Some use terms like flint and chert interchangeably. Others see the former as a derivative of the latter. The principal dividing line in the use of these terms is geographic (Luedtke 1992). In New World studies, it is more common to see flint identified as a specific form of chert. By contrast, research in Britain has generally maintained a more marked distinction between the two. Material derived directly or indirectly from Cretaceous chalk deposits is usually referred to as flint, while stone from beds within limestones and shales goes by the name of chert. Occasionally, the term chert is used to indicate that material is relatively coarse grained. This is problematic however, as cherts from within limestone and shale deposits can vary considerably, from fine to coarse grained.

There are other problems too, though some encourage us to ask different questions of our evidence. Despite some success, materials such as flint are difficult to characterize (Aspinall and Feather 1972, Craddock *et al.* 1983). In other cases, such as some of the fine grained volcanics used for axe-making in the Neolithic, there can be considerable variation in the structure and trace element composition of stone from within what we recognize as a particular source. In such cases, the more precise characterization of variability in trace element composition could be integrated with studies of techniques and products. This may be particularly important where sources were used over protracted periods of time, and/or their products were distributed over wide areas. The integration of different techniques may allow us to link specific areas or ways of working within a source to particular clusters or phases within broader distributions.

These sources of variation need to be remembered and accounted for in the design of sampling and analysis programmes, not just to avoid confusion, but to open up new lines of enquiry. Although it may still be difficult to source flint artifacts, we could use trace element analyses to look at the intra- and inter-regional structure of assemblages. Here, the questions shift from tying objects to their specific geological sources, towards assessing the range of sources that are represented in specific areas at particular times (see similar arguments in Chapter 41). As long as flint remains difficult to source with a high degree of confidence, such analyses may be difficult to take very far. But where characterization is possible, we can begin to explore patterns of interaction and change over time in the regional structure of assemblages.

Above all, we should remember that our classifications work in very different ways to those that people recognized in the past. Where we see a vein of workable quartz, others may have seen the bones, blood or semen of an ancestral being. Where we see a source comprising one type of stone, others may have recognized many, using practical and social criteria in their determinations (Burton 1984, Taçon 1991). There may be much that we cannot know. But research needs to be sensitive to this difference, and to the possibility that social relations and perceptions shaped the variability that we encounter in raw material selection and working traditions.

PROCUREMENT AND PRODUCTION

Though the identification of certain sites goes back considerably further, characterization studies over the past 50 years or so have added an extraordinary number of sources to our inventories. This has led to renewed interest in mines, quarries and other extraction sites, as places worthy of study in their own right, and as sources of data to set against the evidence of dispersal patterns.

At a basic level, the nature of the raw material at a particular source influences the range of analyses that are likely to be applied. Where rock was pecked, ground, polished or sawn into shape, attention will often focus on the identification of extraction areas,

on the distribution of tools used in stoneworking and on pieces discarded during the production process. Sites of this nature may have little in the way of waste assemblages that allow the detailed study of reduction sequences – often all that remains are hammers and dust. Where stone was worked by flaking, the potential for more detailed technological analysis is far greater. As well as rejects, or objects broken during manufacture, there may be large volumes of flakes, chips, chunks and spalls generated during both extraction and flaking. In other words, there is a lot more evidence and a far greater potential for exploring specific techniques.

The study of sources can be undertaken with a range of questions in mind. Beyond chronology, we can ask what was being made at particular sites, or at different locations within a source. We can also explore how working was organized, highlighting questions of scale, duration and the arrangement of people (Cleghorn 1986, Ericson and Purdy 1984, Seiveking and Newcomer 1987). And where sources have long histories, we inevitably want to know how, and in what ways, exploitation may have changed over time. Work on these issues has prompted an increasing concern with the detailed description of extractive and stoneworking techniques, and with the intimate and often subtle choices made in following particular reduction sequences. This concern is not entirely new. Some of the earliest studies of sources reflect a sophisticated grasp of the analytical potential of waste material that matches more recent work (Warren 1922).

Along with the refitting of artifacts, experimental stoneworking has prompted a series of important developments in technological research (Flenniken 1984). Under laboratory conditions, experiments have generated valuable, if basic, information on the mechanics of flaking (Cotterell and Kaminga 1987). To these can be added experiments that have dramatically increased our ability to 'read' waste assemblages in technological terms. Replication has provided data on the character of different reduction sequences, and on the nature, frequency and spatial patterning of classes of waste generated during specific forms of stoneworking (Amick and Maudlin 1989, Newcomer and Seiveking 1980, Inizan et al. 1992). These insights shed light on the spatial and temporal variability of working; prerequisites for exploring how production was organized in practical and social terms. Work on hand axe manufacture led Mark Newcomer to identify the debitage signatures of distinct forms of flaking engaged at various points in the process (Newcomer 1971). Similar work on material from the mines at

Grimes Graves in Norfolk, provided the basis for determining specific forms of working as well as different classes of waste identifiable in archaeological assemblages through multivariate analysis (Burton 1980).

Technological analyses at stone sources have been used to address a variety of problems. On Melos, a major source of obsidian in the Aegean, Robin Torrence used the quantitative analysis of cores and waste, and of error rates, to explore levels of standardization and specialization in blade core production (Torrence 1986). Crucial to her work was the idea that different levels of specialization and standardization in both artifacts and ways of working might be equated with different forms of exchange and with specific levels of social complexity. In south-east Ireland, work at a rhyolite source related the organization of working to the broader regimes of settlement and movement followed by prehistoric communities. Here, the range of artifacts at the source and the extent to which they had been worked, were compared with evidence collected from field survey elsewhere in the region (Zvelebil *et al.* 1987, 1992). Differences in stoneworking between different places were used in models of how procurement was organized within broader mobility regimes (see also Parry and Kelly 1987, Torrence 1989). Around Great Langdale in Cumbria, the detailed characterization of waste identified significant changes in the spatial and technical organization of Neolithic axe making (Bradley and Edmonds 1993). Even though the source was used almost exclusively for the production of axes (classified as Group VI by the implement petrology programme), ways of working changed. In this case, these changes were understood as a function of shifts in the perception and use of axes, both as practical tools, and as tokens of identity and value.

Similar work in other settings has addressed rather different concerns. In Palaeolithic research, the detailed assessment of working practices has opened up debate concerning the cognitive abilities of hominids and the persistence of technical traditions (Schlanger 1996). It has also been used to differentiate forms of technical know-how, shifting attention towards learning, skill and the social relations of working (Pigeot 1990). Much of this work has been inspired by the concept of the '*chaîne opératoire*' and by a view of techniques as complex social practices (Lemmonier 1993). Central to this is the recognition that the character and significance of techniques varies according to context. For example, we cannot assume *a priori* that specialization in working can necessarily be equated with the emergence of particular levels or forms of social complexity.

This may hold in certain cases, but in others, differentiation in skill, or in the range of techniques learnt and engaged by people, may arise for very different reasons (Edmonds 1990, Pigeot 1990). Inevitably, the questions that we ask of sources and techniques will themselves have to vary according to context.

DISTRIBUTION, MOBILITY AND EXCHANGE

In addition to the identification of sources, characterization studies have played a major role in recognizing broad patterns of artifact distribution. Again, the level of success achieved in this field tends to vary as a function of the distinctiveness of raw materials. Long established, our ability to recognize these patterns has underwritten research on a wide range of archaeological issues.

Two themes have dominated the interpretation of artifact dispersal patterns: mobility and exchange. For the most part, prehistorians working with particular distributions have tended to explain patterns as a consequence of the movement of artifacts and materials either with or between people. The choice of explanation has often varied according to period, and to assumptions about the nature and organization of past societies. In Mesolithic studies, for example, it is common to find an emphasis on the movement of people, with dispersal patterns related to the seasonal rounds followed by communities of gatherers and hunters. By contrast, research on the Neolithic and Bronze Age often sees a more marked concern with the circulation of goods in varied exchange spheres (Bradley 1984). This common opposition is to some extent a product of distinct traditions of enquiry and of different research priorities. We must be careful however, to avoid setting that opposition in stone. Complex cycles of exchange may operate amongst gathererhunters, and movement is still an important theme for communities reliant on domesticates. Whatever the context, it is important to explore how the two are articulated.

Distribution studies have changed a great deal. A common criticism of some early work was that it remained relatively superficial – concerning itself with putting 'dots on maps' and little more (see Chapter 53). This may apply in certain cases but is not entirely accurate. Our perspectives have changed, and this has led us to ask new questions of our evidence. In the first few decades of the twentieth century, a common response to extensive distributions was to recognize the signature of the large scale movement or migration of distinct cultures. Where this could not be postulated, the movement of artifacts and materials tended to be explained in terms of relatively general notions of trade (but see Clark 1965 for an early interest in gift exchange). Such approaches came in for criticism in Anglo-American and Scandinavian archaeology in the 1960s and 1970s, and research shifted towards establishing more general links between patterns and processes.

In mobility studies, this prompted the search for regularities in the organization of residence, movement and tool use, and for the signatures that these might leave in the archaeological record (Bamforth 1986, Kelly 1995, Torrence 1989). Research also explored how the development of sedentism – however defined – might impact upon traditions of procurement and production (Andrefsky 1998). In work on exchange, these developments encouraged a concern with linking specific dispersal patterns to particular exchange processes, and a related desire to tie forms of circulation to different levels of social complexity. Research based on these premises made increasing use of formal, mathematical approaches to distribution, in an attempt to relate different patterns of fall-off to distinct exchange mechanisms. Refined over more than a decade, formal models were developed for a spectrum of exchange relations; from balanced to negative reciprocity, and from down-the-line trade to redistribution and prestige goods (Earle and Ericson 1977, Ericson and Earle 1982).

Much of this work has been valuable, prompting us to recognize the complexity of the problems we face in interpretation. However, we have had to limit at least some of our early ambitions. There are few powerful cross-cultural correlations between dispersal patterns and either mobility regimes or exchange processes. The same pattern can result from a variety of processes and vice versa. We have also come to question the idea that particular types of exchange can be correlated exclusively with particular levels of social complexity. Criticism has also stressed the generality of many accounts, and this has gone hand in hand with a shift of theoretical focus. Although there remains a considerable diversity in approaches, recent work has seen an increased concern with the articulation of different forms of exchange in social reproduction, and with the wider variety of values given to objects and materials (Appadurai 1985, Edmonds 1995). Approaches to mobility have also continued to develop. Questions of sedentism and the broad models of settlement remain on many agendas. Now though, these issues are complemented by a more historical concern with how

particular traditions of routine landscape use were themselves caught up in social reproduction (Ingold 1993, Whittle 1997, Pollard 1999).

A consequence of these developments has been that it is nowadays more common to place distributions in some form of context. Attention is now routinely paid to the character and treatment of material in different settings away from its source as well as to calculations of distance. When interrogating distributions or 'fall-off curves', we can ask a range of questions of our evidence. Did stone move as raw material or as finished artifacts? Were a range of artifacts in circulation from a particular source, or only restricted forms? What can we say about the manner of treatment; about curation, or the settings in which objects were circulated, deposited or discarded? (Some of these issues are considered further in Chapter 57.) And beyond everything else, what lengths of time were involved in the development of our patterns? Difficulties with sourcing will sometimes make it difficult to furnish answers. But these and other questions provide at least part of the basis for exploring both the circulation of goods and traditions of landscape occupation in the past. Once again, the integration of characterization studies with detailed technological analysis is crucial. Establishing how the working of stone was organized at a site, landscape or regional scale is a prerequisite for asking about the practices that shaped its dispersal.

USE WEAR STUDIES

Alongside chronology, an interest in the practical function of tools has perhaps the longest history in lithic studies. Informed since the nineteenth century by ethnographic analogy, studies of function have also made a persistent use of observations of wear sustained on stone artifacts during use (Evans 1872).

Use wear analysis takes a range of forms. A distinction can be made between approaches based on low and high powered microscopy, and those which characterize residues on tool surfaces. The initial development of microwear research is often attributed to the work of the Semenov laboratory in the first half of the twentieth century (Semenov 1964). Though this was by no means the first attempt to link the uses of tools to wear traces, Semenov's research laid the foundations for work based on systematic experiment and microscopy (Keeley 1980, Tringham et al. 1974). Fundamental to all of this pioneering work was the assumption of a consistent relationship between the ways in which tools were used, the materials to which they were applied, and the wear traces they sustained. Actions could be differentiated, as could the processing of materials as diverse as wood, bone, flesh, hide and plants.

Identification of these different uses is dependent upon characterizing specific traces. Using low power microscopy, at magnifications of less than ×100, experiments suggest that we can often determine the direction and sometimes the intensity of particular actions such as slicing, piercing or scraping (Hayden 1979, Odell and Odell-Vereecken 1980). It is also possible to distinguish between use on soft or hard materials. The situation can become confusing where tools are used in a variety of ways and on a range of materials. However, low power use wear studies are reliable, and less time-consuming than their high powered counterparts. This increases the range of material that can be sampled and the scale of the issues that can be addressed.

Low powered approaches place a particular emphasis on patterns of edge damage, using the character, extent and direction of scars and scratches (or 'macrowear') as indicators of use. These also have their part to play in more high powered (up to ×500) approaches, though here the range of attributes studied is wider and rather more contentious. A common focus at this level is the characterization of polishes and striations, formed on the edges of tools during use (Vaughan 1985). Use of the scanning electron microscope and microprobe has also led to the identification of distinctive residues such as plant phytoliths and perhaps even blood (Anderson 1980, Fullagar 1988, Loy 1983; see Chapter 26). Here again, it is argued that there are consistent relationships between forms of use and the appearance, intensity and extent of polishes created where the immediate surface of a tool forms a silica gel (Keeley 1980, Moss 1983).

A measure of debate still surrounds the identification of particular 'microwear' traces at these scales of magnification. Though some appear relatively confident in the assignment of tasks to particular traces, others are more cautious, or even critical (Grace 1989, Hurcombe 1988, Juel-Jensen 1988). There is also confusion about the genesis of polishes themselves, as well as their vulnerability in the face of various forms of post-depositional attrition (Plisson and Mauger 1988). Some suggest that polishes form as a result of the friction generated when a tool is used, largely as a function of abrasion. Others see polish formation as a chemical, rather than mechanical process (Anderson 1980), citing the incorporation of opaline plant residues to support their argument. This debate has yet to be

fully resolved, though the balance of evidence seems to support the latter view (Van Gijn 1989).

Despite these uncertainties, use wear analysis at a variety of scales remains an important component of our analytical repertoire. After all, the fact that polishes are not absolutely determined and completely understood does not really set use wear studies apart from much other research in archaeology! Problems aside, what is important in the final analysis are the archaeological questions that are asked of sampled assemblages. Many studies have demonstrated a capacity to catch some of the tasks undertaken in particular settings (Donahue 1994, Juel-Jensen 1988). Others have explored how these tasks vary within and between sites, and how use relates to the morphology/typology of tools themselves (Beyries 1987). Such work opens up a range of issues about the spatial organization of action and the classification of artifacts that lie at the heart of current debate (e.g., Hurcombe 1994, Van Gijn 1989). It can also highlight biases in research. It has been use wear research that has led us to place as much attention on apparently unmodified flakes as upon retouched tools (Gero 1989). This shift has implications not only for the range of tasks that can be traced, but also for our grasp of the ways those tasks may have been perceived in terms of particular divisions of labour.

LITHICS IN CONTEXT

If there is a common thread to be traced through this discussion, it is that the successful application of any technique is as much (if not more) a function of the questions that are asked as a product of reliability or accuracy in description. Both are crucial. In determining our questions, we have to ask about the limits and potentials of particular techniques. But we are also drawn into broader debates about the way that technology and social life are bound up with each other. In the past, as in the present, that relationship was both complex and historical. That is why we cannot assume that understanding will necessarily flow in some straightforward and simple way from the gradual accumulation of descriptions or from the application of what we call common sense.

Other issues have also been stressed, among them questions of context and scale. Context here is taken to mean three things: the empirical record with which we work, contemporary debate, and the past social practices in which the materials we study were once engaged. Things were different, and if we want to move beyond description, we have to acknowledge all three. Scale is also crucial, whether we are studying the variable nature of reduction strategies across a region, the character of working around a dwelling or the uses of different edges on tools. Over 20 years ago, it was suggested that in lithic studies, as in many areas of research, we were in danger of losing our sense of scale; studying twigs at the expense of branches, trees and forests (Cross 1982). Much of the work referenced here suggests that this problem is being tackled through the integration of analyses. There is, however, some way still to go.

REFERENCES

*Recommended for further reading

Amick, D. and Maudlin, R. (1989). *Experiments in Lithic Technology*. BAR International Series 528, British Archaeological Reports: Oxford.

Anderson, P. (1980). A testimony of prehistoric tasks: diagnostic residues on stone tool working edges. *World Archaeology*, **12**:181–194.

*Andrefsky, W. (1998). *Lithics*. Cambridge University Press: Cambridge.

Appadurai, A. (ed.) (1985). *The Social Life of Things*. Cambridge University Press: Cambridge.

Aspinall, A. and Feather, S.W. (1972). Neutron activation analysis of prehistoric flint mine products. *Archaeometry*, **14**:41–53.

Bamforth, D. (1986). Technological efficiency and tool curation. *American Antiquity*, **51**:38–50.

Beyries, S. (1987). *Variabilité de l'Industrie Lithique au Moustérien*. BAR International Series 328, British Archaeological Reports: Oxford.

Bradley, R. (1984). *The Social Foundations of Prehistoric Britain*. Longmans: London.

Bradley, R. and Edmonds, M. (1993). *Interpreting the Axe Trade*. Cambridge University Press: Cambridge.

Brooks, I. (1989). Debugging the system: the characterization of flint by micropalaeontology. In Brooks, I. and Phillips, P. (eds) *Breaking the Stony Silence*, 53–72. BAR 213, British Archaeological Reports: Oxford.

Burton, J. (1980). Making sense of waste flakes. *Journal of Archaeological Science*, **7**:131–148.

Burton, J. (1984). Quarrying in a tribal society. *World Archaeology*, **16**:234–247.

Clark, J.G.D. (1965). Traffic in stone axe and adze blades. *Economic History Review*, **18**:1–28.

Cleghorn, P. (1986). Organisational structure at the Mauna Kea Adze quarry complex, Hawaii. *Journal of Archaeological Science*, **13**:375–387.

*Clough, T. and Cummins, W. (eds) (1979). *Stone Axe Studies*. Research Report 23, Council for British Archaeology: London.

*Clough, T. and Cummins, W. (eds) (1988). *Stone Axe Studies 2*. Research Report 67, Council for British Archaeology: London.

*Cooney, G. and Mandal, S. (1998). *The Irish Stone Axe Project*. Wordwell: Bray.

Cotterell, B. and Kamminga, J. (1987). The formation of flakes. *American Antiquity*, **52**:675–708.

Crabtree, D.E. (1972). *An Introduction to Flintworking*. Occasional Paper 28, Idaho State Museum: Pocatello.

Craddock, P., Cowell, M., Leese, M. and Hughes, M. (1983). The trace element composition of polished flint axes as indicator of sources. *Archaeometry*, **25**:135–163.

Cross, J. (1982). Twigs, branches, trees and forests: problems of scale in lithic analysis. In Moore, J. and Keene, A. (eds) *Archaeological Hammers and Theories*, 87–106. Academic Press: London.

Cunliffe, B.W. and Renfrew, A.C. (eds) (1997). *Science and Stonehenge*. Proceedings of the British Academy 92, Oxford University Press: Oxford.

Dobres, M.A. and Hoffman, C. (1994). Social agency and the dynamics of prehistoric technology. *Journal of Archaeological Method and Theory*, **1**:211–258.

Dobres, M.A. and Hoffman, C. (1998). *Making Culture. Essays on Technological Practice, Politics and World Views*. Cambridge University Press: Cambridge.

Donahue, R. (1994). The current state of lithic microwear research. In Ashton, N. and David, A. (eds) *Stories in Stone*, 156–168. British Museum Press: London.

Earle, T.K. and Ericson, J.E. (1977). *Exchange Systems in Prehistory*. Academic Press: London.

Edmonds, M. (1990). Description, understanding and the *chaîne opératoire*. In Schlanger, N. and Sinclair, A. (eds) *Technology in the Humanities*. Archaeological Review from Cambridge **9.1**, 55–70.

*Edmonds, M. (1995). *Stone Tools and Society*. Batsford: London.

Ericson, J. and Earle, T. (1982). *Contexts for Prehistoric Exchange*. Academic Press: London.

Ericson, J. and Purdy, B. (1984). *Prehistoric Quarries and Lithic Production*. Cambridge University Press: Cambridge.

Evans, J. (1872). *The Ancient Stone Implements, Weapons and Ornaments of Great Britain*. Longmans, Green, Reader and Dyer: London.

Flenniken, J.J. (1984). The past, present and future of flint knapping. *Annual Review of Anthropology*, **13**:187–203.

Fullagar, R. (1988). Recent developments in Australian use wear and residue studies. In Beyries, S. (ed.) *Industries Lithiques: Tracèologie et Technologie*, 133–146. BAR International Series 411, British Archaeological Reports: Oxford.

Gero, J. (1989). Genderlithics. In Conkey, M. and Hastorff, C. (eds) *Engendering Archaeology*, 163–193. Blackwells: Oxford.

Grace, R. (1989). *Interpreting the Function of Stone Tools. The Quantification and Computerisation of Microwear Analysis*. BAR International Series 474, British Archaeological Reports: Oxford.

Hayden, B. (1979). *Lithic Use Wear Analysis*. Academic Press: New York.

Hurcombe, L. (1988). Some criticisms and suggestions in response to Newcomer *et al.* (1986). *Journal of Archaeological Science*, **15**:1–10.

Hurcombe, L. (1994). From functional interpretation to cultural choices in tool use: The behaviour-function link. In Ashton, N. and David, A. (eds) *Stories in Stone*, 145–155. British Museum Press: London.

Ingold, T. (1993). The temporality of landscape. *World Archaeology*, **25**:152–174.

Inizan, M.-L., Roche, H. and Tixier, J. (1992). *Technology of Knapped Stone*. Préhistoire de la Pierre Taillée 3, C.R.E.P.: Meudon.

Juel-Jensen, H. (1988). Functional analysis of stone tools – a review. *Journal of World Prehistory*, **2**:53–88.

Keeley, L. (1980). *The Experimental Determination of Stone Tool Uses*. Chicago University Press: Chicago.

Kelly, R. (1995). *The Foraging Spectrum*. Smithsonian Institution Press: Washington DC.

Kempe, D. and Harvey, A. (eds) (1983). *The Petrology of Archaeological Artefacts*. Clarendon Press: Oxford.

Kempe, D. and Templeman, J.A. (1983). Techniques. In Kempe, D. and Harvey, A. (eds) *The Petrology of Archaeological Artefacts*, 26–53. Clarendon Press: Oxford.

Lemmonier, P. (1993). *Technological Choices*. Routledge: London.

Loy, T. (1983). Prehistoric blood residues: detection on tool surfaces and identification of species of origin. *Science*, **220**:1269–1271.

*Luedtke, B. (1992). *An Archaeologist's Guide to Flint and Chert*. UCLA Archaeological Research Tools 7, University of Los Angeles: California.

Masson, A. (1984). Analyse petrographique des silex utilisés par les néolithiques de L'Ile de Corrège a Leucate. In Guilaine, J., Freises, A. and Montjardin, R. (eds) *Leucate-Correge: Habitat Noye du Neolithique Cardial*, 59–71. Musee Paul Valery: Toulouse.

Mauger, M. (1984). L'apport des microfossiles dans l'identification des silex. Example du Magdalénien de L'Ile de france. *Bulletin de la Societé de Préhistorique Française*, **81**:216–220.

McBryde, I. (1984). Kulin greenstone quarries: the social contexts of production and distribution for the Mount William site. *World Archaeology*, **16**:267–285.

Moss, E. (1983). *The Functional Analysis of Flint Implements*. BAR International Series 177, British Archaeological Reports: Oxford.

Newcomer, M. (1971). Some quantitative experiments in hand axe manufacture. *World Archaeology*, **3**:85–94.

Newcomer, M. and Seiveking, G. de G. (1980). Experimental flake scatter patterns, a new interpretative technique. *Journal of Field Archaeology*, **7**:335–352.

Odell, G. and Odell-Vereecken, F. (1980). Verifying the reliability of lithic usewear assessments by 'blind tests': the low power approach. *Journal of Field Archaeology*, **7**:87–120.

Olsen, A. and Alsaker, S. (1984). Greenstone and diabase utilisation in the stone age of western Norway: technological and socio-cultural aspects of axe and adze production and distribution. *Norwegian Archaeological Review*, **17**:71–103.

Parry, W. and Kelly, J. (1987). Expedient core technology and sedentism. In Johnson, J. and Morrow, C. (eds) *The Organisation of Core Technology*, 285–304. Westview Press: Boulder, Colorado.

Pelegrin, J. (1990). Prehistoric lithic technology: some aspects of research. In Schlanger, N. and Sinclair, A. (eds) *Technology in the Humanities*. Archaeological Review from Cambridge **9.1**:116–125.

Petrequin, P. and Petrequin, A. (1993). *Écologie d'un Outil: la Hache de Pierre en Irian Jaya (Indonesie)*. Monograph du CRA 12, CNRS: Paris.

Pigeot, N. (1990). Technical and social actors: flintknapping specialists at Magdalenian Etiolles. In Schlanger, N. and Sinclair, A. (eds) *Technology in the Humanities*. Archaeological Review from Cambridge **9.1**, 126–141.

Plisson, H. and Mauger, M. (1988). Chemical and mechanical alteration of microwear polishes: an experimental approach. *Helinium*, **28**:3–16.

Pollard, A.M. and Heron, C. (1996). *Archaeological Chemistry*. Royal Society of Chemistry: Cambridge.

Pollard, J. (1999). These places have their moments. Occupation practices in the British Neolithic. In Bruck, J. and Goodman, M. (eds) *Making Places in the Prehistoric World: Themes in Settlement Archaeology*, 76–93. Longmans: London.

Schlanger, N. (1996). Understanding Levallois: lithic technology and cognitive archaeology. *Cambridge Archaeological Journal*, **6**:231–254.

Schlanger, N. and Sinclair, A. (eds) (1990). *Technology in the Humanities*. Archaeological Review from Cambridge, **9.1**.

Seiveking, G. and Hart, M.B. (1986). *The Scientific Study of Flint and Chert*. Cambridge University Press: Cambridge.

Seiveking, G. and Newcomer, M. (1987). *The Human Uses of Flint and Chert*. Cambridge University Press: Cambridge.

Semenov, S. (1964). *Prehistoric Technology*. Cory, Adams and Mackay: London.

Taçon, P. (1991). The power of stone: symbolic aspects of stone use and tool development in western Arnhem Land, Australia. *Antiquity*, **65**:192–207.

Thorpe, R.S., Williams-Thorpe, O., Jenkins, D.G. and Watson, J.S. (1991). The geological sources and transport of the Bluestones of Stonehenge, Wiltshire, UK. *Proceedings of the Prehistoric Society*, **57**:103–157.

Tilley, C. (1999). *Metaphor and Material Culture*. Blackwell: Oxford.

Torrence, R. (1986). *The Production and Exchange of Stone Tools*. Cambridge University Press: Cambridge.

Torrence, R. (1989). *Time, Energy and Stone Tools*. Cambridge University Press: Cambridge.

Tringham, R., Cooper, G., Odell, G., Voytek, R. and Whitman, A. (1974). Experimentation in the formation of edge damage: a new approach to lithic analysis. *Journal of Field Archaeology*, **1**:171–196.

Van Gijn, A.L. (1989). *The Wear and Tear of Flint*. Annalecta Praehistoria Leidensia 22, University of Leiden: Leiden.

Vaughan, P. (1985). *Usewear Analysis of Flaked Stone Tools*. University of Arizona Press: Tucson.

Warren, S.H. (1922). The Neolithic stone axes of Graig Lwyd, Penmaenmawr. *Archaeologia Cambrensis*, **77**:1–35.

Whittle, A.W.R. (1997). Moving on and moving around: Neolithic settlement mobility. In Topping, P. (ed.) *Neolithic Landscapes*, 15–22. Neolithic Studies Group Seminar Papers 2, Oxbow: Oxford.

Zvelebil, M., Moore, J.A., Green, S.W. and Henson, D. (1987). Regional survey and analysis of lithic scatters: a case study from southeast Ireland. In Rowley-Conwy, P., Zvelebil, M. and Blankholm, H.P. (eds) *Mesolithic Northwest Europe: Recent Trends*, 9–32. University of Sheffield: Sheffield.

Zvelebil, M., Green, S.W. and Macklin, M. (1992). Archaeological landscapes, lithic scatters and human behaviour. In Rossignol, J. and Wandsnider, L. (eds) *Space, Time and Archaeological Landscapes*, 193–226. Plenum: New York.

38

Glass and Glazes

J. HENDERSON

Department of Archaeology, University of Nottingham.

Glasses and glazes are amorphous solids; they are essentially the same but are distinguished by the functions that they perform. A solid is a rigid material and does not flow when it is subjected to moderate forces. Glass lacks the long-range order which characterizes crystalline materials like metals and there is no regularity in the arrangement of its molecular constituents on a scale larger than a few times the size of these groups (Doremus 1994:1). This means that its constituents (largely oxides) are only arranged in a regular way in small volumes. Although Jones (1956:1) defines glass as 'an inorganic product of fusion which has been cooled to a rigid condition without crystallisation', Doremus (1994:1) notes that glasses can be prepared without cooling from the liquid state. Nevertheless ancient glasses all fall into the definition proposed by Jones. Glass is also a super-cooled liquid. This means that when soda-lime-silica glass cools from temperatures above 1100°C to a temperature at which potential changes could occur (the *transition temperature*, T_g), and at which an abrupt change of volume occurs, the rate of cooling must be controlled carefully. If the melt cools too slowly a crystalline silicate can be produced; by cooling at an appropriate rate this can be avoided, and a true glass which contains no crystals is formed.

The chemical constituents in the glass, the oxides, are arranged in an open network; in a soda-lime-silica glass, the glass used for the longest period in the ancient world, the oxides in the network are sodium oxide (Na_2O), calcium oxide (CaO) and silica (SiO_2). In structural terms glasses can be defined by the relationships between network-formers (e.g., Si^{4+}) and network-modifiers (e.g., Na^+). Examples of network stabilizers, which improve the durability of the glass, include Mg^{2+} and Ca^{2+}. There is a wide range of combinations of these network sub-units which produce a correspondingly wide range of compositions

RITUAL AND SOCIO-CULTURAL APPROACHES

We only have hints as to how glass production was organized before the Medieval period. One source of information are the cuneiform texts which derived from the palace of Asurbanipal, King of Assyria (664–627 BC) at Kuyunjik (Nineveh), Mesopotamia. These are thought to describe much earlier procedures as well as those carried out in the seventh century BC (Oppenheim *et al.* 1970:28). The texts include a description of the ritual aspects of glass production including a reverence for the material (Peltenburg 1971), when solids are transformed into a glowing liquid and, on cooling, back to a translucent 'solid'. Clearly translations can vary according to the translator. However, there are several ritual characteristics which shed

Handbook of Archaeological Sciences. Edited by D.R. Brothwell and A.M. Pollard.

fascinating light on the procedures at a time when Mesopotamia saw a fluorescence of glass vessel production. The time and place of glass-making was considered to be critical to its success (Oppenheim *et al.* 1970:32): 'When you set up the foundation of a kiln to (make) glass, you (first) search in a favourable month for a propitious day, and (then only) you set up the foundation of the kiln.'

'Kubu' images were set up in the building in which the glass furnace was constructed – no outsider or stranger should thereafter enter the building and no unclean person should pass in front of the images. Regular libation offerings were made before the kubu images and a sheep was sacrificed before the images on the day the glass was made. Clearly, evidence for this aspect of glass production would normally be absent from excavated glass-working and glass-making sites, though as Oppenheim *et al.* (1970:33) have pointed out, these procedures were an accepted practice in Mesopotamia. It is nevertheless an interesting reflection of the awareness that the glassmakers must have had of the limitations of their skills and technological knowledge.

In total contrast to these textual references, other, much later, historical evidence can be drawn on to highlight features of the social and practical organization of glass production. In the Medieval and into the post-Medieval periods information about the social status of glass makers and the organization of glass houses is available (Polak 1997). In a glass house there tended to be a Master of the glass house who generally *owned* the secret of how to make glass and sometimes owned the glasshouse. He was responsible for dividing his team of men and positioning them around the glass furnace, for keeping the fuel supply going, for providing clay for the glass pots (crucibles), 'stone' for the furnace and potash (alkali), and for ensuring a supply of other materials. The master was picked from the glassworkers and, by the seventeenth century generally lived in his own house, while the glass blowers rented their accommodation. In addition to the master, the glasshouse was ranked into craftsmen (such as the glass blowers) and below them students. In addition, a range of *specialists* were involved in keeping the glasshouse going. Separate specialists (many of whom were peripatetic) constructed the glass pots and the furnaces, smiths were used to make the tools used and keep them in good condition, carpenters were used for making the moulds, others (only) provided the fuel, and stoked the furnace. The Master was responsible for co-ordinating these specialists; the glass makers were often in the minority. This arrangement is similar to the organization of a lot

of other crafts, based on the Medieval guild system where a series of specialists serviced the production processes. Nevertheless, in early fourteenth century Florence, for example, glass blowers were not numerous enough to form a guild. They eventually joined with the metal workers and then became a member of the all-encompassing association of craftsmen in arts and medicine. However, by 1594 in Barcelona, for example, glass craftsmen had their own guild. In the Medieval period there was also a division amongst glass vessel makers. In thirteenth century Venice the *violorio* (bottle maker) actually made both bottles and beakers; by the early fourteenth century in Florence there was a further degree of specialization: bottle and beaker makers had become separate specialists.

Much of this historical information is especially relevant to Medieval spheres of production and is often associated with an urban society. However, given that glass production (especially glass making from raw materials and glass blowing) in any period involves the same principles, co-operation between the artisans would (obviously) have been involved. For earlier periods, we are not, however, able to refer to the historical evidence of rules such as the *Ordnung* for glassmakers in the Spessart Forest dated 1406 or the *Bundesbrief* for glass makers in Hesse dated 1537, with a later version dated 1559.

THE CHEMICAL COMPOSITIONS OF ANCIENT GLASSES

Turner (1956) and Caley (1962) assembled some of the early chemical analyses of glass, and as early as 1957 Forbes noted some chronological changes in the use of glass raw materials. It was not until the early 1960s when Sayre and Smith (1961) first published neutron activation analyses of groups of glasses that definable compositional groupings were identified, which could be correlated to both geographical and chronological criteria. These compositional types were based on the occurrence of five oxides: manganese, antimony, lead, magnesium and potassium. The first two were used in a discriminatory way in their role as decolourants, lead oxide as a major component, magnesia as an impurity in the alkalis used, and potassium as either an impurity in the principal alkali or as the principal alkali itself.

The glass types which Sayre and Smith defined are found at different times:

(i) high magnesia soda-lime glasses between *c.* 1500 and 800 BC,

(ii) low magnesia soda-lime glasses between *c.* 800 BC and AD 1000,

(iii) high antimony soda-lime glasses between *c.* 600 BC and 200 BC,

(iv) Islamic high lead glasses between *c.* AD 1000 and 1400, and

(v) Islamic high magnesia between *c.* AD 840 and 1400.

The time ranges associated with these compositions are approximate, but are, in general, valid, and have withstood the test of time. Sayre (1967:145) also noted that ancient soda-lime glasses can be divided into those which contain either high or low magnesia levels (HMG and LMG respectively). It was found that a correlation between potassium and magnesium oxides reflected the exploitation of mineral (low magnesia) or plant-ash (high magnesia) sources of alkali in ancient glasses. Within the HMG compositional group Sayre (1967:146) noted very close similarities in standard deviation ranges of a number of non-colourant oxides in second millennium BC Egyptian, Mycenaean–Minoan and Sumerian–Elamite glasses, underlining the innate conservatism of the glass technology at the time.

Ancient glasses of other compositions can now be added to the five compositional types defined in 1961. The first is a low magnesia, high potassium oxide glass (LMHK) which occurs between *c.* 1150 and 700 BC in Europe (Henderson 1988a, Brill 1992). This was an unexpected discovery which strongly suggested innovation with new raw materials in early Europe. A second compositional type is high potassium (and high barium) oxide glasses of the Chinese Han Dynasty (206 BC–AD 221: Jiazhi and Xianqiu 1987), a Chinese invention. Thirdly, high alumina glasses from the first millennium AD in India (Brill 1987), again reflecting the use of new raw materials. Fourthly, lead oxide-silica glasses from *c.* tenth to the fourteenth centuries AD are the earliest example of the use of a high level of lead oxide as a glass former; some lead oxide levels are as high as 65 per cent (Henderson and Warren 1986, Wedepohl *et al.* 1995). 'Potash' glasses of the High Medieval period (Pollard and Heron 1996:149) were frequently, though not exclusively (Cox and Gillies 1986), used for the production of Medieval church and cathedral windows and vessel glass in the West. A range of post-Medieval glasses of mixed-alkali, low alkali – high calcium and soda-lime silica compositions have been identified (Henderson 1998a). There are, undoubtedly, other glass compositional types yet to be discovered which will also be

characteristic of their time of production. Occasionally glass compositions can be characteristic of their place of production, such as is apparently the case for the glass found in large quantities at Frattesina in northern Italy of *c.* eleventh to the ninth centuries BC (Bietti-Sestierri 1980, Henderson 1988b), of a mixed-alkali composition. Generally, though, it can be difficult to be confident that the glass found at a factory site is compositionally characteristic of that site.

ANCIENT POTTERY GLAZES AND THEIR CHEMICAL COMPOSITIONS

Glazes have the same material characteristics as glasses – they are amorphous, can be coloured by adding transition metal ions and can be opacified with various crystalline compounds. As with glasses, their chemical composition affects the temperatures at which they become viscous – an important property in relation to the rate at which the pottery substrate is contracting as it cools – and the absorption of light. However, glazes are used specifically for attachment to pottery surfaces. This difference in function has led to glaze compositions which are not found amongst ancient glasses at all. To coat a pottery body with glass and make it stick is quite an achievement, since the expansion coefficient of the clay is normally much lower than that of the glaze. If the relative contraction and expansion of the glaze and the pottery do not match, then either the glaze will separate and fall off, or the glaze will craze on cooling. Various flaws can be created in the glaze if it is fired at the wrong temperature.

The earliest pottery glazes date to around the middle of the second millennium BC in the Middle East (Moorey 1994, Peltenburg 1971). Their basic composition was alkali-lime-silica. This is consistent with glass technology at the time – the principal alkali used was also soda. However, the use of a soda-rich glaze tended to produce cracks in the glaze as it shrunk on to the pot (i.e., the glaze *fit* was poor). Indeed Hedges and Moorey (1975) were (at the time) surprised to find that all of the pre-Islamic glazed pottery dating to between 600 BC and AD 600 from Kish and Nineveh they analysed had been made in the soda-lime tradition because they expected that problems with glaze fit would have been encountered. Freestone (1991) reports finding the same soda-lime technology in ninth century BC glazes from the Neo-Assyrian sites of Nimrud, Ba'shiqa and Arban.

Some of the first lead-rich glazes were introduced by the Chinese in the Warring States period (475–221 BC);

these were either lead oxide-silica or lead oxide-baria-silica (Wood and Freestone 1995). Slightly later, in the Han Dynasty, glazes contained significantly higher lead oxide levels of typically *c.* 53 to 60 per cent (Wood 1999:table 78) which, with the balance of 29 to 33 per cent silica and 3.5 to 6.7 per cent alumina, is close to the eutectic. The Romans possibly introduced lead glazes independently (Tite *et al.* 1998:242), but it seems likely that the Chinese were the first to introduce lead-silica glaze technology. These lead-rich glazes continued to be manufactured in the Byzantine and Islamic worlds. A lead-alkali glaze technology was first added to the alkali glaze technology, probably in Iraq, in the eighth century AD (Mason and Tite 1994). While the Romans produced lead glazes in various shades of green due to the presence of iron, the use of lead by Islamic potters tended to be associated with the introduction of the earliest tin opacifiers in pottery glazes – a gap of some 900 years since the introduction of tin as an opacifier in glasses (see below); lead-tin was also used by late Roman glass makers as an opacifier.

In the Medieval West the familiar olive green colour of so many of the wares is due to the presence of iron in the pottery which interacted with the lead-silica glaze under reducing conditions. In addition to this, yellow and colourless glazes were produced under oxidizing conditions (Newell 1995). The darker green hues found in this Medieval pottery were produced by using copper and brass filings. The addition of iron oxide produced a darker brown colour in the glaze under reducing conditions. Because these glazes sometimes contained high (~ 60 per cent) lead oxide levels, the potter had to be careful not to reduce the glaze to the extent that the lead was reduced to metal which would have produced a matt metallic finish.

Another glaze type is salt (NaCl) glaze. This was produced by introducing salt into the kiln at high temperature. A proportion of the salt decomposes with the alkali (Na) combining with the aluminium and silica in the pottery to produce a high temperature soda-rich glaze; the chlorine combines with hydrogen from the water in the pot to produce an acidic hydrogen chloride gas (Starkey 1977:2). In the Far East the glazes used on stoneware and porcelain tended to mature at high temperatures (up to 1350°C), having different chemical compositions from the soda-lime and lead-rich glazes used in the West. The principal compositional difference is the inclusion of a high alumina content with relatively low levels of calcium oxide, soda and potassium oxide. In some Chinese pottery the alkali used was provided by wood ash applied to the surface which interacted with silica in the pot and produced a mottled

colour. Some glazes contained elevated magnesia which increased their durability; this was certainly necessary given the low calcium oxide levels.

THE RAW MATERIALS

Early glass makers must have passed through a period of technological experiment and innovation both in the selection of appropriate raw materials and in the discovery of the properties that the raw materials imparted to the glasses. In some cases the addition of a small quantity of a compound which was designed to modify the appearance of the glass would also change the working properties – a very important consideration when making a complex glass vessel or object.

The alkalis, silica and lime

It is generally agreed that the principal source of alkali used to make glasses of the second millennium BC was ashes of the plants of the genus *Salicornia* or *Salsola*, both of which grow in the desert or maritime environments found in Egypt and the Middle East (Brill 1970a). The compositional characteristics of these halophytic plants, high soda with relatively high impurity levels of magnesia and potassium oxide, are carried through into the glass made from them.

A different alkali would have been used for the manufacture of later soda glasses. In the West from *c.* 800 BC the chemical compositions of most glasses changed from a glass which contained a high magnesia impurity to one which contained a low magnesia impurity (LMGs: Sayre 1967). The most likely source of the soda alkali used to produce these in the European Iron Age, Hellenistic and Roman glasses is an evaporite mineral which occurs at Wadi el-Natrun in Egypt (Forbes 1957:142). The mineral itself is *trona*, a sodium sesquicarbonate, $Na_2CO_3.NaHCO_3.2H_2O$ (Brill pers. comm.), and has a variable composition of 22.4 to 75 per cent sodium carbonate, 5 to 32.4 per cent sodium bicarbonate and impurities of 2.2 to 26.8 per cent sodium chloride and 2.3 to 29.9 per cent sodium sulfate (Turner 1956:table IV).

The alkali source most frequently-used by Medieval glass makers to make church and cathedral windows appears to have been beech wood, characterized by elevated manganese concentrations (Royce-Roll 1994); but other woods were also used, such as oak and elm. Bezborodov (1975) published a long list of possible plant sources that could have been used, which also includes bracken and seaweed.

Silica in glass-making is provided by sand or quartz pebbles. Iron impurities in sand produce the common greenish colour often observed; lower iron and other impurity levels are found in quartz. At the fourth century AD Jalame glass factory in Palestine, the coastal landscape was studied in order to assess the possible sources of sand which introduced impurities in the glasses excavated from the site. Though no direct evidence for glass-making was found at Jalame, it was suggested that a local sand source was used (Brill 1988).

Soda-lime glasses typically contain calcium oxide ('lime') levels of 6.5 to 9.0 per cent, a range found in soda-lime glasses into the first millennium AD (Turner 1956:45, Henderson 1985:277). Calcium oxide is essential as a network stabilizer; without it a soda-silica glass would dissolve easily in water. Pliny (Natural History XXXVI:66; Eichholz 1989) refers to the use of 'shells' as a glass-maker's raw material, for which the obvious source would be beach sand. The suggestion has been made that the proportion of shell fragments is always the same in the sand source, resulting in a repeatable glass composition (Brill 1970b). It is however much more likely that, as with ancient metallurgy, where consistent proportions of mineral-bearing ores would have been purified and melted, the different constituents of the sand were separated, perhaps by using a centrifugal device, so that the shell fragments could be used as a calcium source, which could have been added in measured quantities.

Lead

Brill (1970a) has reviewed the earliest use of lead in ancient glass. From the Eighteenth Dynasty (1550–1307 BC) lead was used in Egyptian glasses, specifically for decorative opaque yellow glasses which were normally applied to core-formed vessels, in the form of lead antimonate, $Pb_2Sb_2O_7$ (Lilyquist and Brill 1993). Translucent high lead glasses are unusual until c. ninth to tenth centuries AD when they were used for the manufacture of beads and rings (Henderson and Warren 1986), and somewhat later in the manufacture of generally prestigious yellow, emerald green and opaque red Medieval vessel glasses (Wedepohl et al. 1995).

Glass colouration

The parameters which effect the colouration of glass are complex. Although the oxides of transition metal ions, such as cobalt and copper can, under the right circumstances, produce the familiar deep blue and turquoise blue colours respectively, a range of other factors play an important part (Pollard and Heron 1996:168, Henderson 2000). Glass colour is dependent on the glass absorbing part of the visible wavelengths of light through interaction with colourant oxides in the glass and the reflection of the balance of light wavelengths; it is the reflected light wavelengths that we observe as colour (Doremus 1994:306). These factors include:

(i)   the occurrence of transition metal ions,
(ii)   the use of crystalline opacifiers,
(iii) the chemical environment in which colouration is achieved,
(iv)   the furnace atmosphere (redox), and
(v)   the heating cycle which is clearly affected and controlled by the kind of furnace and fuels used.

Cobalt blue glass

One of the few colourant minerals which has been used in ancient glass, and for which it is (apparently) possible to link associated impurities with its geological origin, is cobalt. Cobalt is commonly found in association with other minerals, such as copper (Henderson 1985:278). The chemical analysis of cobalt in ancient Egyptian glasses has produced an interesting discussion in the literature. Kaczmarczyk and Hedges (1983:46) discovered that cobalt is associated with manganese, zinc, nickel and alumina in New Kingdom cobalt blue faience and other cobalt blue objects, which contain abnormally high alumina concentrations. Kaczmarczyk (1986) suggested that an Egyptian source of alum with a significant cobalt impurity was used for Egyptian New Kingdom glass colouration. Shortland and Tite (2000) have noted that a natron-based blue glass was used in fifteenth and fourteenth century BC Egyptian glasses, as distinct from the balance of (plant ash) glass in use at the time. Chemical analyses of Iron Age European blue glasses have revealed that the source of cobalt changed c. second century BC from an antimony-rich source to a manganese-rich source, which is no coincidence given the important changes in the industrial and social centralization which occurred at the time (Henderson 1991b).

Chemical analysis of Medieval European blue glasses by Gratuze et al. (1995) has shown that there were discrete chronological changes in the use of cobalt sources according to a range of impurities such as lead and zinc. The work is still preliminary, but, nevertheless, it has already been possible to suggest that a cobalt-rich colourant was exported from the Islamic world to High Medieval western Europe to be incorporated in glass of typical High Medieval ('forest') composition as distinct from Islamic Middle Eastern soda-lime glasses (Henderson 1998b).

Turquoise blue, opaque red and translucent red glasses

The two ionic states of copper produce two correspondingly different colours in ancient glasses: a turquoise blue colour when the copper(II) ion is present (Brill 1970b) and a bright sealing-wax red or a dull brown-red colour when the copper(I) ion is present (Hughes 1972, Freestone 1987). When crystalline forms of copper are produced in the reddish glasses, the presence of lead oxide in the glass at 1 per cent or more greatly facilitates the precipitation of the crystals out of the glass melt. 'Striking' the copper or copper(I) oxide crystals out of solution is essential to the development of the colour. This involves heat treating (re-heating) the glasses at temperatures at which the crystals can form (Freestone 1987). The bright sealing-wax red colour is caused by the development of branching dendritic copper(I) oxide crystals.

Archaeological inference from the chemical analysis of opaque sealing-wax red enamels used in the European later Iron Age has shown how some compositional distinctions between the enamels used (and presumably manufactured) in western and eastern Britain after the second century BC (Henderson 1989a:47) suggest that different workshop zones existed in which somewhat different recipes were employed for making opaque red enamels. A duller red colour generally containing lower lead and copper levels was introduced by the Romans in the first century AD and used for the manufacture of tesserae and enamels (Hughes 1972, Henderson 1989a:48, 1991a). Opaque reddish-brown crystals of iron(III) oxide have been found in Egyptian faience (Kaczmarczyk and Hedges 1983) and in Islamic glasses (Freestone 1999).

Translucent red glasses and enamels contain particles of a copper-rich composition, and are known as 'copper-ruby' glasses (Weyl 1951:428). Andreas Cussins (1630–1705) studied the formation of gold ruby glass (the purple of Cassius) which consisted of colloidal gold and tin(IV) oxide; these glasses were not dichroic. Johann Kunkel successfully produced gold ruby glass commercially. The ruby colour is due to light being absorbed at a particular wavelength (0.53 nm; Doremus 1994:315). This absorption

band comes from the spherical geometry of the particles and the particular optical properties of the gold. The particle size involved is c. 200–400 nm; the size of the gold particles influences the colour produced. Crystals in opaque glasses normally measure between c. 1 nm and 10 nm.

Translucent iron green, purple and brown glasses

One of the principal colourant impurities in sand is iron. This can produce a range of translucent colours, ranging from pale blue, brown, to yellowish-green and dark olive green, depending on the furnace conditions (Sellner et al. 1979). Iron oxide is invariably present in early glasses, and can be used deliberately to produce a translucent dark brown colour, but generally it occurs only as an impurity which is eclipsed by the addition of colourants like cobalt and copper to the glass melt. The common iron-green glass of later periods is produced by a mixture of iron(II) and iron(III) ions in the melt (Weyl 1951:91). Later (Medieval) 'forest' glasses often contain manganese and iron together, introduced as impurities in the wood ash used as an alkali. The presence of elevated manganese oxide levels in ancient glasses implies that a relatively pure mineral source of colourant, like pyrolusite, was used. The unwanted pale colours caused by impurities in translucent glasses can be removed by using glass decolourizers, antimony trioxide and manganese oxide (Henderson 1985:284).

Opaque white, turquoise, blue and yellow glasses

Opacity in ancient glasses is due to the presence of dispersed crystals in a translucent glass matrix. Opaque red glasses have already been discussed; other early opacifiers in white, turquoise, blue and yellow glasses all contain compounds based on antimony (Turner and Rooksby 1961, 1963, Rooksby 1962, Henderson 1985).

Opaque white glass in early Egypt is coloured by masses of white calcium antimonate crystals which cause the light to be reflected and refracted from the glass. Calcium antimonate ($Ca_2Sb_2O_7$ or $Ca_2Sb_2O_6$) does not occur naturally as a mineral, so the antimony added to the glass would react with the calcium to produce crystals (Turner and Rooksby 1961) and was still used in Venice in the nineteenth century. In order to produce opaque turquoise and blue glasses the same procedure is followed as for white glasses, but the antimony is added to a translucent turquoise or blue glass instead of a weakly-tinted glass.

From the second millennium BC opaque yellow glasses were coloured and opacified by lead antimonate crystals (Rooksby 1962:23). Since lead antimonate occurs naturally as bindheimite [$Pb_2(Sb,Bi)_2O_6(O, OH)$], if an impurity of bismuth is found in ancient lead antimonate opacified glasses this might show that bindheimite had been used as an opacifier. In the process of heat-treating lead-containing batches, a reaction between lead and antimony would also produce opaque yellow lead pyroantimonate $Pb_2Sb_2O_7$ which would remain incompletely dissolved in the glass under oxidizing conditions; in this case the shapes of the lead antimonate crystals would reflect the heat treatment of the glass batch.

Another class of opacifiers are tin compounds. No tin-based glass opacifiers have been detected in ancient glasses until after the second century BC, and the earliest have been found in Iron Age Europe (Henderson 1985, 1989a). Tin oxide crystals were used to produce opaque white glass; lead stannate to produce an opaque yellow colour. The earliest tin-opacified glazes were developed in the eighth century AD in the Middle East (Mason and Tite 1997; see above).

Opacifiers used in seventeenth century AD glass include lead arsenate crystals which cause a somewhat 'milky' colour in glass. The opacifier was probably first introduced by Venetian glass workers. Calcium phosphate can also act as an opacifier, as indeed can sodium phosphate (Turner and Rooksby 1961, 1963, Bezborodov 1975:73). Calcium fluoride was used especially by the Chinese (Henderson *et al.* 1989). Incompletely dissolved raw materials (like silica) or partial devitrification of the glass can also cause opacity. Crystalline soda-lime-silicates, which may be produced by incomplete vitrification, or formed out of solution when the glass was being worked, will have the same effect. Masses of air bubbles will reduce the transmission of light through the glass as well.

Similar colourants are used in glazes as those found in glasses. Discrete changes in the use of cobalt-rich colourants have been identified in the glazes produced between c. 1430 and 1650 in Turkey, including Iznik (Henderson 1989b). Both manganese-rich and arsenic-rich cobalt ores were used at different times. The use of colourants not found in glasses can be noted: in Neo-Assyrian ninth century BC pottery Freestone (1991) found that a black colour was caused by a Mn (Fe) pigment, in addition to white calcium antimonate, yellow lead antimonate and a green glaze opacified with calcium antimonate. In Partho-Sasanian glazes Hedges (1976) found that a blue colour was due

to reduced iron, green was due to iron (with or without copper), darker browns were due to iron and manganese and a black colour due to iron sulfide which had been produced under reducing conditions.

GLASS PRODUCTION: THE EVIDENCE OF FURNACE TYPES

The reviews by Charleston (1978) and by Newton and Davison (1989) of the forms of ancient glass furnaces give an impression that it is relatively easy to classify them into 'southern' and 'northern' types. For the production of glass in both of these furnace types there is a tacit assumption that the glass raw materials were first fritted either in the furnace itself or (in the case of the 'northern' type) in a separate small furnace or 'oven' at the lower temperatures required. The frit, often combined with recycled glass (cullet) and/or additional colourant material would then have been melted in the crucible. As mentioned below, this is not always the case. Moreover there are several complicating factors in the interpretation of excavated furnace, and for that matter any industrial, remains. The most common (inevitable) problem is that only partial furnace remains survive to be excavated so that archaeologists are forced to infer what the original structure, and functions of the structure, might have been. Once the furnaces have been located, it can be very difficult to find the evidence for specific processes of glass production. Even if the debris from glass production is found in the glass workshop or furnace, there is always the possibility that it was re-deposited from (for example) another glass furnace: there is no guarantee at all that the (examples of) products and by-products from a specific furnace would be dumped in the remains of the furnace that produced them, or indeed that they can be located at all (see Chapter 40).

The so-called 'southern' type of glass furnace is thought to be a beehive shape, divided into three compartments: the lower chamber for the fuel, the middle chamber for melting the glass in pots (crucibles) and the top chamber for annealing glass vessels (see Figure 38.1). The 'northern' type has chambers which are horizontally disposed instead. In 'northern' furnaces the firing chamber is in the form of a 'trench' with sieges (broad shelves) at both sides on which the crucibles containing the glass melt are placed (see Figure 38.2). The whole structure is roofed over and is a tunnel shape. The small annealing ovens are often separated. In the 'southern' furnace the heat rises through holes in the dividing floors between the chambers; in the

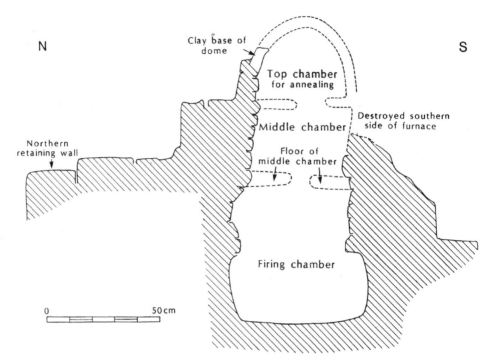

Figure 38.1   Cross section through an early ninth century three-chambered 'southern' glass furnace found at al-Raqqa, northern Syria.

'northern' type the heat reverberates off the roof of the structure down on to the glass melt.

The 'southern' glass furnace type has been found in various locations south of the Alps (but also north of the Alps); the 'northern' type seems to be located exclusively to the north of the Alps, where it formed part of the 'forest' glass-making tradition. There is, however, another type of glass furnace, the tank furnace (see Figure 38.3). The most likely way that this furnace was used would have been for mass-production of glass with a single melt. The furnace is fired at one end with a through draught being drawn up through a vent at the opposite end to the fuel. The melt would have been loaded into the chamber and fired (probably once); the product would not, necessarily, have been of a high quality, but it could be produced in vast quantities.

Some of the earliest possible evidence for glass production has been found at Tell el-Amarna in Egypt. In the remains of a New Kingdom, eighteenth Dynasty industrial estate in the Dynastic capital of Akhenaten (1353–1337 BC) Flinders Petrie (1894:26) described a 'brickwork furnace in a glazing factory'. Petrie's excavations, and subsequent excavations by Nicholson (1995) have produced the evidence of glass-working

in the form of spills of glass, vessel and rod fragments and drips of glass adhering to cylindrical ceramic vessel fragments. Evidence for the glass *working* at Tell el-Amarna is indisputable, but there is currently no published primary archaeological evidence for the elusive process of *making* glass from raw materials there. The scientific investigation of Egyptian cobalt blue glass by Shortland and Tite (2000) helps to bolster the case for the Egyptian manufacture of glass from primary raw materials, but does not show that it was made at Tell el-Amarna (Henderson 2000).

Although evidence of working glass with a distinctive composition has survived, such as in eleventh to ninth century BC contexts at Frattesina in northern Italy (Brill 1992) and on Hellenistic Rhodes (Weinberg 1969), it is difficult to point to the remains of glass furnaces for this period. For later periods Price (1998:333) has reviewed the evidence of Roman glass furnaces in Britain and noted the small (0.9 m diameter) furnaces with keyhole-shaped plans which have been found at sites like Mancetter, Warwickshire and Leicester of the 'southern' type. A *rectangular* structure from Caistor by Norwich appears to have been larger but, like those at Mancetter and Leicester, probably held one pot; this again shows that the simple

ROSEDALE

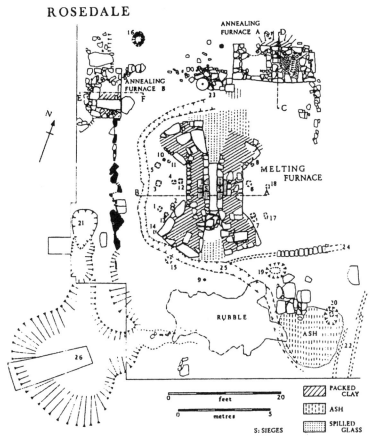

Figure 38.2 Plan of a 'northern' glass furnace with associated structures found at Rosedale, UK, showing a distinction between functional areas within the workshop (after Crossley and Aberg 1972). Reproduced by kind permission of the Society of Post-Medieval Archaeology.

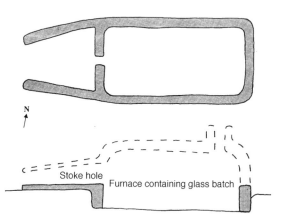

Figure 38.3 A schematic cross-section through a tank furnace (re-drawn with permission of Y. Gorin-Rosen).

distinction between 'northern' and 'southern' furnaces does not work. A further exception is the discovery of Roman tank furnace fragments from London (Shepard and Heyworth 1991). At Autun, France excavations have revealed the plan of a Roman tank furnace measuring 1.9×0.88 metres with an apsidal end (Rebourg 1989) and in Cologne, Germany first century Roman circular and rectangular structures have been found together (Seibel 1998:43). Extensive excavations have been carried out at a fourth century AD glass factory at Jalame in Palestine (Weinberg 1988), near where, according to the Roman historian Pliny (AD 23–79), glass-making was first discovered. The excavations at Jalame are important because the entire workshop and all the glass found has been fully published. The excavations revealed somewhat ambiguous structural evidence for a furnace with the discovery of a firing trench. The comprehensive scientific report by Brill makes an especially important contribution.

The evidence for glass furnaces in early Medieval Italy (seventh to eighth centuries) on the island of Torcello in the Venetian lagoon is strong. Excavations revealed a glass house (Tabaczynska 1987) with clear evidence for functionally discrete structures which can be related to different glass making/production processes. In Israel the impressive remains of 16 early Byzantine tank furnaces at Hadera (Freestone and Gorin-Rosen 1999) is a reflection of the massive scale of production of raw glass there. It is estimated that between 8 and 10 tons of glass were produced each time the furnace was fired; perhaps ingots were also produced (Foy and Jézégou 1998:124).

The classification of 'southern' and 'northern' types breaks down with the discovery north of the Alps of a Medieval glass furnace type which is circular in plan. At Cadrix, France, Foy (1989) discovered a stoke hole and the base of the middle chamber of a presumed three-chambered furnace. Examples of the Medieval 'northern' furnace type have been found across the full range of 'forest' glass production sites in Europe (Wood 1965, Lappe and Möbes 1984). The early fifteenth century manuscript depicting Sir John de Mandeville's *Travels* (1963), shows a furnace with an *oval* plan and domed roof. It has a stoke hole below, two glory holes containing glass pots on the upper level and an annealing oven at the 'back' of the furnace. It is difficult to tell whether there was a separate fire pit for the annealing oven, but this again shows that it is difficult to generalize about the form which furnaces took. The post-Medieval examples from Hutton-le-Hole and especially Rosedale, north Yorkshire, England (Crossley and Aberg 1972) revealed evidence for the process of annealing occurring in separate annealing ovens and 'wings' (extensions) on the four corners of the furnace, a technological development which is thought to have been introduced by immigrant glass-workers from Lorraine (Crossley 1990:229). One aspect of glass production which would have impacted on the environment in a significant way is the enormous amount of wood that would have been used as an alkali source and as fuel (Cable 1998).

FUTURE DIRECTIONS IN RESEARCH

An ideal way of studying the production of ancient glass and glaze is a combination of archaeological excavation of production sites, the scientific analysis of the

debris from production, an attempt to characterize the raw materials used and research into the historical evidence for glass/glaze production at the site(s). The chemical analysis of glass will continue to provide evidence for discrete chronological changes in ancient glass technology, and may still reveal new and interesting compositions in the future. Associated with these areas of study, an experimental approach to melting glass allows researchers to establish how variations in the levels of raw materials used in glass production can influence strongly working properties and can inform us as to how raw materials may have behaved under different conditions when being melted. Of course this holistic approach should also include a study of the effects that the glass industry had on the environment (levels of pollution and exploitation of fuel resources). Where glass and glaze production form part of a range of other high temperature industries, they should not be studied in isolation.

REFERENCES

*Recommended for further reading

Bezborodov, M.A. (1975). *Chemie und Technologie der antiken und mittelalterlichen Glaser*. P. von Zabern: Mainz.

Bietti-Sestierri, A.M.B. (1980). Lo scavo del'abitato protostorico di Frattesina, Fratta Polesine (Rovigo). *Bulletino di Paletnologia Italiana*, 21:221–256.

Brill, R.H. (1970a). Lead and oxygen isotopes in ancient objects. *Philosophical Transactions of the Royal Society of London*, A269:143–164.

Brill, R.H. (1970b). The chemical interpretation of the texts. In Oppenheim, A.L., Brill, R.H., Barag, D. and von Saldern, A. (eds) *Glass and Glassmaking in Ancient Mesopotamia*, 105–128. Corning Museum of Glass: Corning.

Brill, R.H. (1987). Chemical analyses of some early Indian glasses. In Bhardwaj, H.C. (ed.) *Archaeometry of Glass*, 1–25. Indian Ceramic Society: Calcutta.

Brill, R.H. (1988). Scientific investigations of the Jalame glass and related finds. In Weinberg, G.D. (ed.) *Excavations at Jalame: Site of a Glass Factory in Late Roman Palestine*, 257–294. University of Missouri Press: Columbia.

Brill, R.H. (1992). Chemical analyses of some glasses from Frattesina. *Journal of Glass Studies*, 11:11–22.

Cable, M. (1998). The operation of wood fired glass melting furnaces. In McCray, P. (ed.) *The Prehistory and History of Glassmaking Technology*, 315–331. American Ceramic Society: Columbus, Ohio.

Caley, E.R. (1962). *Analysis of Ancient Glasses 1790–1957*. Corning Museum of Glass: New York.

*Charleston, R.J. (1978) Glass furnaces through the ages. *Journal of Glass Studies*, 20:9–34.

Cox, G.A. and Gillies, K.J.S. (1986). The X-ray fluorescence analysis of Medieval durable blue soda glass from York Minster. *Archaeometry*, **28**:57–68.

Crossley, D. (1990) *Post-Medieval Archaeology in Britain*. Leicester University Press: London.

Crossley, D. and Aberg, A. (1972). Sixteenth century glass-making in Yorkshire: excavations of furnaces at Hutton and Rosedale, North Riding, 1968–71. *Post-Medieval Archaeology*, **6**:107–159.

de Mandeville, J. (1963). *The Bodley Version of Mandeville's Travels*. Early English Text Society 253, Oxford University Press: Oxford.

*Doremus, R.H. (1994). *Glass Science*. John Wiley: New York.

Eichholz, D.E. (trans.) (1989). *Pliny the Elder, Natural History, Books XXXVI–XXXVII*. Loeb Classical Library 419, Harvard University Press: Cambridge, Mass.

Forbes, R.J. (1957). Glass. In Forbes, R.J. (ed.) *Studies in Ancient Technology Vol. 5*, 110–231. Brill: Leiden.

Foy, D. (1989). *Le Verre Médiéval et Son Artisanat en France Méditerranienne*. CNRS: Paris.

Foy, D. and Jézégou, M.-P. (1998). Commerce et technologie du verre antique le témoignage de l'épave 'ouest embies 1'. In Rieth, E. (ed.) *Méditerranée Antique. Pêche, Navigation, Commerce*, 121–134. Comité des Travaux Historiques et Scientifiques: Nice.

Freestone, I.C. (1987). Composition and microstructure of early opaque red glass. In Bimson, M. and Freestone, I.C. (eds) *Early Vitreous Materials*, 173–191. Occasional Paper No. 56, British Museum Press: London.

Freestone, I.C. (1991). Technical examination of Neo-Assyrian glazed wall plaques. *Iraq*, **53**:55–58.

Freestone, I.C. and Gorin-Rozen, Y. (1999). The great glass slab at Bet-She'Arim, Israel: an early Islamic glassmaking experiment? *Journal of Glass Studies*, **41**:105–116

Gratuze, B., Soulier, I., Barrandon, J.N. and Foy, D. (1995). The origin of the cobalt blue pigment in French glass from the thirteenth to the eighteenth centuries. In Hook, D.R. and Gaimster, D.R.M. (eds) *Trade and Discovery. The Scientific Study of Artefacts from Post-Medieval Europe and Beyond*, 123–134. Occasional Paper 109, British Museum Press: London.

Hedges, R.E.M. (1976). Pre-Islamic glazes in Mesopotamia – Nippur. *Archaeometry*, **18**:209–213.

Hedges, R.E.M. and Moorey, P.R.S. (1975). Pre-Islamic ceramic glazes at Kish and Nineveh in Iraq. *Archaeometry*, **17**:25–43.

*Henderson, J. (1985). The raw materials of early glass production. *Oxford Journal of Archaeology*, **4**:267–291.

Henderson, J. (1988a). Electron-probe microanalysis of mixed-alkali glasses. *Archaeometry*, **30**:77–91.

Henderson, J. (1988b). Glass production and Bronze Age Europe. *Antiquity*, **62**:435–451.

*Henderson, J. (1989a). The scientific analysis of ancient glass and its archaeological interpretation. In Henderson, J. (ed.) *Scientific Analysis in Archaeology and its Interpretation*, 30–62. OUCA Monograph 19/UCLA

Institute of Archaeology Research Tools 5, Oxbow Books: Oxford.

Henderson, J. (1989b). Iznik pottery: a technical examination. In Attasoy, N. and Raby, J. (eds) *Iznik, the Pottery of Ottoman Turkey*, 65–69, 84–87. Alexandria Press: London.

Henderson, J. (1991a). Technological characteristics of Roman enamels. *Jewellery Studies*, **5**:65–76.

Henderson, J. (1991b). Industrial specialisation in Late Iron Age Europe: organisation, location and distribution. *Archaeological Journal*, **148**:104–148.

Henderson, J. (1998a). Post-Medieval glass: production, characterisation and value. In Kingery, D. and McCray, P. (eds) *The Prehistory and History of Glass and Glass Technology*, 33–59. American Ceramic Society: Columbus, Ohio.

Henderson, J. (1998b) Technological aspects of Islamic blue glasses. In Ward, R. (ed.) *Gilded and Enamelled Glass from the Middle East*, 116–121. British Museum Press: London.

*Henderson, J. (2000). *The Science and Archaeology of Materials*. Routledge: London.

Henderson, J. and Warren, S.E. (1986). Beads and rings; scientific analysis of the glass. In Tweddle, D. (ed.) *Finds from Parliament Street and Other Sites in the City Centre*, 209–226. The Archaeology of York Fascicule 17/4, Council for British Archaeology: London.

Henderson, J., Tregear, M. and Wood, N. (1989). The technology of sixteenth- and seventeenth-century Chinese cloisonné enamels. *Archaeometry*, **31**:133–146.

Hughes, M.J. (1972). A technical study of opaque red glass of the Iron Age in Britain. *Proceedings of the Prehistoric Society*, **38**:98–107.

Jiazhi, L. and Xianqiu, C. (1987). A study on West Han PbO-BaO-SiO_2 glass and its corroded layer unearthed at Yang Zhou. In Bhardwaj, H.C. (ed.) *Archaeometry of Glass*, 21–26. Indian Ceramic Society: Calcutta.

Jones, G.O. (1956). *Glass*. Methuen: London.

Kaczmarczyk, A. (1986). The source of cobalt in ancient Egyptian pigments. In Olin, J.S. and Blackman, J. (eds) *Proceedings of the 24th International Symposium on Archaeometry*, 369–376. Smithsonian Institution Press: Washington DC.

Kaczmarczyk, A. and Hedges, R.E.M. (1983). *Ancient Egyptian Faience: an Analytical Survey of Egyptian Faience from Predynastic to Roman Times*. Aris and Phillips: Warminster.

Lappe, U. and Möbes, G. (1984). Glashütten im Eichsfeld. *Alt-Thuringen*, **20**:207–232.

Lilyquist, C. and Brill, R.H. (1993). *Studies in Early Egyptian Glass*. Metropolitan Museum of Art: New York.

Mason, R.B. and Tite, M.S. (1994). The beginnings of Islamic stonepaste technology. *Archaeometry*, **36**:77–91.

Mason, R.B. and Tite, M.S. (1997). The beginnings of tin opacification of pottery glazes. *Archaeometry*, **39**:41–58.

Moorey, P.R.S. (1994). *Ancient Mesopotamian Materials and Industries. The Archaeological Evidence*. Clarendon Press: Oxford.

Newell, R.W. (1995). Some notes on 'Splashed Glazes'. *Medieval Ceramics*, **19**:77–88.

*Newton, R. and Davison, S. (1989). *Conservation of Glass*. Butterworths: London.

Nicholson, P.T. (1995). Recent excavations at an ancient Egyptian glassworks – Tell el-Amarna 1993. *Glass Technology*, **36**:125–128.

*Oppenheim, A.L., Brill, R.H., Barag, D. and von Saldern, A. (1970). *Glass and Glassmaking in Ancient Mesopotamia*. Corning Museum of Glass: New York.

Peltenburg, E. (1971). Some early developments of vitreous materials. *World Archaeology*, **3**:6–12.

Petrie, W.F.M. (1894). *Tell el-Amarna*. Methuen: London.

Polak, A. (1997). Glas en glasmakers. In Brand, J., de Muijnck, C. and van der Sande, B. (eds) *Het drinkglas*. Waanders: Zwolle.

Pollard, A.M. and Heron, C. (1996). *Archaeological Chemistry*. Royal Society of Chemistry: Cambridge.

Price, J. (1998). The social context for glass production in Roman Britain. In McCray, P. and Kingery, D. (eds) *The Prehistory and History of Glass and Glass Technology*, 331–348. American Ceramic Society: Columbus, Ohio.

Rebourg, A. (1989). Un atelier de verrier Gallo-Romain à Autun. *Revue Archéologique de l'Est et du Centre*, **156**:12–23.

Rooksby, H.P. (1962). Opacifiers in opal glasses. *GEC Journal of Science and Technology*, **29**:20–26.

Royce-Roll, D. (1994). The colors of Romanesque stained glass. *Journal of Glass Studies*, **36**:71–80.

Sayre, E.V. (1967). Summary of the Brookhaven program of analysis of ancient glass. In Young, W.J. (ed.) *Application of Science in Examination of Works of Art*, 145–154. Museum of Fine Arts: Boston.

Sayre, E.V. and Smith, R.W. (1961). Compositional categories of ancient glass. *Science*, **133**:1824–1826.

Seibel, F. (1998). *Technologie und Fertigungstechniken römischer Glashütten am Beispiel der Ausgrabungen im Hambacher Forst: aktualistische Vergleiche und Modelle*. Galda and Wilch: Berlin.

Sellner, C., Oel, H.J. and Camera, B. (1979). Untersuchung alter Gläser (Waldglas) auf Zusammenhang von Zusammensetzung, Farbe und Schmelzatmosphäre mit der Elektronenspektroskopie und der Elektronenspin-resonanz (ESR). *Glastechnische Berichte*, **52**:255–264.

Shepard, J. and Heyworth, M. (1991). Le travail du verre dans London Romain (Londinium): un état de la question. In

Foy, D. and Sennequier, G. (eds) *Ateliers de Verriers de l'Antiquité á la Période Pré-Industrielle*, 13–22. Association Française pour l'Archéologie du Verre: Rouen.

Shortland, A.J. and Tite, M.S. (2000). Raw materials of glass from Amarna and implications for the origins of Egyptian glass. *Archaeometry*, **42**:141–152.

Starkey, P. (1977). *Saltglaze*. Pitman: London.

Tabaczynska, E. (1987). The early medieval glass-works on the Torcello Island on the Venetia Lagoon: technological interpretations. *Archaeologia*, **12**:63–88.

Tite, M.S., Freestone, I.C., Mason, R., Molera, J., Vendrell-Saz, M. and Wood, N. (1998). Lead glazes in antiquity – methods of production and reasons for use. *Archaeometry*, **40**:241–260.

Turner, W.E.S. (1956). Studies of ancient glass and glass-making processes. Part III: the chronology of glass-making constituents. *Journal of the Society of Glass Technology*, **40**:39–52.

Turner, W.E.S. and Rooksby, H.P. (1961). Further historical studies based on X-ray diffraction methods of the reagents employed in making opal and opaque glasses. *Jahrbuch des Römisch-Germanischen Zentralmuseums*, **8**:1–16.

Turner, W.E.S. and Rooksby, H.P. (1963). A study of the opalising agents in ancient glasses throughout 3400 years, part II. In Matson, F.R. and Rindone, G.E. (eds) *Advances in Glass Technology*, 306–307. Plenum Press: New York.

Wedepohl, K.H., Krueger, I. and Hartmann, G. (1995). Medieval lead glass from north western Europe. *Journal of Glass Studies*, **37**:65–82.

Weinberg, G.D. (1969). Glass manufacture of Hellenistic Rhodes. *Archaiologikon Deltion*, **24**:143–151.

Weinberg, G.D. (ed.) (1988). *Excavations at Jalame: Site of a Glass Factory in Late Roman Palestine*. University of Missouri Press: Columbia.

*Weyl, W.A. (1951). *Coloured Glasses*. Society of Glass Technology: Sheffield.

Wood, E.S. (1965). A medieval glasshouse at Blunden's Wood, Hambledon, Surrey. *Surrey Archaeological Collections*, **62**:54–79.

*Wood, N. (1999). *Chinese Glazes*. Black: London.

Wood, N. and Freestone, I.C. (1995). A preliminary examination of a Warring States pottery jar with so-called 'glass paste' decoration. In Guo Yanyi (ed.) *Science and Technology of Ancient Ceramics 3*, 12–17, Science Press: Beijing.

39

Science, Speculation and the Origins of Extractive Metallurgy

D. KILLICK

Department of Anthropology, University of Arizona.

The study of the origins of extractive metallurgy – the winning of metals from their oxide, carbonate, or sulfide ores – is complicated by a basic epistemological problem. All students of the subject live, or lived, in societies utterly dependent upon the unique mechanical, electrical and magnetic properties of metals. This fact is so embedded in our unconscious that it has often led scholars to make inappropriate assumptions about the social and economic impact of the earliest use of metals. Many of the foremost students of the subject have had extensive training in materials science, engineering, chemistry or geology. This knowledge is invaluable in the interpretation of the material remains of prehistoric metallurgy, but it can also be a liability, since modern scientists and engineers are channelled by their education and their professional experience into particular ways of viewing metallurgical technology and value systems. Archaeologists and ethnographers have however documented a number of instances of unexpected extractive technologies, often over the initial objections of archaeometallurgists and other scientists (Killick 1991, Juleff 1996).

Thus the central problem for historians of metallurgy, as for all historians and prehistorians, is to avoid reading the present into the past – what historians call the 'presentist fallacy'.

Some archaeologists, influenced by critical theorists of the Frankfurt School, have argued that the presentist fallacy cannot be avoided, so that all archaeological reconstructions are merely fables serving present political ends (e.g., Shanks and Tilley 1987). This extreme pessimism has been effectively countered by Bruce Trigger: 'Yet, if subjective factors intervene at every level in the interpretation of the past, so too does archaeological evidence, which, at least within the bounds of a commitment to scientific methodology, partially constrains and limits what it is possible to believe about the past' (Trigger 1989:407).

If we broaden this conclusion to include ethnographic, historical, chemical, geological and experimental evidence, it applies exactly to research on early extractive metallurgy. We cannot unlearn what we know from the present, but the accumulation of material evidence puts ever tighter constraints on our quite legitimate speculation about the past. We can also develop the habit of examining our own working assumptions for ethnocentric bias.

With these caveats firmly in mind we can turn to the main questions concerning the origins of extractive metallurgy:

(i) When, how, and why were metals first smelted from their ores?

(ii) Was metallurgy invented in a single region, from which the technology spread by diffusion, or was

---

it independently developed in two or more different regions?

(iii) What immediate economic and social consequences came of this innovation?

(iv) Why did metallurgy begin with some of the rarer metals, rather than with the more abundant?

This chapter briefly examines the history of thought on these topics, concentrating particularly upon the role of scientific evidence in limiting what it is possible to believe about the past.

THE ERA OF UNRESTRAINED SPECULATION

Scholarly interest in the origins and course of metallurgy can be traced back to the work of the Danish scholar Christian Thomsen (1788–1865). Through study of the contents of excavated hoards stored in the National Museum of Denmark, Thomsen deduced that there had been five successive stages of technology in Danish prehistory. In the earliest stage no metals were found, most edged tools being made of chipped stone. This was followed by a stage in which stone and copper tools co-existed. In the succeeding Bronze Age the use of stone tools ceased and alloyed copper was employed. The Bronze Age was followed by two divisions of the Iron Age, the later of which extended into the period of the earliest historic records in Scandinavia. This inferred sequence was subsequently confirmed by the stratigraphic excavations of Jens Worsaae (1821–1885) (see Trigger 1989:73).

These five stages were subsequently condensed to a 'Three Age' succession of Stone, Bronze and Iron Ages, soon replicated in other parts of Europe. This striking finding fed the growing interest in social evolution during the second half of the nineteenth century. Henry Morgan drew upon the Three Age system for his monumental *Ancient Society* (1877), and Morgan's work greatly influenced Karl Marx and Frederick Engels, who considered the Three Age system important evidence in favour of their theory of historical materialism. Marx did not make any specific comment on the origins of metallurgy, but Engels gave the matter some consideration in his *Origins of the Family, Private Property and the State*, published in 1884. In Morgan's stage of 'lower barbarism', 'Bronze provided serviceable tools and weapons though it could not displace stone tools; only iron could do that, and the method of obtaining iron was not yet understood. Gold and silver were beginning to be used for ornament and decoration and must have already acquired a high value with respect to copper and bronze' (Engels 1972:220).

Even the innovation of iron was not seen to have immediate effect. With the arrival of the stage of 'upper barbarism', 'Iron was now at the service of man, the last and most important of all the raw materials which played a historically revolutionary role – until the potato. Iron brought about the tillage of large areas, the clearing of wide tracts of virgin forest; iron gave to the handicraftsman tools so hard and sharp that no stone, no other known metal could resist them. All this came gradually; the first iron was often even softer than bronze' (Engels 1972:222).

Engels wrote at a time when the Bessemer and Siemens-Martin processes for the production of cheap bulk steel were revolutionizing transportation, agriculture, industry and architecture, and he may have been unconsciously imposing his awareness of this revolution on to his reconstruction of the remote past. If so, he was expressing a belief in the transformative powers of iron that was widely held in Europe in the late nineteenth and early twentieth centuries. Other examples of this are Sir Harry Johnston's view that it was the acquisition of iron that enabled the speakers of Bantu languages to rapidly spread over one-third of the African continent (Vansina 1979), and this stanza from Rudyard Kipling's 'Cold Iron' (Kipling 1982:642):

'Gold is for the mistress – silver for the maid –
Copper for the craftsman cunning at his trade.
"Good!" said the baron, sitting in his hall
But Iron – Cold Iron – is master of them all.'

The fact that this early scholarly fixation with iron is now forgotten is testament to the influence of V. Gordon Childe, whose views on the origins and social impact of early metallurgy dominated all discussion of the subject between the late 1920s and the mid-1960s. Like Engels, Childe was a technological determinist, but his views on the impact of early metallurgy were very different. Bronze tools, he argued, were manifestly superior to stone tools in agriculture and in warfare, and must therefore have been in great demand. Childe was convinced that the technical skills required to manufacture bronze were difficult to master and thus would have been in short supply; early metalworkers would therefore have enjoyed high status and an unprecedented degree of independence. He saw early bronze workers as full-time specialists, migrating from group to group. By breaking free of the bonds of kinship, Childe argued, these early craft specialists precipitated the transition from societies based upon kinship to societies based upon class.

Whilst he agreed with Engels that the subsequent mastery of ferrous metallurgy transformed prehistoric economies – iron being much more abundant, and thus more affordable than bronze – Childe did not see it as having had revolutionary social consequences (Childe 1930:4, 1985:85, 1944). On the spread of metallurgy, he was unequivocal; it had diffused outward in all directions from a region of invention somewhere in the Near East – *ex Oriente lux*.

INITIAL RESTRAINTS ON SPECULATION

The eloquence of Childe's arguments obscured for a long time the lack of empirical support for his views. The ethnographic data then available (e.g., Cline 1937) showed that metalworkers in societies below the level of states were rarely full-time specialists. Nor did their essential economic function necessarily accord them independence, wealth or high status. But no European archaeologists of that period were much interested in world ethnography, and it was not until the early 1970s that these records were used to undermine Childe's views (Rowlands 1971).

In an important review article on the state of research on the origins of metallurgy, Wertime (1964:1262) bemoaned the lack of empirical field research, the inability of current chemical methods 'to detect the very minute trace elements which might indicate more precisely the mother ores from which an artifact is made', and the great difficulty of dating past mines, furnaces and slag heaps (which rarely provide diagnostic pottery types). Metal artifacts excavated from Near Eastern tells could however be dated by association, and chemical analysis of them revealed a more complicated sequence of alloys than considered in Childe's account; between unalloyed copper and tin bronze occurred 'long and often unintentional trials with impurities such as arsenic and antimony' (Wertime 1964:1257).

Wertime also provided the earliest clear exposition (much influenced by the metallurgist Cyril Stanley Smith) of what we can call the *Standard Model* of early extractive metallurgy, which would be the dominant paradigm for the next 25 years. In the Standard Model, metallurgy began with cold forging of native copper, followed by hot-working (annealing), melting together of small pieces in a fire, and then casting in an open mould after melting in a crucible. Enlargement of crucibles led to the smelting of pure

carbonate ores of copper (malachite and azurite) and lead (cerussite) in small furnaces.

As pure ores were exhausted, early metalworkers discovered that if iron oxide flux was added to the charge of low grade ore, the gangue minerals (clays, silicates and aluminosilicates) could be induced to form a liquid slag that would separate from the smelted metal in a furnace. Through experimentation, more complex technologies were developed to recover copper from sulfide ores. Some of these sulfide ores contained antimony and arsenic, giving rise to copper-arsenic-antimony alloys (Wertime 1964:1260). Since the proportion of these elements was largely beyond the control of the metalworkers, they turned in time to the use of tin to produce bronze of consistent alloy content – a development long delayed by the scarcity of tin ores in the Near East. Along with the development of these alloys came improvements in casting technology such as two-piece closed moulds and the lost-wax (*cire perdue*) process.

It is strange that Wertime's review made no mention of radiocarbon dating, which by 1964 was beginning to be widely employed in archaeology. The fuel for smelting, casting and smithing the earliest metals was almost inevitably charcoal, while the combustion of wood was also used to crack rock underground ('fire-setting') and to light the miner's work. Radiocarbon dating was therefore ideally suited to the study of prehistoric mines, furnaces and forges, and archaeologists moved swiftly to take advantage of this new method. By the late 1960s major projects were under way on prehistoric mines and metallurgical sites in Israel, the USSR, western and eastern Europe, the Balkans, China and sub-Saharan Africa.

THE MAKING OF MODERN ARCHAEOMETALLURGY

On some projects (notably the Timna project directed by Beno Rothenberg in Israel) metallurgists, chemists and mineralogists were invited to participate in field survey and excavation. This was a development of the utmost importance. The scientific study of prehistoric metal artifacts was nothing new; chemical analyses of archaeological metals had been made sporadically since the late 1700s (Pollard and Heron 1996:3), whilst optical metallography had been used to infer the manufacturing technology of ancient metals from the 1910s (e.g., Mathewson 1915). These studies had thrown little light on the early history of extractive metallurgy, since archaeologists were unfamiliar with the field evidence (ores, slags and refractory ceramics), and in any case could not date them, so samples were rarely brought home for laboratory scientists to study. Collaboration in the field lead to the mutual education of archaeologists and metallurgists, and so to rapid advance in the pace of discovery. Many scholars made important contributions in the 1960s and 1970s, but two above all were responsible for transforming the study of early metallurgy. Both were professional metallurgists, but their approaches could hardly have been more different.

Ronald Tylecote (1916–1991) developed the integrated approach that is the core of modern archaeometallurgy, combining archaeological fieldwork, scientific analysis and experimental reconstruction. Apart from his work with Rothenberg's Timna project, in the course of which he personally trained many of the senior European scholars now active, he undertook archaeometallurgical fieldwork in western and eastern Europe, Cyprus, Sardinia, Nigeria and Sudan. He also undertook archaeometallurgical tours of China and Japan, and was an extraordinarily prolific writer on the subjects of past mining and metallurgy; his two editions of *A History of Metallurgy* (Tylecote 1991) served as the definitive reference work on the subject for more than two decades. His work was squarely empirical, focused upon the reconstruction of past techniques in metallurgy, but largely unconcerned with the questions of *why* humans domesticated metals, and what social impact this may have had.

These questions were central to the thought of the second founding figure of modern archaeometallurgy. Cyril Stanley Smith (1903–1992) was an eminent solid state physicist who developed in mid-career a passionate interest in the history of metallurgy. Smith's early ventures, beginning in 1940, were a series of annotated translations of early European texts on pyrotechnology, including those of Theophilus (*c.* 1125; Hawthorne and Smith 1979) and Biringuccio (1540; Smith and Gnudi 1966). From 1949 he began to apply the analytical methods of materials science to the study of historic and prehistoric artifacts, mostly in museum collections. Though he never took part in field excavation of metallurgical sites, he did make a notable archaeometallurgical field trip through Iran in 1967 with Theodore Wertime, and studied many of the oldest samples of metal recovered in American excavations in the Near East.

Smith drew on all of these experiences to propose a truly radical theory of the invention of pyrotechnologies (Smith 1970, 1976, 1981). Noting that the earliest examples of these artificial materials tended to be beads, figurines, pendants and other ornaments rather than functional tools or weapons, Smith argued that the origins of pyrotechnology lay more in aesthetics than in economics. Subsequent research in the Old World on the origins of metallurgy (Stech 1990, Eleuère and Mohen 1991, Chernykh 1992), lime plaster (Kingery *et al.* 1988), ceramics (Vandiver *et al.* 1989) and glass (Charleston 1991) has largely confirmed his theory. In the New World, as in the Old, the earliest known metal objects were made for displays of status and as grave goods, not for hunting, agriculture or warfare (Binford 1962).

Smith's views have profoundly influenced subsequent American work on the origins of pyrotechnology, and are certainly well known to European archaeometallurgists. Unfortunately the latter have rarely ventured any opinion on the social context of early metallurgy, preferring to stick closely to technical interpretation. The lack of communication between archaeometallurgists and archaeologists in Europe is glaringly evident in Colin Renfrew's much-cited analysis of the Varna cemetery in Bulgaria (*c.* 4300 BC), which is notable for its precocious wealth of gold and copper burial goods (Renfrew 1986). Not only does Renfrew present as novel the claim that the earliest metallurgy was developed for display rather than for economic utility, but he is also led, as Muhly (1988:15) has noted, into serious error through ignorance of the properties of metals.

NEW PERSPECTIVES

The main challenge before archaeometallurgy in the 1970s and 1980s was how to interpret the archive of material remains recovered by fieldwork. Part of the problem lay in the unfamiliar nature of the remains and materials, and part with the range of expertise required to do it justice. Native copper, clay refractory ceramics, crucible smelting, hand-blown furnaces, iron-rich smelting slags and copper-antimony-arsenic alloys are all foreign territory to modern materials scientists; nor is there much in the older scientific literature that is directly relevant. The hyper-specialization of modern science and technology was, and is, an acute problem. To fully understand these lost technologies, the analyst needs advanced training in metallurgy, ceramics and geology, practical knowledge of the construction and operation of furnaces, and an encyclopaedic knowledge of the range of historic, ethnographic and archaeological data on pre-industrial metallurgy. No scholar can be expert in all these areas.

Faced with this dilemma, archaeometallurgists divided into two camps. Both were intimately involved in the analysis of archaeological materials, but they differed in their approach to interpretation. One side took existing analytical and conceptual tools and literature, and applied them to the analysis of the prehistoric remains. The other, with Tylecote to the fore, sought understanding primarily through experiment, using actual archaeological evidence as the constraint.

SUCCESS AND FAILURE OF ARMCHAIR ARCHAEOMETALLURGY

The benefits and pitfalls of reliance upon existing scientific approaches and literature are well illustrated in the theories of the Cambridge metallurgist Jim Charles. During the 1960s geochemists produced the first reliable estimate of the geochemical abundance of the elements in the Earth's crust. Inspection of the abundance data for the major metals (Table 39.1) immediately raises the question of why some of the least abundant metals – gold, silver, lead and copper – were the first to be exploited, whilst some of the most abundant – aluminium, titanium and manganese – were not obtained in metallic form until the nineteenth or twentieth centuries. Charles (1985) showed that this is easily explained by the thermodynamics of reactions between these metals and oxygen, as graphically expressed in an Ellingham diagram (Figure 39.1).

This Ellingham diagram is a plot of the stability of metal oxides with increasing temperature in the presence of carbon monoxide, which was invariably the reducing agent in pre-industrial furnaces. Above each line the oxide is stable; below the line the metal is stable. The point of intersection between the line of each metal:metal oxide and the line for carbon:carbon monoxide marks the minimum condition for reduction of that metal oxide by carbon monoxide. The more negative the free energy of formation, the more difficult it is to reduce the metal with carbon monoxide. As Charles showed, this diagram solves the paradox in Table 39.1, which is that the most abundant metals (aluminium, iron, titanium) were among the last to be obtained in metallic form. These metals are the most difficult to reduce from their oxides. Conversely, some of the rarest metals are easily reduced to the metallic state. (Gold is not plotted on this diagram because it has positive free energy of formation, and is therefore almost always found in the metallic state.) With only minor exceptions (e.g., mercury), the historical sequence of the wide-

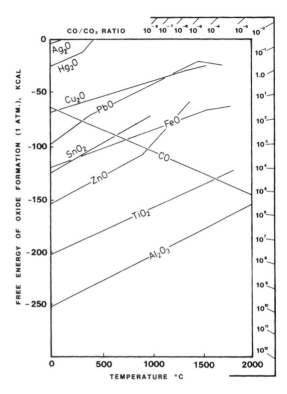

Figure 39.1 Ellingham diagram showing the free energy of formation of common metal oxides to their constituent metals over a range of absolute temperature. The free energy of formation of carbon monoxide is also shown.

spread use of these metals corresponds to the relative strength of their chemical bonds to oxygen. The sequence in which the metals were used is therefore a direct expression of the growth of human technological expertise through time. More specifically, it reflects the ability of metalworkers to achieve higher temperatures and more reducing gaseous atmospheres in their furnaces.

Much less successful was Charles' attempt to explain trends in copper alloy composition in terms of the mineralogy and structure of an idealized copper deposit (Charles 1980, 1985:158). His argument was that the sequence of alloy use was a natural consequence of progressively mining down through a vertically stratified copper ore body. In his model native copper co-exists with copper oxide, copper carbonates, and iron oxides in the oxidized gossans above a primary sulfide ore body containing arsenic (producing easily-reduced arsenates in the oxidized zone). The metallurgical sequence of the Standard Model was, in Charles' view, driven by progressive exhaustion of resources.

Diminishing native copper resources promoted experimentation with the associated carbonates; scarcity of pure carbonate ores led in turn to the discovery of the fluxing powers of iron oxide, permitting exploitation of impure ores; the mining away of the oxide layer necessitated the invention of more complex techniques for smelting sulfides, which led naturally to the co-smelting of complex ores, producing copper-arsenic-antimony alloys; and exhaustion of these led to the discovery of a substitute, tin bronze.

Unfortunately this idealized scheme corresponds to neither geological nor archaeological reality. Some of the earliest worked ore deposits in formerly glaciated parts of Europe, such as Ross Island in Eire, Cwmystwth in Wales and the Mitterberg in Austria, have no oxidized zone; sulfides were smelted there from the start (Craddock 1995:126, O'Brien 1996). Nor is there any reason to believe that the quantities of ore mined in Europe during the Chalcolithic and Bronze Age were sufficient to exhaust the oxide zones (Budd and Taylor 1995). Nor is the exhaustion of native copper a plausible reason for the development of smelting. Even in Iran, where native copper has been used for eight millennia, it was still available in quantity in the 1930s (Pigott 1996:154).

Problems have also arisen in the application of modern engineering conceptual tools to the residues of prehistoric extractive metallurgy. Slags are the most important source of evidence for prehistoric smelting technology because (i) unlike the metal produced, the slags were usually left at the smelting site, and (ii) because the slag preserves in its chemical composition and mineral assemblage a record of the temperature and the furnace atmosphere at the time of solidification from the molten state. Slags can therefore provide valuable evidence of the knowledge and skill of the prehistoric metalworker (see Chapter 40). Many of the early archaeometallurgists had professional experience in the British iron and steel industry, and thus tried to adapt techniques used in the analysis of blast furnace slags to the interpretation of prehistoric slags. Bulk chemical analyses of these slags were obtained, and the temperatures of solidification inferred by plotting the simplified chemical data on to published ternary equilibrium phase diagrams (e.g., Tylecote and Boydell 1979:41).

Equilibrium phase diagrams are extremely useful when used appropriately, but may not be suitable for the interpretation of early slags, which are frequently not near chemical equilibrium, or are chemically more complex than the three-component phase diagrams. Techniques from mineralogy, especially optical petrography and electron probe microanalysis, provide more direct (and hence more reliable) evidence. Unfortunately relatively few archaeometallurgists have extensive training in mineralogy, so the interpretation of pre-industrial slags is still an area in need of considerable development.

Table 39.1   Estimated abundance (in parts per million) of the major metals in the Earth's crust and approximate date of first widespread use. Abundance data from Krauskopf and Bird (1995:589).

Element	Crustal abundance (ppm)	First widespread use
Aluminium	81 300	19th C. AD (Europe/USA)
Iron	50 000	Early 1st millennium BC (Near East)
Titanium	4400	20th C. AD (Europe/USA)
Manganese	950	19th C. AD (Europe)
Vanadium	135	20th C. AD (Europe)
Chromium	100	20th C AD (Europe)
Nickel	75	Cu/Ni alloys, 2nd millennium BC (Near East)
Zinc	70	Brass, 2nd C. AD (Rome); Zn metal, 10th C. AD (India)
Copper	55	Native, *c.* 7000 BC; smelted, *c.* 5000 BC (Near East)
Cobalt	25	20th C. AD (Europe/U.S.A)
Lead	13	6th millennium BC (Near East/Balkans)
Tin	2	4th millennium BC (Near East)
Arsenic	1.8	As/Cu alloys, 5th millennium BC (Near East/Balkans)
Antimony	0.2	Sb/Cu alloys, 5th millennium BC (Near East)
Bismuth	0.2	Bi/Cu alloys, 2nd millennium AD (Peru)
Mercury	0.08	1st millennium BC (China)
Silver	0.07	4th millennium BC (Balkans/Near East)
Platinum	0.01	*c.* AD 100 (South America)
Gold	<0.01	5th millennium BC (Balkans)

THE EXPERIMENTAL APPROACH

The most fruitful approach to the study of the earliest extractive metallurgy has been the close integration of archaeology, archaeometallurgy and experimental archaeology. Although experimental reconstruction of smelting procedures, based upon archaeological or ethnographic evidence, have been made on occasion since 1894 (for references see Tylecote and Merkel 1985), it was only in the 1970s that the modern protocol for experiments was developed, largely by Tylecote and his collaborators (e.g., Tylecote *et al.* 1971, Tylecote and Boydell 1979). The essential elements of this protocol are the full recording of relevant technical data (timed logs of temperatures and gas composition, additions of fuel and ore, etc.), systematic series of trials with controlled variation of parameters, and full archaeometallurgical analysis of the inputs and products.

This integrated approach has advanced our understanding of early metallurgical processes far beyond the straightjacket of the Standard Model. The mutual co-reduction of mixtures of sulfide and oxide ore (Rostoker *et al.* 1989) has been shown to be a viable alternative explanation for the earliest sulfide smelting, whilst experiments with the production of copper arsenic alloys suggest that the earliest copper-arsenic alloys in the British Isles may have been produced by relatively simple low temperature co-smelting of oxide minerals, rather than from the more elaborate technologies required for the smelting of sulfide minerals (Budd *et al.* 1992). By successive iteration – from the archaeological record to experiment, comparison of the experimental product to the archaeological evidence, adjusting the experiment, and so on – the restraints upon speculation become more and more confining.

DIFFUSION OR INDEPENDENT INVENTION?

One of the earliest shots fired in the radiocarbon revolution was aimed at Childe's belief that metallurgy had been invented in the Near East, and had diffused from there to all other parts of the Old World. (The independent invention of copper smelting in the New World, now dated to the mid-second millennium BC, has not been seriously disputed.) In the late 1960s Colin Renfrew argued that the available radiocarbon dates hinted at the independent invention of metallurgy in the Balkans, in Italy and in the Iberian Peninsula (Renfrew 1969). Strong supporting evidence has since emerged from independent archaeometallurgical data

in each of these regions, and strong arguments made for independent invention in western Europe as well (Muhly 1988, Craddock 1995:126, Ruiz-Taboada and Montero-Ruiz 1999).

In western Europe, Italy and Iberia the earliest evidence of extractive metallurgy is of very inefficient but quite variable processes. All involve some form of crucible smelting, using relatively pure copper ores, that produces little or no slag. This is not at all what one would expect if extractive metallurgy had been introduced directly from the Near East, where such crude processes had by this time (in the fourth and third millennia BC) been long abandoned. Even in Britain, the last region of western Europe to begin extractive metallurgy (around 2200 cal BC) no evidence has yet been found of furnaces or slags in the earliest phases. Nor was metallic lead, smelted since the sixth millennium in the Near East, known in the early Chalcolithic of Iberia or Western Europe (Craddock 1995:145).

Independent invention of copper metallurgy has been claimed for Thailand in the fourth millennium BC and for Niger, West Africa, in the early second millennium BC. The current consensus is that there was no metallurgy in Thailand before 2000 BC (Muhly 1988:12), whilst the evidence for metallurgy in Niger before the early first millennium BC has been discredited (Killick *et al.* 1988). The case for independent invention of copper metallurgy in China is complicated by doubts about the context of metal objects dated 5000–3000 cal BC, many of which are brass – and thus automatically suspect (Muhly 1988:13). Copper smelting crucibles previously attributed to the Neolithic Hongshan Culture (4500–3000 cal BC) have recently been directly dated by thermoluminescence to the interval 1500–700 BC (Chen *et al.* 1998). Although there is a great deal of ongoing research on this topic in China, very little information is available at present (D. Wagner, pers. comm.).

DISCUSSION AND CONCLUSIONS

This brief review emphatically supports Trigger's contention that empirical evidence constrains what it is possible to believe about the past. The speculative theories of Engels, Childe, Wertime, Smith and Charles have been repeatedly re-examined in the light of new evidence from archaeology, archaeometallurgy and experiment, and have been found wanting in many respects. It is no longer possible to believe, as Childe did, that the earliest metalworking brought about revolutionary changes in economic and social organization.

It is also increasingly unlikely (if not absolutely disproven) that knowledge of metallurgy originated in the Near East and diffused to all other regions of the Old World. Independent invention is proven in the New World, is very probable in the Balkans and in Iberia, is increasingly likely in western Europe; East Asia is still uncertain. These regional sequences of metal production cannot all be made to fit Wertime's Standard Model; nor do they support the geological determinism of Charles. On the other hand, some bold speculation has found empirical confirmation, most notably Smith's view that the invention of the pyrotechnologies was motivated more by aesthetics than economics.

The combination of archaeology, archaeometallurgy and experimental replication has become an extremely powerful engine for discovery. As its explanatory power has grown, so some of its leading European practitioners seem to feel that speculation on the social setting of early metallurgy is unscientific and thus best left to others (e.g., Craddock 1995:2). This is a point of view with which I strongly disagree, and I therefore feel it appropriate to close with a defence of speculation.

Extractive metallurgy is human behaviour – metals do not mine or smelt themselves, though it would appear so in much of the recent European literature on the subject. However naive the grand theories of Childe, Smith and Wertime may appear from our present vantage point, each represented a huge advance in thought on metallurgical origins, and together they have defined the central questions for the field for much of the previous century. If those who now possess the deepest scientific understanding of the evidence will not speculate on the social significance of their research, then those who are less well informed on technological matters must do so (e.g., Renfrew 1986).

One of the few exceptions to the recent dearth of speculation on the social setting of early European metalworking is a collaboration between an archaeometallurgist and a theoretically-inclined archaeologist (Budd and Taylor 1995). This accuses Childe, Wertime and their successors of greatly exaggerating both the scale of metal production and the evidence for economic specialization in metal working in Europe during the Bronze Age, and also of projecting a false picture of a 'scientific, experimenting, specialized, industrial and necessarily male metallurgist' into prehistory (Budd and Taylor 1995:141). They favour instead a 'minimalist' model of small scale, unspecialized metal workers more concerned with achieving 'a generalized kind of magico-religious power' (Budd and Taylor 1995:139) – though what this might be is left unspecified.

Ironically, their argument suffers from exactly the same deficiency as Childe's own, which is ignorance of the anthropological literature on the role of ritual in pre-industrial metalworking (e.g., Childs and Killick 1993, Herbert 1993). This literature shows that the opposition between 'magical' and 'economic' production is mistaken; where metalworkers were credited with magical powers, this did not generally prevent them from acting as rational, self-interested, experimental economic agents. Indeed, Shennan (1999) has recently presented a detailed argument, drawing on both African ethnography and Ricardo's Law of Comparative Advantage, for highly specialized copper production operating within a complex system of exchange in the eastern Alps during the Bronze Age. Any argument for 'uneconomic' production will have to be made at a comparable level of theoretical and empirical sophistication. This can be done, as is well demonstrated by Steven Epstein's elegant explanation for the almost complete lack of technological change in copper smelting over more than six centuries on the north coast of Peru (Epstein 1993, 1996). This research is the product of archaeological fieldwork, archaeometallurgical analysis and experimental replication, as in the best European research. To these Epstein adds an anthropological sophistication and a willingness to speculate about the meaning of metallurgy that are largely absent in contemporary research on the origins of metallurgy in European and Asian archaeometallurgy.

REFERENCES

*Recommended for further reading

Binford, L.R. (1962). Archaeology as anthropology. *American Antiquity*, **28**:217–225.

Budd, P. and Taylor, T. (1995). The faerie smith meets the bronze industry: magic versus science in the interpretation of prehistoric metalworking. *World Archaeology*, **27**:133–143.

Budd, P., Gale, D., Pollard, A.M., Thomas, R.G. and Williams, P.A. (1992). The early development of metallurgy in the British Isles. *Antiquity*, **66**:677–686.

Charles, J.A. (1980). The coming of copper and copper-based alloys and iron: a metallurgical sequence. In Wertime, T.A. and Muhly, J.D. (eds) *The Coming of the Age of Iron*, 151–182. Yale University Press: New Haven.

Charles, J.A. (1985). Determinative mineralogy and the origins of metallurgy. In Craddock, P.T. and Hughes, M.J. (eds) *Furnaces and Smelting Technology in Antiquity*, 21–28. Occasional Paper 48. British Museum Publications: London.

Charleston, R. (1991). *Glass – 5000 Years*. British Museum Publications: London.

Chernykh, E.N. (1992). *Ancient Metallurgy in the USSR*. Cambridge University Press: Cambridge.

Chen Tiemei, Li Yanxiang and Bao Wenbo (1998). Dating of the copper-smelting remains found at Niuheliang site. In *Proceedings of the Fourth International Conference on the Beginnings of the Use of Metals and Alloys (BUMA-IV)*, 231–232. Japan Institute of Metals: Sendai.

Childe, V.G. (1930). *The Bronze Age*. Cambridge University Press: Cambridge.

Childe, V.G. (1944). Archaeological ages as technological stages. *Journal of the Royal Anthropological Institute*, **74**:7–24.

Childe, V.G. (1985). *What Happened in History*. Penguin: London (reprint).

Childs, S.T. and Killick, D.J. (1993). Indigenous African metallurgy: nature and culture. *Annual Review of Anthropology*, **22**:317–337.

Cline, W.W. (1937). *Mining and Metallurgy in Negro Africa*. General Series in Anthropology No. 5, George Banta: Menasha.

*Craddock, P.T. (1995). *Early Metal Mining and Production*. Edinburgh University Press: Edinburgh.

Eluère, C. and Mohen, J.-P. (eds) (1991). *Découverte du Métal*. Picard: Paris.

Engels, F. (1972). *The Origins of the Family, Private Property and the State*. International Publishers: New York (reprint).

Epstein, S.M. (1993). *Cultural Choice and Technological Consequences: Constraint of Innovation in the Late Prehistoric Copper Industry of Cerro Huaringa, Peru*. Unpublished PhD Dissertation, University of Pennsylvania.

Epstein, S. (1996). Le cuivre, le fer, et le souffle humain: culture et technique dans la fonte andine préhispanique. *Techniques et Culture*, **27**:125–126.

Hawthorne, J.G. and Smith, C.S. (1979). *Theophilus. On Divers Arts*. Dover: New York.

Herbert, E.W. (1993). *Iron, Gender and Power: Rituals of Transformation in African Societies*. University of Indiana Press: Bloomington.

Juleff, G. (1996). An ancient wind-powered iron smelting technology in Sri Lanka. *Nature*, **379**:60–63.

Killick, D. (1991). The relevance of recent African iron-smelting practice to reconstructions of prehistoric smelting technology. In Glumac, P.D. (ed.) *Recent Trends in Archaeometallurgical Research*, 47–54. MASCA Research Papers in Science and Archaeology 8(1), University Museum: Philadelphia.

Killick, D., van der Merwe, N.J., Gordon, R.B. and Grébénart, D. (1988). Reassessment of the evidence for early metallurgy in Niger, West Africa. *Journal of Archaeological Science*, **15**:367–394.

Kingery, W.D., Vandiver, P. and Prickett, M. (1988). The beginnings of pyrotechnology, Part II: production and use of lime and gypsum plaster in the pre-pottery Neolithic Near East. *Journal of Field Archaeology*, **15**:219–244.

Kipling, R. (1982). *The Portable Kipling*. Penguin Books: London.

Krauskopf, K.B. and Bird, D.K. (1995). *Introduction to Geochemistry*, (3rd edn). McGraw-Hill: New York.

Mathewson, C.H. (1915). A metallographic description of some ancient Peruvian bronzes from Machu Picchu. *American Journal of Science*, **40**:525–616.

Morgan, L.H. (1877). *Ancient Society*. Henry Holt: New York.

*Muhly, J.D. (1988). The beginnings of metallurgy in the Old World. In Maddin, R. (ed.) *The Beginning of the Use of Metals and Alloys*, 2–20. MIT Press: Cambridge, Mass.

O'Brien, W. (1996). *Bronze Age Copper Mining in Britain and Ireland*. Shire Books: Princes Risborough.

Pigott, V.C. (1996). Near Eastern archaeometallurgy: modern research and future directions. In Cooper, J.S. and Schwarz, G.M. (eds) *The Study of the Ancient Near East in the Twenty First Century*, 139–176. Eisenbrauns: New York.

Pollard, A.M. and Heron, C. (1996). *Archaeological Chemistry*. Royal Society of Chemistry: Cambridge.

Renfrew, C. (1969). The autonomy of the south-east European Copper Age. *Proceedings of the Prehistoric Society*, **35**:12–47.

Renfrew, C. (1986). Varna and the emergence of wealth in prehistoric Europe. In Appadurai, A. (ed.) *The Social Life of Things*, 141–168. Cambridge University Press: Cambridge.

Rostoker, W., Pigott, V.C. and Dvorak, J.R. (1989). Direct reduction to copper metal by oxide-sulfide mineral interaction. *Archeomaterials*, **3**:69–87.

Rowlands, M.J. (1971). The archaeological interpretation of prehistoric metalworking. *World Archaeology*, **3**:210–224.

Ruiz-Taboada, A. and Montero-Ruiz, I. (1999). The oldest metallurgy in western Europe. *Antiquity*, **73**:897–903.

Shanks, M. and Tilley, C. (1987). *Re-constructing Archaeology: Theory and Practice*. Cambridge University Press: Cambridge.

*Shennan, S. (1999). Cost, benefit and value in the organization of early European copper production. *Antiquity*, **73**:352–363.

Smith, C.S. (1970). Art, technology and science: notes on their historical interaction. *Technology and Culture*, **11**:493–549.

Smith, C.S. (1976). On art, invention and technology. *Technology Review*, **78**:2–7.

*Smith, C.S. (1981). *A Search for Structure: Selected Essays on Science, Art and History*. MIT Press: Cambridge, Mass.

Smith, C.S. and Gnudi, M.T. (1966). *The Pirotechnia of Vannoccio Biringuccio*. MIT Press: Cambridge, Mass.

Stech, T. (1990). Neolithic copper metallurgy in Southwest Asia. *Archeomaterials*, **4**:55–61.

Trigger, B. (1989). *A History of Archaeological Thought*. Cambridge University Press: Cambridge.

*Tylecote, R.F. (1991). *A History of Metallurgy*, (2nd edn). Institute of Metals: London.

Tylecote, R.F. and Boydell, P.J. (1979). Experiments on copper smelting based on early furnaces found at Timna. In Rothenberg, B., Tylecote, R.F. and Boydell, P.J. (eds) *Chalcolithic Copper Smelting: Excavations and Experiments*, 27–49. Monograph No. 1, Institute for Archaeometallurgical Studies: London.

Tylecote, R.F. and Merkel, J. (1985). Experimental smelting techniques: achievements and future. In Craddock, P.T. and Hughes, M.J. (eds) *Furnaces and Smelting Technology in Antiquity*, 3–20. Occasional Paper 48, British Museum Publications: London.

Tylecote, R.F., Austin, J.N. and Wraith, A.E. (1971). The mechanism of the bloomery process in shaft furnaces. *Journal of the Iron and Steel Institute*, **209**:342–363.

Vandiver, P., Soffer, O., Klima, B. and Svoboda, J. (1989). The origins of ceramic technology at Dolní Věstonice, Czechoslovakia. *Science*, **246**:1002–1008.

Vansina, J. (1979). Bantu in the crystal ball, 1. *History in Africa*, **6**:287–333.

Wertime, T. (1964). Man's first encounters with metallurgy. *Science*, **146**:1257–1267.

40

Pyrotechnology

J.G. McDONNELL

Department of Archaeological Sciences, University of Bradford.

The development and manipulation of high temperature processes produced some of the finest and most technologically-advanced artifacts recoverable from the archaeological record. These include ceramics, glass and metals, each of which displays chronological and geographical variations in the levels of technological achievement. They are normally studied by materials specialists, from a technological, regional or chronological perspective. This chapter attempts to consider their production through an examination of the pyrotechnological characteristics of a range of different processes, including a consideration of some processes applicable to organic materials

·Any study of this nature is hampered by problems such as poor representation in the archaeological record, inadequate excavation and recording techniques, absence of appropriate sampling strategies, and recovery or analysis of only components of the processes. Equally, a myriad of technological terms have been used in the description of pyrotechnological features, evidence and structures. Many of these have been adopted from modern processes, and applied incorrectly to the archaeological record. When examined in detail some of these terms are inconsistent, such as the use of the term *smelting hearth* to describe a furnace. The term *hearth* has equal validity when applied to the domestic hearth, the blacksmith's hearth or the lead ore/slag hearth used in lead smelting.

However, pyrotechnological considerations show that very different temperatures, atmospheres and chemical processes are occurring in each of these three cases, and the terminology should reflect this fact. Similarly, the term *furnace* is widely used, especially with reference to glass-making and metal smelting, yet the two processes, although operating in the same temperature range, have radically different atmospheric conditions – highly oxidizing in the former and highly reducing in the latter.

This chapter considers a theoretical approach to these technologies, examining commonalities across technologies, rather than within technologies. The study of any individual technology requires synthesis of archaeological data (which is in most cases incomplete), historical records and texts, experimental data and detailed analyses of the materials used in or produced by the process. These include the primary inputs (e.g., raw clays used for ceramics), the waste by-products (e.g., the slags, residues and waste debris), as well as the finished products. It is probably only in the case of certain ceramics that all these stages have been adequately studied.

Pyrotechnology is a term that has evolved to mean deliberate processes utilizing the control and manipulation of fire. Invariably it refers to high temperature processes in the manufacture of inorganic artifacts. Fire is a chemical reaction that occurs when fuel, heat

Handbook of Archaeological Sciences. Edited by D.R. Brothwell and A.M. Pollard.

and oxygen are present in the proper ratio and in suffcent amounts to produce energy (both light and heat; Rossotti 1993:3). This chemical reaction is a 'chain reaction', limited by the amount of fuel, oxygen or heat available. If the ratio of fuel to oxygen is changed there will be a consequent effect upon the heat generated.

THE THREE COMPONENTS

To generate the chemical reactions needed for pyro-technology, three factors must be considered; fuel, temperature and atmosphere.

Fuel

A wide range of fuels have been used in antiquity – wood, charcoal, coal, peat, turves, gorse (furze), dung (Smith 1998, Thompson and Young 1999). The selection of fuel is often dominated by environmental factors. For example, in Shetland, peat charcoal may have been employed for ironworking although charcoal would be a better fuel (Bond 1998:82). The fuels all have different calorific values, ash contents, and physical attributes such as strength under load, etc. There is also variation within one fuel type, e.g., different types of wood will burn differently.

Oxygen is also a fuel and consideration must be given to its method of introduction into the pyrotech-nological process. Some technologies rely on 'natural draft', which may be enhanced by the 'chimney effect'. These are usually simple processes, but an exceptional example is the iron smelting furnaces of Sri Lanka which rely on indirect wind pressure rather than natural draft (Juleff 1998). Most advanced technologies require the use of a forced draft (bellows), not necessarily to enable greater volumes of air to be introduced into the process, but more importantly to control the quantity of air (oxygen) in the system. The adoption of motive power, firstly water power, did however enable increased volumes and pressures of air to be utilized.

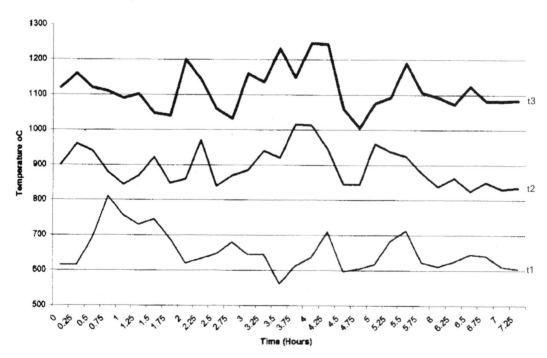

Figure 40.1   Temperature profile of an iron smelting experimental furnace conducted at Old Scatness, Shetland, August 1999. The furnace was approximately 1.5 metres tall. Thermocouples were located 0.2 metres from top (t1), 0.4 metres from top (t2) and 0.75 metres from top at tuyere level (t3), 20 cm above tapping arch in front of the furnace. The tuyere was on the sides. The furnace was lit at 07.30 and preheated until 12.15 (time = 0) when the first ore was added. Total ore added 10.5 kg, final addition at 16:40.

Temperature

The control of temperature is crucial in many processes. It is essential to appreciate that no single temperature defines the operation of a bonfire, kiln, hearth or furnace. These processes are dynamic and so the temperature changes throughout the time of the operation and at different points within the process (Figure 40.1). Particular processes may require certain temperatures for particular periods of the operation. In this chapter the temperature discussed or used in any process is the temperature required for the (chemical) reaction or physical change to proceed, e.g., the firing of coarse pottery, reduction of a metal oxide or melting of an alloy (e.g., Table 40.2). In the past in order to control temperatures, reliance was inevitably placed on the human senses – touch on the furnace wall, or colour of the flame or the metal being worked in the hearth. The ability to see these colours (ranging from dull red at 500°C to white above 1400°C) is essential in many pyrotechnological processes. Such control cannot be achieved in daylight, therefore low light levels are needed, as in the traditional smithy.

Atmosphere

The atmosphere generated in many pyrotechnological processes is of equal importance to the temperature attained. The atmosphere can either be oxidizing, reducing or neutral. In all processes the nature of the atmosphere may change through either the time of the operation or in different zones of the process. The balance between oxidizing and reducing conditions is defined as the *redox*. Under oxidizing conditions the atmosphere has excess oxygen. In reducing conditions the atmosphere is oxygen-deficient and the reducing gas is normally carbon monoxide (CO), generated by a reaction between limited oxygen and carbon from the fuel. Formally, redox is quantified in terms of the partial pressure of oxygen available, expressed as $p[O_2]$. Under normal atmospheric conditions, $p[O_2] = 0.2$, since approximately 20 per cent of the atmosphere is oxygen. Under strongly oxidizing conditions, the partial pressure of oxygen will remain at 0.2, but the temperature is higher, causing reactions to occur more quickly. Under reducing conditions the partial pressure of oxygen decreases and tends to zero, i.e., values of the order of 10^{-6}, whereas the partial pressure of CO increases. To ensure the reduction of metallic oxides to metal in smelting processes requires a minimum temperature and a minimum partial pressure of CO (Parker 1978:271).

The need to control these three parameters depends on the nature of the technological process. The development of technology can be viewed as evidence for increasing control over these parameters. This is manifested as changes to the physical structures represented by a bonfire, kiln, or furnace. These structures particularly relate to *primary production processes*, e.g., firing ceramics, making glass, or smelting ores. In developed technologies, especially metal production, there are *secondary processes*, which inevitably involve the use of a hearth. This structure is dealt with separately below since the term encompasses many different meanings.

THE PROCESSES AND STRUCTURES

Each of the four classes of pyrotechnological processes considered here (bonfire, hearth, kiln, furnace) is associated with different structures that may survive in the archaeological record. A bonfire lacks physical structural remains, operating at low temperatures and having no means of controlling atmosphere. This lack of structure makes it virtually invisible in the archaeological record. In contrast, a furnace gives a high degree of control of fuel, temperature, and atmosphere, and the remains (bases) of iron smelting furnaces are readily identified and excavated in the archaeological record, e.g., Kyloe Cow Beck, Bilsdale, North Yorkshire (Figure 40.2). This physical structure is, however, only part of the archaeological record, and the visibility of these processes is more commonly

Figure 40.2 Iron smelting furnace, Kyloe Cow Beck, Bilsdale, North Yorkshire. It is a clay built shaft furnace built into the slope, with structure surviving to near tuyere level. The tapping arch and channel for slag can be seen. Archaeomagnetic date late fourteenth century AD.

through the recovery of the associated debris and residues rather than the structures themselves.

The term 'organic processes' is used here to encompass a wide range of activities involving the action of fire on organic materials. Most are involved with food production, e.g., corn drying, cooking, baking, smoking fish and meats. These processes may be assumed to have occurred, but there is often little evidence for them in the archaeological record (Kemp 1999). With a few exceptions (e.g., corn driers), they lack diagnostic residues, and also have no diagnostic structural evidence. The inorganic processes are much better defined both by structure and associated residues, but there are still major gaps in the inorganic record (e.g., prehistoric non-ferrous smelting sites). The following discussion is structured effectively in terms of the maximum temperature achievable in the four processes, but also in terms of the degree of control which can be exerted during each process (Table 40.1).

The bonfire

Bonfires can utilize different fuels, probably with wood being the most common, but peat and dung are also viable. There is little or no control over temperature or redox conditions either within the bonfire or during the life of the bonfire.

Organic processes

The *clamp*, which gives some control over the bonfire, was used extensively for the production of charcoal, inhibiting high temperatures and oxidizing conditions (Tilman 1978). Also included (technologically speaking) within these processes are funeral pyres, which have been extensively discussed by McKinley (see Chapter 24). Her experiments show that the construction of the pyre imparts some control over the cremation process, such as orienting the long axis of the pyre into the wind. The maximum temperatures achievable

are in excess of 1000°C, but only for short periods, and in particular places, but temperatures of *c.* 700–800°C could easily be maintained for some time. Despite some control through the construction, however, fluctuation in the strength or direction of the wind has a dramatic effect on the pyre process.

Inorganic processes

Bonfire firing of ceramics, or open firing (Orton *et al.* 1997:127), is common among traditional potters, and was undoubtedly used in antiquity. The open firing of ceramics is characterized by the production of small quantities of pots, rapid changes in temperature and redox, and the short duration of firing. Open firing of pottery is only rarely recognized in the archaeological record (Peacock 1982:67), although it can be inferred from a technological analysis of the products (see Chapter 36). It is normally though not exclusively associated with the production of hand-made coarsewares (Orton *et al.* 1997:130). Clamp firing of bricks is discussed by Mayes (1965:91), and these products are considered burnt rather than the fully-fired brick or tile.

Ore roasting (Figure 40.3) was an essential preliminary stage in most copper and iron smelting technologies. The roasting process had a vital chemical and physical effect upon the ore; it converted ores such as carbonates to oxides, and caused micro-cracking within ore particles to facilitate the penetration of reduction gases during smelting. It has also been argued that bonfires were the earliest pyrotechnology used in metal smelting (e.g., Craddock 1996:135). Timberlake undertook experimental tin smelting at Flag Fen utilizing a bonfire. The smelts were successful, but the quantities produced were small (Timberlake 1994). Pollard *et al.* (1990) argued that the early use of bonfire technology may have accounted for the minor and trace element signatures (especially arsenic) in early Bronze Age metalwork. A classic example of bonfires used in metallurgy is the use of *bales* or *boles* for lead smelting (Raistrick 1927, Murphy 1992, Barker and White 1992,

Table 40.1 High temperature structures.

Type	'Effective Operating Temperature range' (°C)	Maximum Temperature (°C)	Redox	Control
Bonfire	600–800	*c.* 1000	predominantly oxidizing	none
Hearth	800–1000	1300	predominantly oxidizing	medium
Kiln	600–900	1300	predominantly oxidizing	medium
Furnace	800–1100	1500	reducing	high

Figure 40.3 Box section through top 1 metre of 3 metre of build-up of ore roasting bonfire debris at Rievaulx Abbey, North Yorkshire. The ore was prepared for the blast furnace which operated from *c.* AD 1570–1670.

Hamilton *et al.* 1999). The most frequently-quoted example is Wintering's Edge, Gunnerside, North Yorkshire, often cited as the classic bale (e.g., Raistrick 1927, Tylecote 1986:57). Unfortunately, despite extensive searching this site has never been located since Raistrick's original work, and some doubt must be placed on such sites until other examples are properly excavated and recorded.

The archaeological evidence for bale smelting of lead is primarily the slags and evidence of burning, since there is an absence of structures. Recent work utilizing geophysics has raised a number of questions concerning the simple explanation of bales (Hamilton *et al.* 1999). The smelting of lead ore (galena, PbS) in bonfires could be achieved because the process is an exothermic relatively low temperature oxidation process which does not require a reducing atmosphere (Murphy 1992). It is interesting to note that lead beads are the earliest dated smelted metal in Britain (Hunter and Davis 1994).

Hearths and hearth processes

The term 'hearth' is probably one of the most common technological terms used in archaeology. It is diagnostically domestic, and the recognition of a hearth within a building immediately suggests the focus of domestic occupation in that area, e.g., in long houses (where humans and domestic animals occupy the same structure) it may distinguish human activity and occupation from that of animals (Figure 40.4). The hearth is essentially a controlled bonfire – the controls including space (i.e., within a structure), control of fuel and hence some control over temperature.

Organic processes

The domestic hearth was used within the home to provide heat, light, and for cooking; it operated at low temperatures (300–500°C), and under oxidizing conditions. It is usually assumed that if there is no evidence for an inorganic processes (e.g., slag – see below) then the hearths were associated with an organic process, such as smoking food, etc.

Inorganic processes

The *technological hearth* can be defined as a hearth used for pyrotechnological inorganic processes. With the exception of lead smelting, all technological hearths were used for secondary processes, e.g., iron smithing or secondary copper alloy working. In the following discussion it is assumed that there is some additional evidence for the relevant technological processes.

(i) Smelting hearths

The use of the term 'smelting hearth' must be considered inaccurate in all cases except the Medieval lead smelting process, the lead ore hearth and the slag hearth. In these cases the process is carried out in an open hearth, and in the lead ore hearth probably with oxidizing conditions prevailing (Willies 1991, Bassham 1992). These two processes were effectively one step up in control of the conditions used in bole smelting, and utilized water powered bellows.

(ii) The secondary metalworking hearth

The secondary metalworking hearth is the essential requirement of the blacksmith (and associated trades), copper and precious metalworking crafts. The requirements were fuel, usually charcoal although peat would also be suitable, and a forced draft. Two levels of secondary metalworking must be distinguished, (a) the permanent forge or smithy and (b) temporary metalworking. In the former it would be expected that there would be both a building and a permanent hearth structure. In the latter case, any hearth could be adopted to work the metal.

(iii) Non-ferrous secondary metalworking hearths

Non-ferrous metals could be alloyed, cast, and hot and cold worked. The melting points of metals and alloys are given in Table 40.2, and show that these range from low melting point alloys, e.g., pewter (Sn/Pb eutectic 185°C), pure metals such as tin (232°C) to high melting

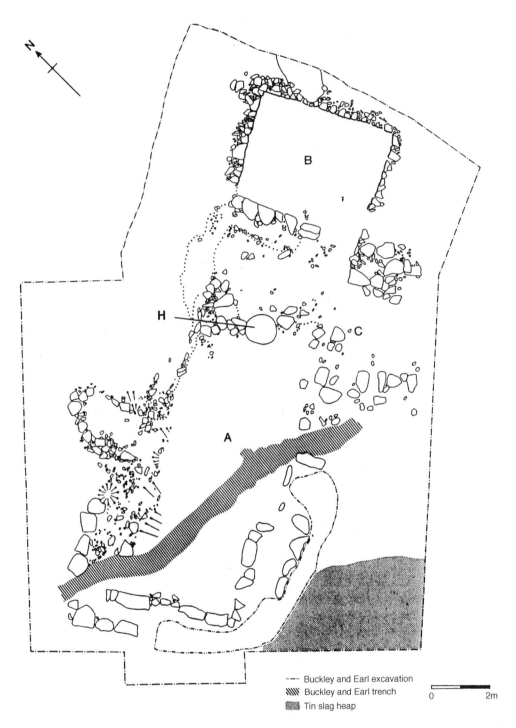

N

B

H

C

A

- - - Buckley and Earl excavation
\\\\\ Buckley and Earl trench
▒▒▒ Tin slag heap

0   2m

Figure 40.4 Plan of twelfth century AD longhouse at Crift Farm, Lanlivery, Bodmin, Cornwall. The domestic occupation is at the northeast end, focused on the circular domestic hearth. Originally the lower part had a central drain for animal waste. This longhouse was adapted for metallurgy – the waist-high forge constructed against the south-east wall, and tin smelting slag was dumped outside the south wall.

Table 40.2 Temperatures of various processes.

Process	Temperature °C	Redox
Sawdust ignition temperature	120	oxidizing
Baked clay	200	oxidizing
Reduction of copper oxide to copper	200	reducing
Melting point of tin	232	reducing/neutral
Wood ignition temperature	245	oxidizing
Charcoal ignition temperature	300	oxidizing
Melting point of lead	327	reducing/neutral
Reduction of lead oxide to lead	600	oxidizing
Fired clay	700	oxidizing
Reduction of tin oxide to tin	700	reducing
Lime kiln – dissociation of $CaCO_3$ to CaO	700–800	oxidizing
Firing coarseware pottery	800	oxidizing
Reduction of iron oxide to iron	>800	reducing
Volatilization of zinc	917	reducing/neutral
Glass transition temperature	~1000	oxidizing
Liquidus temperature of 10% Sn bronze	1020	reducing/neutral
Melting point of gold	1064	reducing/neutral
Melting point of copper	1086	reducing/neutral
Melting temperature of metal smelting slags	1000–1100	reducing(?)
Firing stoneware pottery	1400	oxidizing
Fusion of glass raw materials	1500	oxidizing
Vitrification of clays	>1500	oxidizing

point pure metals, such as copper (1086°C) and alloys (10 per cent tin bronze 950°C). There are some hearths that are readily identified as non-ferrous working hearths by the association of metalworking debris (Bayley 1993:213). Special hearths were utilized for *cupellation* (separation of gold and silver from base metals) and *parting* (separation of gold from silver; see Bayley 1991).

(iv) Ferrous secondary metalworking
Unlike the other metals used in antiquity, nearly all iron was either hot or cold worked, and joined by welding. Close to the tuyere (air inlet) the conditions in the hearth were high temperature (1500°C) and strongly oxidizing. Away from the tuyere the temperature drops and the atmospheric conditions become less oxidizing moving to neutral or slightly reducing. The iron smith required different temperatures depending on the process being carried out ranging from simple forging and shaping (a few hundred degrees), through cutting to fire welding at more than 1000°C.

Past excavations of sites interpreted as smithies have failed to recover the residue assemblage, and therefore doubt must prevail over their interpretation. The slag distribution data from Wharram Percy (McDonnell 2000) or Hamwic (Andrews 1997:222) has made identification of the smithy building possible, but not the location of the forge. A major difficulty is that some smithies, in some periods probably the majority, were waist-high forges, e.g., Burton Dassett, Warwickshire; Crift Farm, Bodmin, Cornwall (Mills and McDonnell 1992, McDonnell forthcoming). In these cases there is no obvious 'burnt' or heated structure and the interpretation of these two forges relies solely on the presence and distribution of hammerscale recovered from floor levels. Ground level examples do exist, e.g., a Pictish smithing hearth at Birsay, Orkney (McDonnell 1986a). Classically, Crew (1985) has excavated a snail-shaped smithy building at the Late Iron Age Hillfort of Bryn-y-Castell, Snowdonia, North Wales. The shape reduced the light, further confirming that smiths need to work in low light levels.

Kilns and ovens

The oven is an enclosed reverbatory structure used solely for domestic processing of organic material such as bread. Reverbatory structures utilize the roof, often a barrel vault construction, to reflect the heat (hot flames and gases) downwards. The kiln was used for a variety of organic and inorganic processes. Kilns used different methods of transferring the heat to the process, e.g., directly or by reverbatory methods. Kilns did not normally reach high operating temperatures (i.e., in excess of 1000°C) and were predominantly oxidizing. They utilized a wide variety of fuels, including wood, charcoal, and coal.

Organic processes

Kilns have a range of applications for organic processes, such as corn dryers, and malting. Corn and barley (malting) were dried to preserve the grains, and required gentle heating to c. 100°C, the corn being dried on a surface heated from below. Corn driers are well-represented in the archaeological record notably in the Roman and Medieval periods (Gibson 1988, Heaton 1992, van der Veen 1989).

Inorganic processes

Inorganic processes include lime, potash, brick, tile and pottery production. In most cases the critical control is that of temperature. Slaked lime (CaO) production requires the dissociation of either calcium or magnesium carbonate to oxide, at about 700–800°C (Table 40.2) under oxidizing conditions. Lime was produced for two main purposes, either agricultural, for liming fields or for mortars and plasters. Limekilns are known from the Roman and later periods (Palmer and Neaverson 1998:53). Less well-studied are the remains of the alum industry (Millard 1999). Alum (a hydrated double sulfate of potassium, ammonia or sodium) was an important mordant in the dyeing industry, and was extracted (in England at least) by calcining alum shales in large clamps, followed by further extraction and purification to aluminium sulfate.

Brick and tile production are usually discussed together, and are well attested in both the Roman and Medieval periods (e.g., Drury 1981, McWhirr 1979, Stopford 1993). The temperatures achieved were c. 1200°C, (presumably under oxidizing conditions) and the kilns were taken up to temperature slowly to dispel remaining moisture. The temperature was held for some time (unspecified) and then allowed to cool, the whole process taking several days, although the source of this information is not given (Drury 1981:137).

The largest and most studied group of kilns are pottery kilns. The earliest pottery kilns in Britain derive from the Late Iron Age (Morris 1994). Roman kiln technology was reviewed by Swann (1984) and Medieval pottery production including kiln data was discussed by Moorhouse (1981). Orton et al. (1997)

argues that domestic ovens could be utilized to make pottery. Ethnographic studies have provided a wealth of information (e.g., Orton et al. 1997). The archaeological investigation of pottery kilns has revealed considerable detail regarding their structure and operation. Moorhouse (1981:97) argues that it was not the type of structure which produced the distinctive fabric types but the potters' method of firing the kiln that was the major influence (e.g., see Chapter 36). A wide range of fuels have been used in pottery production, with wood and coal predominating. The temperatures achieved would depend on the type of ceramic produced, from vessel fabrics requiring temperatures of the order of 800°C to the highly fired stonewares and porcelains requiring temperatures of more than 1400°C. In the majority of kilns the redox conditions were predominantly oxidizing, although specialist production of reduced wares, (e.g., Terra Nigra) requiring reducing conditions were produced, by burning wood as fuel under restricted air flow. Technological studies of pottery such as Classical Greek black figure vases have shown exceptional control over firing conditions (Maniatis et al. 1993).

There are two processes that require the operation of kilns as predominantly oxidizing, but at much higher temperatures. These are glass making furnaces (Hunter 1991), and steel cementation furnaces (Barraclough 1984:34, Cranstone 1997) for the conversion of malleable wrought iron into steel. Both of these technologies do not fully satisfy the term furnace (see below) in that the atmospheric conditions are predominantly oxidizing. In glass making (Pollard and Heron 1996:149) the glass furnace (kiln) is used to fuse the raw materials together in a crucible at temperatures of the order of 1500°C under oxidizing conditions. Subsequent glass working, i.e., making vessels and annealing artifacts, was carried out at lower temperatures but still under oxidizing conditions.

The cementation furnace/kiln was a reverbatory furnace used to convert bars of malleable wrought iron into (blister) steel bars. About 10–14 tonnes of (usually) Swedish bar iron were packed together with carbonaceous material in sandstone chests. The top 20 cm of the chest was covered by a mixture of sand and hammer scale, termed grozel, to seal the chests. A coal fire was lit in the grate between the chests and fired for about two weeks. The hot flames and gasses surged around the chests achieving temperatures of the order of 900°C within the chests, where the highly reducing conditions enabled carbon to diffuse into the iron bars (Barraclough 1984:34). After about two weeks firing and one week cooling the bars were fully carburized, showing a coarse pearlite microstructure (McDonnell 1997).

Furnaces

Furnaces operate under high degrees of fuel, temperature and atmosphere control. They therefore require substantial structures to be successful. The problem faced by the early furnace operator was to achieve high temperatures yet maintain control over the atmosphere.

The primary use of furnaces is in the smelting of ores to metal. Although the temperatures required for reducing oxides to metal are relatively low, e.g., for copper temperatures of the order of 300°C are needed, whereas iron requires 800°C, the atmospheric conditions must be strongly reducing (p[O] $\sim 10^{-6}$). Critically very high temperatures (>1100°C) are required to liquate the slags that remove the gangue component, and for copper the metal also needs to melt (1086°C). There is clearly a conflict between high temperatures and reducing conditions, since the former are achieved by increased air (oxygen) flow, the latter by restricted air flow. The only solution to this is to have good thermal properties of the furnace structure to reduce heat loss; hence furnaces were constructed of clay, often with walls of $c.$ 10–20 cm thick. Non-ferrous metal smelting furnaces have been excavated, e.g., in Israel and southern Spain (Craddock 1996:122). Tin smelting furnaces of the later Medieval period (blowing houses) have been investigated (Greeves 1994), but the only pre-blowing house smelting site known in Britain is Crift Farm (McDonnell 1995). Here no furnace structure has been identified although approximately five tonnes of slag are in a slag heap adjacent to the buildings where the furnace is believed to have been.

Numerous iron smelting furnaces have been excavated, and this has resulted in a chronologically-based furnace typology of western Europe (Cleere 1972, Calissendorff 1979). These typologies are fundamentally flawed, because the greater part of the furnace superstructure that often defines the typology rarely survives. These furnace typologies have been used to date other sites and reinforce the typology. Thus the published furnaces at Berkhamsted were dated, at the time, as Roman because they were identified as shaft furnaces; the assumption from the published typologies being that shaft furnaces were a Roman introduction, although all other data from the site indicates an Iron Age date (Thompson and Holland 1976). It is now assumed, by this author, that most furnaces are a variation on the basic shaft furnace. Scholars have often confused furnace typology with slag typology. Thus, in a shaft furnace, there were a number of possibilities for how the slag was removed. It could be tapped, giving classic tap slag (McDonnell 1986b), or the slag was tapped into a pit below the furnace, resulting in the characteristic slag pit furnaces of Poland, North Germany and Denmark (Voss 1995), or the slag remained in the base of the furnace, i.e., a furnace slag. There is no strict or tight relationship between furnace typologies and slag typologies.

The temperature profile of an experimental furnace is illustrated in Figure 40.1. The temperature recorded at tuyere level, but not near the tuyere, exceeds 1200°C, whilst the temperature near the top of the furnace fluctuates around $c.$ 600°C. The atmosphere ranges from reducing at the top (blue flame, indicative of the burning of carbon monoxide), to highly oxidizing conditions just above the tuyere, generated by the incoming air. The furnaces exhibit temperature and atmosphere stability for long periods of time (seven hours; Figure 40.1), which is in sharp contrast to the fluctuations of these components shown by bonfire technologies, e.g., the funeral pyre (Chapter 24).

Complex technologies

A sophisticated manufacturing technology normally encompasses more than one process. The more complex the technology, the more processes are involved. Thus the complete cycle of manufacturing a metal artefact from the ore may include bonfire technology at the ore processing stage, furnace technology to smelt the ore to metal and hearth process to manufacture the artefact from the stock metal.

The visibility of these processes in the archaeological record will depend on the level of activity. A one-off operation is virtually invisible. Permanent operations will figure in the record either through survival of the structures but more likely through recovery of the associated residues. Thus at Rievaulx Abbey the seventeenth century iron blast furnace structure has not yet been located, although its position can be postulated from the location of the 2–3 metre depth of ore roasting debris (Figure 40.3), the blast furnace slag heap, and the watercourses used to power the bellows (McDonnell 1999).

THE RESIDUES AND SLAGS OF PYROTECHNOLOGICAL PROCESSES

The recovery of slags and residues associated with the pyrotechnological process enables the archaeological scientist to confirm the presence of that process on the site/settlement, although not necessarily on the area excavated. The slags and residues can only be used for positive identification – the absence of inorganic residues can only suggest (but not prove) that the pyrotechnological structures were used for organic processes. However the association between the residues and the structure must be rigorous. The temptation to interpret evidence for burning plus a few grams of 'slag' as a smelting site must be resisted.

Slags and residues are divided into two broad groups; diagnostic and non-diagnostic. Diagnostic slags can be attributed to a particular industrial process. These comprise the ironworking slags, i.e., smelting or smithing slags, and the non-ferrous residues, e.g., crucibles, or other residues derived from, for example, lime burning. Non-diagnostic residues cannot be directly ascribed to a process, but may be identified with a process by association with diagnostic residues, e.g., clay furnace lining with smelting slag.

The identification, characterization and discussion of the diagnostic and non-diagnostic residues associated with all the organic and inorganic pyrotechnological processes is beyond the scope of this chapter. For example, there are probably five to ten different 'types' of iron smelting slags, but the discipline is still in its infancy, and the author recognizes that the classifications previously proposed (e.g., McDonnell 1986b, 1988) are too simplistic. A brief overview of the slags and residues associated with some technologies are given in Table 40.3, and some more detailed examples for ironworking are given in Table 40.4. Within these

Table 40.3 Examples of diagnostic and non-diagnostic residues.

Process	Diagnostic residues	Associated non-diagnostic residues	Confirmed in the archaeological record
Organic Processes			
Domestic hearth	none	?	Y
Smoking food	none	?	N
Charcoal production	?	charcoal	Y
Corn drying	burnt grain	fired clay, daub etc	Y
Cremation	burnt bone?	charcoal/ash	Y
Inorganic Processes			
Bonfire Technologies			
Ore roasting	ore fines	charcoal	Y
Bale lead smelting	lead slags	fuel?, fired clay?	Y
Other metal smelting	slag?	fuel?, fired clay?	N
Pottery production	wasters?	fuel?, fuel ash slag(?)	Y
Hearths			
Domestic	none		
Lead, Slag/Ore	slags	hearth lining, fuel	Y
Non ferrous secondary metalworking	crucibles, metal spill, etc	hearth lining, fuel, fuel ash slag(?), cinder(?)	Y
Ferrous Secondary metalworking	hammerscale, smithing slags	hearth lining, fuel, fuel ash slag(?), cinder(?)	Y
Kilns			
Lime	limestone	fuel, kiln structure, fuel ash slag(?), cinder(?)	Y
Tile/Pot	wasters	Fuel, fuel ash slag(?), cinder(?)	Y
Glass	glass waste	Fuel, fuel ash slag(?), cinder(?)	Y
Cementation	crozzel, bar iron/steel	fuel	Y
Furnaces			
Copper smelting	smelting slags	fuel, furnace lining	Y
Tin smelting	smelting slags	fuel, furnace lining	Y
Iron smelting	smelting slags	fuel, furnace lining	Y

Table 40.4   Examples of slags and residues specific to ironworking.

Process	Structure	Diagnostic Residues (General)	Diagnostic Residues (Slag Types)	Non-Diagnostic Residues
Ore processing	bonfire	ore, ore fines (roasted)	tap slags	fuel, fired clay
Iron smelting	furnace	ore fines, smelting slags, metallic iron/steel, bloom	furnace slags slag blocks gromps	fuel, fired clay
Bloom smithing	hearth(?)	bloom, slags(?), billet	undefined in the archaeological record	fuel, fired clay, cinder(?)
Iron smithing	hearth	slags, stock iron, products	hearth bottoms or PCBs (Plano-Convex bases), smithing slag lumps, hammerscale (flake and spheroidal)	fuel, fired clay, fuel ash slag(?), cinder(?)

tables there are a number of terms, such as fuel ash slag and cinder, which describe certain types of residue, but because they are non-diagnostic there must be some doubt as to whether they are generated by particular processes. Furthermore, there is no strict definition of terms, and different researchers use different terminologies, although in the analysis of the ironworking debris from Scole in Norfolk some attempt was made to more clearly define certain slag types (Cowgill *et al.* forthcoming).

The fact that slags and residues are waste products has led to two inevitable results. Firstly when these residues were generated they were considered as waste products and therefore disposed of as such, although Hingley (1998) has argued for ritual deposition of ironworking slags. If they were disposed of as waste products then they occur in secondary, tertiary or higher contexts, and therefore may bear no direct relation to the place of working. Critically the microslags, e.g., hammerscale in ironworking, recovered during sieving, are potentially better indicators of the place of working. The second outcome of the nature of slags and residue is that archaeologists also considered them as useless and rarely bothered to keep them, or at best kept some 'representative' sample, without the expertise to decide what was or was not representative. This situation still continues today, with few conscious policies for the recovery of micro-residues.

The diagnostic slags and residues for most technologies can be readily identified through scientific analysis. The characterization and identification of non-diagnostic residues is more complex. Thus vitrified hearth lining could derive from any number of pyrotechnological processes, and even the presence of some copper alloy residues adhering only shows that copper working was potentially one, but not the sole process associated with that debris.

CONCLUSIONS

Pyrotechnological processes were fundamental to early societies and cultures. The organic processes provided food, heat and light. The food manufacturing processes are poorly represented in the archaeological record save for the corn dryers due to the lack of associated diagnostic residues. These processes, although involving fire and heat, are relatively low temperature and therefore less likely to manifest themselves as high temperature features. They required little control and therefore lacked substantial structures. Many of the processes could utilize the domestic hearth, and would not require the construction of a specialist hearth, kiln or oven. Such structures would only be needed where there was intense activity.

The inorganic pyrotechnological processes span the complete range of structures from bonfire technologies lacking structure and control through to the carefully constructed, highly controlled smelting furnaces. As the process becomes more complex, needing higher temperatures, etc., so the levels of control increase and more infrastructure is required. Thus the change from the use of hand or foot bellows to waterpowered bellows needs the construction of dams, leats and wheel pits. These changes will manifest themselves in the archaeological record of the site but may also be represented by changes in slag or residue composition. Thus there are clear differences between iron bloomery slags (50–60 per cent FeO content, crystalline structures of iron silicate, iron oxide and a non-crystalline glassy phase), high bloomery slags (10 per cent FeO, predominantly glassy phase), and blast furnace slags (5 per cent iron oxide, wholly glassy phase).

Future research and understanding of pyrotechnological processes will rely on the full excavation of features and structures and the recovery of raw materials, residues and products of these processes. Certainly, in the case of ironworking, these criteria have not been met. Our current interpretation is based on poor excavation techniques, and incomplete recovery of all products and waste-products. There is a failure to integrate the data recovered from structures (such as the correct identification of waist high forges), with residues (e.g., recovery of hammerscale), and products (such as stock iron bars and rods). At the post-excavation stage there is often poor interpretation and integration of the data (the tendency to distribute the different categories of material (metal artefact, slag, fired clay) to different specialists). The fragmented data is rarely re-constituted to provide an overview of the pyrotechnological process. Recognizing these problems will enable future researchers to establish rigorous methodologies prior to excavation.

REFERENCES

*Recommended for further reading

Andrews, P.A. (ed.) (1997). *Excavations at Hamwic: Vol 2. Excavations at Six Dials.* Research Report 109, Council for British Archaeology: York.

Barraclough, K.C. (1984). *Steelmaking before Bessemer. Volume 1 Blister Steel, the Birth of an Industry.* Metals Society: London.

Barker, L. and White, R. (1992). Early smelting in Swaledale and Arkengarthdale: a further look. In Willies, L. and Cranstone, D. (eds) *Boles and Smeltmills*, 15–18. Historical Metallurgy Society: London.

Bassham, S. (1992). Wharfedale lead smelt mills and fume condensation. In Willies, L. and Cranstone, D. (eds) *Boles and Smeltmills*, 37–39. Historical Metallurgy Society: London.

Bayley, J. (1991). Archaeological evidence for parting. In Pernicka, E. and Wagner, G.A. (eds) *Archaeometry '90*, 19–28. Birkhäuser Verlag: Berlin.

Bayley, J. (1993). *Non-Ferrous Metalworking in England – Late Iron Age to Medieval.* Unpublished PhD Thesis, University College, London.

Bond, J. (1998). Ashes to earth: the making of a settlement mound. In Nicholson, R.A. and Dockrill, S.J. (eds) *Old Scatness Broch, Shetland: Restrospect and Prospect*, 81–96. University of Bradford/Shetland Amenity Trust/North Altantic Biocultural Organisation: Bradford and Lerwick.

Calissendorff, K. (1979). *Iron and Man in Prehistoric Sweden.* Jernkontoret: Stockholm. (trans. H. Clarke).

Cleere, H.F. (1972). The classification of early iron-smelting furnaces. *Antiquaries Journal*, 52:8–23.

Cowgill, J., McDonnell, G. and Mills, J.M. (forthcoming). Ironworking analysis for the Scole and Oakley Road Improvement Project. In Ashwin, T. and Tester, A. (eds) *Excavations Along A140/A143 By-Pass, Scole, Norfolk.* East Anglian Archaeology.

*Craddock, P.T. (1996). *Early Metal Mining and Production.* Edinburgh University Press: Edinburgh.

Cranstone, D. (1997). *Derwentcote Steel Furnace: An Industrial Monument in County Durham.* Lancaster Imprints No. 6, Lancaster University Archaeological Unit: Lancaster.

Crew, P. (1985). *Bryn-Y-Castel 1979–1985 Interim Reports.* Snowdonia National Park: Plas Tan y Bwlch.

Drury, P.J. (1981). The production of brick and tile in Medieval kilns. In Crossley, D. (ed.) *Medieval Industry*, 126–142. Monograph No. 40, Council of British Archaeology: London.

Gibson, A. (1988). Medieval corn-drying kilns at Capo, Kincardineshire and Abercairns, Perthshire. *Proceedings of the Prehistoric Society of Scotland*, 118:219–230.

Greeves, T. (1994). Stamping and smelting at Upper Merivale Tin Mill: preliminary results 1991–1993. In Ford, T.D. and Willies, L. (eds) *Mining Before Powder.* Bulletin of the Peak District Mines Historical Society, 12:76–80.

Hamilton, K., McDonnell, J.G. and Schmidt, A. (1999). Assessment of early lead working sites in the Yorkshire Dales by geophysical prospection. *British Mining: Memoirs of the Northern Mine Research Society*, 63:158–164.

Heaton, M.J. (1992). Two mid-Saxon grain-driers and later Medieval features at Chantry Fields, Gillingham, Dorset. *Proceedings of the Dorset Natural History and Archaeological Society*, 114:97–126.

Hingley, R. (1998). Iron and ironworking and regeneration: a study of the symbolic meaning of metalworking in Iron Age Britain. In Gwilt, A. and Haselgrove, C. (eds) *Reconstructions of Iron Age Societies*, 9–18. Monograph 71, Oxbow: Oxford.

Hunter, F. and Davis, M. (1994). Early Bronze Age lead; a unique necklace from southeast Scotland. *Antiquity*, 68:824–830.

Hunter, J. (1991). The Medieval glass industry. In Crossley, D. (ed.) *Medieval Industry*, 143–150. Monograph No. 40, Council for British Archaeology: London.

Juleff, G. (1998). *Early Iron and Steel in Sri Lanka: a Study of the Samanalawewa Area.* Deutsche Archaologische Institut, Von Zabern: Mainz.

Kemp, R. (1999). The excavation of a monastic fishing establishment at Oldstead Grange, North Yorkshire. *Internet Archaeology*, 7 (http://intarch.ac.uk/).

Maniatis, Y., Aloupi, E. and Stalios, A.D. (1993). New evidence for the nature of Attic black gloss. *Archaeometry*, 35:23–34.

Mayes, P. (1965). Medieval tile-kiln at Boston, Lincs. *Journal of the British Archaeological Association*, 28:86–106.

McDonnell, G. (1995). The Crift Farm project; second interim report. *Journal of the Trevithick Society*, 22:50–57.

McDonnell, G. (1999). Monks and Miners, the ironworking industries of Rievaulx and Bilsdale. *Medieval Life*, **6**:16–21.

McDonnell, G. (2000). The smithy. In Stamper, P.A. and Croft, R.A. (eds) *Wharram Percy, the South Manor Area*. York University Archaeological Publications 10, English Heritage: London.

McDonnell, G. (forthcoming). The identification of smithies through hammerscale distribution. *Journal of Historical Metallurgy*.

McDonnell, J.G. (1986a). Copper alloy and iron, including evidence of production. In Hunter, J.R. (ed.) *Rescue Excavations on the Brough of Birsay 1974–82*, 196–207. Monograph Series 4, Society of Antiquaries of Scotland: Edinburgh.

McDonnell, J.G. (1986b). *The Classification of Early Ironworking Slags*. Unpublished PhD Dissertation, Aston University.

McDonnell, J.G. (1988). Ore to artefact – a study of early ironworking technology. In Slater, E.A. and Tate, J.O. (eds) *Science and Archaeology, Glasgow 1987*, 193–207. BAR 196, British Archaeological Reports: Oxford.

McDonnell, J.G. (1997). The slags and residues, and metallographic analysis of metallic samples. In Cranstone, D. (ed.) *Derwentcote Steel Furnace: an Industrial Monument in County Durham*, 93–102. Lancaster Imprints No. 6, Lancaster University Archaeology Unit: Lancaster.

McWhirr, A. (1979). *Roman Brick and Tile: Studies in Manufacture, Distribution and Use in the Western Empire*. BAR International Series 68, British Archaeological Reports: Oxford.

Millard, A.R. (1999). Geochemistry and the early alum industry. In Pollard, A.M. (ed.) *Geoarchaeology: Exploration, Environments, Resources*, 139–146. Special Publication 165, Geological Society: London.

Mills, A. and McDonnell, G. (1992). *The Identification and Analysis of the Hammerscale from Burton Dassett, Warwickshire*. Report Number 47/92, English Heritage Ancient Monuments Laboratory: London.

Moorhouse, S.A. (1981). The Medieval pottery industry and its markets. In Crossley, D. (ed.) *Medieval Industry*, 96–125. Monograph No. 40, Council of British Archaeology: London.

Morris, E.L. (1994). Production and distribution of pottery and salt in Iron Age Britain. *Proceedings of the Prehistoric Society*, **60**:371–394.

Murphy, S. (1992). Smelting residues from boles and simple smeltmills. In Willies, L. and Cranstone, D. (eds) *Boles and Smeltmills*, 43–47. Historical Metallurgy Society: London.

Orton, C., Tyers, P. and Vince, A. (1997). *Pottery in Archaeology*. Cambridge University Press: Cambridge.

Palmer, M. and Neaverson, P. (1998). *Industrial Archaeology – Principles and Practice*. Routledge: London.

*Parker, R.H. (1978). *An Introduction to Chemical Metallurgy*. Pergamon: Oxford.

Peacock, D.P.S. (1982). *Pottery in the Roman world: an Ethnoarchaeological Approach*. Longman: London.

Pollard, A.M. and Heron, C. (1996). *Archaeological Chemistry*. Royal Society of Chemistry: Cambridge.

Pollard, A.M., Thomas, R.G. and Williams, P.A. (1990). Experimental smelting of secondary copper minerals: implications for Early Bronze Age metallurgy in Britain. In Pernicka, E. and Wagner, G.A. (eds) *Archaeometry '90*, 127–136. Birkhäuser Verlag: Berlin.

Raistrick, A. (1927). Notes on lead mining and smelting in West Yorkshire. *Transactions of the Newcomen Society*, **7**:81–96.

Rossotti, H. (1993). *Fire*. Oxford University Press: Oxford.

Smith, W. (1998). Fuel for thought: archaeobotanical evidence for the use of alternatives to wood fuel in Late Antique North Africa. *Journal of Mediterranean Archaeology*, **11**:191–205.

Stopford, J. (1993). Modes of production among Medieval tilers. *Medieval Archaeology*, **37**:93–100.

Swann, V. (1984). *The Pottery Kilns of Roman Britain*. Royal Commission on Historical Monuments Supplementary Series 5, HMSO: London.

Thompson, A. and Holland, E. (1976). Excavations at an Iron Age site at Dellfield, Berkhamsted. *Hertfordshire Archaeology*, **4**:137–148.

Thompson, G.B. and Young, R.L. (1999). Fuels for the furnace: recent and prehistoric ironworking in Uganda and beyond. In van der Veen, M. (ed.) *The Exploitation of Plant Resources in Ancient Africa*, 221–239. Plenum Press: New York.

Tilman, D.A. (1978). *Wood as an Energy Source*. Academic Press: New York.

Timberlake, S. (1994). An experimental tin smelt at Flag Fen. *Journal of the Historical Metallurgy Society*, **28**:122–129.

*Tylecote, R.F. (1986). *The Prehistory of Metallurgy in the British Isles*. Institute of Metals: London.

van der Veen, M. (1989). Charred grain assemblages from Roman period corn dries in Britain. *Archaeological Journal*, **146**:302–319.

Voss, O. (1995). Snorup – an iron producing settlement in West Jutland 1st–7th Century AD. In Magnusson, G. (ed.) *The Importance of Ironmaking; Technical Innovation and Social Change*, 132–139. Jernkontorets Bergshistoriska Utskott: Stockholm.

Willies, L. (1991). Lead: ore preparation and smelting. In Tylecote, R.F. and Day, J. (eds) *Industrial Revolution in Metals*, 84–130. Institute of Metals: London.

41

The Provenance Hypothesis

L. WILSON and A.M. POLLARD

Department of Archaeological Sciences, University of Bradford.

The concept of provenance (or *provenience*) has been current in archaeology for at least a century and a half. As originally conceived, the term provenance is relatively undefined – often it is used to denote the findspot of an object (a definition which is still accepted in the world of fine art and antiquities), or to imply the source of manufacture of an artifact in very general terms (a production 'workshop' or 'school'). With the advent of instrumental methods of chemical analysis in the middle of the twentieth century (and subsequently the widespread availability of methods of isotopic analysis) the term provenance has taken on a more precise meaning within scientific archaeology. As early as the 1840s and 1850s, pioneering work by European chemists (see Pollard and Heron 1996:5) led to the scientific acceptance that some chemical property of an archaeological artifact (almost invariably an inorganic artifact) could be considered characteristic of the raw material source of the object – the 'chemical fingerprint' was born.

From the 1960s onwards, a 'golden age' of archaeological chemistry was established (Pollard and Heron 1996, 2000), in which an ever-expanding portfolio of archaeological artifacts were subjected to chemical provenancing – ceramics, non-ferrous metals, lithics, glasses and faience, and a select range of organic raw materials, including amber and jet. In order to accommodate the need to analyse large numbers of samples, and a large number of characteristics on each sample,

increasing attention was paid through the 1970s to statistical manipulation of multivariate data (in fact the approaches are not strictly statistical, in that they are not based on established mathematical models, but are empirical). Mathematical treatment of data sets rapidly became an integral feature of provenance work and systematic methodologies were advocated (e.g., Ward 1974, Harbottle 1982, Pollard 1986). Such approaches proliferated to the extent that almost every continent can demonstrate successful studies of ceramics and metals (see Pollard and Heron 1996: chapters 4 and 9).

ASSUMPTIONS OF SCIENTIFIC PROVENANCE

Before discussing the specific considerations appropriate to some of the key categories of materials, a few fundamental observations should be made about the general methodology of scientific provenance. The major assumptions underlying every provenance study can be summarized as follows:

(i) The prime requirement is that some chemical (or isotopic) characteristic of the geological raw material(s) is carried through (unchanged, or predictably relatable) into the finished object.

Handbook of Archaeological Sciences. Edited by D.R. Brothwell and A.M. Pollard.

(ii)   That this 'fingerprint' varies between potential geological sources available in the past, and that this variation can be related to the geographical (as opposed to perhaps a broad depositional environment) occurrences of the raw material. *Inter*-source variation must be greater than *intra*-source variation for successful source discrimination.

(iii) That such characteristic 'fingerprints' can be measured with sufficient precision in the finished artifacts to enable discrimination between competing potential sources.

(iv)   That no 'mixing' of raw materials occurs (either before or during processing, or as a result of recycling of material), or that any such mixing can be adequately accounted for.

(v)   That post-depositional processes either have negligible effect on the characteristic fingerprint, or that such alteration can either be detected (and the altered elements or sample be discounted), or that some satisfactory allowance can be made.

(vi)   That any observed patterns of trade or exchange of finished materials are interpretable in terms of human behaviour. This pre-supposes that the outcome of a scientific provenance study can be interfaced with an existing appropriate socioeconomic model, so that such results do not exist *in vacuo*.

The degree to which these assumptions are met varies from material to material, as discussed below. It is perhaps surprising, with hindsight, that the provenance hypothesis has been so successful – if these *ab initio* requirements had been explicitly stated before any such work had been attempted, it might be that no reasonable researcher would have embarked on the quest! The fact that it has been so successful is a tribute to the triumph of empiricism over rationalism. It is also, indirectly, a tribute to the skill and control exerted by ancient craftspeople over the vagaries of inherent variations in raw material and process-induced differentiation.

CHOICE OF ELEMENTS AND INSTRUMENTATION

There has been a substantial literature devoted to the elucidation of the 'best' elements to use when determining provenance, particularly for ceramics (see Chapter 36). Indirectly (and occasionally explicitly) this has been reduced to the proposition that a particular analytical technique is more appropriate to the study of particular materials (see Renfrew and Bahn 1996:346 for a summary of materials and choice of techniques for characterization). In ceramic provenancing, for instance, it is widely (and reasonably) argued that trace elements are more useful than major and minor elements, on the grounds that these are more variable in clay sources. Also, trace elements are less susceptible to anthropogenic control than the major and minor elements, which are more likely to influence the firing and performance characteristics of the pot. It has even been argued that there exists some universal but restricted suite of elements, which invariably give an adequate characterization of clay source (e.g., Mallory-Greenough and Greenough 1998). In the late 1970s, this debate focused on the relative advantages of neutron activation analysis (NAA) over the newer technique of inductively coupled plasma emission spectrometry (ICP-OES). Thankfully, these somewhat sterile debates have largely diminished in recent years and it is now recognized that determination of as wide an elemental and isotopic range as possible is desirable. Although certain procedures and equipment tend to be used most commonly with a view to source discrimination, a range of instruments and analytical protocols exist which may fulfil provenance objectives, often non-destructively (see Ciliberto and Spoto (2000) for an overview of analytical techniques). Specific consideration of an individual project's aims and the nature of the materials involved should determine the optimum strategy. If a single element discriminates between pottery from two sources, and that is the goal of the research, then analysis of that element by whatever means is adequate in this context. It is recognized, however, that a fuller analysis might allow additional information to be inferred (e.g., technological choices of raw materials). Since most analytical techniques now give multiple elemental information from a single sample at little extra cost, such a strategy might always be regarded as beneficial.

MATHEMATICAL CONSIDERATIONS

Early attempts to manipulate and interpret the profiles of chemical compositions of analysed materials, without the benefit of significant computational power, usually involved the graphical display of analytical data in some empirical format, with the comparison being carried out by eye, or subsequently by the derivation of some 'rule-of-thumb' formula for determining similarity (e.g., Catling *et al.* 1963).

The advent of (relatively) powerful computers in the late 1970s enabled the construction of large databanks of analytical information, which could be automatically interrogated to identify similarities. It also signalled the arrival of automated pattern recognition procedures, based on the treatment of data as points in multivariate space, whose dimensions were defined by the chemical components measured (Baxter 1994:2; see also Chapter 54).

The desire to create databanks is entirely reasonable, for both practical and financial reasons. It is self-evident that it is unrealistic and wasteful of resources to expect every analytical programme to include examples of all possible raw material sources, or examples of all related types of object. Ideally, if a self-consistent database of all related analyses could be created (e.g., of Roman *terra sigillata*, European Bronze Age metalwork, or Mayan fine ceramics), then new projects could simply key in to these data and answer sophisticated questions of trade and exchange without endless duplication of effort. Such projects were facilitated by the dissemination of a limited number of internationally accepted standard reference materials, but ultimately have been limited by the very nature of ever-improving analytical technologies. It soon became apparent, for example, that the analyses of Aegean ceramics produced by optical emission analysis (OES) could not be rigorously compared with those produced by the successor techniques of atomic absorption spectrometry (AAS) (e.g., Jones 1986:43). Not only do the suites of elements satisfactorily quantified by each technique not always overlap, but more importantly the precision (and accuracy) of each technique varies substantially from element to element. Any automated classification of such a mixed database is almost certain to produce a classification based more on analytical technique than on any underlying geochemical variation. Even with databanks created using a single analytical technique (such as the large NAA databases produced during the 1970s, e.g., Sayre 1982), it is unrealistic to automatically expect that quality control of the analyses produced over a period of years or even decades could be sufficient to eliminate long-term trends in the data. Similar comments also apply to databases of lead isotopic measurements, where proponents have expressly stated that some data produced in the 1970s and 1980s should not be compared with those produced more recently (Stos-Gale *et al.* 1996:381). Furthermore, inter-laboratory data discrepancies, possibly the result of differential analytical capability and technical expertise, suggest that any archaeological inferences drawn

from such data should be applied with caution (e.g., Stos-Gale *et al.* 1998, Amov 2000). The relative failure of such approaches, against the optimistic claims made by proponents in the early days, has probably been responsible for the relative decline of interest in large-scale provenance studies.

Within a single study, when all the analyses have been obtained under reasonably reproducible conditions so that comparability can be assumed, it has become the norm to use commercially available multivariate computer packages to determine similarity and difference between samples (e.g., SPSS, Minitab or Clustan). If each analysis is considered as a point in multivariate space defined by the measured variables, then it is reasonable to assume that samples which are chemically similar will lie close together in this multi-dimensional space. Samples, which are substantially 'the same', can be agglomerated into chemically coherent 'groups' which will 'characterize' a single 'source'. Different 'sources' can then be distinguished as discrete clouds of points in multivariate space (see Chapter 54).

Several empirical approaches have been used to derive these discrete clouds, depending on how much additional information is available. Baxter (1994) provides a concise introduction to the variety of statistical methods applicable to archaeological data. As a purely exploratory technique, suitable to address the question of how many sources are represented in an assemblage, principal components analysis (PCA) has been used extensively. The number of dimensions defined by the variables measured is reduced to a smaller set which can be more easily displayed, and plotting the first two components and looking for separation can often detect between-group variation. Hierarchical cluster analysis, by which groups are assembled sequentially using some pre-defined algorithm that combines adjacent points, has also been routinely employed. A number of procedures have been invoked to define at which point the separation of clusters becomes significant, thus determining how many 'groups' are contained in the analysis. This is a useful exploratory tool which allows classification when little or nothing is known about the structure of the data set (Bray 1994:99), and the resultant dendrograms are a common sight in archaeological provenance interpretations. More sophisticated still, discriminant analysis (DA) has been used to quantify the probability of group integrity, and the likelihood of a particular object belonging to a pre-specified group. This procedure is similar to cluster analysis, with the exception that control groups must be pre-defined on some external criterion (either using archaeological information, or 'control groups' obtained from production sites or raw material sources).

It was observed (and demonstrated) many years ago that all these techniques only offer empirical solutions. In the case of cluster analysis, for example, the decision as to which of the many clustering algorithms are employed (e.g., average linkage, Ward's method) can have a profound effect on the nature of the outcome (e.g., Pollard 1983). Perhaps because this introduces a measure of personal preference into the analysis, there has been a tendency in recent years to move away from this automated approach, and to revert to simpler techniques such as bivariate scatter plots, selected on the basis of some geochemical understanding of the systems involved.

CHARACTERIZATION OF SOURCE MATERIAL

The vast majority of provenance studies, on all materials, have had as their goal the creation of a chemical link between a group of objects and a geographically defined source of raw material. In order to achieve this, it is necessary to have examples of source materials with which to compare the chemical composition of the objects. The nature of this source material varies substantially between classes of material – it could be, for example, quantities of ore collected from known mineral outcrops in the case of non-ferrous metal studies, or samples of clays from known deposits in the case of ceramic studies. In some cases, it has proved practical to use objects (or debris from the production process), rather than the raw materials themselves, which are believed on other grounds to represent a particular raw material source (e.g., ceramic kiln wasters to represent a particular production site, rather than the raw clay itself). It has always been axiomatic in chemical provenance studies that only mis-matches between source material and test object can be conclusively demonstrated. In other words, provenancing proceeds by systematic elimination of possible sources, rather than by positive attribution. If a traded pot does not match chemically with a vessel of similar appearance from a particular source, then it is reasonable to assume that the vessel in question was not manufactured at that kiln (always assuming contemporaneity of the two samples, and technological equivalence). If, however, a 'statistical' match is demonstrated, then one can only say it is *possible* that the two may derive from the same source. In all cases there may be an exactly similar source of material in another place

(geographically close or remote) which happens to have an identical geochemical fingerprint, but which has not been identified or is not represented in the analysis.

Misuse of the terms 'sourcing' and 'provenance' is considered by some to be a serious problem (Shackley 1998:261). Even the most comprehensive study, utilizing the most advanced analytical equipment can, at best, only realistically provide a chemical characterization and the statistical probability of an artifact originating from a particular source (the probability only being defined in terms of all the sources studied). The definition of a provenance study must therefore first identify the attainable outcomes.

SPECIFIC CONSIDERATIONS

Lithics

Theoretically, lithics provide the best possible material by which to test the hypothesis of provenance, since the extraction and production techniques of lithic artifacts are unlikely to alter the chemical composition significantly, and post-depositional processes are also unlikely to greatly modify the bulk composition. Exposure to heat, either during mining by firesetting, or as part of the manufacturing process to facilitate flaking, is unlikely to modify the composition unduly. Similarly, although re-use of lithics might be practised by reduction or re-sharpening, these processes are chemically insignificant. Lithic heterogeneity can be introduced as the result of diagenesis episodes over geological timescales (Andrefsky 1998:41), yet there is an extremely good chance that the chemical composition of an excavated lithic object is closely related to that of the source rock. The success of geochemical provenancing therefore depends on the degree of elemental variability *within* a particular deposit, and the degree of variation *between* geographically separated outcrops (Luedtke 1978:414).

Several successful chemical studies have been carried out on flint (or chert) and obsidian. With flints, the chemical composition of the raw material is controlled by the geochemistry of the solution and re-depositional microenvironment and complex diagenetic cycles (Andrefsky 1998:41). Luedtke (1992:appendix A) has undertaken extensive provenancing on cherts, employing a scientific protocol often used as a model for later studies:

(i) define the problem,

(ii) determine which chert types are possible sources for the artifact(s) of interest, by consulting the relevant geological literature,

(iii) learn as much as possible about regional chert sources, from archaeological and geological literature and about potential post-depositional alteration,

(iv) determine the best analytical procedure to use,

(v) perform analysis, and

(vi) match artifacts to sources, with emphasis on the value of blind testing. Statistical interpretation is of utmost importance at this stage.

More recent approaches have combined geological and geochemical analyses based on the assumption that both artifact and source have diagnostic chemical and petrological signatures (Malyk-Selivanova et al. 1998). Following strict discriminatory criteria, apparently secure correlations have been achieved for several lithic tools. In combination with visual, petrographic and chemical analyses, neodymium isotope ratios have recently been used to significantly increase the precision of provenance determinations (Brady and Coleman 2000).

The formation of obsidian, being a volcanic glass, is controlled by the magma composition, amongst other factors (see Chapter 7). Mediterranean and Near Eastern sources have been the focus of numerous studies (e.g., Renfrew 1982, Torrence 1986) and characterization has produced positive archaeological results. For a full discussion of obsidian geochemistry and provenance investigations in the Eastern Mediterranean, readers are referred to Pollard and Heron (1996:chapter 3).

Isotopic studies have been carried out successfully on marble, where the oxygen and carbon isotope signals in the carbonates are indicative of the (inorganic or biogenic) metamorphic environment (Kempe and Harvey 1983). The research of Herz (1987) resulted in the compilation of a database of isotopic fingerprints for classical Greek and Roman marbles. Many archaeological samples have subsequently been sourced with apparent success.

Steatite (soapstone) vessels and beads are common finds in archaeological contexts, and consequently have been the subject of numerous provenance studies. Investigations of North American sources (Allen and Pennell 1978, Rogers et al. 1983) and British sources (Moffat and Butler 1986, Bray 1994) have had some successes, utilizing trace elements, ultra trace elements (notably the rare earth elements) and strontium isotope signals.

Exceptionally, other rock properties have been used to provenance lithic materials, such as the magnetic susceptibility (McDougall et al. 1983; see Chapter 6), or the geological age of the raw material deposit (Mitchell et al. 1984). These techniques provide a crucial independent test of the provenance predicted geochemically, and should be used more often.

Ceramics

Provenance studies of ceramics, along with those on metals, probably account for the vast majority of all studies undertaken (see Neff 1992 for a review). Ceramics provide a greater challenge than lithics, in that there is a much greater degree of anthropogenic manipulation of the raw material in converting clay into pottery (see Rice 1987:419 and Chapter 36 for a full discussion). Clay deposits, unlike most technologically important lithic sources, are extremely common and widely dispersed, although clays of a quality suitable for the manufacture of sophisticated vessels are more restricted. To first order, the chemical composition of a clay deposit is a complex product of the mineralogy of the rocks from which the clay is derived, the weathering and transport processes responsible for producing the clay deposit, and the chemical environment in which the clay is deposited and matured. In all but the simplest of ceramic production procedures, clay sources are carefully selected to give the correct physical and chemical properties required for the finished product. This might involve washing, weathering, levigating, mixing clays from more than one deposit and adding temper. Ceramics are fired, depending on kiln technology, at temperatures between 700 and 800° in a simple bonfire, to upwards of 1400° in an oriental porcelain kiln. Within the kiln, a wide range of chemical reactions take place, depending on the mineralogy of the clay and the exact conditions and temperature of the firing (see Chapter 40). Conceivably, the use to which the vessel is put (or any particular post-firing treatments for decorative or functional purposes) might further affect particular components of the chemical composition. Finally, post-depositional geochemical and mineralogical alteration, after having been observed sporadically in the past, is now receiving more systematic attention (see Chapter 49).

Not surprisingly, therefore, it is fair to report that very few chemical studies of pottery have successfully and unambiguously linked vessels with raw clay sources, or even attempted to do so. The highest likelihood of such success comes in simpler production systems, probably on a small scale, when suitable clay is extracted and made into vessels with little processing (see Chapter 36 for descriptions of such studies). Invaluable information on the processing technology of pottery production can be obtained by ceramic petrology and details of prehistoric pottery trade may be revealed (Peacock 1982). Furthermore, intensive study of particular production areas can yield spectacular success when such studies are combined e.g., Greek and Cypriot pottery (Jones 1986, Knapp and Cherry 1994); Islamic ceramics (Mason and Tite 1994); Egyptian pottery (Redmount and Morgenstein 1996).

At the other extreme of scales of production, it appears that 'industrial' manufacture of fine ceramics (e.g., the great *terra sigillata* factories in Roman Gaul) also lend themselves to chemical provenancing (e.g., Picon *et al.* 1971). At first sight this might seem unlikely, since the scale, variety and longevity of production suggests that the sheer volume of processed clay would mitigate against it. Nevertheless, experience shows that it is exactly this scale of production which allows the method to succeed – a tribute to the quality control of the pottery makers. Some caveats are necessary. Only the foolhardy would believe that a sample of even several hundred vessels from one workshop could adequately characterize the complete range of production over a period of many tens or even hundreds of years (remembering that a large kiln might fire many hundreds of vessels at a time, and the firing cycle could be repeated every few weeks). It is also likely that large kilns were employed to make a wide range of vessel types, either firing them together so that variation in the heat and redox distribution of the kiln could be exploited to the full, or perhaps in sequential firing campaigns. Given also that fabric composition might be varied to accommodate the differing needs of different shapes, sizes and functionalities of vessel, as well as the different 'qualities' of output, it is likely that pottery of quite different compositions could be fired in the same kiln at the same time. It is therefore necessary to match as closely as possible the form and fabric of the vessels being provenanced with those of the kiln control groups. The widespread practice of using kiln wasters (misshapen ceramics recovered by excavation of the kiln or nearby waste dumps) has much to recommend it – it is highly unlikely that such material would be transported any distance – but it must be remembered that such material *failed* in the firing. (Perhaps because the composition was not matched to the firing cycle?)

Several issues which have been seen at various times as complications, or insurmountable obstacles, have

extended the literature of this area. One which sometimes reappears is the concept of the transport of raw clay over great distances (Jones 1986:53). The principal raw materials required to make pottery are wood, water and clay, and about 10 times the weight of wood is required compared to the weight of the clay. Thus, if deforestation occurs due to over-exploitation of the local woodland, it could be easier to take the clay to the wood rather than vice versa. Although this makes some sense, all that can be said is that there is no good evidence for such trade on any large scale prior to the industrial era. It is known, for instance, that stamps and moulds for making terra sigillata moved around Roman Europe (thus potentially deceiving the stylistic attribution of provenance), but as yet there is no decisive evidence for the movement of clay.

A second area of discussion has been the dilution effect of various tempers added to the clay fabric, to improve thermal or other physical properties. If trace element analysis alone were used for characterization purposes, then the effect of the addition of substantial quantities of pure quartz (SiO_2) would simply be to reduce the quantities of all of the other elements measured. Impure quartz might show an overall dilution effect, with enrichment of a few elements (e.g., TiO_2). By chemical analysis alone, two otherwise identical clay fabrics might then appear dissimilar if slightly different amounts of temper were added to each, unless independent petrological studies were carried out to detect this fact. Plots of chemical composition in this case would reveal strings of points rather than tight clusters. Several efforts have been made to resolve this difficulty mathematically (e.g., Mommsen *et al.* 1992), but it still seems to represent a limitation to the technique.

Bridging the gap between pottery and glass provenance studies, some research has been conducted on ceramic glazes (e.g., Mason *et al.* 1992). Primarily determining chemical composition and utilizing lead isotopes in the glaze to assign provenance, initial results appear promising.

Glasses

Glasses and other vitreous silicates such as faience have proved particularly intransigent to chemical provenancing. In large measure this is a reflection of the chemical complexity of vitreous silicates (see Chapter 38). Both primary raw materials (quartz sand and plant ash) might be expected to be highly heterogeneous in composition, despite the fact that only high purity sands can produce transparent glass, and that any ashes used are likely to have been washed before use. Added to this is the expectation that the molten glass is likely to partially flux any container used to hold it, and that any colourant added is likely to bring in further impurities. Finally, the recyclability of glass is a further disadvantage – most known recipes for ancient glass, such as Theophilus' twelfth century survey of glassmaking technology (Hawthorne and Smith 1963), prescribe the use of substantial quantities of *cullet* (broken recycled glass). Taken together, it is not surprising that glass has been the least successful ancient material to be studied from the provenance perspective.

Broad compositional categories have long been established, which might have geographical or cultural significance (e.g., Sayre and Smith 1961), and lead-containing glasses were a relatively early success of the lead isotope technique (Brill 1970, Brill *et al.* 1973) but on the whole little further progress has been reported. This might change in the near future, if the promising pilot studies carried out using strontium isotopes are shown to have broad applicability (Freestone pers. comm.). Glass may also be suitable for the well-established techniques of rare earth geochemistry (see Henderson 1984 and Allen and Pennell 1978 for theories and methodologies) which can now be carried out relatively easily using inductively coupled plasma mass spectrometry (ICP-MS).

Metals

Metal objects from the European Bronze Age were the first group of artifacts to be subjected to systematic provenance studies (Junghans *et al.* 1960, 1968), and metals continue to receive a great deal of attention. Initially such studies used trace element analysis by optical emission spectrometry (OES), and nearly all subsequent analytical techniques have been applied to metals at some stage. The big contribution, however, was the application of the lead isotope technique to archaeological materials, including non-ferrous metals, beginning in the late 1960s with the work of Brill and Wampler (1967) (see Gale and Stos-Gale 1989 for a review of the development of lead isotope archaeology). Any metal which contains traces of lead derived from the original ore source is susceptible to the technique, but principal interest focused initially on silver alloys, and subsequently copper alloys (Gale and Stos-Gale 1982, Gale 1991). Considerable quantities of ink have been spilt debating the interpretation of lead isotope data, particularly in the elucidation of metal trade in

the Bronze Age Aegean (e.g., Budd *et al.* 1995a, 1995b, Gale and Stos-Gale 1995, Muhly 1995 to name but a few). These disputes have not focused on the applicability of the method or the precision of the analyses, but largely on the ways in which the data have been presented (which represent underlying differences of belief in the mathematical nature of the data), and the degree to which precise geographical interpretations can (or should) be made (Scaife *et al.* 1999).

Metals intrinsically suffer from all of the disadvantages listed above for glass as a material for provenance studies. In particular, high temperature processing is usually required to win a metal from its ore, and to purify it for use. Fluxes are often necessary to ensure that unwanted material (gangue) is removed as slag, thus introducing further sources of impurity variation. Small changes in temperature and furnace conditions (primarily redox) could affect the high temperature chemical reactions in such a way as to alter the trace element composition of the melt without varying the input charge. Metals are also, in theory, infinitely recyclable. When it was introduced, the use of lead isotopes was felt to circumvent at least some of these problems. It was implicitly believed that lead isotopes are not fractionated during anthropogenic processing (Gale and Stos-Gale 1982). This was subsequently challenged from a theoretical standpoint (Budd *et al.* 1995c), but there has since been no experimental evidence to support this theory (other metal systems of archaeological interest, particularly zinc, do appear to show measurable fractionation during processing; Budd *et al.* 1999). In fact, the only likely major drawback to the lead isotope technique is if significant quantities of lead are introduced from a different source to the primary metal, either by recycling or deliberate addition of lead to control the fluidity during casting.

In principle, therefore, lead isotope provenancing provides an ideal method to relate a metal object to the geological source of that metal. Many significant results have been reported (e.g., Aegean isotope applications reviewed by Gale and Stos-Gale 1992), but it has been repeatedly emphasized that successful studies require adequate geochemical characterization of all sources available to the ancient miner. This has been resource intensive in terms of sample collection and measurement (until recently all lead isotope measurements have been obtained using the technique of thermal ionization mass spectrometry (TIMS), which is relatively slow and laborious).

Irrespective of these considerations, the method has some limitations. In a recent extensive lead isotope study of British sources of copper in the Bronze Age

(Rohl and Needham 1998), it has been demonstrated that all the sources in the UK (as well as Eire and the near Continent) substantially overlap in terms of lead isotope ratios. Some attributions can be made (e.g., certain parts of Cornwall have excessive uranium, which gives a highly distinctive lead isotope signature), but it seems clear that isotope data in this case is insufficient to uniquely characterize the material. Attempts have been made to combine isotope data with trace element information, but the results are often contradictory and difficult to interpret, thus giving only limited success to date (Rohl and Needham 1998).

Amber, jet and bone

Flushed by the early success of the large analytical programmes on inorganic materials, some workers turned to geological raw materials of organic origin, particularly amber and jet. Amber characterization has been highly successful, largely due to the work of Beck (1986) using infrared spectroscopy. Baltic amber was found to have a highly characteristic spectrum shared by no other source of the resin. Baltic and non-Baltic sources can easily be differentiated on this basis, and it appears that widespread trade or exchange in this resin existed throughout prehistory (Lambert 1997:161). In an attempt to assign geographical provenance more specifically, carbon-13 nuclear magnetic resonance spectroscopy was employed, and has successfully established distinctions on a worldwide scale, based on structural information and the identification of carbon functionalities within the resins (Lambert et al. 1996).

Jet characterization has been somewhat less rewarding than amber, although more recently, when jet and other black lithic materials were analysed using the appropriate organic techniques of GC-MS rather than the earlier attempts which essentially considered them as 'honorary inorganic' substances, some success has been reported (Watts et al. 1999). Part of the rationale behind the earlier studies, however, was to aid discrimination between jet and other black lithic materials, which have been extensively misclassified in the archaeological literature (Bussell et al. 1981), and this more limited goal has shown good results.

In recent years, some interest has been aroused by the potential to 'provenance people' by the chemical or isotopic study of bone and teeth. The first successes were obtained by using stable isotopes of carbon and nitrogen in bones and teeth, which reflect different stages of an individual's life (Sealy et al. 1995). More recently the fact that certain stable and radiogenic isotopes found in geological contexts (primarily strontium and lead) vary systematically with geographical location has been exploited. Over time, these isotopic signals enter the food chain (via soils, plants and animals) or the water supply, and become manifest in human apatite and enamel through dietary intake. Ancient human migration has been investigated on this theoretical basis (e.g., Ezzo et al. 1997, Price et al. 1998, Budd et al. 2000, Montgomery et al. forthcoming) with significant successes claimed to date. This appears to be a promising avenue for future provenance research, although one in which the complications of post-mortem diagenesis must be addressed directly (see Chapters 23 and 51).

EVALUATION AND PROSPECTS

There can be little question that the application of chemical and isotopic analysis to archaeological materials for provenance purposes has yielded some impressive successes – particularly with those materials such as obsidian and amber, which are relatively chemically unaltered from geological source to finished object. More complex materials, especially metals, have often generated more controversy than insight. Ceramics, however, generally remain an outstanding success story, in spite of the inherent complications of the production cycle.

The inevitable question to ask after nearly fifty years of scientific provenance studies is 'has it been worthwhile'? There are too many studies which have given definitive and valuable conclusions to dismiss the endeavour, and yet scepticism, sometimes highly dismissive, is still abroad. The main criticism seems to be that scientific studies do not in general engage and articulate with broader archaeological understanding. This suggests that the sixth requirement listed in the introduction is not being adequately met. Moreover, this implies at least a lack of communication, and, at worst, a disregard or disinterest (Shackley 1998:259) between archaeologists concerned with the reconstruction of ancient trade and exchange systems, and those involved in provenancing. It has occasionally been suggested that provenance studies are sometimes misdirected – asking the wrong question. Much effort, particularly in the field of metal studies, has been expended on identifying the exact source of raw materials, even down to particular mines. In general it might be said that the archaeological framework within which these studies need to be interpreted is not sufficiently well-developed to accommodate such precise information – models of social structure, trade specialization, and modes of exchange are often singularly lacking.

Perhaps in certain cases less specific information may be of more immediate relevance – a concept encapsulated by the term *processual provenance* (Pollard forthcoming). Particularly in the case of metals, it could be argued that many factors might be responsible for a change in the trace element or isotopic signature, in addition to a simple change in ore source – e.g., smelting technology, recycling regime. An observed change in trace element or isotopic pattern may not automatically therefore signify the exploitation of a new source of raw material. Perhaps what is actually of greater archaeological significance, at least in the short term, is the knowledge that *something* has changed, rather than the specifics of *what* has changed. Although moving away from the original concept of provenance, it might be argued that the relatively simple detection of change in the material record is a valuable adjunct when interpreting the archaeological record. This is particularly the case if such a change is contemporaneous with other changes observed in the archaeological record – stylistic influences, mortuary patterns, stratigraphic sequence, or whatever. In such cases, it might be reasonable to observe that some variation has occurred to the metal in circulation as a result of social change, rather than necessarily assuming a simplistic shift in raw material extraction patterns or technological change (e.g., Begemann *et al.* 1995). Similar considerations might apply in some circumstances to ceramic and glass production, but, as noted above, it is more realistic to assume that changes in the composition of lithics directly reflects the exploitation of a new source of raw material.

Despite the fact that provenance studies are not currently the most 'fashionable' branch of archaeological science, on a more positive and practical note, it is certainly the case that the capacity to carry out large-scale studies of this type is now more widely available than ever before. Continual advances in analytical instrumentation, and specifically the high throughput capacity and multi-element sensitivity of the current generation of inductively coupled plasma machines (of both optical and mass spectrometry types) means that capacity is no longer limited by analytical restrictions. In particular, the next generation of multi-collector ICP mass spectrometers, with sensitivities and resolution for isotopic ratios such as lead, comparable to (if not better than) that of conventional TIMS instrumentation (e.g., Gale *et al.* 1999, Rehkamper and Halliday 1998, Halliday *et al.* 1998), may herald a new age of relatively rapid and cheap isotopic and chemical studies of archaeological material. We may look forward to a future when the utility of such studies is not limited by analytical capability, but more by the quality of the definition of the archaeological problem.

REFERENCES

*Recommended for further reading

Allen, R.O. and Pennell, S.E. (1978). Rare earth element distribution patterns to characterise soapstone artefacts. In Carter, G.F. (ed.) *Archaeological Chemistry II*, 230–257, Advances in Chemistry 171, American Chemical Society: Washington DC.

Amov, B.G. (2000). Comment on Z.A. Stos-Gale, N.H. Gale, N. Annetts, T. Todorov, P. Lilov, A. Raduncheva and I. Panayotov, 'Lead isotope data from the Isotrace Laboratory, Oxford: *Archaeometry* database 5, ores from Bulgaria', *Archaeometry*, **42**:237–241.

Andrefsky, W. (1998). *Lithics: Macroscopic Approaches to Analysis*. Cambridge University Press: Cambridge.

*Baxter, M.J. (1994). *Exploratory Multivariate Analysis in Archaeology*. Edinburgh University Press: Edinburgh.

Beck, C.W. (1986). Spectroscopic studies of amber. *Applied Spectroscopy Review*, **22**:57–110.

Begemann, F., Pernicka, E. and Schmitt-Strecker, S. (1995). Thermi on Lesbos: a case study of changing trade patterns. *Oxford Journal of Archaeology*, **14**:123–136.

Brady, M. and Coleman, D. (2000). Determining the source of felsitic lithic material in southeastern New England using neodymium isotope ratios. *Geoarchaeology*, **15**:1–19.

Bray, I.S.J. (1994). *Geochemical Methods for Provenance Studies of Steatite*. Unpublished PhD Thesis, University of Glasgow.

Brill, R.H. (1970). Lead and oxygen isotopes in ancient objects. *Philosophical Transactions of the Royal Society*, **A269**:143–164.

Brill, R.H. and Wampler, J.M. (1967). Isotope studies of ancient lead. *American Journal of Archaeology*, **71**:63–77.

Brill, R.H., Shields, W.R. and Wampler, J.M. (1973). New directions in lead isotope research. In Young, W.J. (ed.) *Application of Science in Examination of Works of Art*, 73–83. Boston Museum of Fine Arts: Boston.

Budd, P., Pollard, A.M., Scaife, B. and Thomas, R.G. (1995a). Oxhide ingots, recycling and the Mediterranean metals trade. *Journal of Mediterranean Archaeology*, **8**:1–32.

Budd, P., Pollard, A.M., Scaife, B. and Thomas, R.G. (1995b). Lead isotope analysis and oxhide ingots: a final comment. *Journal of Mediterranean Archaeology*, **8**:70–75.

Budd, P., Pollard, A.M., Scaife, B. and Thomas, R.G. (1995c). The possible fractionation of lead isotopes in ancient metallurgical processes. *Archaeometry*, **37**:143–150.

Budd, P.D., Lythgoe, P., McGill, R.A.R., Pollard, A.M. and Scaife, B. (1999). Zinc fractionation in liquid brass (Cu/Zn) alloy: potential environmental and archaeological applications. In Pollard, A.M. (ed.) *Geoarchaeology: Exploration, Environments, Resources*, 147–153, Special Publication 165, Geological Society: London.

Budd, P.D., Montgomery, J., Barreiro, B. and Thomas, R.G. (2000). Differential diagenesis of strontium in archaeological human dental tissues. *Applied Geochemistry*, 15:687–694.

Bussell, G.D., Pollard, A.M. and Baird, D.C. (1981). The characterisation of Early Bronze Age jet and jet-like material by X-ray fluorescence. *Wiltshire Archaeological Magazine*, 76:27–32.

Catling, H.W., Richards, E.E. and Blin-Stoyle, A.E. (1963). Correlations between composition and provenance of Mycenaean and Minoan pottery. *Annual of the British School at Athens*, 58:94–115.

*Ciliberto, E. and Spoto, G. (2000). *Modern Analytical Methods in Art and Archaeology*. John Wiley: New York.

Ezzo, J.A., Johnson, C.M. and Price, T.D. (1997). Analytical perspectives on prehistoric migration: a case study from East-Central Arizona. *Journal of Archaeological Science*, 24:447–466.

Gale, N.H. (1991). Copper oxhide ingots: their origin and their place in the Bronze Age metals trade in the Mediterranean. In Gale, N.H. (ed.) *Bronze Age Trade in the Mediterranean*, 197–239. Studies in Mediterranean Archaeology 90. Paul Aströms Förlag: Jönsered.

Gale, N.H. and Stos-Gale, Z.A. (1982). Bronze Age copper sources in the Mediterranean: a new approach. *Science*, 216:11–19.

Gale, N.H. and Stos-Gale, Z.A. (1989). Bronze Age archaeometallurgy of the Mediterranean: The impact of lead isotope studies. In Allen, R.O. (ed.) *Archaeological Chemistry IV*, 159–198, Advances in Chemistry Series 220, American Chemical Society: Washington DC.

*Gale, N.H. and Stos-Gale, Z.A. (1992). Lead isotope studies in the Aegean (The British Academy Project). In Pollard, A.M. (ed.) *New Developments in Archaeological Science*, 63–108, Proceedings of the British Academy 77, Oxford University Press: Oxford.

Gale, N.H. and Stos-Gale, Z.A. (1995). Comments on 'Oxhide ingots, recycling and the Mediterranean metals trade'. *Journal of Mediterranean Archaeology*, 8:33–41.

Gale, N.H., Woodhead, A.P., Stos-Gale, Z.A., Walder, A. and Bowen, I. (1999). Natural variations in the isotopic composition of copper: possible applications to archaeology and geochemistry. *International Journal of Mass Spectrometry*, 184:1–9.

Halliday, A.N., Lee, D.C., Christensen, J.N., Rehkamper, M., Yi, W., Luo, XZ., Hall, C.M., Ballentine, C.J., Pettke, T. and Stirling, C. (1998). Applications of multiple collector ICPMS to cosmochemistry, geochemistry and paleoceanography. *Geochimica et Cosmochimica Acta*, 62:919–940.

Harbottle, G. (1982). Chemical characterization in archaeology. In Ericson, J.E. and Earle, T.K. (eds) *Contexts for Prehistoric Exchange*, 13–51. Academic Press: New York.

Hawthorne, J.G. and Smith, C.S. (1963). *On Divers Arts: The Treatise of Theophilus*. University of Chicago Press: Chicago.

Henderson, P. (1984). General geochemical properties and abundances of the rare earth elements. In Henderson, P. (ed.) *Developments in Geochemistry 2: Rare Earth Element Geochemistry*, 1–32. Elsevier Science: Amsterdam.

Herz, N. (1987). Carbon and oxygen isotopic ratios: a database for classical Greek and Roman marbles. *Archaeometry*, 29:35–43.

Jones, R.E. (ed.) (1986). *Greek and Cypriot Pottery: A Review of Scientific Studies*. Fitch Laboratory Occasional Paper 1, British School at Athens: Athens.

Junghans, S., Sangmeister, E. and Schröder, M. (1960). *Metallanalysen kupferzeitlicher und frühbronzezeitlicher Bodenfunde aus Europa*. Gebr. Mann: Berlin.

Junghans, S., Sangmeister, E. and Schröder, M. (1968). *Kupfer und Bronze in der frühen Metallzeit Europas. Katalog der Analysen Nr. 985–10040*. Gebr. Mann: Berlin.

Kempe, D.R.C. and Harvey, A.P. (1983). *The Petrology of Archaeological Artefacts*. Clarendon: Oxford.

Knapp, A.B. and Cherry, J.F. (1994). *Provenience Studies and Bronze Age Cyprus: Production, Exchange and Politico-Economic Change*. Prehistory Press: Madison, Wisconsin.

Lambert, J.B. (1997). *Traces of the Past: Unravelling the Secrets of Archaeology through Chemistry*. Addison-Wesley: Reading, Massachusetts.

Lambert, J.B., Johnson, S.C. and Poinar, G.O. Jr (1996). Nuclear magnetic resonance characterization of Cretaceous amber. *Archaeometry*, 38:325–335.

Luedtke, B.E. (1978). Chert sources and trace element analysis. *American Antiquity*, 43:413–423.

Luedtke, B.E. (1992). *An Archaeologist's Guide to Flint and Chert*. Archaeological Research Tools 7, Institute of Archaeology, University of California: Los Angeles.

Mallory-Greenough, L.M. and Greenough, J.D. (1998). New data for old pots: trace element characterization of ancient Egyptian pottery using ICP-MS. *Journal of Archaeological Science*, 25:85–97.

Malyk-Selivanova, N., Ashley, G.M., Gal, R., Glascock, M.D. and Neff, H. (1998). Geological-geochemical approach to 'sourcing' of prehistoric chert artefacts, northwestern Alaska. *Geoarchaeology*, 13:673–708.

Mason, R.B. and Tite, M.S. (1994). Islamic pottery: a tale of men and migrations. *Museum International*, 46:33–37.

Mason, R.B., Farquhar, R.M. and Smith, P.E. (1992). Lead-isotope analysis of Islamic glazes: an exploratory study. *Muqarnas*, 9:67–71.

McDougall, J.M., Tarling, D.H. and Warren, S.E. (1983). The magnetic sourcing of obsidian samples from Mediterranean and Near Eastern sources. *Journal of Archaeological Science*, 10:441–452.

Mitchell, J.G., Askvik, H. and Resi, H.G. (1984). Potassium-argon ages of schist honestones from the Viking-Age sites at Kaupang (Norway), Aggersborg (Denmark), Hedeby (West-Germany) and Wolin (Poland), and their archaeological implications. *Journal of Archaeological Science*, **11**:171–176.

Moffat, D. and Butler, S.J. (1986). Rare earth element distribution patterns in Shetland steatite – consequences for artifact provenancing studies. *Archaeometry*, **28**:101–115.

Mommsen, H., Beier, T., Diehl, U. and Podzuweit, C. (1992). Provenance determination of Mycenaean sherds found in Tell el Amarna by NAA. *Journal of Archaeological Science*, **19**:295–302.

Montgomery, J., Budd, P. and Evans, J. (forthcoming). Reconstructing the lifetime movements of ancient people: a Neolithic case study from southern England.

Muhly, J.D. (1995). Lead isotope analysis and the archaeologist. *Journal of Mediterranean Archaeology*, **8**:54–58.

*Neff, H. (ed.) (1992). *Chemical Characterization of Ceramic Pastes in Archaeology*. Monographs in World Archaeology, Prehistory Press: Madison, Wisconsin.

Peacock, D.P.S. (1982). *Pottery in the Roman World: an Ethnoarchaeological Approach*. Longman: London.

Picon, M., Vichy, M. and Meille, E. (1971). Composition of the Lezoux, Lyon and Arezzo samian ware. *Archaeometry*, **13**:191–208.

Pollard, A.M. (1983). A critical study of multivariate methods as applied to provenance data. In Aspinall, A. and Warren, S.E. (eds) *Proceedings of the 22nd Symposium on Archaeometry*, 56–66, University of Bradford Press: Bradford.

Pollard, A.M. (1986). Multivariate methods of data analysis. In Jones, R.E. (ed.) *Greek and Cypriot Pottery: A Review of Scientific Studies*, 56–83. Fitch Laboratory Occasional Paper 1, British School at Athens: Athens.

Pollard, A.M. (forthcoming). Review of 'The Circulation of Metal in the British Bronze Age: the application of lead isotope analysis', Rohl, B. and Needham, S., British Museum Occasional Paper **102** (1998). *The Archaeological Journal*.

*Pollard, A.M. and Heron, C. (1996). *Archaeological Chemistry*. Royal Society of Chemistry: Cambridge.

Pollard, A.M. and Heron, C. (2000). Analytical chemistry in archaeology. In Meyers, R.A. (ed.) *Encyclopaedia of Analytical Chemistry*, Vol. 15, 13455–13477, John Wiley: Chichester.

Price, T.D., Grupe, G. and Schröter, P. (1998). Migration in the Bell Beaker period of central Europe. *Antiquity*, **72**:405–411.

Redmount, C.A. and Morgenstein, M.E. (1996). Major and trace element analysis of modern Egyptian pottery. *Journal of Archaeological Science*, **23**:741–762.

Rehkamper, M. and Halliday, A.N. (1998). Accuracy and long-term reproducibility of lead isotopic measurements by multiple-collector inductively coupled plasma mass spectrometry using an external method for correction of mass discrimination. *International Journal of Mass Spectrometry*, **181**:123–133.

Renfrew, C. (1982). Bronze Age Melos. In Renfrew, C. and Wagstaff, M. (eds) *An Island Polity*, 35–43. Cambridge University Press: Cambridge.

Renfrew, C. and Bahn, P. (1996). *Archaeology: Theories, Methods and Practice*, (2nd edn). Thames and Hudson: London.

Rice, P.M. (1987). *Pottery Analysis: A Sourcebook*. University of Chicago Press: Chicago.

Rogers, M., Allen, R., Nagle, C. and Fitzhugh, W. (1983). The utilization of rare earth element concentrations for the characterization of soapstone quarries. *Archaeometry*, **25**:186–195.

Rohl, B. and Needham, S. (1998). *The Circulation of Metal in the British Bronze Age: The Application of Lead Isotope Analysis*. Occasional Paper 102, British Museum Publications: London.

Sayre, E.V. (1982). Preservation and coordination of archaeometric data: the whole is greater than the sum of its parts. In Olin, J.S. (ed.) *Future Directions in Archaeometry: a Round Table*, 116–120. Smithsonian Institution: Washington DC.

Sayre, E.V. and Smith, R.W. (1961). Compositional categories of ancient glass. *Science*, **133**:1824–1826.

Scaife, B., Budd, P., McDonnell, J.G. and Pollard, A.M. (1999). Lead isotope analysis, oxhide ingots and the presentation of scientific data in archaeology. In Young, S.M.M., Pollard, A.M., Budd, P. and Ixer, R.A. (eds) *Metals in Antiquity*, 122–133, BAR International Series 792, Archaeopress: Oxford.

Sealy, J.C., Armstrong, R. and Schrire, C. (1995). Beyond lifetime averages: tracing life histories through isotopic analysis of different calcified tissues from archaeological human skeletons. *Antiquity*, **69**:290–300.

Shackley, M.S. (1998). Gamma rays, X-rays and stone tools: some recent advances in archaeological geochemistry. *Journal of Archaeological Science*, **25**:259–270.

Stos-Gale, Z.A., Gale, N.H. and Annetts, N. (1996). Lead isotope data from the Isotrace Laboratory, Oxford: *Archaeometry* database 3, ores from the Aegean, Part 1. *Archaeometry*, **38**:381–390.

Stos-Gale, Z.A., Gale, N.H., Annetts, N., Todorov, T., Lilov, P., Raduncheva, A. and Panayotov, I. (1998). Lead isotope data from the Isotrace Laboratory, Oxford: *Archaeometry* database 5, ores from Bulgaria. *Archaeometry*, **40**:217–226.

Torrence, R. (1986). *Production and Exchange of Stone Tools: Prehistoric Obsidian in the Aegean*. Cambridge University Press: Cambridge.

Ward, G.K. (1974). A systematic approach to the definition of sources of raw material. *Archaeometry*, **16**:41–53.

Watts, S., Pollard, A.M. and Wolff, G.A. (1999). The organic geochemistry of jet: pyrolysis-gas chromatography/mass spectrometry (Py-GCMS) applied to identifying jet and similar black lithic materials – preliminary results. *Journal of Archaeological Science*, **26**:923–933.

SECTION 7

Archaeological Prospection

Overview—The Role and Practice of Archaeological Prospection

A. DAVID

English Heritage Centre for Archaeology, Portsmouth.

The need to search out and characterize the remains of our past has always been a fundamental part of archaeological endeavour, helping to satisfy a curiosity about our past. Archaeological prospection is a relatively new term which draws together the many non-destructive methods used to locate and characterize the surviving physical evidence of past human activity. These vary from the fundamental observation and mapping of artifact distributions and topography, to the analysis of anthropogenic chemical and geochemical signatures in the soil, and to ground-based, aerial and underwater remote sensing. The term thus embraces both the more traditional methods of archaeology, such as surface collection and aerial photography, as well as those technical applications more recently adapted from the physical and chemical sciences. Linking them all is the gathering pace of the digital revolution which is allowing unprecedented advances in the display, analysis and interpretation of a very wide range of past human phenomena.

In recent decades a growing incentive for the development of prospecting technologies has also been the widespread realization that archaeological remains are a finite resource endangered by modern encroachment. The concept of cultural resource management (CRM) recognizes the need to identify and conserve dwindling archaeological remains, and this has increased the emphasis on the development and application of prospecting technologies. In England, for instance, an assessment of the archaeological potential of land proposed for development has to be provided prior to a decision by the planning authority and this has resulted in the widespread deployment of geophysical prospecting techniques. Whilst such technologies will continue to be devoted to the resolution of the particular objectives of archaeological research, it therefore shares this role with the often more demanding need to provide information for cultural resource management.

This context, together with the impetus from new technical developments and the need to engage both archaeologists and scientists on the same agenda, led to the inauguration in 1994 of a specially-dedicated international journal *Archaeological Prospection*. From 1995 this has been supplemented by a continuing series of bi-annual conferences. Whilst the large majority of contributions to these outlets have been devoted to geophysics and geophysical data, the wider span of prospecting interests has been demonstrated by papers such as those on soil phosphate survey (Crowther 1997), aerial reconnaissance (e.g., Featherstone *et al.* 1999), digital elevation modelling (Redfern *et al.* 1999), dowsing (Locock 1995, van Leusen 1998), vegetation (Herbich 1996) and satellite remote sensing (e.g., Carr and Turner 1996). Probably the most up-to-date

---

Handbook of Archaeological Sciences. Edited by D.R. Brothwell and A.M. Pollard.
© 2001 John Wiley & Sons, Ltd.

compilation of recent work is that published to coincide with the third and most recent conference on archaeological prospection (Fassbinder and Irlinger 1999).

Undoubtedly the single most productive suite of tools for archaeological prospecting is that derived from remote sensing (Chapter 44). Optical (and near-infrared) aerial photography in particular has been very widely applied. Even for Britain however, where aerial photographic coverage might be considered to be substantial (Figure S7.1), campaigns of flying produce hundreds of new discoveries each year. A National Mapping Programme, designed to provide overall coverage of England within the next 10–12 years will provide a major source of information on the national archaeological resource. The increased use of colour and digital photography, of automated image enhancement, rectification and data storage, are each to be welcomed, as is the incorporation of such data (including digital elevation models, DEMs) as a contribution to a more holistic archaeological analysis within Geographic Information Systems (GIS; see Chapter 53).

Figure S7.1 Distribution map of specialist oblique aerial photographs held by English Heritage, December 1999. © English Heritage.

Optical aerial photography is nevertheless rather expensive to achieve and the visibility of archaeological features is heavily dependent on many factors outside the operators' control. Here, the potential of satellite imaging seems to be cause for optimism, both by providing greatly expanded, even global, coverage and by increasingly useful ground resolutions for panchromatic digital imagery (to < 1.0 metre for some of the new generation of commercial satellites). Multispectral (MSS) data obtained both from space and from lower altitudes is also very promising, being more flexible than conventional aerial photographic data and readily manipulated by computers for integration with other datasets. MSS resolution, currently at 1–2 metres from aircraft (3–5 metres for some satellites), must be increased, but recent case studies suggest, for instance, that images at infrared wavelengths both complement optical imagery and detect archaeology over areas such as permanent pasture where the potential of aerial photography is much more limited. Airborne sensors are also contributing to the construction of large scale DTMs which may come to have archaeological potential: Laser Induced Direction And Range (LIDAR) systems are currently able to construct terrain maps with a height accuracy of 10–15 cm and a typical horizontal resolution of 1–4 metres on the land surface.

The term remote sensing is also often applied to those ground-based methods which make use of geophysical principles (Chapter 43), and it is these techniques which constitute what most people usually understand to be archaeological prospecting. Sessions on the subject have been a regular feature of *Archaeometry* conferences worldwide, and related papers appear within the journal of the same name. An early florescence in the subject was marked by the journal of the Lerici Foundation, *Prospezione Archeologiche* (1966–86). The history of archaeological geophysics, and an exposition of its applications, from a largely British perspective, is given by Clark (1990). A more theoretical overview of the subject, and of other remote sensing technologies, is provided by Scollar *et al.* (1990). Whilst initially pioneered in Europe, archaeological geophysics has been taken up by research teams worldwide, notably in Japan. Archaeologically-dedicated instruments and software have been commercially available for some years.

In both editions of the landmark text on *Science in Archaeology* (Brothwell and Higgs 1963, 1969), the section on prospecting included just two contributions: on magnetic location (Aitken 1969) and resistivity surveying (Clark 1969). Over 30 years on it remains true that these two basic methods, considerably refined and developed in their applications, probably remain the most significant within the discipline. Magnetic properties, already of notable value to dating (Chapter 6), have proved of immense benefit to prospecting. Today's fluxgate and total field instruments are capable of remarkable sensitivity (± 10 picotesla for some caesium instruments; better than ± 1 nanoTesla for fluxgates; Becker 1995), and survey teams can now cover very large areas at high sample density, at rates in excess of 1 hectare/day. The deployment of wheeled multiple arrays of sensors is a growing development combining both increased speed and ground resolutions of at least 0.5 m $\times$ 0.5 m, close enough to locate smaller features such as gulleys, palisade trenches and post-holes (Becker 1999). Where soils and surface conditions are favourable, images of extraordinary clarity can be achieved, complementing and often extending evidence from other methods such as aerial photography (Figure S7.2: Stanton Drew). The factors of speed and the magnetic definition of a wide range of archaeological features have ensured that magnetometer survey is often the preferred method both of reconnaissance and of very detailed survey.

A related method of site reconnaissance is magnetic susceptibility survey, which can indicate areas where detailed magnetometer survey may be profitable, as well as having interpretational value in its own right (Chapter 45). Magnetic susceptibility values, when obtained from sediments within and adjacent to archaeological features can also be used in combination with magnetic anomaly data to model those features in three dimensions (e.g., Neubauer and Eder-Hinterleitner 1997, Eder-Hinterleitner et al. 1999), and to obtain estimates of depth (e.g., Dittrich and Koppelt 1997). Research is also taking place into developing estimations of the depth and shape of magnetic targets utilizing signal processing techniques (Tabbagh et al. 1997) and complex attribute analysis (Tsokas and Hansen 2000). Instrumental advances which have yet to be assessed in mainstream archaeological geophysics include triple-axis magnetometers for enhanced target characterization (see Chapter 43). One important requirement to take forward such experimentation, throughout the discipline, is the construction of appropriate artificial test sites.

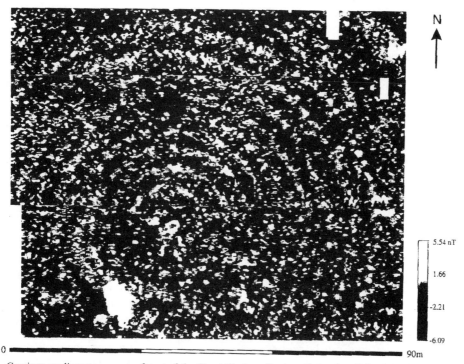

Figure S7.2   Caesium gradiometer survey of part of the Great Circle at Stanton Drew, near Bristol, England. Nine concentric rings of pits have been located within the second largest stone circle in Britain. The pits, registering as anomalies as slight as 1/100000th of the Earth's magnetic field, are assumed to be the foundations of a vast prehistoric timber temple. © English Heritage.

Methods of resistivity survey are still most effectively applied to the detection and definition of the two-dimensional plans of building foundations but are slower to undertake than magnetometry. Commercially available equipment now includes facilities for the measurement of resistivity at varying probe spacings, allowing a degree of depth estimation; also, experimental mobile wheeled arrays with variable electrode spacing, and mobile electrostatic arrays (Panissod *et al.* 1998) are being developed with a view to speedier and more flexible coverage. Generally, more attention is being devoted to the use of multiprobe arrays where successive measurements from increasingly separated electrodes are plotted as pseudosections or mathematically reconstructed as tomographic profiles. If such profiles are surveyed in closely spaced succession across a site followed by their conversion into horizontal depth 'slices', an approximation to three-dimensional reconstruction can be achieved. However, these techniques have yet to demonstrate more than a coarse resolution at depth and require further research (e.g., Meyer and Danckwardt 1999).

If magnetic and resistivity methods remain the mainstays of routine geophysical survey, enlivened by research into three dimensional reconstruction, it is this latter goal which has fostered the emergence of a third technique which is currently receiving much attention: ground penetrating radar or GPR (Conyers and Goodman 1997; see Chapter 43). Radar technology has reached a very high level of sophistication as a consequence of its other commercial and military uses, but has only relatively recently been applied in archaeological prospecting – with results that initially both excited and confused archaeologists (Stove and Addyman 1989, McCann 1995). With an increasing rapport between archaeologists and radar technicians, fuelled as well by necessary developments in computational power, it has become apparent that GPR, used with caution on carefully selected targets can be highly effective. Early applications involving the assessment of individual profiles, which are very difficult to interpret in isolation, are now being superseded by the surveying of closely spaced multiple transects providing an equivalence of coverage to that normally expected of magnetic and resistivity surveys. The GPR data can then be processed to minimize spurious effects, and interpolated to create a matrix through which a succession of horizontal 'time slices' can be created, each corresponding to a particular 'window' of two-way travel time or estimated depth (Goodman *et al.* 1995). Each slice allows the continuity of anomalous reflectors to become more apparent across the entire survey area

and for significant patterns to be more readily recognized. Furthermore, the computerized animation of successive time slices helps the viewer to trace such continuities throughout the vertical dimension, providing a valuable guide to the relative depth and preservation of structural remains. Time slicing methods have been used to particularly good effect in the study of Roman buildings (e.g., Kandler *et al.* 1999, Goodman and Nishimura 2000 see Figure S7.3 in colour plates) and seem sure to find much wider application in the near future. Other methods under investigation include the automated calculation of isosurfaces in blocks of GPR data for the more direct extraction of 3D information (Leckebusch and Peikert 1999).

Other electromagnetic (EM) methods have a less prominent role in archaeological geophysics although it is curious that more advantage has not been taken of their versatility, with instruments such as the EM38 allowing measurement of both conductivity (in two depth modes) as well as magnetic susceptibility (Cole *et al.* 1995). Vehicle-mounted instruments with global positioning systems (GPS), already in use for agricultural mapping, invite an archaeological application. New variable-frequency EM instruments have yet to be fully tested in archaeological conditions.

Other methods, such as gravity survey and seismics have so far seen very limited application on terrestrial sites. Acoustic methods are however the staple of offshore prospecting with echo-sounding and side-scan sonar providing often highly detailed images of the sea (or lake) bed, and of features such as wreck sites lying upon it. Lower frequency sub-bottom profilers can distinguish landforms and stratigraphy below the seabed, and in the last few years very high resolution, digital, frequency modulated sub-bottom profilers have come into use. These are capable of resolving sediment layers as close as 7.5 cm apart and can generate images of the seabed from all depths up to 30 cm. Case studies have shown that such systems can successfully image buried wooden objects on wreck sites and can profile underlying geomorphological structures (Quinn *et al.* 1997). Together with new dual frequency digitally recorded side-scan sonar such developments are timely in view of the increasing need to bring offshore cultural resource management into line with that inland. Sites under freshwater can also be imaged using GPR (Blake 1995).

Archaeological prospecting is of course not limited only to the discovery and identification of buried or drowned structures, but also includes their characterization in terms of human use. Aerial and ground-based methods can now map sites in two and even three dimensions, and their morphology, so defined, can be analysed together with topographic detail and other surface evidence such as artifact type and distribution (Chapter 42). Surviving fabric can be productively examined with remote sensing technologies (Brooke 1994). Depending on the availability of additional data for instance from boreholes, as well as excavation and documentary sources, many sites can be characterized in precise detail. Where interpretation is more constrained a further source of evidence which is available both from the ground surface and at depth during the course of excavation, is geochemical analysis (Chapter 45). In phosphate analysis, with its origins in the 1920s and with sporadic continuing attention, this branch of prospection has a greater longevity than most. It seems unfortunate, therefore, that the method remains problematic and still in need of a more critical approach requiring input of new research (e.g., Crowther 1997 and Chapter 45). However, phosphate is only one element the distribution of which can be informative, and multi-element assays have now been conducted on a number of sites (e.g., Entwhistle *et al.* 2000, Aston *et al.* 1998), with results warranting cautious optimism. Critical fine-tuning to exclude non-anthropogenic influences, the better comprehension of the 'taphonomy' of particular trace elements, and the need for increased spatial resolution coupled with speedier sampling and laboratory analysis remain areas for further improvements. In recent years the interpretative possibilities of lipid and other biomarkers, which have been shown to have considerable longevity in the soil, have been explored with rather more positive indications (e.g., Bull *et al.* 1999; see Chapters 28 and 45). Although still very time-consuming, molecular and isotopic methods are allowing the secure identification of former manuring activities (where other visible evidence is lacking) and allowing the functional interpretation of particular archaeological features (cess pits). The relevance of this to prospecting, as such, is necessarily very limited at present, but, when linked with geophysical information (for instance), these methods together offer a valuable continuum between identification and functional interpretation.

Integration is, after all, an overarching requirement of the multidisciplinary effort that constitutes most archaeological research. For archaeological prospection perhaps the main thrust must be towards the use of multiple technologies, followed by an increasingly seamless (digital) integration with all other relevant datasets (Chapter 46). The location and characterization of sites is best achieved using several detection methods; for instance in the right circumstances aerial photographs, magnetics, resistivity and GPR can all provide differing but highly complementary information on buried structural remains such as Roman buildings. Test pits and excavation can provide 'ground truth'. Together, such information can be imported into a GIS (Chapter 53) and subjected to a wide range of comparative analyses at any appropriate scale. Ultimately, perhaps, virtual reality techniques offer the opportunity to use geophysical and other data to 're-construct' archaeological scenarios for testing against independent data, and for interactive presentation to others. Excavation is both expensive and destructive; the increasingly refined application of geophysical and other methods, whilst not removing the need to excavate, can at least ensure that a maximum of information can be gained non-destructively and – if excavation is necessary – that this is both informed and precisely targeted.

Geophysical and other prospecting techniques of course have significant limitations and these should be a goad to further research. Deep overburden (>1 m) can be particularly intractable to both aerial and ground-based geophysical techniques; urban and suburban situations also conceal rich, complex and deep archaeological deposits which seem impossible to resolve except where a high degree of expectation, or foreknowledge, already exists. In these and indeed in many other situations it must be accepted that geophysics needs to proceed in close conjunction with ground truthing – the one informing the other. Borehole information can be critical in this exchange, and the potential of cross-hole resistivity and GPR surveys has yet to be assessed.

Beyond the nearly impenetrable constraints of the urban environment, rural areas offer continued promise, where alluvial and other covers are not excessive. Recent years have seen the application of geophysical and geochemical surveys at scales of coverage which allow inter- as well as intra-site exploration, approaching comparability with the sort of landscape coverage taken for granted by aerial archaeologists. The integrated survey of Roman sites, with the ultimate aim of the virtual reconstruction of entire cityscapes within their settings is becoming a reality (Gaffney *et al.* 2000, Kandler *et al.* 1999). The potential of combined geophysical and multispectral data is further exemplified by a recent project in the Vale of Pickering (Powlesland *et al.* 1997). The use of mobile sensor arrays will see the size of such surveys growing and integration within GIS must become routine, subject to appropriate data standards (e.g., English Heritage 1995, Schmidt and Wise forthcoming). New software utilizing developments in artificial intelligence will no doubt eventually allow the automated recognition of features in large arrays of geophysical data, eliminating subjectivity and speeding the interpretation process.

The role of archaeological prospecting has never been clearer, nor more in demand than at present. 'One might be forgiven for thinking that the peak of development in archaeological prospecting had been reached. Experience teaches that it has not' (Clark 1990:26). Ten years further on, into a new millennium, the horizons seem broader still.

REFERENCES

Aitken, M. (1969). Magnetic location. In Brothwell, D. and Higgs, E. (eds) *Science in Archaeology*, 681–694 (2nd edn). Thames and Hudson: London.

Aston, M.A., Martin, M.H. and Jackson, A.W. (1998). The potential for heavy metal soil analysis on low status archaeological sites at Shapwick, Somerset. *Antiquity*, 72:838–846.

Becker, H. (1995). From nanoTesla to picoTesla – a new window for magnetic prospecting in archaeology. *Archaeological Prospection*, 2:217–228.

Becker, H. (1999). Prospecting in Ostia Antica (Italy) and the discovery of the basilica of Constantinus I in 1996. In Fassbinder, J.W.E and Irlinger, W.E. (eds) *Archaeological Prospection: Third International Conference on Archaeological Prospection*, 139–143. Bavarian State Conservation Office: Munich.

Blake, V.S. (1995). Image processing and interpretation of ground penetrating radar data. In Huggett, J. and Ryan, N. (eds) *Computer Applications and Quantitative Methods in Archaeology 1994*, 175–180. BAR International Series 600, British Archaeological Reports: Oxford.

Brooke, C.J. (1994). Ground based remote sensing of buildings and archaeological sites: ten years research to operation. *Archaeological Prospection*, 1:105–119.

Brothwell, D. and Higgs, E. (1963). *Science in Archaeology*. Thames and Hudson: London.

Brothwell, D. and Higgs, E. (1969). *Science in Archaeology*, (2nd edn). Thames and Hudson: London.

Bull, I.D., Simpson, I.A., van Bergen, P.F. and Evershed, R.P. (1999). Muck 'n' molecules: organic geochemical methods for detecting ancient manuring. *Antiquity*, 73:86–96.

Carr, T.L. and Turner, M.D. (1996). Investigating regional lithic procurement using multi-spectral imagery and geophysical exploration. *Archaeological Prospection*, 3:109–128.

Clark, A.J. (1969). Resistivity surveying. In Brothwell, D. and Higgs, E. (eds) *Science in Archaeology*, 695–707 (2nd edn). Thames and Hudson: London.

Clark, A.J. (1990). *Seeing Beneath the Soil*. Batsford: London.

Cole, M.A., Linford, N.T., Payne, A.W. and Linford, P.K. (1995). Soil magnetic susceptibility measurements and their application to archaeological site investigation. In Beavis, J. and Barker, K. (eds) *Science and Site*, 144–162. Occasional Paper 1, School of Conservation Sciences, Bournemouth University: Bournemouth.

Conyers, L.B. and Goodman, D. (1997). *Ground-Penetrating Radar: an Introduction for Archaeologists*. Altamira Press: Walnut Creek, Ca.

Crowther, J. (1997). Soil phosphate surveys: critical approaches to sampling, analysis and interpretation. *Archaeological Prospection*, 4:93–102.

Dittrich, G. and Koppelt, U. (1997). Quantitative interpretation of magnetic data over settlement structures by inverse modelling. *Archaeological Prospection*, 4:165–178.

Eder-Hinterleitner, A., Neubauer, W. and Melichar, P. (1999). Magnetic modelling for the 3D reconstruction of the Neolithic circular ditch system of Steinabrunn/Austria. In Fassbinder, J.W.E. and Irlinger, W.E. (eds) *Archaeological Prospection: Third International Conference on Archaeological Prospection*, 32–33. Bavarian State Conservation Office: Munich.

English Heritage (1995). *Geophysical Survey in Archaeological Field Evaluation*. Research and Professional Services Guideline No. 1, English Heritage: London.

Entwhistle, J.A., Abrahams, P.W. and Dodgshon, R.A. (2000). The geoarchaeological significance and spatial variability of a range of physical and chemical soil properties from a former habitation site, Isle of Skye. *Journal of Archaeological Science*, 27:287–303.

Fassbinder, J.W.E. and Irlinger, W.E. (eds) (1999). *Archaeological Prospection: Third International Conference on Archaeological Prospection*. Bavarian State Conservation Office: Munich.

Featherstone, R., Horne, P., Macleod, D. and Bewley, R. (1999). Aerial reconnaissance over England in summer 1996. *Archaeological Prospection*, 6:47–62.

Gaffney, C., Gater, J., Linford, P., Gaffney, V. and White, R. (2000). Large scale systematic fluxgate gradiometry at the Roman city of Wroxeter. *Archaeological Prospection*, 7:81–99.

Goodman, D. and Nishimura, Y. (2000). Ground penetrating radar survey at Wroxeter. *Archaeological Prospection*, 7:101–105.

Goodman, D., Nishimura, Y. and Rogers, J.D. (1995). GPR time slices in archaeological prospection. *Archaeological Prospection*, 2:85–90.

Herbich, J. (1996). Relationships between the contemporary distribution of weed types and earlier settlements along the lower Vistula banks (northern Poland). *Archaeological Prospection*, 3:1–12.

Kandler, M., Doneus, M., Eder-Hinterleitner, A., Melichar, P., Neubauer, W. and Seren, S.S. (1999). Carnuntum – the largest archaeological landscape in Austria and the impact of archaeological prospection. In Fassbinder, J.W.E. and Irlinger, W.E. (eds) *Archaeological Prospection: Third*

International Conference on Archaeological Prospection, 48–49. Bavarian State Conservation Office: Munich.

Leckebusch, J. and Peikert, R. (1999). Automated extraction of 3-D features from georadar data for interpretation and visualization. In Fassbinder, J.W.E. and Irlinger, W.E. (eds) *Archaeological Prospection: Third International Conference on Archaeological Prospection*, 52. Bavarian State Conservation Office: Munich.

Locock, M. (1995). The effectiveness of dowsing as a method of determining the nature and location of buried features on historic garden sites. *Archaeological Prospection*, **2**:15–18.

McCann, W.A. (1995). GPR and archaeology in central London. *Archaeological Prospection*, **2**:155–166.

Meyer, C. and Danckwardt, E. (1999). DC tensor geoelectrics – now applicable to archaeological prospection! In Fassbinder, J.W.E. and Irlinger, W.E. (eds) *Archaeological Prospection: Third International Conference on Archaeological Prospection*, 58. Bavarian State Conservation Office: Munich.

Neubauer, W. and Eder-Hinterleitner, A. (1997). 3D-interpretation of postprocessed archaeological magnetic prospection data. *Archaeological Prospection*, **4**:191–206.

Panissod, G., Dabas, M., Florsch, N., Hesse, A., Jolivet, A., Tabbagh, A. and Tabbagh, J. (1998). Archaeological prospecting using electric and electrostatic mobile arrays. *Archaeological Prospection*, **5**:239–252.

Powlesland, D., Lyall, J. and Donoghue, D.N.M. (1997). Enhancing the record through remote sensing. The application and integration of multi-sensor, non-invasive remote sensing techniques for the enhancement of the Sites and Monuments record. Heslerton Parish Project, N. Yorkshire, England. *Internet Archaeology*, **2**: [http://intarch.ac.uk/journal/issue2/pld_toc.html]

Quinn, R., Bull, J.M. and Dix, J.K. (1997). Imaging wooden artifacts using Chirp sources. *Archaeological Prospection*, **4**:25–35.

Redfern, S., Lyons, G. and Redfern, R.M. (1999). Digital elevation modelling of individual monuments from aerial photographs. *Archaeological Prospection*, **6**:211–224.

Scollar, I., Tabbagh, A., Hesse, A. and Herzog, I. (1990). *Archaeological Prospecting and Remote Sensing*. Cambridge University Press: Cambridge.

Schmidt, A. and Wise, A. (forthcoming). *Archaeological Geophysics: Guide to Good Practice*. AHDS Guides to Good Practice. AHDS: York. http://ads.ahds.ac.uk/project/goodguides/g2gp.html

Stove, G.C. and Addyman, P.V. (1989). Ground probing impulse radar: an experiment in archaeological remote sensing at York. *Antiquity*, **63**:337–342.

Tabbagh, A., Desvignes, G. and Dabas, M. (1997). Processing of Z gradiometer magnetic data using linear transforms and analytical signal. *Archaeological Prospection*, **4**:1–14.

Tsokas, G.N. and Hansen, R.O. (2000). On the use of complex attribute analysis and the inferred source parameter estimates in the exploration of archaeological sites. *Archaeological Prospection*, **7**:17–30.

van Leusen, M. (1998). Dowsing and archaeology. *Archaeological Prospection*, **5**:123–138.

42

Surface Collection Techniques in Field Archaeology: Theory and Practice

T.J. WILKINSON

Oriental Institute, University of Chicago.

Even in the early twenty-first century, many people still consider that archaeology is largely driven by excavation. However, the regional scale often provides the most appropriate arena for the analysis of archaeological problems and cultural processes, a point that was driven home by Binford (1964). Not only do many of the materials recovered during excavation, such as ceramics, stone tools, faunal and carbonized plant remains, originate beyond the limits of the settlement, but similarly the cultural record frequently includes a constellation of occupation sites in the region of any excavated site. In addition there is the cultural landscape of fields, field boundaries, roads, quarries and other installations all of which provide a wealth of information bearing upon our understanding of the site. Also many 'big questions', such as the development of urbanism, subsistence strategies, state formation, economic exchange, and ritual matters, are best examined from a regional perspective. For example, in recent decades archaeological survey has revolutionized our understanding of the development of ancient states, e.g., Adams (1981) for Mesopotamia; Alcock (1993) for Greece; Blanton *et al.* (1981) and Sanders *et al.* (1979) for Mesoamerica; for a general review see Ammerman (1981). This chapter outlines methodologies and theoretical issues that relate to the recording and collecting of cultural material at the regional level. There are two basic ways of recording material at this level; one is prospecting, the

intuitive search for a particular goal, be it site, culture, or feature (e.g., mining sites in a metal-rich zone); the second is sampling, which is the more specific survey of a region (Zubrow and Harbaugh 1978:109; but see Nance 1983:292). Within this scheme sampling is concerned with using information from a part of something to make inferences about the whole (Shennan 1997:361).

Archaeological surveys provide a description of settlement location and a history of changes of settlement and landscape which can ultimately provide rough estimates of population levels. Surveys can also amplify and complement historical data and provide a range of information on economic, social and environmental conditions (Hole 1980). By explicitly structuring investigations to include large scale and long-term cultural and environmental records, we are therefore more likely to successfully tackle some of the many facets of human-environment interactions. It should be emphasized however that the surface record of past cultures varies considerably from place to place, so that no single survey recipe can be applied world-wide, or even within a single region. The record of past settlement ranges from major multi-period *tells* (in the Middle East and parts of the Old World) accumulated from millennia of sedentary occupation, to sparse traces of hunter-gatherer groups, either elsewhere, or in the same regions but at much earlier periods. Consequently sampling techniques must be tailored to suit these varied circumstances, and it continues to be necessary for archaeologists to be realistic and practical in the choice of survey design.

Haselgrove *et al.* (1985) and Schofield (1991) give a good review of off-site and ploughzone archaeology. Cherry *et al.* (1978) and Mueller (1975) discuss sampling in archaeology but both are now updated by Nance (1983) and Shennan (1997), the latter being an excellent guide to statistical methods in sampling. Field walking is covered in Hayfield (1980) and a critical review of the interpretation of off-site scatters can be found in Alcock *et al.* (1994). General issues of archaeological survey in the Mediterranean, with much discussion of concepts and issues, can be found in Keller and Rupp (1983).

GEOARCHAEOLOGY AND LANDSCAPE TAPHONOMY

Both natural and cultural processes may have biased the record of surface archaeological remains, therefore it is necessary to undertake a geoarchaeological appraisal during the early stages of any sampling programme. In addition in most parts of the world cultural processes, as well as leaving a palimpsest of former occupation, will have erased traces of previous occupations (Taylor 1972). Thus we often witness so-called landscapes of destruction (usually the areas most attractive for long-term settlement) beyond which, in more marginal areas, the archaeological record is more complete because cultural processes are less likely to have removed them. These processes of landscape taphonomy may result in biases in the surface record of artifacts that include the preferential sorting of pottery associated with stone clearance mounds, as well as the gross disturbance of the archaeological record such as by the excavation of bedding trenches for vines (Gaffney *et al.* 1991). Even the effect of ploughing can have a more radical effect on the form of sites than was hitherto anticipated. Recent simulation studies show that ploughzone artifact distributions become more spread out and of lower density through time, and have a tendency to be more circular (on flat land) or elongated (on slopes), with the record losing progressively more information with time (Boismier 1997:238). As tillage events increase cumulatively through time, information on intra-site patterning (e.g., functional areas or specific building areas) is lost and spurious tillage-induced arrangements take their place. Furthermore on slopes, artifact patterning can then become determined more by topographic features, such as footslopes or field boundaries, than by their original configuration. In upland areas the construction of terraced fields can result in pre-existing sites being partly destroyed, the artifacts of which are then further dispersed by slope processes.

More obvious is the role of natural processes which can deposit a considerable depth of sediment over earlier landscapes and their sites (Brookes *et al.* 1982), or can erode the sites away entirely (Allen 1991, Zangger *et al.* 1997). Such biasing processes rarely affect the landscape evenly; rather some areas may be buried or eroded, whereas others will remain stable and appear as windows within an archaeological record that has otherwise disappeared. Unless geoarchaeological studies proceed before or during the early stages of survey, such biases may not be recognized. Furthermore, to understand gaps in the cultural record it may be necessary to insert a systematic programme of valley floor sampling into the regional strategy in order to recover the more subtle traces of settlement (Banning 1996).

Increased use of ceramic petrology and trace element analysis (see Chapter 36) for fingerprinting pottery and other artifacts will in future make it advisable to conduct some form of regional geochemical assessment alongside archaeological survey. These assessments can then be integrated within the mapping framework of the survey. Although a complete geochemical assay of an entire region may be inappropriate for most archaeological purposes, some form of spatial control on soil geochemistry is advisable. Such techniques, if formalized into a regional sampling scheme, can provide valuable control data for artifact sourcing, identification of human impacts in the landscape (e.g., soil magnetism; Allen 1988), key trace elements and metallic pollutants (Willis *et al.* 1998), and agricultural intensification (Bintliff *et al.* 1992). Sampling procedures are best integrated with cultural elements by means of a Geographical Information System (see below, and Chapter 53).

THE CONCEPT OF THE CONTINUOUS LANDSCAPE

The archaeological landscape does not solely consist of discrete sites or site clusters, but in many areas of the world it is evident that there exists a virtually continuous spread of artifacts across the terrain (Cherry 1983). If always interpreted as individual sedentary sites, these artifact scatters could inflate estimates of the occupied area. Sampling techniques have therefore been devised to deal with the differentiation of occupied areas from 'background noise', and various theories proposed to explain the various forms of scatter (e.g., Foley 1981, Wilkinson 1982, Gallant 1986, Alcock *et al.* 1994). Alternatively, the term 'site' is sometimes regarded as being almost meaningless (Haselgrove 1985:14, Thomas 1975) and it has been maintained that by restricting field work to well-defined entities known as sites, much cultural information will be lost (Dunnell and Dancey 1983:271).

Sites, their recognition and definition

Traces of sedentary occupation are usually more visible than those of nomadic pastoralists. This is because sedentary sites frequently comprise permanent buildings and because more sustained use of such sites will have allowed more time for rubbish to accumulate. Pottery and lithics are not the only remains to be expected, and frequently a wider range of criteria can be employed for site recognition. These include:

(i)   stone scatters (from the remains of foundations),
(ii) other artifacts, such as door sockets, quernstones, etc.,
(iii) soil colour, (soils of greyer hue, being indicative of ash and other occupation debris in the soil),
(iv) cut features: pits and ditches, and
(v)   geophysical traces of occupation (see Chapter 43).

In addition, the presence of a network of modern canals or drains across a landscape can provide valuable insights into the archaeological record by providing sites and features in section, as well as locations for sampling environmental data (Crowther *et al.* 1985; see Jones (1995) for the use of borehole transects in the Nile valley). Furthermore, even if the actual cut faces of canals are not clean, it is possible by walking along the upcast of such cuts to obtain a good record of completely buried sites from the presence of sherds and other materials thrown up from buried cultural deposits. In the Near East, where sites are frequently represented by surface mounding, the more subtle traces of settlement are often best distinguished by microtopographic surveying of the mounded area or any adjacent enclosed depressions that resulted from the excavation of mud brick for buildings.

Components of the off-site record

It is often inappropriate to categorize the record of surface remains into on-site and off-site components because in many cases it is difficult to recognize and define sites and distinguish them from the background scatter. Nevertheless, Plog's (1978) definition proves expedient: a site is a discrete and potentially interpretable locus of material with spatial boundaries marked by at least relative changes in artifact densities (but see also Haselgrove 1985, Schofield 1991:3, and Figure 42.1). In areas where sites are more elusive, however, surveys examine the relative levels of variation of artifacts between collection units or fields, between ecological zones, and between regions. Thus the study of artifact distributions becomes a study in its own right. Where it is possible to define living sites, off-site material may then be classified as material that is scattered widely across the terrain, is without clear boundaries, and which lacks a discernible relative change in artifact densities (see also Gallant 1986). Factors that contribute to the accumulation of the continuous record are as follows, in no order of priority:

(i)   Cemeteries, if they contain grave goods, can contribute to the surface scatter, if the burials are sufficiently shallow, have been plundered, or the ground is heavily eroded.
(ii) Special-purpose sites, which have less domestic rubbish than would normally be expected. Such sites include rural religious sites, temporary activity areas and some military installations (Murray and Kardulias 1986).
(iii) Pastoral/hunter gatherer sites can yield varying amounts of surface material depending upon the nature of the nomadic population. Some, such as the Turkman nomads cited by Cribb (1991), leave substantial traces, whereas others leave virtually nothing behind (Frendo 1996). In East Africa, Foley (1981) recognized pastoral nomadic and hunter-gatherer components, each of which left a characteristic signature of artifact scatters on the land surface. In terms of hunter-gatherers Foley divided the record into a behavioural component and an accumulative component, scatters of both being potentially transformed by sedimentation, erosion and other taphonomic or geoarchaeological processes. The behavioural component is formed because, outside the home base but within the home range of the group, a range of activities such as butchering, tool-manufacture and so

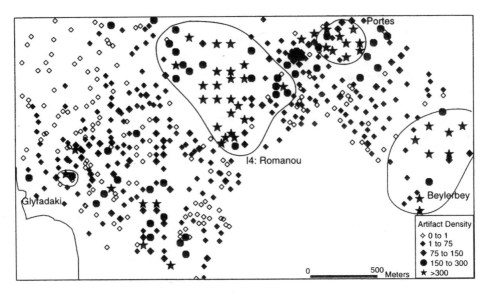

Figure 42.1 Artifact densities at POSI (Places of Special Interest) 14 and in its vicinity (by Sebastian Heath, from Davis *et al.* 1997:fig. 7; courtesy of the American School of Classical Studies at Athens).

on, can result in different discard patterns which result in a sparse and variable lithic scatter over the terrain. The accumulative component results because home bases are changed frequently (often being occupied for only a few days) and the occupants do not return to the same location. As a result, home base debris forms a scatter which accumulates roughly in proportion to the degree of occupation in the area. Combined, the behavioural and accumulative components result in a broad scatter of material over the landscape, which can then be sampled by a regional sample design (see below).

(iv) Ploughed-out sites and sites transformed by subsequent activities have already been discussed under taphonomic processes. Such processes of ploughing, deep cultivation and terrace construction may result in the form of the original site being lost. Nevertheless, the existence of the site can still be confirmed by careful survey.

(v) The random arrival of pottery, for example, pieces that drop off passing pack animals or remains from field labour, although contributing to surface scatters in the New World (Santley 1992:166), seems unlikely to account for the widespread and often quite dense scatters of surface material in the Old World (Bintliff and Snodgrass 1988, Alcock *et al.* 1994:143).

(vi) Because people do not necessarily enjoy living in their own accumulated rubbish, it should not be assumed that middens will be the preferred living area (Schofield 1991:6, 117). In the Vera Cruz and Gulf Coast areas of Mexico, management of household debris can result in scatters of material off-site. Configurations of artifacts conform to a houseplot model (Killion 1992) in which certain areas remain free of household refuse, but other areas beyond receive more secondary refuse, in some cases as fertilizer (Santley 1992:166). In the Old World, secondary use of household refuse as fertilizer can also result in artifacts being re-distributed into the landscape. The application of settlement-derived wastes on fields as fertilizer can result in the incorporation of artifacts into field soils (Foard 1978:363, Wilkinson 1982, Gallant 1986, Bintliff and Snodgrass 1988, Alcock *et al.* 1994). Scatters usually comprise pottery, but also specialized materials such as vitrified kiln lining can become incorporated into kiln ash which is then applied to fields (Wilkinson and Tucker 1995:56, fig. 40). Sherds in such 'field scatters' tend to decrease in density away from sites thereby forming zones which probably relate to declining applications of manure and therefore land-use intensity away from the central site. In Central Asia and the Middle East scatters can extend over hundreds of square kilometres and can be concentrated by aeolian activity (Stein 1921, Wilkinson 1988:100), whereas in western Europe where both deflation and gross pottery production may be less, surface scatter densities can be much more sparse (Bintliff and Snodgrass 1988, Williamson 1984, Gaffney and Tingle 1985). In addition to influencing inter-regional differences, gross-pottery circulation or input into the system can also entail certain periods (such as the pagan Saxon period in Britain) being under-represented (Foard 1978, Millett 1985). If surface scatters are to be interpreted as resulting from manure applications, it is necessary to demonstrate that they are continuous, of low density compared with on-site scatters, are dispersed through the plough-soil, and that they cannot reasonably be explained as resulting from sites that have been destroyed by ploughing. Although recognized as contributing to off-site material since 1950, the debate as to what processes have contributed to such scatters continues (Alcock et al. 1994).

In summary, the surface record can be classified into a number of general categories: accidental losses, primary refuse (material discarded at its point of use), secondary refuse such as that discarded away from its point of use (e.g., dumped in pits), and deliberate deposition, e.g., burials, hoards (Haselgrove 1985:14). Thus after its useful life an artifact can appear in a number of locations, as a result of accidental dropping, by the transport of refuse to form a midden, and then by additional transport on to the fields as fertilizer.

SURVEY METHODS

Owing to limitations of staff and finances it is not always practicable for the entirety of any survey area to be examined at an intensity that would enable all archaeological sites to be recovered. Nevertheless, the more time that is expended upon survey the greater is the recovery of sites per unit area (Plog 1978:fig. 10.1, Cherry 1983:fig. 1). This is especially so for the smaller dispersed settlements, be they either sedentary, pastoral or hunter-gatherer sites. Whereas increased intensity of survey within a sampled area can result in greater recovery of archaeological sites and other surface information, coverage of the entire region of interest (often a natural or economic region) can result in a more structured record, especially if ancient settlement was

nucleated. The latter approach or 'full coverage survey' is the systematic observation of entire areas as opposed to specifiable parts as in sample surveys, or unspecifiable parts as in reconnaissance surveys (Kowalewski and Fish 1990:263). By being able to find most larger and medium sites and many smaller sites full-coverage survey provides a top down structure of the settlement. This is, however, at the expense of the recovery of smaller sites, which may be under-represented. Full-coverage survey is therefore better for providing structural properties of the archaeological record that can be used for locational analyses such as nearest-neighbour analysis and rank-size curves. Such data cannot be recovered using sampling survey strategies (Sumner 1990). On the other hand, in order to estimate the full range of sites and artifact scatters, sample survey is a more appropriate technique. To be pragmatic it is suggested that during fieldwork there is an initial concentration upon full coverage survey, followed by intensive survey and then, as appropriate, controlled surface collection from individual sites. Excavation can then form a later part of such a strategy as outlined by Redman (1973:64).

Sampling of surface material comprises the collection of all surface artifacts, or specific diagnostic classes of artifacts from the available ground surface (Flannery 1976a). *Accessibility sampling* is where samples are taken convenient to access routes, other areas being under-represented; this is often undertaken as *haphazard* or *grab sampling* of sites without any given sampling procedure being followed. *Judgemental* or *purposive* sampling builds on the surveyor's knowledge in order to sample surface material. Although this may be very successful at pinpointing sites or even making a representative sample of an area, there is no way of knowing how representative such samples are of the entire population. Finally, *probabilistic sampling* entails collecting part of the archaeological record in such a way that probability theory can be used to make estimates of the whole from which it was selected (Shennan 1997:361; for a useful glossary of sampling terms see Cherry et al. 1978:409).

If it is possible to survey 100 per cent of the area of interest, this should be done, but if this is impossible for reasons of time, money, or logistics, then it is recommended that probabilistic sampling is conducted according to a design that will enable some assessment to be made of the reliability of the result (Flannery 1976b:132, Plog 1978:284). However, many field workers now question whether it is even possible to speak of 100 per cent survey coverage (Sundstrom 1993:91). Sampling techniques are best based on intensive survey techniques using probabilistic sample designs (Cherry 1983:393). In the case of smaller sites, site visibility can vary from year to year (Ammerman 1995), and the soil itself acts as a reservoir for a large number of artifacts (much larger than is on the surface; Haselgrove 1985:8). As a result, a single sweep through an area will not necessarily recover all traces of cultural activity. In order to obtain a more representative record of archaeological data, it is therefore better to employ a multi-stage survey design (Cherry 1983:394). When sample survey is initiated it can take the form of one of the following regional sampling designs (based on Berry and Baker 1968:91 and Plog 1976:137). Here sampling units, that is the definable entities which contain the items of interest, are drawn from an overall list of sampling units in the population that forms the sample frame. The sample unit (an area or quadrat) is selected to encompass an area that is sufficiently large to contain a site or a number of sites, but itself forms only a fraction of the total area of interest. In this case the sample frame consists of the total number of, for example grid squares, in the area. From this, the sample fraction is the percentage of sample units selected from the overall population for collection. Usually the sampling fraction can comprise perhaps 5–25 per cent of the total area, but in certain intensive surveys almost complete coverage of an entire (but small) area is attempted (see below: field walking). This percentage is insufficient on its own however to plan a sample collection strategy and it is crucial that the number of artifacts collected is large also (Haselgrove 1985:11) because precision of sample survey increases as both sample size and sample fraction increase (Plog 1978:284).

The following sample schemes can be applied to a given region (adapted from Clark and Hosking 1986:164, Shennan 1997:361):

(i) To obtain a *random sample* of a region, using an existing co-ordinate system, one takes two random numbers to establish the location of each sample point, the first might apply to the N–S axis, the second to the E–W. Both are independent so that the resulting intersections provide a simple random sample within the grid (Clark and Hosking 1986:165). Although this methodology should give an unbiased and truly representative sample of the population being investigated (Whallon 1979:14), a true random sample may leave gaps which could thereby leave significant areas unsampled. An alternative approach therefore is to employ a systematic design.

(ii) *Systematic samples*, on the other hand, establish from a given point (usually chosen at random x and y co-ordinates) sample points at fixed intervals (Figure 42.2). The disadvantage of this is that if there is regular periodicity in the population being sampled, such as a grid pattern of buildings, the sampling may only reproduce part of that periodicity.

(iii) For a given grid comprising a fixed number of points, a *stratified spatial sample* can entail randomly sampling a set number of samples from each cell of the grid (e.g., Redman and Watson 1970). Alternatively, the region can be *stratified* according to natural regions (clay plain, steep scarp slopes, etc.), each stratum of which has sample squares selected at random in proportion to the area of each sub-region.

(iv) Limitations of the above sampling designs include the appearance of voids and unsampled areas in the random system and the problem of periodicities in the systematic system. A *stratified, systematic, unaligned design* can therefore be employed to provide both an even coverage and a random distribution of sampling points (this is described in more detail in Berry and Baker (1968:93) and Clark and Hosking (1986:167)).

Systematic and stratified systematic unaligned techniques ensure an even coverage of the region. On the other hand the stratified systematic unaligned design avoids the periodicities of systematic sampling, gives good areal coverage, is efficient and deals with most distributions. Because however it can be difficult in the field to accurately locate and physically reach random sample areas, transects can be more convenient to use, and this is often the chosen methodology for many surveys (see below).

With quadrat sampling it is important to appreciate that there are three different populations being examined (Nance 1983): (i) sample units (that is the quadrats themselves), (ii) sites and (iii) artifacts. Of these, sites and artifacts are sampling *elements*, that is they are basic members of the population of interest, a sampling *unit* is an entity such as a quadrat which contains the elements (e.g., sites) themselves (Nance 1983:297). A fundamental characteristic among sampling models is the properties which distinguish element sampling from cluster sampling, the latter being 'a sample in which each sampling unit is a collection, or cluster of elements' (Schaeffer *et al.* 1979:141). Because sites usually occur dispersed within quadrats, the sample universe is not the same as the number of quadrats. In fact some

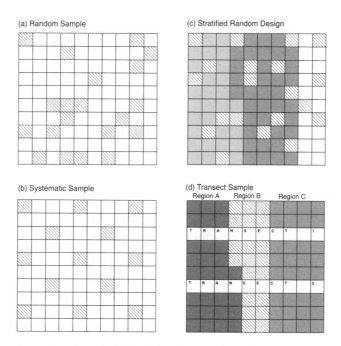

Figure 42.2   Commonly used examples of sample designs: (a) random quadrats, (b) systematic quadrats, (c) stratified quadrats, (d) systematic transects (adapted from Shennan 1997).

squares may contain many sites, while others will be blank; also the distribution of these sites will not necessarily conform to a normal distribution. Unfortunately, because of this clustering, and because discovery probability varies directly with site abundance and inversely with the degree of clustering, as clustering increases sample size needs to be increased (Schiffer *et al.* 1978:4). According to Nance (1983:297), one of the most frequently made statistical errors in archaeology is the use of simple random sample statistics in the analysis of data which was assembled by cluster sampling. Cluster sampling, however, requires that sample populations be rather large, and it is often unrealistic to satisfy this assumption in many survey situations. Furthermore the samples from quadrats or transects are likely to be from skewed distributions (Nance 1983:302). A useful example of probabilistic sample methodology is given by Read (1986), and for more details on sample methodologies see Plog (1976:fig. 5.2, 1978), Mueller (1975), Redman and Watson (1970), Clark and Hosking (1986), Redman (1987) and Shennan (1997).

Both element and cluster sampling techniques can be employed during an archaeological survey. When it is the properties of the sample space that are of interest, data are gathered by element sampling, but when the data of interest are sites, artifacts or features contained in these sampling units, data should be collected by various cluster sampling designs. Although cluster sampling is more complex than element sampling this technique is more frequently required for probabilistic survey (Nance 1983:348). Finally, in order to design sample strategy and estimate target parameters one actually needs to know the total population of archaeological materials (e.g. sites; Schiffer *et al.* 1978:3). Although this 'sampling paradox' may be partially sidestepped by the use of estimates, these will not necessarily be accurate, therefore it is better for any survey to be conducted over a number of years or stages so that target parameters can be estimated more accurately. Furthermore, if sites are aggregated into clusters, this increases the standard error of the estimate. Since larger survey quadrats reveal more clustering than small sampling units, one way to reduce the effects of aggregation is to use smaller quadrats. However this further results in problems of locating and reaching the sample areas as noted above. Another approach for dealing with clustered distributions of sites or artifacts is adaptive sampling (Shennan 1997). This multi-stage procedure improves the estimation of sample parameters by introducing a second sampling stage which increases the number of sample quadrats around any given cluster. If any of the initial stage of random quadrats intersects with the item of interest, the adjacent squares, above, below, to the right and to the left, are also collected. Sample parameters can then be estimated for the entire 'network' of sample squares that relate to the cluster in question (for further details see Shennan 1997:385). In spite of the problems posed by clustered distributions, if sample conditions are good and the survey universe is sufficiently large, sample survey can be used to efficiently estimate the number and distribution of sites (see Judge *et al.* 1975).

Although regional sample designs using the above techniques can enable regional settlement to be estimated with greater accuracy, transect survey can provide clear advantages. Transects can be set out across the sample region either at random or, more commonly, systematically (i.e., at regular intervals), but from a randomly selected starting point (e.g., Plog 1976:fig. 5.4, Batovic and Chapman 1985). If evenly spaced, transects can provide a reasonable estimate of the distribution of cultural material. Transects are much better than sample quadrats at providing information across natural or geological boundaries and it is better to position them to go across the full range of geological variation (Shennan 1985:11, fig. 2.7). Although transect sampling may only provide a partial record (frequently in the range of 5–20 per cent of the survey area), when tested against the pattern of modern settlement it has been shown that it can provide a reasonable approximation of the true pattern of settlement (Shennan 1985:fig. 2.6). For conventional large scale surveys in the Middle East transect spacing of 200 metres may recognize most sites (Redman 1982), but for more specialist surveys, the spacing of transects as little as 11 metres apart is recommended. Such a spacing would for example, provide, a 90 per cent probability of recovering all sites larger than 10 metres in diameter (Sundstrom 1993:93).

Because many archaeological surveys are undertaken within cultivated areas, in such cases sampling schemes should take into account the fact that collection will be within fields, and therefore the field may form the most pragmatic collection unit. In 'field walking' every field within the sample area is walked usually along regular transects, and the data recovered are recorded by both collection and by estimation using clickers or tally counters (Foard 1978, Taylor 1974, Hayfield 1980). Sampling techniques can be those described above, for example in the case of transects, each field along a particular transect is individually walked. In the case of the Hvar survey in Dalmatia, a 180 × 180 metres grid was defined by the pre-existing

Greek centuriation of rectilinear fields (Gaffney *et al.* 1991:61). Within each grid square north-south traverses were walked at 10 metre intervals, each traverse being sub-divided into four recording units of 45 metres. All artifacts (except tile) were retained from each 45 metre long collection unit (72 units per 180 metres square). This collection system (defined as 'extensive' by the fieldworkers) was then followed by an intensive system in areas where artifact concentrations and suspected habitation were noted. This entailed total collection of all artifacts from the surface within a 10 × 10 metres grid. In other surveys field walking entails making virtually a total coverage of all fields within the designated area, which is however usually rather small (Cherry *et al.* 1991). Such methodologies then can provide a remarkable picture of both occupation sites and off-site materials (Figure 42.1).

Where initial surveys have revealed that recognizable bounded sites are present (or form clustered and usually mounded features, as in parts of the Middle East), the following strategy can be employed. Within the site itself quadrats can be laid out according to probabilistic or systematic techniques (as above) to provide a means of localizing occupations of specific periods (Redman and Watson 1970). More pragmatically, strips can be laid out across the mound along the two axes, and along each strip individual sample squares can be collected. Although not as comprehensive as techniques that sample from the entire mound surface, this gridded strip technique (Whallon 1979) provides a fast and efficient means of defining areas of occupations for various periods. In landscapes of tells, before embarking on this relatively time consuming technique, however, it is crucial to ascertain whether a lower or outer town exists in the form of a subtle spread of low mounding, foundation stones or cultural debris. This is because the utility of detailed sampling is nullified if it is only confined to a fraction of the site. Such on-site sampling programmes can then be undertaken in tandem with other techniques such as the collection of surface ceramics and lithics, geomagnetic mapping of sub-surface features and excavation of test trenches (Zettler 1997, Peregrine *et al.* 1997). On the *c.* 40 ha Bronze Age lower town of Tell Sweyhat, it has therefore been possible to produce a nested set of data which can be mutually inter-related and analysed.

Alternatively, where there is a significant amount of material off-site, transects can then be set out across the terrain between sites. For example, in several Middle Eastern study areas transects were laid out either radially from tells, or with reference to field boundaries, if these were known from maps (Wilkinson 1989). With

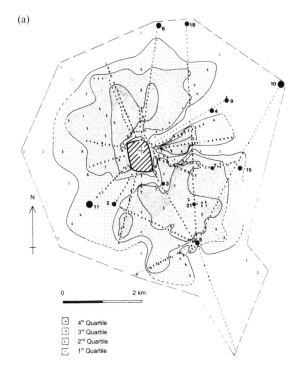

(a)

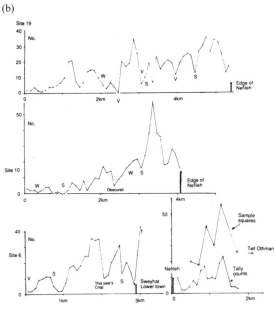

(b)

Figure 42.3   (a) Map of sherd distributions around Early Bronze Age Tell Sweyhat, Syria, with sherd scatter densities derived from tally counter transects and 10 by 10 m sample quadrats expressed as quartile distributions. (b) Tally counter transect and sample square data from a single transect at Tell es-Sweyhat, Syria.

the technology of the time, this was the most rapid technique to use, but now Global Positioning Systems (GPS), make it much easier to position sampling points on grids. When transects are employed, sample squares can be set out at intervals along them. To estimate continuity of scatter, tally counters are used to count the number of surface sherds per unit length walked (usually 100 metres) between squares (Figure 42.3). Such procedures demonstrate that surface material in many parts of the Near East forms a virtually continuous scatter rather than the beaded cluster characteristic of sedentary sites. However, scatter density can vary depending upon patterns of sedimentation, with lower densities occurring where local sedimentation has overlapped the scatters. In order to determine if such sedimentation has obscured field scatters, it is necessary to dig soil pits and collect the pottery within arbitrary excavation units of 10 or 20 cm depth (Wilkinson 1988:fig. 7.3). Test pits, shovel tests, or auger holes can also be employed during conventional surveys where visibility of surface artifacts is low or where completely buried sites are anticipated. Unfortunately if sites are small and the sample area is large, this technique can entail the excavation of an inordinate number of subsurface tests. However, with the application of more rigorous sampling techniques, it is now possible to estimate with greater accuracy the probability of intersecting and detecting otherwise invisible sites (Kintigh 1988, Shennan 1997:393). Similar data, but more qualitative, can also be obtained by inspection of canal cuts or other drains cut across the terrain, and such investigations provide a cross check to determine whether, for example, surface artifact scatters represent *in situ* occupation or are the remains of agricultural practices such as manuring.

MAP COVERAGE

Until recently, in many parts of the world, good maps were a rarity, but now commercial satellite images, and maps generated therefrom, can be used in tandem with a hand-held GPS, or for greater accuracy a differential GPS arrangement. If the images are geographically corrected the two systems can provide a convenient and relatively accurate way of fixing sites within a geographical framework. For convenience of plotting, UTM (Universal Transverse Mercator) co-ordinates are to be preferred over traditional latitude and longitude. A particular advantage of image-based maps is that they can show field boundaries which enables field walking transects to be mapped in terms of recognizable landscape divisions.

ARTIFACT AND SITE VISIBILITY

The size of sites and spacing of transects or sample areas all influence the likelihood of site discovery (Sundstrom 1993). In addition, operator differences between survey crew members or variations in land use can significantly influence the interpretation of results. Surface cover (crops or straw) can obscure sherds, and freshly ploughed fields can provide lower artifact visibility than fields that have had some weeks to be weathered and washed by rain (Foard 1978:360). Therefore if meaningful quantitative comparisons are to be made, these are best made between samples taken from a comparable land use. If it is not possible to sample from a single land use type it may be necessary to compensate for such differences by first applying scores to ground surface visibility and then by correcting the raw data by multiplying by a certain score (Gaffney et al. 1991:fig. 6.11). Because land use and therefore site visibility will change from season to season or year to year, it is advisable that site survey is not limited to a single visit because many minor sites will only be recognized after repeated visits to an area (Ammerman 1995; for a different view see Davis and Sutton 1995).

INTEGRATION OF SAMPLE STRATEGIES WITH SITE CATCHMENT ANALYSIS, ENVIRONMENTAL AND LANDSCAPE ARCHAEOLOGY

Site catchment analysis, defined as the study of the relationships between technology and natural resources that lie within the economic range of individual sites (Vita-Finzi and Higgs 1970:5), is primarily aimed at providing a context for the analysis of site economies. If this methodology is to be used it should therefore be incorporated into any regional study and sample design, because by incorporating data on modern land use, site catchment analysis can be seen as providing a new data layer for regional analysis. Good contexts for environmental analysis (e.g., organic deposits for pollen analysis) occur only episodically through the landscape (if at all!) and it is therefore not usually possible to initiate a formal sampling scheme for investigations of the palaeoenvironment. Nevertheless it is valuable to incorporate palaeoenvironmental investigations into the formal research design and integrate data from such work into an overall regional synthesis.

The foregoing suggests that a programme of full-coverage extensive survey combined with a carefully nested sequence of probabilistic sample survey will provide the most pragmatic methodology for regional studies. However, what have been described as methodologically unlovely approaches must also be included in regional studies (Schiffer et al. 1978), otherwise much crucial information will be lost. Thus there remains a need for purposive (or biased) sampling techniques, which can supply additional data. Such techniques become even more important in specialized environments where adherence to a formal grid would limit the results of survey. For example, in surveys below high water mark along tidal river estuaries or coasts where the complex, variable and dynamic range of environments make probabilistic sampling an impossibility, it is necessary to focus the survey on key localities. In such places, broad expanses of terrain such as, for example, an emergent palaeosol on the foreshore of an estuary, may provide a suitable environment for small-scale sub-sampling programmes (see Fulford et al. 1997:74 for a review of intertidal survey techniques). Therefore if surveys are to be used to maximum effect it is crucial that prior experience and knowledge are incorporated into survey design.

For convenience of manipulation and analysis, data from regional sampling should be stored and manipulated using a single data management system, preferably being integrated with data from nearby excavated sites. Any regional project will include many layers of information, such as sites of different occupation periods, artifact types, site classes, etc., but in addition we can assume that non-systematic features (stray finds, data from sites and monuments records), other economic data (e.g., Domesday 'woodland in terms of swine'), land-use classes, soil data, environmental sequences, data from regional geochemical assay, stone and sediment source materials, and so on, can all supply meaningful information which can be included in the overall data handling system and can be manipulated by means of a GIS (Davis et al. 1997:411; see Chapters 46 and 53). Although not as methodologically 'clean' as data culled from statistically rigorous sampling techniques, non-systematic data especially that from sites and monuments records (Gilman 1996, Massagrande 1995) provide a crucial but under-appreciated part of the record which can provide numerous supplementary insights into patterns of settlement and human activities (e.g., the occurrence of Neolithic polished stone axes). Therefore in future more effort should be made to explicitly integrate sampling of cultural data, geophysical and geochemical prospection methodologies at the regional level.

REFERENCES

*Recommended for further reading

Adams, R. McC. (1981). *Heartland of Cities*. University of Chicago Press: Chicago.

Alcock, S. (1993). *Graecia Capta: an Archaeological and Historical Study of Roman Greece*. Cambridge University Press: Cambridge.

Alcock, S.E., Cherry, J.F. and Davis, J.L. (1994). Intensive survey, agricultural practice and the classical landscape of Greece. In Morris, I. (ed.) *Classical Greece: Ancient Histories and New Archaeologies*, 137–170. Cambridge University Press: Cambridge.

Allen, M.J. (1988). Archaeological and environmental aspects of colluviation in south-east England. In Groenman-van-Waateringe, W. and Robinson, M. (eds) *Man-Made Soils*, 67–92. BAR International Series 410, British Archaeological Reports: Oxford.

Allen, M.J. (1991). Analysing the landscape: a geographical approach to archaeological problems. In Schofield, A.J. (ed.) *Interpreting Artefact Scatters: Contributions to Ploughzone Archaeology*, 39–57. Oxbow: Oxford.

*Ammerman, A.J. (1981). Surveys and archaeological research. *Annual Review of Anthropology*, **10**:63–88.

Ammerman, A.J. (1995). The dynamics of modern land use and the Acconia survey. *Journal of Mediterranean Archaeology*, **8**:77–92.

Banning, E.B. (1996). Highlands and lowlands: problems and survey frameworks for rural archaeology in the Near East. *Bulletin of the American Schools of Oriental Research*, **301**:25–45.

Batovic, Í. and Chapman, J.C. (1985). The 'Neothermal Dalmatia' project. In Macready, S. and Thompson, F.H. (eds) *Archaeological Field Survey in Britain and Abroad*, 158–195. Society of Antiquaries: London.

Berry, B.J.L. and Baker, A.M. (1968). Geographical sampling. In Berry, B.J.L. and Marble, D.F. (eds) *Spatial Analysis: a Reader in Statistical Geography*, 91–100. Prentice: New Jersey.

Binford, L.R. (1964). A consideration of archaeological research design. *American Antiquity*, **29**:425–441.

Bintliff, J. and Snodgrass, A. (1988). Off-site pottery distributions: a regional and inter-regional perspective. *Current Anthropology*, **29**:506–513.

Bintliff, J., Davies, B., Gaffney, C., Snodgrass, A. and Waters, A. (1992). Trace metal accumulations in soils on and around ancient settlement in Greece. In Spoerry, P. (ed.) *Geoprospection in the Archaeological Landscape*, 9–24. Monograph 18, Oxbow: Oxford.

Blanton, R.E., Kowalewski, S.A., Feinman, G. and Appel, J. (1981). *Ancient Mesoamerica: a Comparison of Change in Three Regions*. Cambridge University Press: Cambridge.

Boismier, W.A. (1997). *Modelling the Effects of Tillage Processes on Artefact Distributions in the Ploughzone: a Simulation of Tillage-induced Pattern Formation*. BAR British Series 259, British Archaeological Reports: Oxford.

Brookes, I., Levine, L.D. and Dennell, R.W. (1982). Alluvial sequences in central western Iran and implications for archaeological survey. *Journal of Field Archaeology*, 9:285–299.

Cherry, J. (1983). Frogs around the pond: perspectives on current archaeological survey projects in the Mediterranean region. In Keller, D.R. and Rupp, D.W. (eds) *Archaeological Survey in the Mediterranean Area*, 375–416. BAR International Series 155, British Archaeological Reports: Oxford.

Cherry, J., Gamble, C. and Shennan, S. (eds) (1978). *Sampling in Contemporary British Archaeology*. BAR British Series 50, British Archaeological Reports: Oxford.

Cherry, J.F., Davis, J.L. and Mantzourani, E. (1991). *Landscape Archaeology as Long-term History. Northern Keos in the Cycladic Islands*. UCLA Press: Los Angeles.

Clark, W.A.V. and Hosking, P.L. (1986). *Statistical Methods for Geographers*. John Wiley: New York.

Cribb, R (1991). *Nomads in Archaeology*. Cambridge University Press: Cambridge.

Crowther, D., French, C. and Pryor, F. (1985). Approaching the Fens the flexible way. In Haselgrove, C., Millett, M. and Smith, I. (eds) *Archaeology from the Ploughsoil. Studies in the Collection and Interpretation of Field Survey Data*, 59–76. University of Sheffield Press: Sheffield.

Davis, J.L. and Sutton, S.B. (1995). Response to Ammerman, A.J. 'The dynamics of modern land use and the Acconia survey'. *Journal of Mediterranean Archaeology*, **8**:113–123.

Davis, J.L., Alcock, S.E., Bennet, J., Lolos, Y.G. and Shelmerdine, C.W. (1997). The Pylos Regional Archaeological Project, Part 1: overview and the archaeological survey. *Hesperia*, **66**:391–494.

Dunnell, R.C. and Dancey, W.S. (1983). The siteless survey: a regional scale data collection strategy. *Advances in Archaeological Method and Theory*, **6**:267–287.

Flannery, K.V. (1976a). Sampling by intensive surface collection. In Flannery, K.V. (ed.) *The Early Mesoamerican Village*, 49–62. Academic Press: New York.

Flannery, K.V. (ed.) (1976b). *The Early Mesoamerican Village*. Academic Press: New York.

Foard, G. (1978). Systematic fieldwalking and the investigation of Saxon settlement in Northamptonshire. *World Archaeology*, **9**:357–374.

Foley, R. (1981). *Off-site Archaeology and Human Adaptation in Eastern Africa*. BAR International Series 97, British Archaeological Reports: Oxford.

Frendo, A.J. (1996). The capabilities and limitations of ancient Near Eastern nomadic archaeology. *Orientalia*, **65**:1–23.

Fulford, M., Champion, T. and Lang, A. (1997). *England's Coastal Heritage. A Survey for English Heritage and the RCHME*. Report 15, English Heritage: London.

Gaffney, V. and Tingle, M. (1985). The Maddle Farm (Berks.) Project and micro-regional analysis. In McReady, S. and Thompson, F.H. (eds) *Archaeological Field Survey in Britain and Abroad*, 67–73. Society of Antiquaries: London.

Gaffney, V., Bintliff, J. and Slapsak, B. (1991). Site formation processes and the Hvar Survey Project, Yugoslavia. In Schofield, A.J. (ed.) *Interpreting Artefact Scatters: Contributions to Ploughzone Archaeology*, 59–77. Oxbow Books: Oxford.

Gallant, T.W. (1986). Background noise and site definition: a contribution to survey methodology. *Journal of Field Archaeology*, **13**:403–418.

Gilman, P.J. (1996). Archaeological research and the Essex SMR. In Bedwin, O. (ed.) *The Archaeology of Essex*, 181–191. Essex County Council Planning Department: Chelmsford.

Haselgrove, C. (1985). Inference from ploughsoil artefact scatters. In Haselgrove, C., Millett, M. and Smith, I. (eds) *Archaeology from the Ploughsoil. Studies in the Collection and Interpretation of Field Survey Data*, 7–29. University of Sheffield Press: Sheffield.

Haselgrove, C., Millett, M. and Smith, I. (eds) (1985). *Archaeology from the Ploughsoil. Studies in the Collection and Interpretation of Field Survey Data*. University of Sheffield Press: Sheffield.

Hayfield, C. (ed.) (1980). *Fieldwalking as a Method for Archaeological Research*. Occasional Paper No. 2, Department of the Environment: London

Hole, F. (1980). Archaeological survey in Southwest Asia. *Paléorient*, **6**:21–44.

Jones, M. (1995). A New Old Kingdom settlement near Ausim: report of the archaeological discoveries made in the Barakat Drain Improvements Project. *Mitteilungen des Deutschen Archäologischen Instituts Abteilung Kairo*, **51**:85–98.

Judge, W., Ebert, J.I. and Hitchcock, R.K. (1975). Sampling in regional archaeological survey. In Mueller, J.W. (ed.) *Sampling in Archaeology*, 82–123. University of Arizona Press: Tucson.

Keller, D.R. and Rupp, D.W. (1983). *Archaeological Survey in the Mediterranean Area*. BAR International Series 155, British Archaeological Reports: Oxford.

Killion, T.W. (1992). Residential ethnoarchaeology and ancient site structures. In Killion, T.W. (ed.) *Gardens in Prehistory. The Archaeology of Settlement Agriculture in Greater Mesoamerica*, 119–149. University of Alabama Press: Tuscaloosa.

Kintigh, K.W. (1988). The effectiveness of sub-surface testing: a simulation approach. *American Antiquity*, **53**:686–707.

Kowalewski, S.A. and Fish, S.K. (1990). Conclusions. In Fish, S.K. and Kowalewski, S.A. (eds) *The Archaeology of Regions. A Case for Full-Coverage Survey*, 261–277. Smithsonian Institution Press: Washington DC.

Massagrande, F. (1995). Using GIS with non-systematic survey data: the Mediterranean data. In Lock, G. and Stancic, Z. (eds) *Archaeology and Geographic Information Systems: a European Perspective*, 55-65. Taylor and Francis: London.

Millett, M. (1985). Field survey calibration: a contribution. In Haselgrove, C., Millett, M. and Smith, I. (eds) *Archaeology from the Ploughsoil. Studies in the Collection and Interpretation of Field Survey Data*, 31–37. University of Sheffield Press: Sheffield.

Mueller, J.W. (ed.) (1975). *Sampling in Archaeology*. University of Arizona Press: Tucson.

Murray, P. and Kardulias, P.N. (1986). A modern-site survey in the S. Argolid, Greece. *Journal of Field Archaeology*, **13**:21–41.

*Nance, J.D. (1983). Regional sampling in archaeological survey. The statistical perspective. *Advances in Archaeological Method and Theory*, **6**:289–356.

Peregrine, P.N., Bell, A., Braithwaite, M. and Danti, M.D. (1997). Geomagnetic mapping of the Outer Town. In Zettler, R. (ed.) *Subsistence and Settlement in a Marginal Environment: Tell es-Sweyhat, 1989–1995: Preliminary Report*, 73–84. Research Papers in Science and Archaeology 14, MASCA: Philadelphia.

Plog, S. (1976). Relative efficiencies of sampling techniques for archaeological surveys. In Flannery, K.V. (ed.) *The Early Mesoamerican Village*, 136–158. Academic Press: New York.

Plog, S. (1978). Sampling in archaeological surveys: a critique. *American Antiquity*, **43**:280–285.

Read, D.W. (1986). Sampling procedures for regional surveys: a problem of representativeness and effectiveness. *Journal of Field Archaeology*, **13**:477–491.

Redman, C.L. (1973). Multistage fieldwork and analytical techniques. *American Antiquity*, **38**:61–79.

Redman, C.L. (1982). Archaeological survey and the study of Mesopotamian urban systems. *Journal of Field Archaeology*, **9**:375–382.

Redman, C.L. (1987). Surface collection, sampling and research design: a retrospective. *American Antiquity*, **52**:249–265.

Redman, C.L. and Watson, P.J. (1970). Systematic, intensive, surface collection. *American Antiquity*, **35**:279–291.

Sanders, W.T., Parsons, J.R. and Santley, R.S. (1979). *The Basin of Mexico, Ecological Processes in the Evolution of a Civilization*. Academic Press: New York.

Santley, R.S. (1992). A consideration of the Olmec phenomenon in the Tuxtlas, Early Formative settlement pattern, land use and refuse disposal at Matacapan, Veracruz, Mexico. In Killion, T. (ed.) *Gardens of Prehistory. The Archaeology of Settlement Agriculture in Greater Mesoamerica*, 150–183. University of Alabama Press: Tuscaloosa.

Schaeffer, R., Mendenhall, W. and Lott, L. (1979). *Elementary Survey Sampling*. Duxbury Press: North Scituate, Mass.

Schiffer, M.B., Sullivan, A.P. and Klinger, T.C. (1978). The design of archaeological surveys. *World Archaeology*, **10**:1–28.

Schofield, A.J. (1991). Interpreting artefact scatters: an introduction. In Schofield, A.J. (ed.) *Interpreting Artefact Scatters: Contributions to Ploughzone Archaeology*, 3–8. Oxbow: Oxford.

Shennan, S. (1985). *Experiments in the Collection and Analysis of Archaeological Survey Data: the East Hampshire Survey*. University of Sheffield Press: Sheffield.

*Shennan, S. (1997). *Quantifying Archaeology* (2nd edn). Edinburgh University Press: Edinburgh.

Stein, M.A. (1921). *Serindia: Detailed Report of Explorations in Central Asia and Westernmost China (5 vols)*. Clarendon Press: Oxford.

Sumner, W.M. (1990). Full-coverage regional archaeological survey in the Near East: an example from Iran. In Fish, S.K. and Kowalewski, S.A. (eds) *The Archaeology of Regions. A Case for Full-Coverage Survey*, 87–115. Smithsonian Institution Press: Washington DC.

Sundstrom, L. (1993). A simple mathematical procedure for estimating the adequacy of site survey strategies. *Journal of Field Archaeology*, **20**:91–96.

Taylor, C.C. (1972). The study of settlement patterns on Pre-Saxon Britain. In Ucko, P.J., Tringham, R. and Dimbleby, G.W. (eds) *Man, Settlement and Urbanism*, 109–113. Duckworth: London.

Taylor, C.C. (1974). *Fieldwork in Medieval Archaeology*. Batsford: London.

Thomas, D.H. (1975). Nonsite sampling in archaeology: up the creek without a site. In Mueller, J.W. (ed.) *Sampling in Archaeology*, 61–81. University of Arizona Press: Tucson.

Vita-Finzi, C. and Higgs, E.H. (1970). Prehistoric economy in the Mount Carmel area of Palestine. *Proceedings of the Prehistoric Society*, **36**:1–37.

Whallon, R. (1979). *An Archaeological Survey of the Keban Reservoir Area of East-Central Turkey*. Memoirs of the Museum of Anthropology No 11, University of Michigan: Ann Arbor.

Wilkinson, T.J. (1982). The definition of ancient manured zones by means of extensive sherd-sampling techniques. *Journal of Field Archaeology*, **9**:323–333.

Wilkinson, T.J. (1988). The archaeological component of agricultural soils in the Middle East: the effects of manuring in antiquity. In Groenman-van-Waateringe, W. and Robinson, M. (eds) *Man-made Soils*, 93–114. BAR International Series 410, British Archaeological Reports: Oxford.

Wilkinson, T.J. (1989). Extensive sherd scatters and land use intensity: some recent results. *Journal of Field Archaeology*, **16**:31–46.

Wilkinson, T.J. and Tucker, D.J. (1995). *Settlement Development in the North Jazira, Iraq. A Study of the Archaeological Landscape*. Aris and Phillips: Warminster.

Williamson, T. (1984). The Roman countryside. Settlement and agriculture in NW Essex. *Britannia*, **15**:225–230.

Willis, K.J., Sümegi, P., Braun, M., Bennett, K.D. and Tóth, V. (1998). Prehistoric land degradation in Hungary: who, how and why? *Antiquity*, **72**:101–113.

Zangger, E., Timpson, M.E., Yazvenko, S.B., Kuhnke, F. and Knauss, J. (1997). The Pylos regional archaeological project. Part II: landscape evolution and site preservation. *Hesperia*, **66**:549–641.

Zettler, R. (1997). Surface collections and excavations in the Lower Town. In Zettler, R. (ed.) *Subsistence and Settlement in a Marginal Environment: Tell es-Sweyhat, 1989-1995: Preliminary Report*, 35–72. Research Papers in Science and Archaeology 14, MASCA: Philadelphia.

Zubrow, E.B.W. and Harbaugh, J.W. (1978). Archaeological prospecting: kriging and simulation. In Hodder, I. (ed.) *Simulation Studies in Archaeology*, 109–122. Cambridge University Press: Cambridge.

43

Geophysical Prospection in Archaeology

Y. NISHIMURA

Centre for Archaeological Operations, Nara National Cultural Properties Research Institute.

This chapter introduces archaeological geophysical prospection, or the nondestructive methods of searching from above the ground for artifacts and features buried below, without making any changes to the ground surface itself. Recently, however, this field is coming to be thought of more broadly as 'cultural properties prospection', including not only the study of subsurface features, but also the diagnosis of the internal structure of above-ground wood or stone edifices. Additionally, the method of analysing soil, in order to learn the nature of a feature after it has been uncovered through excavation, might be called 'chemical prospection' (see Chapter 45). If a pit has been detected, for example, but its nature is not well understood, the method of identifying whether it is a rubbish pit, a mortuary feature, or a simple depression in the soil through chemical analysis could also be called a form of prospection, according to the perspective currently being advanced.

GENERAL PRINCIPLES

Archaeological prospection assumes that subterranean conditions, namely differences in the soil and the presence of foreign objects, may be elicited through differences in some kind of physical property. The ground surface might, for example, be pounded with a hammer; as an acoustic pulse travels faster through hard strata, but more slowly through soft ones, it may be possible to distinguish between subsurface strata by its speed of transmission alone. Or when an electric current is applied to the ground, it does not conduct well in dry soil. In other words, the electrical resistivity is high. But in damp soil the current conducts well and the resistivity is low. Such phenomena make it possible to differentiate between soil strata and to detect foreign objects in the soil, based on differences in electrical resistivity.

In this manner, with regards to subterranean features alone, it is possible to differentiate between soils, and to detect objects of an alien nature, based on a variety of their physical properties. Archaeological prospection is a nondestructive means of probing for artifacts and features from above ground, by searching out the sizes, shapes, and extents of differences detectable to the physical sciences.

Generally speaking, when trying to infer the existence of foreign objects or differences in the soil, efforts are made to emphasize the data so that anomalies, thought to show artifacts and features, are rendered more readily understandable. This process simultaneously amplifies noise, however, requiring care in the actual treatment of the data. Also, in investigations of limited geographical extent, it becomes impossible to distinguish between those portions of the data

Handbook of Archaeological Sciences. Edited by D.R. Brothwell and A.M. Pollard.

representing the average ground conditions for the location, and those that are anomalous. For this reason, it is desirable to measure the widest area possible.

It goes without saying that archaeological geophysical prospection differs from general prospection for ground water or mineral resources. One aspect of this difference is that prospection for underground resources normally involves the probing of considerable depths (many tens of metres). If such methods of measurement and analysis are applied directly to the shallower depths of interest in archaeological prospection (often less than one or two metres), the results will be insufficient. From the perspective of these deeper geological investigations, the regions of archaeological interest fall within the range of noise associated with the Earth's crust.

Of great importance for understanding the results of prospection, since it is being conducted for archaeological sites and artifacts, is the need to refer to the results of previous investigations of the site in question and the immediate environs. It is necessary to consult sufficiently with the archaeologists investigating the site in question. When a geophysical anomaly is detected, if previous archaeological findings for that site and those of the surrounding area are taken into consideration, this should enhance understanding of what is causing the anomaly.

If the site and surroundings are totally unknown archaeologically, and moreover there is no general information about the site, it may be possible nevertheless to distinguish between different soils on the basis of some inherent property, and to determine the extent of such differences. But in such an area it is not possible to link the results of prospection with particular types of artifacts or features. If prospection is conducted at a location where not even a distribution survey has been undertaken, and where no record exists of the recovery of artifacts, the prospection results will be of little validity.

EARTH RESISTANCE SURVEYS

This method consists of passing an electric current through the ground, and then inferring the presence of artifacts and features from differences in electric resistivity produced by different soils or by foreign objects. There are many methods, using different configurations of electrodes, for measuring resistance to an electric current flowing through the ground. These include the Wenner, Double Dipole, Schlumberger, twin electrode configurations, and so forth (Clark

1990:37). The basis of measurement for these configurations is the use of four electrodes, two for the current ('C') and two for measuring the potential difference ('P') (Figure 43.1).

The difference between the various electrode configurations is one of measurement sensitivity. Double Dipole is the most sensitive, followed by Schlumberger, Wenner, and then twin electrode (Aspinall and Lynam 1970). Of these, the Double Dipole and Schlumberger configurations are seldom used for archaeology. This is because variations in the contact resistance, between the electrodes and the soil in which they are inserted, greatly affect the resulting measurements (Scollar *et al.* 1990:346). When using these configurations on poorly conducting ground, salt water is often poured at the points of contact in

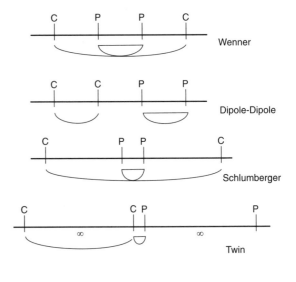

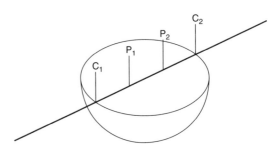

Figure 43.1 Configuration of electrodes for a variety of electrical resistivity survey techniques. C indicates the current probe positions, and P the position of the probes which measure the potential. The solid hemispheres indicate the volume of subsurface sampled.

order to obtain sufficient conductivity between the electrodes and the soil. Another reason why these configurations are not used archaeologically may be because they are greatly affected by differences in surface topography (Fox *et al.* 1980, Sutherland *et al.* 1998), making the results difficult to interpret.

In archaeological prospection, use of the Wenner and twin electrode configurations is common. This appears to be because, unlike geological prospection which aims at producing a *pseudo-section* (i.e., a vertical cross-section), and takes measurements with a large number of fixed electrodes, in order to obtain information showing the sizes and shapes of features extending over a horizontal area, archaeological prospection uses a method in which the electrodes have to be moved between each measurement. Even though the contact resistance changes slightly with each measurement as the electrodes are moved, since the modern instrument impedance is high the effect on the measurement is not great (Scollar *et al.* 1990:347). Another reason why these configurations are commonly used is the commercial availability of such equipment adapted for these methods.

Survey equipment

Equipment employed in archaeological prospection includes all-purpose instruments used for generalized surveying, and those developed especially for archaeological applications. Generally speaking, all-purpose instruments must be capable of greatly increasing the electric current, when prospecting in deep strata, for which the electrodes must be spread widely apart. These instruments therefore have the benefit of being able to increase the signal/noise ratio by elevating the current. Since they are capable of high-voltage electric output (currents of 20 mA or greater), caution must be exercised to prevent harmful effects to the operator, and careless contact with the electrodes should be avoided. Because it is not possible to use these instruments in a portable fashion, the power unit location is fixed, and wires are run to the electrodes. In geological prospection, the electrodes are not moved for each measurement once they have been initially set. Accordingly, this method is used mainly in archaeological prospection when the objective is to produce a vertical *pseudo-section*.

The RM15 Resistance Meter (Geoscan Research, England), is an example of equipment widely used in archaeological prospection. Designed for use mainly with the twin electrode configuration, the instrument is mounted on a portable rectangular frame, with the two mobile probes (C1, P1) fixed to the bottom of the frame. The remote probes (C2, P2), set at a position sufficiently removed so that the flow between the current probes (C1, C2) is radial, are connected to the instrument by wires (see Figure 43.1). When the electrodes are pushed into the ground at each measurement position, data are automatically recorded and saved on a mobile data-logger. The system is one permitting very speedy measurement – typically ∼ 0.7 hectares per day with experienced operators in suitable locations.

The mobile probes on the frame sold with the RM4, a prototype of this model, were fixed at an interval of 0.5 metres, but with the RM15 the probe interval can be selected from 0.5, 0.75, 1.0, 1.25, and 1.5 metres. Also, using several of these intervals, it is possible to take measurements for a *pseudo-section* (Figure 43.2 in colour plates).

Survey methods

Survey methods can be divided into two types. One aims to produce a *pseudo-section* as a vertical profile, the other seeks to find the horizontal distribution of electrical resistance variations. If the mobile probe interval is widened in earth resistance prospection, it is possible to obtain information from deeper strata in the soil. In three-dimensional terms, each measurement roughly represents the average electrical resistivity of a hemispherical volume in the soil. If the probe interval is widened, proportionately greater volumes of soil are averaged (Figure 43.1), but small objects become difficult to detect. From experience, the greater portion of the information is obtained from a depth up to half the probe interval; if the latter is 1 metre, for example, the readings typically reflect conditions down to 0.5 metres in depth.

Vertical profiling

By traversing a single line several times, and increasing the electrode interval on each traverse, followed by displaying the results as a series of rows laid next to each other (with the smaller intervals toward the top), the result has the appearance of a vertical profile cut through the soil. This is referred to as an *apparent* or *pseudo-section* (Aspinall and Crummett 1997). While research on analytical techniques for converting this approximate section into a true section has been underway for some time (Szymanski and Tsourlos 1993), it is still a matter of trial and error, and an appropriate method has yet to be developed. It is particularly difficult to analyse the soils lying underneath a stratum of high electrical resistivity near the surface.

Horizontal surveying

Surveys made over a horizontal area are more common in archaeological prospection than those made to obtain vertical profiles. This is because the purpose of prospection is more often to determine the location of artifacts and features, by observing the distribution of electrical resistance, and attempting to infer the nature of anomalies from their shapes, sizes, positions, and relative strengths.

In this type of survey, measurements are often displayed as maps showing the horizontal distribution of earth resistance, with collected data often averaged by dedicated software over a number of adjacent measurement points. In other words, the value for any point is replaced with the average of its own measured value plus those of the four nearest measurement points. Since this is the smallest area for which averaged values can be calculated, the use of this method is common. This is because there may be anomalies in the process of taking any individual measurement, or discrepancies in the actual measurement interval; making the averaged area small is intended to minimize the resulting disparities.

If vertical profiling as described above is conducted over a large number of parallel lines, it is possible to obtain results similar to those from a horizontal survey (Panissod *et al*. 1998). These data may first be processed to approximate a series of true vertical sections, and then it is possible to compile a horizontal plan for specific depths. This is similar to the *time slice technique* used with ground-penetrating radar data (see below). Further, it becomes possible to produce three-dimensional renderings which approximate the particular object under study, using only resistivity data (Chambers *et al*. 1999). Research aimed at developing this type of three-dimensional resistivity representation is likely to advance in the near future.

MAGNETOMETER SURVEYS

This method infers the presence of subterranean artifacts and features by measuring magnetic fields. If there is a difference in magnetism between a feature and the surrounding soil, there will also be a slight difference in their effect on the Earth's magnetic field, which can be detected by magnetometer surveys (Leute 1987:14).

Iron oxides (Fe_2O_3, Fe_3O_4) are the most widely-distributed strongly magnetic substances on the Earth's surface.

Apart from searching for features which may be detected by slight differences in magnetism, magnetometer surveys have the unique characteristic of being a very powerful method for the prospection of kilns and hearths which display thermoremanent magnetism (see Chapter 6). Even though a hearth may have turned visibly red as a result of being heated, as the soils making the hearth and those around it are essentially the same, it is very difficult to detect a difference in electrical resistivity. Because of the physical phenomenon of thermoremanence, in which the magnetic domains within the feature are re-aligned by heating, the hearth produces a large anomaly by greatly distorting the Earth's magnetic field, which is possible to detect with magnetometers (Aitken *et al*. 1958).

In contrast to other, more active, survey methods, magnetometer survey consists of a passive measurement of the Earth's magnetic field, which is a drawback in conducting the survey. When railroads, motor vehicles, houses, or other objects containing masses of iron which produce magnetic anomalies greater than those of archaeological features, are near the survey site, the small variations caused by the features are masked by these larger disturbances, and are impossible to detect. Moving objects such as trains and motor vehicles are especially disruptive for magnetic survey work. In addition to these human influences, variations in the magnetic field surrounding the Earth also produce disturbances. These include diurnal changes in the Earth's magnetic field, as well as those which take place over the space of hours, and others occurring in a matter of minutes (Telford *et al*. 1990:72). All these disturbances are labelled 'noise'.

Survey methods and equipment

At present, there are two methods utilized in archaeological magnetic prospection. One measures the total intensity of the magnetic field, while the other measures its component on the vertical axis. For measuring total intensity, *proton magnetometers* are most popular, but recently *caesium magnetometers* have also become available. For vertical axis measurement, the *fluxgate gradiometer*, developed especially for archaeological applications, has become universal. Because these instruments measure different components of the Earth's magnetic field, it is necessary to exercise caution regarding the results they display.

In a proton magnetometer, it is necessary to excite the protons in heavy water or kerosene enclosed within the sensor, during which time the device must be fixed in place. This interval is short, only about one second, but this still means that more time is required for measurement than with fluxgate gradiometers or caesium magnetometers, which provide constant excitation and make continuous measurements possible.

When making a survey, measures are taken to reduce the effects of noise. For example, in total intensity surveying with a proton magnetometer, measurements can be made simultaneously using two sensors attached to the upper and lower portions of a pole (gradiometer), or using some other arrangement of two measuring devices, one of which serves as a reference station while the other is moved from point to point over the target area. In either case, assuming that both devices are subject to the same background noise, then by taking the difference between the two values, only the effects due to artifacts and features are obtained. The same method is followed when using the newer caesium magnetometers. As noted above, the fluxgate gradiometer was devised specifically for archaeological prospection. The FM18 and FM36 are two models developed by Geoscan Research, which have two sensors stacked vertically 50 cm apart, and record the differences between their readings.

For both proton magnetometers and fluxgate gradiometers using sensors positioned 50 cm apart vertically, the effective depth of reading is about 1.5 metres. Any attempt to increase the sensitivity and collect data from a greater depth would require setting the sensors farther apart. Since these are placed vertically on the same pole, it becomes difficult to maintain a vertical orientation while moving, making the arrangement impractical. A tri-axial fluxgate gradiometer, which measures independently each of the three directional components of the magnetic field, has been developed (Kamei et al. 1992), but it cannot be said to have been used widely yet. Analytical methods utilizing the three components independently may be a future development in this field.

GROUND-PENETRATING RADAR (GPR)

This type of prospection applies the system and methods utilized in general survey work, such as investigations of buried pipes and underground cavities, and accordingly there is no equipment developed specifically for archaeological research. As applied research in this area is rapidly advancing, there is much information which should be given consideration for archaeological prospection. GPR in archaeology is necessarily connected with this research (Conyers and Goodman 1997).

Principles

If an electromagnetic wave is propagated towards the ground, about 40 per cent of the energy is reflected at the ground surface, but the remainder penetrates into the ground, with a portion subsequently bouncing back to the surface from any buried interface. If the returning signal is displayed in temporal sequence, in different colours or shades on a grey scale according to its strength, an image looking very much like a section of the strata in the ground may be obtained. Making inferences about subterranean conditions, namely the presence of artifacts and features, by observing these images is the basis of this method.

The electromagnetic waves utilized fall within the band known as microwaves, and the antennae used in archaeology are nearly all within the range of several tens to several hundreds of Megahertz (MHz). As this band overlaps the VHF and UHF ranges used for ordinary television broadcasts, lifting the antenna unduly when surveying in the vicinity of houses may produce noise in their reception. Electromagnetic waves also tend to leak out from the gap between the antenna and the ground surface. It is accordingly necessary to take precautions while surveying, such as maintaining a sufficient distance from dwellings.

The waves travel freely through a medium of uniform density, but if there is a difference between soils, for example, they will reflect or refract at the soil interface, where different media come together. If radical density differences, such as those offered by metals, rock, or cavities, are encountered, these will cause strong reflections. Even in cases such as postholes, where the difference between the soil within the feature and that comprising it is not great, nonetheless there will be reflections according to the degree of difference, which may allow detection of the feature.

As the waves reflect most strongly where media of very different densities come together, the largest reflection in GPR is produced between the antenna and the ground, or where the waves encounter an air and soil boundary. This is especially pronounced in pulsed radar. For this reason, any variation produced by shallow soil differences or the presence of artifacts can be obliterated by the saturated condition of the signal from the region immediately below the ground surface.

It is advisable to think that this condition will apply to the first 30 cm or so from the surface, a point of caution associated with this method of prospection.

Instrumental considerations

At present, the most widely-used method compresses the electromagnetic waves into pulses for transmission and reception. As the compressed wave strikes an object and is reflected by it, resonances are produced, which cause a succession of similar reflections to show below the object as a characteristic of this method. At a particular soil interface, for example, because of the reflection occurring there, a pattern of horizontal stripes continues from that point on. The occurrence of this phenomenon can be misinterpreted as a series of thin soil layers. In extremely large reflections caused by metals or subterranean cavities, these repetitive reflections continue downward for a considerable extent. In such cases, the distinctive pattern of reflection enables the inference of the object as being of metal or a similar material.

A single wave or scan can be displayed in the manner shown in Figure 43.3. In displaying images made from such data as a vertical section, portions of the scan falling within specific ranges are assigned different colours or grey scale intensities. The lowermost values of these ranges are called the threshold levels.

During actual survey work, these scans are lined up across the display image, and as the number of scans taken per second varies from several tens to more than a hundred, if the antenna is moved at a pace of about 8–10 sec/m, the number of scans representing the data for 1 metre ranges from 100 to more than 1000. Because of this, one characteristic of GPR is that large amounts of data are obtained in comparison with other prospection methods. In most other surveys it is normal to take only one measurement over a 50 cm or 1 metre interval, hence GPR is noteworthy as a prospection method which may enable studying subterranean conditions in great detail (Conyers and Goodman 1997).

Antennae

There are two types of antennae for sending and receiving the pulses. In the *combined* or *unitary antenna* arrangement, the same antenna is used for transmission and reception, while the *split* or *dual arrangement* uses separate antennae for sending and receiving signals. With the split arrangement it is possible to combine the two antennae into a single bundle. Where a gap separates the two in a split arrangement, an angle is produced in the signal path which may be better suited to detecting certain objects, but the vertical path travelled by the signal going upwards and downwards in the unitary arrangement provides more potential for detecting an object in detail. Perhaps because only one antenna is used for sending and receiving, frequencies are generally lower in the unitary arrangement. In fact, it is difficult to distinguish between the results of the two arrangements in actual use.

Methods for moving the antenna over the survey area include pulling a unit fitted with wheels, dragging one mounted on a sled, and carrying one by hand. The use of a sled keeps the unit in contact with the ground, minimizing energy loss of the pulse. The method of carrying an antenna suspended from the shoulders by ropes is used with low frequency antennae of 70 or even 40 MHz. In low-frequency surveying, the disturbance arising from the interval between the antenna and the ground surface does not greatly affect the data.

With the dual arrangement, in which the antennae can be separated by fixing the transmitter and moving the receiving antenna, it is possible to measure the velocity of the signal to a particular stratum (Pipan *et al.* 1999). The initial and final receiving times for a wave reflecting from the top of the stratum can be read

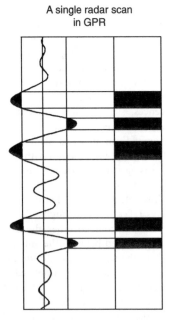

A single radar scan in GPR

Figure 43.3 A single radar scan in GPR.

from an image recorded over a specific period of time, and therefore the wave velocity calculated from the distance travelled by the receiving antenna. The only requirements in this case is information about the distance travelled by the antenna and the travel times of the waves. In this manner, by having the transmitter and receiver in separate locations, it is possible to calculate the actual depth of subterranean features.

Angle of transmission

The wave radiating from the transmitting antenna is generally taken to be wider than 90°, although it depends on the frequency. With this wide an angle of transmission, even before the antenna arrives directly over an object, its presence may be detected from (albeit weak) reflections, travelling diagonally and being displayed on the resulting image. For this reason, objects such as pipes or even isolated stones may be displayed on the screen before the antenna reaches their actual position, and their images may appear larger than reality. These images typically describe a parabolic form below the object in the radar image (Vaughan 1986). In a separate phenomenon, a V-shaped ditch may be displayed with an inverted V-shaped form extending downward from its bottom. Also, the edges of ditches or post holes are sometimes seen to assume sharp angles, with reflections centring upon the edge. This phenomenon, known as the *edge effect*, is seen not only in GPR, but also in magnetometer surveys and other methods. For all of the above phenomena, the reflection is not an expression of the actual condition of the soil or features.

Wave frequency and resolution

The wavelength of the emitted pulse is related to antenna size and frequency. A large antenna with a low frequency emits a pulse with a long wavelength, whereas that from a high-frequency antenna is short. Furthermore, the ability of the antenna to discriminate objects, or its power of resolution, is related to the wavelength, with longer wavelengths lacking the ability to detect smaller objects. Generally speaking, antennae used in archaeological prospection with frequencies around 500 to 900 MHz are called high frequency, and those of 300 MHz or less called low. This difference in frequency is also related to the penetrating power of the wave. High frequency antennae are able to survey only shallow strata, while lower frequencies may work at deeper levels (Daniels 1996:39). With high frequency

antennae of 500 to 700 MHz, it is difficult to survey depths of 1 metre in wet paddy soils as seen in southeast Asia, but it is possible to obtain data for nearly 2 metres with antennae of 200 to 400 MHz. However, for dry soils such as sand or volcanic ash, it is not difficult to obtain data up to 4 metres below the surface with antennae of around 300 MHz. The electric resistivity of the soil is of some value as a criterion for judging the penetration of the wave. If the overall resistivity is low, radar prospection at deep levels is not hopeful. Conversely, if the resistivity is high, then prospects for deeper radar prospection are good. Generally speaking, if the relative dielectric constant of the soil is around 27, prospection to a depth of about 2 metres should be possible with a 300 MHz antenna.

Surveying

GPR equipment consists of an antenna (or antennae) for transmitting and receiving signals (see above), a control unit which sends the signals to the transmitter, and a device to record data picked up by the receiver. It is common for the control unit and data recorder to be combined into a single device. Electric generators and batteries are used as the power source; batteries range from large items made for vehicles, to specially-designed smaller ones.

The antenna or antennae are connected to the control unit by cables, but caution must be exercised with these in operation. Since the cables themselves are capable of acting as antennae, they should be kept as far from the receiving antenna as possible. If such measures are not taken during the survey, the cables may produce noise, making it impossible to obtain good data. Similarly, when surveying with long wavelength antennae (300 or 400 MHz), there is danger of noise from nearby dwellings or other structures. At these frequencies, the antenna's reception will be greatly affected when close to structures containing steel piping spaced less than 1 metre apart, for example. Also, in large-scale surveys, if a vehicle serves as the power source, or the control unit is mounted on a vehicle which follows the antenna, it is conceivable that reflections will be received from the metallic body of the vehicle itself.

Ordinarily, the receiving antenna is scanned over the survey area along lines separated by a set interval. This interval is determined by the size of the object being sought. If the object is small (e.g., of the order of 50 cm), the space between scan lines must be smaller than this. But no matter how narrow the interval, if the wavelength is too long for the object being sought it cannot be detected. Moreover, as discussed above with regard to resolution, since higher frequency antennae are unable to survey deeper strata, deeply-lying small items cannot be found. This is true regardless of the method of prospection employed.

Even though the signal radiates over a wide angle, if the object being sought is shallow, depending upon the scan interval used, it may fall between scan lines, and only a small portion of it may be detected. Accordingly, there are instances when it is necessary to make the interval very close. Also, depending on the characteristics of the particular antenna used, the angle of transmission may be rather narrow, making it possible that even deep lying objects will not be picked up in detail with wider scan intervals.

Another vital practical aspect of surveying is to run the scans in zigzag fashion, with each line being measured in the opposite direction from the previous one. If a feature such as a ditch presents a symmetric V-shaped or U-shaped section the direction of the scan will not matter, but if one side has a different angle from the other, it is likely that the reflection of the signal will vary between the two sides. If this feature is surveyed from both directions, each directional set will obtain a different type of data, and by comparing both sets it may be possible to learn more accurately the actual shape. With scans taken from a single direction only, there is a risk of losing important data. On the other hand, some linear features may be detected accurately when the antenna makes a traverse perpendicular to the feature, whereas the reflection obtained when the scan direction is parallel to the object is insufficient. Accordingly, it is ideally preferable to cover the survey area twice, with one set of scans running at right angles to the other. From limitations of time, however, this method often cannot be followed. As the next best measure, scans should be made at as fine an interval as possible.

Displaying the results

As stated above, displaying GPR results in a manner resembling a vertical section is the basis of this surveying method. A variety of techniques are used for this, such as displaying in different colours or grey scale values, or showing the outline of the wave trace itself. In examining such displays, caution must be paid to special patterns of reflection such as ringing or the edge effects described above. Also, as a characteristic of wave transmission, the velocity will be slower for wet

soils, and faster in dry ones. Accordingly, should there be a feature presenting a straight line in actuality, if the soil above varies locally from drier to wetter, the object will be displayed as a curved line because the time of travel to and from the object varies with the overlying soil conditions (Goodman 1994). Generally speaking, no matter what the topography of the ground surface surveyed, the results will be displayed with the surface shown as a horizontal line. Accordingly, the topography must be kept in mind when interpreting the results. Also, when scans are taken with the antenna run up or down a slope, the waves are transmitted and received at angles perpendicular to the slope, and it must be borne in mind that the results will differ in nature from those taken along a level surface.

Compiling a horizontal plan

The technique of making horizontal plans using data taken from apparent profiles, previously mentioned for resistivity, is widely gaining popularity in GPR (Figure 43.4). Data from profiles taken at a set interval are entered into a computer, and data for a particular period of travel time are extracted from each profile and arranged horizontally. This produces a horizontal plan of the distribution of the reflection, refraction, and attenuation in wave strength for a particular time period, and is called a 'time slice' (Goodman *et al.* 1995). When transposing the results of the wave behaviour on to a horizontal plan, the data must be converted to numeric values; as large differences between the greatest and smallest values make computation

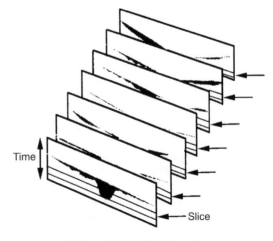

Figure 43.4 A GPR time slice.

difficult, measures are ordinarily taken to reduce the order of magnitude of this difference.

The reason for producing these horizontal plans is because the shape and size of an anomaly thus observed becomes the basis for making inferences about the nature of artifacts and features of interest to archaeology. If supplemental information about the physical properties of the anomaly in question is available, the inference may draw closer to the actual condition. If GPR shows a feature extending in a straight line, for example, and from the archaeology of the surrounding region this is thought to be perhaps a ditch or a moat, a road, a rampart, a roofed earthen wall, etc., then it becomes easier to infer the nature of the feature if the physical properties of the object can be brought into consideration, such as very low readings in a resistivity survey, or high signal attenuation in the radar survey. Low resistivity would suggest a feature associated with wetter soils, such as a ditch or moat; high resistivity would indicate a different sort of feature, such as a stone wall or earthen rampart. However, should a ditch with low resistivity, or a road with high resistivity be encountered in a GPR survey, if the soil above such a feature is different, this may cause a strong radar reflection. Accordingly, the reflection provides no way to determine the nature of the feature. But by utilizing the results of a resistivity survey over the same area, it is possible to specify certain physical properties of a particular locus, and it becomes possible to infer the nature of the feature.

By making a horizontal plan, at times it becomes possible not only to infer the existence of features, but also to observe historical changes in the strata they occupy. As shown in Figure 43.5 in colour plates for example, in a survey in search of subterranean chamber graves, from the stratigraphic positions of graves where the chamber still survives, differences may be inferred in the direction of cultivation and in the boundaries of cultivation. These differences are thought to be associated with changes over time in land ownership. As another example, in the Roman urban site of Wroxeter, UK, it was possible to detect patterns thought to be the traces of Medieval cultivation, in the strata above the Roman buildings.

In the time slice method, when the intent is to differentiate and display separately features in overlying layers from different periods, it may not be possible to depict the desired features adequately unless the proper time slice is selected. At times it is necessary to proceed in trial-and-error fashion. Also, although data are taken continuously along the lines surveyed, as the interval between lines is ordinarily 50 cm or 1 metre, it is necessary to interpolate for these regions to display the same amount of data along both the vertical and horizontal axes of the plan. Accordingly, when averaging the data in the interpolations, some definition is lost for the finer details of features, such as the corners of a square feature being displayed as rounded. Some method of preventing this effect will be needed in the future.

Topographically-modified time slices

As stated above, in GPR profiles the ground surface is normally displayed as a flat horizon. In actual survey work, such as a mound of earth covering a stone burial chamber, the ground surface rises and falls, yet the structure underneath was built with a level surface as its base. If the normal time slice procedure is followed, the slices will be made parallel to the ground surface, and the structure will not be accurately represented. For such cases some means of modifying the profile is required, so that they conform with the actual topography prior to making the slices. It is also possible to use topographically-modified time slice techniques not just where the surface level varies, but also when the ground surface itself may be flat, but the buried features are on an incline. In this case, the slices need to be taken parallel to a reflective layer in the profile images.

In comparison with other prospection methods, GPR is characterized by an abundance of data. As a tool for archaeological prospection, it is still in need of further research. It should also be borne in mind that, under certain topographic conditions, it may not be possible to use an antenna effectively, and that there is also a limit on the depth that can be surveyed.

OTHER PROSPECTION METHODS

While the three methods described above are those most widely used in archaeological prospection, other techniques are also employed, including electromagnetic (EM) and seismic methods, and occasionally microgravity. The following account introduces EM.

Electromagnetic prospection (EM)

If an electric current is passed through a coil this sets up a primary magnetic field, and when this passes over substances such as soil or metals with high conductivity, a secondary magnetic field is generated (Reynolds 1997:566). The EM method of prospection is performed by observing the strength of the latter, and the size of the secondary field is often expressed in units of conductance (mho or Siemens), the inverse of the ohm used for earth resistance measurements. This type of survey can therefore be used to the same effect as an earth resistance survey, and is thus classed as a non-contact type of resistivity prospection. As the characteristic of this method is the generation of a magnetic field during measurement, it has the drawback that accurate readings cannot be taken if more powerful magnetic fields or other types of noise interfere. But as there is no need to set up electrodes, it has the advantage of being easy to perform.

In addition to being utilized for the same purpose as resistivity surveying, EM is often employed in the detection of metals. Using it in parallel with magnetometer surveys for this purpose increases the effectiveness (Tabbagh 1984). By surveying the same area with both methods, should any location show an anomaly in both surveys, this means there is some form of iron object present. But should an anomaly be detected by EM but not be picked up by the magnetometer, it is likely that some non-ferrous metal is buried at that location.

Equipment

It is generally agreed that the greater the spacing between the transmitting and receiving coils, the deeper the penetration of the survey (Scollar *et al.* 1990:549). Among equipment utilized archaeologically there are models designed for detecting shallow-lying metals with a spacing of 1 metre, and those intended for searching out large deep structures such as ditches and moats, with a coil spacing of 3.6 metres. The EM38 produced by the Canadian firm Geonics is an example of an instrument with a 1 metre spacing, where the measuring coil can be used in two modes, one with the coil vertical to the ground surface and the other with it horizontal. The depth of information detectable in the two modes is 1.5 metres for the vertical, and 0.75 metres for the horizontal position. Also, by taking data in both modes, it can be used for analysing the conditions of buried strata.

SUMMARY: ESSENTIAL POINTS OF GEOPHYSICAL PROSPECTION

In archaeological geophysical prospection, since the purpose is to detect the presence of subterranean features and artifacts, collecting information on previous site investigations, and historic information on the surrounding region, and making use of these in interpreting the survey are essential elements of the process. In addition, it is necessary to utilize different types of survey on the same target area, and to compare the results. The various geophysical prospection methods reviewed here such as earth resistance, magnetometer, GPR surveys, and so forth, all detect different physical characteristics of the soil. If any of these detect an anomaly, it is highly possible that an artifact or archaeological feature of some kind lies buried at that spot. Experience over the past 50 years has shown that these techniques, alone or (preferably) in combination, can provide rapid and reliable information on the location, depth and nature of buried features without the need for excavation. Not only does this reduce expense in archaeological research but it offers a uniquely powerful tool in the broader area of cultural heritage management.

ACKNOWLEDGEMENT

The author and editors are extremely grateful to Professor Walter Edwards, Department of Japanese Studies, Tenri University, Nara, for providing an excellent translation of this manuscript, and to Dr Armin Schmidt, University of Bradford, for greatly assisting in the editorial process.

REFERENCES

*Recommended for further reading

Aitken, M.J., Webster, G. and Rees, A. (1958). Magnetic prospecting. *Antiquity*, **32**:270–271.

Aspinall, A. and Crummett, J.G. (1997). The electrical pseudo-section. *Archaeological Prospection*, **4**:37–47.

Aspinall, A. and Lynam, J. (1970). An induced polarization instrument for the detection of near-surface features. *Prospezioni Archeologiche*, **5**:67–75.

Chambers, J., Ogilvy, R., Meldrum, P. and Nissen, J. (1999). 3D resistivity imaging of buried oil- and tar-contaminated waste deposits. *European Journal of Environmental and Engineering Geophysics*, **4**:3–14.

*Clark, A.J. (1990). *Seeing Beneath the Soil*. Batsford: London.

*Conyers, L.B. and Goodman, D. (1997). *Ground-Penetrating Radar: an Introduction for Archaeologists*. Altamira Press: Walnut Creek, Ca.

Daniels, D. (1996). *Surface Penetrating Radar*. Institution of Electrical Engineers: Stevenage.

Fox, R.C., Hohmann, G.W., Killpack, T.J. and Rijo, L. (1980). Topographic effects in resistivity and induced-polarization surveys. *Geophysics*, **45**:75–93.

Goodman, D. (1994). Ground-penetrating radar simulation in engineering and archaeology. *Geophysics*, **59**:224–232.

Goodman, D., Nishimura, Y. and Rogers, J.D. (1995). GPR time slices in archaeological prospection. *Archaeological Prospection*, **2**:85–90.

Kamei, H., Nishimura, Y., Komatsu, M. and Saito, M. (1992). A new instrument: a three-component fluxgate gradiometer. Abstract for the *28th International Symposium on Archaeometry*, 171. 23–27 March, Los Angeles.

Leute, U. (1987). *Archaeometry*. VCH: Weinheim.

Panissod, G., Dabas, M., Florsch, N., Hesse, A., Jolivet, A., Tabbagh, A. and Tabbagh, J. (1998). Archaeological prospecting using electric and electrostatic mobile arrays. *Archaeological Prospection*, **5**:239–252.

Pipan, M., Baradello, L., Forte, E., Prizzon, A. and Finetti, I. (1999). 2-D and 3-D processing and interpretation of multi-fold ground penetrating radar data: a case history from an archaeological site. *Journal of Applied Geophysics*, **41**:271–292.

Reynolds, J.M. (1997). *An Introduction to Applied and Environmental Geophysics*. John Wiley: Chichester.

*Scollar, I., Tabbagh, A., Hesse, A. and Herzog, I. (1990). *Archaeological Prospecting and Remote Sensing*. Cambridge University Press: Cambridge.

Sutherland, T.L., Schmidt, A. and Dockrill, S. (1998). Resistivity pseudosections and their topographic correction: a report on a case study at Scatness, Shetland. *Archaeological Prospection*, **5**:229–237.

Szymanski, J.E. and Tsourlos, P. (1993). The resistive tomography technique for archaeology: an introduction and review. *Archaeologia Polona*, **31**:5–32.

Tabbagh, A. (1984). On the comparison between magnetic and electromagnetic prospection methods for magnetic features detection. *Archaeometry*, **26**:171–182.

Telford, W.M., Geldart, L.P. and Sheriff, R.E. (1990). *Applied Geophysics*, (2nd edn). Cambridge University Press: Cambridge.

Vaughan, C.J. (1986). Ground-penetrating radar surveys used in archaeological investigations. *Geophysics*, **51**:595–604.

44

Remote Sensing

D.N.M. DONOGHUE

Department of Geography, University of Durham.

The science of remote sensing is concerned with the measurement and interpretation of electromagnetic radiation reflected or emitted by a target from a receiver located at a distance from the target. Remote sensing instruments that are familiar to archaeologists include photographic cameras and geophysical instruments such as magnetometers that make no contact with the ground. This chapter focuses only on instruments that image the ground at visible, infrared and microwave wavelengths and include conventional and digital cameras, multispectral scanners, thermographic scanners and synthetic aperture RADAR sensors. For an introduction to photography and aerial photographic interpretation see Avery and Berlin (1982), Avery and Lyons (1981); for background information on the physics and techniques of remote sensing see Sabins (1996), Lillesand and Kiefer (1999) or Elachi (1987).

AERIAL PHOTOGRAPHY

Historically, the practice of using remote sensing techniques for archaeological prospection has been based on low altitude aerial survey at optical and near infrared wavelengths. In the 1920s O.S.G. Crawford, the archaeological officer of the British Ordnance Survey, demonstrated that archaeological structures could be delineated from shadow, soil and crop markings on panchromatic aerial photography (Crawford 1923, 1928, 1929, Crawford and Keiller 1928). Since that time, both oblique and vertical aerial photography have been used extensively for archaeological reconnaissance and mapping all over the world. Among the very first practitioners of aerial archaeology were Crawford and Allen, who undertook extensive surveys in Britain and the Middle East, and the Frenchman Antoine Poidebard who surveyed a large part of Syria. These pioneers helped to refine the instruments and establish methods that are still in use today. Crawford in particular established methods of site classification and wrote about the effects of weather, season, soil moisture and crop type on photographic return (Crawford 1923, 1928, 1929). Poidebard undertook experiments to evaluate the influence of photographic scale, illumination effects and infrared film as he surveyed hundreds of miles of Syrian desert landscape (Poidebard 1929, 1934). It is also interesting to note that Charles Lindbergh became interested in using air photography for recording the presence of Anasazi sites in New Mexico and Mayan sites buried under the forests of the Yucatan in Mexico. He did much to stimulate interest in the USA in airborne survey techniques and inspired others such as Paul Kosok who made extensive use of photography to survey pre-Colombian sites in the Moche valley and Nazca regions of Peru in the 1940s (Deuel 1969).

Handbook of Archaeological Sciences. Edited by D.R. Brothwell and A.M. Pollard.

The physical size of the camera (format), the focal length of its lens, the sensitivity of the film and external factors such as atmospheric attenuation and scattering determine the quality of aerial photographs. The Second World War saw considerable technical advances in reconnaissance photography and in its interpretation. In particular, large format cameras were developed with lenses specially calibrated for aerial survey. Film technology saw the introduction of fast film suitable for photogrammetric survey work and new films reduced atmospheric attenuation by blocking sensitivity to the ultra-violet and blue parts of the electromagnetic spectrum that are most affected by water vapour.

After the war Jean Baradez, a specialist in military reconnaissance with the French air force, used his considerable expertise in the interpretation of vertical photography to map an extensive network of Roman military remains in North Africa (Deuel 1969). Vertical photography including stereoscopic viewing was used by workers like John Bradford who embraced aerial techniques in an extensive career of archaeological survey in Italy (Bradford 1957). From the 1950s onward, aerial survey was well established in archaeology and able to yield a tremendous amount of evidence for new features as well as providing a tool to help map specific sites and extensive landscapes. In the post-war period, important work by Riley, St Joseph, Bradford, Williams-Hunt, Valvassori, Scollar, Kosok and Wilson established beyond doubt the importance of aerial archaeology in Europe and the wider world (e.g., Riley 1987, St Joseph 1977, Wilson 1982). Today, aerial photography is accepted as a cost-effective, non-invasive technique for the reconnaissance and survey of monuments. Interpretation is guided by classification schemes that distinguish between description and interpretation of observed features (Edis *et al.* 1989).

However, airborne survey can be expensive and so there are still relatively few surveys undertaken by archaeologists for purely archaeological purposes. In Britain, important exceptions include the work of the Cambridge University Committee for Aerial Photography, the English Heritage (formerly RCHME) Air Photographic Unit and sister units in Scotland and Wales and a number of regional surveys (Palmer 1984). English Heritage established a National Mapping Programme in 1994 that continues to yield extensive amounts of data from crop and soil mark evidence (Bewley 1993, NAPLIB 1993, Stoertz 1997). There is also a growing interest in ground-based photography for the investigation and conservation of standing structures (Brooke 1989, 1994).

Computer data processing techniques

Irwin Scollar was among the first to demonstrate how computer processing could be used to digitally enhance archaeological images, geometrically rectify oblique aerial photography, produce photo mosaics, and create digital terrain models (Scollar 1965, Scollar *et al.* 1990). The computer hardware and software needed to perform digital image processing have improved significantly in recent years and there are now several powerful software packages available at a reasonable cost for desktop personal computers. It is no longer necessary to be expert in the mathematics of image manipulation to make use of this technology.

It is important to note that photographic film is a complex physical and chemical material that degrades with time at a rate that depends on the environment in which it is stored. Digital image storage, on the other hand, should not degrade and is an attractive method of archiving unique photographic records. The disadvantage of digital storage has been the loss of detail that results from the digitizing process itself and the amount of computer space required. However, optical scanning technology is now extremely good and conversion need not result in significant loss of quality. Also, the cost of computer storage space has reduced to such an extent that this is no longer a major limitation. Air photography can now be acquired directly in digital form using specialist digital cameras. The absolute resolving power of the best digital cameras almost matches that of photographic film.

Once images are stored in a digital form there are a wide range of processing techniques that can be used to enhance them. These include *contrast enhancement* to improve the visual appearance of both panchromatic and colour imagery, methods to remove defects introduced by the imaging device and methods to highlight geometric patterns such as edges or circular features within an image. Some image processing systems contain methods to manipulate image geometry that allows an image to be warped on to different map projections. Scollar (1965) adapted standard photogrammetric techniques to transform both vertical and oblique air photographs to map projections. An alternative approach is to transform features that are interpreted from oblique photographs (Palmer 1976). Haigh developed a specialist software package (AERIAL) to warp the cartographic interpretations from image data in a format that can be incorporated into CAD and Geographical Information Systems (GIS) (Haigh 2000). The problem with transforming only the interpretation is that it is difficult to reinterpret the original record if the photograph is lost or degraded in quality. In future, it would be ideal if both the original photograph and the interpreted feature were archived in a digital form (Bewley *et al.* 1998).

Advances in digital photogrammetry mean that it is now possible to derive height information and produce *Digital Terrain Models* (DTM) on low-cost desktop computers. An accurate DTM can only be produced from vertical photography acquired with a calibrated camera flown with 60 per cent frame overlap. Although the imagery may be expensive to acquire, height information can be extracted on a desktop computer relatively cheaply and used to produce digital orthophotographs that can be of considerable benefit in interpreting features in the landscape.

AIRBORNE MULTISPECTRAL SCANNERS (MSS)

Archaeological structures such as buildings, walls and ditches can usually be seen on conventional air photography at an appropriate scale and viewing angle. On the other hand, crop and soil marks are more difficult to detect with certainty. The visibility of crop marks often depends on vegetation type, soil conditions, sun-sensor geometry and film sensitivity, and so it is extremely difficult to obtain photographs under optimal conditions. Multispectral sensors address some of these problems because they are able to look simultaneously at a wide range of different wavelengths, many of which are more sensitive to vegetation status than either the human eye or photographic film. The limited spectral range of photographic film (350–1100 nm) is overcome by the use of photoelectric sensing devices where image data is recorded in a digital form. These devices are able to separate electromagnetic radiation into a number of discrete narrow wavebands, hence the term *multispectral*. Narrow band spectral imaging can often help to enhance or distinguish different features on the ground according to their particular absorption and reflectance properties. Multispectral scanners (MSS) make it possible to study wavelength bands that are particularly sensitive to vegetation growth, moisture and temperature. These bands can be viewed individually or combined in colour composite images. Another major advantage of multispectral imaging is that the data is produced in a digital form that can be modified using computer-based image processing techniques. Photographic film can only be developed once but the effect of image enhancement is to allow the user to experiment with different ways of development in an

interactive way and to adjust the contrast of different parts of the picture to assist interpretation.

MSS were first developed to test sensors designed for spacecraft. However, a number of studies have now used a low altitude airborne platform to evaluate these instruments for archaeological purposes. In Britain, airborne multispectral scanners managed by the Natural Environment Research Council (NERC) have been used to assess the archaeological potential of multispectral data at a number of sites. In former wetland environments such as the Fenlands of eastern England and the Vale of Pickering, multispectral imagery has complimented vertical photography and revealed new information at infrared wavelengths (Donoghue and Shennan 1988a, 1988b, Shennan and Donoghue 1992, Powlesland and Donoghue 1993, Powlesland *et al.* 1997). In the United States, a number of studies have been undertaken to assess multispectral data for recording the Pueblo archaeology and its environmental setting at Chaco Canyon in New Mexico and other sites (Lyons and Avery 1977, Lyons and Mathien 1980, Avery and Lyons 1981). The archaeological examination of standing structures, such as historic buildings and monuments, may be aided by the use of ground-based multispectral imaging to provide geological and construction phase differentiation in walls and related building features.

Multispectral case study

The first evaluation of multispectral data in Britain was conducted over the former wetland environment of Morton Fen in Lincolnshire (Shennan and Donoghue 1992). This study concluded that MSS data offer considerable potential for landscape assessment because: (i) crop marks were readily detected in the near infrared (760–900 nm), (ii) soil marks were well defined at the wavelength range of red light (630–690 nm), and (iii) the thermal infrared band (8000–12 000 nm) was able to detect some features not visible at any other wavelength. In addition, computer enhancement of the digital data placed less dependency on the time of year for revealing archaeological features. This study was undertaken on a flat landscape that consisted of marine and freshwater sediments traversed by ancient drainage channels, some of which were modified by humans for agricultural and industrial purposes. These sediments produced particularly clear crop and soil marks and the MSS data added detail and precision to traditional aerial and ground based surveys. Morton Fen is a reclaimed wetland environment where land drainage and deep ploughing are causing rapid destruction of the archaeological record. MSS data may provide a rapid and cost-effective tool for monitoring change.

A more recent study in the Vale of Pickering in North Yorkshire brought together a multi-sensor data set that included oblique air photographs, large scale vertical colour photography, digital MSS data and ground-based geophysics to help establish the value of the MSS data (Powlesland *et al.* 1997). Vertical colour photography and Daedalus 1268 eleven band, 2 metre ground resolution, MSS imagery was acquired from an altitude of 800 metres by NERC in June 1992. The MSS data were enhanced on a desktop computer using standard image processing routines such as contrast stretching, density slicing and colour composite production.

The Daedalus scanner has eleven bands that range from 420 to 12 000 nm, although not all are equally useful. The Morton Fen study concluded that four bands (5, 7, 10, 11) contained the most information and two independent interpreters studying the Vale of Pickering data arrived at the same conclusion that 'bands 4, 5, 7, 10 and 11 have shown the most potential for feature recognition' (Powlesland *et al.* 1997). These 'best' bands represent wavelengths in the red (4 and 5), near infrared (7), short-wave infrared (10) and thermal infrared (11) parts of the electromagnetic spectrum. Wavelength bands in the 420 to 520 nm range often suffer from atmospheric attenuation and scattering that degrades definition. Red and infrared images are less affected by atmospheric water vapour and usually provide good definition of soil marks and crop marks. The near and short wave infrared bands are particularly sensitive to plant health and can often detect water stress in vegetation before it can be seen by the naked eye. The thermal infrared region detects emitted rather than reflected radiation and is basically measuring ground surface temperature. It is the only waveband that is responding in part to the sub-surface properties of the ground. A fuller discussion of thermal imagery is given below.

Analysis of MSS data has much in common with analysis of aerial photographs, in that experience is necessary in order to separate out archaeology from natural or modern anthropogenic features. The sensitivity of MSS imagery to the relative moisture status of vegetation and soils can help to detail geomorphological features such as relict fluvial channels, potential peat deposits which could assist in identifying areas for palaeo-environmental research and gravel islands which may have supported human habitation or ritual sites.

MSS imagery is normally acquired as long swathes about 1.5 km wide and up to 10 km long. If the aircraft collects Global Positioning Satellite navigation data in conjunction with the imagery it is a simple process to mosaic these strips into a wide synoptic view of the study area. It is then possible to follow features across the landscape and to see associations between apparently discrete sites, a process that is difficult using discrete oblique photographic prints. In the Vale of Pickering a number of isolated features were shown to be previously unidentified trackways across the valley, enclosure systems and extensive barrow cemeteries. Areas that had previously been identified as small islands appeared to be more extensive, linear ridges running parallel to the valley edge. For example, the imagery reveals that a cemetery of round and square barrows on a gravel ridge is linked to the dry land by a ditched trackway.

Of particular interest was an area of *Ladder Settlement*, a sequence of overlying enclosures following a trackway (of late Iron Age to Romano-British date, *c.* 200 BC–AD 200). Although the *Ladder Settlement* is believed to be a continuous landscape feature running along the southern margin of the Vale, aerial photographic plots had left a number of apparent 'gaps' in the line of the settlement, particularly in areas of pasture. Two areas in particular were investigated (see Figures 44.1 and 44.2), where the line of the *Ladder Settlement* was believed to exist, but where there was no evidence of the settlement from either the oblique or the vertical colour photographs. In addition, the known line of the *Ladder Settlement* was also visible in the multi-spectral imagery, in many cases equalling the definition obtained by the combined aerial photographic plots.

This work (Powlesland and Donoghue 1993, Powlesland *et al.* 1997) shows the picture of human occupation and activity in the Vale of Pickering, pieced together from the oblique aerial photographic record, to be flawed, particularly because of the lack of continuous cover and the variable return provided by the oblique air photographs. The site-centred interpretation that the oblique record generates makes the overall assessment of the landscape both difficult and biased in favour of 'good-sites'. The large scale vertical photography and multi-spectral imagery acquired over the study area on a single date by the NERC instruments proved to be a very effective method of enhancing the detail and the breadth of coverage of the conventional record collected over more than a decade. This study reinforces the conclusions reached from the Fenlands (Donoghue and Shennan 1988a, 1988b) and demon-

Figure 44.1 Daedalus Multispectral imagery from the Vale of Pickering showing crop marks in multispectral image data extending across the landscape through different crop types (Copyright NERC).

Figure 44.2 The same Daedalus Multispectral image shown in Figure 44.1 with a magnetometry survey superimposed within a field of grass (Copyright NERC/Landscape Research Centre).

strates the effectiveness of the combined use of colour air photographs and MSS data for fields under crop and permanent pasture. The broad swathe width (1.5 km), continuous coverage and speed of data collection provided by the MSS make this an ideal tool for assessment of areas subject to pipeline and road schemes, as well as former wetland landscapes at risk from land drainage and deep ploughing (Shennan and Donoghue 1992).

AIRBORNE THERMOGRAPHY

Thermal prospection techniques have many important applications in geology, archaeology and environmental monitoring. Tabbagh and Hesse pioneered the evaluation of airborne thermography for archaeology and conducted a number of trial flights over different soil types in France (Hesse 1970, Perisset and Tabbagh 1981, Tabbagh 1976, 1979, Scollar *et al.* 1990). Both pre-dawn and daytime thermal imagery proved valuable in detecting archaeology from surface soil patterns or from the thermal effect of a buried structure. The French group used a two-channel Aries thermal line scanner sensitive to temperature differences of 0.1°C. Although this instrument provided promising results for several soil types, the relatively uniform temperature of the ground surface hides much of the information content in thermal imagery. This is a particular problem for vegetated surfaces where the plants regulate their own temperature through evapotranspiration which acts to create uniform canopy temperatures. However, archaeology is sometimes visible through vegetation at thermal wavelengths and invisible at other wavelengths (Bellerby *et al.* 1990). This suggests that the sub-surface affects evapotranspiration or that the thermal energy emitted by the soil is greater than the thermal 'blanket' provided by the vegetation. This effect is still poorly understood but is important since crop marks are rarely seen in permanent pasture land and a great deal of land is being set aside as permanent pasture in Europe.

Heat flow in soils is governed by time, depth, density, heat capacity and thermal conductivity, all properties relevant to ground disturbance. Pre-dawn and midday images can be combined to compute the diurnal heat capacity (otherwise termed the *thermal resistance to temperature change* or *apparent thermal inertia*) of the ground. Apparent thermal inertia (ATI) offers considerable potential for the detection of buried archaeology. Figure 44.3 shows an example of a thermal image acquired by NERC's airborne Daedalus scanner over the site of Bosworth battlefield in Leicestershire where an experiment is being conducted to quantify the value of apparent thermal inertia data.

Other sources of thermal imagery include analogue sensors flown by the Royal Air Force and the Police. Although not widely available, these data have been used to detect ground disturbance associated with archaeology (Small 1994). Thermal prospection has also been shown to reveal features hidden under plaster on historic buildings and monuments. In Germany, von Cramer (1981) has employed this technique very

Figure 44.3 Daytime thermal imagery from Bosworth Battlefield, Leicestershire showing former field boundaries and possible ditch structures in the vicinity of the heritage centre located on Ambion Hill thought to be the camp site of the army of Richard III before the battle (Copyright NERC Airborne Remote Sensing Facility).

successfully for many years to reveal hidden construction and concealed features in buildings.

SATELLITE IMAGERY

Optical space photography dates back to the first manned space flights. However, regular coverage of the Earth is obtained from sensors on orbiting satellites that use conventional film or digital imaging devices. Until very recently, the optical satellite imagery available to the public has been of low spatial resolution and of limited use for archaeology. On the other hand, there have been several studies that have demonstrated the capability of satellite imagery to derive important environmental information that is of considerable value in archaeological landscape assessment. For example, the North-west Wetlands Project used Landsat TM image data to help define the extent of peat deposits and former wetland environments. The satellite data identified a considerably larger area of wetland than could be confidently identified from aerial photography or Soil Survey data (Cox 1992). A similar application saw satellite data used to predict possible wetland sites for archaeological investigation along the

Delaware coast (Custer *et al.* 1986). In Mediterranean landscapes, Landsat and SPOT satellite data have helped to identify both modern and relict agricultural systems and land use patterns (Gaffney *et al.* 1995, Urwin and Ireland 1992, Stein and Cullen 1994, Madry and Crumley 1990, Sussman *et al.* 1994, Wiseman 1992). In tropical forests, where ground survey is extremely difficult, satellite data have proved valuable for both characterizing the environment and for visualizing the rate and patterns of change (Behrens and Sever 1991). Many countries lack large scale topographic maps and so satellite remote sensing can play an important role in providing these data in support of archaeological surveys.

At present, relatively high ground resolution panchromatic imagery can be obtained from the French SPOT satellite (10 metres) and the Indian IRS system (5 metres). The best available Russian photography is from the KVR-1000 declassified spy camera where the photographic film is digitized to provide 2 metre resolution over a 40 km by 40 km footprint. Fowler (1996) gives an illustration of KVR imagery for the area around Stonehenge in Wiltshire. The equivalent American declassified spy satellite data comes from the CORONA programme although the declassified archive is limited to the period 1959–1972 at present. These data are now commercially available at relatively low cost from the United States Geological Survey. Kennedy (1998), in a study of the archaeology of part of the Euphrates Valley in Turkey, points out that the availability of these data helps to address problems of restricted access to aerial photography in many countries. The CORONA programme experimented with several different panoramic cameras and it is important to know that the KH4B camera that operated from September 1967 to May 1972 acquired the most detailed pictures. The KH4B camera gives approximately 2 metre resolution but other cameras give resolutions that vary from 3–8 metres on the ground (McDonald 1995).

The IKONOS space camera sensor was launched on 24 September 1999. This is the first of a series of very high spatial resolution civilian satellite sensors where the data is available commercially (IKONOS [1 m], Orbview-3 [1–2 m] and Quickbird [0.82 m]). Some of these new systems also have a multispectral capability at 3–5 metres spatial resolution. Such digital imagery will offer considerable potential for landscape assessment and the monitoring of sites and landscapes. It will be particularly valuable when combined with the historical declassified military images to assess landscape change.

RADAR IMAGERY FROM SPACE

RADAR is an acronym for Radio Detection and Ranging. Radar operates in the microwave region of the electromagnetic spectrum over the frequency range from 40 000 to 300 megahertz. Radar sensors generate their own energy to illuminate the ground rather like a flash camera in the dark. The Radar system measures distances as a function of round trip travel times (at light speed) of a directed beam of pulses spread out over specific distances. The pulses received by the Radar antenna are reconstructed into an image according to the direction and modification of the signal. The frequency and direction of the energy transmitted determine the resolution of the sensor. Radar images show microwave scattering and attenuation for the frequency and geometric configuration of the sensor. Rough surfaces such as urban areas scatter microwaves strongly and appear bright on radar images, smooth surfaces such as calm water reflect the microwaves away from the sensor and appear dark (Elachi 1982, 1987).

By supplying its own illumination, radar can function during both day and night and the beam passes though cloud without significant interference. Imaging radar mounted on air- or spaceborne platforms is particularly useful for mapping regions with high levels of cloud cover. An unexpected benefit of spaceborne radar imagery is its ability to penetrate hyper-arid, smooth desert sand and tropical forest canopies to reveal the archaeology beneath. Data from NASA's Shuttle Imaging Radar (SIR) system have been used to demonstrate the existence of palaeo-channels in desert areas of the USA, North Africa and the Middle East (El-Baz 1989, 1997, McCauley et al. 1982; see Figure 44.4 in colour plates). The same system has been used to reveal important archaeology hidden under dense forest canopy, such as Mayan canals in Mexico and Guatemala and around the city of Angkor in Cambodia. There have only been four SIR missions. The last was in 1994, and so the data is only available for limited time periods and for that part of the Earth covered by the Space Shuttle's orbit path. Other spaceborne radar sensors have poor spatial resolution and are not useful for detecting archaeology directly. However, they are good at many forms of environmental mapping.

FUTURE DEVELOPMENTS

Remote sensing for archaeology is both a well established and a rapidly expanding field. The existing archive of aerial imagery is widely distributed throughout the world and photographs are often very difficult to access. At present, it is almost impossible to retrieve information about the historical photographic record for any given location. The world-wide-web has stimulated the development of internet-based image catalogues and metadata systems that should help to make information more accessible. Therefore, existing image archives will become much more valuable and useful.

Digital cameras may begin to replace conventional photography as their quality improves and prices fall. Advances in computer technology can now provide excellent image enhancement, geometric correction and digital storage capability that can be afforded by archaeological research and management organizations.

'The potential offered by the combination of a seamless mosaic of digital MSS imagery, draped on to a three-dimensional landscape model and superimposed with geophysical surveys, vector plots of plans, and databases linked to photographic images, field notes and spot find information in a Geographic Data Management System is tremendous; providing for the first time the facility for detailed landscape management and assessment on the desktop.'

(Powlesland et al. 1997).

Remote sensing can provide an impressive picture of the archaeological landscape without the need for invasive or expensive survey methods. On the other hand, it can be used inappropriately, it can be wrongly interpreted and it is not necessarily a substitute for ground-based investigation. The true potential of multispectral remote sensing, including thermal imaging, is still not clear and it needs to be evaluated to test responsiveness under a broad range of climatic and ground conditions. Further research is likely to produce sensors capable of resolving small features such as post-holes and shallow pits. Advances in thermal imaging will hopefully help to distinguish sub-surface features associated with shallow ground disturbance such as graves, which are particularly difficult to detect. When used appropriately, remote sensing provides a basis for testing hypotheses of landscape evolution that may be tested by ground survey, geophysical survey or excavation. Large-scale airborne survey may even provide the framework on which planning policy and excavation strategies can be established.

Finally, the number of researchers interested in archaeological applications of remote sensing techniques is growing steadily and there are now several special interest groups that meet to discuss new developments and research. The Archaeological Data Service recently launched a guide to good practice for air photography and remote sensing and this is available on the world-wide-web and provides an excellent starting point for those interested in obtaining data and further information (Bewley *et al.* 1998, 1999).

REFERENCES

*Recommended for further reading

*Avery, T.E. and Berlin, G.L. (1982). *Fundamentals of Remote Sensing and Airphoto Interpretation*, (5th edn). Prentice Hall: New Jersey.

Avery, T.E. and Lyons, T.R. (1981). *Remote Sensing: Aerial and Terrestrial Photography for Archaeologists*. National Park Service: Washington DC.

Behrens, C.A. and Sever, T.L. (eds) (1991). *Proceedings of the Applications of Space Age Technology in Anthropology Conference*. NASA: Mississippi.

Bellerby, T.J., Noel, M. and Branigan, K. (1990). A thermal method for archaeological prospection: preliminary investigations. *Archaeometry*, **32**:191–203.

Bewley, R.H. (1993). Aerial photography for archaeology. In Hunter, J.R. and Ralston, I. (eds) *Archaeological Resource Management in the UK: an Introduction*, 197–204. Alan Sutton: Stroud.

Bewley, R.H., Donoghue, D.N.M., Gaffney, V., Van Leusen, M. and Wise, A. (1998). *Air Photography and Remote Sensing: a Guide to Good Practice*. Archaeological Data Service: York. (http://ads.ahds.ac.uk/public/guides/apandrs).

Bewley, R.H., Donoghue, D.N.M., Gaffney, V., Van Leusen, M. and Wise, A. (1999). *Archiving Aerial Photography and Remote Sensing Data: a Guide to Good Practice*. Archaeological Data Service, Oxbow: Oxford.

Bradford, J.S.P. (1957). *Ancient Landscapes*. G. Bell and Sons: London.

Brooke, C.J. (1989). *Ground Based Remote Sensing*. Technical Paper No. 7, Institute of Field Archaeologists: Birmingham.

Brooke, C.J. (1994). Ground based remote sensing of buildings and archaeological sites: ten years research to operation. *Archaeological Prospection*, **1**:105–119.

Cox, C. (1992). Satellite imagery, aerial photography and wetland archaeology – an interim report on an application of remote sensing to wetland archaeology: the pilot study in Cumbria, England. *World Archaeology*, **24**:249–267.

Crawford, O.G.S. (1923). Air survey and archaeology. *Geographical Journal*, May:324–366.

Crawford, OGS (1928). *Air Survey and Archaeology*. Professional Papers, New Series 7, Ordnance Survey: Southampton.

Crawford, O.G.S. (1929). *Air Photography for Archaeologists*. Professional Papers, New Series 12, Ordnance Survey: Southampton.

Crawford, O.G.S. and Keiller, A. (1928). *Wessex from the Air*. Oxford University Press: Oxford.

Custer, J.F., Eveleigh, T., Klemas, V. and Wells, I. (1986). Application of LANDSAT data and synoptic remote sensing to predictive models for prehistoric archaeological sites: an example from the Delaware coastal plain. *American Antiquity*, **51**:572–588.

Deuel, L. (1969). *Flights into Yesterday*. Macdonald: London.

Donoghue, D.N.M. and Shennan, I. (1988a). The application of remote sensing to wetland archaeology. *Geoarchaeology*, **3**:275–285.

Donoghue, D.N.M. and Shennan, I. (1988b). The application of multispectral remote sensing techniques to wetland archaeology. In Murphy, P. and French, C. (eds) *The Exploitation of Wetlands*, 47–59. BAR British Series 186, British Archaeological Reports: Oxford.

Edis, J., Macleod, D. and Bewley, R. (1989). An archaeologists guide to the classification of cropmarks and soilmarks. *Antiquity*, **63**:112–126.

El-Baz, F. (1989). Remote sensing in archaeology: a case study. *Sensors*, **6**:33–38.

El-Baz, F. (1997). Space age archaeology. *Scientific American*, **277**:60–65.

Elachi, C. (1982). Radar images from space. *Scientific American*, **247**:54–61.

*Elachi, C. (1987). *Introduction to the Physics and Techniques of Remote Sensing*. John Wiley: New York.

Fowler, M. (1996). High-resolution satellite imagery in archaeological application – a Russian satellite photograph of the Stonehenge region. *Antiquity*, **70**:667–671.

Gaffney, V., Ostir, K. and Stančič, Z. (1995). Environmental monitoring in Central Dalmatia. *International Society for Photogrammetry and Remote Sensing*, **31(B7)**:563–567.

Haigh, J.G.B. (2000). Developing rectification programs for small computers. *Archaeological Prospection*, **7**:1–16.

Hesse, A. (1970). La prospection géophysique en archaeologie, problemes, resultats et perspectives. *Mis à Jours*, **5**:369–390.

Kennedy, D. (1998). Declassified satellite photographs and archaeology in the Middle East: case studies from Turkey. *Antiquity*, **72**:553–561.

*Lillesand, T.M. and Kiefer, R.W. (1999). *Remote Sensing and Image Interpretation*, (4th edn). John Wiley: New York.

Lyons, T.R. and Avery, T.E. (1977). *Remote Sensing: A Handbook for Archaeologists and Cultural Resource Managers*. National Park Service: Washington DC.

Lyons, T.R. and Mathien, F.J. (eds) (1980). *Cultural Resources Remote Sensing*. National Park Service Cultural Resources Management Division: Washington DC.

Madry, S.L.H. and Crumley, C.L. (1990). An application of remote sensing and GIS in a regional archaeological settlement analysis: the Arroux River Valley, Burgundy, France. In Allen, K.M.S., Green, S.W. and Zubrow, E.B.W. (eds) *Interpreting Space: GIS and Archaeology*, 364–381. Taylor and Francis: London.

McCauley, J.F., Schaber, G.G., Breed, C.S., Grolier, M.J., Haynes, C.V., Issawi, B., Elachi, C. and Blom, R. (1982).

Subsurface valleys and geoarchaeology of the eastern Sahara revealed by Shuttle Radar. *Science*, **218**:1004–1020.

McDonald, R.A. (1995). CORONA: success for space reconnaissance. A look into the Cold War, and a revolution for intelligence. *Photogrammetric Engineering and Remote Sensing*, **61**:689–720.

NAPLIB (1993). *National Association of Aerial Photographic Libraries. Directory of Aerial Photographic Collections in the United Kingdom.* Association for Information Management: London.

Palmer, R. (1976). A computer technique of transcribing information graphically from oblique aerial photographs. *Journal of Archaeological Science*, **4**:283–290.

Palmer, R. (1984). *Danebury: an Aerial Photographic Interpretation of its Environs.* Supplementary Series 6, Royal Commission on the Historical Monuments of England: London.

Perisset, M.C. and Tabbagh, A. (1981). Interpretation of thermal prospection on bare soils. *Archaeometry*, **23**:169–187.

Poidebard, A. (1929). Les revelations archaeologiques de la photographie aerienne – une nouvelle méthode de récherches et d'observation en region de steppe. *L'Illustration*, 25 May: 660–662.

Poidebard, A. (1934). *La trace de Rome dans le desert de Syrie. Le limes de Trajan a la conquête arabe. Récherche aeriennes (1925–1932).* Paul Geuthner: Paris.

Powlesland, D. and Donoghue, D. (1993). A multi-sensor approach to mapping the prehistoric landscape. In *Proceedings of the 9th NERC Airborne Symposium*, 88–96. NERC: Swindon.

Powlesland, D., Lyall, J. and Donoghue, D.N.M. (1997). Enhancing the record through remote sensing. The application and integration of multi-sensor, non-invasive remote sensing techniques for the enhancement of the Sites and Monuments Record. Heslerton Parish Project, N. Yorkshire, England. *Internet Archaeology*, **2**. (http://intarch.ac.uk/journal/issue2/pld_toc.html)

Riley, D.N. (1987). *Aerial Photography and Archaeology.* Duckworth: London.

*Sabins, F.F. (1996). *Principles and Interpretation of Remote Sensing*, (3rd edn). Freeman: New York.

St Joseph, J.K.S. (ed.) (1977). *Uses of Air Photography*, (2nd edn). Baker: London.

Scollar, I. (1965). *Archäologie aus der Luft.* Rheinland Verlag: Köln.

*Scollar, I., Tabbagh, A., Hesse, A. and Herzog, I. (1990). *Archaeological Prospecting and Remote Sensing.* Cambridge University Press: Cambridge.

*Shennan, I. and Donoghue, D.N.M. (1992). Remote sensing in archaeological research. In Pollard, A.M. (ed.) *New Developments in Archaeological Science*, 223–232. Oxford University Press: Oxford.

Small, F. (1994). *Royal Air Force Infrared Linescan Imagery: an Analysis and Evaluation.* Royal Commission on the Historical Monuments of England: Swindon.

Stein, C.A. and Cullen, B.C. (1994). Satellite imagery and archaeology – a case-study from Nikopolis. *American Journal of Archaeology*, **98**:316.

Stoertz, C. (1997). *The Ancient Landscapes of the Yorkshire Wolds.* Royal Commission on the Historical Monuments of England: Swindon.

Sussman, R., Green, G. and Sussman, I. (1994). Satellite imagery, human-ecology, anthropology, and deforestation in Madagascar. *Human Ecology*, **22**:333–354.

Tabbagh, A. (1976). Les proprietes thermiques des sols. *Archaeo-Physica*, **6**:128–148.

Tabbagh, A. (1979). Prospection thermique aeroportée du site de Prepoux. *Revue d'Archaéométrie*, **7**:11–25.

Urwin, N. and Ireland, T. (1992). Satellite imagery and landscape archaeology: an interim report on the environmental component of the Vinhais Landscape Archaeology Project, North Portugal. *Mediterranean Archaeology*, **5**:121–131.

von Cramer, J. (1981). Thermografie in der Bauforschung. *Archäologie und Naturwissenschaft*, **2**:44–54.

Wilson, D.R. (1982). *Air Photo Interpretation for Archaeologists.* Batsford: London.

Wiseman, J. (1992). Archaeology and remote sensing in the region of Nikopolis, Greece. *Context*, **9**:1–4.

45

Geochemical Prospecting

C. HERON

Department of Archaeological Sciences, University of Bradford.

The archaeological record is much more than distinct features, such as habitation surfaces, hearths, ditches, pits, and portable artifacts/ecofacts, such as potsherds, stone tools, and botanical/faunal remains. It has long been appreciated that human activity can cause subtle changes in soils and sediments resulting from inputs of organic and inorganic matter. Identifying the presence, source and spatial extent of anthropogenic inputs forms the basis of geochemical prospecting. Geochemical prospecting can be deployed in a variety of settings from the sampling of topsoil or the collection of samples from excavated horizons, such as floor surfaces, grave fills, courtyards, buried soils and so on. Considerable effort has been directed at the recognition of domestic activity, although there has been increasing interest in the accumulation and persistence of heavy metals around mining sites and in agricultural soils. Food debris, waste products and human remains constitute the most common categories of matter deposited. The chemical species present in these samples are nearly always present in the soil environment; thus the simple identity of a specific chemical element is not normally sufficient to confirm an anthropogenic input. Rather it is the superimposition of a *fixed* anthropogenic signal over that of the soil chemical environment that must be identified and interpreted. By and large, chemical species in the soil are far from homogeneous. This makes geochemical prospecting a challenging and complicated endeavour.

Geochemical prospecting has emerged as a complement to methods of soil science with a well-established pedigree (e.g., Limbrey 1975). As a survey method, it is rarely carried out in isolation from other approaches to archaeological prospecting. At one level, the determination of chemical species in the soil can be undertaken in parallel with pH measurements, loss-on-ignition, organic carbon, particle size analysis and so on. These supplementary datasets offer opportunities for comparison and correlation. Chemical data are also commonly undertaken allied to the measurement of soil magnetic properties (typically magnetic susceptibility), surface and subsurface evidence from artefact distributions or visible features, soil micromorphology, geophysical survey data, as well as documentary and ecological evidence. The aim of this chapter is to assess the utility of chemical methods of survey currently available to the archaeologist and to review examples from the recent literature. A detailed overview of the relevant chemical principles is beyond the scope of this chapter, but readers are referred to the appropriate literature.

PHOSPHATE ANALYSIS

Phosphorus is an essential plant nutrient and is taken up by plants in the form of inorganic phosphate ions in the soil solution: $H_2PO_4^-$ and HPO_4^{2-} (see Chapter 16). Getting adequate phosphorus into plants is a

Handbook of Archaeological Sciences. Edited by D.R. Brothwell and A.M. Pollard.

widespread problem and this consideration has prompted a considerable amount of soil chemical research (see Brady and Weil 1999:540, Rowell 1994). Essentially the problem is that soil phosphates are insoluble (or at least have very low solubility). Added soluble phosphates will readily combine with cations in the soil solution to form low-solubility compounds. The formation of insoluble phosphates is known as *fixation* and includes the processes of precipitation and adsorption. The total quantity of phosphorus in an average soil is approximately 0.05 per cent by weight (400–2000 kg/ha), of which only a negligible proportion is available to the plants at any one time.

Phosphate in soils at relatively high pH is combined with calcium ions forming the apatite group of calcium phosphate minerals. Apatite is the most abundant and widespread natural phosphorus compound on Earth. The simpler compounds of calcium are quite soluble and readily available for plant growth (fertilizers contain large amounts of these soluble calcium phosphates). However, these compounds are present in soil in extremely small quantities and they are converted readily into the more insoluble forms. Soluble phosphates also adsorb on solid calcium carbonate surfaces. At lower soil pH, calcium phosphates do dissolve liberating the phosphate ions, but ions of aluminium and iron are available to form aluminium phosphate (variscite) or iron phosphate (strengite). Phosphate ions also adsorb on to the surfaces of insoluble iron, aluminium and manganese hydrous oxides. Phosphorus is most available near pH 6.5 for mineral soils and about pH 5.5 for organic ones. Even at this pH, phosphate adsorption onto clay mineral surfaces is possible.

Inorganic phosphate may be changed from insoluble to soluble forms in the soil, although the speed of the process is often much too slow to provide adequate phosphorus for optimum plant growth. Much of the phosphate taken up by plants (apart from that supplied by phosphate fertilizers) is believed to come from organic phosphates released by decomposition of organic matter. Research into the mobility of soluble phosphates added to soil suggests that it rarely travels more than 2–3 cm from the fertilizer granule before reaction with the soil.

The precise chemical nature of the organic phosphorus fraction in soil remains an active area of investigation in soil chemistry. The proportion of phosphorus bound to organic chemical species varies widely depending on a range of factors. Organic phosphorus compounds, present in all living organisms, are found in nucleic acids and certain forms of lipid. Many plants are rich in organic phosphate compounds (e.g., phytin). Phosphorus can be released from dead plant and animal residues by bacteria and other organisms capable of secreting phosphatases. These enzymes split off inorganic phosphate ions which are then in a form available to plants in the soil solution. This process is known as mineralization. However, the fate of most of the ions is fixation with the inorganic fraction of the soil.

Archaeological geochemical prospecting has, until recently, been synonymous with phosphate (or phosphorus) analysis, beginning with the agronomic observations by Olof Arrhenius in the 1920s, through the spot tests of Lorch on archaeological sites to the systematic work of Cook and Heizer (1965) and Eidt (1977, 1984). A comprehensive and critical essay by Bethell and Máté (1989) remains the most important summary and covers the development of phosphate analysis in detail.

The application of soil phosphorus surveys to archaeology is based upon the premise that higher than 'background' quantities of phosphorus are associated with occupation areas (organic waste and refuse and ashes), with burials (due to the presence of calcium phosphate in bone and organic phosphorus containing compounds in soft tissue), or intensive land use (for example, resulting from manuring). Applications have varied from the study of discrete archaeological features or horizons, such as the characterization of an excavated burial or buried soil, to intra-settlement study, to surveys of several hectares with topsoil samples taken on a regular, albeit rather coarse, grid often at 5–10 metre intervals. This latter larger-scale application has found favour in the general trend towards landscape archaeology, which considers settlements in their wider environmental context. As long ago as 1977, Robert Eidt (1977:1327) identified a 'valuable if somewhat disorganized body of knowledge' generated by case studies in the detection of soil phosphate in archaeological contexts.

Laboratory (and field) protocols for quantifying soil P vary widely, making comparisons of soil P data problematical. One of the more common is the determination of *inorganic phosphate* following treatment of the soil with weak (e.g., 2M) acid (e.g., Craddock *et al.* 1985). Once extracted, the concentration of phosphate is determined in solution by absorption spectrophotometry or colorimetry via the formation of the blue phosphomolybdate complex. Most 'spot' tests conducted in the field rely upon a similar weak acid extraction of inorganic phosphate. Methods of fractionation into different categories of inorganic phosphate are derived from the fundamental work of Chang and Jackson (1957), and others. Eidt (1977, 1984) pioneered the fractionation of inorganic phosphate into (i) non-occluded Fe and Al phosphates, (ii) occluded Fe and Al phosphates, and (iii) calcium phosphates for archaeological application. These methods are still employed (e.g., Lillios 1992), but the precise archaeological value of this approach remains difficult to verify (Bethell and Máté 1989). An alternative is to extract the *total phosphorus* component of the soil using standard complete digestion methods such as hydrofluoric acid. These methods produce a result that is insensitive to the state of mineralization of the soil (Crowther 1997). Alternatively, conversion of organic phosphorus-containing compounds to inorganic phosphate by ignition of the soil can be performed prior to a 2M acid extraction, thus rendering a value for the *bulk phosphorus* signal (Bethell and Máté 1989). In principle, this offers a simple protocol to yield both inorganic and organic components in a soil, by determining inorganic phosphorus via weak acid extraction, and inorganic plus organic from an ignited duplicate sample (and thus organic by subtraction), but experience suggests that this rarely works satisfactorily, perhaps because of inherent inhomogeneity. The potential of the information derivable from the organic phosphorus fraction therefore remains largely untapped in archaeology. Ottaway (1984) identified the persistence of organic phosphorus in soils from a Tell site in the former Yugoslavia, although the precise form and origin could not be ascertained. More sophisticated diagnostic techniques offer promising avenues for the study of organic phosphorus compounds in archaeological soils and sediments.

RECENT TRENDS

In favour of the optimists is the empirical appeal of a large number of published phosphate surveys (see Bethell and Máté 1989), particularly where other evidence is deployed, especially the presumed relationship between the distribution of phosphate and recognizable archaeological features (e.g., Craddock *et al.* 1985). Combined phosphate and soil magnetic susceptibility surveys have sometimes produced intriguing mutually exclusive patterns (Craddock *et al.* 1985, Heron and Gaffney 1987:75). Clark (1987:39) identified the value of such surveys, especially since magnetic susceptibility highlights soils and sediments enhanced magnetically by burning, whereas high phosphate values were considered to show areas of stock enclosure. However, he

cautioned against behavioural interpretation without considering 'interference between the two phenomena'. However, little fundamental research has been reported to date.

Soil magnetic susceptibility is a valuable prospecting tool in its own right and relies upon the conversion of weakly magnetic oxides and hydroxides to more strongly magnetic forms (Dalan and Banerjee 1998). Following the classic work of Le Borgne in the 1950s and 1960s, Tite and Mullins (1971) conducted a series of heating experiments on a range of soils to investigate the degree of magnetic enhancement, and to inform on the likely outcomes of magnetic prospecting as a function of geological origin of the soil. A considerable body of work has been reported since then (reviewed in Dalan and Banerjee 1998). Burning is well established as an important mechanism, although the identification of high concentrations of magnetotactic bacteria in a posthole has renewed interest in the organic 'fermentation' mechanism (Fassbinder and Stanjek 1993). There are increasingly sophisticated methods of laboratory studies aimed at characterizing magnetic minerals in soils (e.g., Dalan and Banerjee 1998, Peters and Thompson 1999, Linford 1994), as well as practical comparisons aimed at distinguishing natural from anthropogenic enhancements (Crowther and Barker 1995), and at improving field and laboratory recording methods, with sampling interval an important consideration (e.g., Batt *et al.* 1995).

According to Bethell and Máté (1989:17), 'It is hard to say that P analysis has done more than confirm site interpretation; the cautiously judicious might say that it has failed in even this role'. Phosphorus determinations have, to a certain extent, remained on the fringe of archaeological prospecting. There are many interesting case studies presented in the archaeological literature but many questions remain. The critical one is the extent to which a cultural signal can be recognized as part of a dynamic soil chemical system based upon the accumulation, fixation or loss of soil P from the soil. Variations in the natural 'background' levels of soil phosphate, variable retention capacities of phosphate in soil, vertical variations within soil profiles and the difficulties in disentangling this from more recent applications of fertilizers, manure, grazing animals and so on are factors which are readily acknowledged but rarely investigated (Crowther 1997). Through three case studies, Crowther (1997) has shown that correlating soil phosphorus data with determinations such as loss-on-ignition and particle size analysis can produce a better understanding of the phosphate signal persisting in the sedimentary matrix. Furthermore, due care in sampling specific horizons across archaeological sites is emphasized and the need for a fuller consideration of the pedological context has been made. In the UK, phosphate analysis has not been widely employed as a non-invasive prospecting tool in the context of archaeological evaluation following the publication of Planning Policy Guidance Note 16 (Department of Environment 1990). This is in stark contrast to the rapid growth of archaeological geophysics (David 1995, Gaffney *et al.* 1998; see Chapter 43). Conventional case studies in soil phosphate analysis continue to appear (e.g., Vizcaino and Cañabate 1999), yet few of these venture much beyond a routine phosphate assay. There has been continued interest in rapid on-site tests for phosphate (e.g., Farswan and Nautiyal 1997, Terry *et al.* 2000). An agenda, sensitive to the archaeological potential of phosphate analysis, with the opportunity to embrace the long-standing uncertainties identified by Crowther (1997) and, with a view to exploring standardized methods of phosphate extraction and detection, is required to reinvigorate this aspect of archaeological geochemistry.

MULTI-ELEMENTAL ASSAYS OF SOILS AND SEDIMENTS

During the 1990s, there has been a discernible shift away from the assay of a single soil chemical species, such as phosphorus, to the determination of a number of soil elements. In part, this has resulted from the wider availability and suitability of analytical techniques capable of assaying a wide range of elements in solution. Phosphorus can be assayed as one of a range of elements enhancing the possibility of recognizing a cultural signal. However, the obvious risk is that, in scaling up to analyse many more elements, the long-term fate of many of them is poorly understood. Many of these studies have yet to produce convincing datasets with immediate appeal for archaeological interpretation.

Bethell and Smith (1989) used inductively coupled plasma emission spectrometry to determine the quantities of 25 elements in the fill of a grave at Sutton Hoo. The grave contained a crouched inhumation, preserved as a 'pseudomorph' of stained sand, and the remains of a wooden coffin. A number of elements were shown to be enhanced in the body samples over that of the surrounding sandy matrix, although the greatest difference was seen in the levels of phosphorus (determined as %P_2O_5). Using previously published examples, the authors cautioned against a distinctive elemental 'signature' that could be used irrespective of the precise soil chemical context.

Entwistle and Abrahams (1997) and Entwistle *et al.* (1998, 2000) have explored the value of multi-element assays using inductively coupled plasma mass spectrometry for the study of historic settlement patterns on the Isle of Skye. Topsoil samples were collected from two adjacent croft farmsteads and associated enclosures or kailyards, used for growing vegetables and storing compost. Analyses of bulked soils from 60 fields and 30 'off-site' locations were also incorporated into the sampling strategy. Sensibly, despite the absence of historical evidence, the off-site soils were not considered to be unaffected by human activity. Over the presumed location of a nucleated farming complex or clachan, the soil samples showed, relative to the off-site control samples, elevated (up to 3.5 times) potassium, caesium, rubidium and thorium and 'enrichments' of barium, lanthanum, cerium and praseodymium. Although promising, the relationship between these elements and specific anthropogenic sources is extremely difficult to determine, although high potassium levels in excreta, seaweed and wood ash could explain the distribution of this element. As is commonly the case in multi-element assays in archaeological soil geochemistry, the phosphorus distributions provoke more discussion than all other elements. Somewhat surprisingly, only 'minor enrichment' relative to the 'control' samples was observed at the site of the former clachan and in most of the remaining fields. In contrast, 10 of the 11 kailyards associated with the later crofting landscape were interpreted as displaying 'significant enrichment'. Quoting a study by Edwards (1983), the low phosphorus enrichments are considered to be due to regular depletions caused by removal to the growing crops or to topsoil erosion. Similarly, depletions of organic matter determined by loss-on-ignition adjacent to the croft buildings were explained by the accelerated decomposition of organic residues caused by regular cultivation and cropping. Curiously, this application of inorganic geochemistry, with its references to animal manure, turf and peat, and seaweed, makes no mention of the advances in biomarker work reported below. Trace element assays of topsoils have also been undertaken in other contexts, including their correlation with surface pottery scatters in central Greece (Bintliff *et al.* 1992), yet the enhanced copper and lead in topsoils associated with dense surface scatters of pottery from the likely habitation sites was not reflected in the Scottish surveys. Aston *et al.* (1998) have produced a series of clear enhancements in phosphorus, lead and zinc associated with a settlement pattern at Shapwick,

Somerset. Sampling of soils from excavated horizons has been carried out at a Bronze Age site in southeast Sweden (Linderholm and Lundberg 1994). Middleton and Price (1996) sampled floor surfaces in both ethnographic and archaeological contexts.

LIPID BIOMARKERS AND THE RECOGNITION OF CESS AND MANURING PATTERNS

Chemical prospecting has not been overlooked by the expansion of biomolecular and isotopic investigations in archaeology. In particular, interest has focused upon the extraction, identification and quantification of lipid molecules and amino acids in soils (see Chapter 28). Whilst the latter has yet to grow into sustained archaeological investigation, the former has become a recognized and powerful tool; notably, the identification of lipid biomarkers, such as coprostanol (5β-cholestanol) and 5β-stigmastanol, and even bile acids could represent a paradigm shift away from the easy-to-measure but difficult-to-interpret phosphate survey.

The most promising development in the last decade and a half of geochemical prospecting has been the identification of lipid biomarker compounds in soils and sediments. A summary of recent work carried out by the research group led by Richard Evershed (Bull et al. 1999a) reviews the biochemical origin, geochemical occurrence and recent archaeological applications. These studies have confirmed the persistence of certain biomarkers in soils and this offers opportunities for identifying manuring distributions and confirming identification of discrete features, such as cesspits. The approach is based on the conversion, mediated by microbial populations, of sterol molecules in animals and plants to β-stanols as food is passed through the mammalian gastrointestinal tract. The identification of coprostanol (5β-cholestan-3β-ol) relative to other sterol degradation products formed under normal conditions of environmental modification (5α-stanols) has been used as a contemporary indicator of faecal infiltration into marine environments (e.g., Grimalt et al. 1990, Jeng and Han 1994). Coprostanol is a reduction product of cholesterol. The major stanol present in herbivorous animals is 5β-stigmastanol, produced when the principal plant sterol, sitosterol, is similarly reduced in the gut. Additional data indicates that bile acids also persist in archaeological soils (Evershed and Bethell 1996). Furthermore, patterns of bile acid distribution offer greater specificity of the source of the faecal material.

The persistence of sterols and β-stanols from aggregated and desiccated faecal samples from Loveluck Cave, Arizona was first established by Lin and co-workers (Lin et al. 1978). The archaeological potential of β-stanol biomarkers of disaggregated faecal deposits was first explored by Knights et al. (1983) who demonstrated the presence of coprostanol and other β-stanols in a Roman ditch adjacent to a bathhouse at Bearsden Roman fort. Pepe and co-workers (Pepe et al. 1989, Pepe and Dizabo 1990) evaluated the potential of a range of lipid biomarkers, including alkanes, fatty acids and sterols in Gallo-Roman and Medieval deposits from the Louvre excavations in Paris and considered the impact of bacterial reworking on the molecular residues of cultural activity. Bethell et al. (1994) published data on Medieval and Roman pitfills and obtained samples from the fill of a latrine used by an excavation team over several seasons whilst digging a site at Galgenberg, Germany. Of the two Roman pitfills sample, one (Pit 1), strongly suggested use as a cesspit (see also Bethell et al. 1993:fig. 3 for another dataset). Bethell and co-workers established a set of criteria to identify the presence of human faecal matter in soil, independent of the simple occurrence of coprostanol, using ratios of the $5\beta/5\alpha$-stanols. These criteria have been modified to take account of epicoprostanol (Bull et al. 1999a:92), as the suggested criteria for assessing contemporary faecal pollution (Grimalt et al. 1990) are too stringent given that coprostanol is a more unstable compound relative to 5α-stanols (Bull et al. 1999a:92).

Assessment of the 5β-stigmastanol contribution to a plot of land subjected to a 14-year manuring experiment was carried out by Evershed et al. (1997). Within a 30×30 metre wheat field at the Butser Ancient Farm, Hampshire, a 15 metre wide central strip was treated with cattle manure (10 tons wet weight per acre per year). Topsoil samples were taken at one metre intervals across a 30 metre transect, with a further three soil samples taken from a non-manured location nearby. The concentration of 25 elements, including phosphorus, was also determined by inductively-coupled plasma atomic emission spectroscopy, using partial digestion procedures. Levels of coprostanol, 5β-campestanol and 5β-stigmastanol were quantified using the selected ion monitoring mode of the GC/MS. The manured strip was found to be enhanced in 5β-stanols, with edge blurring considered to be the result of annual ploughing and natural biological processes in the soil. Of the inorganic elements, phosphorus displayed a 'complete lack of enhancement' (Evershed et al. 1997:493). This was considered to be the result of a range of factors, including the high background concentration of phosphorus in the soil, depletion caused by cropping, and leaching of the soluble phosphate ions. The lack of a total phosphorus assay and an assessment of variation in phosphorus in the vertical soil profile were factors not considered in this preliminary study.

Simpson *et al.* (1999) have recently applied lipid biomarker techniques at a Medieval farmstead (twelfth to nineteenth century, West Mainland, Orkney). The sampling strategy was based upon an earlier total phosphate survey. Six soil samples were investigated from three excavated profiles along a transect extending from the site. Total lipid extracts and the analysis of the sterol/stanol fraction confirmed higher levels in the anthropogenic deep top soil adjacent to the farmstead. Furthermore these data confirmed earlier suggestions based on other soil and documentary sources that composted turf and ruminant animal manure had been applied to the topsoil. Bile acid data suggested an input from pig manure for which there is no specific reference in documentary sources (see also Bull *et al.* 1999b).

The relationship between specific marker compounds (lipids, amino acids) of soils and 'fingerprint' data obtained from pyrolysis-gas chromatography/mass spectrometry of insoluble organic matter and previous vegetation cover/land use has been used in a series of investigations at the Rothamsted Experimental Station, UK (van Bergen *et al.* 1997, 1998a, 1998b; Bull *et al.* 1998). Beavis and Mott (1996, 1999) have also used plots at Rothamsted to test the detection of an amino acid 'fingerprint' in soils to distinguish between known vegetation and between different treatments, such as manured versus unmanured areas. Although preliminary, even further resolution might be possible using either carbon or nitrogen isotopes, combined with the recognition and identification of individual compounds (Simpson *et al.* 1997). There are many other examples of promising research avenues. Farrimond and Flanagan (1996) have compared pollen evidence and lipids in a Flandrian peat bed suggesting that the lipids represented localized additions of plant debris, whereas the pollen sequence derived from plants from a wider area. Barba *et al.* (1996) have explored a range of techniques for determining the presence of organic accumulations in lime plaster floor samples in the Hall of the Eagle Warriors, Templo Mayor, Mexico. Analysis of soil profiles from Tofts Ness, Sanday, Orkney made use of molecular and isotopic studies of the bulk lipid fraction to confirm an input of grassy turf to the

anthropogenic soil formation, and to identify specific manure inputs (Bull *et al.* 1999b).

Although the number of samples assayed to date is very small (the four case studies briefly reviewed in Bull *et al.* (1999a) amount to just over 50 samples in total), the diagnostic potential appears to be very great. Continued attention needs to be given to the formation and preservation of 5β-stanols in the environment (e.g., Grimalt *et al.* 1990) so that natural 'background' variation in soils and sediments can be monitored. Similarly, the relative degradation of individual stanol compounds and the subtlety of archaeological interpretation based upon differences in less than 1–2 micrograms of stanols per gram of soil will be addressed by wider sampling strategies. Many of the recent case studies have been carried out on buried soil horizons from the Northern Isles, where farming relied upon sustained additions of manure and other products to maintain soil fertility. For some years, phosphate survey has, in these circumstances, been successful in confirming considerable inputs of organic matter. Whilst the biomolecular investigations have expanded the knowledge base, more challenging situations in other archaeological landscapes where buried soils do not persist will need to be tackled. In terms of archaeological interpretation, the recognition of ancient manuring regimes has to be appreciated against a wider backdrop of land used at different times for other activities, such as grazing livestock. The latter would also be expected to produce elevated 5β-stanols. Here, other evidence, especially sherd scatters, might be invoked in support of manuring (e.g., Bull *et al.* 1999a:94). There are no published studies of the concentration and spatial variation of 5β-stanols from land used for grazing animals, as opposed to deliberate additions of manure. Just as we should not necessarily always equate 'off-site' pottery scatters as the inorganic remains of past manuring activity (Alcock *et al.* 1994), neither should we do the same with small differences in the concentration of 5β-stanols from a small sample.

CONCLUSIONS

To some, geochemical analysis of soils and sediments remains the Cinderella of archaeological prospecting. The confidence with which an anthropogenic signal can be separated from natural variations in the soil matrix remains a critical factor. Most surveys endeavour to identify 'control' or 'off-site' samples taken away from presumed areas of archaeological interest. Such soils and sediments may not, of course, be unaffected by human impact. The recent impact of biomarker and isotopic approaches on geochemical prospecting has revitalized this field and with further progress in multi-element investigations (including phosphorus) offer considerable potential. In addition to the detection of manure and other organic and mineral inputs into soils, the recognition and delimitation of specific activities such as food processing, tanning, dyeing and other practices envisages an expanded role in the future.

REFERENCES

*Recommended for further reading

Alcock, S.E., Cherry, J.F. and Davis, J.L. (1994). Intensive survey, agricultural practice and the classical landscape of Greece. In Morris, I. (ed.) *Classical Greece: Ancient Histories and Modern Archaeologies*, 137–170. Cambridge University Press: Cambridge.

Aston, M.A., Martin, M.H. and Jackson, A.W. (1998). The potential for heavy metal soil analysis on low status archaeological sites at Shapwick, Somerset. *Antiquity*, **72**:838–847.

Barba, L.A., Ortiz, A., Link, K.F., López Luján, L. and Lazos, L. (1996). Chemical analysis of residues in floors and the reconstruction of ritual activities at the Templo Mayor, Mexico. In Orna, M.V. (ed.) *Archaeological Chemistry: Organic, Inorganic and Biochemical Analysis*, 139–156. ACS Symposium Series 625, American Chemical Society: Washington DC.

Batt, C., Fear, S. and Heron, C. (1995). The role of magnetic susceptibility as a geophysical survey technique: a site assessment at High Cayton, North Yorkshire. *Archaeological Prospection*, **2**:179–196.

Beavis, J. and Mott, C.J.B. (1996). Effects of land use on the amino acid composition of soils: 1. manured and un-manured soils from the Broadbalk continuous wheat experiment, Rothamsted, England. *Geoderma*, **72**:259–270.

Beavis, J. and Mott, C.J.B. (1999). Effects of land use on the amino acid composition of soils: 2. Soils from the Park Grass experiment and Broadbalk Wilderness, Rothamsted, England. *Geoderma*, **91**:173–190.

*Bethell, P.H. and Máté, I. (1989). The use of soil phosphate analysis in archaeology: a critique. In Henderson, J. (ed.) *Scientific Analysis in Archaeology*, 1–29. Monograph 19, Oxford University Committee for Archaeology: Oxford.

Bethell, P.H. and Smith, J.U. (1989). Trace element analysis of an inhumation from Sutton Hoo, using inductively coupled plasma emission spectrometry: an evaluation of the technique applied to analysis of organic residues. *Journal of Archaeological Science*, **16**:47–55.

Bethell, P.H., Evershed, R.P. and Goad, L.J. (1993). The investigation of lipids in organic residues by gas chromatography/mass spectrometry: applications to palaeodietary studies. In Lambert, J.B. and Grupe, G. (eds) *Prehistoric Human Bone: Archaeology at the Molecular Level*, 229–255. Springer-Verlag: Berlin.

Bethell, P.H., Goad, L.J., Evershed, R.P. and Ottaway, J. (1994). The study of molecular markers of human activity: the use of coprostanol in the soil as an indicator of human faecal material. *Journal of Archaeological Science*, **21**:619–632.

Bintliff, J., Davis, B., Gaffney, C., Snodgrass, A. and Waters, A. (1992). Trace metal accumulations in soils on and around ancient settlement in Greece. In Spoerry, P. (ed.) *Geoprospection in the Archaeological Landscape*, 9–24. Monograph 18, Oxbow: Oxford.

*Brady, N.C. and Weil, R.R. (1999). *The Nature and Properties of Soils* (12th edn). Macmillan: London.

Bull, I.D., van Bergen, P.F., Poulton, P.R. and Evershed, R.P. (1998). Organic geochemical studies of soils from the Rothamsted Classical Experiments – II. Soils from the Hoosfield Spring Barley Experiment treated with different quantities of manure. *Organic Geochemistry*, **28**:11–26.

Bull, I.D., Simpson, I.A., van Bergen, P.F. and Evershed, R.P. (1999a). Muck 'n' molecules: organic geochemical methods for detecting ancient manuring. *Antiquity*, **73**:86–96.

Bull, I.D., Simpson, I.A., Dockrill, S.J. and Evershed, R.P. (1999b). Organic geochemical evidence for the origin of ancient anthropogenic soil deposits at Tofts Ness, Sanday, Orkney. *Organic Geochemistry*, **30**:535–556.

*Chang, S.C. and Jackson, M.L. (1957). Fractionation of soil phosphorus. *Soil Science*, **84**:133–144.

Clark, A.J. (1987). Site prospecting. In Mellars, P. (ed.) *Research Priorities in Archaeological Science*, 38–39. Council for British Archaeology: London.

Cook, S.F. and Heizer, R.F. (1965). *Studies on the Chemical Analysis of Archaeological Sites*. Publications in Anthropology No 2, University of California: Berkeley.

Craddock, P.T., Gurney, D., Pryor, F. and Hughes, M.J. (1985). The application of phosphate analysis to the location and interpretation of archaeological sites. *Archaeological Journal*, **142**:361–376.

*Crowther, J. (1997). Soil phosphate surveys: critical approaches to sampling, analysis and interpretation. *Archaeological Prospection*, **4**:93–102.

Crowther, J. and Barker, P. (1995) Magnetic susceptibility: distinguishing anthropogenic effects from natural. *Archaeological Prospection*, **2**:207–215.

*Dalan, R.A. and Banerjee, S.K. (1998). Solving archaeological problems using techniques of soil magnetism. *Geoarchaeology*, **13**:3–36.

David, A. (1995). *Geophysical Survey in Archaeological Field Evaluation*. English Heritage Research and Professional Guideline No. 1, English Heritage: London.

Department of the Environment (1990). *Archaeology and Planning*. PPG16, DoE: London.

Edwards, K.J. (1983). Phosphate analysis of soils associated with the Old Kinord field and settlement system, Muir of Dinnet, Aberdeenshire. *Proceedings of the Society of Antiquaries of Scotland*, 113:620–627.

Eidt, R.C. (1977). Detection and examination of anthrosols by phosphate analysis. *Science*, 197:1327–1333.

Eidt, R.C. (1984). *Advances in Abandoned Settlement Analysis: Application to Prehistoric Anthrosols in Colombia, South America*. University of Wisconsin: Milwaukee.

Entwistle, J.A. and Abrahams, P.W. (1997). Multi-element analysis of soils and sediments from Scottish historical sites: the potential of inductively coupled plasma-mass spectrometry for rapid site investigation. *Journal of Archaeological Science*, 24:407–416.

Entwistle, J.A., Abrahams, P.W. and Dodgshon, R.A. (1998). Multi-element analysis of soils from Scottish historical sites: interpreting land-use history through the physical and geochemical analysis of soil. *Journal of Archaeological Science*, 25:53–68.

Entwistle, J.A., Abrahams, P.W. and Dodgshon, R.A. (2000). The geoarchaeological significance and spatial variability of a range of physical and chemical soil properties from a former habitation site, Isle of Skye. *Journal of Archaeological Science*, 27:287–303.

Evershed, R.P. and Bethell, P.H. (1996). Application of multimolecular biomarker techniques to the identification of fecal material in archaeological soils and sediments. In Orna, M.V. (ed.) *Archaeological Chemistry: Organic, Inorganic and Biochemical Analysis*, 157–172. ACS Symposium Series 625, American Chemical Society: Washington DC.

Evershed, R.P., Bethell, P.H., Reynolds, P.J. and Walsh, N.J. (1997). 5β-Stigmastanol and related 5β-stanols as biomarkers of manuring: analysis of modern experimental material and assessment of the archaeological potential. *Journal of Archaeological Science*, 24:485–495.

Farrimond, P. and Flanagan, R.L. (1996). Lipid stratigraphy of a Flandrian peat bed (Northumberland, UK): comparison with the pollen record. *The Holocene*, 6:69–74.

Farswan, Y.S. and Nautiyal, V. (1997). Investigation of phosphorus enrichment in the burial soils of Kumaun, mid-central Himalaya, India. *Journal of Archaeological Science*, 24:251–258.

Fassbinder, J.W.E. and Stanjek, H. (1993). Occurrence of bacterial magnetite in soils from archaeological sites. *Archaeologia Polona*, 31:117–128.

Gaffney, V.J., Gaffney, C.F. and Corney, M. (1998). Changing the Roman landscape: the role of geophysics and remote sensing. In Bayley, J. (ed.) *Science in Archaeology: an Agenda for the Future*, 145–156. English Heritage: London.

Grimalt, J.O., Fernández, P., Bayona, J.M. and Albaigés, J. (1990). Assessment of faecal sterols and ketones as indicators of urban sewage inputs to coastal waters. *Environmental Science and Technology*, 24:357–363.

Heron, C.P. and Gaffney, C.F. (1987). Archaeogeophysics and the site: ohm sweet ohm? In Gaffney, C.F. and Gaffney,

V.L. (eds) *Pragmatic Archaeology: Theory in Crisis?*, 71–81. BAR British Series 167, British Archaeological Reports: Oxford.

Jeng, W.L. and Han, B.C. (1994). Sedimentary coprostanol in Kaohsiung Harbour and the An-Shui estuary, Taiwan. *Marine Pollution Bulletin*, 28:494–499.

Knights, B.A., Dickson, C.A., Dickson, J.H. and Breeze, D.J. (1983). Evidence concerning the Roman military diet at Bearsden, Scotland, in the 2nd Century AD. *Journal of Archaeological Science*, 10:139–152.

Lillios, K.T. (1992). Phosphate fractionation of soils at Agroal, Portugal. *American Antiquity*, 57:495–506.

Limbrey, S. (1975). *Soil Science and Archaeology*. Academic Press: London.

Lin, D.S., Connor, W.E., Napton, L.K. and Heizer, R.F. (1978). The steroids of 2000-year-old human coprolites. *Journal of Lipid Research*, 19:215–221.

Linderholm, J. and Lundberg, E. (1994). Chemical characterization of various archaeological soil samples using main and trace elements determined by inductively coupled plasma atomic emission spectrometry. *Journal of Archaeological Science*, 21:303-314.

Linford, N. (1994). Mineral magnetic profiling of archaeological sediments. *Archaeological Prospection*, 1:37–52.

Middleton, W.D. and Price, T.D. (1996). Identification of activity areas by multi-element characterization of sediments from modern and archaeological house floors using inductively coupled plasma-atomic emission spectroscopy. *Journal of Archaeological Science*, 23:673–687.

Ottaway, J.H. (1984). Persistence of organic phosphate in buried soils. *Nature*, 307:257–259.

Pepe, C. and Dizabo, P. (1990). Étude d'une fosse du 13ème siècle par les marqueurs biogéochimiques: chantier archéologique du Louvre (Paris). *Revue d'Archéométrie*, 14:23–28.

Pepe, C., Dizabo, P., Scribe, P., Dagaut, J., Fillaux, J. and Saliot, A. (1989). Les marqueurs biogéochimiques: application à l'archéologie. *Revue d'Archéométrie*, 13:1–12.

Peters, C. and Thompson, R. (1999). Supermagnetic enhancement, superparamagnetism, and archaeological soils. *Geoarchaeology*, 14:401–413.

Rowell, D.L. (1994). *Soil Science: Methods and Applications*. Longman: London.

Simpson, I.A., Bol, R., Dockrill, S.J., Petzke, K.-J. and Evershed, R.P. (1997). Compound-specific $\delta^{15}N$ amino acid signals in palaeosols as indicators of early land use: a preliminary study. *Archaeological Prospection*, 4:147–152.

Simpson, I.A., Dockrill, S.J., Bull, I.D. and Evershed, R.P. (1999). Lipid biomarkers of manuring practice in relict anthropogenic soils. *The Holocene*, 9:223–229.

Terry, R.E., Hardin, P.J., Houston, S.D., Nelson, S.D., Jackson, M.W., Carr, J. and Parnell, J. (2000). Quantitative phosphorus measurement: a field test procedure for archaeological site analysis at Piedras Negras, Guatemala. *Geoarchaeology*, 15:151–166.

*Tite, M.S. and Mullins, C. (1971). Enhancement of the magnetic susceptibility of soils on archaeological sites. *Archaeometry*, **13**:209–219.

van Bergen, P.F., Bull, I.D., Poulton, P.R. and Evershed, R.P. (1997). Organic geochemical studies of soils from the Rothamsted Classical Experiments – I. Total lipid extracts, solvent insoluble residues and humic acids from Broadbalk Wilderness. *Organic Geochemistry*, **26**:117–135.

van Bergen, P.F., Flannery, M.B., Poulton, P.R. and Evershed, R.P. (1998a). Organic geochemical studies of soils from Rothamsted Experimental Station – III. Nitrogen-containing organic matter in soil from Geescroft Wilderness. In Stankiewicz, B.A. and van Bergen, P.F. (eds) *Nitrogen-containing Macromolecules in the Bio- and Geosphere*, 321–338. ACS Symposium Series 707, American Chemical Society: Washington DC.

van Bergen, P.F., Nott, C.J., Bull, I.D., Poulton, P.R. and Evershed, R.P. (1998b). Organic geochemical studies of soils from the Rothamsted Classical Experiments – IV. Preliminary results from a study of the effect of soil pH on organic matter decay. *Organic Geochemistry*, **29**:1779–1795.

Vizcaino, A.S. and Cañabate, M.L. (1999). Identification of activity areas by soil phosphorus and organic matter analysis in two rooms of the Iberia Sanctuary 'Cerro El Pajarillo'. *Geoarchaeology*, **14**:47–62.

46

Archaeological Data Integration

M. VAN LEUSEN

Groningen Institute for Archaeology.

There are many different archaeological sciences, but all ultimately serve the science of Archaeology. It is the job of the archaeologist to integrate data supplied by each of the sciences into one interpretative scheme – an archaeological *understanding*. By successfully integrating archaeological data sets, you will have created a whole that is larger than its constituent parts. For example, radiocarbon dates can be used to date single objects, but put into the context of site *stratigraphy* they can date many objects and features in the site. If objects dated in this way are used in conjunction with, say, a ceramic *typology*, objects and features in other sites can be dated too – even if these are far removed in space and time from the original dated objects. In other words, by integrating data from several sources the value of each is increased (and conversely, by *not* integrating data from these sources, much of their value remains unrealized).

Although everyone will agree that data integration is a good thing in principle, in practice there has been little concerted and effective effort by archaeologists to bring it about. However, developments since the early 1990s in the ways archaeological data are being collected, stored, described, and communicated are improving our ability to integrate and analyse archaeological data generated from a wide variety of sources. This chapter briefly reviews the historical background to current data integration issues, and introduces the two main types of data – geographical and alphanumeric – which archaeologists would like to be able to integrate. These two types are discussed in more detail, with examples, below. A final section summarizes the current state of the field and looks at some new developments which are likely to be of great significance in the future. A recurrent theme throughout this chapter will be the fact that much archaeological data produced nowadays is *digital* data, intimately linking the goal of data integration to the means provided by information technology.

Providing a useful reference list for a subject that is changing all the time is difficult. Some sources, such as Burrough (1989, but available in a new edition by Burrough and MacDonnell 1998) and Dana Tomlin (1990) on GIS, have remained valuable for over a decade. Other sources, such as the proceedings of successive Computer Applications in Archaeology (CAA) conferences, provide information on current research and developments. The published proceedings of the 1997 CAA conference (Dingwall *et al.* 1999) provide a very useful section on the history of archaeological computing, including efforts to integrate data from different sources and the authors' views on where the remaining hurdles lie. In addition to this, a recent review article on the integration of GIS and remote sensing applications (Hinton 1996) can be recommended. Finally, a lot of the latest and most accessible

Handbook of Archaeological Sciences. Edited by D.R. Brothwell and A.M. Pollard.
© 2001 John Wiley & Sons, Ltd.

material appears on the Internet. The Archaeological Data Service (ADS), based in York, maintains a web site at http://ads.ahds.ac.uk with many documents relating to issues in data integration, for example:

AHDS Guides to Good Practice
(http://ads.ahds.ac.uk/project/goodguides/g2gp.html)
AHDS Standards web page
(http://ads.ahds.ac.uk/project/userinfo/standards.html)
ArchSearch catalogue
(http://ads.ahds.ac.uk/catalogue/)

The guides to good practice are also available in hard copy (Gillings and Wise 1999, Bewley *et al.* 1999).

HISTORICAL BACKGROUND: SPECIALIZATION AND FRAGMENTATION

Archaeology is an unusual science, not just because it destroys much of its own evidence during examination, but also because it does not limit itself to any particular aspect of the past. Whereas the study of modern societies is conducted by many different kinds of scientists, from sociologists to economists, an archaeologist is expected to study all aspects of past societies. This burden was not so keenly felt in the days of the gentleman antiquarian, who would be relying mostly on folklore, historical, and epigraphic sources for his interpretation of archaeological finds. But starting in the late nineteenth century the realization came that archaeological finds might have their own independent story to tell, and the study of our remote past became increasingly sophisticated as a result.

This, and the huge increase in levels of academic funding (translated into academic research positions) since the late 1960s, coupled to the rise of the New Archaeology, led to the spawning of a large number of specialisms, especially where archaeology touches on the 'hard' physical, chemical, and biological sciences. As a direct result, there are now archaeological scientists studying only pollen, tree rings, plant macrofossils, pedology, geomorphology, or various types of geophysical and geochemical data – to list only a very few examples. This fragmentation of archaeological expertise is reflected in the structure of the current volume – each sub-section dealing with some specialist subject and written by an appropriate specialist contributor.

As a side effect of the expansion and professionalization of archaeology in the 1960s and 1970s, archaeological specialists have tended to drift further and

further apart. Increasing computerization during the 1970s was partly to blame. Each specialism began to generate its own tools and software programs which at the time were very expensive and required the hiring of non-archaeologist programmers. Initially no effort was made to integrate the data generated by these tools – indeed, the need to do this was not recognized. This fragmentation of archaeological research also had unexpected negative effects in the teaching curricula, which simply did not have enough room for more than a cursory treatment of most of the specialist sub-disciplines.

By the early 1980s, data sets produced by specialists could no longer even be handled, let alone analysed, by the archaeologist responsible for overall analysis and interpretation. Not only did the digestion and synthesis of the full range of data encountered by archaeologists require a level of specialist knowledge that a generalist could no longer muster; the *format* of these data had also become increasingly digital, i.e., physically 'untouchable' and accessible only by using specialist software and hardware tools. Thus, a typical excavation report by this time had come to include various appendices containing the details of particular specialist scientific analyses – say, mollusc studies. This in turn led to fears of the disintegration of archaeology as a unified science, with specialists no longer willing or able to talk to each other, and higher education no longer able to produce archaeological 'generalists'. By the early 1980s, therefore, the archaeological generalist, whose task it is to integrate all the available and relevant data, was faced with *two* challenges instead of one: that of finding and accessing such data, and that of digesting it. As will be shown below, large strides have been made in dealing with the former, whereas the latter has proved to be much more resistant to our efforts. But first we must briefly consider some basic concepts of archaeological data integration.

How do we know that two or more sets of archaeological data can be integrated? There must be a common denominator which will provide the link between the data sets. Two such denominators can be identified – *location* and *identity*. *Location* provides the link when we want to integrate two or more spatial data sets. To be precise, the data sets must be made to fit into one single map projection and co-ordinate system. *Identity* provides the link when we try to integrate two alphanumeric (text/numbers) data sets; when we work with database management systems identity is provided by one or more 'key fields' which typically contain such items as site IDs, find, context, or feature numbers. We must be sure that such key fields have unambiguous definitions. The next two sections deal with these two types of common denominator in turn.

INTEGRATING GEOGRAPHICAL DATA

Archaeologists and mapping

It is not by accident that Geographical Information Systems (GIS) have been at the forefront of archaeological data integration effort since the mid-1980s. Archaeology has always had a strong cartographic tradition, and has stressed the importance of recording the location of any finds and features encountered. Regional archaeological projects, designed to integrate streams of incoming data from such diverse sources as field walking campaigns, air photographic study, historical maps, and soil surveys, demonstrate its unifying power. Such data in turn provide the 'landscape archaeology' background against which more detailed and small-scale investigations (geophysical, geochemical, and excavation) are conducted. Strikingly, almost all such data can be (re-)formatted as a raster of digital numbers – a characteristic that is the main driving force behind data integration efforts employing GIS.

GIS may have been an important contributing factor in much of the recent work in landscape archaeology, but in its turn the development of GIS is certainly not driven by relatively poorly-funded archaeology. Rather we can recognize independent forces in the wider society – in particular the increasing convergence of tools and technologies and the increased availability of map data and software – which allow archaeologists to 'hitch a ride', as it were.

Convergence of hardware systems is illustrated by field survey instruments (e.g., those used for 'total station' and satellite positioning, and for geophysical surveying). Such instruments nowadays carry integrated computers and software which produce data formats compatible with those used on the desktop. Site plans, elevation values, and soil resistivity data all end up on the fieldwork director's desktop PC within an hour or two after initial acquisition – fast enough to allow corrective changes to the fieldwork strategy, exemplified by the work of Lyall and Powlesland (1996) at North Heslerton. Conversely, computerized handheld field work 'assistants' are now being developed to bring an integrated data environment out into field situations – a gratifying development in which 'executive toys' are converted for serious research (Ryan *et al.* 1999). In the software arena, packages such as those for GIS, Computer Aided Design/

Mapping (CAD/CAM), and image processing have evolved to handle data formats coming in from an ever greater range of remote sensing platforms, and are themselves merging into generic management and processing tools. New raster and vector data formats (hierarchical data format or HDF, used mainly for multiband remote sensing data; geographic tagged image file format or geoTIFF, Portable Network Graphics or PNG; Windows MetaFile or WMF) have been adopted to further facilitate the integration of information from the former domains of GIS, remote sensing, and image processing.

Developments in software and data accessibility since the early 1990s have further facilitated data integration. Software that was once available only on arcane and expensive computing platforms has now become much cheaper, user-friendly, and packaged into the Windows-like visual interfaces we are all acquainted with. There is also the increasing availability of generic digital data sets such as detailed topographic and soil maps, and even free small-scale thematic world maps. Most countries now have their standard scale topographic maps and elevation models available as digital files; a good overview of data sources is provided in the ADS *GIS Guide to Good Practice* (Gillings and Wise 1998). Such data potentially provide a common basis for the more specialist and higher resolution data sets being generated by archaeologists, and they are essential for one of the basic integrative operations, geo-referencing, to take place. This development is still ongoing, and digital topographic data unfortunately are still very expensive in most countries, limiting access by archaeologists (except for the USA and Belgium, where the philosophy is that the taxpayer has already paid for the data to be produced, so shouldn't have to pay again to use it!). The following explains some of the basis of integrating geographical data (for a fuller treatment, see Chapter 53).

The *what* and *where* of geographical data integration

For a successful integration of data coming in from multiple sources (data producers) and platforms (instruments), we need a common basis to the data. This is as true at the local scale to combine, say, geophysical, aerial photographic, elevation and excavation data on a site, as it is on a regional scale – say, combining radar and topographic map data to find cities and roads hidden under rainforest canopy or desert sands (as in the 1992 discovery of the lost caravan trade city of Ubar in the Oman desert; Fiennes (1993), Fisher and Fisher (1999)). As already mentioned above, this common basis has been found in *identity* and in geographic *location*. In other words, before we can successfully integrate archaeological data sets we must ask ourselves two questions: *what* do the data represent and *where* are they located?

Archaeologists deal with the first question by using site names or numbers, feature and layer numbers, find and sample numbers, etc., in order to *identify* data. This allows an archaeological scientist to link all sorts of information in a (computerized) database. In the 1970s relational database programs (RDBMS) were the first focus for integration of alphanumeric (text and numbers) data. Geographical *location* as a way to combine different data sets has also been around for a long time, maps being one of the main tools for archaeological research. Since the mid-1980s computer screens have been able to handle complex graphic displays and geographic location has come to the fore as an integrative factor. Integration of two-dimensional geographical data can occur when two preconditions are met. Firstly, the data should be locatable and the precision/accuracy of the given locations should be known; secondly, appropriate conversion and transformation systems should be used to bring all data into one reference system. In other words, we must know where everything is and how certain we are of that, and we must be able to put everything within one geographical frame of reference. Whereas the former is normally taken care of in archaeology by appropriate field work, the latter often requires specific digital transformations of the data – usually called *geo-referencing*, *co-registering*, or *rectification* (for photos).

An example – Wroxeter

The integration of data from different sources in a GIS can benefit the archaeologist on a number of levels. First and very important is the possibility of visually inspecting and mapping data that can now be put on screen together ('overlaid') for the first time – an ability enhanced by the application of image enhancement techniques. A good example of this is the overlaying of geophysical data and aerial photographs at the Romano-British civitas capital of Viroconium (present-day Wroxeter in Shropshire), which has been studied in the setting of its late Pre-Roman Iron Age and early Roman hinterland (Gaffney and Van Leusen 1996). A second benefit of digital data integration in a GIS is that, rather than having to analyse each data set

individually, it allows very powerful multivariate analytical techniques to be used to search for patterns in the integrated data. This is an area of research that is, unfortunately, still largely unexplored by archaeologists, and no examples are given here.

While the Wroxeter Hinterland study area is nearly 1300 km^2 in size and GIS has been used in many types of analysis of the landscape and its archaeology, the project is used here as an example because it encompasses a detailed aerial photographic and geophysical study of Wroxeter itself (Gaffney *et al.* 2000, Van Leusen 1999). Oblique aerial photographs of the site taken in the late 1950s and 1960s, and vertical aerial photographs taken in 1976 – a very dry year – just after the site was ploughed, provide exquisite detail of the urban buildings and underlying legionary fortress at Wroxeter. Mapping these by traditional means meant using the relatively poor spatial control supplied by Ordnance Survey 1:2500 scale mapping, and the combination of map errors, limited precision, and the lack of recognizable fixed points on a site that is largely given over to short pasture has led to mapping errors of the order of several metres. The new mapping by members of the Wroxeter Hinterland Project was based on a network of control points independently measured by satellite positioning (GPS) to an accuracy of a few millimetres (Figure 46.1).

A series of geophysical surveys were then conducted at the site, whose location was measured directly from the GPS points. The magnetometry survey data covered nearly all the site and allowed the location of many new control points such as angles of Roman walls and modern water pipes, but they were still relatively coarse-grained at a horizontal resolution of 25 by 100 cm. However, at this stage of the data integration it was possible, thanks to the new control points, to tie the aerial photographs directly to the geophysical data and therefore to the GPS network (Figure 46.2). This in turn allowed the full detail of the photographs to become available for the mapping of the town, and a much more detailed interpretation of the geophysical data than would otherwise have been possible (Van Leusen 1999; Figure 46.3).

Integrating geographical data in a GIS has in this case not only produced a superior map of the subsurface archaeological features at Wroxeter in terms of accuracy and detail, but it has also allowed us to begin exploring the multivariate data, with questions such as:

(i) What does it mean when we encounter linear features with a high resistivity but consistently

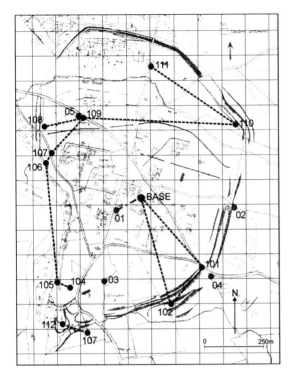

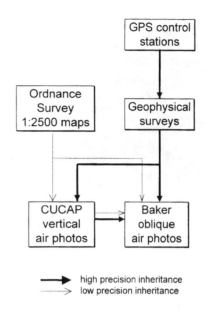

high precision inheritance
low precision inheritance

Figure 46.2   The inheritance of locational information during integration of Wroxeter datasets, using GIS, has followed pathways guaranteeing high precision wherever possible, with lower precision pathways used as backup.

Figure 46.1   Establishing the high accuracy site grid at Wroxeter. A system of GPS control stations was put in place at Wroxeter in order to allow accurate and absolute location of the geophysical survey data. This would have been impossible to obtain using just the Ordnance Survey 1:2500 maps (the method used by Wilson (1984); figure background).

lower-than-average magnetic field gradient? (Answer: at Wroxeter, part of the town centre was apparently burnt in a large fire which caused a high background magnetism; stone wall foundations therefore show up as low magnetic anomalies while still having a high resistivity.)

(ii)   How was the flow of water and sewage within the Roman town organized? (Answer: by combining the known water supply and sewage lines with depth information from ground penetrating radar data and with surface elevation data, we can calculate the absolute depth, vertical angles, and flow direction of the aqueducts and sewers.)

So, GIS has allowed us to integrate archaeological data sets on the basis of their common geographical frame of reference; but how can we integrate non-spatial data? For example, how can we integrate data from several pollen cores taken and analysed by different people using different procedures? How, out of hundreds of

publications on Beaker pottery, can we distil a picture of typo-chronological change across western Europe if each country uses its own preferred typologies and chronologies? These exemplify the problems involved in integrating alphanumeric data.

INTEGRATING ALPHANUMERIC DATA

Off the shelf and on to the Net

Archaeological data that can be written down (rather than being represented graphically as in a GIS) are called *alphanumeric* data. The lion's share of field and laboratory records are likely to be alphanumeric, and integration of such data usually takes place with the help of database management software. To get access to other people's data sets, you can use the Internet. A very important part of a database is the specification of its structure (*metadata*) and of the allowed terms for each field (*standards*).

In the early 1980s much effort was put into ultimately failed attempts to create dedicated archaeological database applications. In contrast, nowadays many archaeologists can use an off-the-shelf *relational database management system* (RDBMS) with little training. In addition, current RDBMS can allow objects such as

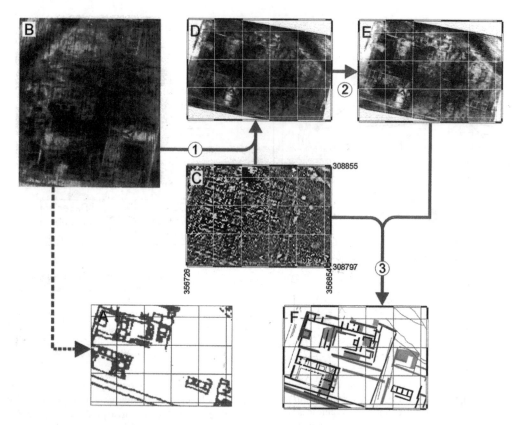

Figure 46.3   Creating highly accurate maps of Roman Wroxeter by combining the high spatial accuracy of the geophysical data with the high spatial resolution of the aerial photographs. Oblique aerial photograph B is ortho-rectified and georeferenced using recognizable features in the magnetometric map C. The resulting ortho-photo map D is enhanced to bring out more archaeological detail (E). The nature of the features in both C and E can be surmised from their morphology in combination with the type of soil and magnetometric response. These are mapped and interpreted on-screen, resulting in one or more very accurate and detailed interpretative plans of Wroxeter (F; compare the previous mapping (A)). The spacing of all grid lines is 25 metres.

photographs, drawings, reports, sound files and video to be handled just the same as the traditional text and number fields. This development is further simplified by the availability of so-called Object-Oriented (OO) database management systems, which use a more intuitive system for organizing data. Simply by bringing together items that used to be (and to a large extent still are) stored separately in slide rooms, drawing archives, and libraries, an archaeologist stands a better chance of producing an integrated analysis of all available data.

Increased networking of data also leads to convergence of tools and techniques. Even archaeological publications can now allow readers to exploit digital data integration, as in the 'papers' published in the electronic journal *Internet Archaeology*, which have

become interactive resources rather than static presentations (http://intarch.ac.uk/journal/).

Standards and metadata

One of the basic requirements for scientific work in any discipline is that both analytical results and raw data must be made available for peer review, so that others can see whether they agree with your interpretations. For this to happen, standards are necessary. In fact, nearly everything in science is standardized in some way – from the methods for collecting data to the format for publication. In archaeology like in most other fields in the humaniora, one of the most difficult things to standardize is terminology. There is such a great variation in the words (to say nothing of the languages) that people use to describe things, that we must collectively decide to use only a small subset of these words, and must agree on their meaning. From the fact that so many such standards are being proposed by various groups (see the overview of standards for British and international archaeology on the ADS web pages at http://ads.ahds.ac.uk/project/userinfo/standards.html) it can be inferred, however, that we are still far from reaching a general agreement on standard terminology.

Yet another development that has taken place since the early 1990s as a direct result of the increased availability of networked information is the call for, and construction of, so-called *metadata*. These are data descriptors like the ones used in a library to find books – 'data about data'. Why are these metadata so important for data integration? If you have ever had to analyse data collected by other people you will understand why. In order to integrate two equivalent data sets – say, two databases containing site data – you would have to know the exact structure of each database, an exact description of what each field contains, and the exact meaning of all the prescribed words that are used in each of the two databases. Does 'site' in the first database mean exactly the same as it does in the second? Is 'Late Neolithic' in the first database the same as 'Chalcolithic' in the second? The same kinds of questions arise if you want to search two or more library catalogues at once. In order to look for an author, the search programme must know which fields in both catalogues hold the 'author' information even if this is called LASTNAME and FIRSTNAMES in one, and AUTH_NAME in the other. So metadata tells you what the data mean, and therefore if (and how) you can integrate them. One of the best known current systems for recording metadata is named the 'Dublin Core', to which extensions covering archaeological requirements have recently been proposed (see Dublin Core Metadata Initiative at http://purl.org/dc/).

The Internet

Even with sufficient metadata it is not always practically possible to integrate data sets. They may still be inaccessible because of their geographic distance, for instance. The advent of the Internet is again beginning to provide solutions to this problem. Data sets can now be held anywhere in the world and still be accessible to the end user; and the end user may not even be aware that the data reside elsewhere, or that what he/she perceives to be one dataset is in fact a composite of multiple data sets from around the world, seamlessly integrated by their metadata.

One could easily imagine a study that uses a typological classification developed and held by an American university to classify, map, and analyse the distribution of palaeolithic flint knives in southern and western Europe. The data for this could come from a large number of separate digital publications of single finds, and from databases held by governments, museums and universities throughout Europe. Even though these would use different languages and even vocabularies to describe the knives, metadata catalogues would ensure that all knives satisfy the criteria given in the American typology.

CONCLUSIONS AND FUTURE DEVELOPMENTS

User responsibility

Archaeology is not about collecting data – it is about using data to understand and explain the past. The archaeological sciences are generally seen to be 'helper' sciences to this central aim. The archaeological generalist must therefore be able to integrate the data and interpretations generated by the specialists. One of the most important tasks facing an academic researcher is to attempt to integrate the data that are available in his or her field of expertise. Whereas the availability and accessibility of data and the user-friendliness of tools and techniques have steadily increased since the 1980s, that cannot guarantee that analysis and interpretation of the integrated data will be conducted properly – this remains the user's responsibility.

This theme of user responsibility can also be cast in the form of a quantity/quality trade-off. In order to integrate data we must look for a common denominator. In database applications this denominator is *identity*, in GIS applications combined with geographic *location*. In networked applications the common denominator is formed by *metadata* standards. Such standards can be used to integrate data sets that are deemed to be of sufficient quality or interest. 'Substandard' data fall by the wayside, and integration is limited to those data sets that qualify. The user is therefore faced with a dilemma: the more data sets he/she wants to integrate, the lower must be the standards required and the less scope there is for interesting types of analysis. Conversely, setting the metadata standards higher means that fewer data sets will qualify. In other words, when we apply standards to data, the best we can obtain is the highest common denominator. There is always a trade-off between depth (quality of integration) and width (number of data sets to be integrated).

The role of Information Technology

The role information technology (IT) plays in archaeological research has, in the late 1980s and 1990s, shifted from a negative (or at best neutral) one, to one conducive to the integration of data that may be distributed around the world. Whereas IT during the 1970s and early 1980s probably contributed to the fragmentation of archaeological analysis, the exponential growth in the number and availability of IT applications over the last decade is having the opposite effect. The functionality of tools and technologies originally developed for the needs of disparate fields are now converging. Software and data that once were in the domain of highly specialized operators have now become available to, and manageable by, most researchers. An increasing awareness of the importance of data standards and metadata means increased quality and usefulness of the data recorded by archaeologists. One only needs to remember the boxes filled with computer punch-cards, common until the late 1970s but now relegated to departmental basements or worse, to appreciate how much influence this technological shift has already had on the conduct of archaeology. Leading the way have been applications dealing with data that have a spatial (geographic) component. But IT has also brought increasing communication (through the Internet) and data integration (through the creation of metadata descriptive archives).

Future developments

We are perhaps only at the very beginning of a development that may take another few decades to bear full fruit. The growth and development of the Internet, while unpredictable in detail, is certain to lead to further improvements in the availability and accessibility of archaeological (or archaeologically-relevant) data sets, and this in turn is likely to force the general acceptance of tools for the creation and accessing of metadata. The limiting factor to such developments will be social – the slow process of agreeing on international standards, the continued need to learn foreign languages, the perception that some archaeological data should not be made available to the general public.

Specific to the future development of GIS will be a drive to allow storage and analysis of four-dimensional data, i.e., extending current GIS with the third spatial dimension of depth, and the fourth dimension of time. As has happened with database management software, GIS-like software will become part of everyone's standard desktop software set before long. The next stage will then be for other specialist applications on the desktop (such as those needed for statistical analysis, web searching, and probabilistic reasoning/expert systems) to become integrated with the GIS.

The future of data integration in archaeology will also lie in the development of new and improved Internet protocols. For example, the provision of Dublin Core metadata (Gillings and Wise 1999: section 5.4) for digital data sets opens the way for these to be recorded in meta-databases, and searched and accessed over the Internet. The *Archaeological Holdings Search System* (ArchSearch) database operated since 1997 by the Archaeology Data Service (ADS) is the first such meta-database in British archaeology (http://ads.ahds.ac.uk/catalogue/). Traditionally, meta-data are kept separate from the data themselves, as in a library where the catalogue is kept separate from the books, but recent work on the Extensible Mark-up Language (XML; Bosak and Bray 1999) seems likely to change this. Under XML, each single data element in a digital document is tagged so that cataloguing software (and your Internet browser) can recognize it. The cataloguing software will simply lift certain elements from the book (such as author name, abstract, and number of pages). If the XML coding was properly done, this means that another step in the data integration process – that of retrieving data based on their metadata – will have been automated. The UK government has pledged to carry through precisely this policy (termed 'Interoperability Framework') for the integration of its own information systems by 2005, and Higher Education (including Archaeology) will follow in its footsteps – if perhaps at a slower pace.

The future is also bringing increased international standardization, although here standardization of the tools (for example, the web browsers) is happening much more quickly than standardization of content (which requires large numbers of archaeologists to agree). One good example of the former is current browsers' impaired ability to handle more than one character set, such as Latin or Cyrillic, at a time. In the near future almost all software applications are likely to adopt the international Unicode (ISO/IEC 10646) standard, which uses 16 bits rather than the current 8 bits to record one digital character and can therefore accommodate all scripts and numbering systems ever invented by humans – including the 6000 or so characters of classical Chinese! To find out more, see http://www.unicode.org.

It is down to you

Obviously, being able to read all these characters does not mean that you will understand them – in fact, the language barrier will be the single most important factor preventing further data integration in the future. Native English speakers, though they are in a relatively privileged position in this respect, will still have to master at least one foreign language if they want to work with original data from any country of continental Europe, Asia, Africa, or Central and South America. In the same fashion, the increased availability of tools and data from around the globe may not be put to good use unless students acquire a high level of specialist knowledge in the technologies involved in data integration. Academic and professional training will have to adapt to these changing needs.

REFERENCES

*Recommended for further reading

Bewley, R., Donaghue, D., Gaffney, V., Van Leusen, M. and Wise, A. (1999). *Archiving Aerial Photography and Remote Sensing Data*. Arts and Humanities Data Service: York.

Bosak, J. and Bray, T. (1999). XML and the second-generation. *Scientific American*, **280**(5):89–93. (http://www.sciam.com/1999/0599issue/0599bosak.html).

*Burrough, P.A. and MacDonnell, R.A. (1998). *Principles of Geographical Information Systems*. Oxford University Press: Oxford.

Dingwall, L., Exon, S., Gaffney, V., Laflin, S. and Van Leusen, M. (1999). *Archaeology in the Age of the Internet, Computer Applications and Quantitative Methods in Archaeology 1997*. BAR International Series 750, Oxbow: Oxford.

Fiennes, R. (1993). *Atlantis of the Sands: the Search for the Lost City of Ubar*. Signet: London.

Fisher, J. and Fisher, B. (1999). The use of KidSat images in the further pursuit of the frankincense roads to Ubar. *IEEE Transactions on Geoscience and Remote Sensing*, **37**:1841–1847.

Gaffney, C., Gater, J., Linford, P., Gaffney, V. and White, R. (2000). Large scale systematic fluxgate gradiometry at the Roman city of Wroxeter. *Archaeological Prospection*, **7**:81–99.

Gaffney, V.L. and Van Leusen, P.M. (1996). Extending GIS methods for regional archaeology: the Wroxeter Hinterland Project. In Kamermans, H. and Fennema, K. (eds) *Interfacing the Past. Computer Applications and Quantitative Methods in Archaeology 1995*, 297–305. Analecta Praehistorica Leidensia 28, Leiden University Press: Leiden.

Gillings, M. and Wise, A. (1999). *GIS Guide to Good Practice*. Arts and Humanities Data Service: York.

*Hinton, J.C. (1996). GIS and remote sensing integration for environmental applications. *International Journal of Geographical Information Systems*, **10**:877–890.

Lyall, J. and Powlesland, D. (1996). The application of high resolution fluxgate gradiometery as an aid to excavation planning and strategy formulation. *Internet Archaeology* 1 (http://intarch.ac.uk/journal/issue1/lyall_index.html).

Ryan, N., Pascoe, J. and Morse, D. (1999). Enhanced reality fieldwork: the context aware archaeological assistant. In Dingwall, L., Exon, S., Gaffney, V., Laflin, S. and Van Leusen, M. (eds) *Archaeology in the Age of the Internet, Computer Applications and Quantitative Methods in Archaeology 1997*, 269–274. BAR International Series 750, Oxbow: Oxford.

*Tomlin, C.D. (1990). *Geographic Information Systems and Cartographic Modeling*. Prentice Hall: Englewood Cliffs, NJ.

Van Leusen, P.M. (1999). The Viroconium Cornoviorum atlas. *European Journal of Archaeology*, **2**:313–325.

Wilson, D.M. (1984). The plan of Viroconium Cornoviorum. *Antiquity*, **58**:117–120.

SECTION 8

Burial, Decay and Archaeological Conservation

Overview—Degradation, Investigation and Preservation of Archaeological Evidence

C. CAPLE

Department of Archaeology, University of Durham.

The museums of the present are filled with stone and bronze axe heads, mineralized metal tools, cracked pots and glass fragments. This does not accurately define our past, but reflects what has survived burial for hundreds or thousands of years, and has been recognized as an antiquity and recovered by archaeologists. This surviving evidence led early antiquarians such as C.J. Thompson to classify prehistory into the ages of stone, bronze and iron. This is a misleading categorization by which the prehistoric past is still known. In reality, the vast majority of the objects of the past were made of wood, textile, skin and other organic materials. The only opportunity we have to gain a more 'holistic' glimpse of the past is when we find remains in the frozen, desiccated or waterlogged anoxic conditions which preserve organic and other materials. Examples such as Ötze the ice man (Spindler 1995), Tutankhamen's tomb (Carter and Mace 1922–33) and the Glastonbury Lake Villages (Bulleid and Gray 1911) demonstrate the rich complexity and diversity of the material culture of the past.

DEGRADATION

That some objects survive well in some soil layers but not in others was noted by nineteenth century archae-

ologists such as Augustus Henry Lane Fox (Thompson 1977). Over the succeeding years archaeologists, using field observations, traditional knowledge about the nature of decay e.g., from food preservation, and information from soil scientists, have explained the differences in survival of archaeological artifacts in terms of soil pH and the activity of soil microbes. The first substantial scientific experiments to provide accurate data to confirm these observations did not occur until the construction of the experimental earthworks at Overton Down, established in 1960 (Jewell and Dimbleby 1966), and Mordon Bog, Wareham, established in 1963 (Evans and Limbrey 1974). These experimental earthworks placed a variety of materials used in antiquity in and under an earthen bank. The materials were then recovered by excavation at intervals of 2, 4, 8, 16 and 32 years. The recovery after 64 years has yet to occur. This experiment was intended to reveal information on the speed and nature of the degradation processes of archaeological materials and thus indicate what materials the archaeologist might expect to survive and what were the crucial factors in the survival of such material. The quality of the subsequent recovery excavations, the lack of scientific measurement of factors such as the quality of the groundwater or the soil microbe populations at the start of the experiment and the lack of replicates has meant that there have been

Handbook of Archaeological Sciences. Edited by D.R. Brothwell and A.M. Pollard.

limitations on the information which has come from these experiments (Bell *et al.* 1996). Though the importance of the burial environment on the survival of archaeological materials and thus the interpretation of archaeological deposits was noted in 1969 (Biek 1969), there has been little systematic research into the burial environment, its effects on the archaeological materials buried within it and consequently on our understanding of the past.

The interaction between the burial environment and archaeological evidence (*diagenesis*) is initially observed at the interface between the object and its environment. Since the vast majority of the information about the formation and use of the object is present at its surface (Caple 2000), as well as the true visual form of the object, there is a substantial loss of information in the initial period of degradation. As the interaction continues, the decay zone increases in thickness, only stopping when the archaeological material has been completely transformed into minerals which are stable within the burial environment and equilibrium is reached. It is essential to accurately characterize the interaction between the object and its burial environment in order to understand the loss of information which has occurred at this interface. As a result of degradation the object's original surface can be the fragile exposed outer layer of a decayed zone, as in the case of glass (see Chapter 49) or the original surface can be buried deep within layers of corrosion, only capable of being detected by X-radiography and revealed through careful physical cleaning, as in the case of iron (Cronyn 1990). The depth and complexity of the interaction zone are shown in a cross section through the corrosion layers of a copper alloy object and the differential distribution of selected elements (Figure S8.1).

INVESTIGATION

Modelling

Using the basic principles of chemistry, physics, mineralogy and materials science, mathematical models are formed of how one material reacts with another. Through comparing factors such as mineral solubilities, standard electrode potentials and diffusion models, a picture of the interaction of pure materials in a purely chemical world can be established. This approach is exemplified in Chapter 47, describing the nature of the soil environment, and Chapter 48 describing the basis of metal corrosion. As greater realism is sought in these studies greater complexity emerges, making such modelling increasingly reliant upon computers (Pollard 1998).

Models or hypotheses have been widely used in archaeological science in order to relate elemental and molecular composition with information about ancient diet, provenance, ancient technologies or even the date of artifacts. Simple models were initially created to describe the natural environment, such as that originally envisaging constant levels of ^{14}C production or of incorporation of Sr into bone purely through the diet (see Chapters 51 and 23). These models are subsequently modified as the complexity of the natural world has begun to be appreciated and in particular as the diagenetic influence of the burial environment upon archaeological materials has been documented.

Measurement

This involves the description of the burial environment and archaeological materials in chemical, physical and biological terms and their interpretation in terms of the archaeology of the site, landscape geography, hydrology and ancient technology as well as the principles of chemistry, biology and physics. This usually establishes an accurate, though broad brush, picture of what is present and indicates the level of the complexity and natural variability of such environments and materials. A holistic example of this type of research has recently been undertaken in Sweden where the systematic mapping of corroded copper alloy artifacts and their correlation to the underlying geology, soil conditions and human activities has provided the first coherent picture of the extent to which soil conditions and anthropogenic activities affect the survival of archaeological artifacts in the ground (Fjaestad *et al.* 1996). In general there has been little accurate measurement or characterization of archaeological burial environments. Recent work in the UK on this subject has focused on relating the preservation of archaeological organic materials to the presence of the water table (Corfield 1994) and the definition of the chemistry of the burial environment in terms of oxidizing/reducing potential (Eh) and pH (Caple *et al.* 1997; Figure 47.02). This permits us to define the minerals which could form and would be stable in such an environment and thus the likelihood of corrosion of specific metals or the likelihood of organisms to survive and thus organic materials to decay.

There is a long history of analysing the degraded zones of archaeological material, from nineteenth century investigation of weathered glass (Fowler 1880) to

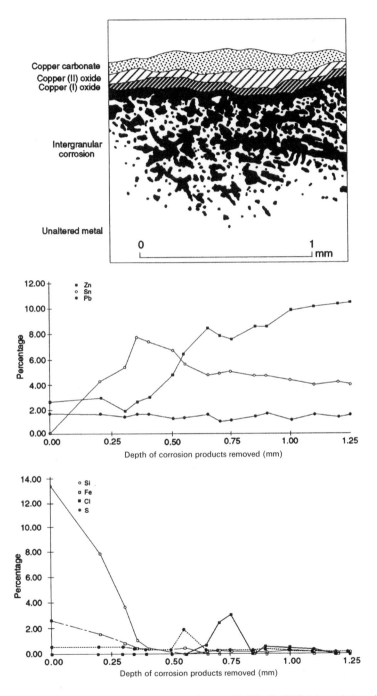

Figure S8.1   Copper corrosion: the principal layers, copper carbonate (CuCO₃.Cu(OH)₂) (green), tenorite (CuO) (black) and cuprite (Cu₂O) (red), are visible as layers. Note the deep penetration of corrosion into the object; any elemental analysis of the surface, even if corrosion is removed, will not accurately represent the composition of the metal. The elemental composition through the corrosion layers reveals that the competing decay mechanisms and mineral solubilities of the copper, zinc, tin and lead have resulted in a very inhomogeneous distribution of the elements within the crust. It also indicates the incorporation of elements such as iron, silica, sulfur and chlorine from the soil into the corrosion zone (Dungworth 1995).

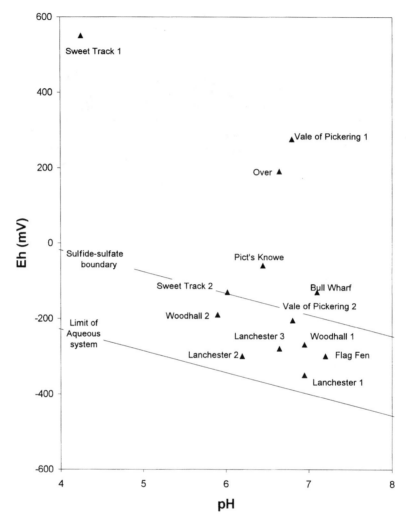

Figure S8.2   An Eh/pH diagram indicating the chemical conditions of a number of waterlogged archaeological sites in the UK, from which organic remains have been recovered (Caple *et al.* 1997). Sites such as Lanchester, Woodhall, Flag Fen, and the lower levels of the Sweet Track and the Vale of Pickering have good preservation, Picts Knowe and Bull Wharf have intermediate levels of preservations, whilst Over and the upper levels of the Sweet Track and the Vale of Pickering have poor preservation. The correlation of good organic preservation with highly reducing conditions is clearly confirmed.

modern analysis of degraded wood (Grattan and Mathias 1986, Rowell and Barbour 1990) and metals (Graedel and Franey 1990, Selwyn *et al.* 1999). The lack of data to correlate these decay products with the chemistry and biology of the environments which produce them continues to limit the wider applicability of measurement research for modelling purposes though it provides essential information to conservators seeking to preserve this type of decayed material as shown in Chapters 50 and 52.

These two methodologies constructively interact with each other and are both struggling to cope with:

(i)   the level of complexity of the burial environment,

(ii)   the fact that burial environments change with time, and thus what is measured now is not necessarily applicable to 100, 1000 or 10 000 years ago, and

(iii)   the problems of surface chemistry and biological organisms, which add levels of variability to the chemical and physical systems where research has initially been concentrated.

As Chapter 52 shows, even when working in the relatively stable environments of museums, attempts to model and thus predict the stability of relatively pure polymers used for conservation work, using the Arrhenius equation to extrapolate from short term high temperature information to the long term low temperature conditions which are of interest has proved difficult to achieve (Bilz and Grattan 1996).

EVIDENCE

Objects of all forms, including ecofacts such as bones, contain information on their construction and use. Elemental compositions are related to the raw materials from which the object was created, the microstructure can reflect the method of formation whilst the surface often bears the marks and imprints from tools used in the object's formation as well as scratches and wear from use. In this sense any and every object is a *historic document*; the myriad of facts it contains merely has to be read or investigated using appropriate analytical techniques in order to reveal the truth about the object's past, its construction, use or discard (Pollard and Heron 1996, Caple 2000).

The property of an object as a historic document is exemplified by the scant remaining traces of dyes present in the earth-coloured fragments of textile recovered from waterlogged sites such as Coppergate in York and the High Street excavations in Dublin. The extraction of the dyes through treating sample threads with solvents and then analysing the extract using UV/ visible spectrophotometry has revealed a range of dyes: madder/bedstraw (red), lichen (purple), woad (blue), and a yellow of unknown origin, used to colour the fabrics of the eighth to eleventh century Anglo-Scandinavian population of NW Europe. These data have shown the preference of the inhabitants of Dublin for purple coloured garments, whilst those of York and the Saxons of London preferred red. Those textile fragments recovered from Scandinavian graves indicate a marked preference for blue coloured garments (Walton 1989).

Objects were not, however, created to provide information on their origin, method of manufacture, use or discard. They were created to perform a function within society and through their form, colour and decoration reflect the aesthetic values and beliefs of that society (Hodder 1994, Pearce 1994, Caple 2000). As such these objects can be regarded as *aesthetic entities* which impinge on the senses of any viewer and evoke (as they were intended to) a response. It is, therefore, important to reveal the holistic form of the object in order to aesthetically appreciate the object and how the society which created it wanted to see and represent itself.

The power and aesthetic expression of the whole is conveyed by an object such as the Sutton Hoo helmet, which was originally recovered as hundreds of small corroded iron fragments from the degraded remains of a ship burial within Mound X at Sutton Hoo in East Anglia in 1939. The burial was probably that of King Readwald who died around AD 625. Meaningless in its fragments, the mineralized pieces of helmet were carefully cleaned and assembled into the form of the original helmet. This initial restoration of 1946 was subsequently seen to have many practical faults and the helmet was consequently re-restored in 1968 when a much more accurate restoration was achieved. This revealed that the Sutton Hoo helmet was originally a burnished steel helm having a face mask with stylized features, earflaps and neck guard to protect the wearer, with the whole helmet covered in decorative bronze plaques of interlace design, with fighting and dancing figures. This object has provided the primary image of an Anglo-Saxon warrior king of the seventh century from the first reconstruction in 1946 to the present day and is one of the main ways in which we picture and thus understand the Anglo-Saxons (Williams 1992).

PRESERVATION

Buried objects interact with their surroundings and change chemically and physically as they seek to come to equilibrium with their burial environment (Chapter 52). When excavated they seek to come to terms with the new dry oxygen rich environment of the museum. The chemical and physical changes they undergo during burial and after recovery we describe as decay or corrosion. If waterlogged organic materials are uncovered by excavation they may desiccate and shrivel, if metals they may actively corrode, if frozen or desiccated organic materials they may thaw or re-hydrate and subsequently be attacked by insects or fungi. Thus there is a need to preserve such objects and mitigate the forces of decay so that the object remains valuable, both as an aesthetic entity, a whole object, and as a source of information about the past – a historic document. The task of preservation is primarily undertaken by conservators: 'the activity of the conservator (restorer) consists of technical examination, preservation and conservation/restoration of cultural property' (ICOM-CC 1984).

The need for specialized skills and expertise to preserve an object which if untreated would have crumbled to dust is demonstrated by the body of a man, recovered from the peat deposits of Lindow Moss in Cheshire in 1984. After radiocarbon dating an autopsy and full scientific investigation revealed that this was an individual who lived in the first century AD and who had been deliberately killed by being strangled, hit on the head with an axe and then had his jugular vein cut. This is almost certainly a deliberate sacrifice similar to many other 'bog bodies' found in wetlands over much of NW Europe c. 800 BC–AD 200. Analysis has provided considerable evidence about his diet, death and lifestyle (Stead et al. 1986). The tissues of the body, especially the skin and hair, were physically well preserved though chemically degraded and fully waterlogged. If allowed to dry these tissues would have shrunk, desiccated and eventually turned to dust. To preserve both the physical form of the body and the evidence it contains it was preserved through soaking in a carefully calculated concentration of a specific molecular weight polymer, polyethylene glycol (PEG), then frozen and freeze dried. This both replaced some of the water in the degraded proteins of the skin and hair so avoiding shrinkage, and removed the remaining water avoiding evaporation from the liquid state which collapses soft waterlogged organic materials. The body preserved in this way has retained its original texture and shape and has become one of the most popular exhibits in the British Museum (Stead et al. 1986, Omar et al. 1989).

We understand the past through the events which occurred there (history) and the physical remains, material culture, which has come down to us from that past (archaeology). Through these mediums we create a picture and understanding of the past. Into this image we place the additional information revealed by archaeological science to provide a more accurate, detailed or corrected view of the past. The fact that archaeology is still primarily a discipline which uses information on the physical form of artifacts for typologies for dating and cultural definition is often unstated. Thus, although the information which can be obtained from DNA analysis is crucially important in determining the origins of mankind, only a few tens of bones of the many tens or hundreds of millions of bones recovered from archaeological excavations will be analysed in this way. All the rest are, however, examined to determine the species, size, sex and age of the animal from which they derive. Archaeological conservation has principally developed techniques to preserve this physical form information, and is still developing and refining its techniques in order to preserve DNA and other molecular level information potentially contained within the bone. This means balancing the requirements of objects as both aesthetic entities and historic objects. Samples and other material of the past which are not objects have no requirement to have their physical form preserved, and can, therefore, be preserved, frozen, or desiccated as a small volume sample so that the historic evidence is preserved for future study.

REFERENCES

Bell, M., Fowler, P.J. and Hillson, S.W. (1996). *The Experimental Earthwork Project 1960–1992*. Council for British Archaeology: York.

Biek, L., (1969). Soil silhouettes. In Brothwell, D. and Higgs, E. (eds) *Science in Archaeology*, (2nd edn) 118–123. Thames and Hudson: London.

Bilz, M. and Grattan, D.W. (1996). The ageing of parylene: difficulties with the Arrhenius approach. In Bridgland, J. (ed.) *ICOM-CC 11th Meeting, Edinburgh*, 925–929. James and James: London.

Bulleid, A. and Gray, H. St G. (1911, 1917). *The Glastonbury Lake Village Vols. 1 and 2*. Antiquarian Society: Glastonbury.

Caple, C. (2000). *Conservation Skills: Judgement, Method and Decision Making*. Routledge: London.

Caple, C., Dungworth, D. and Clogg, P. (1997). The assessment and protection of archaeological organic materials in waterlogged burial environments. In Hoffmann, P., Grant, T., Spriggs, J.A. and Daley, T. (eds) *Proceedings of the 6th Waterlogged Organic Archaeological Materials Conference*, 57–72. ICOM-CC: Bremerhaven.

Carter, H. and Mace, A.C. (1922–33). *The Tomb of Tut-ankh Amen Discovered by the late Earl of Caernarvon and Howard Carter, Vols. 1–3*. Cassell: London.

Corfield, M. (1994). Monitoring the condition of wet archaeological sites. In Hoffmann, P., Daley, T. and Grant, T. (eds) *Proceedings of the 5th Waterlogged Organic Archaeological Materials Conference*, 423–436. ICOM: Bremerhaven.

Cronyn, J.M. (1990). *The Elements of Archaeological Conservation*. Routledge: London.

Dungworth, D. (1995). *Iron Age and Roman Copper Alloys from Northern Britain*. Unpublished PhD Thesis, University of Durham.

Evans, J.G. and Limbrey, S. (1974). The experimental earthwork on Morden Bog, Wareham, Dorset: 1963–1972. *Proceedings of the Prehistoric Society*, **40**:170–202.

Fjaestad, M., Nord, A.G., Tronner, K., Ullen, I. and Lagerlof, A. (1996). Environmental threats to archaeological artefacts. In Bridgland, J. (ed.) *ICOM-CC 11th Meeting, Edinburgh*, 870–875. James and James: London.

Fowler, J. (1880). On the processes of decay and, incidentally, on the composition and texture of glass at different periods, and the history of its manufacture. *Archaeologia*, **46**:65–162.

Graedel, T.E. and Franey, J.P. (1990). Formation and characteristics of the Statue of Liberty patina. In Baboian, R., Cliver, E.B. and Bellante, E.L. (eds) *The Statue of Liberty Restoration*, 101–110. National Association of Corrosion Engineers: Texas.

Grattan, D.W. and Mathias, C. (1986). Analysis of waterlogged wood: the value of chemical analysis and other simple methods in evaluating condition. *Somerset Levels Papers*, **12**:6–12.

Hodder, I. (1994). The contextual analysis of symbolic meanings. In Pearce, S.M. (ed.) *Interpreting Objects and Collections*. Routledge: London.

ICOM-CC (1984). *The Conservator-Restorer: A Definition of the Profession*. International Council of Museums Conservation Committee: Copenhagen.

Jewell, P.A. and Dimbleby, G.W. (1966). The experimental earthwork on Overton Down, Wiltshire, England: the first four years. *Proceedings of the Prehistoric Society*, **32**:313–342.

Omar, S., McCord, M. and Daniels, V. (1989). The conservation of Bog Bodies by freeze-drying. *Studies in Conservation*, **34**:101–109.

Pearce, S.M. (ed.) (1994). *Interpreting Objects and Collections*. Routledge: London.

Pollard, A.M. (1998). The chemical nature of the burial environment. In Corfield, M., Hinton, P., Nixon, T. and Pollard, A.M. (eds) *Preserving Archaeological Remains In Situ*, 60–65. Museum of London Archaeological Service: London.

Pollard, A.M. and Heron, C. (1996). *Archaeological Chemistry*. Royal Society of Chemistry: Cambridge.

Rowell, R.M. and Barbour, R.J. (eds) (1990). *Archaeological Wood, Properties, Chemistry and Preservation*. Advances in Chemistry Series 225, American Chemical Society: Washington DC.

Selwyn, L.S., Sirois, P.J. and Argyropoulos, V. (1999). The corrosion of excavated archaeological iron with details on weeping and akaganeite. *Studies in Conservation*, **44**:217–232.

Spindler, K. (1995). *The Man in the Ice*. Phoenix: London.

Stead, I.M., Bourke, J.B. and Brothwell, D. (1986). *Lindow Man. The Body in the Bog*. British Museum Press: London.

Thompson, M.W. (1977). *General Pitt Rivers*. Moonraker Press: Bradford on Avon.

Walton, P. (1989). Dyes of the Viking Age: a summary of recent work. *Dyes in History and Archaeology*, **7**:14–20.

Williams, N. (1992). The Sutton Hoo helmet. In Oddy, W.A. (ed.) *The Art of the Conservator*. British Museum Press: London.

47

Defining the Burial Environment

R. RAISWELL

Department of Earth Sciences, University of Leeds.

Burial environments can be spatially and temporally variable; artifacts may spend time exposed to the atmosphere and surface weathering processes, may be buried in soils which can be dry, intermittently or permanently water-saturated, and may be deposited on to (and buried within) lake, estuarine or marine sediments. This diversity significantly affects both the nature and extent of degradation processes.

Degradation processes arise because artifacts are unstable in contact with air or water, or both. Such lack of stability does not necessarily lead to rapid reaction, and in fact nature is adept at building complex organic materials (e.g., hair, bark) which are designed to resist the effects of decay, although being unstable from an energetic viewpoint. This apparent contradiction arises because stability is defined thermodynamically by the energy difference between artifact composition and the equilibrium state (where there is no tendency for any net chemical change; see below). Materials may however remain far from equilibrium for very long periods; a large energy difference indicates a considerable driving force for chemical reaction but the rate of the reaction by which equilibrium is approached may still be exceedingly slow. For example, most metals are far from equilibrium under normal conditions, and their approach to equilibrium requires conversion to metal oxides. Clearly, however, metal objects can survive for prolonged periods before being completely oxidized. Thus the key factor in degradation is not so much thermodynamic stability as the rates of reaction. In general thermodynamics predict what *should* happen whereas the study of reaction rates predicts what *actually* does happen over a given period of time.

The study of reaction rates or kinetics forms the basis of many commonly used dating techniques in archaeology, e.g., obsidian hydration (Chapter 7) and isotope dating (Chapter 2) through quantifying the mechanisms by which reactions occur. However reaction mechanisms are often complex and poorly understood, so that precise mathematical description of reaction rates is difficult. By contrast the thermodynamic treatment of chemical reactions is relatively well-understood, and is more suitable for a preliminary treatment of environmental systems. This approach is mainly adopted here, and further details can be found in many geochemical textbooks with simple (Raiswell *et al.* 1980) to more advanced treatments (Drever 1997, Langmuir 1997).

Most degradation reactions in the burial environment involve reactions between solids and either gases or water, or both. A thermodynamic treatment of these reactions first requires an accurate description of all the solid, gaseous and dissolved species involved.

Handbook of Archaeological Sciences. Edited by D.R. Brothwell and A.M. Pollard.

GASES

The concentrations of gases are usually described in terms of partial pressures, which are defined as that fraction of the total pressure which is exerted by the gas in question. Gas mixtures are assumed to be *ideal*, which implies that each gas behaves independently of all the others. Dry air at 25°C and 1 atmosphere pressure (= 1 bar) contains a partial pressure of nitrogen of 0.78, oxygen 0.21 and carbon dioxide 0.00033 (usually written as $pCO_2 = 10^{-3.3}$ bar). Many soil systems contain levels of CO_2 of more than 10^{-2} bar because the microbial breakdown of organic matter is able to produce CO_2 faster than it can be lost from the soil by diffusion to the atmosphere.

The solubilities of gases are described by Henry's Law, which states that the solubility at a given temperature is proportional to the partial pressure. Thus:

$$\text{Solubility} = K_H \times p \qquad (1)$$

where K_H is the Henry's Law constant, values of which can be found in geochemical texts (e.g., Langmuir 1997). At 25°C K_H for CO_2 is 3.39×10^{-2} moles bar^{-1}, so the solubility of atmospheric CO_2 in pure water is:

$$\text{Solubility} = 3.39 \times 10^{-2} \times 0.00033$$
$$= 1.1 \times 10^{-5} \text{ moles litre}^{-1}.$$

Similarly the solubility of oxygen ($K_H = 1.26 \times 10^{-3}$ at 25°C) is 2.7×10^{-4} moles litre^{-1}.

WATER AND SOLUTES

Pure water is rarely found in natural systems, and generally dissolved species are present. The presence of solutes introduces a significant degree of complexity into the thermodynamic treatment of reactions in solution. Above we assumed that mixtures of gases behaved ideally (i.e., different gases exert no influence on each other). This is also a reasonable assumption for uncharged species in solution, but it is clearly unlikely for dissolved ions. In fact the electrostatic repulsions experienced by similarly-charged ions, and the attractions between oppositely charged species, are sufficiently strong to prevent a proportion of ions from exhibiting their true chemical behaviour. These interactions become stronger in more concentrated solutions where ions are forced into close proximity. Thus a solution of NaCl can be envisaged as containing oppositely charged Na^+ and Cl^- ions some of which are electrostatically attracted to each other sufficiently strongly to prevent them behaving independently, and thus participating in chemical reactions. Chemical behaviour is controlled by the active ions only, and thermodynamic expressions are therefore written in terms of the concentrations of active ions (or *activities*) rather than total concentrations. Unfortunately most analytical methods measure only total concentrations and not activities, and the latter are derived from the former by defining:

$$\text{Activity} = \gamma \times \text{Concentration} \qquad (2)$$

where γ is an activity coefficient representing the proportion of active ions. Activity coefficients can be calculated by summing all the possible electrostatic interactions between different species in solution, and simple approaches for this can be found in Drever (1997) and Langmuir (1997). For the present purposes we will assume that solutions are sufficiently dilute that activity and concentration are equal, but this is actually a poor approximation even in dilute freshwaters. Activities, like concentrations, can be expressed in molarities (moles litre^{-1}) in most near-surface dilute solutions.

EQUILIBRIUM

The concept of equilibrium can be illustrated by reference to the dissolution of calcium sulfate, $CaSO_4$, in water:

$$CaSO_4 \rightarrow Ca^{2+} + SO_4^{2-}$$

The addition of solid $CaSO_4$ to water causes the left to right, or forward reaction, to occur as $CaSO_4$ dissolves. Provided sufficient $CaSO_4$ is present, the dissolution reaction will proceed until no further $CaSO_4$ dissolves and the solution is saturated. This is the equilibrium point for this reaction, where undissolved $CaSO_4$ is in contact with a solution of Ca^{2+} and SO_4^{2-} ions. Although there is no further overall dissolution, all equilibria are dynamic and forward and backward reactions both occur (albeit at identical rates).

The behaviour of solutes at equilibrium is governed by the Law of Mass Action. Consider a chemical reaction between a moles of A and b moles of B to form c moles of C and d moles of D:

$$aA + bB \rightarrow cC + dD$$

Initially, with A and B only present, reaction is rapid but as A and B are consumed the reactions slows down. The rate of the forward reaction can be expressed as:

$$\text{Rate} = k_1[A]^a \times [B]^b \qquad (3)$$

and the rate of the back reaction is:

$$\text{Rate} = k_2[C]^c \times [D]^d$$

where k_1 and k_2 are rate constants.

Equilibrium occurs when the rates of the forward and backward reaction are equal, and thus:

$$k_1/k_2 = [C]^c \times [D]^d/[A]^a \times [B]^b = K \qquad (4)$$

where K is the *equilibrium constant* and square brackets are used to indicate activities. The equilibrium constant has a finite value which reflects the existence of a fixed ratio of the activities of the products to that of the reactants. For the dissolution of $CaSO_4$:

$$K = [Ca^{2+}][SO_4^{2-}]/[CaSO_4] = 10^{-4.5}$$

However the activity of pure solids is regarded as unity because the equilibrium position is not affected by the amount of undissolved $CaSO_4$. Thus:

$$K_{sp} = [Ca^{2+}][SO_4^{2-}] = 10^{-4.5} \qquad (5)$$

The value of K for a dissolution reaction is known as the *solubility product* (K_{sp}) and Table 47.1 lists values for some common minerals. Suppose that a solution of $MgSO_4$ is added to the saturated solution of $CaSO_4$. The addition of $MgSO_4$ causes $CaSO_4$ to precipitate because the activity of sulfate in (5) must include the

sulfate ions from both sources. The resulting increase in $[SO_4^{2-}]$ causes the solubility product of $CaSO_4$ to be exceeded and thus $CaSO_4$ precipitates. The sulfate ion is common to both $CaSO_4$ and $MgSO_4$ and hence precipitation by this mechanism is termed the *common ion effect*. This example demonstrates two important features of equilibrium expressions. Firstly, the ion activities in an equilibrium expression refer to the total activities of that ion whatever their source. Secondly, reactions at equilibrium are reversible. The addition of more sulfate causes the backward reaction to occur until the product of $[Ca^{2+}]$ and $[SO_4^{2-}]$ again reaches the solubility product (note that the solution will now contain more $[Ca^{2+}]$ than $[SO_4^{2-}]$).

The solubility product expression can be used to derive an important parameter termed the *Saturation Index*. The solubility product represents the activity values for the component ions which are in equilibrium with the solid phase, where there is no tendency for the solution to precipitate or dissolve. However solutions can be undersaturated, where the product of the ion activities is less than the solubility product (for example where the solutions have not had an opportunity to dissolve sufficient $CaSO_4$). Equally solutions may also be over-saturated where the product of the ion activities exceeds the solubility product, but precipitation has not yet had time to occur. These situations can be recognized by defining a Saturation Index (SI):

$$SI = \log_{10}([Ca^{2+}][SO_4^{2-}]/K_{sp}) \qquad (6)$$

In effect SI measures the extent to which a solution deviates from equilibrium with respect to $CaSO_4$. Positive values of SI indicate that a solution is over-saturated and has the potential to precipitate $CaSO_4$, whereas negative SI values indicate undersaturation and the potential to dissolve $CaSO_4$. Values of SI = 0 indicate equilibrium with $CaSO_4$. SI values are extremely important because they show whether a solution is likely to dissolve or precipitate a given mineral.

All equilibrium constants have a finite value, hence there must always be some reactants present, thus the concentrations of [A] and [B] in equation (4) cannot be zero at equilibrium. So how is it that some reactions appear to go to completion, with little or no reactant left? This situation usually arises where one of the reactants is consumed before equilibrium can be reached. Consider the environmentally important reaction of the dissolution of limestone in acid:

$$CaCO_3 + 2H^+ \rightarrow Ca^{2+} + CO_2 + 2H_2O$$

Table 47.1 Solubility products for some common minerals.

Calcite	$CaCO_3$	-8.4
Siderite	$FeCO_3$	-10.7
Magnesite	$MgCO_3$	-7.5
Strontianite	$SrCO_3$	-9.0
Dolomite	$CaMg(CO_3)_2$	-17.9
Gypsum	$CaSO_4.2H_2O$	-4.6
Barite	$BaSO_4$	-10.0
Anglesite	$PbSO_4$	-7.8
Celestite	$SrSO_4$	-6.5
Pyrite	FeS_2	-42.5
Galena	PbS	-17.5
Sphalerite	ZnS	-24.7
Apatite	$Ca_3(PO_4)_2$	-25.5

Values form Faure (1998) expressed as logarithms to the base 10 at 25°C.

which has an equilibrium constant:

$$K = [Ca^{2+}]pCO_2/[H^+]^2 = 10^{-9.9} \qquad (7)$$

However the CO_2 escapes to the atmosphere (which is fixed at $pCO_2 = 10^{-3.3}$; see above), to which it makes a negligible additional contribution, so equation (7) simplifies to:

$$[Ca^{2+}]/[H^+]^2 = 10^{-13.2}$$

Thus any acidic solution with $[H^+] < 10^{-7}$ (i.e., with a pH of less than 7; see below) requires large concentrations of Ca^{2+} ($>10^{0.8}$ or approximately 6.3 moles litre^{-1}) to attain equilibrium. Carrying out the reaction in a closed vessel would allow the CO_2 to accumulate to above atmospheric levels, and equilibrium could then be reached such that $CaCO_3$ would remain in contact with strong acid without reaction.

HYDROGEN ION AND pH

The dissolution of limestone by acid first requires that the acid dissociates to release H^+ which is consumed. The activity of H^+ is a useful parameter because it reflects the progress of this reaction and many others of environmental significance. The conventional measurement of H^+ by electrodes does in fact measure hydrogen ion activity, and is usually reported on a logarithmic scale:

$$pH = -\log_{10}[H^+]$$

A pH of 7 indicates $[H^+] = 10^{-7}$ moles litre^{-1} and pH values < 7 are characteristic of acid solutions, whereas alkaline solutions have pH > 7. This distinction arises because water dissociates such that:

$$H_2O = H^+ + OH^-$$

and the Law of Mass Action for this equation is:

$$K = [H^+][OH^-] = 10^{-14} \text{ moles}^2 \text{ litres}^{-2}$$

Pure water has $[H^+] = [OH^-] = 10^{-7}$ and acid solutions with $[H^+] > 10^{-7}$ are so defined because there is an excess of $[H^+]$ over $[OH^-]$. Burial environments can vary widely in their pH. Extremely acidic conditions (pH < 2) may be encountered where sulfuric acid is generated by pyrite oxidation, and also in marshes and waterlogged soils (pH 3–6). Marine environments are alkaline (seawater pH ~ 8), as also are saline soils (pH 10–12).

OXIDATION AND REDUCTION

In addition to pH, natural environments can also vary widely in their *oxidizing* capacity (defined as their ability to accept electrons) and *reducing* capacity (ability to donate electrons). The tendency of elements to be oxidized or reduced can be quantified through their *Standard Electrode Potentials* (E^o) expressed in volts. Table 47.2 shows the E^o values for some common species. There are unfortunately several different conventions and that adopted here is the IUPAC (International Union of Pure and Applied Chemistry) convention, where oxidation-reduction (or *redox*) reactions are written with the oxidized species accepting electrons on the left, and with reaction producing the reduced form. Other conventions write these equations the other way round – in this case, the numerical values are the same, but the sign differs. These reactions, which contain electrons, are known as *half-reactions* because a complete redox reaction must contain one reaction which generates electrons, and another reaction which exactly consumes all the electrons (free electrons cannot survive and each oxidation must be accompanied by a reduction). Species high in Table 47.2 are readily oxidized, and are stronger oxidizing reagents than species lower in Table 47.2, and are therefore able to reduce these species by compelling them to accept electrons.

Table 47.2 Standard Electrode Potentials.

Reaction	Electrode Potential (volts)
$Li^+ + e^- \rightarrow Li(s)$	−3.04
$K^+ + e^- \rightarrow K(s)$	−2.92
$Ca^{2+} + 2e^- \rightarrow Ca(s)$	−2.87
$Na^+ + e^- \rightarrow Na(s)$	−2.71
$Mg^{2+} + 2e^- \rightarrow Mg(s)$	−2.36
$Mn^{2+} + 2e^- \rightarrow Mn(s)$	−1.18
$Zn^{2+} + 2e^- \rightarrow Zn(s)$	−0.76
$Cr^{3+} + 3e^- \rightarrow Cr(s)$	−0.74
$Fe^{2+} + 2e^- \rightarrow Fe(s)$	−0.41
$Co^{2+} + 2e^- \rightarrow Co(s)$	−0.28
$Ni^{2+} + 2e^- \rightarrow Ni(s)$	−0.23
$Sn^{2+} + 2e^- \rightarrow Sn(s)$	−0.14
$Pb^{2+} + 2e^- \rightarrow Pb(s)$	−0.13
$Fe^{3+} + 3e^- \rightarrow Fe(s)$	−0.02
$H^+ + e^- \rightarrow 1/2H_2(g)$	0.00
$Cu^{2+} + 2e^- \rightarrow Cu(s)$	+0.35
$Cu^+ + e^- \rightarrow Cu(s)$	+0.52
$Ag^+ + e^- \rightarrow Ag(s)$	+0.80
$O_2 + 4H^+ + 4e^- \rightarrow 2H_2O$	+1.23

All dissolved species except where brackets indicate s = solid, g = gas.

The E^o values refer to the voltages generated when that species is used in an electromotive cell with a hydrogen electrode (constructed by bubbling hydrogen over an inert platinum plate). This reaction:

$$2H^+ + 2e^- \rightarrow H_2$$

is arbitrarily given a potential of 0.0 volts at 25°C and 1 bar for a solution which has unit activity of H^+.

Consider an electrical cell made by inserting a Zn metal plate into a 1 mole litre^{-1} solution of $ZnSO_4$, and a Cu electrode into a 1 mole litre^{-1} solution of $CuSO_4$ (Figure 47.1). The two electrodes are connected by a wire (which allows the transfer of electrons) passing through a voltmeter, and the two electrode vessels are connected by a salt bridge (which allows the transfer of anions). Once connected it is observed that Cu metal is deposited on the Cu electrode whereas Zn dissolves and enters the solution. Clearly Cu is reduced from the solution and Zn is oxidized, dissolving into the solution. These observations can be confirmed by considering the E^o values from Table 47.2:

$$Zn^{2+} + 2e^- \rightarrow Zn \quad E^o = -0.76 \text{ volts}$$

$$Cu^{2+} + 2e^- \rightarrow Cu \quad E^o = +0.35 \text{ volts}$$

To ascertain how this electrical cell behaves, one half-reaction must be reversed so that the electrons supplied by this reaction are exactly consumed in the other half-reaction:

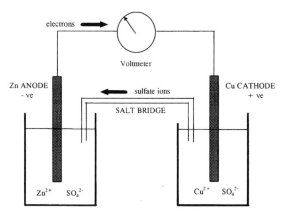

Figure 47.1 A Zn-Cu electrochemical cell. The metallic Zn and Cu electrodes are immersed in solutions of $ZnSO_4$ and $CuSO_4$ respectively, which are connected through a salt bridge. Sulfate ions migrate through the salt bridge to balance the flow of electrons through the wire connecting the electrodes and the voltmeter.

$$Cu^{2+} + 2e^- \rightarrow Cu \quad +0.35 \text{ volts}$$

$$Zn \rightarrow Zn^{2+} + 2e^- \quad +0.76 \text{ volts}$$

adding gives:

$$Zn^{2+} + Cu \rightarrow Zn + Cu^{2+} \quad E^o = 1.11 \text{ volts}$$

The electrons must cancel out, which in some redox reactions may entail multiplying one half-reaction by an integer (the E^o values are not so multiplied). The convention used here means that the overall reaction is spontaneous when the E^o value is positive, and the voltmeter would thus read +1.11 volts. Note that had the Cu half-reaction been reversed (instead of the Zn) the overall E^o would then be negative, indicating that the left to right reaction was not spontaneous. Thus the sign indicates the spontaneous direction of the reaction, and no prior knowledge of the system is necessary.

The E^o values in Table 47.2 are however only of very limited use since they assume unit activity of all dissolved species, whereas most burial environments typically have lower activities of dissolved species. Use of the Nernst equation is necessary for a realistic view of redox reactions:

$$Eh = E^o - RT(\ln K)/nF$$

where Eh is the *redox potential* under the chosen conditions, R is the Gas Constant, T is temperature in degrees Kelvin (degrees centigrade + 273), F is the Faraday constant, n is the number of electrons involved in the reaction, and K is the equilibrium constant. At 25°C (T = 298°K) with R = 8.31 joules deg^{-1} mole^{-1}, F = 96 487 coulombs mole^{-1} and converting natural logarithms to the base 10 gives:

$$Eh = E^o - 0.059 \log K/n \quad (8)$$

The Nernst equation can be used to derive some important limits of Eh and pH variations in natural environments. Consider the reduction of water to hydrogen:

$$2H_2O + 2e^- \rightarrow H_2 + 2OH^- \quad (9)$$

and substitute in:

$$2H_2O \rightarrow 2H^+ + 2OH^-$$

to give:

$$2H^+ + 2e^- \rightarrow H_2$$

and:

$$Eh = E^o - 0.059 \times 1/2 \times \log(pH_2/[H^+]^2) \quad (10)$$

Equation 10 therefore represents the reduction of water to hydrogen, and experience tells us that this does not commonly occur (i.e., there are no naturally-occurring species which are strong enough reducing agents to achieve this). The lowest Eh at which this could occur is given by $pH_2 = 1$ bar and then (10) simplifies to:

$$Eh = -0.059 \log pH \qquad (11)$$

Also consider the oxidation of water to oxygen gas:

$$2H_2O \rightarrow 2H_2 + O_2$$

and putting:

$$2H^+ + 2e^- \rightarrow H_2$$
$$2H_2O \rightarrow 4H^+ + O_2 + 4e^-$$

gives:

$$4H^+ + O_2 + 4e^- \rightarrow 2H_2O$$
$$E^\circ = 1.23 \text{ volts (Table 47.2)}$$

and:

$$Eh = 1.23 - \frac{0.059}{4} \log 1/(pO_2 \times [H^+]^4) \qquad (12)$$

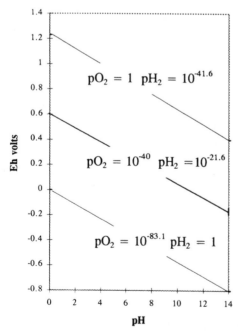

Figure 47.2 The stability field of water as a function of Eh and pH at 25°C and 1 bar pressure. Contours show partial pressures of hydrogen and oxygen.

Again we argue that natural systems contain no oxidizing agents strong enough to break water down to oxygen and thus the upper limit of the stability of water is given when pO_2 is 1 bar. Equations (11) and (12) can be plotted on an Eh-pH diagram (Figure 47.2) which also shows intermediate values of pH_2 and pO_2. Environments having negative Eh are reducing and those with positive Eh are oxidizing. Note that some oxygen is present even in reducing environments (because the equilibrium of water requires the presence of both species), however reducing conditions exist because $pH_2 > pO_2$. The Eh of a burial environment is mainly a function of the rates of supply of oxidizing agents (mainly oxygen) relative to reducing agents (mainly organic matter). In porous sediments the penetration of water carrying dissolved oxygen is facilitated and oxidizing conditions prevail. Conversely, if the supply of organic matter exceeds that of oxygen (as in poorly-drained peat-bogs), reducing conditions are established.

KINETICS

Kinetic models provide information on the pathways or time taken to reach equilibrium. The rates of chemical reactions are usually expressed in terms of the consumption of one of the products, and rate laws are defined by reference to the number of species involved in the rate-limiting step of the reaction. Thus the order of equation (3) is 'a' with respect to A, and 'b' with respect to B. These exponents are always integers and most reactions in natural systems are zero or first order. A *zero order* reaction is one where the reaction rate (dC/dt) is independent of concentration (C) and is constant:

$$dC/dt = -k$$

and integrating gives:

$$C = C_0 - kt$$

In a *first order reaction* the rate is directly proportional to the concentration C, thus:

$$dC/dt = -kC$$

and integrating gives:

$$C = C_0 e^{-kt}$$

Clearly reaction order can only be obtained by measuring the rates of change of the reactants, and cannot be predicted from the number of moles involved in the reaction equation. Laboratory and field studies have been used to give empirical rate laws for many important reactions in natural systems, but identifying the precise reaction mechanism is difficult. It is however often possible to identify the nature of the rate controlling step. For example rates of mineral dissolution or precipitation are usually controlled by either transport or surface reactions. A mineral which dissolves readily will release component ions into the surrounding water more rapidly than these ions can be transported away. These ions build up around the mineral surface, which becomes surrounded by a layer of water enriched in solutes (with which it is closer to equilibrium than with the bulk fluid). Rates of dissolution then slow down, and may be controlled by the rates at which ions are transported away by flow or diffusion. Conversely, where a mineral dissolves slowly, the component ions can be transported away as quickly as they are released, and the mineral surface is always in contact with fresh solution. Dissolution is then surface-reaction controlled. Most common minerals are relatively insoluble and dissolve by surface-reaction controlled mechanisms (see Berner 1980).

PROCESSES IN SOILS

Soils are derived from the weathering of rock by a variable combination of physical, chemical and biological processes, the interactions of which are mainly controlled by climate, vegetation, soil composition and water chemistry. Synthesizing these interactions to explain the global variation in soil types has presented a major challenge to soil scientists. However our concern is only to define the burial environment in terms of potential weathering reactions, and reconciling the influence of these reactions on soil composition is beyond our scope (see Lindsay 1979). This permits an important simplification by allowing us to concentrate on water composition.

Figure 47.3 (from Chesworth 1992) shows an Eh-pH diagram with a central shield-shaped area drawn around all the most common weathering environments. A few extreme environments are excluded from this area, notably the very acid soils developed from the weathering of abundant iron sulfides (see below), which is thus a restricted version of Figure 47.2. The arrows on Figure 47.3 define three main weathering trends (acid, alkaline and reducing), which are related to the behaviour of water. Measurements of soil Eh and pH plotted on Figure 47.3 can therefore provide

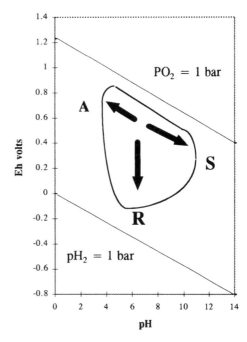

Figure 47.3 The Eh-pH framework of alteration under Earth surface conditions. The outline area represents most weathering environments. A is the acid weathering trend, S is the alkaline trend and R is the reduced trend. From Chesworth (1992) by permission of Elsevier Press.

a simple indication of how the burial environment may influence artifact weathering.

The acid trend

The acid trend is the most common weathering trend and is characteristic of humid climates where the drainage of water is downward through the soil profile (Chesworth 1992). The main weathering reaction is acid hydrolysis, where the cations Ca^{2+}, Mg^{2+}, Na^+ and K^+ (the most soluble components) are progressively displaced by hydrogen ions. The most important sources of H^+ are from the solution of CO_2, the oxidation of sulfides, and the formation of organic acids. Carbon dioxide is produced from the aerobic decay of organic matter, and dissolves in water to produce the weak acid H_2CO_3 which dissociates to produce H^+:

$$CO_2 + H_2O \rightarrow H_2CO_3 \rightarrow H^+ + HCO_3^-$$

The HCO_3^- may also dissociate to CO_3^{2-} to produce another H^+, but this only occurs significantly above pH 10. A soil water in equilibrium with $pCO_2 = 10^{-2}$

bar has a pH of 4.9, which is significantly more acidic than that of rainwater in equilibrium with the atmosphere (pH 5.6). The oxidation of iron sulfides generates sulfuric acid and can produce extremely acidic solutions in mineralized areas where pyrite is abundant:

$$FeS_2 + 15/4O_2 + 7/2H_2O$$
$$\rightarrow Fe(OH)_3 + 2SO_4^{2-} + 4H^+$$

and in poorly drained peaty soils organic acids may be significant.

Acid hydrolysis can be considered to occur in two stages. The first stage of attack occurs rapidly on surfaces, where there are broken bonds or defects in the lattice structure. For example, silicates have three dimensional lattices so that any mineral surface represents a disruption of lattice continuity. The broken bonds exposed on the surfaces are the focus for attack by H^+ or OH^-, depending on whether the exposed sites are negatively or positively charged. The phenomenon of abrasion pH is an example of surface hydrolysis, where the grinding of minerals produces fresh surfaces which readily react with hydrogen ions and produce the characteristic increase in pH. Cations at the surface are also leached and replaced by H^+.

The second stage of attack occurs more slowly as the mineral lattice is partially or wholly dissolved. Aluminosilicate lattices can be broken down slowly because silica, although only poorly soluble under acid conditions, can be preferentially removed to aluminium. The low solubility of silica however requires that relatively large volumes of water are flushed through the system; the larger the volumes of water, the more silica can be removed and the lower the Si/Al ratio of the residual material. Continued removal of silica in this way ultimately leaves only residual iron and aluminium.

The acid weathering trend will affect glass and pottery in the same way as mineral silicates, first causing the surface removal of cations and their replacement by H^+ and then producing a surface leached layer (see Chapters 7 and 45). Next more extensive breakdown of the lattice will be initiated. The acid oxidizing trend will also encourage the oxidation of metals and, in very acidic conditions, even their dissolution. Organic materials are likely to be relatively rapidly degraded as rapid flushing supplies oxygen for microbial decay.

The alkaline trend

Chesworth (1992) describes this trend (Figure 47.3) as occurring in relatively arid regions with a net annual water deficit. The net direction of water movement is upwards through the soil profile, although this may be reversed during periods of seasonally high rainfall. The upward movement of water leads to evaporation at the soil surface, and the precipitation of soluble salts such as Na, K, Mg and Ca carbonates and sulfates (and even chlorides under very arid conditions). The order of mineral precipitation is dictated initially by solubility products, such that the minerals with the highest SI values will precipitate first. However the relative abundances and rates of removal of ions will continuously modify the soil solution and the composition of the precipitating minerals.

Alkaline conditions can favour the rapid breakdown of aluminosilicate lattices because silica solubility increases with increasing pH. However much depends on the rates of water movement; variable flushing rates are likely to lead to cation and silica leaching but with these dissolved materials re-precipitated nearby. Thus artifacts are likely to be encrusted with salts. Most metals are poorly soluble under these conditions but surface oxidation and alteration to metal carbonates and sulfates is probable. Organic materials can also be degraded by microbial oxidation, aided by the attack of alkalis.

The reduced trend

This trend (Figure 47.3) requires the presence of excess water to produce partial or complete submergence (Chesworth 1992). Waterlogged conditions essentially prevent ready access to oxygen (which is only poorly soluble in water; see above), and hence relatively small concentrations of organic matter are able to consume oxygen and maintain anaerobic conditions. These conditions allow the reduction of metals (e.g., Fe, Mn), and thus their dissolution. The mobility of reduced metals is the main feature of this weathering trend, and is in marked contrast to the lack of mobility of metals in their oxidized states, in either of the other weathering trends. Note that variations in the water table may cause any given soil horizon to fluctuate between oxidizing and reducing. Reduced conditions then produce dissolved metals, which may be fixed as carbonates or sulfides (as these anions are the product of anaerobic microbial activity). Subsequent oxidation produces acid solutions (see above), and results in the precipitation of iron as red-brown iron hydroxides.

The reduced trend still produces weathering of aluminosilicates by acid hydrolysis, which proceeds at fairly uniform rates except under very acid or very alkaline conditions. However there is significantly increased potential for the weathering of artifacts which contain reducible metals, and dissolution is likely to produce pitting and etching.

SYNTHESIS

The present treatment of interactions between artifacts and their environment is drawn substantially from geochemistry. There are however fundamental differences in the perspective of the two disciplines. The study of geochemistry, and geology as a whole, is underpinned by the Principle of Uniformitarianism. The present is the key to the past invites geologists to study modern water-rock interactions to identify the nature of the changes which occur, and quantify the rates of reaction. These data can then be extrapolated back in time to understand ancient rocks, and allow the nature of past processes and environments to be described. However substantial difficulties arise where ancient rocks have no modern analogues. Herein also lies one of the unique difficulties which face archaeologists examining post-burial artifact–environment processes. The composition of artifacts has varied through time; more recent artifacts inevitably reflect technological advances as materials and construction methods evolve. Such differences between older and newer arti-facts make it much more difficult to isolate the effects of time from post-burial change. There is no magic bullet which can eliminate these difficulties. In a young and rapidly evolving science, like archaeology, the emphasis on understanding post-burial artefact–environment interactions must lie in thorough observation, careful experimentation and the informed use of thermodynamic and kinetic models.

REFERENCES

Berner, R.A. (1980). *Early Diagenesis – A Theoretical Approach*. Princeton University Press: Princeton.

Chesworth, W. (1992). Weathering systems. In Martin, I.P. and Chesworth, W. (eds) *Weathering, Soils and Paleosols*, 19–40. Developments in Earth Surface Processes No. 2, Elsevier: Amsterdam.

Drever, J.I. (1997). *The Geochemistry of Natural Waters*. Prentice Hall: New Jersey.

Faure, G. (1998). *Principles and Applications of Geochemistry*. Prentice Hall: New Jersey.

Langmuir, D.L. (1997). *Aqueous Environmental Geochemistry*. Prentice Hall: New Jersey.

Lindsay, W.L. (1979). *Chemical Equilibria in Soils*. John Wiley: New York.

Raiswell, R.W., Brimblecombe, P., Dent, D.L. and Liss, P.S. (1980). *Environmental Chemistry: the Earth-Air-Water Factory*. Edward Arnold: London.

48

Electrochemical Processes in Metallic Corrosion

M. McNEIL

US Nuclear Regulatory Commission, and Department of Materials Science, University of Toronto

and L.S. SELWYN

Canadian Conservation Institute, Ottawa.

The usual definition of corrosion (as opposed to mineral alteration and other forms of environmental degradation) is that it is an electrochemical reaction between an electrically conductive material, usually a metal, and its environment, usually water, that produces a deterioration of the material and its properties. The electrochemical reaction can be separated into *anodic* and *cathodic* reactions; oxidation reactions occur at the anode, and reduction reactions occur at the cathode. Metal ions enter the solution from the anode to form either dissolved species or solid corrosion products. The free energy of the system is lowered as the metal converts to a lower-energy form and the change in free energy is the driving force for corrosion. The best known example of corrosion is the rusting of steel where the metal (iron) is converted into a non-metallic corrosion product (rust).

Corrosion is of interest to archaeologists in three separate questions. First, it is desirable to know what can be learned from the artifact as recovered by examining the corrosion phenomenology. One class of questions includes the original form and composition, perhaps some information about fabrication techniques, and the chemical history of the site, which could provide insights into the activities associated with the artifact. A second class of questions relates to authentication: to what extent can examination of the corrosion structure prove that an artifact is at least not a recent fake? A third class of questions relates to preservation: how does one prevent corrosion processes from destroying the retrieved artifact? In this review an effort will be made to outline some points related to all three questions, though of course the third issue is the one which has received most attention from conservators.

THERMODYNAMICS

The natural starting point in describing electrochemical processes in metallic corrosion is the thermodynamic basis for electrochemical reactions. For a more

Handbook of Archaeological Sciences. Edited by D.R. Brothwell and A.M. Pollard.

comprehensive review of electrochemical processes, the reader is referred to corrosion textbooks (Kaesche 1985, Scully 1975, Uhlig and Revie 1985).

Associated with every reaction at a fixed temperature and pressure is a change in the thermodynamic quantity known as the *Gibbs free energy*, G. For an electrochemical or corrosion reaction, ΔG can be calculated from the cell potential E_{cell} of the reaction. The corrosion of copper in water containing dissolved oxygen can be used as an example:

$$Cu + \tfrac{1}{2}O_2 + H_2O \rightarrow Cu^{2+} + 2OH^- \qquad (1)$$

This reaction can be separated into half-reactions, with the anodic half-reaction given by:

$$Cu \rightarrow Cu^{2+} + 2e^- \qquad (2)$$

and the cathodic half-reaction given by:

$$\tfrac{1}{2}O_2 + H_2O + 2e^- \rightarrow 2OH^- \qquad (3)$$

The Nernst equation (Skoog *et al.* 1988:293) is used to calculate the half-cell potential, E_h, for a half-reaction relative to the *standard hydrogen electrode* (SHE); E_h is also referred to as the oxidation-reduction (redox) potential or simply as the electrode potential. The half-cell potentials of the cathodic half-reaction, $E_{h,cathode}$, and the anodic half-reaction, $E_{h,anode}$, are:

$$E_{h,cathode} = E^o - (0.0592/n) \log \{[OH^-]^2/[O_2]^{1/2}\} \qquad (4)$$

and

$$E_{h,anode} = E^o + (0.0592/n) \log [Cu^{2+}] \qquad (5)$$

where n is the number of electrons in the reaction, $[OH^-]$, $[Cu^{2+}]$, and $[O_2]$ are the activities of the hydroxyl ions, copper ions, and oxygen gas, and E^o is the standard reduction potential for the half-reaction ($E^o = 0.34V$ for the anodic half-reaction and $E^o = 0.40V$ for the cathodic half-reaction). Standard reduction potentials for many half-reactions can be looked up in tables (Lide and Frederikse 1997; see also Chapter 47, Table 1) or calculated from free energies (Wagman *et al.* 1982, Lide and Frederikse 1997). Activity is a measure of concentration in liquids or partial pressure in gases; for dilute solutions, the activity is equal to the concentration.

Once the half-cell potentials have been calculated, the cell potential is calculated from:

$$E_{cell} = E_{h,cathode} - E_{h,anode} \qquad (6)$$

In the copper corrosion example, the cell potential would be 0.06 V if the activities were unity. The cell potential is important because it contains thermodynamic information about the reaction. The change in free energy, ΔG, for this reaction can be calculated from:

$$\Delta G = -nFE_{cell} \qquad (7)$$

where n is the number of electrons involved in the reaction and F is the Faraday constant. In this example, ΔG is negative which means the reaction will proceed spontaneously in the direction as written because the system is moving toward a lower free energy. In other words, copper will corrode if it is placed in water containing (in this example) dissolved species at unit activity.

The cell potential is important on a practical level because it can be measured if one were to construct a reversible electrochemical cell containing a copper electrode and an oxygen electrode. Thus, in the above example, the potential difference measured between an oxygen electrode and a copper electrode when no current was flowing (open-circuit conditions) would be $E_{cell} = 0.06$ V. If some current was allowed to flow, the measured potential would be less than the maximum predicted value. If the cell was short-circuited, the potential measured between the two electrodes would be zero.

The individual half-cell potentials, $E_{h,cathode}$ and $E_{h,anode}$, can also be measured using a reference electrode. One then measures the potential difference between the reference electrode and one of the electrodes in the electrochemical cell. The potential is then corrected to be relative to SHE (ASTM 1992). If current was allowed to flow, then the measured values would be different from their predicted ones. If the cell were short-circuited and current allowed to flow freely, the measured potential of each electrode would be identical. This potential is called the corrosion potential, E_c, and it must lie between the two equilibrium half-cell potentials.

Corroding metals are not at equilibrium; when a metal is corroding in a solution, the resulting system is equivalent to a short-circuited electrochemical cell. The thermodynamic driving force is the difference between $E_{h,cathode}$ and $E_{h,anode}$ but when corrosion is taking place the anodic and cathodic reactions are no longer separated electrically with no current flowing. Instead, current is flowing and the potential of the metal is the corrosion potential, E_c, which lies somewhere between the equilibrium potentials for the anodic and cathodic reactions (i.e., $E_{h,anode} < E_c < E_{h,cathode}$).

The corrosion potential can be measured using a reference electrode, as mentioned above. It must be kept in mind that E_c reflects only the value at which the rates of anodic and cathodic reactions are equal and does not reflect a metal corrosion rate (i.e., the metal dissolution rate). More information on corrosion potential and corrosion rates can be found in corrosion textbooks such as Scully (1975), Kaesche (1985) or Uhlig and Revie (1985).

POURBAIX (STABILITY) DIAGRAMS

Pourbaix (Pourbaix 1974) and Garrels (Garrels and Christ 1965) more or less independently developed a graphical method to generalize the application of thermodynamics to corrosion and mineral alteration by drawing diagrams of electrode potential (E_h) versus the concentration of hydrogen ions (pH). These diagrams, called Pourbaix diagrams or sometimes simply *stability diagrams*, are calculated for a given element in an aqueous solution at a specified temperature and pressure. Within each diagram, the form of the element with the lowest free energy state is shown, the form being the metal, a soluble ion or an insoluble compound. The calculations use the Nernst equation, and solubility and thermodynamic data for the metal, its ions and its compounds (Marek *et al.* 1987). The calculations and assumptions involved in constructing these diagrams are discussed in modern corrosion textbooks; there is also a software package (HSC Chemistry for Windows, developed by Outokumpu Research Oy in Finland, http://www.outokumpu.com/hsc/index.htm) which can be used to generate Pourbaix diagrams.

Figure 48.1 shows a simple example of a Pourbaix diagram for a Cu-water system. The concentration of Cu^+ is fixed at 10^{-6} molar. This is a common convention in the application of Pourbaix diagrams to corrosion processes, though a different concentration could easily be chosen. Regions labelled with ions (e.g., Cu^{2+}(aq)) represent active regions where copper corrodes because the thermodynamically stable species are copper ions in solution, not copper metal. Those regions labelled as containing only solid phases are regions where Cu would either not corrode (i.e., the solid phase is Cu) or corrode more slowly (i.e., the solid phase is a protective oxide). Of importance is that Pourbaix diagrams show regions where solid films can form and regions where they cannot. One cannot tell, however, from the diagram whether a solid film is protective (the phenomenon of *passivity*) and corrosion is limited, or is non-protective (either

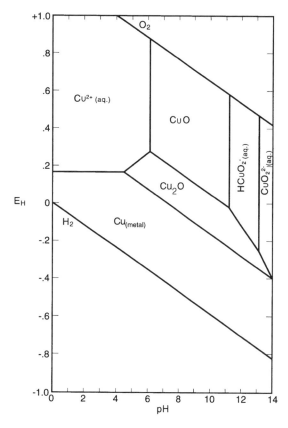

Figure 48.1 Cu-H_2O Pourbaix diagram at 298 K and atmospheric pressure.

because it is non-adherent or for other reasons discussed in corrosion textbooks) and corrosion continues.

A range of conditions can be found in natural environments. The pH typically falls between an acidic pH 4 (e.g., water in peat bogs) and an alkaline pH 9 (e.g., water flowing over limestone; see Chapter 47). The potential scale can usually be correlated with the oxygen concentration with more aerated conditions corresponding to a higher potential. In a burial environment where there is free-flowing water (e.g., in sandy soil) the environment is oxidizing but where there is restricted access of oxygen (e.g., in mud) the environment is reducing. The potential scale is limited in a natural environment by the stability of water. Above the line marked O_2 in Figure 48.1, water will tend to decompose to produce gaseous oxygen; and below the line marked H_2 it will tend to decompose to produce gaseous hydrogen. Electrochemical conditions above the O_2 line almost never occur in the natural world, but conditions below the H_2 line can occur if the potential is depressed by the action of micro-organisms, for example. The water is unstable but may not actually generate H_2 if there is no material present to act as a catalyst for the hydrogen generation reaction. For descriptions of E_h levels in various environments and their relation to dissolved oxygen and sulfur species, see Garrels and Christ (1965).

As mentioned earlier, it is possible, in practice, to measure a corrosion potential E_c (relative to a reference electrode) of a buried metal. The pH of the aqueous phase next to the metal surface can also be measured. These values can then be placed on the appropriate Pourbaix diagram and used to see where the metal lies and therefore predict the surface condition of the metal.

Pourbaix diagrams can be modified to include dissolved species in the water; such species are often included if they are capable of forming soluble species or insoluble salts with the metal (e.g., anions such as chlorides, sulfides, carbonates, or phosphates). The calculations must be re-done to include these new species. For example, Pourbaix diagrams can be developed to predict the effects of microbiological corrosion on artifacts. Figure 48.2 shows a Pourbaix diagram similar to that of Figure 48.1, but with sulfur present; it is assumed that the total sulfur concentration is 1 molar. This might be characteristic of a copper surface covered with a biofilm containing sulfate-reducing bacteria, which reduce sulfate ions to sulfide and sulfur, in an environment containing sulfates. This diagram shows the presence of copper sulfides. Sulfiding attack on copper alloys is common both in seawater and in burials, as sulfate-reducing bacteria are ubiquitous in the biosphere (McNeil *et al.* 1991), though tin bronzes in general are fairly resistant and severe damage to buried tin bronzes from microbiological sulfiding attack is rare (Tylecote 1979).

Pourbaix diagrams do have limitations because they reveal nothing about the kinetics of the reactions (i.e., the corrosion rates) or about the structural stability or porosity of insoluble corrosion products. Thermodynamics may predict the formation of an insoluble material such as malachite, $Cu_2CO_3(OH)_2$, on buried copper when carbonate ions are available. When a copper-alloy artifact corrodes under conditions that produce a uniform malachite layer, the underlying surface is protected and the corrosion rate is relatively slow compared to the corrosion rate of copper without such a layer. On the other hand, if the corrosion conditions result in a corrosion product which does not precipitate on the metal surface or which is physically

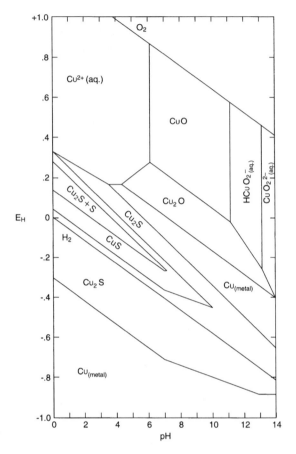

Figure 48.2 Cu-H_2O Pourbaix diagram at 298 K and atmospheric pressure. Total concentration of sulfur species 1 mole litre^{-1}.

unstable (e.g., chalcocite, Cu_2S, which erodes easily in circulating water) then the corrosion rate will be faster than if the uniform layer had precipitated. In the case of (almost always microbiological) sulfiding corrosion of Cu alloys, the non-protectiveness of chalcocite, Cu_2S, and the (relative) protectiveness of djurleite, $Cu_{31}S_{16}$, are not predicted by thermodynamics. Therefore, it is not sufficient for the Pourbaix diagram to show that in a particular area the corrosion product is a solid to predict the corrosion rate.

A second type of diagram is the so-called '*modified stability diagram*'. This type of diagram can be used to understand why one corrosion product forms under certain circumstances while another, involving the same elements in the same valence states, forms under others. Pourbaix diagrams and modified stability diagrams are in a sense opposite sides of the same coin.

Imagine, for example, a four-dimensional figure showing regions of stability of various species as a function of E_h, pH, cation activity (for example, the concentration of the dominant Cu-containing ion) and the critical anion activity (frequently the concentration of Cl^-, which is the dominant chloride-containing anion in almost all situations involving chlorides). One can then obtain Pourbaix diagrams by taking sections normal to the anion and cation axes. However, sections taken in other directions produce other types of diagrams; in particular, one can make a projection on a plane normal to the E_h and pH planes, and this produces a modified stability diagram. The applications of these diagrams are described in Mohr and McNeil (1992).

CORROSION DURING BURIAL

The dominant form of corrosion on buried objects is the more or less general attack on the surface of an artifact. This includes both uniform corrosion and various types of localized corrosion in which parts of the surface corrode at different rates, producing a moon-crater appearance ('Muldenkorrosion') or in which deposition of corrosion products produces 'botryoidal' growths on the surface.

Localized corrosion is concentrated in small areas, especially grain boundaries and pits. Localized chloride attack arises from accumulation of chloride ions at anodic sites. This accumulation is a consequence of the physical separation of the anodic and cathodic processes caused by the formation of corrosion products on the buried object. The anodic process, that is, dissolution of the metal, takes place at the metal/corrosion interface. The cathodic reaction, usually oxygen reduction, takes place at the outermost electrically conducting material, such as cuprite (Cu_2O) on the surface of copper or magnetite (Fe_3O_4) on the surface of iron. The physical separation of the anodic and cathodic reactions prevents the mixing of the reaction products and results in pH changes at the anodic and cathodic regions. This is illustrated in Figure 48.3 for iron. In a case where the surface is a very good insulator the cathodic process depends on fractures or porosity and associated paths for conduction through water.

In the anodic region, metal ions go into solution, accumulate, and undergo hydrolysis, thereby locally acidifying the region. Electrical neutrality must be maintained and charge balance of the cations is achieved by diffusion of anions from the surrounding environment. Chloride ions tend to concentrate because of their high mobility and because they are often the predominant environmental anion. As the metal corrodes and chloride ions accumulate, the

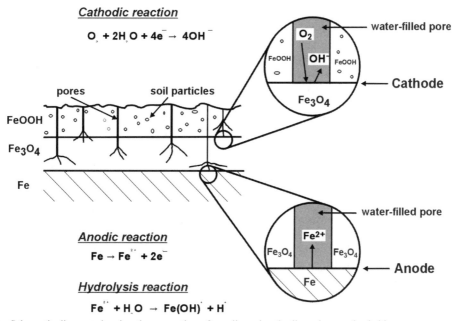

Figure 48.3 Schematic diagram showing the separation of anodic and cathodic regions on buried iron.

local conditions in the anodic region favour localized attack. The processes occurring in the anodic region are equivalent to those within a pit or crevice, where the anodic dissolution of the metal is accelerated by the presence of both hydrogen and chloride ions. Increased metal dissolution then leads to an increase in the local concentration of hydrogen ions (by hydrolysis) and chloride ions (by electromigration), causing accelerated attack. Limiting factors include the plugging of anodic sites with non-conducting minerals, other mass transport limitations, and resistive effects (ultimately a pit can get so deep that the bottom is effectively decoupled from cathodic sites). For buried objects, or objects in the sea, the environmental chemistry and the structures and chemistry of the corrosion products play critical roles by limiting the rate at which reacting species can reach cathodic regions.

Pourbaix diagrams can be used to predict the corrosion products of a metal (soluble or insoluble) that are thermodynamically stable under burial conditions. This knowledge is helpful in distinguishing between corrosion products formed during burial and those formed after an excavated artifact has been exposed to air. The diagram for copper in the presence of carbonate ions predicts the formation of malachite, $Cu_2CO_3(OH)_2$, in conditions which are oxidizing and alkaline. In practice, a dense layer of this compound is frequently identified on buried copper objects. The diagram for iron predicts the presence of two stable solids, goethite (α-FeOOH) under oxidizing conditions and magnetite (Fe_3O_4) under more reducing conditions and these are both common on archaeological iron. If one introduces other anions such as carbonates, sulfides, or phosphates in the calculation of the iron stability diagram, a few more solid corrosion products are predicted: iron carbonate (siderite, $FeCO_3$) and iron phosphate (vivianite, $Fe_3(PO_4)_2.8H_2O$) are predicted under more reducing conditions than needed for magnetite; and iron sulfides (e.g., pyrite, FeS_2) under anaerobic conditions (Garrels and Christ 1965, Turgoose 1982).

Vivianite forms if there is a source of phosphate ions such as bones found in cemeteries, fish waste sites, or garbage dumps. Haematite (α-Fe$_2$O$_3$) does not normally form as a corrosion product under burial conditions, but is sometimes identified on archaeological iron. Because haematite forms when goethite is heated, its presence is usually attributed to exposure to fire before the object was buried.

These diagrams are also useful in predicting whether or not solid metal chlorides will form during burial. In copper-based alloys, solid nantokite (CuCl) may form

under reducing conditions but in iron-based alloys, iron chloride salts, with their high solubility in water, tend to remain in solution and are present on freshly excavated iron only as an acidic iron(II) chloride solution filling the pores of archaeological iron (Turgoose 1993). The presence of CuCl or an acidic iron(II) chloride solution have important consequences for corrosion on metal artifacts after they are excavated. The most important form of attack in the archaeological context is the type of localized chloride attack which leads, after excavation, to 'bronze disease' on copper-based alloys or to 'active corrosion' on iron artifacts. This is discussed in more detail below.

CORROSION AFTER EXCAVATION

When an excavated object is exposed to an indoor environment, it usually experiences a decrease in relative humidity and an increase in available oxygen relative to burial. Water evaporates from any solution filling the pores, cracks and spaces within solid corrosion products and the solution therefore concentrates. Solids or ions in solution that were thermodynamically stable in the burial environment may no longer be stable in air and may oxidize to new corrosion products or to new ions in solution. These transformations can cause chemical damage and/or physical damage to the object.

Three examples of damage to excavated objects on exposure to air (and sufficient moisture) are active corrosion on iron, bronze disease on copper alloys, and the oxidation of pyrite (pyrite disease) or other metal sulfides. Maintaining a sufficiently low level of relative humidity usually minimizes these damaging reactions.

Active corrosion on iron is caused by chloride ion contamination and often is revealed through two symptoms, 'weeping' and akaganéite (β-FeOOH) formation (Selwyn et al. 1999). Weeping is the formation of drops of acidic liquid that, on drying, leave hollow shells of rust-coloured corrosion. Akaganéite formation involves growth of bright red-brown, elongated particles with a crystal structure stabilized by chloride ions within tunnels (Post and Buchwald 1991). Both symptoms are associated with the iron(II) chloride solution in freshly excavated iron, and they are partly explained by the oxidation of the iron(II) ions in solution, given by:

$$4Fe^{2+} + O_2 + 6H_2O = 4FeOOH + 8H^+ \tag{8}$$

Iron oxyhydroxides (FeOOH) precipitate when iron(II) ions are oxidized and hydrolysed; the three common forms are goethite (α-FeOOH), the form which is thermodynamically stable, lepidocrocite (γ-FeOOH) and akaganéite (β-FeOOH). When the solution contains low concentrations of chloride ions, goethite and/or lepidocrocite precipitate; when the chloride concentration is high, akaganéite forms (Refait and Génin 1997). The precipitation of any of these iron oxyhydroxides can physically damage the artifact because their molar volumes are about three times greater than the molar volume of iron. Akaganéite is usually considered a symptom of active corrosion because the characteristic bright red-brown elongated particles of β-FeOOH are easily recognized at the metal/corrosion interface and its presence indicates a high chloride ion level within the object.

Weeping is another symptom of active corrosion. Weeping is attributed to the hygroscopic nature of iron chloride salts. Iron(II) chloride tetrahydrate crystals ($FeCl_2.4H_2O$) form when an iron(II) chloride solution dries rapidly. If these crystals are then exposed to a relative humidity above about 56 per cent, the salt deliquesces and forms bubbles of liquid referred to as weeping. As oxygen diffuses into the liquid of the bubble, iron(II) ions are oxidized to iron(III) ions which have low solubility and precipitate as one of the forms of iron oxyhydroxide. Precipitation around the outer boundary of the sphere leads to the hollow shells remaining after weeping has occurred.

So far, the discussion has focused on the formation of solid phases in equation (8). The other consequence of equation (8) is the formation of hydrogen ions and the resulting chemical damage they cause. When the occluded solution is iron(II) chloride and there is remaining iron metal in the artifact, a corrosion cycle can consume the remaining iron and totally destroy the object. Askey et al. (1993) proposed the following corrosion cycle for iron contaminated with HCl:

$$2Fe(s) + 4HCl(aq) + O_2(g) = 2FeCl_2(aq) + 2H_2O \tag{9}$$

$$2FeCl_2(aq) + 3H_2O + \tfrac{1}{2}O_2(g)$$
$$= 2FeOOH(s) + 4HCl(aq) \tag{10}$$

The designations are (s) for solids, (aq) for aqueous, and (g) for gas. The crucial point about this cycle is that the chloride ion forms a soluble salt with iron(II) ions and it is this solubility in equations (9) and (10) which allows the cycle to proceed. If the iron chloride salt were insoluble, it would precipitate and the cycle would be broken.

Instability in excavated bronze objects is due to the existence of chloride-containing species, mainly copper(I) chloride (nantokite, CuCl), formed during burial as chloride ions accumulate. Nantokite usually forms close to the metal/corrosion interface and is present as a grey or grey-green, translucent waxy solid. It remains stable if it is sealed within a corrosion crust and thus protected from water and oxygen. If, however, it is exposed to moist air as a result of handling, cleaning, or cracking (from temperature fluctuations), then nantokite reacts to form light green, powdery corrosion products. The reaction of CuCl with water and oxygen involves oxidation and hydrolysis. Two proposed reactions are given below:

$$4CuCl(s) + O_2(g) + 4H_2O$$
$$= 2Cu_2(OH)_3Cl(s) + 2H^+(aq) + 2Cl^-(aq) \tag{11}$$
$$3CuCl(s) + 3/4O_2(g) + 3/2H_2O$$
$$= Cu_2(OH)_3Cl(s) + Cu^{2+}(aq) + 2Cl^-(aq) \tag{12}$$

Scott (1990) proposed reaction (11) and Strandberg and Johansson (1998) proposed reaction (12) as the dominant reaction.

The reaction products are one of the basic copper chloride isomers (e.g., atacamite, paratacamite, clinoatacamite (Pollard et al. 1989, Jambor et al. 1996)) and hydrochloric acid. Because nantokite usually resides close to the metal/corrosion interface, its reaction products cause physical damage to the overlying corrosion products. Eventually, the basic copper chlorides erupt on the surface where they become visible. It is this process of CuCl (or other chloride-containing species) interacting with moisture and oxygen to form light green corrosion products that is called bronze disease (Scott 1990). The formation of an electrolyte, especially an acidic one, can cause continued corrosion of any remaining copper metal (Strandberg and Johansson 1998). Unlike the iron corrosion cycle, where the chloride ions are released back into solution to continue participating in the corrosion cycle, the reactions giving rise to bronze disease only continue until all of the CuCl is consumed; the chloride ions are gradually removed as they become incorporated into the solid basic copper chlorides.

The final damaging reaction to be discussed is the oxidation of metal sulfides formed during burial under anaerobic conditions. Metal sulfides are generally less stable than their corresponding oxides. Oxidation of metal sulfides has been observed on archaeological copper (Duncan and Ganiaris 1987) and archaeological wood stained with iron sulfides (MacLeod and Kenna

1991, Jespersen 1989). The oxidation of pyrite (described as *pyrite disease* when observed in geological and palaeontological collections) provides a good example. Pyrite is unstable in moist air and the oxidation reactions are complex; for more information, see the review by Lowson (1982). A simplified description of the initial reaction is:

$$2FeS_2 + 7O_2 + 2H_2O = 2FeSO_4 + 2H_2SO_4 \qquad (13)$$

The main products of this oxidation reaction are sulfuric acid and an iron(II) sulfate that exists in various hydrated forms. The phase change from sulfide to sulfate causes physical damage because of the volume increase. The production of sulfuric acid can cause further damage to the underlying metal or to associated material; sulfuric acid is deliquescent at all levels of relative humidity. Crystals of iron(II) sulfate (rozenite, $FeSO_4.4H_2O$) have been observed on water-logged wood impregnated with iron sulfides (Jespersen 1989). The iron(II) sulfates can be oxidized to iron(III) sulfates. Examples of a range of iron sulfates identified on archaeological wood include roemerite, bilinite, butlerite, natrojarosite, and jarosite (MacLeod and Kenna 1991).

CORROSION PROCESSES ON FORGERIES

Relatively little work has been done on using studies of corrosion products to detect forgeries, or more precisely to validate legitimate items. There are corrosion phenomena, however, which are very rarely replicated on modern reproductions.

The isotope Cl^{36} is produced by nuclear explosions, and a chloride mineral showing the Cl^{36} abundance characteristic of modern chlorides is very likely to have formed after 1945. Presence of the nuclear Cl^{36} is not absolute proof of the modernity of a chloride mineral (for example, a porous mineral could have been exposed to modern chloride electrolytes and have been enriched in Cl^{36} through ion exchange); but its absence from a chloride mineral corrosion product is proof positive that the mineral was not formed in recent times. In principle one could use carbon isotopic analysis to date carbonate corrosion products. However, isotopic analysis of corrosion products is rarely if ever used for a number of reasons, not least that it requires that a substantial amount of corrosion product be removed, and that it cannot distinguish a modern fake from a genuine piece which had been cleaned and repatinated in more recent times.

Presence of embrittlement of silver alloys due to discontinuous precipitation (Thompson and Chatterjee 1954, Ravich 1993) is an almost certain proof of a high degree of antiquity. In fact silver embrittlement by discontinuous precipitation can be produced in a few weeks under proper conditions. The process is unpublished (though it would be made accessible to a curator with a serious forgery question), and it requires a proper scientific laboratory rather than a forger's workshop. In any event it may not give precisely the correct precipitate morphology on the crack surfaces.

It appears at present that duplication of bronze disease implies that the artifact is not modern. Some symptoms of mild bronze disease could probably be synthesized by a knowledgeable scientist in a laboratory, but the severe generalized problem frequently found in artifacts would be extraordinarily difficult to synthesize – and anyway, the chlorides would all have modern nuclear Cl^{36} signatures.

Dealloying is a process whereby the surface (and sometimes the entire structure) of an alloy is depleted of one of the elements (Scully 1975). Of particular interest is the dealloying of bronzes, which has been studied by Geilmann (1956). Dealloying can occur either from exposure to high temperatures or from long-time exposure to water; the latter is common in archaeology. Dealloying can be accelerated by the use of elevated temperatures and more aggressive water chemistry, but presuming antiquity for a seriously dealloyed object is probably reasonable if the dealloyed element is not zinc (which is peculiarly susceptible to dealloying). Probably measurement of concentration profiles would be a useful way of confirming antiquity, but one must be willing to cut a hole in the specimen!

SUMMARY

The corrosion of metals is an electrochemical process, with oxidation reactions occurring at the anode (i.e., the metal surface) and reduction reactions occurring at the cathode. Pourbaix diagrams (graphs of electrode potential versus pH) are a convenient way to apply thermodynamics to the electrochemistry of corrosion. We have used the corrosion of copper in water as an example, but could have chosen any metal.

The corrosion of archaeological metals after they are excavated is determined by how they corroded during burial. Chloride ions, which often concentrate at the surface of the corroding metal, can play a crucial role. Our examples highlight the importance of solubility and oxidation state of the corrosion products formed under burial conditions: in corroding iron,

iron(II) chloride remains in solution because of its high solubility, whereas in corroding copper alloys, copper(I) chloride precipitates because of its low solubility.

After metal objects are excavated, corrosion problems arise mainly because corrosion products that were stable in the burial environment (with its usually low oxygen level) are no longer stable after excavation (where the oxygen levels are usually higher). We have emphasized iron because of its susceptibility to severe damage after excavation, particularly when iron(II) chloride salts are present (active corrosion). We also described bronze disease, observed on copper alloys when copper(I) chloride is oxidized in moist air, and pyrite disease, when pyrite that has contaminated materials such as wood reacts with water and oxygen.

The corrosion of archaeological metals, both during burial and after excavation, is evidence of their history, and distinguishes these metals from forgeries. We have reviewed the corrosion processes to stress the differences.

REFERENCES

*Recommended for further reading

Askey, A., Lyon, S.B., Thompson, G.E., Johnson, J.B., Wood, G.C., Cooke, M. and Sage, P. (1993). The corrosion of iron and zinc by atmospheric hydrogen chloride. *Corrosion Science*, **34**:233–247.

ASTM (1992). Designation G3-89. Standard practice for conventions applicable to electrochemical measurements in corrosion testing. *1992 Annual Book of ASTM Standards*, Vol. 03.02, 56–64. American Society for Testing and Materials: Philadelphia.

Duncan, S.J. and Ganiaris, H. (1987). Some sulphide corrosion products on copper alloys and lead alloys from London waterfront sites. In Black, J. (ed.) *Recent Advances in the Conservation and Analysis of Artifacts*, 77–93. University of London Summer Schools Press: London.

*Garrels, R.M. and Christ, J.L. (1965). *Solutions, Minerals and Equilibria*. Freeman Cooper: San Francisco.

Geilmann, W. (1956). Verwitterung von Bronzen im Sandbogen. *Angewandte Chemie*, **68**:201–212.

Jambor, J.L., Dutrizac, J.E., Roberts, A.C., Grice, J.D. and Szymanski, J.T. (1996). Clinoatacamite, a new polymorph of $Cu_2(OH)_3Cl$, and its relationship to paratacamite and 'anarakite'. *The Canadian Mineralogist*, **34**:61–72.

Jespersen, K. (1989). Precipitation of iron-corrosion products on peg-treated wood. In MacLeod, I.D. and Grattan, D.W. (eds) *Conservation of Wet Wood and Metal*, 141–152. Western Australian Museum: Perth, Australia.

*Kaesche, H (1985). *Metallic Corrosion*. National Association of Corrosion Engineers: Houston.

Lide, D.R. and Frederikse, H.P.R. (eds) (1997). *The Handbook of Chemistry and Physics* (77th edn). CRC Press: New York.

Lowson, R.T. (1982). Aqueous oxidation of pyrite by molecular oxygen. *Chemical Reviews*, **82**:461–497.

MacLeod, I.D. and Kenna, C. (1991). Degradation of archaeological timbers by pyrite: oxidation of iron and sulphur species. In Hoffmann, P. (ed.) *Proceedings of the 4th ICOM-Group on Wet Organic Archaeological Materials*, 133–142. International Council of Museums: Bremerhaven.

Marek, M.I., Natalie, C.A. and Piron, D.L. (1987). Thermodynamics of aqueous corrosion. In Davis, J.R. (ed.) *Metals Handbook: Vol. 13 Corrosion*, 18–28 (9th edn). American Society for Metals: Metals Park, OH.

*McNeil, M.B., Mohr, D.W. and Little, B.J. (1991). Correlation of laboratory results with observations on long-term corrosion of iron and copper alloys. In Vandiver, P.B., Druzik, J. and Wheeler, G.S. (eds) *Materials Issues in Art and Archaeology II*, 753–759. Symposium Proceedings 185, Materials Research Society: Pittsburg PA.

Mohr, D.W. and McNeil, M.B. (1992). Modified log-activity diagrams as a tool for modelling corrosion of nuclear waste containers, with particular reference to copper. *Journal of Nuclear Materials*, **190**:329–342.

Pollard, A.M., Thomas, R.G. and Williams, P.A. (1989). Synthesis and stabilities of the basic copper(II) chlorides atacamite, paratacamite and botallackite. *Mineralogical Magazine*, **53**:557–563.

Post, J.E. and Buchwald, V.F. (1991). Crystal structure refinement of akaganéite. *American Mineralogist*, **76**:272–277.

*Pourbaix, M. (1974). *Atlas of Electrochemical Equilibria*. National Association of Corrosion Engineers: Houston.

Ravich, I.G. (1993). Annealing of brittle archaeological silver: microstructural and technological study. In Bridgland, J. (ed.) *ICOM Committee for Conservation 10th Triennial Meeting, Washington, DC*, 792–795. International Council of Museums: Paris.

Refait, P. and Génin, J.-M.R. (1997). The mechanisms of oxidation of ferrous hydroxychloride β-$Fe_2(OH)_3Cl$ in aqueous solution: the formation of akaganeite vs goethite. *Corrosion Science*, **39**:539–553.

Scott, D.A. (1990). Bronze disease: a review of some chemical problems and the role of relative humidity. *Journal of the American Institute for Conservation*, **29**:193–206.

Scully, J.C. (1975). *The Fundamentals of Corrosion* (2nd edn). Pergamon Press: Oxford.

Selwyn, L.S., Sirois, P.J. and Argyropoulos, V. (1999). The corrosion of excavated archaeological iron with details on weeping and akaganéite. *Studies in Conservation*, **44**:217–232.

Skoog, D.A., West, D.M. and Holler, F.J. (1988). *Fundamentals of Analytical Chemistry* (5th edn). Saunders College Publishing: New York.

Strandberg, H. and Johansson, L.-G. (1998). Some aspects of the atmospheric corrosion of copper in the presence of sodium chloride. *Journal of the Electrochemical Society*, **145**:1093–1100.

Thompson, F.C. and Chatterjee, A.K. (1954). The age embrittlement of silver coins. *Studies in Conservation*, **1**:115–125.

Turgoose, S. (1982). The nature of surviving iron objects. In Clarke, R.W. and Blackshaw, S.M. (eds) *Conservation of Iron*, 1–7. Monographs and Reports No. 53, National Maritime Museum: Greenwich.

Turgoose, S. (1993). Structure, composition and deterioration of unearthed iron objects. In Aoki, A. (ed.) *Current Problems in the Conservation of Metal Antiquities*, 35–52. Tokyo National Research Institute of Cultural Properties: Tokyo.

Tylecote, R.F. (1979). The effect of soil conditions on the long-term corrosion of buried tin bronzes and copper. *Journal of Archaeological Science*, **6**:345–368.

*Uhlig, H.H. and Revie, R.W. (1985). *Corrosion and Corrosion Control*. John Wiley: New York.

Wagman, D.D., Evans, W.H., Parker, V.B., Schumm, R.H., Halow, I., Bailey, S.M., Churney, K.L. and Nuttall, R.L. (1982). The NBS table of chemical thermodynamic properties. *Journal of Physical and Chemical Reference Data*, **11**, supplement 2.

49

Post-depositional Changes in Archaeological Ceramics and Glasses

I.C. FREESTONE

Department of Scientific Research, British Museum.

Ceramic artifacts are well represented in the archaeological record, so that there is a tendency to regard them as stable materials. However, they have commonly undergone a degree of alteration during burial, although this may be less apparent than in the case of glass, which often has a surface 'skin' of altered material. In fact, weathering can have a serious effect upon the interpretation of an assemblage, and investigations involving the analysis or testing of excavated ceramics and glasses should allow for this possibility.

The post-depositional changes undergone by inorganic materials in archaeology have attracted interest for a number of reasons:

(i)   they offer a potential dating tool – in principle, if the rate of change is known, then the amount of change can give the date of deposition,

(ii) modifications of the physical properties of artifacts, for example, colour or strength, complicate their interpretation,

(iii) changes in chemical and mineralogical composition may interfere with the investigation of the provenance, technology and use of an artifact,

(iv) weathering may adversely affect the *in situ* preservation of archaeological materials, leading to a gross distortion of the material record, and

(v)   archaeological materials have been studied as potential analogues of nuclear waste disposal glasses.

Deterioration, and the factors that control it, is also of over-riding interest to conservators concerned with preserving the cultural heritage in museums and historic buildings. However, this substantial field (Newton and Davison 1989) is not the immediate concern of the present chapter, which is concerned with deterioration of buried artifacts in the ground.

Archaeological ceramics are predominantly silicate materials, in that compounds of silica make up the majority of the phases present (see Chapter 36). In this respect, they resemble the rocks that make up the Earth's crust. Indeed, many of the same minerals occur in both ceramics and rocks. However, the chemistries, phase compositions and microstructures of many archaeological ceramics ensure that they deteriorate at a much faster rate than most rocks and minerals. They are commonly fine-grained and very porous, with a high internal surface area, which can react with environmental solutions. They may contain metastable phases, which react very rapidly. The particles in the ceramic are often bound together with very fine films and filaments of glass, and, as these corrode, the strength of the material deteriorates, eventually resulting in disaggregation.

In a similar way, while natural glasses, or obsidians, may be seen as analogues for artificial archaeological glasses, their chemistries differ in important respects so that the kinetics of their interactions with low temperature solutions differ by orders of magnitude. Synthetic, or human-made, glasses are very much less stable than obsidian (see Chapter 7).

There are substantial literatures dealing with the weathering of silicate minerals and the corrosion of container glasses but these do not translate easily to archaeological materials, although the same chemical principles control the interactions with the environment. Our understanding of weathering processes in archaeological ceramics and glasses is limited at the present time. Indeed, the possibility of weathering changes in ceramics has often been neglected in investigations that purport to describe or measure some physical, or chemical, property of a material before it was buried.

This short account deals with the two material types in turn. Glass, as a single-phase material, which can itself be an important component of a ceramic, is considered first. The main chemical and structural characteristics of the materials are summarized to allow a generalized understanding of the corrosion process. These are followed by brief reviews of the information on weathering of the materials from the archaeological literature.

GLASS

Early glassworkers made glass by melting silica (from sand or pebbles) with a flux, which was typically rich in sodium but which, in some cultures, was predominantly of potassium or lead (see Chapter 38). Outlines of the structures of glass suitable for the non-specialist are provided by Brill (1962) and Pollard and Heron (1996:150). Pure silica (SiO_2) glass is composed of a *network* of silicon atoms, cross-linked by 'bridges' of oxygen. The structure of vitreous (glassy) silica is compared schematically with that of crystalline silica in Figures 49.1a and 49.1b. They differ in that the arrangement of the atoms in the glass is not regular, but has variable bond lengths and bond angles. This disordered atomic arrangement resembles that of molten silica and for this reason glass has commonly been referred to as a *supercooled liquid*. This is a very convenient way to conceptualize glass, although it is probable that some ordering of the structure does occur as the glass is quenched from the melt. This three dimensional 'random network' is modified by the solution of basic oxides, such as soda (Na_2O), potash (K_2O) and lime (CaO), which are often known as *network modifiers*:

$$\equiv Si\text{–}O\text{–}Si \equiv \; + Na_2O \rightarrow 2 \equiv Si\text{–}O^- Na^+$$

By eliminating the bridging oxygen bond between the silicon atoms, the network modifier lowers the melting temperature and viscosity of the glass, making it easier to melt and work. The structures of pure silica glass, and a soda-silica glass are compared schematically in Figures 49.1b and 49.1c.

Ancient glass invariably contained a flux, usually soda and/or potash, to allow it to be made and worked using the furnaces and techniques available. In addition to an alkali oxide, early glass also contains calcium oxide (lime). The alkaline earth oxides, lime (CaO)

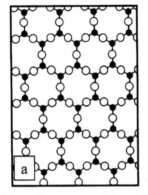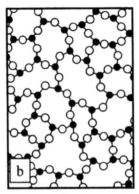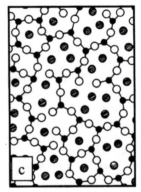

Figure 49.1 Schematic structures of (a) crystalline SiO_2 with regular bond lengths and bond angles, (b) glassy SiO_2 with variable bond lengths and angles, (c) $Na_2O\text{-}SiO_2$ glass, with broken Si-O-Si bridges. Black circles represent Si atoms, open circles O atoms and shaded circles Na atoms. Note that for simplicity, each silicon atom is shown bound to three oxygens; in reality it would be bound to four, the fourth effectively above the plane of the diagram. After Brill (1962), with permission of the Corning Museum of Glass.

and magnesia (MgO) are sometimes referred to as glass stabilizers, as they render the glass less soluble in water.

Typical ancient glass compositions are reviewed in Chapter 38. Soda-lime-silica glasses are by far the most common. In the Bronze Age and early Iron Age of Europe and the Near East, these typically contain several percent potassium oxide (potash) and magnesium oxide (magnesia). The source of alkali in these glasses was a relatively impure sodium-rich plant ash. Roman, Byzantine, early Medieval and early Islamic glasses (up to ninth and tenth centuries AD) contain very low potash and magnesia, as the alkali used was a relatively pure mineral soda (trona, commonly called natron). From the ninth century, glasses in the Mediterranean and the Near East reverted to the use of soda-rich plant ash as a flux, while in Europe wood and plants from temperate inland areas were burned to produce potassium-rich ashes and potash-lime-silica glasses. Lead-rich glasses are relatively uncommon; in addition to China, lead-rich glasses were used in the West to produce red and yellow opaque glasses in antiquity, and certain transparent glasses in the Medieval period.

Glass corrosion

The corrosion of buried glass takes place primarily through the action of water, via two main mechanisms (Scholze 1982, 1988), de-alkalization and network dissolution.

De-alkalization (ion exchange)

Hydronium ions (H_3O^+) from the environment exchange a hydrogen ion for an alkali in the glass network:

$$H_3O^+ + \equiv Si-O^-Na^+ \rightarrow \equiv Si-OH + H_2O + Na^+$$

This process leaves a hydrated silica-rich layer, sometimes termed the leached layer or 'gel' layer, at the surface of the glass. The hydrogen is much smaller than the sodium that it replaces, and furthermore has a strong covalent bond with oxygen. The result is a contraction and weakening of the network.

Network dissolution (silica hydrolysis)

Under alkaline conditions, the oxygen bridges of the network itself may be broken down and silica dissolve:

$$\equiv Si-O-Si \equiv +OH^- \rightarrow \equiv Si-OH + \equiv Si-O^-$$

It follows that, in addition to humidity, the acidity, or pH, of the burial environment will have a strong effect

upon the corrosion process, as the breakdown of the network and solution of silica are strongly pH dependent (e.g., Adams 1984, Heimann 1986).

The composition of glass is a crucial factor in determining the rate of deterioration (Newton 1985). Pure sodium silicate glasses are water soluble, and require the presence of 5 per cent or more lime to render them stable. Virtually all ancient soda-rich glasses contain significant amounts of lime; it is unclear, however, if low-lime soda glasses were made in significant quantities but have been dissolved away, so that we have no evidence of this practice. Verità (1998) has reported extant but corroded examples of low-lime archaeological glass, for example.

The concentration of silica is also an important control of corrosion. For example, El-Shamy (1973) found that the tendency of glass to corrode was greatly reduced when the mole percentage SiO_2 in glass was greater than 66 per cent, and Cox et al. (1979) found that the durability of Medieval window glass depended upon silica content. However, silica concentration is not the only compositional factor controlling glass corrosion. Minor amounts of metal oxides may have a dramatic effect (e.g., Scholze 1982), while recent work on Renaissance enamel glasses by Biron (1999) suggests that silica is not the major factor in distinguishing those glasses which are apparently stable from those that are apparently unstable.

Some minor components, such as Al_2O_3 and Fe_2O_3, have low solubilities, and therefore their presence in the glass will increase its resistance to corrosion. However, they may have an apparently disproportionate effect due to their position in the glass structure. To understand this, it is useful to refine the structural model of glass outlined above, where alkali (and alkaline earth) cations are assumed associated with randomly distributed non-bridging ($\equiv Si-O^-$) oxygens in the glass network. Aluminium, a trivalent cation (Al^{3+}), behaves as a network former, like tetravalent silicon (Si^{4+}), in the glass structure. However, to do this, it requires an associated alkali cation (e.g. Na^+) for charge balance purposes, so that $NaAlO_2$ may be regarded as effectively equivalent to SiO_2. An addition of a small amount of aluminium in the glass may therefore tend to distribute the alkalis on a set of sites that are different from those associated with non-bridging oxygens. Fe^{3+} is likely to show similar behaviour to Al^{3+}.

Recent structural work has suggested that the distributions of alkalis and non-bridging oxygens are not random, but that they may be concentrated in channels (e.g., Greaves et al. 1991). This 'modified random network model' has implications for the diffusion and exchange of hydronium and alkali metal ions near the glass surface, because it allows less impeded access into the glass structure. The role of aluminium in associating the alkali cations with network forming sites is likely to reduce such diffusion channels and enhance the durability of the glass in this way.

The corrosion layer

From the foregoing, we see that there are two glass corrosion effects, ion exchange and network dissolution. In principle, these effects are in competition. If de-alkalization proceeds more rapidly than network dissolution, then the corroding glass will have a leached surface layer composed of hydrated silica. On the other hand, if network dissolution is the major mechanism, then there will be no hydrated silica layer and the surface of the glass will be progressively etched away. In practice, most groundwater is of intermediate pH, so that ion exchange appears to be the dominant mechanism, and a hydrated silica-rich layer is present on many archaeological glasses.

The development of such a layer is shown schematically in Figure 49.2. The structural re-arrangement that occurs when Na^+ is replaced by H^+ results in a porosity on a very fine scale, so that the hydrated layer behaves as a gel. Hydronium ions are able to diffuse through it to the glass surface and attack fresh glass, while dissolved alkali and alkaline earth cations diffuse out. In general, there does not appear to be a marked compositional gradient in this layer. The examination of numerous ancient glasses in the scanning electron microscope indicates that the boundary between the pristine glass and the hydrated layer is typically sharp down to at least one micrometre. However, detailed studies of corroded glass surfaces indicate the presence of a very thin zone at this boundary, which is characterized by a very steep compositional profile, of the order of $1\,\mu m$ thick (Scholze 1982:fig.1, Anovitz et al. 1999). This appears to be a region of diffusion of alkali cations out of the glass structure and is labelled diffusion zone in Figure 49.2. If network dissolution proceeds more rapidly, then there will be no hydrated layer, and the volume of glass will be severely diminished. In practice, the great majority of excavated glass has a hydrated silica surface layer, or shows little evidence of corrosion.

Macroscopically, the weathered (de-alkalized) layer on the glass surface may appear as a thin iridescent skin or as an opaque dull buff to brown coating. The thickness ranges dramatically from a few micrometres to

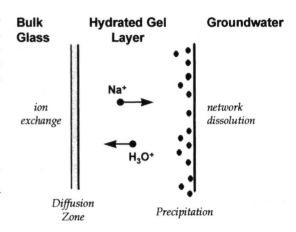

Figure 49.2   Schematic diagram showing corrosion of a soda-lime-silica glass. A simplified version of the model shown by Schulz et al. (1992).

millimetres, depending on composition, time since burial and environmental conditions. The glassy nature of the original material may be unrecognizable, fresh glass being preserved only as a core. The integrity of the weathered layer may vary considerably – in some cases, it is a flaky, exfoliating skin, readily detached from the glass, while in others it may be fully coherent with the underlying fresh glass, a de-alkalized pseudomorph of the original artifact. Vandiver (1992, 1995) has drawn attention to the marked changes in the appearance of the weathered layer that may occur after excavation. What may appear to be a relatively coherent and translucent material may undergo marked changes as it dries, becoming opaque and fragmentary, which she found were due to the loss of up to 23.5 per cent water by weight. Experimental work on model glass compositions (Scholze 1988) suggests that the water in the weathered layer is present as H_2O molecules, as well as hydroxyl groups (OH) bound to silicon atoms, and these are probably lost on drying. The amount of molecular water present may be variable and this may be one explanation for the variable behaviour of glass weathering layers after excavation.

In cross-section under the microscope, the weathered layer is readily identified due to its difference in refractive index (light microscopy) or electron back-scattering coefficient (as seen in the scanning electron microscope; Figure 49.3). A periodic structure, consisting of numerous bands, typically sub-parallel to the original surface, is often present (Figure 49.3). In many weathering products, SiO_2 and H_2O are virtually the only components present thus, by elimination, the layered structures are likely to represent variations in

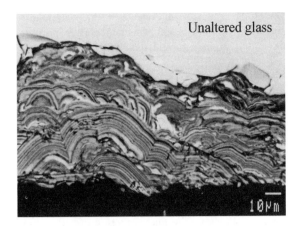

Figure 49.3 Scanning electron microscope cross section of a corroded soda-lime-silica glass showing the characteristic banding in the hydrated silica layer. British Museum photograph by C.P. Stapleton.

the SiO_2/H_2O concentration. Some years ago, it was observed that the number of bands in the weathered layers on some glasses was close to their calendar ages in years and it was suggested that this might offer a method of dating, analogous to dendrochronology. However, further work revealed substantial deviations from this pattern, and work in this area was not continued (Newton 1966). It is clear that the processes producing the banded structure of the glass have a complex dependency on a whole range of environmental factors; furthermore, even if there was a direct chronological relationship, the weathered layer may be thinned by physical and chemical processes (e.g., network dissolution). The thicknesses of the bands in the weathered layer may be of the order of hundreds of nanometres, and this interferes with light, causing the vivid iridescent colours – such as gold, purple and pink – that are sometimes shown by corroded glass.

In addition to the removal of soluble chemical components from the glass, principally the alkalis and alkaline earths, less soluble components may be concentrated in the weathered layers. For example, where the glass contained lead, even in low concentrations, lead salts (phosphates, sulfates and carbonates) may be precipitated near the surface of the weathered layer, apparently the result of lead leaching out of the glass and anionic components diffusing in (e.g., Freestone *et al.* 1985). Similarly, iron, aluminium, manganese, tin and antimony oxides commonly occur in ancient glasses, and may be enriched by weathering in the surface layer. Clearly, if an understanding of the original composition of a glass is required, then even

a qualitative analysis of a weathered glass surface may give misleading information.

Weathering of glasses above the ground, for example in church windows, or museums, may sometimes appear very different from buried glasses which are subject to frequent runoff of soil solutions. Hydrated silica layers can be very thin. It appears that network dissolution is a more aggressive phenomenon in such conditions. Whereas in the soil, the alkalis leached from the glass surface are washed away, in the atmosphere, they tend to remain as salts on the surface, creating alkaline conditions which favour breakdown of the network (e.g., Sterpenich and Libourel 1997).

Cultural factors influencing corrosion

The rate of weathering of archaeological glass varies substantially according to production technology. Some of the major groups are:

(i) Roman glass – a soda-lime-silica glass with 15–20 per cent Na_2O, 5–10 per cent CaO, 2–3 per cent Al_2O_3 and *c.* 70 per cent SiO_2, Roman glass is remarkably stable. The hydrated layer on much Roman glass is typically of the order of a few tens of micrometres or negligible, depending on the environment (e.g., Cox and Ford 1993).

(ii) Near Eastern plant ash glass. Soda-lime-silica glass differing from Roman glass primarily in terms of a slightly reduced silica content, lower alumina and higher alkaline earths $(CaO + MgO)$, glass of this type is far less stable than Roman glass. For example, Sasanian glass (*c.* fourth century AD) can be recovered from excavations in Mesopotamia with opaque weathering crusts several millimetres thick, while the accompanying Roman glass has a thin iridescent skin. Glass of this type recovered from the Egyptian desert, however, may be extremely well preserved, because of the very low ambient humidity. The poor preservation of glass from Bronze Age Mesopotamia (*c.* 1500 BC) is a major impediment to our understanding of the development of early glass technology.

(iii) Medieval European 'forest' glass. Low in silica, high in alkali (potash) and alkaline earths, Medieval glass is notoriously susceptible to weathering, and typically develops substantial hydrated layers, even after a few centuries.

(vi) Lead glasses. There are insufficient data on the corrosion of archaeological lead-silica glasses but Han dynasty $BaO–PbO–SiO_2$ glasses often have a thick weathered layer, while the lead-rich opaque red enamels on early Medieval Celtic metalwork are often extremely corroded relative to other (low lead) colours.

(v) Renaissance 'cristallo' glasses. Very clear glasses were produced in Venice from the fifteenth century, using plant ashes, which had been purified by solution and re-precipitation of the alkalis. Unfortunately, the alkaline earths were also removed from the ash by this technique, resulting in an unstable low-lime glass.

Quantification/prediction of corrosion

Attempts have been made, with some success, to use thermodynamic approaches to predict the corrosion rates of glasses from their compositions. One of the most successful has been the use of the free energies of hydration of the oxides making up the glass. Suggested by Paul (1977) and developed by Jantzen and Plodinec (1984) this relates the corrosion loss from the glass with a calculated free energy of hydration for the glass composition concerned. Where compositional differences are high, for example between obsidian and soda-lime-silica glass, there is a good correlation. However, it should be noted that for the differences of interest to archaeologists, the method is at present less useful. For example, Cox and Ford (1993) calculate similar free energies of hydration for Roman glasses excavated from Wroxeter, which show apparent corrosion rates (derived from the thicknesses of the hydrated layers) differing by factors approaching an order of magnitude. However, a difference in corrosion rate of this order is crucial – it can determine whether a thin glass vessel, of 1–2 mm wall thickness, has a thin corrosion layer or is totally destroyed. Thus local environmental factors, or minor differences in glass composition, are likely to be of greater significance than free energies of hydration, calculated using present models, in determining the relative corrosion rates of compositionally similar archaeological glasses.

CERAMICS

Archaeological ceramic bodies are generally made from fired clay, although there are some notable exceptions, such as the quartz-rich faience and stonepaste bodies of the ancient and Islamic worlds, and the soft-paste porcelains of early modern Europe. Unlike glass, ceramics are polycrystalline, and typically consist of

two or more phases (discrete chemical compounds). Depending primarily upon firing temperature, porosity may vary dramatically, from high-fired stoneware bodies, with porosities of less than 2 per cent, to low-fired earthenwares, with porosities of several tens of per cent.

Porosity is a key factor in the weathering of ceramics, as it provides access to soil solutions. A dried clay body may have 50 per cent pores by volume, and these pores are open or interlinked, allowing access to groundwater. As the clay body is fired, shrinkage occurs, but the porosity remains high until small amounts of melt begin to form at the contacts of the clay minerals, at temperatures in the range 600–800°C. Figure 49.4a shows the microstructure of a Romano-British earthenware, which has been fired so that a small amount of melting, or *vitrification*, has occurred. The pores appear black and it can be readily appreciated that the interior of this vessel was very accessible to soil solutions after burial. In addition to the very fine pores, seen in Figure 49.4a, coarser pores, resulting from shrinkage around coarse mineral particles and from forming processes such as coiling, are also present in low fired earthenwares. These allow easy ingress of soil solutions. As the firing temperature of a ceramic is increased, the amount of melt formed increases and the body shrinks until the pores are closed and the ceramic is essentially a suspension of crystals in a glass, as shown in Figure 49.4b for an eighteenth century English porcelain. The pores in this ceramic are closed, preventing access to water.

Low-fired ceramics

As has been observed, porosity provides access for corrosive soil solutions, and it follows that very low-fired earthenware ceramics with a high porosity are relatively unstable. A comparison of modern pottery fired in a bonfire and a prehistoric sherd demonstrates this very well; when struck a modern sherd will emit a high pitched sound while an ancient ceramic will often sound dull; a sample will break from an ancient sherd in a less brittle manner. The degree of deterioration of the ceramics clearly varies, dependent on a range of factors, including burial environment. For example, Allen (1991) measured the hardness of prehistoric potsherds from a number of British Bronze Age sites. On the basis of her data, she suggested that the hardness of the pottery was related to the acidity of the burial environment. Sherds from acidic deposits (pH 4.5) were softer than those from neutral or moderately alkaline

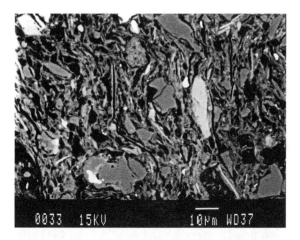

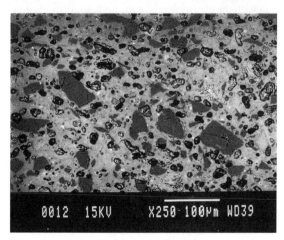

Figure 49.4 Cross sections, in the scanning electron microscope, of (a) low-fired Romano-British pottery flagon, showing very high porosity (black) and the very fine nature of the interparticle bonds, (b) largely vitrified eighteenth century porcelain, with large quartz particles (grey) and closed pores (black) in a continuous glass matrix. British Museum photographs by I.C. Freestone.

environments. Allen's findings, although very suggestive, are not well constrained, because of the nature of the archaeological materials. It is not clear, for example, if the pots from the different sites differed in terms of initial firing temperature or bulk composition. They do indicate, however, the need for more investigations of this type.

Microstructures of low-fired ceramics consist essentially of a framework of fired clay particles, bonded at edges and corners by a small amount of melting or solid state sintering. The clay particles will have partially or wholly lost their structurally bound water (−OH groups; de-hydroxylization), and be partially amorphous, consisting of collapsed aluminosilicate structures. It is probable that the corrosion of low-fired ceramics depends upon two main mechanisms. Firstly, particle contacts involving glass will be especially vulnerable to attack and weakening, due to glass corrosion processes (see above). Secondly, fired clay minerals are prone to re-hydration, and will slowly revert to clay. Kingery (1974) reports laboratory evidence for the re-hydroxylization of ancient ceramic clays, while Vandiver (1992) refers to observations and experiments on Upper Palaeolithic fired clay figurines which indicate that their clays have partially re-hydroxylated. Furthermore, there is an abundance of verbal anecdotal evidence (but little formal reporting) of the 'clay-like' consistency of ceramics retrieved from excavation.

Perhaps the simplest mechanism of ceramic corrosion is the dissolution of very soluble phases that occur naturally in the clay or which were added as temper. Calcite ($CaCO_3$) is the most obvious of these, and pottery which was originally tempered with limestone or shell often shows large angular voids, where the lime has been leached out in a moderately acidic environment. Ceramic petrographers frequently need to infer the character of leached calcite inclusions from the form of the remaining void. Voids left by the dissolution of gypsum ($CaSO_4.2H_2O$), naturally included in the clay, may sometimes also be recognized in thin section by their characteristic 'swallow-tailed' morphology.

The scaly deposits of calcium carbonate on the surfaces of many excavated ceramics are well-known, but it is less well appreciated that soil solutions may deposit new minerals internally, in the pores. These include calcite, which may be visible in large pores using the optical microscope, but also includes material precipitated on a very fine scale in the matrix of the ceramic, or possibly adsorbed on the mineral phases in the matrix. Figure 49.5 shows the distribution of phosphorus, calcium and iron oxides across the cross section of a sherd of Romano-British pottery (Freestone et al. 1985). The deposition of material within the sherd is demonstrated by the characteristic U-shaped diffusion profiles across the wall of a vessel. There is a clear enrichment towards the surfaces of the sherd, reflecting penetration by soil solutions. Such profiles clearly indicate that even the cores of low-fired pottery are accessible to contaminants from the burial environment. Calcium and phosphorus oxides are particularly well correlated, suggesting that a calcium phosphate phase is being precipitated. Later

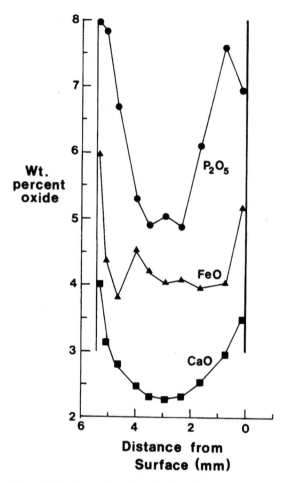

Figure 49.5 Compositional profiles for phosphorus, calcium and iron oxides across a sherd of Roman red-slipped pottery (Freestone *et al.* 1985).

work has reported similar effects for phosphate (Dunnell and Hunt 1990) and other components including oxides of manganese (Walter and Besnus 1989) and strontium and barium (Picon 1991). De Paepe (1979) noted the absorption of transition metals, such as zinc and lead, in domestic ceramics associated with early metallurgical activity. Lemoine and Picon (1982) detected large changes in major element composition which would be likely to affect provenance investigations of ceramics (see Chapter 41); Buxeda i Garrigós (1999) has advocated the use of statistical procedures to minimize any problems.

It was at one time suggested that the diffusion of material into ancient ceramics might offer a dating method (Waddell and Fountain 1974). However, cera-

mics are so varied in their microstructure (even the products of a single kiln have a range of firing temperatures) that derivation of a diffusion coefficient applicable to more than a single sherd is impracticable at the present time.

Calcareous ceramics

Calcareous ceramics, made using clays containing CaO in the range 5–25 weight per cent, may be particularly affected by weathering even where porosity is relatively low. The lime is originally present in the clay as calcite, $CaCO_3$, but if the ceramic is fired to temperatures above about 800°C, the calcite decomposes to calcium oxide, CaO, losing CO_2 as a gaseous phase. Depending upon firing temperature and duration, this CaO may react with the clay minerals in the body to form silicates and aluminosilicates. Any unreacted lime will eventually re-carbonate to $CaCO_3$ and be liable to dissolution, but some of the lime-rich silicates formed are also vulnerable to corrosion.

Calcareous clays of this type were widely used in the ancient world to produce relatively vitrified ceramic domestic wares, typified by Roman *terra sigillata*. These were commonly fired in the temperature range 800–1050°C, and developed an extensive glass phase as well as high temperature silicates such as gehlenite ($Ca_2Al_2Si_2O_7$). Heimann and Maggetti (1981) drew attention to the observation that, while gehlenite is commonly found in modern ceramics, it is rare in ancient ceramics of similar composition. They were able to show that the absence of gehlenite in the ancient material is due to its decomposition by soil solutions, and confirmed the presence of characteristic decomposition products in ancient terra sigillata sherds.

Extensive alteration was observed by Middleton and Cowell (1993) and Owen and Day (1998) in calcareous porcelain sherds from the mid-eighteenth century Longton Hall factory, Staffordshire, UK. In these ceramics the lime was largely present as crystals of wollastonite, $CaSiO_3$, which decomposed and was partially leached from the sherds. Owen and Day estimated that the weathered samples had undergone a mass loss of 17–44 per cent, mainly due to the depletion of 75–80 per cent of the total CaO and up to 45 per cent of the SiO_2.

Glazes and surface coats

It might be anticipated that the application of a glaze coating to a ceramic would prevent ingress of soil solutions and inhibit corrosion. This is generally the case but the degree of protection varies. Vandiver (1992) draws attention to the importance of the 'fit' between the glaze and the ceramic body; how well they are fused together and whether crazing has developed due to differential contraction. McCarthy *et al.* (1997) show that heterogeneities in the glaze, particularly silica particles, may significantly affect its deterioration. Early ceramic glazes are of a limited number of types; each of these has a characteristic weathering behaviour. They include:

(i) Alkaline glazes, composed primarily of alkali oxides and silica, have a long history in the Near East, beginning in the sixteenth century BC. They are commonly low in silica, lime and alumina, similar to plant ash glasses, and are very susceptible to weathering. Indeed, it can be difficult to find sufficient unweathered glazes from Mesopotamian contexts that can give a representative sample of compositional variation. Freestone (1991) shows examples of such glazes which are completely deteriorated, being composed of hydrated silica, similar to the porous layer found on the surface of weathered glasses.

(ii) Lead glazes. The production of lead glazes began in the late first millennium BC, apparently independently in the Near East and in China; their use grew in the West in the Medieval period. Lead glazes commonly show some vulnerability to weathering, dependent upon how they were made. In Medieval Europe, lead glazes were often produced by reacting a lead compound directly with a pottery body, yielding a glaze with up to 10 per cent alumina, which promotes glaze stability. On the other hand, eighteenth century English porcelain glazes which were applied as a lead-silica frit have low alumina, and were found by Middleton and Cowell (1993) to be extensively weathered after 250 years.

(iii) The glossy clay slips on ancient Greek and Roman pottery, such as Attic wares and terra sigillata are essentially dense, vitrified clays similar in composition to the body clay. Thus they form a protective layer on the vessel surface. However, they are thin, and were frequently damaged due to physical abrasion, during use and site formation processes. The compositional profiles in Figure 49.5 were derived from a sherd with such a 'clay glaze' on one surface; however, the poor preservation of the 'glaze', which was not well-bonded to the body, has resulted in little protection of the ceramic.

(iv) Stoneware and porcelain glazes. The glazes on Far Eastern porcelain and stoneware, and upon European salt-glazed stoneware, have high alumina contents and low porosities, which render them very durable. They act as good protection for the ceramic bodies, but the bodies themselves are, in any case, relatively stable.

CONCLUSIONS

The overall impression that emerges from a review of the corrosion of ancient ceramics and glasses is one of complexity. The processes that occur are complex not only because of the nature of the chemical reactions that occur, and their dependence upon very variable environmental factors – average humidity, pH, temperature and so on, but also because of the great variability of these synthetic materials. Glasses show a wide range of compositional variability, in minor elements as well as major ones, while ceramics based upon a single clay may show a wide range of mineralogies and porosities, depending upon firing temperature. Simple relationships are unlikely to emerge from the study of such materials, so that the possibility of using their corrosion as a basis for dating, which has been suggested from time to time (see above) is very unlikely.

The compositional changes undergone by glass during the corrosion process are commonly recognized macroscopically and are very apparent upon analysis with a modern micro-analytical technique that involves imaging, for example the electron microprobe. However, the changes undergone by ceramics are often far from evident, detectable only by detailed analysis (Bearat *et al.* 1992). However, they may affect the physical properties of the material, so that tests of the physical properties of early ceramics, such as fracture strength and thermal shock resistance, should be undertaken upon replica materials, as the original materials may give very misleading results. There is also a possibility that compositional alteration may modify the elemental analysis of a ceramic to the extent that provenance determination becomes seriously affected. While the success of such techniques in many cases suggests that this may not be a ubiquitous problem, the analyst would be wise to watch for suggestive variations of likely contaminants, such as P, Ba, Mn and Na and to reject heavily affected sherds. The common practice of taking a sample for analysis from the centre of sherds is likely to reduce, but not eliminate, the problem.

Archaeological materials, particularly glasses, have been widely seen as potential analogues for nuclear waste disposal glasses (Heimann 1986, Vandiver 1995, Macquet and Thomassin 1982, Trocellier 1997). As noted by Heimann, however, the relationship is, at best, a qualitative one, as the conditions in nuclear waste repositories are likely to be very different from those encountered in archaeological deposits. However, the large body of work generated by the investigation of glasses as host media for nuclear waste is invaluable in facilitating an understanding of the processes involved in the corrosion of archaeological materials.

Finally, the relationship of corrosion mechanisms and rates with environmental factors needs to be better understood if we are to be able to confidently preserve archaeological remains *in situ*. Not only may environmental changes affect the rate of corrosion of the original material, but alterations in conditions such as average humidity may have a marked effect on the weathering products which are already present, for example, by dehydrating glass corrosion layers, causing exfoliation or disaggregation. There is a clear need for much more work to be done, aimed specifically at archaeological materials.

REFERENCES

*Recommended for further reading

Adams, P.B. (1984). Glass corrosion. *Journal of Non-Crystalline Solids*, **67**:193–205.

Allen, C.S.M. (1991). Thin sections of Bronze Age pottery from the East Midlands of England. In Middleton, A. and Freestone, I. (eds) *Recent Developments in Ceramic Petrology*, 1–15. Occasional Paper 81, British Museum Press: London.

Anovitz, L.M., Elam, J.M., Riciputi, L.R. and Cole, D.R. (1999). The failure of obsidian hydration dating: sources, implications and new directions. *Journal of Archaeological Science*, **26**:735–752.

Bearat, H., Dufournier, D. and Nouet, Y. (1992). Alteration of ceramics due to contact with sea water. *Archaeologia Polona*, **30**:151–162.

Biron, I. (1999). Study of XVth and XVIth century painted enamels through scientific analysis: causes of glass deterioration. *Berliner Beiträge zur Archäometrie*, **16**:163–179.

Brill, R.H. (1962). A note on the scientist's definition of glass. *Journal of Glass Studies*, **4**:127–138.

Buxeda i Garrigós, J. (1999). Alteration and contamination of archaeological ceramics. The perturbation problem. *Journal of Archaeological Science*, **26**:295–313.

Cox, G.A. and Ford, B.A. (1993). The long term corrosion of glass by ground water. *Journal of Materials Science*, **28**:5637–5647.

Cox, G.A., Heavens, O.S., Newton, R.G. and Pollard, A.M. (1979). A study of the weathering behaviour of Mediaeval glass from York Minster. *Journal of Glass Studies*, **21**:54–75.

De Paepe, P. (1979). Chemical characteristics of archaic and classical coarse wares from Tharikos, SE Attica (Greece). *Miscellanea Graeca*, **2**:89–112.

Dunnell, R.C. and Hunt, T.L. (1990). Elemental composition and inference of ceramic vessel function. *Current Anthropology*, **31**:330–336.

El-Shamy, T.M. (1973). The chemical durability of K_2O–CaO–MgO–SiO_2 glasses. *Physics and Chemistry of Glasses*, **14**:1–5.

Freestone, I.C. (1991). Technical examination of neo-Assyrian wall plaques. *Iraq*, **53**:55–58.

Freestone, I.C., Meeks, N.D. and Middleton, A.P. (1985). Retention of phosphate in buried ceramics: an electron microbeam approach. *Archaeometry*, **27**:161–177.

Greaves, G.N., Gurman, S.J., Catlow, C.R.A., Chardwick, A.V., Howde-Walter, S., Henderson, C.M.B. and Dobson, B.R. (1991). A structural basis for ionic diffusion in oxide glasses. *Philosophical Magazine*, A **64**:1059–1072.

Heimann, R.B. (1986). Nuclear fuel waste management and archaeology: are ancient glasses indicators of long term durability of man made materials? *Glass Technology*, **27**:96–101.

Heimann, R.B. and Maggetti, M. (1981). Experiments on simulated burial of calcareous terra sigillata. In Hughes, M.J. (ed.) *Scientific Studies in Ancient Ceramics*, 163–177. Occasional Paper 19, British Museum: London.

Jantzen, C.M. and Plodinec, M.J. (1984). Thermodynamic model of natural, Medieval and nuclear waste glass durability. *Journal of Non-Crystalline Solids*, **67**:207–223.

Kingery, W.D. (1974). A note on the differential thermal analysis of archaeological ceramics. *Archaeometry*, **16**:109–112.

Lemoine, C. and Picon, M. (1982). La fixation du phosphore par les céramiques lors leur enfouissement et ses incidences analytiques. *Revue d'Archéométrie*, **6**:101–112.

Macquet, C. and Thomassin, J.H. (1982). Archaeological glasses as modelling of the behaviour of buried nuclear waste glass. *Applied Clay Science*, **7**:17–31.

McCarthy, B.E., Vandiver, P.B. and Kruger, J. (1997). A study of the role of heterogeneities in the initial stages of corrosion of glazes using dynamic imaging microellipsometry. In Vandiver, P.B., Druzik, J.R., Merkel, J.F. and Stewart, J. (eds) *Materials Issues in Art and Archaeology V*, 31–38. Symposia Proceedings 462, Materials Research Society: Pittsburgh.

Middleton, A.P. and Cowell, M.R. (1993). Report on the examination and analysis of some porcelains from Longton Hall and West Pans. *Post-Medieval Archaeology*, **27**:94–109.

Newton, R.G. (1966). Some problems in the dating of ancient glass by counting the layers in the weathering crust. *Glass Technology*, **7**:22–25.

Newton, R.G. (1985). The durability of glass – a review. *Glass Technology*, **26**:21–38.

*Newton, R.G. and Davison, S. (1989). *Conservation of Glass*. London: Butterworths.

Owen, J.V. and Day, T.E. (1998). Assessing and correcting the effects of the chemical weathering of potsherds: a case study using soft-paste porcelain wastes from the Longton Hall (Staffordshire) factory site. *Geoarchaeology*, **13**:265–286.

Paul, A. (1977). Chemical durability of glasses: a thermodynamic approach. *Journal of Materials Science*, **12**:2246–2268.

Picon, M. (1991). Quelques observations complémentaires sur les alterations de composition des céramiques au cours de temps: cas de quelques alcalins et alcalino-terreux. *Revue d'Archéométrie*, **15**:117–122.

Pollard, A.M. and Heron, C. (1996). *Archaeological Chemistry*. Royal Society of Chemistry: Cambridge.

*Scholze, H. (1982). Chemical durability of glasses. *Journal of Non-Crystalline Solids*, **52**:91–103.

Scholze, H. (1988). Glass-water interaction. *Journal of Non-Crystalline Solids*, **102**:1–10.

Schulz, R.L., Clark, D.E. and Folz, D.C. (1992). Theories of corrosion as applied to preservation of archaeological ceramics. In Vandiver, P.B., Druzik, J.R., Wheeler, G.S. and Freestone, I.C. (eds) *Materials Issues in Art and Archaeology III*, 1015–1029. MRS Symposium Proceedings 267, Material Research Society: Pittsburgh.

Sterpenich, J. and Libourel, G. (1997). Les vitraux médiévaux: caractérisation physico-chimique de l'alteration. *TECHNE*, **6**:70–678.

Trocellier, P. (1997). Les verres nucléaires. *TECHNE*, **6**:85–92.

*Vandiver, P.B. (1992). Corrosion and conservation of ancient glass and ceramics. In Clark, D.E. and Zoitos, B.K. (eds) *Corrosion of Glass Ceramics and Ceramic Superconductors*, 393–430. Noyes Publication: Park Ridge, New Jersey.

Vandiver, P.B. (1995). Corrosion of synthesised glasses and glazes as analogues for nuclear waste glass degradation. In Vandiver, P.B., Druzik, J.R., Madrid, J.L.G., Freestone, I.C. and Wheeler, G.S. (eds) *Materials Issues in Art and Archaeology IV*, 395–412. Symposium Proceedings 352, Materials Research Society: Pittsburgh.

Verità, M. (1998). Deterioration mechanisms of ancient soda-lime-silica mosaic tesserae. In *Proceedings of 18th International Congress on Glass, San Francisco*. American Ceramic Society: Ohio Westerville.

Waddell, C. and Fountain, J.C. (1984). Calcium diffusion: a new dating method for archaeological ceramics. *Geology*, **12**:24–26.

Walter, V. and Besnus, Y. (1989). Un example de pollution en phosphore et en manganese de céramiques anciennes. *Revue d'Archéométrie*, **13**:55–64.

Zachariasen, W.H. (1932). The atomic arrangement in glass. *Journal of the American Chemical Society*, **54**:3841–3851.

50

The Deterioration of Organic Materials

J.M. CRONYN

Institute of Archaeology, University College London.

There are a number of reasons why an understanding of the deterioration of the organic materials of artifacts both during burial (taphonomy) and when exposed is important to archaeology, an understanding which is largely effected through the specialism of conservation. Conservation in this context aims to understand why and how archaeological materials deteriorate and how this can be prevented (e.g., Berdacou 1990, Caple 2000, Cronyn 1990). It seeks to address a range of archaeological questions, including the following:

(i) Can we predict where organic material may still be surviving in order to protect it or to inform excavation strategy?

(ii) Can the absence or condition of material tell us something of its environment prior to and immediately after burial, or is this survival/loss more to do with the nature of the original material?

(iii) What effect will excavation have on organic material?

(iv) How can damage to the material be prevented whilst it is being excavated, lifted, stored and examined?

(v) Can it be preserved *in situ*?

(vi) How can it be preserved for long-term study and for meaningful display?

(vii) Can close examination of this deteriorated material tell us something about its original appearance, use and manufacture?

Thirty years ago the literature on this subject was not extensive. It was written either by non-archaeological scientists in answer to specific characterization queries or to make use of a particular analytical technique, or else by conservators empirically testing practical solutions of conservation. By the mid-1970s, following the great expansion in wet-site and marine excavation, the subject was beginning to develop with scientists working more closely with archaeology and conservators using science more robustly. The literature of the last 10 years looks more towards systems than a static view, linking characterization of condition with complex interrelating causes and treatments. It remains patchy, with, for example, the post-excavation 'museum' environment receiving wider study than that of burial, and is published largely in conference proceedings rather than refereed journals. These developments are set in the context of a vast literature in 'biodegradation', the useful destruction of organic waste, as well as 'biodeterioration' (Allsopp and Seal 1986), the unwanted biological decay of materials useful to society. Whilst these sciences are a major reference source for the deterioration of archaeological organics, care needs to be taken in extrapolating

Handbook of Archaeological Sciences. Edited by D.R. Brothwell and A.M. Pollard.

inferences to extended time periods and to already badly-deteriorated materials. These sciences in return have found data from archaeological studies useful; e.g., Hedges (1990) welcomed dated archaeological wood to help calibrate geochemical data sets.

DETERIORATION OF ORGANIC ARTIFACTS

Broadly, deterioration of artifacts is caused by physical, chemical or biological agents in burial sites (Chapter 47) or post-excavation environments (Chapter 52), which result in physical and chemical changes to the material. These changes also depend on the intrinsic nature of a particular material; thus in wet sites oak is inherently more robust than ash, and parts of a leather shoe may survive only because it has iron nails. Given the variables both within the burial environment and within specific artifacts, it is extremely difficult to predict with certainty which materials will survive and in what condition, but certain generalizations can be made. As organic materials are part of the natural carbon cycle (Chapter 16), they are most unlikely to survive burial unless the activity of biological organisms is constrained.

The most common constraint is the restriction of oxygen whereby only anaerobic bacteria or those tolerant of very low oxygen levels can flourish. Typical examples of this are the waterlogged native North American sites, and compacted urban sites such as the Elizabethan Rose Theatre in London (Corfield 1998). The other major constraint is desiccation, where the water needed for microbial activity is absent. Examples include the dry tombs of Egypt and the frozen Iron Age tombs in Siberia. Other causes of restricted micro-organism growth are high saline levels as in arid soils or localized toxins such as copper salts from corroding artifacts. But even if biological deterioration has been reduced to a minimum, material is most unlikely to be found in its pre-burial condition. Not only will the remaining bacteria have an effect on its physico-chemical nature, but chemical agents will also be active in wet sites. Hydrolysis of the fibrous polymers which make up most of the organic materials used in artifacts will ensue; broadly that of plant materials is increased by acidic pH and that of animal materials in an alkaline pH. In dry sites there is the possibility of oxidation. Finally, in both wet and dry sites there are physical agents which can cause changes to materials, whether this is the crushing weight of overburden on an urban site, or desiccation and sub-

sequent loss of volume of cellular and fibrous tissue in a dry vault.

On excavation there is an alteration in the variables of the deteriorating agents, most noticeably a change in humidity. Material becomes physically unstable; that from wet sites shrinks and distorts as water is lost; that from dry sites swells or disintegrates as moisture is taken up. As moisture levels rise, hydrolysis of the latter may occur, as may oxidation of the former as oxygen levels increase. From any burial, organics may suffer oxidation from increased light levels and more rapid chemical reactions because of increased temperatures. The levels of oxygen, moisture and temperature now allow for aerobic microbial activity and even that of insects and molluscs. But a major agent of physical deterioration at this juncture is often simply poor handling. This understanding of deterioration is underpinned by considerable knowledge, knowledge which continues to develop. For example, recent research suggests that in peat bogs preservation of bodies may be a result of insufficient nutrients rather than low oxygen levels as previously thought (Painter 1995).

DETERIORATION OF WOOD

Because wood is the major organic material found on wet archaeological excavations, it is the major concern of research. Before the 1950s there are only a few examples of even partially successful attempts to preserve wet wood artifacts. These tend to be extremely important and massive finds, such as the Viking Oseberg boat in Norway (Christensen 1970). Better conservation techniques were first developed in Scandinavia for projects such as the raising of the seventeenth century warship *Vasa*, now on display in Stockholm harbour (Barkman 1975), and were based on an analysis of deteriorated wood. Since then conservation has developed techniques not only to provide further impressive displays such as the Viking timber buildings at York (Spriggs 1991), but also for a growing archive for study and future use.

Wet site taphonomy

On excavation, wood can appear in what looks like remarkably good condition with little sign of deterioration. The real situation is revealed as soon as the moisture content falls: the 'wood' can rapidly crack, warp and shrink alarmingly and irreversibly. Whilst there is a long tradition of research in wood and timber preservation, the timescales and environments discussed there are inappropriate for archaeological wood. The fruits of the first 20 years of conservation-related research were drawn together by Florian (1990), Grattan (1987), Grattan and Clarke (1987), and Rowell and Barbour (1990) where discussion is also contributed by wood scientists, microbiologists and geochemists.

Wet archaeological wood has lost much of the cellulose fibrils which make up its cell walls, but the original lignin, a polyphenol which strengthens and protects living wood, remains. This reinforces and cements together the deteriorated skeletal cells whose dimensions are retained bulked out by water and, on occasion, extraneous deposits. Thus on excavation wet wood can appear in excellent condition complete with delicate tool marks such as those on rare Anglo-Saxon wooden coffins (Park 1997). But as soon as moisture is lost, the cells collapse and the cellulose molecules shrink.

Recent work has shown that the major cause of the deterioration of wood during burial is due to micro-organisms (Blanchette *et al.* 1990). Little success has been found using culture techniques to identify which organisms have caused this decay: more has been found by examining the micromorphology using both light and electron microscopy to match the pattern of cell wall deterioration with that of known fungi and bacteria. When an understanding of the biochemical requirements of these micro-organisms is also brought into play, a picture emerges of the absence of deterioration by micro-organisms where a deposit is completely anoxic, but evidence of aerobic bacterial attack eroding the cell walls even in near anoxic conditions (Blanchette *et al.* 1990, Blanchette and Hoffmann 1994, Nilsson 1999). Where conditions are less anoxic, the activity of these bacteria increases and when conditions allow for greater aerobic activity, there is evidence of attack by soft rot fungi. If oxygen levels are high enough to allow brown and white rot fungi to flourish for any length of time, no wood will survive (Blanchette *et al.* 1990). There are of course other environmental as well as material parameters which affect the activity of micro-organisms, but certainly in these wet environments, E_h (a measure of redox: see Chapter 47) appears to be the major discriminator in relation to the survival of wet wood. The degree of abiotic deterioration that occurs is still unclear (Hedges 1990). It is likely that there is hydrolysis of the hemi-cellulose components of the cell walls and possibly some of the cellulose itself, resulting in shortened polymers which may cause physical disruption (Hoffmann and Jones 1990).

These authors make it clear that the degree of deterioration of wet wood can vary enormously both between species and between zones in wood, with the core often being barely degraded compared to the external surface, something which has long been known to cause problems in treatment.

In situ preservation

This information, together with research in engineering and in environmental management and chemistry, is currently being put to use in an attempt to preserve wet wood *in situ* and to predict its survival (Chapter 47). But reburial of large wooden artifacts in particular has been a long-standing consideration: in an attempt to cope with large quantities of ships' timbers in Denmark, some were reburied (Jespersen 1985), whilst attempts to retain the level of the water table on the polders of the Netherlands around excavated or exposed ships has a similar pedigree (de Jong 1981). The renewed interest has triggered a series of laboratory experiments related to the reburial of timber (Bjordal and Nilsson 1999, Gregory 1999).

Storage of wet wood

Deterioration studies are also addressing the problem of successful storage of wet wood, at least in the short term. During storage raised oxygen levels are inevitable and evidence has been produced of considerable deterioration by aerobic bacteria, as well as brown and white rot fungi, for example on the stored timbers of Henry VIII's flagship *Mary Rose* raised from the seabed in 1982 (Mouzouras 1994). Early methodologies for storage drawn from timber preservation research suggested the use of particular biocides. These have been refined over the years to take account of problems of disposal of mass quantities of biocide, its interference in analysis and treatments, as well as its possible toxicity during treatment and later handling and display. Other supplementary, less toxic, means to control organisms have been sought, including cooled water (Mouzouras 1994), surfactants (Yoshimura and Omura 1995), gamma-ray irradiation (Pointing *et al.* 1997) and copper-silver ion sterilization (Vere-Stevens *et al.* 1999).

Long-term preservation of wet wood

The question of how to preserve wet wood in the long term received considerable attention in the 1970s and 1980s, both in north-west Europe and in North America where wrecks and wet prehistoric sites were being widely excavated. Deterioration studies are crucial to characterize deteriorated material so that this can be linked to specific treatments, and treatments can be evaluated. This characterization has been attempted in numerous ways including chemically (Grattan and Mathias 1986), and morphologically (Blanchette and Hoffmann 1994). But that which has been most widely used is the assessment of physical condition, especially calculation of the maximum water content (Grattan 1987, Schniewind 1989). For small objects such as the Maori bowls of New Zealand (Johns 1998), because it can be overly destructive to take samples, completely non-destructive methods of testing are of paramount interest. At present, rather than one single discriminator, workers rely on a holistic assessment of condition using a number of modes of characterization (Panter and Spriggs 1997).

Treatments for the long-term preservation of wet wood (Grattan and Clarke 1987) have two major aims: (i) to overcome the surface tension of the retreating columns of water in the cells as it is often greater than the tensile strength of the deteriorated cells, and (ii) to introduce enough strength into the dried-out cells to withstand handling and display (Barbour 1990).

For large objects, treatments are usually designed to replace the water with a non-toxic, water soluble substance which solidifies on drying thereby supporting the cells. The substance which has replaced the alum previously used is PEG (polyethylene glycol). Examples of its large scale use are the immersion of the entire *Bremen Cog* (Hoffmann 1997) and spraying the *Mary Rose*. One of the problems with PEG is cost and possible cheaper alternatives have been investigated, including impregnation with sucrose (Hoffmann and Kühn 1999), natural freeze-drying in an arctic environment (Ambrose *et al.* 1994) and simply careful air-drying. For some time, smaller items have been treated using freeze-drying chambers (Ambrose 1990). Before being frozen, the wet wood is immersed in a solution of a cryoprotector which counteracts the increase in volume of water when it freezes and subsequent destruction. The ice is sublimed from the wood under reduced pressure thereby avoiding surface tension problems. Low molecular weight PEGs are used both as a cryoprotector and as a humectant which buffers the degraded cellulose against moisture changes after treatment (Watson 1997). This method has been successful at treating both very degraded wood such as the prehistoric trackways of Somerset (Coles 1981) and wood

with delicate detail such as Roman writing tablets where the imprint of the stylus alone retains the message (Ganiaris 1990).

New treatments are constantly being mooted such as the use of supercritical-drying (Kaye and Cole-Hamilton 1998) and PAGs (polyalkylene glycols – less biodegradable hygroscopic alternatives to PEG; Pouman *et al.* 1999). But these are usually too expensive for anything on a routine practical scale. Any treatment has numerous parameters which must be matched against the many characteristics of degraded wood when choosing which method to use. Making these connections is not easy and still needs much development. Before any wood, particularly in the case of large objects, is treated, wider discussion is also necessary: not only is the treatment expensive but also the later care and curation is costly. In some countries where there are agreed guidelines (e.g., Brunning 1995 for the UK), it is thought ethical to consider disposing of timbers once they have been studied and recorded (e.g., Fry 1996).

Dry archaeological wood

Dry wood is found in archaeological contexts to a much lesser extent than wet wood, but it is part of many museum collections, especially those with collections from Egyptian tombs (e.g. Watkinson and Brown 1995). Here the wood is often in remarkably good condition often only requiring treatment to provide strength for handling and display. The lack of moisture in such tombs and in other desert regions where even prehistoric basketry can be found, inhibits microorganisms and insects. Only in recent years (Schniewind 1989) have attempts been made to investigate the nature of degraded dry wood to develop and match more appropriate treatments. Blanchette *et al.* (1994) has found morphological evidence for attack by soft rot and brown rot fungi, but also for abiotic deterioration, possibly chemical, leading to cracking of the cell walls and separation of cells. Again in conjunction with polymer chemistry and wood science (Schniewind and Eastman 1994), conservation is looking to improve the success of reversible treatments which consolidate dry wood as in the case of the seventh century AD coffin of St Cuthbert in Durham (Cronyn and Horie 1985).

Deterioration of textiles

The fibres in archaeological textiles can be from either a cellulosic plant source such as the bast fibres of flax (linen) or nettles, or an animal proteinaceous source such as wool (keratin) or the silk moth larval cocoons (sericin) (Tímár-Balázsy and Eastop 1998). Not only do these fibres have implications for economic and environmental interpretation, there is also interest in the dyes (e.g., Gillard *et al.* 1994a), the fabric into which the fibres are spun and woven (Wild 1990) and evidence of use, such as the possible pre-burial washing of Tutankhamun's shroud (Cooke 1990).

Effects of burial environments on deterioration

As fibres made into textiles are not treated to extend their life, it is not surprising that almost all textiles once buried deteriorate extremely quickly; cellulosics, for example, losing much of their strength within just three weeks (Cooke 1990). It is only the rapid formation of stable and extreme conditions of anoxia in rubbish tips or cesspits, or desiccation in desert burials or frozen tombs, which will preserve them. Apart from a general understanding that hydrolysis of cellulosic fibres is faster in acidic environments and that of proteins is faster in alkaline, there is little direct evidence for the processes of deterioration during burial. These might include bacterial attack in wet environments and oxidation in arid environments (Cooke 1990). Keratin, the protein of wool, has a particularly complex pattern of deterioration because of the disulfide bonds which cross-link the polymer chains (Tarleton and Ordoñez 1995), usually rendering it particularly resistant to hydrolysis and enzyme attack in all except extremely alkaline wet sites. Certainly in particular waterlogged sites differential deterioration of fibre types occurs, as is shown by fabrics of mixed types (Pritchard 1990). Some evidence of physical deterioration has also been found caused by freezing and thawing of ice in fragments of woollen textile of seventeenth and eighteenth century Arctic fur trappers or whalers (Peacock 1999). Dyes too are subject to deterioration during wet burial; some study has been made of the change in colour due to redox reactions of mordants (Needles and Regazzi 1987).

Preservation of organic materials as pseudomorphs

Apart from anoxic or desiccated sites, textiles can be preserved where micro-organisms are inhibited in other ways such as in salt-laden soils or adjacent to corroding copper alloy objects. In aerated damp environments, a phenomenon known as replacement can 'preserve' the morphology if not the chemistry of textile fibres, or

indeed wood and skins (Cameron 1990). Here rapid corrosion of iron or sometimes copper allows the precipitation of the corrosion products in or around the fibres whilst they decay. What is retrieved later is a pseudomorph, either a cast of the outside of the fibre or a replica of the fibre itself. There has been considerable interest (e.g., Chen *et al.* 1998) in the mechanisms of this phenomenon, and recently it has been shown that more often than not chemical traces of the fibres and even dyes can be found within these pseudomorphs (Gillard *et al.* 1994b).

Long-term preservation and presentation

There has been less interest and success in the characterization of deteriorated fibres in relation to treatment. The post-excavation survival of wet textile fragments again primarily concerns dimensional stabilization and strengthening of weakened tissue: on rapid air-drying the fibres collapse allowing the polymeric molecules to bond irreversibly to one another (Tímár-Balázsy and Eastop 1998), leading to shrinkage and embrittlement. The low research activity in this area is partly because textile fragments can often be treated simply, and apparently successfully, by air-drying and careful storage; there is not the dramatic deterioration experienced on exposing wet wood. A belief has perhaps developed that no better treatments are needed. A dearth of research may also be due to the low esteem in which, until recently, textiles in archaeology have been held, as well as the difficulty of researching the material (Cooke and Peacock 1992). Research is also hampered by the very small quantities of wet textile found on excavation, and also by its diversity. But new treatments are needed; air dried textiles are often extremely brittle and impossible to study or display without damage (Tarleton and Ordoñez 1995).

To counteract the collapse of fibres on drying due to the surface tension of the retreating water, freeze-drying including the addition of cryoprotectors, consolidants, plasticizers and humectants is now often used (Peacock 1990). Work continues to determine whether this is the least damaging means for drying wet textiles or whether dehydrating through solvents or slow air-drying from the frozen state might be preferable (Peacock 1990, Jakes and Mitchell 1992, Peacock 1999, Tarleton and Ordoñez 1995).

Research is also needed on the presentation of excavated textiles. These are often either blackened like wet wood, or encrusted with brown-red iron corrosion products as is found in some marine sites (Jenssen 1987).

Techniques are needed to remove these discolorations without stripping out dyes, causing very fragile material to disintegrate (Peacock 1990), or soiling which is considered as 'evidence' rather than 'dirt' to be removed (Brooks *et al.* 1996).

DETERIORATION OF SKIN MATERIALS

Effects of manufacture

Understanding the deterioration of archaeological skin materials is complicated by the material added during their preparation for use. Preparation broadly consists of the removal of readily putrescible matter and excess water, and their replacement with tanning agents and possibly lubricants, thereby producing 'leather'. Tanning agents prevent the collagen fibres collapsing in on themselves, causing the skins to shrink and lose their flexibility when they are dried out. Tanning agents also block the re-entry of water so preventing the putrefaction normally associated with untreated dead skin. Those agents which are removable and thus less successful at tanning create what are known as 'semi-tanned' leathers: examples are cod oil in 'chamois' leathers, and alum in 'tawed' leathers. But certain tanning agents, particularly plant tannins, are able to bond with the collagen molecules and are less easily removed. This bonding also raises the temperature at which the collagen denatures causing the irreversible shrinkage of the molecule. This raised shrinkage temperature gives leather greater durability during use. The components of leather artifacts may be further complicated by a final post-tanning lubrication with fats, waxes or oils to further increase flexibility and durability. Overviews of the physico-chemical nature of both the fibrous protein polymer collagen and tanning can be found in Calnan and Haines (1991), Florian (1987), and Rahme (1996). There is also a large literature on the manufacture of archaeological skin materials *per se* and the choice of tanning agent in relation to period and geography (e.g., Rahme 1996, Reed 1972, Thomson 1998).

Apart from a greater understanding of this technology, the study of skin materials can also provide information in relation to animal husbandry as well as faunal and floral environments. Examination of leather artifacts, particularly shoes which are one of the most common but complex finds, can offer much. To allow for future study, details such as tooling, stitching, dyes, paint and foot impressions must all be retained by the conservation process. Another benefit of well conserved

leather artifacts is for displays of great immediacy to the museum visitor.

Past approaches to preservation

There has not been the same amount of research into the deterioration of archaeological skin materials as there has been of wood but a few projects have tried to characterize the deteriorated and treated materials in order to get away from 'cookbook' treatments (e.g., Jenssen 1987). In the past skin materials have been seen as 'forgiving' (Godfrey and Kasi 1999), in that they do not collapse on excavation to the same extent as wood, and they respond reasonably well to a great variety of empirical treatments. The early development of skin conservation was by leather historians and craftsmen (e.g., Waterer 1973) who proposed adaptations of craft techniques. When leather chemists were involved (e.g., Reed 1972) there was a tendency to adapt modern manufacturing techniques, including those for chromium tanned leather developed only in the mid-nineteenth century. Both these approaches can be problematic in that the techniques were originally designed for undeteriorated material, and excavated leather is undoubtedly deteriorated.

Taphonomy and survival

It is generally accepted that, from wet sites, usually the only skin materials to survive will be those tanned with vegetable tans. The tanning agents of semi-tanned leathers are either leached out or else subject to deterioration themselves. As in untanned skins (e.g., 'rawhide'), this leaves the unprotected collagen subject to chemical hydrolysis which breaks down both cross-links between the strands of its triple helix, and the peptide bonds along its length. There may be some anaerobic bacteria which can assimilate undeteriorated collagen (Caneva *et al.* 1991) but once hydrolysis has set in, biodeterioration by organisms which produce only general protease enzymes can be rapid. Only in arctic or arid conditions do semi-tanned skins seem to be preserved. In the latter conditions even untanned skin materials such as the parchment of the Dead Sea Scrolls can survive, in this case aided by salts introduced during manufacture which inhibit the activity of organisms (Wallert 1996). In wet sites even vegetable tanned leather deteriorates to some extent – unbound tannins are leached out and some hydrolysis of the collagen occurs, particularly at alkaline pHs, reducing the length of the molecules until, ultimately, the protein is more akin to gelatin than skin. An additional complication is the ingress of mineral particles and salts from the burial environment, whether soil particles or iron corrosion products. Unlike wood, being by nature an open 3D woven structure, leather offers less of a barrier to these contaminants.

On excavation, bulked out by water and held together by surface tension, leather from wet sites can appear in good condition. As water is lost, it shrinks, fragments and becomes extremely hard, depending, apparently, on the degree of tannin loss, the extent of collagen hydrolysis and mineral contamination, and the rate at which water is lost. One aspect of deterioration apparent on excavation is the dark colour of the leather, possibly due to the formation of metallic sulfides by anaerobic sulfate-reducing bacteria, or iron tannate complexes.

New approaches to understanding and treatment

In the last few years fresh effort, mostly but not all on historic leathers in relation to environmental pollution (e.g., Larsen 1996), has been put into characterizing deteriorated skin materials and using this to improve conservation techniques. Whilst the measurement of the lowering of collagen fibre shrinkage temperature (FST) has been used to estimate the degree of deterioration, it is difficult to relate this quantitative data to what can be seen in archaeological leather with the SEM. It may be that mineral contamination is causing interference (Wallace 1997). FTIR shows differences in the molecular state of collagen from different samples of deteriorated leather but as yet it has not been possible to associate these states with any visible state of condition or type of treatment (Godfrey and Kasi 1999). Considerable work has gone into adapting medical epidemiological and statistical methodologies to the condition assessment of both untreated and treated leather using simple non-invasive techniques to gain quantitative data (Sully and Suenson-Taylor 1999), but there is still much to be done to link visible deterioration with any measurable characteristics. Treatments therefore are still based on empirical findings. Tests in the 1980s found that the freeze-drying techniques derived for wood were the most satisfactory, but recent dissatisfaction with long term results may arise from the choice of cryoprotector-humectant. Some workers use a low molecular PEG (e.g., Bonnot-Diconne and Barthez 1999), whilst others have used glycerol (e.g., Sully and Suenson-Taylor 1999). The exact role of these materials and possible alternatives remains to be investigated. Recent tests have shown that the use of

'craft' materials such as immersion in castor oil followed by air drying is not the way forward (Williams and Harnett 1999). Debate still surrounds the removal (Jenssen 1987) or otherwise of mineral contaminants: do they cause deterioration in oxygenated environments or are they blocking treatments, leaving the leather unnecessarily discoloured, or in fact holding the decayed collagen together?

FUTURE DIRECTIONS

Deterioration studies in conservation have used a great many different methodologies and techniques, drawn from different sciences, from pharmacology to geochemistry. This is both a great strength and a real problem. The strength is that interdisciplinarity is recognized as essential to produce robust research which does not 'reinvent the wheel'. The problem is how to engender this interdisciplinarity and how to obtain funding for it. Research proposals tend to fall between funding bodies; a way forward may be to analyse the defined problem into phases, each addressable by a particular area of science (Seeley 1997). Multidisciplinary research teams could then be assembled, resulting from careful planning rather than happenstance (Price 1997). Real understanding and collaboration between science and conservation (Peterson 1990) is absolutely crucial to ensure research actually addresses real archaeological conservation problems. A crucial forum for galvanizing such research internationally has been the International Council of Museums Conservation Committee: Working Group On Wet Organic Materials known as WOAM (Bonnot-Diconne et al. 1999).

In general, new directions in quantitative methodologies are being sought, a recent example being the development of techniques based on epidemiological studies to evaluate the condition of materials (Suenson-Taylor et al. 1999). The understanding of deterioration in relation to conservation has long been recognized as a challenging if difficult area of research given the variables of both the archaeological material, the burial environment, and the possible treatments. But it is an area of research that can lead to real tangible benefits to archaeology in the form of both information and preserved artifacts.

REFERENCES

*Recommended for further reading

Allsopp, D. and Seal, K.J. (1986). *Introduction to Biodeterioration*. Edward Arnold: London.

Ambrose, W.R. (1990). Application of freeze-drying to archaeological wood. In Rowell, R.M. and Barbour, R.J. (eds) *Archaeological Wood Properties, Chemistry, and Preservation*, 235–261. Advances in Chemistry Series 225, American Chemical Society: Washington DC.

Ambrose, W.R., Neale, J.L. and Godfrey, I.M. (1994). Antarctic freeze-drying of waterlogged timbers: a feasibility report. In Hoffmann, P. (ed.) *Proceedings of the 5th ICOM Group on Wet Organic Archaeological Materials Conference*, 231–252. ICOM: Bremerhaven.

Barbour, R.J. (1990). Treatments for waterlogged and dry archaeological wood. In Rowell, R.M. and Barbour, R.J. (eds) *Archaeological Wood Properties, Chemistry, and Preservation*, 177–192. Advances in Chemistry Series 225, American Chemical Society: Washington DC.

Barkman, L. (1975). The preservation of the warship *Wasa*. In Oddy, W.A. (ed.) *Problems in the Conservation of Waterlogged Wood*, 65–66. National Maritime Museum: London.

Berducou, M.C. (ed.) (1990). *La Conservation en Archéologie: Méthods et Practiques de la Conservation-Restauration des Vestiges Archéologiques*. Masson: Paris.

Bjordal, C. and Nilsson, T. (1999). Laboratory reburial experiments. In Bonnot-Diconne, C., Hiron, X., Khoi Tran, Q. and Hoffmann, P. (eds) *WOAM 98 Proceedings of the 7th ICOM Group on Wet Organic Archaeological Materials Conference*, 71–77. ARC-Nucléart: Grenoble.

*Blanchette, R.A. and Hoffmann, P. (1994). Degradation processes in waterlogged archaeological wood. In Hoffmann, P. (ed.) *Proceedings of the 5th ICOM Group on Wet Organic Archaeological Materials Conference*, 111–137. ICOM: Bremerhaven.

*Blanchette, R.A., Haight, J.E., Koestler, R.J., Hatchfield, P.B. and Arnold, D. (1994). Assessment of deterioration in archaeological wood from ancient Egypt. *Journal of the American Institute of Conservation*, 33:55–70.

Blanchette, R.A., Nilsson, T., Daniel, G. and Abad, A. (1990). Biological degradation of wood. In Rowell, R.M. and Barbour, R.J. (eds) *Archaeological Wood Properties, Chemistry, and Preservation*, 141–176. Advances in Chemistry Series 225, American Chemical Society: Washington DC.

Bonnot-Diconne, C. and Barthez, J. (1999). Study of the ageing of waterlogged archaeological leather after conservation treatment. In Bonnot-Diconne, C., Hiron, X., Khoi Tran, Q. and Hoffmann, P. (eds) *WOAM 98 Proceedings of the 7th ICOM Group on Wet Organic Archaeological Materials Conference*, 232–237. ARC-Nucléart: Grenoble.

*Bonnot-Diconne, C., Hiron, X., Khoi Tran, Q. and Hoffmann, P. (eds) (1999). *WOAM 98 Proceedings of the 7th ICOM Group on Wet Organic Archaeological Materials Conference*. ARC-Nucléart: Grenoble.

Brooks, M.M., Lister, A., Eastop, E. and Bennett, T. (1996). Artifacts of information? Articulating the conflicts in conserving archaeological textiles. In Roy, A. and Smith, P. (eds) *Archaeological Conservation and its Consequences*, 16–21. International Institute for Conservation: London.

Brunning, R. (1995). *Waterlogged Wood: Guidelines on the Recording, Sampling, Conservation, and Curation of Waterlogged Wood*. English Heritage: London.

*Calnan, C. and Haines, B. (eds) (1991). *Leather: its Composition and Changes with Time*. Leather Conservation Centre: Northampton.

Cameron, E. (1990). Identification of skin and leather preserved by iron corrosion products. *Journal of Archaeological Science*, 18:25–33.

Caneva, G., Nugari, M.P. and Salvadori, O. (1991). *Biology in the Conservation of Works of Art*. ICCROM: Rome.

Caple, C. (2000). *Conservation Skills: Judgement, Method and Decision Making*. Routledge: London.

Chen, H.L., Jakes, K.A. and Foreman, D.W. (1998). Preservation of archaeological textiles through fibre mineralisation. *Journal of Archaeological Science*, 25:1015–1021.

Christensen, B.B. (1970). *The Conservation of Waterlogged Wood in the National Museum of Denmark*. Studies in Museum Technology 1, National Museum of Denmark: Copenhagen.

Coles, J.M. (1981). Conservation of wooden artifacts from the Somerset levels: 3. *Somerset Level Papers*, 7:70–80.

Cooke, W.D. (1990). Fibre damage in archaeological textiles. In O'Connor, S.A. and Brooks, M.M. (eds) *Archaeological Textiles*, 5–14. Occasional Papers No. 10, United Kingdom Institute for Conservation: London.

*Cooke, W.D. and Peacock, E. (1992). Quantitative research in ancient textiles and freeze drying. In Bender Jørgensen, L. and Munksgaard, E. (eds) *Archaeological Textiles in Northern Europe*, 218–228. School of Conservation: Copenhagen.

Corfield, M. (1998). The role of monitoring in the assessment and management of archaeological sites. In Bernick, K. (ed.) *Hidden Dimensions: the Cultural Significance of Wetland Archaeology*, 302–316. University of British Columbia Press: Vancouver.

*Cronyn, J.M. (1990). *The Elements of Archaeological Conservation*. Routledge: London.

Cronyn, J.M. and Horie, C.V. (1985). *St Cuthbert's Coffin: Its History, Technology and Conservation*. Dean and Chapter of Durham Cathedral: Durham.

de Jong, J. (1981). The deterioration of waterlogged wood and its protection in the soil. In *Conservation of Waterlogged Wood*, 31–40. Government Printing and Publishing Office: The Hague.

*Florian, M. (1987). Deterioration of organic materials other than wood. In Pearson, C. (ed.) *Conservation of Marine Archaeological Objects*, 21–54. Butterworths: London.

Florian, M.E. (1990). Scope and history of archaeological wood. In Rowell, R.M. and Barbour, R.J. (eds) *Archaeological Wood Properties, Chemistry, and Preservation*, 3–32. Advances in Chemistry Series 225, American Chemical Society: Washington DC.

Fry, M.F. (1996). Buried but not forgotten: sensitivity in disposing of major archaeological timbers. In Roy, A. and Smith, P. (eds) *Archaeological Conservation and its Consequences*, 52–54. International Institute for Conservation: London.

Ganiaris, H. (1990). Examination and treatment of a wooden tablet from London. *The Conservator*, **14**:3–9.

Gillard, R.D., Hardman, S.M., Thomas, R.G. and Watkinson, D.E. (1994a). Detection of dyes by FTIR microscopy. *Studies in Conservation*, **39**:187–192.

Gillard, R.D., Hardman, S.M., Thomas, R.G. and Watkinson, D.E. (1994b). The mineralization of fibres in burial environments. *Studies in Conservation*, **39**:132–140.

Godfrey, I. and Kasi, K. (1999). The analysis and treatment of waterlogged leather I: denaturation and defibrillisation studies. In Bonnot-Diconne, C., Hiron, X., Khoi Tran, Q. and Hoffmann, P. (eds) *WOAM 98 Proceedings of the 7th ICOM Group on Wet Organic Archaeological Materials Conference*, 217–223. ARC-Nucléart: Grenoble.

*Grattan, D.W. and Clarke, R.W. (1987). Conservation of waterlogged wood. In Pearson, C. (ed.) *Conservation of Marine Archaeological Objects*, 164–206. Butterworths: London.

*Grattan, D.W. (1987). Waterlogged wood. In Pearson, C. (ed.) *Conservation of Marine Archaeological Objects*, 55–67. Butterworths: London.

Grattan, D.W. and Mathias, C. (1986). Analysis of waterlogged wood: the value of chemical analysis and other simple methods in evaluating condition. *Somerset Levels Papers*, **12**:6–12.

Gregory, D. (1999). Re-burial of ship timbers in the marine environment as a method of in-situ preservation. In Bonnot-Diconne, C., Hiron, X., Khoi Tran, Q. and Hoffmann, P. (eds) *WOAM 98 Proceedings of the 7th ICOM Group on Wet Organic Archaeological Materials Conference*, 78–86, ARC-Nucléart: Grenoble.

Hedges, J.I. (1990). The chemistry of archaeological wood. In Rowell, R.M. and Barbour, R.J. (eds) *Archaeological Wood Properties, Chemistry, and Preservation*, 111–140. Advances in Chemistry Series 225, American Chemical Society: Washington DC.

Hoffmann, P. (1997). Conservation of the Bremen Cog: between the steps. In Hoffmann, P., Daley, T., Grant, T. and Spriggs, J.A. (eds) *Proceedings of the 6th ICOM Group on Wet Organic Archaeological Materials Conference*, 527–543. ICOM: Bremerhaven.

Hoffmann, P. and Jones, M.A. (1990). Structure and degradation process for waterlogged archaeological wood. In Rowell, R.M. and Barbour, R.J. (eds) *Archaeological Wood Properties, Chemistry, and Preservation*, 35–65. Advances in Chemistry Series 225, American Chemical Society: Washington DC.

Hoffmann, P. and Kühn, H.J. (1999). The candy ship from Friesland. In Bonnot-Diconne, C., Hiron, X., Khoi Tran, Q. and Hoffmann, P. (eds) *WOAM 98 Proceedings of the 7th ICOM Group on Wet Organic Archaeological Materials Conference*, 196–203. ARC-Nucléart: Grenoble.

Jakes, K.A. and Mitchell, J.C. (1992). Recovery and drying of textiles from a deep ocean historic shipwreck. *Journal of the American Institute for Conservation*, **31**:343–353.

*Jenssen, V. (1987). Conservation of wet organic artefacts excluding wood. In Pearson, C. (ed.) *Conservation of Marine Archaeological Objects*, 122–163. Butterworths: London.

Jespersen, K. (1985). Extended storage of waterlogged wood in nature. In *Waterlogged Wood: Study and Conservation*, 39–54. Centre d'étude et de Traitement des Bois Gorgés d'Eau: Grenoble.

Johns, D.A. (1998). Observations resulting from the treatment of waterlogged wood bowls in Aotearoa, New Zealand. In Bernick, K. (ed.) *Hidden Dimensions: The Cultural Significance of Wetland Archaeology*, 317–328. University of British Columbia Press: Vancouver.

Kaye, B. and Cole-Hamilton, D.J. (1998). Supercritical drying of waterlogged archaeological wood. In Bernick, K. (ed.) *Hidden Dimensions: The Cultural Significance of Wetland Archaeology*, 329–339. University of British Columbia Press: Vancouver.

Larsen, R. (ed.) (1996). *Environmental Leather Project: Deterioration and Conservation of Vegetable Tanned Leather*. Protection and Conservation of European Cultural Heritage Research Report No 6, Nielsen: Copenhagen.

Mouzouras, R. (1994). Micro-organisms: mechanisms of control. In Spriggs, J.A. (ed.) *A Celebration of Wood*, 21–34. York Archaeological Wood Centre: York.

Needles, H.L. and Regazzi, M.E. (1987). Burial induced color changes in unmordanted and mordanted madder-dyed cotton and wool fabrics. In *Preprints of Papers Presented at the Fifteenth Annual Meeting of the American Institute for Conservation of Historic and Artistic Works*, 78–84. American Institute for Conservation: Washington DC.

Nilsson, T. (1999). Microbial degradation of wood: an overview with special emphasis on waterlogged wood. In Bonnot-Diconne, C., Hiron, X., Khoi Tran, Q. and Hoffmann, P. (eds) *WOAM 98 Proceedings of the 7th ICOM Group on Wet Organic Archaeological Materials Conference*, 65–70. ARC-Nucléart: Grenoble.

Painter, T.J. (1995). Chemical and microbial aspects of the preservation process in Sphagnum peat. In Turner, R.C. and Scaife, R.G. (eds) *Bog Bodies: New Discoveries and New Perspectives*, 88–99. British Museum Press: London.

*Panter, I. and Spriggs, J. (1997). Condition assessments and conservation strategies for waterlogged wood assemblages. In Hoffmann, P., Daley, T., Grant, T. and Spriggs, J.A. (eds) *Proceedings of the 6th ICOM Group on Wet Organic Archaeological Materials Conference*, 185–200. ICOM: Bremerhaven.

Park, J. (1997). The Barton on Humber project: a large collection of waterlogged wood. Data retrieval, storage, pre- and post-treatment methods. In Hoffmann, P., Daley, T., Grant, T. and Spriggs, J.A. (eds) *Proceedings of the 6th ICOM Group on Wet Organic Archaeological Materials Conference*, 503–515. ICOM: Bremerhaven.

Peacock, E.E. (1990). Freeze-drying archaeological textiles: the need for basic research. In O'Connor, S.A. and Brooks, M.M. (eds) *Archaeological Textiles*, 22–30. Occasional Papers No. 10, United Kingdom Institute for Conservation: London.

Peacock, E.E. (1999). A note on the effect of multiple freeze-thaw treatment on natural fibre fabrics. *Studies in Conservation*, **44**:12–19.

Peterson, C.E. (1990). New directions in the conservation of archaeological wood. In Rowell, R.M. and Barbour, R.J. (eds) *Archaeological Wood Properties, Chemistry, and Preservation*, 433–449. Advances in Chemistry Series 225, American Chemical Society: Washington DC.

Pointing, S.B., Jones, A.M. and Jones, E.B.G. (1997). Practical considerations for gamma radiation sterilisation of waterlogged archaeological wood. In Hoffmann, P., Daley, T., Grant, T. and Spriggs, J.A. (eds) *Proceedings of the 6th ICOM Group on Wet Organic Archaeological Materials Conference*, 317–327. ICOM: Bremerhaven.

Pouman, A., Jones, A.J. and Moss, S.T. (1999). Preliminary studies on polyalkylene glycols (PAGs) as a pretreatment to the freeze-drying of waterlogged archaeological wood. In Bonnot-Diconne, C., Hiron, X., Khoi Tran, Q. and Hoffmann, P. (eds) *WOAM 98 Proceedings of the 7th ICOM Group on Wet Organic Archaeological Materials Conference*, 104–110, ARC-Nucléart: Grenoble.

Price, C. (1997). Attracting partners: increasing the effectiveness of research. In Foley, K. and Shacklock, V. (eds) *Conservation Research: Needs and Priorities*, 51–54. De Montfort University: Leicester.

Pritchard, F. (1990) Missing threads from Medieval textiles in north west Europe. In O'Connor, S.A. and Brooks, M.M. (eds) *Archaeological Textiles*, 15–17. Occasional Papers No. 10, United Kingdom Institute for Conservation: London.

Rahme, L. (1996). *Leather: Preparation and Tanning by Traditional Methods*. Caber Press: Portland, Or.

Reed, R. (1972). *Ancient Skins, Parchments and Leathers*. Academic Press: London.

*Rowell, R.M. and Barbour, R.J. (eds) (1990). *Archaeological Wood Properties, Chemistry, and Preservation*. Advances in Chemistry Series 225, American Chemical Society: Washington DC.

*Schniewind, A.P. (1989). Archaeological wood. In Schniewind, A.P. (ed.) *Concise Encyclopedia of Wood and Wood-Based Materials*, 14–18. Pergamon Press: Oxford.

Schniewind, A.P. and Eastman, P.Y. (1994). Consolidant distribution in deteriorated wood treated with soluble resin. *Journal of the American Institute of Conservation*, 33:247–256.

Seeley, N. (1997). Contexts for conservation research. In Foley, K. and Shacklock, V. (eds) *Conservation Research: Needs and Priorities*, 45–50. De Montfort University: Leicester.

Spriggs, J.A. (1991). The treatment, monitoring and display of Viking structures at York. In Hoffmann, P. (ed.) *Proceedings of the 4th ICOM-Group on Wet Organic Archaeological Materials Conference*, 49–60. ICOM: Bremerhaven.

*Suenson-Taylor, K., Sully, D. and Orton, C. (1999). Data in conservation: the missing link in the process. *Studies in Conservation*, 44:184–194.

Sully, D. and Suenson-Taylor, K. (1999). An interventive study of glycerol treated freeze dried leather. In Bonnot-Diconne, C., Hiron, X., Khoi Tran, Q. and Hoffmann, P. (eds) *WOAM 98 Proceedings of the 7th ICOM Group on Wet Organic Archaeological Materials Conference*, 224–231. ARC-Nucléart: Grenoble.

Tarleton, K.S. and Ordoñez, M.T. (1995). Stabilization methods for textiles from wet sites. *Journal of Field Archaeology*, 22:81–95.

Thomson, R. (1998). Leather working processes. In Cameron, E. (ed.) *Leather and Fur: Aspects of Early Medieval Trade and Technology*, 1–9. Archetype Press: London.

*Tímár-Balázsy, A. and Eastop, E. (1998). *Chemical Principles of Textile Conservation*. Butterworth-Heinemann: Oxford.

Vere-Strevens, L., Crawshaw, A., Panter, I. and Spriggs, J. (1999). Further research into the copper/silver ion sterilisation system as applied to treatment of archaeological oak wood in PEG solutions. In Bonnot-Diconne, C., Hiron, X., Khoi Tran, Q. and Hoffmann, P. (eds) *WOAM 98 Proceedings of the 7th ICOM Group on Wet Organic Archaeological Materials Conference*, 95–103. ARC-Nucléart: Grenoble.

Wallace, A. (1997). Scanning electron microscopy and fibre shrinkage temperature analysis of archaeological waterlogged leather: observations on Medieval leather from Swinegate, York. In Hoffmann, P., Daley, T., Grant, T. and Spriggs, J.A. (eds) *Proceedings of the 6th ICOM Group on Wet Organic Archaeological Materials Conference*, 137–152. ICOM: Bremerhaven.

Wallert, A. (1996). Deliquescence and recrystallization of salts in the Dead Sea Scrolls. In Roy, A. and Smith, P. (eds) *Archaeological Conservation and its Consequences*, 198–202. International Institute for Conservation: London.

Waterer, J. (1973). *A Guide to the Conservation and Restoration of Objects made Wholly or in Part of Leather* (2nd edn). Museum of Leathercraft: Northampton.

Watkinson, D. and Brown, J. (1995). Conservation of the polychrome wooden sarcophagus of Praise Mut. In Brown, C., Macalister, F. and Wright, M. (eds) *Conservation in Ancient Egyptian Collections*, 37–46. Archetype Press: London.

*Watson, J. (1997). Freeze-drying highly degraded waterlogged wood. In Hoffmann, P., Daley, T., Grant, T. and Spriggs, J.A. (eds) *Proceedings of the 6th ICOM Group on Wet Organic Archaeological Materials Conference*, 9–21. ICOM: Bremerhaven.

Wild, J.P. (1990). Introduction to archaeological textile studies. In O'Connor, S.A. and Brooks, M.M. (eds) *Archaeological Textiles*, 3–4. Occasional Papers No. 10, United Kingdom Institute for Conservation: London.

Williams, E. and Harnett, L. (1999). Castor oil: re-assessing an old treatment for archaeological leather. In Bonnot-Diconne, C., Hiron, X., Khoi Tran, Q. and Hoffmann, P. (eds) *WOAM 98 Proceedings of the 7th ICOM Group on Wet Organic Archaeological Materials Conference*, 238–243. ARC-Nucléart: Grenoble.

Yoshimura, S. and Omura, M. (1995). Inhibition of biodeterioration of excavated waterlogged wood using cationic surfactants. In *Biodeterioration of Cultural Property 3*, 187–192. Office of Archaeology and National Museums: Bangkok.

51

The Deterioration of Bone

A. MILLARD

Department of Archaeology, University of Durham.

Bone is popularly regarded as a dry, inanimate, uncomplicated and robust material. In fact, it is a complex biological material which can undergo a variety of pre-depositional and post-depositional processes, causing physical and chemical changes which can both destroy and add to archaeological information potential. These *taphonomic* processes can also lead to bone being unstable when removed from the ground, or even unstable in the face of changing environmental conditions (see Chapter 15). Together these factors mean that a full understanding of bone deterioration requires an understanding of bone structure and chemistry, possible pre-depositional physical and chemical changes, and interactions with the geochemistry of the burial environment (Millard 1998). These issues have been considered in a series of conferences on paleodiet (van Klinken and Hedges (1995a), Bocherens and Denys (1998), Bocherens *et al.* (1999)).

THE STRUCTURE OF BONE

Living bone is a complex, dynamic tissue, composed of approximately 80 per cent mineral and 20 per cent protein by dry weight. It exhibits a hierarchical structure with a number of different scales of organization (Figure 51.1), which gives it the mechanical properties required of a skeletal material (Weiner and Wagner 1998). The major bone protein is *collagen*, a long chain structural protein which coils in a left-handed helix; three molecules of collagen supercoil in a right-handed manner to form a *tropocollagen triple helix*. Tropocollagen molecules combine into *fibrils* with spaces between the molecules, within which crystals of bone mineral form (Weiner and Wagner 1998). Mineral also occurs between the fibrils of mature bone.

Bone mineral is a carbonate-hydroxyapatite (mineralogically termed *dahllite*) which can accommodate a large number of trace elements by surface and lattice substitutions. It differs from geological apatites, so it has been termed 'bioapatite'. The crystals are very small, and shaped like a book with dimensions typically $2-5 \times 40-50 \times 20-25$ nm. Their small size gives bone mineral a very large and chemically reactive surface of $85-170$ m^2 g^{-1} (Lowenstam and Weiner 1989).

The collagen fibrils combine to form three structures:

(i) in *woven bone* the fibrils have no preferred orientation and are randomly distributed over distances of more than a few microns,

(ii) in *lamellar bone* the fibrils are aligned over distances of tens of microns to form sheets of thickness about 3 μm, and

(iii) in *parallel-fibred bone* the structure is intermediate between the other two (the least common structure).

At the next structural level there are four types of bone (Currey 1984). The first two are simply woven and lamellar bone structures which extend over much

Handbook of Archaeological Sciences. Edited by D.R. Brothwell and A.M. Pollard.

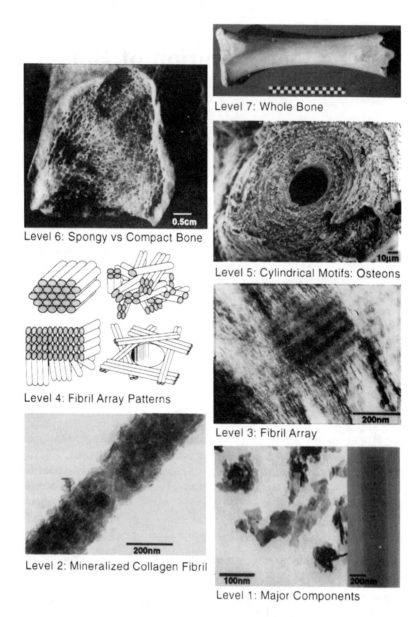

Figure 51.1 The seven hierarchical levels of organization of bone. Level 1: isolated crystals from human bone (left side) and part of an unmineralized and unstained collagen fibril from turkey tendon observed in a transmission electron microscope (TEM) (right side); Level 2: TEM micrograph of a mineralized collagen fibril from turkey tendon; Level 3: TEM micrograph of a thin section of mineralized turkey tendon; Level 4: Four fibril array patterns of organization found in the bone family of materials; Level 5: SEM micrograph of a single osteon from human bone; Level 6: fractured section through an ancient human femur (about 5500 years old); Level 7: whole bovine bone (scale 10 cm). From Weiner and Wagner (1998) used with permission, from *Annual Review of Material Science*, Volume 28, © 1998 by Annual Reviews http://www.AnnualReviews.org

greater distances; the third is the *Haversian system* which consists of concentric lamellae around a blood vessel; the fourth is *fibrolamellar* bone where a scaffold of parallel-fibred bone has its cavities filled by lamellar bone – this is found on rapidly growing bone surfaces.

The next level of organization is into *compact* (or *cortical*) and *cancellous* (or *trabecular*) bone. Cancellous bone is spongy, consisting of fine interlacing partitions (trabeculae) which contain marrow; it is found in vertebrae, flat bones and the ends of long bones. Cortical bone is hard and compact, found in the shafts of long bones surrounding the marrow cavity. The final level of organization is the arrangement of cancellous and cortical bone into the skeleton, forming macroscopic structures which allow the skeleton to be a flexible mechanical framework.

INFORMATION AND TAPHONOMY

Each level of organization of bone carries information of use in archaeology, from morphology allowing species identification, to isotopic information on diet (see Chapter 23). It is important therefore to consider deterioration at the various levels, since bone destroyed at one level may still provide useful information at another.

After death and burial bone interacts with highly variable burial environments. This leads to an extremely complex series of processes, which are currently categorized and characterized to a certain extent but not completely understood. The history of a bone from death to recovery is its *taphonomy*, the pre- and syn-burial part is termed *biostratinomy* and the post-burial part *diagenesis* (following Lyman 1994; see Chapter 15). Broadly, biostratinomic processes are macroscopic, influencing species and skeletal element composition of assemblages, whilst diagenesis is microscopic, including chemical changes and microbial attack.

Biostratinomy

Biostratinomic processes influence the preservation or destruction of a bone, via its state when it is buried, and, indeed, *whether* it gets buried at all (see Chapter 15). The major natural destructive processes include:

(i) *digestion* – although bones can survive passage through the digestive tract, their surfaces are frequently etched, and they are vulnerable to further changes (Andrews and Armour-Chelu 1998),

(ii) *trampling* – causes fragmentation and reduces the chances of survival, and

(iii) *exposure* – bones on the ground surface can be affected by heat, fragmented by freeze-thaw cycles, or etched by plant roots.

Additionally, archaeologists must consider pre-burial anthropogenic influences, including:

(i) *Butchery and defleshing* – the marks produced by these processes and how to distinguish them from bite and trample marks, are well-known (Lyman 1994) but little or no work has been done on how well they survive, and whether they influence a bone's survival.

(ii) *Cooking* – little is known about the effect of cooking on bones, with claims of unchanged (Chaplin 1971:81) and decreased survival (Speth 1999). Boiling changes the 'crystallinity' of bone mineral (Sillen 1989), and racemizes amino acids in collagen (Bada *et al.* 1989). Clearly, cooking has fundamental effects on the structure of bone.

(iii) *Burning and cremation* – these processes are fairly well studied, with a number of experimental studies and archaeological comparisons (see Shipman *et al.* 1984, Stiner *et al.* 1995, and Chapter 24). However, we still know little of their effect on the deterioration of bones.

(iv) *Excarnation* is known in a number of cultures, but its effect on bones is rarely considered. Disarticulation and loss of small bones is expected, but there are no studies of changes to microscopic preservation. These effects might be similar to natural exposure, but curation of excarnated remains could cause differences.

(v) *Deliberate burial* – bones on archaeological sites are often deliberately buried, whether animal bones in refuse pits or human bones in graves. In each case there are specific factors to consider, such as the influence of the other contents of the pit on the burial environment or, for human burials, the influence of a coffin or shroud or of organic matter added to speed decay, and of grave goods on the burial environment (Henderson 1987).

It is clear that when bone becomes buried it is not pristine, and that biostratinomy influences the initial state of the bone, and possibly the whole course of its diagenesis. This factor is not often considered in diagenetic studies.

Diagenesis

Bone diagenesis covers a multitude of processes which are responsible for the destruction of bone, although they can also add information about burial. They are controlled by different environmental factors, and respond differently to environmental change. Diagenetic processes are intimately linked to one another, although we tend to study them independently. Following this practice, individual processes are described before outlining how we can understand this complex picture.

Microbiological attack

Within a very short time of death microbiological decay takes over a body (see Chapter 29). The organisms involved include both fungi and bacteria, but few have been identified to species. Initially they attack soft tissues, but bones have been histologically altered by microbiological attack within three months of death (Bell *et al.* 1996).

The changes to bone have been classified by Hackett (1981) and Garland (1989). Four types of 'focal destructive' change are identified, named as *centrifugal Wedl foci*, *linear longitudinal foci*, *budded foci* and *lamellate foci*. The different types may, in part, be caused by different organisms. Garland (1989) and Millard (1993) observed mostly linear longitudinal and lamellate foci, with examples of Wedl foci only in bones from marine environments. These destructive foci are surrounded by, and sometimes in-filled by, mineral which is denser than unaltered bone mineral. Generalized destructive change is also observed in some bones.

The extent of alteration of a bone by microbiological attack can be summarized using the 'histological index' of Hedges *et al.* (1995); see Table 51.1 and Figure 51.2. Using this scale it has been shown (Millard and Hedges 1995) that bone from waterlogged terrestrial sites is well preserved, suggesting that the agents of change require an aerobic environment. Bones tend to have a histological index of either 0–1 or 5, with a much smaller proportion lying in between (Hedges *et al.* 1995, Nielsen-Marsh 1997, Millard 1993), suggesting that histological alteration tends to go more or less to completion if it happens. The distribution of histological index with date, however, does not vary significantly, suggesting that histological change occurs rapidly in comparison with the date range of the current dataset, i.e., in less than 500 years. Understanding which factors con-

Table 51.1 Histological index, modified from Millard (1993) and Hedges *et al.* (1995).

Index	Approximate % of intact bone	Description
0	< 5	No original features identifiable, except that Haversian canals may be present
1	< 15	Haversian canals present, small areas of well-preserved bone present, or lamellate structure is preserved by the pattern of destructive foci
2	< 50	some lamellate structure is preserved between the destructive foci
3	> 50	Some osteocyte lacunae preserved
4	> 85	Bone is fairly well preserved, with minor amounts of destructive foci
5	> 95	Very well preserved, virtually indistinguishable from modern bone

trol the type and extent of microbiological attack will require studies of bone on this shorter timescale.

Organic diagenesis

Collagen decay and loss is the major diagenetic change to the organic phase of bone. A number of workers have attempted to characterize the changes undergone by collagen, in order to assess its integrity for isotopic studies. For example, DeNiro and Weiner (1988) extracted that component of archaeological bones with the same solubility characteristics as collagen, and used stable isotope analysis, C/N ratio, amino-acid composition, and infra-red spectroscopy to examine its integrity. They concluded that some changes which alter collagen to the extent of providing unreliable isotopic measurements are subtle and can only be detected by a combination of these measurements.

Humic substances move from soil to bone during burial, and may chemically link to collagen, affecting its isotope composition. The collagen-humic reaction was investigated by van Klinken and Hedges (1995b), and whether purified collagen could be recovered from its products. They found that humic acids react rapidly with collagen *in vitro*, and that some standard chemical

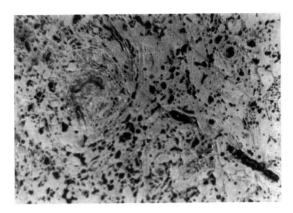 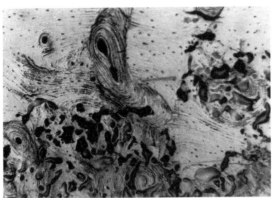

Figure 51.2   Variation in histological index, on the left an index of 1 and on the right an index of 4.

treatments do not entirely remove them. The rapidity of the initial reaction rules out Maillard-type condensation reactions: most likely is the initial formation of a hydrogen-bonded complex which undergoes further reactions.

Amino acid racemization has been investigated for dating and ageing (Pollard and Heron 1996), but has proved unreliable for both. Collins *et al.* (1999) showed that racemization of amino-acids in collagen is impossible while the triple helix structure is maintained, except in the telopeptide regions. Using a kinetic model they showed that in archaeological bone racemization is a function of collagen degradation rather than directly of time and temperature.

Lipid survival has only recently been investigated. Cholesterol and its degradation products are found in bones, but acyl lipids do not survive well (Evershed *et al.* 1995). Steroids from soil bacteria and disease bacteria (Gernaey *et al.* 1998) are also detectable. The presence of cholesterol oxidation and reduction products correlates with aerobic and anaerobic environments. Lipids with preserved carbon skeletons offer an alternative to collagen for $\delta^{13}C$ measurements for palaeodietary reconstruction (see Chapter 28; Stott *et al.* 1997, Jim *et al.* in press).

DNA is only detected in archaeological specimens in short fragments of the original molecule, and at millionths of the *in vivo* concentration (Richards *et al.* 1995, Handt *et al.* 1994); even so, much information is available from ancient DNA (Chapter 25). The preservation of DNA is little understood, though its preservation correlates well with the histological index (Colson *et al.* 1997). DNA preservation has been linked to the extent of amino-acid racemization, but a study of the reaction kinetics suggests that there should only be a weak correlation between the two measurements (Collins *et al.* 1999).

Inorganic diagenesis

Diagenesis of the inorganic phase of bone can be divided into three groups of processes: loss, gain and internal changes. Processes of mineral loss are difficult to study as concentrations are usually expressed relative to bone mass or a major ion. Loss of trace elements could in principle be studied, but little has been done.

Most work has focused on uptake and exchange of material. A large number of elements not substantially present in living bone can be shown to be present in excavated bone (see Whitmer *et al.* 1989); of particular interest are uranium and fluorine as they are used for dating. Uranium uptake in bone frequently follows a pattern consistent with diffusion and adsorption by mineral surfaces (Millard and Hedges 1995, 1996) and this has been confirmed by uranium-series dating studies (Millard and Pike 1999, Pike 2000). Fluorine uptake also appears to be diffusive (Coote *et al.* 1982). Secondary (authigenic) minerals can form in voids in archaeological bone, and in some cases replace bone mineral itself. Calcite is often deposited in calcareous environments and pyrite in reducing environments, where it can become a problem for conservation (see below).

Elements and ions endogenous to bone are also gained from or exchanged with the environment. Exchange of carbonate and phosphate compromises oxygen and carbon isotope signals (Wang and Cerling 1994). Strontium has long been recognized as undergoing diagenesis, which causes problems in palaeodiet studies (Chapter 23) and techniques such as Sillen's (1986) solubility profile method have been developed to overcome diagenesis. However, Budd *et al.* (2000) present strontium isotope measurements suggesting that complete exchange of strontium may occur, so that no method could possibly recover a biogenic signal. Despite more than 25 years of bone strontium analysis, strontium diagenesis still needs to be understood before strontium dietary reconstruction can be reliably applied. Similarly the use of lead concentrations and isotope ratios is hampered by lack of detailed chemical studies of diagenetic lead uptake. However, lead isotope analysis is a useful tool to discriminate between diagenetic and non-diagenetic lead (Budd *et al.* 1998).

Internal changes are expressed by changes in crystallinity, representing a reordering of material in the bone, which can be monitored by a 'crystallinity index' based on X-ray diffraction or infra-red spectra (e.g., Sillen 1989, Weiner and Bar-Yosef 1990). The different measures of crystallinity correlate well (Hedges *et al.* 1995), but their precise structural implications are unclear.

Understanding and predicting diagenesis

Certain diagenetic processes might be described as partly understood, e.g., uranium uptake (Millard and Hedges 1995, 1996), and exchange of carbonate (Wang and Cerling 1994), but most cannot, though some are the study of active research, e.g., amino acid racemization (Collins *et al.* 1999). It is clear however that water as the agent of transport and hydrolysis is crucial to diagenesis. Hedges and Millard (1995) classified water movement regimes, in order to model diagenetic processes:

(i)   *flow* where hydraulic flow through the bone is the dominant process,

(ii) *recharge* where water alternately moves in and out of the bone, and

(iii) *diffusion* where there is no water movement and the dominant transport process is diffusion.

Calculation of the rates of various processes using this classification and simplified assumptions yielded results of the appropriate magnitude. This work also shows that the porosity of bone is a key factor in determining water movements. Further work by Pike *et al.* (in press) demonstrates that the effect of flow and dissolution on bone can lead to catastrophic changes.

Collagen is almost certainly demineralized before it is altered and hydrolysed. It is not susceptible to enzymatic degradation, except by a limited number of collagenase-producing organisms (Child and Pollard 1991). Non-enzymatic hydrolysis, followed by loss, must therefore be a major degradation pathway, and progress has been made in modelling this process (Nielsen-Marsh *et al.* 2000), to the extent that minimum collagen loss can be reliably predicted. Again water is the key agent in change.

Further understanding is likely to come from studies of the chemistry of the interaction of specific elements with bioapatite and kinetic modelling studies of molecules such as DNA. More work is also needed on the variation of crystallinity and solubility characteristics of bone mineral with variation in minor ion concentrations.

CONSERVATION OF BONE

As discussed above, excavated bone is not pristine. This means that it has frequently lost the mechanical strength of fresh bone, and requires conservation treatment to promote its long-term curation. Bones from waterlogged and/or acidic environments appear to require more intervention than others, because their collagen-mineral interaction is altered by loss of mineral and/or swelling of collagen. In particular bones from reducing environments may contain salts such as pyrite which expand upon oxidation by air, thus cracking the bone.

Conservation (consolidation) treatments have been applied to excavated bones for at least 150 years, in some cases routinely to all bones from a site, and in others on the basis of need. The history of bone consolidation treatments is well covered by Johnson (1994).

Mechanical treatment

The ideal treatment for mechanical instability in bones would give long term stability and would be removable, but such a treatment has not been, and probably will not be, found. Shelton and Johnson (1995) note that the current situation is unchanged from that described by Lepper and Lewis (1941):

'[T]he techniques employed by each individual institution have been determined by field and laboratory experience leading to empiric conclusions without precise experimental control and quantitative evaluations . . . [i]n some cases, methods of preparation and materials employed have been determined only on a basis of personal opinion unsupported by empiric or theoretical evidence.'

Problems can arise from the use of proprietary materials which may have unspecified compositions or additives which can change at the whim of the manufacturer. However a number of workers are now approaching the topic from an understanding of the properties of bone, including possible diagenetic alteration. Bunn (1987) identified humidity change as a major factor in the deterioration of stored bone (compare Hedges and Millard 1995, Hedges *et al.* 1995 for buried bone). She investigated which consolidants buffer bone against humidity-induced weight changes. She compared a polyvinyledene chloride (PVdC) latex marketed as SARAN with polyvinylacetate (PVAc) and the acrylic resin Paraloid. SARAN did indeed provide a better buffer, though it has disadvantages in terms of toxicity, and a low pH for the wet latex, and is predicted to degrade after five years.

Other studies are more empirical. For example Kres and Lovell (1995) investigated several acrylic resins and a polyvinyl butyral resin for the consolidation of dry bone. The polyvinyl butyral resin proved superior in terms of penetration, drying time and matt finish, however nothing is known about its long-term stability (Table 51.2; Johnson 1994). For wet bone, Stone *et al.* (1990) compared polyethylene glycol (as PEG 3350) and acrylic emulsion (Rhoplex AC-33), on bones from the Windover, Florida, site, concluding that

Rhoplex had better penetrating power and when used at sufficient dilution did not exacerbate existing cracks and exfoliation. However this successful conservation for mechanical integrity compromised the chemical integrity of the bones, as discussed below.

The latter two cases exemplify the *ad hoc* nature of the selection of consolidants for many sites, with emphasis on ease of use, particularly in a 'field' situation, rather than removability and long-term stability. Johnson (1994) and Shelton and Johnson (1995) review the materials which have been and are used, with their advantages and disadvantages. Consideration of the reversibility and long-term properties of these consolidants means that conservators will only use a small number of those used by archaeologists (Table 51.2). Care must also be taken during the consolidation process to ensure that surface marks on the bone, e.g., butchery marks, are not obscured (Johnson 1994).

Chemical integrity

All consolidants introduce new material into bone which could either add material which is inseparable from endogenous material, destroy some endogenous component or make some component difficult to extract. The effect of consolidants on chemical integrity is dependent on the consolidant and the chemical species of interest. For example, a nineteenth century treatment with a collagen-based fish glue adds material which is chemically inseparable from endogenous

Table 51.2   Polymers in use for the consolidation of archaeological bone (from Johnson 1994). Reproduced with the permission of *Journal of Field Archaeology* and Trustees of Boston University. All rights reserved.

Polymer name	Used by conservators?	Field conditions	Problems
Natural resins	No	Not used	Poor penetration, poor consolidation
Cellulose nitrate resins	No	Not used	Not stable
Poly(vinyl) acetal resins	No	Not used	No longer available
Poly(vinyl) butyral resins	Yes	Dry, solvents available	Mostly used in paleontology, no testing on long-term stability, solvent toxicity
Poly(vinyl) acetate resins	Yes	Dry, solvents available	Need proper molecular wt., can soften in heat, solvent toxicity
Poly(vinyl) acetate emulsions	No	Not used	Often unstable
Acrylic emulsions (Rhoplex AC-33)	Yes	Wet, damp	Questions about long-term stability and effects of high pH
Acrylic colloidal dispersion (Acrysol WS-24)	Yes	Wet, damp	Questions about long-term stability
Acrylic resin (Acryloid B-72)	Yes	Dry, solvents available	Solvent toxicity, may soften in high temperatures
Epoxies	No	Not used	Staining, not reversible
Cyanoacrylate resins	No	Not used	May stain, not stable

collagen, thus nullifying radiocarbon dating, but is unlikely to alter the isotopic composition of lead in a bone. Scientists undertaking chemical and biochemical analysis of bones have avoided conserved or consolidated specimens wherever possible. However there are a few examples of analyses of treated bones which illustrate the need for care with consolidation treatments.

The oldest conservation treatment which has been successfully removed for biochemical analysis is probably that of the Neanderthal type specimen (Krings *et al.* 1997). The bone had been surface treated at least twice with an unidentified varnish. As it was a surface treatment it could be physically removed. Tests demonstrated that it had a low amino-acid content and hence was unlikely to be biasing amino-acid racemization measurements on the bone. Subsequently the oldest and one of the longest ancient DNA sequences known was extracted from the bone.

Other attempts to extract DNA from treated bones have fared less well. Tuross and Fogel (1994) examined the extraction of DNA from bones with a variety of conservation treatments. Some bones from a historic cemetery in New Orleans had been immersed in PVAc solution to stabilize them for transport. Left and right femurs from the same individual were compared and it was found that less DNA could be extracted from the treated bone using a non-destructive washing method. Whether PVAc had destroyed DNA or merely blocked its extraction is unclear.

The same paper also examined the effect of Stone *et al.*'s (1990) Rhoplex treatment on the collagen stable isotope values of material from Windover. Comparison of treated and untreated bones showed that $\delta^{15}N$ values were unaltered by Rhoplex treatment, but $\delta^{13}C$ values were altered and very variable. It proved impossible to completely remove Rhoplex from extracted collagen. PVAc treated bones from another collection did prove to produce reliable stable isotope results. This confirms the earlier study of Moore *et al.* (1989) which demonstrated that, for isotopic analysis of collagen, acetone was effective at removing polyvinyl-acetaldehyde acetal from bones, even several decades after treatment.

Radiocarbon dating is much more sensitive than stable isotopy to the introduction of extraneous carbon. Even so, Law *et al.* (1991) have demonstrated that careful extraction procedures can recover collagen free of PVAc/PVOH consolidant. An attempt to date bone from Cuello, Belize, had failed because standard extraction procedures did not remove all the consolidant. By applying more rigorous extraction procedures, culminating in hydrolysis of the protein to its constituent amino-acids, and their purification, as well as monitoring of each stage of extraction using infra-red spectroscopy, it was possible to arrive at reliable radiocarbon dates. Even so, there remains a small possibility of contamination.

For each of these examples the presence of consolidants necessitated extra steps in extraction protocols to guarantee the purity of the extracted compounds. The easiest treatment to remove for analytical purposes is the surface varnish, and of the soaking treatments, PVAc appears easier to remove than acrylic resin, though the effect of PVAc on DNA extraction appears detrimental. On the current evidence, it would seem that surface treatments are to be preferred over penetrating treatments and PVAc over acrylic resin, if the chemical integrity of the organic component of bone is to be preserved. However, no work appears to have been done on the effect of consolidation treatments on the inorganic component, and thus we should be wary of using them indiscriminately.

One case study stands out as a model of minimal conservation treatment combined with understanding of the physical and chemical state of the bone. Turner-Walker's (1998) pre-conservation evaluation of the West Runton elephant carefully considered and combined information on the burial environment, investigation of the diagenesis of selected skeletal elements, and ageing tests on small samples to determine the most appropriate conservation strategy. The strategy adopted was one of limited consolidation of friable and weakened areas, combined with controlled storage, below 55 per cent RH to prevent hydration with subsequent oxidation of pyrite and above 45 per cent RH to prevent cracking and warping due to collagen dehydration. This on-going strategy contrasts with a one-off treatment and enables mechanical stabilization whilst maximizing the potential for future chemical and biochemical analyses.

OVERCOMING DETERIORATION

A number of methods have been devised to overcome deterioration which adversely affects chemical and biochemical extractions. They can be divided into three groups:

(i) *Screening* of samples leads to rejection of some samples before full analysis. This may include rejection of samples on visual inspection e.g., if consolidant is observed, or preliminary analysis followed by full analysis only of promising samples, e.g. examining histological preservation before ancient DNA extraction (Colson *et al.* 1997).

(ii) *More specific extraction* methods, depending on the aim of the analysis, e.g., Sillen's (1986) solubility profile technique for strontium, or extraction of hydroxyproline rather than acid insoluble residue for radiocarbon dating (Stafford *et al.* 1982).

(iii) *Physical or chemical cleaning* – most analytical protocols involve mild surface cleaning of bone but more rigorous cleaning has been advocated, e.g., extensive surface removal (Lambert *et al.* 1991).

FUTURE DIRECTIONS

Conservation and consolidation treatments need to be improved by further implementation of protocols similar to Turner-Walker's (1998) example. More work is needed to investigate the long-term stability of consolidants applied to bone, and to understand their interactions with the compounds present in bone. In future it may prove necessary to use different consolidants on different bones from a site to ensure that different classes of (bio)chemical information are each preserved in some of the bones.

In understanding diagenesis a two-pronged approach is necessary, encompassing both modelling and experimental studies. Without models we cannot predict what is likely to happen under new conditions; without experimental measurements we will not have the data to build and test models.

The *hydrological* model of Hedges and Millard (1995) shows promise for categorizing and describing transport processes, but it needs further elaboration and testing. A *geochemical* modelling approach has been advocated by Pollard (1995), but as yet has not been pursued fully. Kinetic modelling needs to be further developed for collagen and extended to DNA.

More experimental data is needed which is accompanied by the information on a burial environment which is necessary for modelling. Advances will be made most rapidly if as many analyses as possible are made on the same bones, and on bones of similar origin but in differing environments, notably studies of multiple environments on single sites (e.g., Bocherens *et al.* 1997).

This chapter has concentrated on the deterioration of cortical bone as less is known about the diagenesis of other skeletal components such as ivory, dentine, and enamel, let alone the differential diagenesis of woven versus lamellar bone or young osteons compared to older, more mineralized osteons. There is much still to do in understanding, overcoming and using bone deterioration to gain archaeological information.

REFERENCES

*Recommended for further reading

Andrews, P. and Armour-Chelu, M. (1998). Taphonomic observations on a surface bone assemblage in a temperate environment. *Bulletin de la Société Géologique de France*, **169**:433–442.

Bada, J.L., Herrman, B., Payan, T.L. and Man, E.H. (1989). Amino acid racemization in bone and the boiling of the German Emperor Lothar I. *Applied Geochemistry*, **4**:325–327.

Bell, L.S., Skinner, M.F. and Jones, S.J. (1996). The speed of post-mortem change to the human skeleton and its taphonomic significance. *Forensic Science International*, **82**:129–140.

*Bocherens, H. and Denys, C. (eds) (1998). *Actes de la Troisième Conférence Internationale sur la Diagenèse de l'Os*. Société Géologique de France: Paris.

Bocherens, H., Tresset, A., Wiedemann, F., Giligny, F., Lafage, F., Lanchon, Y. and Mariotti, A. (1997). Diagenetic evolution of bone in two French Neolithic sites. *Bulletin de la Société Géologique de France*, **168**:555–564.

*Bocherens, H., van Klinken, G.J. and Pollard, A.M. (eds) (1999). Proceedings of the 5th Advanced Seminar on Paleodiet. *Journal of Archaeological Science*, **26**(2).

Budd, P., Montgomery, J., Cox, A., Krause, P., Barreiro, B. and Thomas, R.G. (1998). The distribution of lead within ancient and modern human teeth: implications for long-term and historical exposure monitoring. *Science of the Total Environment*, **220**:121–136.

Budd, P., Montgomery, J., Barreiro, B. and Thomas, R.G. (2000). Differential diagenesis of strontium in archaeological human dental tissues. *Applied Geochemistry*, **15**:687–694.

Bunn, M. (1987). SARAN as a treatment for bone. In Starling, K. and Watkinson, D. (eds) *Archaeological Bone Antler and Ivory*, 28–33. UK Institute for Conservation: London.

Chaplin, R.E. (1971). *The Study of Animal Bones from Archaeological Sites*. Seminar Press: London.

Child, A.M. and Pollard, A.M. (1991). Microbial attack on collagen. In Pernicka, E. and Wagner, G.A. (eds) *Archaeometry '90*, 617–624. Birkhäuser Verlag: Basel.

Collins, M.J., Waite, E.R., and van Duin, A.C.T. (1999). Predicting protein decomposition: the case of aspartic-acid racemization kinetics. *Philosophical Transactions of the Royal Society B*, **354**:51–64.

Colson, I.B., Bailey, J.F., Vercauteren, M. and Sykes, B.C. (1997). The preservation of ancient DNA and bone diagenesis. *Ancient Biomolecules*, **1**:109–117.

Coote, G.E., Sparks, R.J. and Blattner, P. (1982). Nuclear microprobe measurement of fluorine concentration profiles, with application in archaeology and geology. *Nuclear Instruments and Methods*, **197**:213–221.

Currey, J. (1984). *The Mechanical Adaptations of Bones*. Princeton University Press: Princeton.

DeNiro, M.J. and Weiner, S. (1988). Chemical, enzymatic and spectroscopic characterisation of 'collagen' and other organic fractions from prehistoric bones. *Geochimica et Cosmochimica Acta*, **52**:2197–2206.

Evershed, R.P. Turner-Walker, G., Hedges, R.E.M., Tuross, N. and Leiden, A. (1995). Preliminary results for the analysis of lipids in ancient bone. *Journal of Archaeological Science*, **22**:277–290.

Garland, A.N. (1989). Microscopical analysis of fossil bone. *Applied Geochemistry*, **4**:215–229.

Gernaey, A.M., Minnikin, D.E., Copley, M.S., Power, J.J., Ahmed, A.M.S., Dixon, R.A., Roberts, C.A., Robertson, D.J., Nolan, J. and Chamberlain, A. (1998). Detecting ancient tuberculosis. *Internet Archaeology*, **5** http://intarch.ac.uk/journal/issue5/gernaey_toc.html.

Hackett, C.J. (1981). Microscopical focal destruction (tunnels) in exhumed human bones. *Medicine, Science and the Law*, **21**:243–265.

Handt, O., Richards, M., Trommsdorff, M., Kilger, C., Simanainen, J., Georgiev, O., Bauer, K., Stone, A., Hedges, R., Schaffner, W., Utermann, G., Sykes, B. and Pääbo, S. (1994). Molecular genetic analyses of the Tyrolean Ice Man. *Science*, **264**:1775–1778.

Hedges, R.E.M. and Millard A.R. (1995). Bones and groundwater: towards the modelling of diagenetic processes. *Journal of Archaeological Science*, **22**:147–154.

Hedges, R.E.M., Millard, A.R. and Pike, A.W.G. (1995). Measurements and relationships of diagenetic alteration of bone from three archaeological sites. *Journal of Archaeological Science*, **22**:201–209.

Henderson, J. (1987). Factors determining the state of preservation of human remains. In Boddington, A., Garland, A.N. and Janaway, R.C. (eds) *Death Decay and Reconstruction*, 43–54. Manchester University Press: Manchester.

Jims, S., Stott, A.W., Evershed, R.P., Rogers, J.M. and Ambrose, S.H. (in press). Animal feeding experiments in the development of cholesterol as a palaeodietary indicator. In Millard, A.R. (ed.) *Proceedings of Archaeological Sciences '97*, 68–77. BAR British Series, Archaeopress: Oxford.

*Johnson, J.S. (1994). Consolidation of archaeological bone: a conservation perspective. *Journal of Field Archaeology*, **21**:221–233.

Kres, L.A. and Lovell, N.C. (1995). A comparison of consolidants for archaeological bone. *Journal of Field Archaeology*, **22**:508–515.

Krings, M., Stone, A., Schmitz, R.W., Krainitz, H., Stoneking, M. and Pääbo, S. (1997). Neanderthal DNA sequences and the origin of modern humans. *Cell*, **90**:19–30.

Lambert, J.B., Xue, L. and Buikstra, J.E. (1991). Inorganic analysis of excavated human bone after surface removal. *Journal of Archaeological Science*, **18**:363–383.

Law, I.A., Housley, R.A., Hammond, N. and Hedges, R.E.M. (1991). Cuello – resolving the chronology through direct dating of conserved and low-collagen bone by AMS. *Radiocarbon*, **33**:303–315.

Lepper, H.A. and Lewis, G.E. (1941). Materials for conservation of vertebrate fossils: an analysis of their effectiveness. *American Journal of Science*, **239**:17–24.

Lowenstam, H.A. and Weiner, S. (1989). *On Biomineralization*. Oxford University Press: Oxford.

*Lyman, R.L. (1994). *Vertebrate Taphonomy*. Cambridge University Press: Cambridge.

Millard, A.R. (1993). *Diagenesis of Archaeological Bone: the Case of Uranium Uptake*. Unpublished D.Phil. Thesis, University of Oxford.

*Millard, A.R. (1998). Bone in the burial environment. In Corfield, M., Hinton, P., Nixon, T. and Pollard, A.M. (eds) *Preserving Archaeological Remains in Situ*, 93–102. Museum of London Archaeology Service: London.

Millard, A.R. and Hedges, R.E.M. (1995). The role of the environment in uranium uptake by buried bone. *Journal of Archaeological Science*, **22**:239–250.

Millard, A.R. and Hedges, R.E.M. (1996). A diffusion-adsorption model of uranium uptake by archaeological bone. *Geochimica et Cosmochimica Acta*, **60**:2139–2152.

Millard, A.R. and Pike, A.W.G. (1999). Uranium-series dating of the Tabun Neanderthal: a cautionary note. *Journal of Human Evolution*, **36**:581–585.

Moore, K.M., Murray, M.L. and Schoeninger, M.J. (1989). Dietary reconstruction from bones treated with preservatives. *Journal of Archaeological Science*, **16**:437–446.

Nielsen-Marsh, C. (1997). *Studies in Archaeological Bone Diagenesis*. Unpublished DPhil. Thesis, University of Oxford.

Nielsen-Marsh, C.M., Gernaey, A.M., Turner-Walker, G., Hedges, R.E.M., Pike, A.W.G. and Collins, M.J. (2000). The chemical degradation of bone. In Cox, M. and Mays, S. (eds) *Human Osteology in Archaeology and Forensic Science*, 439–454. Greenwich Medical Media: London.

Pike, A.W.G., Nielsen-Marsh, C. and Hedges, R.E.M. (in press). Modelling bone dissolution under different hydrological regimes. In Millard, A.R. (ed.) *Proceedings of Archaeological Sciences '97*, 127–132. BAR British Series, British Archaeological Reports: Oxford.

Pike, A.W.G. (2000). *Uranium Series Dating of Archaeological Bone by Thermal Ionization Mass-Spectrometry*. Unpublished DPhil. Thesis, University of Oxford.

Pollard, A.M. (1995). Groundwater modelling in archaeology – the need and the potential. In Beavis, J. and Barker, K. (eds) *Science and Site*, 93–98. Occasional Paper 1, School of Conservation Sciences, Bournemouth University: Bournemouth.

Pollard, A.M. and Heron, C. (1996). *Archaeological Chemistry*. Royal Society of Chemistry: Cambridge.

Richards, M.B., Sykes, B.C. and Hedges, R.E.M. (1995). Authenticating DNA extracted from ancient skeletal remains. *Journal of Archaeological Science*, **22**:291–300.

Shelton, S.Y. and Johnson, J.S. (1995). The conservation of sub-fossil bone. In Collins, C. (ed.) *The Care and Conservation of Palaeontological Material*, 59–71. Butterworth-Heineman: Oxford.

Shipman, P., Foster, G. and Schoeninger, M. (1984). Burnt bones and teeth: an experimental study of colour, morphology, crystal structure and shrinkage. *Journal of Archaeological Science*, **11**:307–325.

Sillen, A. (1986). Biogenic and diagenetic Sr/Ca in Plio-Pleistocene fossils of the Omo Shungura formation. *Paleobiology*, **12**:311–323.

Sillen, A. (1989). Diagenesis of the inorganic phase of cortical bone. In Price, T.D. (ed.) *The Chemistry of Prehistoric Human Bone*, 211–229. Cambridge University Press: Cambridge.

Speth, J.D. (1999). Boiling vs. baking and roasting: a taphonomic approach to the recognition of cooking techniques in small mammals. In Rowley-Conwy, P. (ed.) *Animal Bones and Human Societies*, 89–105. Oxbow Books: Oxford.

Stafford, T.W., Duhamel, R.C., Haynes, C.V. and Brendel, K. (1982). Isolation of proline and hydroxyproline from fossil bone. *Life Sciences*, **31**:931–938.

Stiner, M.C., Kuhn, S.L., Weiner, S. and Bar-Yosef, O. (1995). Differential burning, recrystallization and fragmentation of archaeological bone. *Journal of Archaeological Science*, **22**:223-238.

Stone, T.T., Dickel, D.N. and Doran, G.H. (1990). The preservation and conservation of waterlogged bone from the Windover Site, Florida: a comparison of methods. *Journal of Field Archaeology*, **17**:177–186.

Stott, A.W., Evershed, R.P. and Tuross, N. (1997). Compound-specific approach to the $\delta^{13}C$ analysis of cholesterol in fossil bones. *Organic Geochemistry*, **26**:99–103.

*Turner-Walker, G. (1998). The West Runton fossil elephant: a pre-conservation evaluation of its condition, chemistry and burial environment. *The Conservator*, **22**:26–35.

Tuross, N. and Fogel, M.L. (1994). Exceptional molecular preservation in the fossil record: the archaeological, conservation and scientific challenge. In Scott, D.A. and Meyers, P. (eds) *Archaeometry of Pre-Columbian Sites and Artefacts*, 367–380. Getty Conservation Institute: Marina del Rey.

*van Klinken, G.J. and Hedges, R.E.M. (eds) (1995a). Special issue on bone diagenesis. *Journal of Archaeological Science*, **22**(2).

van Klinken, G.J. and Hedges, R.E.M. (1995b). Experiments on collagen-humic interactions: speed of humic uptake and effects of diverse chemical treatments. *Journal of Archaeological Science*, **22**:263–270.

Wang, Y. and Cerling, T.E. (1994). A model of fossil tooth and bone diagenesis – implications for paleodiet reconstruction from stable isotopes. *Palaeogeography, Palaeoclimatology, Palaeoecology*, **107**:281–289.

Weiner, S. and Bar-Yosef, O. (1990). States of preservation of bones from prehistoric sites in the Near East: a survey. *Journal of Archaeological Science*, **17**:187–196.

*Weiner, S. and Wagner, H.D. (1998). The material bone: structure-mechanical function relations. *Annual Review of Material Science*, **28**:271–298.

Whitmer, A.M., Ramenofsky, A.F., Thomas, J., Thibodeaux, L.J., Field, S.D. and Miller, B.J. (1989). Stability or instability: the role of diffusion in trace element studies. In Schiffer, M.B. (ed.) *Archaeological Method and Theory 1*, 205–273. University of Arizona Press: Tucson.

52

Maximizing the Life Span of Archaeological Objects

D. WATKINSON

School of History and Archaeology, Cardiff University.

Buried objects are considered to reach equilibrium with their burial environment according to their composition and the nature of the burial environment (Cronyn 1990). Thus aerated damp environments are likely to convert non-noble metals into their corrosion products, whereas low oxygen environments with no microbial activity may produce only superficial corrosion of the same metals. Kinetic factors have a major influence on metals corrosion, with extensive polarization of the electrode processes significantly reducing corrosion rate. This situation may persist, as many burial environments retain fairly constant moisture, temperature, oxygen, carbon dioxide, soluble ion levels and biodeterioration rates. The biggest environmental change for any buried artifact is its excavation and consequent exposure to the atmosphere, which is normally richer in oxygen, drier, warmer and brighter than the burial environment, with a different range of active microbes and significant moisture and temperature fluctuations. Objects undergo chemical and physical change as they strive to reach a new equilibrium by interacting with their new environment. Since this results in the loss of archaeological evidence, then conservation should begin at the moment of excavation.

THE CONSERVATION PROCESS – AN OVERVIEW

The long-term preservation of an object can be divided into a number of distinct stages:

(i)   *on-site conservation* – prevents immediate deterioration of excavated material,
(ii) *investigative conservation* – reveals technological and other information,
(iii) *interventive conservation* – maintains the physical integrity of weakened unstable material using treatments that increase physical and chemical stability, and
(iv) *preventative conservation* – reduces continued decay by control of the ambient environment.

Management decisions determine which objects to retain, analyse and conserve (Andrews 1991). Ethics and available conservation techniques are used to decide if these goals are attainable (UKIC 1990). Conservation regimes develop from research which:

(i)   determines the structure and decay of cultural material,

---

Handbook of Archaeological Sciences. Edited by D.R. Brothwell and A.M. Pollard.
© 2001 John Wiley & Sons, Ltd.

(ii)   investigates, designs and quantifies preservation techniques, and

(iii)   assesses the long-term performance of conservation materials.

Successful conservation is underpinned by science and requires adequate resources and good long-term management. Before 1960 individual scientists, such as Rathgen and Plenderleith, gradually laid the foundations of archaeological conservation (Gilberg 1987, Oddy and Windsor 1998). Conservation research now encompasses a wide range of materials and scientific disciplines, with input from pure and applied scientists, conservators and conservation scientists. Its remit includes testing materials for conservation practice, developing conservation techniques and investigating the structure and decay of artifactual materials. Most conservation research is located at dedicated centres, such as National Museums, government institutions and universities.

ON-SITE PRESERVATION

Unless immediate steps are taken to preserve excavated unstable archaeological objects, it is unlikely that subsequent long-term care or conservation will reverse the initial damage they sustain if left unattended (Watkinson and Neal 1998, Pearson 1987). Specifying suitable temporary post-excavation storage environments relies upon research into decay mechanisms to identify an environment that will either arrest or slow decay. Research is often hampered by non-availability of standardized archaeological samples. Consequently testing standardized non-archaeological materials and projecting experimental results to archaeological contexts is often employed. Weak waterlogged archaeological glass used to be stored within custom cut insets in polyethylene foam, which were then kept in a high relative humidity to prevent drying and collapse of the wet laminated silica-rich glass matrix. Experiments using simulated Medieval glass, with FT-IR microscopy and SEM/EDX analysis, showed that entrapment of leached alkalis between the glass surface and the polyethylene foam led to increased pH and localized surface corrosion, which was considerably worse in high humidity, as compared to immersion systems (Earl and Watkinson 1997).

Simple technical questions, such as 'how air-tight are the lids on commercially available polyethylene boxes?' can be of critical importance for the successful design of a storage microclimate. Successful physical packing

procedures rely on research into the structure and decay of both the materials comprising the object and the packing materials, including labelling techniques that ensure objects remain a valid study resource.

Past empirical use of materials, such as biocides to prevent biodeterioration of waterlogged wood, provided poor or hazardous storage conditions (Dawson 1982) but more recent approaches use low oxygen levels, vacuum storage and refrigeration, in preference to biocides (Jensen et al. 1996). Some storage problems appear less complex, as they rely on preventing a single reaction, such as identifying the critical humidity for the formation of a damaging soluble salt in porous stone, then providing storage below this value. However, even this can be complicated when a mixture of salts is present.

INVESTIGATIVE, INTERVENTIVE AND NON-INTERVENTIVE CONSERVATION

Archaeological conservation seeks to preserve excavated material and reveal information about its past. Investigative cleaning procedures (Cronyn 1990) and analysis (Pollard and Heron 1996) are used to reveal details of object composition, technology and life history. Understanding how decay and corrosion change the structure of materials is essential for determining the appearance and positioning of original surfaces on archaeological objects. Adhesives, consolidants and surface coatings may be applied during investigative cleaning to provide physical integrity to an object. Scientific testing of these materials is essential to ensure that they meet practical and ethical conservation goals.

In the past physical and chemical interventions were used to preserve archaeological objects, with little attention to the nature and quality of post-treatment storage and display conditions. Although these interventive treatments were often considered to be 'one-off' stabilization methods, it is now recognized that few treatments can prevent an object reacting with its ambient environment, even though interventive treatments may enhance object stability. Understanding and controlling environment interaction with archaeological objects is now considered important to ensure their long-term preservation.

Preventive conservation involves storing an object in an environment that will maintain its condition by limiting its physical and/or chemical change. It is now a favoured conservation technique, although it may be preceded by interventive conservation treatments that are essential for the physical well being of an object and analysis. Preventive conservation encompasses planning to combat threats such as disasters, theft and fire, as well as implementation of appropriate management structures, which leads to an overall holistic concept termed *collection care* (Michalski 1990a). Although limited intervention followed by preventive conservation is the preferred conservation route, it is often only a realistic consideration for historical objects and fairly stable and non-reactive archaeological materials that retain their physical and chemical integrity. Much archaeological material is sufficiently weakened and altered that it will need to undergo substantial intervention followed by controlled long-term storage.

Examining the physical stabilization of waterlogged wood and reviewing attempts to chemically stabilize iron will provide some idea of the differences in the development of interventive treatment techniques within conservation.

The empirical relationship between the degradation of waterlogged wood and its degree of distortion, warping, shrinkage and collapse upon drying was known since the beginning of the twentieth century (Rathgen 1905). High profile ship finds created pressure to develop successful treatments and stimulated research into the mechanisms of treatments (Hafors 1990). The formation of the International Council of Museums Working Group on Waterlogged Archaeological Materials (ICOM/WOAM) brought together many scientists and conservators actively interested in wood decay and conservation. Over the past 20 years this has created an interchange of ideas, rationalized research and disseminated information. Progress was aided by the creation of research-based government institutions, such as the Canadian Conservation Institute. Work by botanists, wood scientists and wet wood conservators provided an understanding of the structure and cellular decay of waterlogged wood, which was essential for designing and understanding treatments (Barbour 1984, Hoffman and Jones 1990, Blanchette and Hoffman 1993). The action of polyethylene glycol as a consolidant for waterlogged wood was revealed by research that located both its position and its chemical action within wet wood. This led to treatments employing low molecular weight PEG impregnation followed by high molecular weight PEG; the first to satisfy and control the response of the wood substance to moisture and the second to physically support it (Young and Simms 1987, Hoffman 1984). Currently freeze-drying is used in conjunction with PEG to remove the water from wet wood but leave behind the PEG consolidants. Research into the stability and chemical properties of

PEG (Brownstein 1982, Bilz *et al.* 1993, Geymayer *et al.* 1990) and its influence on the moisture response of treated wood (Grattan 1982), provides understanding of its performance as a long-term treatment material and guidance for storage and display (MacLeod 1987). Although PEG is the favoured treatment material, work continues on developing cheap, easy-to-use alternatives, such as sugars (Hoffman 1996).

The thrust and structure of research into the corrosion and conservation of archaeological iron over the same time period is different to that of waterlogged wood. Specialist scientists and conservators have been involved in iron research but the balance of research has been directed towards understanding corrosion mechanisms, rather than developing effective treatment methods. This may be influenced by the fact that archaeological iron often retains its physical integrity upon excavation. It can be successfully cleaned to reveal its shape and then stored in a desiccated environment to prevent continued corrosion (Turgoose 1982). In this form it is readily accessible for study. In contrast the need to remove its water and physically support waterlogged wood, before it can undergo long-term storage, polarized research towards devising suitable stabilization techniques in tandem with structure and decay studies.

Current understanding of iron corrosion has benefited from the input of corrosion scientists over the past 20 years, who utilized much existing work within corrosion science and supplemented it by experiment (Selwyn *et al.* 1999). Their work has swept away the simple picture of iron corrosion that had existed in conservation for over 50 years until the late 1970s.

Research into treatment methods for iron lags behind understanding of the corrosion process. The limited success of coatings and inhibitors (Turgoose 1985) has meant that stabilization techniques for chloride contaminated archaeological iron has centred on the removal of the chloride corrosion accelerators (Knight 1997). Whilst many chloride extraction methods have been advocated, quantifiable assessments of their success and understanding of how they work is limited (Watkinson 1996). Other than desiccation, no practical methods of preventing corrosion of iron in store have been adequately explored (Green and Bradley 1997). Although desiccation is effective it remains unreliable, as the usual method of microclimate control utilizes desiccated silica gel in sealed boxes, which requires the support of good management and adequate resources for long-term effectiveness (Dollery 1994). To date, research into the conservation of iron has lacked the co-ordination, internationalism and funding input of the waterlogged wood research. The immediacy and lure of large evocative ships as display items is not duplicated by small iron objects, yet ongoing corrosion of archaeological iron in store remains chronic.

Not all metals present the same problems as iron. Benzotriazole, a commercial inhibitor, has been found to be effective in the stabilization of chloride-infested unstable archaeological copper alloys (Madsen 1985), although its exact chemical action remains unclear (Brostoff 1997). Only when there is high acidity does it fail to stabilize objects and treatment modifications deal with this problem (Drayman-Weisser 1987). Consequently the storage and long-term survival of copper alloys is more readily and successfully achieved.

MATERIALS FOR CONSERVATION

Conservation practice utilizes a wide range of synthetic polymers (Horie 1987), whose properties change with their ageing (McNeil 1992). In the past, the properties of conservation materials received little or no scientific investigation unless empirical assessment of treated objects suggested that they were failing. Thus the empirical use of soluble nylon in the 1960s as a consolidant was discontinued due to its poor ageing properties (Sease 1981, Fromageot and Le Marie 1990). Testing conservation materials is central to conservation ethics, especially for continued reversibility. In theory all treatments and materials applied to objects should be reversible, to allow for their future removal; in reality this is impracticable (Horie 1983). Reversible consolidants added to friable objects cannot be successfully removed, as breaking down the secondary forces between the consolidant and its substrate would severely damage or destroy the weak object. This places greater importance on the use of materials that retain their properties in the long term. Feller (1994) classified conservation polymers according to their stability; with those showing no undesirable property changes for 100 years as 'stable', but those with changes after six months as 'temporary'. Determining whether a material will be stable in 100 years time presents many difficulties. Using the Ahrrenius equation to extrapolate results of accelerated ageing tests is of limited use, as it often produces an overestimation of decay (Feller 1994, Shashoua et al. 1992). Elevated temperatures or high light levels during testing can produce new reaction routes or favour decay mechanisms, which either do not occur or are of little importance at room temperature, especially if thermoplastic polymers are tested

above their glass transition temperature. Only long-term test procedures can provide meaningful results within a conservation context.

Down et al. (1996) presented results of an exhaustive 10-year test programme involving a large number of acrylic and polyvinyl acetate resins and emulsions. Studies that do not rely upon accelerated ageing are an invaluable aid to conservators selecting polymers for conservation practice. Unfortunately their vast scope and in-depth analysis make them rare and expensive to fund, unless they are supported by large national institutions, such as the Canadian Conservation Institute, or international project funding. Whilst an understanding of how ageing changes the chemistry of polymers and modifies their physical properties is essential to good conservation practice, a knowledge of the physical properties of conservation materials allows for informed decisions regarding their suitability for a particular task. There are many established methods for doing this, from simple bending techniques to sophisticated test rigs for hardness and strength, although results can be of limited practical use when the properties of the object are unknown and impractical to measure (Shashoua 1993).

Even products specifically designed for conservation practice, such as the epoxy resin adhesive Hxtal NYL-1 (polyoxypropylene triamine), have shortcomings and require testing within the context of their use (Bradley 1990). The chemical properties of materials are not always the primary factor in deciding whether to use them. Although Hxtal NYL-1 produces limited numbers of conjugated C=C bonds upon ageing and so yellows only slightly, its refractive index is not as suitable for glass adhesion as the less stable Ablebond 321 (Tennent and Townsend 1984). Many conservators may choose to bond glass using the highly reversible Paraloid B72 (methyl acrylate/methyl ethacrylate), with added fumed silica to improve bond technology, rather than the difficult to reverse epoxy resins. Operational environments may influence the selection of conservation materials. Charola et al. (1984) revealed that ambient relative humidity influenced the degree of polymerization and properties of methyl trimethoxy silane stone consolidant.

LONG-TERM STORAGE IN THE MUSEUM ENVIRONMENT – COLLECTIONS CARE

Indefinite survival of museum objects is a rather unrealistic long-term conservation goal in contrast to minimizing physical and chemical change to objects. Collections care encompasses everything that influences the survival of cultural collections and includes environmental control, finance, political posture, management structures, disaster planning, human error, equipment failure and building fabric. The successful design and implementation of a well-researched conservation strategy should consider all of these factors and quantify and prioritize the threat they pose to the survival of museum objects (Fahy 1994, Knell 1994, Murray 1991, Thompson 1992).

Assessing the museum environment centres on the identification, detection and quantitative measurement of environmental parameters, which affect the longevity of museum objects (Thomson 1986, Cassar 1995). Measures can then be taken to control them and prevent detrimental chemical and physical changes to collections. Science underpins this exercise. As with conservation treatments, understanding and quantifying decay mechanisms is essential for advocating favourable storage environments. Solutions for controlling environments cannot ignore management, finance and other factors that will influence their design, implementation and maintenance. A pro-active approach to environmental control is preferred but this may be limited to commissioning of new or refurbished museums, where budgets are large and building structure can be changed. A reactive approach may be dictated by existing collections with limited budgets. This often involves assessing the environment, tracing and quantifying the causes of visible damage to objects and exploring possibilities for damage control. Additionally, remedial interventive conservation methods may be required to repair and reinforce the physical integrity of objects.

It is recognized that constantly responding to problems is an inappropriate strategy for the ongoing care of collections and long-term planning is preferred. This requires an assessment of the condition and conservation needs of a collection, which would be prohibitively time consuming and expensive if a whole collection was surveyed. Collection surveys were designed to avoid this problem. They assess the condition and needs of a statistically viable range of objects, then extrapolate results to predict the needs of the collection as a whole (Keene 1991). Although they are a recent innovation, their worth has already been questioned, as they rely on subjective judgements and limited data ranges (Taylor 1996). In addition, there is more than a hint that these are a bureaucratic tool for presenting quantified data to grant-aiding bodies. Even in this form they aid preservation by procuring financial aid. Resource management and a policy for gaining grant aid must rank alongside scientific research as important factors for the long-term preservation of collections.

ASSESSING THE MUSEUM ENVIRONMENT

To understand the aggressiveness of an environment it must be assessed qualitatively and quantitatively, preferably using reliable, cheap and accurate detection and quantification techniques for the various agencies of decay. Moisture can be accurately spot recorded using the sling psycrometer (Thomson 1986) or an approximate value can be read off a cobalt impregnated paper scale (Daniels and Wilthew 1983). Continuous recording systems that determine environmental trends over long time periods facilitate forward planning and range from cheap clockwork thermohygrographs, which record moisture levels and temperature (Pragnell 1990), to expensive telemetric computer data logging systems that utilize capacitance measurements in their detectors (Pragnell 1993). Successful interpretation of environmental data must take into account its limitations (Brown 1993). A knowledge of the building, its structure, air exchanges, numbers of visitors, heating system(s), lighting quality and routines, buffering effects, building and showcase materials are all essential to interpret relative humidity trends and plan for change and control (Cassar 1995). A wide range of pollutants may be present within museums and their origins may be external or internal (Baer and Banks 1985). Their detection at low concentrations within museums presents problems and both active and passive monitoring systems have been tested for their accuracy, reproducibility and suitability for museum contexts (Knight 1994, Grzywacz 1993). Damage caused by pollutants and the amounts required to cause damage to materials, continues to be a focus for research (Thickett et al. 1998). Light quality and quantity is a problem for susceptible materials, especially high-energy short wavelength ultra-violet light (Michalski 1987). Reliable techniques exist for spot and cumulative recording of light quantity and quality (Thomson 1986) and its action must be considered in relation to moisture and temperature levels, which influence the nature and extent of damage it can produce.

Damage due to environment

Understanding how agencies of decay produce damage and how damage is related to quantity or quality of the agency is a prerequisite to controlling their action. Moisture is a major cause of damage to many museum materials. It facilitates chemical reactions, dissolves acidic gases and promotes physical change.

Fluctuating relative humidity can cause physical damage to organic materials that are in dynamic equilibrium with it. Weak organic archaeological material is likely to be at greater physical risk than slightly decayed historical material, as it is less able to sustain stresses accompanying water loss or gain (Michalski 1993). Polymers used to treat objects must be carefully selected as they may modify the response of a material to moisture and it has to be assessed whether the change is advantageous. Measuring the response of organic materials to various fixed and fluctuating relative humidities provides a guide to how quickly damage is likely to occur and how extensive it is likely to be (Erhardt and Mecklenberg 1994).

Recommended relative humidity values normally fall into two categories. The first category comprises materials which should be stored below an experimentally determined critical value for a reaction that causes their decay (Erhardt and Mecklenberg 1994). For example hygroscopic salts on metals absorb water and provide electrolyte that has a long dwell-time on the metal surface and facilitates corrosion, which is more extensive than corrosion occurring in a 100 per cent relative humidity without dissolved salts. The critical humidity of corrosion products or contaminating salts determines safe storage values for metals. Turgoose (1982) identified the need for chloride-contaminated archaeological iron to be stored in a relative humidity below 20 per cent, as this favoured the formation of $FeCl_2.2H_2O$ in preference to $FeCl_2.4H_2O$, which is hygroscopic and promotes corrosion. In contrast, iron contaminated with sulfate ions (normally from polluted atmospheric environments), can be safely stored below 60 per cent relative humidity, which is the critical humidity for change from $FeSO_4.4H_2O$ to the hygroscopic $FeSO_4.7H_2O$ (Jones 1992).

A second category comprises mainly organic materials, where water is an integral part of their structure and loss or gain of water will cause physical stress. These materials should be stored in a relative humidity that is static and not so low that it dehydrates them nor so high that it swells them and supports biodeterioration. Regular fluctuations in moisture levels cause the most damage to these objects, as they strive to lose or gain water to equilibrate with the moisture content of the environment. For many years recommendations were stringently set at an ideal 55 ± 5 per cent (Thomson 1986). Recent work has identified a central relative humidity range (25 per cent to 65 per cent), within which it is suggested quite large fluctuations around a central point will cause minimal or no

damage, provided the nature of the material is taken into account when setting the allowable fluctuation range (Michalski 1993). More research would clarify the picture, as outcomes depend upon the equilibrium moisture content/relative humidity response time of a material, its geometry, the longevity of the fluctuation and its condition. Naturally it is preferable to store material in a static relative humidity, but the cost of achieving this may be high and present difficult decisions regarding prioritizing budget allocation. Threats to *in situ* archaeological material are often moisture related. Wilson-Yang and Burns (1989) assessed the environment in the tomb of Nefertari in Egypt and Maekawa and Preusser (1993) suggested pragmatic steps to protect it.

Linking damage to particular pollutants involves identifying decay mechanisms and products, measuring pollutants and tracing their source. Black spots occurring on archaeological copper alloys were linked to sulfurous gases within closed showcases (Eggert and Subotta-Brown 1999). Adhesives and other materials used to construct showcases and storage containers must be tested to determine whether they emit significant quantities of pollutants that will react with cultural material stored within them (Green and Thickett 1995, Eremin and Wilthew 1996). Conservation materials can also present a threat to the objects that they are applied to. Significant off-gassing of acetic acid from polyvinyl acetate emulsion adhesives and consolidants, during the first three months after their application, make them a threat to many metals (Down *et al.* 1996, Thickett *et al.* 1998).

Controlling the museum environment

Controlling environments to meet set criteria can be difficult. Active control using air conditioning has been advocated as the only way to provide reliable and accurate environmental control (Thomson 1986). Other workers point to air conditioning limitations such as installation and running cost, limited plant life and an inability to meet stringent environmental control parameters (Oreszczyn *et al.* 1994, Padfield and Jensen 1994). Buildings housing cultural material may be historical monuments or may not lend themselves to the installation of air conditioning. In these instances active control may be effected by designs using humidifiers and dehumidifiers, aided by natural ventilation systems in the building (Cassar and Clark 1993). Limited environmental control is provided on a smaller scale by actively conditioning showcases using humidifiers and dehumidifiers (Bradley 1996). The natural moisture and temperature buffering properties of buildings and their furnishings is considered when designing control systems which do not rely on air conditioning (Padfield and Jensen 1990, Eshoj and Padfield 1993), but the nature of a building limits this approach (Padfield 1996). For sensitive materials, control systems that deal with pollution, relative humidity, temperature and light have been developed and are controlled by computers (Saunders 1993). These are necessarily expensive to establish and run.

Studies on the rate of air and moisture exchange (hygrometric half-life) in showcases (Thomson 1986), along with the natural buffering effects of construction materials and contents, have contributed to the safer display of objects and the use of passive control systems (Stolow 1987), that rely upon a high quality of showcase design to succeed. Cracks a millimetre wide are capable of causing major leakage to the exterior (Michalski 1994). Checking whether showcases meet design standards is challenging and has been achieved using tracer gases to determine leakage (Cassar and Martin 1994). Using desiccating agents, such as silica gel, to passively control microenvironments is common for long-term storage of archaeological metals (Cassar 1985, Weintraub 1982). Minimal fluctuation around a mid-range relative humidity has been passively achieved in display cases, using conditioned silica gel to act as a moisture reservoir to buffer changes in the relative humidity within showcases, caused by external temperature fluctuations or ingress of water (Brimblecombe and Ramer 1983). Such microclimates are suitable for organic materials, where fluctuations in relative humidity are to be avoided. Unfortunately, control systems can only be expected to meet and maintain their design parameters if they are supported by a suitable management structure and trained staff with sufficient financial backing (Dollery 1994).

Although most materials surviving from archaeological contexts are not particularly light sensitive, many of the polymers used to conserve them are prone to light damage (Feller 1994). Metals, stone, ceramics and glass are essentially unaffected by light but organic materials, dyes and many pigments suffer damage (Michalski 1987). For sensitive materials both the quality and quantity of light must be controlled (Michalski 1990b). Since the damage caused by light is governed by reciprocity, damage resulting from exposure to a specific quality of light for a given number of hours, is independent of the intensity of the lighting. Thus exposure for 10 hours at 200 lux intensity is the same as 20 hours at 100 lux, for the same quality of light, but the relationship between damage and exposure is not linear, so doubling exposure times does not double the damage caused (Saunders and Kirkby 1996). A certain quality of light is required to institute decay mechanisms and is related to the structure of the material in question and the impurities it contains. Light damage usually occurs via free radical mechanisms and often involves oxidation of polymers, which will continue in the dark if the reaction is autocatalytic (McNeil 1992). Although the removal of oxygen from storage environments would prevent oxidation, limit the range of aggressive chemical reactions and prevent aerobic biodeterioration systems, it is costly, difficult to achieve and limits access to the material. Small-scale oxygen elimination has been examined using the chemical Ageless(T), but at present this is not a viable option for long-term storage (Gilberg and Grattan 1994). In order to be seen objects must be lit and damage is likely to result but may be minimized by controlling light quality and limiting exposure times. Light sensitive materials should be stored in the dark.

SUMMARY

The idea of simple interventive stabilization treatments is outdated and conservation is recognized as comprising many parts. Together, interventive and preventative conservation methods aid the survival of archaeological objects and they rely upon materials science, research and organizational issues to succeed. No matter how complete the results of research, they can only be useful to conservation if they are practicable and supported by good management and adequate finance. Importantly, conservation must be a continuous process if objects are to survive. The process can be summarized as:

(i)   identify conservation problems,
(ii) formation of research teams – conservators, conservation scientists and specialist scientists (e.g., botanists, metallurgists, and corrosion scientists),
(iii) research finance – government money supporting the primary objectives of various institutions, or from external grant giving bodies,
(iv) location of research – practical conservation laboratories, conservation research laboratories, universities,
(v)   co-operation – national and international working groups,

(vi) research into the structure and decay of the materials,

(vii) influence of environment on decay rate,

(viii) design, evaluate and field test interventive and non-interventive treatment techniques,

(ix) evaluate conservation materials,

(x) design and implement suitable storage and display environments,

(xi) monitor environments, and

(xii) publication – ICOM Triennials, IIC Conferences, specialist conferences, wide range of specialist scientific journals.

REFERENCES

*Recommended for further reading

Andrews, G. (1991). *Management of Archaeological Projects.* English Heritage: London.

Baer, S. and Banks, P.N. (1985). Indoor pollution: effects on cultural and historic material. *International Journal of Museum Management and Curatorship*, **4**:9–20.

Barbour, J. (1984). The condition and dimensional stabilization of highly deteriorated waterlogged hardwood. In Ramiere, R. and Colardette, M. (eds) *Proceedings of 2nd meeting of ICOM Committee for Conservation Wet Organic Archaeological Materials Working Group*, 23–38. CETBGE: Grenoble.

Bilz, M., Dean, L., Grattan, D., McCawley, C., McMillan, J. and Cook, C. (1993). A study of the thermal breakdown of PEG. In Hoffman, P. (ed.) *Proceedings of 5th Meeting of ICOM Committee for Conservation Wet Organic Archaeological Materials Working Group*, 213–230. International Council of Museums: Bremerhaven.

Blanchette, R. and Hoffman, P. (1993). Degradation processes in waterlogged archaeological wood. In Hoffman, P. (ed.) *Proceedings of 5th meeting of ICOM Committee for Conservation Wet Organic Archaeological Materials Working Group*, 111–142. International Council of Museums: Bremerhaven.

Bradley, S.M. (1990). Evaluation of Hxtal NYL-l and Loctite 350 Adhesives for glass conservation. In Grimstard, K. (ed.) *Preprints ICOM Committee for Conservation 9th Triennial Dresden*, 669–674. International Council of Museums: Los Angeles.

Bradley, S. (1996). Development of an environmental policy for the British Museum. In Bridgland, J. (ed.) *ICOM Committee for Conservation 12th Triennial Meeting Edinburgh*, 8–13. James and James: London.

Brimblecombe, P. and Ramer, B. (1983). Museum display cases and the exchange of water vapour. *Studies in Conservation*, **28**:179–188.

Brostoff, L.B. (1997). Investigation into the interaction of benzotriazole with copper corrosion minerals and surfaces. In Macleod, I.D., Pennec, S. and Robbiola, L. (eds) *Metals 95. Proceedings of Metals in Conservation Conference*, 95–98. James and James: London.

Brown, J.P. (1993). What can psychrometric data tell us? In Child, R.E. (ed.) *Electronic Environmental Monitoring in Museums*, 37–59. United Kingdom Institute for Conservation: London.

Brownstein, A. (1982). The chemistry of PEG. In Grattan, D. (ed.) *Proceedings of 1st meeting of ICOM Committee for Conservation Wet Organic Archaeological Materials Working Group*, 279–285. International Council of Museums: Ottawa.

Cassar, M. (1985). Checklist for the establishment of a microclimate. *The Conservator*, **9**:14–16.

*Cassar, M. (1995). *Environmental Management: Guidelines for Museums and Galleries.* Routledge: London.

Cassar, M. and Clarke, W.O. (1993). A pragmatic approach to environmental improvements at the Courtauld Institute Galleries in Somerset House. In Bridgland, J. (ed.) *Preprints of the ICOM Committee for Conservation, 10th Triennial Meeting, Washington DC*, 595–600. International Council of Museums: Paris.

Cassar, M. and Martin, G. (1994). The environmental performance of museum display cases. In Roy, A. and Smith, P. (eds) *Preventive Conservation Practices, Theory and Research*, 171–173. International Institute for Conservation: London.

Charola, A.E., Wheeler, G.E. and Freund, G.G. (l984). The influence of relative humidity in the polymerisation of methyl trimethoxy silane. In Bromelle, N.S., Pye, E., Smith, P. and Thomson, G. (eds) *Adhesives and Consolidants*, 177–181. International Institute for Conservation: London.

*Cronyn, J. (1990). *The Elements of Archaeological Conservation.* Butterworths: London.

Daniels, V.D. and Wilthew, S.E. (1983). An investigation into the use of cobalt salt impregnated papers for the measurement of relative humidity. *Studies in Conservation*, **28**:80–84.

Dawson, J. (1982). Some considerations in choosing a biocide. In Grattan, D. (ed.) *Proceedings of 1st meeting of ICOM Wet Organic Archaeological Materials Working Group*, 269–276. International Council of Museums: Ottawa.

Dollery, D. (1994). A methodology of preventive conservation for a large, expanding and mixed archaeological collection. In Roy, A. and Smith, P. (eds) *Preventive Conservation Practice, Theory and Research*, 69–72. International Institute for Conservation: London.

Down, J., MacDonald, M.A., Teterault, J. and Williams, S. (1996). Adhesive testing at the Canadian Conservation Institute – an evaluation of selected poly(vinylacetate) and acrylic resins. *Studies in Conservation*, **41**:19–44.

Drayman-Weisser, T. (1987). The use of sodium carbonate as a pretreatment on difficult to stabilize bronzes. In Black, J. (ed.) *Recent Advances in Conservation and Analysis*, 105–108. Institute of Archaeology Summer Schools Press: London.

Earl, N.J. and Watkinson, D.E. (1997). Assessment of post-excavation systems for archaeological glass using FT-IR Microscopy. In Sinclair, A., Slater, E. and Gowlett, J.A.J. (eds) *Archaeological Sciences 1995*, 19–30. Oxbow: Oxford.

Eggert, G. and Subotta-Brown, U. (1999). Black spots on bronzes and elemental sulphur. In Bridgland, J. (ed.) *ICOM CC 12th Triennial Lyons*, 283–287. James and James: London.

Eremin, K. and Wilthew, P. (1996). The effectiveness of barrier materials in reducing emissions of organic gases from fireboard: results of preliminary tests. In Bridgland, J. (ed.) *Preprints of the ICOM CC 12th Triennial Meeting Lyons*, 27–35. James and James: London.

Erhardt, D. and Mecklenburg, M. (1994). Relative humidity re-examined. In Roy, A. and Smith, P. (eds) *Preventive Conservation: Practice, Theory and Research*, 32–38. International Institute for Conservation: London.

Eshoj, B. and Padfield, T. (1993). The use of porous building materials to provide a stable relative humidity. In Bridgland, J. (ed.) *ICOM Committee for Conservation 10th Triennial Meeting Washington DC*, 605–609. International Council for Museums: Paris.

Fahy, A. (ed.) (1994). *Collections Management*. Routledge: London.

Feller, R.L. (1994). *Accelerated Ageing. Photochemical and Thermal Aspects*. Getty Conservation Institute: Los Angeles.

Fromageot, D. and Le Marie, J. (1990). The prediction of the long-term photo-ageing of soluble polyamides used in conservation. *Studies in Conservation*, 36:1–8.

Geymayer, P., Glass, B. and Leidl, E. (1990). Oxidative degradation of polyethylene glycols. In Hoffman, P. (ed.) *Proceedings of 4th meeting of ICOM Wet Organic Archaeological Materials Working Group*, 83–90. International Council of Museums: Bremerhaven.

Gilberg, M. (1987). Friedrich Rathgen: the father of modern conservation. *Journal of the American Institute for Conservation*, 26:105–120.

Gilberg, M. and Grattan, D. (1994). Oxygen-free storage using Ageless oxygen absorber. In Roy, A. and Smith, P. (eds) *Preventive Conservation Practice, Theory and Research: IIC Ottawa Congress*, 177–180. International Institute for Conservation: London.

Grattan, D. (1982). A practical comparative study of treatments for waterlogged wood. *Studies in Conservation*, 27:124–136.

Green, L. and Bradley, S. (1997) An investigation of strategies for the long-term storage of archaeological iron. In MacLeod, I.D., Pennec, S. and Robbiola, L. (eds) *Metal 95. Proceedings of Metals in Conservation Conference*, 205–209. James and James: London.

Green, L. and Thickett, D. (1995). Testing materials for use in the storage and display of artifacts – a revised methodology. *Studies in Conservation*, 40:145–152.

Grzywacz, S. (1993). Using passive sampling devices to detect pollutants in museum environments. In Bridgland, J. (ed.) *ICOM Committee for Conservation 10th Triennial Meeting Washington DC*, 610–615, International Institute for Conservation: Paris.

Hafors, B. (1990). The role of the Wasa in the development of the polyethylene glycol preservation method. In Barbour, J. and Rowell, R.M. (eds) *Archaeological Wood: Properties, Chemistry and Preservation*, 177–194. Advances in Chemistry Series 225, American Chemical Society: Washington DC.

Hoffman, P. (1984). On the stabilization of waterlogged oakwood with PEG – molecular size versus degree degradation. In Ramiere, R. and Colardelle, M. (eds) *Proceedings of 2nd meeting of ICOM Committee for Conservation Wet Organic Archaeological Materials Working Group*, 95–116. CETGBE: Grenoble.

Hoffman, P. (1996). Sucrose for waterlogged wood – not so simple at all. In Bridgland, J. (ed.) *ICOM CC 11th triennial Edinburgh*, 657–663. James and James: London.

Hoffman, P. and Jones, M. (1990). Structure and degredation process for waterlogged archaeological wood. In Barbour, J. and Rowell, R.M. (eds) *Archaeological Wood: Properties, Chemistry and Preservation*, 33–66. Advances in Chemistry Series 225, American Chemical Society: Washington DC.

Horie, V. (1983). Reversibility of polymer treatments. In Tate, J.O., Tennent, N.H. and Townsend, J.H. (eds) *Resins in Conservation*, 3.1–3.6. Scottish Society for Conservation and Restoration: Edinburgh.

*Horie, C.V. (1987). *Materials for Conservation, Organic Consolidants, Adhesives and Coatings*. Butterworths: London.

Jensen, E.L., Salmonsen, E. and Straetkvern, K. (1996). From waterlogged site to archaeologist's desk – new packing methods with minimum of handling. In Roy, A. and Smith, P. (eds) *Archaeological Conservation and its Consequences, IIC Copenhagen Congress*, 89–93. International Institute for Conservation: London.

Jones, D. (1992). *Principles and Prevention of Corrosion*. Macmillan: New York.

Keene, S. (1991). Audits of care: a framework for collections condition surveys. In Norman, M. and Todd, V. (eds) *Storage: Preprints for UKIC conference Restoration '91*. United Kingdom Institute for Conservation: London.

Knell, S. (ed.) (1994). *Collections Care*. Routledge: London.

Knight, B. (1994). Passive monitoring for museum showcase pollutants. In Roy, A. and Smith, P. (eds) *Preventive Conservation Practice, Theory and Research, IIC Ottawa Congress*, 174–176. International Institute for Conservation: London.

Knight, B. (1997). The stabilisation of archaeological iron: past, present and future. In Macleod, I.D., Pennec, S. and Robbiola, L. (eds) *Metal 95. Proceedings of Metals in Conservation Conference*, 36–42. James and James: London.

MacLeod, I.D. (1987). Hygroscopicity of archaeological timber: effects of molecular weights of impregnant and degree of degradation. In MacLeod, I.D. (ed.) *Conservation of*

Wet Wood and Metal, 211–214. Western Australia Museum: Perth.

Madsen, B. (1985). Benzotriozole: a perspective. In Keene, S. (ed.) *Corrosion Inhibitors in Conservation*, 19–20. Occasional Paper 4, UKIC: London.

Maekawa, S. and Preusser, F. (1993). Environmental monitoring at the tomb of Nefertari. In Bridgland, J. (ed.) *Preprints of ICOM Committee for Conservation 10th Triennial Meeting Washington DC*, 616–623. International Council of Museums: London.

McNeill, I.C. (1992). Fundamental aspects of polymer degradation. In Allen, N.S., Edge, M. and Horie, C.V. (eds) *Polymers in Conservation*, 14–31. Special Publications No. 105, Royal Society of Chemistry: Cambridge.

Michalski, S. (1987). Damage to museum objects by visible radiation (light) and ultra-violet radiation (UV). In *Lighting Preprint: a Conference on Lighting in Museums, Art Galleries and Historic Houses*, 3–16. United Kingdom Institute for Conservation/Museums Association: London.

Michalski, S. (1990a). An overall framework for preventive conservation and remedial conservation. In Grimstard, K. (ed.) *Preprints of ICOM Committee for Conservation 9th Triennial Meeting Dresden*. ICOM: Los Angeles.

Michalski, S. (1990b). Towards specific lighting guide-lines. In Grimstard, K. (ed.) *Preprints of ICOM Committee for Conservation 9th Triennial Meeting Dresden*, 585–588. ICOM: Los Angeles.

Michalski, S. (1993). Relative humidity: a discussion of correct and incorrect values. In Bridgland, J. (ed.) *Preprints of ICOM Committee for Conservation 10th Triennial Meeting Washington DC*, 624–629. International Institute for Conservation: Paris.

Michalski, S (1994). Leakage prediction for buildings, cases, bags and bottles. *Studies in Conservation*, **39**:169–192.

Murray, F. (1991). Planning for preventive conservation. In Lord, G. and Lord, D.B. (eds) *The Manual of Museum Planning*, 127–160. HMSO: Norwich.

Oddy, A. and Winsor, P. (1998). A provisional bibliography of Harold Plenderleith. *Studies in Conservation*, **43**:144–149.

Oreszczyn, T., Cassar, M. and Fernandez, K. (1994). Comparative study of air-conditioned and non air-conditioned museums. In Roy, A. and Smith, P. (eds) *Preventive Conservation Practice, Theory and Research*. IIC Ottawa Congress, 144–148. International Institute for Conservation: London.

Padfield, T. (1996). Low energy climate control in museum stores: a post script. In Bridgland, J. (ed.) *Preprints of ICOM Committee for Conservation 11th Triennial Meeting Edinburgh*, 68–71. James and James: London.

Padfield, T. and Jensen, P. (1990). Low energy climate control in museum store. In Grimstard, K. (ed.) *Preprints of ICOM Committee for Conservaton 9th Triennial Meeting*, 596–601. International Council of Museums: Los Angeles.

Padfield, T. and Jensen, P. (1994). Comparative study of air-conditioned and non air-conditioned museums. In Roy, A. and Smith, P. (eds) *Preventive Conservation: Practice,*

Theory and Research: IIC Ottawa Congress, 144–148. International Institute for Conservation: London.

Pearson, C. (1987). *Conservation of Marine Archaeological Objects*. Butterworths: London.

Pragnell, R.F. (1990). Recording humidity: no need to lose your hair. *Environmental Engineering*, **X**:15–18.

Pragnell, R.F. (1993). Measuring humidity in normal ambient environments: the role of the electronic relative humidity hygrometer. In Child, R.E. (ed.) *Electronic Environmental Monitoring in Museums*, 15–29. United Kingdom Institute for Conservation: London.

Pollard, A.M. and Heron, C. (1996) *Archaeological Chemistry*. Royal Society of Chemistry: Cambridge.

Rathgen, F. (1905). *The Preservation of Antiquities: A Handbook for Curators*. Cambridge University Press: Cambridge.

Saunders, D. (1993). The environment and lighting in the Sainsbury Wing of the National Gallery. In Bridgland, J. (ed.) *Preprints of ICOM Committee for Conservation 10th Triennial Meeting Washington DC*, 630–638. International Council of Museums: Paris.

Saunders, D. and Kirby, J. (1996). Light-induced damage: investigating the reciprocity principle. In Bridgland, J. (ed.) *Preprints of ICOM Committee for Conservation 11th Triennial Meeting Edinburgh*, 87–90. James and James: London.

Sease, C. (1981). The case against using soluble nylon in conservation work. *Studies in Conservation*, **26**:102–110.

Selwyn, L.S., Siris, P.J. and Argyropoulos, V. (1999). The corrosion of archaeological iron with details on weeping and akaganeite. *Studies in Conservation*, **44**:217–232.

Shashoua, Y. (1993). Mechanical testing of resins for use in conservation. In Bridgland, J. (ed.) *Preprints of ICOM Committee for Conservation 10th Triennial Meeting Washington DC*, 580–585. International Council of Museums: Paris.

Shashoua, Y., Bradley, S.M. and Daniels, V.D. (1992). Degradation of cellulose nitrate adhesive. *Studies in Conservation*, **37**:120–131.

Stolow, N. (1987). *Conservation and Exhibitions*. Butterworths: London.

Taylor, J. (1996). *An Assessment of Condition Surveys as Objective Tools of Analysis*. Unpublished BSc Dissertation, Cardiff University.

Tennent, N. and Townsend, J. (1984). The significance of refractive index of adhesives for glass repair. In Bromelle, N., Pye, E., Smith, P. and Thomson, G. (eds) *Adhesives and Consolidants. Preprints of IIC Paris Conference*, 205–208. International Institute for Conservation: London.

Thickett, D., Bradley, S. and Lee, L. (1998). Assessment of the risks to metal artifacts by volatile carbonyl pollutants. In Mourney, W. and Robbiola, L. (eds) *Metals 98. Proceedings of the International Conference on Metals Corrosion*, 260–264. James and James: London.

*Thompson, J.M.A. (ed.) (1992). *Manual of Curatorship: A Guide to Museum Practice* (2nd edn). Butterworth Heinman: London.

*Thomson, G. (1986). *Museum Environment* (2nd edn). Butterworths: London.

Turgoose, S. (1982). Post excavation changes in iron antiquities. *Studies in Conservation*, **27**:97–101.

Turgoose, S. (1985). Corrosion inhibitors for conservation. In Keene, S. (ed.) *Corrosion Inhibitors in Conservation*, 313–318. United Kingdom Institute for Conservation: London.

UKIC Archaeology Section (1990). *Guidance for Conservation Practice*. United Kingdom Institute for Conservation: London.

Watkinson, D.E. (1996). Chloride extraction from archaeological iron: comparative treatment efficiencies. In Roy, A. and Smith, P. (eds) *Archaeological Conservation and its Consequences, IIC Copenhagen Congress*, 208–212. International Institute for Conservation: London.

*Watkinson, D.E. and Neal, V. (1998). *First Aid for Finds* (3rd edn). RESCUE/UKIC: Southampton.

Weintraub, S. (1982). Studies on the behaviour of RH within an exhibition case. Part I: measuring the effectiveness of sorbents for use in an enclosed show-case. In van Aspern de Boer, J.R.J. (ed.) *Preprints ICOM Committee for Conservation 6th Triennial, Ottawa*, 1–11. International Council of Museums.

Wilson-Yang, K.M. and Burns, G. (1989). The stability of the Tomb of Nefertari 1904-1987. *Studies in Conservation*, **34**:153–170.

Young, G.S. and Simms, R. (1987). Microscopical determination of PEG in treated wood – the effect of distribution on dimensional stabilization. In MacLeod, I.D. (ed.) *Conservation of Wet Wood and Metal*, 109–140. Western Australian Museum: Perth.

SECTION 9

Statistical and Computational Methods

Overview – Numbers, Models, Maps: Computers and Archaeology

R.D. DRENNAN

Department of Anthropology, University of Pittsburgh.

In the first edition of *Science in Archaeology* (Brothwell and Higgs 1963) there was no section on statistical and computer applications. By the second edition, Brothwell and Higgs (1969:17) noted that 'the application of statistical methods to archaeology is becoming such an important matter for consideration, that we have considered the subject worthy of an entirely new section'. It was still the case in 1969 that computers were accessible to and utilized by only a few archaeologists. One of the four chapters in that new section, however, did deal with computer applications. Both statistics and computers were then viewed as novel and unusual in archaeology; it was common to wonder whether they would have much impact on the field and, if they did, whether it would be for good or ill. Brothwell (1969:678) was fully confident that statistics and computers would both come to be widely used in archaeology, although his 'plea for statistical caution' revealed considerable ambivalence about the likely nature of the result.

Brothwell's (1969) view of the future has certainly proved accurate in that computers and statistics have come to be exceedingly common archeological tools. Not at all surprisingly, many of the ways in which they have come to be central elements in archaeological research were beyond almost everyone's imagination in 1969. Reading what was written thirty years ago about the future of statistics and computers in archaeology is not at all unlike watching science fiction movies from the mid-twentieth century. Human travel into space certainly does now exist, as movie makers imagined, although it has by no means become common. It is Earth-orbiting satellites and the work that they do that have had a massive impact on the lives of many more people. Looking at those movies, one is struck by how immediately recognizable they are as mid-twentieth century visions of the late twentieth century. Focused on the idea of human voyagers into space, movie makers showed remarkable lack of imagination with regard to the myriad impacts of changing technology and human customs. Computer monitors are nowhere to be seen; the telephones are clunky black devices with rotary dials; and ash trays are everywhere. Similarly, in archaeology, word processors and email have had a bigger impact on how we do our work than the analytical applications on which more attention was focused in the 1960s. Few, if any, archaeologists imagined then how scarce typewriters would become by the end of the century.

Handbook of Archaeological Sciences. Edited by D.R. Brothwell and A.M. Pollard.

STATISTICS AND TRAINING

As Brothwell (1969:669) noted, quantitative or numerical analysis was not entirely new to archaeology in 1969, but archaeologists were rapidly becoming much more sophisticated and self-conscious about such analysis. Some were pressing eagerly beyond percentages, means, and other common fare of grade-school arithmetic, toward tools that required special statistical training to master – training that the vast majority of archaeologists practising in 1969 did not have. Brothwell worried about the damage that could be done if such tools were not properly used. The archaeological literature had, of course, long had its share of preposterous conclusions reached by flawed logic and inaccurate observation in no way involving numbers or statistics. Somehow, though, abuse of the specialized tools of statistical analysis has seemed a particularly grave danger, and a series of articles has critiqued ill-conceived or poorly executed analyses (e.g., Thomas 1978). Whether this steady criticism has produced much improvement is open to question; it may only have exacerbated the mathematical anxiety still felt by many.

Over the past 30 years it has become much more common for archaeological training to include statistics, and the last decade or so has seen a proliferation of textbooks that attempt to explain both basic principles and advanced analytical topics in specifically archaeological applications (e.g., Shennan 1997, Fletcher and Lock 1991, Baxter 1994, Drennan 1996). At the close of the twentieth century, using statistics has become 'normal science' in archaeology, and no review of basic principles was deemed necessary to this volume. Instead, three chapters review more advanced topics in statistical analysis: geographic information systems (Chapter 53), multivariate analysis (Chapter 54), and Bayesian approaches (Chapter 55); and one chapter illustrates the successful integration of an assortment of statistical analyses, both basic and advanced, to support conclusions (Chapter 59). This last may superficially seem out of place in this section, because Neff's subject is clearly not statistics or computers but pottery production and distribution on the Pacific coastal plain of Guatemala. It is in this chapter, however, that the reader sees data, conclusions, and statistical analyses in their 'real' relationship to each other. For obvious reasons, chapters focusing on statistical methods and computer applications tend to use data just as brief examples to show analytical approaches in action. We do need constant reminders of how peculiar an impression this gives of research.

The fact is that statistical analyses are regularly incorporated into archaeological studies in very routine ways, and the archaeological community has clearly become much more statistically literate than it was a few decades ago. At the same time, one still does not have to look far to find examples of badly done statistical analysis in archaeology. Significance tests, for example, are used ineffectively or erroneously because an author's grasp of the basic concept of significance is tenuous. Some archaeologists seem especially unsure of this aspect of their work, and at least some readers of the archaeological literature still seem to have enough fear and distrust of statistics that they automatically disbelieve whatever results they are presented with – or enough awe that they automatically trust whatever they read (which is just as bad). I do not dare predict whether this will continue to be the case after another 30 years have passed. I certainly hope not.

If, however, statistical analysis has become and will continue to be part of the archaeologist's normal tool kit, it is worth paying attention to how successive generations of archaeologists learn to use these tools, especially if archaeologists' hands are not yet as steady as one might hope when they wield them. It is heartening that basic training in statistical analysis is more commonly offered (and indeed frequently required) in archaeology programmes than it was 30 years ago, at both graduate and undergraduate levels. On the other hand, training in statistics does not always fully produce the desired results.

In the introductory course I teach on archaeological data analysis, the number of students (especially graduate students) confessing to a previous introduction to statistics has increased over the years. Over half the 30 to 40 students now fall in this category. Very few of these students who have already taken statistics, however, feel confident of their ability to use basic statistics effectively in their archaeological work. College statistics courses, like college language courses, although successful for some students, seem also to produce too many students unable to put what they have studied into practice. Three elements of successful statistical training for archaeologists are worth mentioning in this context.

First, archaeology students (and professionals as well) need to be introduced to basic principles of statistical analysis explicitly (it will not happen by osmosis), and this introduction works best if it occurs in a specifically archaeological context that makes clear from the very beginning just how statistical tools are useful in archaeology. The conceptual leap from basic statistical principles to how they can be useful to archaeologists is substantial, and it is not realistic to expect that many instructors in general applied statistics courses will have enough familiarity with archaeological applications to provide much guidance. Budding archaeologists get off to a much stronger start at effective use of basic statistical tools if they are introduced to them specifically in the context of their application to archaeological data analysis.

Part of the reason for this is that archaeological data analysis calls for a somewhat different application of statistical tools than that provided in most basic applied statistics courses or texts. To cite only a single example, questions of sampling and sample bias work out differently in archaeology than in most other disciplines. For psychologists, sociologists, and others, sample selection is of vital importance for avoiding bias, and stratified sampling designs of considerable complexity are commonly used to minimize sample size. Archaeologists can sometimes work this way, but we often have no choice but to work with samples known to result from strongly biased selection procedures. This is often the case when existing museum collections are studied, and such collections may provide much larger and better samples than could be collected anew even though methods better suited to avoiding bias could be adopted in new field research. Even when new field research is carried out and appropriate random sampling techniques are employed, the population available to sample from may already and unavoidably be a biased sample from the population the archaeologist really needs to characterize. An obvious instance is when an entire sector of a site has been eroded away by a river before archaeologists get to it. It is all well and good to say we should not work with such a site but rather select one that is intact so as to avoid this sample bias, but no archaeologist who has actually worked in the field is naive enough to think this can often (or perhaps ever) be done. In such situations, archaeologists must be able to identify likely sources of bias and think clearly about the nature and analytical implications of this bias. As Cowgill (1977:351) has pointed out, this problem is not unique to statistical inference. Whenever we make conclusions of whatever kind about a whole on the basis of a study of some part of that whole (which, in archaeology, is to say almost always), issues of sample bias arise.

In the Americas, for example, much is made of the fluted Clovis points manufactured by some of the hemisphere's earliest inhabitants. The known sample of Clovis points available for study is not large, and most of these are known only because collectors own or have owned them. This is clearly a very biased sample, but it is not possible to simply go out and collect a better one. To make any conclusions at all about fluted points requires careful consideration of the nature and impact of bias. This is the case whether our interest is regional variation in the mean point length or the aesthetic values of the flaking patterns. Fortunately, there are ways to use such a sample, and the powerful concepts for thinking about sampling bias that statisticians have developed can help us interpret meaningfully both the estimates of mean length we may make and our qualitative aesthetic judgements of flaking patterns. That is to say, both kinds of conclusions must take seriously the implication that some kinds of Clovis points are absent or under-represented in the sample available for study as a consequence of sampling bias. Archaeology students cannot be expected to be introduced to using concepts involving sample bias constructively in situations like this except in archaeology, because the quite proper way to deal with such difficulties in most disciplines is simply to avoid them through proper sample selection in the first place.

A second element in effective statistical training in archaeology has to do with the nature of the approach taken. Introductory statistics courses (and textbooks) sometimes take an abstractly mathematical approach, attempting to demonstrate the validity of equations by deriving them algebraically from a long series of other equations. The formal language of mathematics is powerful, efficient, elegant – and totally incomprehensible to a substantial majority of the world's archaeologists. Some thoughts can best be expressed in Arabic, but not to an audience that does not understand the language. It makes no more sense to express in abstract mathematical notation things that can be conveyed in other ways if the intended audience mostly just do not speak this language.

At the opposite extreme are 'cookbooks' that make no effort to convey principles but instead reduce them to simple recipes or sets of instructions to be followed by rote. Whatever else may be said in favour of or against such an approach, it is altogether unsatisfactory in archaeology, where data idiosyncrasy is the rule. The cookie-cutter approaches to sampling and experimental design that appear to work in some disciplines may produce data sets that are analysable by following standard recipes, but this does not happen in archaeology. No two data sets present exactly the same opportunities or difficulties. Real understanding of principles is required, and there are ways to convey the necessary understanding without resorting to a mathematical language that only adds to the difficulty of communication. Most introductory books on statistics written especially for archaeologists strive for such approaches, and we are fortunate that there are now several different flavours to choose from.

A third element in successful statistical training is to put the techniques to real work immediately. For students, this means not only in a data analysis course, but also in projects, in other courses, and wherever they can apply what they have learned to the analysis of varied data sets to answer real questions of intrinsic interest and importance. Lack of such opportunities vitiates the aims of statistical training as surely as lack of opportunity to put a foreign language to practical use leads inevitably and relatively quickly to serious erosion of what has been accomplished in the classroom. Students must meet the principles of statistical analysis early enough in their training that they have multiple opportunities (indeed necessities) to put them into practice before they arrive at the stage of writing a thesis. Making the application of statistical techniques to archaeological analysis not only normal science but consistently healthy science will require continued attention to making sure that training in the use of statistical tools is effective. This is a problem not faced by lumberjacks or rock climbers – in these fields natural selection strongly favours those who use the tools of the trade well. In archaeology we must devise our own (and hopefully more humane) solutions.

COUNTING

Two of the chapters that follow call much-needed attention to counting (Chapters 56 and 57). It is a measure of how archaeological use of statistics has advanced that we can recognize what a vexing and important basic issue this is. The complexity inherent in initial quantification in archaeology is yet another way in which statistical applications in archaeology differ from those in other disciplines. Specialists in faunal analysis have a longer history of awareness of the complexities of counting than the rest of us do, but many similar concerns arise with ceramic and lithic artifacts, exactly as Shott points out. Floral remains are the most difficult major category of archaeological materials to analyse quantitatively, precisely because it is so hard to figure out what is a meaningful way to count them in the first place.

Faunal analysts quickly recognized that counting the number of bone fragments of each species recovered carries with it the risk of counting the same animal many times, since each individual animal can produce many bone fragments in the archaeological record. Analysts of ceramics and lithics have only sporadically recognized that a similar risk adheres to counting pot sherds and lithic artifact fragments. Minimum numbers of individuals have often been used in faunal analysis; the estimated vessel equivalents and minimum numbers of tools discussed by Shott are the equivalent for ceramics and lithics, respectively. It is important to recognize, whether we are talking about bones, sherds, or lithics, that counting the total number of fragments and counting the minimum number of individual things that must have been fragmented to produce that number of fragments are the opposite ends of a continuum of quantification techniques. Minimum numbers of things are based on the assumption that any two fragments that *could* have come from the *same* thing *did* come from the same thing. Another way to say this is that minimum number quantification assumes maximal *interdependence* of fragments observed (interdependence in the sense that fragments originating from the same thing are interdependent). Using total numbers of fragments is based on the assumption that any two fragments that *could* have come from *different* things *did* come from different things. This is an assumption of maximum *independence* of fragments observed. As such, total numbers of fragments amount to estimates of the *maximum* number of individual things.

As both Shott and O'Connor recognize, taphonomy is at the crux of the issue. Consider a hypothetical assemblage that comes from the excavation of a single pit feature: the sherds of a single reconstructable and nearly complete cooking pot and the bones of virtually every part of the right and left sides of a rabbit's body with no duplication of elements whatever. In such an extreme case, the conclusion is obvious: the most meaningful way to quantify this assemblage is as one cooking pot and the bones of one rabbit. It seems excessive even to bother to say it, but the reason for this is that any two fragments that *could* have come from the *same* thing, clearly *did*. Now consider a hypothetical assemblage that comes from a small test pit excavated in the middle of an extensive area of jumbled-up midden debris deposited over the course of several hundred years. Since the sample is small we attempt to fit artifacts together and discover that sherds are highly varied in terms of ceramic type, vessel form, size, colour, decoration, etc., and that no two of them can fit together. Bones are a motley assortment of widely differing numbers of different body parts of several different species. In this assemblage, it seems quite likely that the sherds may really not include any two from the same vessel, and the bones may really not include any two from the same individual animal. The fundamental assumption of quantifying by minimum number of things is seriously violated. The fundamental assumption of quantifying by maximum number of things, on the other hand, seems quite likely to be valid in this case, and the real number of separate things represented by the fragments seems likely to be close to the maximum (i.e., the total number of fragments).

Neither minimum numbers nor maximum numbers provide a single best approach for all situations. In some cases, the taphonomic situation may approximate the assumptions of one or the other closely enough to justify its use, given the research objectives. Here it is easy to follow O'Connor's concluding advice to select the approach to quantification that best suits the particulars of the case. In many cases, it will be clear that the real number of things represented lies somewhere in the middle zone between the minimum and maximum numbers, and one may be faced with the unhappy conclusion that neither is very applicable. It is not out of the question to invent a systematic scheme for using a particular assemblage's characteristics to position it precisely on a scale of appropriate quantification between the maximum and minimum numbers. For example, an assemblage in which a modest proportion of sherds can be fitted together might be appropriately quantified by the median of the minimum and maximum numbers; one in which only a small proportion of sherds can be fit might be quantified by a number halfway between the maximum and the median of the minimum and maximum, etc. Pursuing refinement of such a scheme might produce something like the 'unified theory of quantification' called for by Shott.

On the other hand, such numbers would still fall short of the goal of finding one correct way to count everything, because there *is* no single correct way to count anything. Even if such a scheme did work satisfactorily, we would still need to count things in a variety of different ways, depending on both the taphonomic conditions and the research aims, just as O'Connor concludes. If, for example, we wish to investigate whether the results of the hunt were shared between households, with meatier parts going to higher status families, neither minimum numbers of individuals nor maximum numbers nor something in between will do. The faunal remains will need to be quantified in a way tailored specifically to this research question.

As O'Connor observes, simply counting numbers of bone fragments is a simple and straightforward way to describe faunal assemblages. The same is true of sherds and of lithic tool fragments. For some research aims

and with some assemblages, the problems both O'Connor and Shott note with this procedure just do not matter. Often it is sufficient for us to be able to say things like 'Deer was a similarly important source of meat at sites X and Y' or 'Deer was a slightly more important source of meat at site X than at site Y' or 'Deer was a much more important source of meat at site X than at site Y'. If the nature of the deposits suggests similar taphonomic processes operating at both sites, then there seems no reason not to base statements such as these simply on proportions calculated from the total number of fragments. As long as we do not need statements of the absolute quantities of deer meat at either site, but only conclusions about how its importance, relative to the meat of other species, differs from one site to another, and taphonomic conditions are similar, then the worries about the validity of counts of total numbers of fragments are just not relevant.

The same can be said for other kinds of artifacts. If two sites are taphonomically similar, then a higher proportion of decorated sherds from one means that decorated pottery was in more common use there. It makes no difference that decorated pottery may be finer and break more readily into smaller fragments than undecorated pottery, as long as the two assemblages have been subject to the same kinds of pottery-breaking factors operating at about the same intensity. This is an issue of sampling bias in disguise (see above). As long as two samples have been collected with the same kinds of bias operating at similar intensities, then there are many ways in which they are fully comparable. This is one of several productive ways to approach samples known to be biased. We can often make comparisons in relative terms with samples or techniques of quantification that would not sustain conclusions framed in absolute numbers. Such comparisons will often enable us to achieve our research aims; we do not always need absolute numbers, which are usually much more difficult to produce reliably, for reasons elaborated upon by both O'Connor and Shott.

COMPUTING

If computers have become the tools of choice for even very simple statistical analyses involving only one or two variables at a time, they are the *sine qua non* of most spatial analysis (Chapter 53), of multivariate analysis (Chapter 54), and of the vast majority of specialized applications like the Bayesian approaches to various tasks discussed by Buck (Chapter 55). All three of these chapters raise even more challenging issues of the same kind discussed above with regard to the application of basic statistical principles. The analyses discussed in these chapters involve computations of considerable complexity and staggering quantity. They are inconceivable without the aid of computers and are, thus, realizations of the expectations of the 1960s, which focused on a future filled with kinds of analysis that would not be practicable without computers.

With such complex computational underpinnings, those carrying out such analyses (not to mention those reading about them) can lose sight of the principles upon which the analyses are based. It is by no means necessary to understand the principles in order to carry out the analyses, since knowing how to use the programs written to carry them out is not the same as understanding the principles upon which the programs are based, and explanations of principle are even more divorced from explanations of how to carry out the analyses than is the case with more basic statistical manipulations. Results of multivariate analyses and spatial analyses are now quintessentially graphical: compelling pictures of relationships between variables and/or cases and visually appealing maps of spatial distributions. One of the criteria by which programs to perform such analyses are judged to be good is that they produce such results almost automatically, requiring as little effort as possible from the user. The close of the twentieth century has brought us to an especially awkward moment in this regard. It is much less work to carry out such analyses than to learn to understand what the results mean. The limitations to effective implementation of such analyses are no longer technological but, in fact, cultural.

The forms of multivariate analysis summarized by Baxter (Chapter 53) are applied in a wide variety of disciplines. All are available in many general purpose statistical analysis programs. All have been in use for some time. One of them (cluster analysis) was the subject of a chapter in the 1969 edition of *Science in Archaeology* (Hodson 1969). Despite all this, the majority of archaeologists do not now understand any of the four multivariate approaches Baxter presents well enough either to carry out an analysis or critically evaluate one found in the literature. The Bayesian applications discussed by Buck (Chapter 55) are tailor-made for particular archaeological situations and much more novel. They offer to bring considerable power to archaeological analysis, but their potential is clearly still being explored.

Geographical Information Systems (Chapter 53) are, of course, all the rage, not only in archaeology

but also in a number of other disciplines. Their obvious power to manage complicated spatial data bases and the compelling graphical displays they produce make it very easy to understand their popularity, despite the enormous investment of time and energy that may be required to create an archaeological GIS data base. Quite a lot of the literature on GIS in archaeology is programmatic; articles often describe basic principles of one GIS program or another, discuss the creation of a data base, provide a display or two, and conclude with an optimistic statement about the useful analyses that the author is now in a position to carry out. As Gillings observes, true spatial data analysis capabilities, as opposed to data display or summarizing, are underdeveloped in most GIS programs. This results largely from the fact that most buyers of GIS packages do not use them for answering research questions but rather for data base purposes in support of management functions – keeping track of road maintenance, utilities, zoning regulations, and the like in cities, for instance. It is no accident, then, that some of the most fully realized successes in the application of GIS in archaeology come not from research at all but from cultural resource management.

Moore and Keene (1983) discussed the 'law of the hammer' in archaeology, likening new methodologies to a new hammer given to a child, who, of course, immediately begins to pound everything in sight. It takes a while to learn what to pound and just how to pound it in order to produce useful results. We seem to still be in this stage with GIS. The techniques themselves occupy centre stage when GIS appear in the archaeological literature, rather than the results of applying the techniques. This is normal when a new methodology comes along, but one expects eventually to see the focus shift from the techniques to the results they have produced. This will not happen until the appeal of using the hammer, just because it is new and shiny, has diminished, and we learn to tell when things really do need pounding and only then pick up the GIS hammer.

The example GIS analysis Gillings provides demonstrates some of the things GIS programs, as they exist now, are very good at. Figure 53.3 shows quite clearly a pattern of avoidance of flood-prone areas for locating settlements, and Gillings applies a conventional significance test effectively to demonstrate that settlements are not evenly located across flood-prone and non-flood-prone areas. No one, of course, will be very surprised at the conclusion that people avoided locating their settlements in flood-prone areas, but a potentially much more interesting unevenness in settlement distribution is evident in the map – an unevenness that occurs entirely within the zone not subject to flooding, where virtually all the sites are found. The sites clearly group themselves into seven or eight clusters separated by substantial swathes of unoccupied (but unflooded) territory. The implications of this pattern for reconstructing social and political organization are much more exciting. These implications might or might not be pursuable with common GIS tools, however, depending on whether the pattern corresponds to any available GIS layer or not. Some of the most valuable results of GIS analysis may be produced when it fails to account for observed settlement patterning, since this is likely to mean that the patterns are not simple responses to the sorts of environmental variables it is easy to incorporate into GIS data bases, but indicate instead more purely social, political, and economic forces at work (e.g., Drennan and Quattrin 1995).

This is an example of what Gillings refers to as 'the often uncritical and problematic relationship between GIS and archaeological theory'. Resolving the problems in the relationship between GIS and archaeological theory will involve figuring out just what things can be pounded productively with GIS and what things need to be pounded with different tools, and this merits high priority in the ongoing effort to realize the enormous potential of GIS. As in the history of other new research methodologies, we will need to move beyond the stage of doing what GIS programs do to our data, just because GIS programs do it, and then justifying the effort after the fact by creating a (sometimes quite trivial) research question that was answered. Along the lines urged by Moore and Keene (1983), we will need to focus clearly on intrinsically interesting and important research questions and frame our analysis agendas in terms of what we need to do to our data in order to answer those questions.

GIS analysis, like Bayesian approaches and multivariate analysis, are not really practicable without computers, and we are accustomed to the thought that advances in computer technology open new analytical horizons to us annually (if not daily). On the other hand, all four multivariate approaches discussed by Baxter in Chapter 54 were in use in archaeology 30 years ago. Bayesian approaches were also being used, although archaeologists had not yet found out about them. There were no programs identified as 'geographic information systems', but there were programs that produced maps of spatial distributions, including overlays of different distributions. The maps were crude things, printed on line printers with peculiar combinations of text characters creating monochrome quasi-

halftones, but they accomplished the same thing that Gillings identifies as the principal current result of GIS analysis.

The computing power available to an archaeologist who sought it out thirty years ago was laughable compared to what many of us are now accustomed to having on our own desks (or laps). But much of the difference between the analyses we are able to perform now and those we were able to carry out 30 years ago has to do with appealing graphical output and user convenience. Dramatic increases in computing power have, to a very large extent, been sopped up by graphical user interfaces. Computer curmudgeons (anyone who has actually keypunched a card qualifies) are entitled to raise sceptical questions about the nature of this advance. We now accompany lectures with projections of bulleted lists of points to be made, in chartreuse Times Roman type on a puce background, instead of writing in chalk on a blackboard. We use ARC-INFO to render site distribution on a map of soil fertility in 256 colours, instead of SYMAP to produce a crude version of the same thing on a line printer. We are beginning to use three-dimensional GIS and rendering techniques, but do the results give us analytical tools qualitatively different from the graphics produced by generations of *National Geographic* artists?

We do live in a very different world of archaeological analysis than we did 30 years ago, one with a much wider range of analytical opportunities. Some of the changes represent substantive advances, some are only cosmetic. Most especially, phenomenal increases in the accessibility and ease of use of computers have put analytical approaches that existed 30 years ago within the reach of large numbers of practitioners instead of just a few with the fortitude to invade their universities' 'computer centres' (even the phrase has become quaint). It has become easier to carry out often quite complicated and advanced statistical analyses than to learn how to interpret the results effectively. Widespread availability of powerful, versatile, standardized software and the hardware to run it on, together with the Internet, have qualitatively changed the possibilities for sharing information and collaborating with other archaeologists scattered around the globe. These advances, however, have not diminished the ego-involvement and ethnocentrism that have always bedeviled such collaborations, and the potential exists for widening the gap between the haves and the have-nots among archaeologists, particularly those on opposite sides of the major economic divides in an increasingly global economy.

BEYOND DATA ANALYSIS

Numerical modelling and simulation studies (Chapter 58) take us to quite a different realm from that of data analysis, and Doran and Hodson (1975:265) also used the phrase 'beyond data analysis' to denote it. Numerical models may be directly and abstractly theoretical, defining and quantifying the socio-cultural variables we seek to understand and specifying their relationships. Such models may have nothing whatever to do with archaeological data or they may derive input from the results of archaeological research and/or produce output for comparison with the conclusions of archaeological research. As Lake observes, a second main current in numerical modelling in archaeology is more accurately characterized as methodological. It relates quite clearly to data analysis, but it is not, itself, data analysis. It involves the same kind of modelling and simulation, but the processes modelled are not the socio-cultural processes archaeologists seek ultimately to understand better, but rather the processes that produce the archaeological record. The contribution such modelling makes is to data analysis, or at least to the interpretation of analytical results.

While data analysis, broadly defined at least, is an activity that must be engaged in by any archaeologist involved in primary research, numerical modelling is not. As such, it is quite reasonable to expect it to be a specialized activity engaged in by only a small number of archaeologists, just as Lake predicts, and in contrast to the enthusiastic pronouncements of some proponents a few decades ago. In Moore and Keene's (1983) terms, numerical modelling is an approach that has passed through its phase of being a shiny new hammer to try pounding different things with. It has been replaced, perhaps by GIS analysis, as the appealing new toy.

Advances in computer technology also have considerable relevance to numerical modelling. The simulations that are usually required to bring the numerical models that have interested archaeologists to life require substantial computing power. More important, they are often extremely involved programming tasks that have exceeded the patience, energy, and resources of many of the archaeologists who have undertaken them. Computer games like Civilization and SimCity have in some ways realized the dreams of archaeologists involved in what Lake calls heuristic modelling. Here variables, archaeologists have long toyed with in studying the development of urbanism, are combined into a genuine toy, and an extraordinarily slick and sophisticated toy at that. This kind of programming can be achieved with the resources that the market for computer games makes available but not with those made available for archaeological research.

Of course, much of the programming effort required for these games is needed for the production of engaging graphical output, and this would not be necessary for a 'serious' simulation. On the other hand, we have come, like everyone else, to expect a very polished and glitzy output from our computers. Precisely this capacity of the software that we use, offers us powerful data analyses and simulations by presenting complicated patterns and relationships in ways that we can perceive them easily. It also offers us such technologically impressive renditions of trivia or outright falsehood that it becomes more difficult to recognize the substance for what it is. Counter to the computer mass market trend toward increasing ease of use, putting more powerful analytical tools to work well tends to require ever higher levels of skill.

REFERENCES

Baxter, M.J. (1994). *Exploratory Multivariate Analysis in Archaeology*. Edinburgh University Press: Edinburgh.

Brothwell, D. (1969). Stones, pots and people: a plea for statistical caution. In Brothwell, D. and Higgs, E. (eds) *Science in Archaeology*, 669–679 (2nd edn). Thames and Hudson: London.

Brothwell, D. and Higgs, E. (eds) (1963). *Science in Archaeology*. Thames and Hudson: London.

Brothwell, D. and Higgs, E. (eds) (1969). *Science in Archaeology* (2nd edn). Thames and Hudson: London.

Cowgill, G.L. (1977). The trouble with significance tests and what we can do about it. *American Antiquity*, **42**:350–368.

Doran, J.E. and Hodson, F.R. (1975). *Mathematics and Computers in Archaeology*. Edinburgh University Press: Edinburgh.

Drennan, R.D. (1996). *Statistics for Archaeologists: A Commonsense Approach*. Plenum Press: New York.

Drennan, R.D. and Quattrin, D.W. (1975). Social inequality and agricultural resources in the Valle de la Plata, Colombia. In Price, T.D. and Feinman, G.M. (eds) *Foundations of Social Inequality*, 207–233. Plenum Press: New York.

Fletcher, M. and Lock, G.R. (1991). *Digging Numbers: Elementary Statistics for Archaeologists*. Oxford University Committee for Archaeology: Oxford.

Hodson, F.R. (1969). Classification by computer. In Brothwell, D. and Higgs, E. (eds) *Science in Archaeology*, (2nd edn) 649–660. Thames and Hudson: London.

Moore, J.A. and Keene, A.S. (1983). Archaeology and the Law of the Hammer. In Moore, J.A. and Keene, A.S. (eds) *Archaeological Hammers and Theories*, 3–13. Academic Press: New York.

Shennan, S. (1997). *Quantifying Archaeology*, (2nd edn). Edinburgh University Press: Edinburgh.

Thomas, D.H. (1978). The awful truth about statistics in archaeology. *American Antiquity*, **43**:231–244.

53

Spatial Information and Archaeology

M. GILLINGS

School of Archaeological Studies, University of Leicester.

Spatial data is information that describes the distribution of things upon the surface of the Earth – any information concerning the location, shape of, and relationship between, geographical features (AGI 1996, DeMers 1997). Archaeology routinely deals with an enormous amount of spatial data, varying in scale from the locations of archaeological sites on a continental landmass, down to the position of individual artifacts in an excavated context. Arguably, much, if not all, archaeological data is spatial in nature or has an important spatial component. All artifacts, from monuments to ploughsoil scatters, are found *somewhere*, often in a position seemingly patterned relative to other things. Realization as to the importance of this spatial component has led over the years to the development of ever more precise techniques of recording: from plane tables and compasses to Total Stations and Global Positioning Systems (GPS).

Given this importance, and the considerable methodological developments that have taken place in recording, it is noteworthy that until very recently the mechanisms used for the presentation, analysis and interpretation of spatial data have remained largely static. For example, in seeking to explain observed spatial patterns and structure in the material remains of the past, archaeologists have considered factors as diverse as:

(i) adaptation to environmental conditions,

(ii)   territorial control and economic rationality,
(iii) perception, experience and memory,
(iv) carefully structured and formalized intent,
(v)   the physical manifestation of a cosmological or symbolic-ideological design,
(vi) the result of a number of quasi-random post-depositional forces, and
(vii) the unplanned, accumulated and embedded product of everyday social practice.

The means by which such diverse hypotheses have been explored has been remarkably uniform – the visual perusal of simple distribution maps. Whilst such maps are undoubtedly useful, as mechanisms for exploring the full complexity of the archaeological record they are often far from satisfactory. We are rarely interested solely in where things are. We often have a wealth of information *about* the artifacts under study, which needs to be integrated for the purposes of interpretation. We term this information *attribute* data. By simply plotting a distribution map we can show the spatial location of a series of objects but say little about them. Traditional strategies for integrating such information have relied upon multiple distribution maps, the use of symbols, or both. These are satisfactory until large volumes of information or complex datasets need to be examined. In such cases researchers can rapidly find themselves dealing with hundreds of separate plots or a bewildering array of symbols. Further

Handbook of Archaeological Sciences. Edited by D.R. Brothwell and A.M. Pollard.

problems arise if we want to incorporate information outside the artifactual sphere, e.g., environmental factors, such as soil types, or cultural and ideological factors, such as political boundaries or the optimum alignment to catch the last rays of the setting midsummer sun. To compound this problem the actual interpretation of such maps is often uncritical and subjective, with the level of subjectivity increasing with the amount of information to process.

What is needed to make best use of the carefully recorded spatial and attribute information recovered by archaeologists, is a dynamic and flexible environment within which to integrate, express, analyse and explore the full range of data, both spatial and nonspatial. Ideally, such an environment would permit the vast quantities of data to be managed, enable visual summaries to be generated and provide a firm platform upon which more sophisticated exploratory and statistical investigations could take place. Geographical Information Systems (GIS) have the potential to provide precisely this type of environment.

WHAT IS A GIS?

A GIS is a computerized system for collecting, checking, integrating and analysing information related to the surface of the Earth (Rhind 1988). More specifically, it is an integrated set of computer-based techniques for the storage, manipulation, analysis and display of spatial, often map-based, data. A GIS does not represent a single computer programme – more a myriad of specific task-oriented programmes. This has given rise to the popular concept of the GIS as a 'tool-box'. The tools can be structured loosely into four subsystems (after DeMers 1997), presented with archaeological analogues in Table 53.1. Of critical

importance is the subsystem entitled 'data manipulation and analysis'. This enables the GIS to compare, contrast, combine and analyse the data held within it, often generating new information in the process. Presence of such tools gives GIS its unique identity, distinguishing it from *Computer Aided Mapping* (CAM) and *Computer Aided Design* (CAD) software.

HOW DOES GIS WORK?

The concepts of thematic mapping and geo-referencing

The entire collection of data held within the GIS for a specific region or problem area is referred to as the 'spatial database'. Rather than storing information in the form of a traditional map, the GIS stores spatial information thematically. Any map contains information relating to a host of specific themes – e.g., topography (spot-heights and contours), hydrology (rivers and streams), communications (roads, tracks and pathways), land-use (woods, houses, industrial areas) and archaeology (locations of sites). Although we think of maps as a simple and familiar way of representing the spatial arrangement of the world, maps are highly complex entities. GIS does not conceptualize, store and manage spatial information in such a holistic form. Although it is convenient to talk of spatial information held within the GIS as 'GIS-maps', it is formally incorrect. The GIS relies instead upon the concept of thematic mapping (Figure 53.1). Rather than a single, complex, multiply-themed map sheet, the GIS stores and manages a collection of individual sheets, each themed to a particular facet of the region. These are variously referred to as *themes*, *layers*, *images* or *coverages*. What is important to acknowledge is that after incorporation into the spatial database we no longer

Table 53.1 The basic subsystems of GIS.

Subsystem of the GIS	Archaeological Example
Data input and preparation	Digitizing a survey transect map. Reading lists of finds co-ordinates and converting those co-ordinates from the survey grid to a national system.
Data storage and retrieval	Creating a set of spatial layers containing survey transect maps; location of visible structural remains; existing sites recorded in the regional Sites and Monuments Register (SMR). Creating a series of attribute databases relating to the contents of each transect unit (i.e., ceramic, lithic, tile counts, surface visibility, etc.) and the regional SMR.
Data manipulation and analysis	Converting a contour map into an elevation model from which slope information can be derived. Combining this with surface artifact density trends to explore possible biasing effects due to preferential exposure/masking as a result of down-slope erosion.
Reporting and data output	Output of tabular data for input into an exploratory statistics package. For example intervisibility patterns for sites located during surface survey. In addition plotting a hardcopy map summarizing the visibility trends for final publication.

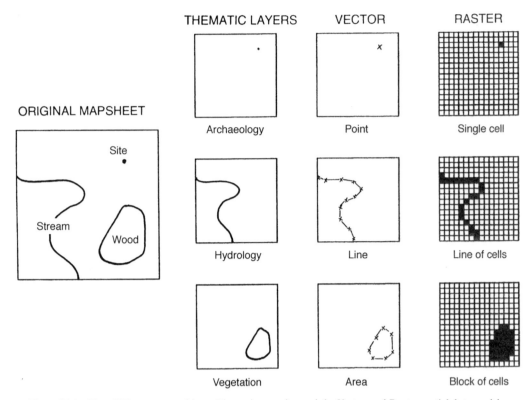

THEMATIC LAYERS   VECTOR   RASTER

ORIGINAL MAPSHEET

Site

Stream

Wood

Archaeology   Point   Single cell

Hydrology   Line   Line of cells

Vegetation   Area   Block of cells

Figure 53.1 How GIS represents objects. Thematic mapping and the Vector and Raster spatial data models.

have a single map but a group of themed layers – topography (holding contours), hydrology (showing rivers and streams), communications (roads and paths), landuse (areas of woods, houses, etc.), and archaeology (site locations). A GIS-based spatial database and a traditional map-sheet contain the same information but are structured in a very different way.

For this concept to work we must be able to combine and overlay the individual component themes whilst maintaining the original spatial relationships between the features. For example, if on the map an archaeological site is 23 metres from a river and sits on the 92.5 metre contour, then when the GIS overlays three layers (showing site location, contours and hydrology) the same relationship must hold. For this the GIS relies on *geo-referencing*, which refers to the location of a thematic layer in space as defined by a co-ordinate system. Two types of co-ordinate system are currently in widespread use. The oldest is the *geographical co-ordinate system*, based upon measurements of latitude and longitude. The other is the *rectangular* or *planar co-ordinate system*. Modern plane co-ordinate systems have evolved from Cartesian co-ordinates, a mathema-

tical construct defined by an origin and a unit of distance. In a plane, two axes are established running through the origin perpendicular to each other, and subdivided into units of the specified distance from the origin. Good examples are the international UTM grid system and the Ordnance Survey grid covering the United Kingdom (Gillings and Wise 1998). If all spatial features, in all component layers, are referenced using the same co-ordinate system, then they can be overlaid and combined maintaining the accuracy and spatial integrity of the source map.

THE PRINCIPAL TYPES OF GIS

There is no single, generic GIS. Two types are in common archaeological usage, which differ in their spatial data model, i.e., the way in which they conceptualize and represent the spatial locations of features. These are termed *Vector–GIS* and *Raster–GIS*. There are a variety of vector and raster data structures, i.e., the precise way in which the data model is implemented, which are often tied to specific software packages. The following discussion concentrates on more generic features and issues.

Vector-GIS

In vector GIS, the spatial locations of features are represented in one of three ways (Figure 53.1). The first, and simplest, is as discrete X, Y co-ordinates – in effect single points. The second builds upon this, representing features as a series of ordered X, Y co-ordinates to define a line (referred to as an *arc*). The third method is composed of a series of lines which close to define a discrete area (or polygon). Any thematic layer in a vector system can contain either points, lines or area features. In a vector system, to effectively manage and manipulate the features held within each layer, the GIS has to establish *topology* for them. Topology is concerned with order, contiguity and relative position in the spatial arrangement of objects rather than with actual linear dimensions. The most familiar topological map in the United Kingdom is the London Underground metro system. Here the individual stations are in the correct order for each line, but their indicated positions bear no relation to their true spatial locations. Topology is useful in GIS because many spatial modelling operations do not require co-ordinates, only topological information. For example, to find out which archaeological sites fall within a certain soil zone requires the GIS to determine whether a series of points are contained by a polygon – a topological relationship. To determine the optimal path between two points on a Roman road network requires a list of the lines or arcs that connect to each other – once again a topological relationship. Topology can be calculated and stored with each data layer (for example ArcInfo) or calculated as and when needed (systems such as Arcview).

When spatial objects are input into a vector GIS it is possible to assign an identification code to each distinct feature. For example, when digitizing a map of intensive survey transects, a code for each transect is entered at the same time as the individual lines defining each transect box. When reading in a list of co-ordinates, perhaps relating to sites in a Sites and Monuments Register, each can have a code directly associated with its defining co-ordinate pair. This code may be unique or shared between features of a single type. For example in a landscape all sites in the region can be assigned a unique identifier, perhaps their Sites and Monuments Register code, or all Iron Age enclosures can be given one shared code and all Romano–British

field systems another. This identifier code is crucially important as it provides the 'hook' that can be utilized by a relational database to link the spatial features in the vector data layer directly to any external database of attribute information we wish to integrate into the system.

Raster–GIS

In the vector model, the spatial representation of features and their non-spatial attributes are kept separate, linked via a relational database. In the raster model they are merged into a single unified data file. The spatial-database once again comprises a series of discrete thematic layers, sometimes referred to as *images* because they can be thought of as images of some aspect of the environment. In practice the study area is covered by a fine mesh or matrix of grid cells, like a chess-board (Figure 53.1). The specific attribute value of the ground surface at each cell point is recorded as the value for each cell. The value assigned to each grid-cell is dictated by the specific attribute we want to record. It can correspond to a feature identifier (e.g., 1 = woodland, 2 = urban, 3 = lake, etc., or 0 = no archaeological site, 1 = site), a qualitative attribute code (soil type 1, 2, 3 etc.), or a quantitative value (e.g., 73.56 metres above sea level). Whereas in the vector model attribute data was separated from the spatial information, attributes are here encoded directly into the thematic layer. It should be noted that most modern commercial raster systems, for example IDRISI, incorporate some degree of database functionality through the data frame concept. This is the ability to treat cell values as identifier codes that can be used to link the raster data layer to a database table of attribute information.

To illustrate the raster spatial data model we can look at the way it represents the three basic types of feature present in vector coverages. Points are represented by single grid-cells, lines by a set of connecting cells and areas by contiguous blocks of adjoining cells. To record where individual cells are in space, each is referenced according to its position within the rows and columns of the grid. To geo-reference the overall theme or image, the left, right, top and bottom co-ordinates of the grid are recorded, as is the resolution of each cell. For example, if the grid-cells are 30 metres square and the corner co-ordinates are known, the spatial location of any given cell is determined by simply counting along from a corner in increments of 30 metres. Returning briefly to the topic of topology, in raster systems there are no implicit topological relationships in the data; we are, after all, not recording individual spatial features but the behaviour of attributes in space.

Comparing the two

There is no clear-cut answer to the question 'which is best?', with both approaches being adept at dealing with different kinds of problems. Given the trend within commercially available systems such as ArcInfo, Arcview, IDRISI and GRASS to incorporate both vector and raster capabilities, such questions are rapidly becoming redundant. However, some important generic issues do remain and the most important of these are discussed below.

Raster data structures tend to be more data intensive. Take the example of five site locations identified during fieldwalking a study area. If a 100×100 raster layer for the area is established with a cell resolution of 10 metres, then only five of the 10 000 cells record the locations of sites – 9995 cells record the absence of information. In the vector model the five sites would be represented by five single co-ordinate points. In addition, the choice of grid-cell resolution is critical to any analysis (Figure 53.2). The finer the resolution, the closer and more detailed the representation. There are no rules to guide us, only the requirements and tolerances of the desired analysis. Increasing resolution dramatically increases file size, and the more unwieldy and slow layers become to store, manipulate and integrate (Gaffney and Stančič 1991:28). The question of size is critical in deciding upon the optimum resolution for a raster database.

Unlike the vector model, the raster representation defines geographical space in a simple and predictable way. Spatial attributes are always represented as rectangular grids. Hence they are ideally suited to problems requiring the overlay, comparison and combination of thematic layers. As satellite and aerial-photographic data sources are themselves stored in a raster format (as *picture elements*, abbreviated to *pixels*), raster systems are ideally suited to such data. In addition, the raster model copes better with data which changes continuously across a study area, i.e., data which is not discrete, having no clear-cut edges or boundaries, e.g., surface topography.

The vector model, with its topologically defined points, lines and areas, and flexible database linkages, is better at defining bounded entities, describing networks, and handling database-intensive enquiries. Vector systems are suited to tasks such as identifying

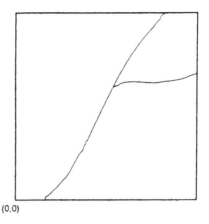

(0,0)

Original Mapsheet

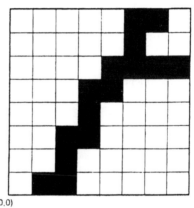

(0,0)

10 m Resolution Raster Grid

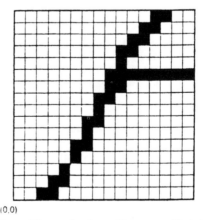

(0,0)

5 m Resolution Raster Grid

Figure 53.2   The issue of resolution in Raster GIS.

and isolating all coin finds of a late Roman date and containing over 40 per cent silver, or finding the shortest distance between points on a frontier. Problems arise in having to 'shoe-horn' uncertain and fuzzy archaeological entities (e.g., a site location based on an increasing density of ceramics against a continuous background spread of manuring material) into the rigorous and unambiguous point, line and area categories required.

Affecting both systems are a number of important generic issues such as the accumulation and propagation of spatial and attribute error (e.g., Heywood *et al.* 1998:177) and the effects of factors such as generalization, i.e., the way in which the spatial representation of a given feature depends heavily upon the scales at which it is both acquired and analysed (e.g., Müller *et al.* 1995).

GIS AND SPATIAL ANALYSIS

Spatial Analysis comprises 'a set of techniques whose results are dependent on the locations of the objects of analysis' (Goodchild 1996:241). This encompasses a variety of approaches ranging from the statistically complex and computer intensive to the simple visual appraisal of a distribution map. What distinguishes GIS from CAM and CAD packages is the presence of analytical capabilities that enable existing information to be explored and analysed and new information to be generated in the process.

There are a wide variety of analytical tools available within the GIS, which can be grouped into the following broad categories; simple measurement, querying, map overlay, interpolation, reclassification, and network analysis. It should be noted that there is a degree of overlap between certain classes, such as query and reclassification, and, in addition, the functionality of GIS often depends upon groups of tools working closely and seamlessly together, e.g., query, reclassification and map overlay. The sheer breadth of analytical functions precludes any discussion here beyond identifying and characterizing the main areas. For more comprehensive accounts readers are referred to recent introductory texts (e.g., DeMers 1997, Heywood *et al.* 1998).

Simple measurement

In both vector and raster GIS it is a relatively routine task to measure the dimensions and properties of spatial features within the database, e.g., the number of point features in a layer, the summed area of a group of polygons, the length of a network of lines, and so on. Depending on the precise system, more advanced measurements such as shape, sinuosity and spatial integrity are also possible. In the case of raster approaches, the accuracy of the results is highly dependant upon the resolution of the underlying grid, as calculations of length and area are based upon counting cells.

Querying

With vector GIS it is straightforward to query the full database of spatial and attribute information to extract or isolate specific features. For example, given a layer of chance coin finds, only those of a late Roman date and certain percentage of silver may be isolated. With raster GIS, the same task involves reclassification (see below). In both cases, when combined with features such as map overlay, GIS offers a very powerful approach for extracting information from the overall project database.

Map overlay

One of the most powerful capabilities of GIS is the ability to compare and combine variables between discrete thematic layers. Raster systems are particularly adept at adding, subtracting, dividing and multiplying data layers as a result of the consistent, cell-based data representation. In such systems this process is termed '*Map Algebra*' or '*Mapematics*'. In vector systems map overlay takes one of three basic forms; point-in-polygon, line-in-polygon and polygon-on-polygon. The first two are relatively straightforward, for example overlaying a point layer of site locations with a polygon layer of soil types to examine the agricultural potential of site location. Polygon-on-polygon overlay is a much more complex operation, taking one of three forms corresponding to the Boolean AND (referred to in vector GIS terminology as 'intersect'), OR ('union') and NOT ('intersect') operators.

Map overlay is frequently used in archaeological analyses. A common example is the combination of environmental layers to construct a predictive model of site location (e.g., van Leusen 1993). Another is the addition of a series of binary *viewsheds* (in-view, out-of-view layers), to create a more useful archaeological heuristic, the *Cumulative Viewshed* (Wheatley 1995).

Interpolation

Interpolation is estimating the value of a property between the locations at which it has been sampled (Heywood *et al.* 1998:117). It is most commonly used to generate representations of the continuously changing surface topography of a region. Surface elevation is sampled and recorded at a number of points, for example with a total station survey instrument. Interpolation is used to determine the elevation between the sampled points to produce a continuous *Digital Elevation Model* (DEM). Raster systems contain a number of interpolation techniques ranging from a simple linear option, which assumes the values change in a smooth linear fashion, to highly sophisticated geostatistical techniques, such as Kriging (Bailey and Gattrill 1995:183).

In vector systems interpolation is most commonly used in the construction of Thiessen polygons and, in an exact form, to generate *Triangulated Irregular Networks* (TINs). This is a vector-based representation of continuous variables such as elevation, where the sampled elevation points are linked directly to form a mosaic of triangles whose surfaces summarize the area, slope and aspect of the portion of terrain represented. Interpolation is however not restricted to elevation data – a TIN can be generated for any continuous variable. For example, recent work by Wheatley (1996) has used a number of raster interpolation techniques to extend surface artifact counts into areas not covered by intensive survey.

Reclassification

A GIS not only stores spatial and attribute data, but can re-express it in a number of ways. For example a DEM or TIN can be reclassified to produce layers encoding slope, aspect or zones of visibility from a fixed point. A slope layer could in turn be reclassified to show zones of the landscape shallow enough to be cultivable with oxen and a simple plough, and zones that were too steep. One common reclassification task is the generation of *buffer zones*, e.g., identification of all land within 500 metres of a spring or water source. As well as simple reclassification, a number of what are termed *neighbourhood functions* are also available. In raster systems these can re-classify the value of a cell on the basis of the attributes of neighbouring cells. In archaeology these commonly involve the use of filters to enhance or smooth facets of the data, for example a high-pass filter to enhance the edges of house founda-

tions present in micro-topographic survey data (Gillings in press).

Network analysis

This is a set of techniques for exploring network issues such shortest path analysis and allocation modelling. Such approaches make full use of topological information and tend to be restricted to vector systems. For some applications in archaeology see Allen (1990) and Ruggles and Church (1996).

SPATIAL DATA ANALYSIS

As a group, the capabilities discussed above enable the GIS to routinely identify, extract and re-express the information held within the spatial database. However, it can be argued that whilst all fall within the general rubric of spatial analysis, as defined earlier, none of these techniques tell us whether any of the trends or patterns identified are statistically significant or not. A clear distinction can be drawn between techniques which identify and summarize spatial patterns, and those which investigate these patterns. In a recent review the term spatial analysis was re-defined to draw an explicit distinction between the techniques of spatial summarization on the one hand and those of spatial analysis proper on the other (Bailey 1994:15). Inherent in the latter is the importance of statistical description and modelling. In this formulation the GIS capabilities outlined above (query, reclassification, mapematics, etc.) are *summarization* techniques that are prerequisites of spatial analysis but do not formally constitute it (Kvamme 1994:1). More recently the term '*Spatial Data Analysis*' has been used to further distinguish between applications of conventional statistical tests to spatial data, i.e., where the objects being analysed could be moved in space without affecting the outcome of the test, and those statistical techniques which take into account the locational component of the datasets (Bailey and Gattrell 1995). This distinction has been elegantly illustrated in an archaeological context by Kvamme (1993). It is clear from this that spatial analysis represents much more than query and map overlay, and that within it some very distinct sub-fields can be identified.

A detailed discussion of the techniques involved in Spatial Analysis is beyond the scope of the current discussion, but luckily several good introductory texts exist (e.g., Hodder and Orton 1976, Bailey and

Gattrell 1995). In addition, detailed accounts of specific application areas such as Exploratory Data Analysis (Hartwig and Dearing 1979), and key issues such as Spatial Autocorrelation, i.e., the tendency of objects close in space to be more alike (Goodchild 1986), and the Modifiable Areal Unit Problem, where the precise choice of boundary for an analysis directly influences its outcome (Openshaw 1984), are readily available.

The relationship between GIS and Spatial Analysis has been discussed by Fotheringham and Rogerson (1994) and the broader issue of GIS, spatial analysis and the social sciences by Goodchild (1996). In the archaeological context Kvamme has been at the fore-front of attempts to expand the range of spatial data analyses undertaken (e.g., Kvamme 1993, 1996). Specific archaeological applications of techniques such as EDA and logistic regression have been explored in some detail (e.g., Farley *et al.* 1990, Williams *et al.* 1990, Warren 1990).

Although most researchers equate GIS directly with spatial data analysis, commercial GIS packages have been notable for the paucity of intrinsic statistical capabilities. This is improving as new releases of packages such as IDRISI contain enhanced statistical functionality, and the flexible programming languages associated with packages such as Arcview enable statistical routines to be readily incorporated. Despite such developments, at present GIS is perhaps better thought of as a platform or environment from which spatial analyses can be undertaken, rather than a spatial data analysis engine.

ARCHAEOLOGY AND GIS

Archaeologists have been using GIS since the mid-1980s and a number of publications have charted both the history and developing relationship between GIS and archaeology (e.g., Kvamme 1995, Harris and Lock 1995, Wansleeben and Verhart 1997, Lock 1998). The earliest archaeological application of a GIS was in 1982 as part of the Granite Reef archaeological project, in the south-west United States, where a home-grown raster system was used to store layers relating to environmental factors such as soils, rainfall and temperature. These layers were combined to examine questions such as environmental suitability for early hunters, desert travel and prehistoric agriculture. This approach was so novel that it predated the term GIS, being referred to as a 'computer-based cartographic analysis system'.

The first conference was held in the United States in 1985 and the first major textbook was published as recently as 1990 (Allen *et al.* 1990). Subsequent years have witnessed the publication of a number of extended case-studies which illustrate the breadth and diversity of applications (Gaffney and Stančič 1991, Lock and Stančič 1995, Maschner 1996, Aldenderfer and Maschner 1996, Peterson 1998). This growth has served to greatly increase levels of awareness of the archaeological potential of GIS. Falling hardware and software costs have also brought practical GIS within the reach of the majority of archaeological units, agencies and institutions.

Where does GIS fit in?

At first glance, current applications of GIS appear highly diverse but on closer examination the vast majority share a regional landscape focus. This is perhaps not surprising given the traditional emphasis within landscape archaeology upon mapping and the importance of spatial information.

Although intra-site and excavation-based studies exist, their successful application has been severely hampered by two fundamental shortcomings of most GIS systems. The first is the inability of GIS to handle truly three-dimensional information. Excavation-based recording is invariably undertaken in 3D and yet the best the GIS can manage is 2.5D, where features can have any location in the X, Y dimensions but the third dimension is present only as a fixed attribute (Harris and Lock 1996). A further fundamental problem is the lack of a truly temporal dimension to GIS. It can handle patterns in 2D space but not time except via highly simplistic snapshot-based strategies such as time-slices e.g., the distribution of sites of a specific period identified during field survey. Although commercial 3D systems exist and research is underway to develop fully spatio-temporal (in effect 4D) systems, these are not routinely available to archaeologists. As a result, at present the limitations described above greatly inhibit the broader application of GIS to intra-site and excavation contexts.

Regional landscape-based applications can be broken down into two broad areas: those concerned with Cultural Resource Management (CRM) in the present, and those concerned with the analysis and study of landscapes in the past (which might be termed 'research').

CRM applications have been both reactive and proactive. In the reactive case, national agencies have used GIS to integrate data over a range of spatial scales in an attempt to structure and archive enormous and complex databases of archaeological information (e.g., Bosqued *et al.* 1996). Proactively, the analytical and map overlay capabilities of GIS are used to assess the impact of proposed developments on the archaeological resource and to predict the extent of archaeological remains in areas which have not been intensively studied (e.g., Altschul 1990).

Research applications of GIS can be broken down further into a number of distinctive sub-classes. Some studies focus upon environmental information, whether concerned with modelling post-depositional change in landscape morphology, or the construction of deterministic models to describe observed patterning in the archaeological record. A key feature of such studies is the renaissance of interest in formal statistical approaches characteristic of the spatial archaeology of the 1970s. This involved the adoption and application of a series of statistical and explanatory approaches to the study of spatiality imported into archaeology from disciplines such as plant ecology, economics and geography (Clarke 1977). Many of these techniques, for example Site Catchment and Thiessen polygon analyses (e.g., Hunt 1992), have been re-applied using GIS along with the development of enriched alternatives such as cost-surface modelling and the construction of highly complex inductive/deductive predictive models of site location (e.g., Westcott and Brandon 2000).

An interesting sub-class has questioned the primacy afforded to purely environmental factors in these studies, and has attempted to incorporate instead cultural or humanistic factors. These studies often make use of the GIS technique of viewshed analysis, i.e., the reclassification of a DEM to show all areas which would have been visible from a given point, in an attempt to include human perceptual factors into the analytical environment. Attempts are also being made to integrate more fully experiential and cognitive factors into GIS (e.g., Zubrow 1994). The point to stress is the diversity and breadth of application. Far from finding a comfortable niche within landscape archaeology or CRM, the impact and potential of GIS is being felt right across these sub-disciplines.

A CASE STUDY: TISZA, HUNGARY

The data derives from an intensive survey project undertaken in and around the flood-plain of the river Tisza in northeast Hungary. One of the questions raised concerned the degree of influence ancient flood events may have exerted on the human exploitation of the environment. Since effective flood control prevented any direct measurements of flood impact, the GIS package ArcInfo was used to investigate this phenomenon. Fuller accounts of the GIS programme can be found in Gillings (1995, 1997, 1998).

For the current analysis the following layers were selected from the GIS database; (i) topography (a vector line layer containing contours was digitized from 1:5000 base-maps – each contour was allocated an identifier code corresponding to its elevation value), (ii) site location (a vector point layer that was input as co-ordinates from the site register – each point feature was labelled using its unique project site code).

The first stage was to generate a DEM for the study area, using a raster interpolation procedure designed to generate hydrologically correct elevation grids from contour information. Given that the overall study area is 481 kilometres square, a grid resolution of 30 metres was chosen as a compromise between file size and accuracy. Once generated the raster DEM was then reclassified to identify potentially flooded zones in the landscape, based on a typical inundation level of 91.5 metres suggested by earlier geomorphological appraisal. A simple approach would have been to reclassify all land below 91.5 metres as flooded and all land above as dry. Instead, to acknowledge that flood events would have varied in their precise impact, a fuzzy reclassification was undertaken. All land under 91 metres was classified as unambiguously flooded (cell-value 0) and all land above 92 metres as unambiguously dry (cell-value 1). Intermediate zones, around the 91.5 metres level, were assigned a value between 0 and 1 depending upon their precise elevations. The result was a layer encoding new information – a crude index of the possibility of inundation in a typical flood event.

The next stage was to examine the distribution of archaeological sites and determine whether the potential flood zone exerted any influence on their location. Visual examination of a simple overlay of the raster flood zones with the vector site layer strongly suggested that sites were located so as to avoid the zones of flooding. This apparent patterning was investigated by constructing a null hypothesis: *the flood zone has no effect upon the distribution of sites*, and testing its statistical significance. If the null hypothesis were true we would expect sites to be distributed evenly across the study area. A simple non-parametric significance test was used, the Chi-square test (see Shennan 1990).

To facilitate testing a further reclassification was undertaken, simplifying the fuzzy flood-zone into three distinct zones: areas that would have been flooded (cells = 0); areas that may have been flooded (cells > 0 and < 1); and areas that would have remained dry (cells = 1). To establish the frequency of sites falling in each zone two options were available: either the vector site distribution of points could be converted to a raster and then cross-tabulated with the existing raster

layer of flood zones, or the flood zones could be converted to a series of vector areas and a simple point-in-polygon map overlay performed (Figure 53.3). In this study the first option was selected. To calculate the portion of the total study area of 481 kilometres square represented by each zone, the GIS was queried to determine the cell frequency for each. Since each cell represents 30 metres square it was a routine task to calculate the areas and relative proportions of each zone. With these calculated, the expected number of sites from the overall total of 142 we would expect to find within each was determined, assuming the null hypothesis to be true. A Chi-square test was then performed (Table 53.2). Although not a problem in the present analysis, it is a requirement of the Chi-square test that the expected cell frequencies should not be too small, with the general rule that no expected frequency should be less than five (Levin and Fox 1988:290).

The result clearly rejects the null hypothesis, suggesting that the observed tendency to avoid areas liable to flood is significant. We then need to explain why that might be so. The analysis acts as a springboard to further investigation and in this sense GIS is best thought of as providing a flexible analytical environment rather than a black-box giving specific answers. For example, we could undertake further queries to sub-divide the distribution of sites by period to see whether the pattern varies with time. We could also explore the effects of altering the suggested flood thresholds. We also have to explain the fact that despite the overall trend, sites still occur in flood-prone areas. We could compare them to the fuzzy zone layer to estimate the level of risk involved, and examine the attributes of these sites to look for indications of ritual usage or seasonality.

Flood Zones
■ Flooded
▨ Uncertain
□ Dry

N

Figure 53.3 An overlay of the archaeological sites and potential flood zones.

Table 53.2 The results of the Chi-square test.

Total number of sites = 142
Total study area = 481 km^2

Zone	% proportion of study area	Expected site frequency (f_e)	Observed site frequency (f_o)	$(f_o - f_e)^2/f_e$
Flooded	17.7	25.134	2	21.293
Prone to flooding	22.9	32.518	5	23.287
Dry	59.4	84.348	137	32.867

Calculated Chi-square = 77.447
Value of Chi-square with 1 degree of freedom at 0.05 significance level = 3.841
Value of Chi-square with 1 degree of freedom at 0.01 significance level = 6.635
The null hypothesis can therefore be rejected.

FUTURE DIRECTIONS

Looking forward, three trends can be identified. The first concerns the development and integration of fully 3D GIS and temporal or TGIS into everyday archaeological research (Harris and Lock 1996). The second concerns the often uncritical and problematic relationship between GIS and archaeological theory. A number of researchers are exploring links between the rigid data models offered by the GIS and new theoretical perspectives concerning the nature of space, human perception and cognition, and the relationship between people and their environments. As GIS becomes embedded within archaeological research such trends will inevitably gather pace (Gaffney *et al.* 1995, Llobera 1996, Wheatley 1993). The final trend concerns the blending of GIS techniques with emerging technologies such as *Virtual Reality* (VR) modelling, *Artificial Intelligence* (AI) and the dynamic capabilities of the Internet and World Wide Web. Such developments are already challenging current reliance upon the static mapsheet to mediate between the researcher and the data under investigation, leading to greatly enriched analyses and studies (Gillings and Goodrick 1996).

REFERENCES

*Recommended for further reading

AGI (Association for Geographic Information) (1996) *AGI Standards Committee GIS Dictionary*.
http://www.geo.ed.ac.uk/agidict/welcome.html.
Association for Geographic Information/University of Edinburgh: Edinburgh.

Aldenderfer, M. and Maschner, H.D.G. (eds) (1996). *Anthropology, Space, and Geographic Information Systems*. Oxford University Press: New York.

Allen, K.M.S. (1990). Modelling early historic trade in the eastern Great Lakes using geographic information systems. In Allen, K.M.S., Green, S.W. and Zubrow, E.B.W. (eds) *Interpreting Space: GIS and Archaeology*, 319–329. Taylor and Francis: New York.

*Allen, K.M.S., Green, S.W. and Zubrow, E.B.W. (eds) (1990). *Interpreting Space: GIS and Archaeology*. Taylor and Francis: New York.

Altschul, J.H. (1990). Red flag models: the use of modelling in management contexts. In Allen, K.M.S., Green, S.W. and Zubrow, E.B.W. (eds) *Interpreting Space: GIS and archaeology*, 226–238. Taylor and Francis: New York.

Bailey, T.C. (1994). A review of statistical spatial analysis in geographical information systems. In Fotheringham, S.

and Rogerson, P. (eds) *Spatial Analysis and GIS*, 13–44. Taylor and Francis: London.

*Bailey, T.C. and Gatrell, A.C. (1995). *Interactive Spatial Data Analysis*. Longmans: New York.

Bosqued, C.B., Preysler, J.B. and Expiago, J. (1996). The role of GIS in the management of archaeological data: an example of application for the Spanish administration. In Aldenderfer, M. and Maschner, H.D.G. (eds) *Anthropology, Space, and Geographic Information Systems*, 190–201. Oxford University Press: New York.

Clarke, D.L. (ed.) (1977). *Spatial Archaeology*. Academic Press: London.

*DeMers, M.N. (1997). *Fundamentals of Geographic Information Systems*. John Wiley: New York.

Farley, J.A., Limp, W.F. and Lockhart, J. (1990). The archaeologist's workbench: integrating GIS, remote sensing, EDA and database management. In Allen, K.M.S., Green, S.W. and Zubrow, E.B.W. (eds) *Interpreting Space: GIS and Archaeology*, 141–164. Taylor and Francis: New York.

*Fotheringham, S. and Rogerson, P. (1994). *Spatial Analysis and GIS*. Taylor and Francis: London.

*Gaffney, V. and Stančič, Z. (1991). *GIS Approaches to Regional Analysis: a Case Study of the Island of Hvar*. Znanstveni institut Filozoske fakultete: Ljubljana.

Gaffney, V., Stančič, Z. and Watson, H. (1995). Moving from catchments to cognition: tentative steps towards a larger archaeological context for GIS. *Scottish Archaeological Review*, **9–10**:51–64.

Gillings, M. (1995). GIS and the Tisza flood-plain: landscape and settlement evolution in north-eastern Hungary. In Lock, G. and Stančič, Z. (eds) *The Impact of Geographic Information Systems on Archaeology: a European Perspective*, 67–84. Taylor and Francis: New York.

Gillings, M. (1997). Spatial organization in the Tisza flood-plain: landscape dynamics and GIS. In Chapman, J. and Dolukhanov, P. (eds) *Landscape in Flux. Central and Eastern Europe in Antiquity*, 163–178. Colloquia Pontica 3, Oxbow: Oxford.

Gillings, M. (1998). Embracing uncertainty and challenging dualism in the GIS-based study of a palaeo flood-plain. *European Journal of Archaeology*, **1**:117–144.

Gillings, M. (in press). The utility of the GIS approach in the collection, storage and analysis of surface survey data. In Bintliff, J., Kuna, M. and Venclova, N. (eds) *The Future of Archaeological Field Survey in Europe*. Sheffield Academic Press: Sheffield.

Gillings, M. and Goodrick, G.T. (1996). Sensuous and reflexive GIS: exploring visualization and VRML. *Internet Archaeology*, **1** (http://intarch.ac.uk/).

*Gillings, M. and Wise, A. (1998). *GIS Guide to Good Practice*. Archaeology Data Service: York
(http://ads.ahds.ac.uk/project/goodguides/gis/).

Goodchild, M.F. (1986). *Spatial Autocorrelation*. Concepts and Techniques in Modern Geography 47, GeoBooks: Norwich.

Goodchild, M.F. (1996). Geographic Information Systems and Spatial Analysis in the social sciences. In Aldenderfer, M. and Maschner H.D.G. (eds) *Anthropology, Space, and Geographic Information Systems*, 241–250. Oxford University Press: New York.

Harris, T. and Lock, G. (1995). Toward an evaluation of GIS in European archaeology: the past, present and future of theory and applications. In Lock, G. and Stančič, Z. (eds) *Archaeology and Geographical Information Systems: a European Perspective*, 349–366. Taylor and Francis: London.

Harris, T.M. and Lock, G.R. (1996). Multi-dimensional GIS: exploratory approaches to spatial and temporal relationships within archaeological stratigraphy. In Kamermans, H. and Fennema, K. (eds) *Interfacing the Past: Computer Applications and Quantitative Methods in Archaeology CAA95*, 307–316. Analecta Praehistorica Leidensia 28, University of Leiden Press: Leiden.

Hartwig, F. and Dearing, B.E. (1979). *Exploratory Data Analysis*. Sage: California.

*Heywood, I., Cornelius, S. and Carver, S. (1998). *An Introduction to Geographical Information Systems*. Longmans: New York.

*Hodder, I. and Orton, C. (1976). *Spatial Analysis in Archaeology*. Cambridge University Press: Cambridge.

Hunt, E.D. (1992). Upgrading site-catchment analyses with the use of GIS: investigating the settlement patterns of horticulturalists. *World Archaeology*, 24:283–309.

Kvamme, K.L. (1993). Spatial statistics and GIS: an integrated approach. In Andresen, J., Madsen, T. and Scollar, I. (eds) *Computing the Past: Computing Applications and Quantitative Methods in Archaeology*, 91–104. Aarhus University Press: Aarhus.

Kvamme, K.L. (1994). GIS graphics vs. spatial statistics: how do they fit together? *Archaeological Computing Newsletter*, 38:1–2.

Kvamme, K.L. (1995). A view from across the water: the North American experience in archaeological GIS. In Lock, G. and Stančič, Z. (eds) *Archaeology and Geographical Information Systems: a European Perspective*, 1–14. Taylor and Francis: London.

Kvamme, K.L. (1996). Investigating chipping debris scatters: GIS as an analytical engine. In Aldenderfer, M. and Maschner, H.D.G. (eds) *Anthropology, Space, and Geographic Information Systems*, 38–71. Oxford University Press: New York.

Levin, J. and Fox, J.A. (1988). *Elementary Statistics in Social Research*. Harper and Row: New York.

Llobera, M. (1996). Exploring the topography of mind: GIS, social space and archaeology. *Antiquity*, 70:612–622.

Lock, G. (1998). The past, present and future of GIS-based cultural landscape research. In Peterson, J. (ed.) *The Use of Geographic Information Systems in the Study of Ancient Landscapes and Features Related to Ancient Land Use*, 31–35. European Commission: Brussels.

*Lock, G. and Stančič, Z. (eds) (1995). *Archaeology and Geographical Information Systems: A European Perspective*. Taylor and Francis: London.

*Maschner, H.D.G. (ed.) (1996). *New Methods, Old Problems: Geographic Information Systems in Modern Archaeological Research*. Center for Archaeological Investigations Occasional Paper 23, Southern Illinois University: Carbondale.

Müller, J., Lagrange, J. and Weibel, R. (eds) (1995). *GIS and Generalization: Methodology and Practice*. Taylor and Francis: London.

Openshaw, S. (1984). *The Modifiable Areal Unit Problem*. Concepts and Techniques in Modern Geography 38, GeoBooks: Norwich.

Peterson, J. (ed.) (1998). *The Use of Geographic Information Systems in the Study of Ancient Landscapes and Features Related to Ancient Land Use*. European Commission: Brussels.

Rhind, H.D. (1988). A GIS research agenda. *International Journal of Geographical Information Systems*, 2:23–28.

Ruggles, A.J. and Church, R.L. (1996). Spatial allocation in archaeology: an opportunity for re-evaluation. In Maschner, H.D.G. (ed.) *New Methods, Old Problems: Geographic Information Systems in Modern Archaeological Research*, 147–173. Center for Archaeological Investigations Occasional Paper 23, Southern Illinois University: Carbondale.

Shennan, S. (1990). *Quantifying Archaeology*. Edinburgh University Press: Edinburgh.

van Leusen, P.M. (1993). Cartographic modelling in a cell-based GIS. In Andresen, J., Madsen, T. and Scollar, I. (eds) *Computing the Past: Computing Applications and Quantitative Methods in Archaeology*, 105–124. Aarhus University Press: Aarhus.

Wansleeben, M. and Verhart, L. (1997). Geographical Information Systems: methodological progress and theoretical decline. *Archaeological Dialogues*, 1:53–70.

Warren, R.E. (1990). Predictive modelling of archaeological site location: a case study in the Midwest. In Allen, K.M.S., Green, S.W. and Zubrow, E.B.W. (eds) *Interpreting Space: GIS and Archaeology*, 201–215. Taylor and Francis: New York.

Westcott, K.L. and Brandon, R.J. (2000). *Practical Applications of GIS for Archaeologists: a Predictive Modelling Kit*. Taylor and Francis: New York.

Wheatley, D.W. (1993). Going over old ground: GIS, archaeological theory and the act of perception. In Andresen, J., Madsen, T. and Scollar, I. (eds) *Computing the Past: Computing Applications and Quantitative Methods in Archaeology*, 133–138. Aarhus University Press: Aarhus.

Wheatley, D.W. (1995). Cumulative viewshed analysis: a GIS-based method for investigating intervisibility, and its archaeological application. In Lock, G. and Stančič, Z. (eds) *Archaeology and Geographical Information Systems: a European Perspective*, 171–186. Taylor and Francis: London.

Wheatley, D. (1996). Between the lines: the role of GIS-based predictive modelling in the interpretation of extensive survey data. In Kamermans, H. and Fennema, K. (eds) *Interfacing the Past: Computer Applications and Quantitative Methods in Archaeology*, 275–292. Analecta Praehistorica Leidensia 28, University of Leiden Press: Leiden.

Williams, I., Limp, W.F. and Briuer, F.L. (1990). Using Geographic Information Systems and exploratory data analysis for archaeological site classification and analysis. In Allen, K.M.S., Green, W.S. and Zubrow, E.B.W. (eds) *Interpreting Space: GIS and Archaeology*, 239–273. Taylor and Francis: New York.

Zubrow, E.B.W. (1994). Knowledge representation and archaeology: a cognitive example using GIS. In Renfrew, C. and Zubrow, E.B.W. (eds) *The Ancient Mind: Elements of Cognitive Archaeology*, 107–118. Cambridge University Press: Cambridge.

54

Multivariate Analysis in Archaeology

M.J. BAXTER

Department of Mathematics, Statistics and OR, Nottingham Trent University.

Archaeological data are frequently presented in the form of a table of n rows and p columns, where we assume n is larger than p. Such data are said to be p-dimensional. Patterns in the data are not always readily seen using methods appropriate for one (univariate) or two (bivariate) variables (e.g., Drennan 1996, Shennan 1997) and recourse is often had to methods of multivariate analysis (Baxter 1994a). These methods aim to transform the data so that lower-dimensional displays (usually two) can be used to examine the data for structure, by which is commonly meant the existence of grouping within the data.

Baxter (1994a) covers the main multivariate techniques used in archaeology and has an extensive bibliography of archaeological applications. In this chapter four multivariate methods that have found widespread use are discussed. The view is taken that, with modern computer software, implementation of these methods is as easy as calculating a mean, and their intention (if not the underlying mathematics) is readily understood. Other than the brief section on notation no attempt is made to discuss the detail of the underlying mathematics, which can be pursued in the references indicated. What is important is an understanding of the purpose of different methods, interpretation of their output, and their limitations.

TERMINOLOGY AND NOTATION

The rows and columns of a table of data will be referred to as *cases* and *variables* respectively. If there are n cases and p variables the table can also be referred to as an n by p data matrix and denoted by $\mathbf{X}$, with the observation in the ith row and jth column denoted by x_{ij}. The mean and standard deviation of the ith variable are $\bar{x}_i$ and s_i. The variables are denoted by X_1, X_2 etc.

It is usual to modify the data in $\mathbf{X}$ before multivariate analysis. Most commonly, the data are either standardized using $y_{ij} = (x_{ij} - \bar{x}_i)/s_i$ or transformed to (base 10) logarithms, $y_{ij} = \log x_{ij}$. Sometimes data are standardized after first transforming. The reasons for standardization and/or transformation are that some statistical techniques (e.g., PCA and cluster analysis) produce results that depend on the scale of measurement of the data. If the raw data are used, variables with larger values will tend to have more weight, to the extent that they may totally dominate an analysis. Standardization gives each variable equal weight. Logarithmic transformation, which requires all $x_{ij} > 0$, will produce a more nearly equal weighting (though not exact equality). It may also convert a variable with a skew distribution to one having a more nearly symmetrical distribution. This is considered by some to be important in analyses – of ceramic compositions, for example – where the variables are trace elements that may have a naturally skewed distribution.

After standardization or transformation, variables $Y_1, Y_2, \ldots, Y_p$ are obtained. These can be further transformed to new variables that are linear combinations of the form:

$$Z = a_1 Y_1 + a_2 Y_2 + \cdots + a_p Y_p$$

where the coefficients a_i depend on the technique used.

Another important concept is that of (squared) Euclidean distance between two cases, i and j, which is defined as:

$$d_{ij}^2 = \sum_k (y_{ik} - y_{jk})^2$$

where d_{ij} is a generalization, to p dimensions, of the familiar 'ruler' distance.

THE MAIN MULTIVARIATE TECHNIQUES

In the general statistical literature most texts on multivariate analysis cover the subjects dealt with here. Kraznowski and Marriott (1994, 1995) is a good starting point with extensive references. Everitt and Dunn (1991) and Manly (1994) are introductory texts, the latter including some archaeological examples. All the main techniques have texts entirely devoted to them, including PCA (Jolliffe 1986), cluster analysis (Everitt 1993), correspondence analysis (Greenacre 1993) and discriminant analysis (McLachlan 1992). Shennan (1997) has an introduction to PCA, cluster and correspondence analysis.

As an introductory example, Table 54.1 is extracted from Pollard and Hatcher (1986) and shows the chemical composition of specimens of Chinese ceramics (greenwares) dating from the third to fifteenth centuries AD. The first and last few rows from the full sample of 133 specimens are shown and the data are eight-dimensional. In the original paper multivariate statistical methods were used to investigate the relationship between the chemistry of the specimens and their origin and date. Figure 54.1 shows the results of a technique known as principal component analysis (PCA) applied to the full data set. In the left-hand diagram the components plotted are linear combinations of the original variables. The plot shows that there are two main groups in the data. That to the left consists mainly of early, northern specimens and contrasts with the later, southern specimens to the right. This establishes that

Table 54.1 Data extracted from that given in Pollard and Hatcher (1986) showing the first and last few entries in their table of the chemical composition of 133 specimens of oriental greenware.

Id.	Al_2O_3	CaO	MgO	Fe_2O_3	TiO_2	Na_2O	MnO	K_2O
1	17.42	0.46	0.75	2.65	0.98	1.35	0.010	2.66
2	16.41	0.39	0.54	1.90	0.78	0.93	0.010	2.98
3	16.19	0.43	0.56	2.08	0.92	0.80	0.010	2.48
4	17.42	0.39	0.54	1.90	0.76	0.88	0.010	2.83
5	21.24	0.22	0.33	2.65	1.20	0.21	0.010	3.06
...	...	...	...	...	...	...	...	...
129	20.03	0.02	0.15	1.76	0.07	0.15	0.041	5.60
130	19.66	0.20	0.15	1.97	0.01	0.19	0.039	4.34
131	27.97	0.95	0.40	1.77	1.09	0.28	0.005	1.69
132	23.06	0.05	0.21	8.87	0.08	0.48	0.017	5.02
133	20.24	0.20	0.41	2.25	0.09	0.51	0.146	5.22

these archaeologically distinct groups are also chemically distinct. The plot also identifies a chemically unusual specimen to the bottom right of the plot. The right-hand diagram is discussed later.

Principal component analysis (PCA)

As often used, PCA has the aim of taking the original p variables, converting these to p new variables (principal components) that are linear combinations of the (usually) standardized or transformed originals, and investigating structure in the data by using the first few components.

The p components, $Z_1, Z_2, \ldots, Z_p$, are defined to be uncorrelated, such that Z_1 is most important (in the sense of having the maximum variance possible), Z_2 is the second most important, and so on. The hope is that most of these components are unimportant, so that examination of plots based on the first two or three will suffice to determine the important structure in the data. If PCA works well then the distances between points on a plot will be a good approximation to the true distances between cases, d_{ij}, in p-dimensional space.

This brief summary begs the question of what is meant by terms such as 'important' and 'good approximation', and this is not easily answered. The sum of the variances of the Z_i is the same as the sum of the variances of the Y_i; if the proportion of total variance accounted for by the first two or three components is high (e.g., 70–80 per cent or better) an analysis would often be accounted a good one. Such rules, of which there are several, should not be interpreted rigidly. Data sets such as that in Table 54.1 often give rise to values for the first two components in the range 50–60

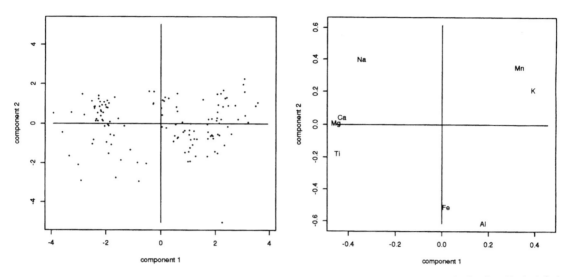

Figure 54.1 The outcome of a principal component analysis of the data from Table 54.1, after standardization. To the left the plot of cases shows two main chemical groups in the data. The plot to the right is of the variables. Taken together this is a form of biplot, the interpretation of which is discussed in the text.

per cent that, nevertheless, produce useful and interpretable plots. In such cases inspection of plots based on the third, fourth, etc., components may, however, be useful.

Software implementations of PCA should include information on the variances of the Z_i (for mathematical reasons often called *eigenvalues*) and their cumulative proportion. Figure 54.1 is based on standardized data for which the total variance is p. The variance of the first two components is 3.90 and 1.36 respectively. Expressed as a percentage of the total these account for 49 per cent and 17 per cent of the variance, or a cumulative value of 66 per cent, which is reasonable.

Interpretation of a PCA is often based solely on inspection of a plot such as Figure 54.1. If archaeological information is available (e.g., provenance, type, date), but not used in the analysis, the hope might be that distinct groups correspond to distinct provenances, for example. It is often helpful to label points in plots according to the archaeological information available.

What is actually plotted in the left-hand diagram of Figure 54.1 is Z_1 against Z_2 where:

$$Z_1 = 0.18Al - 0.43Ca - 0.45Mg + 0.02Fe$$
$$- 0.45Ti - 0.34Na + 0.33Mn + 0.39K$$
$$Z_2 = -0.61Al + 0.04Ca + 0.01Mg - 0.51Fe$$
$$- 0.18Ti + 0.40Na + 0.35Mn + 0.21K$$

and the variables are standardized. It is sometimes possible to give such linear combinations a useful interpretation, but this is not essential. In the present example the second component is determined largely by Al_2O_3 and Fe_2O_3, for example. The right-hand diagram shows the coefficients in the form of a bivariate plot based on the pairs (0.18, -0.61), (-0.43, 0.04), (-0.45, 0.01), etc. Figure 54.1 as a whole is an example of a biplot or RQ-mode plot (often the two diagrams would be superimposed). Cases to the left of the left-hand diagram will be relatively rich in those elements (e.g., Ca, Mg, Ti) that occupy a similar position in the right-hand diagram, and relatively poor in elements (e.g., Mn, K) occupying a diametrically opposite position. Further aspects of interpretation are discussed in Baxter (1994a) and Neff (1994).

This example raises an issue of general interest in the application of multivariate methods, and that is the treatment of outliers. The PCA analysis shows one case (132) to be outlying, and other forms of analysis show that cases 131 and 133 are also outliers. These were omitted in the analyses presented in Pollard and Hatcher (1986) and, where outliers are obvious and the aim of an analysis is to determine the main patterns in the data, this is a sensible course of action. The decision is not a critical one in this example because the same two groups are evident, and the coefficients are similar, after omission of the three cases.

The scale dependence of PCA might be regarded as a limitation, but it is not easy to advise on whether to standardize, transform or both. The issue is discussed in Pollard (1986), Bishop and Neff (1989) and Baxter (1994a, 1995). Another limitation of PCA is that it may miss important features of the data if the effective dimensionality is much greater than two or three, and for this reason it is often used in conjunction with the technique of cluster analysis.

Cluster analysis

Main ideas

Cluster analysis is a generic term for a range of methods that have as a common aim the subdivision of cases into groups, such that cases are similar to those within the group to which they are allocated, and different from cases within other groups. It is the most widely used multivariate technique in archaeology, and only the most important ideas and commonly used methods are discussed here. The same considerations concerning data standardization or transformation that arise in PCA apply, and standardization is usual.

A cluster analysis has two main components; (i) a measure of (dis)similarity between cases is defined, (ii) a method (algorithm) for grouping cases is specified. As (i) and (ii) can be determined and combined in many different ways this gives rise to the numerous different methods of cluster analysis available. The measure of dissimilarity used most in practice is Euclidean distance, d_{ij}, or its square. Hierarchical agglomerative algorithms are most commonly used to group cases. In such an algorithm each individual case is considered as a cluster, so that there are n clusters in all. The two most similar cases are amalgamated to get $(n-1)$ clusters. Amalgamation proceeds until all cases are contained in a single cluster. Results are usually presented in the form of a dendrogram (see Figure 54.2).

Once a cluster contains two or more cases, algorithms differ in the way similarity between clusters is defined. Perhaps the most widely used algorithm is the average linkage method. If two clusters contain n_1 and n_2 members there are $n_1 n_2$ distances that can be measured, taking one case from each cluster. The average of these distances defines the dissimilarity between two clusters, and the most similar (least dissimilar) clusters are merged at any given stage. The complete linkage method has also found some favour. In this method the dissimilarity between two clusters is defined as the maximum distance between two cases, one from each cluster.

The other method that has competed with average linkage in terms of popularity is Ward's method. If, at a given point, there are k clusters a measure of the variation within each cluster, S_i say, is defined, and the total variation of the clustering is:

$$S = S_1 + S_2 + \cdots + S_k.$$

Any amalgamation to $(k-1)$ clusters, and a recalculation of the S_i, will result in an increase in S. Those clusters are amalgamated for which this increase is the least.

An alternative to hierarchical agglomerative methods is partitioning (or k-means or relocation) methods. In hierarchical methods once two cases or clusters have been merged the merge cannot be 'undone'. In Ward's method S can be regarded as a measure of how good the clustering is, but for given k the method does not necessarily optimize (minimize) this because it cannot 'go back' on earlier merges. In partitioning methods an attempt is made to minimize S (or some similar criterion) by iteratively relocating cases between clusters until a minimum is achieved. A starting position can be obtained either from a hierarchical method or randomly.

Example

Pollard and Hatcher's (1986) cluster analysis of their standardized data using Ward's method, after omitting the three outliers, showed two main groups in the data. The upper diagram in Figure 54.2 is the dendrogram for the same data analysed using average linkage. This admits a similar interpretation, with the additional identification of case 92 as a possible outlier (in the top left). If the dendrogram is cut to give three clusters of 1, 52 and 77 specimens, and this is taken as the starting position for a k-means analysis (that available in the S-Plus package), three cases are reallocated to give groups of 1, 54 and 75 cases. If the four group solution, with clusters of size 1, 4, 52 and 73, is used k-means results in clusters of size 1, 17, 38 and 74. In both cases the final singleton cluster (case 129) is different from that used to initiate the iteration.

When analysis reveals clear groups it is often sensible to conduct separate analysis on the different groups, as detail may be obscured in the global analysis. For illustration this is done here using the smaller and earlier group of 52 cases (case 92 is not used) obtained in the original average link analysis. The lower diagram in Figure 54.2 shows the dendrogram from an average linkage cluster analysis of the standardized data. It is

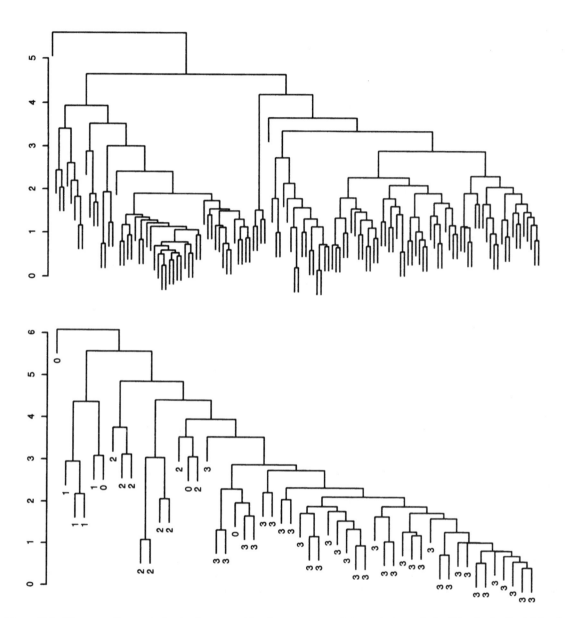

Figure 54.2   The upper diagram is the dendrogram arising from an average linkage cluster analysis of the standardized data of Table 54.1, suggesting two main groups and a possible outlier. The lower diagram is based on a similar cluster analysis of the smaller of the two groups suggested, with points labelled (1, 2, 3) or as outliers (0) according to the grouping determined by Pollard and Hatcher (1986).

hard to interpret, and indicative of a problem that can arise with cluster analysis output. The stepped appearance is characteristic of a phenomenon known as chaining which makes the identification of distinct clusters difficult. Pollard and Hatcher's (1986) analysis, based on Ward's method and a form of relocation, identified

three groups of 4, 9 and 35 specimens, labelled 1, 2 and 3 in Figure 54.2, and a small number of outliers, labelled 0. Ignoring outliers, if the dendrogram is cut at 5 on the vertical axis the small group 1 is separated out; if it is cut at about 3.75 the large group 3 is separated out from the other two, which are sub-divided into small groups of between one and four cases. Given a knowledge of the grouping obtained by Pollard and Hatcher, Figure 54.2 can be seen to be compatible with their analysis. Approached 'cold' it is hard to discern clear groups.

Problems and practicalities

This example raises a number of issues that need to be addressed in any application of cluster analysis. The first is 'which method should be used?'. There is no easy answer to this; one suspects many practitioners are guided by precedent, software availability and what appears to 'work'. It is often sensible to apply more than one algorithm and compare results (Pollard 1983). Dendrograms obtained using Ward's method, particularly with squared Euclidean distance as the dissimilarity measure, are often apparently easier to interpret than those obtained with other methods. The drawback is that the method can artificially suggest groups even if the data are random, so it is advisable to confirm them against other methods.

Determining an appropriate number of clusters is also not easy. Formal methods of deciding on the numbers of clusters exist but have not been widely used in archaeology, and do not always work well, so that informal methods are more common. Some check is desirable since the appearance of a dendrogram, even if apparently clear-cut, can mislead. One useful approach is to decide on the number of clusters, and then label a PCA plot according to cluster membership. If the clustering is 'real' clusters should appear as disjoint groups on the plot. It can be helpful to use components in addition to the first two for this purpose since, with several clusters, separation may exist but not necessarily in the first two dimensions. Experimentation with different numbers of clusters can also be informative. Another technique sometimes used with the same aim is discriminant analysis, discussed below.

A major problem with cluster analysis, as applied to much archaeological data, is that the methods in common use tend to find spherical clusters. The clusters, if any, that exist may, however, be elongated or spherical because of correlations that exist between the variables and many methods can fail to recognize this. This problem has been known for a long time but no really satisfactory solution has emerged. For this reason some researchers now place less reliance on cluster analysis than was the case, say, 10–15 years ago.

Discriminant analysis

The third multivariate technique that has seen widespread use in scientific archaeology is discriminant analysis. It is assumed in advance of analysis that each case belongs to one of g groups, where we assume $g < p$. It is then possible to derive $(g - 1)$ uncorrelated linear combinations of the original variables that maximize the separation between groups, and this is often displayed on a plot using just the first two combinations. This contrasts with PCA where the linear combinations are derived to successively maximize variance, and no assumptions about the existence of groups are made. Figure 54.3 contrasts the two approaches; the data used for the lower diagram in Figure 54.2 have been used, excluding outliers, and cases have been labelled according to which of Pollard and Hatcher's (1986) groups they belong to. The separation of the groups is much clearer in the discriminant analysis than in the PCA.

The version of discriminant analysis just used is (Fisher's) linear discriminant analysis (LDA). Many other approaches exist but LDA dominates archaeological usage. One generalization is quadratic discriminant analysis (QDA), in which terms in Y_i^2 may be included in the definition of the linear combinations. This has potential advantages over LDA, but is also far more demanding of data and is rarely used. It is not necessary to standardize data in LDA or QDA, since this is taken care of by the mathematics of the method, but transformation is always an option.

Stepwise versions of LDA are sometimes used, and Pollard and Hatcher provide an example. In stepwise LDA a subset of the available variables is selected as the best discriminators, usually by deleting variables sequentially until all remaining ones are needed. This can be achieved in various ways which, in general, give different results and are not guaranteed to produce a selection that is 'optimal' in any sense. This is discussed in Baxter (1994b).

The success of a discriminant analysis can be assessed in various ways. After an LDA, group centroids can be calculated and the 'distance' of each case to each group centroid calculated. Cases are allocated to the group whose centroid is nearest, and the success of the LDA is measured by the percentage of cases correctly allocated to the group to which they were assumed to belong. This is the re-substitution approach. The same idea may also be used to allocate cases not used in the analysis to a group.

Although the re-substitution approach is widely used it has limitations. One is that a case influences the outcome of an LDA, and hence the group it is allocated to.

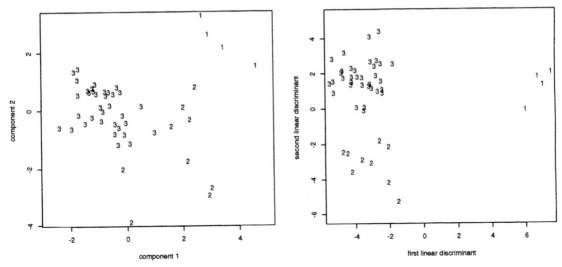

Figure 54.3 The left diagram is based on a principal component analysis of the data used for the lower diagram in Figure 54.2, after omitting outliers, and with points labelled according to the grouping determined by Pollard and Hatcher (1986). This may be contrasted with the discriminant analysis of the same data in the right diagram.

This produces an optimistic assessment of the success of an analysis. A better approach is cross-validation, in which allocation is based on an LDA that omits the case to be allocated. For the example being used here re-substitution and cross-validation both give success rates of 100 per cent, but differences of 10–20 per cent can occur. It should be remarked that the initial definition of groups using cluster analysis, or other multivariate methods, leads one to expect a 'good' result. If purely archaeological criteria are used to define groups the success of an LDA would generally be lower.

A second limitation of either allocatory procedure is that cases are allocated even if they are not very close to any group. A more sensitive procedure is possible. If it is assumed that groups have a (multivariate) normal distribution the 'distances' of cases to groups can be converted to probabilities, and cases only allocated if some limit (e.g., 0.05) is exceeded for at least one group. A warning must also be issued here. Such calculations often assume that groups have the same covariance matrix (i.e., same shape and size) and inspection of plots such as the left-hand diagram in Figure 54.3 will often show that this is manifestly untrue, so 'exact' probability calculations must be viewed with circumspection.

Finally, the use of the term 'distance' has been glossed over in the discussion of LDA. This is not, in fact, the Euclidean distance introduced earlier but Mahalanobis distance, a generalization of Euclidean distance that allows for correlation between variables. A full discussion requires mathematics at a higher level than is being assumed here, but it is discussed a little further below.

Correspondence analysis

The methods discussed so far have been popular since multivariate methods began to be widely used in archaeology, in the 1970s. By contrast the next technique to be discussed, correspondence analysis, has only really come into its own in the last 10 years or so. It can be thought of as a form of PCA that is particularly appropriate for tables of counted data (e.g., counts of artifact type by site) and results in a display of data similar to that of a PCA biplot. Mathematical details, which are quite complicated, are given in the references cited in the final section and here the method will be illustrated by example only.

Cool and Baxter (1999) present data on the abundance of six different glass vessel types for 18 Romano–British assemblages dated to the first–second, second–third and fourth centuries AD. Figure 54.4 shows the outcome of a correspondence analysis of these data. The left-hand diagram, which is analogous to the left-hand diagram in Figure 54.1, plots the assemblages labelled by date. The late assemblages clearly separate out from the earlier ones and there is a hint that first–

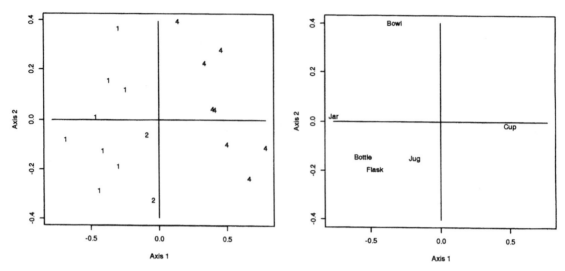

Figure 54.4 The correspondence analysis shown in this figure is of Table 1 in Cool and Baxter (1999) which shows the abundance of six glass vessel types within 18 assemblages. The left diagram plots the assemblages, labelled by date (1 = first–second century; 2 = second–third century; 4 = fourth century). The right diagram plots the vessel types. Interpretation is discussed in the text.

second and second–third century assemblages differ, a possibility which is explored in the original paper. The right hand diagram suggests that, relative to early assemblages, late assemblages are characterized by an abundance of cups and a dearth of jars and other types.

Correspondence analysis has most often been used for assemblage data of this type, often with the aim of chronologically ordering or seriating assemblages. Applications to data generated by the more traditionally 'scientific' disciplines within archaeology are less common; biological data has, perhaps, attracted the greatest usage (see the bibliography in Baxter 1994a). This reflects the facts that different techniques are appropriate for different kinds of data, and different approaches to generating 'archaeologically informative' data lead naturally to different data types. For example, PCA and many methods of cluster analysis are best suited to continuous data, such as the elemental concentrations generated in the measurement of artifact compositions. In this section the similarities between PCA and correspondence analysis have been emphasized; their differences are discussed in technical detail by Gower and Hand (1996).

Other methods

The four methods discussed account for the vast majority of applications of multivariate analysis in archaeol-

ogy, scientific or otherwise. Both PCA and correspondence analysis can be thought of as particular examples of multidimensional scaling methods that lead to low dimensional representations of high dimensional data. Other approaches exist (Cox and Cox 1994) but have had limited archaeological use. Correspondence analysis has links to canonical correlation analysis, which is appropriate if one wishes to explore the relationships that exist between two predefined sets of variables and also has had little use.

Nearly all the techniques discussed are examples of exploratory methodologies, where no distributional assumptions are made about the population sampled, and there is no explicit formulation of a statistical model. Some statisticians would see this as a limitation and would like to see more use made of model-based methods. The Bayesian approach is a potentially attractive model-based methodology whose archaeological potential has been explored most fully by Buck, Litton and co-workers (Buck et al. 1996; see also Chapter 55). An attraction is that archaeological knowledge can be incorporated into a statistical analysis in a 'natural' fashion. Potential drawbacks are that it is mathematically heavy going for the non-initiated and, like all model-based approaches, relies on assumptions that may not apply or be difficult to verify. Great success has been achieved in tackling dating problems, but multivariate applications have received less attention, though an outline of what might be done is given in Buck *et al.* (1996) with examples.

CURRENT AND FUTURE PROSPECTS

The use of multivariate analysis in archaeology is conservative in the sense that it is mostly established techniques, widely available in software packages, that are used, and recent developments (say the last 10–15 years) in the statistical literature have had limited impact. Other than correspondence analysis the methods presented in this chapter are essentially those discussed in Bieber *et al.* (1976) and Pollard (1986).

Methods that, on the surface, seem worth investigating with archaeological data include projection pursuit (Jones and Sibson 1987), model-based clustering (e.g., Banfield and Raftery 1993, McLachlan and Basford 1988), classification trees and forms of discriminant analysis other than LDA (Ripley 1996), neural networks (Ripley 1996, Bell and Croson 1998), and graphical modelling (Scott *et al.* 1991). The last of these is capable of dealing with data of more than one type, and this is a general topic also worth further investigation. Books that deal with more recent developments in the field of multivariate analysis include Krzanowski (1995) and Ripley (1996). Venables and Ripley (1997) contains material on some aspects of multivariate analysis, with details of implementation in the package S-Plus. This package also contains functions for brush-and-spin plots, biplots, k-means clustering, Mahalanobis distance calculations, model-based cluster analysis, and classification trees as well as the 'standard' methods. Given that S-Plus also has powerful programming facilities, and is regularly updated, use of this or any package with similar facilities is probably preferable to the writing of 'special purpose' packages that was necessary in the past.

That these and other methods have not been more widely used could be attributed to factors such as their unfamiliarity, complexity (in some cases) and lack of availability in 'user-friendly' software packages. Other, and more fundamental, reasons may limit their use in scientific archaeology. To work well (or at all) many of these methods require large sample sizes and/or relatively small numbers of variables. In certain areas of scientific archaeology, such as artifact compositional analysis, analytical techniques can generate measurements for 20–30 variables without there being a commensurate increase in the sample size. Under these circumstances, unless one is prepared to make unrealistic assumptions about the data or be highly selective

about the variables used, it is likely that these newer methodologies may have limited application.

Apart from the ease with which multivariate methods can be applied, what has changed over the last 20 years or so is the way in which some researchers approach multivariate analysis. The limitations of cluster analysis, for example, are now well understood and in some laboratories (e.g., Glascock 1992, Beier and Mommsen 1994) it is regarded simply as an initial exploratory method, the results of which are to be treated with extreme caution, and modified by application of other methodologies. In some approaches PCA is used as the major analytical tool, rather than as a supplement to cluster analysis. Where sample sizes permit, greater use is also being made of Mahalanobis distance than has possibly been the case in the past, for evaluating groups produced by methods such as cluster analysis (Glascock 1992), or as an integral part of grouping procedures. The strengths and limitations of this usage are discussed in Baxter and Buck (2000), which is a recent review, specifically about methods used for handling analytical data, including discussion of topics such as Mahalanobis distance, Bayesian methods and outlier detection mentioned only briefly here.

The journals *Archaeometry*, *Journal of Archaeological Science*, *American Antiquity* and *Archeologia e Calcolatori* are all good sources of articles where multivariate statistics are used, with the last of these producing an annual round-up of publications in quantitative archaeology that includes multivariate applications. For discussions of the way statistics are, or have been, used in particular laboratories or for specific problems (such as the analysis of ceramic compositions) see Bieber *et al.* (1976), Harbottle (1976), Pollard (1986), Neff (1992) and Beier and Mommsen (1994). That the main techniques covered in this chapter have been extensively used over the last 20 years or so and continue to enjoy widespread application reflects, one hopes, their usefulness in making sense of complex archaeological data. It is likely, therefore, that while newer techniques will be explored, the exploratory multivariate methods discussed here will continue to see wide service in the analysis of archaeological data.

REFERENCES

*Recommended for further reading

Banfield, J.D. and Raftery, A.E. (1993). Model-based Gaussian and non-Gaussian clustering. *Biometrics*, **49**:803–821.

*Baxter, M.J. (1994a). *Exploratory Multivariate Analysis in Archaeology*. Edinburgh University Press: Edinburgh.

Baxter, M.J. (1994b). Stepwise discriminant analysis in archaeology – a critique. *Journal of Archaeological Science*, **21**:659–666.

Baxter, M.J. (1995). Standardization and transformation in principal component analysis, with applications to archaeometry. *Applied Statistics*, **44**:513–527.

*Baxter, M.J. and Buck, C.E. (2000). Data handling and statistical analysis. In Ciliberto, E. and Spoto, G. (eds) *Modern Analytical Methods in Art and Archaeology*, 681–746. John Wiley: New York.

Beier, T. and Mommsen, H. (1994). Modified Mahalanobis filters for grouping pottery by chemical composition. *Archaeometry*, **36**:287–306.

Bell, S. and Croson, C. (1998). Artificial neural networks as a tool for archaeological data analysis. *Archaeometry*, **40**:139–151.

Bieber, A.M., Brooks, D.W., Harbottle, G. and Sayre, E.V. (1976). Application of multivariate techniques to analytical data on Aegean ceramics. *Archaeometry*, **18**:59–74.

Bishop, R.L. and Neff, H. (1989). Compositional data analysis in archaeology. In Allen, R.O. (ed.) *Archaeological Chemistry IV*, 57–86. Advances in Chemistry Series 220, American Chemical Society: Washington DC.

*Buck, C.E., Cavanagh, W.G. and Litton, C.D. (1996). *The Bayesian Approach to Archaeological Data Interpretation*. John Wiley: Chichester.

Cool, H.E.M. and Baxter, M.J. (1999). Glass vessel assemblages in Roman Britain: an aspect of Romanization. *Journal of Roman Archaeology*, **12**:72–100.

Cox, T.F. and Cox, M.A.A. (1994). *Multidimensional Scaling*. Chapman and Hall: London.

*Drennan, R.D. (1996). *Statistics for Archaeologists*. Plenum Press: New York.

Everitt, B.S. (1993). *Cluster Analysis* (3rd edn). Edward Arnold: London.

Everitt, B.S. and Dunn, G. (1991). *Applied Multivariate Data Analysis*. Edward Arnold: London.

Glascock, M.D. (1992). Characterization of archaeological ceramics at MURR by neutron activation analysis and multivariate statistics. In Neff, H. (ed.) *Chemical Characterization of Ceramic Pastes in Archaeology*, 11–26. Prehistory Press: Madison, Wisconsin.

Gower, J.C. and Hand, D.J. (1996). *Biplots*. Chapman and Hall: London.

Greenacre M.J. (1993). *Correspondence Analysis in Practice*. Academic Press: London.

Harbottle, G. (1976). Activation analysis in archaeology. *Radiochemistry*, **3**:33–72.

Jolliffe, I.T. (1986). *Principal Component Analysis*. Springer-Verlag: New York.

Jones, M.C. and Sibson, R .(1987). What is projection pursuit? *Journal of The Royal Statistical Society Series A*, **150**:1–36.

Krzanowski, W.J. (1995). *Recent Advances in Descriptive Multivariate Analysis*. Oxford University Press: Oxford.

Krzanowski, W.J. and Marriott, F.H.C. (1994). *Multivariate Analysis: Part 1 – Distributions, Ordination and Inference*. Edward Arnold: London.

Krzanowski, W.J. and Marriott, F.H.C. (1995). *Multivariate Analysis: Part 2 – Classification, Covariance Structures and Repeated Measurements*. Edward Arnold: London.

Manly, B.F.J. (1994). *Multivariate Statistical Methods* (2nd edn). Chapman and Hall: London.

McLachlan, G.J. (1992). *Discriminant Analysis and Statistical Pattern Recognition*. John Wiley: New York.

McLachlan, G.J. and Basford, K.E. (1988). *Mixture Models*. Marcel Dekker: New York.

Neff, H. (ed.) (1992). *Chemical Characterization of Ceramic Pastes in Archaeology*. Prehistory Press: Madison, Wisconsin.

Neff, H. (1994). RQ-mode principal components analysis of ceramic compositional data. *Archaeometry*, **36**:115–130.

Pollard, A.M. (1983). A critical study of multivariate methods as applied to provenance data. In Aspinall, A. and Warren, S.E. (eds) *Proceedings of the 22nd Symposium on Archaeometry*, 56–66. University of Bradford: Bradford.

Pollard, A.M. (1986). Data analysis. In Jones, R.E. (ed.) *Greek and Cypriot Pottery: A Review of Scientific Studies*, 56–83. Fitch Laboratory Occasional Paper 1, British School at Athens: Athens.

Pollard, A.M. and Hatcher, H. (1986). The chemical analysis of oriental ceramic body compositions: part 2 – greenwares. *Journal of Archaeological Science*, **13**:261–287.

Ripley, B.D. (1996). *Pattern Recognition and Neural Networks*. Cambridge University Press: Cambridge.

Scott, A., Whittaker, J., Green, M. and Hillson, S. (1991). Graphical modelling of archaeological data. In Lockyear, K. and Rahtz, S.P.Q. (eds) *Computer Applications and Quantitative Methods in Archaeology 1990*, 111–116. BAR International Series 565, British Archaeological Reports: Oxford.

*Shennan, S. (1997). *Quantifying Archaeology*, (2nd edn). Edinburgh University Press: Edinburgh.

Venables, W.N. and Ripley, B.D. (1997). *Modern Applied Statistics with S-Plus*, (2nd edn). Springer-Verlag: New York.

55

Applications of the Bayesian Statistical Paradigm

C.E. BUCK

School of History and Archaeology, Cardiff University.

In this section, we look at a framework for statistical data interpretation that some people feel has particular advantages for archaeology. This approach is based on the work of Thomas Bayes (1763) and allows for prior information (available before the research was undertaken) to be incorporated with the current data and integrated coherently into the interpretation process. Since much archaeological research builds on work that has gone before it, the ability to make use of prior information is seen by some as a distinct advantage.

The Bayesian approach to data analysis is model-based, rather than exploratory, and is not usually adopted in the early stages of research in a given subject area. When investigating a new type of data for the first time, we are commonly most interested in summarizing or illustrating our findings and are not seeking statistical tools that will play a formal part in the interpretation process. In such situations, we adopt a range of standard tools (such as histograms, x-y plots and means and standard deviations) that are now available by adopting spreadsheets and other software commonly installed on desktop computers.

In order to move beyond data exploration and towards interpretation, however, archaeologists sometimes seek to build statistical models that will form the core of formal statistical procedures. To do this we must understand (or have formal hypotheses about) at least something of the processes that gave rise to the data we observe today. Statistical modelling provides a well defined framework for setting down the relationship between what we understand and what we wish to learn about.

Although in much of archaeological research our understanding of such relationships is poor, there are some cases in archaeological science where substantial research has resulted in us being able to build quite reasonable models that can be used in the interpretative process. A Bayesian statistician would argue that, in such situations, any available prior information should be explicitly included as part of the statistical investigation and, thus, be allowed to have a bearing on the results obtained. Clearly, there are both philosophical and theoretical issues associated with adopting such a framework. References to theoretical works are given below, but readers interested in the philosophical aspects will find Howson and Urbach (1993) interesting.

THE USE OF PROBABILITY FOR FORMALIZING IDEAS

In order to formalize our ideas about what we know and what we want to learn about, statisticians (amongst others) commonly use the concept of probability. This is necessary since almost nothing of what we observe in the real world can ever be measured or recorded with

Handbook of Archaeological Sciences. Edited by D.R. Brothwell and A.M. Pollard.

certainty. Thus, we can only represent the features of the world we are studying (past, present or future) if we have a formal framework for reporting and calculating uncertainties. This is exactly what formal probability theory is used for. The details of the theory (indeed its basics) are beyond the scope of this chapter, but are described from a Bayesian perspective (in an introductory fashion) in Lee (1997) and in more detail in O'Hagan (1988) and Bernardo and Smith (1994). Here we simply discuss probability, outlining in an intuitive manner how and why it is important in Bayesian interpretation.

Most people use at least some probability concepts in their everyday language and are even used to interpreting other people's probability statements. The most common of these is the weather forecast in which we are told, for example, that there is a 75 per cent chance of rain tomorrow in the town in which we live. Most people feel that they can usefully interpret such statements and are likely to be aware that the forecaster is telling us that (s)he believes that there is a 3 in 4 chance of rain and only a 1 in 4 chance that it will stay dry. This assessment is based upon the skill, judgement and experience of the weather forecaster, the current data from satellites and ground-based weather stations, the skill of the other workers in the meteorology office, etc.

There are an enormous number of mechanisms for arriving at probability assessments and the specific ones selected depend upon the nature of the available information and the use to which it will be put. No matter how they are obtained, however, probabilities should always be quoted in units that are scalable to the range zero to one. Once on that scale, the sum of the probabilities for all possible events should be one.

As with most measurements made to help us understand the world, having an agreed scale on which observations are recorded is really helpful, but is certainly not sufficient to make it an interpretative tool. All assessments of probability are only as useful as the precision with which they have been obtained. When the weather forecaster tells us that there is a 75 per cent chance of rain tomorrow, what do they really mean? In reality, of course, there is some error that is not being reported. We are all used to assuming that there is error associated with weather forecasting and we simply allow for that, in some heuristic way, when utilizing the probability assessment supplied.

When using probability assessment to aid in the interpretation of data from archaeology we must be prepared to consider the uncertainty, estimate it where possible, and make use of it in any interpretations we undertake. This is true regardless of whether we are assessing prior probability or interpreting probability statements which arise from calculations based upon field or laboratory data that we wish to interpret.

AN OUTLINE OF THE FRAMEWORK

Bayesian statisticians believe that the concepts of uncertainty, probability and subjectivity are all interrelated and are not usefully separated when we come to make interpretations. The Bayesian statistical framework has at its core just one theorem, known as Bayes' theorem, which is intuitively very simple. If we represent the data that we have collected using the symbol x and use θ to represent the feature(s) of our model that we are trying to learn about, then θ is usually referred to as the parameter(s) of the model. Given x and a model with parameter(s) θ, Bayes' theorem then has three components which need exploration: the *likelihood*, the *prior*, and the *posterior*.

The *likelihood* is a statistical function whose form is determined by the specific statistical model we are using but which can, in general terms, be represented by $P(x|\theta)$. Here, P represents probability and $|$ is read as 'given'. Consequently, the likelihood is the probability of observing particular data values given some specific values of the unknown parameters. Thus this is a formal statement of the relationship between what we want to learn about and the data we collect.

The *prior* is also a function and can be represented by $P(\theta)$. In simple terms, we can think of this as the probability we attach to observing specified values of the unknown parameters before (*a priori*) we observe the data. In other words, this is a formal statement of what we knew before the latest data were collected.

The *posterior* is what we want to obtain (a combination of the information contained in the data, the likelihood and the prior) and can be represented by $P(\theta|x)$. In simple terms, we can think of this as the probability we attach to specified values of the unknown parameters after observing the data.

Bayes' theorem relates these three components thus:

Posterior $\propto$ likelihood $\times$ prior

or:

$$P(\theta|x) \propto P(x|\theta) \times P(\theta)$$

Here $\propto$ means 'proportional to' and, since the sum of all possible posterior values must be one, we can scale the results to provide posterior information on the probability scale.

Bayes' theorem thus provides a mechanism for obtaining *a posteriori* information about the parameter values of interest based upon the data, a model and appropriately formulated prior information. In other words, given an explicit statement of our *a priori* information, a clearly defined statistical model and a desire to obtain *a posteriori* understanding, Bayes' theorem provides us with a probabilistic framework within which to make interpretations.

In addition to the coherent and explicit nature of the framework, there is another attractive feature of adopting the Bayesian paradigm in that it allows us to learn from experience. Today's posterior information (based on current data and prior information) is in a suitable form to become the prior for further work if and when more data become available. Few other interpretative frameworks offer a clear structure for updating belief in the light of new information and yet it is such an important part of most intuitive approaches to learning about the world in which we live.

By way of an intuitive explanation, consider what is involved in arriving at an understanding of the chronology of a newly excavated site. There are many types of information that have a bearing on the calendar dates attributed to activity at a site, but one common method is to seek organic material that can be radiocarbon dated. Suppose that in the first season at a newly discovered site we obtain little in the way of stratified deposits, but do find a collection of charred grains associated with a cooking fire. These grains are the best chance for obtaining a calendar date estimate for the site and so they are submitted to a dating laboratory.

When interpreting the radiocarbon determination obtained, we have very little *a priori* information about the likely date except the broad chronological period on the basis of other evidence. Thus, provided the calendar date estimate is from the appropriate broad time period we can do little more than accept it at face value. In subsequent seasons, however, this estimate could be used as *a priori* information to inform further programmes of dating. Over several seasons we would hope that a range of evidence might lead to a refined chronological picture of the site, with each season's results being used to aid the interpretation of those obtained in subsequent years. As shown below, the mathematical methods required to integrate such complex sources of information can be quite sophisticated, but the basic philosophical framework remains the same throughout.

RADIOCARBON DATING

Consider a single archaeological event which relates directly to the death of an organic object (for example

the burning of a seed). By dating this object we hope to obtain information about the calendar date for the archaeological event; we denote this date by θ. Associated with θ is a unique 'radiocarbon age', $\mu(\theta)$, which relates to the amount of ^{14}C present in the sample when it is measured by the radiocarbon dating laboratory (see Chapter 2). Unfortunately, $\mu(\theta)$ is not available precisely, in fact what the radiocarbon laboratory provides is x which is an estimate of $\mu(\theta)$. As explained in Chapter 2, x can be seen as a particular realization of a random variable X where:

$$X = \mu(\theta) + \text{noise}.$$

The model

The *noise* is assumed to have a normal distribution with mean zero and standard deviation σ which is conventionally represented as:

$$X \sim N(\mu(\theta), \sigma^2).$$

The exact form of $\mu(\theta)$ is not known and this is why a calibration curve is needed (again see Chapter 2). The calibration data usually take the form of decadal or bidecadal measurements of known-age material which provide us with piecewise linear calibration curves of the sort used by archaeologists all over the world (an example extracted from such a curve is shown in Figure 55.1). To complete our model, we need a formal statement of the calibration curve thus:

$$\mu(\theta) = \begin{cases} a_1 + b_1\theta & (\theta \geq t_0) \\ a_k + b_k\theta & (t_k - 1 \geq \theta < t_k, \ k = 1, 2, \ldots, K) \\ a_K = b_K\theta & (\theta > t_K) \end{cases}$$

where t_k are called the 'knots' of the calibration curve, $K + 1$ is the number of bi-decadal measurements (or knots) used to define the calibration curve and the a_ks and b_ks are known constants for each straight line that makes up the piecewise linear curve.

The likelihood

Given the piecewise linear model formulation for the calibration curve, and the normal distribution used to model the relationship between the radiocarbon determination and the calibration data, the likelihood takes the form:

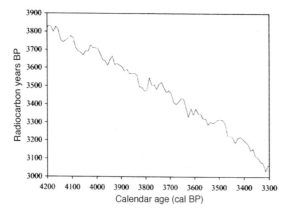

Figure 55.1   Plot of the terrestrial radiocarbon calibration curve between 4200 and 3300 cal BP (Stuiver *et al.* 1998).

$$\text{for } \theta \leq t_0 \qquad \frac{1}{\sqrt{2\pi}\sigma}\exp-\frac{(x-a_1-b_1\theta)^2}{2\sigma^2},$$

$$\text{for } t_{k-1} \geq \theta < t_k \qquad \frac{1}{\sqrt{2\pi}\sigma}\exp-\frac{(x-a_k-b_k\theta)^2}{2\sigma^2},$$

$$\text{for } \theta > t_K \qquad \frac{1}{\sqrt{2\pi}\sigma}\exp-\frac{(x-a_K-b_K\theta)^2}{2\sigma^2},$$

The prior

There are very many different types of prior information that can be important in radiocarbon calibration. Here we use a simple example, but much more complex types of information can also be utilized. Since most archaeological samples submitted for radiocarbon dating arise from excavation, it is quite common for us to have stratigraphic information that provides prior information about the order in which events occurred. Consider, for example, a situation in which we know *a priori* that θ_1 occurred before θ_2. Assuming that the calendar dates will be quoted as 'before present' (cal BP), we know that:

$$\theta_1 > \theta_2$$

Thus, *a priori*, all pairs of calendar dates, θ_1 and θ_2 are equally likely provided that the value of θ_1 is larger than θ_2. This can be represented formally thus:

$$P(\theta_1, \theta_2) = \begin{cases} 1 & \theta_1 > \theta_2 \\ 0 & \text{otherwise.} \end{cases}$$

The data

Each radiocarbon determination is composed of an estimate of the radiocarbon age (x) and the associated laboratory error (σ). In most situations, we will have just one radiocarbon determination associated with each archaeological event to be dated, but sometimes we will have more – we assume here that there is just one determination available for each of the two events, taken as 3470 ± 50 and 3480 ± 50 respectively.

The posteriors

Potentially, the posteriors are complex since the dates of many samples may all be related to one another. In our example, however, the posterior for each of the calendar dates of interest is simply restricted so that it does not contravene the restriction $\theta_1 > \theta_2$. Thus the posterior for θ_1 is:

$$P(\theta_1|x_1, x_2) = \sum_{\vartheta_1 > \vartheta_2} P(\theta_1, \theta_2|x_1, x_2)$$

and similarly for the posterior probability of θ_2.

Consider first what happens if the two determinations are calibrated separately (until recently the only way that this calibration could be undertaken). In this situation, the values of θ_1 and θ_2 are not dependent upon one another and can lie anywhere within the range of the calibration curve. Upon calibration, we obtain the calendar date distributions shown in Figure 55.2. The two distributions are almost the same, unsurprisingly, since the radiocarbon determinations themselves are very similar, and the reported standard errors are large by comparison with the difference between the estimated means.

Now, implementing the Bayesian paradigm allows us to incorporate the stratigraphic information into the calibration process. The calendar date distributions that result are shown in Figure 55.3. Notice that the distributions cover shorter time periods (when compared to Figure 55.2) because all pairs of dates that contravene the stated relationship $\theta_1 > \theta_2$ are excluded.

Although this example is simple, it shows that including the stratigraphic information as part of the calibration process does produce noticeably different posterior calendar date distributions. Often, this will lead to quite a different understanding of the chronology of the site or landscape under study. In situations where the available prior information is more complex (or there are more events or phases involved), computing the posteriors can be time consuming and require

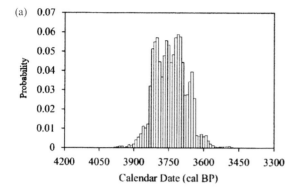

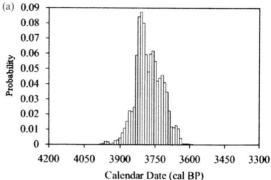

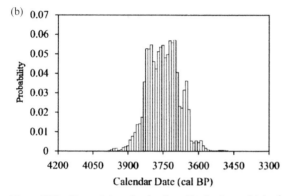

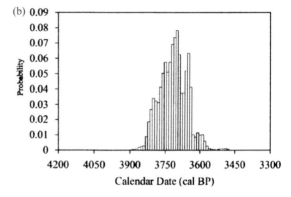

Figure 55.2 Plots of the calendar date distributions obtained for (a) θ_1 and (b) θ_2 when the stratigraphic relationship between the samples is ignored.

considerable computing power. Nonetheless, the same basic framework holds and can be shown to be appropriate for even very complex relative temporal information. Further basic information about Bayesian radiocarbon calibration is given by Buck *et al.* (1996), and more detailed discussions in Buck *et al.* (1991, 1992, 1994a, 1994b), Christen (1994a, 1994b), Christen and Litton (1995) and Zeidler *et al.* (1998). There is software available for undertaking Bayesian radiocarbon calibration, for example, OxCal by Bronk Ramsey (1995) and BCal at http://bcal.cf.ac.uk.

OTHER ARCHAEOLOGICAL APPLICATIONS

Although radiocarbon calibration is thus far the most well-known use of Bayesian statistics in archaeology, there have been a number of other published case studies, which are briefly summarized here.

The megalithic yard

The very first published application of Bayesian statistics in archaeology was that of Freeman (1976).

Figure 55.3 Plots of the calendar date distributions obtained for (a) θ_1 and (b) θ_2 when the prior information that θ_1 is older than θ_2 is included in the calibration process.

Freeman took the work of Thom (1967) and reconsidered the possibility of the existence of a megalithic unit of measurement known as the 'megalithic yard'. From surveys of an enormous number of megalithic stone circles, Thom had suggested that such a unit did exist, but Freeman felt that this claim was worthy of reassessment within the Bayesian framework. Freeman's results did not concur with those of Thom, as he did not find any evidence for a single quantum used for all monuments in the UK. He did, however, look at regional data and found some evidence for local quanta, particularly for the west of Scotland.

Image processing

Bayesian image processing is a huge area of research in its own right. Here we simply draw the reader's attention to the fact that these procedures exist and note that there can be great advantages to including prior information in the analysis of noisy image data (any digital data that contains a spatial component we wish to plot and interpret). In archaeology, such data commonly arise from geophysical, chemical and field surveys of archaeological sites or landscapes. Exploratory methods for investigating such data (such as dot density plots, grey scales and contours) have been widely and successfully used by archaeologists and geophysicists, but they do not always lead directly to archaeological interpretations.

Typically, archaeological survey data have a low signal to noise ratio which means that the information can be masked. As a consequence, reliable interpretations are only possible if the signal can be enhanced and/or the noise reduced. There are a large number of procedures for doing this, but if there is some *a priori* information about the nature of the image we are looking for, a Bayesian approach can be enormously helpful. Such methodologies are discussed from an archaeological perspective in Buck *et al.* (1996) and in more general terms by Besag and Green (1993) and Ripley (1988).

Cluster analysis

Commonly archaeologists seek to identify groupings in their data that relate to archaeological phenomena. Usually such groupings are identified by the use of one or other of the many techniques of cluster analysis (see Chapter 54). Some of these are exploratory in nature and others are model-based. In order to adopt model-based approaches, we must have some understanding of the processes that gave rise to the data we observe, or have a clear hypothesis that can be represented in statistical terms. Many researchers feel that this is not possible with archaeological data and use almost exclusively exploratory methods, but others feel there is much to gain from model-based approaches.

If we adopt a model-based approach, then there will be some situations in which prior information is available about the nature of the clusters we are trying to locate, and thus a Bayesian cluster analysis might be used. Buck (1994) suggests an approach which is suitable for aiding in the interpretation of continuous data (such as chemical compositional data from ceramics) and Dellaportas (1998) describes an approach which is suitable for both continuous and categorical data (such as observations of the physical characteristics of stone tools). A number of illustrative examples have been published, e.g., Buck *et al.* (1996), Buck and Litton (1996), Baxter and Buck (2000) and

Dellaportas (1998). Note, however, that a Bayesian cluster analysis gives rise to posterior probability assessments about which samples are likely to form a coherent cluster on the basis of the data, the model and any prior information that is available. A great deal of information is built into the analyses and it is vital to be open minded about other possible models, whether the data are of sufficiently high quality, and the nature of the prior information included. Re-analyses using different models, data and/or priors must be undertaken in order to establish the sensitivity of the results, before using them to make inferences.

Seriation

Seriation is a technique for chronologically ordering archaeological contexts, such as graves, on the basis of the presence/absence or frequencies of particular artifacts found in them. A range of statistical approaches to seriation have been developed over many years (see Buck *et al.* 1996). Most of these approaches result in a single 'best' ordering of the contexts, but do not suggest other likely orderings that are feasible given that minor errors in recording the information are inevitable, or that some objects have been lost through decay or lack of retrieval. Buck and Litton (1991) and Buck *et al.* (1996) suggest a Bayesian approach to seriation which overcomes both of these shortcomings and, of course, allows prior information (where available) to be included in the interpretative process. The methodology has, however, not been widely tested and further research is in progress to devise a flexible and robust Bayesian approach to seriation, e.g., Halekoh and Vach (forthcoming) and Buck and Sahu (forthcoming).

Human age estimation

Human age estimates can usefully be made on the basis of morphological changes in teeth. Traditionally, a range of indicators have been scored on individuals of known and unknown age and a regression analysis adopted to establish the age of each of the unknown individuals. Lucy *et al.* (1996) provide a literature review of previous work in this area and reassess the statistical techniques adopted. They suggest that advances could be made by formulating the problem within the Bayesian framework. Their results are not substantially different from those obtained using the previous methods, but they are probabilistic and allow for the possibility of the inclusion of prior information and the coherent updating of information in the light of new data.

SOME PRACTICALITIES

Modelling

Due to features like the piecewise linear calibration curve adopted for radiocarbon calibration, many archaeological problems are statistically non-standard. This has often meant that close collaboration is required between a number of specialists including statisticians if useful models are to be built. Fortunately, statisticians have often found archaeological problems interesting and challenging and so this kind of collaboration is not too unusual. Nonetheless, applications of Bayesian analysis to archaeology have been around for more than 20 years and they are by no means standard; further collaboration is certainly still needed.

Specifying the prior

One of the major stumbling blocks to more widespread use of Bayesian techniques in archaeology is the perceived difficulty of specifying prior information. Some archaeologists do not acknowledge that reliable prior information exists and prefer to continue using exploratory methods or traditional model-based ones. Others have difficulty expressing their ideas in a suitable form because of their lack of knowledge about the mathematics which underlies the models they wish to use. Tackling this problem requires further collaboration, clear communication and an acceptance that different researchers will have varying views about which interpretative framework to use or which specific model to adopt. Most importantly, there is no need for everyone to agree. Researchers who adopt the Bayesian framework are forced to be explicit about what they believe and thus different workers can compute posteriors based on their own prior information and then compare the posterior probability distributions obtained.

Evaluating the posteriors

Early applications of the Bayesian framework to archaeology (as with other disciplines) were restricted to likelihoods and priors for which the necessary calculations could easily be undertaken. Since the mathematical integrations required for some models are not analytically soluble, however, quite a lot of real questions simply could not be tackled. These problems are now rapidly being overcome with recent advances in numerical techniques which allow the posterior information to be sampled rather than obtained exactly. Some of the earliest illustrations of the use of these techniques for evaluating Bayesian posteriors were in Bayesian radiocarbon calibration (see above). Indeed, one particularly successful form of sampling known as the Gibbs sampler (a type of Markov chain Monte Carlo simulation) is at the core of many of the widely used Bayesian radiocarbon calibration techniques and is described in Litton and Buck (1996). For those interested in the use of Markov chains for undertaking Bayesian inference in general, there are now a number of books including Gilks et al. (1996) and Gamerman (1997).

Interpretation

Ultimately, the most important part of any statistical investigation is the interpretation of the results obtained. The posterior distributions that arise from Bayesian analyses can be very complex and are sometimes not directly interpretable in terms of the original problem. This means that exploratory methods of data analysis may be needed to help investigate, interpret and report upon the posterior distributions obtained. When making such interpretations, the level of our confidence in the posteriors should be affected by their sensitivity to changes in the data, prior or model parameterization. Such sensitivity should be investigated as part of the interpretation of all posterior information. It is always useful to relax some of the prior assumptions and re-compute the posteriors to see what effect this has. All reports of Bayesian analyses should make reference to sensitivity analysis of this type, since without them we cannot be at all sure how robust the results are and thus how reliable they are as prior information for future research.

LOOKING AHEAD

The use of modern statistical methods to aid in archaeological interpretation is growing. There has been much success in terms of acceptance of the potentials by both statisticians and archaeologists. For example, the Bayesian radiocarbon framework is now widely accepted as a powerful tool in archaeological interpretation. Indeed, some funding agencies will not fund new radiocarbon dating projects unless researchers commit to undertake interpretations in this way. Greater understanding of the complexities of the issues involved is still needed by members of both disciplines. The need for modelling skills, programming skills and powerful computers means that archaeologists will, for the time being at least, need to collaborate with statisticians. However, statisticians are usually very keen to work on the interesting problems that arise from cutting edge archaeological research and so both disciplines stand to gain by collaboration. In order to do this successfully, however, experts on both sides now need to look at their own disciplines from a slightly different perspective and start to look for further useful areas of collaboration.

REFERENCES

*Recommended for further reading

Baxter, M.J. and Buck, C.E. (2000). Data handling and statistical analysis. In Ciliberto, E. and Spoto, G. (eds) *Modern Analytical Methods in Art and Archaeology*, 681–746. John Wiley: New York.

Bayes, T.R. (1763). An essay towards solving a problem in the doctrine of chances. *Philosophical Transactions of the Royal Society*, **53**:370–418.

*Bernardo, J.M. and Smith, A.F.M. (1994) *Bayesian Theory*. John Wiley: Chichester.

Besag, J. and Green, P.J. (1993). Spatial statistics and Bayesian computation. *Journal of the Royal Statistical Society*, **B55**:25–37.

Bronk Ramsey, C. (1995). Radiocarbon calibration and analysis of stratigraphy: the OxCal program. *Radiocarbon*, **37**:425–430.

Buck, C.E. (1994). *Towards Bayesian Archaeology*. Unpublished PhD Dissertation, University of Nottingham.

Buck, C.E. and Litton, C.D. (1991). A computational Bayes approach to some common archaeological problems. In Lockyear, K. and Rahtz, S.P.Q. (eds) *Computer Applications and Quantitative Methods in Archaeology 1990*, 93–99. Tempus Reparatum: Oxford.

Buck, C.E. and Litton, C.D. (1996). Mixtures, Bayes and archaeology. In Bernardo, J.M., Berger, J., David, A.P. and Smith, A.F.M. (eds) *Bayesian Statistics 5*, 499–506. Oxford University Press: Oxford.

Buck, C.E. and Sahu, S.K. (forthcoming). Bayesian model selection for relative chronology building. *Applied Statistics*.

Buck, C.E., Kenworthy, J.B., Litton, C.D. and Smith, A.F.M. (1991). Combining archaeological and radiocarbon information: a Bayesian approach to calibration. *Antiquity*, **65**:808–821.

Buck, C.E., Litton, C.D. and Smith, A.F.M. (1992). Calibration of radiocarbon results pertaining to related archaeological events. *Journal of Archaeological Science*, **19**:497–512.

Buck, C.E., Christen, J.A., Kenworthy, J.B. and Litton, C.D (1994a). Estimating the duration of archaeological activity using ^{14}C determinations. *Oxford Journal of Archaeology*, **13**:229–240.

Buck, C.E., Litton, C.D. and Shennan, S.J. (1994b). A case study in combining radiocarbon and archaeological information: the early Bronze Age settlement of St Veit-Klinglberg, Land Salzburg, Austria. *Germania*, **2**:427–447.

*Buck, C.E., Cavanagh, W.G. and Litton, C.D. (1996). *The Bayesian Approach to Interpreting Archaeological Data*. John Wiley: Chichester.

Christen, J.A. (1994a). *Bayesian Interpretation of ^{14}C Results*. Unpublished PhD Dissertation, University of Nottingham.

Christen, J.A. (1994b). Summarising a set of radiocarbon determinations: a robust approach. *Applied Statistics*, **43**:489–503.

Christen, J.A. and Litton, C.D. (1995). A Bayesian approach to wiggle-matching. *Journal of Archaeological Science*, **22**:719–725.

Dellaportas, P. (1998). Bayesian classification of Neolithic tools. *Applied Statistics*, **47**:279–297.

Freeman, P.R. (1976). A Bayesian approach to the megalithic yard. *Journal of the Royal Statistical Society*, **A139**:20–55.

Gamerman, D. (1997). *Markov Chain Monte Carlo: Stochastic Simulation for Bayesian Inference*. Chapman and Hall: London.

Gilks, W., Richardson, S. and Spiegelhalter, D.J. (1996). *Markov Chain Monte Carlo in Practice*. Chapman and Hall: London.

Halekoh, U. and Vach, W. (forthcoming). A Bayesian approach to seriation problems in archaeology. *Applied Statistics*.

Howson, C. and Urbach, P. (1993). *Scientific Reasoning: the Bayesian Approach*, (2nd edn). Open Court: Illinois.

*Lee, P.M. (1997) *Bayesian Statistics: an Introduction*, (2nd edn). Arnold: London.

Litton, C.D. and Buck, C.E. (1996). An archaeological example: radiocarbon dating. In Gilks, W., Richardson, S. and Spiegelhalter, D. (eds) *Markov Chain Monte Carlo in Practice*, 465–480. Chapman and Hall: London.

Lucy, D., Aykroyd, R.G., Pollard, A.M. and Solheim, T. (1996). A Bayesian approach to adult human age estimation from dental observations by Gustafson's method. *Journal of Forensic Sciences*, **41**:189–194.

O'Hagan, A. (1988). *Probability: Methods and Measurements*. Chapman and Hall: London.

Ripley, B.D. (1988). *Statistical Inference for Spatial Processes*. Cambridge University Press: Cambridge.

Stuiver, M., Reimer, P.J., Bard, E., Beck, J.W., Burr, G.S., Hughes, K.A., Kromer, B., McCormac, F.G., van der Plicht, J. and Spurk, M. (1998). INTCAL98 radiocarbon age calibration 24 000–0 cal BP. *Radiocarbon*, **40**:1041–1083.

Thom, A. (1967). *Megalithic Sites in Britain*. Clarendon Press: Oxford.

Zeidler, J.A., Buck, C.E. and Litton, C.D. (1998). The integration of archaeological phase information and radiocarbon results from the Jama River Valley, Ecuador: a Bayesian approach. *Latin American Antiquity*, **9**:135–159.

56

Animal Bone Quantification

T.P. O'CONNOR

Department of Archaeology, University of York.

This chapter reviews the principal methods used for quantifying the taxa present in archaeological animal bone assemblages. A technique which is satisfactory as a means of describing the recovered assemblage may be a poor means of inferring information about the death assemblage from which it derives, and techniques which focus on the death assemblage may not give useful information about the original population. Most quantification methods can be shown to be closely inter-correlated, and many are correlated with sample size. Sample size is also closely, but non-linearly, correlated with taxonomic diversity. Iterative simulations can show how different techniques behave under limiting conditions, though their main value is in showing the degree of stochastic variability inherent in most of the commonly-used procedures. NISP (*Number of Identified Specimens*) techniques have the merit of being simply descriptive. MNI-based procedures (*Minimum Number of Individuals*) suffer from arbitrary subjectivity in their original estimation, and the data cannot be subjected to further numerical analysis. Weight methods are compromised by, amongst other things, the inevitable inclusion of silt and clay. Killed-population estimates are of some heuristic value, but raise the problem of defining the killed population which is being estimated. Semi-quantitative procedures are briefly reviewed, and are particularly recommended for material recovered by sieving.

ANIMAL BONE QUANTIFICATION

The purpose of quantifying archaeological bone assemblages is to establish 'how much' there is of different identified taxa in each of, or all of, a series of samples. This simple statement obviously begs the question of what constitutes an identifiable taxon, and what constitutes the 'sample'. The first matter is a significant question in its own right, but is beyond the remit of the present chapter (see O'Connor 2000:36). For the present purposes, the sample comprises the bones recovered by whatever means from whatever stratigraphic unit or volume of sediment has been taken as the unit of study.

Animal bone quantification can be undertaken in a number of different ways, and this chapter starts from the premise that there is no 'right' way; rather that different techniques have their strengths and weaknesses. There have been almost as many different quantification methods applied to bone assemblages as there have been specialists analysing them. Although this approach may appear to compromise inter-observer comparisons, there is much to be said for adapting an essentially imperfect methodology to suit the research in hand. This chapter sets out to consider some of the more commonly used procedures, based on;

(i)   raw counts of identified specimens (NISP, TNF),

Handbook of Archaeological Sciences. Edited by D.R. Brothwell and A.M. Pollard.
© 2001 John Wiley & Sons, Ltd.

(ii)   the weight of identified fragments,

(iii) the estimation of the minimum number of individuals in the identified sample (MNI), and

(iv)   those methods which seek to estimate the 'killed population' which has contributed to the sample.

The most detailed treatment of the subject to date remains that of Grayson (1984). Ringrose (1993) gives a statistician's view, and raises a number of important points, and Moreno-Garcia *et al.* (1996) demonstrate a quite different approach to the problem.

DESCRIBING THE SAMPLE

The simplest way of quantifying an animal bone sample is to count up the number of specimens attributed to each taxon in the sample. These procedures are often described either as *Number of Identified Specimens* (NISP) or *Total Number of Fragments* (TNF) methods. They are measures of abundance, telling us 'how much' we have of each taxon in each sample. The raw count is the *absolute abundance*, and the raw counts converted to a percentage or proportion of the total number of specimens in the sample can be regarded as the *relative abundance*. NISP methods have the twin merits of simplicity, and of providing a quantified description of what the analyst recorded in that sample (O'Connor 1985a).

NISP methods tend to be used in different ways by different analysts, and the working method should be defined for each published analysis. For example, a 'specimen' may be a single bone or a fragment, but there is an obvious choice to be made with material which has undergone fragmentation during storage and handling. A group of fragments obviously derived from the same freshly-broken bone could comprise one specimen. Whether NISP data convey information about the death assemblage or the living population is questionable. Some individual animals could each be counted many times over in any set of NISP data, yet NISP methods implicitly treat each recorded specimen as a separate individual. When NISP data are used only as a description of the recovered sample, the repeated counting of individual animals is not a problem. However, the interdependence of fragments becomes significant when the interpretation of NISP data steps across the line between the recovered sample and the death assemblage from which it is derived. Gautier (1984) has suggested that the assumption of each fragment representing a different individual may often be valid because taphonomic attrition is so high.

He argues that the higher the degree of taphonomic attrition, the lower the probability of any one individual contributing more than one fragment to the recovered assemblage. Whilst there is an appealing logic in this argument, it assumes that taphonomic factors at the point of death and sedimentation act evenly on each individual in the death assemblage. Actualistic data, and a little speculative thought, suggests that this is seldom the case.

Grayson (1979:201, 1984:20) discusses this problem of interdependence at some length, and also reviews the effect which the degree of fragmentation may have on the data, complicating comparison between samples where the degree and pattern of fragmentation differ. The distorting effects of fragmentation are also discussed by Chase and Hagaman (1987) and by Ringrose (1993). Noe-Nygaard (1979) discusses a case in which bones have been processed for marrow, and the resulting fragmentation has a marked effect on the quantification of the assemblage. Faced with highly-fragmented material from Neolithic sites in Greece, Watson (1979) developed an interesting alternative to NISP, shifting the quantification away from Linnaean taxonomy towards a typology of fragment categories. His recommended procedure has not been generally adopted, despite its utility in overcoming some of the problems caused by fragmentation. Fragmentation is particularly high in material recovered by sieving (screening) and the improved recovery of small elements such as carpals and loose teeth accentuates the interdependence problem. The simulations undertaken by Gilbert *et al.* (1982) showed that small samples of identified bones will represent the relative abundance of the more common taxa in the sampled population with lower precision than they will the less common taxa. In order for precision for all taxa to be about the same, these authors found that sample size had to be at least 2000 identified specimens. In this author's experience, obtaining 2000 identified specimens in a sample sieved on a 2 mm aperture mesh is likely to require the retrieval of at least 10 000 fragments. Unless deposits are exceptionally bone-rich, this could require processing sediment samples of the order of 500–1000 kg in weight. This is unlikely to be practicable for more than the occasional, exceptional sample.

NISP data are also distorted if some of the taxa involved have more identifiable bones per individual than others. For example, pigs have more toes and teeth than bovids, and unmodified NISP data systematically over-estimate pig remains relative to bovids. This effect is obviously more pronounced when comparing between mammals, birds and fishes, because of the big anatomical differences between these classes of vertebrate. Identification protocols may also be significant, as some taxa may be identifiable on a greater number of elements of the skeleton than others. Goats, for example, may only be confidently identifiable on a limited number of skeletal elements, so reducing the effective number of potential 'specimens' in the goat skeleton.

The most thorough published reviews of quantification methods dismiss NISP methods (Grayson 1984, Ringrose 1993, 1995, Pilgram and Marshall 1995, O'Connor 2000:54). Grayson (1984:96) shows that NISP (and MNI, below) data may be useful as an ordinal measure, and Winder (1991) also allows that NISP may serve to show the rank order of taxa. If that is the limit of utility of NISP methods, then much of the discussion regarding definition of 'countable specimens', and interdependence, would seem to be otiose. The fact remains, however, that NISP data are readily obtained, and do serve to describe the size and composition (scale and profile, *sensu* Winder 1991) of the sample. NISP data are valid for intersample comparisons in circumstances where biasing factors such as differential decay and recovery can be shown to have been of the same order and magnitude in all of the samples concerned. As estimators of the profiles of the original death assemblage, however, NISP data lack validity.

An alternative procedure is to weigh all of the fragments attributed to each taxon. Obviously, 100 fragments of cattle bone are likely to weigh much more than 100 similarly-fragmented fragments of cat bone. However, the weight of the skeleton is proportional to the weight of the whole live animal, and herein lies the attraction of quantification by weighing. Kubasiewicz (1956) introduced the procedure, applying quantification by weight in order to quantify the relative dietary contribution of hunted mammal taxa. Kubasiewicz argued that as a predictable and sufficiently constant proportion of the weight of a mammal is its skeleton, and another is potentially edible muscle, then comparing the relative abundance of taxa by weight of bone fragments gives an estimate of their potential meat contribution.

Chaplin (1971) and Casteel (1978) set about rejecting quantification by weight with commendable vigour and clarity. There is the obvious problem of weighing bone fragments, rather than bones plus soil. Large volumes of cancellous tissue, such as longbone epiphyses or vertebral centra, may contain substantial amounts of sediment which resists washing, and may persist even through water-sieving. Differential destruction and

transport of bone fragments of different densities may cause a sample to contain a disproportionate amount of dense fragments, thus distorting the meat:bone weight comparison. There is also a difference between potential meat yield and actual meat usage. Differing cultural practices will result in more or less of the carcass of an animal being used, and so quantification by weight can only, at best, quantify potential yield.

Furthermore, bone weight does not comprise a constant proportion of the total body weight of an animal. A consequence of body-size allometry is that bigger animals require proportionally bigger bones to support their weight. Although this allometric scaling effect is quite minor within a narrow range of body weight, it becomes very marked in comparisons of taxa which differ substantially in body size. The relationship between bone weight (y) and body weight (x) is a power relationship of the form $y = a.x^b$ (Alexander *et al.* 1979, Prange *et al.* 1979, Jackson 1989). The exponent b may only be small, but this power relationship none the less precludes comparing the meat yield of, say, cattle, sheep, and chickens by direct comparison of the weight of fragments identified to those three taxa. Barrett (1993) has modified the weight method to take account of allometric scaling, but the problems of taphonomic effects and of cultural variation in utilization still remain, and quantification by weight must be seen as applicable only in rather particular circumstances.

ESTIMATING THE DEATH ASSEMBLAGE

NISP and weight methods clearly have their inherent problems, and many bone analysts prefer to estimate *Minimum Numbers of Individuals* (MNI). The aim of this procedure is to overcome the problem of interdependence and multiple counting of individual animals by making the individual animal, not the individual specimen, the counting unit. The MNI for a particular taxon is generally estimated by counting the most abundant non-reproducible element in the sample, usually with some adjustment being made for apparent left-right pairs (see below). The introduction of MNI methods to archaeology is generally credited to White (1953), although Casteel (1977a, 1977b) cites much earlier application in Russian sources. The procedure was popularized within archaeology by Chaplin (1971), and refined somewhat to take account of young and old individuals by Bökönyi (1970). In effect, Bökönyi suggested that separate MNI estimations should be made for each of several readily recognizable age categories, summing these estimates to give an overall MNI estimate for that taxon. One fundamental problem with MNI estimation is the necessity of 'pairing' left and right side specimens. This requires the construction of enantiomorphic pairs, as one can seldom be absolutely certain that a left-right pair definitely derived from one individual animal. Mammal and bird species show differing degrees of bilateral symmetry, and asymmetry within an individual may be of the same order as variation between individuals. Different observers will take a different view on the pairs present in a given sample, and quite minor inter-observer variations in the estimation of pairs can make a substantial difference to the eventual MNI estimate (O'Connor 1985b; see below). White (1953:397) rejected reconstruction of pairs as 'the expenditure of a great deal of effort with small return', presumably realizing how little information might be gained from the laborious reconstruction of pairs that might not be pairs.

Although many papers have been written on MNI estimation, only a few authors have stressed that MNI is only an estimate, as the real number of individuals represented in the sample cannot be calculated (e.g., Clason 1972). Grayson (1981, 1984:28) has been especially critical of MNI calculation, clearly doubting that it is measuring what we think it is measuring. He shows that MNI may be closely correlated with sample size (Grayson 1981), and thus with NISP, though Cruz-Uribe (1988) has cited examples to the contrary. Grayson's point is really that MNI *can* be closely correlated with sample size, whilst Cruz-Uribe shows that it may not *always* be so: the two positions are not mutually exclusive, nor does Cruz-Uribe's paper gainsay the original point. Grayson (1984:62) also shows that MNI values can be tightly predicted from NISP counts. Therefore, whatever information resides in MNI data also resides in NISP, so why take the extra step of calculating MNI? The answer is that MNI estimates are not biased in the same way as NISP by factors such as fragmentation. MNI has its own biases. For example, rare taxa are always over-estimated with MNI methods, and taxa with many identifiable specimens per individual are overestimated in highly fragmented assemblages, but under-estimated in assemblages with little fragmentation (Holzman 1979). Gilbert *et al.* (1982) showed by simulation that MNI values may need to be based on samples as large as 60–70 000 bones in order to achieve the same consistency in replicate sampling as is achieved by NISP (termed TNF in their paper) on samples of 2000 bones. Their figure of 60 000 fragments is clearly not intended as a realistic recommendation, but the simulation does serve to show

the sensitivity of MNI estimates to stochastic factors, and thus that the estimates obtained from archaeological samples are not robust.

Aggregation of sedimentary units is a problem with MNI. For example, if one phase of a site is represented by six refuse pits, the MNI estimate for sheep could be calculated by pooling all of the bones from the six pits and examining them as one sample, or by examining each pit as a separate sample, and then summing the six sheep MNI estimates. The latter procedure will almost invariably produce a much higher MNI estimate than the former. If bones from one individual are dispersed among two or more of the sampled pits, that individual will be counted in each separate MNI estimate, thus increasing the aggregated MNI estimate. This problem has been discussed by Grayson (1979, 1984:29) and Watson (1979), and is particularly well criticized by Ringrose (1993:126). This inflation of MNI estimates gives us some information about the origins of the recovered assemblage, by showing that different sediment catchments have sampled the life-space of the individual animal. An understanding of temporal and spatial catchments is obviously essential to an understanding of bone taphonomy (Winder 1991, O'Connor 1996). However, the analyst still has to decide how to subdivide material prior to making MNI estimates, and how to aggregate the data afterwards. Furthermore, in order to use the inflation of numbers analytically, one would have to know a baseline value, a 'minimum MNI', against which to quantify the degree of inflation. The best estimate for that figure would be the MNI estimate for the aggregated sample.

In fact, further numerical analysis or modification of MNI estimates is mathematically indefensible. MNI values are not finite integers, but minimum estimates (Plug and Plug 1990) – 'more than 20' cannot be added to 'more than 10' in any sensible way. It follows that MNI values from one sample cannot be added to those from another, and that MNI estimates for the taxa within one sample cannot be summed to obtain a total to convert MNI estimates to relative abundance measures. This resolves the problem of aggregation: the data cannot be arithmetically aggregated, so any aggregation of sedimentary units requires physical aggregation of the bone samples and complete re-analysis. Plug and Plug's concise paper leaves MNI estimation looking decidedly fragile. It is one of the more remarkable features of zooarchaeological methodology that MNI estimates continue to be used, despite serious inherent flaws, and two decades of detailed criticism.

ESTIMATING THE MISSING INDIVIDUALS

Other quantification procedures seek to estimate not only the individuals present in the recovered sample, but those which have been lost altogether, in order to estimate numbers in the original death assemblage. The point of 'killed population' (or 'Probable Number of Individuals' – PNI) estimates is that what matters for archaeological interpretation is what was, rather than what is, so in quantifying the recovered sample, we are quantifying the wrong thing (Winder 1993). Just as the interpretation of an occupation site will put posts which no longer exist into extant post-holes, so killed population procedures reconstruct missing animals through quantified inference from extant data.

Killed-population procedures are based on paired skeletal elements, and the premise that equal numbers of left and right side elements will have entered the death assemblage, and that taphonomic attrition will not be selective to body side. The larger the observed disparity in the abundance of contra-laterally paired elements, therefore, the larger the number of pairs of bones which must have entered the death assemblage in order for the disparity to have arisen by chance elimination of left or right side elements. Krantz (1968) based a procedure on counts of left and right side elements and apparent pairs – the basic data of MNI estimation, and subject to the same problem of pairing. Fieller and Turner (1982) and Turner (1983) based their simpler method on the logic of biologists' mark-and-recapture methods for population estimation (the Lincoln or Petersen Index), and Poplin (1981) has proposed the same index. The calculation of these indices is illustrated below. Wild and Nichol (1983) give a good example of the practical use of killed-population methods, and Ringrose (1993) is unusually positive about these methods as estimators of the death assemblage. However, for each sample we have to decide what killed population the sample represents. This requires informal modelling of the depositional processes which brought the bones together in the first place. It is not unlikely that different taxa arrived through quite different depositional processes, and so comparison of killed population estimates for several taxa within one sample may have little validity. The estimates may have some value in phase-to-phase comparisons of the abundance of one taxon, or in circumstances where it is clear that all taxa have undergone the same taphonomic trajectory. More mundanely, both the Krantz and Fieller/Turner algorithms are sensitive to quite small variations in the number of pairs, so the inaccuracy inherent in reconstructing pairs becomes multiplied to give considerable inaccuracy to the killed population estimates.

A matter that has received little attention in the zooarchaeological literature is the likely accuracy of killed population estimates based on Lincoln Index procedures. The accuracy of this Index has been examined using numerical simulation by Roff (1973). Where the 'true' population size is small (i.e., where $PNI < 100$), the sampling intensity for acceptable levels of accuracy becomes quite large. For example, for accuracy within 10 per cent, if PNI is 100, the sample size (MNI) needs to be 83 (Smith et al. 1975:34). Given that zooarchaeological investigations often involve estimating abundance from what were probably quite small original death assemblages, this is a serious limitation. In fact, we have a circular argument: since we cannot know the killed population size with certainty, we cannot estimate the accuracy by observation. In field applications of the Lincoln Index to mark-and-recapture experiments, some ecologists have argued that the commonly-used algorithm (in our terms $PNI = (LR)/P$; for definitions see below) consistently over-estimates PNI by $1/P$. This tendency can be corrected by applying $PNI = L(R + 1)/(P + 1)$ (Smith et al. 1975).

To illustrate the calculation of MNI and killed-population estimates, the following conventions are used:

L = the number of left-side specimens,
R = the number of right-side specimens,
P = the number of enantiomorphic pairs,
MNI = estimated minimum number of individuals in the sample,
N = estimated killed-population number.

Estimation of MNI

As originally used by White (1953), the procedure was to separate specimens of the most abundant element of a given species into left- and right-side specimens, and to take the larger of L and R as the estimate of MNI. Subsequent analysts have incorporated pairing, arguing that the best estimate of MNI is the total of pairs plus unpaired lefts plus unpaired rights, i.e.,

$$MNI = P + (L - P) + (R - P)$$

which can be simplified to:

$$MNI = (L + R) - P$$

To show the susceptibility of this calculation to inter-observer variation in reconstructing pairs, let $L = 20$

and $R = 12$. If $P = 2$, $MNI = 30$, whereas if $P = 8$, $MNI = 24$.

Killed-population estimates

Krantz (1968) recommends:

$$N = (R^2 + L^2)/2P$$

Basing their work on ecologists' Lincoln (Petersen) Index, Fieller and Turner (1982) recommend:

$$N = (RL)/P$$

For small samples, Wild and Nichol (1983) prefer:

$$N = \{((R + 1)(L + 1))/(P + 1)\} - 1$$

Taking the same data as above, the Lincoln Index gives $N = 120$ when $P = 2$, and $N = 30$ when $P = 8$. For comparison, Krantz's index gives $N = 133.5$ when $P = 2$, and 34 when $P = 8$. The corresponding values for Wild and Nichol's index are 90 and 29.3. All three indices are clearly vulnerable to inter-observer variability, Krantz's most of all.

EVALUATION AND PROSPECT

Animal bone quantification is deeply problematic. There is information to be inferred from the different numbers of specimens identifiable to different taxa, but different quantification methods will introduce their own distinctive 'noise' to mask that signal. We might hope that the signal will be of greater amplitude than the noise, and, for example, regard as significant only quite large variations and differences in NISP values. However, we have no idea what the amplitude of the noise is likely to be. If the relative abundance of a taxon changes by 5 per cent between phases is that significant? What about 10 per cent, or 15 per cent? The second problem is one of scale. Our interpretation of groups of samples may tend to be over-focused on the numerically abundant taxa, at the cost of missing informative variation in the less abundant taxa. One way around this problem is to depress the higher values through log-transformation of the data. Table 56.1 gives an example of such a procedure. The data are from Medieval samples from 16–22 Coppergate, York (Bond and O'Connor 1999:table 91). Relative abundances of major taxa are listed as %NISP and $\log_e$(%NISP), showing the use of a logarithmic transformation making clearer trends in the less abundant taxa. The increase in bird bones through time is rendered particularly clear by the log transformation,

Table 56.1 Relative abundance of major taxa plotted as (above) %NISP and (below) $\log_e$%NISP (from Bond and O'Connor 1999:table 91).

Date	Cattle	Sheep	Pig	OM	Bird	Total NISP
Late 9th C.	69.2	18.6	7.0	3.2	1.9	3259
Early 10th C.	57.2	27.3	9.6	1.3	4.4	9678
Mid 10th C.	61.2	18.2	14.5	1.8	4.1	5518
Late 10th C.	52.1	19.8	18.8	1.3	7.5	13866
Early 11th C.	59.5	21.1	13.2	1.2	5.0	4214
11th C.	56.5	20.4	15.6	2.5	5.2	2374
12th C.	49.4	25.2	14.4	2.6	8.3	8294
13th C.	47.9	26.5	13.4	1.8	10.4	24089

Date	Cattle	Sheep	Pig	OM	Bird
Late 9th C.	4.24	2.92	1.95	1.16	0.64
Early 10th C.	4.05	3.31	2.26	0.26	1.48
Mid 10th C.	3.95	2.94	2.93	0.26	2.01
Late 10th C.	4.11	2.90	2.67	0.59	1.41
Early 11th C.	4.09	3.05	2.58	0.18	1.61
11th C.	4.03	3.02	2.75	0.92	1.65
12th C.	3.90	3.23	2.67	0.96	2.12
13th C.	3.87	3.28	2.60	0.59	2.34

OM = Other mammals

and the high proportion of bird bones in the late tenth century sample stands out. 'Other mammals' (OM) shows a marked increase in the eleventh and twelfth century samples.

An alternative is to use semi-quantitative categories, whether vernacular (*few*, *some*, *many...*) or locally defined numeric classes. We might, for example, reduce raw NISP figures to semi-quantitative categories (< 5, 5–20, 20–100, 100+). Semi-quantitative scaling removes the need to count every last fragment of rib, or small diaphysis fragments, as the specimens attributed to each taxon can be placed in a category without exact counting. This may seem highly subjective, but the degree of comparability of data from one analyst to another is probably no worse than when two analysts have taken slightly different decisions when calculating NISP or MNI values. We may decide to define categories on different criteria for different taxa. Taxa which are only confidently identifiable on a few elements of the skeleton may be recorded as 'abundant' on the basis of fewer identified specimens than another taxon in the same sample, thus getting around the quantifying-goats problem identified above. The context of the sample will also be relevant. In a northern European Medieval context, a sample in which cattle bones comprise 40 per cent of identified fragments would be unremarkable, whereas red deer bones comprising 40 per cent of fragments would seem unusually abundant. At a Mesolithic site in the same region, red deer comprising 40 per cent NISP would be unremarkable. The ecology of different species will also affect our perceptions of abundance. Herbivores should always be more abundant than carnivores of similar body size, on the simple grounds of energy attenuation through successive trophic levels.

The first necessity in taking forward animal bone quantification may be to admit that none of the techniques currently in use is entirely satisfactory. NISP counts have their place as a description of the sample rather than as an estimator of any population parameters. MNI values have little to recommend them, and killed population estimates may raise more questions than they resolve. In the absence of one generally applicable ideal technique, we might instead focus our attention on devising the best means of answering the questions pertinent to each assemblage, given the condition and completeness of the material, and the aims of the research. It is, after all, generally good science to match the techniques to the research aims, not the other way about.

REFERENCES

*Recommended for further reading

Alexander, R.M., Jayes, A.S., Maloiy, G.M.O. and Wathuta, E.M. (1979). Allometry of the limb bones of mammals from shrews (*Sorex*) to elephants (*Loxodonta*). *Journal of Zoology, London*, **189**:305–314.

Barrett, J.H. (1993). Bone weight, meat yield estimates and cod (*Gadus morhua*): a preliminary study of the weight method. *International Journal of Osteoarchaeology*, **3**:1–18.

Bökönyi, S. (1970). A new method for the determination of the number of individuals in animal bone material. *American Journal of Archaeology*, **74**:291–292.

Bond, J.M. and O'Connor, T.P. (1999). *Bones from Medieval Deposits at 16–22 Coppergate and Other Sites in York*. Archaeology of York Fascicule 15/5, Council for British Archaeology: York.

Casteel, R.W. (1977a). A consideration of the behaviour of the Minimum Number of Individuals index: a problem in faunal characterisation. *Ossa*, **3/4**:141–151.

Casteel, R.W. (1977b). Characterisation of faunal assemblages and the Minimum Number of Individuals determined from paired elements: continuing problems in archaeology. *Journal of Archaeological Science*, **4**:125–134.

Casteel, R.W. (1978). Faunal assemblages and the 'Wiegemethode' or weight method. *Journal of Field Archaeology*, **5**:71–77.

Chaplin, R.E. (1971). *The Study of Animal Bones from Archaeological Sites*. Seminar Press: London.

Chase, P.G. and Hagaman, R.M. (1987). Minimum number of individuals and its alternatives: a probability theory perspective. *Ossa*, **13**:75–86.

Clason, A.T. (1972). Some remarks on the presentation of archaeozoological data. *Helinium*, **12**:139–153.

Cruz-Uribe, K. (1988). The use and meaning of species diversity and richness in archaeological faunas. *Journal of Archaeological Science*, **15**:179–196.

Fieller, N.R.J. and Turner, A. (1982). Number estimation in vertebrate samples. *Journal of Archaeological Science*, **9**:49–62.

Gautier, A. (1984). How do I count you, let me count the ways? Problems of archaeozoological quantification. In Grigson, C. and Clutton-Brock, J. (eds) *Animals and Archaeology 4. Husbandry in Europe*, 237–251. BAR International Series 227, British Archaeological Reports: Oxford.

Gilbert, A.S., Singer, B.H. and Perkins, D. Jr. (1982). Quantification experiments in computer-simulated faunal collections. *Ossa*, **8**:79–94.

Grayson, D.K. (1979). On the quantification of vertebrate archaeofaunas. In Schiffer, M.B. (ed.) *Advances in Archaeological Method and Theory vol 2*, 199–237. Academic Press: New York.

Grayson, D.K. (1981). The effects of sample size on some derived measures in vertebrate faunal analysis. *Journal of Archaeological Science*, **8**:77–88.

*Grayson, D.K. (1984). *Quantitative Zooarchaeology*. Academic Press: London.

Holzman, R.C. (1979). Maximum likelihood estimation of the fossil assemblage composition. *Paleobiology*, **5**:77–89.

Jackson, H.E. (1989). The trouble with transformations: the effects of sample size and sample composition on weight estimates based on skeletal mass allometry. *Journal of Archaeological Science*, **16**:601–610.

Krantz, G.S. (1968). A new method of counting mammal bones. *American Journal of Archaeology*, **72**:286–288.

Kubasiewicz, M. (1956). O metodyce badan wykopaliskowych szczatow kostynch zwierzecych. *Materialy Zachodnio-Pomorskie*, **2**:235–244.

Moreno-Garcia, M., Orton, C. and Rackham, J. (1996). A new statistical tool for comparing animal bone assemblages. *Journal of Archaeological Science*, **23**:437–453.

Noe-Nygaard, N. (1979). Problems of quantification of archaeozoological material caused by differences in butchering and marrow fracturing techniques. In Kubasiewicz, M. (ed.) *Archaeozoology*, 109–119. Agricultural Academy: Sczeczin.

O'Connor, T.P. (1985a). On the presentation of results in environmental archaeology. In Fieller, N.R.J., Gilbertson, D.D. and Ralph, N.G.A. (eds) *Palaeoenvironmental Investigations. Research Design, Methods and Data Analysis*, 147–152. BAR International Series 258, British Archaeological Reports: Oxford.

O'Connor, T.P. (1985b). On quantifying vertebrates – some sceptical observations. *Circaea*, **3**:27–30.

O'Connor, T.P. (1996). A critical overview of archaeological animal bone studies. *World Archaeology*, **28**:5–19.

*O'Connor, T.P. (2000). *The Archaeology of Animal Bones*. Sutton Publishing: Stroud.

Pilgram, T. and Marshall, F. (1995). Bone counts and statisticians: a reply to Ringrose. *Journal of Archaeological Science*, **22**:93–97.

Plug, C. and Plug, I. (1990). MNI counts as estimates of species abundance. *South African Archaeological Bulletin*, **45**:53–57.

Poplin, F. (1981). Une probléme d'ostéologie quantitative: calcul d'effectif inital d'après appariements. Généralisation aux autres types de remontages et d'autre materiels archéologiques. *Revue d'Archéométrie*, **5**:159–165.

Prange, H.D., Anderson, J.F. and Rahn, H. (1979). Scaling of skeletal mass to body mass in birds and mammals. *American Naturalist*, **113**:103–122.

*Ringrose, T.J. (1993). Bone counts and statistics: a critique. *Journal of Archaeological Science*, **20**:121–157.

Ringrose, T.J. (1995). Response to Pilgram and Marshall 'Bone counts and statisticians: a reply to Ringrose'. *Journal of Archaeological Science*, **22**:99–102.

Roff, D.A. (1973). On the accuracy of some mark-recapture experiments. *Oecologia*, **12**:15–34.

Smith, M.H., Gardner, R.H., Gentry, J.B., Kaufmann, D.W. and O'Farrell, M.H. (1975). Density estimations of small mammal populations. In Golley, F.B., Petrusiewicz, K. and Ryszkowski, L. (eds) *Small Mammals, their Productivity and Population Dynamics*, 25–53. Cambridge University Press: Cambridge.

Turner, A. (1983). The quantification of relative abundances in fossil and subfossil bone assemblages. *Annals of the Transvaal Museum*, **33**:311–321.

Watson, J.P.N. (1979). The estimation of the relative frequencies of mammalian species: Khirokitia 1972. *Journal of Archaeological Science*, **6**:127–137.

White, T.E. (1953). A method for calculating the dietary percentages of various food animals utilized by aboriginal peoples. *American Antiquity*, **18**:386–398.

Wild, C.J. and Nichol, R.K. (1983). Estimation of the original number of individuals from paired bone counts using estimators of the Krantz type. *Journal of Field Archaeology*, **10**:337–344.

Winder, N.P. (1991). How many bones make five? The art and science of guesstimation in archaeozoology. *International Journal of Osteoarchaeology*, **1**:111–126.

Winder, N.P. (1993). Using modern bone assemblages to estimate ancient populations. *Circaea*, **10**:63–68.

57

Quantification of Broken Objects

M.J. SHOTT

Department of Sociology, Anthropology and Criminology, University of Northern Iowa.

Archaeologists are fond of observing that they play in the garbage of past cultures. Garbage, by definition, is discarded because it has no value. Many objects that ancient people used became garbage upon breaking, and others broke after being thrown out. Because archaeologists deal with garbage, of necessity they deal with broken objects. Counting objects found is a basic archaeological practice. To judge from the scant reflection occasioned by the issues that counting engages, however, archaeologists seem to consider it the refuge of small minds. Yet counting is as problematic and complex as it is fundamental and for a simple, even banal, reason: people made and used objects as wholes, but archaeologists ordinarily recover them in pieces. Counting broken objects is a simple task but not so determining the number of original wholes from multitudinous fragments of widely varying size and form that comprise widely varying fractions of the wholes. In this perspective, counting is no refuge but instead a complex issue at once fascinating and critical to an archaeology that entertains serious scientific pretensions. The question is not whether to count, since counting is necessary for many archaeological problems, but why and especially how to count.

This chapter reviews recent archaeological thought on the problems of counting broken objects. Virtually everything that people made or consumed in the past could break, but coverage emphasizes the familiar troika of chipped stone, pottery and bones (for a more extended treatment of the latter, see Chapter 56), because these are abundant in the archaeological record. These and other kinds of objects are 'material categories' for this chapter's purposes. Similar methods apply to these abundant categories but their salient differences, identified in course, may justify unique treatment at times.

The chapter is not about quantitative methods, whether descriptive, inferential or multivariate. Quantitative methods are valid manipulations of counts and measurements, and Chapter 54 treats that subject. Instead, the chapter is about quantity or count, and how archaeologists arrive at the figures that they then analyse using statistics. It is about how much, not how different or how significant.

WHY COUNT?

Before discussing how to count broken objects we must consider why we count in the first place. The reasons are many and varied; only a few major ones are discussed here. Frequency seriation is a popular method to order pottery assemblages in time. At least in detail, its results can be influenced by using sherds as units of observation, because pottery types that differ in size, fragility and context of use – common factors of variation – can produce different numbers of sherds from the same number of original vessels. If the frequency seriated is sherds, not vessels, results are compounded by these factors independent of time or order.

Size and composition are fundamental assemblage properties. Composition especially is thought to register meaning, behaviour or action, and other important qualities in the archaeological record. Ordinarily, size and composition are treated as independent properties. Often, however, they are not independent but related because of the joint effects of assemblage accumulation span and the use rates and use lives of artifacts. The relationship of assemblage size and composition is demonstrated in theory (Schiffer 1975) by regular changes in composition as size increases, and ethnographically in pottery assemblages where the proportional representation of short-lived vessel types increases regularly with assemblage size (David 1972). It is inferred in archaeological lithic assemblages from North America and Europe by size-dependent variation in composition across types (Shott 1997, in press). Because assemblage size and composition are related, size – quantity of specimens – must be taken into account before analysis and interpretation of composition.

More generally, within assemblages simple description of quantity found bears on questions like activity, scale of production and use and their sociopolitical implications, as well as on formation questions like occupation span and resident population. Between assemblages, legitimate comparison occurs only when counting is in equivalent units, not the fragments whose number is affected by taphonomy and other factors apart from cultural context. Indeed, virtually all interpretive questions that archaeologists pose engage quantity of ancient things in some way.

WHAT TO COUNT?

Ancient people used pots, not sherds, and hunted animals, not bones. Ceramic and faunal analysts long since abandoned the simple counting of fragments for other measures approximating the original units they wished to infer (Lyman 1994, Orton 1993). These measures link fragments to original wholes; often, they also require considerable mathematical effort in the calculation. Obviously, stone tools can break like other artifacts, so lithic analysts too are beginning to consider the problematics of counting.

Breakage is obvious, but its archaeological implications are not, or at least they are not widely appreciated. Categories like stone, pottery and bone differ in their probability of breakage and in the number and size of pieces into which they break. Thus, equal numbers of original wholes may yield very different numbers of pieces. Within each category similar variation exists. Bifaces, for instance, were likelier to break and into more pieces than were unifaces, owing to their comparative thinness and the greater variety and strength of stresses they experienced, especially those used as projectile tips. Thick-walled vessels were more resistant to breakage than delicate ones.

Sometimes entire objects are less important than their salient parts. For example, flake tools, common in ethnographic and archaeological assemblages, are fashioned only on the edges used and lack distinct form. Counting flakes as tools is questionable in the best of circumstances because intact and broken flake tools can be impossible to distinguish (did a broken flake break before or after use?) and because the used edge, not the whole tool, was the area of value. In contrast, it is often (but not always) easier to determine if a used edge is complete or not (White 1969:23); counting edges obviates the difference between intact and broken flake tools and emphasizes the unit of common value to the user in the past and the archaeologist today.

HOW TO COUNT?

Asking how much a tool or sherd is (Shott 1995) sounds frivolous or nonsensical; tools are tools. Yet how and how much we count are at once more important and problematic than it may seem for reasons noted above. To further complicate matters, objects like stone tools were reduced in use by what amounts to controlled, fine-scaled breakage. Objects also could be transported between locations, so sometimes were used where they were not discarded. After discard, natural and cultural factors further broke objects and fragments. Considering the vagaries of discard and recovery, what was used originally may relate in kind and number only indirectly to what is found. As a result, identical counts between assemblages do not necessarily register identical numbers of objects discarded, let alone amounts of behaviour connected with their use.

The central problem in counting broken objects is to somehow link the number of fragments to numbers of original objects. Refitting alone would solve the problem only if we had the virtually infinite time and resources that it demands and if some fragments or original objects were not destroyed (e.g., sherds ground to powder for grog temper, bone reduced to ash or crushed to extract marrow, broken but refurbished stone tools further reduced by re-sharpening) or deposited in places or contexts impractical to refit. Without refitting, linking fragments to wholes requires prior knowledge of properties of the wholes preserved in the fragments. Using pottery as an example, fragments reduce to wholes if we know in advance properties of the wholes like surface area, weight, rim diameter or diagnostic elements (e.g., rims, necks, shoulders, bases).

QUANTIFICATION METHODS

The statistical requirements for the valid analysis of collections of broken objects are daunting, but Orton (1993) and Orton and Tyers (1990) began the effort in pottery. Moreno-Garcia *et al.* (1996) extended it to broken animal bones.

Pottery

When interest is in taphonomy or how pots are reduced to sherds and the manifest complexities that govern their deposition (e.g., Deal 1998, Hayden and Cannon 1983), sherds are valid units of observation. For most purposes, however, sherd count is a poor measure of quantity for a host of taphonomic reasons; aggregate weight and surface area are better but less than ideal (Orton 1993:175). Miller (1986) applied to pottery the Lincoln Index used in faunal studies (see below) and argued, among other things, that the method is unaffected by varying breakage rates. Orton advocated instead quantification by *estimated vessel equivalent* (EVE).

In any event, the first step in valid quantification is to sort sherds into 'families' (Orton and Tyers 1990:83), the nearest approximation to distinct vessels that fragmentation and similarity of original vessels permit. Orton and Tyers (1990:84) measured EVEs by vessel rim circumference but also identified other measures. Childress (1992) and Miller (1986) used vessel surface area, Byrd and Owens (1997) its near-equivalent 'effective area'. Cool and Baxter (1996:2) preferred diagnostic elements, defining up to seven mutually exclusive elements in glass vessels (Cool and Baxter 1996:fig. 1) much as zooarchaeologists define diagnostic bone elements. Orton (1993:181) disliked diagnostic elements for pottery because elements 'themselves may be broken', complicating measurement.

Unlike rim diameter, surface area conceivably applies to other categories like stone and bone, certainly to the copper kettles of European origin that native Americans often flattened to sheets (e.g., Bradley 1987:fig. 13) before reducing the metal to a range of objects unforeseen by the suppliers. So too do diagnostic elements. Yet these measures require at least one intact (or nearly so) vessel of each type to calculate the measure, so require prior knowledge that fragments alone cannot provide. Rim diameter requires only one intact (or nearly so) rim, or much less if rims are circular. Surface area and rim diameter work best on pottery that is moulded or thrown and so varies little within types. Diagnostic elements should work equally well no matter how pottery is made.

EVEs are adequate for describing assemblages and Baxter and Cool (1994) considered them suitable also for some comparisons between assemblages. But EVEs do not directly equal vessels and their values are not equivalent to vessel counts for statistical purposes. Comparative analysis of assemblages using methods that presume counts are illegitimate using EVEs. Orton and Tyers' (1990:90; see also Baxter and Cool 1994:2) ingenious statistical reasoning defined *pottery information equivalents* (PIEs) that can be treated as counts for assemblage comparisons, and Orton and Tyers (1993) devised an algorithm to perform the comparisons.

Fauna

Lyman (1994) treated faunal quantification at length. Faunal analysts sometimes also use ecology's Lincoln Index of capture-recapture to estimate original quantity (e.g., Fieller and Turner 1982). This measure exploits the obvious symmetry of animal skeletons. In effect, the percentage of matching left-right articulating pairs of elements among all identifiable elements gives an estimate of original quantity. Lincoln's Index is valid subject to rather severe assumptions that include statistical dependence of anatomical pairs, and equal fragmentation rates. It also is imprecise at low matching rates and yields estimates from various element pairs that may differ among one another (Ringrose 1993:129).

Lithics

The nearest lithic equivalent to 'sherd families' is Larson and Kornfeld's (1997) *minimum analytical nodules* (MAN) that includes all cores, debris and tools linked by conjoining or virtual identity in raw material. Ideally, MANs are individual nodules but this ideal can be as difficult to attain as the equivalence of sherd families with distinct vessels. Visual difference in raw material, for instance, is not always proof of difference nor similarity proof of origin in the same nodule (Simpson 1996). This is no criticism of MAN, merely a recognition of its limitation. MANs are sufficient units of quantity for analysis of reduction sequences, but a single nodule can yield many tools so MAN is not a valid measure of tool quantity.

For stone tools, quantification begins with diagnostic elements like proximal, medial and distal fragments. Portnoy (1987) (Mayer-Oakes and Portnoy 1993) may be the first explicitly to consider lithic quantification. She called her measure 'minimum number of intact tools' (MNIT; here, MNT), found by adding the number of complete specimens to the largest value among proximal, medial and distal fragments. This is a lithic equivalent to MNI. In stone, Orton's quantities can be redefined as estimated tool equivalents (ETEs) and tool information equivalents (TIEs).

There is no equivalent to rim circumference in stone tools, although tool perimeter might approximate it when practical. Tools possess diagnostic elements; for instance, a hypothetical end scraper might possess three (proximal, medial, distal as flake-diagnostic elements or butt, blade, and bit as tool-diagnostic elements), a stemmed point as many as eight (Figure 57.1).

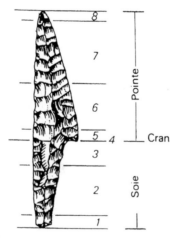

Figure 57.1 Diagnostic zones or elements identified in Solutrean Pointes à Cran (Chadelle *et al.* 1991:277). Reproduced with permission by the publisher APDCA, Antibes, France.

Alternatively some lithic types like bifaces might be measured by surface area or length.

A strength of Orton and Tyers' (1993) algorithm is its ability to use PIE counts to analyse interaction between attributes via log-linear methods. Orton and Tyers emphasize pottery form, fabric and context in their applications. Lithic equivalents might be tool type, raw material and context, although analysts could use other attributes depending on their interests. Interactions between these attributes, both within and between assemblages, then could be analysed.

Equivalence of pottery, stone and bone

EVEs and PIEs are worth considering, but so are salient differences between pottery and other categories. Stone yields production debris easily confused with re-sharpening debris and, in some cases, with tools themselves. Only the latter debris type is relevant to tool quantification, but the two are not easily distinguished and often were discarded together. Pottery and bone do not yield production debris that is easily mistaken for the finished product. Pottery is an object, stone (usually) forms one part of a compound object, and bone occurs naturally in bundles of objects known as skeletons. Stone and bone are apt to move during use, so re-sharpening debris and fragments of recycled tools and an animal's bones are scattered across the landscape, often widely. With rare exceptions, pottery is used and discarded in one place. Stone tools change in size and form during use as a product of ordinary re-sharpening. Animal skeletons certainly do the same, and at times so do individual bones. In original use, pottery does not, although sherds of broken pots often do. Pottery is brittle and tends to break into many small pieces. So too does bone, depending on its use. Stone is brittle but breaks less often than pottery and bone and, when it does, into fewer, relatively larger pieces. In Orton and Tyers' (1990:86) terms, stone generally is less broken than are pots and more complete as fragments than are sherds. Moreover, many stone and bone fragments are recognizable as diagnostic elements; most sherds are not recognizable as diagnostic elements like rims or shoulders. In sum, pottery was used as relatively few irreducible wholes but is recovered in many small pieces. Tools were used as reducible wholes and are recovered whole or in fewer, larger pieces. Bones fall between the other categories in some respects, and beyond them in others. A method designed to quantify pottery may not work as well on other categories, depending on how these properties affect the measures that result.

Other categories

As above, EVEs apply to categories like kettles. They also apply to tobacco pipes, abundant in European assemblages dating to between *c.* AD 1600 and 1900 by considering each pipe bowl equivalent to a vessel mouth. Quantity bears on dating accuracy and other questions in pipe assemblages (Nöel Hume 1963). In most sources, it is given by number of bowl and stem fragments, without regard to original number of intact specimens. If types or size classes of pipes having time-dependent properties typically broke into different numbers of fragments (i.e., if types, however defined, differed in Orton's 'chunkiness'), then quantity given by number of fragments is biased.

Pipes combine the valuable properties of linearity (in stems), sphericity (in bowls), and diagnostic elaboration (in possessing elements like rims, bowls, stems and mouthpieces). Quantity in pipe assemblages can be estimated separately by EVEs using stems, bowls and diagnostic elements. For instance, MNV by diagnostic element and quantity by total stem length over average length per specimen yielded similar estimates in an Australian assemblage (Dana and Morrison 1979:3).

STONE TOOL QUANTIFICATION: A WORKED EXAMPLE

No single quantification measure is best in all conditions, which are apt to vary in manufacturing, use, deposition and taphonomy. Only comparison on the same assemblages will identify the strengths and weaknesses of the various measures. Raw counts, minimum number of objects, object equivalents, and object information equivalents can be compared in worked examples. There are many pottery examples and, recently, faunal ones (Moreno-Garcia *et al.* 1996). As yet, there are no examples in stone.

As in bone and pottery, simple counts of tool quantity can be misleading. If we exclude fragments, counts probably are too low and we fail to use the information inherent in the fragments. If we count all fragments, whatever their size, we risk multiple counting that would especially inflate the counts of brittle specimens that break into many pieces. As in pottery, deposited tool assemblages of identical original size and composition that are subject to different kinds and degrees of

post-occupational stress can yield very different counts. Exhaustive refitting can reduce the problems, but requires much time and effort.

Anyway, refitting shows that fragments belonged to the same original tool, but failure to refit is inconclusive. It means either that the fragments were from different tools, that they were from the same tool but that an intervening section is missing, or that circumstances do not permit systematic refitting. Only the first of the latter three possibilities is certain, useful knowledge. The other two can be minimized by careful attention to differences in raw material and unambiguous indications of incompatibility like great differences in tool dimensions. But dimensions, even thickness in extreme cases, can differ in fragments of the same original tool owing to reworking. Refitting is a partial answer, but so may be quantification methods developed for other material categories. A worked example demonstrates the point.

Bull Brook

The example is unifacial flakeshavers in the Bull Brook Paleoindian assemblage of eastern North America (*c.* 11 000 BP uncalibrated). Grimes and Grimes (1985) found that many specimens broke in use and that fragments sufficiently long were reworked to continue in use; indeed, their flakeshaver life-cycle model is quite involved (Figure 57.2) and by itself illustrates the challenges of quantification. They measured the length of intact tools, the pieces of conjoined ones, and unconjoined fragments.

Flakeshavers are distinctive in size and form and therefore are fairly easy if time-consuming to conjoin. Grimes and Grimes (1985:figs. 2, 5) showed that some tools broke into two or more fragments, that some such fragments were reworked and continued in use, and that reworked specimens themselves could break into fragments. Their flakeshaver life-cycle model (Grimes and Grimes 1985:fig. 5) shows the various permutations linking an original tool to varying number and types of fragments or depleted specimens and makes a wonderful if daunting case for the need to quantify systematically.

Table 57.1 describes the Bull Brook assemblage (ignoring two anomalous 'irregular ends'; Grimes and Grimes 1985:39) by count of intact specimens and various fragments. It also shows MNT calculations. The assemblage contains 41 intact flakeshavers and 113 fragments, but what is the best estimate of quantity of original intact flakeshavers in the Bull

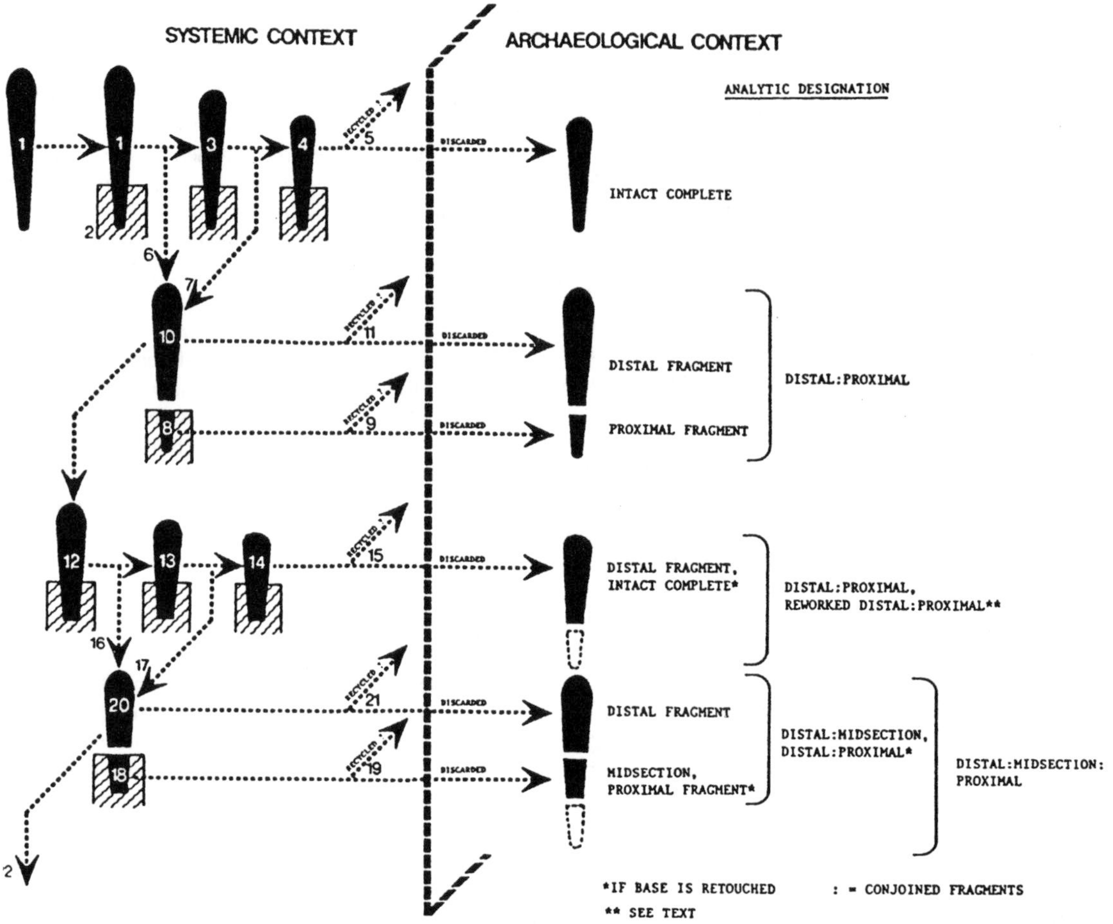

Figure 57.2 Model of Paleoindian flakeshaver life history. Reproduced from Grimes and Grimes (1985:figure 5) in *Archaeology of Eastern North America*, with permission of the Maine Historic Preservation Commission.

Brook assemblage? An overly strict estimate is the 41 intact specimens, which fails to take account of fragments. A liberal figure treats each fragment as a tool, yielding $41 + 113 = 154$ specimens. Distal fragments outnumber others so $MNT = 41 + 69 = 110$ tools whether or not fragments are conjoined, which is nearer the higher figure.

Some intact flakeshavers actually are reworked from long fragments of even longer original specimens (e.g., Grimes and Grimes 1985:fig. 2c,d). Discarded proximal sections of the original long flakeshavers raise the spectre of double-counting. But distal fragments outnumber proximals at Bull Brook, so MNT is unaffected. But the life-cycle model shows how a single original specimen can yield from one to six discarded tools or fragments, even assuming a maximum of only three fragments per fracture. Where assemblages' size and nature make impractical the refitting conducted at Bull Brook, even MNT could seriously exaggerate quantity. Therefore, ETE also should be calculated.

Cool and Baxter (1996) used diagnostic elements to calculate ETE. Vessels and animal bones may contain many such elements, but flakeshavers minimally possess three: proximal or haft, medial, and distal or bit elements. Some specimens possess a shoulder at the proximal:medial juncture but many do not (e.g., Grimes and Grimes 1985:plate 1), so shoulders are eliminated. Without examining each specimen, all fragments are assumed to include only one element (i.e., to be strictly proximal, medial or distal pieces). This is unsatisfactory because many specimens probably retain two elements but is ignored here for illustration.

Table 57.1 Flakeshaver MNT at Bull Brook (Grimes and Grimes 1985).

Fragment	Without conjoining n	With conjoining n
intact	41	53
proximal	24	12
medial	20	9
distal	69	57
MNT	$= 41 + 69 = 110$	$= 53 + 57 = 110$

MNT = Intact + highest fragment total

Essentially, ETE parses tools as the sum of diagnostic elements. By definition, intact specimens possess all elements; following Baxter and Cool (1994:4) their ETE = 100. A specimen possessing half of all elements has an ETE value of 50, one possessing one-quarter of all elements an ETE value of 25, and so on. Intact Bull Brook flakeshavers retain all three original elements. Therefore, their ETE = 100 (3 elements retained/3 original elements = 1.0×100). Fragments retain one original element each, so ETE = 33 (1 element retained/3 original elements = 0.33×100). Table 57.2 shows ETE values and calculations necessary for TIE, also following Baxter and Cool's format and notation, yielding measures of stone-tool quantity using Orton and Tyers' (1990) method. Specimen ETE values are multiplied by n and summed across the assemblage, yielding ΣETE$*$n or ΣW_j in Baxter and Cool's (1994) notation. Separately, ETEs are squared, the result also multiplied by n, and summed as well. This yields ΣETE^{2*}n or ΣS_j^2 in Baxter and Cool's notation.

Table 57.2 ETE Calculations for Bull Brook Flakeshavers.

element	n	ETE (W_i)	ETE$*$n (W_j)	ETE^2 (S_i^2)	ETE^{2*}n (S_j^2)
with joins					
intact	53	100	5300	10 000	530 000
proximal	12	33	396	1089	13 068
medial	9	33	297	1089	9801
distal	57	33	1881	1089	62 073
Σ	131		7874		614 942
TIE $= (130/131)*(7874^2/614942) = 100.1$					
without joins					
intact	41	100	4100	10 000	410 000
proximal	24	33	792	1089	26 136
medial	20	33	660	1089	21 780
distal	69	33	2277	1089	75 141
Σ	154		7829		533 057
TIE $= (153/154)*(7829^2/533057) = 114.2$					

TIE is found as $((n - 1)/n) * ((\Sigma W_j)^2/\Sigma S_j^2)$ (Baxter and Cool 1994:4), which here = 100.1. Ignoring joins, TIE = 114.2. These figures are gratifyingly near MNT, which tends to justify both measures.

Thus, MNT and two TIE measures yield values between 100 and 114 at Bull Brook. The insignificant difference between original and derived measures of quantity suggest that the mathematical exertions demanded by Orton's method may be unnecessary in lithic assemblages. Perhaps this owes to stone tools' great completeness and low brokenness noted above. However, it is equally possible that very small fragments simply were omitted from counting. If they were numerous, their inclusion might significantly alter original counts. Indeed, ETE and TIE calculated over several tool classes and in several lithic assemblages do not always agree with MNT (Dibble and Shott in preparation). ETE and TIE may be worth the effort to calculate in some cases, but much work remains to identify the conditions for which they are best suited.

There is no statistical requirement to use only one measure at a time (Orton 1993:181) and we may find that different ones work best with different types. For instance, ETE using tool length might serve best in unifaces reduced mostly in length but little in other dimensions like end scrapers (Shott 1995), flakeshavers (Grimes and Grimes 1985) and microliths (Hiscock 1996). Metric attributes like length might also be best where distinct diagnostic elements are hard to define, as in microlithic blade industries. Similarly, MNT may prove best for many purposes but suffers from MNI's aggregation effects (Lyman 1994). ETE and PIE are more derived and require much calculation, albeit automated (Orton and Tyers 1993); they too suffer aggregation effects. Yet ETE and TIE force attention to the existence and therefore the meaning of fragments and may help unravel the taphonomic history of assemblages. In theory, TIE reduces fragmented tool assemblages to valid original counts as PIE reduces sherd assemblages to pots.

THE POPULATIONS COUNTED

Since Cowgill (1970), archaeologists have known that recovered assemblages are a small and not necessarily representative sample of the original populations of objects, meaning and actions that interest us. Zooarchaeologists (Lyman 1994) and ceramicists (Orton 1993:178) contemplated at length the various populations from which their samples derive and the quantification methods best suited for their estimations. How we quantify depends on the questions that interest us and the original populations we wish to estimate. For most questions assemblages are samples, but of what?

Leaving aside the stages that follow discard and preservation (what intervenes between Cowgill's (1970:163) *physical finds* population and the recovered assemblage), our *physical finds* populations might be (i) all object-using activity conducted at a site, some of which involved objects themselves not discarded but retained for further use elsewhere, i.e., 'curation' in common if imprecise parlance (Shott 1996), or (ii) all objects discarded at a site. The first is Orton and Tyers' (1990:175) Level i Life Assemblage, the second their Level ii Death Assemblage. Orton (1993:178) considered the former unattainable in pottery because vessels used at, but taken from, a location leave no evidence of their presence. Such transport in pottery seems uncommon. In any event, the debris of stone tools and bone can be scattered in many places. In theory, then, both populations are attainable in these categories. Most quantification methods characterize samples of the first population but methods unique to material categories may be needed to characterize samples of the second.

Consider stone tools. Trivially, a tool's presence in an assemblage is a register of its discard and presumably its use there. Two tools of the same type therefore register equal amounts of use. But if the tools are reduced to different degrees, they register equal amounts of discard but not of use; each counts as one item but not one unit of use. Generalizing, tools can be used in many places but only discarded in one. Ordinarily, they and their use count only where they were discarded.

If our estimation goal is Orton and Tyer's (1993) death assemblage, there is no problem. If, however, it is their life assemblage then we face an apparent dilemma because there seems no way to estimate the number of tools taken from the place. Fortunately, however, tools leave evidence of their use in re-sharpening debris. The prospects of conjoining flakes from different places to one another or the parent tool are absurdly remote. But we know how small tools are upon discard. If we also know or can estimate how large they were at first use and how large re-sharpening flakes struck from them were, then we can calculate the number of flakes struck in the tools' reduction. In this way we can count tool use, if not tools themselves, from re-sharpening flakes.

Thus, debris can suggest that more or less tool use occurred in an assemblage than the number of tools

would indicate. For instance, the number of uniface re-sharpening flakes in a Paleoindian assemblage accounted for only an estimated 25 per cent of the total reduction of unifaces found there (Shott 1995). In that case, tools discarded (Level ii Death Assemblage) considerably exaggerate amounts of tool use (Level i Life assemblage). The broad estimates necessary in our current state of knowledge make this case merely illustrative but the method should yield valid results with better recovery and data on flake size and number, data that experiments can provide.

Consider again Bull Brook flakeshavers. Suppose we could distinguish their re-sharpening flakes from those of other types and that we knew or could estimate the number of such flakes struck over the lifespan of a typical specimen. (Alternatively, we might estimate total platform area of resharpening flakes and then measure the same in debris assemblages.) Generously assuming a representative sample, if we find only half as many re-sharpening flakes as expected from the number of specimens found we conclude that, on average, flakeshavers were brought there already half reduced. If we find twice as many re-sharpening flakes as expected, we conclude that twice as many specimens were used as were found. MNT and TIE would be inaccurate in either case unless we accounted for tool movement via re-sharpening debris. Until this problem is solved, even ETE and TIE can be poor estimates of the Level i assemblage. One solution redefines the quantities to include the number of re-sharpening flakes sufficient to account for observed degrees of reduction from original to discarded size. Another separately estimates quantity from tools and debris and compares the estimates for agreement. Assemblages can contain many tool types but re-sharpening flakes rarely can be distinguished at levels finer than between biface and uniface. At least, however, they can help quantify tool use at this admittedly crude level.

THE NEED FOR DATA

Most archaeologists neglect object fracture and its effect upon quantification. Even now we have little systematic data on type-specific probabilities of fracture in use and the number, mean size and variance of the resulting fragments, let alone on how post-occupational factors like trampling and ploughing compound breakage. Some experiments are useful starts for stone tools (e.g., Dockall 1997), but our ignorance justifies an urgent experimental programme in all material categories as well as more empirical studies.

TYPOLOGY AND QUANTIFICATION

The integrity of defined lithic types is compromised if the types arbitrarily apportion the reduction continuum. Distinguishing, for example, Middle Paleolithic single and double scrapers is no more valid than treating tadpoles and frogs as different taxa (Dibble 1987, Dibble and Shott in preparation). Typological integrity is relevant to quantification because the reduction that compromises it cross-cuts the traditional tool types that are the subjects of quantification. Thus, if we wish to know how many side scrapers, for instance, were used at a site, we must consider not only 'curation' and tool fracture but also the possibility that a specimen that began as one type was discarded as another and passed through other types during its use life. Should the discarded specimen count as one of each type or just its final one? To the extent that types are analytical contrivances and not revealed categories the problem is illusory. But types are useful contrivances and, in any event, many published sources assume their validity and so cannot be used in comparative studies without engaging the assumption. Thus, the problem is both theoretical and practical.

Neeley and Barton's (1994) Levantine Epipaleolithic bladelet/microlith reduction sequence is a good example of typological dilemmas. Its validity is questioned (e.g., Henry 1996:136) as part of a broader critique reminiscent of the Bordean perspective in the never-resolved Mousterian debate, wherein Perigordian Middle Paleolithic assemblage variation was attributed variously to identity-conscious social groups making and using different kinds or proportions of tools (e.g., Bordes and de Sonneville Bordes 1970) or task group differences within a single culture (e.g., Binford 1973). Whatever the validity of the respective views in the Mousterian controversy, recent criticism is irrelevant to the illustrative value of Neeley and Barton's (1994) argument. In the inferred sequence, one blank can yield four or more discarded specimens of different recognized types. Should all be counted as distinct tools? Perhaps only the original blank should be counted? Tool fragments will not always be possible to assign to a defined type, a further complication. Fortunately, finished types are formed by the fracture or reduction of long, narrow blanks. Like channel flakes, perhaps mean original blank length could serve as a measure of one unit for blanks. If so, quantification is accomplished only at the highest typological and technological level.

THE NEED FOR A UNIFIED THEORY OF QUANTIFICATION

Assemblage analysis is one of archaeology's most fundamental tasks, with importance greater than many archaeologists realize. It has a long pedigree in lithic studies, an inexplicably shorter and less developed one in ceramics and other categories. Uncommon is the simultaneous treatment of stone, pottery and other categories as components of larger assemblages. If lithic analysis regularly interprets assemblages composed, say, 20 per cent of scrapers, 30 per cent of bifaces and 50 per cent of retouched flakes, only rarely do archaeologists interpret assemblages composed 20 per cent of scrapers, 30 per cent of bone tools and 50 per cent of cord-marked earthenware cooking-pot sherds.

We define material categories with some practical legitimacy but at once erect boundaries lacking meaning or legitimacy to those who made and used the categories. People used stone *and* pottery *and* meat *and* many other things and archaeologists should study assemblages of all such materials combined. To do so requires units of counting and observation – specimens – that possess integral meaning common to the material categories. This means tools, pots, and cuts of meat, not fragments, sherds and MNI. In all material categories we require common units of measurement grounded in common theory of quantification of broken objects. Only with such method and theory can archaeologists treat and analyse assemblages as ancient people made and used them. Only then can we legitimately speak of unified assemblages of stone, pottery and other categories, not contrived assemblages separately of stone, of pottery, of other categories.

CONCLUSION

Archaeology is assemblage analysis as much as it is anything else. Because original wholes are found mostly in pieces, archaeology requires a theory of counting of broken objects. In this perspective, counting is no mere technical matter but a problem that goes to the heart of all archaeological interpretation. It emerges as part of a broader and vital – if neglected (Shott 1998) – theory of how the archaeological record formed. This apparent refuge of small minds has large implications for the practice of archaeology and the validity of interpretation.

ACKNOWLEDGEMENTS

The research for this chapter was supported in part by a Summer Research Fellowship from the University of Northern Iowa. I thank Jean-Pierre Chadelle and the Association pour la Promotion et la Diffusion des Connaissances Archéologiques for permission to reprint Figure 57.1, and Arthur Spiess and *Archaeology of Eastern North America* for permission to reprint Figure 57.2.

REFERENCES

*Recommended for further reading

Baxter, M.J. and Cool, H.E. (1994). *Notes on Some Statistical Aspects of Pottery Quantification*. Research Report 15/94, Nottingham Trent University, Department of Mathematics, Statistics and OR.

Binford, L.R. (1973). Interassemblage variability: the Mousterian and the 'Functional' argument. In Renfrew, C. (ed.) *The Explanation of Culture Change: Models in Prehistory*, 227–254. Duckworth: London.

Bordes, F. and de Sonneville-Bordes, D. (1970). The significance of variability in Palaeolithic assemblages. *World Archaeology*, 2:61–73.

Bradley, J.W. (1987). *Evolution of the Onondaga Iroquois: Accommodating Change, 1500–1655*. Syracuse University Press: Syracuse, New York.

Byrd, J.E. and Owens, D.D. (1997). A method for measuring relative abundance of fragmented archaeological ceramics. *Journal of Field Archaeology*, 24:315–320.

Chadelle, J.-P., Geneste, J.-M. and Plisson, H. (1991). Processus fonctionnels de formation des assemblages technologiques dans les sites du Paléolithique Supérieur: les pointes de projectiles lithiques du Solutréen de la Grotte de Combe Saunière (Dordogne, France). In *25 Ans d'Études Technologiques en Préhistoire, Xie Rencontres Internationales d'Archéologie et d'Histoire d'Antibes*, 275–287. Éditions APDCA: Juan-les-Pins.

Childress, M.R. (1992). Mortuary vessels and comparative ceramic analysis: an example from the Chucalissa site. *Southeastern Archaeology*, 11:31–50.

Cool, H.E. and Baxter, M.J. (1996). *Quantifying Glass Assemblages*. Research Report 5/96, Nottingham Trent University, Department of Mathematics, Statistics and OR.

Cowgill, G.L. (1970). Some sampling and reliability problems in archaeology. In *Archéologie et Calculateurs: Problèmes Sémiologiques et Mathématiques*, 161–172. Centre National de la Recherche Scientifique: Paris.

Dana, A. and Morrison, R. (1979). *Clay Pipes from Port Arthur 1830–1877*. Research School of Pacific Studies Technical Bulletin 2, Australian National University: Canberra.

David, N. (1972). On the life span of pottery, type frequencies, and archaeological inference. *American Antiquity*, 37:141–142.

Deal, M. (1998). *Pottery Ethnoarchaeology in the Central Maya Highlands*. University of Utah Press: Salt Lake City.

Dibble, H.L. (1987). The interpretation of Middle Paleolithic scraper morphology. *American Antiquity*, 52:109–117.

Dibble, H.L. and Shott, M.J. (in preparation). *Lithic Analysis: The Study of Stone Tools and Assemblages*. Princeton University Press.

Dockall, J.E. (1997). Wear traces and projectile impact: a review of the experimental and archaeological evidence. *Journal of Field Archaeology*, 24:321–331.

Fieller, N.R. and Turner, A. (1982). Number estimation in vertebrate samples. *Journal of Archaeological Science*, 9:49–62.

Grimes, J.R. and Grimes, B.G. (1985). Flakeshavers: morphometric, functional and life-cycle analyses of a Paleoindian unifacial tool class. *Archaeology of Eastern North America*, 13:35–57.

Hayden, B. and Cannon, A. (1983). Where the garbage goes: refuse disposal in the Maya Highlands. *Journal of Anthropological Archaeology*, 2:117–163.

Henry, D.O. (1996). Functional minimalism versus ethnicity in explaining lithic patterns in the Levantine Epipaleolithic. *Antiquity*, 70:135–136.

Hiscock, P. (1996). Transformations of Upper Paleolithic implements in the Dabba industry from Haua Fteah (Libya). *Antiquity*, 70:657–664.

Larson, M.L. and Kornfeld, M. (1997). Chipped stone nodules: theory, method, and examples. *Lithic Technology*, 22:4–18.

*Lyman, R.L. (1994). Quantitative units and terminology in zooarchaeology. *American Antiquity*, 59:36–71.

Mayer-Oakes, W.J. and Portnoy, A.W. (1993). Paleo-Indian studies at San José, Ecuador. *Lithic Technology*, 18:28–36.

Miller, G.L. (1986). Of fish and sherds: a model for estimating vessel populations from minimal vessel counts. *Historical Archaeology*, 20:59–85.

Moreno-Garcia, M., Orton, C. and Rackham, J. (1996). A new statistical tool for comparing animal bone assemblages. *Journal of Archaeological Science*, 23:437–453.

Neeley, M.P. and Barton, C.M. (1994). A new approach to interpreting Late Pleistocene microlith industries in southwest Asia. *Antiquity*, 68:275–288.

Nöel Hume, A. (1963). Clay tobacco pipe dating in the light of recent excavations. *Quarterly Bulletin of the Archaeological Society of Virginia*, 18:22–25.

*Orton, C. (1993). How many pots make five? – an historical review of pottery quantification. *Archaeometry*, 35:169–184.

Orton, C.R. and Tyers, P.A. (1990). Statistical analysis of ceramic assemblages. *Archeologia e Calcolatori*, 1:81–110.

Orton, C.R. and Tyers, P.A. (1993). *A User's Guide to Pieslice*. Unpublished Ms., Institute of Archaeology, University College London.

Portnoy, A.W. (1987). A formula for estimating the minimum number of individual lithic tools. Paper presented at the 52nd Annual Meeting of the Society for American Archaeology, Toronto.

*Ringrose, T.J. (1993). Bone counts and statistics: a critique. *Journal of Archaeological Science*, **20**:121–157.

Schiffer, M.B. (1975). The effects of occupation span on site content. In Schiffer, M.B. and House, J.H. (eds) *The Cache River Archeological Project: an Experiment in Contract Archeology*, 265–269. Research Series No. 8, Arkansas Archeological Survey: Fayetteville.

Shott, M.J. (1995). How much is a scraper? Curation, use rates, and the formation of scraper assemblages. *Lithic Technology*, **20**:53–72.

Shott, M.J. (1996). An exegesis of the curation concept. *Journal of Anthropological Research*, **52**:259–280.

Shott, M.J. (1997). Activity and formation as sources of variation in Great Lakes Paleoindian assemblages. *Midcontinental Journal of Archaeology*, **22**:197–236.

*Shott, M.J. (1998). Status and role of formation theory in current archaeological practice. *Journal of Archaeological Research*, **6**:299–329.

Shott, M.J. (in press). Size as a factor in Old World Middle Paleolithic assemblage variation: a North American perspective. In Moloney, N. and Shott, M.J. (eds) *Lithic Analysis at the Millennium*. Institute of Archaeology, University College London: London.

Simpson, D.N. (1996). Aspects of weathering of rhyolite and typological and technological considerations of this material based on the results of refitting. *Norwegian Archaeological Review*, **29**:79–87.

White, J.P. (1969). Typologies for some prehistoric flaked stone artefacts of the Australian New Guinea Highlands. *Archaeology and Physical Anthropology in Oceania*, **4**:18–46.

58

Numerical Modelling in Archaeology

M.W. LAKE

Institute of Archaeology, University College London.

Numerical modelling is generally a complex process that is, and will probably remain, a highly specialized area of archaeological research. Consequently this chapter does not attempt to provide a recipe for successful modelling. Instead it aims to provide an overview of when, why and how numerical modelling has been used in archaeology, and what future directions it might take. Sabloff (1981) remains a useful, if now slightly dated, introduction to modelling in archaeology. It includes Aldenderfer's (1981a) helpful essay on the steps involved in building a model. For a review (with examples) of the current state of the art, see Kohler and Gumerman (2000). On a more practical tack, those interested in simulating human behaviour should consult Gilbert and Troitzsch (1999).

NUMERICAL MODELLING DEFINED

If, as David Clarke suggested, 'models are pieces of machinery that relate observations to theoretical ideas' (Clarke 1972:2), then modelling includes activities as diverse as the reconstruction of an Iron Age roundhouse and the use of mathematical equations to study the rise of urbanism. The reader will doubtless readily accept that the former is not an example of numerical modelling, but may be more surprised to discover that the latter need not be either (although it often is). To pursue Clarke's metaphor further, numerical modelling may be defined on the basis of both

machine type and mode of operation: according to his scheme (Figure 58.1) the machines are abstract non-iconic analogues and the mode of operation is iterative. As non-iconic analogues, numerical models represent the real world as a set of variables linked by mathematical or logical conditions; they are iterative because they must be solved or studied by repeatedly replacing those variables with numbers until the specified conditions are met. Some mathematical models and all simulation models fall into this category.

Following Doran and Hodson, a mathematical model is 'an attempted specification in exact mathematical terms ... of the variables which characterize a real world situation or process, and of the relationships that hold between them' (Doran and Hodson 1975:26). Mathematical models in archaeology range in complexity from a simple equation linking floor area and settlement population (Naroll 1962) to a set of literally hundreds of equations describing the growth of Rome (Zubrow 1981). Very complex models are often numerical simply because they cannot be solved by mathematical reasoning, but this is also true of simpler models based on nonlinear differential equations. A nonlinear differential equation is a differential equation that cannot be written in the form (Nagle and Saff 1989):

$$F(x) = a_0(x)y + a_1(x)\frac{dy}{dx} + \cdots + a_{n-1}(x)\frac{d^{n-1}y}{dx^{n-1}}$$
$$+ a_n(x)\frac{d^n y}{dx^n}$$

Handbook of Archaeological Sciences. Edited by D.R. Brothwell and A.M. Pollard.

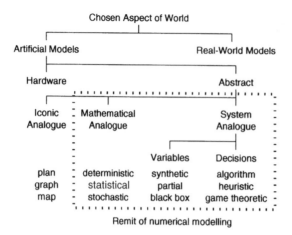

Figure 58.1 Types of model. Based on Clarke (1972:fig. 12), by permission of Methuen.

Such equations are frequently found in systemic models that deal with the rates of change of one variable with respect to another, for example in McGlade's (1997) model of prehistoric exchange in Wessex. Irrespective of whether the mathematical insolubility stems from complexity or nonlinearity, an approximate solution can often be obtained by iteratively changing the values of variables until the condition linking them is met to an acceptable degree of accuracy; it is this iterative process that renders such models numerical.

Simulation is more difficult to define. Aldenderfer (1981a:13) suggests that simulation involves using a computer to study the behaviour of a model over time, where that model is generally a mathematical, logical or quantitative representation of a system or process. In addition, Doran and Hodson (1975:286) note that simulation models one process by another which 'is itself an abstracted representation of the target real-world process'. This insight is particularly useful because it allows simulation to be defined as the subset of numerical modelling containing those models in which the process of change in the model mirrors the process of change in the real world. Such models are numerical because they are iterative, and simulations because similar iterations occur in the real world. It is largely inconsequential whether one reserves the term simulation to refer to models that fulfil this criterion, or additionally admits the process of iteration itself. The term is used in both senses here, so that 'computer simulation' is simply the use of a computer to experiment with a simulation model, which itself is a 'computer simulation'.

MODEL BUILDING AND USE

Aldenderfer (1981a:22) provides a comprehensive account of the process of computer simulation. The following discussion largely summarizes his scheme (Figure 58.2), but with an emphasis on those aspects relevant to numerical modelling in general. Usually the first step is to consider whether the archaeological problem at hand will benefit from the application of numerical modelling. This will obviously be so if one has already constructed a mathematical model that is not soluble by mathematical reasoning. Less obvious, but perhaps more interesting, are cases where the rationale for numerical modelling is more directly archaeological, and where computer simulation is likely to be particularly appropriate. These include situations where one wishes to study the progress or outcome of a process that has no analogue in the modern world, or where experimentation with that process might be too slow, dangerous, unethical or costly.

The first step in any explicit modelling process, numerical or otherwise, is to define the problem and, if appropriate, the hypothesis to be tested. A very simple problem may prove to be soluble by numerical

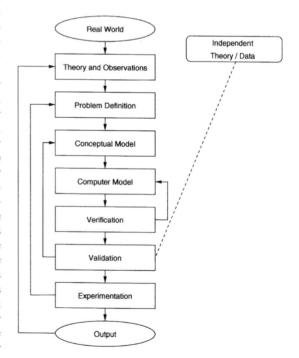

Figure 58.2 The process of computer simulation. Based on Sabloff (1981:24), by permission of the University of New Mexico Press, Albequerque.

modelling and that will be the end of the matter. More often, problem definition and modelling occur in feedback, with the results of the first round of modelling prompting a refinement of the original problem; such circularity should not, however, be allowed to cloud the clarity of the problem definition during any one cycle of the process. Once armed with a clearly stated problem and an assessment of data availability it should become clear whether and which type of numerical modelling is appropriate.

The next step is to construct a conceptual model. This usually constitutes a verbal or mathematical description of the boundary, components, causality and logic of the model. System bounding determines what should be included in the model and what can be omitted. Unfortunately there is no well-established method of system bounding, so each researcher must be prepared to look critically at any preconceptions concerning what is and is not relevant. The task of identifying the components of the model is largely a question of deciding how detailed it needs to be. All models necessarily simplify real world systems since their purpose is to 'replace situations or systems or entities which we cannot understand or investigate or predict by those that we can understand, investigate or predict' (Doran and Hodson 1975:287). In general the most useful models are the simplest that include all relevant aspects of the real world system. Simplification may require the modification, combination or aggregation of components, and must be undertaken with reference to the problem definition since it is likely to alter the locus of causality. The flow of causality through the model is ultimately determined by the logic with which components are connected. This may be specified verbally, by means of a flowchart, or as a set of mathematical equations.

The conceptual model must be converted into a form in which it can be used, whether for further study or simply to obtain a solution to a mathematically insoluble equation. For purely pragmatic reasons this usually entails implementing the model on a computer. The simplest case of solving an equation may involve nothing more than entering the formula in one of the widely available mathematical software packages. It may be possible to code more complex models using the macro language provided by appropriate software such as a mathematical, geographical information system, or simulation package. In other cases it may be necessary to write a new computer program specifically for the model. This last course of action is best avoided unless absolutely necessary since it is extremely time consuming and often frustrating. The models most likely to require dedicated programs are simulations, particularly those based on networks of decisions rather than ensembles of linked variables.

Computerized models must be verified to ensure that they function as intended – in other words, that a given input produces the output predicted by the rules of the conceptual model. In the case of complex models that include random variables one may have little option but to settle for a statistical assessment rather than an absolute verification.

Once it is clear that the computer model accurately implements the conceptual model the next step is to establish the validity of the latter. Quite what this entails, and indeed means, depends on the type and purpose of the model. The validity of a model designed to solve a mathematically insoluble equation will be ensured by correct mathematical reasoning. The validity of other models created solely to produce an end result will be judged on whether their output is sufficiently realistic. For example, the validity of the XTENT model (Renfrew and Level 1979) of territorial division must be assessed in terms of how accurately the resulting maps fit the relevant archaeological data. In contrast, the validity of most simulation models will be judged on whether the modelled process is realistic, not on the realism of the output alone. The realism of the process may be assessed by investigating whether the model produces reasonable output for a wide range of input values, which should include some extreme examples. This approach was followed during validation of a model of the evolution of cultural learning among early hominids (Lake 1995). Theoretical considerations indicated that cultural learning should evolve in a stable environment, but not in a rapidly fluctuating environment. By conducting a series of simulations with artificially constructed environmental regimes of known stability it was possible to check whether the model produced plausible results. Note, however, that it would have been tautologous to use the same input both to validate the model and simultaneously test the archaeological hypothesis.

The immediate purpose of simulation is usually to conduct a series of experiments that could not otherwise be performed, for whatever reason. There are four main experimental strategies that can be used depending on the archaeological problem at hand. Two of these may be used for hypothesis testing. The first varies the model input until the output matches an observed state. This is the appropriate strategy when one is reasonably confident about the nature of some process and wishes to determine what conditions were required for it to have produced the observed state. For example, one might attempt to determine the distribution of artifacts at a site prior to its transformation by some relatively well understood physical process. The second strategy varies the modelled process until it successfully produces output matching one observed state in response to input matching another. This is appropriate if the aim is to identify what process was operating in the past. For example, given knowledge of relative prey abundances it might be possible to identify past human hunting strategies by running a number of computer simulations to establish which would result in the observed faunal assemblage composition. When using either of these strategies it is important to be aware of the problem of *equifinality*: that more than one state or process may produce the desired output. The other two experimental strategies may be used for heuristic purposes. The first of these attempts to hold constant a given output, which may or may not match an observed state, while varying the input and possibly also the process. The aim of this strategy is to identify the sensitivity of the model to variations in input or process, perhaps with a view to establishing the best use of limited resources for increasing the accuracy of predictions. For example, there would be little point in attempting to improve the estimation of prehistoric rainfall in some study if it could be shown that the most extreme values permitted by the present error terms do not alter the predicted settlement pattern. The second heuristic strategy simply varies the model input in order to examine the range of outputs that can be produced by the modelled process. This approach is most likely to be used in the context of theory building. One might, for example, wish to ascertain whether a proposed model of urban growth is actually capable of producing urban collapse and, if so, under what circumstances.

Numerical modelling can have conceptual, developmental or output utility (Aldenderfer 1981a:20). A model has *output utility* when it produces results that are potentially of value to others who were not party to the modelling process. Numerical models used to solve mathematically insoluble equations have output utility, as do those that have been used successfully for hypothesis testing. Models used for heuristic purposes are normally said to have *developmental utility*, because their purpose is to help the modeller learn more about the modelled process. Finally, nearly all models have *conceptual utility*: the requirement for some kind of logical description, mathematical or otherwise, forces the modeller to clarify his or her thinking. Needless to say, any given model may have more than one type of utility.

HISTORY AND CURRENT STATUS

The history presented here is largely, although not exclusively, that of simulation modelling, since it is this activity which has received the greatest exposure in the literature. It is likely that the use of other numerical techniques to solve a variety of mathematical problems has often gone unreported owing to its lack of specifically archaeological content.

The use of numerical models is inextricably bound up with the use of computers, since it is the latter which make numerical modelling a practical proposition. Consequently it is not surprising that anthropologists (Hays 1965) and archaeologists (Doran 1970) were introduced to simulation in the late 1960s and early 1970s, when computers first became available outside the fledgling computer sciences. A 1972 survey of the use of computers in archaeology listed two simulation studies and predicted that 'because of its real suitability to many of the current problems of archaeology and for working in a systemic frame of reference, [simulation] will be one of the burgeoning fields of activity in the next few years' (Whallon 1972:39). Initially it appeared that this prediction might prove accurate: at least five simulation studies were either published or started in the following two years, and four of these more or less explicitly treated culture as an adaptive system. The subject matter of the latter ranged from Palaeolithic social systems (Wobst 1974) through hunter-gatherer subsistence strategies (Thomas 1972) and Anasazi settlement (Cordell 1972) to the colonization of Polynesia (Levison *et al.* 1973). The fifth study was of tribal exchange (Wright and Zeder 1977).

Doran and Hodson, however, were not impressed with the early archaeological uses of simulation. They argued that: 'The established value of computer simulation techniques in other fields, together with the complexity of many archaeological problems, suggests that such techniques have archaeological potential. But it must be admitted that there is virtually no direct evidence in support of the suggestion' (Doran and Hodson 1975:203). Existing models were either so simplistic that they barely warranted the use of simulation, or else they required more input data than was available. Despite continued optimism in some quarters (Hodder 1978:viii) many of the additional 15 or so studies that had appeared by 1981 (Ammerman *et al.* 1978, Chadwick 1979, Elliott *et al.* 1978, Mosimann and Martin 1975, and references below) seemed to others to confirm Doran and Hodson's earlier pessimism. Aldenderfer, himself an advocate of simulation, was forced to concede that '... a majority of archaeologists consider simulation mildly interesting but on the whole not particularly useful in the conduct of archaeological research' (Aldenderfer 1981a:12). It is, then, hardly surprising that the use of simulation lapsed during the 1980s, with just a few exceptions (Mithen 1986, Yiannouli and Mithen 1986, Potts 1988, Reynolds 1986).

The majority view reported by Aldenderfer suggests that archaeologists had found simulation wanting as a technique, but Hodder's optimism shows that this was not universally the case. In fact, it appears that there are two different reasons why simulation had ceased to be regarded as useful: one more applicable to North America and one to Britain. Doran and Hodson's critique did little to alter the trajectory of simulation modelling in North America, and most studies from the second half of the 1970s continued the attempt to operationalize the systems approach to social organization and culture change, usually in the context of settlement pattern. Some claimed an element of hypothesis testing as their function (Gunn 1979, O'Shea 1978, Zubrow 1975), whilst others had largely heuristic aims (Black 1978, Cooke and Renfrew 1979, Zimmerman 1977, Zubrow 1981). In both cases simulation was seen to lack output utility: the former failed to convince, often through a lack of data, whilst the latter only benefited the model developer, and then only in the context of a theoretical framework whose validity was increasingly questioned. In contrast (but see Aldenderfer 1981b, Ammerman *et al.* 1978), most of the modelling undertaken in Britain during the second half of the 1970s was explicitly methodological (e.g., Donnelly 1978) and often did have output utility. Hodder's optimism in 1978 no doubt stemmed from his involvement in a number of these projects, which included modelling the nature of rank size relationships (Hodder 1979), artifact dispersal (Hodder and Orton 1976) and association between distributions (Hodder and Okell 1978). Indeed, his subsequent change of theoretical heart (Hodder 1982) goes a considerable way to explaining why such studies ceased in the 1980s. It was not that simulation itself had been found wanting, but that the broader methodology to which it contributed was not considered appropriate for the new task of elucidating systems of meanings.

The 1990s have seen a revival of interest in simulation. This has been fuelled by at least three developments. First, those simulations whose function is largely hypothesis testing have seen a narrowing of focus (e.g., Mithen 1990), so that they no longer attempt to model whole social systems, but instead much more specific aspects of human behaviour. This increases the likelihood of obtaining appropriate test data and so producing output utility. Second, a number of recent simulations have drawn on theories or principles borrowed from the biological sciences, especially behavioural ecology (e.g., Mithen 1990, Lake 1995, Kohler *et al.* 2000) and population biology (Steele *et al.* 1998, Zubrow 1990). Perhaps the most important virtue of this borrowing is that it eases the process of validation: if the principles in question are widely accepted to have validity in the biological sciences then, since their integrity can be assumed, it simply remains to demonstrate their relevance. In a third development, models whose function is purely or largely heuristic are now able to draw on a greatly enriched set of concepts and methods for studying complex systems. These range from the rise of agent-based modelling (DeAngelis and Gross 1992), which enables archaeologists to explicitly model individuals (e.g., Doran 1997, Lake 2000), to the mathematics of catastrophe (Zeeman 1977) and chaos (Thompson and Stewart 1986), which provide a means to study the often endogenous origins and inherent unpredictability of systemic change (e.g., McGlade 1997, van der Leeuw and McGlade 1997a).

PROPERTIES OF MODELS

Numerical models can be categorized on the basis of many different properties, ranging from their purpose through to the programming language in which they are written. Five properties are considered here: purpose, timescale, predictability, causality and morphogenesis. Issues related to specific computer software are not considered owing to their limited 'shelf-life'.

Purpose

The purposes for which archaeologists have used numerical models can be subsumed under three headings: tactical, explanatory and heuristic. Numerical models have been used tactically (Orton 1973) to develop archaeological method. For example, Aldenderfer (1981b) built a model of artifact discard to test whether multivariate statistical methods are capable of identifying relevant patterning in assemblages. The model of sampling created by Ammerman *et al.* (1978), Hodder and Okell's (1978) model of association between distributions, and Hodder and Orton's (1976) model of artifact dispersal also fall into this category. Other numerical models have been used in an explanatory role to test hypotheses. Examples include the spread of Neolithic axes (Elliott *et al.* 1978), Mesolithic hunting strategies (Mithen 1990) and Pawnee site development (O'Shea 1978). All these models simulated the formation of an archaeological record which could then be compared with real data. The boundary separating explanatory and heuristic modelling is more ambiguous. Indeed, it is not uncommon for authors to claim both functions for one model (e.g., Kohler *et al.* 2000). Simulations such as that of Mithen (1993b) to model Late Pleistocene mammoth hunting fall at the hypothesis-testing end of the spectrum. Mithen's use of this model was heuristic to the extent that he used it to explore the effect of changing the hunting strategy, but was weakly hypothesis-testing in that he also used it to assess the plausibility that certain scenarios led to mammoth extinction. In contrast, Cooke and Renfrew's (1979) use of their simulation of the emergence and development of early Aegean Civilization was almost entirely heuristic. They wished to explore the dynamics of the system and, unlike Mithen, used 'highly hypothetical' (Renfrew 1981:298) initial values.

Timescale

Whilst all numerical models are iterative they nevertheless differ in the time interval represented by each iteration. The values used in published models range from minutes (Mithen 1990) to units of five years (O'Shea 1978). In addition there are a number of models where the interval of each iteration is not specified (e.g., van der Leeuw and McGlade 1997a). Short intervals, such as minutes or activity 'slots', are usually found in models that explicitly capture aspects of individual decision making (e.g., Aldenderfer 1981b, Lake 1995, Mithen 1990). In contrast, long intervals, such as years (e.g., Wobst 1974), are mostly found in models that treat their subject matter as a system of interdependent variables. Intermediate intervals, such as 10 day blocks (Reynolds 1986) or seasons (e.g., Kohler *et al.* 2000), are typically found where agency is invested in groups rather than individual human beings. To the extent that there is any discernible trend it is towards short and intermediate intervals on the one hand and relatively abstract intervals on the other.

Predictability

Numerical models differ in the certainty with which their results can be predicted from the specified initial conditions. The results of deterministic models are either completely predictable or completely unpredictable. The results of stochastic models are predictable to varying degrees of probability. Stochastic models incorporate one or more processes that involve random variables, either because the modelled behaviour includes a genuinely random process, or more usually to circumvent a problem of inadequate data. The results of such models are not completely determined by the algorithm operating on the initial conditions because they also depend on the specific values of the random variables. A probabilistic prediction may be obtained by repeatedly running the model with different values for the random variables. Many simulation models have a stochastic element, e.g., the probabilistic encounter of game during hunting (Mithen 1990), the simulation of movement as a random walk (Ammerman and Cavalli-Sforza 1979, Elliott *et al.* 1978) and the use of Markov chains to control the sequence of climatic conditions (e.g., Thomas 1972, Aldenderfer 1981b). In contrast, the results of deterministic models are completely determined by the algorithm operating on the initial conditions and are therefore in principle predictable. In practice, however, unpredictability can arise when the results are extremely sensitive to the initial conditions, which is often the case in models based on systems of non-linear differential equations (e.g., McGlade 1997). Although the equations are deterministic, the results cannot be calculated exactly owing to the arbitrary precision with which the computer stores the initial conditions and intermediate values.

Causality

Causality is a difficult concept but one of great relevance to simulation models. The locus of causality may be conceived in at least two ways. One is as those components of a model that determine the nature of change in all others. In the case of tactical and explanatory models these are usually readily identifiable. In the case of heuristic models that comprise systems of components connected by feedback loops it is frequently neither possible nor desirable to locate absolute or root causes of system behaviour. Indeed, the aim of such modelling is often precisely to explore the interdependencies among system components and so avoid the distortions required by monocausal explanation. An alternative view conceives of the locus of causality as the lowest level in a hierarchy of simulation components. Once again, there is a potential problem with feedback: if lower level entities create higher level entities that in turn alters the possible states or actions available to the lower level entities then the locus of causality becomes blurred. At present, however, this problem remains largely theoretical since very few archaeological simulations include feedback between hierarchical levels (for an exception see Doran 1989). Instead, the locus of causality is closely correlated with timescale. As already noted, short iteration intervals generally imply that explanation will be couched in terms of the thoughts and actions of individual human beings, whereas long intervals imply explanation at the supra-individual systemic level.

Morphogenesis

Morphogenesis refers to structural change and is again of greatest relevance to simulation. All simulations model change in the sense that the values of individual variables change over the course of the simulation. Far fewer model structural change, that is, change in the behaviour of the system as a whole. Since many of the most important questions tackled by archaeologists concern morphogenesis, for example the transition to farming or the rise of urbanism, it is not surprising that early models were criticized for their inability to generate novel system behaviours (Renfrew and Cooke 1979). Some recent models can undergo morphogenesis. It occurs in agent-based models when agents change the rules governing their own behaviour, in other words when they make so-called 'meta decisions' about the decision-making process itself (e.g., Reynolds 1997), and it occurs in systems models as a result of a non-linearity in the rules (e.g., van der Leeuw and McGlade 1997a). The sense in which the new system behaviours are novel varies, however. When meta decision-making simply chooses between fixed rules then the novelty is relatively shallow: the modeller simply learns about the conditions under which known behaviours can occur. For example, during the *Emergence of Society* project's simulations (Doran 1997) individuals from an unstructured community eventually co-ordinate their activities as group members, but it seems that the rules governing this increased complexity were written into the model at the outset (van der Leeuw and McGlade 1997b:149). In another variant of meta decision-making the simulation itself generates new rules (Reynolds 1997). Of course, the modeller must still supply an algorithm for generating the new rules, but because his or her involvement is now one step further removed the novelty is deeper. Non-linear systems models are not strictly capable of generating

novelty because their behavioural repertoire is fully determined by the initial equations. Often, however, that repertoire will not have been mapped for all possible parameter values so, even though the system does not generate new rules, novelty is possible in the limited sense that the modeller may observe behaviours that were not expected.

THE FUTURE

Great claims were made for numerical modelling when it was first used by archaeologists in the early 1970s. A quarter of a century later it looks highly unlikely that 'archaeological data and ideas will soon be examined regularly by fitting together sets of conceptions into computerized models that imitate the real world and simulate the dynamic operations of past systems' (Schwartz 1981). Instead it seems most likely that numerical modelling, and computer simulation in particular, will remain the preserve of specialists and even then not their full time preoccupation. It would, however, be a serious loss if the technique were dropped altogether, so it is worth sketching possible developments in the three uses of simulation identified above.

Although tactical modelling has generally proved successful it is now seldom used, largely because there is currently very little active research into the adequacy of archaeological quantitative methods. There is, however, one nascent body of thought that might change this situation. This is the growing suspicion that the current practice of producing explanatory narratives from an essentially ethnographic viewpoint is undermined by, or at best fails to exploit, the peculiar properties of much of the archaeological record. In particular, it is recognized that the individual behaviours about which such narratives are built are often simply not visible in the archaeological 'record' because it is a palimpsest. This is especially clear in the case of the Palaeolithic (Stern 1993), but equally, if less dramatically, true for later periods. In order to overcome this problem some researchers (e.g., Clark 1992, Murray and Walker 1988) will probably attempt to build explanations that ascribe causality to higher level entities, whilst others (e.g., Mithen 1993a, Shennan 1989) will try to gain a better understanding of how local events give rise to observable aggregate phenomena. In either case computer simulation could play an important role in helping to develop quantitative methods for teasing apart separate signals in the archaeological evidence, or at least determining the extent to which this is a realistic aim. Recent moves to integrate multi-agent simulation and geographical information systems (Lake and Mithen 1998, Lake 2000) may prove especially useful in this endeavour (see Chapter 53).

The use of numerical models for hypothesis testing has often been undermined by the poor quality of many archaeological data sets. Nevertheless, recent studies suggest that the technique can be of use if the scope of the hypotheses under test is narrowed in response to data availability. Of course, there is a risk that by considering fewer causal influences this approach is likely to produce overly simplistic explanations. One solution may be to ensure that sufficient attention is given to those instances where predictions made on the basis of narrowly focused, but (relatively) secure input data do not match observations from the archaeological record. If it can be shown that such mismatches are robust, in other words that extreme values from the error range associated with the input are unable to produce the desired outcome, then there is good reason to suppose that other causal factors were also relevant. Ideally such a conclusion should provide a catalyst for further research, but this will require either unusual theoretical agility on the part of the modeller, or that the modelling process is part of a larger project which is not wedded to a single line of enquiry. It is perhaps noteworthy in this respect that funding councils seem increasingly to favour applications for larger projects.

The value of heuristic modelling is likely to remain contentious because it is so difficult to assess. No doubt many modellers have gained important insights by building and experimenting with numerical models, but there will always be a suspicion that this is the last available claim when all else has failed. It could be argued that the real test is whether the insights gained from heuristic modelling have proved useful to others, in which case the conclusion is largely negative. There are two answers to this charge. The first is that new software technologies will allow modelling to become more closely aligned with current theoretical concerns. As discussed above, many early computer simulations were built and deployed within a systems-thinking framework that has since been found wanting. The use of agent-based programming techniques has already made it possible to put individuals back in the picture, whilst new methods for modelling emergent phenomena, such as those being developed at the Santa Fe Institute (Minar et al. 1996), should soon allow exploration of the relationship between agency and structure. The second answer to the charge that heuristic modelling is irrelevant points to the unwillingness of archaeologists to confront the inadequacy of existing explanatory frameworks, especially for dealing with change. It is particularly notable that recent simulation models based on nonlinear mathematics have been criticized for their failure to make good contact with the content of the archaeological record. This would indeed be a serious charge if these models had been constructed to test hypotheses, but they were not. Instead their purpose was to study the behaviour of complex systems (e.g., exchange systems: McGlade 1997), with a view to establishing the kinds of change that our narratives need to encompass. That this process may go against the grain of habitual thought does not make it irrelevant and certainly provides no grounds for rejecting simulation.

ACKNOWLEDGEMENTS

I am especially grateful to Clive Orton and Stephen Shennan, who both provided useful comments on an earlier version of this chapter. Needless to say, neither are responsible for any deficiencies that remain. My understanding of the practicalities and role of simulation in archaeology has also benefited from discussions with many people, notably Steven Mithen and James McGlade – I'm sure that each will find something to disagree with here!

REFERENCES

*Recommended for further reading

*Aldenderfer, M.S. (1981a). Simulation for archaeology: an introductory essay. In Sabloff, J.A. (ed.) *Simulations in Archaeology*, 11–49. University of New Mexico Press: Albuquerque.

Aldenderfer, M.S. (1981b). Creating assemblages by computer simulation: the development and use of ABSIM. In Sabloff, J.A. (ed.) *Simulations in Archaeology*, 67–118. University of New Mexico Press: Albuquerque.

Ammerman, A.J. and Cavalli-Sforza, L.L. (1979). The wave of advance model for the spread of agriculture in Europe. In Renfrew, C. and Cooke, K.L. (eds) *Transformations: Mathematical Approaches to Culture Change*, 275–294. Academic Press: New York.

Ammerman, A., Gifford, D. and Voorrips, A. (1978). Towards an evaluation of sampling strategies: simulated excavations of a Kenyan pastoralist site. In Hodder, I. (ed.) *Simulation Studies in Archaeology*, 123–132. Cambridge University Press: Cambridge.

Black, S. (1978). Polynesian outliers: a study in the survival of small populations. In Hodder, I. (ed.) *Simulation Studies in Archaeology*, 63–76. Cambridge University Press: Cambridge.

Chadwick, A.J. (1979). Settlement simulation. In Renfrew, C. and Cooke, K.L. (eds) *Transformations: Mathematical Approaches to Culture Change*, 237–256. Academic Press: New York.

Clark, G.A. (1992). A comment on Mithen's ecological interpretation of Palaeolithic art. *Proceedings of the Prehistoric Society*, **58**:107–109.

Clarke, D.L. (ed.) (1972). *Models in Archaeology*. Methuen: London.

Cooke, K.L. and Renfrew, C. (1979). An experiment on the simulation of culture changes. In Renfrew, C. and Cooke, K.L. (eds) *Transformations: Mathematical Approaches to Culture Change*, 327–348. Academic Press: New York.

Cordell, L.S. (1972). *Settlement Pattern Changes at Wetherill Mesa, Colorado: a Test Case for Computer Simulation in Archaeology*. Unpublished PhD thesis, University of California, Santa Barbara.

DeAngelis, D.L. and Gross, L.J. (1992). *Individual-Based Models and Approaches in Ecology: Populations, Communities and Ecosystems*. Chapman and Hall: New York.

Donnelly, K.P. (1978). Simulations to determine the variance and edge effect of total nearest-neighbour distance. In Hodder, I. (ed.) *Simulation Studies in Archaeology*, 91–96. Cambridge University Press: Cambridge.

Doran, J.E. (1970). Systems theory, computer simulations, and archaeology. *World Archaeology*, **1**:289–298.

Doran, J.E. (1989). Distributed AI based modelling of the emergence of social complexity. *Science and Archaeology*, **31**:3–11.

Doran, J. (1997). Distributed artificial intelligence and emergent social complexity. In van der Leeuw, S.E. and McGlade, J. (eds) *Time, Process and Structured Transformation in Archaeology*, 283–297. Routledge: London.

Doran, J.E. and Hodson, F.R. (1975). *Mathematics and Computers in Archaeology*. Edinburgh University Press: Edinburgh.

Elliott, K., Ellman, D. and Hodder, I. (1978). The simulation of Neolithic axe dispersal in Britain. In Hodder, I. (ed.) *Simulation Studies in Archaeology*, 79–87. Cambridge University Press: Cambridge.

*Gilbert, N. and Troitzsch, K.G. (1999). *Simulation for the Social Scientist*. Open University Press: Buckingham.

Gunn, J. (1979). Occupation frequency simulation on a broad ecotone. In Renfrew, C. and Cooke, K.L. (eds) *Transformations: Mathematical Approaches to Culture Change*, 257–274. Academic Press: New York.

Hays, D.G. (1965). Simulation: an introduction for anthropologists. In Hymes, D. (ed.) *The Use of Computers in Anthropology*, 401–426. Mouton: The Hague.

Hodder, I. (ed.) (1978). *Simulation Studies in Archaeology*. Cambridge University Press: Cambridge.

Hodder, I. (1979). Simulating the growth of hierarchies. In Renfrew, C. and Cooke, K.L. (eds) *Transformations: Mathematical Approaches to Culture Change*, 117–144. Academic Press: New York.

Hodder, I. (1982). *Symbols in Action*. Cambridge University Press: Cambridge.

Hodder, I. and Okell, E. (1978). An index for assessing the association between distributions of points in archaeology. In Hodder, I. (ed.) *Simulation Studies in Archaeology*, 97–108. Cambridge University Press: Cambridge.

Hodder, I. and Orton, C. (1976). *Spatial Analysis in Archaeology*. Cambridge University Press: Cambridge.

*Kohler, T.A. and Gumerman, G.J. (eds) (2000). *Dynamics in Human and Primate Societies: Agent-Based Modeling of Social and Spatial Processes*. Oxford University Press: Oxford.

Kohler, T.A., Kresl, J., van West, C., Carr, E. and Wilshusen, R. (2000). Be there then: a modelling approach to settlement determinants and spatial efficiency among Late Ancestral Pueblo populations of the Mesa Verde region, U.S. Southwest. In Kohler, T.A. and Gumerman, G.J. (eds) *Dynamics in Human and Primate Societies: Agent-Based Modeling of Social and Spatial Processes*, 145–178. Oxford University Press: Oxford.

Lake, M.W. (1995). *Computer Simulation Modelling of Early Hominid Subsistence Activities*. Unpublished PhD thesis, University of Cambridge.

Lake, M.W. (2000). MAGICAL computer simulation of Mesolithic foraging. In Kohler, T.A. and Gumerman, G.J. (eds) *Dynamics in Human and Primate Societies: Agent-Based Modeling of Social and Spatial Processes*, 107–144. Oxford University Press: Oxford.

Lake, M.W. and Mithen, S.J. (1998). The MAGICAL project: integrating simulation modelling and GIS analysis in archaeology with an application to Mesolithic Scotland. Unpublished ms.

Levison, M., Ward, R. and Webb, J. (1973). *The Settlement of Polynesia: a Computer Simulation*. University of Minnesota Press: Minneapolis.

McGlade, J. (1997). The limits of social control: coherence and chaos in a prestige goods economy. In van der Leeuw, S.E. and McGlade, J. (eds) *Time, Process and Structured Transformation in Archaeology*, 298–330. Routledge: London.

Minar, N., Burkhart, R., Langton, C. and Askenazi, M. (1996). The Swarm simulation system: a toolkit for building multi-agent simulations. http://www.santafe.edu/projects/swarm/overview/overview.html.

Mithen, S.J. (1986). The application of Leslie Matrix models in archaeology. *Science in Archaeology*, **28**:24–31.

Mithen, S.J. (1990). *Thoughtful Foragers: A Study of Prehistoric Decision Making*. Cambridge University Press: Cambridge.

Mithen, S.J. (1993a). Individuals, groups and the Palaeolithic record: a reply to Clark. *Proceedings of the Prehistoric Society*, **59**:393–398.

Mithen, S.J. (1993b). Simulating mammoth hunting and extinction: Implications for the Late Pleistocene of the Central Russian Plain. In Petersen, G.L., Bricker, H.M. and Mellars, P. (eds) *Hunting and Animal Exploitation in the Later Palaeolithic and Mesolithic of Eurasia*, 163–178.

Archaeological Papers No. 4, American Anthropological Association: Washington DC.

Mosimann, J.E. and Martin, P.S. (1975). Simulating overkill by Palaeoindians. *American Scientist*, **63**:304–313.

Murray, T. and Walker, M. (1988). Like what? A practical question of analogical inference and archaeological meaningfulness. *Journal of Anthropological Archaeology*, 7:248–287.

Nagle, R.K. and Saff, E.B. (1989). *Fundamentals of Differential Equations* (2nd edn). Benjamin/Cummings: Redwood City, California.

Naroll, R. (1962). Floor area and settlement population. *American Antiquity*, **27**:587–589.

Orton, C. (1973). The tactical use of models in archaeology – the sherd project. In Renfrew, C. (ed.) *The Explanation of Culture Change*, 137–139. Duckworth: London.

O'Shea, J.M. (1978). The simulation of Pawnee site development. In Hodder, I. (ed.) *Simulation Studies in Archaeology*, 39–46. Cambridge University Press: Cambridge.

Potts, R. (1988). *Early Hominid Activities at Olduvai*. Aldine de Gruyter: New York.

Renfrew, C. (1981). The simulator as demiurge. In Sabloff, J.A. (ed.) *Simulations in Archaeology*, 283–306. University of New Mexico Press: Albuquerque.

Renfrew, C. and Cooke, K.L. (eds) (1979). *Transformations: Mathematical Approaches to Culture Change*. Academic Press: New York.

Renfrew, C. and Level, E. (1979). Exploring dominance: predicting polities from centers. In Renfrew, C. and Cooke, K.L. (eds) *Transformations: Mathematical Approaches to Culture Change*, 145–168. Academic Press: New York.

Reynolds R.G. (1986). An adaptive computer model for the evolution of plant collecting and early agriculture in the eastern valley of Oaxaca. In Flannery, K.V. (ed.) *Guilá Naquitz: Archaic Foraging and Early Agriculture in Oaxaca, Mexico*, 439–507. Academic Press: London.

Reynolds, R.G. (1997). Why does cultural evolution proceed at a faster rate than biological evolution? In van der Leeuw, S.E. and McGlade, J. (eds) *Time, Process and Structured Transformation in Archaeology*, 269–282. Routledge: London.

*Sabloff, J.A. (ed.) (1981). *Simulations in Archaeology*. University of New Mexico Press: Albuquerque.

Schwartz, D.W. (1981). Foreword. In Sabloff, J.A. (ed.) *Simulations in Archaeology*, ix–xi. University of New Mexico Press: Albuquerque.

Shennan, S.J. (1989). Cultural transmission and cultural change. In van der Leeuw, S.E. and Torrence, R. (eds)

What's New: A Closer Look at the Processes of Innovation, 330–346. Unwin Hyman: London.

Steele, J., Adams, J. and Sluckin, T. (1998). Modelling Palaeoindian dispersals. *World Archaeology*, 30:286–305.

Stern, N. (1993). The structure of the Lower Pleistocene archaeological record: a case study from the Koobi Fora formation. *Current Anthropology*, **34**:201–225.

Thomas, D.H. (1972). A computer simulation model of Great Basin Shoshonean subsistance and settlement. In Clarke, D.L. (ed.) *Models in Archaeology*, 671–704. Methuen: London.

Thompson, J.M.T. and Stewart, H.B. (1986). *Nonlinear Dynamics and Chaos*. John Wiley: Chichester.

van der Leeuw, S.E. and McGlade, J. (1997a). Structural change and bifurcation in urban evolution: a non linear dynamical perspective. In van der Leeuw, S.E. and McGlade, J. (eds) *Time, Process and Structured Transformation in Archaeology*, 331–372. Routledge: London.

van der Leeuw, S.E. and McGlade, J. (eds) (1997b). *Time, Process and Structured Transformation in Archaeology*. Routledge: London.

Whallon, R. (1972). The computer in archaeology: a critical survey. *Computers and the Humanities*, 7:29–45.

Wobst, H.M. (1974). Boundary conditions for Palaeolithic social systems: a simulation approach. *American Antiquity*, **39**:147–178.

Wright, H.T. and Zeder, M. (1977). The simulation of a linear exchange system under equilibrium conditions. In Earle, T.K. and Ericson, J.E. (eds) *Exchange Systems in Prehistory*, 233–253. Academic Press: New York.

Yiannouli, E. and Mithen, S.J. (1986). The real and the random architecture of Siphnos: analysing house plans using simulation. *Archaeological Review from Cambridge*, **5**:167–180.

Zeeman, E.C. (ed.) (1977). *Readings in Catastrophe Theory*. Addison-Wesley: Reading, Mass.

Zimmerman, L.J. (1977). *Prehistoric Locational Behaviour: A Computer Simulation*. Reports of the State Archaeologist of Iowa Number 10. University of Iowa Press: Iowa.

Zubrow, E. (1975). *Prehistoric Carrying Capacity: A Model*. Cummings: Menlo Park.

Zubrow, E. (1981). Simulation as a heuristic device in archaeology. In Sabloff, J.A. (ed.) *Simulations in Archaeology*, 143–188. University of New Mexico Press: Albuquerque.

Zubrow, E. (1990). The depopulation of Native America. *Antiquity*, **64**:754–765.

59

Synthesizing Analytical Data – Spatial Results from Pottery Provenance Investigation

H. NEFF

Research Reactor Center, University of Missouri-Columbia.

Based on the discussions of inorganic resource exploitation in Section 6, one can contrast two ideal approaches to provenance determination, one applicable to materials that occur in discrete, localized outcrops and one applicable to materials whose natural sources are spatially widespread. In the first case, sampling most of the relevant sources is a practical goal. Once the raw materials have been sampled, the sources of artifacts can be determined by comparing their compositions to the ranges of compositional variation of reference groups defined for each source. Obsidian and other lithic materials exemplify materials in this first category.

The second category of material is epitomized by ceramics, the raw materials for which can be obtained almost anywhere. Not only are clays nearly ubiquitous, but their compositions may be expected to change gradually through space, as the relative contributions of different parent rocks and weathering regimes gradually change. Even specifying what constitutes a 'clay source' may be problematic in many environments. Although observations such as these are sometimes cited (mainly in informal rather than peer-reviewed contexts) as a basis for regarding raw clay sampling as a waste of time, their real import is to place special demands on the design of ceramic provenance research. Rather than sampling and characterizing groups of 'knowns' (source samples), a ceramic

provenance investigation usually begins by analysing 'unknowns' (artifacts) and then using various pattern-recognition and statistical techniques (Chapter 54) to identify groups in the unknown data. The second step is to link these groups of unknowns to locations on the ground, which is accomplished most directly by sampling raw materials (knowns) and then comparing the raw materials to the groups identified among the unknowns.

The ubiquity of potential ceramic raw material sources also complicates the task of summarizing and recognizing patterns in ceramic source usage data. Whereas comparison of lithic source usage may involve a straightforward comparison of source frequencies across assemblages, comparison of ceramic source usage has to take into consideration the possibility that ceramics in an assemblage might have originated in many different locations in a series of partially overlapping resource zones. Simplifying the comparison by merely tabulating frequencies of 'local' vs. 'non-local' ceramics begs the question of where one places the arbitrary dividing line between 'local' and 'non-local' and masks all variation in source usage within the two categories.

All of these considerations highlight the fact that material characterization-based ceramic provenance determination must be considered not as a separate undertaking from spatial analysis but as part and parcel of a single, integrated analytical strategy. The rest of this chapter describes how the basic approach to ceramic source determination just outlined can be tailored to yield valuable and sometimes surprising results about past interaction patterns, even in an environment that presents significant challenges.

CERAMIC PROVENANCE RESEARCH IN PACIFIC COASTAL GUATEMALA

The examples discussed here all involve ceramic provenance investigations on the Pacific coast of southern Guatemala. This is a highly fertile agricultural region, which apparently saw population maxima during the Late through Terminal Formative Periods (400 BC–AD 200) and Middle through Terminal Classic Period (400 AD–1000 AD). An absence of geographic barriers helped make the region a nexus of cultural interactions that were crucial in the development of prehistoric southern Mesoamerican societies. For instance, Late Formative sculptural art and hieroglyphic writing of this region were ancestral to later achievements by the Classic Maya in the lowlands to the north. A highlight of the Early Classic period was the arrival of emissaries of the central Mexican empire of Teotihuacán, whose presence is attested by ceramic art (Berlo 1980, Medrano 1994) as well as the presence of green obsidian from the central Mexican source at Pachuca (Bove 1993). During Middle and Late Classic times, a Mexican-influenced sculptural style known as Cotzumalguapa spread across much of the central Pacific piedmont and into the neighbouring highlands (Chinchilla 1996, Parsons 1969).

Speculation about interaction patterns on the Guatemalan coast has depended largely on ceramic typological similarities (e.g., Demarest and Sharer 1986, de Hatch 1989). Some time ago, however, Frederick J. Bove recognized that provenance investigation of ceramics via instrumental neutron activation analysis (INAA) could provide a more secure basis for inference. Bove initiated collaborations with Bishop and Neff to secure the necessary analytical resources. INAA was undertaken at Brookhaven National Laboratory (BNL) during the early 1980s and later at the Missouri University Research Reactor (MURR). Procedures used at BNL are described by Bishop et al. (1982a), and those used at MURR are described by Glascock (1992).

A standard approach to ceramic provenance investigation, in which groups of unknowns are defined by pattern recognition techniques, met with only limited

success when applied to the Pacific Guatemalan data (e.g., Neff et al. 1989a). The basic problem is that, to define chemical groups in this data set, one must arbitrarily partition a continuum of compositional variation in the ceramics (Neff and Bove 1999). The continuum of compositions in the ceramic data arises, of course, from conditions in the natural geological environment. Soils and sediments of the Pacific coast originate in the chain of Quaternary volcanoes that lies just north of the coastal plain. The volcanoes supply primary volcanic material (rhyolitic air-fall and ash-flow tuffs) as well as alluvial sediments that are transported by a series of rivers that drain north to south out of the highlands (Figure 59.1). The rivers terminate in a mangrove-estuarine zone immediately behind the beach, where they deposit a large part of their fine sediment load. Clay deposits include primary clays developing on volcanic tuffs, which predominate along the upper edge of the coastal plain and to the west of the Tiquisate zone, and sedimentary clays, which predominate below about 100 metres elevation and to the east of the Tiquisate zone. Clays are widely available, and there are few natural compositional discontinuities (Neff et al. 1992, Neff and Bove 1999).

Motivated in part by the limited success of our initial attempts to make sense of the Pacific coast ceramic compositional data, we have undertaken an extensive ceramic raw materials survey of the region. Beginning in 1990 in the central coastal department of Escuintla, we gradually expanded our sampling coverage to include the entire coastal plain from the western border with Mexico to the eastern border with El Salvador. The bulk of the sample consists of clays (sampling locations shown in Figure 59.1), but volcanic sand and volcanic ash tempers were collected as well. Although sampling coverage is still uneven, analysis of the raw material data clearly documents systematic east-west variation in sediment mineralogy and chemistry that appears to reflect the origin of river-borne sediments in different highland catchments (Neff 1998, Neff et al. 1992). These results are important because they show that, in principle, ceramic source determination is possible on the Guatemalan Pacific coast despite our disappointing initial results.

The INAA undertaken at BNL and MURR yielded a highly complex database of over 3500 analyses of ceramics representing tens of different types and from tens of sites scattered across the Pacific coastal plain and adjacent highland regions of Guatemala and El Salvador. The raw material component of the database is also complex, consisting of 290 clay samples from 146 locations together with 29 volcanic sand samples and 21

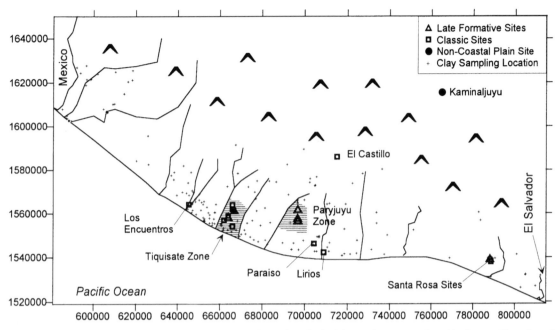

Figure 59.1   Map of the Pacific coast of Guatemala showing archaeological sites and zones mentioned in the text. The axis scales are metres (UTM coordinates), and grid north is parallel to the y-axis.

volcanic ash samples. As shown in the following sections, several complementary approaches to data analysis have proved useful for extracting information about ceramic provenance from this large and complex database.

THE STANDARD APPROACH TO SOURCE DETERMINATION: LATE FORMATIVE FINE RED POTTERY

Despite the difficulties posed by the size of the database and the absence of clear compositional discontinuities in Pacific Guatemalan raw materials, a standard, group-based approach to ceramic source determination has yielded some clear and useful source attributions. As discussed above, the 'standard approach' involves definition of compositional groups among the unknowns followed by assignment of the unknown groups to sources or source zones. The second step may be based on various lines of evidence, including the 'criterion of abundance' (Bishop *et al.* 1982b), arguments based on characteristics of regional geology (e.g., Steponaitis *et al.* 1996), or comparison of the groups to an extensive sample of raw materials (e.g., Neff 1998). In the first example to be discussed here, a source zone

initially suggested by the criterion of abundance was ultimately confirmed by direct comparison with our Pacific coastal raw material sample. In effect, successive applications of the standard approach produced increasingly refined and specific provenance inferences.

Fine Red pottery of the Late Formative period has been recognized as an important component of highland ceramic assemblages both in Guatemala (e.g., Kaminaljuyu; see Figure 59.1) and in neighbouring western El Salvador (Demarest and Sharer 1986, Sharer 1978, Wetherington 1978). On the central Pacific coast of Guatemala, it is present in fairly low frequencies (e.g., Parsons 1967). Efforts to determine the provenance of Fine Red began with the INAA study undertaken at BNL in the 1980s. Bishop *et al.* (1989) concluded that a number of types, including Fine Red, were made locally in both El Salvador and Guatemala. Neff *et al.* (1988a) found that the differences between coastal and highland Guatemalan Fine Red were subtle enough that they might be due to the addition of a distinct volcanic ash temper to clays from a single source. Neither of these studies identified a specific region or regions where Fine Red might have been produced. However, archaeological reconnaissance carried out by Arthur Demarest, Barbara Arroyo, and Sonia Medrano during the late 1980s had encountered substantial quantities of Fine Red pottery at sites on the eastern Pacific coast of Guatemala. The criterion of abundance would therefore suggest that Fine Red pottery from both highland and Pacific coastal sites in Guatemala probably originated on the eastern coast, near the Salvadoran border (Neff *et al.* 1994).

An opportunity to test the hypothesis that Fine Red originated in eastern Pacific coastal Guatemala arose in the mid-1990s, when Francisco Estrada Belli carried out archaeological surveys and excavations in the department of Santa Rosa, near the Salvadoran border. Estrada Belli sampled both raw materials (locations shown in Figure 59.1) and various Formative and

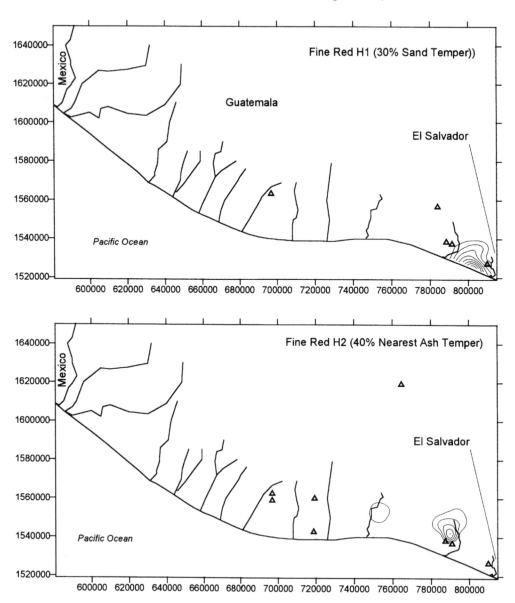

Figure 59.2 Topographic maps indicating variation in the probability that raw materials from various Pacific Guatemalan locations would be included in two Fine Red reference groups. For the sand tempered group (top) raw clays were mixed with 30 per cent of the nearest sampled sand sample. For the ash tempered group (bottom) raw clays were mixed with 40 per cent of the nearest volcanic ash sample. Scale and orientation as before.

Classic pottery types recovered in his surveys and excavations. As reported by Kosakowsky et al. (1999), Fine Red and other pottery types from Santa Rosa are chemically consistent with Fine Red from other Salvadoran and Guatemalan sites, there being a total of three recognizable compositional groups. The two largest groups are Fine Red-H1, which is sand tempered, and Fine Red-H2, which is tempered with volcanic ash. Both groups are represented among the sampled pottery from the Santa Rosa sites.

In a bulk analysis, of course, elemental concentrations are determined not just by the clay component but also by the added non-plastic component (Arnold et al. 1991, Neff et al. 1988a, 1988b, 1989b). Therefore, before comparing raw clay data to the two main Fine Red reference groups allowance must be made for the effect of volcanic ash or volcanic sand temper. New clay data were calculated by pairing each raw clay sample with the nearest sampled temper of the appropriate type (sand or volcanic ash) and then calculating the elemental concentrations for a mixture of the two components.

Comparisons of the 'tempered' clays to a reference group can be represented by a 'probability surface', on which elevation corresponds to the probability that raw materials from a particular location belong to the group (Neff 1995, 1998, Neff and Bove 1999). The probabilities are derived from Mahalanobis distances of the individual raw material data points from the group centroid, taking into account the group's variance-covariance structure (Beier and Mommsen 1994, Bishop and Neff 1989, Leese et al. 1989, Sayre 1975). For both the sand- and ash-tempered Fine Red groups, probability is maximum (and Mahalanobis distance reaches a minimum) on the eastern Pacific coast near the contemporary border with El Salvador (Figure 59.2). (The probability maps in this paper were generated using the program Surfer (Golden Software 1997). The kriging option (see Chapter 53) was used to interpolate a grid of evenly-spaced elevations from the original, unevenly distributed probabilities for the individual raw material sampling locations.) Maximum clay probabilities of around 22 per cent in the case of the sand-tempered group (Fine Red-H1) and 4.4 per cent in the case of the ash-tempered group (Fine Red-H2) easily qualify the raw materials for group membership based on the 1 per cent p-value criterion used for assigning the pottery (Kosakowsky et al. 1999). Direct comparison of raw materials to the Fine Red reference groups thus provides strong support for the hypothesis suggested by the criterion of abundance, namely that Fine Red pottery originated on the eastern Pacific coast

of Guatemala, near the current border with El Salvador.

Comparison of find spots with source zone locations shown in Figure 59.2 indicates that there was substantial movement of Fine Red pottery out of its production zone on the eastern Pacific coast of Guatemala. Ash-tempered Fine Red H2, in particular, was distributed far from its production region (find spots in El Salvador are not shown). This information casts a new light on Demarest and Sharer's (1986) observation that Late Formative ceramic assemblages from southeastern Guatemala and western El Salvador share many types and modes. Based on initial INAA results, these ceramic similarities were previously argued to arise from the wide dissemination of cultural preferences and ceramic production practices (Bishop et al. 1989). It now appears, however, that this 'ceramic sphere' was created as much by movement of pots as by movement of ideas on how to make pots (Kosakowsky et al. 1999, Neff et al. 1999). This case illustrates how a growing database of ceramics and raw material coupled with increasingly refined application of the standard, group-based approach to ceramic source determination yields increasingly secure and specific inferences about interaction amongst past populations.

EXPANDING THE STANDARD APPROACH TO SOURCE DETERMINATION

The standard approach works well in cases, like that of Fine Red pottery, where the focus is on one or a few ceramic types that turn out to show a limited range of compositional variation. Deficiencies become apparent as the number of production centres likely to be represented in a collection of analysed ceramics grows. These deficiencies are especially acute in regions, such as the Pacific coast of Guatemala, where natural ceramic raw materials define a continuum of compositional variation with few clear discontinuities. As demonstrated elsewhere (Neff and Bove 1999), efforts to define compositional groups in such an environment yield arbitrary partitions of the compositional continuum, and the geographic meanings of these partitions shift as marginal specimens are moved into and out of the group. The group-based approach can, however, be reformulated to incorporate more realistic assumptions about how ceramic production patterns and natural raw material variation might have interacted to produce compositional variation in the accumulated ceramic assemblages.

One axiomatic assumption that can be made about any collection of analysed ceramics is that each analysed pot comes from a single source (e.g., a clay pit). Subsets of the collection might come from the same or nearby sources, of course; this is assumed in the group-based approach. But in cases such as coastal Guatemala, where raw materials define a compositional continuum, there is no straightforward way to determine how many true source-related groups might exist in the collection or where the dividing lines between the groups might lie. Since, logically, there is no reason why each and every pot could not come from a unique source, methods for extracting information from the database of ceramic and raw material analyses should allow for this extreme possibility.

Such an allowance can be incorporated into source-usage models by viewing each analysed ceramic as the centroid of a hypothetical group, to which raw materials can be compared in a manner analogous to the standard approach illustrated above with the Fine Red groups. The variance-covariance structure of this hypothetical group must be estimated somehow, and the most obvious means is to sample the elemental concentration space in the immediate vicinity of the focal specimen. Here, the first step is to calculate Euclidean distances to all analysed ceramics from the region in order to identify the 100 specimens that are most similar to the focal specimen. Next, from this group, the 30 specimens with the smallest Mahalanobis distances from the focal specimen (i.e., the hypothetical group centroid) are extracted. These 30 specimens provide the basis for estimating the variance-covariance matrix of the 'group' centred on the focal specimen. The sample sizes used at each stage in this estimation are, of course, arbitrary; they were chosen by experimentation, and they reflect a compromise between the desirability of achieving stable parameter estimates and the desirability of obtaining estimates applicable to a localized source rather than a very extensive source zone.

Like the Fine Red pottery discussed above, most Pacific Guatemalan ceramics are tempered with either volcanic ash or volcanic sand. Therefore, comparison of the raw materials to the hypothetical groups centred on each specimen usually should incorporate the effect of temper, as was done in the Fine Red case. But what tempering proportion should be used? Some time ago, Ed Sayre (Kaplan et al. 1982) suggested using least squares to solve a two-parameter linear equation in which the elemental concentrations in the focal ceramic are regressed on the elemental concentrations in the clay and temper, respectively. With the parameters constrained to sum to 1, the least-squares solution provides

mixing proportions that achieve the closest fit of two given paste components (clays and tempers) to a given ceramic. As in the Fine Red example discussed above, each clay sample is paired with the closest temper of the appropriate type (sand or volcanic ash). The mixture of the two components that best approximates the focal specimen is then calculated, and the resulting elemental concentrations are then substituted for the raw clay data for that sampling location. If the focal ceramic specimen is untempered, raw clay elemental concentrations are retained for each location.

Using the focal specimen as the centroid and the estimated group variance-covariance matrix obtained for that specimen, Mahalanobis distances and associated probabilities of group membership can now be calculated for each ceramic paste in the sample. The Mahalanobis distances indicate how closely a given ceramic paste (i.e., the focal specimen composition) could have been approximated using the raw materials accessible at each location sampled on the raw materials survey. The Hotelling's T^2 probabilities associated with the Mahalanobis distances define for each individual specimen a probability surface analogous to the probability surfaces for the Fine Red groups discussed above (Figure 59.2). Elsewhere (Neff and Bove 1999) probability surfaces are actually based on the inverse of the Mahalanobis distances rather than the probabilities obtained from the Hotelling's T^2 distribution. The two measures are related to one another monotonically. The inverse Mahalanobis distance is a direct indication of similarity of raw materials to the focal specimen, whereas the probabilities incorporate assumptions about the underlying distribution of Mahalanobis distances. The probabilities, however, have a more intuitively accessible interpretation and are used here for that reason.

The purpose of individual-specimen source determination is to provide a basis for comparing source usage between collections of analysed ceramics without imposing an arbitrary group structure on a continuum of compositional variation (Neff and Bove 1999). In effect, each collection is described by a series of probability surfaces, one for each analysed specimen in the collection. To be useful, however, this information must be summarized in some way, so that the collections can be compared.

Here, source usage is summarized for each collection as follows. First, the raw material Hotelling's T^2 probabilities generated for each single-specimen 'group' in the collection are expressed as percentages of the maximum probability for that specimen; this gives equivalent weights to all ceramic specimens in the collection. Next, average scores are calculated across all of the single specimen 'groups' in the collection. When a probability surface is calculated based on the averages for each raw material sampling location, elevation expresses how closely raw materials from a location can be expected to approximate ceramic compositions in the collection. These source-usage surfaces are expected to have multiple peaks and plateaus, since ceramics in the collection are expected to come from a number of distinct locations and, secondarily, because there is some noise in the determination of sources for individual specimens (Neff and Bove 1999).

The summary source-usage data obtained by the above means can be arranged into a matrix in which the collections are represented by successive columns and the raw material sampling locations are represented by successive rows. Each row–column intersection indicates the strength of the compositional connection between a collection and a particular sampling location. Patterns of resemblance in this matrix can be recognized by RQ-mode PCA (Neff 1994), which simultaneously scales the sampling locations (rows) and the collections (columns), the latter being of greatest interest here. The first principal component tends to arrange the sampling locations according to how much they resemble *any* of the pottery, and all of the collections tend to have positive scores of approximately the same magnitude. This 'size' component (Baxter 1994:71) is of little use for recognizing spatial patterning. The second and third components provide the best available two-dimensional representation of source-usage similarities among the collections (Neff and Bove 1999).

LATE FORMATIVE AND CLASSIC PERIOD ASSEMBLAGES FROM THE GUATEMALAN PACIFIC COAST

Three Late Formative and six Classic period collections were extracted from the Pacific coastal Guatemalan database in order to exemplify the individual-specimen source determination methods described above. Locations of the sites or zones from which the collections were drawn are shown in Figure 59.1. Some of these collections were also used in other studies reporting results of individual-specimen source determination (Neff and Bove 1999, Neff *et al.* in prep.). Previously, however, Plumbate, a tradeware known to originate near the present border between Mexico and Guatemala (Neff 1984, Neff and Bishop 1988), was omitted from the collections because the raw material

sample did not extend west to the presumed source region. Recently, a few raw material samples have been analysed from the region adjacent to the Mexican border, and this addition makes it possible to include the analysed Plumbate in the study presented here, albeit by reducing the number of elements to 19 to reconcile different analytical strategies employed. It should be remembered, however, that the raw material sample from the central coast is still much better than that from either the far west or the far east (see Figure 59.1).

PCA-based scaling of the collection summary data yields the configuration of collections and raw material data points shown in Figure 59.3. The clustering of the collections in this 'source-usage space' largely parallels their spatial proximity (Figure 59.1), suggesting that spatially proximate communities tended to obtain pottery from the same sources. This is not surprising, since such a pattern tends to minimize the energetic costs of transporting heavy and breakable ceramic vessels. Collections on the periphery of the PCA space have convincing linkages with comparatively few raw clays, while those with more central positions have links to a greater diversity of clays. The clay data points, meanwhile, diverge from the main point cloud toward the collections in which the approximations of their compositions are best represented. Overall, PCA-based scaling of clays and collections appears to extract systematic geographic variation in raw material composition together with least cost procurement patterns that define dominant zones of ceramic supply for each site or site cluster. The similarities and differences summarized in Figure 59.3 can, however, be examined in more detail and in relation to other information about the prehistoric societies of the Guatemalan coast.

The points on the upper right in Figure 59.3 represent Late Formative and Classic period collections from the eastern coastal department of Santa Rosa. Source usage surfaces for both Santa Rosa collections show probability peaks on the eastern coast, in the immediate vicinity of the sites from which the collections are derived (Figure 59.4). For the Formative collection, this result is expected, since the Fine Red reference groups that are now tied securely to the eastern Guatemalan coast (see above and Kosakowsky *et al.* 1999) are dominated by Fine Red from Nueve Cerros and other sites in Santa Rosa. Ceramics used during the Classic period in this region also seem to have been derived in large part from local sources. Interestingly, both the Formative and Classic source-usage surfaces show minor peaks lying west of Santa Rosa, which may suggest a west-to-east flow of

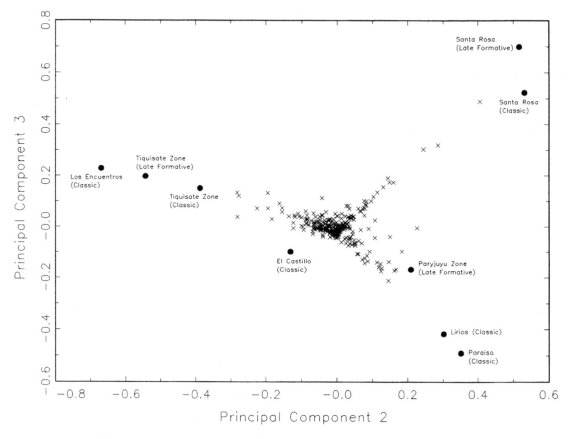

Figure 59.3 Variable and object coordinates on Principal Components 2 and 3 derived from a PCA of the composite source-usage maps for the nine ceramic collections studied (locations in Figure 59.1). The underlying data matrix has clay sampling locations in successive rows and the nine ceramic collections in successive columns. Each cell represents the average strength of the linkage between the clay sampling location and the ceramics in a collection.

ceramics. This possibility requires further investigation, but it is noteworthy that a small number of the Classic period specimens from La Maquina are macroscopically similar to Tiquisate White ware from the central coastal piedmont (discussed below).

The collections on the lower right in Figure 59.3 are from Lirios and Paraiso, two Classic period sites on the lower part of the central coast (Figure 59.1). Both sites are very close to the highest points on their respective source-usage surfaces (Figure 59.5), in accord with hypothesis that ceramic consumption at these sites emphasized local products. The similarity in source usage of these two sites has been noted previously (Neff and Bove 1999). The main difference between the two source usage surfaces is that Paraiso's shows a peak along the upper reaches of the Nahualate River. This peak corresponds to one of the most important

production centres for Tiquisate White ware (Neff 1995), which is represented by a number of specimens in the Paraiso collection and not by any in the Lirios collection. Another difference is that the Paraiso collection has a larger area of high elevation on the far western coast, near the border with Mexico; this reflects the presence in the Paraiso collection of several San Juan Plumbate specimens, which originate near the present Mexico–Guatemala border.

The collection from the Late Formative Paryjuyu zone and that from the Classic period site of El Castillo fall closest to the main scatter of raw material data points in the PCA space (Figure 59.3). This indicates that relatively more of the sampled raw materials are similar to ceramics in each collection. In the case of Paryjuyu, the high number of raw material linkages appears to reflect the general similarity of clays from

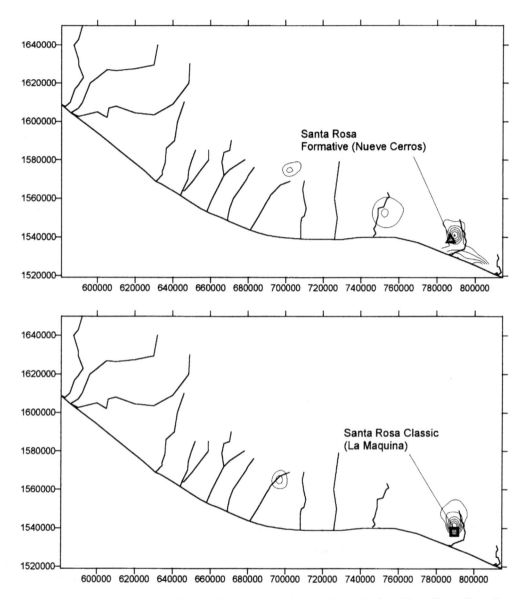

Figure 59.4 Composite source usage maps for Late Formative period analysed ceramics from Nueve Cerros, Santa Rosa (top) and Classic period ceramics from La Maquina, Santa Rosa (bottom). Contours represent the average percentage of the maximum clay probability calculated relative to each single-specimen group in the collection. Contour intervals 2 per cent, minimum contour 6 per cent. Scale and orientation as before.

along the Coyolate River to Paryjuyu zone ceramics: the three sites represented in the collection are located more or less at the summit of the probability surface. Additionally, eight of the 69 Paryjuyu specimens are members of the Fine Red reference group, and these constituents define a smaller eastern peak on the source-usage surface.

The collection from the Classic period piedmont site of El Castillo also shows similarities to a large number of raw material samples (Figure 59.3), but in this case linkages are spread across a broad area of the coastal plain. The source usage map for El Castillo (Figure 59.6) shows a large area of high-probability terrain extending out to the south, southwest, and southeast,

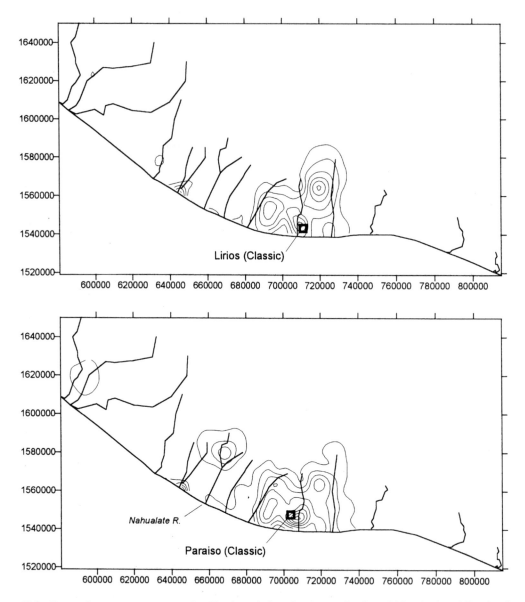

Figure 59.5 Composite source usage maps for Classic period analysed ceramics from Lirios (top) and Paraiso (bottom). Contours represent the average percentage of the maximum clay probability calculated relative to each single-specimen group in the collection. Contour intervals 2 per cent, minimum contours 2 per cent (top) and 1 per cent (bottom). Scale and orientation as before.

suggesting that the site drew ceramics from a broad area of the coastal plain and piedmont. Prominent peaks on the upper coastal plain to the southwest of the site correspond to the major sources of Tiquisate White ware, which came to dominate serving vessel production during the Classic period (Neff 1995). Although there are a few analysed Plumbate specimens in the El Castillo collection, they do not define a peak in the Plumbate source region along the Mexican border; this reflects both the small number of Plumbate analyses and the poor quality of the raw material sample from the far west. On the other hand, the probability surface does show a peak on the far eastern coast, which suggests the possibility that part of the El

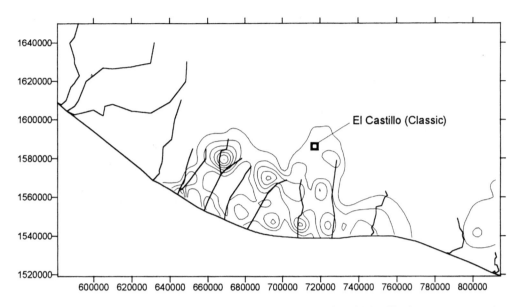

Figure 59.6 Composite source usage map for Classic period analysed ceramics from El Castillo. Contours represent the average percentage of the maximum clay probability calculated relative to each single-specimen group in the collection. Contour interval 1 per cent, minimum contour 1.5 per cent. Scale and orientation as before.

Castillo collection originated there. The latter result is especially important in light of: (i) the possibility that some Classic period ceramics may also have flowed in the other direction (see above), and (ii) the recent discovery of Cotzumalguapa-style stone sculpture at several sites on the eastern coast (Estrada Belli and Kosakowsky 1998).

El Castillo and its neighbours, El Baul and Bilbao, are at the epicentre of the Cotzumalguapa style. The ceramic provenance data presented here thus indicate that stone sculptural canons and ceramics circulated along the same channels. The accumulating evidence strongly suggests that a large part of the Guatemalan Pacific coast was integrated during the Classic period into an interaction sphere that may have been centred in the Cotzumalguapa zone, near El Castillo (Chinchilla 1996, Estrada Belli and Kosakowsky 1998, Parsons 1967, 1969).

The large scale of the Cotzumalguapa interaction sphere can be appreciated by contrasting the ceramic source usage pattern for El Castillo, in the Cotzumalguapa core zone, with ceramic source usage at other Classic period sites. Two source usage maps can be contrasted by subtracting the grid estimated for one collection from the grid estimated for the other, so that the resulting surface shows extreme values (positive or negative) where the differences between the two grids are greatest. (The program

Surfer (Golden Software 1997) has options for performing mathematical operations (subtraction in this case) on grids of the same size). When the grid for Paraiso is subtracted from the grid for El Castillo, the resulting surface (Figure 59.7) identifies the lower central coast as much more strongly linked to Paraiso. Surrounding Paraiso's relatively localized ceramic supply zone is a more extensive area that was more strongly linked to El Castillo. The transition between Paraiso-dominated and Castillo-dominated zones falls very close to midway between the two sites. Figure 59.8 thus suggests that the spheres of influence controlled by Paraiso and El Castillo were largely complementary and that El Castillo's was substantially larger than Paraiso's. Stone sculptural distributions are again relevant here: the distinctive Cotzumalguapa sculpture found at El Castillo and other piedmont sites as far east as Santa Rosa (Estrada Belli and Kosakowsky 1998) is completely absent at Paraiso, Lirios, and other lower coastal sites. Multiple lines of evidence thus depict a competitive situation, with the Cotzumalguapa core zone sites dominating a large area of the piedmont together with far eastern parts of the coastal plain, and Paraiso together with Lirios controlling a circumscribed zone on the lower part of the central coast.

The individual-specimen source determination approach also facilitates identification of trends in

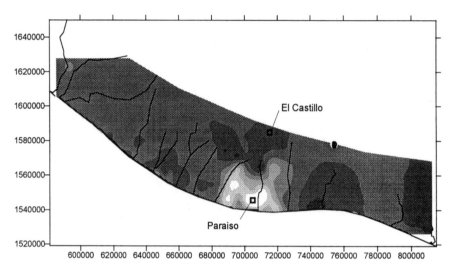

Figure 59.7   Map showing the result of subtracting the Paraiso probability surface grid (Figure 59.5, bottom) from the El Castillo probability surface grid (Figure 59.6). Extreme positive values (dark) indicate regions where the average percentage of the maximum clay probability calculated relative to each single-specimen group in the El Castillo collection is large compared to the Paraiso collection. Extreme negative values (unshaded) indicate regions where the average percentage of the maximum clay probability calculated relative to each single-specimen group in the Paraiso collection is large compared to the El Castillo collection. Contour interval 2 per cent, minimum contour −9 per cent, maximum contour, 3 per cent. Scale and orientation as before.

resource procurement and economic interaction over time (Neff *et al.* in prep.). This can be illustrated by source usage data for two Late Formative sites and five Classic period sites in the Tiquisate zone. The sites all lie within about 10 kilometres of one another on the lower coastal plain (Figure 59.1). These collections together with the Classic period collection from Los Encuentros form a cluster at the low end of Principal Component 2 in the PCA source-usage space (Figure 59.3). The source usage summaries for the two collections (Figure 59.8) show some overlap in sources, as would be expected given their spatial proximity and their proximity in the PCA source-usage space. Nonetheless, there is a clear contrast between Late Formative and Classic period procurement patterns, which can be highlighted by subtracting the Late Formative grid from the Classic period grid (Figure 59.9). Whereas Late Formative source usage was focused on lower coastal resources in the immediate vicinity of the collection sites, Classic period source usage shifted to residual clay sources of the upper coastal plain, where Tiquisate White ware production was centred (Neff 1995, Neff *et al.* in prep.). Thus, the cost of obtaining ceramics in the Tiquisate zone increased between Late Formative and Classic times: more vessels came from greater distances. Elsewhere (Neff 1995, Neff *et al.* in prep.), I have argued that

this shift in ceramic circulation patterns reflects an evolutionary process in which specialized ceramic production and regional exchange were concurrently favoured by selection associated with growing differentials in comparative advantage.

CONCLUSION

The archaeological record is recognizable as the product of human activity in large part because those activities displaced materials in space. It follows that archaeologists concerned with providing a scientific account of the archaeological record must seek objective means to describe the kinds and amounts of materials that were moved and the directions and distances over which they travelled. The basic data are measurements of the discrepancy between where objects occur in the archaeological record and where they resided prior to human intervention. Provenance investigation provides these data.

Application of chemistry-based provenance methods to ceramic circulation is complicated by the fact that ceramic raw materials are widely available and by the fact that the chemical profile of clays often changes gradually through space. The first condition means that the ceramics in an assemblage may originate

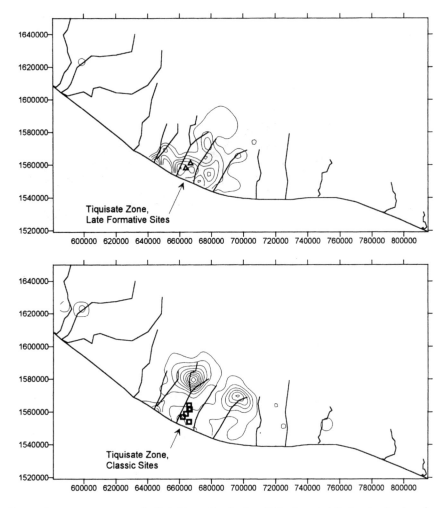

Figure 59.8 Composite source usage maps for Late Formative (top) and Classic period (bottom) collections from the Tiquisate zone. Contours represent the average percentage of the maximum clay probability calculated relative to each single-specimen group in the collection. Contour intervals 1 per cent (top), 2 per cent (bottom), minimum contours 2 per cent (top) and 1 per cent (bottom). Scale and orientation as before.

in numerous locations, while the second condition complicates the task of mapping composition on to geographic space. Because of these problems, extracting information about ceramic circulation patterns from ceramic compositional data may loom as a substantial challenge. The Pacific Guatemalan examples discussed here show how these problems can be circumvented by investing heavily in raw material sampling and by explicitly incorporating space into the quantitative analysis of compositional data. Substantive implications of these Guatemalan ceramic provenance studies have not yet been explored completely. Already it is clear, however, that our investment in raw material sampling

and methodological refinement is paying off in the form of new insights into ancient political and economic relations and their evolution over time.

ACKNOWLEDGEMENTS

Fred Bove has contributed immeasurably to the research reported in this paper. I thank him especially for trusting that a substantial investment in chemistry-based ceramic provenance determination would eventually pay off. The work has also depended on contributions of time, energy, and expertise from Barbara

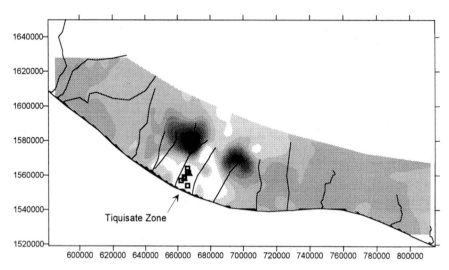

Figure 59.9   Map showing the result of subtracting the Tiquisate zone Late Formative probability surface grid (Figure 59.8, top) from the Tiquisate zone Classic period probability surface grid (Figure 59.8, bottom). Extreme positive values (dark) indicate regions where the average percentage of the maximum clay probability calculated relative to each single-specimen group in the Classic period collection is large compared to the Late Formative collection. Extreme negative values (unshaded) indicate regions where the average percentage of the maximum clay probability calculated relative to each single-specimen group in the Late Formative collection is large compared to the Classic period collection. Contour interval 1 per cent, minimum contour −3 per cent, maximum contour, 8 per cent. Scale and orientation as before.

Arroyo, Ron Bishop, Jessica Child, Jim Cogswell, Arthur Demarest, Francisco Estrada Belli, Mike Glascock, Marion Hatch, Cynthia Hays-Lewis, Carlos Herman, Sergio Herrera, Laura Kosakowsky, Enrique Urisas, Brenda Lou, Mike Love, Sonia Medrano, Genie Robinson, Sergio Rodas, Claudia Wolley, and certainly others whom I have failed to remember. The US National Science Foundation provided support for many aspects of the research reported here, including raw material sampling (BNS89-11580) and INAA at MURR (BNS91-02016, SBR95-03035).

REFERENCES

*Recommended for further reading

Arnold, D.E., Neff, H. and Bishop, R.L. (1991). Compositional analysis and 'sources' of pottery: an ethnoarchaeological approach. *American Anthropologist*, **93**:70–90.

Baxter, M.J. (1994). *Exploratory Multivariate Analysis in Archaeology*. Edinburgh University Press: Edinburgh.

Beier, T. and Mommsen, H. (1994). Modified Mahalanobis filters for grouping pottery by chemical composition. *Archaeometry*, **36**:287–306.

Berlo, J.C. (1980). *Teotihuacán Art Abroad: A Study of Metropolitan Style and Provincial Transformation in Incensario Workshops*. Unpublished Ph.D. Dissertation, Yale University.

Bishop, R.L. and Neff, H. (1989). Multivariate analysis of compositional data in archaeology. In Allen, R.O. (ed.) *Archaeological Chemistry IV*, 576–586. Advances in Chemistry Series 220, American Chemical Society: Washington DC.

Bishop, R.L., Harbottle, G. and Sayre, E.V. (1982a). Chemical and mathematical procedures employed in the Maya Fine Paste ceramics project. In Sabloff, J.A. (ed.) *Excavations at Seibal: Analyses of Fine Paste Ceramics*, 272–282. Memoir 15(2), Peabody Museum: Cambridge, Mass.

Bishop, R.L., Rand, R.L. and Holley, G.R. (1982b). Ceramic compositional analysis in archaeological perspective. In Schiffer, M.B. (ed.) *Advances in Archaeological Method and Theory 5*, 276–329. Academic Press: New York.

Bishop, R.L., Demarest, A.A. and Sharer, R.J. (1989). Chemical analysis and the interpretation of Late Preclassic intersite ceramic patterns in the southeast highlands of Mesoamerica. In Bove, F.J. and Heller, L. (ed.) *New Frontiers in the Archaeology of the Pacific Coast of Southern Mesoamerica*, 135–145. Anthropological Research Papers No. 39, Arizona State University: Tempe, AZ.

Bove, F.J. (1993). The terminal Formative–Early Classic transition. In Bove, F.J., Medrano, S., Arroyo, B. and Lou, B. (eds) *The Balberta Project: The Terminal Formative–Early Classic Transition on the Pacific Coast of Guatemala*, 177–194. Memoirs in Latin American Archaeology No. 6, University of Pittsburgh: Pittsburgh.

Chinchilla, O.F. (1996). *Settlement Patterns and Monumental Art at a Major Pre-Columbian Polity: Cotzumalguapa, Guatemala.* Unpublished Ph.D. Dissertation, Vanderbilt University, Nashville.

de Hatch, M.P. (1989). Observaciones sobre el desarollo cultural prehistórico en la costa sur de Guatemala. In Whitley, D.S. and Beaudry, M.P. (eds) *Investigaciones Arqueológicos en la Costa Sur de Guatemala,* 38–81. Institute of Archaeology Monograph 31, UCLA: Los Angeles.

Demarest, A.A. and Sharer, R.J. (1986). Late Preclassic ceramic spheres, culture areas, and cultural evolution in the Southeastern highlands of Mesoamerica. In Urban, P. and Schortman, E.M. (eds) *The Southeast Maya Periphery,* 194–223. University of Texas Press: Austin.

Estrada Belli, F. and Kosakowsky, L.J. (1998). Survey in Jutiapa, southeastern Pacific Guatemala, 1997. *Mexicon,* **20**:55–64.

Golden Software (1997). *Surfer for Windows,* version 6.04. (http://www.golden.com/).

Glascock, M.D. (1992). Characterization of archaeological ceramics at MURR by neutron activation analysis and multivariate statistics. In Neff, H. (ed.) *Chemical Characterization of Ceramic Pastes in Archaeology,* 11–30. Monographs in World Archaeology No. 7, Prehistory Press: Madison, WI.

Kaplan, M.F., Harbottle, G. and Sayre, E.V. (1982). Multi-disciplinary analysis of Tell el Yahudiyeh ware. *Archaeometry,* **24**:127–142.

Kosakowsky, L.J., Estrada Belli, F. and Neff, H. (1999). Late Preclassic ceramic industries of eastern Pacific Guatemala and western El Salvador: the Pacific Coast of Santa Rosa as core, not periphery. *Journal of Field Archaeology,* **26**:377–390.

Leese, M.N., Hughes, M.J. and Stopford, J. (1989). The chemical composition of tiles from Bordesley: a case study in data treatment. In Rahtz, S.P.Q. and Richards, J. (eds) *Computer Applications and Quantitative Methods in Archaeology 1989,* 241–249. BAR International Series 548, British Archaeological Reports: Oxford.

Medrano, S. (1994). *Un incensario estilo – Teotihuacano de Escuintla,* 131–143. VIII Simposio de Investigaciones Arqueológicas en Guatemala, 1993. IDEAH and Asociación Tikal: Guatemala.

Neff, H. (1984). *Developmental History of the Plumbate Pottery Industry in the Eastern Soconusco Region, A.D. 600–A.D. 1250.* Unpublished Ph.D. Dissertation, University of California, Santa Barbara.

Neff, H. (1994). RQ-mode principal components analysis of ceramic compositional data. *Archaeometry,* **36**:115–130.

Neff, H. (1995). A role for 'sourcing' in evolutionary archaeology. In Teltser, P. (ed.) *Evolutionary Archaeology: Methodological Issues,* 69–112. University of Arizona Press: Tucson.

Neff, H. (1998). Units in chemistry-based provenance investigations of ceramics. In Ramenofsky, A.F. and Steffen, A. (eds) *Measuring Time, Space, and Material: Unit Issues in Archaeology,* 115–127. University of Utah Press: Provo, UT.

Neff, H. and Bishop, R.L. (1988). Plumbate origins and development. *American Antiquity,* **53**:505–522.

*Neff, H. and Bove, F.J. (1999). Mapping ceramic compositional variation and prehistoric interaction in Pacific coastal Guatemala. *Journal of Archaeological Science,* **26**:1037–1051.

Neff, H., Bishop, R.L. and Arnold, D.E. (1988a). Reconstructing ceramic production from ceramic compositional data: a Guatemalan example. *Journal of Field Archaeology,* **15**:339–348.

Neff, H., Bishop, R.L. and Sayre, E.V. (1988b). Simulation approach to the problem of tempering in compositional studies of archaeological ceramics. *Journal of Archaeological Science,* **15**:159–172.

Neff, H., Bishop, R.L. and Bove, F.J. (1989a). Compositional patterning in ceramics from Pacific coastal and highland Guatemala. *Archeomaterials,* **3**:97–109.

Neff, H., Bishop, R.L. and Sayre, E.V. (1989b). More observations on the problem of tempering in compositional studies of archaeological ceramics. *Journal of Archaeological Science,* **16**:57–69.

*Neff, H., Bove, F.J., Lou, B. and Piechowski, M.F. (1992). Ceramic raw materials survey in Pacific coastal Guatemala. In Neff, H. (ed.) *Chemical Characterization of Ceramic Pastes in Archaeology,* 59–84. Prehistory Press: Madison WI.

Neff, H., Bove, F.J., Robinson, E. and Arroyo, B. (1994). A ceramic compositional perspective on the Formative to Classic transition in southern Mesoamerica. *Latin American Antiquity,* **5**:333–358.

Neff, H., Cogswell, J.W., Kosakowsky, L.J., Estrada Belli, F. and Bove, F.J. (1999). A new perspective on the relationships among cream-paste ceramic traditions of southeastern Mesoamerica. *Latin American Antiquity,* **10**:281–299.

Neff, H., Bove, F.J. and Arroyo, B. (in prep). Evolution of ceramic resource procurement on the Guatemalan central Pacific coast. In Dunnell, R.C. and Leonard, R.D. (eds) *Applications of Evolutionary Theory in Archaeology.*

Parsons, L.A. (1967). *Bilbao, Guatemala: An Archaeological Study of the Pacific Coast Cotzumalguapa Region, vol. 1.* Publications in Anthropology No. 11, Milwaukee Public Museum: Milwaukee.

Parsons, L.A. (1969). *Bilbao, Guatemala: An Archaeological Study of the Pacific Coast Cotzumalguapa Region, vol. 2.* Publications in Anthropology No. 12, Milwaukee Public Museum: Milwaukee.

Sayre, E.V. (1975). *Brookhaven Procedures for Statistical Analyses of Multivariate Archaeometric Data.* Report BNL-23128, Brookhaven National Laboratory: New York.

Sharer, R.J. (1978). Pottery and conclusions. In Sharer, R.J. (ed.) *The Prehistory of Chalchuapa, El Salvador, Vol. 3,* 1–226. University of Pennsylvania Press: Philadelphia.

Steponaitis, V.P., Blackman, M.J. and Neff, H. (1996). Large-scale patterns in the chemical composition of Mississippian pottery. *American Antiquity,* **61**:555–572.

Wetherington, R.K. (1978). Descriptive taxonomy of Kaminaljuyú ceramics. In Wetherington, R.K. (ed.) *The Ceramics of Kaminaljuyú, Guatemala,* 3–50. Monograph Series on Kaminaljuyú, Pennsylvania State University: University Park.

General Index

Abietic acid   343
Abundance Estimate of
    macrofossils   162
Accelerator Mass Spectrometry
    (AMS)   25, 27–30, 98, 332
Acid hydrolysis   602
Acid rain   198
Acid trend in soils   601
Acoustic microscopy   84
Activity, thermodynamic   596
Actuopalaeontology   181
Additive dose method, in TCD   48, 51
Adenine   302
    see also DNA
aDNA (ancient DNA)   207, 219, 297,
    306
Aerial photography   522, 555
Aerial reconnaissance   521
Age at death
    in animals   419
    in human skeletons   207, 239–243,
        251, 263, 285, 700
Age structure of population   260
Agent–based modelling   727
Agricultural practices   174, 338
Agriculture, origins of   393
Airborne multispectral scanners
    (MSS)   522, 557–559
Airborne thermography   559
^{26}Al   94, 98
Albumin   318
Alkaline glaze – degradation   623
Alkaline trend in soils   602
Alleles   304
Alum industry   500
Amber   295, 514
Amino acid racemization   6, 242, 325–
    326, 641
Amino acids   355
Anaemia   232, 308
Anaerobic bacteria   628

Anasazi sites, New Mexico, air
    photography   555
Anatomically modern humans   63
Ancient Biomolecules Initiative
    (ABI)   xix, 297
Animal fodder   371
Annales school   112
Annual water deficit   602
Anodic reaction in
    electrochemistry   605
Anomalous fading in TL   51
Anopheles mosquitoes   232
Antennae – radar   547
    frequency of   548
Anthracosis   253, 254, 255
Antigen   317
Archaeobotany   395–397
    and agriculture   393–399
Archaeological chemistry – golden
    age   507
Archaeological Data Service
    (ADS)   561, 576
Archaeological prospection   521–528
Archaeological science,
    introduction   xvii–xx
Archaeomagnetism   73–79
    dating applications   74–76
Archaeometallurgy   485–487
Archaic hominids   63, 214
Archangelos potters, Rhodes   453
Arctic Fox   148
Armadillo   149, 423
'Armchair archaeometallurgy'   487
Artificial intelligence   681
Atherosclerosis   252, 253, 254, 255
Atmosphere, in biogeochemical
    cycles   191
Atomic Absorption Spectrometry
    (AAS)   463, 509
Attic black and read figure vases –
    technology   456

'Australian slide' technique (in
    TCD)   52
Australopithecines   214
Autopsy   250, 410
Average Linkage Cluster Analysis   688

Bacterial denitrification   198
Bale hearth   496
Bayesian statistical approaches   25,
    208, 263–265, 669, 692, 695–702
    image processing   699
    theorem   696
^{10}Be   94, 98
Bear   69, 148
Bed Bug   130
Beekeeping   122, 430
Beeswax   333–334, 435
Bejel   232
    see also treponematosis
Bering land bridge   150
Berkhamstead furnaces   501
Bilateral symmetry in animals   706
Bile acids   566
Biochemical pathways   275
Biodegradation   351, 627
Biodeterioration   351, 627
Biogeochemical cycles   106, 191–199,
    297
    carbon cycle   195–197
    'mean residence time' (MRT)   192
    nitrogen cycle   197–198
    phosphorus and sulfur cycles   198–
        199
    water cycle   192–195
Biogeography   124, 135
Biological resources, see resource
    exploitation
Biomarkers   175, 331, 345, 526
Biominerals   174
Biomolecular studies   266–267, 295–
    299, 396
    see also DNA

Biopurification   274
Biosphere   191
Biostratinomy   180, 181, 184, 639
   experimental   184–186
   see also taphonomy
Birch bark tar   343
Bitumins   343, 345
Blood residues   313–322
   see also haemoglobin
Bloomery slag   503
Blue Whale   416
'Bog bodies'   404, 592
Bole hearth   496
Bomb carbon   25
Bone
   conservation   642–646
      consolidation polymers   643
   cremated   281–290
   diagenesis   182–186, 325, 637–647
      chewing   185
      exposure   184
      heating   185
      transport   184
   estimation of MNI   707–708
   quantification   703–710
      by weight   705
   structure   637–639
Bonfire   495
Bordes-Binford debate   719
Breakage of objects   712
Bremen Cog   630
Brewing   371
British Atmospheric Data Centre   114
British Oceanic Data Centre   114
Bronze disease in conservation   610
Brucellosis   227, 229
Brunhes/Matuyama boundary   15, 76
Burial environment   595–603
Buried soils   143
Burnt bone   281–290
   colour   282, 288
   histological ageing   285
   shrinkage   281
   size of fragments   289

^{14}C (in-situ cosmogenic nuclei)   94, 98
C_3 photosynthesis   270
C_4 photosynthesis   270
^{41}Ca dating   5, 98
Caesium gradiometer   523
Calcined bone   287
Calibrated radiocarbon age   6, 25–27
Calvin–Benson photosynthetic pathway
   (C_3)   270
Cambridge University Committee for
   Aerial Photography   556

Canadian Conservation Institute   652
Cancer   254
Cannibalism   233
   molluscan   434
Canonical Correspondence Analysis
   (CCA)   161
Carbon cycle   191, 195–197, 628
Carbon isotopes ratios   208, 271, 334,
   336, 399
   and diet   208, 269, 270–272
   diet to collagen shift   271
   in collagen   326
Carbonized plant remains   396
Caries   251
Cat Louse   130
Cathodic reaction in
   electrochemistry   605
Causality   728
Cave deposits   183
Cell potential in electrochemistry   606
Cementation furnace   500
Ceramics   449–457
   firing   456, 530
   petrology   449–459, 530
   porosity   620
   post-depositional changes   615–625
   provenance   508, 511–512, 733–747
   quantification   713
   vitrification   620
Cesspits   131
Chagas disease   410
Châine opératoire   443, 450, 455, 465
Chert   463
Childe, V.G.   484
Chitin   123, 131
Chloride ions in metal corrosion   609
Cholesterol   296, 340
   carbon isotope values   342
Chromatography   295, 331, 332, 333,
   341, 345, 435, 436,
   447
Chromosomes   239
   see also DNA
Citrate cycle   355
^{36}Cl   94, 98, 99
   in forgeries   612
Clamp (firing)   496
Classic Maya, decline   193
Classification trees   693
Clay
   geochemistry   451
   minerals   450
   slip – degradation   623
   sources   733
Climate change   9, 17, 153, 155–166,
   193
   and human evolution   17

Climate models   103–104, 112–118
   Energy Budget Models (EBM)   114–
      115, 118
   General Circulation Models
      (GCM)   113–114, 118
   quaternary environments   111–119
Climate Response Model   163
Climate system   113
Cluster Analysis   407, 688–689, 700
Cochineal insect   435
Cockroach   129
Co-evolution   233, 422
Colitis, acute bacterial   410
Collagen   298, 323, 342, 354–355
   experimental decomposition   355
   structure   637
Collagenase activity   353
Collections care   652
Colonization of Polynesia   726
Colorimetric analysis   161
Compact bone   638
Compound specific Isotope Ratio Mass
   Spectrometry   298
Computed tomography   408
Computer Aided Design (CAD)   672
Computer Aided Mapping
   (CAM)   672
Computerized animation   524
Computing   667–669
   see also statistics, multivariate data
      analysis, cluster analysis
Conceptual model   725
Conceptual utility in modelling   726
Connate water in obsidian   85
Conservation and life span of
   objects   649–659
   on-site   650
Conservation, materials   652
Consolidants   643
Cooking vessels – residues   333
Copper corrosion   589
Copper deposit, idealized   487
Copper–silver ion sterilization   629
Coprolites
   and diet   403–411, 436
   composition   404
   food identification   405
      ritual foods   409
   intestinal parasites   405
Coprostanol   569
Coral   438
   calibration of radiocarbon   26, 69
Coronary artery disease   252
   see also atherosclerosis
Correspondence Analysis   161, 691
Corrosion potential   606
Cortical bone   638

Cosmogenic isotopes   93–100
Coventional radiocarbon age   23
Craft specialization   446
Craniometry   205
Cremation   281–292, 639
   animal bone   287–288
   combustion rates   284
   modern cremation   283
   pathology of cremated bone   287
Cribra orbitalia   308
Cro-Magnon   213
Crop marks   557
Crossdating in dendrochronology   35
Crossover-immuno-electrophoresis
   (CIEP)   315, 316, 318, 319, 320
Crystallinity index in bone   642
Culinary practices   371
Cultural Resource Management
   (CRM)   521, 543, 678
Cumulative viewshed   676
Cytosine   302
   see also DNA

δ notation   194, 270
Dahlite   637
Darwin, C.   214, 215, 365, 393
Data integration   575–583
   alphanumeric data   579
   geographical data   577–578
De Vries effects in radiocarbon   25, 26,
   27
Dead Sea Scrolls   632
De-alkalization of glass   617
Dealloying of metals   612
Debitage, lithics   464
Degradation and preservation   587–
   591
   bone   637–647
   diagenesis   588
   fats   334
      laboratory experiments   334
   preservation   591–592
Delta notation in isotopes   194, 270
Demography   221–222, 231, 259–268
Dendrochronology   3, 4, 26, 35–46, 75
   and radiocarbon time   42
   techniques   37–38
Dendroclimatology   42, 193
Dendrogram   688, 689
Dendroprovenancing   41
Denitrification   198, 272
Dental attrition   240, 241
Dental microwear   371
Dentine transparency   241
Deoxyribonucleic acid, see DNA
Desiccated bodies   251

Detrended Correspondance Analysis
   (DCA)   155, 159, 164
Detrital remanent magnetism   14
Developmental utility, models   726
Devensian   137, 139
Diagenesis   180, 186–187,640–642
   see also taphonomy
Diagnostic slags   502
Diamagnetism   73
Diatom analysis   168
Diet
   human   220–221
   palaeodiet   269–276, 297, 340–343,
      403–411
   and isotopes   269–273
   and trace elements   274–275
Digital camera   556
Digital Elevation Modelling
   (DEM)   521, 522, 677
Digital photogrammetry   557
Digital Terrain Models (DTM)   557
Discriminant analysis   509, 690
Disease, human   222, 225–234
   and culture   232–233
   and coprolites   410
DNA   7, 131, 206, 208, 219, 223, 225,
   228, 232, 239, 266, 267, 297, 298,
   301–311, 313, 319, 320, 321, 352,
   363, 368, 395, 396, 397, 407, 592,
   641, 642, 644
   and disease   308
   burnt bone   287
   dog   310
   horse   310
   kinship studies   308
   population studies   309–310
   structure   302–305
   wheat   310
Dog   xix, 231, 318
Dog Cockle   431, 432
Domesday   538
Domestication
   animal   225, 227, 368, 420, 422
   plant   373, 383, 386, 393–399
Dose rate determination in TCD   52
Dose response curve in TCD   48
Double dipole array in resistivity
   survey   544
Douglass, A.E.   37, 38
Down's Syndrome   255
Dripping dishes   334
Dublin Core Metadata Initiative   581
Duck   420
Dyes   591

Early uranium uptake (EU)   56, 67
Earth's magnetic field   13

Earthworms   172
Eccentricity of Earth's orbit   10
Echinococcosis   227, 230
Ecology, human   219
Economic archaeology   365–375
Ecosystem, human   220
Edge effect in GPR   549
Eemian interglacial   13
Effective Hydration Temperature in
   obsidian (EHT)   83, 88, 89
Egyptian mummies   251
Eigenvalues in PCA   687
El Salvador, ceramics   735
Electrical resistivity surveying   524,
   544–546
Electrochemical cell   599
Electromagnetic prospection   524,
   551–552
Electromagnetic radiation   547, 558
Electron microprobe analysis
   (EMPA)   463, 488
Electron spectroscopy for chemical
   analysis (ESCA)   435
Electron spin resonance (ESR)   6, 47–
   60, 52–53, 69, 404, 409
'Elf shot'   461
Elk   148
Ellingham diagram   487
Elm decline (Neolithic)   128, 379, 390
Embrittlement of silver alloy   612
Emic information   450
Emphysema   255
Endoscopy   408
Endotherms   147
Energy Budget Models (EBM)   114–
   115, 118
Engels, F.   484
Environmental reconstruction   103–
   110
Enzyme Linked Immunosorbent Assay
   (ELISA)   313,
   316–317, 318, 319, 320, 327
'Eoliths'   461
Epitopes   318
Epoxy resin adhesive   652
Equifinality   183, 368, 374, 726
Equilibrium constant   597
Equilibrium phase diagrams   488
Equivalent dose in TCD   49
Estimated Tool Equivalents
   (ETE)   714, 717
Estimated Vessel Equivalent
   (EVE)   713
Ethnoarchaeology   455, 466
Ethnography   174
Ethology   xviii
   brain and behaviour   215

Etic information   450
'*Ex oriente lux*'   485
Exchange system models   730
Exoskeleton   122
Experimental archaeology   105, 282
   earthworks   105, 173
   taphonomic   184–187
Exposure dating   6, 96
External dose rate in TCD   53, 54
Extractive metallurgy   483
   'Standard Model'   485

Faience   475, 620
Fallow Deer   151
Farquhar equation   196
Fats   331
Fatty acids   332
Ferromagnetism   73
Fertilizer   532, 566
Fibrils, collagen   637
Field survey   529
Field walking   536
Fine Red pottery   736
First radiocarbon revolution   25
Fish bones   288
Fishing   170, 422
Fixation of phosphorus   566
Flag Fen
   chemical conditions   590
   experimental tin smelting   496
Flakeshaver   715
   life-cycle model   716
Flint   463
Flood-plain survey   679
Fluxgate magnetometer   523
Focal destruction, bone   640
Food webs   197, 220, 223
Foraminifera   463
Forest (potash) glass   473, 619
Fossil fuel emission   198
Fossilization   186, 187, 352
Fourier-Transform Infra-red
   Spectroscopy (FTIR)   84, 435,
   451, 633, 650
Fox   149
Fractionation, isotopic   11, 271
   anthropogenic   513
Fragmented assemblages, bone   706
Frostbite   251
Frozen mummies   254
Full coverage survey   533
Fungi   352
Furnace   495
   forced draft   494
   glass   477–480
   natural draft   494

typology   501
water power   494
Fuzzy zone   680
Gamma-ray irradiation   629
Gamma spectroscopy, in U-series
   dating   67
Garbage   711
Garden hunting   420
Gas chromatography-combustion-
   isotope ratio mass spectrometry
   (GC-C-IRMS)   332
Gas chromatography/mass
   spectrometry (GC-MS)   331
Gender and sex   235
General Circulation Models
   (GCM)   113–114, 118
Genetic analysis   6
Genetic diseases   308
Geoarchaeology   530
   see also lithics, resource exploitation,
   soil, petrology, ceramic
   petrology, geochemistry,
   metallurgy, alum
Geochemical prospection   565–573
Geochemistry
   clay   450–452
   stone artifacts   462
Geographic Information Systems
   (GIS)   522, 524, 530, 538, 556,
   577, 578, 664, 668, 669, 672–681
Geomorphology   106
Geophysical prospection   522–525,
   543–552
   earth resistance surveys   544–546
   Ground Penetrating Radar
   (GPR)   547–551
   magnetometer surveys   546–547
Geo-referencing   672
Geosphere   191
Ghat   284
GISP2 ice core   195
Glass   471–482, 512–513
   ancient compositions   472, 617
   cobalt blue glass   475
   colour   475–477
   decolourizers   476
   definition   471
   provenance   512
   ritual   471–472
Glass furnaces   477, 500
   'northern' type   477
   'southern' type   477
   tank furnace   479
Glass network formers   86, 616
Glass network modifiers   86, 616
Glass transition temperature T_g 471
Glasshouses, Medieval   472

Glaze   473–474, 622–623
Global cooling   18
Global Positioning Systems
   (GPS)   524, 537, 558, 578
Glow curve (TL)   50
Grain Beetle   124, 129
Grauballe bog body   409, 410
Great Langdale stone axe factory   465
Greenhouse gases   111
GRIP ice core   18, 195
Grog in pottery   453
Ground Penetrating Radar
   (GPR)   524, 525, 526, 547–551
   satellite radar imagery   561
Guanaco   419
Guanine   302
   see also DNA
Guatemala – ceramics   734
Guinea Pig   420

Hadley Centre   114
Haemoglobin   296, 314
   abnormal   232
   thalassaemia   308
Half-cell reactions   598
Hamann-Todd collection   243
Hammerscale   503
Haplotypes   304
Hatch-Slack photosynthetic pathway
   (C_4)   270
^{3}He   94
Hearth   495
Heated bone   185
Heather   157, 380, 382
Hemastix technique   314, 320
Henry's Law   596
Herd mammals, domestication   419,
   420
Heuristic modelling   730
Hierarchical cluster analysis   509, 510
High Performance Liquid
   Chromatography (HPLC)   435
Histological index, bone   640
Histology of bone   324
Histoplasmosis   252
Holly   141
Holocene de Vries effects in
   radiocarbon   27
Hominid evolution   18, 213–218, 423
   bipedalism   215
   dating   214
   disease   216
   environmental contrasts   214–215
Hominids   206, 213–218
Homo economicus   366
Homo erectus   213–217, 309

Honey Bee   131
Hongshan culture   489
Hoola hoop   xviii
Horse   421
    DNA   310
Hotelling's T^2 probability   738
House Fly   130
Hoxnian Interglacial   151
Huldremose Woman   407, 408, 410
Human faeces   340, 403
    composition   404
Human Flea   130
Human genome   303
Human Genome Project   295, 304,
    308
Human Louse   129
Human migration   514
Human palaeobiology   205–209
    as human ecology   219–223
Human tissue preservation, see
    mummified tissue
Hunter/gatherer subsistence   231, 726
Hyaena   147, 150
Hydrated gel layer in glass
    corrosion   618
Hydration thickness in obsidian   87
Hydrological model in bone
    degradation   645
Hydrosphere   191
Hydroxyapatite   282, 637
Hypothyrodism   232
Hypsodont   151

Ice cores   4, 18, 191, 195
'Ice man' ('Ötzi')   323, 587
Immunochemical detection   326–327
Immunoelectrophoresis   313
Immunoglobulin G (IgG)   318
Immunology   296, 327
In situ preservation   615, 629, 654
Incremental growth in animal
    tissue   419
Inductively Coupled Plasma Emission
    Spectroscopy (ICP-OES)   463,
    508
Inductively Coupled Plasma Mass
    Spectrometry (ICP-MS)   513, 515,
    568
Infants – under-representation in
    skeletal assemblages   262
Infra-red spectroscopy   295, 514
Inorganic phosphorus
    determination   566
Insects   121–132, 427–429, 433–434
    as palaeoenvironmental
        indicators   121–132

dyes   435
pests   438
taxonomic orders   121–123
In-situ cosmogenic isotopes   94–99
    accumulation rate   96
    production   93
    production rate   95
Instrumental Neutron Activation
    Analysis (INAA)   734
Internal dose rate in TCD   53, 55
International Tree Ring Data Bank
    (ITRDB)   39
Internet   581
Interpolation in GIS   677
Interventive conservation   649, 650
Intra-site patterning   530
Invertebrate resources   427–440
    and trade   436–438
    insect dyes   435
    main groups exploited   428
    medicines and poisons   436
    shell tools   430
    silk   433–434
Investigative conservation   649, 659
Ion exchange in glass   617
Ipswichian interglacial   13, 138
Iron corrosion   651
Ironworking   503
Irrigation   233
Island biotas   421
Isochron   65
Isoelectric focusing (IEF)   319
Isoelectric point (pI)   319
Isotope
    dilution   66
    fractionation   195
    standards   195
    systematics   191–199
Isotopes and diet   270–273

Jet   514
'Jurassic Park'   297

Kalinga potters   452
Kentri potters, Crete   453–454
Keratin   631
Kermes insect   435
Ketones   338
'Killed population'   704, 707, 708
    see also Probable Number of
        Individuals
Kiln, pottery   495
Kiln wasters   510, 512
Kinetics   595
Kinship, DNA   302
K-means analysis   688

Kriging   677, 737
K-strategists   420, 421
'Kubu' images   472
Kuru   233

Lac insect   435
Lacustrine sequences   142
Lamps   334
Landnam clearance model   380
Landsat   560
Laser Induced Direction And Range
    (LIDAR)   522
Late Formative Fine Pottery –
    provenance   735
Late-glacial   139, 149
Latrine   131, 569
Law of Mass Action   596
'Law of the Hammer'   668
Layer in GIS   672
Lead glaze – degradation   623
Lead isotope analysis, metals   513
Leather   632
Leech anticoagulants ('hirudins')   436
Lemming   148
Leslie Matrix   262
Level i Life Assemblage   718
Level ii Death Assemblage   718
Life cycle of inorganic artifacts   444
Life table   260
Light sensitivity   655
Likelihood in Bayesian analysis   696
Lincoln index   707, 713
Lindow Man   162
Linear discriminant analysis   690
Linear uranium uptake (LU)   56, 67
Lipid biomarkers   526
Lipids   296, 331–348, 354, 369, 566
    analytical techniques   331
    animal fats   334–336
    beeswax   333–334, 435
    biomarkers   569, 570
    plant waxes   333
    survival   641
Lithic assemblages   712
Lithics   461–468, 510
    characterization   461–464
    distribution   465–466
    procurement and production   464–
        465
    provenance   510–511
    quantification   713–717
    use wear studies   466–467
Little Ice Age   104, 163, 273
Livestock husbandry   422
Localized corrosion, metal   609
Loess   9, 17

Long chronologies in
    dendrochronology   38
Longue durée   373
Lumpfish   416
Lycopodium spores   162

Macrofossils (plants)   156–159, 395,
    396
Magnetic dating   74–76
Magnetic epoch   18
Magnetic properties of materials   73–
    74
Magnetic reversals   10, 13–15, 74
Magnetic survey   76, 546–547
Magnetic susceptibility   14, 73, 76, 511,
    523, 565
Magnetometer surveys   76, 546–547,
    559
Mahalanobis distance   691, 737, 738
Maize agriculture   271
Mammals as climatic indicators   147–
    154
Mammoth hunting model   728
Manure   338, 533, 568, 569
Manuring   174, 296
Map overlay in GIS   676
Mapematics   676
Marine cores   10, 12
Market economies   366
Markov Chain   701
Mary Rose
    coniferous resin   343, 344
    wet wood   629, 630
Mass spectrometry   66, 67, 295, 332,
    338, 343, 344, 345, 435, 444, 447
Materials science paradigm   444
Maya sites, Yucatan   555
'Mean Residence Time' (MRT)   192
Megafaunal extinction   421
Megalithic yard   699
Mesolithic hunting strategies   728
Metals   483–490, 497–504
    Abundance   488
    forgeries   612
    provenance   513–514
Metal corrosion   605–613
    burial corrosion   609–610
    Pourbaix diagrams   607–609
    thermodynamics   605–607
Metallurgy
    archaeometallurgy   485–487
    experimental   489
    origins   483–491
    Timna project   485, 486
Microbial activity   297, 324, 351, 355,
    640
    peroxidases   314

Microbiology
    and archaeology   351–357
    in corpse decomposition   352
    influence on archaeometric data   355
    of mineralized tissue   353–354
Micro-organisms   181, 351, 629, 631
Micropalaeontology   463
Microtopographic survey   531
Microwave energy (in ESR)   48
Middens   185
Milankovitch cycles   10, 11, 15, 17,
    103, 113, 118
Milk   369
Milk fats   336
Mineralization   186, 198, 566
Minimum Analytical Nodules
    (MAN)   713
Minimum Number of Individuals
    (MNI)   666, 703, 705
Minimum Number of Intact Tools
    (MNT)   714
Mistletoe   141, 409
Mode of production, inorganic
    materials   443
Model
    building   724
    of radiocarbon dating   23–4
Model-based clustering   693
Modelling   723–732
    Bayesian   701
    collagen degradation   298
Modified random network model of
    glass   618
Modified stability diagram   608
Molluscs   135–143, 427–438
    and deposit age   138
    as climatic indicators   140
    environmental responses   136–142
    Non-marine   135–145
Monoclonal antibodies   318
Morbidity   226
Morphogenesis in modelling   729
Mortality   226
Mössbauer spectroscopy   456
Muldenkorrosion   609
Multicollector Inductively Coupled
    Plasma Mass Spectrometer   515
Multispectral (MSS) data   522, 557–559
Multivariate data analysis   159, 238,
    243, 509, 664, 668, 686–694
    see also Principal Components
        Analysis, Hierarchical Cluster
        Analysis, Discriminant Analysis
Mummified tissue   207, 249
    DNA   320
    Rehydration   250
Museum environment   653–655

Mussel   429
Mutual Climatic Range (MCR)   127
Myocardial infarction   252

NASA   561
Nasopharyngeal carcinoma   255
Native copper   488
Natural Environment Research Council
    (NERC)   xix, 114, 297, 557
Natural intensity in TCD   48
^{21}Ne   94
Neanderthals   7, 63, 206, 213, 216
    DNA   206
Nearctic   148
Nefertari, tomb of   654
Neoplasms   253
Nernst equation   599, 606
Network dissolution in glasses   618
Neural networks   693
Neutron Activation Analysis (NAA)
    295, 438, 444, 463, 508, 734
'New Archaeology'   209, 365, 576
Nile valley, climate   115
Nitrogen cycle   197–198
Nitrogen isotopes   272–273, 326
    and diet   208, 272
North West Wetlands Survey   162
Nuclear Magnetic Resonance
    (NMR)   514
Nuclear waste glass   86
Nucleotide sequence   303
Number of Identified Specimens
    (NISP)   703, 704
Numerical modelling   670, 723–732

Obliquity of ecliptic   10
Obsidian   616, 733
    Chemistry   83
    sources   77, 511
    weathering   86
Obsidian hydration dating   81–92
    effective hydration temperature   83,
        88, 89
Ochronosis   251
Oils   331
Old Woodland Fauna   127
Olive oil   334
On-site conservation   649, 650
Open-system behaviour   66, 356
Optical Emission Spectroscopy
    (OES)   463, 509, 513
Optically Stimulated Luminescence
    (OSL)   47–50, 58
Opuntia cactus seed   407, 410
Oral pathology   217
Orbital tuning   16
Ordnance Survey   555, 673

Ore roasting   496
Organic materials, deterioration   627–633
Organic phosphorus compounds in soils   566
Origins of agriculture   393–399
Oseberg Viking ship   628
Osteoarthritis   252
Osteocalcin   324
Osteomyelitis   251
Osteoporosis   254, 287
Otitis media   255
Otoliths ('ear stones')   416
'Ötze'   323, 587
Ouchterlony technique   315–316
Output utility in modelling   726
Oxygen isotopes   4, 10–13, 142, 195
  and diet   269, 273
  and stratigraphy   4, 10–13, 68
  climatology   273
  in spondylus shells   437
Oxygen Isotope Stages (OIS)   11
Oxygen partial pressure in pyrotechnology   495
Oyster   429

Packrat middens   123, 127
PAGs (polyalkylene glycols)   630
Palaeobiology   179, 415–423
  human   205–256, 403–411
Palaeobotany   155–165, 379–390
  taphonomic considerations   181
Palaeoclimatology   124, 126, 297
Palaeodemography   259–268
  methods   260–262
  migration   265–266
Palaeodiet   208, 269–276, 297, 340–343, 403–411
  and bone chemistry   208, 269
  and isotopes   269–273
  and trace elements   274–275
Palaeoeconomy, see resource exploitation
Palaeoentomology, see insects
Palaeoepidemiology   205
Palaeointensities, magnetic   75
Palaeomagnetic reversals   76
Palaeomagnetism   73
Palaeopathology   207, 219, 253
Palaeotemperatures   106, 191, 195
Palearctic   148
Paleoindian   30, 422, 715
Palynology   106, 379–390
Paraloid B72   652
Paramagnetic centres   48
Paramagnetism   73
Parasitic infection   252

Partial pressures   596
  oxygen (p[O_2])   495
Parting, metals   499
Pathogens   225
Peat bogs   105, 123, 155–166
  blanket bogs   156
  humification   159
  ombrotrophic   105, 155, 156
  stratigraphy   155–166
Pedology   167
Peedee Belemnite (PDB)   195, 270
PEG (polyethylene glycol)   610, 633, 643, 651
Periodontal disease   251
Perlite   81, 86
Peterson index   707
Petrology, see ceramic petrology
pH, definition   588
Phenice's criteria   238
Phosphate
  analysis   565–569
  mineralization   123
  survey   525, 566
Phosphorus cycle   198
Photosynthesis   196, 197, 270
Photosynthetic pathways   270, 296
Phytoarchaeology, see archaeobotany
Phytoliths   397, 399, 467
Pike   420
Pimaric acid   343
Pinta   232
  see also treponematosis
Pitch   343
Pixel   84, 675
Places of Special Interest (POSI)   532
Plaggen soils   174
Plague   227
Planning Policy Guidelines   16   568
Plasma, blood   313
Plateau test, in TCD   52, 53
Pliny   475
Ploughsoil scatter   671
Plumbate ware   739
Pneumonia   251, 253, 254
Polar wandering   14
Poliomyelitis   251
Pollen analysis   379–392
  modelling   384
  off-site   383
  on site   383
Pollen grains   173
Polyclonal antibodies   318
Polymerase Chain Reaction (PCR)   239, 228, 305, 306, 319, 320
Polyvinylacetate (PVAc)   643, 644
Polyvinyledene chloride (PVdC)   643
Population size   265

Population structure   259
Porcelain   474, 622
Porotic hyperostosis   252
Post-depositional changes
  bone   637–647
  ceramics and glass   615–625
  metals   605–613
Posterior probability, Bayesian   696
Potassium–argon dating (K-Ar)   5, 14, 16, 18
Pottery Information Equivalents (PIE)   713
Pottery kiln   500
Precession of the equinoxes   10
Pre-Clovis   30
Predator-prey system   420
Pre-Pottery Neolithic   397
'Presentist fallacy'   483
Preventative conservation   649
Principal Components Analysis (PCA)   127, 509, 686–688, 690, 691, 740
Prior probability, Bayesian   696
Probability   695
Probability surface   738
Probable Number of Individuals (PNI)   704, 707, 708
'Processual provenance'   515
Production technology, inorganic materials   444–447
Prospection, see archaeological prospection
Protein A   318
Proteins   323–329
  environment and survival   325
  mineral interactions   324
  rate of diagenesis   325
  role of temperature in survival   323–324
Proton Induced X-ray Emission (PIXE)   171, 435
Provenance postulate   445, 507–517
Proxy climate signals   156
Pseudosections in prospection   524, 545
Punctuated equilibria   137
Pyrite disease   611
Pyrolosis Gas Chromatography/Mass Spectrometry (py-GC/MS)   570
Pyrotechnology   486, 493–505
  cupellation   499
  experimental furnace   494
  fuel   494
  inorganic processes   496–497, 500
  iron smelting furnace   495, 501
  kilns and ovens   499–500
  organic processes   496, 497, 500
  residues and slags   502–503

Quadratic discriminant analysis   690
Quantification
  bone   703–710, 713
  broken objects   711–721
Quaternary   9, 17, 18, 30, 68, 103, 104, 106
  fossil record   182
  geochronology   9–20, 30
  mammalian fauna   147
  soils   169
Quaternary environments   23, 103–107, 135
  climate models   112–117
    Energy Budget Models (EBM)   114–115, 118
    General Circulation Models (GCM)   113–114, 118
  modelling   111–119, 126
Querying in GIS   676

Rabbit   151
Radar, see Ground Penetrating Radar
Radiocalcium dating   98
Radiocarbon dating   xvii, 3, 6, 7, 23–33, 75, 82, 131, 191, 296, 313, 319, 697–699
  calibration   6,25
    Bayesian approach   697
  effect of microbial activity   355
Radio-immunoassay (RIA)   315, 316, 318, 319, 320, 327
Radish oil   337
Raman spectroscopy   444, 447
Random network model, glass   616
Raster-GIS   673
Raw materials, inorganic – physical properties   445
Rawhide   632
Reaction kinetics in corrosion   600
Re-burial   222
Reclassification in GIS   676
Red Deer   148
Red enamel glass   476
Redox   598, 629
  conditions   495
  potential Eh   588
Reduced trend in soils   602
Refitting, lithics   464, 712
Regeneration technique in TCD   52
Rehydration of mummies   250
Reindeer   147, 148
Relative humidity   654
Remote sensing   555–564
Renaissance paintings, dendrochronology   36

Reproductive strategies   420
Reservoir corrected radiocarbon age   25
Residue analysis   332
Resins   331, 343
Resistance meter, archaeological prospection   545
Resource exploitation   361–363, 365–378
  'cultivation' of invertebrates   429
  'domestication' of invertebrates   429–430
  faunal analysis   666
  inorganic   443
  invertebrates   427
  vertebrates   415–425
Reverbatory structures   499
Reversed polarity, palaeomagnetism   14
Ricardo's Law of Comparative Advantage   490
Ritual deposition   374
Roe Deer   148
Root dentine transparency   241
Rothamsted Experimental Station   570
RQ-mode PCA   687, 739
R-strategists   421
Ruffer's technique   250

Sahara   115, 150, 193
Sahel   117
St Cuthbert's coffin, Durham   630
Salmon   416
Salt glaze   474
Salting out (proteins)   314
Sample bias   665
  in skeletal populations   262
Sample selection   665
Sampling paradox   535
Sand temper   736
Satellite remote sensing   521
  imagery   560
  radar imagery   561
Saturation Index (SI)   597
Scanning Electron Microscopy (SEM)   124, 168, 405, 407, 447, 455, 456, 467, 619, 621, 633, 650
Schlumberger array   544
Seasonality – diet   275
Seaweed Fly   131
Second Radiocarbon revolution   25
Secular variation   14, 74, 75
Sedge   162
Sediment dating by OSL   58
Seismic survey   524

Semi-quantitative categories in bone quantification   709
Sexing human skeletons   237–239
  by DNA   307
  cremations   286–287
Sexual dimorphism   418
Sheep Louse   130
Shine-down curve (OSL)   50
Showcases   655
Shrew   149
Shuttle Imaging Radar (SIR)   561
Sickle cell anaemia   232
Side-scan sonar   524
Significance tests   664
Silicate weathering   616
Silk   433
Simulation   670, 724
Site catchment analysis   538
Site formation processes   170
Skeletal anatomy
  human   237–247
  mammalian   151
  vertebrate   415
Skin, deterioration   632
Slags   502–503
  bloomery   503
  diagnostic   502
Smith, C.S.   486
Soapstone, provenancing   511
Social ranking   372
Socio-cultural factors
  in disease   232
  in human ecology   220, 221
Soil lipids   338–340
Soil magnetic susceptibility   567–568
Soil micromorphology   105, 106, 167–177
  experimentation   173
  faecal spherulites   174
  pollen   172
  terminology   168–169
Soil phosphate survey   565–568
Soil processes, chemical   601–603
Solubility product (K_{sp})   597
Solubility profile, bone   274
Space shuttle   561
Spatial analysis   676–678
Spatial information   671–683
SPECMAP timescale   9, 10, 15–17
Spectral analysis of time series   11
Speleothems   63, 68
Spina bifida   251
S-Plus   693
SPOT satellite   560
Sr/Ca ratio in bone   269, 274
Stability field (Eh/pH) diagram   590, 600, 601, 607

Standard Hydrogen Electrode
    (SHE) 606
Standard Light Arctic Precipitation
    (SLAP) 195
Standard Mean Ocean Water
    (SMOW) 195, 270
5β-Stanols 339
Statistical training 665
Statistics and computing in
    archaeology 663–670
Status and diet 274
Steatite, provenancing 511
Steel cementation 500
Sterile procedures 321
Sterols 569
Stimulus-diffusion model 394
Stochastic models 728
Stockholm tar 343
Stratigraphic correlation 4
Strontium isotope ratios 269, 275
    and diet 270, 275, 437
    in glass 513
Sub-Milankovitch events 18
Subsistence economies 367
'Suess wiggles' 95
Sulfate reducing bacteria 199, 608
Sulfide oxidation in corrosion 611
Sulfur cycle 198–199
Sulfur isotope ratios 199
Surface collection techniques in field
    archaeology 529–541
Surface exposure dating 96–98
Surface scatter 531, 533
Survey methods, field 533–537
Syphilis 232
    see also treponematosis

Tapeworm 229
Taphonomy 106, 135–136, 179–190,
    374, 666
    assemblage distinctions 182
    bone 637–647
    diagenesis 135, 270
    invertebrates 183, 186
    plants 183–184, 186
    skin 632–633
    terminology 179–181
    vertebrates 182–183, 186
Tattoos 250
Technological
    choices 449
    determinism 484
    hearth 497
    'minimalism' 490
    style 445, 450
Technology, discovery of new 443

Temper, ceramic 453, 512
Tephra 163
Tephrochronology 106
Terminations, Quaternary 13, 16
Testate amoeba analysis 161, 163
Textiles 591
    deterioration 630–631
    Tutankhamun's shroud 631
Thallassaemia 232, 308
Thematic mapping in GIS 672
Thera, eruption 4, 75
Thermal imaging 559
Thermal Ionization Mass Spectrometry
    (TIMS) 5, 513
Thermal neutrons 94
Thermodynamic equilibrium 595
Thermoluminescence (TL) 47–50, 56
Thermoremanent magnetism 76
Third radiocarbon revolution 25
'Three Age system' 484, 587
Thymine 302
    see also DNA
Time Series Analysis (TSA) 155
Time slice, in GPR 546, 550
Tin opacifiers, in glass 474, 477
Tiquisate White ware 740
Tobacco pipes 715
Tollund Man 323, 409, 410
Tomography 444
Tool Information Equivalents
    (TIE) 714, 717
Topology 674
Total Number of Fragments
    (TNF) 704
Total phosphorus determination 567
Total station survey 577
Trace elements
    in bone 274
    in soils 564
Trade and exchange 447, 466
Transects 536
Trapped Charge Dating (TCD) 47–60
    see also electron spin resonance,
    optically stimulated luminescence,
    thermoluminescence
Treponematosis 226, 231, 232, 252
Triacylglycerols 334
    degradation pathways 335
Triangulated Irregular Networks
    (TIN) 677
Trophic level 272
Tropocollagen 637
Tsunami 40, 75
Tuberculosis 227, 309
Tunnelling, bone 352
Turin Shroud 29
Tylecote, R.F. 486

Tyrian purple 434, 435

Uncalibrated radiocarbon dates 7, 23
Unicode 582
Unified theory of quantification 719
Uniformitarianism 181, 367, 603
Universal Transverse Mercator (UTM)
    co-ordinates 537, 538, 673
Uranium series dating 6, 60, 63–71
    techniques 66
Uranium uptake 55
Urea 272
UV/Visible spectroscopy 435, 591

Vale of Pickering survey 557
Variance-covariance matrix 738
Vasa warship, Stockholm 628
Vector-GIS 673
Vegetation
    human impact 379–392
    mesolithic 386
    neolithic elm decline 390
Venom 436
Vertebrate resources 415–425
Vienna Standard Mean Ocean Water
    (VSMOW) 195
Viewsheds 676
Virtual reality modelling 681

Ward's method, cluster analysis 688
Warps in radiocarbon ages 25, 26,
    27
Water cycle 11, 192–195
Waterlogged environments 602
Waterlogged wood 651
Water Vole 149
'Wave of advance' model 266
Waxes 331, 333
    beeswax 333
    plant waxes 333
Weed floras 369
Weeping (iron corrosion) 610
Weevil 127
Weighted Average Ordination
    (WAO) 155, 161
Wenner array 544
West Runton elephant 644
Western blot 327
White-tailed Deer 148
Wiggle matching, radiocarbon 6, 42
Wild Boar 148
Wood, deterioration 628
Wood-boring Beetle 438
Woodworm 128

Woolly Mammoth   147, 153
Woolly Rhinoceros   147
Wroxeter Hinterland Project   551, 578

XML   582

X-ray Diffraction (XRD)   314–315,
      430, 444, 451, 642
   tomography   444
X-ray Fluorescence (XRF)   295, 444,
      463
X-ray radiography   444, 588
XTENT model   725

Y chromosome   237, 307
Yaws   232
   see also treponematosis
Younger Dryas   141, 149

Zeroing event in TCD   47

Site Index

Abingdon Vineyard, Oxfordshire, UK   341, 342
Abri Pataud, France   419
Abu Hureyra, Syria   394
Akrotiri, Thera, Greece   75, 433, 434
Al-Aqsa Mosque, Jerusalem   29
Alcester, Warwickshire, UK   438
Aleutian Islands, Alaska   255
Al-Raqqa, Syria   478
Anasazi sites, New Mexico   555
Antelope House, Arizona   407
Antonine Wall, Scotland   385
Anzick, Montana, USA   30
Archangelos, Rhodes, Greece   453
Arroyo Frias River, Argentina   30
Atapuerca, Spain   69, 76, 206
Autun, France   479
Azapa, Chile   406, 410

Bab edh-Dhra', Jordan   228
Baleshare, Scotland   374
Ban Chiang, Thailand   362
Ban Lum Khao, Thailand   362
Bar Hill fort, Scotland   385
Barton-on-Humber, Lincolnshire, UK   341, 342
Bearsden Fort, Scotland   385, 569
Bellville, Ontario, Canada   242
Bercy, Paris, France   324
Berkhamstead, Hertfordshire, UK   501
Betatakin, Arizona, USA   40
Bir Kiseiba, Egypt   115, 117
Birsay, Orkney, Scotland   499
Boxgrove, Sussex, UK   4, 136
Bryn-y-Castell, Snowdonia, Wales   499
Bodensee lake settlement, Switzerland   40, 41
Bolton Fell Moss, Cumbria, UK   159–161, 385, 386, 387

Bosworth battlefield, Leicester, UK   560
Buhl, Idaho, USA   30
Bull Brook, USA   715–718
Bull Wharf, UK   590
Burton Dassett, Warwickshire, UK   499

Cadrix, France   480
Caistor by Norwich, UK   478
Camarones, Chile   406
Carlston Annis, USA   261
Carnuntum, Austria   525
Catal Höyük, Turkey   41
Caverna da Pedra Pintada, Brazil   30
Chaco Canyon, New Mexico   557
Christ Church, Spitalfields, London   242
Copán, Honduras   84, 88
Coppergate, York, UK   130, 430, 433, 435, 591, 708
Cotzumalguapa, Guatemala   743
Coxcatlan Cave, Mexico   29
Crift Farm, Cornwall, UK   498, 499, 501
Cuzco, Peru   453

Dahkla Oasis, Egypt   116, 117
Dead Sea   632
Deaf Adder Gorge, NT, Australia   58, 59
Dereivka, Ukraine   421
Dirty Shame Rockshelter, Oregon, USA   131
Dublin, High Street   591
Dubrovnik, Croatia   41

El Morro, Chile   405, 410
Engis Cave   213

Falkland Islands   104
Flag Fen, Cambridgeshire, UK   496, 590
Franchthi Cave, Greece   373
Frattesina, Italy   473, 478
Frourio Vardari, Greece   36

Garnsey, New Mexico   368
Gough's Cave, Somerset, UK   29
Gran Dolina, Spain   69
Great Langdale, Cumbria, UK   465
Greenland   4, 255, 420
Guila Naquitz, Mexico   394

Hadar, Ethiopia   215
Hadera, Isreal   480
Hamel, Oxford   130
Hampstead Heath, London, UK   127
Hamwic, Hampshire, UK   499
Hayonim Cave, Israel   274
Herculaneum, Italy   36, 41
Hexian, China   56
High Street, Dublin   591
Holywell Coombe, Folkestone, UK   135, 139
Hutton-le-Hole, Yorkshire, UK   480
Huaca Prieta, Peru   404

Jalame, Palestine   475, 479
Jericho, Jordan   431, 432
Jerusalem, Al-Aqsa Mosque   29
Jinmium, NT, Australia   59
Joint Mitnor Cave, UK   323

Kagamil Island, Aleutians   255
Kebara cave, Israel   58, 69

Kentri, Crete, Greece   453–454
Kerma, Nubia   273
Khok Phanom Di   362
Kiet Siel, Arizona, USA   40
Kish, Mesopotamia   473
Kodiak Island, Alaska, USA   230
Krapina, Croatia   206
Kyloe Cow Beck, Yorkshire   495

Lake Mungo, Australia   26, 59
Langenesværet, Norway   171, 172
Lavagnone di Brescia, Italy   42
Lindow Moss, Cheshire, UK   158, 406,
   409, 592
Lovelock Cave, Arizona, USA   569

Makhadma, Egypt   419
Malakunanja, NT, Australia   58
Mary Rose, Portsmouth, UK   343,
   344, 629, 630
Matacapan, Mexico   452
Melos, Greece   465
Monte Verde, Chile   30
Mordon Bog, Wareham, UK   587
Morton Fen, UK   558
Mostin, California, USA   30
Moundville, Alabama, USA   453
Mount Etna, Sicily   36

Nabta Playa, Egypt   115, 117
Nazca sites, Peru   555
Nefertari, tomb of   654
Newstead (Trimontium), Scotland   114
Niger River, Mali   431
Nimrud (Assyria)   473
Nineveh, Mesopotamia   471, 473
Nipisat I, Greenland   420
Non Nok Tha, Thailand   362
Northern Isles, Scotland   170
Novgorod, Russia   41

Ocampo Caves, Mexico   131
Old Scatness broch, Shetland,
   Scotland   185, 494
Olduvai, Tanzania   215
Omo, Ethiopia   215
Oseberg, Norway   628
Overton Down, Wiltshire, UK   105,
   174, 187, 587
Oxford, the Hamel   130

Pamwak, Papua New Guinea   86

Paviland Cave, Gower, Wales   213
Pazyryk, W. Russia   41
Picts Knowe, UK   590
Point Hope, Alaska, USA   40
Pompeii, Italy   41, 434
Pot Creek Pueblo, USA   84
Poundbury Camp, Dorset, UK   271
Pueblo Bonito, New Mexico   40

Qafzeh, Israel   58, 69
Qasr Ibrim, Egypt   305, 345
Qilakitsoq, Greenland   255
Quoygrew, Westray   171

Raversijde, Belgium   374
Rievaulx Abbey, Yorkshire, UK   497,
   501
Ringkloster, Denmark   370
Robert's Haven, Caithness,
   Scotland   171
Rosedale, Yorkshire, UK   479, 480
Rose Theatre, London, UK   628

Safsaf Oasis, Egypt   562
St Cuthbert's coffin, Durham, UK   630
St Lawrence Island, Canada   252
San Marcos Cave, Mexico   29
Santa Rosa, Guatemala   739–744
Sarepta, Levant   435
Sasi, Manus Islands   87
Scole, Norfolk, UK   503
Sháráfabad, Iran   373
Shetland, Scotland   174
Skhul, Israel   58, 69
Snake Hill Cemetery, Ontario,
   Canada   273
South Georgia   104
Sphinx, Egypt   99
Spitalfields, London, UK   242
Stanton Drew, Bristol, UK   523
Stellmoor, Germany   421
Sterkfontein, South Africa   70
Stonehenge, Wilshire, UK   3, 437
Sutton Hoo, Suffolk, UK   568, 591
Swanscombe, Kent, UK   67, 138
Swartkrans Cave, South Africa   275
Sweet Track, Somerset, UK   41, 590,
   630

Tabun, Israel   58, 69
Tarapacá, Chile   406, 410
Tehuacán Valley, Mexico   29, 390
Tell Aswad, Syria   397

Tell el-Amarna, Egypt   370, 478
Tell Ghoraife, Syria   397
Tell Mureybit, Syria   397
Tell Ramad, Syria   397
Tell Sweyhat, Syria   536, 537
Temple Hill Moss, Scotland   159, 163,
   164
Templo Mayor, Mexico   570
Teotehuacán, Mexico   273, 734
Theopetra Cave, Greece   170
Thera, Greece   4, 75
Thessaloniki, Greece   41
Thorne Moors, Humberside, UK   127
Ticul, Yucatan, Mexico   450
Tisza, Hungary   679
Tofts Ness, Orkney, Scotland   175,
   340, 570
Trimontium (Newstead), Scotland   114
Tulán, Chile   406, 407, 410
Turkana basin, Tanzania   137
Tysfjord, Norway   229

Ubar, Oman   577
Utqiagvik, Alaska, USA   254

Varna, Bulgaria   486
Vera Cruz, Mexico   532
Vertesszöllos, Hungary   68
Vesterålen, Norway   170, 171
Viroconium (Wroxeter), Shropshire,
   UK   578–580, 620
Vore, Wyoming, USA   421

Wadi el-Natrun, Egypt   474
Wadi Jilat, Jordan   397, 399
Walton Moss, Cumbria, UK   386
West Cotton, Northamptonshire,
   UK   333, 336, 337, 436
West Heath Spa, Hampstead Heath,
   UK   129
Wharram Percy, Yorkshire, UK   499
Whitrig Bog, Scotland   104
Wintering's Edge, Yorkshire, UK   497
Wroxeter, Shropshire, UK   578–580,
   620

Yarnton Refectory Farm, Oxfordshire,
   UK   341
York, UK   129, 130, 430, 433, 435, 591

Zhoukoudian, China   56
Zweeloo Moss, Denmark   406, 409

Species Names and Taxonomic Groups Index

Abida secale   141
Abies spp.   38, 39
Achatina fulica   136
Achromobacter iophagus   351
Acipenseridae (sturgeons)   416
Aegilops spp.   381
Aglenus brunneus   130
Alces alces   148
Alkaligenes piechaudii   355
Alopex lagopus   148
Ancylostoma duodenale   252
Anisus leucostoma   139
Anobium punctatum   128
Anodonta spp.   136
Aphodius holdereri   125, 128, 137
Apis mellifera   131
Apodemus sylvaticus   149
Apodes (eels)   416
Arianta arburstorum   141
Arvicola terrestris   149
Ascaris lumbricoides   252
Aspergillus spp.   351
Australopithecus   214
   A. africanus   272
   A. robustus   272, 274
Avena spp.   377, 378, 402

Bacillus subtilis   355
Balaenoptera musculus   416
Belgrandia marginata   137
Betula spp.   39
Blatta orientalis   129
Bos primigenius   419
Brassica oleracea   333
Brucella melitensis   228

Calluna vulgaris   157, 380, 382
Candidula intersecta   140
   C. gigaxii   140

Capparis spp.   397
Capreolus capreolus   148
Cardium spp.   430
Carychium tridentatum   139
Cavia aperea   420
Cedrus sp.   39
Centaurea spp.   397
Cepaea nemoralis   137
   C. hortensis   137
Cerastoderma spp.   430
Cernuella virgata   140
Cervus elaphus   148
Chlorostoma spp.   405, 410
Choromytilus meridionalis   429
Cimex columbarius   130
Clausilia pumila   141
Clethrionomys glareolus 149
Clostridium histolyticum   353
   C. welchii   357
Cochlicopa lubricella   136
Coelodonta antiquitatis   147
Coleoptera   104, 122, 126
Columella columella   137
Condylura cristata   149
Conus geographicus   436
   C. textile   436
Corbicula fluminalis   136
Corylus spp.   380
   C. avellana   406
Cricetus cricetus   149
Crocidura suaveolens   149
Crocuta crocuta   147, 150
Cyclopterus lumpus   416

Dactylopius coccus   435
Dama dama   151
Damalinia ovis   130
Dasypus novemcinctus   423
Dasypus spetemcinctum   149
Dentalium spp.   431, 437

Desmana moschata   149
Dicrostonyx torquatus   148
Dimetrodon   417
Diptera   104, 122
Discus ruderatus   139
Dryophthorus corticalis   127

Echinococcus granulosis   229
Ena montana   141
Eriophorum vaginatum   162
Erodium spp.   397
Esox lucius   420
Eunapius nitens   430

Felicola subrostratus   130
Felis pardalis   149
Fitzroya cupressoides   39
Fraxinus spp.   380

Glycymeris glycymeris   431, 432
   G. violascens   431, 432
Gyraulus laevis   139

Haematopinus apri   130
Hedera helix   141
Helicella itala   136
Helicodonta obvoluta   141
Helix aspersa   139
   H. pomatia   140
Helophorus glacialis   125
Hesperophanes fasciculatus   438
Hippopotamus amphibius   147
Homo economicus   366
   H. erectus   213–217, 309
   H. heidelbergensis   76
Hordeum spp.   380, 382

Ilex aquilinum   141
Isorhipis melasoides   127, 128

Juniperus spp.   37

Kermococcus vermilio   435
Kerria lacca   435

Lagarostrobus spp.   39
    L. colensoi   39
    L. franklinii   39
Laminifera pauli   139
Larix spp.   39
Lasius brunneus   127
Lauria cylindracea   141
Lemmus trimucronatus   148
Leipsosteidae (gars)   416
Lycopodium spp.   162

Malva spp.   397
Mammuthus primigenius   147, 153
    M. trogontherii   153
Melophagus ovinus   129
Mercenaria mercenaria   438
Microtus agrestis   149
    M. gregalis   150
Monacha cantiana   140
Musca domestica   130
Murex   434
Mycobacterium bovis   227
    M. tuberculosis   227, 252, 352
Myomimus personatus   149
Mytilus edulis   429

Nasua nasua   149
Neotoma spp.   123
Nesovitrea hammonis   137

Odocoileus virginianus   148
    O. hemionus   148
Ondatra zibethica   149
Opuntia spp.   407, 410
Oreochromis niloticus   419
Oryctolagus cuniculus   151
Oryzaephilus surinamensis   129
Ostrea edulis   429
Ovibos moschatus   148

Oxychilus cellarius   139

Pachypasa otus   429
Pandaka pygmaea   416
Panicum miliaceum   409
Panthera onca   149
Paranthropus spp.   214
Pediculosis capitis   255
Pediculus humanus humanus   129
Phalacrocorax spp.   420
Phaseolus spp.   410
Picea spp.   39
Pinna nobilis   434
Pinus spp.   38, 39
    P. longaeva   38
    P. silvestris   38
Pisidium clessini   138
    P. obtusale   139
    P. stewarti   139
Plantago lanceolata   380, 381, 382
Plasmodium falciparum   309
    P. malaria   232, 252
Platyla similis   141
Plesianthropus sp.   214
Populus spp.   37
Prosopis spp.   410
Pseudomonas fluorescens   355
Pthirius pubis   130
Ptinus fur   128
Pulex irritans   130
Pupilla muscorum   137
    P. sterri   139
Pycmomerus terebrans   127

Quercus spp.   38, 39, 380

Rangifer tarandus   147, 148
Rheum palaestinum   398
Rubus spp.   409
Rumex acetosa   380, 381, 382
Ruthenica filograna   141

Saiga tatarica   149
Salmo salar   416
Schistosoma haematobium   252
Scirpus americanus   410, 411
Scorzonera judaica   398
Secale cereale   381, 407, 409
Sitophilus granarius   129

S. linearis   130
Sorex caecutiens   149
    S. araneus   149
Spalax leucodon   149
Spergula arvensis   407, 409
Sphagnum spp.   124, 156, 157, 187
    S. imbricatum   162
Spondylus gaederopus   437
Stomoxys calcitrans   130
Streptomyces spp.   353
Succinea oblonga   139
Succisa spp.   380, 382
Sus scrofa   148

Tachardiella larrede   435
Tachyeres pteneres   420
Taenia solium   252
Tanousia runtoniana   138
Tayassu tajacu   149
Theodoxus danubialis   138
Thoracochaeta zosterae   131
Tilapia spp.   423
Tilia spp.   380
Triticum spp.   380, 381, 382
Truncatellina cylindrica   141
Tsuga spp.   39

Ulmus spp.   380
Unio spp.   136
Uria lomvia   420
Ursus deningeri   69
    U. arctos   149
    U. maritimus   148
Urtica spp.   380, 382

Vallonia tenuilabris   139
    V. enniensis   141
Valvata naticina   138
Vertigo genesii   137
Viscum album   141, 409
Vitrinobrachium breve   136
Viviparus diluvianus   138
Vulpes vulpes   149

Widdringtonia cedarbergensis   39

Yersinia pestis (plague)   227

Zea mays   29, 399